KT-441-848

READER'S DIGEST COMPLETE

MANUAL

READER'S DIGEST COMPLETE

MANUAL

Published by the
Reader's Digest Association Ltd
London • New York • Sydney • Montreal

contributors

Editors

Noel Buchanan

Art editors

Julie Bennett • Kate Harris • Iain Stuart • John Vigurs • Joanna Walker

Consultant editors

Nicholas J. Frewing, Des.RCA, FSIAD • Mike Lawrence • Tony Wilkins

Contributors and specialist consultants

Roger Bisby • Anthony Byers • Roger DuBern • Nicholas J. Frewing, Des.RCA, FSIAD • Simon J. Gilham • Ernest Hall, FRSH • Colin D. Kinloch, DFH, C.Eng, MIEE • John McGowan • Helen O'Leary • Colin M.J. Sutherland, C.Eng, F.Inst. E, MCIBSE • Bob Tattersall • Tony Wilkins • Jacqui Woodford

Technical organiser

Simon J. Gilham

Photographers

Colin Bowling • Martin Cameron • Andrew Long • Malkolm Warrington • Les Wies

Demonstrators

Simon J. Gilham • Joanne Hemsley, BA(Hons) • Caroline Stansfield

Illustrators

Richard Bonson • Kuo Kang Chen • Brian Delf • John Erwood • Andy Green • Mike Grey • Grose Thurston Industrial and Commercial Artists • Peter Harper • Hayward and Martin • Inkwell Design and Art • Kevin Jones Associates • Pavel Kostal • Norman Lacey • Janos Marffy • Precision Illustration • Barry Salter Associates • Lee Tucker • Edward Williams Arts

In addition to the organisations listed on page 511, the publishers wish to give their special thanks to the following companies for providing equipment and facilities:
Armitage Shanks Ltd • Buck & Ryan Ltd • H. Burbidge & Son Ltd • Marley Roof Tile Co. Ltd • Pegler Ltd • Vitrex Ltd

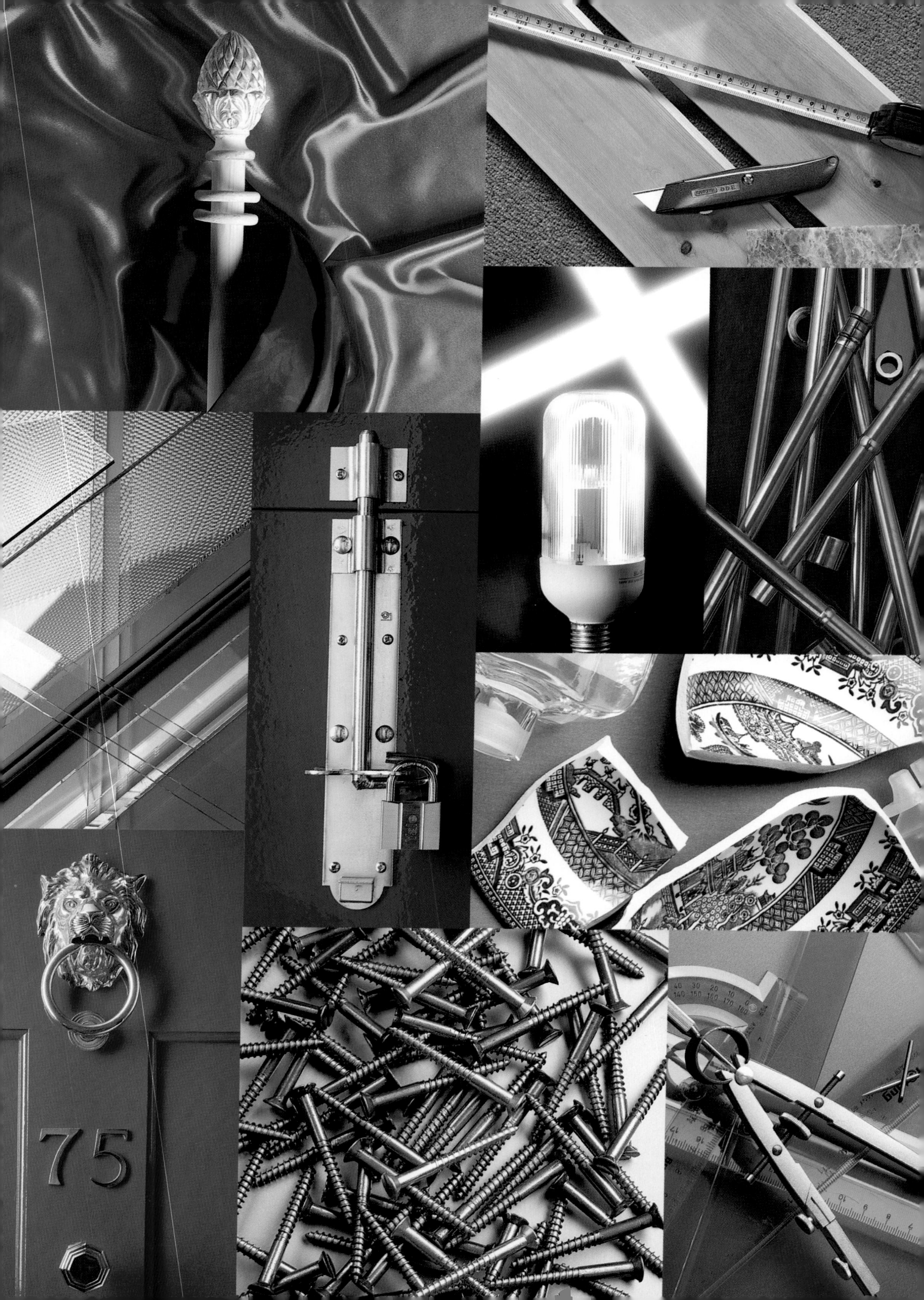
75

Contents

Home Survey
97

Home survey

Before starting to do any work on your house, you need to identify the areas of your home that need attention. This might include structural problems such as subsidence, damp and a leaky roof as well as cosmetic improvements such as rearranging a room to give it more pleasing proportions or to let in more light.

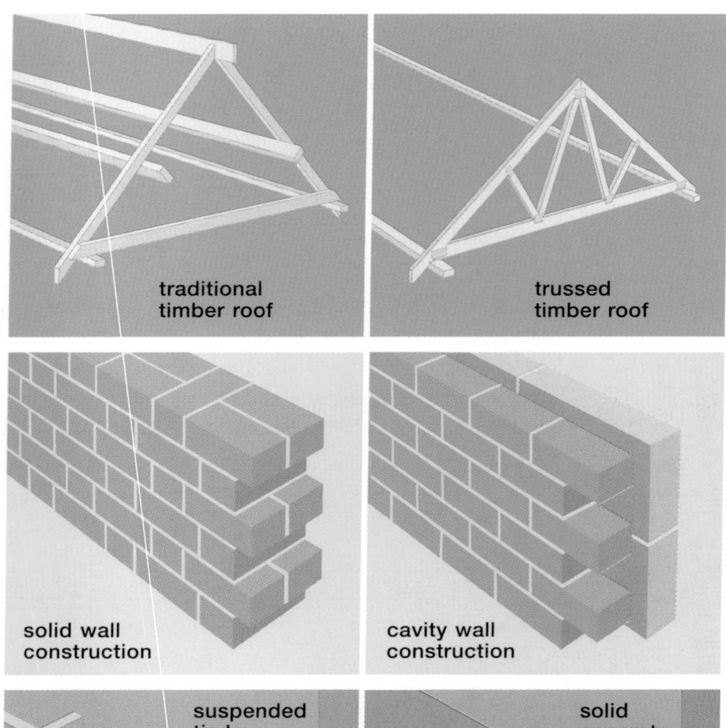

How your home was built

Generation of change

The age of your home will dictate how it has been built. The construction of houses built in the last half-century differs markedly from those put up before about 1920. Houses built during the intervening generation of change incorporate both traditional building techniques and some of the new methods of construction that were being introduced.

Before picking up the tools

Knowing how your home is built before embarking on DIY jobs can save you time and money. Understanding how the roof, walls and floors are put together and what they're made of will help you to plan improvements and alterations, and to deal with any faults that may develop as time goes by.

Look in the loft

A glance in the loft will tell you what sort of roof you have. Traditional timber roofs, assembled on site, have open space below the rafters for storage. Roofs constructed in the past 50 years usually have roof trusses—prefabricated timber frames incorporating rafters and ceiling joists. These are factory-made so the roof structure can be erected quickly, but the design and number of the trusses leaves little room for storage.

Save boarding on a roof

If you live in an older house with a boarded roof—one with planking laid across the tops of the rafters—don't have it stripped off if you ever have a new roof put on the property. The boarding insulates the roof space far better than a layer of roofing felt alone, and areas which are rotten can be replaced easily with sections of new pressure-treated wood.

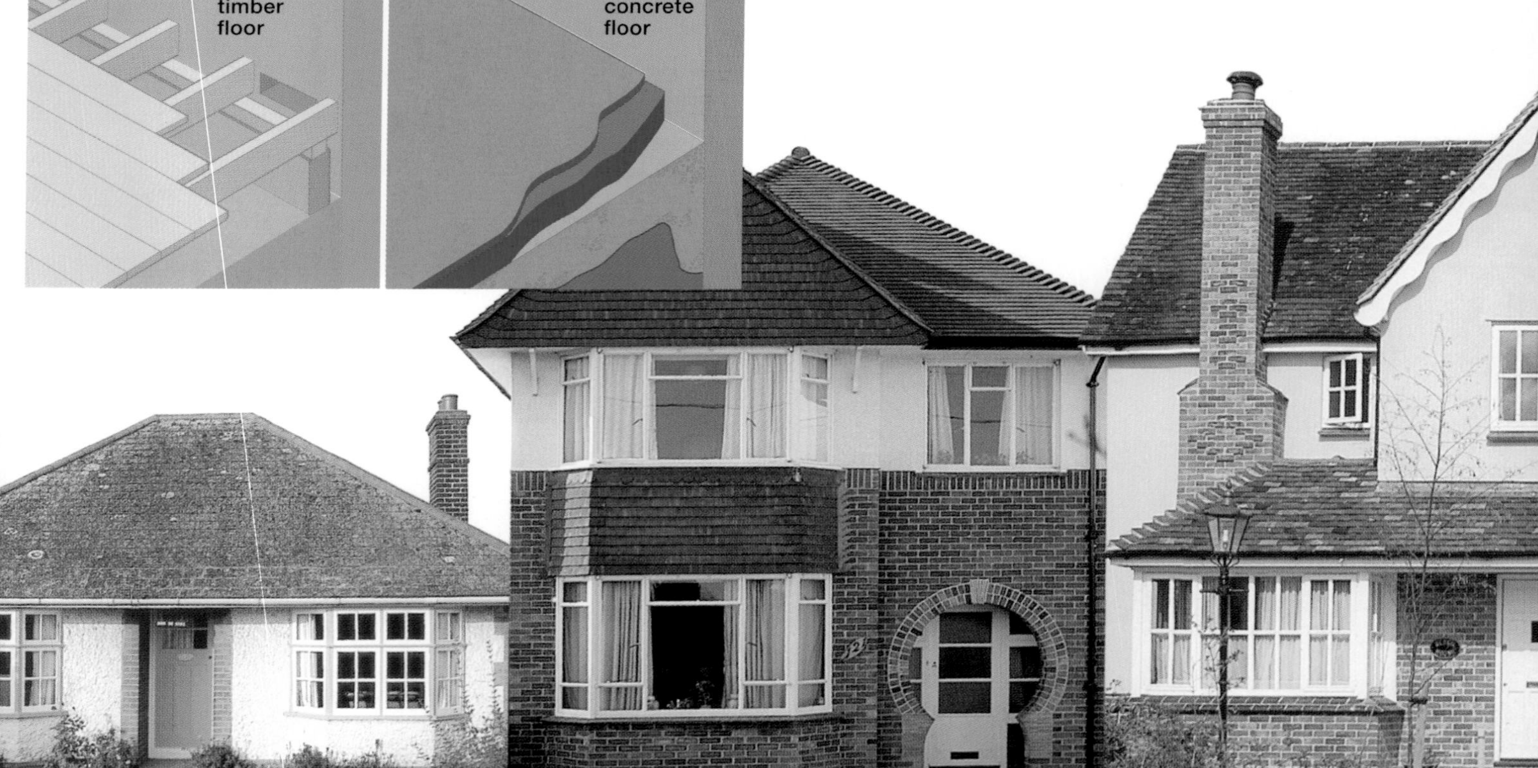

Strong enough to bear the weight?

Old roofs are usually covered with natural slates or clay tiles, and were designed to take the weight of these. Before you replace them with concrete tiles, which are usually much heavier, ask an expert whether the roof timbers will need to be strengthened. If the timbers do need reinforcing, the cost is likely to cancel out any saving you might make by re-roofing with manufactured tiles—in which case, you're better off leaving the roof structure alone and replacing like with like.

Two kinds of external brick walls

Solid all the way through

The bricks in solid walls are laid in patterns known as bonds. What they all have in common are headers—bricks laid end-on so that they pass right through the wall to give it strength. A solid wall will be as thick as the length of a brick 8½in (215mm) plus the thickness of plaster inside and any rendering outside. You can measure the wall at a door or window opening.

A cavity in the middle

Only the long faces of bricks, known as stretchers, are on view if your house has cavity walls. The walls are a minimum of 10⅖in (255mm) thick (two single leaves of brickwork, each 4in (102.5mm) thick, separated by a 2in (50mm) wide cavity) and more if the cavity is wider or the internal leaf is built of thicker blockwork.

Suspended and solid ground floors

What lies beneath your feet?

Ground floors in most houses built before about 1950 are usually covered with floorboards laid over timber joists which are suspended over an underfloor airspace. In the past 50 years solid concrete ground floors have become the norm, although they may be overlaid with timber strip flooring or chipboard. Accessing and altering plumbing and heating pipework under a timber floor is a relatively simple matter; getting at pipes buried in concrete is much more difficult.

No more damp and better insulation

Concrete floors in the kitchens and sculleries of old houses are prone to rising damp because they were laid straight onto the earth, with no separating damp-proof membrane (DPM). Inherent dampness in a solid floor also makes it cold and liable to condensation. Where concrete floors have been laid next to wooden ones, they can hinder ventilation of the underfloor space, increasing the risk of rot in the wood floor. Nowadays, building regulations ensure that concrete ground floors are underlaid with a DPM of heavy-grade polythene, and since 1990 they must be insulated.

Prone to rot and draughts

In older homes, the ends of the joists supporting timber ground floors are embedded in external walls, making them prone to rot if the walls are damp. The square-edge floorboards used until the 1930s let in underfloor draughts—a problem largely cured by the use of tongue-and-groove boards, although at the cost of making the boards more difficult to lift.

Assessing the condition of your property

Get your priorities right

Carry out a survey to make sure your home is weathertight, safe and thief-proof before you do anything else. There's no point in decorating if the roof is letting in rain, or installing new light fittings if the wiring is dangerous and needs replacing. And if the house isn't secure, filling it with expensive fixtures and fittings before making sure that all the exterior doors and windows have good locks is also getting your priorities wrong.

Take it from the top

Start your home survey with the roof. A pair of binoculars is useful for inspecting it without having to climb a ladder. If you can't see the whole roof surface from your garden or the street, ask to view it from a neighbour's property.

Check the controls

Before you start any DIY, make sure you know where the water and gas stoptaps and main electricity supply switch are located. Keep a torch by the electricity meter, plus some fuse wire if the system has fuses. You will need to locate all drain inspection chambers (manholes) and check that the covers can be lifted easily if a drain becomes blocked.

Inspect the loft

Go into the loft to inspect the underside of the roof. Look for water stains on the timbers, or wait until there's a heavy downpour and then look for signs of rain getting in. There should be ventilators along the eaves, at the ridge, in gable walls or on the roof slope. Shine a light along the eaves if there are none to be seen, because

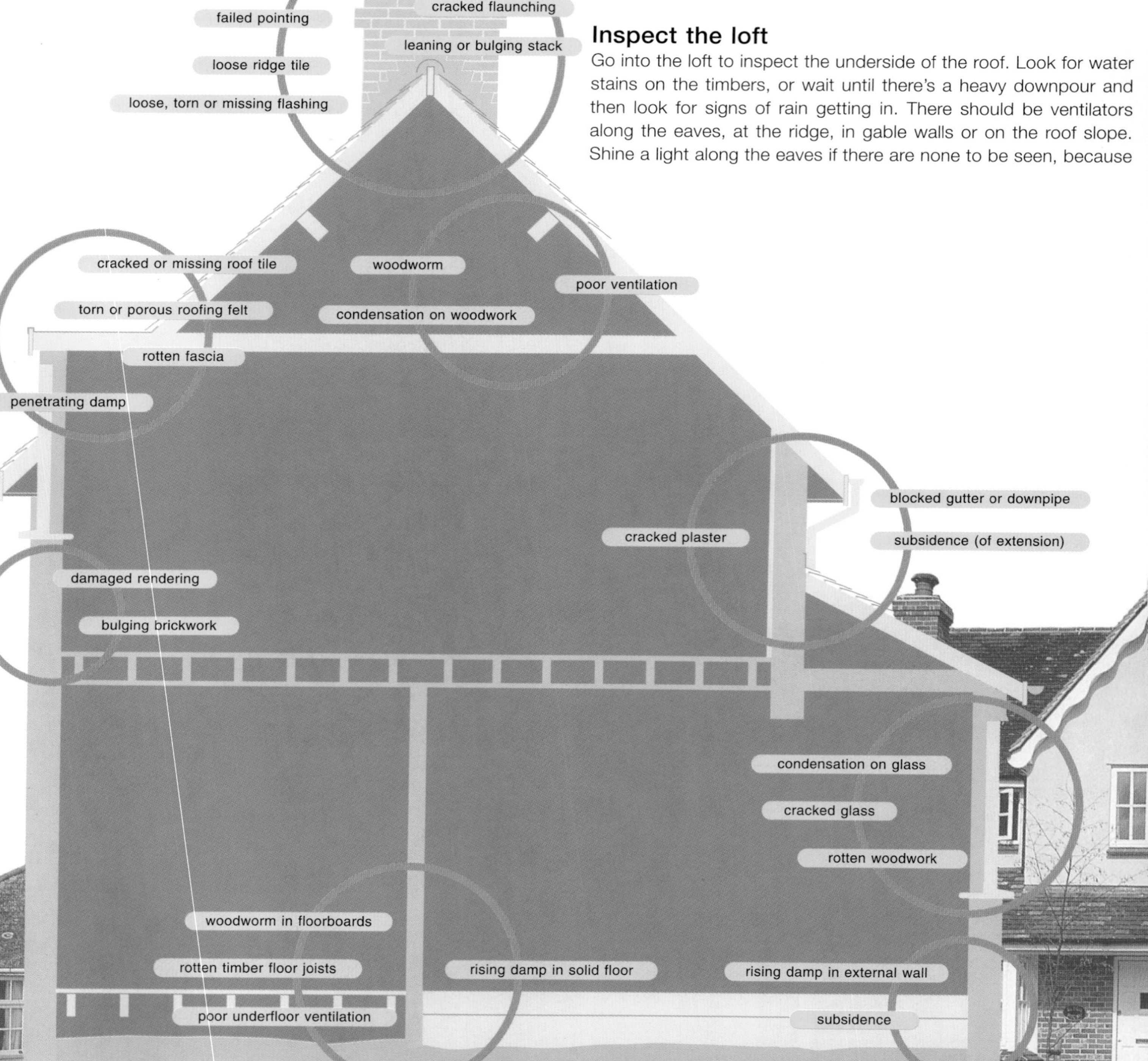

a badly ventilated roof space can be liable to dry rot, and this often sets in along the eaves. Lastly, carefully examine the roof timbers for signs of woodworm.

Stacks of trouble

Chimneys are the most exposed part of your house, so check them closely for signs of damage. Look for cracks in the pots and in the flaunching—the mortar bed in which the pots are embedded. If a stack is built against an outside wall, examine it for straightness. The combination of coal gases condensing inside the flue and rain soaking through the mortar joints can set up a chemical reaction which makes the brickwork bulge outwards. Repointing the brickwork and lining the flue can arrest the problem, but a severely damaged stack may have to be completely rebuilt.

Include the garden

Remember to survey the garden at the same time as the rest of your home. Fences may be in poor condition, a shed roof may be leaking, garden paths may need lighting, and nearby trees may be undermining boundary walls. A gate or door into the garden might need a lock fitting to it.

Look for overflows

Check the gutters and downpipes for blockages. Stains on the house walls can reveal where previous overflows have occurred. The next time it rains, check where gutters are overflowing or where water is leaking from downpipe joints.

Is the woodwork sound?

Prod the external woodwork with a bradawl to detect rot under the paintwork and look round the edges of door and window frames for gaps where rainwater can penetrate—especially on north and west-facing walls, which are the most exposed to the weather.

Safe and secure

As you work your way around the house checking the woodwork, look at how windows and external doors are secured. You may need to fit new locks or upgrade existing ones.

That sinking feeling

Subsidence is the most serious problem you might detect. It occurs most commonly on clay soil, which expands when wet and then contracts as it dries out. Look at the corners of your house and at the door and window openings. Are they vertical and square?

Zigzag cracks running down the walls from the corners of door and window frames, and between the main house and an extension, are signs of possible subsidence. Inside, doors and windows may start jamming for no apparent reason, and wallpaper can crease or tear.

Barriers to rising damp

Look for a damp-proof course (DPC)—visible outside between the second and third courses of brickwork above ground level. This is a horizontal band of slate, bituminous felt or black polythene. In an older house built before DPCs were introduced, you may see a row of small mortar or rubber plugs indicating that a chemical DPC has been injected into the walls in recent years.

Where the air gets in

Airbricks or grilles are built into the outside walls, just above ground level, in houses with suspended timber ground floors. These allow air to circulate in the underfloor space, helping to keep it dry and to discourage rot. Make sure they are not blocked or obstructed in any way.

Testing timber floors

Jump up and down on timber ground floors. If they sag noticeably, the joists may be rotten because their ends are built into walls suffering from rising damp. Prod the skirting boards with a bradawl to see if they're rotten—another indication that there may be problems beneath the floor.

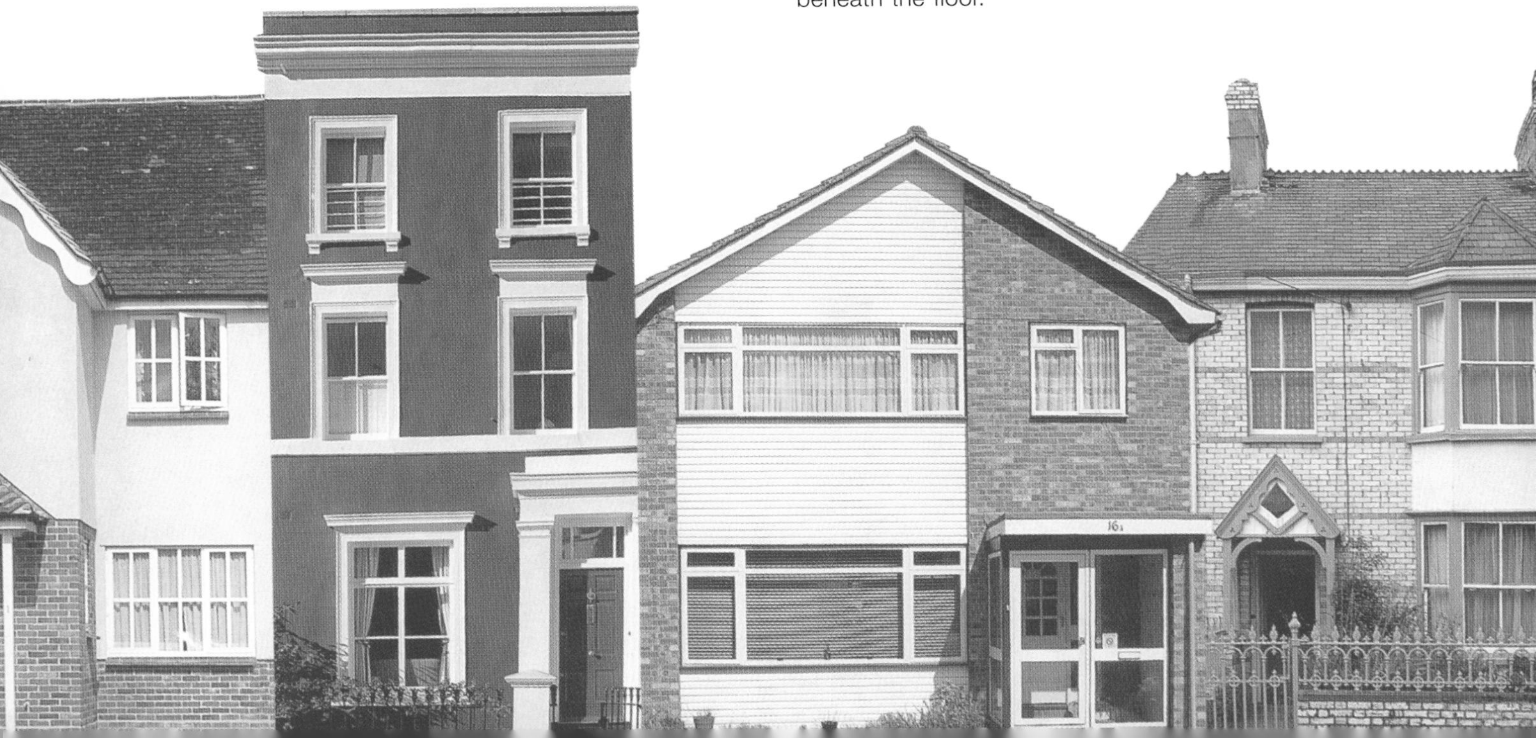

Diagnosing damp and tracing the causes

mould growth in built-in wardrobe

penetrating damp above window

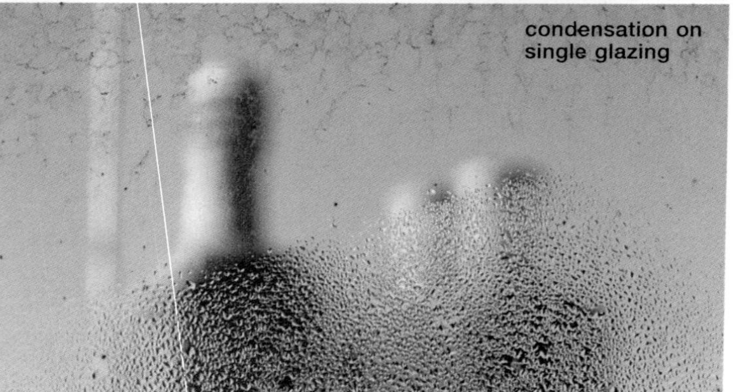
condensation on single glazing

Find the reason before trying a remedy

Damp problems in a house can be due to a number of causes—rain getting through the walls or roof, moisture being absorbed from the ground, condensation settling on cold surfaces, or a mixture of these. Make sure you know what the cause of dampness is before trying to cure it, otherwise you may be dealing only with part of the problem, or worse still adopting the wrong remedy for the sort of damp involved.

Spot the tell-tale semicircles

In an old house with a slate damp-proof course (DPC), slight movement of the building can crack the slates, allowing damp from the ground to rise into the masonry above the crack. A single point failure will cause a semicircular patch of damp up to 3ft 3in (1m) or so across, while multiple cracks will lead to an almost continuous band across the affected wall.

Try the foil test

If you're not sure of the cause of a damp patch on a wall, try the foil test. Dry the wall surface with a fan heater, then tape some kitchen foil tightly over the damp area. If the surface of the foil is wet after 24 hours, you have condensation. If the foil is dry but the wall surface beneath it is damp, you have rising or penetrating damp. Discount rising damp if the moisture is more than 3ft 3in (1m) above outside ground level.

Getting through the gaps

Patches of dampness on walls around windows and doors are usually caused by rain getting through gaps between their frames and the surrounding masonry. Where the damp is below the opening, it may be because there is no drip groove to stop the water creeping under a projecting sill or threshold. If there is a drip groove, make sure the rain is not passing across it because it is blocked with paint or mortar.

Looking for a leak in the roof

Discovering exactly where a pitched roof is leaking can be difficult. Rain can trickle down the roofing felt and along the sides of rafters before it drips onto the loft floor. Clues such as dampness on a party wall or chimney stack in the loft, may indicate that flashings are defective or missing. Getting someone to play a hose on the roof, area by area, while you remain inside the loft can also help to reveal where the water is getting in.

Woodworm at work

At the same time as checking lofts, underfloor spaces and built-in cupboards for signs of dampness, inspect structural timbers and joinery for evidence of woodworm, which thrives in slightly damp environments. Look for the small flight holes made by the beetles when they emerge from the wood and the fine wood dust created by the pest. Check the untreated backs of all freestanding chests and wardrobes, and the unpainted top and bottom edges of doors at the same time.

Prod the paintwork

Use a bradawl to test the soundness of skirting boards if there are signs of damp in downstairs walls or the underfloor space. The backs of skirting boards are usually left unpainted, so they readily absorb moisture from the masonry. However, severe deterioration of the boards is often not apparent because of paint applied to their face sides.

Crossing the bridge

If you think you have rising damp in your house, locate the damp-proof course (DPC) and make sure it isn't covered by a flowerbed, path, drive or patio. Look for rendering that has been applied over the DPC. Check whether there is a vertical DPC sandwiched between the house wall and the end of a garden wall built up against it. Curing these common causes of rising damp will solve the problem for little or no cost.

Check out the plumbing

Leaks in plumbing and central-heating pipework can cause damp patches which could be misinterpreted as rising or penetrating damp. This is especially common where the pipes are run beneath a floor or are buried in wall plaster. Here a pinhole leak or a weeping fitting can release surprisingly large volumes of water as time goes by, especially if it has no chance to dry out naturally.

If this is the cause of the problem, you have two possible courses of action. You can either expose the fault and then replace the affected pipes, which will cause a lot of disruption. Alternatively, you can simply leave them where they are and bypass them by installing new ones.

Suspect condensation

If the roof isn't leaking but the timbers and loft insulation are damp, the most likely culprit is condensation. This is caused by warm. moisture-laden air rising into the loft from the rooms below and condensing on cold surfaces within the loft space. In serious cases, roof timbers can start to rot and saturated insulation materials can stain ceilings.

Letting of steam

The kitchen and bathroom are the main sources of condensation in the home. Bathing, cooking and washing up, and washing and drying clothes all pour large volumes of steam into the air. Portable gas space heaters and paraffin stoves also create a lot of moisture.

The problem is often made worse by a combination of poor room ventilation and over-efficient draught-proofing, both of which stop warm moisture-laden air inside the house being replaced with cooler drier air from outside.

Unventilated fitted cupboards built against outside walls can suffer badly from condensation. This can lead to unsightly mould growth, which will quickly spoil clothes stored there.

Prepare a plan and visualise your options

Measure and draw

Experiment with your ideas for alterations by drawing a floor plan on graph paper. An ultrasonic estimator is the most accurate tool for quickly taking measurements. The larger the scale of your drawing, the more detail can be included on it, so use the whole sheet of graph paper, or tape a couple of sheets together if necessary. Be sure to take lots of photocopies before you start sketching out and modifying your ideas. Mark which way the doors open—this is very important for the positioning of light switches—and include other features on your plan such as radiators, light fittings and socket outlets.

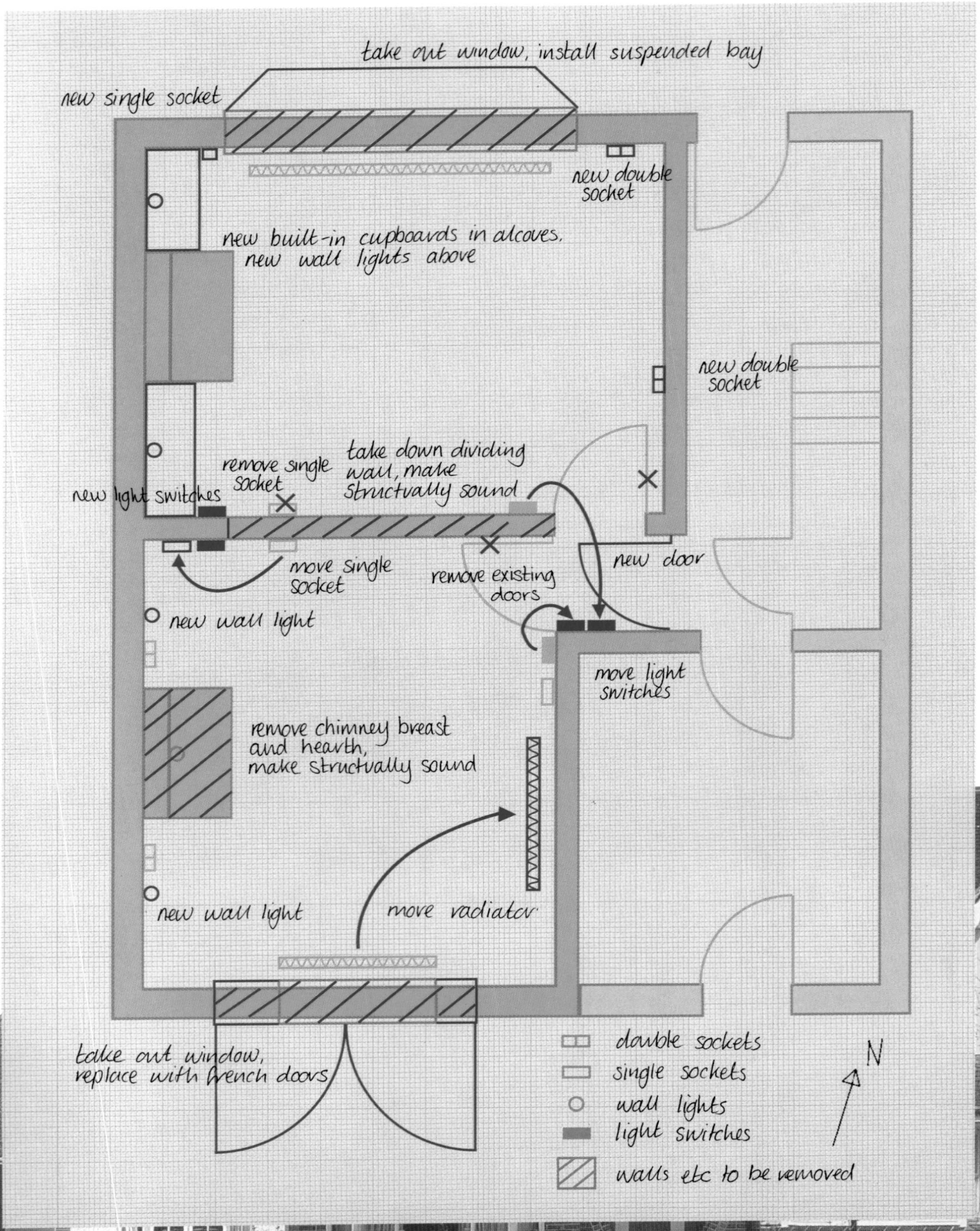

take out window, install suspended bay
new single socket
new double socket
new built-in cupboards in alcoves, new wall lights above
new double socket
take down dividing wall, make structurally sound
remove single socket
new light switches
move single socket
remove existing doors
new door
new wall light
move light switches
remove chimney breast and hearth, make structurally sound
new wall light
move radiator
take out window, replace with french doors
double sockets
single sockets
wall lights
light switches
walls etc to be removed
N

Consider the alternatives before making changes

A sense of direction
Find out in which direction north lies and mark it on your plan. Aspect can be vital if you're thinking of building a conservatory, or having skylights or new windows put in the house—all of which need to face south or west to get most sunshine and daylight.

Envisage the impact
If you decide to have new openings made in a wall, or an existing one enlarged, you can get an idea of the overall impact by sketching them full-size on sheets of lining paper, then taping these in position on the wall surface.

Change without disruption
Instead of altering the size of rooms by knocking them into one another to create bigger spaces or putting up stud walls to make them smaller, consider creating change by illusion. Using colour, lighting, furniture and furnishings to create different effects is cheaper and less disruptive than undertaking building work.

Illusions of space
Several design tricks can be used to make a room feel bigger than it really is. For example, brightly lit rooms with pale walls, bare floors, simple furniture and sheer curtains feel spacious. Strategically hung mirrors also add an illusion of extra space, reflecting what lies through a window, around a corner or beyond an open doorway.

That shrinking feeling
A room can be made to feel smaller too. Dark walls and ceilings seem to advance. A picture rail also makes a ceiling feel lower, especially if the wall above the rail is painted to match the ceiling colour. Heavy, patterned fabrics, dark furniture and focused lighting emphasise the shrinking effect.

Structural considerations
Make sure a dividing wall is non-loadbearing before you knock it down to turn two rooms into one. One way to tell is to look at floorboards in the room above—if they run parallel to the wall, the joists they're laid on must be supported by the wall—but seek expert advice if you're in any doubt.

Counting the potential costs
One room made from two will have more light if both the originals had windows, but the bigger area will be more expensive to heat. A sense of comfort may be lost if the new room feels too long, too narrow or too low. In addition, there will now be space where there were two surfaces to stand furniture against and hang things on.

New uses for existing areas
You can make your home suit your lifestyle better by changing the way you use rooms. For example, an understairs cupboard could be converted into a downstairs toilet. You could house the washing machine, tumble drier and airer in an old walk-in larder and increase food storage in the kitchen.

An integral garage is an obvious candidate for conversion into a playroom, a home office or a teenager's room if you're prepared to leave the car on the drive or street.

Rooms with a view
Glass creates an impression of space. Glazing a solid door at the end of a claustrophobic hall introduces a view of the outside or into a room, lets in light and makes the hall feel more spacious. Creating or emphasising a view of the garden through a window or french doors makes a room appear larger, especially if tall plants are kept away from the other side of the glass.

Lofty thoughts
Don't forget the loft when you're looking for extra space. Although the roof trusses used in most properties since about 1950 usually involve too much structural work to make loft conversion practical, roof spaces in older houses can often be turned into an extra room.

Making the most of your abilities

Risks not worth the saving

Always err on the side of caution if you're not confident about your DIY skills—especially if the job involves working at height. All the equipment needed for carrying out roof repairs and alterations can be hired, but if you are unsure about whether you can do the job safely, paying professional contractors is preferable to risking injury or worse.

Opportunity to tackle other tasks

Scaffolding forms a substantial part of the total cost of having a house re-roofed. Try to take advantage of it by having other jobs, such as painting the outside woodwork or repointing the brickwork, carried out while the scaffolding is in place. It will have to satisfy the requirements of different tradespeople (for example, providing planking and access ladders for painters). You will probably have to pay extra to keep the scaffolding beyond the four weeks usually negotiated by roofers. Remember that you will not be covered by the contractor's insurance if you work from the scaffolding yourself.

A sensible division of labour

Many building jobs involve an element of unskilled work. For example, having a room replastered involves hacking off and carting away the old plaster. Tradespeople will often agree to you doing this sort of work yourself to save money before they come in to carry out the skilled part of the job.

Time and patience

Before you tackle a large project yourself, estimate how long it will take and how disruptive it will be. Can you and others living in the house put up with a long period of disorder if you're able to devote only weekends to the project?

Nothing kills enthusiasm more quickly than apparent lack of progress. You may conclude that the solution is to employ others to do the major disruptive work while devoting your input to just the finishing stages.

Get an expert opinion

Consult a professional surveyor or building engineer if your home survey alerts you to a serious problem—subsidence, for example—that could require major structural work. An expert will assess whether the problem has stabilised and requires no action, if it can be arrested without major building work, or if extensive remedial work is needed.

Strategies to combat damp problems

Let your house breathe

There are a number of simple but effective remedies for condensation. Open windows when the weather is suitable so that drier air can get into the room. Fit extractor fans with humidity detectors in kitchens and bathrooms to remove moist air automatically, or else plug in a dehumidifer. Lastly, remember that sealing up doors, windows and unused flues to eliminate draughts will increase the likelihood of condensation.

Is a guarantee required?

Installing a damp-proof course (DPC) in an older house usually involves drilling holes into the second or third course of brickwork above outdoor ground level, then pumping a chemical waterproofer into the walls. You can hire the equipment and do the job yourself if you don't need the guarantee.

Easy ways to cut humidity

Create less moisture by drying clothes outdoors whenever possible. If you have a tumble drier, vent it to the outside.

Keep lids on boiling saucepans and shut bathroom and kitchen doors to stop steam spreading through the house.

Use dehumidifiers in damp, enclosed areas and avoid heaters that run on paraffin or oil—both fuels produce large quantities of water vapour when they are burned.

Allow time for drying out

If your home needs a damp-proof course (DPC), schedule it into the order of work as early as possible. The plaster on damp walls will have absorbed salts from the masonry and will have to be hacked off to a height of about 3ft 3in (1m) before the DPC is installed. Then the masonry will need to be left bare for several months so that it can dry out before the walls are recovered—either with a traditional sand and cement plaster, or with one recommended by the damp-proofing company.

Raising the floor

Always seek advice about the best way to tackle rising damp in a solid floor, which is caused by the absence or failure of a damp-proof membrane (DPM) between the floor and the ground beneath.

Low levels of damp can be tackled by coating the floor with a heavy-duty damp-proofing liquid to create a new DPM, then applying a thin sand and cement screed on top.

If you cannot afford to raise the floor level much, you can lay a self-levelling compound instead of a traditional screed to provide a new floor surface. If, however, the damp problem is very severe, you may be advised to have the whole floor lifted and replaced.

Made to absorb moisture

Decorate kitchens and bathrooms with paint specially made for these rooms. Ordinary emulsion paint will flake or develop mould if it gets damp frequently, but anti-condensation paint is designed to absorb moisture from damp air and release it back into the atmosphere when the air is drier.

Damp-proof plaster

If condensation is severe, on north-facing walls for example, have them replastered with an anti-condensation plaster. Like kitchen and bathroom paint, this product absorbs moisture when the atmosphere is damp and releases it when it is dry. The plaster also contains small air bubbles which insulate the surface, helping to further reduce the risk of condensation.

Try small adjustments first

You can hold condensation at bay by spending more on keeping the house warm—turning up the central heating and improving the insulation. Often, however, marginal adjustments—slightly more ventilation combined with a low but constant level of background heat—are just as effective, and cheaper.

Solutions for accident black spots

Minimise fire danger

Buy a fire blanket and keep it somewhere accessible in the kitchen, which is where most fires start. Fit smoke detectors in the hall and on landings. Don't store tins of paint or other flammable materials under the stairs; move them to a garage or shed so they won't pose a risk to a main line of escape if you're unlucky enough to have a fire. Finally, if there are locks fitted to patio doors or upstairs windows, keep the keys nearby and make sure that everyone knows where they are.

Lighting the way

Falls tend to occur at entrance doorways, on stairs and in kitchens and bathrooms, often because people cannot see clearly where they are going.

Wire in two-way light switches so that nobody has to negotiate the stairs in the dark. Put up a hand rail if necessary and if there are babies or toddlers in the house, fit stair gates at the top and bottom of the flight. Fit outside lights to illuminate the route to your front door at night.

Stop slipping and sliding

Put down non-slip mats in shower cubicles and in baths used for showering. Fit wall-mounted grab handles in the bathroom for extra safety, especially if you have someone elderly or disabled living in the house.

A fabric bath mat soaks up water and stops the bathroom floor from being slippery when wet. If you are replacing the bathroom flooring, choose a slip-resistant material.

Warning sticker

Place a colourful label at eye level on patio doors to warn people of their existence. It's easy to walk into the glass, especially in fine weather when you might expect the doors to be open. Replace ordinary glass with toughened or laminated glass in all full-length glazed timber doors. Then, if someone should fall against a pane, it won't break into lethal shards.

Use tools safely

Many DIY tools need sharp blades or powerful motors to be able to do their jobs properly. This means that they can cause injury if they are not used correctly and with care. When using bladed tools, keep them sharp so they will cut without effort, and make sure that your hands are behind the cutting direction and out of the cutting line. Read the instructions before using any power tool for the first time, and never bypass or de-activate any safety guard that is specially fitted to the tool.

Wear the right gear

Assemble a safety kit before embarking on DIY. For many jobs you'll need safety goggles, a face mask, a hard hat, a pair of tough gloves and some sturdy footwear. Different items offer varying degrees of protection. A dust mask, for example, won't protect you against solvent vapours and fine droplets of paint in the air, so buy a specialist spray mask or a respirator made to at least approved standard BSEN405 if you're going to tackle jobs such as respraying car bodywork. If you anticipate using noisy power tools such as a concrete breaker or floor sander for long periods, buy some ear defenders.

Invest in a first-aid kit for your workshop that meets Health and Safety Executive standards for workplace use. These are available from tool and equipment hire shops.

Reducing the risks from power in the home

Secure shelves
If you have an adjustable shelving system on an open wall, rather than in an alcove, secure the shelves to their brackets with screws. This will stop an accidental collision from dislodging a shelf or its contents. It is also a good idea to round off any sharp shelf corners in this situation.

Fit castor cups
Move chairs and sofas fitted with castors away from patio doors and other low-level glazing, so there's no chance of them being propelled through the glass when people sit down on them. Alternatively, fit castor cups beneath the castors to stop the furniture from moving so easily.

Backs against the wall
Secure the tops of tall bookcases and display units to the wall with L-shaped brackets so they cannot topple over if they are unevenly loaded or if a child tries to climb up the shelves.

Remove or tape down
Loose rugs laid on polished wooden hall floors and landings pose a serious hazard, especially near the top of stairs. Either remove them, or fix special non-slip tape to the underside.

Make an appointment
If you have no record of when a gas or oil-fired central-heating boiler or water heater was last serviced, arrange for a service straight away. This will ensure that the appliance burns its fuel properly and is adequately ventilated.

If you experience drowsiness or headaches in the room when an appliance is on, don't use it until it's been checked.

Choose coiled leads
Swap long flexes on kettles, toasters and other appliances for coiled or short straight leads that cannot dangle over the edge of worktops where a small child could reach and pull them.

Prevent a heat surge
The water temperature in a shower can rise suddenly and cause scalding if a cold tap is turned on elsewhere in the house. You can eliminate the risk by replacing the shower mixer with a thermostatically controlled model or by fitting a mains-fed electric shower unit.

Baby-safe sockets
Plug socket guards into all unused electric sockets if you have small children in the family; this prevents tiny fingers or metal objects from being poked into socket holes. It is also worth making sure that all plugs have sleeved live and neutral pins, so they are safe even if partly pulled out of their sockets.

Fully bonded
For total electrical safety, all exposed metalwork in the bathroom and kitchen should be linked (bonded) to earth by special cables covered in green-and-yellow PVC insulation. If there is no evidence of these vital links in your home (they may have been concealed under the floor, for example), call in an electrician to find out and to install them if necessary.

rotring

1 Ideas for the home

Kitchens

Planning your kitchen

The shape and size of a kitchen largely govern the siting of worktops and units, and the amount of space that can be devoted to them. But whatever the shape or size, the major appliances such as the oven, hob and refrigerator will need to be installed within easy reach of each other and of the sink.

The sink itself is best placed near a window, which gives a view and a good light for washing up. Avoid having it jammed into a corner, which reduces access and makes it difficult for anyone to help with the washing up.

If possible, have a work surface on each side of the cooker and the sink, giving an uninterrupted sequence of worktop, sink, worktop, cooker, worktop.

Deciding on a place for the cooker

Ideally the cooker or hob should be against an outside wall so that it can be vented by a cooker hood or extractor fan.

Avoid placing a hob beneath a window; there is a risk of curtains catching fire. And accidents can be caused by people leaning across the hob in order to open or clean the window.

For the same reason, do not place the cooker near a door; there is an extra risk of pan handles being knocked by people going in and out of the room.

If a corner is the only place where the cooker can go, fit it across the angle. Otherwise only one side is left free for a worktop, and access is difficult.

The placing of the refrigerator is less critical, but ideally it should not be next to the cooker or in a position where it will be exposed to the heat of the sun for long periods during the day.

Cooking ingredients that are used frequently, such as salt, flour, stock cubes and herbs, should be kept on a shelf or in a cupboard near the cooker. Keep tea, coffee and sugar near the kettle.

Use the wall space between a worktop and wall cupboards for hanging utensils or to fit narrow shelves for storing herb jars.

These pages illustrate how other people have coped with a variety of problems in their kitchen planning and should help you to make the best of the space you have.

Using the existing space

Most proprietary ranges of kitchen furniture are manufactured in standard sizes, usually in metric measurements. Kitchens, however, are not built to standard measurements and rarely will a run of these standard base units fit exactly between the walls.

NARROW WORKTOPS (*left*) Tall, shallow units and narrow worktops on the right-hand wall of a very limited space have made this U-shaped layout possible. Bright paintwork and plenty of lights on the ceiling and above the units make up for the small amount of natural light.

The problem can be dealt with by cutting the worktop to the exact length required and leaving a gap between two of the units. The gap can then be used to store trays or a waste bin, or for fitting a towel rail. Some manufacturers sell narrow units for dealing with these gaps. Alternatively, you could cut down a full-size unit to fit or custom build something.

Another point to remember is that the positioning of some appliances will be governed by the location of the services. For example, washing machines and dishwashers need to be near the water supply and drainage system. While the relocation of these services is within the scope of the handyman, any changes should be planned and carried out before worktops and base cupboards are fitted. Relocation of gas points, however, must be carried out by the local gas company, or by an approved CORGI gas fitter.

Also at an early stage decide where the electricity socket outlets should be, and how many you will need. In a kitchen many of the sockets should be fitted on the wall above the worktop for appliances such as kettle, toaster and food mixer. Bear in mind that you will probably be adding other appliances in the future. If extra sockets on a spur are to be added, the wiring should be recessed into the wall, and this must be done before fitting wall coverings. Similarly a ventilation fan or cooker hood, unless it is the recirculating type, will require a hole to be made in an outside wall or window.

Altering the space

Often more space can be gained, and a different shape acquired, by structural alterations such as removing a wall to make one room out of two. In old houses the removal of a disused chimney breast will give extra space, and if there is an adjoining brick-built coal shed, scullery or outside wc, it may be possible to convert these buildings in order to extend the kitchen. Such alterations, however, should be planned properly and carried out by a qualified builder. Find out from your local council whether the planned alterations require planning permission before starting work.

Relocating the kitchen

Where it is not possible to enlarge a kitchen it may be worth considering adapting another room, especially if you want to incorporate an eating area. The abandoned kitchen may then be suitable to be turned into a playroom or a utility room, housing a washing machine, a tumble dryer and a chest freezer.

Large Victorian or Edwardian houses are particularly suitable for relocating the kitchen. One of the larger ground-floor rooms will often have space for a dining table and chairs, or an island or peninsular unit. Another advantage is that if you turn the front room into a kitchen-living room, you will have a view of the street as you prepare a meal.

WHITE SPACE (*left*)
White units and wall tiles in an L-shaped configuration, combined with a neutral grey vinyl floor, create a bright atmosphere. Appliances are built-in for maximum neatness, while under-unit worktop lighting and recessed ceiling lights mean that night lighting is good too.

WOOD WORKS (*below*)
In a large farmhouse the kitchen units have been contained in one corner. A hanging rack which includes additional lighting is suspended over a butcher's block. The microwave is built-in under the hob to save worktop space, while floral tiles lend decoration.

Planning your kitchen (continued)

CULINARY CORNER (*above left*) In a limited space every centimetre has been wisely planned. Triangular units make the best use of space in a compact kitchen built in to the corner of a room. The sink unit extends into a worktop.

WINDOW STORAGE (*above right*) Tall windows in a small space are the perfect place for ceiling-mounted suspended shelves. Simple white units have been placed under the windows.

FOLDING DOORS (*right*) Cheerily painted concertina-style doors disguise a run of kitchen units at the end of a room. Deep shelves either side of the sink provide extra storage.

COUNTRY COMFORT (*left*) Painted units integrate the cooking and eating areas in a combination of cream and wood, which is used to edge a tiled work surface. Quarry tiles are both practical and easy to clean.

CO-ORDINATED CORNER (*below left*) Uniform floor-to-ceiling grey units combined with pale green shelving display a modern, efficient use of a small area. A microwave oven is built into a tower unit to create more cupboard space.

ROOM DIVIDER (*below right*) A complete Shaker-style kitchen is fitted into an upstairs landing by means of an irregular U-shaped layout. Runs of painted shelves are used for both food and china storage.

Style: your personal choice

The style or 'mood' of your kitchen will reflect your own likes and dislikes. Choosing the units and equipment that you want will probably establish the basis of a theme that can be used all over the room. It may be a country look of natural timber, the bright efficiency of coloured plastics, or the earthy feel of ceramic surfaces.

Whatever your choice, try to keep the style consistent throughout – in the walls, flooring, cupboards, and even down to pots and crockery. The choice need not be influenced by the type of house. A cottage or farmhouse kitchen will not necessarily look out of place in a suburban semi and a modern kitchen can look fine in a cottage.

Choosing the unit

Ready-assembled or self-assembly kitchen units are available in a range of styles. For a country effect there are moulded wood units, cabinets with leaded-glass fronts and worktops finished in simulated marble or timber.

In the modern style, melamine-fronted and flush-faced units, with their concealed hinges and recessed handles, are both attractive and easy to keep clean. Colours range from plain white to brilliant red.

Creating your own style may take longer than selecting factory-made units, but it can be more fun, and less expensive. You can buy cheap, easily adaptable articles of furniture never intended for use in the kitchen from secondhand furniture shops, auctions and even jumble sales. Victorian washstands, chests of drawers and bedside cabinets make fine base units. Over the years they will probably have acquired layers of paint, but that can be stripped back to the natural solid wood.

Decorating the room

Paint is the most practical and least expensive wall covering. Vinyl emulsion, with either a silk or matt finish, is easy to apply and to clean.

Paintwork needs a smooth surface, so if the plasterwork is in poor condition it may be better to use a good quality wallpaper, preferably vinyl coated so that it can be wiped over. Alternatively, decorative wallboards, with simulated wood, tile or stone finishes, can be used. They are easy to apply with adhesives. Tongued-and-grooved wood panelling will cover an uneven wall.

Ceramic tiles are the most durable and easy to clean of all wall coverings. If used from floor to ceiling this can give a clinical effect. They are better used in combination with one of the other finishes, in areas most likely to be splashed with water or grease.

Choosing the flooring

Kitchen flooring should be hard-wearing and easy to clean. Vinyl satisfies these requirements, and can be laid in sheet form or as tiles. Vinyl-coated cork tiles also give a durable and washable finish. Quarry tiles are particularly suitable for a cottage or farmhouse-style kitchen, but they need a solid sub-floor for the best results. Kitchen-quality carpeting makes a hard-wearing, warm and noiseless flooring. It is easily washable, especially if laid as carpet squares which can be lifted and washed individually.

For more information

Stripping paintwork	105
Painting a room	115-123
Wallpapering a room	126-135
Tiling a wall	139-146
Building shelves	169-180
Making cupboards	181-185
Fitting a drawer in a cupboard	186
Planning and fitting kitchen worktops	187-188
Filling gaps in built-in cupboards	188
Fitting decorative wallboards	251
Cladding a ceiling with timber	254
Types of flooring	277

PINE CLADDING (*above*) A smart variation on tongue-and-groove timber, the walls in this small kitchen are lined with pine strips that match hand-built units, and a pine and vinyl floor. Metal rails are attached to the front of the units for storing towels and drying cloths.

COOL BLUE (*left*) Ultra-simple cupboard doors are of a size to match the generous scale of these extension windows. A blue-and-white tiled splashback is both practical and decorative. The sink is placed near the window for a good view.

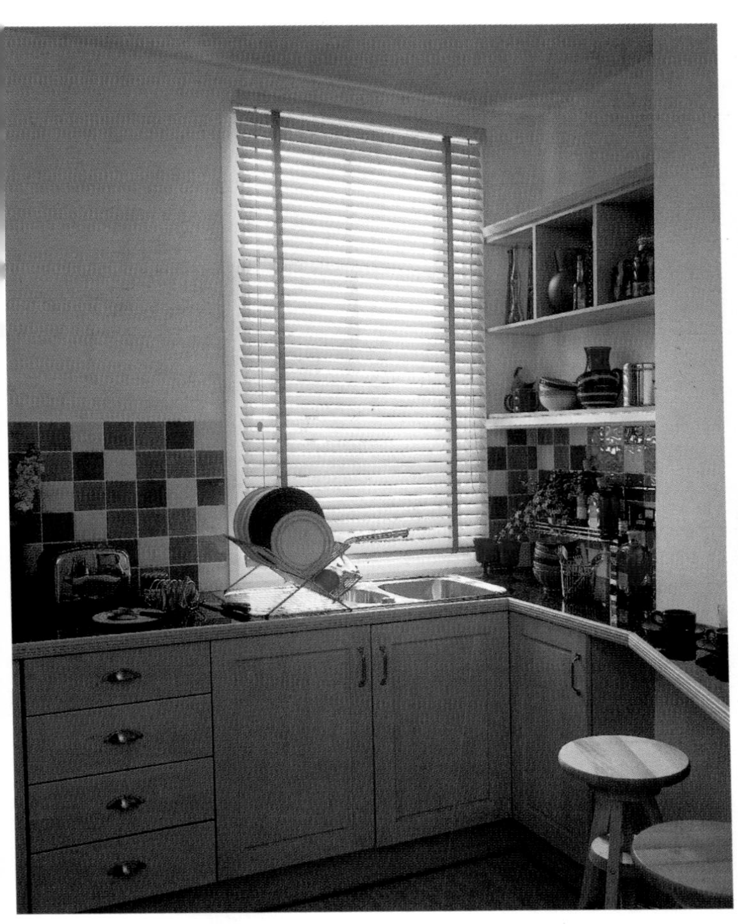

CONTEMPORARY CHIC (*above left*) Pale beech units with two different chrome handles and wood-edged laminated work surface extend around a converted chimney breast. Colourful blue and white tiles, randomly arranged, protect the walls from food splashes.

CLEAN LINES (*above right*) An inventive mix of materials including mosaic tiles, stainless steel and coloured laminate, plus wooden flooring, provide a softening effect in a scrupulously minimal kitchen. Open shelving acts as a room divider in an otherwise open space.

CLASSIC COLOUR (*left*) Blue and yellow are favourite colours for making a bright, inviting kitchen. The colour scheme extends to painted units and a blue-tiled worktop as well as complementary tones in the splashback and accessories.

Style: your personal choice (continued)

OPEN DISPLAY (*above left*) Custom-made open shelving is used here instead of units to make a virtue out of displaying china, food and cooking equipment.

GALLEY RUN (*above right*) A narrow run of units in a light and airy dining room provide a sink, food preparation and cooking space. Unobtrusive yet practical.

SHAKER RANGE (*left*) An Aga range is built into an adapted opening, providing a room divider and a view from a dining area into a neat selection of Shaker-inspired painted units. Utensils are suspended from the ceiling on a metal rail.

QUIRKY COUNTRY (*above left*)
A hugely inventive trompe l oeil cat and mouse design is applied to two cupboards for a unique touch. A versatile tall wall unit incorporates extractor fan, pots and pans and display storage as well as lighting.

MODERN RETRO (*above*)
A clean and contemporary arrangement of simple units fashioned from stone pillars and marble worktops creates an unfitted atmosphere, with the island unit housing the sink, storage space and doubling up as room divider.

INVISIBLE KITCHEN (*left*)
Hidden behind floor-to-ceiling pillars which are in fact cupboards, this discreet kitchen area uses wooden work surfaces that match the floor, and units that are colour-linked to the walls.

Space to eat in

In a small house or flat, the kitchen is often the main room for eating. Even if a house has a separate dining room, the kitchen is a handy place to eat at least some meals, particularly breakfast. When the family is in a rush, time is saved by getting the food straight from the cooker to the table, and back to the sink afterwards. Dirty plates and cooking utensils are limited to one room, rather than being spread over two. And the heat from the cooking helps to warm up the kitchen first thing on a winter's morning.

If space is limited, a small eating area may be created as part of the worktop layout, especially where the worktop is accessible from both sides. A peninsular unit can be provided with enough overhang on one side to allow knee room for people sitting on high stools or chairs. The other side is used for serving.

A small table top, which can be stowed away when not in use, can provide an eating area for two or three people. It can be designed to fold down against a wall or slide into a recess in a worktop base. Folding chairs or stackable stools can be stored under a worktop or in a cupboard when they are not being used.

Planning for comfort

In tiny kitchens convenience is the first priority, but in a larger kitchen where all meals are eaten, comfort should also be planned. If the kitchen is large enough, the eating and working areas can be separated by kitchen units which will act as a sideboard and serving counter. A 'ladder' of open shelves above the units can be used to keep decorative storage jars, and will make an even more definite divider between the two parts of the room.

The dining area can be given greater warmth with a rug or carpet on the floor, and a lamp suspended over the dining table. A dimmer switch fitted in the working area will make it unobtrusive when you are eating, and pictures and plants around the dining area will give a relaxed and friendly atmosphere.

TABLE TALK (*below*) A generously proportioned eating area is given its own distinction by means of a tiled patterned floor which complements quarry tiles in the kitchen area.

SPACE AT TABLE (*left above*) A knocked-through room houses a kitchen area at one end and a spacious dining table at the other. The flooring is tough vinyl which apes the styles of wooden boards.

MEDITERRANEAN EATING (*left below*) A long narrow kitchen incorporates a peninsular unit, painted cupboards and rustic tiles, together with a Provençal table setting to evoke a Mediterranean atmosphere.

POT STORE (*right*) A beam that marks the division between two former rooms is carefully disguised with a ceiling-mounted metal pole and dangling pots and pans. A tiled work surface echoes the floor tiles and blends in with the natural brickwork.

WHITE ELEGANCE (*left*) Simple units, stainless steel and beech floorboards make for a light and breezy room, where a peninsular unit provides the backdrop for a built-in seating area.

ISLAND LIFE (*above*) An interesting combination of breakfast bar, utility area, room divider and plant box shows the versatility of arranging units in the centre of a room. Every corner has been used to good effect.

Fitting the main equipment

Before designing a kitchen, a major choice lies between a combined cooker and a split-level oven and hob.

Combined cookers can be obtained in three different styles. A conventional free-standing cooker is not an integral part of the kitchen units. A flush-fitting (also called slip-in) cooker fits exactly into the space between two kitchen units so that food cannot fall in between. A built-in cooker is similar but is fitted into the kitchen units, so that the worktop surrounds the hob.

A split-level oven and hob give the convenience of an eye-level oven and the choice of either gas or electricity for each component. But having both oven and hob at working level takes up valuable space in a small kitchen. They also cost more than a combined cooker.

Some ovens incorporate the grill, so that the two cannot be used at the same time – a considerable disadvantage if you do a lot of cooking. However, double ovens are available, one incorporating the grill, and other models have a microwave oven as well.

Refrigerators, freezers and sinks

Refrigerators can be fitted beneath a worktop or built into a stack of kitchen cupboards. A panel that matches the kitchen units can be fitted to the refrigerator door, giving an unbroken surface of the same colour.

There are two types of freezer – chest and upright. Chest freezers are usually larger than upright models and are best installed in a garage or an outhouse. Upright freezers often fit below a work surface, but combined fridge-freezers are available which are much taller.

When buying a sink, consider if you have space for a double-bowl model which allows two jobs to be done at once. Make sure that one of the bowls is big enough to wash large saucepans and roasting tins.

Fitting the equipment

Most kitchen equipment can be fitted by the handyman, though gas connections must be done by an approved gas fitter – it is illegal to do it yourself.

Electric cookers or split-level electric ovens and hobs need a separate 30 or 45amp circuit taken from the consumer unit; they cannot be connected to the power circuit supplying socket outlets.

Washing machines and dishwashers also need to be connected to the plumbing system, a task made easier by using self-boring taps which can be fitted without turning off the water supply. A drain kit attached to the sink waste pipe is fitted in a similar way.

If a sink is to be fitted some distance away from the old position, the plumbing will need to be extended, but slight repositioning of taps can be carried out using flexible copper pipes.

COOKING RANGE (*left*) A redundant chimney breast is happily used to house the family range, a freestanding oven placed within a tiled recess. Display shelves have also been incorporated above the hearth.

FARMHOUSE UNITS (*below*) Dresser-like units flank a traditional farmhouse Aga in a cosy, informal kitchen where a stable door and wall-mounted shelves are also custom built.

MODERN SHAKER (*opposite below*) An Aga is included in a strictly fitted scheme, softening the sleek modern units which include an island work station and floor-standing larder cupboard.

For more information

Choosing kitchen taps	307
Fitting a waste pipe and trap	318
Fitting a lay-on sink	320
Fitting an inset sink	321
Plumbing-in a washing machine or dishwasher	342
Installing a fixed appliance	370
Installing an electric cooker circuit	375

TRADITIONAL SINK (*right*) A deep butler's sink fits neatly in a run of hand-built cupboards. Two-tone tiles and a wooden plate rack evoke the simplicity of a country larder.

OVERHEAD CUPBOARDS (*far right*) Classic tongue-and-groove panelling used as a splashback is an easy way to disguise uneven walls and blends well with simple Shaker-style wall units. A butler's sink rests on top of a cupboard and below a wooden work surface which has been cut away with a jigsaw.

Fitting in the main equipment (continued)

DOUBLE OVEN (*above*) Two ovens are better than one, especially when placed in a tower unit. Easy to use and safely out of reach of young children, this classical style model is also placed conveniently close to the kitchen sink.

HIGH MICROWAVE (*above right*) Building in a microwave above or below the main oven saves worktop space and makes it easy to transfer food from one form of cooker to another.

LOOSE ARRANGEMENT (*right*) An informal combination of fitted and freestanding units and appliances is both retro and contemporary in style. The worktops are placed in three different spaces rather than being run around the walls.

FRIDGE-FREEZER (*far left*) In a busy family kitchen, a generous-sized fridge combined with an adequate freezer has been integrated into the kitchen units.

HIDDEN LAUNDRY (*left*) Large appliances can be disguised by placing them behind a specially built or adapted cupboard door.

STORING DIRTY DISHES (*above*) Dishwashers are often integrated into a kitchen plan rather than left freestanding.

SIDE BY SIDE (*left*) When there is no room for tall units, small under-counter fridges and freezers may be built in under a worktop.

Creating good work surfaces

In a well-planned kitchen there should be three main work surfaces; one for food preparation and washing up, one for food mixing, and one for cooking.

Ideally, each area should have adjacent storage for items needed for each function – for example, the vegetable rack and refrigerator near the food-preparation area, and pots and pans above or below the cooking area.

A heatproof work surface is needed beside the cooker or hob. Cooker makers produce metal worktop inserts, but wood or cork mats can also be used.

Types of worktops

Most proprietary worktops are made of chipboard laminated with heat and scratch resistant materials such as melamine.

There are two standard thicknesses, $1\frac{3}{16}$ in (30mm) and $1\frac{1}{2}$ in (40mm) – though some manufacturers' sizes vary. The front edge can be square or round. The standard width is 24in (600mm), though other widths are available. Lengths range from 8in (200mm) to 13ft (4m).

In addition to the standard rectangular shapes, some specialist firms supply L-shaped worktops and even banjo-shaped worktops for peninsular units. Worktops can also be obtained with cut-outs for a sink or hob.

Lighting the kitchen

An even spread of light with no shadows is essential in a kitchen, and this is best achieved with fluorescent lamps. A centrally fitted lamp – the wattage will depend on the size of the kitchen – will give good general illumination, but may cast the shadow of anyone standing in front of a work surface. This can be overcome by fitting tubular fluorescent lights beneath the front edges of wall-mounted cupboards.

For more information

Tiling a work surface	145
Planning worktops for a kitchen	187
Filling gaps between kitchen units	188
Fitting a strip light under a shelf	394
Wiring a lighting circuit	395

CORIAN DRAINER (*above*) Tough, durable and elegant, this piece of Corian work surface has been grooved at each side of a butler's sink to provide drainage.

EXTRA SPACE (*far left*) In a busy kitchen, additional work space is provided by a traditional butcher's block.

WOOD FINISH (*left*) Rounded, thick beech worktops soften a run of painted units in a galley-style kitchen.

BRIGHT WHITE (*far left*)
Clean living is inevitable on this white laminate work surface with grey accents. It wipes clean and is a durable option.

RUSTIC PARLOUR (*left*)
A porcelain basin has been countersunk into a wooden surface in this cosy country kitchen.

CERAMIC BLUE (*above*)
Colour and practicality combine in this cheerful worktop which is edged with a thick lip of beech.

A place for everything

Cupboards fitted below worktops or mounted on walls will provide a generous amount of storage space, but they are not always practical in a small or awkwardly shaped kitchen. Sometimes there is insufficient room to fit more than one or two standard size wall cupboards, in which case shelving may be the only answer, or perhaps a combination of cupboards and shelving.

When choosing cupboards look for a rigid design, strong hinges and handles, and a tough surface finish that will not scratch easily. Shelving should be thick enough to support the weight of items placed on it without bowing. The kitchen needs to be kept clean so both cupboards and shelving should have easy-to-wipe surfaces. Coated or laminated chipboard can be bought in a range of lengths, widths and thicknesses, and needs no final finishing. Timber can be finished with polyurethane varnish or Danish oil.

Avoiding wasted space

In planning your kitchen you will have decided the best places for cupboards and shelving, but there will almost certainly be areas of wasted space, especially in corners where units meet at right angles and on walls where cupboards and shelving cannot be fitted. There are a number of ways of overcoming the problems. For example, corner cupboard doors can be fitted with semicircular baskets so that when the door is closed the baskets swing into the corner space. And wire mesh grids can be attached to a wall above a sink or cooker hob for hanging kitchen tools and small utensils.

Keeping things accessible

The contents of shelves and cupboards are not always easily accessible. Tins and packets of foodstuffs in particular may get pushed to the back and forgotten. Pull-out units with wire trays, pull-out larders and wire baskets fitted on the inside of cupboard doors are some of the ways in which storage space can be made more accessible and easier to organise.

Storing awkward items

Large items such as frying pans, colanders and preserving pans often will not fit easily, if at all, in a cupboard or on a shelf. A simple answer is to hang them on a rail fitted somewhere they can be reached easily but will not obstruct a working area. Brass curtain rails or shower curtain rails are easily adaptable for the purpose.

Keeping perishable food

A larder or a ventilated cupboard is ideal for storing fresh fruit and vegetables, cheese, eggs and preserves. It needs to be cool so it should be built against a north-facing wall to avoid direct sun.

A larder should have an open window covered with wire mesh to keep out flies. A cupboard can be ventilated by fitting an airbrick in the wall.

UTENSIL RACK (*left*)
A deep metal rail is shaped to fit underneath cupboard units and above the sink in a recessed splashback. The utensils are suspended from butcher's hooks for easy access.

SHOP FITTING (*below*)
A bank of old shop drawers is given a new role in a kitchen, surmounted by a modern work surface. The original label holders on the drawer fronts can be used to indicate the new contents.

For more information

Fixing things to tiles	145
Choosing timber	148-150
Choosing man-made board	151
Sanding and finishing timber	167-168
How to make shelves	169-180
How to make cupboards	181-188
Installing an airbrick	236
Choosing curtain rails	404

HANGING RACK (*above left*) An ingenious combination of plate rack, utensil storage and pot shelf, this small handmade wooden rack slots neatly onto a sloping ceiling by means of heavy-duty screws.

WOOD AND STONE (*above right*) Neat open storage in the form of a dresser, a ceiling-mounted hanging rack and wall shelves make an attractive display in a quarry-tiled kitchen.

FULL LARDER (*left*) A contemporary update of a classic food store, this larder cupboard door incorporates a wire mesh panel to both air and view the contents.

A place for everything (continued)

INTEGRAL LARDER (*above left*) A purpose-built food cupboard is fitted out with wire shelving to store different-sized bottles, jars and cans, as well as space for recycling bottles and newspapers at the bottom.

BUDGET SHELVING (*above right*) An economical shelving system has been incorporated into a basic kitchen arrangement to provide storage and display space.

RECLAIMED CUPBOARDS (*right above*) Simple reclaimed floorboards are subtly distressed and transformed into cupboard fronts and shelves in this rustic kitchen.

GLASS LIGHTING (*right below*) Halogen spotlights in the top of a built-in wall unit throw pleasing pools of light onto glassware stored on adjustable glass shelves.

DIY DRESSER (*far right*) By resting a glass-fronted cupboard on top of a simple pot table a dresser effect is instantly achieved in a contained space.

BASKET DRAWERS (*left*) A carefully constructed apothecary-style dresser includes a variety of large baskets for storing fresh fruit and vegetables in the dark, while allowing air to circulate.

CUTLERY STORE (*below left*) Integral cutlery drawers, one sliding over the other are a sensible solution when there is a shortage of drawer space.

OPEN STORAGE (*below right*) Deep shelves are constructed under a hob to house all manner of kitchen paraphernalia. Similar shelves on each side of the chimney breast serve the same purpose.

A place for everything (continued)

GREEN ON WOOD (*above*)
A tartan-etched glass panel in a wall unit hides any unruly contents while cups can be stored on hooks underneath.

CLEAR VIEW (*far left*) Ingenious see-through shelving can be accessed from both sides of this kitchen counter.

POTS AND PANS (*left*) A carousel fitted into a corner unit is invaluable for maximising the available space.

FROSTED GLASS (*opposite*) Sleek lines abound in this counter-to-ceiling cupboard with frosted glass fronts. The units form a V-shape to provide a worktop that allows two people to use it at the same time.

Living areas

Creating a style with colour and furnishings

The character of a living room depends on the relationship between its size and the way it is decorated and furnished. Large rooms with big windows and high ceilings, such as are found in many Victorian and Edwardian houses, can take larger furniture, strong colours and dramatic swathes of curtains. They may even need them to stop people rattling around.

In contrast, the smaller rooms and low ceilings of a terraced house or a modern 'semi' can be made to feel more spacious by decorating in pale colours and scaling the furniture to be in keeping with the space available.

It is possible to change the structure of the room by taking out a fireplace, replacing old windows or removing a dividing wall to make one room out of two. But the personality and taste of the people who use it are reflected most strongly in the way the room is furnished and decorated. A living room has to serve several functions; it is a place to watch television, listen to the radio or the hi-fi, read, entertain friends and, in some cases, eat dinner.

Above all, it is a place to relax in, and so its essential quality is comfort – not only in the choice of chairs, settees and side tables, but also in the decoration, the carpets, the rugs and the curtains on the windows.

Colours play an important part in the comfort of a room, and they can be used in various ways. Bright colours will bring cheer to a room with little natural light; pastel shades will soften the harshness of a large, angular room. Contrasts, too, can be used to good effect; in a room with rich coloured furnishings, a paler shade of the same colour, or a neutral colour, will make the furniture stand out boldly rather than merge with the decor.

If part of the room is to be used as a dining area, try to make it partly separate from the rest of the room, perhaps by the use of a folding screen, a room divider or a trough of tall-growing house plants.

Lighting the room

When decorating the room, remember that colours look different in the evening under electric light than they do in daylight. A normal filament bulb makes red and yellow walls and furnishings appear brighter, and green and blue objects look darker.

In a living room, a single light from an overhead fitting is likely to make the room appear flat and uninteresting. It always helps to add more lighting at different points of the room to create highlights and shadows, and to direct light where it is most needed – for reading or sewing, for example.

For general lighting, allow 2 watts per square foot (20 watts per square metre) of floor space if you are using filament lamps. So for a room of 180 square feet (17 square metres) use lamps totalling 360 watts for overall lighting, plus lamps for close work.

DRAWING ROOM (*left*) In a traditional front room one alcove has an integral glass-fronted bookcase and cupboard while the other is home to the family piano.

For more information

SIMPLY BRIGHT (*above*) Neutral walls and a recessed fireplace provide a simple backdrop for brightly coloured sofas and cushions, a practical tiled floor and unfussy wooden Venetian blinds.

TIMBERED ELEGANCE (*left*) A classic country living room boasts a brass fender, upholstered window seat and tailored pelmet and curtains for a comfortable atmosphere.

Creating a style with colour and furnishings (continued)

PERIOD COLOUR (*above*) A sense of the contemporary is evident in this period living room, where a uniform colour is applied to walls, fireplace and cupboards. A striking mirror is placed above the fireplace to enlarge the room.

FLORAL CHINTZ (*left*) A dramatic wallpaper border and imposing fringed pelmet and curtains give definition to this Victorian-style living room.

BOOK STORE (*right*) Painted original plasterwork is the backdrop for tailor-made bookcases in this welcoming beamed sitting room. Further comfort is provided with a generous quantity of cushions.

WICKERWORK (*left*) This leafy outdoor room combines Scandinavian elegance in the form of formal wallpaper and candle sconces with quintessential country style: white wicker furniture and rustic wooden floorboards.

The fireplace as a focal point

The old-fashioned open fire may not be very good for heating a room – but there is nothing better for making a place look cheerful. Many people keep a fireplace just for cosy evenings at home, while relying on central heating for overall background warmth.

Some modern houses have been built without fireplaces, but the tradition of the fire as a focus of family life is so strong that many people are putting new ones in. Others are installing freestanding stoves of the continental type, with a duct instead of a chimney to carry away the smoke.

If you have a fireplace, there are a number of efficient substitutes for the old-fashioned open fire which offer a compromise between tradition and convenience. There are controlled-draught, slow-burning fires with easy-to-clean ash pits, enclosed stoves that fit into the fireplace, and gas or electric fires. Some of the gas models offer realistic simulations of open fires, with flames leaping from 'coal' or 'logs'. Most fires, except electric, can be used to provide hot water and to heat radiators.

If any of these appliances are being fitted into an existing fireplace, it may be necessary to remove the surround or alter the cavity.

Alternatively, an old fireplace can be removed altogether and the space used to display an attractive object such as a bowl of flowers or a statuette. A strip light concealed in the opening would enhance the effect and – even without the fire – the fireplace remains the focal point of the room.

For more information

Removing an old fire surround	257
Removing a raised hearth	258
Sealing off a fireplace	258
Creating a wall recess	258

VICTORIAN FORMALITY (*above*) A traditional wood surround frames pictorial tiles and a cast-iron grate. The original hearth is replaced with bricks and each alcove is enclosed by a shelving and storage unit.

ORNATE GRATE (*far left*) A cast-iron fireplace surround comprises ornate moulded decoration echoed in highly decorative tilework.

WOODBURNING STOVE (*left*) A cast-iron stove fits snugly in a brick fireplace surrounded by a stencilled diamond wall decoration.

SWEDISH FIRE (*above*) Nestling in the corner of a sizeable entranceway, this ledged fireplace is both focal point and welcoming feature.

SMALL INGLENOOK (*far left*) A compact wood-burning stove juts out from a charming original cottage inglenook fireplace.

PAINTED SURROUND (*left*) Gently colourwashed walls provide a framework for a painted and gilded fireplace surround in deep burgundy, highlighted with burnished gold paint.

Deciding on the window dressing

Curtains can transform a window into one of the main features of the living room. They will not only improve the shape of the window, but the colour and texture of the fabric can be major elements of the room's decor.

The shape of the window can be either enhanced or disguised by curtains. The slender outline of a sash window in a tall room is emphasised by floor-to-ceiling curtains topped by a deep-pleated heading.

A window at the narrow end of a room can be made to look wider by hanging the curtains to sill level only, and making the track wide enough for the curtains to hang clear of the glass when they are open.

Curved windows increase the space inside a room, so do not reduce the effect by hanging curtains directly from one side to the other. Fit flexible track following the curve.

Two windows of different sizes on the same wall can be covered by one sweep of curtain, covering the windows and the wall in between, and uniting them into a single feature.

The elegant curve of an arched window could – if there is no need for privacy – be left uncurtained, as an architectural feature.

Blinds: attractive alternative

Blinds are attractive alternatives to curtains, with several variations in style. Roller blinds have an appealing simplicity and allow maximum light to enter the room. Roman, festoon and vertical louvred blinds can each play a part in creating a particular style of room.

STRIPED SWAG (*left*) This graduated pelmet shows restrained elegance in a traditional room. Generous tie-backs in a plain colour complement the wide striped fabric and provide a colour reference which is also found in the antique armchair.

GARDEN VIEW (*below left*) Simple French windows are made more interesting by the addition of gingham curtains and swag.

METAL SYMMETRY (*below right*) A curled metal curtain pole defines the window space in a recess which includes a seat and bolsters. The curtains have tab headings embellished with hand-tied bows.

For more information

The right curtains for your windows	403
Choosing the style of heading	404
Making your own curtains	410-424
Pelmets, tie-backs and valances	419-422
Making curtains without sewing	422
How to make blinds	424-427

COMPREHENSIVE BLINDS (*left*) Tall, floor-to-ceiling Venetian blinds give uncluttered elegance to shuttered windows in a period room which is furnished in the comtemporary manner.

TIED BACK (*below left*) Voluminous chintz curtains are secured on each side of a recess with a thick tasselled tie-back looped behind a large brass hold-back. Distressed paintwork in lemon yellow blends nicely with the curtains.

COLOURFUL CURTAINS (*above*) A blue pelmet and side curtains make a dramatic, sophisticated statement when combined with satin-style inner curtains.

ARCHED FESTOON (*below right*) Curved windows are often difficult to dress, but here a shaped festoon blind has been created to fill the space exactly, providing a touch of elegance during the day or at night.

Deciding on the window dressing (continued)

BAY BLINDS (*top*) Bay windows lend themselves well to a series of blinds. Here transparent muslin is made up into tie blinds to good effect.

CAFE BLIND (*above left*) This cafe-style edging enables the blind to be pulled down right along the bottom edge rather than by a central pull. A brass rod is threaded through fabric which doubles back on itself.

BLIND IDEA (*above right*) Blind kits enable you to make your blinds using the fabric and finish of your choice. Here scalloped edges soften the effect of neutral colours.

METAL DEFINITION (*above*) A simple cast-iron curtain rail has been moulded to fit a shallow bay. Pencil-pleat curtains are suspended on rings whose visibility adds to the appeal.

GARLAND VIEW (*left*) Generous folds of yellow curtains are kept neatly in place with a painted pelmet adorned with classical garlands. The motifs are echoed with a trained ivy on the windowsill.

LOOSELY FORMAL (*opposite*) Delicate cream curtains with tab tops on a metal curtain pole are held up in soft drapes by a rope tie back to give a glimpse of bright sunflowers on the windowsill.

Ideas for storage and shelving

Everyone in the family uses the living room, putting extra demands on the available storage and display space. The best way to work out how much shelving and storage you will need and where it should be placed is to make a list of items, not forgetting to allow for future additions, and to put them in three categories: items frequently used; items used only occasionally; and objects which are purely decorative.

From that list you can then decide which items should be stored in cupboards or drawers and which should be on open shelving. For example, if the living room has a dining area you will need drawers for cutlery and cupboards or shelves for crockery. You may also want a drinks cupboard, but if a set of decanters and glasses are worth displaying they could go on open shelving where they will be both decorative and convenient.

Books, also, can be decorative if they are arranged neatly on shelves or in a bookcase, but valuable books are best kept in a glass-fronted cupboard to protect them from dust.

In addition, most living rooms need surfaces for television, video and hi-fi systems or radio. Since the backs of the electrical equipment are unsightly they are best placed close to a wall or in a semi-enclosed recess, but make sure that there is adequate ventilation to prevent them from overheating. Records, cassettes and CDs should be stored away from any heat source, but near the playing equipment.

Buying storage units

Furniture manufacturers offer a good range of freestanding storage units, often compactly designed with combinations of open and glass-fronted shelves, drinks cupboard, record storage compartment and drawers. Freestanding units have the advantage that they can be moved if you wish to rearrange the room.

Units are widely available in kit form for assembly at home. Before buying, make sure that you see the unit assembled in the shop, and when you get it home check that none of the pieces are missing and that nothing is damaged.

If a room has alcoves – perhaps either side of a chimney breast or a built-in cupboard – they can be adapted for shelving or tailor-made storage units. Shelves can be permanently fixed on supporting battens, or they can be mounted on adjustable track. The choice of shelving material will depend on the items to be stored – glassware, for example, looks particularly well on glass shelves – but the shelves must be thick enough to support the weight without bowing or breaking.

For more information

FOSSIL CHIC (*below*) An impressive collection of geological finds is beautifully displayed on delicate glass shelves within an all-white alcove. The metal shelf supports protrude from the wall to provide a resting place for each shelf.

DOUBLE VISION (*above*) A whole wall of shelving is supplemented with an extra bookcase on castors which glides along the main shelves on aluminium runners.

RECESSED DISPLAY (*right*) Alcoves are the obvious place for storage and display. Here a simple timber framework houses slim shelves that are lip-edged for neatness.

CHROME TOWER (*far right*) A freestanding unit on castors provides a versatile place for safeguarding precious oversized books and breakables. The same unit can be used for hi-fi or even a television when space is at a premium.

Ideas for storage and shelving (continued)

STORAGE UNIT (*above*)
Custom-made for the room, this ingenious unit houses the hi-fi, television, tapes and CDs as well as some books. The television sits on an extending bracket which folds back behind wooden doors when not in use.

GLASS ON GLASS (*right*)
An old glass-fronted cabinet has been repainted, fitted with glass shelves and lit from inside to display glasses and crockery.

COSY CORNER (*far right*)
In a tight corner, small triangular shelves make an engaging space for displaying precious china. They are secured with small wooden supports.

GEORGIAN ELEGANCE (*above*) In a welcoming period living room traditional colour has been applied to woodwork on and around the fireplace so that the alcove shelves become integral to the panelled effect often found in homes of this era.

SPACE MAKER (*far left*) Shelves that fit perfectly in an awkward place have a satisfying symmetry of their own.

INVISIBLE SUPPORT (*left*) Glass shelves appear to emerge seamlessly from a wall to highlight a delicate display of glassware. They are supported by flat metal brackets, driven into a solid wall.

Ideas for storage and shelving (continued)

CHIC LAMINATE (*above*)
A stylish unit comprising coloured laminate-faced board and integral lighting is both furniture and decorative object, housing a collection of large books in a simply decorated space.

BOOK STORE (*left*)
For a large number of books, the best solution can often be to devote a whole wall to them, making a feature of the display. Painted wood or MDF (medium-density fibreboard) are strong and durable materials to use.

WALL SPACE (*opposite*)
A combination of closed cupboards, open shelves and television swivel shelf makes for practicality and efficiency on a subtle scale.

Ideas for storage and shelving (continued)

RESTRAINED ELEGANCE (*left*) Built-in units beside a fireplace with panelled cupboards and display shelves fall short of the ceiling to make way for more display space.

SMALL DISPLAY (*right*) A bookcase backed with tongue-and-groove panelling instantly evokes the country.

GLASS SUSPENSION (*left*) Tensioned wire has been drilled into the floor and ceiling and through glass shelves to form a floating display area for a collection of china.

LIBRARY LOOK (*below*) In a room dominated by books, an area has been devoted to displaying objects in glass fronted, internally lit cupboards. Elsewhere, open shelves also house a television and storage boxes.

Bathrooms

Function and style

PULL-OUT CUPBOARD (*below*) This unit is similar to a pull-out kitchen larder, except that it comprises shelves instead of wire baskets. It is large enough to hold most things you need in a bathroom.

The bathroom is a difficult room to plan imaginatively. It has to contain at least two major items, the bath and washbasin, probably a wc and perhaps a shower and bidet. And the siting of all these is governed by the plumbing and waste pipes. There must also be necessary fitments such as towel rails, mirrors, wall cabinets and shelving. And the space available is usually less than in the kitchen.

As all the plumbed-in fittings will be permanent fixtures, they need to be chosen to look well for a long time. Fancy shapes and fashionable colours may be in vogue when they are chosen but can look very outdated after a few years.

But do consider what modern developments will make a useful contribution to the room. Many baths, basins and toilets incorporate space-saving and useful refinements. There are wall-hung basins, close-coupled wc suites, and baths with grab handles and taps at the side instead of the end. Complete shower cabinets can be bought to fit in a corner – or in a small space in a different part of the house. Alternatively, a shower cubicle can be built over a shower tray, surrounded by a curtain hung from a rail.

As with the fittings, permanent wall finishes such as tiles and decorative wallboards are likely to be part of the room for some years. So in choosing them try to forecast how long they will be visually pleasing. If you want to do something unusual, striking effects can be obtained with paint or wallpaper, which can be changed easily once you tire of the idea.

In a small bathroom, shelves and a small mirrored wall cabinet should be sufficient for cosmetics, shaving tackle and toothbrushes, with a large rail for bath towels and a smaller one, or a ring, for hand towels. For a large room, wall cabinets are available that will hold all the bathroom requirements, including towels, as well as being fitted with a mirror, strip light and shaver socket.

A vanity unit, perhaps with the luxury of two hand basins, will hide unsightly pipework and provide a cupboard for storing bathroom cleaning materials.

For more information

Ceramic tiling on walls	139-146
Fixing things to ceramic tiles	145
Making shelves of all types	169-180
Making cupboards	181-186
Hanging a mirror	235
Fitting decorative wallboards	251
Laying vinyl or cork floor tiles	279
Laying ceramic floor tiles	281
Laying sheet vinyl	283-285
Choosing bathroom taps	307
Installing a washbasin, bidet, bath and shower	323-330

TILE STYLE (*far left*) Shimmering blue floor tiles are a cheerful addition to a part-tiled bathroom with a neat vanity storage unit.

RUSTIC PANELLING (*left*) In a colour-coordinated bathroom a narrow, awkward space has been adapted with panelling to provide storage space as well as the usual fixtures and fittings.

EAVES BATHING (*below*) A small eaves corner includes an unobtrusive bath within a run of painted tongue-and-groove panelling which conceals pipework.

Function and style (continued)

TILED BATHROOM (*above left*) A loft space has been completely tiled in white, including a half-wall to divide up the space and echo the shape of the bath. Practical, clean and different.

STAGE MANAGED (*above right*) With all fittings built in to provide plenty of storage, a corner bath is slotted into the remaining space by means of a stepped plinth.

HEAT AND LIGHT (*right*) Bold, coloured tiles, a heated chrome towel rail and eminently practical linoleum flooring are cheerful yet functional companions in a modern bathroom.

VANITY UNIT (*above left*)
Traditional units that include a sink and surround can store cleaning materials, towels and bath toys.

CORNER SHOWER (*above right*) An unobtrusive shower has doors that slide back from one corner so that the space on each side of the unit can be fully exploited.

COOL BLUE (*left*)
A Mediterranean feel is achieved by using blue tiles and painting specially fitted window shutters, bath panelling and a built-in cupboard.

DISCREET CHARM (*below*)
Understated bathroom fittings slip happily into this country cottage by means of a tiled support structure finished with a wooden shelf.

Function and style (continued)

SHOWER TIME (*opposite*) When there is insufficient space for a shower cubicle as well as a bath, a shower above the bath is a good compromise. Curtains prevent water splashes.

VICTORIAN SPLENDOUR (*above right*) If space exists, traditional fittings can become decorative as well as practical. An armchair is a luxurious addition if bathing with company.

CAST IRON (*right*) Metal curtain poles and shelving are easy care options in a bathroom and can be echoed with metal accessories. A stencilled border of leaves softens the black found elsewhere in the room.

Bedrooms

What style for such a personal room?

Choosing the style of a bedroom gives more scope for indulging your ideas than any other room in the house. This is a room used almost exclusively by the people who sleep there, so it can fully reflect their personal tastes, however simple or outlandish they may be. Different bedrooms in the same house may convey totally different personalities without detracting from any overall theme in the other rooms.

A bedroom has more functions than just for sleeping – it can be a refuge from the rest of the family, a work place for adults, a study room for teenagers and a playroom for children.

Whatever style you choose, you will have to live with it at both ends of the day when moods can be very different. So ask yourself if you are creating a room you will be able to face first thing on a winter's morning.

Begin by planning the layout, with wardrobe, dressing table and chest of drawers placed where they are most convenient, and a work or play area blended in with the conventional bedroom furniture.

The bed sets the theme for the rest of the room, be it a modern divan or an ornate four-poster, and so too do the pattern and colours of the bedding. If you decide on an historical style, such as Regency or Victorian, a four-poster or a brass bedstead will establish the mood. Both types of bed are made by modern manufacturers. There is no need to follow the theme to uncomfortable extremes – a modern sprung mattress and duvet can be fitted to a traditional bed.

For a modern look, select plain furniture and let patterns and colours provide highlights. Duvet covers are available in a wide range of designs including stripes, patchwork and floral. And the pattern of the bedcovering can be repeated in the curtains and even in the wallpaper. Alternatively, combine strongly patterned furnishings with pastel shades or small-patterned paper on the walls.

There is no reason why styles should not be mixed. A stripped pine dressing table or chest of drawers can look as well in a modern setting as in a period one.

While furnishings and decor create a room's mood, it is the smaller and personal items that provide the finishing touches. In a bedroom, you can display favourite possessions, such as decorative hairbrushes, a pretty hand mirror or an inlaid jewellery box.

Hang old prints, watercolours and photographs in a room with a Victorian or Edwardian theme. In a modern room plain walls often go better with plain furniture, but a few pictures that pick up the main colour of the decor can provide interesting highlights.

ROMANTIC BED (*left*) A wrought-iron bedhead is further defined with a wall-mounted fabric hanging secured with rings. It can be easily removed for washing.

FRENCH COUNTRY (*above left*)
In an evocation of French country style, fabric and wallpaper are as one. The wallpaper is applied to built-in cupboard doors in a continuation of the curtains to give the impression of a wall rather than a storage area.

CURTAIN SCREEN (*above right*)
Temporarily dividing off an area of a bedroom or guest room means you can hide away a sleeping zone during the day. Curtains can be formal as here, or simple muslin for a more casual look.

TRAVELLER'S TALE (*left*)
Journeys can inspire an ethnic approach to surroundings. This combination of earth colours and primitive fabrics transports and relaxes at the same time.

What style for such a personal room? (continued)

FITTED ELEGANCE (*above*) The panelled wardrobe doors and integral recessed ceiling lights are sleek additions to this blue and cream bedroom. The bedhead is immersed in an alcove that provides light and storage space, doing away with a need for bedside tables.

ARCHITECTURAL MOULDING (*right*) This wardrobe-cum-cupboard has the advantage of being portable while retaining the feel of a built-in unit. The curtain behind the glass can be replaced from time to time to ring the changes in a room.

NATURAL LIGHT (*left*) Neutral tones and natural wood create a peaceful harmony of colour and materials in this Shaker-inspired bedroom. A charming four-poster bed can be draped simply or dramatically according to mood.

HEALTHY SLEEP (*below*) Wooden floorboards can be stripped and varnished in a weekend and are a healthy, dust-free alternative to carpet. Closed storage and simple window treatments are also helpful for asthma sufferers.

UNDERSTATED CHIC (*bottom*) A simple iron bedhead can be softened with a variety of pillows and cushions. Matching bedside tables, lamps, and even pictures, produce perfect symmetry in an ordered environment.

CLASSIC STRIPES (*above*) Regency-style wallpaper is echoed in the stripes of a period sofa. Curtains are kept plain, as is the bedspread, to provide visual relief.

ECLECTIC PELMET (*right*) An ornate gilded picture frame has been salvaged and converted into a delightful pelmet for simple cotton drapes in a small bedroom.

COTTAGE CHARM (*opposite*) Country style is often loosely coordinated. Here handmade patchwork sits happily against a neatly tailored upholstered bedhead. A matching curtain hides clutter in an alcove.

What style for such a personal room? (continued)

SOFT COLOUR (*top left*) Different tones of the same colour produce a pleasing warmth when used on walls and fabric.

WINDOW SOLUTION (*above*) When windows are positioned in a confined space, curtain rods on hinged brackets can be swung open to let in the light.

SMALL STORAGE (*top right*) A cupboard, wall shelves and alcove are used to good effect and are finished off with blue-and-white accessories.

MELLOW YELLOW (*right*) Carefully colour-washed walls and soft ochres and oranges combine to make a sunny, restful bedroom. Curtains of crushed silk and muslin are merely clipped onto a metal pole.

FLORAL THEME (*above*) Blue-on-white floral motifs on bedhead and curtains are echoed in botanical prints hung on the wall and delicate floral embroidery on the bedcover.

RESTFUL CORNER (*left*) Coordinating the colour and theme of the soft furnishings in a tiny room creates a comfortable atmosphere. Any round table can be enhanced by draping it with fabric.

Fitting in shelves and wardrobes

You may need storage in a bedroom for books, television, radio, cosmetics or knick-knacks – but the greatest amount of space will be for clothes. Fitted wardrobes are best as they can be designed for your needs and to the shape of the room, often making use of otherwise wasted space.

A fitted wardrobe can be built from floor to ceiling along the entire length of one wall, or it can be built into a recess. The space can then be divided into compartments for hanging, shelving, drawers, shoe racks, and space for blankets and suitcases.

Self-assembly fitted wardrobes can be bought cheaply, but one built to your own design can be tailor-made to your exact requirements.

First calculate how much space you need, remembering to make allowance for the future. Generally, a man will need a hanging rail of about 3ft 6in (1.1m), and a woman about 5ft 6in (1.6m). Jackets, shirts and skirts need a hanging depth of about 3ft 3in (1m), dresses and overcoats about 4ft 6in (1.4m). Suspend the hanging rails at a convenient height, say 5ft 6in (1.7m), and about 1ft (300mm) from the back of the unit. The unit needs to be about 2ft (610mm) deep from front to back.

Avoid building fitted wardrobes against an outside wall. If damp should begin to penetrate the wall because of some external problem, such as damaged guttering, it may be some time before you notice it.

Make sure that the door you choose is suitable for the space in front of the unit. Hinged doors are fairly easy to fit and give maximum access, but there must be enough space for them to open fully. Sliding doors overcome the space problem, but are less convenient as only half the unit is accessible at a time. Another idea is to fit roller blinds which can be raised to uncover part or all of each section. Curtains can be used in a similar way. Or the wardrobe could be left without any doors at all – dust is not a particular problem in modern houses.

Many proprietary wardrobe units come with a matching range of other furniture, such as dressing tables and chests of drawers. If you are building your own wardrobe to a simple design, a few old pieces of furniture may go well with it. Some can have a dual purpose, such as a trunk for storing bed linen which also serves as a seat; a bedside table for lamp and clock can also have drawers for small personal items.

Open shelving is the simplest form of storage space in any room, and in the bedroom its best use is for books, a portable television, radio, plants, photographs and the other odds and ends that give the room character.

Recesses too small for a wardrobe make good shelving space. And a disused fireplace can be removed to open up an aperture where shelves can be mounted on battens or on bricks.

For more information

Woodworking techniques	148-168
Shelf brackets in an alcove	169
Track shelving systems	172-173
Glass shelves	174
Tailor-made shelves	176-177
Making cupboards	181
Fitting doors to cupboards	182-185
Fitting drawers to cupboards	186

BEAMED UP (*above*) A timber beam provides a graphic heading for a curtained clothes store. A metal hanging rail is screwed to the wall and floor space is used for keeping shoes and other accessories tidy.

CLOSED DOOR (*left*) Original timber has been used in conjunction with a new door to construct a deep and generous wardrobe in an alcove.The bare wood complements the wooden floor and pine bed.

WICKER WARDROBE (*opposite*) A pleasing combination of hanging rails and runs of wicker baskets mean that shirts, dresses and shoes as well as sweaters and underwear can all be neatly accommodated.

Children's rooms

A place to play

SLEEPING BAY (*below*) A platform bed protrudes from a built-in unit which is at once bedhead, cupboard and bedside table. Deep drawers below the bed accommodate clothes and spare bedding.

In designing a child's bedroom one important factor overrides all others – children grow up rapidly. The furniture, decor and storage space that was adequate one year becomes outgrown, outmoded or inappropriate the next.

The room itself takes on new functions as the years go by. It starts as a playroom, but later becomes a place for doing homework, entertaining friends, playing pop music and perhaps mastering a home computer. The design, therefore, should be flexible, with furniture, shelves and worktops that can be easily extended, converted or discarded as time goes by. In the early days, keep the decor simple and easy to change as it may quickly become damaged or dirty. As soon as they are able, the children can have a say in choosing their own style – and eventually do their own decorating.

It is essential to look well ahead when deciding on the size and type of bed for a child. For two or more children sharing a room, bunk beds save space and should last until the children have separate rooms, when they can be split up into two singles.

Finding space for clothes, books and toys

Storage space is always a problem in a child's bedroom. Space has to be found for clothes, books and toys – which all accumulate rapidly as the child grows up. A simply constructed wardrobe should cope with most storage problems, especially if it has plenty of adjustable shelving which can be rearranged as the needs arise. For example, young children, particularly boys, need little hanging space for clothes, but when dresses, jackets and blouses become part of their wardrobe the shelves can be removed and a hanging rail fitted. Plastic trays and wire baskets are excellent for storing small items of clothing and toys. They can stand on lower shelves or be fitted on runners beneath the shelves.

Additional shelving can be arranged around the walls of the room, fitted on adjustable brackets so that the height can be increased as the child grows taller.

A long work surface will serve changing interests, from crayoning and painting to model-making, homework and electronic games. Plastic laminated kitchen worktops, hard-wearing and easy to clean, are perfect for this purpose, and can be bought at DIY stores.

The floor covering, too, should be chosen carefully. A tough, washable carpet will withstand the wear and tear, but makes a poor surface for push-along cars, whereas vinyl or cork flooring is easy to keep clean, makes a good base for model train sets and racetracks, and can be covered with rugs or carpeting when the time comes to put away childish things.

For more information

Painting a room	115-123
Hanging wallpaper	126-138
Woodwork techniques	148-168
Making shelves	169-180
Shelves from slotted steel angle	178
Laying vinyl or cork flooring tiles	279
Laying sheet vinyl flooring	283-285

PAINTED STORAGE (*left above*)
Junk-shop finds or unappealing furniture can be revived beyond recognition by painting, then applying stencils or decoupaged motifs to the surface.

FANTASY WIGWAM (*left below*)
Dramatic colourwashes and bed drapes fashioned from a tilted teepee make an enclosed retreat. Deep storage drawers are slotted under the bed and a floor-to-ceiling wardrobe holds toys and clothes.

NURSERY ROOM (*above*)
A bold fabric at the window and colourful walls produce an interesting view for a baby. Changing facilities are incorporated into a traditional bookcase adapted for use as a towel and nappy store.

CORNER STORE (*below*)
Shelves built into a corner are deep enough to be used as a writing place. Curtains fixed on with cup hooks mean that clothes and toys can be stored tidily.

A place to play (continued)

GIRL'S ROOM (*top*) A bed tucked neatly into an alcove can be curtained off when homework or playing are going on. Freestanding open shelves and a wicker basket hold clutter, and draped fabric at the window echoes the bed curtain.

BOY'S ROOM (*above*) Zen-like simplicity is complemented with streetwise artworks on a wall-hung canvas and on fabric used as a wardrobe front. The mix of calm and chaos is an interesting one in an understated multilevel bedroom.

TWIN CAPACITY (*right*) Two indentical raised bed units placed end to end are multi-functional and very economical with space. The rest of the room can be given over to serious playing.

BUNKED DOWN (*above left*) Built-in bunks include a deep drawer on castors, together with a walk-in wardrobe and wall space for coat hooks, a mirror and sports equipment. Neat and functional.

HEARTH STORE (*above right*) A disused fireplace is used for storage, while the mantelpiece houses toys. When the child is older the fireplace can be reclaimed once again.

PINBOARD DISPLAY (*left*) A huge wall-mounted cork pinboard is both practical and decorative. It can be painted or left plain and is easily removed when necessary.

RACE TRACK (*below*) This pair of bunk beds has a pull-out bottom section which can be fitted with a model racetrack.

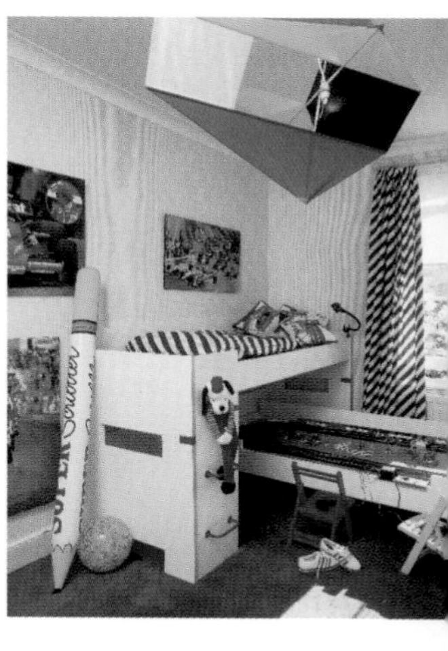

Halls and stairs

Passageways with panache

CERAMIC AND WOOD (*below*) Sturdy and colourful ceramic tiles provide a cheerful welcome in an open hallway that leads directly to the stairs and the kitchen. A wooden chest of drawers echoes the ceiling beams.

The entrance hall gives the first impression of a house as people come through the front door, so it should be warm and welcoming. As space is limited it needs only to be sparsely but practically furnished – a table and coat stand are the only essential items. And because the hall is the main thoroughfare of the house, and possibly the only escape route in case of fire, it should be left clear of clutter. In a narrow hallway, space can be saved by fixing coat hooks to a wall and having a shelf instead of a table.

Most hallways tend to be dark, but the amount of natural light can be increased by fitting a door with glass panels. Glass in a front door can reduce security, but the risk of a break-in will be minimised by fitting a lock that can be opened only with a key from either side, or by glazing the door with safety glass. Preferably use laminated glass which has a plastic interlayer, making it very difficult to break.

Flooring for the hall

Flooring should be hard-wearing and easy to clean. Ceramic tiles, wood mosaic or vinyl are ideal, but if you prefer carpeting choose a heavy-duty grade. Remember that you will probably want to continue it up the stairs and onto the landing, which could be expensive.

Wall decoration and paintwork will also usually need to be the same for the hall, stairway and landing as there is seldom a clearly defined dividing line between them. Emulsion paint in warm colours is the best choice for walls. Apart from the difficulty in papering a stairway, wallpaper can suffer permanent damage from knocks, whereas damaged paintwork can easily be touched in. And wallpaper is quickly dirtied by children running their hands down the stairway wall, which they frequently do if it is fitted with a dado rail.

Depending on the available space, try to add interest to your hall and stairs with a few finishing touches. An old trunk or chest will make an attractive showpiece in the hall and there will probably be an odd corner that can be brightened by a floor-standing house plant, a display of flowers or a standard lamp. The walls can be hung with paintings, prints or photographs, perhaps in a series up the stairs. A large mirror in the hall will give the effect of extra space, as well as being useful for a final check on your appearance before leaving the house.

For more information

Stripping paint from wood	105
Painting walls	115
Painting woodwork	116-119
Hanging wallpaper	126-138
Putting up shelves	169-180
Hanging a new front door	196
Locks and bolts for a front door	201
Laying vinyl tiles	279
Laying ceramic tiles	281
Laying sheet vinyl	283-285
Laying floor carpet	286-289
Laying stair carpet	290-292
Laying wood mosaic flooring	295
Repairing staircases	296-298

REFLECTED LIGHT (*left*) A carefully chosen colour scheme makes the best use of natural light. Neutral-coloured walls pick up daylight filtered by the textured and stained-glass panels.

ORIENTAL CRAFT (*above*) Arts and Crafts meets the Orient on this polished timber staircase that is surrounded with Oriental artefacts.

ANTIQUE SPLENDOUR (*below left*) Huge paintings and solid antique furniture are perfectly at home in a narrow hallway which is opened up with a white tiled floor and a stone-like wall which has been treated with a paint effect.

SPACE ENHANCEMENT (*below right*) Natural light floods into a hallway where pale colours maximise the space. Star wallpaper is echoed in the star-shaped ceiling lamp, and a radiator cover provides table space.

Passageways with panache (continued)

TILED FLOOR (*above left*) In a contemporary update of the classic tiled hall floor, black and white tiles are boldly teamed with white woodwork and deep blue walls.

ENTRANCE ROOM (*above right*) This wide hallway looks more like a living room with its generous curtains, comfortable sofa and sea-grass matting. There is even room for a bicycle.

OPEN STAIRS (*far left*) This simplest of staircases means that the living room space is little disturbed by open stairs leading to the first floor.

UNDERSTAIRS STORAGE (*left*) A cupboard and floor-to-ceiling fitted shelves maximise the space in a narrow hallway which has had half the understairs cupboard removed to widen the passageway.

MATERIAL MATCH (*opposite*) Mosaic tiling on the floor, a wrought-iron table, wicker basket and painted wooden pigeonhole shelves are a successful blend of materials in this sunny hallway.

Radices
Radices

Working areas

Planning thinking space

WORK AND PLAY (*below*) A laundry room doubles as a small workshop for model-making. Each area has its own adjustable light, with general lighting provided by spotlights fitted beneath a wide shelf across the room.

The average family may well include a student, a musician or model-maker, a dressmaker and a DIY enthusiast – or any other combination of individuals with their own interests. Finding space for all of them to pursue their activities within the ordinary family home requires ingenuity and careful planning.

A student's homework requires at least a table or desk, and shelves for books and files. Creative hobbies such as painting and pottery need space where things can be left when not being worked on. Sewing demands a large worktop for the sewing machine and for spreading out fabric, and also storage space for fabrics and accessories. Model-making or repair work need a permanent workbench and plenty of wall space for keeping tools.

The amount of space needed will depend on the activity, and one activity may be able to share its space with another. For example, a spare bedroom could be used for sewing during the day and homework in the evening. A study area, however, need not actually be a room of its own. It could be a corner or alcove of a living room, a space under the stairs, or a little-used passageway.

If someone in the family has a hobby that creates mess and there is no room that can be entirely devoted to it, consider converting a cellar, loft or conservatory. Alternatively, you could have a small extension built onto the house, or you could put up a shed in the garden. With good insulation and a small bottled-gas or paraffin heater, a shed can be used all year round.

What extra facilities are needed?

Once you have decided on your work area, consider what additions it will need to make it as useful as possible. Almost any work space will need a worktop, shelves and cupboards. A worktop containing electrical appliances such as a drill, circular saw, lathe or other machinery will need plenty of power points, and possibly a separate circuit from the consumer unit.

Soundproofing may also be necessary to avoid disturbing other members of the family or the neighbours. Partition walls between rooms or party walls between houses may have to be soundproofed with plasterboard on battens.

Good lighting is essential for most activities, especially painting, sewing and anything involving tools. Daylight is best, and will be most consistent throughout the day if the window faces north. Fluorescent tubes give the best artificial lighting, and can be combined with adjustable spotlights to focus light exactly on the work.

Ventilation is essential in a room where toxic materials like glues, resins or acids are used. Do not rely on windows and air bricks, fit an extractor fan big enough for the size of the room.

For more information

Making shelves	169-180
Making shelves from slotted metal angle	178
Making cupboards	181-188
Using pegboard for storage	184
Fitting an extractor fan	237
Insulating a room against noise	268
Adding an extra power socket	372
Installing a ring circuit	379
Adding a new lighting point	390
Choosing a fluorescent lamp	394

DESK TIDY (*far left*) A minimal desk includes a recessed filing system and a clip-on task light for practicality, while the surface of a filing cabinet provides additional work space.

WOOD AND WHITE (*left*) Open wooden shelving is fixed to the far wall. A freestanding unit carves up the space and provides a divider between work activity and a quiet desk.

DOUBLE THE WORK (*below*) Two work stations have been formed by placing two strips of laminate on two sets of metal trestles for an unbroken run of work space. A filing cabinet on castors slips neatly underneath, while the table top is sturdy enough for a computer.

Planning thinking space (continued)

INTERESTING ANGLES (*above left*) A complete home office includes a triangular worktop where computer work or a two-person meeting can take place. A shelf behind the worktop provides room for a fax machine. A kitchen area allows office entertaining to take place too.

BEDROOM WORK (*above right*) A computer and discreet filing cabinet are placed unobtrusively against a window and softened with two table lamps and an informal work chair.

SEWING ROOM (*right*) In a generous-sized living room a corner has been devoted to sewing, with a machine and table placed next to the window for maximum daylight.

QUIET WORK (*above*)
Shelves fitted above and around a doorway are the perfect backdrop for a quiet desk by the window. Bleached floorboards and pale woodwork give a Scandinavian feel.

INFORMAL DESK (*below*)
Cast iron and wood form this hallway table which doubles as a work station in a family home. Stencilled walls and wide shelves are home to toys and reminders in the absence of a proper notice board.

HOMEWORK (*left*)
Using the space below a platform bed to full effect, a desk and shelves fit snugly underneath and within this wooden framework.

OFFICE CORNER
(*above*) Separate from the living room but linked by an open doorway, this small home office comprises matching wall units and desk but has a painting and flowers to soften its purpose.

CORNER PLOT (*below*) Two adjoining windows have been pinpointed as the natural place for a workdesk in this airy room. Shelves abut the window so that books are easily to hand, and a floor-standing lamp provides night time illumination.

FLORAL STUDY (*left*) An armchair for visitors and storage space on the window ledge are plus points in this cosy work area which is decorated with cheerfully bright citrus colours.

CLOSE TO HOME (*below left*) A desk at the end of the bed is convenient in case of sudden inspiration at the end of the day. A screen shields the work area from view so that sleep is not disturbed.

HEAVY METAL (*below right*) Industrial aluminium shelving is put to practical use as work storage and a desk. Paperwork is stored on open shelves under the work station.

REFLECTIVE WORK (*above left*) An ornate carved mirror frame dominates a wall above a simple glass-topped table. Deep wooden alcove shelves store books as well as a collection of ceramics at a safe height.

AWKWARD CORNER (*above right*) A difficult space has been used to full advantage in this bedroom so that it incorporates a desktop and two small filing cabinets near the window.

SEW ALONE (*left*) A quiet corner is used as a sewing space which joins onto a glass-topped table. A freestanding tower on castors houses hi-fi and CDs as well as precious items.

Lofts and attics

Innovation overhead

The loft space in many houses can be converted to gain an extra room, provided there is enough headroom and the roof is of a type suitable for conversion.

But stronger joists will have to be fitted in order to carry the floor since in most lofts the joists were designed only to support the ceiling beneath and not the weight of furniture and people. Loft conversion work should be done by expert builders and there are many firms that specialise in it.

If the size and construction of your roof will allow a room to be built there, consider next how to get to it from the floor below. If the room is to be constantly in use, a fixed staircase is the best answer if there is room for one.

Staircases are subject to building regulations which lay down the size of the steps, the angle of ascent, the minimum headroom and the height of the balusters. Retractable ladders, however, are not subject to regulations, and there are lightweight types that can be extended or retracted easily by one person.

A habitable room made in a loft space must have adequate ventilation and window space. Details are laid down in the building regulations. A dormer window will usually meet these needs, and will give extra headroom. If headroom is not an important consideration, nor the view from the window, then a roof light will give adequate light and ventilation and will cost less to fit than a dormer window.

DIY work in a loft

Although loft conversion is a job for professionals, most of the additional work, such as lining the roof, laying the floor and erecting partition walls, is within the scope of the handyman. Plasterboard can be used for lining the roof and partition walls. For the floor, use floorboards with tongued-and-grooved edges, which prevent draughts. Flooring-grade chipboard is also available tongued-and-grooved.

If you wish to put a bathroom in the loft, the plumbing may present problems, and the cold-water cistern, normally mounted on the ceiling joists, will not be high enough to give a sufficient head of water to supply the taps. It may be possible to connect the cold-water supply direct to the rising main, but a pump will be needed for the hot-water supply. First consult your local water board. A shower unit in the loft will present less of a problem if it has a built-in pump.

For more information

Building a stud partition wall 245
Fitting a plasterboard ceiling 247
Lining a wall with wallboards 251
Lining a wall or ceiling with timber cladding 254
Laying a chipboard floor 274
Choosing a floor covering 277
Fitting a loft ladder 298
Installing a vanity basin in a bedroom 325
Fitting a shower 328-330
Installing a ring circuit 379
Wiring a lighting circuit 395

TIDY EAVES (*left*) Low individual book shelves are slotted together under the eaves to house files and other office paraphernalia, while tall adjustable shelves hold books. Spotlights are suspended from the ceiling

RAISED BED (*above left*) A cosy platform sits above hand built architectural shelves which themselves form a backdrop for a reading corner.

WHITE LIGHT (*above right*) Roof and walls blur into one where white tiles and painted tongue-and-groove boarding meet in this attic bathroom, which contains a shower as well as two sinks and a bath.

VAULTED CEILING (*left*) Dramatic roof timbers are set off with floral curtains and white fittings in this rustic attic.

Innovation overhead (continued)

TRADITIONAL ROMANCE (*left*) Classic white bedding and a brass bedstead are always at home in a loft room. There is plenty of space under the bed for storing out-of-season clothes or seldom-used clutter.

ROOF KITCHEN (*below left*) Ingenious metal rails are secured with clips to a sloping wall in such a way that cups, pans and cloths can be suspended on butcher's hooks. A simple and timeless solution for a loft kitchen.

LIGHT LOFT (*below right*) A large room has been painted white to increase the sense of space. The use of low-level furniture helps to disguise the low ceiling.

AQUATIC BATHROOM (*above*) Ceramic tiles on the floor and bath surround abound with watery creatures in a roof space which contains both a shower and a bath.

WINDOW VIEW (*left*) A window placed directly underneath a roof's apex lends definition and a feeling of height to this enclosed bedroom.

Outside the house

Improving the exterior

Regular exterior decorating is essential to protect rendered and wooden surfaces, and it also provides a chance to revive the house's appearance. Colour can be used to emphasise some of its attractive features, such as window frames, decorative lintels or an ornate porch, or to brighten up an overall shabby exterior.

A warm dry spell in September or October is the best time to paint the outside of a house. The wood is likely to be at its driest. It is best to phase the work so that one year the wall, gutters and downpipes are painted and another year the doors and windows. This will spread the workload and help to keep the exterior looking fresh.

Shabby brickwork can be disguised, and effectively weatherproofed, by the application of rendering – a coating of sand and cement. Sometimes small stones or stone chippings are added to the mix, and it is called roughcast. If the stones are thrown onto the mix after it is applied to the wall, the finish is called pebbledash. These types of rendering are best carried out by experts, but there is a dry-mix type – Tyrolean rendering – that can be applied by the handyman. The rendering can then be painted with masonry paint.

Brickwork which is in good condition but has acquired a film of dirt can be restored with a brick-cleaning fluid. Apply the fluid with a brush and then hose it off. It is acid-based, so follow the maker's instructions and wear protective gloves and goggles.

Stonework can also be improved by cleaning, but do not use cleaning fluid as it will attack the stone, causing it to crumble. Use clean water only and scrub the surface vigorously with a bristle brush or use a pressure washer from a tool-hire companies.

BOLD STYLE (*below*) Picked out in a deep royal blue, the door of this Victorian house keys in with the tiled paving. A traditional French number plate tones exactly with the colours of the door and the tiles.

Porches, canopies and awnings

A porch can be an attractive addition to the front of a house, as well as a place to hang wet coats, take off muddy shoes and store umbrellas. It will also act as a draught barrier and provide extra heat insulation.

Porches must conform with building regulations to avoid a transfer of damp from porch to house, so you should check your design with the local authority. But planning permission is not required provided the floor area does not exceed 21sq ft (2sq m), the height is not more than 9ft 6in (3m) and the front is not within 6ft 6in (2m) of a boundary alongside a public highway. The simplest type of porch to erect is one of the prefabricated designs that can be bought in kit form.

Outdoor awnings add colour to windows and give shade on a sunny day. There are two basic designs. A Dutch blind, has a hinged frame like a pram hood and may be covered in fabric or wooden slats. The other has a roller mechanism and is often used over shop windows.

Using plants on walls

Plants and flowers improve the appearance of any house. But some climbers grow rapidly and may eventually block gutters and enter the roof space. Be careful where you plant ivy, Virginia creeper, wisteria and Russian vine. You will have to fix trellis, plastic mesh or galvanised wire to the wall to hold most climbers, but ivy and Virginia creeper cling to walls without support. Their 'suckers', however, can damage soft bricks or crumbling mortar.

For further information

Choosing the right paint	110
Decorating the outside of a house	123
Fixing things to walls	232
Repairing a rendered wall	460
Repairing pebbledash	461
Types of garden fencing	466

HANGING GARDEN (*above left*) Window boxes overflowing with ivy-leaved geraniums make up for the lack of a front garden in a Victorian terraced house. Trailing plants always provide a delightful cascade off a high window ledge.

URBAN RAILINGS (*above right*) A riot of colour and foliage in the form of petunias and ivy poke through painted wrought iron railings which lead to a basement flat.

PURPLE BLOOM (*left*) An old wisteria drenches this Georgian country house with flowers and foliage, creating a quintessentially country feel.

Conservatories – joining house and garden

FLINT AND BRICK (*right*) Mediterranean plants such as a grapevine thrive in a timber-framed conservatory constructed against the back wall of a flint cottage. French windows have been added to provide easy access between the two.

GREEN LIVING (*below*) This greenery-soaked conservatory provides a sense of the outdoors but with protection from the wind and winter cold.

BLUE TIMBER (*above*) Built as an extension to a timber-framed house, this conservatory provides an extra room for eating, relaxing and entertaining.

EATING SPACE (*right*) This lean-to extension has provided space enough to extend a kitchen and make a generous eating area at the back of a town house.

DINNER VIEW (*left*) This tall conservatory makes the best of a beautiful view, allowing a panoramic vista on all sides. Brickwork has been sensitively matched with the existing walls of the house.

Paths, patios and steps

There is more to a garden path than a strip of concrete leading down to the gate. Almost any material, from timber to granite, can be used to make paths and steps, but the most suitable surfaces are paving slabs, paving blocks, bricks, gravel and asphalt.

Precast paving slabs are available in many shapes, sizes and shades. Paving blocks shaped like bricks but made of concrete are easy to handle and can be laid in attractive patterns. Bricks provide a particularly attractive surface, especially when they are laid in a herringbone pattern. Gravel is durable, easy to lay and relatively inexpensive, but is not good beside lawns, as the stones can get on the grass and are picked up by the mower which can damage the mower or cause injury. Asphalt is also cheap and easy to lay. The dull grey or black appearance can be brightened with stone chippings applied while the surface is still soft. Conventional concrete strips make a hard-wearing surface, but they are also hard work to lay.

Most of the materials suitable for paths can also be used for drives, though paving slabs will crack if not given a proper foundation, and gravel will spread when constantly driven over.

Choosing the right spot for a patio

Despite the fickleness of British weather, a patio is a worthwhile garden feature which, on fine days, can be an extension of the house. Choose a south or west-facing aspect if possible. If the only available area faces north or east, site the patio away from the house to catch as much sunshine as possible.

The patio can be paved with slabs, bricks or frost-resistant ceramic tiles, perhaps with random patches of cobbles set in cement, and spaces left for plants. A trellis fence, screen wall or hedge around the patio will shelter it from the wind. Or it can be bordered with raised plant beds made of bricks or stone blocks. A pergola over the patio will support climbing plants to provide shade. Further interest can be added with plants in pots or small tubs which can be moved around in different seasons.

Garden steps must be constructed from tough, weather-resistant materials such as paving slabs, bricks, stone, or railway sleepers. On a steep slope, build short flights of steps with landings to make them less tiring. Like paths, steps can be made more attractive by using a variety of materials, such as brick or stone risers with paved treads.

For more information

Choosing a path or drive	488
Planning a patio	490
Laying paving slabs	492
Laying blocks or bricks	493
Mixing and laying concrete	496
Laying cold asphalt or gravel	499
Repairing path and drive surfaces	500
Planning and building garden steps	501

STEPPED PATIO (*below*) Pots and flower beds mingle in this paved garden. Bricks laid in different formations make an interesting pattern and changes of level provide extra variety.

ROOF HAVEN (*above left*) On a narrow urban roof terrace climbers and pots of healthy plants form a cluster around an intimate setting of table and chairs, creating a secluded and quiet meeting point.

SUBTLE PATIO (*top right*) French windows and two levels of simple decking make an undramatic transition between seating area and the rest of the garden.

POND LIFE (*above*) Metal decking and a brick border form the boundaries of this garden pool. A stone bird bath encourages wildlife while hostas and other shade plants thrive in the subdued light and damp earth.

BRICK STEPS (*left*) Paving slabs, bricks and rockery stones combine to form a multi textured walkway flanked by silver green foliage.

Paths, patios and steps (continued)

BASEMENT GLORY (*above left*) Trelliswork supports a mass of greenery and flowers in a confined basement area. Pots are placed on each stone step up to ground level to continue the sense of abundance.

SEA OF GREEN (*above right*) A small courtyard garden is bordered by tall green trees and swathes of shrubs in beds and containers. In the far corner a round pond is sheltered from the elements and surrounded by terracotta pots.

HERB BARROW (*right*) Lavender, basil, thyme and sage are among a collection of scented herbs planted in pots in a traditional wheelbarrow.

POT LAVENDER (*far right*) A galvanised bucket makes a good weatherproof container for the garden. Lavender thrives in such an environment and provides instant scent wherever it is placed.

LEAFY CORNER (*right*) The striking architectural foliage of a gunnera is displayed in a metal bucket. Purple petunias in a wooden plant pot and a tall variegated weigela provide the colour in this highly textured scene.

Paths, patios and steps (continued)

GREEN FEATURE (*above left*) A circular bed edged with brick and slate contains a centrepiece of bergenia and vinca. Through the opening lies a conifer rockery edged in brick and filled with stones.

PEBBLED PATH (*above right*) An intriguing path made with slabs of concrete and pebbles leads the eye along a raised bed of succulent plants to a resting place in the form of a concrete bench.

SLATE AND EARTH (*right*) Terracotta tiles with 3D motifs are placed in parallel lines between slate slabs to form a unique paving. To one side is a herb patch and a collection of big terracotta pots that are inscribed with the same motif as the tiles.

TRACKING A PATH (*above left*) Old railway sleepers are easy to buy and are not expensive. Here they form a curved path which is filled in with gravel and edged in brick.

STEPPING STONES (*above right*) Sawn-off pieces of tree trunk have been dug into the ground to form a neat path through a shaded garden. Rhododendrons, ferns and azaleas pave the way.

RADIAL PATH (*left*) Paving blocks laid in a circular pattern are crisscrossed with natural bricks to form a walkway between two flower beds.

Paths, patios and steps (continued)

VERDANT WALK (*top left*) A pergola made from rustic poles is the high point of this raised walkway which is laid with pebbles and edged with railway sleepers. Tree trunks and dark bricks are also used in bed edging and pathway.

BRIGHT STEPS (*above left*) Glossy, glazed ceramic tiles are divided by sandstone-coloured bricks to make a startling colour contrast against spreading shrubs.

ALHAMBRA STYLE (*above right*) A Mediterranean atmosphere is captured here with pale paving and stones providing a neutral background for ferns, geraniums and a bougainvillea.

EDGED STEPS (*right*) Wide, deep steps edged with railway sleepers give a distinctly Japanese feel to this route between verdant shrubs.

NEAT AND TIDY (*above left*) In a scrupulously disciplined raised gravel patio herbs and hostas intermingle around a small pond and water pump. The area is reached by steps made from logs and textured paving.

TINY TERRACE (*above right*) Between house and fence lies a charming terraced garden which is separated with blue-painted wooden steps. Proud agapanthus and delicate abelia flank the walkway.

CRAZY PAVING (*left*) Shallow steps have been formed with a mixture of crazy paving and small pieces of brick to create a flowing effect.

Fences, walls and gates

The fences and walls around a garden make a major contribution to the appearance of a house. Broken-down, rotting fences or crumbling walls make the whole property look down-at-heel. A well-maintained boundary, clothed with plants, proclaims pride of ownership that reflects favourably on the house as well.

If you are replacing a fence or wall, choose materials and a design that blend comfortably with the architecture of the house, particularly at the front where house, garden and wall (or fence) are seen as a single picture. A stone wall, for example, would complement a stone-built house, but a red-brick wall may clash.

Garden walls – at either front or rear – can be built of brick, stone or concrete blocks. They need not be solid; a honeycomb wall can be built with the bricks spaced apart in a style called open bond. A similar effect can be achieved with decorative concrete blocks that are moulded in open patterns. Low walls with a soil-filled cavity make an attractive setting for rock plants, particularly types such as aubrieta, that will trail over the edges.

Fences are usually made of wood, with wood or concrete posts, but they can also consist of chain-link mesh or plastic-coated wire.

At the front of the house, where privacy is not important, keep the fence low – no higher than about 3ft (1m). A high front fence looks unsightly and will also shelter an intruder from view if he tries to force a door or window.

An easy fence to erect – which also looks attractive – is the railboard type which has parallel horizontal rails. This style of fence is also available in snap-together plastic sections that are almost indistinguishable from painted timber and need no maintenance.

High fences around the back garden, as well as providing privacy, will give shelter from the wind over a distance about three times greater than their height. Ready-made fencing panels, which are fitted between posts, are easy to erect. Panelled fencing, however, is prone to damage from high winds, and in an exposed situation a close-boarded fence is more weather resistant but also more expensive.

Gates – both wooden and metal – are made in many designs. They can be hung on timber or metal posts or on brick or concrete piers. Ornamental metal gates are usually made of steel rods or bars welded together in decorative designs, but traditional wrought-iron gates are still made by blacksmiths who will make them to order as well as in stock sizes.

WOVEN WILLOW (*left*) Traditional hurdle-making techniques have been used here to form a woven fence.

FORMAL DIVISION (*below*) A painted picket-style fence sits on top of a walled garden to provide extra height.

For more information

Putting up fence posts	468
Fixing panel fencing to posts	469
Erecting a close-boarded fence	470
Fence repair and maintenance	471
Methods of hanging a gate	473
Choosing a gate	474
Choosing gate hinges	475
Fitting a gate and gateposts	475
Choosing gate catches	476
Ways of building a garden wall	478
Buying bricks and blocks	480
Building a brick retaining wall	485
Laying a screen block wall	486

ARCH FORMALITY (*above*) Brick arches have been finished off with trelliswork that extends round the garden. A pond is in the middle of the courtyard area surrounded by generously filled pots.

IRON GATE (*far left*) Timber fencing posts hold up a simple iron gate which does not impede the view to a garden bench placed amid cottage plants.

ENTRANCE WAY (*left above*) A curlicued iron gate includes a house name plate and is flanked by brick pillars in between the gate and open wrought iron fencing.

TRELLIS FENCE (*left below*) A continuous run of trellis panels forms openings and arches along a well-planted garden.

Ideas for garden features

Few of the great gardeners were ever content with flowers and shrubs, trees and lawns. They always sought to add something extra to their creations. On the grand scale, they dammed rivers to create lakes, moved hills to improve the view or built ruins to add an element of surprise. But even the smallest garden can be given added character by something as simple as a carefully sited urn.

A pergola entwined with wisteria, clematis or honeysuckle will make a handsome 'roof' for a patio, or will transform a pathway. A garden path, whether straight or winding, will become more exciting if it leads to some attractive display such as an ornamental pond, and can be made even more tantalising if the sound of a fountain or waterfall is heard before it comes into view. Smaller features could include stone statues used to add interest to a dull corner, a garden seat in a shady bower or a bird table that can be watched from the patio.

Pergolas

A pergola consists of a series of linked archways around which climbing plants are trained. It can be freestanding, straddling a path or patio, or it can be attached to a house wall and extend over a patio or side path.

A simple pergola can be built with sawn timber or, for a rustic style, larch poles. As an alternative the uprights can be of brick or stone with timber for the cross rails. To allow headroom, taking into account the hang of overhead plants, the pergola should be at least 6ft 6in (2m) high and about the same width.

Ornamental ponds

Flexible plastic liners and moulded glass-fibre ponds are easy to install, and are available from garden centres. Making a pond with a plastic liner simply entails digging a hole and placing the liner inside, so that the size and shape of the pond can be to your own design. Glass-fibre units vary in shape and size, and require a hole cut roughly to shape.

The sight and sound of moving water adds to the attraction of a garden pond. A fountain will enliven a formal pond, and in a more natural setting where the pond is backed by a rock garden, a waterfall can be delightful. A submersible pump, placed in the pond and connected to the mains electricity supply by a waterproof cable, will eject water through a fountain head, or deliver it through a tube to the head of the waterfall. The waterfall can run down over rocks, or through a series of glass-fibre pools.

Barbecues

Despite our fickle weather, barbecue parties are increasingly popular, and a built-up unit is simple to construct. It should be made of brick, with a metal tray to hold the charcoal and a grill on which to place the food. Site it on a solid foundation in a sheltered position and where it will not be obtrusive when not in use.

Bird tables and nesting boxes

Perhaps the best of all features in a garden are those provided by nature – birds. You can attract more birds to your garden and observe them close at hand by setting up a bird table, which can be made from a piece of plywood about 18in (460mm) square fixed on top of a post about 5ft 6in (1.7m) from the ground. If there are trees in the garden, a nesting box secured to a trunk may attract some of the 30 or so species which use nesting boxes, including tits and robins.

VEGETABLE PLOT (*below*) Runner beans grow quickly and easily up any structure. Here they are trained up trellis attached to a wooden pergola.

BIRD BATH (*above*) Amid a sea of blue campanulas and red centranthus (valerian) sits a stone bird bath which breaks up the riot of colour and is a decorative addition to the garden.

FORMAL SEATING (*left*) A trellised pergola is a formal surround for a quiet garden bench with its outlook onto beds of pink and purple petunias.

JAPANESE GARDEN (*left below*) The formal elements of a Japanese garden are all present in this rural patch, including raked gravel, loose pebbles, bamboo plants and fences and heavy rocks.

CONCRETE BRIDGE (*below*) Slabs of concrete are used for a narrow path in a densely planted area and two more pieces form a footbridge over a large pond.

ARCHED PATHWAY (*above*) A series of rose-laden arches leads to a quiet seating area Paving slabs laid in a hopscotch formation in the gravel path create an informal walkway.

BIRD CENTRE (*below*) An uncovered feeding table is made from a tree trunk topped with a level feeding area. Cup hooks are screwed into one side to hold a hanging feeder.

Ideas for garden features (continued)

SUN FOUNTAIN (*above*) A circular ceramic sun pours water via a concealed electric pump into a small water pool. Established shrubs behind envelope the scene.

RECYCLED WATER (*left*) A butt for collecting rainwater stands beneath the end of a roof gutter. The decorative barrel nestles behind a stone urn filled with marguerites.

STONE CIRCLE (*below*) A herringbone path leads directly to a circular pond whose ledge is wide enough for pots of greenery.

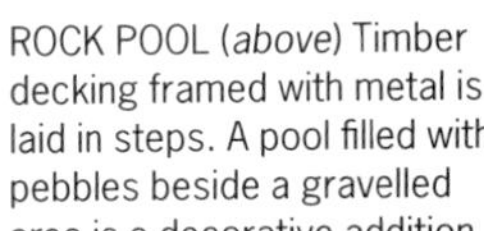

ROCK POOL (*above*) Timber decking framed with metal is laid in steps. A pool filled with pebbles beside a gravelled area is a decorative addition.

OUTDOOR ROOM (*right*) Even the fireplace has been brought outside to enjoy some peace and quiet by a marble-topped table among pots and planters.

BARBECUE AREA (*right below*) A brick-built barbecue has an extension with space for laying down ingredients and utensils.

Painting, wallpapering & tiling

2

Preparation

Painting

Wallpapering

Tiling

Preparing the surface: Tools for the job

Preparing the area to be decorated is nearly always time-consuming, hard work and a chore. But if you have the right tool for a particular job, preparation will be much easier.

Buy the best quality tools you can afford; it may be worth hiring the more expensive tools. Always sharpen scraper blades to a square edge before you start, and keep an old paintbrush handy as a dusting brush.

Make sure you have enough cotton dust sheets or newspapers to protect the floors and furniture, and plenty of rags for mopping up spills.

For smoothing fillers down and removing any roughness on a stripped wall or on woodwork, you need a selection of abrasive papers, including wet-and-dry paper (which can be used dry or damped with water).

Powered sanding tools, such as a disc sander, a flap wheel and a drum sander, will clean stripped surfaces more quickly. But do not try to strip paint off wood with powered sanders, unless the coating is very thin. Abrasives tend to clog when paint or varnish is melted by friction.

Scrapers/strippers

Tools with a flat, slightly sprung blade are called scrapers or stripping knives. The blade may be broad or narrow, according to the area to be scraped.

A broad-blade scraper is the normal tool for removing old wallpaper before redecorating a room. But scrapers are also used to remove old paint that has been softened with a hot-air stripper or a blowtorch. They can only be used on a flat surface. To strip paint from moulded woodwork, such as window and door architraves, use a shave hook.

Before use, sharpen the blade so that it is flat at the end, not like a knife edge.

A wallpaper stripper with a plastic handle and a roller at one end is designed to be used flat against the wall, so that there is less danger of gouging the plaster. The roller can also be used as a seam roller for wallpapering.

For removing paint from window panes, use a special scraper with disposable blades.

Skarsten scraper

Consists of a handle into which a razor-sharp, slightly hooked blade is slotted. It will scrape off paint down to bare wood. On curved surfaces, like banisters, you can strip off paint without heat or a chemical stripper, but the scraper is less effective on flat surfaces or on intricate mouldings. Serrated blades are available for scraping stubborn surfaces.

Shave hooks

Scrapers with a blade set at right angles to the handle, are useful for mouldings and corners. Shave hooks can be triangular, pear-shaped, or a combination of the two. As with scrapers, the edge is designed to scrape rather than dig into the surface.

Filling knife

Closely resembles a scraper but has a more flexible blade. Use it to press filler firmly into holes and cracks and to level it out flush with the surface.

Wire brush

For removing loose or flaking materials before you start decorating. You can use either a hand-held version, or a wire brush or cup brush in a power tool.

Flexible sanding block

A flexible block with an abrasive coating on four sides. Rinse clean and squeeze dry before using to rub down a painted surface in preparation for repainting. Destroys any existing glaze while removing dirt, but cannot be used as a paint stripper.

Blowtorch

An efficient tool for softening paint to be stripped. It is operated by bottled gas which lights immediately you turn a tap and apply a flame to the nozzle.

Blowtorches have replaced blowlamps, which were fired by petrol or paraffin and needed priming before they would light correctly. Torches vary from small units, where the actual container forms the handle, to larger ones with a gas canister and a separate handle. Check that gas refills are freely available before you buy a model – the containers are not interchangeable between makes.

Most blowtorches can be fitted with an attachment that spreads the flame and speeds up the paint-softening process.

The size of a blowtorch does not matter for indoor use, but outdoors the heat from some small units is quickly dissipated in even a gentle breeze. So, for larger jobs and regular outdoor work, use a bigger torch head connected to a large bottle of gas by means of a flexible rubber tube.

A hot-air stripper

Also called a hot-air gun, the tool works like a superheated hair dryer. It is probably the best tool for removing old paint and is much safer than a blowtorch for the amateur because there is no naked flame. An attachment called a spreader will concentrate heat into a smaller area, making the stripper more effective outside.

A steam stripper

Invaluable for removing heavy build-ups of wallpaper or papered surfaces which have been painted. It consists of a water reservoir and a hose, which is connected to a perforated plate. Water is heated by bottled gas or electricity to produce steam. This is forced up the hose and emerges through the perforations in the plate. The steam penetrates the wall covering and softens the adhesive underneath so that the covering can be pulled away by the sheet. Consider buying or hiring one; if all the preparatory work has been done, most rooms can be stripped in a day.

STRIPPING WALLPAPER WITH STEAM

Steam from the perforated plate penetrates the paper and softens the adhesive. Painted paper must first be scored with a serrated scraper or coarse abrasive paper. A special tool may be obtained with the stripper.

PROTECTIVE GEAR

Wear safety goggles to protect your eyes from chemicals, particles of dust or rust. If there is a lot of dust, wear a face mask. If using a chemical stripper, wear rubber gloves to protect your hands. Cotton gloves are cooler when using a hot-air stripper. Wear ear defenders to protect your ears during noisy jobs.

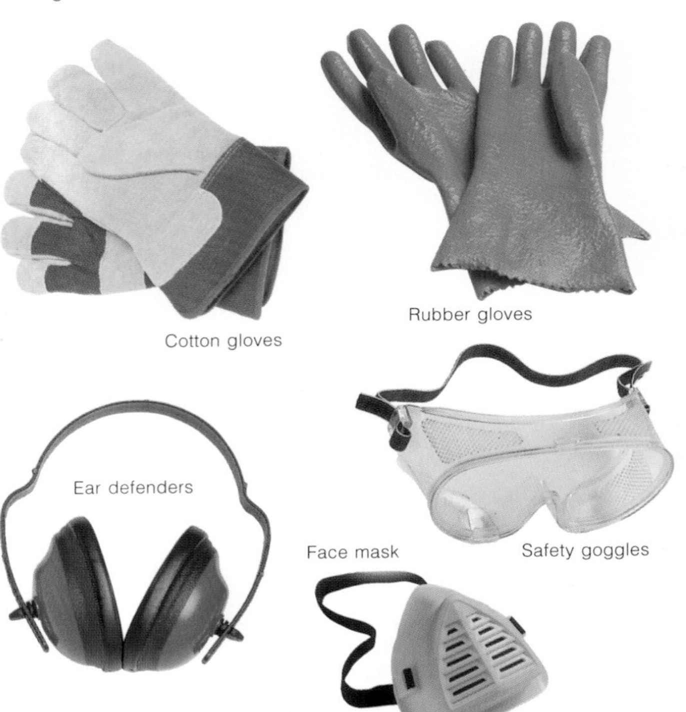

TOOLS FOR PREPARATION

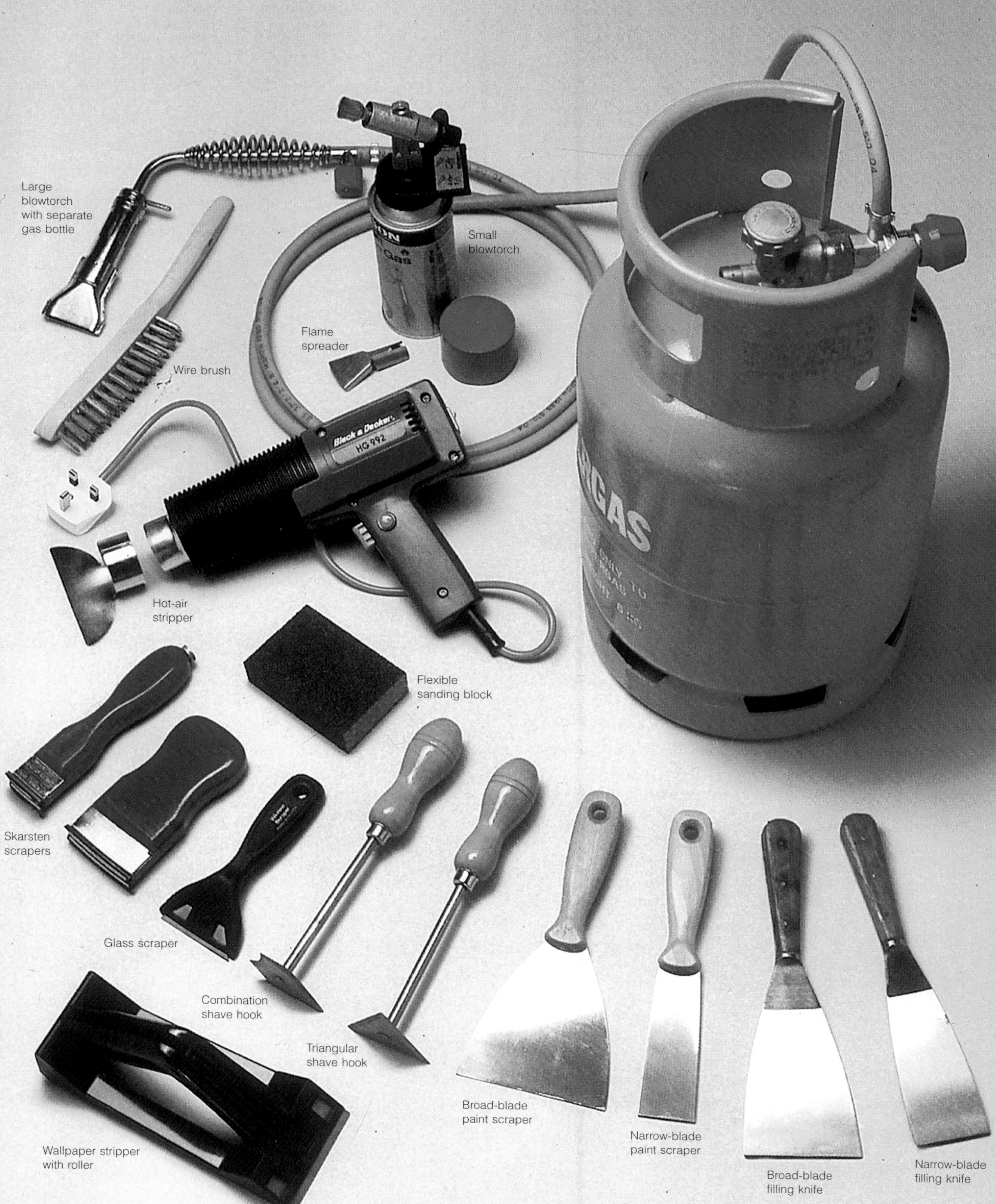

Equipment for working safely at height

Each year thousands of people are injured in falls from insecure ladders and platforms or from chairs and stools. So make sure you have the correct equipment for reaching a height, and use it safely.

A ladder must extend at least three rungs above the work point to give you a secure handhold and allow you to work at waist or chest height. Lash the ladder top to a ring bolt in the fascia board and the foot to a peg in the ground; or use a sandbag to hold the foot. On soft ground stand the ladder on a board pegged in place and with a batten nailed along it.

Use a stepladder indoors and for some outdoor work. Choose one high enough for you to reach the ceiling but not too high to take through doorways easily. Where a stepladder is not high enough, in a stairwell for example, a combination ladder that converts to a stepladder or ladder is useful. A stepladder can act as a trestle for a scaffold board. Borrow another stepladder or hire a trestle for the other end of the board. Boards must be sound timber at least 1½in (38mm) thick.

Scaffold towers can be hired to use outside and in some stairwells. Two people can set up a 13ft (4m) tower in about 10 minutes. The tower must be vertical, so take time to adjust the feet. On soft ground put a plank or paving slab under each foot. Lash the top to a piece of timber across the inside of a window frame or to a ring bolt in the fascia. Always lock any wheels on the tower before climbing it – and always climb up the inside.

Never reach forwards from a scaffold tower, or lean sideways from a ladder or stepladder.

Aluminium ladder A tall ladder made of aluminium is much lighter than one made of wood.

Scaffold tower A toe board around the platform prevents tools from falling off.

Rope and pulley control Makes the ladder easier to raise.

Stepladder The grab rail provides a safety grip.

Combination ladder It must have a locking hinge. A three-way type makes a ladder, a stepladder and a stairwell ladder to stand on two levels.

A 20ft (6m) ladder is long enough for most houses. Two sections are easier to handle than three and a rope and pulley makes extending easier. Aluminium ladders are much lighter than wooden ones. A scaffold tower needs a top guard rail, adjustable feet and a platform of boards that you can move aside to climb through. The safest stepladders have wide steps, a platform and a grab rail.

ACCESSORIES TO FIT ON LADDERS

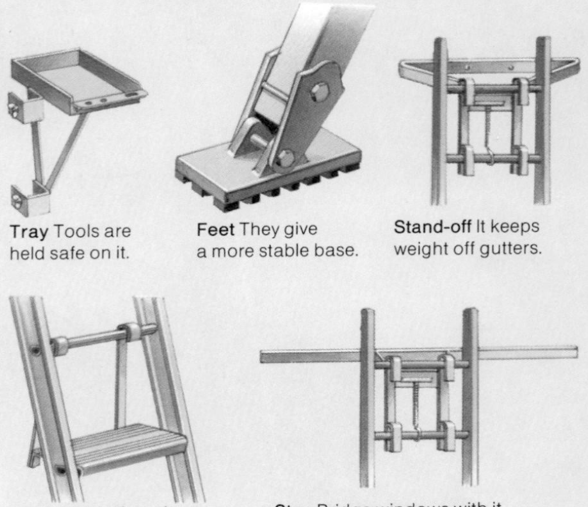

Tray Tools are held safe on it.

Feet They give a more stable base.

Stand-off It keeps weight off gutters.

Hook-on platform It makes standing more comfortable.

Stay Bridge windows with it. Lash on a batten to widen it for windows wider than the stay.

MOVING AND RAISING A LADDER

Carry a ladder vertically with one hand holding a low rung and the other holding a rung just above shoulder height. When you reach the work position, put the ladder's foot in the angle between wall and ground and rest the ladder flat against the wall. Then pull out the foot until the ladder is at an angle of 70 degrees – 1ft (300mm) out for every 4ft (1.2m) up. The foot of a ladder 16ft (5m) high should be 4ft (1.2m) out from the wall. Secure the ladder before you climb it.

Before you start to decorate

Thorough preparation is the key to successful decorating. If you neglect or skimp over the groundwork, the finished surface will always suffer.

First, make ready the area to be decorated. Indoors, isolate the room where you will be working before preparing the surfaces. Most preparatory work creates mess and dust which easily spreads to other areas. Wherever possible, clear out everything movable. Place any remaining furniture in the middle of the room and cover with dustsheets.

Take down curtains and lift carpets (even if they are fitted).

Good-quality carpet – not foam-backed – will need to be restretched when you put it down again (page 288). If you do not want to lift a carpet for this reason, protect it with dustsheets and take extra care not to spill any paint. Using solid emulsion or non-drip gloss paint will reduce the risk of accidents occurring.

Remove shades from lights and take off door furniture. Protect permanent fittings, like wall brackets, with plastic bags.

Next, deal with any damaged woodwork such as rotten window or door frames, badly scratched skirting boards or door panels.

PAINTING OUTSIDE

Not so much advance work can be done outside, but cover porch roofs, tiled sills and even flower borders with protective sheeting. Use dustsheets or old bed sheeting – they hold fine dust and absorb spilt liquid (unlike polythene, which becomes dangerously slippery when wet).

Windows must be open for exterior painting, so take down all the curtains or tie them back.

All surfaces must be clean, dry and stable before decorating can start. Any damaged or problem areas must be treated and old paint and paper stripped off, if necessary. The only exception is that it is easier and less messy to decorate the ceiling before you strip the walls. Use a brush to remove loose dirt, especially on exterior walls. For detailed advice on stripping old wallpaper, tiles and paintwork, see pages 103 – 105.

Preparing walls and ceilings

PAINTED OR WALLPAPERED SURFACES

SURFACE	TREATMENT
Gloss painted	If the wall is to be repainted and the existing paint is sound, wash well with sugar soap and water. If the wall is to be papered, rub it with the smooth side of a flexible sanding pad – damped with clean water – to remove the glaze. Papering over gloss is always risky because the wall is so well sealed, but you have more chance of success if you put up lining paper first (page 133). In steamy areas, like bathrooms, use a vinyl or water-resistant wall covering.
Emulsion painted	If emulsion is peeling, strip it back to ensure a sound base for future decoration. There may be distemper underneath. If the emulsion is sound and well anchored, clean and roughen the surface with sugar soap and water, then redecorate. Emulsioned surfaces can be papered, but use a heavy-duty paste with minimum water. In steamy conditions, use an impervious wall covering, so damp cannot reach the emulsion.
Distemper	Distemper forms a chalky barrier which prevents paint or paper adhering to the wall. Scrub it off with a coarse cloth or a nylon pot scourer and water. If there is a thick coating, damp the whole area, then scrape away with a wide stripping knife. Never scrape bad cases of distemper without wetting it; it makes too much mess. Cover any remaining distemper with stabilising solution. Once dry, the surface can be decorated.

SURFACE	TREATMENT
Standard wallpaper	Soften ordinary wallpaper with water, adding a little liquid detergent. And add a handful of cellulose paste to each bucket of water – it helps to hold the water on the wall. Use a scraper to lift off the paper.
Painted wallpaper	If the wallpaper has been painted, roughen the surface with coarse abrasive paper before you try to strip it off the wall. If the paint is thick, you may have to score the surface with the serrated blade of a wallpaper scraper. Never use a wire brush or wire wool – if slivers of metal become embedded in the plaster, they can rust and cause tiny stains on wall coverings.
Vinyls, washables and wipe-clean papers	Score washable and wipeable wallpapers with a serrated scraper so that water can penetrate. Consider hiring a steam wallpaper stripper to tackle materials that are difficult to remove, or if the wall is covered with layers of old paper. Vinyls are usually easier to strip off a wall – the vinyl skin can be pulled from its backing, then the backing soaked away. With some modern papers and vinyls (called easy-strip), the backing can be left on the wall as the lining paper for the next wall covering. This is only satisfactory if the paper is well stuck. If there are any signs of loose areas, strip it off. If the surface of a stripped wall is rough in places, rub it with coarse abrasive paper mounted on a block.

TILES, TEXTURES AND BRICKS

SURFACE	TREATMENT
Imitation tiling	This type of wall covering, resembling thin rolls of linoleum, was usually stuck on with a strong adhesive, which can make it hard to remove. Pull the top layer from its backing, then soak off the backing and old adhesive with hot water, scraping it away as it softens. If the covering pulls plaster with it, try a steam wallpaper stripper to prevent any more plaster coming off.
Textured coatings	Thick coatings applied by brush or roller on ceilings and walls are difficult to remove. The simplest way is to use a steam wallpaper stripper. Alternatively, you can use a textured-paint remover which works like a chemical paint stripper. If you want to repaint, lightly scrub the coating with a mild solution of sugar soap and water and allow it to dry.
Polystyrene tiles	Expanded polystyrene ceiling tiles may be painted with emulsion but never gloss paint. To remove tiles, lever each one away from the surface and then scrape off the glue (page 104).

SURFACE	TREATMENT
Ceramic tiles	If tiles are to be painted, make sure they are clean and dry, then use enamel or good-quality gloss paint. You cannot hang wallpaper over tiles so you may wish to remove them (page 104). This is very hard work, extremely time-consuming and not a job which can be rushed.
Cork tiles	Cork tiles cannot be successfully painted over, though you may be able to cover them with lining paper and wallpaper. How easy they are to remove from a wall depends on what type of glue has been used to fix them. Prise each tile away from the wall with a wide stripping knife or a bolster chisel. To remove hard lumps of glue, follow the instructions for taking down expanded polystyrene tiles (page 104).
Exposed brick	Brush the bricks to remove dust. Paint interior bricks with emulsion and exterior walls with masonry paint, though good facing brick tends to look better left unpainted.

PROBLEM SURFACES

SURFACE	TREATMENT
Efflorescence	Damp sometimes causes chemicals in mortar or plaster to come to the surface and form whitish fluff, known as efflorescence. Brush efflorescence off the wall, then coat with an alkali-resisting primer or a stabilising solution.

SURFACE	TREATMENT
Stains	Cover any unsightly stains made by tar deposits in a flue or rust marks on a wall, for instance – with an aluminium primer-sealer. This will prevent the stain from bleeding through the new coat of paint.

Preparing walls and ceilings: problem surfaces (continued)

SURFACE	TREATMENT
Damp	Do not isolate damp by applying an impervious coating – this only encourages damp to move elsewhere, creating fresh problems. Hunt out and cure the cause (pages 438, 453).
Uneven plaster	Level out slight irregularities in a wall with a skimming coat of surface plaster (page 239).
Holes and cracks	For small holes and cracks, brush away any loose or crumbling plaster, then repair the area with an appropriate filler (page 106), applied with a filling knife. Larger holes, gaps and cracks in both interior and exterior walls require more extensive treatment involving one of the forms of plaster (page 239).

Preparing and stripping wood and metal

WOODWORK

SURFACE	TREATMENT
New bare wood	Look for cracks and blemishes which need filling. Use fine surface filler for interior wood and a waterproof wood stopping or epoxy-based wood filler for exterior timbers. Apply knotting to all visible knots to stop resin bleeding from them. Smooth the wood by hand, using fine abrasive paper, working only with the grain. Alternatively, use an orbital or multi-purpose power sander, again working with the grain. Be gentle, because with power tools even the finer grades of abrasive paper remove wood very fast.
Old bare wood	If there are signs of damp rot – soft patches easily penetrated by a penknife blade – see pages 210-211. Fill all cracks and gaps with filler as for new wood. When set, smooth with fine abrasive paper. Do not leave wood unprotected for any length of time, especially if it is outside. As soon as preparatory work is complete, apply a coat of wood primer.
Painted wood	If the paint is sound and in good condition, do not strip it unless too many coats are causing an obstruction – making windows hard to open, for instance. Clean down with sugar soap and water. This removes dirt and keys the existing paint so that new paint will adhere to it.
Painted wood (continued)	Keying (roughening a gloss surface very finely) is essential; without it new paint is easily damaged and scratched off. Where the paintwork is slightly damaged but is mainly sound, only work on the damaged areas. Rub with a damp flexible sanding pad to remove all loose material, wipe clean and allow to dry. Prime bare wood where it is exposed. Then lightly rub the whole area with very fine abrasive paper and wash with sugar soap, as for sound paintwork. Fill small chips and stripped patches with fine surface filler. If these are not filled, a depression will show in the finished paintwork, especially when the paint layers are thick.
Varnished wood	Use a chemical paint stripper or varnish remover to get back to bare wood.
Stained wood	If the wood is to be painted and the stain is old, rub down with a flexible sanding pad. If the wood is to be sealed to give a natural finish, remove the stain with a wood bleach. Follow the instructions on the can.
Wood treated with preservative	As long as the preservative is old and dry, paint primer over it.If the coating looks fairly new, unless you know it can be painted, coat the wood with an aluminium primer-sealer. Otherwise the preservative may bleed through.

METALWORK

SURFACE	TREATMENT
New iron and steel	Wipe off any grease with lint-free rag, Then use emery paper to remove rust and wipe clean. Either apply metal primer in as thin a coat as possible, use cold galvanising paint which acts as a rust inhibitor and primer, or apply rust-inhibiting enamel which needs no primer or undercoat.
Old rusted iron and steel	Use wire brushes and emery paper to remove all rust. Always wear safety goggles and leather gloves for protection when preparing metalwork in this way. Fill any serious pitting with epoxy-based filler. If it is left untreated, rust can eat through thin metal, leaving holes. This quite often happens to old steel window frames. Provide an anchor for the filler by backing holes in a window frame with aluminium mesh. Epoxy-based filler is a rust inhibitor, so it can be applied to sound surfaces still showing signs of rust discoloration. Before painting the metal, apply a metal primer, which will prevent further rusting.
Galvanised metal (such as window frames)	Steel window frames are usually in thin sections – only about $\frac{1}{16}$in (2mm) thick – and the galvanised surface has a silvery sheen. Remove dirt and grease with white spirit on lint-free rag. Although a galvanised surface protects steel effectively against rust, it does not afford a good key for paint, and many primers do not grip. Use a zinc chromate primer on a weathered surface. On new galvanised steel, use a mordant solution such as T-Wash, followed by zinc chromate. Clean damaged galvanised areas with white spirit, then apply cold galvanising paint to the damaged parts.
Paint chipped off galvanised metal	Clean bare areas with white spirit, rub the paint edges lightly with emery cloth to soften them. Then either paint with rust-inhibiting enamel or treat with zinc chromate primer and build up coats of gloss level with the original surface. If the whole paint film is unstable strip all the paint and reprime.
Aluminium alloy and anodised aluminium (such as windows and patio doors)	These materials have a very shiny surface and, in good condition, do not need painting. But if you want to match a decorating scheme, clean them with white spirit, dry off and apply enamel paint direct. No primer or undercoat is necessary. Where there are signs of whitish corrosion on weathered surfaces, clean off with flour grade emery paper to avoid scratching. Remove grease and dirt with white spirit, then apply zinc chromate primer.
Copper (such as central heating pipes)	Remove any protective grease with white spirit and rub away any discoloration with fine emery paper. Wipe clean, then apply gloss paint or enamel paint direct. No primer or undercoat is necessary. Ordinary gloss can withstand the heat of water passing through the pipes.
Stainless steel	This should not need painting but, if desired, apply gloss or enamel paint direct after removing any grease with white spirit.
Chromium-plated steel	Like stainless steel, this should not need painting, but it can be coated with enamel applied direct to clean surfaces, which have been degreased with white spirit.
Painted metal (such as window frames)	As with painted woodwork in good condition, do not interfere with sound paint on metal, unless a build-up is making frames too tight. If the paint does not need stripping, clean it down with sugar soap and water. Key the surface with fine abrasive paper, then apply a primer and gloss paint.
Where rust is lifting paint	This may be found in older houses where window frames were not galvanised. Wear safety goggles to protect your eyes. Brush away flaking paint with a wire brush and then scrape back the remaining paint to reveal bright metal. Use an old knife, a Skarsten scraper or, for stubborn areas, a coarse file. Do not ignore any hidden rust; it can lead to a new attack. Treat with rust inhibitor, apply a metal primer, and then build up gloss paint in thin coats until it is level with existing paint.

Stripping wallpaper

You may be able to paper over old wallpaper but it is safer not to – old glue may become reactivated and cause stains, or loosen the old paper. Some wall coverings, including reliefs, washables, wipeables, metallics and flocks, should never be painted or papered over because a covering will not stick to them and any pattern may show through from underneath.

For the best results, strip old wallpaper from the walls before redecorating. If paper is firmly stuck, it is easier to remove with a steam stripper, which can be hired quite cheaply. Alternatively, use a scraper and water following the method given below.

Stripping wallpaper cannot be rushed. If the paper is not left to soak for long enough, it will be very difficult to remove. Put down plenty of cotton dust sheets to protect the floor. To reduce the mess put the larger pieces of stripped paper straight into a large cardboard box, a plastic bag or a bin liner.

STANDARD WALLPAPER

This method for stripping standard wallpaper can also be used for Duplex paper but, because it is thicker, it needs to soak longer.

You will need
Tools Bucket; sponge or old paintbrush; wide stripping knife; water; cellulose paste; liquid detergent or washing-up liquid.

1 Fill a bucket with warm water. Add a handful of cellulose paste and a squirt of liquid detergent or washing-up liquid. The paste helps to hold the water to the wall and the detergent acts as a wetting agent which speeds up the penetration of the water.

2 Wet a whole wall with the water, applying it generously with a large sponge or an old paintbrush.

3 Leave the water to soak into the surface for at least five minutes.

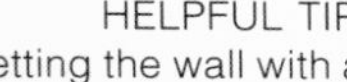

HELPFUL TIP
Wetting the wall with a garden spray is quicker than using a brush or sponge.

4 Test to see whether the paper is ready to be stripped. Slide the edge of a wide stripping knife under the wet paper either at the bottom of the length or at a seam.

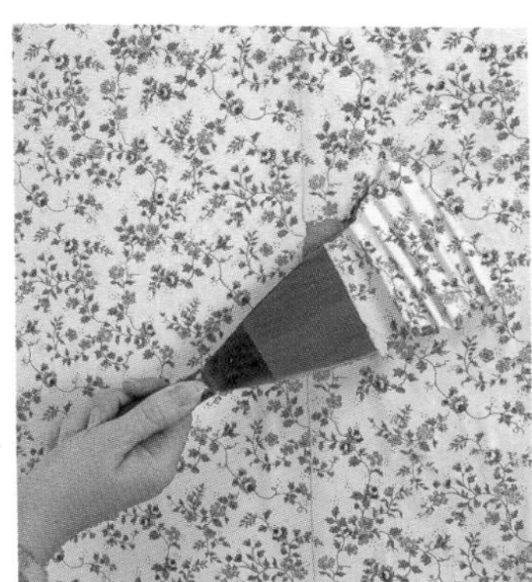

5 Hold the stripper at an angle of about 30 degrees and push it away from you, up the wall. Do not let the blade dig into the plaster. If the paper does not wrinkle and is hard to lift, it needs to soak for longer.

6 Sponge on more water if it is necessary.

7 Try the test again – if the paper wrinkles, pull it away from the wall upwards. It should come away in a fairly big strip.

8 Ease the stripper under the wet covering again and continue to peel away paper.

9 If the paper refuses to come off the wall, despite heavy and lengthy soakings, use a steam wallpaper stripper.

WASHABLES, HEAVY RELIEFS AND PAINTED PAPER

Wallpaper that has been covered with paint can be removed with a chemical stripper designed for textured coatings (page 104). It will be simpler but more expensive than the following method.

You will need
Tools Bucket; sponge or old paintbrush; wide stripping knife; water; cellulose paste; washing-up liquid; serrated scraper or coarse abrasive paper.

1 Roughen the surface with a serrated scraper or coarse abrasive paper so that water can

USING A STEAM STRIPPER

You can save time and energy if you buy or hire a steam stripper to strip wallpaper. Look in *Yellow Pages* under Hire Services – Tools and Equipment, for your nearest hire shop.

You will need
Tools Steam stripper; rubber gloves; safety spectacles; wide stripping knife; water.

1 Ask the hire assistant for an instruction leaflet and follow it carefully.

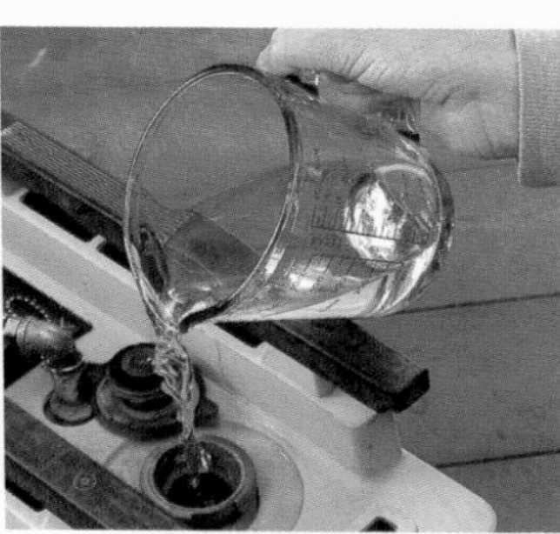

2 Fill the tank with hot or cold water and wait for the light to come on, indicating that the stripper is ready. It usually takes about ten minutes before this happens and steam comes out of the perforated plate.

3 Wear gloves and safety spectacles for protection, especially if stripping paper from a ceiling. Hold the plate at the bottom of the length. Keep it in position until the paper around it shows signs of damp – usually after about a minute.

Strip the paper a length at a time, working on walls from the bottom up.

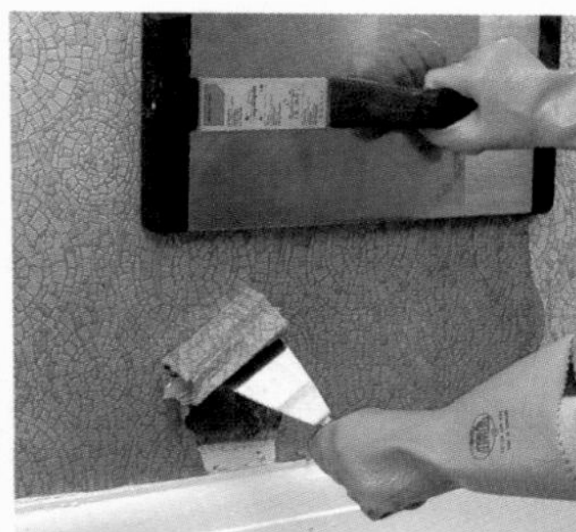

4 Remove the damp wallpaper by pulling it away, loosening stubborn areas with a stripping knife.

At the same time, hold the plate with your other hand on the next area you are going to strip.

5 When you have stripped the first length, return to the bottom of the wall and strip the next length as before. Top up the tank as necessary, first switching off and leaving the stripper for half a minute.

6 Take care when using the stripper on plasterboard. The steam will soften the paper surface, so use a stripping knife as little as possible and do not dig it in. The wallpaper should be easy to peel away from the wall.

Stripping wallpaper (continued)

soak through into the paper. Do not use a wire brush or wire wool – small pieces of metal may become embedded in the plaster underneath and cause stains on the new paper surface.

2 Apply water and strip the covering as for standard wallpaper. If the covering comes off easily, it may be that it was not put up properly. Alternatively, the walls may be damp, in which case find the cause and remedy the problems before redecorating.

VINYLS OR EASY-STRIP PAPERS

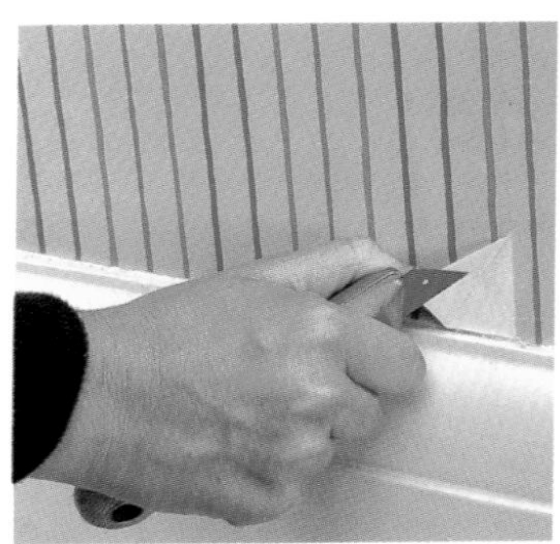

1 With a fingernail or knife blade, lift a corner of the covering away from its backing paper.

2 Peel the covering away from the backing, keeping it as close as possible to the wall. If you pull it towards you, it may pull the backing paper with it.

3 If the backing paper is well stuck to the wall and in good condition, use it as lining paper for the next covering. But if it is damaged, or not stuck firmly to the wall, strip it off as for standard wallpaper.

SAFETY TIP

Switch off electricity at the consumer unit (fuse box) before loosening the screws on a flush mounted switch or socket, if you have to get paper out from behind the fitting.

REMOVING TEXTURED COATINGS

Removing a thick textured coating is a very messy job – especially if a ceiling is involved. There are three possible methods.

Whichever you use, first clear all the furniture out of the room before you start and protect the floor with newspaper, which can be thrown away as it becomes covered with stripped compound.

Artex AX which has not been painted can be soaked with water and then scraped off with a stripping knife. But it is hard work.

The most effective way to remove textured coatings is to use a textured-paint remover. It is available in 4 litre cans – enough to strip 130sq ft (12sq m).

When doing the job wear a cap, protective gloves and goggles. Apply the chemical thickly to the wall or ceiling with a large paintbrush, and leave it to penetrate for the time given on the packet. When the textured surface has softened, strip it off with a wide-bladed wallpaper scraper. Wash down the surface with water and washing-up liquid before redecorating.

Some coatings, including Artex, will need a second scraping after being washed with hot water and washing-up liquid.

Another method of removing a textured coating is to use a steam wallpaper stripper. The heat and steam break through the paint barrier and soften the material underneath so that it can be scraped off the surface with a stripping knife.

Never sand a textured coating – either by power or by hand. Many of the old coatings contain asbestos which should not be inhaled. You do not need to wear a face mask when using the steam stripper because the compound will not produce dust while it is damp.

Removing tiles from walls and ceilings

CERAMIC TILES

Whenever possible, leave old tiles in place. It is much easier to replace damaged tiles, tile over old tiles or brighten them up by recolouring the grout lines than to get them off a wall.

Tiles in older houses may be stuck to the wall with cement mortar – sometimes ½in (13mm) thick. If you remove the tiles you will probably have to repair the wall to make the surface smooth before you can continue to decorate. Tiles which are stuck with adhesive are not quite as difficult to get off a wall, but they may pull plaster with them. In this case the surface should also be made good.

You will need
Tools Heavy duty gloves; safety spectacles; dust mask; wide steel masonry chisel (a bolster); club hammer; hot air stripper; paint scraper.

1 Put on protective clothing – gloves, safety spectacles and mask, and wear a top with long sleeves. Splinters of glass from the glaze will fly in all directions as you chip away at the tiles so you should be well covered. Close doors to prevent dust escaping from the room.

2 Prise the tiles away from the wall one at a time with a wide steel masonry chisel (bolster) and a club hammer. Some tiles will come away in one piece, others may crack and break. There is no easy technique – continue to chisel until you have removed all of the tiles.

3 Use a hot air stripper to soften old adhesive left on the wall and then scrape it off with a paint scraper. Alternatively, a more time-consuming method is to warm the blade of the scraper over a gas cooker or with a blowtorch and then scrape off the adhesive.

Do not allow the blade to become red hot or you will destroy its springiness.

EXPANDED POLYSTYRENE TILES

You will need
Tools Wide stripping knife; safety spectacles. Possibly also a hot air stripper.

1 Lever the tiles away from the ceiling using a wide stripping knife. They are more likely to break into pieces than come off whole. Although the tiles will come away easily, adhesive which is difficult to remove will remain.

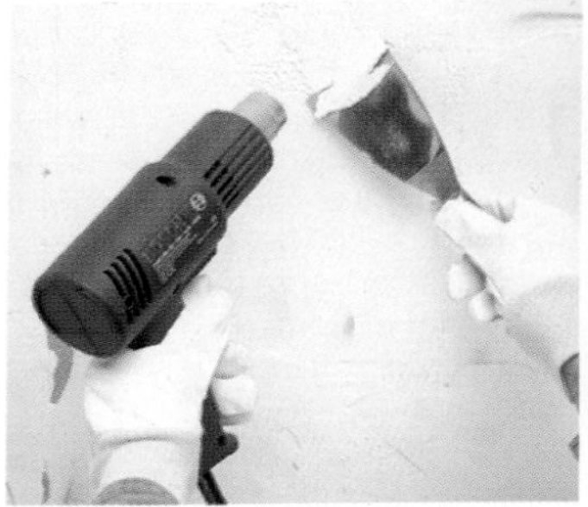

2 Wear safety spectacles for protection. Soften the adhesive left on the ceiling with heat – it will be difficult to remove otherwise. Use a hot air stripper to apply heat direct to the glue and then scrape it off the surface with a stripping knife. Alternatively, heat up the scraper blade and immediately scrape away the glue while the blade is warm.

CORK TILES

You will need
Tools Wide stripping knife. Possibly a hot air stripper.

Cork tiles are mainly used for flooring, but sometimes they are glued to a wall to create a decorative effect or perhaps to make a notice board. If you want to get cork tiles off a wall, follow the same procedure as for removing expanded polystyrene tiles from a ceiling.

Stripping poor paintwork

It is a waste of time and money to put new paint on an unstable surface; you will not achieve a satisfactory or lasting effect. Paint can be stripped dry or with the help of chemicals or heat – often it is best to use a combination of methods. If wood is to be repainted, you will not have to strip off every bit of paint, as you must if you want to varnish the wood.

As a general rule, do not use abrasive paper to strip paint from a surface. Softened paint quickly clogs even open-coat abrasives, making the process expensive. Using power tools only aggravates the problem.

Whichever way you decide to strip the paint, always wear safety spectacles and gloves to protect yourself.

STRIPPING PAINT DRY

On curved surfaces, like handrails, use a Skarsten scraper to remove paint down to bare wood. Keep the hooked blade very sharp and hold it at an angle, so it does not bite into the wood. For best results, pull the scraper towards you.

REMOVING PAINT WITH HEAT

There is a fire hazard when paint is stripped with a heat appliance, so, if you are working indoors, do not leave any newspaper on the floor. Keep a steel tray below to catch paint peelings. Have a bucket of water handy in which to drop any paint which smoulders or catches fire.

Outside, check for birds' nests under the eaves and rotten wood which could smoulder and catch fire if overheated. Keep blowtorches well away from plastic guttering, downpipes and cladding – all are quickly damaged by heat. Remove guttering and brackets if you are working on the fascia boards (the boards which support the gutters).

A hot air gun or a blowtorch will soften paint so that scrapers can remove it more easily. This cuts down the time it would take to strip wood dry. However, beginners should not use a blowtorch to strip paint around windows because the glass is likely to crack.

A hot air gun is much easier for a beginner to use but must still be handled just as carefully as a blowtorch. Some hot air guns have a useful attachment so you can shield glass from the heat when stripping window frames.

1 Soften the paint by moving the hot air gun or blowtorch backwards and forwards. The heat is very strong so do not concentrate in one area or you may burn the surface. The paint should soften in seconds – it may take longer if it is thick.

2 Strip the paint from flat areas with a broad-bladed scraper. Push the tool away from you or upwards. When scraping a vertical surface, make sure your hand is not immediately below the hot paint, which may drip. As an extra safety precaution wear cotton gloves (rubber gloves will make your hands too hot in the heat caused by the gun).

3 When using a shave hook on mouldings, also hold it at an angle, so that hot paint cannot fall onto your hand.

4 With a blowtorch, you may burn the wood through the paint, so do not use one if you want a natural finish.

If you accidentally scorch the surface, rub fine abrasive paper along the grain to remove charred wood. Then apply a wood primer and paint.

USING CHEMICAL STRIPPERS

Applying a chemical stripper is probably the safest method for a beginner and the most effective way of removing paint completely from wood, especially if you want to varnish it. But if you prefer to have a painted door stripped by someone else, see page 199.

Chemical strippers are applied in liquid form or as a paste, mixed from powder and water. They are extremely useful for stripping paint on a window frame, where heat could crack the glass. The drawbacks with chemical strippers are that they can be expensive to use (more than one application is often necessary) and they take up more time than other methods, because you have to wait for the chemicals to work on the paint. Wear safety spectacles and protect your hands from strippers with rubber gloves. If you accidentally spill any on your skin, wash it off immediately with plenty of cold water.

Always neutralise strippers – as directed on the container – before redecorating.

Liquid strippers

1 Use an old paintbrush to apply liquid stripper (which is often clear) onto the surface. The paint wrinkles and breaks up about 15 minutes after application.

Follow the instructions carefully and give the stripper enough time to work. If you try to strip the paint too soon it will not come away and another application of stripper will be needed. If you leave the stripper for too long, it will dry and begin to harden again.

A heavy build-up of paint will almost certainly require more than one application.

2 When the chemicals have had time to work, remove the paint. Use a shave hook on moulded surfaces, pulling the tool towards you.

3 If the surface is flat, lift the softened paint by pushing a wide scraper away from you.

Paste strippers

1 Protect the surrounding area with brown paper or newspaper. Apply the stripper in a thick coat, which will slowly set on the surface while the chemicals work beneath.

2 Follow the manufacturer's instructions; it is usually best to cover the paste with plastic and occasionally spray it with water.

3 After the recommended time (hours rather than minutes), scrape away the paste – it will bring the old paint with it.

Filling small holes and cracks

Small cracks are common in plaster walls. They are usually caused by vibration or by slight structural movement that is quite normal. Or they may appear when plaster is drying out. If there are only a few cracks in isolated patches, repair them with interior filler. Where there are large numbers of cracks, it is cheaper to use a plaster filler (see chart below).

Dents in plasterboard or plaster caused by moving furniture, or gouges made by a wallpaper stripping knife, can be filled with interior filler. So can small holes up to about 1in (25mm) across in plasterboard or about 2in (50mm) across in plaster.

For filling holes up to about 6in (150mm) across and 1in (25mm) deep in plaster, or lots of holes, it is cheaper to use plaster filler.

Larger holes or cracks, or extensive areas of damage, should be repaired with plaster or plasterboard (page 239).

You will need

Tools Hand brush; clean plastic container for mixing; filling knife; mixing stick or wooden spoon; medium or fine abrasive paper and wood block, or an electric sander. Possibly also: trimming knife; large paintbrush; cold chisel; house plant spray; length of wood; plasterer's trowel.

Materials Interior filler or plaster filler; supply of cold water.

USING A POWDER-TYPE INTERIOR FILLER

1 Undercut the edge of the crack by scratching along it with a filling-knife blade to provide a good grip for the filler. This will also dislodge any loose plaster or dirt to leave a firm surface.

If the crack or dent is in plasterboard and the paper surface has been torn, cut off jagged edges with a sharp trimming knife.

2 Brush along the crack with a dry brush to remove dust.

3 Mix the filler with cold water to a stiff paste and load it onto the end of the filling-knife blade.

4 Draw the loaded blade across a crack to press in the filler. Scrape the excess off the blade, then draw it down the crack to remove excess filler from the wall and smooth the surface.

ALTERNATIVELY, fill a hole or dent up to about 2in (50mm) deep by building up the surface in layers, working from the edges. Wait about two hours for each layer to dry before applying the next.

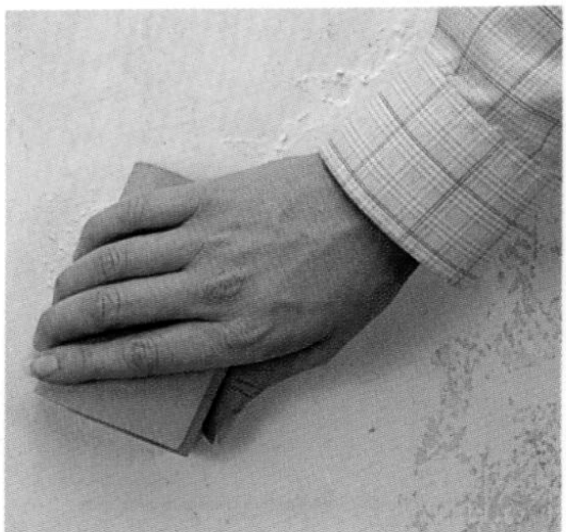

5 When the filler is completely dry, smooth it to the level of the surrounding surface with medium or fine abrasive paper wrapped round a wooden block, or use an electric sander.

CHOOSING A SUITABLE FILLER

Fillers are generally available either as ready-mixed pastes or as powders that are mixed with water. Setting times are given as a guide, but apply to average conditions. In cold weather setting may take longer, but in hot weather or in a heated room it will be faster.

FILLER	WHERE USED	DESCRIPTION
Interior filler (such as Polyfilla Interior Filler)	Cracks or small holes in plaster, wood or masonry inside house.	Available as powder or paste. Cannot be used on damp surfaces. Workable for about 1 hour, sets in 2 hours. When dry can be painted and is strong enough to take screws. Fillers described as 'fine' are stronger and not affected by damp.
One-coat ready-mixed plaster (such as Polyplasta	For all internal plaster repairs, cracks and holes.	A lightweight, tubbed, ready-mixed plaster which can be used to fill holes up to 2in (50mm) deep in one application. Easy to get smooth.
Exterior filler (such as Polyfilla Exterior Filler)	Cracks or holes in outside masonry. Can also be used to repoint brickwork.	Cement-based powder; tough and resistant to weather after about 24 hours. Workable for about 45 minutes, sets in about 2 hours. Can be painted or left bare.
All-purpose filler (such as Tetrion All-purpose Filler)	Cracks and holes in plaster, wood, masonry, glass and metal. Some types are mixed with a diluted adhesive for outside use.	Available as powder or paste. Dries to a tough, slightly flexible, weather-resistant surface that can be painted or left bare, but should not be exposed to permanent wetness or damp. Generally use 2½ parts powder to 1 part water. Workable for up to 1 hour, sets in about 2 hours. Tends to be more expensive than interior or exterior fillers.
Polyester-based metal filler (such as Plastic Padding, Chemical Metal, Isopon)	Cracks in metal such as gutters and downpipes. Can also be used for wood that is to be painted.	Pack contains two ingredients that set chemically when mixed as instructed. Mix only as much as can be applied in 5 minutes. Sets in about 20 minutes in good weather. Use hard types of filler for rigid surfaces, flexible types for bendable.
Epoxy-based wood filler (such as Ronseal High Performance Wood Filler).	Cracks or small holes in wood inside or outside. Flexes with natural expansion and contraction of wood.	Pack contains two ingredients that set chemically when mixed as instructed. Quick-setting, mix only as much as can be applied in about 5 minutes. Sets in 20–30 minutes in good conditions.
Wood filler (such as Rawlplug Plastic Wood)	Cracks or small holes in wood. (For rotton wood, see page 210.)	An adhesive paste that can be used inside or out and will set after about 10 minutes in good conditions. Available in colours to match various woods.
Frame sealant (such as Dow Corning, Unibond)	Gaps between masonry and woodwork.	Flexible, non-setting rubbery paste applied from container fitted into cartridge gun. Forms a skin after about 4 hours and can then be painted. Available in white and various other colours.
Foam filler (such as Unibond, Dow Corning, Manger Fill & Fix expanding foam)	Holes or gaps in most building materials, such as brickwork round pipes through a wall. Used inside or outside. Also suitable for insulating.	Sticky foam applied to dampened surface from pressure spray. Expensive but convenient for filling hard-to-reach areas. Workable for about 5–7 minutes. Expands to about 60 times its original volume and moulds to shape of surroundings. Forms skin in 1–2 hours. Can then be cut, sanded and painted.

USING A PLASTER FILLER

1 Lay dust sheets on the floor, then chip away loose plaster with a cold chisel and club hammer, and brush away dust and debris from the damaged area.

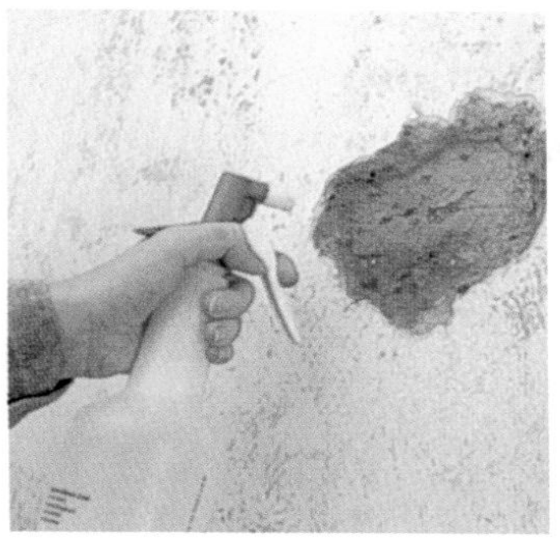

2 Dampen the hole or crack by brushing in water, using a house plant spray or a damp rag.

3 Mix the powder with water to a stiff, creamy consistency. Always use clean utensils, as old set plaster left on them will weaken the plaster and shorten the setting time. Use as soon as possible after mixing.

4 Apply the plaster in layers about ½in (13mm) thick to build up the surface. Wait about an hour for each layer to set before applying the next.

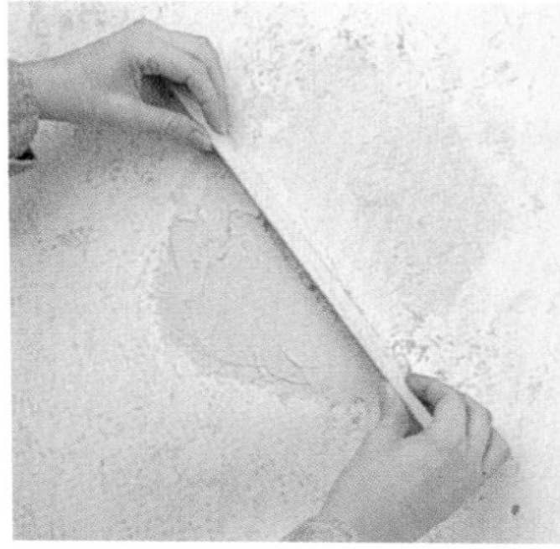

5 Level the last coat by drawing the edge of a flat length of wood across it with a sawing action, or a plasterer's trowel held at an angle.

6 When the surface has nearly set, spray it lightly with water, then smooth it with the flat of a trowel.

Dealing with awkward cracks

A long, fine crack from the top to the bottom of a wall, particularly a stairwell wall (a weak point in many houses), can be filled with interior filler. But if the crack opens again at a later date, get advice from a builder or surveyor in case it is caused by movement or settlement in the foundations.

If the plaster surface is crumbling, the wall may be damp, and this should be remedied (pages 438 and 453) before redecorating. Chip away the plaster area until you reach a firm surround, then fill the damaged area with a suitable filler, or plaster if it is extensive (page 239). Crumbling corners of a wall should be reinforced.

A bulge in the wall surface is a sign that the plaster is coming away from the backing. Break the surface of the bulge and chip it back to sound plaster. Repair with filler or plaster according to the extent of the damage.

Cracks often occur at wall joints or wall-and-ceiling joints. They can be filled with a frame sealant, in the same way as gaps between walls and woodwork (see right). A good way of hiding extensive cracking between wall and ceiling is to fit coving made of plaster or expanded polystyrene to cover it.

USING PRE-MIXED PLASTER

Small holes and cracks can be repaired using one of the pre-mixed lightweight plasters, available in tubs. They are easy to spread, and can be used to fill holes up to 2in (50mm) deep at one application with no risk of sagging.

The plaster is highly adhesive, and will not craze or crack when set. If the surface is going to be painted, apply a skim coat of the plaster to produce a really smooth surface. Wash tools in clean water immediately after use while the plaster on them is still wet.

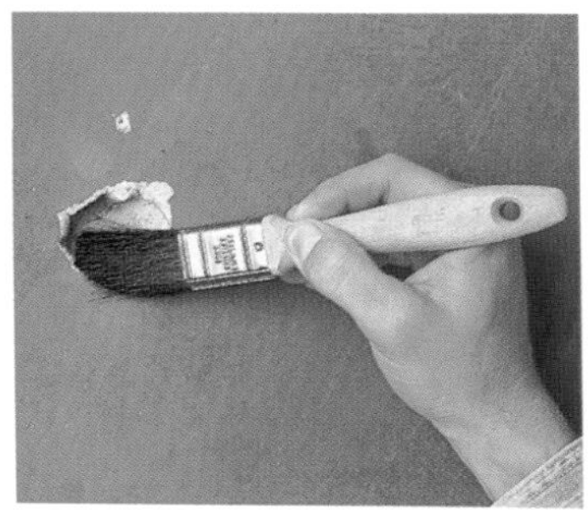

1 Remove all loose material with the point of a trowel. Smooth round the edges of the hole or crack with fine abrasive paper and clean the surface with an old paintbrush.

2 Stir the plaster and use it direct from the tub. Press it firmly into the hole using a filling knife to ensure a good bond.

3 Smooth over with a trowel. When the plaster is dry sand it lightly with a fine grade of sandpaper wrapped around a wooden block.

FILLING GAPS BETWEEN WALLS AND WOODWORK

Gaps between walls and window frames, skirting boards, door frames and staircases, are likely to re-open if filled with interior or plaster filler.

Use a frame sealant, which is a non-setting flexible material that sticks well and resists cracking. It is applied with an applicator gun.

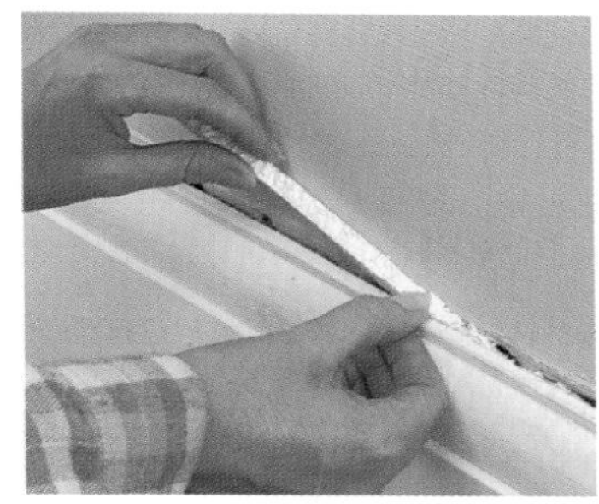

1 If the cracks are deep, half-fill them with thin strips of expanded polystyrene before applying the sealant. On an interior wall, you could use tissue paper instead of expanded polystyrene.

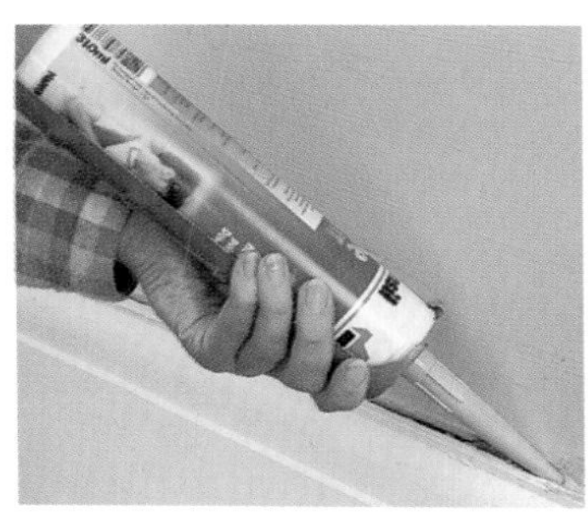

2 Make sure the sealant reaches to both sides of the gap, and press it in and smooth the surface with a wetted fingertip.

USING FOAM FILLER

Deep cavities – around a pipe through a wall, for example – can be difficult to fill but the job is easier if you use foam filler.

Choose a container which can be held at any angle and follow the manufacturer's instructions. Wear the gloves supplied – the foam is very sticky until it sets. Before you start filling a hole, experiment to see how fast the foam comes out of the nozzle and how much it expands.

1 Brush any dust out of the hole. Dampen the surface with water.

2 Allowing for expansion, release foam into the hole. You may only need a thin bead.

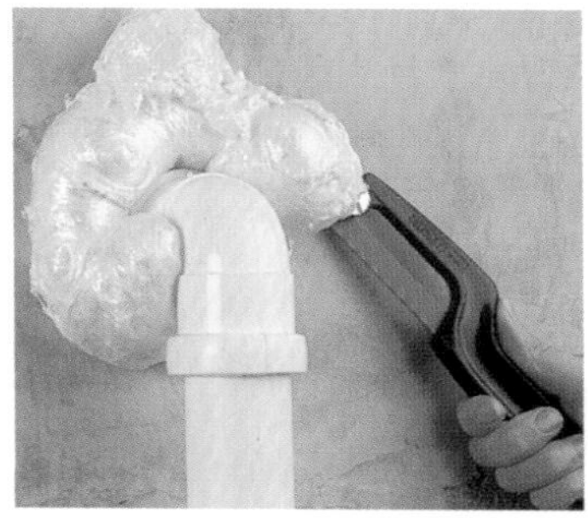

3 Leave the foam for 1 to 2 hours. When it has set, cut any excess away with a hacksaw blade or a sharp knife. Do not inhale the dust.

What goes on before the paint?

Most interior and exterior surfaces require a preparatory coating before you can apply any paint. If a painting surface is stable and sealed, the decorating will be successful. Be sure to choose a coating suitable for the surface.

Take special care with any painted surface that will be exposed to the weather. The end grain of wood must be thoroughly soaked with primer to prevent the rain from penetrating. Primer by itself is not particularly weather resistant, so do not leave a primed surface exposed to rain and wind for long. Cover it with an undercoat and a topcoat as soon as possible.

New windows, doors and other wooden fittings are usually supplied ready primed. Check for scratches and other damage and prime any areas that have become exposed. Give a second coat of primer to any areas that will become hidden by brickwork after the fitting is installed.

When using a microporous paint on bare wood, no primer or undercoat is needed. Do not apply more than two coats.

CHOOSING PRIMERS AND OTHER SEALERS

COATING	WHERE USED	DESCRIPTION	ADVICE
Knotting	Resinous areas, especially knots, in wood.	High in shellac. Prevents resinous areas in wood from discolouring paint.	When dry, coat knotting with primer.
Primer	New or exposed wood, plaster or metal.	Seals pores in absorbent surfaces. Forms a key to which other coats grip.	Buy primer for a specific surface or use all-purpose primer.
Primer-sealer	Stained walls and plaster; old bituminous coatings; areas treated with preservative.	Contains fine scales of aluminium. Forms a barrier to seal the surface.	Apply a second coat if stain is still visible after the first.
Cold galvanising paint	Damaged galvanised metal and new iron and steel.	Zinc-rich coat which acts like a primer and prevents rust.	Stir well before use. Leave to dry thoroughly before applying paint.
Stabilising solution	Mainly on external rendering which has become powdery.	Binds together surfaces to provide a firm support for paint.	Apply fungicide before stabilising solution on a mould-affected surface.
Fungicide	Any affected exterior or interior surface.	Chemical used to kill mould, algae, lichen and moss.	When spores are dead, brush them away and apply another coat.

Painting: Tools for the job

As with all tools, quality counts. Buy the best tools you can afford and take care of them.

Brushes

You really do get what you pay for with a brush. Good quality brushes improve with use, as the tips become rounded and any loose bristles come out. Wear in brushes on undercoats and save your best matured brushes for topcoats.

Cheap brushes usually contain far less bristle for a given width, and they are often badly anchored so that the bristles tend to fall out. Keep cheap brushes for less important work, like applying wood preservatives to rough timber. Cheap brushes are also useful for removing dust after sanding down.

Look out for a new generation of synthetic fibre brushes. They are easy to clean, and the bristles are locked-in. They are especially useful with water-based paints.

For normal jobs, you can manage with 2in, 1in and ½in (50mm, 25mm and 13mm) brushes, with a 4in or 6in (100mm or 150mm) brush for walls and ceilings. An angled ¾in (19mm) cutting-in brush will prove useful for window frames. The angled tip helps to get close to the glass without getting paint on it.

A crevice or radiator brush, with bristles at right angles to the handle, is good for painting awkward places, such as behind radiators and pipes.

A wide brush on a cranked handle (bent at right angles in the middle) is easier on the wrist for work on walls and ceilings, which can be tiring.

Rollers

An easy way to spread paint quickly over large areas is with a paint roller, generally used with a roller tray for holding the paint.

Three main types of roller are available. They are all best with water-based paint, which is easier to clean off than oil-based paint. Where possible, choose a model with a decorating sleeve that can be removed from the core of the roller. This also makes cleaning easier.

FOAM ROLLER A good general-purpose roller if a high finish is not important. It can only be used on smooth and lightly textured surfaces. The foam deteriorates with age, so replace it as soon as there are signs of crumbling.

MOHAIR ROLLER A very fine short pile on a firm backing gives a high finish, making it ideal for large smooth surfaces, such as doors and walls. It is no good on textured surfaces. The pile must always be cleaned thoroughly after use.

SHAGGY PILE ROLLER Lamb's-wool (or imitation) rollers and nylon rollers vary according to their depth of pile. They are well suited to textured and high-relief surfaces because the shaggy pile goes in the crevices. If you are decorating outside walls coated in a pebble dash or stipple, choose a tough exterior grade nylon pile roller.

A small roller on a longer handle is useful for painting areas difficult to reach, such as behind radiators.

Some rollers have a hollow handle to take an extension handle. This means you can reach high areas from ground level.

There is also a range of patterned foam rollers for use with textured coatings – only raised areas on the roller pick up paint. It takes a long time to master the technique of matching the pattern to produce professional results.

Paint pads

A pad consists of a fine layer of mohair bonded to a foam strip, which is mounted on a handle. Pads vary in size from about 1in (25mm) square up to a width of 7in (180mm). You need a tray for the paint, though a baking tin or something similar will do.

Pads are best suited to water-based paints, because most solvents used for cleaning off oil-based paints attack the adhesive between the mohair and the foam. You may think that very small pads are cheap enough to throw away after use, but clean large pads thoroughly – they will last for years. As with rollers, some pads have hollow handles for extension poles.

Aerosols

An aerosol is a pressurised container which forces paint out in a fine spray jet. It is useful for highly textured surfaces, such as basket-weave furniture, and items like wrought-iron gates.

Spray gun

A spray gun has limited uses around the home so it pays to hire spray equipment, rather than buy your own. Cheaper guns – including the type sometimes offered with vacuum cleaners – are best kept for applying wood preservatives. An airless spray gun – operated by a pressure pump – gives the most satisfactory results.

Paint kettle

Pour paint into a paint kettle as required. The kettle usually has a handle, unlike most small paint tins. If you are using more than one colour, line the kettle with foil. This can be removed and thrown away – leaving the kettle clean – when you want to change colour.

Another reason for using a kettle is that should paint become contaminated – perhaps when painting woodwork close to soft mortar or rendering – you have not contaminated all the paint, only what is in the kettle.

Paint shield

Use a plastic or metal shield to keep paint off glass when painting window frames. You can also use one to prevent your paintbrush from picking up dirt from a floor when painting a skirting board.

BRUSHES, ROLLERS, PADS AND SPRAYS

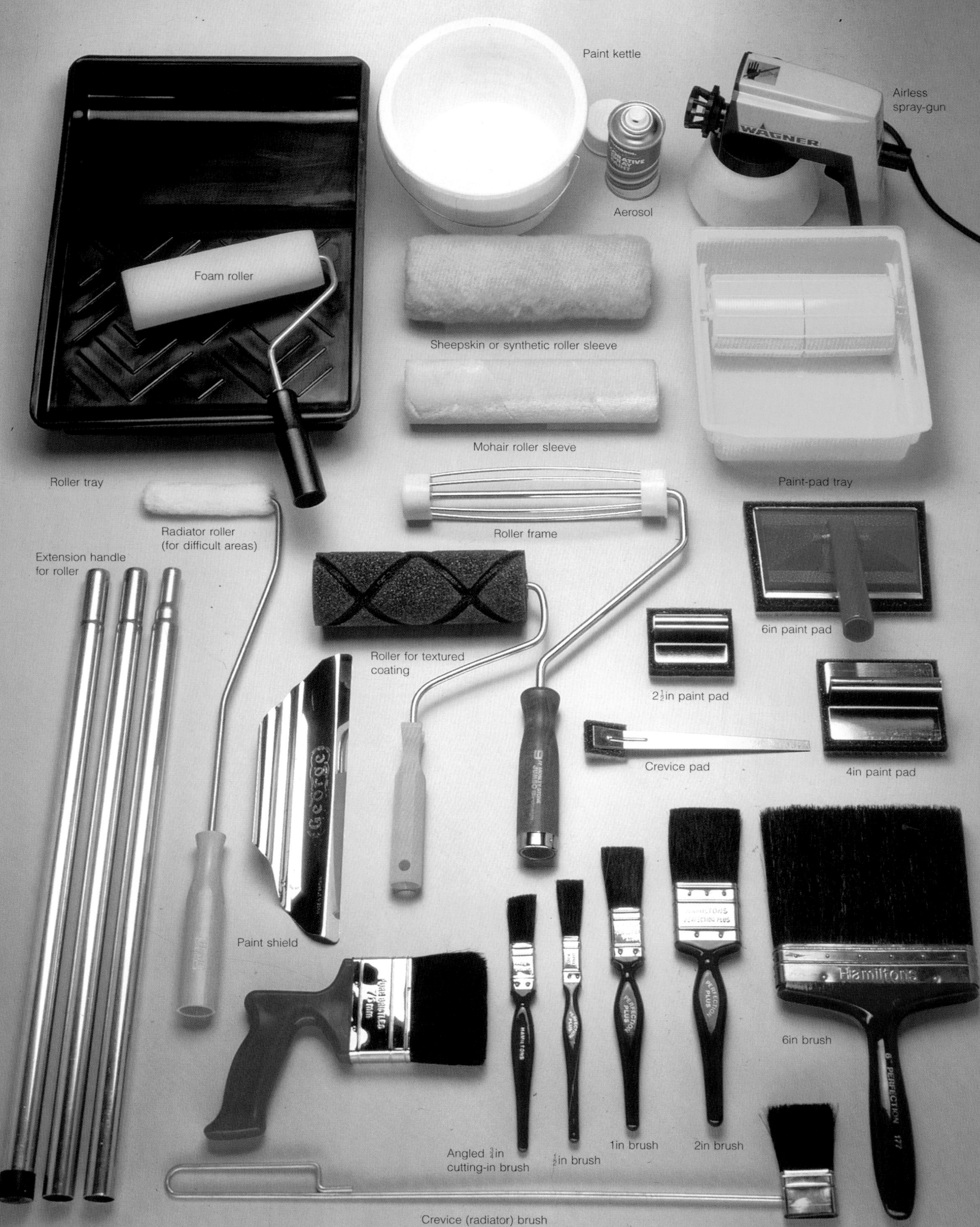

How to decide on the right type of paint

Before you buy paint, make sure that it suits your colour scheme by holding a colour card up against curtain or carpet samples. If possible, take home a tester pot of paint and try it out on a wall. Paint tends to look darker once it is applied to a wall so, if you are doubtful about which shade of a colour to buy, choose the paler one. The colour of paint can vary from batch to batch, so buy as much paint as you need for the job in one purchase to avoid any risk of slight shade differences.

There are two main types of paint. Conventional paints are liquid in consistency. They are sometimes referred to as oil-based (gloss) for wood and metalwork, and water-based (emulsion) for walls and ceilings. Oil-based paint must be used with an undercoat. Emulsion paints do not need an undercoat but two or more coats may be needed to obliterate the colour of the surface. The first coat of emulsion acts as an undercoat.

The second type – specially formulated for beginners – is non-drip paint, which is also called thixotropic, jelly or one-coat paint. The paint looks like jelly in the tin and becomes liquid when it is brushed onto a surface. Then it gels again, making it less prone to drips and runs. Non-drip paint has good covering power, because it is thicker than conventional paints and incorporates the undercoat. For this reason, non-drip paint is no more expensive than other paints in the long run, even though it often costs more per litre.

Non-drip emulsion paints are supplied in both jelly and solid form. The application of a roller to the solid paint – which is sold in a tray – liquefies the paint so that the roller picks up just enough. The non-drip quality makes it ideal for painting a ceiling.

Never stir non-drip paint before use, even if it looks lumpy in the tin. If the paint becomes liquid because it has been accidentally stirred or shaken, leave it to set again before using it.

The final coat of paint – the topcoat – can have a gloss, semi-gloss or matt finish. Alternative names for semi-gloss include eggshell, silk, satin and sheen, depending on the paint manufacturer. The glossier the paint, the tougher and more durable the surface will be. Paints also tend to be stronger and more weather-resistant if they include a synthetic resin, such as polyurethane.

Some paints contain additives which make them more fire-resistant than ordinary paint. They help to reduce the spread of flames, which makes them suitable for painting expanded polystyrene tiles, wood and any combustible surface.

CHOOSING PAINTS FOR EVERY PURPOSE

Follow the manufacturer's advice on the paint tin. This will usually state what surfaces can be coated with the paint, the length of drying time and the expected covering power.

COATING	WHERE USED	DESCRIPTION	ADVICE
Undercoat	Interior and exterior primed surfaces, before applying topcoat. Dark surfaces which are to be painted a paler colour.	A full-bodied paint with more pigment than topcoat. Has good covering power.	Apply a second coat if undercolour shows through the first. Wash tools with white spirit after applying undercoat.
Oil-based, or synthetic, gloss paint (topcoat)	Interior and exterior woodwork and metalwork. Can also be applied to walls and ceilings, if desired.	For both decorative and protective purposes. A relatively thin coating with little covering power.	On wood, always use with an undercoat. This is not necessary on metal. Apply two thin coats of gloss, rather than one thick one. Clean brushes immediately with white spirit.
Non-drip (thixotropic), jelly or one-coat paint	Gloss for interior and exterior woodwork, and emulsion for ceilings.	Combines undercoat and topcoat. Stays on the brush well. Easy for beginners to use.	Two coats may be needed when covering a dark colour. Clean painting tools with white spirit.
Interior emulsion paint	Walls and ceilings.	Water-based, which makes tools easy to clean. Dries quickly and does not leave brushmarks. Acrylic resins are sometimes added to make the paint more hard-wearing.	Does not need an undercoat. Can be diluted with water to form its own primer. Use a roller for fast coverage. Two or three coats may be needed. Clean tools with water and soap or detergent.
Exterior emulsion paint	Outside walls.	Water-based paint but extremely hard-wearing. Keeps the surface looking clean for longer because part of the coating washes away with rain, taking dirt with it.	Fill any fine cracks before painting. Apply with a brush at least 5in (125mm) wide, or a shaggy roller. Clean tools with soap and water.
Microporous paint	Exterior, new, untreated timber.	All-in-one primer, undercoat and topcoat formulated to allow moisture vapour trapped beneath the paint film to pass through it and evaporate without causing the blistering or flaking common to traditional exterior paint systems.	Do not apply over existing paint finishes, as microporous properties work only when paint is applied to new or stripped surfaces. Can be overpainted with minimal preparation as paint film wears by erosion.
Masonry paint	All types of exterior rendering.	Most are strengthened with materials like silica, nylon or sand, which help to form a more durable finish.	Stabilise the surface with stabilising solution and use fungicide as necessary, before applying paint. Clean tools with water.
Bituminous paint	Exterior metal pipes and guttering, and over concrete.	A special paint for waterproofing surfaces.	Other paints will not take over it, so once you have applied it to a surface, continue to use bituminous paint. Clean brushes with paraffin, but even when clean keep only for bituminous paint.
Textured (plastic) coating	Interior walls and ceilings with uneven or unattractive surfaces.	A compound much thicker than paint. Forms a permanent coating which is extremely difficult to remove.	Apply with a shaggy roller, unless the manufacturer specifies otherwise. Coat with emulsion once dry. Will not take a wall covering. Clean tools with white spirit.
Anti-condensation paint	Surfaces in bathrooms, kitchens and any room likely to have a steamy atmosphere.	Semi-porous emulsion which absorbs moisture in the air and allows it to evaporate as the air dries. Prevents droplets forming on the surface. Often contains a fungicide to deter mould.	Apply as interior emulsion. Will not cure condensation, only reduce its effect on the painted surface. Clean tools with water and detergent.
Enamel paint	Metal and wood. Children's toys and furniture.	Non-toxic. Contains very finely ground pigment. May be available with a rust inhibitor.	No primer or undercoat needed. Enamels are best for small jobs. Clean brushes with white spirit.

There are other special paints for specific purposes, including: floor paint for interior and exterior use, garage floor paint, doorstep paint, matt black (for metalwork or decorative timber and blackboards), radiator enamel (which retains its whiteness under heat), anti-damp paint, tile red paint (for window ledges and exterior tiles), and insulation paint (to reduce heat loss).

How much paint do you need?

Calculate how much paint you need before you buy it. Be generous with your calculations and never underestimate.

The porosity, texture and existing colour of a surface affect the amount of paint required to cover it. Highly porous surfaces absorb a considerable amount – especially when priming. Similarly, decorative surfaces, like pebbledash, embossed papers and textured coatings can be very thirsty, perhaps doubling the amount you might expect them to take. Two or three undercoats may be needed to cover a strong colour and, when working outside, always allow for at least two topcoats for good protection against the weather.

Most paint tins indicate average coverage for the amount in the container. You can also use the following table as a general guide.

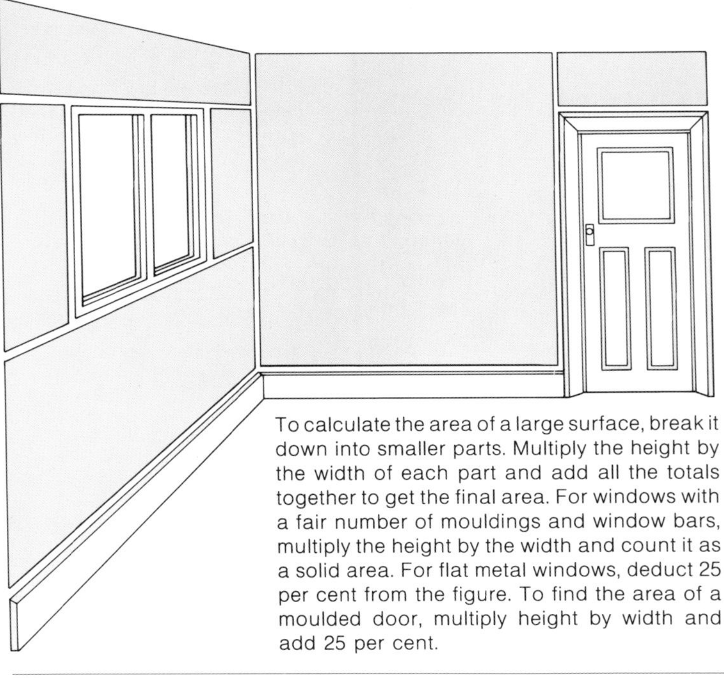

To calculate the area of a large surface, break it down into smaller parts. Multiply the height by the width of each part and add all the totals together to get the final area. For windows with a fair number of mouldings and window bars, multiply the height by the width and count it as a solid area. For flat metal windows, deduct 25 per cent from the figure. To find the area of a moulded door, multiply height by width and add 25 per cent.

THE AREA A LITRE OF PAINT WILL COVER

COATING	COVERAGE PER LITRE
All-purpose primer	130sq ft (12sq m)
Undercoat	170sq ft (16sq m)
Gloss	150sq ft (14sq m)
Non-drip gloss	130sq ft (12sq m)
Emulsion	108–140sq ft (10–13sq m)

LEAD IN PAINT – FACTS ABOUT SAFETY

Paint with a high lead content can cause lead poisoning, so since the 1960s manufacturers have greatly reduced the amount of lead in paint. Most paint now contains little or no lead. Tins of paint that do contain lead must have a warning on them.

The real danger comes from old paint, which should be stripped or, if it is sound, coated with lead-free paint. Always wear a face mask when stripping old paint and open the windows. Never strip the paint dry. It is safest to use a liquid chemical stripper. Keep children out of the way while you work and do not let them chew old painted surfaces – they might be harmful.

Using a paintbrush

Use a paintbrush – the traditional painting tool – to paint any surface with primers, undercoats and varnishes, as well as decorative topcoats. A paintbrush is the best tool for applying gloss to wood and metalwork and for painting where colours or surfaces meet – around windows and doors, for instance. A brush also does a good job on walls and ceilings, provided that you use one at least 4in (100mm) wide. You will get the work done more quickly with a bigger brush but it may become tiring on your wrist.

1 Stir the paint – unless it is non-drip – with a stick or stirrer attachment on a power tool. Make sure any sediment at the bottom of the tin is thoroughly mixed into the paint by lifting the stick as you stir.

2 Line a paint kettle with aluminium foil – to make cleaning easier – and pour in paint to fill about one-third of the kettle. Do not work from the tin; you may contaminate the paint with dried paint, dirt and possibly rust from around the rim.

3 Choose a brush which is the right size for the job and which is also comfortable to work with. Never use one which is wider than the surface you are painting – you will not be able to brush out the paint evenly and may get drips and runs. You may find it most convenient to paint window frames with a 1in (25mm) brush, door panels with a 3in (75mm) brush, and walls with a 4in (100mm) brush – but it is very much a matter of choice. If you find that the brush you are working with is tiring, change to a smaller size.

IF YOU ARE USING OLD PAINT

Wipe away dust and dirt from the rim before you open an old tin. If a skin has formed, cut around the edge and lift it out.

Stir the paint well and then strain it through an old nylon stocking to remove any bits of skin or hardened paint.

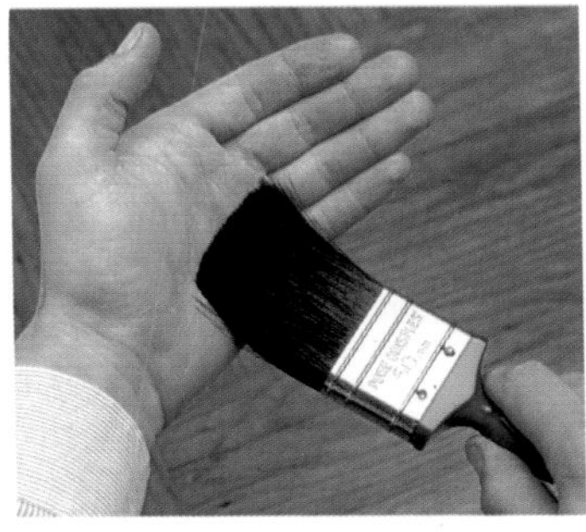

4 Flick the bristles against your hand to remove dust and any loose bristles or dried paint particles.

5 Dip the brush into the kettle to load only about one-third of the bristle depth with paint.

Using a paintbrush (continued)

6 Press the brush against the kettle wall to remove surplus paint. Do not scrape the brush over the rim of the kettle because too much paint will come off.

7 Grip large – 3in (75mm) to 6in (150mm) – brushes around the handle. Hold smaller – 1in (25mm) or 2in (50mm) – brushes more like a pencil.

PAINTING WITH NON-DRIP PAINT

Do not stir non-drip paint and do not remove any excess paint from the brush; it is meant to be heavily loaded. Apply the paint in horizontal bands. Keep the brushing-out to a minimum. Overbrushing will destroy the paint's consistency and make it run.

PAINTING WITH OIL-BASED OR SYNTHETIC GLOSS

1 Start at the top of the surface. Paint three vertical strips parallel to each other. Leave a gap just narrower than the brush width between the strips.

2 When you have exhausted the paint, do not reload the brush. Working from the top, brush across the painted area horizontally to fill the gaps and smooth the paint.

3 With the brush now almost dry, lightly go over the section you have just painted with vertical strokes to ensure an even coating, stopping on an upward stroke. This is termed 'laying off'.

4 Using the same technique, paint a similar sized section underneath the one you have completed. Work the wet paint into the dry, making sure the strips marry into each other. Do not allow the paint to build up where the sections join.

PAINTING WITH EMULSION PAINT

1 Start at the top of the surface. Apply the paint in all directions, working horizontally across the surface and moving down when one band is complete.

2 Lay off the paint with light brush strokes and a fairly dry brush, working in a criss-cross pattern. Lift the paint finally on upward strokes.

3 Do not put the paint on too thickly.

'BEADING' WHERE COLOURS MEET

Where walls meet the ceiling and where adjacent walls are of different colours, keep the meeting edge as straight and as neat as possible. Do not rush the job.

1 Turn the brush edge on, holding the stock with your thumb on one side and your fingers on the other.

2 Load the brush with enough paint to cover about one-third of the bristle depth.

3 Press the brush flat against the surface so that a small amount of paint (the bead) is squeezed from the bristles. Work towards the edge gradually, rather than trying to get close immediately.

4 Draw the brush sideways or downwards along the surface, keeping your hand steady.

CUTTING IN

When using a roller or pad, first paint the edges of a surface (where the tools cannot easily reach) with a brush.

1 Paint four or five overlapping strokes at right angles to the edge.

2 Cross-brush over the painted area in a long, sweeping motion, keeping parallel to the edge.

HELPFUL TIPS

Clean up spills with a damp rag as you go along. Use water for emulsions and white spirit for gloss paints.

Do not apply too thick a coat.

If you have a dark colour to hide, apply two undercoats before the topcoat.

For a fine finish, rub down between coats with fine abrasive paper to remove slight nibs (rough bits). Dust off with a dusting brush, followed by a damp rag.

Do not wear wool when painting. Stray fibres stick to paint.

PAINTING A TEXTURED SURFACE

When you are painting a surface with a heavy texture or relief, load the paintbrush with more paint than for a smooth ceiling or wall. This cuts down the time it takes to coat the surface and fill all the little indentations. But dip to only a third of the bristle depth.

If you are painting a relief wallpaper, Anaglypta for example, use a brush as wide as you can comfortably manage without putting too much strain on your wrist. A 4in (100mm) paintbrush is suitable. Paint the surface as you would an ordinary plaster wall or lining paper, starting at the top right corner and moving down, but work a little more with the bristles so that the paint gets well into the hollowed areas as well as covering the raised parts.

With a textured coating on a wall or a ceiling, you can use a shaggy pile roller – but you may find a brush easier.

Exterior rendered surfaces, such as pebbledash, are best painted with an exterior grade nylon shaggy pile roller or a large exterior grade brush (sometimes called a cement brush) which has firm bristles that hold the paint well. Keep the brush almost at right angles to the surface and apply the paint in a stippling (or stabbing) motion. Because exterior grade emulsion and masonry paint have a thick consistency, you almost have to scoop the paint out of the paint kettle or tin. You will not pick up enough paint just by dipping in.

If the pebbledash is new, wet the surface with water before applying paint to cut down the amount it absorbs.

Painting with other tools

USING A ROLLER

You can cover an area with paint more quickly with a roller than with a brush, but you may need to apply more coats because the paint goes on quite thinly. Always choose a roller which is suited to the surface. Use a foam or mohair pile on a smooth surface and a lamb's-wool or nylon pile on a textured one.

1 Thoroughly stir the paint (unless it is non-drip). Emulsion is particularly suited to rollers because it is easy to clean off.

2 Line the roller tray with aluminium foil, which can be thrown away later to reduce cleaning. Fill about one-third of the tray with paint.

3 Dip the roller into the paint, then run it lightly on the ridged part of the tray. This spreads the paint evenly on the roller sleeve.

4 To apply the paint, push the roller backwards and forwards, alternating diagonal strokes at random.

5 Do not apply too much in one coat. And do not work too fast, or paint will be thrown off the sleeve and spatter. Try not to press the roller too hard or paint will be forced off the ends in ridges.

6 As the paint runs out, go over the painted area to ensure an even spread. Lay off in straight lines on upward strokes.

7 Load the roller with paint again and cover an adjacent area.

8 Cut-in the edges around doors, windows, corners and where walls meet the ceiling as you work. Use a small paintbrush with bristles in good condition for the cutting-in. You will not get a neat finish with a large brush or a roller.

> HELPFUL TIP
>
> Work with the roller a little in front of you to avoid spray, particularly when using liquid emulsion.
>
> Use block (solid) emulsion with a roller to avoid drips and spills.

USING A PAINT PAD

Paint pads quickly cover large areas like walls and ceilings and will cope with lightly textured surfaces. You can also use a pad to paint wood and metalwork.

Do not use them to apply gloss paint because paint cleaning solvents tend to destroy the adhesive which holds the pads to their backing.

1 Stir the paint and pour some into a flat tray or baking dish lined with foil, or into the speed tray supplied with some pads.

2 Select a pad as wide as you can handle for the surface you are painting. The larger the pad, the faster you can cover the area.

3 Run the pad backwards and forwards on the roller in the speed tray to pick up the paint. Alternatively, hold the pad flat against the paint in the tin. Do not let it sink below the pile level. If the pad absorbs too much paint it will drip. A pad needs to be reloaded more often than a brush or roller.

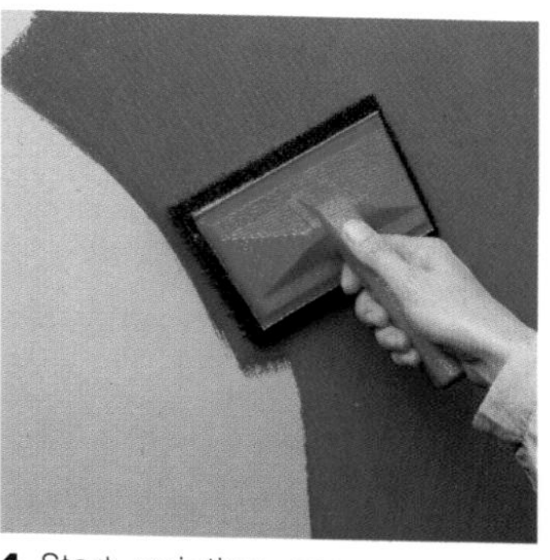

4 Start painting near a corner. Move the pad in all directions with a gentle scrubbing action. Work in strips about four times the width of the pad.

5 Do not press too hard or paint may be forced off the pad in drips. With practice you should get no drips at all.

6 Most pads will get right up to an edge, but use a brush to touch in any areas left uncovered.

> USING AN AEROSOL CAN
>
> An aerosol is ideal for painting an intricate surface which would become clogged with paint if you used a paintbrush. It is only suitable when you need a fairly small amount of paint – for larger jobs use a spray gun.
>
> The key to success with an aerosol is to apply thin coats of paint – possibly as many as ten – because if you spray on a lot of paint in one go it may sag and drip. You do not need to wait for each coat to dry completely before applying the next.
>
> Read the instructions on the can and follow them closely. Shake the can as directed before use and mask off areas you do not want to paint. Hold the aerosol upright and at least 6in (150mm) away from the surface that you are painting.
>
> Always keep the aerosol moving – never concentrate in one area – and hold it parallel to the surface.

USING A SPRAY GUN

It is never as easy to paint with a spray gun as it might look – especially if you have not used one before. Follow the instructions given by the manufacturer closely. Dilute the paint if necessary and mask off areas surrounding the surface to be painted. Wear a face mask so you cannot inhale paint. Hold the gun at right angles to the surface, at a distance of about 12-18in (300-460mm).

Do not hold the gun at one point for any length of time or the paint will build up and cause drips and runs. Always clean out the spray gun thoroughly after use.

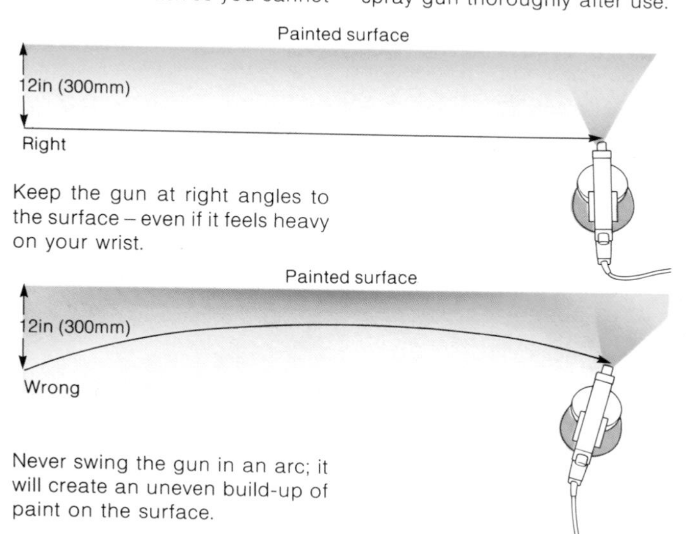

Keep the gun at right angles to the surface – even if it feels heavy on your wrist.

Never swing the gun in an arc; it will create an uneven build-up of paint on the surface.

Looking after brushes, rollers and pads

Always thoroughly clean paintbrushes, rollers and pads after each painting session, otherwise they will soon need replacing. Use cold water to wash off water-based paint immediately and never leave any of your painting tools to soak in water.

Before cleaning a brush, roller or pad, check on the paint tin to see what solvent is needed. Some paints require special thinners to remove them. Buy the necessary solvent at the same time as you buy the paint.

Emulsion and acrylic-based paint need only plenty of clean water. Some paints can be washed off with warm water and detergent, while others need white spirit. You can also use a proprietary brush cleaner, and paraffin will remove oil-based paint.

LEAVING A BRUSH LOADED WITH PAINT

Pads, rollers and trays must not be left loaded with paint, but you can leave a brush for an hour or two so long as you wrap it in a covering which will keep out the air and prevent the paint from drying on the bristles.

Use kitchen foil, a plastic bag or plastic film to wrap the brush as tightly as possible.

You can also leave a brush loaded with gloss paint for longer periods – overnight, for example – if you keep it in a jar of water which prevents the paint from being exposed to the air. Drill a hole in the brush handle, pass a piece of stiff wire through it, and suspend the brush in the jar. Do not allow the bristles to touch the bottom of the jar or they will lose their shape.

CLEANING A BRUSH

1 Gently scrape excess paint from a brush onto paper. Use the back of a knife and work from the heel (the base of the bristles) to the tip.

2 Wash emulsion paint out of a brush under a running tap. Rub a little soap or washing-up liquid into the bristles and rinse in clean water.

ALTERNATIVELY, clean off an oil-based paint, with white spirit, paraffin or brush cleaner.

3 All brushes will benefit from a final wash in soap and a rinse in clean water. Use your fingers to work out any remaining paint.

Once a brush is clean, shake it vigorously to get rid of excess water. Wipe away any remaining water on a lint-free cloth to dry the brush thoroughly, but do not damage the bristles.

4 When the brush is dry, slip a loose rubber band over the tip of the bristles to hold them together – the brush will then keep its shape.

CLEANING A ROLLER

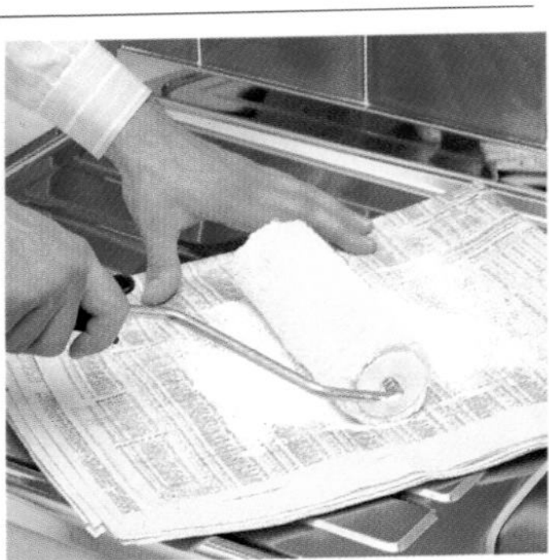

1 Run the roller over the ribbed part of the paint tray and then over sheets of paper to remove excess paint. Keep replacing the paper so that you do not pick up the paint again.

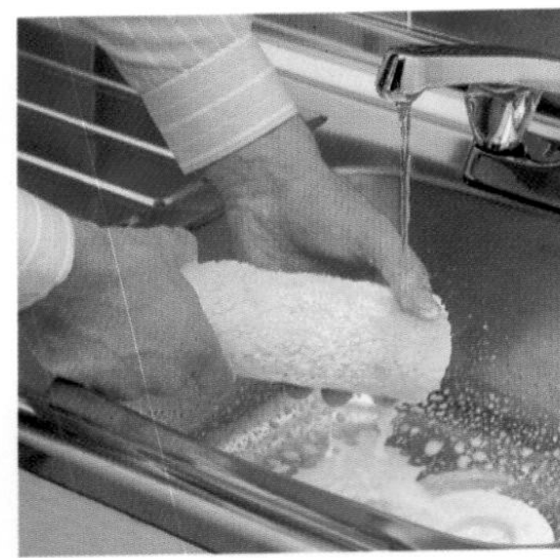

2 Remove the roller sleeve if possible. Wash the roller under running warm water, working the paint out of the sleeve with your hands.

CLEANING A PAINT PAD

Run the pad over paper to get rid of most of the paint. Wash the pad in clean water, taking great care not to separate the mohair from the base. The process will be faster if you use a little soap, but make sure you rinse it all out in clean water.

HOW TO STORE BRUSHES, ROLLERS AND PADS

Leave brushes and rollers to dry and then wrap them in brown paper or lint-free cloth, such as clean old sheeting. Store the tools flat in a warm place where they will not become damp.

Paint pads are an awkward shape to wrap so store them in plastic bags, fastened with rubber bands. This will prevent dust from collecting on the mohair.

HOW TO SOFTEN A NEGLECTED BRUSH

An old brush which has not been cleaned well after use will become hard, with the bristles sticking together in clumps. The best way to soften a brush is to use a proprietary brush cleaner or renovator, following the instructions on the pack.

Tease out any paint particles in the base of the brush with a fine brass bristle brush (normally for cleaning suede). Only use this type of restored paintbrush for rough work, like applying primer.

Painting a ceiling and walls

When you are satisfied that all the preparatory work is complete, you can apply the decorative finish – getting down to the real painting. To avoid spoiling newly painted surfaces with drips and spatters, tackle the ceiling first, then the walls and finally the woodwork. It is a good idea to paint the ceiling (which can be a messy job) before stripping any wall coverings. But this is the only exception to the rule that all preparatory work must be done before you start painting. So check that the surfaces are all stable, as smooth as possible, primed where necessary, clean and dry.

PAINTING A CEILING

1 Make sure that you can safely and comfortably reach the area you are decorating. Set up a scaffold board supported by trestles or stepladders. Your head should be about 3in (75mm) from the ceiling.

If you do not like working at a height, you can use an extension handle (or broomstick) fitted to the hollow handle of a roller or pad, for most of the painting. But you will need to stand on steps or a board to cut-in where the walls and ceiling meet and around the tops of doors and windows.

2 Paint the ceiling in strips starting near the window. If there is more than one window in the room, begin nearest the one where most light comes in.

Cut-in the edges as you work. If possible, remove light fittings mounted on the ceiling before you start painting. Otherwise carefully cut-in around them with a small brush. Paint a ceiling rose after you have painted the ceiling.

> **WHEN TO PAINT COVING**
> If you paint coving after you have painted the ceiling, you will avoid getting splashes on the new paintwork. If coving is to be the same colour as the ceiling, paint it before you paint the walls, otherwise it is easier to paint coving after decorating the walls.

PAINTING THE WALLS

When using a roller on walls, paint horizontal bands about 2ft (610mm) wide across the wall. Work from the top to the bottom. With a brush, paint blocks about 2ft (610mm) square. Start in the top right corner (or the top left one if you are left-handed). Paint the blocks from the top of the wall down and then across.

PAINTING DIFFERENT SURFACES

Bare plaster

Dilute emulsion to half strength with water and use it as a priming and sealing coat. It is difficult to hide the colour of plaster so follow this with at least two coats of neat emulsion. Use a foam or mohair roller or a paintbrush or pad as large as you can comfortably work with. Do any slight touching up with a small paintbrush as work progresses, while the paint is still wet.

Any small blemishes and hairline cracks may show up if they are painted. To avoid this, hang a lining paper or relief wallpaper before painting.

Paper

Lining paper is the ideal surface for painting. You can put on a priming coat but it is not vital. Apply at least two coats of paint and do not expect the first to obliterate any under-colour. Use whichever painting tool you prefer.

Do not worry if small bubbles appear on the paper. They will disappear as the paint dries.

Paint high relief papers, such as Anaglypta, as for lining paper, but use a shaggy pile roller.

Old wallpaper can be painted but does not give ideal results. Test an area first to see that the paper does not bubble or come away from the wall. If it does, you must strip the wall, but if not, apply full-strength emulsion as the first coat. The less water getting onto the wall the better. Use a roller, pad or brush.

Do not paint wallpapers which contain a metallic pattern – the pattern tends to show through the paint.

Paint vinyl wall coverings with a vinyl emulsion, which is more compatible than standard emulsions.

Painted surface

Never paint over distemper – it must be removed (page 101).

New emulsion paint can be applied straight onto old, without a priming coat, provided the surface has been washed down. If there is a drastic colour change, two or three coats will be necessary.

As a general rule, do not paint walls or ceilings with gloss; it enhances blemishes in the surface and is prone to condensation. If you want to paint an old gloss surface, first rub it down with a flexible sanding pad or fine wet-and-dry abrasive paper, damped with clean water. This destroys the glaze on the paint and helps the new paint film to grip the old. Rinse well to remove any deposit. Now apply emulsion, or gloss if you prefer, with the painting tool of your choice.

Textured coatings

Use a brush or shaggy pile roller to put on the paint; emulsion is probably best. These coatings usually have a deep texture and are sometimes abrasive so they will rip foam rollers and can be difficult to coat thoroughly.

Ceiling tiles

Paint expanded polystyrene tiles with emulsion, so long as they are clean. Use a roller, and a small brush for the joins between the tiles. Never use a gloss paint – it creates a fire hazard when it is put on expanded polystyrene.

If you plan to stick polystyrene tiles on the ceiling, it is much easier to paint them before you put them up, especially if they have chamfered edges.

Paint a ceiling in strips, parallel with the main light source – you will need to work from a scaffold board. When one strip is finished, move the scaffold board slightly and work back towards where you began.

You will need to stand on a stepladder to reach the top part of the wall. When you have painted blocks from the top of the wall to the bottom, move the stepladder and start to paint again at the top.

Painting cornices and mouldings

Plaster or imitation plasterwork cornices and ceiling roses can be painted in a plain colour, to match or contrast with the ceiling and walls. Alternatively, you can pick out details in a second colour.

Make sure that the surface is clean and smooth before you start. Fill any small cracks in plaster with interior filler, wait for it to dry and then rub down with fine abrasive paper. If a part of the cornice is broken away, repair it before you do the painting.

These mouldings are usually painted with emulsion. Never use gloss paint on expanded polystyrene coving – it creates a fire hazard.

1 Use a 1in (25mm) brush with no straggly bristles to paint a cornice. Apply the paint in thin coats, so that it does not form drips or runs. Let the paint dry between coats.

2 If you are using two colours, either paint the raised parts first or paint the whole area and fill in the recesses when dry with an artist's sable brush.

3 To keep your hand steady, lean on a mahl stick (a signwriter's rest). To make one, pad the end of a piece of dowel with sponge or cotton wool wrapped in a lint-free rag.

Painting woodwork

Once the ceiling and walls are painted, move on to the woodwork, which should have been well prepared before you started work on the walls and ceiling. Whatever the surface, the order of painting remains the same.

IF THE WALLS ARE TO BE HUNG WITH WALLPAPER

When a room is to be papered, take about ½in (13mm) of paint onto the wall around door and window frames, above skirting boards and below any picture rail or coving.

It is sometimes difficult to hang paper without leaving a small gap – around a door frame, for example. Taking paint onto the wall ensures that, if you do leave any gaps, matching paint will show through, making the imperfection less obvious.

1 Brush knotting over any resinous areas or knots in the wood so they are sealed and cannot seep through.

2 Apply an even coat of primer to bare wood and leave it to dry.

3 Wrap a piece of fine grade abrasive paper around a block of wood, and rub lightly over primed areas to remove any slight nibs (rough bits).

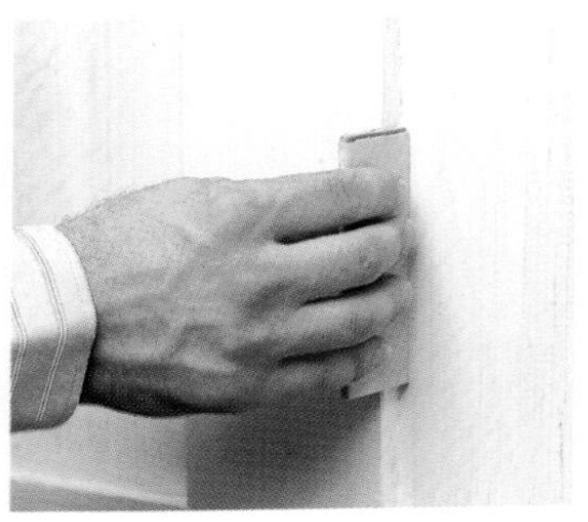

4 Remember to sand moulded areas as well. Use abrasive paper round a thin piece of wood, or a flexible sander.

5 Put one undercoat on light surfaces and two on dark ones. Use an undercoat which matches the colour of the paint.

6 When the undercoat is dry, gently rub over it with abrasive paper.

7 Remove any tiny bits of dust with a dusting brush.

8 Wipe the surface with a damp lint-free cloth (a clean old handkerchief is ideal) or a tacky rag – to pick up any more dust.

9 Apply the topcoat with a brush that is a suitable size for the surface. Gloss paint tends to be the best choice for wood because it is more durable and easier to clean than emulsion.

Painting doors and door frames

Always open a door before you paint it. Leave the door frame until last; that way, any splashes of paint that get on the frame as you paint the door will not matter as you will cover them later.

FLUSH DOORS

1 With a 3in (75mm) brush, work from the top down in horizontal strips, moving about 2ft (610mm) at a time. Work to wet edges – if the paint dries, you will get a paint line which is very difficult to lose.

2 As the brush empties, cross-brush to even out the paint.

3 When a width is complete, brush downwards over the painted area, leaving a wet edge for the next strip to blend into.

PANELLED DOORS

1 Work in the sequence illustrated for best results.

2 Use a brush of a suitable size to paint each part of the door – a smaller one for the mouldings than for the panels, for instance. Do not overload the mouldings with paint; this is a common cause of drips and runs.

GLASS PANELLED DOORS

1 Use a paint shield, an angled cutting-in brush or masking tape to keep paint off the glass. Whichever you use, allow paint to go onto about $\frac{1}{8}$in (3mm) of the glass to seal where the glass and frames meet.

2 Paint the rest of the door with a 3in (75mm) brush.

3 If gloss paint accidentally goes on the glass, remove it with a rag damped with white spirit before it dries. Remove emulsion paint with water. If paint dries on the glass, scrape it off with a razor blade. A scraping tool can be bought for the purpose.

USING TWO COLOURS

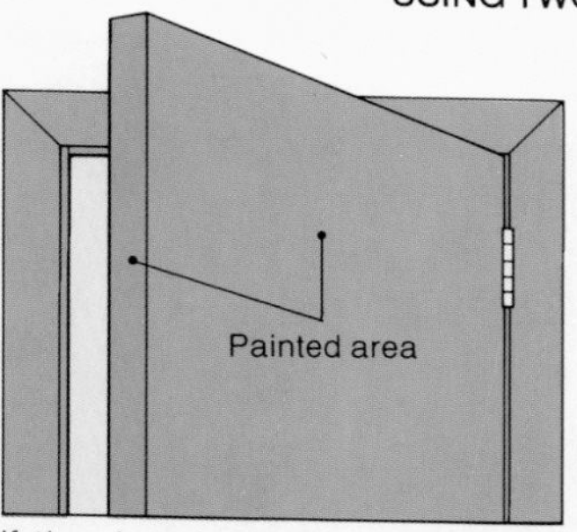

If the door is painted a different colour on each side, paint the lock edge the same colour as the side of the door which opens into the room.

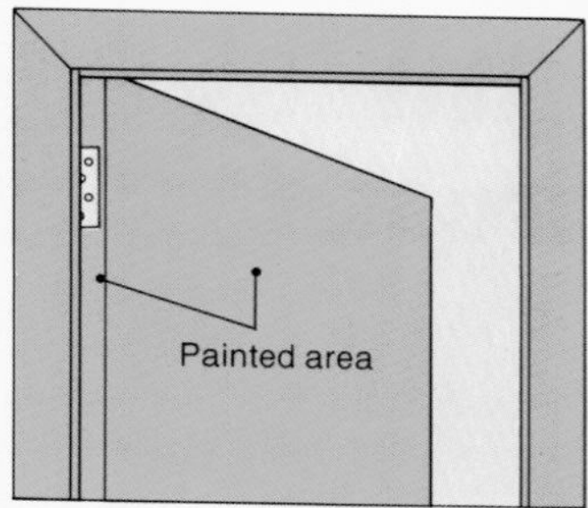

Paint the hinge edge of the door so that it is the same colour as the adjacent, visible face of the door.

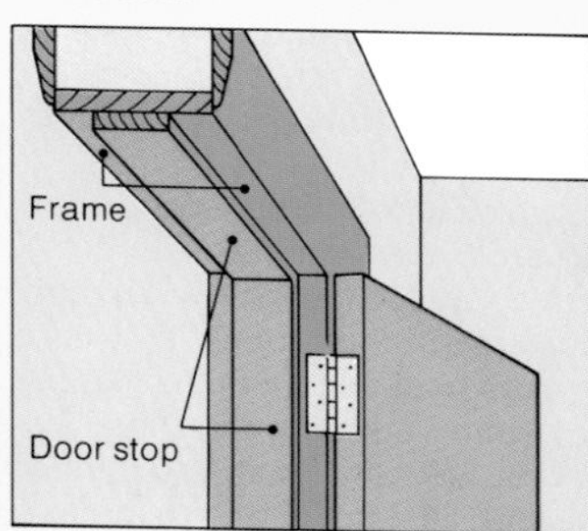

If the door frame is also painted a different colour on each side, all the parts which can be seen from one side when the door is open should be painted the same colour. Paint the door jamb – the side of the door frame – in the same colour as the frame in the room which the door opens into.

In general, you do not have to paint the top and bottom edges of the door. However, if the top is overlooked (from the staircase, for example) paint it, so that it does not stand out as bare wood.

It is not necessary to paint the bottom edge of an interior door. But if an outside door opens out above a step it can be painted to protect it against damp.

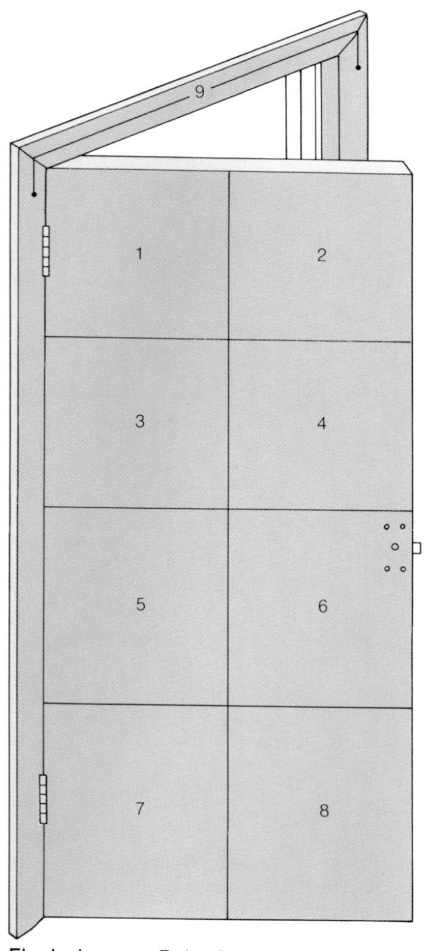

Flush doors Paint from the top down, working to wet edges in horizontal strips.

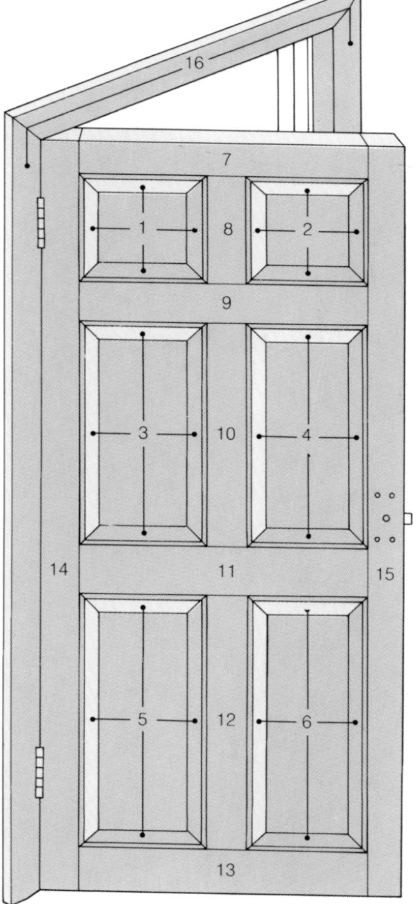

Panelled doors Paint the panels and the mouldings, then the rest.

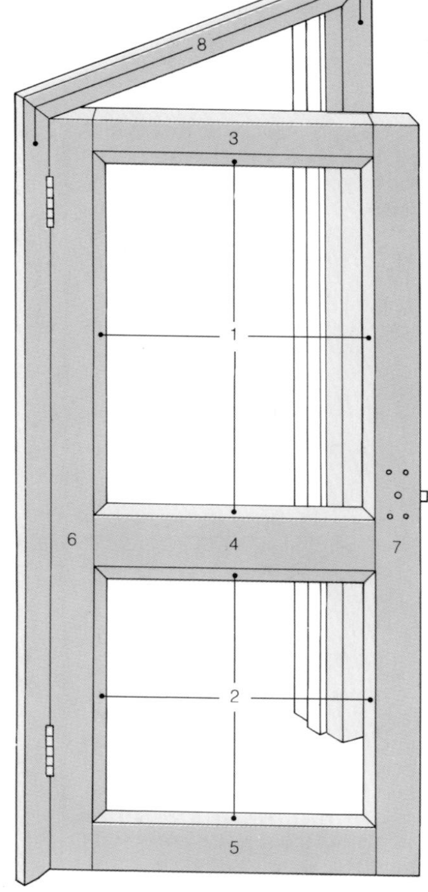

Glass doors Paint the moulding around the glass before the remainder.

Painting skirting boards and picture rails

Although they are not at eye level and so are not the most noticeable parts of a room, paint skirting boards and picture rails with as much care as you take over the rest of the decorating.

Both skirting boards and picture rails are usually painted with gloss paint to match any other painted woodwork in the room. If the walls are to be papered, paint the picture rail before you hang the paper so that you do not splash the paper.

If you lift fitted carpets before painting a skirting board, you will prevent accidents – possibly expensive ones – and will also ensure that no small fibres are picked up and worked into the paint. If you decide not to lift the carpet, protect it well with dust sheets.

SKIRTING BOARDS

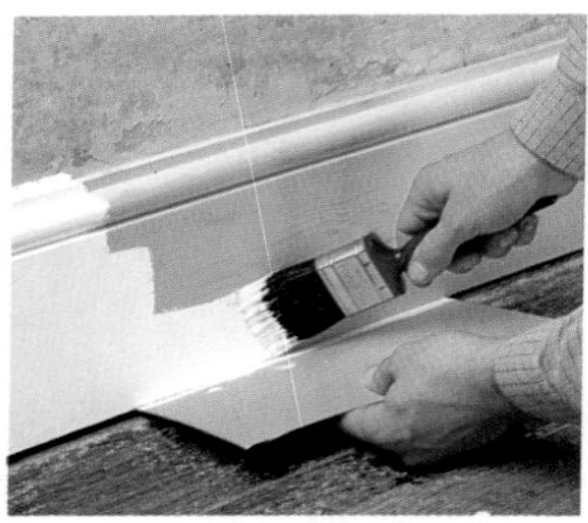

1 Hold a piece of card to prevent the paintbrush from touching the floor, especially if it is concrete or timber – the gap under the skirting board is usually full of fine debris.

2 Apply paint with a 2in or 3in (50mm or 75mm) paintbrush, depending on the height of the skirting board – it is commonly 3in–6in (75mm–150mm) high. Brush out lengthways along the run of the board.

PICTURE RAILS

With a 1in (25mm) brush, paint two or three thin coats, not one thick one, allowing each coat ample time to dry. Finish off brush strokes along the run of the rail.

Painting a staircase

1 Before you start painting, lift the stair carpet and pads. Brush the stairs vigorously – considerable debris collects beneath the carpet and must be cleaned up so that it does not contaminate the paint. If you use a vacuum cleaner, you will pick up dust more effectively.

2 Check for loose or damaged treads and risers, repair them if necessary (page 296), and then prepare the surfaces.

3 The easiest painting sequence to follow is to start with the balusters, newel post and hand rail. Then paint the treads, risers and strings on each side, beginning at the top and working down, painting one stair at a time.

Choose your brush according to which part you are painting; you need a larger brush for the treads than for the balusters, for example.

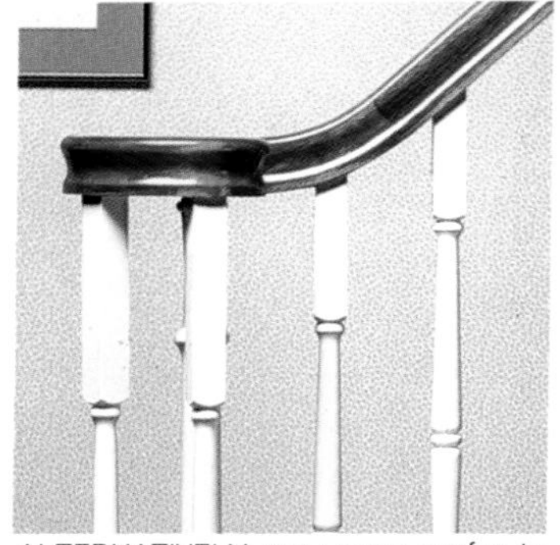

ALTERNATIVELY, you may prefer to varnish the hand rail (or hand rail and balusters), and paint just the treads, risers and strings. It is still best to decorate the hand rail first, so that you do not risk spilling varnish on the new paintwork. If the hand rail was originally painted, remove all traces of old paint before varnishing, either using heat or a chemical stripper (page 105).

4 Rub down the hand rail lightly between coats with flour grade abrasive paper to get a really smooth finish.

5 If you are putting down a stair carpet, you need only paint the parts of the treads that will show. But the paint should extend about 2in (50mm) under the carpet on each side.

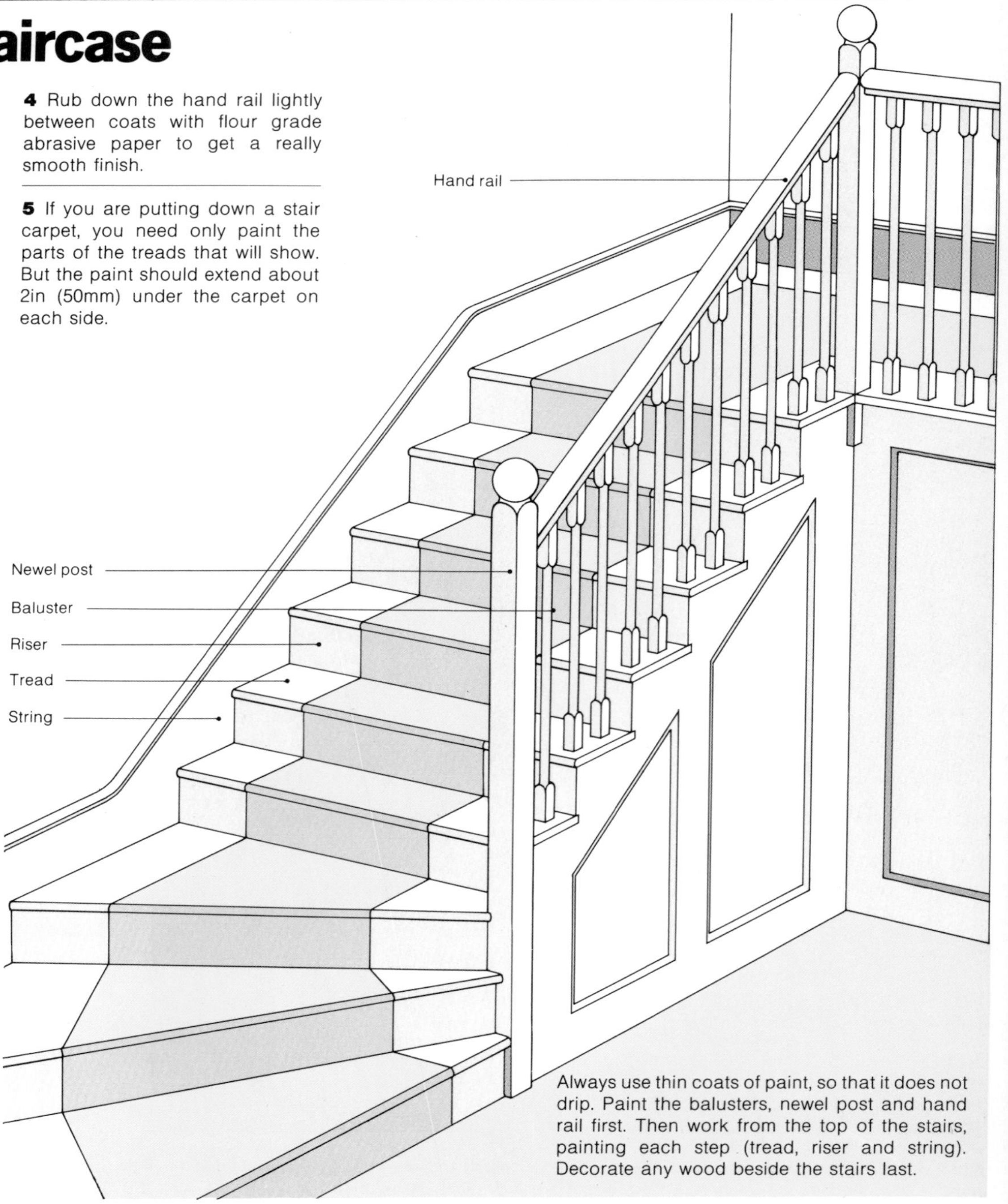

Hand rail

Newel post

Baluster

Riser

Tread

String

Always use thin coats of paint, so that it does not drip. Paint the balusters, newel post and hand rail first. Then work from the top of the stairs, painting each step (tread, riser and string). Decorate any wood beside the stairs last.

Painting interior windows and frames

It nearly always takes more time to paint a window than you think, because of the number of surfaces and because you have to keep paint off the glass. For security reasons, you will probably want to close windows at night, so start work as early as possible.

Protecting the glass

If you use masking tape to keep paint off glass, set it back by about $\frac{1}{16}$in (2mm) so that a thin line of paint goes onto the glass. This will seal any gap between the glass and the frame.

As an alternative to tape, use an aluminium masking shield, moving it along as you paint. Clean the shield regularly – paint tends to creep under it.

CASEMENT FRAMES

1 Open the window. Paint the frame in the order illustrated below left with a 1in or 2in (25mm or 50mm) brush or an angled cutting-in brush. Do not apply too much paint in one coat or it will run and take longer to dry.

The painting sequence is largely determined by the fact that the brush strokes should follow the construction of the joinery; so the vertical brush strokes will 'cut off' the horizontal ones.

2 Keep paint off handles and stays. These look best cleaned up and left natural. Remove any dried paint splashes on metal with wire wool or a wire brush lubricated with white spirit.

3 If you have to close casements and the paint is touch-dry but not absolutely hard, rub a little talc on the meeting surfaces. Alternatively, place a sheet of plastic kitchen film between surfaces likely to stick.

SASH WINDOWS

1 Pull the bottom sash up and the top one down, so that you can paint the meeting rails.

2 Paint the frame following the order illustrated below. You almost need to close the window to paint the inside runners. Give the runners a very thin coat to prevent the surfaces from sticking.

3 Do not let paint get onto the sash cords or they will harden and fail earlier than they should.

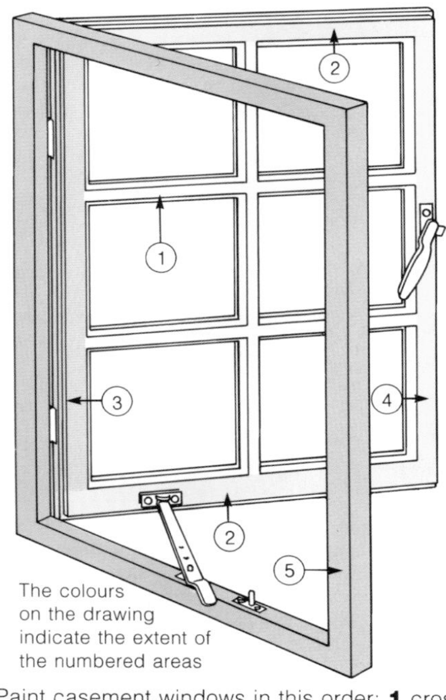

The colours on the drawing indicate the extent of the numbered areas

Paint casement windows in this order: **1** cross-bars and rebates; **2** top and bottom cross-rails; **3** hanging stile and hinge edge; **4** meeting stile; **5** frame.

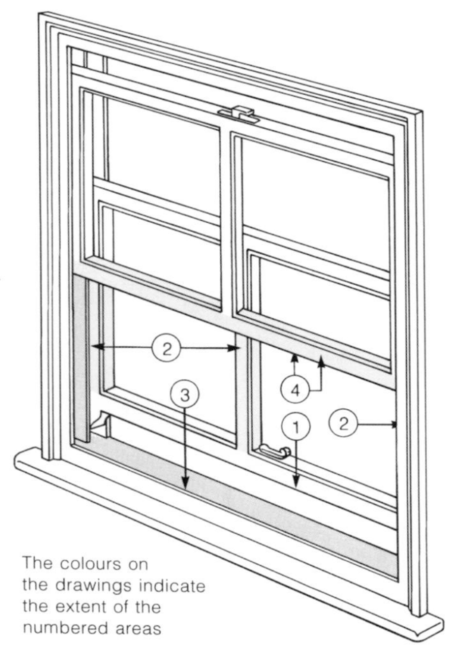

The colours on the drawings indicate the extent of the numbered areas

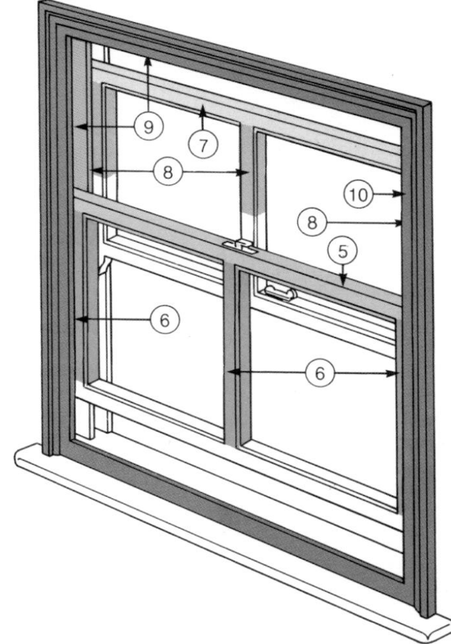

Open sash windows and reverse their positions, then paint them in the following order: **1** meeting rail; **2** vertical bars as far as possible; **3** the area that the inner sash sits on, and lower runners; **4** cross-rail and underside. Reverse the windows, then: **5** cross-rail; **6** vertical bars; **7** cross-rail; **8** rest of vertical bars; **9** soffit, top runners and behind cords; **10** frame.

Painting metalwork

Make sure all metalwork is clean, free from grease before painting.

RADIATORS

Never paint a hot radiator – always let it cool first. Wait for about an hour after you finish painting, then turn on the heating to speed up the drying process. Special radiator paint is available that will keep its whiteness despite the heat.

1 Apply gloss direct to new radiators. Use a 2in (50mm) brush and keep the coat as thin as possible to avoid runs.

2 Put on a second thin coat of gloss when the first coat is dry.

3 Do not paint over control valves; they must be left free to turn.

4 Coat painted radiators with gloss direct, unless there is to be a definite colour change, in which case apply an undercoat first.

PIPES

1 Make sure that steel and copper pipes are clean and free from rust or corrosion (page 102).

2 Apply gloss paint direct with a 1in or 2in (25mm or 50mm) brush, depending on the size of the pipe.

3 Never paint over stop taps or controls or they will not work.

CAST-IRON SURROUNDS AND WROUGHT IRONWORK

1 Remove any rust (page 102). Use a suitably sized brush to coat the surface with gloss or enamel paint direct, without an undercoat.

2 If possible, remove intricate wrought ironwork and take it outside. Then paint it with an aerosol or spray gun, shielding the area behind with dustsheets, paper or cardboard. Always use thin coats to prevent runs. Hold the can or gun at right angles to the ironwork and at a distance of about 12in (300mm). Keep the gun parallel with the surface – moving up and down or from side to side. Never swing the can or gun in an arc or hold it in one position for any length of time.

3 If you cannot move intricate wrought ironwork, put on two thin coats of gloss with a small paintbrush.

WINDOWS

Metal windows tend to be tighter fitting than wooden ones, so do not let paint layers build up on them. If the paint layers are very thick, remove the paint with a chemical stripper (page 105). In all other respects, the painting procedure remains the same as for wooden frames (see above).

> HELPFUL TIP
>
> If you have a small amount of paint left in the tin at the end of a job, pour it into a screw-top jar and label it with the name of the surface it was used for. Paint will keep for years like this and can be used for touching up.

Curing and preventing paint problems

If a paint film breaks down the only remedy is usually to strip off the paint and start again. So prevention of paint faults is the best policy.

The main causes of paint breaking down are incompatible paints being applied on one another, poor preparation of the surface, damp or trapped moisture, grease, rot or rust.

FAULT — CAUSE AND CURE

Flaking

The paint has not been keyed to the surface, which may be too smooth (as with old gloss paint) or may be chalky (as with untreated distemper). Alternatively, rotting timber may be pushing the paint off or rust may have formed underneath. Occasionally, though rarely, paint flakes just because it is inferior quality.

Strip small areas of flaking paint by rubbing with fine abrasive paper, fill with a fine surface filler, apply a primer and repaint. Larger areas must be completely stripped and begun again from scratch.

Blistering

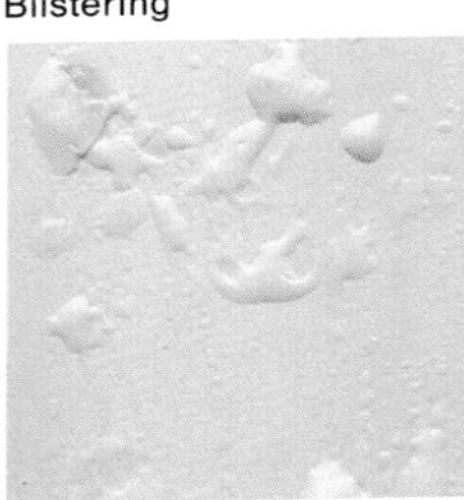

A common problem on painted woodwork. Prick a blister – if water emerges, damp is trapped under the paint film or is finding its way in from behind. The warmth of the sun turns moisture into vapour, which pushes the paint up into a blister. Strip the blistered paint with a hot-air gun and leave the wood until dry. Prime the surface and then repaint the whole of the repaired area.

If there is no sign of water, the wood probably has an open grain and air has been trapped under the paint. Again, the sun's heat expands the air forcing the paint to bubble. Strip the blistered paint, fill the open grain with an epoxy-based filler and repaint. Or omit the filler and use a microporous paint on bare wood.

Crazing (sometimes called orange peel)

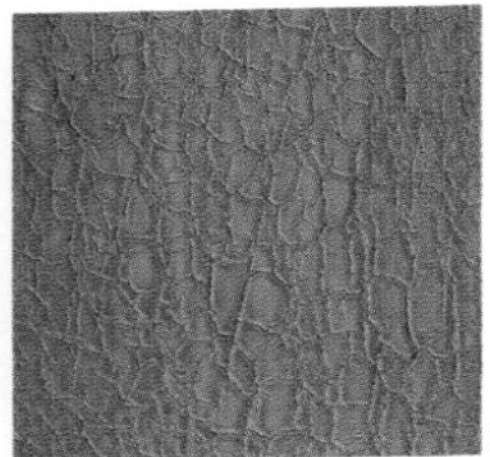

ICI

When a paint surface breaks up like mini crazy paving, incompatible paints have been used. The top layer of paint breaks up because it expands at a different rate from the one underneath. In most cases you must strip the paint with a chemical stripper or heat and start again. However, you can rub down very small areas – only a few inches square – with a flexible sanding pad or with wet-and-dry paper damped with water. When the surface is smooth, fill the stripped area with a fine surface filler, prime and repaint.

Visible under-colour

A topcoat does not have good covering power, so always use undercoat to hide the colour of the surface. Poor coverage is also sometimes the result of using inferior paint (especially emulsion).

To rectify the problem, put on another layer of topcoat, but switch to using one-coat paint, which has more body and covering power than traditional paint.

Runs and tears

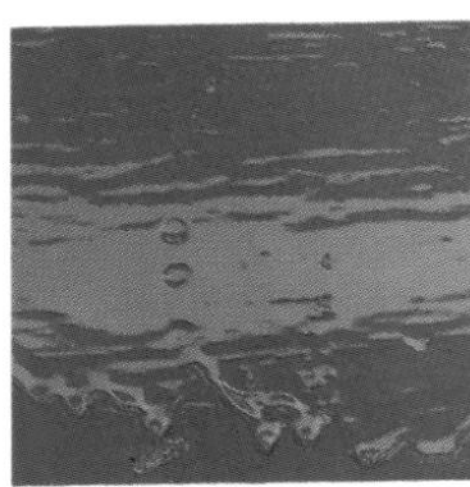

Too much paint applied in a thick coat results in runs and tears which are extremely difficult to disguise or lose. If the paint is still wet, brush out runs but do not do this if the paint has started to dry. Instead, wait until it is completely dry and then rub down with very fine abrasive paper until the surface is smooth. Clean the surface with a dusting brush, followed by a damp rag. Apply a new topcoat, taking care not to put it on too thickly.

Stains

There are a number of reasons why stains occur on a painted surface. For example, water in emulsion may activate impurities in a wall; areas rubbed with a wire brush or wire wool can develop rust stains; deposits in an unlined flue will come through the paint surface. Prevent stains from showing by applying an aluminium primer-sealer before you start painting. If the problem occurs afterwards, brush a primer-sealer over the stain and then repaint.

FAULT — CAUSE AND CURE

Mould and discoloration

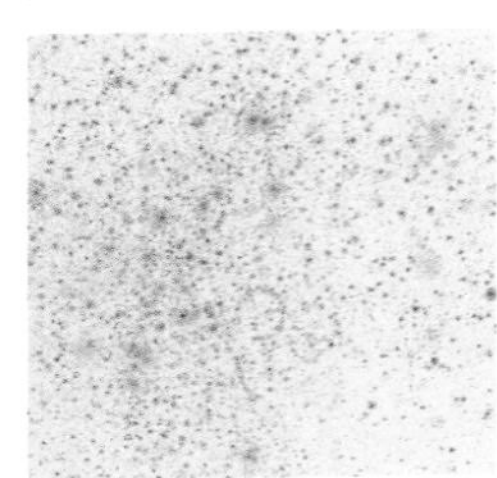

Spores settling on paintwork which is damp – possibly because condensation has been forming on glass or cold metal – often lead to mould and black and brown patches. Treat the affected area with a fungicide as directed by the manufacturer, wash the surface clean, let it dry and then repaint.

Loss of gloss

Gloss paint will sink into the surface and lose its shine if the surface was not primed – or if either primer or undercoat was not left to dry completely. The problem is also a sign of poor quality paint, and it will occur on exterior paintwork in exposed coastal regions where weathering is speeded up.

Make sure the surface is dry, then rub it down with damp wet-and-dry abrasive paper. Brush off the dust, pick up any remaining specks with a clean, damp rag, then apply a new topcoat.

Loss of gloss can also occur if you paint in very cold conditions.

Wrinkled paint

ICI

Usually caused by applying a second coat of paint before the first has dried. Solvents in the wet paint underneath attack the second coat when they try to pass through it and make it wrinkle. Strip the paint with a chemical stripper or heat and redecorate, this time allowing each coat to dry before applying the next.

Gritty paint surface

If a newly painted surface feels rough and has gritty lumps in it, paint has been applied with a dirty brush or has become contaminated by the surrounding areas. Alternatively, there may have been bits of skin in the paint if it was not strained before use and had been left standing for a while. Or it may be that dust has settled on the surface while the paint was still wet.

To ensure that the problem does not arise again, always paint with clean brushes and use a paint kettle. Strain old paint through a paint strainer or a clean, dust-free, old nylon stocking. Use a paint shield or a piece of card to guard against the risk of picking up dirt.

When a gritty surface is dry, rub down with a damp wet-and-dry abrasive paper until it is smooth, wipe clean, then apply a new coat of paint, making sure the brushes are not dirty.

Dark patches on painted wood

Knots in wood which have not been sealed before you decorate may ooze resin when the sun warms them – and the resin will force its way through the paint film. Strip paint away with the edge of a scraper blade, then with fine abrasive paper to expose the knot. Brush knotting over the area to seal it, leave it to dry and repaint.

Paint will not dry

It may be that paint is slow drying because the room is badly ventilated or very cold. Open all the windows and doors to improve the ventilation or put a heater in the room to warm the air. If this does not solve the problem, the paint has been applied to a dirty – and probably greasy – surface. Strip it off with chemical stripper or heat and start again, taking great care to clean the surface thoroughly.

Insects on painted surface

If you can, remove insects which get stuck to fresh paint while the paint is still wet and touch up the surface with a brush and new paint. If the paint has started to dry, wait until it has set hard and then brush away the insects – they make less of a mess that way.

Painting walls with glazes

With a little practice, you can use glazes to create special decorative techniques which will match those of a professional painter. A glaze is a thin, almost transparent film of oil-based colour usually diluted with white spirit. The oil slows the glaze's drying time but you still have to work fast – especially in summer if the weather is hot.

Glazes can be put over surfaces coated with an oil-based paint – undercoat or eggshell – using techniques called sponging, ragging, dragging and stippling. Sponging and ragging take less time to do than the others. Whichever decorative technique you are going to use, thoroughly prepare the surface first (page 101) – dragging, in particular, will otherwise highlight bumps in an uneven wall. Then put on the base coat and leave it to dry. Never use a gloss finish because glaze will not adhere to it.

You can buy transparent oil-based glaze, called scumble glaze, which varies in shade from pale to mid-brown, from specialist paint shops. As a rough guide, a $2\frac{1}{2}$ litre tin of glaze will be enough to cover all the walls in a room 12ft × 12ft × 10ft (3.7m × 3.7m × 3m).

Use artist's oil colours or universal stainers to tint the glaze to the colour you want. Mixing a glaze to achieve a particular colour is a matter of trial and error which becomes easier with practice. Always mix up more glaze than you think you need – it is impossible to match a colour if you run out halfway through the job.

Whether you need to buy special tools depends on which techniques you are using. The brushes traditionally used for stippling and dragging are very expensive, and cheaper versions are a poor substitute as they give very inferior results.

TINTING THE GLAZE

1 Blend a small blob of colour – a little amount goes a long way – with white spirit.

2 Add this to the rest of the glaze in the paint kettle, stirring all the time to mix them well.

3 Test the result on the surface to be painted and repeat the process, if necessary, adding more of the same or a different colour until you are satisfied.

THE TOOLS FOR THE JOB

Paint kettle for glaze

Paint tray

PVC gloves

Flogger (for dragging)

Lint-free rag

Mixing jar for thinning colours

Stippling brush

4in (100mm) paintbrush

Sponge

Artists' oil colours

All the painting techniques with glazes require basic tools and materials – a paint kettle, white spirit and rags for mopping up spills, for example – as well as the particular painting tool needed to achieve the right decorative effect.

Painting walls with glazes (continued)

Glaze is usually diluted with some white spirit before you apply it to a surface. The consistency should be easy to work with – about the same as single cream. If the glaze thickens as you work (because the white spirit has evaporated) stir in some more white spirit – but be careful with the amount because too much will weaken the colour.

ALTERNATIVELY, you can achieve similar painting effects with eggshell or any mid-sheen oil-based paint, although the mixture is not strictly a glaze.

Mix one part paint to two parts white spirit. It is best to choose white paint and then to tint it to the required colour. As with an ordinary glaze, blend a blob of colour with white spirit, add it to the paint mixture and try out the result. Keep blending more colour with the diluted paint until you achieve the colour you want. This 'glaze' dries quickly so it is more suited to sponging and ragging than to dragging or stippling.

You can produce decorative effects with emulsion paint as well – one part diluted with three or four parts water – but this dries even faster.

Always apply an emulsion 'glaze' over an emulsion base coat – not an oil-based one. Similarly, tint it with water-soluble paints – use gouache, acrylic or poster paints. And dilute the emulsion with water, not with white spirit.

Protecting the surface

It is advisable – but not essential – to protect a decorative finish with varnish. Make sure that the glazed surface is completely dry (this may take 24 hours or longer) before you do so.

Choose gloss, semi-gloss or matt varnish, depending on how shiny you want the result to be, and buy varnish with as little colour in it as possible.

Brush on a thin coat, working from the top of the wall down. If you use two coats of varnish, allow the first to dry before you apply the second. Matt varnish, which gives a good flat finish but not a tough one, will not take a second coat.

SPONGING A WALL

Glaze which is applied to the wall with a sponge produces a soft, dappled effect.

You will need
Tools Real (not synthetic) sponge; paint kettle, flat paint tray or baking tin; rags, rubber gloves
Materials Glaze tinted the right colour; white spirit.

1 Thin the glaze with white spirit in the paint kettle, stir well and pour some into the flat tray.

2 Wear rubber gloves to protect your hands. Dip sponge into the glaze and squeeze out the excess.

3 Dab the sponge onto the wall – do not press too hard. Work in a circular pattern to prevent the prints from becoming too regular.

4 Reload the sponge as the glaze runs out. Vary the position of the sponge on the wall so that the impressions it makes are not all the same.

5 Wash the sponge in white spirit when it becomes saturated with glaze. Squeeze it out well or you will over-dilute the glaze.

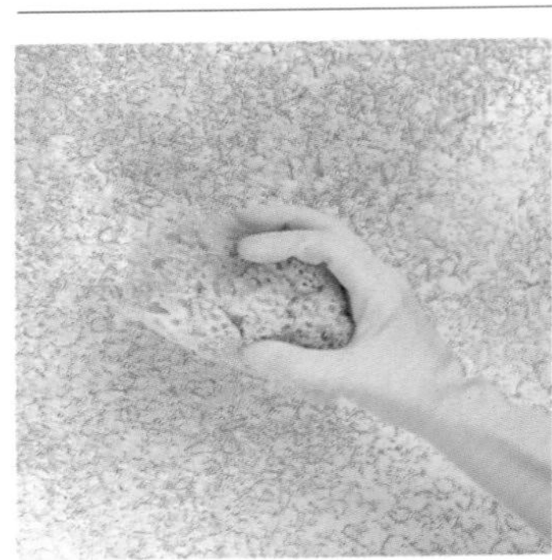

6 For a marbled effect, leave the surface to dry and then sponge on a second colour, using the same technique as before. Sponge over gaps where the base coat shows through and occasionally overlap onto areas sponged with the first colour to create tonal variations.

RAGGING A WALL

With ragging, the pattern is irregular, rather than even, which makes it one of the easiest and fastest decorative techniques.

You will need
Tools A large supply of lint-free rags (all the same texture); 4in (100mm) paintbrush; paint kettle; rubber gloves.
Materials Glaze tinted the right colour; white spirit.

1 Pour the glaze into the paint kettle and thin it with white spirit.

2 Brush glaze onto the surface, beginning at the top of the wall and covering a strip about 2ft (610mm) wide down to the floor.

3 Bunch up a rag into a ball and dab it over the surface to pick up glaze while it is still wet. Use one or both hands to move the rag in all directions. This is a messy job so wear rubber gloves. You may find it easier if you crumple one rag into a ball and then wrap another rag around it.

4 Change the rag whenever it becomes full and too wet to pick up more glaze. It is also a good idea to unwrap the rag and crumple it again in a different way so that the patterns you make are not all the same.

5 Continue to apply and rag off glaze until the whole wall is covered.

> SAFETY TIP
> Glaze is highly flammable. Never leave rags soaked with glaze lying around – they may suddenly burst into flame without warning. When you have finished with a rag, do not keep it to use again – always use a clean rag. Put used rags in a tin with a lid. Make sure the lid is on tight when you throw the tin away. Never put loose used rags straight into a dustbin.

DRAGGING A WALL

This technique will show up the slightest imperfection in a surface, so it is best kept for only the smoothest walls. If possible, try to get someone else to brush the glaze onto the wall, while you drag it off immediately afterwards.

You will need
Tools Paint kettle; 4in (100mm) paintbrush; brush with extra long bristles (called a flogger) or another wide, coarse-haired paintbrush; clean lint-free rags.
Materials Glaze tinted the right colour; white spirit.

1 Thin the glaze with white spirit in the paint kettle. It should be a thin, cream-like consistency – if it is too thick or if one of the bristles is bent – some of the dragged lines of glaze may break into droplets and spoil the effect.

2 Start in a corner and apply a strip of glaze about 2ft (610mm) wide, from the top of the wall to the bottom.

3 Again moving from the top down, drag the dry flogger through the glaze. You will need to stand on steps to reach the top and to climb down carefully as you drag the wall. Keep the movement flowing and as straight as possible. However, the results will be more successful if you relax and do not concentrate too much on keeping the lines steady. Do not worry if the lines are slightly crooked in places – they will not spoil the effect from a distance. Hold the flogger against the wall with light, consistent pressure.

4 If you cannot drag the whole wall in one movement, break off and then brush from the bottom up to where you stopped, overlapping slightly at the join. If you have to do this with the next strip as well, break off at a different height, so that you do not get a line running across the wall where the joins meet.

5 Wipe the flogger frequently on lint-free rag so that the bristles remain as dry as possible and do not lose their shape.

HELPFUL TIP

You can create a similar effect to dragging by using a comb with firm teeth. Special rubber or steel combs are sold by some artists' suppliers but you can also use plastic ones.

You need not confine yourself to vertical lines – experiment with scallop shapes, ticks or criss-cross patterns.

STIPPLING A WALL

With this technique you can create a uniform, soft effect with unobtrusive brushmarks. The special brush required can be bought from specialist paint shops and larger builders' merchants. Cheap brushes with rubber bristles do not last for long because white spirit makes them disintegrate. Use a white or pale base coat for best results. As with dragging, speed is essential so it is easier if you have a helper.

You will need
Tools Paint kettle; stippling brush; 4in (100mm) paintbrush; clean lint-free rags.
Materials Glaze tinted the right colour; white spirit.

1 Pour the glaze into the paint kettle and thin it with white spirit.

2 Brush the glaze onto the wall in a vertical strip about 2ft (610mm) wide.

3 Go over the wet area with the stippling brush, stabbing at the surface. Keep the bristles at right angles to the wall, otherwise the brush will skid.

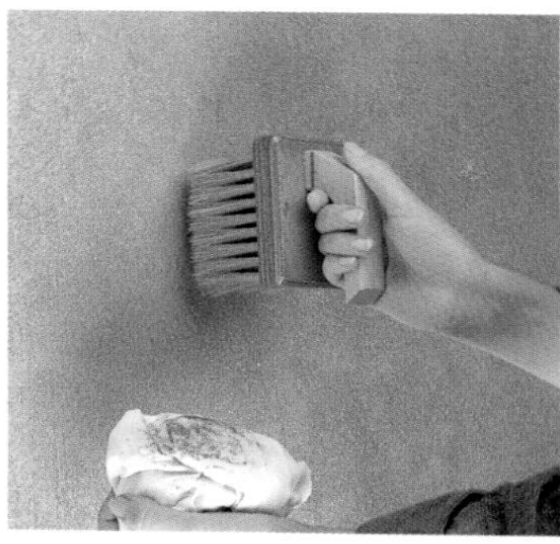

4 Wipe the brush clean on a dry lint-free rag as the picked-up glaze accumulates on the bristles, otherwise they will begin to stick.

5 Continue the process in strips across the wall. Clean the brush immediately after use with white spirit, followed by a little washing-up liquid and warm water.

STENCILLING

Using pre-cut transparent plastic stencils is a quick and easy way of decorating furnishings, walls and floors.

You will need
Tools Stencil brushes.
Materials Plastic stencils; oil-based paint crayon; low-tack (easily detachable) tape; paper towel.

1 Position the first stencil and secure it with tape. Break the seal on the paint crayon by drawing on a paper towel.

2 Having rubbed paint onto an uncut area of the stencil, work the paint well into the brush, using a circular motion.

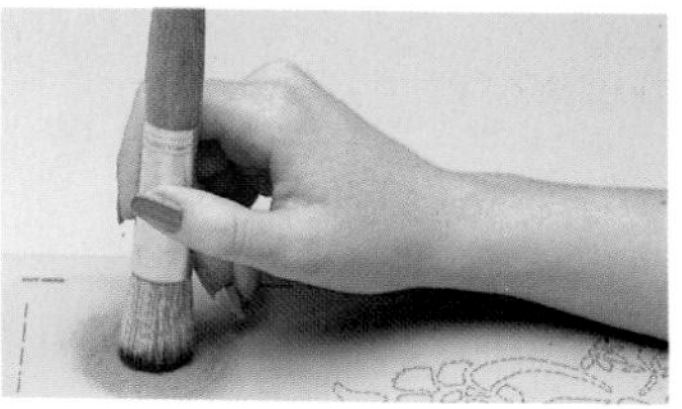

3 Holding the brush at right angles to the stencil, brush paint lightly onto the cut-out areas, using clockwise and anti-clockwise movements.

Repeat the process with the stencils for each additional colour.

Decorating the outside of a house

Exterior paintwork needs repainting every five years or so. Paint deteriorates at different rates, depending on how much it is exposed to wind and rain and the direct heat of the sun and how thoroughly the surface was prepared. The first sign of deterioration is usually when gloss paint loses its shine, or when emulsion becomes over-powdery to the touch.

The best time to start decorating is after a dry spell because paint will not take to a damp surface. Never paint in frosty conditions or rain, and do not paint on a very windy day – or dust and dirt will be blown onto the new paint.

If it starts raining, stop painting at once and do not begin again until after the surface has completely dried out. Similarly do not paint a surface soaked with dew; wait for it to evaporate in the morning and finish work about two hours before sunset, so that the paint has a chance to set before dew forms in the evening.

It is also good practice to follow the sun around the house, working on the east and south sides in the morning and the north and west sides in the afternoon. The surface has then had more time to dry out. Working in direct sunlight can be difficult – especially if you are putting new white paint over old. The glare of the sun makes it almost impossible to see which areas have been painted.

Before you buy the paint
If you are going to change your colour scheme, make sure that the new colours will fit in with the surrounding and neighbouring buildings, especially if the house is semidetached or in a terrace. Bright red paint might look garish next to houses painted in pastel shades, for instance.

Calculate how much paint you need in the same way as for interior decorating, working out the area of each part of the house to be painted (page 111). Remember that rendered surfaces require more paint than smooth ones. If all the walls are to be painted, estimate the total outside area of the house by multiplying the length of the walls by the height. The easiest way to measure the height is to climb a ladder against the wall of the house, drop a ball of string from the eaves to the ground, and then measure the length of the string. Work out the combined area of the doors and windows and deduct this figure from the total outside area, so that you know the area of the walls.

Divide both amounts by the number of square feet (or square metres) 1 litre of paint will cover to find out how many tins of paint you need to buy (consult the manufacturer's recommendations on the tin and see page 111). If you are going to paint the pipes and the outside of gutters, measure their circum-

Decorating the outside of a house (continued)

ference and multiply this by their length in inches (or centimetres). Divide this figure by 144 to give square feet (or by 10,000 to give square metres).

Which paint to use

Choose the paint according to the surface – for the types available see page 110. Buy all the paint of each type from the same batch (check the numbers on each tin) and get any primer and undercoat that you need at the same time.

In general, use exterior grade gloss paint on wood and metal – gutters, downpipes, windows and doors – and use exterior grade emulsion or masonry paint on walls. Alternatively, on bare wood use micro-porous paint, which needs no primer or undercoat. This paint allows trapped air or moisture to evaporate, reducing the risk of flaking associated with hardwoods.

You do not have to use a paint similar to the one previously used with the following exception. Never put gloss paint over surfaces – mainly pipes and guttering – which are coated with bituminous paint. This tends to be less shiny than gloss and often looks thicker and softer than other paint. If you are doubtful about whether old paint contains bitumen, rub a rag soaked with petrol over the surface. If the rag picks up a brownish stain, the paint is bituminous. Either continue to use bituminous paint or, providing it is sound and old, coat it with aluminium primer-sealer. Then paint it with undercoat and gloss.

Where to start

Safe access is most important – your ladder or scaffold tower must be secure and in good condition (page 100). Surfaces should be clean, stable, and stripped if the paintwork is not sound (page 101). Repair damaged areas of a rendered wall and fix gutters if they are not firmly attached to the fascia board. Some weeks before you intend to start painting, check that putty around windows is sound and, if not, replace it (page 217).

Always decorate from the top of the house, working downwards so that the newly painted surfaces cannot be spoilt. Protect climbing plants growing up a wall from any drips or splashes of paint by untying them and covering them with paper or dust sheets. Take care not to weigh down delicate plants with heavy sheets. It is easier to paint exterior walls covered by a well-established climber or creeper after you have pruned the plant, so that you do not have to cope with masses of foliage. Ideally, fix plants to trellis, not to walls direct.

Complete all the preparatory work before you do any painting – this will ensure that flaking old paint does not spoil a freshly painted surface, but never leave a surface exposed. Protect it with at least a primer and, if possible, an undercoat before you stop work at the end of a session.

Most professional house painters redecorate in the following order: bargeboards; fascias; gutters; soffits; walls; downpipes; windows; doors. However, the painting sequence can be varied. If you are working from a scaffold tower, for instance, you may wish to paint all the surfaces you can reach before moving the tower to another site – but try to keep painting a wall until you reach a natural break.

Decide which parts of the outside of the house need to be repainted and where the best place is to start. If you are painting the whole of the outside, there is less chance of new paintwork being damaged if you begin at the top and paint the doors and windows last.

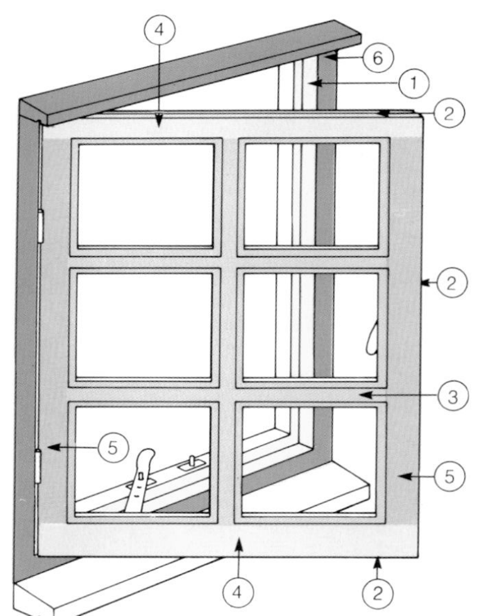

Follow this order when painting the outside of a casement window: **1** rebate; **2** edge of frames; **3** glazing bars and putty; **4** top and bottom rails; **5** vertical bars and hinge edge; **6** frame.

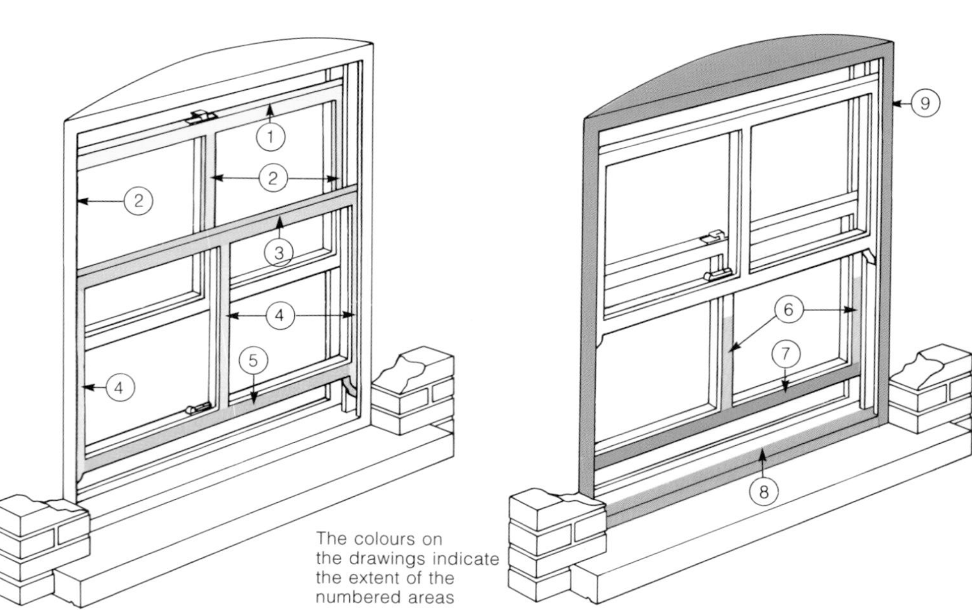

To paint the outside of sash windows, reverse their position and follow this sequence: **1** horizontal rail; **2** accessible surfaces of vertical bars; **3** horizontal rail; **4** vertical bars; **5** horizontal rail and underside. Reverse the sashes, then: **6** remainder of vertical bars; **7** horizontal rail; **8** the wood beneath the window and up the outside runners; **9** frame.

HOW TO TREAT EACH PART OF THE HOUSE

PART	TREATMENT
Bargeboards, fascias and soffits	All these surfaces are painted in the same way, but not necessarily at the same time. Gutters are usually painted the same colour as fascias so it is easiest to paint them immediately afterwards – before soffits, which are often painted to match the walls or windows. **1** Apply knotting, if necessary, and primer to bare wood. Put on an undercoat and leave to dry. Use two undercoats if there is to be a colour change. **2** Lightly sand with fine abrasive paper to remove any rough bits. **3** Apply a coat of gloss with a 3in (75mm) paintbrush, finishing with the grain. Leave it to dry for at least 12 hours. **4** Apply a second coat of gloss. As an alternative to new gloss over old, a stain finish designed to be applied over gloss paint gives a finish resembling natural wood. No base coat or primer is necessary.
Gutters and downpipes	Whether you paint gutters and pipes together or at different times, follow the same painting procedure for both. **1** Clean out debris and wash with water and detergent. **2** Remove rust from the insides of metal gutters with a wire brush. Wipe the surface with a dry cloth and apply rust inhibitor or metal primer. Paint the inside of gutters with any left-over gloss paint. **3** Paint gutters and pipes with exterior gloss using a 2in (50mm) brush. If there is to be a colour change, apply one or more undercoats first. If the surface is coated with bituminous paint see *Paints for every purpose* (page 110). **4** Hold a piece of cardboard as a shield behind pipes as you paint to protect the wall. **5** Apply a second coat of paint when the first is completely dry.
Plastic gutters and pipes	If metal gutters or pipes are in poor condition, consider replacing them with plastic ones, rather than undertake extensive repair work, which can be difficult. Plastic gutters and pipes do not have to be painted, but if you want them to match a colour scheme, apply two coats of exterior grade gloss. Do not use a primer or undercoat. Manufacturers usually advise against painting new plastic because the paint will not adhere perfectly to it. After about a year it is safe to do so. If you are leaving plastic gutters unpainted, unclip and remove them while you are painting the fascia boards.
House walls	**1** Treat new rendering which has not been painted before with a stabilising solution or a primer recommended for such a surface by the manufacturer. **2** On painted rendering – such as pebbledash, spar dash or a textured surface – no undercoat is necessary. Apply two coats of exterior grade emulsion or masonry
House walls (continued)	paint with a 4in or 6in (100mm or 150mm) paintbrush or an exterior grade shaggy pile roller. If you use a brush, work the paint into the surface with the tip of the bristles. **3** Paint the area close to door and window frames with a 2in or 3in (50mm or 75mm) brush. **4** Do not try to paint the whole width of a wall along a house in one go. Instead, divide each wall into sections and paint one section at a time. If you cannot finish painting a wall in one session, stop at a corner of a feature – a window, for instance – so that joins will be less noticeable. Never stop in the middle of a wall. **5** Wrap a collar of paper as protection around a newly painted pipe if you are painting the wall behind it. Move the paper down the pipe as you paint.
Brick walls	**1** Avoid painting good facing brickwork – it is difficult to achieve a satisfactory finish, it cannot be successfully cleaned off later and rarely looks attractive. If you really want to paint it, use exterior grade emulsion and a rough surface paintbrush. Apply at least two coats. **2** To clean dirty bricks, scrub them with a hard bristle brush and plenty of water. Never use soap or detergent because they create permanent white stains.
Windows	If a concrete sill is damaged, repair it before painting the window frame. **1** Strip paint off wooden sills and make good, filling holes and uneven areas with exterior grade wood stopping or epoxy-based filler. **2** Prepare wood and metal frames as for an equivalent inside frame (page 102). **3** Apply knotting to knots and resinous patches in bare wood. Then apply primer, undercoat and exterior grade gloss with a 1in (25mm), 2in (50mm), or angled cutting-in brush. **4** Paint each type of frame following the sequence opposite. **5** Take special care to seal the joint between putty and glass with new paint. This will prevent rain seeping through the window.
Tiled sills	**1** Clean window sills made of clay tiles with a fine wire brush; wash away the dirt with water and dry with a cloth. **2** Alternatively, clay tiles can be painted with special tile paint which is available in a limited colour range. No primer or undercoat is needed. Apply two coats with a 2in (50mm) paintbrush. The mortar joints may be painted or left natural.
Painted doors	**1** Remove metal handles, knockers and other furniture before painting. **2** Replace damaged putty in a glass panelled door (page 217). **3** Prepare the surface as for interior doors (page 102). Use ex-
Painted doors (continued)	terior grade gloss to finish; again follow the same sequence and method as for painting a door inside (page 117).
Varnished doors	**1** To restore a painted door to a natural finish, strip off the paint (page 105). **2** Remove old varnish from a door with a proprietary varnish remover, following the manufacturer's instructions. **3** Fill any scratches and holes in the stripped wood with an exterior grade wood stopping which matches the natural colour. **4** Rub down the whole surface with fine abrasive paper, working with the wood grain. Wipe clean with a damp cloth. **5** If parts of the door have been bleached by the sun – or if you want to enhance the door's natural colour – use water, oil or spirit-based stain to restore or change the colour. Follow the manufacturer's instructions and apply at least two thin coats. **6** Apply three thin coats of exterior grade polyurethane varnish containing an ultraviolet filter and a fungicide. Allow each coat to dry and rub down between coats with fine abrasive paper to remove pimples and to give a key for the next coat. Remove dust with a clean, damp cloth.
Painted weatherboarding	**1** Prepare as for interior painted wood (page 102). Apply knotting, if needed, then wood primer, undercoat and two coats of exterior gloss paint. Alternatively, use a microporous paint (see chart, page 110). **2** Work from the top down, and from left to right if you are right-handed and from right to left if you are left-handed. **3** Paint sections about 3ft (1m) long at a time, using a brush just narrower than the width of one board. **4** Paint the edge of the timber first, then paint the face, finishing with the grain.
Varnished weatherboarding	**1** If the varnish is in good condition, rub over the surface with a flexible sanding pad damped with water to remove the glaze. Wash down with clean water, allow the surface to dry and then apply new varnish. **2** If the varnish is in poor condition, strip it off (page 105). Brush on a wood preservative – stained if you want to change the colour of the wood – and then varnish as for doors above.
Tiled areas	**1** Remove moss and lichen from tiled areas over bays and porches by brushing with a fine wire brush, or scraping with a stripping knife. Then use proprietary fungicide (not bleach) following the manufacturer's instructions. **2** Brighten the tiles by brushing with a fine wire brush or scrubbing with a stiff brush dipped in clean water. Wear safety spectacles against flying particles.

Wallpapering: Tools for the job

Start with the right tools and any decorating job will be easier. Use a stepladder to reach up walls – you cannot hang wallpaper from a ladder. In addition to the tools listed below, you need a steel tape for measuring and you may also need a metal straight-edge to act as a guide when you trim paper. Always use a pencil – not a pen – to make marks.

Depending on the type of wall covering you choose, you may need only some of the tools. For instance, a water trough is necessary only for pre-pasted wallpaper.

Keep a supply of old towels and sponges for general cleaning up – for removing paste from skirting boards, for example. Always wipe paste off immediately or it will harden and be difficult to remove.

Pasting table

A folding table – about 6ft (1.8m) long and 2ft (610mm) wide – is the best type of table to use because it can be easily moved around. As well as being light to carry, the table must be solid enough to stand firmly on the floor. You may be able to improvise a pasting table by laying a flush door across trestles or padded stools – a kitchen table will normally be too wide and slippery to provide a firm base.

Paste brush

Use a 5in or 6in (125mm or 150mm) brush to apply paste to either the paper or the walls. If you use an old paintbrush, make sure that it is clean and free from particles of hardened paint. Always wash the brush well in warm water after use.

Plastic bucket

So long as it is clean, use any household bucket for mixing the paste. Tie a piece of string across the rim, between the handle anchor points, and rest the brush on the string when you are not using it. Wiping the brush across the string will remove surplus paste.

Water trough

If you have chosen a pre-paste[d] wall covering, get a trough for we[t]ting each length before hanging.

Scissors

Paperhanger's scissors with blade[s] of about 10in (250mm) are best fo[r] main cutting work. The longer th[e] blades, the easier it is to cut a straight line, but you may find lon[g] blades difficult to control at first. [If] possible, use stainless steel scissors because they will not rust. Always wipe scissors clean afte[r] each use when cutting paste[d] paper, otherwise the paste will harden on the blades – and they wil[l]

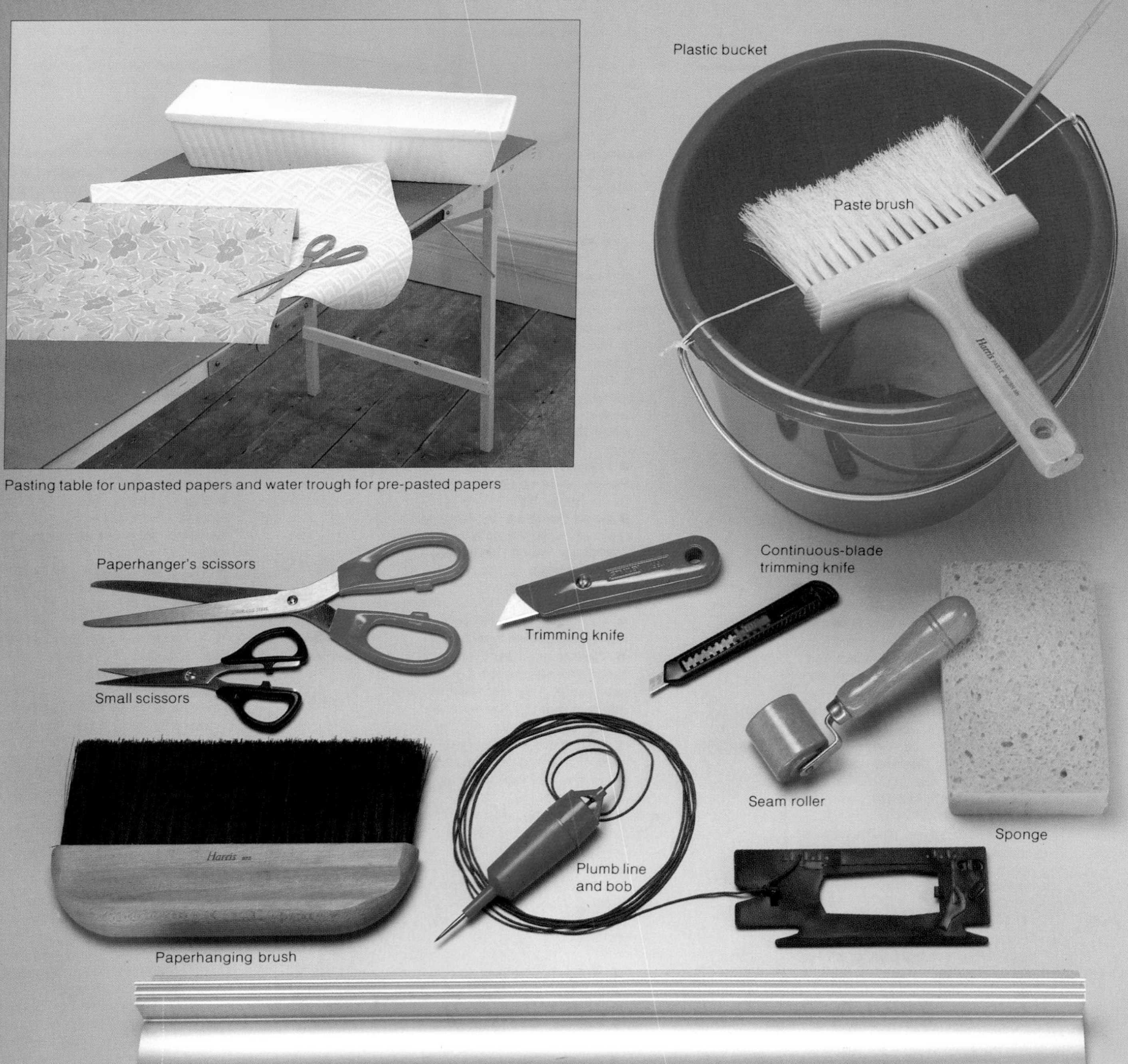

Pasting table for unpasted papers and water trough for pre-pasted papers

tear, rather than cut, the paper in future. If paste has already started to harden on the scissors, stand them in hot water for a couple of minutes and then wipe them dry. Keep a pair of small scissors handy for fine trimming.

Trimming knife
A knife with a razor-sharp blade is useful for trimming and cutting vinyl wall coverings. It is also sometimes easier to trim pasted paper neatly with a knife and straight-edge than with a pair of scissors – provided the paper is not too thin. Keeping the knife sharp is essential so make sure that you have plenty of spare blades. Alternatively, use a knife which has a continuous blade that snaps off at intervals to give a sharp new cutting edge.

Plumb line and bob
Always use a plumb line and bob to mark the true vertical on a wall before hanging the first length of wallpaper – few walls are straight. Most plumb lines are just a length of builder's line, and the bob is a weight attached to the end. You can make your own by tying a small weight – a metal nut or a small screwdriver, for instance – to a length of thin string, but builder's line is preferable because it is less likely to become tangled.

Paperhanging brush
For smoothing out bubbles and creases in newly hung wall coverings. A large brush – between 7in and 10in (180mm and 250mm) wide gives best results and makes the work faster. Never use the brush for anything else and take care not to get paste on the bristles.

Cutting guide
An L-shaped piece of metal about 2ft (610mm) long. Hold it against the skirting board, picture rail or coving when trimming lengths of paper on the wall with a very sharp knife. It is an alternative to creasing the paper and trimming with scissors. The correct length of the paper is achieved by tucking the paper into the crease of the guide, which is slightly shaped so that a little extra paper is left on each length. This reduces the chance of leaving gaps between the paper and the skirting board, picture rail or coving.

Seam roller
For pressing down the seams of wall coverings, once they have been smoothed into place. The handle can be attached to either one or both sides of the roller. The type attached at one side only is more useful because it will reach into corners. Never use a roller on embossed and relief wall coverings because it will spoil the pattern.

Sponge
Use a clean damp sponge to wipe any excess paste away from the surface on vinyls and wipeable wall coverings.

PASTING BY MACHINE
An automatic wallpaper pasting machine will paste 10ft (3m) lengths in seconds, so it may be useful if you have no room for a pasting table or dislike pasting paper in the ordinary way.

Follow the instructions supplied with the machine. It has a trough which is filled with paste, and two rollers. One holds the wallpaper, the other applies paste to the paper when it is passed through the machine.

Hang paper pasted in this way straight onto the wall without cutting it first, as with pre-pasted papers. There is a trimming guide attached so that you can trim the top and bottom of drops accurately – though you still need scissors for cutting to fit in awkward areas.

How many rolls do you need?

When you are buying a wall covering, the number of rolls that you will have to buy is affected by the distance between pattern repeats. You need fewer rolls of paper if it does not have to be matched and has a random pattern, more for paper which has a small drop between the pattern repeats, and even more when the pattern has a large drop. So if you want to keep down the expense, choose either a non-matching paper or a design with a random match.

If the paper you have chosen does have a large repeat, you will probably get one less full length out of each roll, so always buy an extra roll or two. Some stores will allow you to return unused rolls if they are left unopened.

Check that all the rolls come from the same batch, so that there is less chance of colour variation between rolls. If you have to accept rolls with a different batch number – because the store does not have enough from the same batch – plan to use them in areas where any slight shading variations will not show, such as behind furniture or tucked away in a corner.

Even if you managed to buy all the rolls from the same batch, check whether there is any colour variation between them. Open up a number of rolls, lay them side by side partly unrolled, and compare the colour so that you can decide which roll should be hung next to which.

Most British wall coverings are sold fully trimmed in rolls 33ft long × 21in wide (10m × 530mm), though the size may vary by 5 per cent, depending on the manufacturer. If you choose a paper sold in these dimensions, use the chart to calculate how many rolls you need to buy – it is better to have too much paper than to run out and discover that the store no longer has the paper in stock. It is also useful to have spare paper for any future repair work, should the paper ever be ripped or marked.

If you choose from a continental pattern book – or have decided upon a special wall covering, such as hessian – check the size and use the chart provided with the pattern book or by the store to work out how many rolls you need. Rolls may be considerably wider than standard wallpaper.

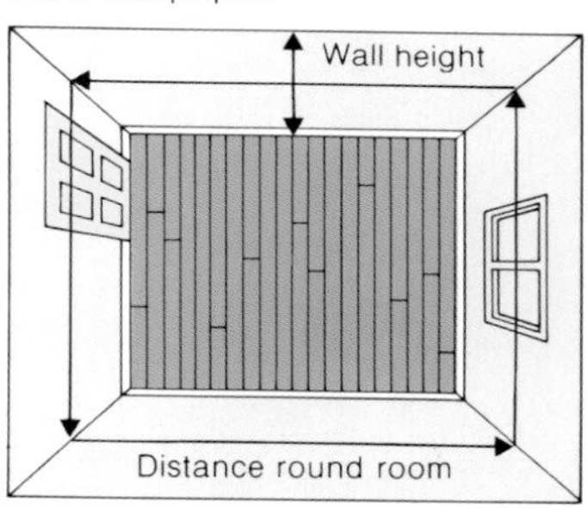

Use a steel tape to measure the height of the walls from the skirting board to the picture rail, coving or ceiling. When measuring the perimeter of the room, include the width of the doors and all standard size windows – the extra paper will be needed for the trimming at the top and bottom of each length. Only deduct the width of a window from your calculations if it is a picture window, or French window, occupying a large part of a wall.

If you are papering a ceiling, measure the perimeter of the room and use the chart.

To find out how much you need to paper the ceiling of a corridor, first measure the width of the ceiling and make sure that it does not vary along the corridor's length; if it does, make a note of the widest part. Divide this measurement by the width of a roll; then measure the corridor length and divide this into 33ft (10m) – the length of a roll. For example, a narrow corridor under 3ft 6in (1.1m) wide needs only two widths of paper to cover it. If the same corridor is under 16ft (5m) long – half the length of a roll – one roll will be enough to paper the whole ceiling. But if the corridor is wider or longer you will need an extra roll.

Standard rolls of wallpaper are approximately 33ft (10m) long and 21in (530mm) wide.

HOW MANY ROLLS FOR THE WALLS?

Wall height	Distance round room (including doors and windows)							
	33ft 10m	39ft 12m	46ft 14m	52ft 16m	59ft 18m	66ft 20m	72ft 22m	79ft 24m
7ft-7ft 6in 2.1-2.3m	5	5	6	7	8	9	10	11
7ft 6in-8ft 2.3-2.4m	5	6	7	8	9	10	10	11
8ft-8ft 6in 2.4-2.6m	5	6	7	9	10	11	12	13
8ft 6in-9ft 2.6-2.7m	5	6	7	9	10	11	12	13
9ft-9ft 6in 2.7-2.9m	6	7	8	9	10	12	12	14

HOW MANY ROLLS FOR A CEILING?

	Distance round room (including doors and windows)						
Feet Metres	30-40 9-12	42-50 13-15	55-60 17-18	65-70 20-21	75-80 22-24	85-90 26-27	95-100 29-30
Number of rolls	2	3	4	6	7	9	10

HELPFUL TIP
If you have a leftover roll of standard wallpaper, use it to make a quick estimate of the rolls you need to decorate a room. Measure the height of a wall and work out how many drops one roll will cover. Then walk around the room, holding the roll of paper against the walls, windows and doors as a measuring stick, to see how many widths you need. Divide the number of drops into the number of widths to give the number of rolls.

CHOOSING A WALL COVERING

TYPE OF WALL COVERING	DESCRIPTION	TIPS TO HELP YOU TO CHOOSE
Lining paper	Plain paper designed to cover poor wall and ceiling surfaces before painting or papering. Sold in five thicknesses. PASTE: cold water; regular; all-purpose	Sometimes supplied in rolls twice the standard length to reduce wastage. The heavier and thicker the paper, the less likely it is to tear when you are hanging it.
Woodchip	Two layers of paper bonded together with a sprinkling of wood chippings between them. Designed to be painted with emulsion. PASTE: heavy-duty; cold water; all-purpose; ready-mixed.	Use to cover uneven walls. Some surfaces feel abrasive to the touch and so are not suitable on walls likely to be rubbed against – narrow hallways, stairs and children's rooms, for example.
Standard wallpaper	A single sheet of paper with a pattern printed on it. Quality of paper varies considerably with the price. PASTE: cold water; regular; all-purpose; ready-mixed.	Cheap papers are thin, and tear easily – especially when damp with paste – and are more difficult to hang than more expensive papers. Papers cannot be washed, so not suitable for kitchens.
Duplex paper	A wallpaper – often with a relief surface – backed by another layer of paper which is bonded to form one sheet. PASTE: heavy-duty; cold water; all-purpose; ready-mixed.	The paper is strong and holds the shape of a relief well. This makes it easier to hang than other relief wallpapers.
Novamura	A foamed polyethylene with relief and a feel of fabric. Available in a wide range of colours and designs. PASTE: cold water; regular; all-purpose; ready-mixed.	The surface springs back into place if it is pressed gently and can be wiped clean. One of the easiest wall coverings to hang and strip. Paste the wall not the covering.
Relief wall coverings	Heavy paper embossed with a pattern during manufacture. The surface may be patterned, coloured or plain for painting. PASTE: cold water; ready-mixed; all-purpose.	Suitable for uneven walls and ceilings. Anaglypta is the best known of these materials, though other manufacturers produce similar coverings.
High relief wall coverings	Made from material resembling hard putty with a strong paper backing. Available in designs including plaster daub effects, brick or stone walling and wood panelling. PASTE: Lincrusta glue (for Lincrusta); heavy-duty; ready-mixed; cold water.	Lincrusta is the best known of these materials. More durable than ordinary relief wall coverings. Soak backing paper with water for about 30 minutes before pasting. Hang as one sheet – do not crease or fold. Trim with a sharp knife and straight-edge, butting joins.
Vinyl	A PVC layer, with a pattern or texture, is bonded to paper. Expanded vinyls have a raised surface, foamed up by heat during manufacture, and a smooth backing. PASTE: vinyl adhesive; ready-mixed (with fungicide); all-purpose (with fungicide).	Their durable and washable surface makes vinyls suitable for kitchens, bathrooms and children's rooms. Special adhesive required if seams overlap. Expanded vinyls need less paste than other relief wallpapers.
Hessian	Available as a roll of unbacked material or bonded to a stout backing paper which helps to keep the hessian from sagging. Dyed hessian is available in a limited colour range. PASTE: heavy-duty; ready-mixed; all-purpose; cold water.	Will hide small cracks in a surface. Hang paper-backed hessian like standard wallpaper. With unbacked hessian, paste the wall not the material. Not a matching material so every join will show, however carefully you hang.
Silk wall covering	Produced by bonding silk to fine backing paper. PASTE: cold water; regular; ready-mixed; all-purpose.	Like hessian, not a matching material so the seams will show. An expensive and delicate wall covering not practical for walls that are likely to be scuffed and knocked.
Japanese grasscloth	Made of real grasses bonded to a fine backing paper and sewn together for strength. PASTE: ready-mixed; all-purpose; heavy-duty; cold water.	Not a matching material so joins will always be visible. Expensive, so best used only for decorative effects – making a feature of one wall, for example. Paste the wall not the paper.
Cork wall coverings	A fine veneer of cork stuck to a plain or painted backing paper. Holes in the cork allow the painted backing to show through, creating a colour contrast. PASTE: heavy-duty; ready-mixed; all-purpose; cold water.	An expensive material best used to make a feature in a room. Apply paste to the wall, not the covering.
Metallic coverings 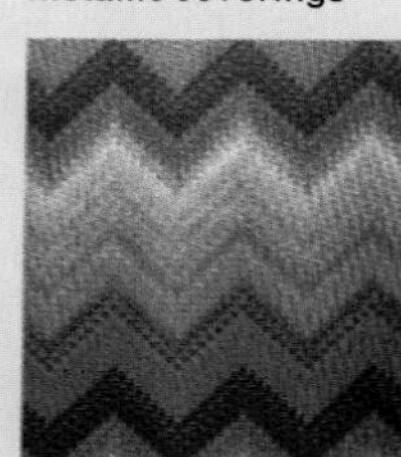	Foil bonded to a paper backing. Fine textures and many colours available. PASTE: heavy-duty; ready-mixed (with fungicide); all-purpose (with fungicide).	Only use on walls with a very smooth surface – bumps and any unevenness will show up. Paste the wall not the covering, and take care not to get paste on the decorative side.
Flocks 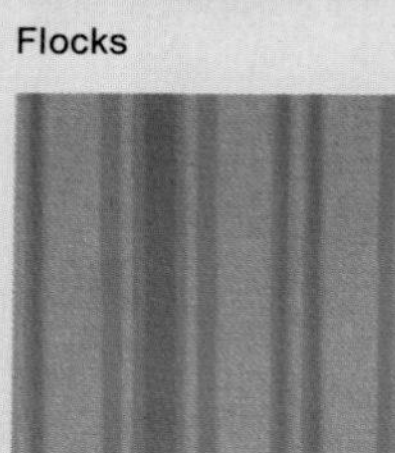	Velvet pile bonded to backing paper. Available in a wide range of colours and designs. PASTE: heavy-duty; ready-mixed; all-purpose; cold water.	Keep splashes of paste off the flocked surface as much as possible – though it should not be permanently stained by marks. Hang as for standard wallpaper. One of the more expensive wall coverings.
Special effects wall coverings	Papers and vinyls in a wide variety of designs which give the impression of real materials like wood, stone, and tiling. PASTE: heavy-duty; ready-mixed; all-purpose; cold water.	Use to create optical illusions and unusual visual effects. Can be overpowering if used on more than one wall in a room. More expensive than other wall coverings.

Hanging standard wallpaper

BEFORE YOU START PAPERING A WALL

Decorate the ceiling before you strip old wallpaper from the walls. Any splashes will go on the old paper and will be removed with it.

The only exception is if you use a steam stripper on the walls. As the steam may damage the ceiling, do all your preparation first.

Thoroughly prepare all the walls, filling cracks and indentations before you hang the first length (page 106). This is particularly important when there are wall lights because they will highlight faults even beneath textured papers.

Clear the room as much as possible before you start. Take down shelves, remove light fittings, if you can, and protect the floor with dustsheets – not polythene, which is slippery when wet.

SIZING THE WALLS

Prime bare walls with size to prevent them from absorbing paste on the wall covering so that it will not stick. Size also makes the surface slippery so that the covering can be slid into place. You can either buy size or use a dilute form of the paste you plan to use to hang the wall covering. Check on the pack for the manufacturer's advice.

Use the paste brush to cover the whole surface and spread the size evenly. If the size gets onto painted woodwork, wipe it off immediately with a damp cloth or sponge. Like all glue it is difficult to remove when dry.

CHOOSING THE RIGHT PASTE

Always use a paste which is recommended by the manufacturer of the wall covering you have chosen. If there is no advice on the roll, consult the retailer.

In general, the heavier the wall covering, the stronger the paste will need to be. Strong, full-bodied wallpaper paste has a thick consistency and contains more solid adhesive than it does water.

Some pastes can be mixed to different strengths to suit both ordinary wallpaper and heavy vinyls by adding more or less water. Follow the instructions on the packet and measure the amount of water and paste carefully – never guess the quantities.

Many wall coverings must be left on one side after they have been pasted while the paste soaks into the paper. The paper expands slightly when it is damp and if it is not left to soak it will continue to expand on the wall – making matching difficult and perhaps forming bubbles. The length of time a covering should be left to soak depends both on which paste you are using and the type of wall covering – though in general heavy, thick coverings need to soak for longer than thin ones.

Vinyls need no soaking time because vinyl does not expand when damp.

TYPE OF PASTE	DESCRIPTION	COVERAGE
Glue size	For all bare surfaces before they are hung with a wall covering. Mix the powder or fine crystals with cold water. Size adds to the adhesive quality of the paste and makes surfaces slippery so that the covering can be slid into place. Some adhesives may be diluted to form size.	A pack which makes just over 1 gallon (5 litres) will cover enough wall for 8 rolls.
Cold-water paste	The traditional starch-based wallpaper paste, still favoured by many professionals because it tends to hold coverings more firmly than regular cellulose paste. For all weights of wallpaper, depending on water content. Mix with cold water, stirring well to avoid lumps. Use with glue size, to provide extra slip and adhesion.	1 gallon (4.5 litre) pack is enough for 5-6 rolls of medium-weight paper.
Regular paste or concentrated	For lining paper and standard wallpaper. Cellulose powder, flakes or concentrated liquid are added to cold water. Easy to mix and spread. Does not mark the surface. Not suitable for heavy materials – they absorb too much water so the paste will not grip.	1 gallon (4.5 litres) is enough for 5-8 rolls.
Heavy-duty paste	For high relief wall coverings; duplex paper; woodchip; corks; flocks; special effects wall coverings like imitation wood panelling; imitation tiling and imitation brick. Will hold heavy materials. Mix with cold water.	1 gallon (4.5 litres) is enough for 4-6 rolls.
Ready-mixed paste	For paper and fabric-backed vinyls; paper-backed hessian; grasscloth; special wall coverings; expanded polystyrene tiles; veneers; coving. A paste containing a fungicide. Usually supplied in a tub. More expensive than powdered paste.	2.5 kilo pack is enough for 3-4 rolls.
All-purpose paste	For all wall coverings. Powder or flakes which must be mixed with varying quantities of cold water to suit the particular wall covering. Follow the instructions on the packet. Contains a fungicide. More expensive than pastes for just one type of wall covering.	Water content varies between 7-12 pints (4-7 litres) per sachet, covering 2-10 rolls.
Vinyl adhesive	For vinyl wall coverings. A powder or ready-mixed paste containing fungicide to discourage mould – essential when hanging impervious materials.	1 gallon (4.5 litres) is enough for 4 rolls.
Lincrusta adhesive	For Lincrusta relief decoration and very heavy relief wall coverings. Thick ready-mixed paste.	1¾ pints (1 litre) will hang one roll. 2 litre can will hang 2-3.

MIXING THE PASTE

Always use a paste suited to the paper and follow any instructions.

1 Fill the bucket with the specified quantity of cold water and slowly add the required amount of powdered paste or liquid, stirring to prevent lumps forming.

2 Most pastes must be left to stand for about 15 minutes, but some are ready immediately.

CUTTING PAPER TO LENGTH

1 Take a roll of paper and check which way the pattern goes. Decide where definite motifs should be in relation to the top of the wall.

2 With a steel tape, measure the wall from the top of the skirting board. The measurement may vary around the room, so measure in a number of places and use the largest figure. Add an extra 4in (100mm) for trimming at the top and bottom.

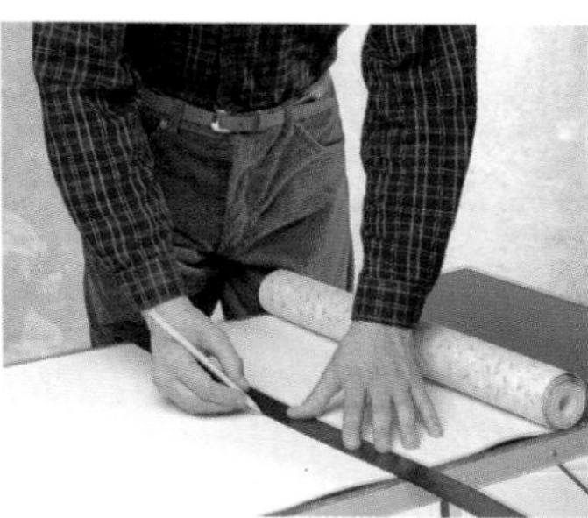

3 Unroll the paper on the pasting table, pattern-side down, measure off the length and draw a line with a pencil and straight-edge across the back.

Hanging standard wallpaper (continued)

4 Cut along the line with a pair of long-bladed scissors.

5 Turn the paper over, unroll the next length and match the pattern by placing it edge to edge with the first length. Using the cut length as a measuring guide, cut off the second length. Continue in this way until several lengths are ready for pasting. Number them on the back so that you know the hanging order.

HELPFUL TIP

If the ceiling is very uneven or sloping, do not cut lengths of paper in advance. It is much easier to hang one piece, and then match the next against it on the wall.

PASTING THE PAPER

1 Lay the cut lengths on the pasting table, pattern down and overlapping the table at each end.

2 Position the top piece of paper so that all the spare paper hangs off the table to the right.

If you are left-handed, work the other way around for all the paper-hanging procedures.

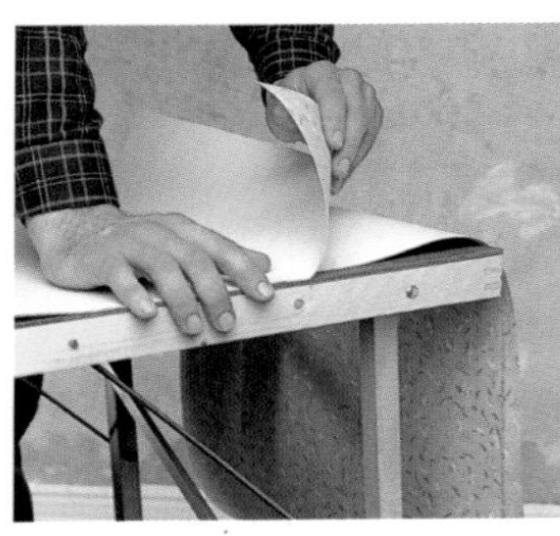

3 Adjust the paper so that it aligns with the edge of the table. If any paste gets onto the surface, wipe it off with a damp cloth. Some decorators let the paper overhang by about ¼in (6mm) to try to prevent paste getting onto the table and pattern – but it is difficult to paste the edges properly without support under them.

4 Load the paste brush and wipe off any excess paste by dragging the brush across the string on the bucket.

5 Brush the paste along the centre of the paper.

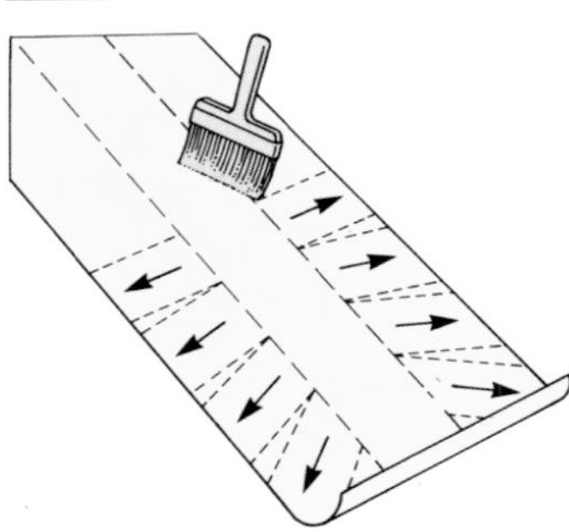

6 Work out from the middle towards the edges, herringbone fashion.

7 Check that all the paper is evenly covered with paste, especially the edges. Holding the left-hand edge, fold the paper over – paste side to paste side – to about the centre of the length. Do not crease the fold.

Slide the paper to the left of the table so that the pasted part hangs off the edge.

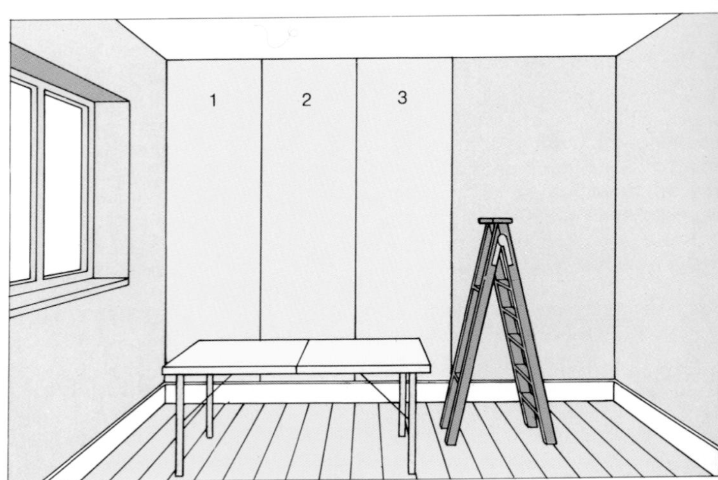

Always start by hanging the first strip of paper on a wall adjoining the main window. If edges overlap, no shadow will be cast.

8 Paste the right-hand end of the paper as you did the left, brushing in a herringbone pattern until the paper is completely pasted.

9 Fold the paper over so that the top and bottom edges meet. Make sure that you know which is the top edge. Either write 'top' on the relevant edge after cutting a length from the roll or always paste the bottom of the length first, so that the final fold will always be the top half.

10 Wipe up any splashes of paste on the table or the other cut lengths of paper with a damp cloth as you work.

11 Leave the pasted paper to soak for as long as the manufacturer recommends. Thin paper and vinyl will be ready for hanging almost immediately but heavier materials need to be left for 10 to 15 minutes.

The paper needs time to expand before it is hung – otherwise bubbles will appear as the paper continues to expand when it is on the wall.

12 Measure, cut and paste the next length while the first is soaking. Leave it to soak for the same amount of time, so it is equally expanded and the pattern will match. Do not allow lengths to soak for too long.

HANGING THE FIRST LENGTH

Start hanging the paper on a wall adjoining the window wall and work away from the light source, so that any slight overlaps will not cast shadows, which make the joins obvious. If there is more than one window in the room, treat the larger one as the main light source.

In the following sequence, the walls are papered in a clockwise direction, beginning at the wall on the right of the window wall. If you are left-handed or prefer to work in an anticlockwise direction, begin on the other side of the room.

1 Make a pencil mark 19in (480mm) out from the corner near the top of the wall, so that adequate paper will turn onto the window wall.

2 Hold the plumb line to the mark and let the bob hang free about 4ft (1.2m) down the wall. When the bob settles, make another pencil mark directly behind the string. Check the distance to the corner all the way down the wall. If it is greater than 19in (480mm) at some point because the corner is not true, not enough paper will turn. So make the top measurement shorter, use the plumb line again and draw new pencil marks.

3 Carry the pasted length to the wall and release the top fold gently, holding it at both sides. Do not let the lower half suddenly drop – it may tear, or stretch and cause matching problems.

4 Hold the top right corner against the wall so that the right-hand edge of the paper aligns with the pencil mark.

Make sure about 2in (50mm) of excess paper is left above the top of the wall for trimming.

5 Keep the left edge of the paper off the wall while you align the right-hand edge on the lower pencil mark.

6 Once the right edge is in place, smooth the paper with your hand or paperhanging brush diagonally up until the top left corner of the paper is on the wall.

7 Let go of the paper and smooth out the top half of the length with the paperhanging brush, working from the centre outwards. Make sure the paper stays on the pencil mark.

8 Release the lower fold. Brush down the centre of the length, then out to the edges as you did when pasting, ensuring that any bubbles are brushed out. Dab down the edges with the tip of the brush or a dry, clean cloth made into a pad.

9 With the length in place, run the back of a pair of scissors along the paper where it meets the skirting board so that it makes a definite crease.

10 Pull the paper gently away from the wall and cut along the crease, with the underside of the paper facing you. Brush the trimmed edge back in place. Repeat at the top.

ALTERNATIVELY, use a trimming guide, which gives a neater edge once you have learnt how to handle it properly.

Slide the guide under the paper and cut off the excess with a trimming knife. The blade must be razor-sharp or it will tear the damp wallpaper. If you feel the knife pulling at the paper, change the blade immediately.

> HELPFUL TIP
> Immediately after trimming, put scraps of pasted paper into a bin liner or large plastic bag to avoid mess and to make cleaning up easier. Wipe paste off woodwork.

HANGING THE NEXT LENGTHS

1 Hang the second length of paper to the right of the piece on the wall, following the same procedure but without using the plumb line. Match the top few feet of the left edge of the new length with the length on the wall, then run your hand diagonally up and to the right to press the top of the paper to the wall.

2 Smooth out the paper from the centre with the paperhanging brush.

3 Release the lower fold, check that the edges match and continue to brush over the paper. Trim top and bottom as before.

4 With two or three pieces hung, run the seam roller lightly down the joins of smooth papers. Do not press down the edges of textured materials, like Anaglypta, or lines will show where the pattern has been flattened.

Wallpapering around corners

All rooms have internal corners which must be negotiated and often external ones as well – on a chimney breast for example.

INTERNAL CORNERS

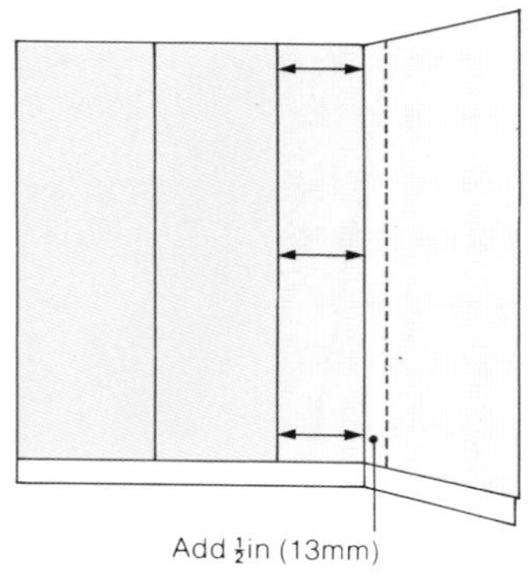

1 Measure the distance between the last length you have hung and the corner at the top, middle and bottom of the wall. Note the widest distance and add ½in (13mm) to allow for the turn onto the next wall.

2 Cut a length to this width. Keep the offcut for papering the first length of the adjoining wall.

3 Paste and hang the length. Take the spare paper around onto the next wall. Use the brush to smooth the paper well into the corner. If creases form, tear the paper – cut vinyl – and overlap the torn pieces so they lie flat.

4 Measure the offcut and hang the plumb line this distance away from the corner to find a vertical. Make pencil marks behind the line at intervals down the wall.

5 Hang the offcut with the right-hand edge aligning with the pencil marks. The length will overlap the paper turned from the previous wall. If the paper is patterned, match the two pieces as closely as possible. Use special vinyl adhesive to make overlapping vinyl stick down firmly.

> HELPFUL TIP
> Standard wallpaper may crease towards the bottom of a length if it is hung on a wall which is out of true. To overcome the problem, tear the paper roughly vertically to just above the point where the crease starts.
>
> One torn edge will be white, the other chamfered with the pattern. Paste the paper back, overlapping the chamfered piece on top of the other. The tear will be almost invisible, whereas a cut in the paper would show.

EXTERNAL CORNERS

Never try to turn more than 1in (25mm) around an external corner – the turned paper is likely to slant and look crooked.

This technique can be applied to rounded walls as well as right-angled corners.

Wallpapering around corners (continued)

1 Paper the wall until there is less than one width to the corner.

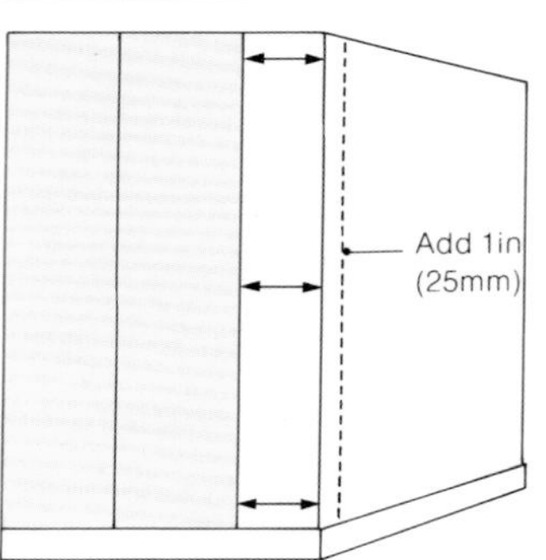

2 Measure the distance between the edge of the last hung length and the corner, at the top, middle and bottom of the wall. Add 1in (25mm) to allow for the turn and cut the paper to this size.

3 Hang the length as far as the corner and take the spare paper around onto the next wall. Smooth away any bubbles with the paper-hanging brush.

4 Hang the offcut from the first length next to the paper on the wall, matching the pattern and butting the joins. Continue to hang lengths until you reach the internal corner. Before you paper the next wall, use the plumb line to get a vertical starting point.

If the walls in the room are more than a little out of true, it is easier to overlap rather than butt the joins – especially if the paper has a vertical pattern. Take the pasted paper around the corner. Then deduct 1in (25mm) from the width of the offcut and mark pencil lines this distance away from the corner, using the plumb line to get a true vertical. Now hang the paper, overlapping the piece turned round the corner.

PUTTING UP A FRIEZE

To enliven a plain colour scheme or to give walls stylish edging, use a wallpaper frieze. There are friezes to match a fabric or the colours or motif of a wallpaper.

With a frieze you can also deceive the eye. A deep frieze at the top of a wall will make the ceiling seem lower. A frame of frieze on the wall, set in about 10in (250mm) from the edge, will help to 'shrink' the long wall of a narrow hall or landing.

APPLYING THE FRIEZE

The frieze must go on a sound, flat surface; a heavily embossed paper is not a suitable surface.

1 For a frieze at the top of a wall, draw a straight pencil guideline; make it slightly lower than the depth of the frieze to allow for an uneven ceiling edge and put a rim of ceiling paint at the top of the wall. If the frieze is to go along the skirting and round a door, no guideline is needed.

2 Cut the frieze to length, using one piece from corner to corner.

3 Paste the frieze, fold it like a concertina and leave it for ten minutes to soak.

4 Apply it along the guideline, brushing it out well and letting out folds as you work along.

MAKING A FRAME

1 Draw guidelines parallel to the nearest wall edge.

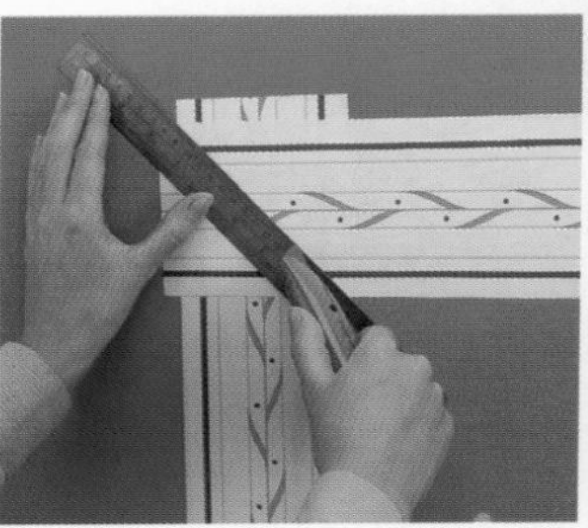

2 Apply the frieze. Cut both layers at the corners with a sharp knife; remove the excess.

Wallpapering around awkward items

CIRCULAR LIGHT SWITCHES

> SAFETY TIP
> Never put metallic or foil wall coverings behind light switches. Always turn off the electricity at the mains (consumer unit) before undoing light switches or sockets.

1 Hang the length of wallpaper in the ordinary way until you reach the fixture. Pierce a hole in the paper over it with a pair of small scissors. Then make star-like cuts out to the edge of the switch so that the paper will go to the wall.

2 Mark the outline of the switch on the paper with the back of a pair of scissors, pressing the cut pieces to the switch.

3 Cut off the surplus paper with small pointed scissors – they must be sharp or you may tear the wet paper. Follow the marked outline but allow for just a fraction of paper to turn onto the fitting so that the wall cannot show through a gap.

4 Smooth the paper flat around the switch with a paperhanging brush. If the paste on the paper immediately around the switch has begun to dry, apply a little more before you brush the paper flat. Then hang the rest of the length.

SQUARE LIGHT SWITCHES OR SOCKETS

1 Turn off the electricity at the mains. Hang the paper from the top of the wall down as far as the switch or socket.

2 Cut the paper to the corners of the switch and pull back the flaps.

3 Partially unscrew the switch cover and pull it about $\frac{1}{4}$in (6mm) away from the wall.

4 Trim away excess paper so that about ⅛in (3mm) of paper will sit behind the cover.

5 Gently ease the switch cover through the hole in the paper.

6 Push the paper behind the switch cover with a piece of flat wood, like a lolly stick, and then brush the paper flat against the wall, smoothing away any remaining air bubbles.

7 Hang the remainder of the length. Rescrew the switch cover and turn on at the mains.

CHIMNEY BREASTS

Because a chimney breast is likely to be the focal point of the room, it is a good idea to centre a strongly patterned wallpaper on it and to hang subsequent lengths from here towards the room corners. If there is no dominant pattern, hang the wallpaper round the chimney breast in the same way as for other corners (page 129).

1 Locate where to hang the first length and plumb a guide line.

2 Hang the centre length and then hang subsequent lengths to turn onto the sides of the alcoves.

FIREPLACES, WINDOWS AND DOOR FRAMES

1 Cut lengths of paper which are to go around large obstructions roughly to size before you apply the paste – so that you do not have to cope with a lot of sticky paper when trimming.

Leave a margin of at least 1in (25mm) of paper for trimming when the paper is on the wall.

2 Paste and hang the paper in the ordinary way as far as you can, then mark the outline of the fixture on the paper using the back of a scissor blade.

3 Peel a little of the paper away from the wall so that you can work comfortably. Cut along the marked outline with scissors.

Use small, sharp scissors if it involves cutting round a lot of small corners, otherwise use normal paperhanging scissors.

4 If the trimming takes some time and the paste on the paper is beginning to dry, apply a little more to the wall rather than the paper.

5 Smooth the wallpaper in place all around the fireplace or door frame, using the points of the bristles to push the paper into awkward corners. Then continue down to the skirting board.

6 Do not cut full lengths of wallpaper to cover small areas – above windows, for example. Use the ends of rolls and any leftover odd lengths, but make sure that the pattern matches.

ARCHWAYS

1 When you are wallpapering an archway between two rooms, turn about 1in (25mm) of paper from the main walls onto the arch.

2 Cut small V nicks in the paper so that it lies flat, curving neatly without any creases.

3 Cut a length of paper to fit the width of the arch. Match it against the pattern on the adjacent wallpaper.

4 Paper the inside of the arch with two pieces of paper. Run one piece of paper up each side to meet at the top centre, overlapping the paper turned from the adjoining walls.

BEHIND RADIATORS

Take lengths of paper only about 6in (150mm) behind a radiator. The wall behind will not show and you will save wallpaper. Do not forget to paper the gap between the bottom of the radiator and the skirting board.

If you really want to paper the wall behind, you may be able to swing the radiator away from the wall so that it rests on the floor.

HOW TO HANG LINING PAPER

Lining paper is plain, cheap wallpaper designed to be either painted or covered with some other type of wall covering, especially unbacked grasscloth, hessian and metallics. There are five grades of thickness – the thicker the lining paper, the less likely it is to tear.

The traditional way to hang lining paper on both ceilings and walls is to form a cross-lining, at right angles to the paper which is being put on top of it. However, this means dealing with long lengths of paper which are difficult to handle when you try to hang them horizontally.

You can safely hang lining paper in the same direction as ordinary wallpaper, if you make certain that the seams in the two papers do not fall in the same place.

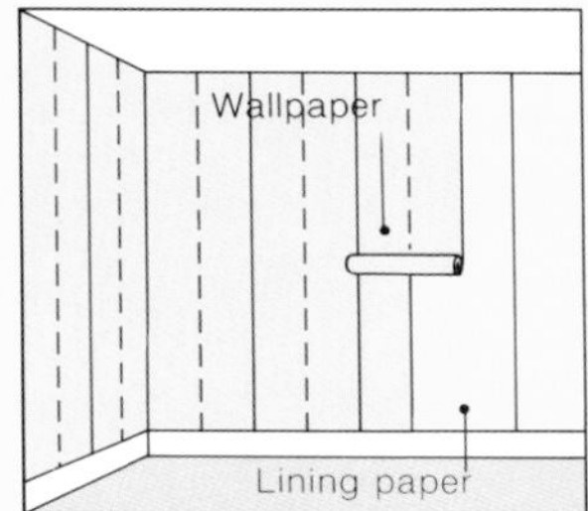

Decide where the first length of wall covering is to go. Then, instead of hanging a full width of lining paper, hang only half a width. The lining paper seams will then occur halfway across each length of the top covering.

Do not overlap the edges because the raised areas may show through the wallcovering. Similarly, do not take lining paper onto adjoining walls. Trim away any excess paper so that the edges fit neatly into corners.

Wait until the lining paper is firmly stuck and dry – at least 12 hours – before hanging paper on top.

Hanging special coverings

NOVAMURA

Novamura differs from standard wallpaper because you do not cut lengths from the roll before you hang it. You also paste the wall and not the covering.

1 Hang a plumb line and mark a true vertical on the wall as for hanging standard wallpaper (page 130).

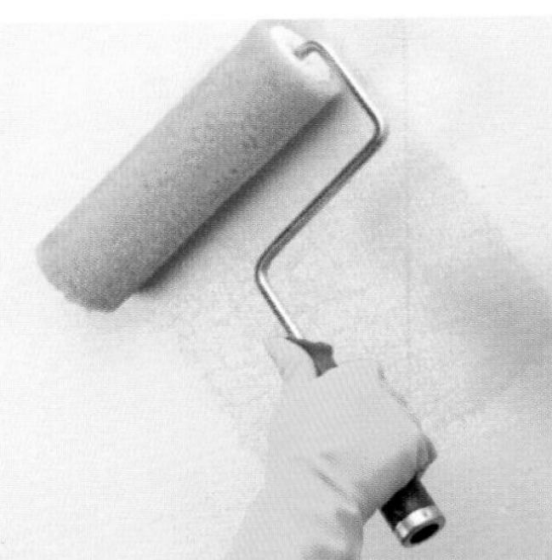

2 Paste the area of the wall which the first length is to cover, taking the paste just beyond the width of the covering. Use an adhesive containing a fungicide and apply it with a paint roller or brush. Wear rubber gloves to protect your hands, if you have sensitive skin.

> HELPFUL TIP
> Use matchsticks to mark where fittings have been taken down from a wall. Push a matchstick into each hole or wallplug, leaving it just proud of the surface. Ease the matchsticks through the paper when you smooth it over the wall. If you are hanging vinyl, make a small cut with a trimming knife for each matchstick.

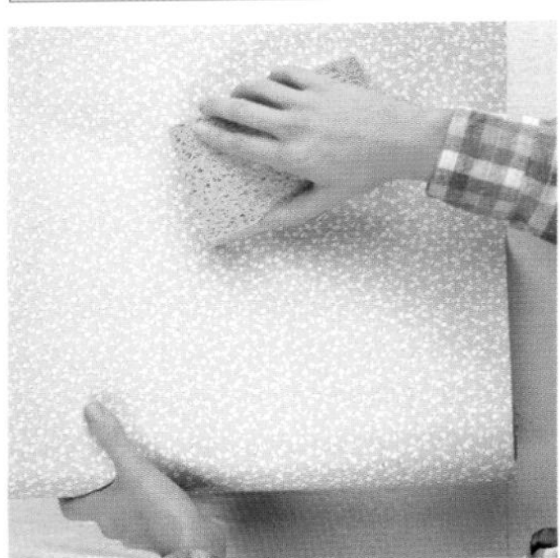

3 Hold a roll of Novamura up to the pasted area. Align the right edge with the pencil marks on the wall. Smooth the covering into place with a damp sponge. Gradually unroll the Novamura as you move down the wall, wiping away any bubbles under the surface as you work. Novamura is light – but you may find it easier if a helper holds the roll.

4 Crease the covering at the top and bottom of the length as for standard wallpaper and trim with a sharp knife or scissors.

5 Paste an adjacent width of the wall and hang the next length as before. Make sure the pattern matches, and butt join the edges of the two pieces.

READY-PASTED PAPERS AND VINYLS

Ready-pasted papers and vinyls are water-resistant so they do not expand in water. This reduces the chance of bubbles forming and means they do not have to be left to soak. Ready-pasteds are convenient – you do not have to bother with a pasting table – but they are more expensive than standard wallpapers or vinyls. You need a water trough for holding each length while it is wetted. Cheap waxed cardboard or polystyrene troughs are usually sold by wall-covering suppliers – but you could improvise with a plastic window box – provided it has no drainage holes.

1 Hang a plumb line to find a true vertical and make pencil marks to act as a guide for the first length as for hanging standard wallpaper (page 130).

> HELPFUL TIP
> Mix a small amount of paste even when you are hanging ready-pasteds. The paste on the covering may begin to dry before the length is hung – while you trim around a fitting for instance. Brush paste onto the dried areas and then smooth the length into place.

2 Fill the water trough with cold water and position it near the wall where you are going to start. Put newspaper underneath and around the trough to soak up any spilled water.

3 Measure the wall height, add 4in (100mm) for trimming and cut a length of the paper or vinyl. Check which way up it is to be hung on the wall.

4 Hold the length by the end which will be at the bottom of the wall and feed the covering into the water trough, rolling it up in the trough so that the pattern faces inwards. The edge by which you finally hold it will be the top one. Make sure it is rolled loosely or water will not wet the whole surface.

5 Use both hands to lift the covering out of the trough. Hold the length above the trough for a few seconds so that surplus water drains into it.

6 Hang the length, smoothing away air bubbles with a clean sponge. Work from the middle of the length out to the edges as for standard wallpaper.

7 Wipe away any excess paste oozing at the seams with a damp rag. The paste will not stain the surface of the covering.

8 Trim the edges as you would standard wallpaper. Then cut the next length. Roll, soak and hang it following the same procedure as for the first length.

9 Keep the water trough topped up with water as you hang the lengths.

10 Use special vinyl seam adhesive to get a good bond where vinyl overlaps vinyl, around corners for example, or where a seam is not lying flat.

11 Cut vinyl with scissors around awkward angles. You cannot tear it. If you have to overlap vinyl, you can make the join less noticeable by reducing the thickness of the vinyl on top by tearing off the backing paper.

12 When you have hung three or four lengths, go over the seams with a seam roller to make sure the edges are firmly stuck.

HESSIAN, GRASSCLOTH AND OTHER SPECIAL COVERINGS

Find out whether paste should be applied to the wall or to the covering – follow manufacturers' instructions and see the chart on page 129. Hessian, silk, grasscloth, cork and heavy relief wall coverings (like Lincrusta) have edges which cannot be matched and are rarely true, so lengths cannot be butt joined. Hang the coverings like standard wallpaper but use the following method to join them.

1 Overlap the edges at each join by about 1in (25mm).

2 Cut through the double thickness down the whole length of the wall with a razor-sharp trimming knife pressed against a metal straight-edge.

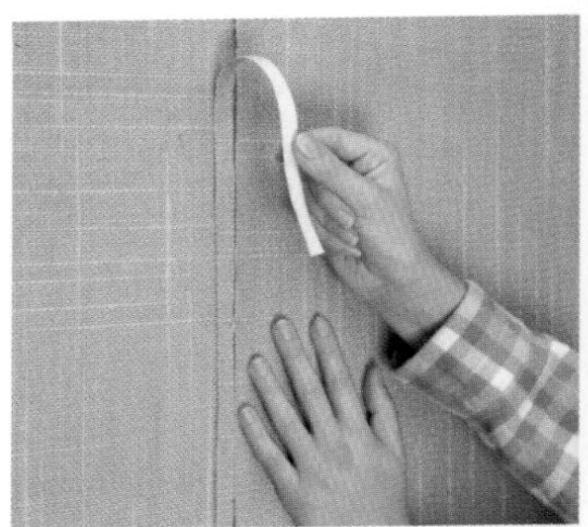

3 Carefully peel the top waste strip of the covering from the wall. Use the trimming knife again if the cut has not gone right through to separate the covering cleanly.

4 Lift up the edge of the covering you have pulled the top strip away from and remove the trimmed strip from underneath.

5 Smooth the covering back into place with a paperhanging brush or damp sponge to form a perfect butt join.

Run a seam roller lightly down the join with hessian, grasscloth and cork coverings. Do not use one on relief wallpapers or any covering likely to be damaged by the wheel.

Wallpapering a ceiling

The ceiling is probably the most difficult area to decorate – you have to work at a height and against gravity. Also, because the ceiling is usually well lit any imperfections will show up. If the ceiling is smooth, you could paint it rather than try to hang paper. Consider applying a textured coating to a very uneven ceiling. This will hide any flaws but has the disadvantage of being hard to remove once it is applied.

You may want to paper a ceiling for a decorative effect or may not be able to avoid doing so. Emulsion paint should not be applied direct to a ceiling with hairline cracks, for instance. You must put up lining paper, otherwise the cracks will absorb the paint.

First cover the floor with plenty of cotton dust sheets. Then set up a safe working platform. Use two trestles or two pairs of steps and arrange a scaffold board between them so that the ceiling clears your head by about 3in (75mm). If possible, the board should allow you to paper the length of the ceiling without rearranging the platform. Use two boards – one on top of the other – to give a firmer support if the trestles are more than 5ft (1.5m) apart. Prepare the surface, filling holes and cracks and sealing any stains. Wear safety spectacles to protect your eyes.

Plan to hang either decorative paper or lining paper beginning at the main window and working away from it. When there are two windows in a room, hang the paper across the narrower width.

If you are hanging lining paper, do not bother to mark a guideline on the ceiling. Align the paper with the wall where you start and butt join the edges so that they do not overlap.

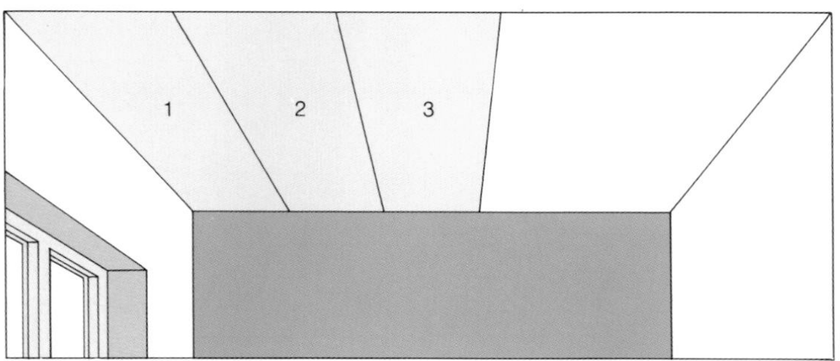

Hang the first length of wallpaper next to the window wall, so that overlapping seams cannot cast shadows and make the joins obvious.

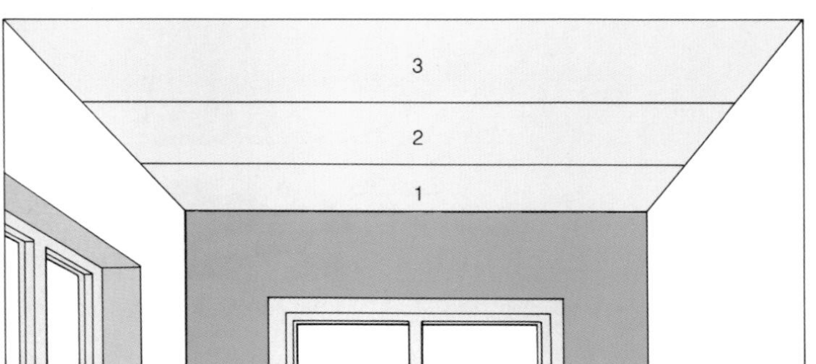

If there are two windows in the room, hang wallpaper across the narrower width of the ceiling. It will make the job easier.

HANGING THE PAPER

1 Brush the whole ceiling with glue size – this gives good slip and helps the adhesion.

2 Measure the ceiling, add a couple of inches for the trimming at each end, and cut the first length.

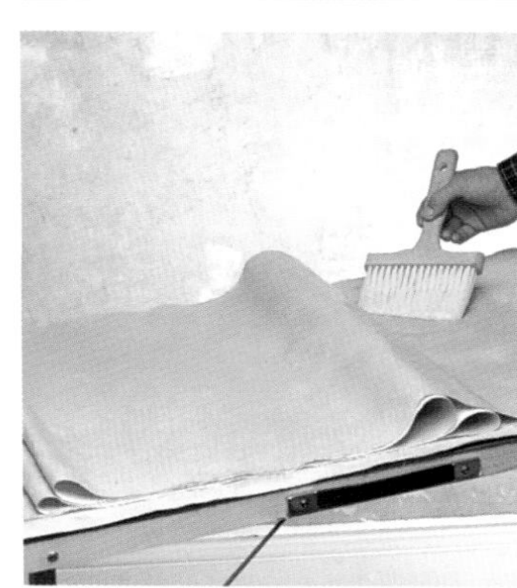

3 Paste as for paper going on a wall but, because of the length of the paper, fold it concertina fashion as you apply the paste. Keep the width of the folds to about 18in (460mm) and do not crease the folds.

4 If you are hanging a decorative wallpaper, make a line parallel with the wall as a guide for the first length. The easiest way is to snap a chalk line with a chalk-line reel (right).

ALTERNATIVELY, hammer two tacks into the ceiling the width of the paper – less ½in (13mm) for trimming – away from the window wall, at the two ends of the ceiling. Tie a piece of string so that it is taut between the tacks and make pencil marks along the line.

5 Check that the scaffold board is under the chalk or pencil marks so that you do not have to lean backwards. If you are right-handed, lay the folded paper over a spare roll and hold it in your left hand so that the paper drapes over the roll. Stand on the end of the board at the right, facing the window. If you are left-handed, hold the roll in your right hand and begin at the other end.

HELPFUL TIP

Papering a ceiling is one of the most difficult decorating jobs – especially if you have never tackled it before. If you can, get a helper to stand on a pair of steps and hold the pile of paper close to the ceiling – at least while you position the first few folds of each length.

6 Release the top fold of paper. Hold it up to the ceiling and position it so that the right-hand edge aligns with the marks. Smooth the paper into the corner with your fingers. When you are satisfied that the paper is positioned correctly, gently go over it with the paperhanging brush.

7 Very carefully move your left hand away to release the next fold of paper. Smooth out the paper with the brush as you move slowly to the left – checking that the paper is following the guideline. If the adhesive is of the correct consistency and the size is doing its job the paper will not pull away from the ceiling – as long as you keep holding the rest of the paper fairly close.

If the paper pulls away easily, the paste is not strong enough, so mix up some more, adding less water. Apply the paste to the ceiling, then smooth the paper back into its position.

SNAPPING A CHALK LINE ON A CEILING

Use a chalk-line reel, which colours the string inside it automatically with powdered chalk, or run a stick of chalk over a piece of string the length of the ceiling. Use coloured chalk if the ceiling is white – unless you are hanging a pale coloured paper, which might be damaged if you got red or blue chalk on it.

The run of the wall is unlikely to be regular so deduct about ½in (13mm) from the paper width to allow for trimming along the wall. Drive a tack into the ceiling this distance away from the window wall at both ends of the ceiling. Attach the chalked string to both tacks so that it is drawn tight.

Hold the string about halfway down its length, pull it down vertically and then let go immediately so that it snaps against the ceiling. Make sure that the chalked line is visible all the way along the ceiling, then remove the tacks and the string.

8 When the whole length is in contact with the ceiling, trim the edges against the wall and the ends. Make a crease with the back of a pair of scissors, pull the paper slightly away from the ceiling and cut away the excess.

9 Continue to hang paper in the same way, butt joining the edges of the pieces.

PAPERING AROUND A CEILING ROSE

1 Hang the first part of the length as far as the ceiling rose.

2 Pierce the paper with scissors or a trimming knife at the point where the fitting has to go through the paper.

3 Make star-shaped cuts out from this hole and pull the fitting through the paper.

4 Hang the remainder of the length. Go back to the rose and trim away the surplus paper with small sharp scissors to make a neat fit.

SAFETY TIP

Turn off the electricity at the consumer unit (the fuse box) before unscrewing a ceiling rose if you plan to remove the fitting so that the paper can go behind it.

Wallpapering a stairwell

Two problems must be overcome when you paper a stairwell – how to reach the walls and how to cope with long lengths of pasted paper.

Reaching the walls

You need to reach both the head wall and the well wall from a safe working platform. With a straight staircase, place a pair of steps on the top landing, lean a ladder against the head wall (so the ladder feet rest against a riser halfway down the stairs) and lay a scaffold board between them. Use one board on top of another for stronger support if the gap between the steps and the ladder is more than 5ft (1.5m).

To paper the head wall, cut and paste the lengths of paper required and paper the top of the wall first, allowing the folded lengths to hang. Then remove the ladder and place one end of the scaffold board on a stair tread and the other on steps at the bottom of the stairs. Adjust the height of the board so that you can comfortably reach the lower half of the head wall and hang the bottom lengths.

When a staircase has a half-landing or there are corners to negotiate, you may be able to rest a scaffold board on two pairs of steps.

You may prefer to reach the walls from a scaffold kit especially if the ceiling is high, although it can be difficult to walk up and down the stairs while it is erected. You can hire a kit designed for use on stairs, with a base only 24in (610mm) wide and adjustable feet.

Hanging the paper

Until you are experienced, choose a good quality wall covering with a non-matching pattern. Matching long lengths is difficult because they tear easily if the paper is thin and tend to stretch.

Hang the paper as on ordinary walls, but take care when cutting lengths to size. Because stairs rise at an angle, each length of paper will be longer at its lower edge.

It is much easier for two people to paper a stairwell. Long lengths of pasted paper are heavy to handle, so if possible get someone to stand on the stairs below where you are hanging the paper and hold the bulk of it while you hang the top.

SAFETY TIP

Make sure that the ladder or platform is firm and safe before you step onto it. If you hire scaffolding obtain advice on how to erect it safely. Always move the platform to get to an area out of reach – you risk overbalancing if you lean or stretch out.

A STRAIGHT STAIRCASE

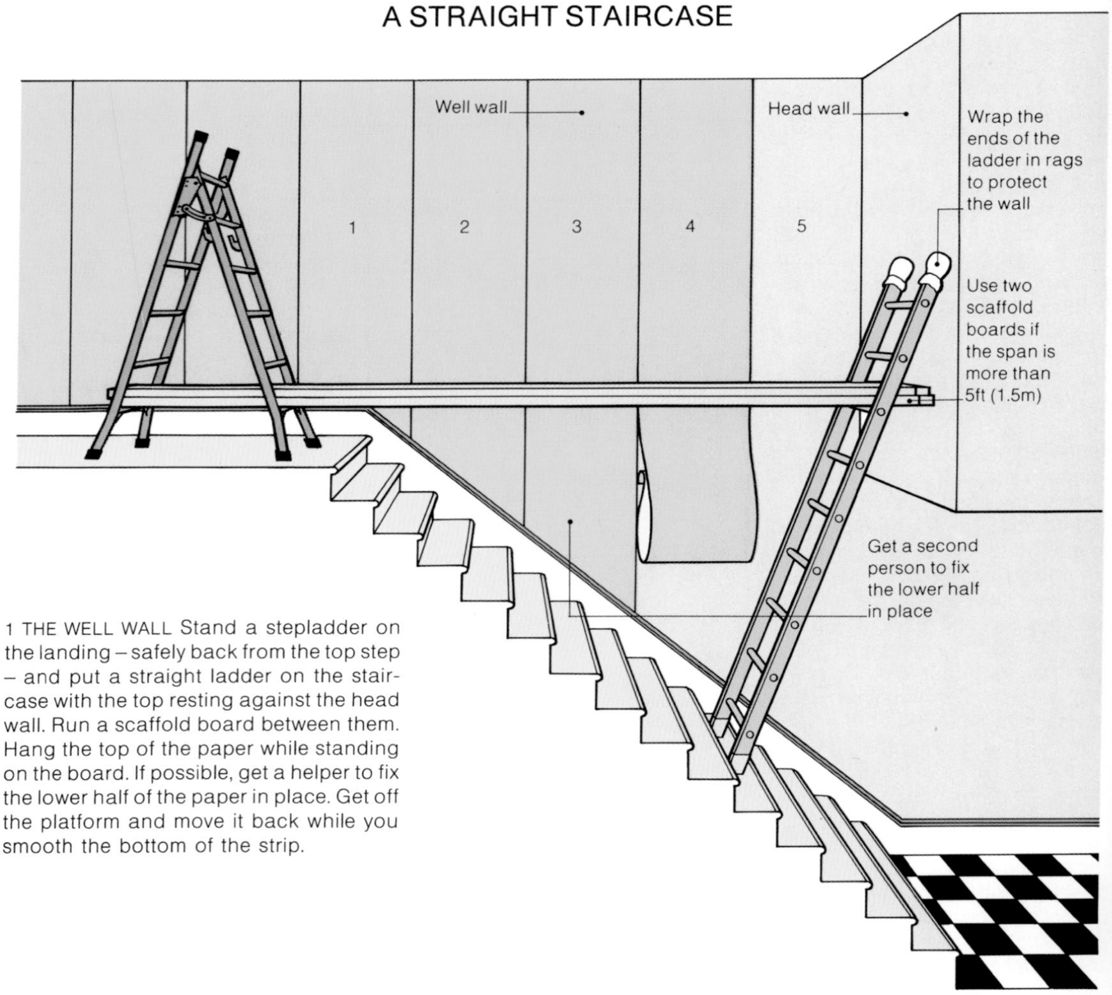

Well wall

Head wall

1 2 3 4 5

Wrap the ends of the ladder in rags to protect the wall

Use two scaffold boards if the span is more than 5ft (1.5m)

Get a second person to fix the lower half in place

1 THE WELL WALL Stand a stepladder on the landing – safely back from the top step – and put a straight ladder on the staircase with the top resting against the head wall. Run a scaffold board between them. Hang the top of the paper while standing on the board. If possible, get a helper to fix the lower half of the paper in place. Get off the platform and move it back while you smooth the bottom of the strip.

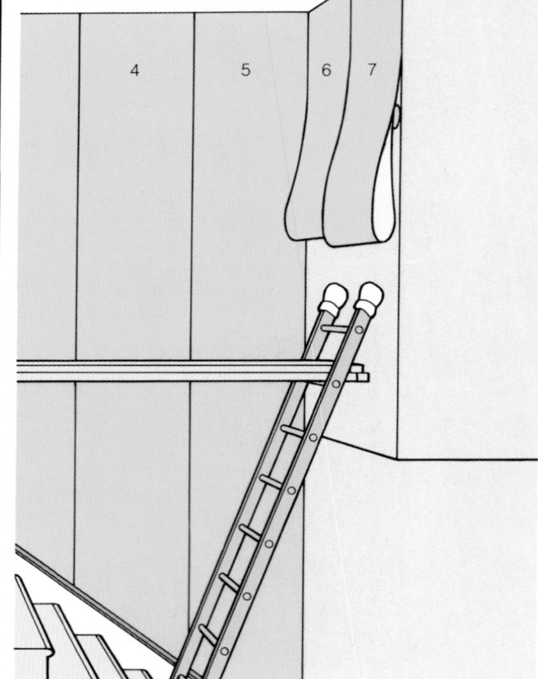

2 UPPER HEAD WALL You will probably need two lengths of paper, perhaps three. Paste and fold them before climbing onto the platform. Get a helper to pass them up one at a time and hang the top of each strip. Let them hang there.

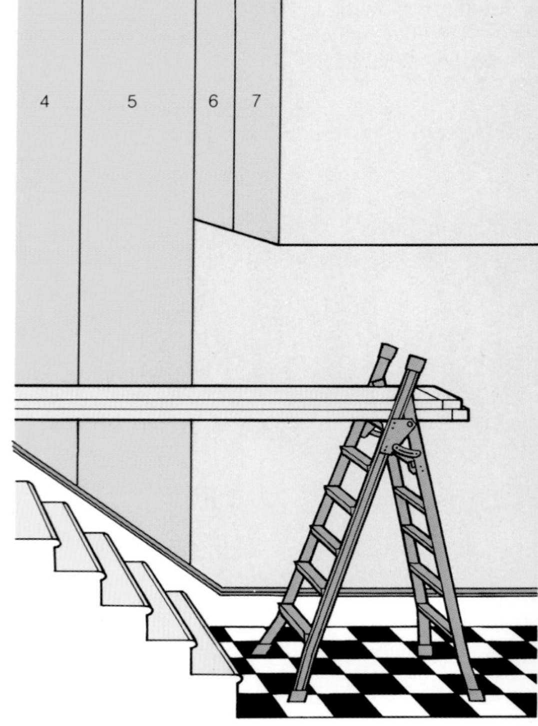

3 LOWER HEAD WALL Dismantle the platform and move the board lower down so that it rests on one of the stairs. A second stepladder at the bottom of the staircase will simplify the rearrangement. Hang the bottom of the paper from the new position.

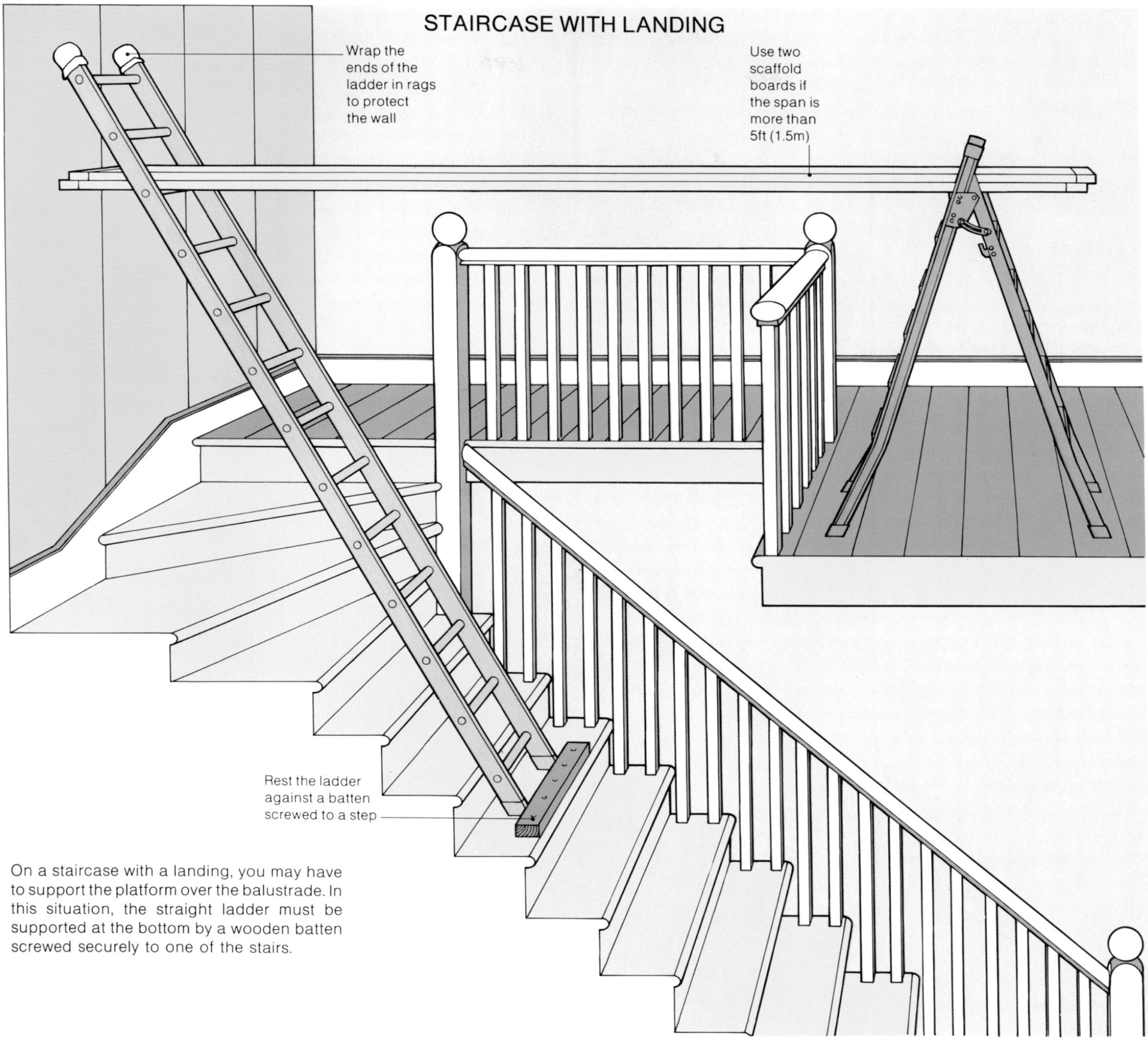

STAIRCASE WITH LANDING

Wrap the ends of the ladder in rags to protect the wall

Use two scaffold boards if the span is more than 5ft (1.5m)

Rest the ladder against a batten screwed to a step

On a staircase with a landing, you may have to support the platform over the balustrade. In this situation, the straight ladder must be supported at the bottom by a wooden batten screwed securely to one of the stairs.

Curing wallpapering problems

POOR PATTERN OR COLOUR MATCH

If you cannot match the edges of the first two or three lengths of a patterned paper, this is because too much has been trimmed off the edges at the factory. Check the whole batch and take all reject rolls to the supplier and exchange them.

Variations in colour shades may occur in different production batches, so always buy all the rolls you need at the same time and make sure they have the same batch number. If there are variations in rolls from the same batch, ask your supplier to replace them if he can. If not, put the poorest match in a place which is not seen very much.

Slight mismatches can be disguised by hanging the offending lengths where they will be partly hidden – behind furniture and in window openings for example – or using them on a separate wall where different light and shade will offset the variation.

PERSISTENT BUBBLES

Small bubbles in wallpaper should disappear as the paper dries out. If they persist the paper has expanded, either because it was not left to soak long enough or because the new paper was applied over old.

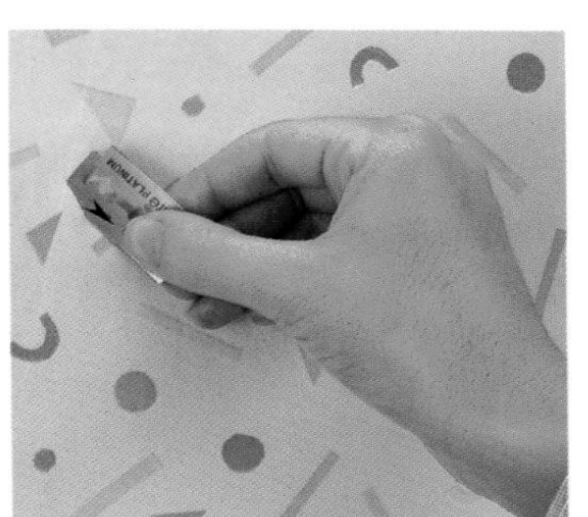

Cut small bubbles with a razor blade and insert new paste behind the flaps with a fine artist's brush. Press the paper into place and wipe away excess paste with a damp rag. If a whole length of paper is badly affected, pull it off and hang another length, increasing the soaking time.

Always strip off old paper before hanging new – moisture in the paste will soften the old paper and cause it to expand. Leave paper to soak for the correct time.

PAPER WILL NOT SLIDE

Water in the paste is being absorbed by the wall, or the paste is drying out too quickly. Either the wall has not been sized or the paste is too watery. Make sure you mix the paste as recommended by the manufacturer, do not add more water to make it go further.

Curing wallpaper problems (continued)

Put the pasted length that will not slide back on the table. Mix a thicker paste and apply it to the wall, then re-hang.

If you suspect that the room temperature is causing the paste to dry quickly, open windows or turn off heating.

Use glue size on the walls; it is more slippery than paste.

FLATTENED RELIEF PATTERN

Caused by too much pressure being applied when pressing the paper into position, particularly at the seams.

Use very gentle pressure when applying relief patterned papers, especially those that are heavily embossed. Do not use a seam roller on the edges; dab with a dry rag.

Expanded vinyls will regain their shape as the foam recovers, but other relief papers will remain flat, and nothing can be done to restore the relief pattern.

SHINY PATCHES ON MATT WALLPAPER

The surface has been rubbed too vigorously when put into place.

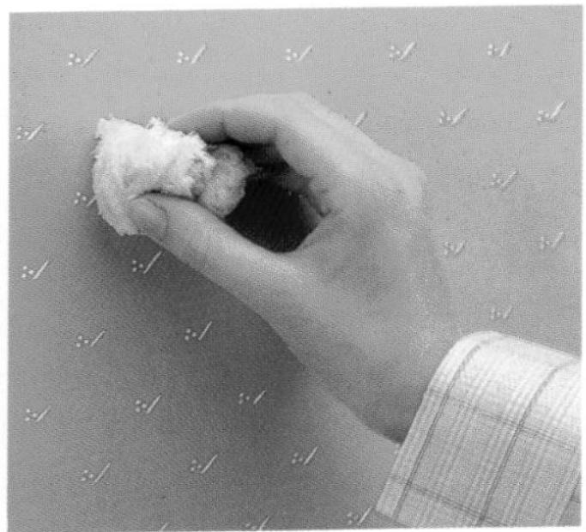

Shine marks cannot usually be removed completely, but rubbing the area with a ball of white bread may lessen the shine. This method can also be used to clean non-washable wallpaper.

Next time, smooth matt papers carefully with a clean, dry sponge or a dry nylon or lambswool paint roller. Or dab with a rag.

STAINING AT THE SEAMS

Old size has been reactivated by the water in the new paste.

Stains cannot be totally removed, but wiping them gently with a clean, damp rag may make them less visible.

To avoid this problem, wash down walls with hot water to remove any old size, and then re-size them.

GAPS AT THE SEAMS

The wallpaper might have shrunk slightly as it dried out, because the paste was not strong enough to hold it in place.

Always use a paste suitable for the type of wallpaper being used (page 129).

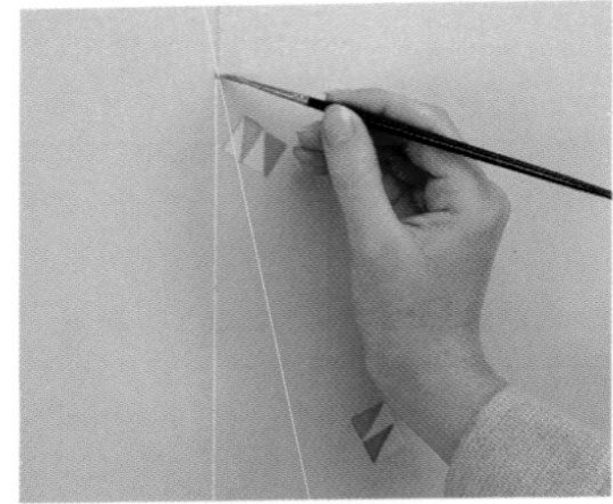

Depending on the colour of the wallpaper, try painting the gap with watercolour, using a fine artist's brush, so that it is less obvious.

SEAMS THAT LIFT

This problem often happens with vinyls and relief papers, and is caused by too little paste being applied to the edges of the paper.

To re-stick the seams, lift the edge gently with a knife blade and apply new paste. For overlapping edges of vinyls use a special vinyl seam adhesive.

Before hanging more lengths, make sure that the paste goes right to the edges.

CREASES IN THE PAPER

Possibly caused by applying paper to a wall which is not perfectly flat, but more often caused by careless hanging.

Creases can be treated in the same way as bubbles. Tear the paper, or cut vinyl, along the crease, re-paste if necessary, and smooth down.

To avoid the problem, fill all indentations with filler or a skimming coat of plaster before papering.

BROWN SPOTS SHOWING THROUGH PAPER

Impurities in the plaster may be the cause, possibly through using a wire brush or wire wool during preparation. Alternatively, the marks may be made by mould which has formed because the surface is cold and damp.

If the spots are excessive and are in areas not likely to be hidden by furniture or pictures, you will have to strip the walls and prepare them thoroughly before redecorating. Treat them with a fungicide before repapering if damp is a problem. And if the wall is cold, line it with expanded polystyrene in roll form.

Next time use abrasive paper – not wire wool or a wire brush – during preparation. Use a fungicide paste on walls likely to attract condensation, such as a bathroom or kitchen.

DAMP PATCHES ON WALLPAPER

If wet patches remain after most of the paper has dried, damp may be striking through the wall, or the patches may be condensation forming on a cold surface.

Do not ignore the problem: find the cause of the damp immediately and cure it (pages 438 and 453). If treated immediately the damp patch will dry out without trace, but if left too long it will leave a stain.

PAPER COMES AWAY FROM THE WALL

There are four possible causes: the paste is too weak to hold the weight of the paper; the surface has not been sized; the paper has been applied over old distemper or gloss paint; condensation has formed on the wall after it has been prepared.

If only small areas of the paper are coming away from the wall, mix a new batch of paste, apply it to the wall and press the paper back into place. If whole sheets are peeling off, strip the walls and prepare the surface thoroughly.

Next time, make sure you use the correct paste, mixed to the manufacturer's instructions, and prepare the surface thoroughly. In a bathroom or kitchen eliminate causes of condensation before papering (page 463).

REPAIRING DAMAGED WALLPAPER

Torn wallpaper can be patched using a piece of matching paper.

1 Tear off the paper from the damaged area, leaving only paper which is firmly attached to the wall.

2 Hold a fresh piece of paper over the hole and adjust it so that the pattern matches the surrounding paper on the wall.

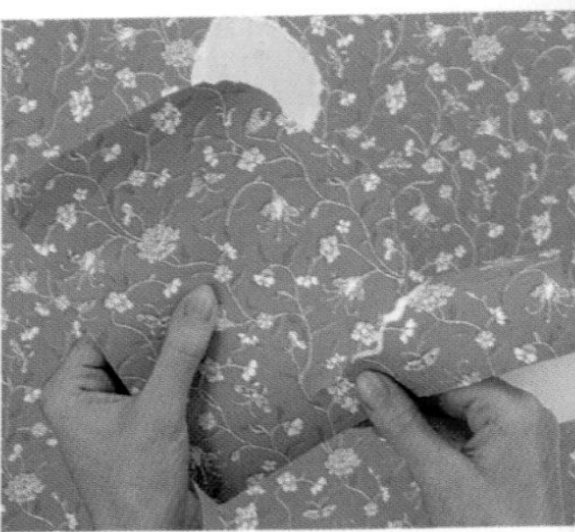

3 Tear (do not cut) a patch from the new paper and peel off a ⅛in (3mm) strip from the back around the edges.

4 Paste the patch and place it over the hole so that the pattern matches all round. Smooth down, working from the centre of the patch to the edges.

PATCHING VINYL WALL COVERING

1 Cut a square piece of vinyl larger than the damaged area. (You cannot tear vinyl wall covering as you can paper.)

2 Tape the square over the hole and with a trimming knife cut a square shape through both layers.

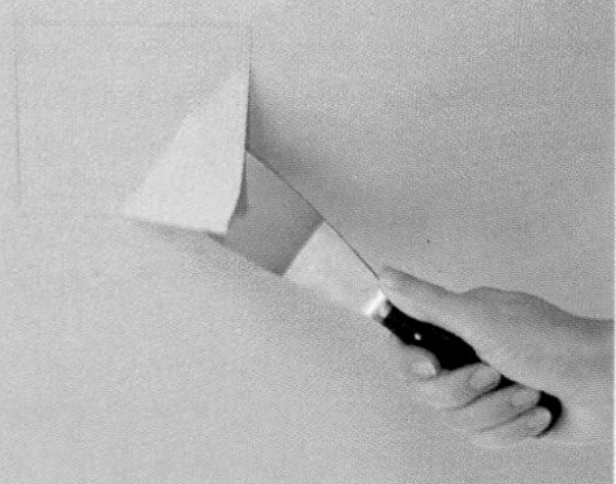

3 Remove the pieces of old vinyl within the square.

4 Coat the patch with vinyl paste and fit it to the wall.

Tiling: Tools for the job

Some of the tools you need, such as pincers or pliers, will probably already be in your tool kit.

Before you start tiling you need a straight batten – with masonry nails and a hammer to fix it – to help you to align the first row of tiles. Similarly, you need a plumb line and spirit level to check that the tiles are put up to a true vertical and horizontal. The tools on this page are also necessary, but instead of the specialist tool it is sometimes possible to substitute something else. If you do not have a tile file, for example, keep abrasive paper handy, wrapped around a sanding block or a piece of wood, to smooth the cut edges of a tile – or you can use a carborundum stone.

Tile cutter
Cutters are used to score a clearly defined scratch across the glaze of a tile – and they vary in size and shape. A cutter may resemble a slim pencil with a cutting tip or have a hardened wheel set into a handle.

Some cutters have two jaws to hold the tile when you break it after it has been scored. Place the scored tile between the jaws and squeeze the handles together. For the toughest tiles, use a platform tile cutter (see right). This can handle tiles up to ⅜in (10mm) thick and both scores and breaks them.

Tile saw
A tungsten-carbide coated rod, mounted in a large metal frame, which acts as a cutting blade. It is the ideal tool for shaping curved tiles to fit around obstructions, such as water pipes, wash basins or baths.

Tile file
A flat strip of metal with an abrasive surface coated with tungsten carbide. It is used to smooth the rough edges of cut tiles. Clean it with a wire brush when the surface has become clogged.

Fine Chinagraph pencil and steel rule
For marking where tiles should be cut. Never use felt-tipped pens to mark a tile – if the ink gets onto the back of the tile it may penetrate and show beneath the glazed surface.

Adhesive spreader
A simple tool made of plastic or metal with one or more notched edges. Large versions are available but small spreaders, usually supplied with tubs of adhesive, are adequate for most jobs.

The notches on the spreader ensure that the adhesive is spread over the wall at a constant depth – and economises on the amount of adhesive used.

Small pointing trowel
Use the trowel to put adhesive on the wall and spread it out to an even consistency.

It is much easier to get adhesive out of the tub with a trowel, though you can do without one if you prefer. If you use a spreader to apply adhesive, the notches tend to become blocked.

Sponge or squeegee
A small piece of synthetic sponge is the best thing for pressing grout into the joins between tiles – some tubs of grout come with a small sponge and a cleaning pad attached.

Alternatively, you can use a rubber squeegee to do the same job. You will get the grouting done more quickly but may not achieve such good results. It is difficult to press a substantial amount of grout between tiles with a squeegee – and thin layers of grout may crack when dry.

Spacers
Small plastic crosses are inserted at the corners of straight-edged tiles as they are applied to the wall. Spacers ensure that there is a constant gap for grout between tiles.

Matchsticks or small pieces of cardboard, provided they are equal in thickness, can be used instead of the plastic crosses on a small job or if you run out.

Tiling gauge
The gauge is a length of batten, wider than any obstruction you need to tile around. Mark the width of the tiles on the wood, plus gaps for spacers if necessary, and use the gauge to position tiles around windows or any similar breaks in the tiling.

PLATFORM TILE CUTTER
A platform tile cutter is an invaluable tool because modern ceramic tiles are so hard that they are more or less impossible to cut using a traditional, hand-held wheel cutter. Some models of platform tile cutter are designed to cut both wall and floor tiles. Simpler, cheaper versions will cut only one thickness of tile.

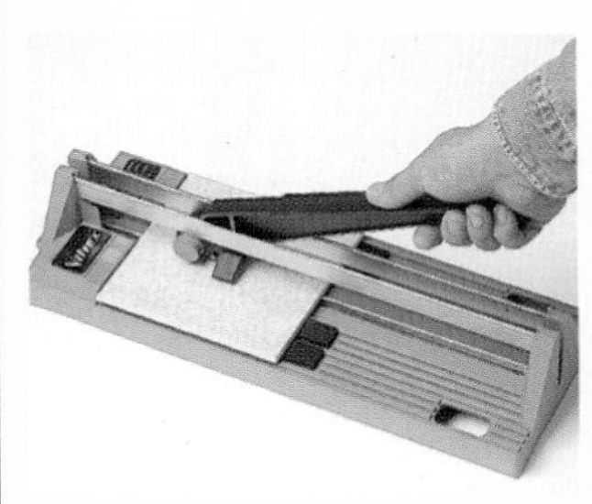

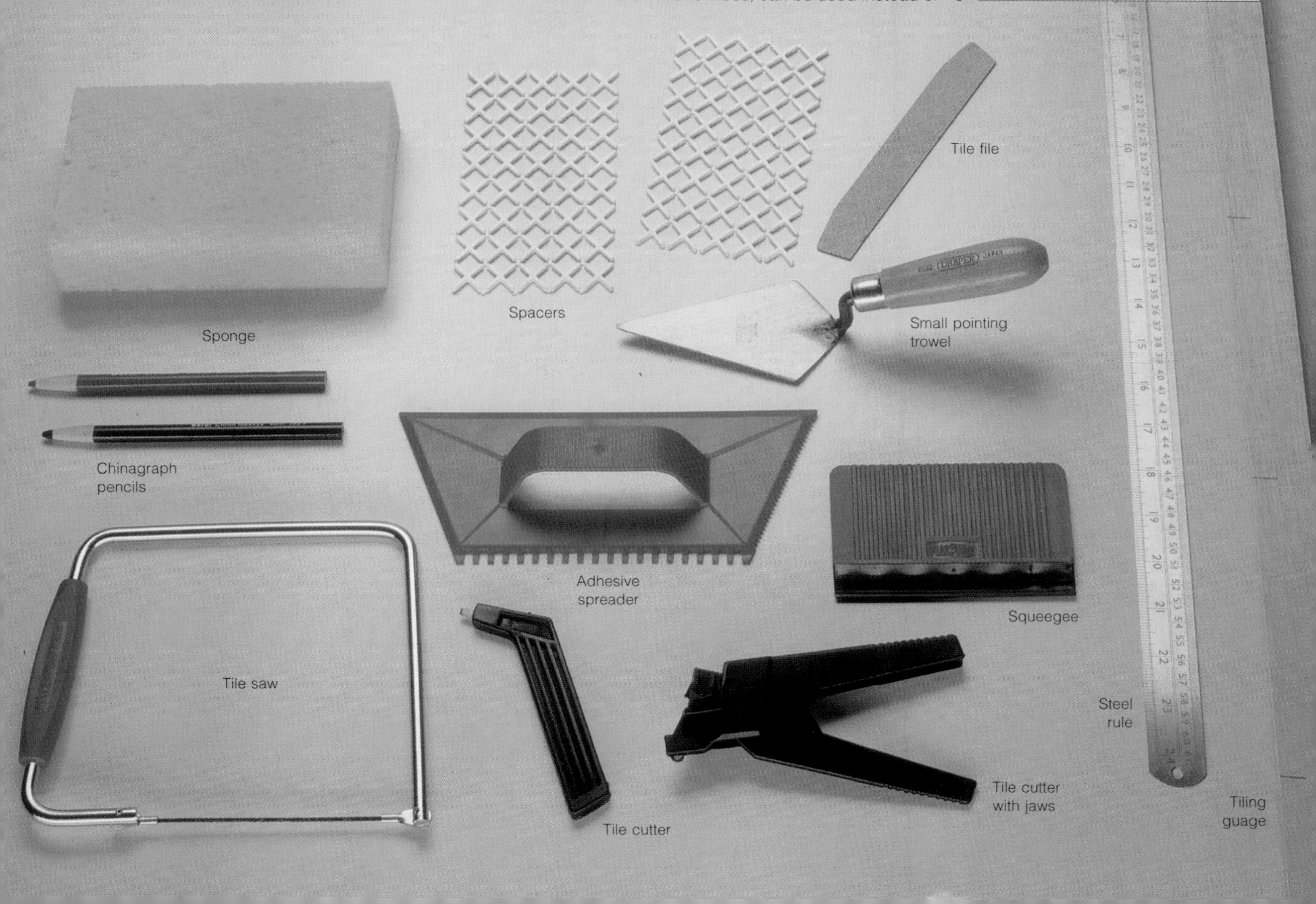

Sponge

Spacers

Tile file

Small pointing trowel

Chinagraph pencils

Adhesive spreader

Squeegee

Tile saw

Tile cutter

Tile cutter with jaws

Steel rule

Tiling guage

CHOOSING CERAMIC WALL TILES AND TRIM

Ceramic tiles are a functional form of wall covering, particularly useful in bathrooms and kitchens. An enormous range is available – prices vary according to size, colour and quality.

Imported tiles are usually made with straight, unglazed edges, calling for glazed border tiles at corners and edges. Most British tiles have one or two glazed edges.

Special plastic edging trim can be inserted under edge tiles as tiling is done. It gives a neat and protective finish.

CERAMIC TILES

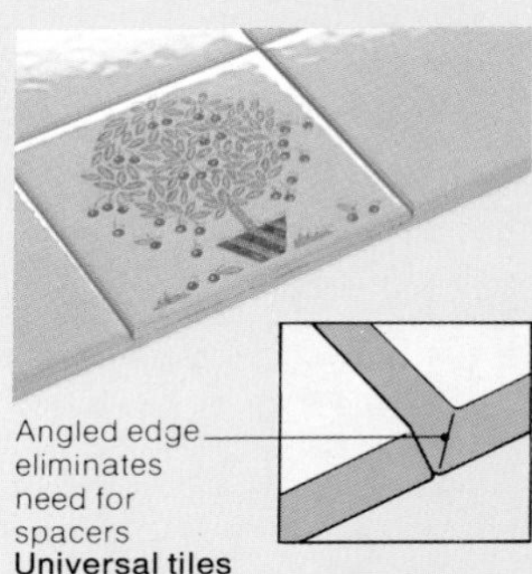

Angled edge eliminates need for spacers

Universal tiles
Tiles with specially angled edges so that when the tiles are stuck next to each other the correct gap is left between them for the grout. Usually sold in boxes of about 25 or 50 and in sizes 4¼in (108mm) and 6in (150mm) square. Each box contains tiles glazed on one or two adjacent sides. Sometimes all the edges are glazed.

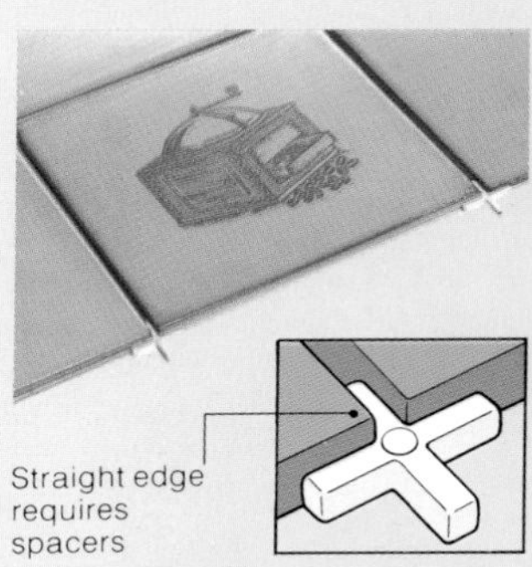

Straight edge requires spacers

Standard field tiles
Tiles with square edges, usually glazed on one or two edges and sometimes on all of them. The most common tiles are 4¼in (108mm) square or 6in (150mm) square and $\frac{5}{32}$in (4mm) thick, but other sizes and shapes are available. Place spacers between tiles as you put them on the wall so there is room for grout. Occasionally you may find square-edged tiles with spacer lugs incorporated into the edges.

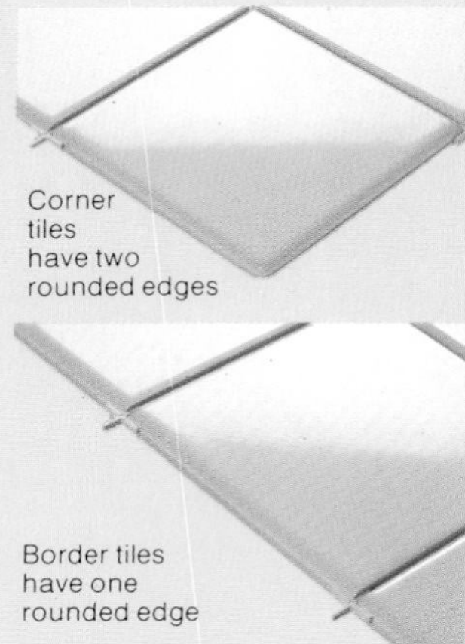

Corner tiles have two rounded edges

Border tiles have one rounded edge

Border tiles
Universal tiles and tiles with glazed edges have greatly reduced the demand for border tiles so they are rarely made today. You will probably have to order them and they are only available in white. Tiles with two rounded edges (sometimes described as REX tiles) are for finishing corners; tiles with one rounded edge (RE tiles) are for bordering the rest of the tiled area.

Imported tiles
Often harder, thicker and heavier than standard ceramic tiles, so experiment on a couple of tiles to see whether you can cut and shape them before you buy in bulk. Occasionally imported tiles are glazed on one or more edges. If the tiles have plain square edges you will need to use spacers.

Heat-resistant tiles
Most tiles will withstand temperatures of 100°C (212°F) without damage because they are fired at great heat during manufacture. The thicker the tile, the less likely it is to crack when it comes in contact with heat. If you are tiling around a fireplace or cooker, check with your supplier that the tiles are suitable.

Insert tiles
In some ranges, manufacturers supply special tiles to which bathroom accessories like towel rails, soap dishes and lavatory-paper holders are attached. Even though they are heavier than ordinary tiles, they can be fixed to the wall with standard adhesive. Check that the particular insert tile you want is available in the colour you have chosen before you buy the tiles.

Mosaic tiles
Small ceramic or glass tiles, known as chips, usually ¾in to 1in (20mm to 25mm) square. They are supplied bonded to string, nylon or paper mesh or faced with paper, about 12in (300mm) square or sometimes in rectangles about 12in × 24in (300mm × 610mm). The netting or paper controls the spacing between the tiles.

BORDERS AND TRIMS

Ceramic trims
You can finish off the top edge of a half-tiled wall with a row of border tiles, or use a slim pencil bead trim in a matching or contrasting colour if you prefer. Border tiles can also be used between areas of field tiles on a fully tiled wall, for example to create the effect of a decorative dado. Border and trim tiles are made in sizes to match standard tile widths so vertical joints will align.

Worktop trim
The neatest way of edging a tiled worktop is to fit a timber moulding to the front and side edges of the worktop. Paint, varnish or stain the moulding first, then screw it to the worktop so it acts as a guide to help you position the tiles and bed them to the correct level. Use epoxy grout to fill all the joints to give the worktop a hard-wearing and hygienic finish.

How many tiles do you need?

Tiles are sold singly, or in boxes containing a specified number, or by the square metre or square yard and sometimes by the half-metre or half-yard.

Before you buy or order tiles, measure the height and width of each part to be tiled and multiply the two figures to give the area in square metres or yards. Add all the figures together to give the total area. Most tile suppliers have charts from which you can read how many tiles you need. With some charts you do not need to know the area – just the height and width measurements. Coverage is also stated on boxes. As a rough guide, a wall 8ft by 10ft (80sq ft) will require 640 4¼in tiles or 320 6in tiles. Add a few tiles to the total to allow for breakages.

If you are going to use contrasting coloured or patterned tiles among plain ones, decide where they are to go and how many you need. This is easier if you make a plan of the wall on graph paper. Alternatively, cut pieces of paper into tile shapes and stick them to the wall to help you to get the height and spacing of the patterned tiles right. It will probably take a couple of hours, but it gives a better impression of how the tiles will look.

There is always a slight colour variation between tiles so mix them thoroughly before you start to tile. If you can, buy tiles which come in boxes with the same batch number.

CHOOSING ADHESIVES, GROUT AND SEALANTS

Standard adhesive
Suitable only for areas unlikely to come into contact with water. Available ready-mixed in tubs, usually with a small plastic spreader provided. Also supplied as a powder to be mixed with water.

Combined adhesive and grout
Does both the sticking and grouting jobs, but is very difficult to remove from the face of tiles when set. Wipe it immediately off the tiles before it dries. If it does harden on a surface, it can be removed with a kitchen scouring pad.

Thick-bed adhesive
Allows tiles to be fixed to an uneven surface – but it is best kept for small areas like splashbacks. Great skill is required to achieve a level surface – it is much easier to make the surface smooth and use standard adhesive.

Waterproof adhesive
Use to fix tiles to shower surrounds and for tiling near a bath, basin or kitchen sink. If you need waterproof adhesive in any part of the room, continue to use it to fix the rest of the tiles as well.

Special adhesive is necessary for fixing tiles which are to be under water constantly – contact an adhesive manufacturer for advice.

Heatproof adhesive
Use to fix tiles to surfaces which will be exposed to unusually high temperatures.

Grout
For filling gaps between tiles. Available ready-mixed or as fine powder to be mixed with water. Use a waterproof grout for areas likely to come into contact with water. You should also use waterproof grout for tiled worktops – germs and dirt will collect in ordinary grout. Apply a heat-resistant grout in high-temperature areas.

Grout is usually white but may be tinted with pigments. Coloured grout is available in a limited range.

Sealants
Flexible mastic, supplied in a tube, can be used to seal gaps between bathroom and kitchen fittings and tiles. Follow the instructions on the tube. Some tubes have small wings which contour the sealant.

Preparing the surface

The glaze on tiles will highlight even tiny undulations in a wall so the area to be tiled must be as flat as possible.

PLASTER

Plaster in good condition is an ideal surface for tiling – but it must be firm and dry. Smooth out any irregularities with a coat of DIY skimming plaster and fill holes and gaps (page 239). Deal with any damp and let the wall dry before you tile. If plaster is crumbling, remove all the loose material and replaster the area.

PLASTERBOARD

You can tile over plasterboard without giving it any special treatment so long as it is firmly anchored to the wall and there are no bulges or gaps in it.

If the plasterboard is around a shower or in any area likely to become damp, seal it with two coats of drywall topcoat (one brand is Gyproc), which is available from builders' merchants.

PAINTED WALLS

Walls painted with either gloss or emulsion paint are not suitable for tiling because the adhesive will only be anchored to the paint – not to the wall. Roughen the paint film by rubbing the surface with coarse abrasive paper so that the adhesive will grip to the wall underneath. Strip off loose or flaking paint with a paint scraper.

PAPERED WALLS

Never apply tiles over any type of wall covering – the adhesive holding the covering will not be strong enough to hold the tiles. Strip the covering to reveal bare plaster (page 103).

OLD CERAMIC TILES

Provided old tiles are firmly stuck to the wall and there is no sign of bulging, new tiles can be stuck over them, using standard tile adhesive. You do not need to roughen the old tiles but make sure that they are clean and dry. Replace any badly cracked tiles.

Stagger new tiles so that their joins do not align with those underneath.

With half-tiled walls there will be a small ledge where the tiling stops. Cover this with strips of tile, cut flush with the ledge. Alternatively, turn the ledge into a feature by finishing it with strips of hardwood moulding, stuck down with the same adhesive as the tiles.

PLAIN BRICKWORK

Tiles can be stuck straight onto exposed brickwork, if you use thick-bed adhesive. However, this is a difficult job best left to experts. As an alternative, line the walls with plasterboard which also acts as insulation.

Check that the bricks are clean and dry, then dab them with panel adhesive every 18in (460mm). Press the plasterboard firmly in position, and leave it to dry before tiling.

PLYWOOD AND CHIPBOARD

Seal ordinary plywood and chipboard with PVA adhesive diluted with an equal amount of water. If you are putting up plywood or chipboard yourself, use exterior grade products which resist damp. The PVA seal is then not necessary.

Tiling a wall

FINDING THE STARTING POINT

The first row of tiles must be straight – otherwise all the tiles will end up crooked – but skirting boards, floors, basin tops or bath edges are rarely level, so you need to establish a horizontal starting line which is true.

If you fix a horizontal batten the height of one tile from the floor, when you come to the bottom row of tiles you may have to cut tiles to fit, but you will not have to cut awkward slivers of tile.

The batten supports the tiles while they are being stuck to the wall as well as providing a true starting point. You can use any strips of wood so long as they have a straight edge. If you find a batten the length of the area to be tiled too unwieldy, use two or more shorter pieces but check with a spirit level to ensure that they have a straight edge.

If you are tiling over a wall already half-tiled or prefer to have complete tiles in the top row see page 144.

You will need
Tools Batten lengths for each area to be tiled; spirit level; hammer; masonry nails; pencil; sample tile (plus spacer if tiles are not self-spacing); steel measuring tape.

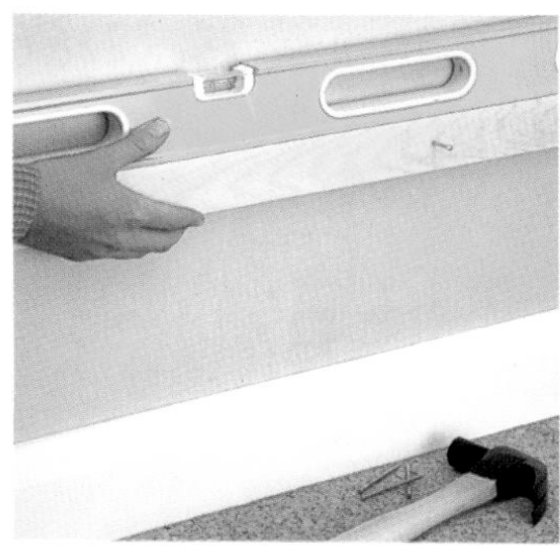

1 Lightly nail a batten to the wall about the height of a tile up from the floor or skirting board, using a spirit level to ensure that it is horizontal.

If you are tiling over old tiles, you will have to drill holes through the tiles with a masonry bit before you can fix the batten. Drill a hole through both ends of the batten and fix one end to the wall. Hold the other end of the batten to the wall and check with a spirit level to make sure that it is horizontal. Mark where to drill the old tiling through the hole in the batten. Drill the hole and then lightly nail the batten to the wall.

2 With the steel tape measure or a ruler, find the spot at which the floor or skirting board is farthest from the batten. This is the lowest point of the floor.

Tiling a wall (continued)

3 Remove the batten, put a tile against the wall at this point, and mark the top of the tile on the wall.

4 Replace the batten so that its upper edge is flush with the top of the tile – but leave a gap for spacers, if you are using them. Use the spirit level again to confirm that the batten is horizontal. Hammer in the nails just far enough to hold the batten firmly in place.

5 If more than one wall is to be tiled, establish the lowest point of the floor and fix battens at the same height on each wall.

POSITIONING TILES ON A PLAIN WALL

If tiles do not exactly fit the width of a wall, pieces of tile must be cut to fill the gap. Space the tiles so that you get a row of cut pieces at each end of the wall – both rows the same width – but try to avoid having thin slivers. Ideally, cut tiles should be at least half a tile wide.

You will need
Tools Steel tape measure; plumb line and bob; pencil; batten; masonry nails; hammer.
Materials Tiles; spacers, if necessary.

1 Place a row of tiles on the floor close to the wall to be tiled – allowing for spacers between each tile if they are to be used.

2 When no more tiles will fit, move the row along so that there is an equal gap at both ends. You might have to remove one tile from the row to get a large enough gap at each end.

3 Mark in pencil the position of the first tile in the row on the batten fixed to the wall. This is where the tiling will start.

4 Drop a plumb line from the top of the wall through the pencil mark on the batten. Mark this true vertical on the wall.

5 Nail a length of batten so that it lies along the vertical line on the wall to make a right angle with the batten already fixed.

6 Place a tile on the horizontal batten and press it close to the vertical one – it should fit the corner perfectly.

If it does not, check your measuring. One of the battens is probably not truly horizontal or vertical, so it will need adjusting.

ARRANGING TILES AROUND OBSTRUCTIONS

Make a simple tiling gauge to position tiles around windows, washbasins, fixed cupboards or similar obstructions. Tiles surrounding a window or any feature in a wall will probably have to be cut to fit. They should be of an equal length all round, otherwise they will attract attention. This means that cut tiles at the ends of the wall will probably not be balanced, but they will be less noticeable there.

You will need
Tools Two lengths of batten; pencil; plumb line and bob; masonry nails; hammer.
Materials Tiles.

1 Make a tiling gauge by marking tile widths along the full length of a piece of straight batten which is about four tiles wider than the obstruction – a window, for example. Allow for spacers, if necessary.

2 Hold the gauge across the window so that an equal length of gauge is overlapping on each side. There will be at least one full tile width and a gap to be filled with a cut tile on each side.

3 Draw a pencil line on the wall to mark where the outer edges of the cut tiles will be.

4 Hang a plumb line from whichever mark is nearer to one end of the wall. Let it drop over the batten on the wall and make a mark.

5 With the gauge as a guide, draw tile widths on the fixed batten between the mark and the wall.

6 Use the plumb line again and draw a true vertical through the pencil mark nearest the wall.

7 Fix a vertical batten along this line with masonry nails, tapped in just firmly enough to hold the batten in position.

8 Place a tile on the horizontal batten, slide it to meet the vertical one and check that it fits.

TILING THE MAIN AREA

Mix the tiles well so that any colour variation in the glaze is not obvious. If you are inserting patterned tiles in the middle of plain tiles, keep a note of where they are to go.

You will need
Tools Pointing trowel; adhesive spreader; spacers, if tiles are not self-spacing; damp cloth.
Materials Tiles, adhesive.

1 Apply adhesive to the wall with the trowel, beginning at the point where the vertical and horizontal battens meet. Spread the adhesive as evenly as possible, keeping the depth to about $\frac{1}{8}$in (3mm). Do not cover more than about 10sq ft (1sq m) at one time.

POSITIONING TILES AROUND A WINDOW

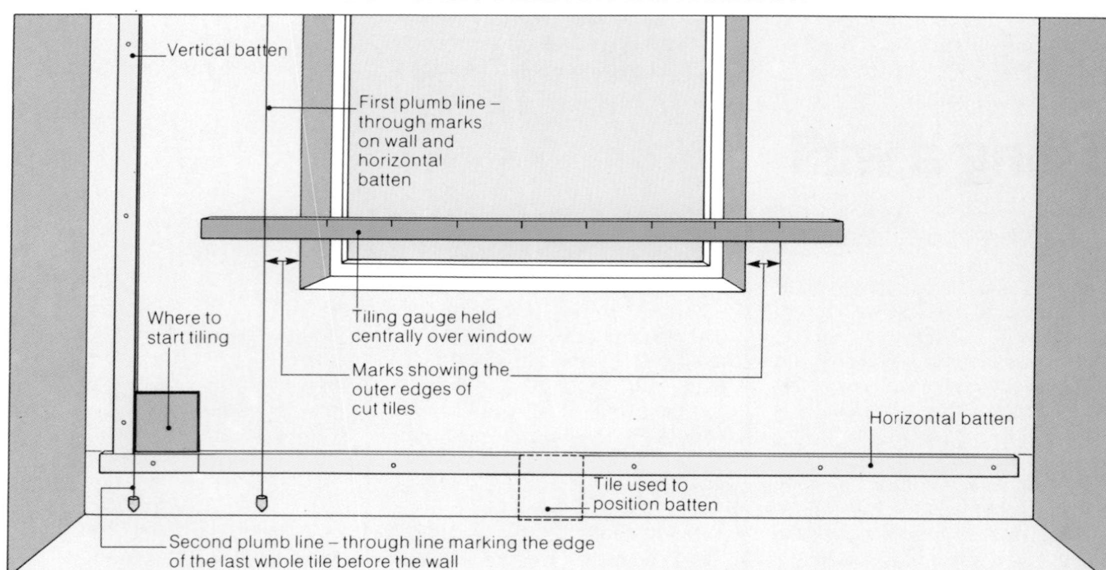

Plan carefully how best to arrange tiles around obstructions, like a window, well in advance of laying the first tile. Work out where tiles which must be cut to fit will look best. Use battens which have a true edge, and check with a spirit level to ensure that they are horizontal or vertical when you fix them to the wall.

2 Hold the spreader at an angle of about 45 degrees and go over the adhesive, so that the notches pull it into ridges. This helps to ensure that the adhesive is applied consistently and it encourages suction between the tiles and the adhesive. You may need to wipe the spreader clean every now and again on a rag or piece of newspaper if it becomes clogged with adhesive.

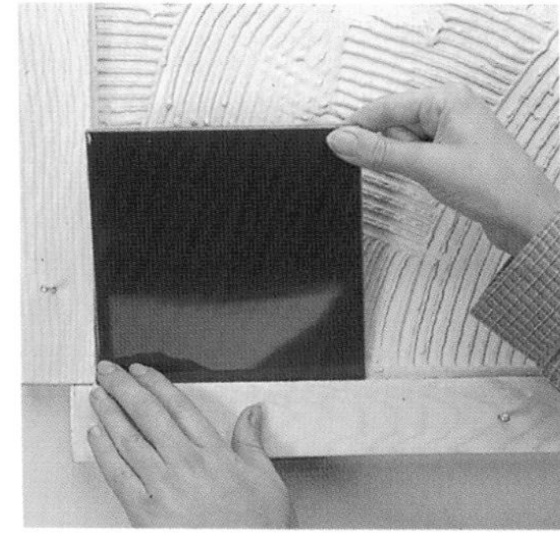

3 Place a tile in the corner where the two battens meet. Apply the bottom edge of the tile first and then lower the rest of it onto the adhesive. Press the tile firmly against the wall using your hand to apply even pressure in the four corners. Try not to allow the tile to slide – this forces adhesive up between the gaps, which will later be filled with grout.

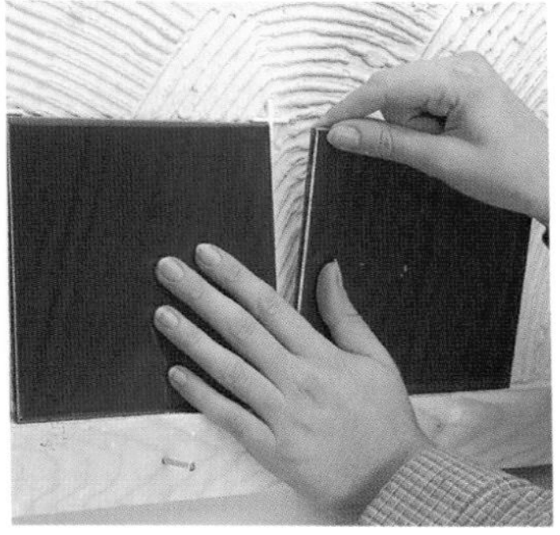

4 Continue tiling, laying the second tile next to the first. Place universal tiles edge to edge and leave a gap between standard field tiles. Press tile spacers, matchsticks or pieces of card between tiles to keep the gaps consistent.

5 As you work, wipe off with a damp cloth any adhesive which gets onto the face of the tiles.

6 Apply more adhesive and continue to lay tiles until you have completed the area which can be covered with whole tiles – ones which do not have to be cut.

7 Remove the battens after about 12 hours. Plastic spacers can be left in place and grouted over, or pulled off the wall – once the adhesive has set – and used again. Always remove matchsticks or card spacers.

HELPFUL TIP

If you are tiling around a shower or anywhere that is likely to become wet frequently or damp with condensation, use acrylic waterproof adhesive and grout. Allow the wall to completely dry out before you start tiling.

Cutting tiles to fit

It is usually necessary to cut tiles to size in order to fill the gaps that are left around the edges of the main tiled area.

For the toughest tiles, you will need to use a platform tile cutter, a tool which is available in most DIY shops. The cutter both scores and breaks the tiles.

You will need

Tools Steel tape measure; fine Chinagraph pencil; steel rule; tile cutter; a carborundum stone or fine abrasive paper wrapped around a block. Possibly: tile saw; pincers or pliers; fine abrasive paper around dowel; pencil; G-cramp.
Materials Tiles; adhesive.

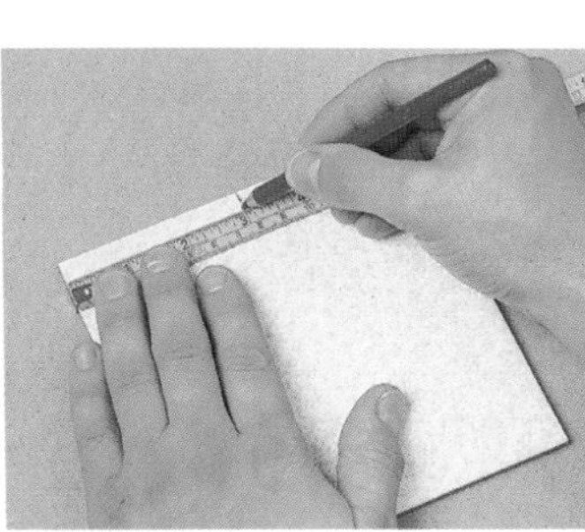

FILLING A GAP

1 Use the steel tape to measure the gap that needs to be filled. If you need to cut more than one tile, take measurements for each tile separately because the size of the gap may vary. Transfer the measurements to the glazed side of the tile and draw a line with the Chinagraph pencil (using the steel rule if the line should be straight).

2 Lay the tile to be cut on the platform and align it. Make sure that the cutter is set for the correct thickness of tile.

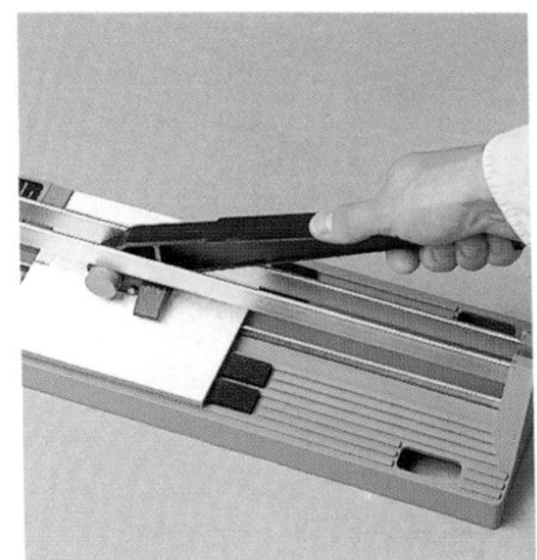

3 Run the cutting wheel over the tile by pushing forward to the end using the knobbed handle.

4 While the tile is still in place on the platform tile cutter, press down lightly on either side of the scored line to snap the tile. It will break cleanly along the scored line.

TAKING A SLIVER OFF A TILE

1 Score the tile much more deeply than you would for an ordinary cut – you must cut right through the glaze to get a clean break.

2 Nibble away at the sliver of tile which is being removed, using pincers or pliers.

SMOOTHING A CUT EDGE

Smooth the rough edge of a cut tile with a tile file held at an angle of about 45 degrees. File in one direction only, moving your hand from the glazed surface downwards, so that you do not damage the face of the tile.

Otherwise, use a piece of fine abrasive paper wrapped around a block of wood, again working in one direction only. Or you can use a small carborundum stone – but make sure that it is clean or you may mark the tile.

CUTTING A CURVED LINE

1 Cut a piece of paper to the size of a tile and make a template to fit around the curved object.

2 Use the paper as a guide to draw the curved line with a Chinagraph pencil onto the glazed tile surface.

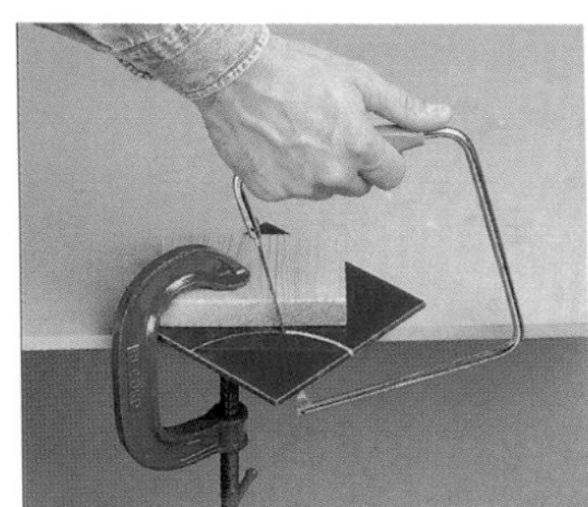

3 Hold the tile securely to a workbench or table with a G-cramp, protecting the glaze with a board offcut sandwiched between tile and cramp Cut along the marked line with a tile saw. Work slowly and with as little pressure as possible to avoid chipping the glaze.

4 Smooth away any rough edges with a carborundum stone, a tile file, or fine abrasive paper wrapped around a piece of dowel.

Cutting tiles to fit (continued)

CUTTING A HOLE

1 If you have to cut a hole in a tile – perhaps to fit around a pipe – imagine the centre point of the hole and draw a line which will pass through it on the tile.

Score the tile and break it in two – one half for each side of the obstruction.

2 Cut a template out of paper or thin cardboard which fits accurately around the obstruction. ALTERNATIVELY, find a round object which is about the same size as the hole that needs to be cut – a coin or small lid might be suitable, for example.

3 Use the paper template or the round object as a guide and score the shape onto both pieces of tile – making two semicircles which fit together to make the hole. Press firmly onto the tile surface as you score the line – you need to make a definite mark on the glazed surface.

4 Nibble away the unwanted pieces of tile with pincers or pliers.

5 Once the hole is cut, remove any roughness with fine abrasive paper wrapped round a piece of dowel or any small object with a curved edge. A tile file will probably be too big for the hole. File in one direction from the glazed surface down.

HELPFUL TIP

If you are filling gaps with cut tiles, apply adhesive to the back of each tile – this is usually easier than trying to apply it to narrow strips of wall. Use the notched spreader as for the walls so that you get the adhesive to a consistent depth.

Tiling in awkward situations

INTERNAL CORNERS

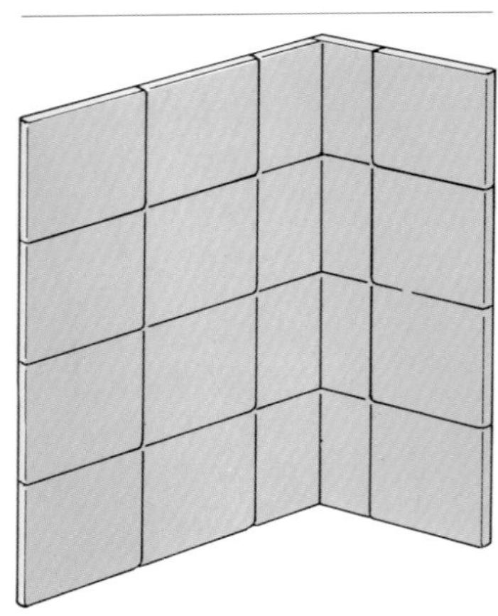

For a neat finish, place the cut edge of a tile in the corner so that the uncut edge is next to an adjacent tile.

EXTERNAL CORNERS

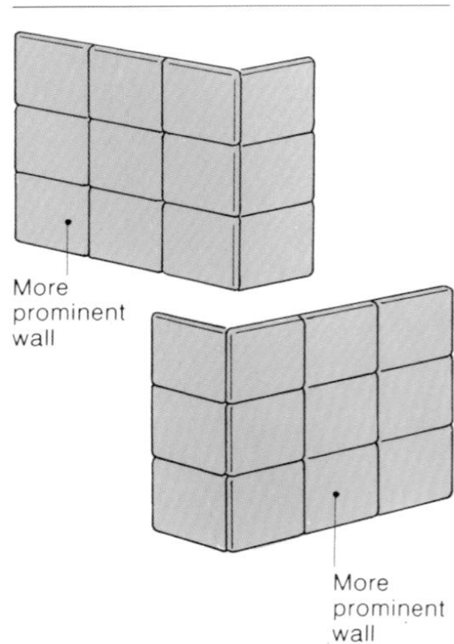

Arrange the edges of tiles at external corners so that the full face of the tile is on the wall which you look at most. For example, fix tiles so that you cannot see any tile edges when you are facing a chimney breast.

A WINDOW RECESS

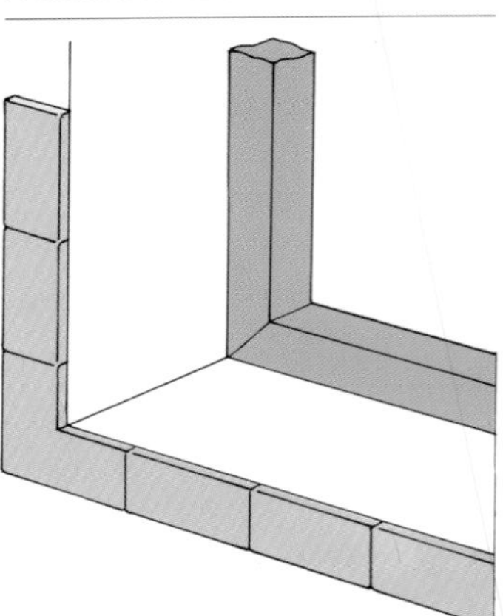

1 Tile the wall as far as the window, cutting tiles to fit. If you have to cut a tile to an L shape, cut a line from the edge to the centre of the tile with a tile saw. Then score a line at right angles to the cut and snap off the unwanted piece.

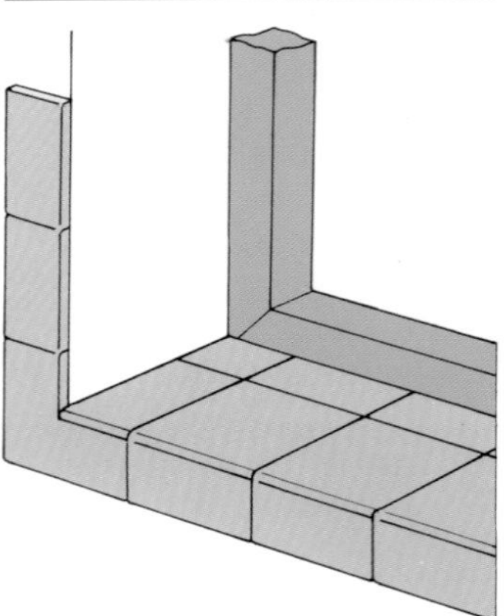

2 Lay the tiles at the bottom of the recess before you do the sides and the top. Put any cut tiles nearest the window, with cut edges against the frame. If possible, arrange the tiles so that glazed edges are visible from the front, or use border tiles with one rounded edge.

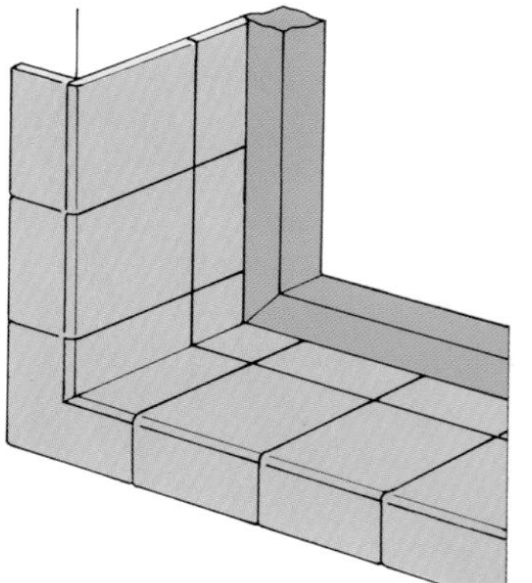

3 Line up the first course of tiles on the side walls with the tiles on the main wall. If the main wall tiles have cut edges, overlap them with the tiles in the recess. If the main wall tiles are uncut, they can overlap the tiles on the side wall.

FIXING AN ACCESSORY TILE

Leave a gap in the tiling for an accessory tile and wipe away the adhesive. Wait 24 hours, then put adhesive on the back of the tile and fit it in the gap.

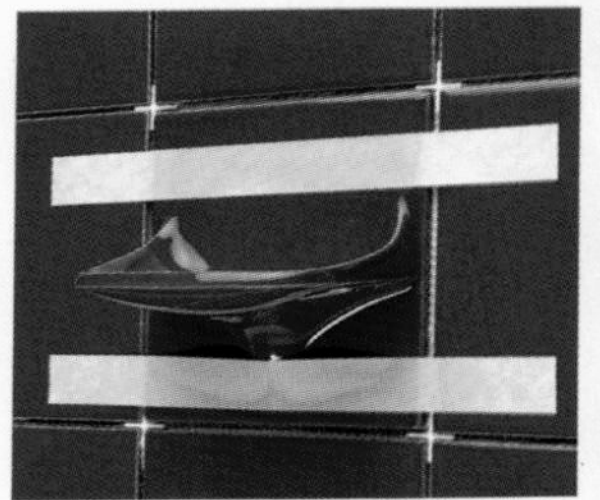

Hold the tile in place until the adhesive has dried, using strips of masking tape going onto the neighbouring tiles.

FINDING THE STARTING POINT FOR A PART-TILED WALL

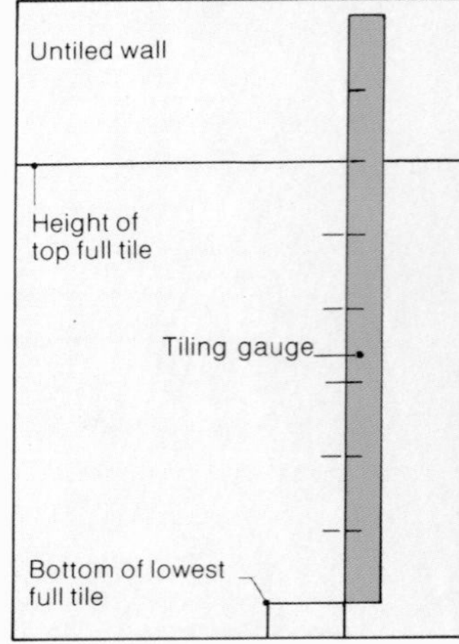

A part-tiled wall looks best if the top row of tiling consists of whole tiles. Use a tiling gauge to mark the height of whole tiles on the wall, beginning where the tiling will stop.

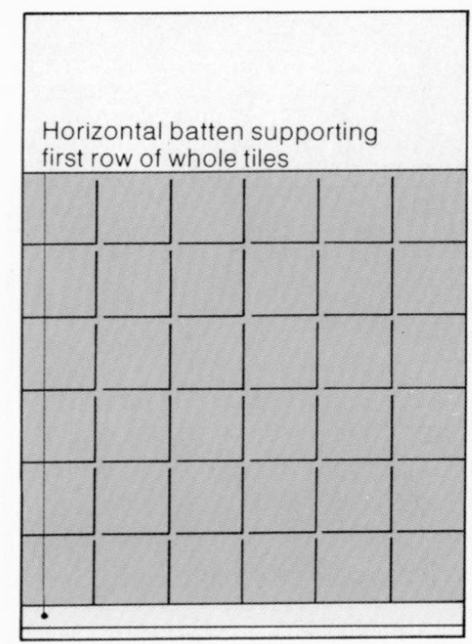

Align a batten with the lowest mark on the wall – where the bottom of the lowest uncut tiles will be – and fix it to the wall along a true horizontal. It will support the first row of tiles.

Grouting between tiles

When the tiles have been in place for at least 12 hours, fill the gaps between them with grout. This gives an attractive finished appearance and prevents dirt from collecting in the cracks.

You will need
Tools Pieces of sponge or a squeegee; larger sponge; thin dowel or something similar for finishing; soft dry cloth.
Material Grout.

PROTECTIVE EDGING

The exposed edges of tiles on external corners and areas like window ledges in kitchens and bathrooms, can be protected from knocks using a special, proprietary plastic edging strip. It is available in a range of standard colours, and is designed to have the perforated section of the strip sandwiched and hidden between the underside of the tile and the base to which the tile is being fixed. Only the protective edging is then visible.

1 If the grout is not ready-mixed, prepare as recommended. With a combined adhesive and grout or a waterproof epoxy-based grout only mix a small quantity – it sets hard quickly.

2 Press the grout firmly into the gaps between the tiles with a small piece of sponge. If you prefer, use a squeegee – this is the professional tool to use but it is difficult to get the grout well into the cracks with it.

3 Wipe away any surplus grout that gets onto the surface of the tiles with another clean, damp sponge while the grout is still wet. Take extra care to wipe away waterproof grout immediately.

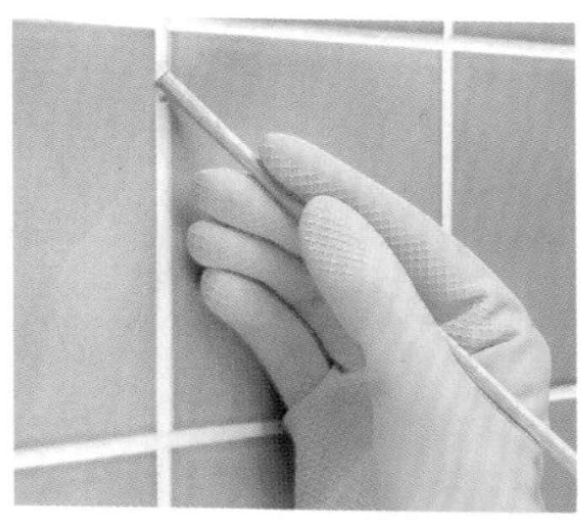

4 To give the tiling a neat professional finish, run a thin piece of dowelling over each grout line. If you do not have a piece of dowel to hand, you can use something of a similar shape – such as the blunt end of a pencil or a lollypop stick.

5 Wipe surplus waterproof grout off the surface of tiles as you go over the lines – it is difficult to remove when dry. Leave ordinary grout to dry then polish it off using a soft, clean, dry cloth. Another way to polish tiles effectively is to use a screwed-up ball of newspaper.

Grout which is discoloured or stained can be brightened by using a proprietary liquid grout whitener. This can be painted over the existing grout with an artist's brush, then any surplus is removed when the whitener has dried.

CREATING A TILED WORK SURFACE

You can tile a work surface using the same method as for tiling walls, but use heavy duty tiles because standard tiles are not strong enough to withstand knocks.

If the tiles you choose are more than about ⅜in (10mm) thick, consider buying or hiring a heavy-duty tile cutter. You could cut quarry tiles with a tile saw but the blade would have to be replaced frequently.

Arrange the tiles so that they look balanced and symmetrical if they have to go round a feature like a sink. If possible, size the worktop so that no cut tiles are needed – but if they are unavoidable, place them to the back of the work surface.

On post-formed worktops, screw on timber lipping all round. Spread the adhesive and start placing the tiles at the front of the worktop, using spacers if necessary. Check that the tiles sit level with the lipping and fill the joints with an epoxy-based grout.

Drilling a hole through a tile

Many bathroom and kitchen accessories, like soap dishes, must be screwed to the wall – in which case you may have to drill holes through ceramic tiles.

This can be a very messy job – a great deal of fine dust is produced which may stain the grouting on the surrounding tiles. To reduce the mess, make a simple disposable tray out of cardboard and stick it to the wall with masking tape below where you plan to drill. Or get someone to hold a vacuum-cleaner nozzle near the drill tip.

You will need
Tools Drill and masonry bit to suit the size of the screws to be used; small masonry bit to make pilot hole in glaze; masking tape; felt tip pen; screwdriver; screws to fix accessory. Possibly steel ruler.

1 Decide where you want to make the screw fixing and mark its position with a felt tip pen.

2 Stick a piece of masking tape over the mark, which should show through it, and re-make the mark on the surface of the tape. If you need to make more than one screw hole, use a strip of tape to cover both hole positions and mark them on the tape. The tape will stop the point of the masonry bit from skating over the smooth tile surface, and will help to ensure that the holes are made precisely where they are required.

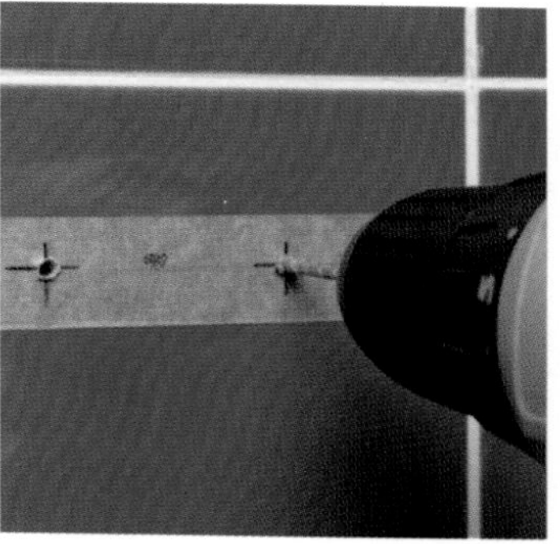

3 Fit a small diameter masonry bit in the drill chuck and press its tip firmly against the first mark on the tape. Start the drill at a low speed and drill slowly and carefully through the glazed surface of the tile. Stop drilling when the bit starts to penetrate the plaster. Using a small bit to do this minimises the risk of cracking the glaze. Repeat the process if necessary to drill a second hole through the other mark on the tape.

4 Switch to a larger diameter bit that matches the size of the screw and wall fixing you intend to use. Position its tip in the hole and proceed to drill slowly and carefully through the tile and the plaster and well into the masonry. Make the hole about 3mm deeper than the length of the wall fixing. Insert the fixing and drive in the screws to attach the accessory. Take care not to overtighten the screws or you may crack the tile.

Replacing a cracked tile

If you work carefully, it is fairly easy to replace a cracked tile or one which has holes that are no longer required. You may consider filling the space with a decorated tile.

You will need

Tools Drill with the largest masonry bit you possess; narrow old woodworking chisel; hammer; safety spectacles; heavy duty gloves; notched adhesive spreader. Tools for applying grout. Possibly a paint scraper.

Materials New tile; adhesive; grout.

1 Wear safety spectacles as protection against slivers of glass likely to splinter away from the glazed tile surface.

2 Drill a hole in the centre of the tile which is to be removed.

3 Work with the chisel and hammer from the hole outwards to get behind the tile. If you need to get more leverage, pack pieces of scrap wood behind the chisel as you work. Remove loose pieces of tile as they break.

4 When you have taken down the tile, carefully chisel out the old adhesive until you reveal bare wall. If the adhesive is very stubborn, try heating the blade of a paint scraper and using it to melt and scrape it. Do not apply heat from a torch direct to the adhesive – you could damage the surrounding tiles

5 Butter the back of a new tile with adhesive, using the notched spreader, and fit it in place.

Do not apply too much adhesive or the tile may sit proud of the rest of the tiles. Put matches or scraps of card around the tile to ensure even spacing.

6 With a damp cloth, wipe away any adhesive on the face of the tile and leave the adhesive to set.

7 After about 12 hours, fill in the gap around the new tile with grout using a small sponge.

COMMON TILING PROBLEMS AND CURES

PROBLEM AND CAUSE	REMEDY
Mould on grout Dark stains on grout lines may be caused by mould, which thrives on the damp and warm conditions often found in kitchens and bathrooms.	Kill mould with a proprietary fungicide, following the manufacturer's instructions. More than one application may be necessary in extreme cases. Do not use bleach – it will kill the mould flowers but will not kill the roots of the mould. When you have brushed away the dead mould you will find that it has left stains on the grout. These can be eliminated with grout whitener. When the whitener is dry, treat the grout with another application of fungicide to prevent further mould.
Dirty grout Grout can become discoloured by grease and dirt.	Clean the grout with a fine scrubbing brush and liquid detergent in warm water. When dry, paint the grout with a grout whitener.
Missing grout Gaps often occur because standard grout has been used instead of waterproof grout in areas prone to water splashing.	Rake out all the old grout with a proprietary grout rake, a small toothed tool designed specifically for the job. Draw the rake along the grout lines, first vertically and then horizontally, to remove the old grout to a depth of about $\frac{1}{8}$in (3mm). Brush out the loose material with an old toothbrush and then re-grout as for new tiling, using waterproof grout in wet areas.
Crazed tiles Tiles may become crazed because they are old, but new tiles may also be affected if water gets behind them.	Nothing can be done to repair tiles damaged by crazing. Either remove the affected tiles or consider painting them, though this will give a surface which is prone to scratches. Enamel gives the best results because it provides a high gloss and dries to a tough surface – but high quality gloss paint will do. No undercoat or primer is needed, but make sure that the surface is clean and dry before painting it.

Laying mosaic tiles

The way sheets of mosaic chips are held together influences how they are put up. A paper covering is fixed to the front of the chips, netting to the back.

MOSAIC TILES BACKED WITH NETTING

1 Apply adhesive to the wall with a notched spreader as for standard ceramic tiling.

2 Lay the sheets onto the adhesive. Cut the net with scissors or a trimming knife when filling awkward areas.

3 Leave for at least 12 hours, then grout as for ordinary tiles.

MOSAIC TILES FACED WITH PAPER

1 Lay each sheet of mosaic chips on a table or the floor with the paper side downwards, and fill the gaps with grout.

2 Wait for the grout to dry off a little and apply adhesive to the wall with a notched spreader.

3 Stick the sheets of chips to the adhesive so that the paper is facing you.

4 Leave overnight so that the adhesive sets hard.

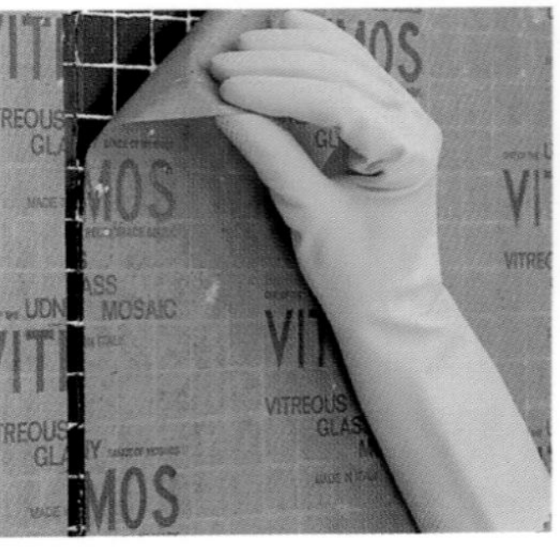

5 To remove the paper from the mosaics, soak it thoroughly with warm water, applied with a sponge or a rag.

Make sure that the paper is completely soaked and then lift it in one corner. It will peel away easily and should come off in one piece.

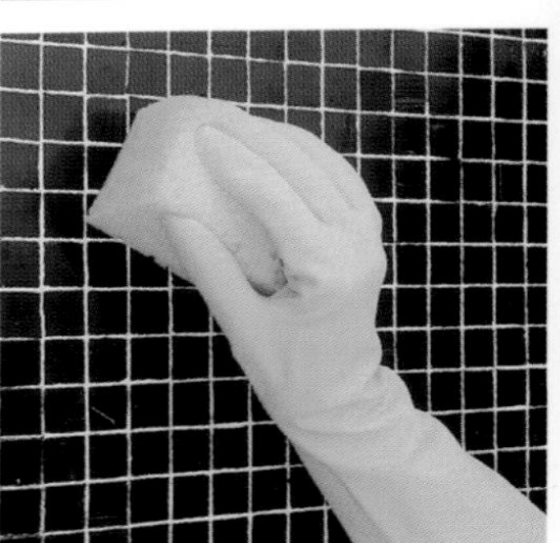

6 When you have soaked off all the facing paper, dry the mosaic by wiping the squeezed-out sponge over the surface.

Apply grout to any gaps which are revealed and to the lines where the sheets of mosaic meet. If you are using a waterproof grout, wipe away any excess immediately. Leave standard grout to dry and then polish off with a cloth.

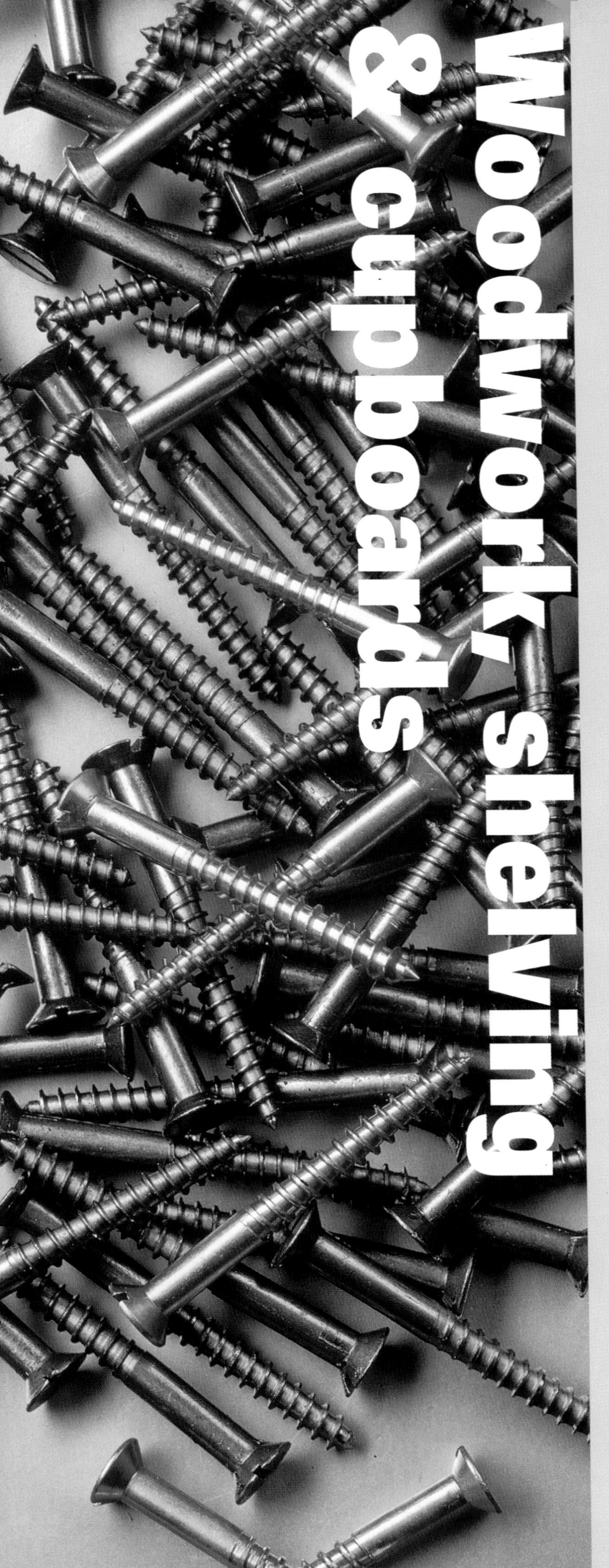

3

Woodwork techniques

Making shelves

Making cupboards

CHOOSING TYPES OF WOOD AND BOARD

These two pages illustrate the main choice of wood and board that is available for DIY work (see also pages 150–151). Some types, pine and chipboard for example, are readily available. Others, such as hardwoods and also waterproof plywood, are generally obtainable only from a timber merchant.

All wood and wood veneers need to be finished with varnish, Danish oil or wax, and their colour will darken with exposure to light. Plastic-coated boards need no finish, and colours do not change.

Pine
Also called deal. A softwood widely used for DIY work, both inside and outside the house. The colour darkens rapidly with exposure to light.

Parana pine
A tough softwood with a fine, even texture, used for interior joinery. Available in wide, long boards, often without knots. It may twist as it dries out, so fix it in place quickly or store it flat with an evenly spread weight on top.

Douglas fir
Also known as British Columbian pine and Oregon pine. A strong and durable softwood with straight, even grain. Used for doors, frames, windows and beams.

Western red cedar
A straight-grained softwood with few knots. Used mainly for external cladding, sheds and greenhouses. Also stands up well to central heating, and can be used close to radiators without warping, but it dents easily.

Oak
A hardwood, used in furniture, doors, frames and sills. Much heavier than softwood. Fittings of steel will stain oak permanently; use brass or iron.

Mahogany
A hardwood widely used for furniture making and as a veneer. Sapele, utile and gaboon are some of the many different types.

Teak
A hardwood containing oils that make it highly resistant to decay. Used for garden furniture, draining boards and for woodblock flooring. Widely found as veneer.

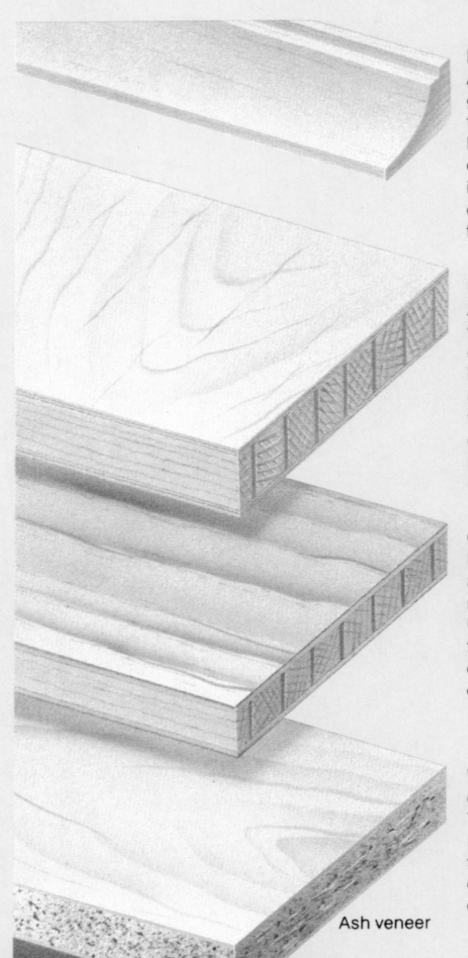

Ramin
A close-textured and even-grained hardwood used for mouldings and small battens. The yellow colour can be improved by staining the ramin to match any other wood being used in the job.

Birch-faced blockboard
A strong man-made board which has a wood-strip core that should be used lengthways. The core is covered on both sides with wood veneer. Birch veneer, one of the most common, may crack in central heating.

Oak-faced blockboard
Decorative veneers, such as oak and mahogany, are more durable than birch. Usually, the decorative face is found on one side only, with a cheaper timber on the other.

Wood-veneered chipboard
Timber veneers, including pine, ash, mahogany and teak, are bonded to standard chipboard to give a decorative surface.

Mahogany veneer

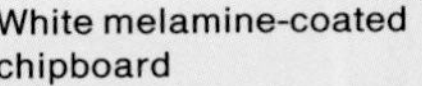

White melamine-coated chipboard
Widely used for furniture-making and DIY. No finishing is needed and it is easily cleaned; the common $\frac{5}{8}$in (16mm) boards are not suitable for work surfaces or for supporting heavy weights.

Wood-effect chipboard
A melamine-coated chipboard printed to resemble wood grain, and available in several colours. Not as attractive as wood-veneered chipboard, but requires no finishing and is easily cleaned.

CHOOSING TYPES OF WOOD AND BOARD

Chipboard worktops
Thick chipboard is coated with a layer of heavyweight melamine for use as worktops. It is sold in a large number of colours and patterns.

Standard chipboard
Wood chips are bonded together to produce a coarse-grained board with a finely sanded face ready for painting or varnishing. Much cheaper than timber, but also weaker. For internal use only.

Medium-density fibreboard
Smooth, fine-faced board that can be both cut and shaped more easily than chipboard, blockboard or plywood. Has to be painted or varnished.

Medium hardboard
Also known as Sundeala. Commonly used as a pinboard for display. Softer and thicker than standard hardboard.

Standard plywood
The most common type has three veneers of wood bonded together at right angles to each other. The sanded surface can be either painted or varnished. Birch is a common outer veneer.

Waterproof plywood
Used for external building work, and sold under the names marine ply or WBP (Weather and Boil Proof). Most often faced with mahogany.

Plastic-faced plywood
A wide range of colours and patterns is available for interior wall-cladding. Heavyweight veneers are also sold for worktops.

Standard hardboard
A thin board with a tough, smooth finish on one side and a textured finish on the other side. Made from compressed wood pulp.

Duo-faced hardboard
A version of hardboard with polished faces on both sides to make it reversible. Useful for making sliding doors for kitchen cabinets.

Oil-tempered hardboard
Oil in the board makes it water-resistant. Used for lining walls and ceilings in outhouses. Also makes a decorative and durable covering over an old floor.

Perforated hardboard
Also called pegboard. The holes may be ¾in (19mm) or 1in (25mm) apart, and are used for fitting hooks for storage or display.

Painted hardboard
The board may be gloss painted, ready for use, or primed for final painting.

Faced hardboard
Plastic coatings on faced standard hardboard are available in several patterns including tile and wood-grain effects.

Softwood and hardwood

Trees that have needle-like leaves and grow cones are the source of softwood, the most commonly used timber for DIY.

Softwood, which is commonly referred to as deal or pine, may come from many different trees, including pine, fir and spruce.

Hardwood comes from trees that grow broad leaves which fall in the autumn. There are many types, including oak, beech, mahogany, teak, sapele and ramin.

Softwood is easily obtained in a wide range of sizes, either in the rough-sawn state or planed on all faces. It can be bought from timber merchants, DIY stores and some builders' merchants. It is easier to work with than hardwood, so the cutting edges of tools last longer. It is graded by quality, with the lower grades used in packing cases, the middle grade for general building work and the top (joinery) grade for stairs, sills and furniture.

Softwood can be damaged more easily than hardwood. However, a coating of paint or varnish increases its resistance to knocks and stains.

Softwood darkens rapidly when exposed to direct sunlight and slowly when shielded from it. It can be stained and varnished easily.

Softwood is easily glued, nailed or screwed into, and a very smooth surface can be achieved.

KNOTS AND SHAKES IN SOFTWOOD

Knots can be either a problem or a desirable feature of softwood. Knots that are dead are often loose and may fall out. Live knots remain firmly attached to the timber.

The occasional knot oozes resin; you can either cut out the section or wipe the knot with white spirit from time to time until the oozing stops, but this may take months. Hard resin must be scraped away.

Most live knots cause no problem and are decorative if the wood is varnished. On painted boards knots will eventually show through as a dark patch if left untreated. Apply knotting fluid over each knot before painting.

Boards that have dried faster at the ends than in the centre may develop splits (called end shakes) at each end. Avoid buying the board, or cut off the split sections.

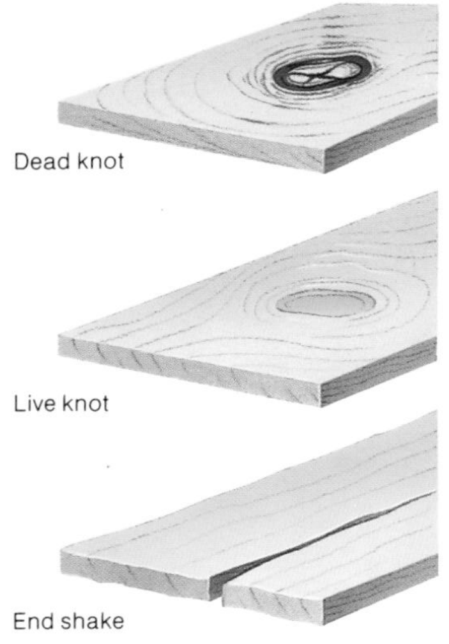
Dead knot

Live knot

End shake

PRESSURE-TREATED TIMBER

Some softwood merchants offer a range of sizes of timber pressure-impregnated against insect and fungal attack. Treated timber is ideal for use in damp conditions – for fencing or outhouses, for example. It is also strongly recommended for all structural work in building, such as floors, roofs, and door and window frames.

If treated timber has to be cut, treat the raw end with preservative applied by brush.

HARDWOOD

Hardwood is mostly stronger than softwood, so will carry a heavier load for a given thickness without bending – useful in shelving.

Hardwoods are harder to obtain than softwoods, except in moulded sections (page 152), because they are mainly supplied by specialist merchants – found in *Yellow Pages* under Timber Merchants.

The range is huge and each has its own characteristics, so ask the supplier about which will be best for a particular job.

Hardwoods glue easily and can be screwed into, using clearance and pilot holes (page 162). But they split if nailed, so pilot holes are also needed for nails.

Most hardwoods resist damage better than softwoods, and they take stain and polish well.

HOW TO BUY TIMBER

Timber and sheet materials are usually sold in metric sizes, although most suppliers will tell you the imperial equivalents or list them in their catalogues.

Timber is sold rough-sawn or planed (prepared). Sawn timber, rough in appearance, is measured as it is cut from the tree, before it dries and shrinks. Consequently sawn sizes are a close guide rather than an accurate measurement.

Planed timber is smooth. It is smaller by about 5mm (3/16in) in both width and thickness than the sawn size, as that amount has been removed during planing. Planed timber is traditionally listed by the original sawn size, followed by the word 'nominal'. Many suppliers now list it by the sawn size, but give a closer approximation of the true size in brackets.

STANDARD SOFTWOOD SIZES

The following sizes of timber are commonly available. All sizes apply to sawn timber. Planed timber will be about 5mm (3/16in) smaller in both width and thickness. If you need timber smaller than is listed here, see page 153.

Thickness \ Width	25mm *1in*	32mm *1¼in*	38mm *1½in*	50mm *2in*	75mm *3in*	100mm *4in*	112mm *4½in*	125mm *5in*	138mm *5 7/16in*	150mm *6in*	175mm *7in*	200mm *8in*	225mm *9in*
12mm *½in*	P		P	SP	SP	SP				P			
16mm *⅝in*	P		P	P	P	P							
19mm *¾in*	SP		SP	SP	SP	SP		SP		SP	SP		S
22mm *⅞in*		P		P	P	P							
25mm *1in*	SP		SP	SP	SP	SP		SP		SP	SP	SP	SP
32mm *1¼in*		P	P	SP	SP	SP	P	SP	P	SP	SP	S	S
38mm *1½in*			SP	SP	SP	SP		S		SP	S	S	SP
50mm *2in*				SP	SP	SP		SP		SP	SP	SP*	SP*
75mm *3in*					SP	SP		S		S	S	S	S

KEY: S = Sawn; P = Planed; P* = Planed to order

LENGTHS OF SOFTWOOD

Softwood is sold in standard metric lengths beginning at 1.8m (5ft 10⅞in) and increasing by stages of 300mm (12in) to 6.3m (20ft 8in). The following lengths are useful for DIY, but not all of them will be available from DIY stores.

1.8m	2.1m	2.4m	2.7m	3.0m	3.3m	3.6m	3.9m
5ft 10⅞in	*6ft 10⅝in*	*7ft 10½in*	*8ft 10¼in*	*9ft 10⅛in*	*10ft 9⅞in*	*11ft 9¾in*	*12ft 9½in*

HOW TO AVOID DISTORTION IN WOOD

Solid timber from a timber yard will normally contain about 17 per cent moisture (by weight). After a few weeks in a centrally heated house, the moisture will drop to 8-10 per cent. As a result, the wood will shrink slightly and may also develop a curve. The wider the board the greater the problem.

Most shrinkage

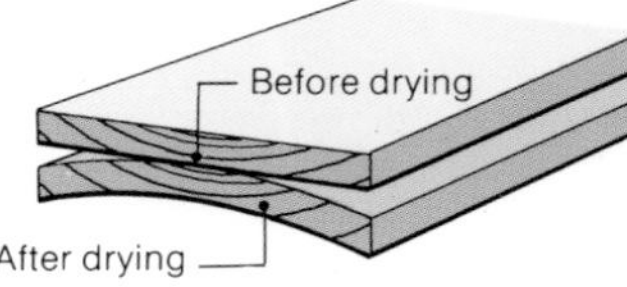

Least shrinkage

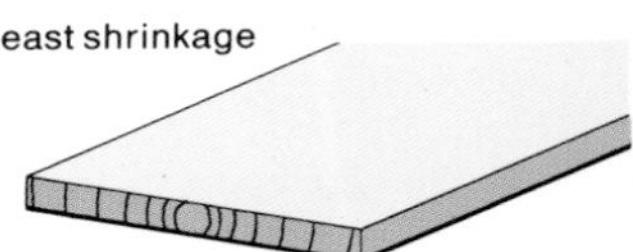

The shrinkage takes place along the length of the annular growth rings which follow the circular shape of the tree trunk. In most cases the rings are much shorter near one face of the board than the other. The longer rings shrink most and the shorter least, causing the board to curve across its width.

The straighter the rings in a board, the less it will curve, so look for boards that have the rings running almost vertically through the thickness.

No matter how carefully something is made, wood that is too wet will develop distortions. So store timber in the house for at least two or three weeks to allow it to dry out.

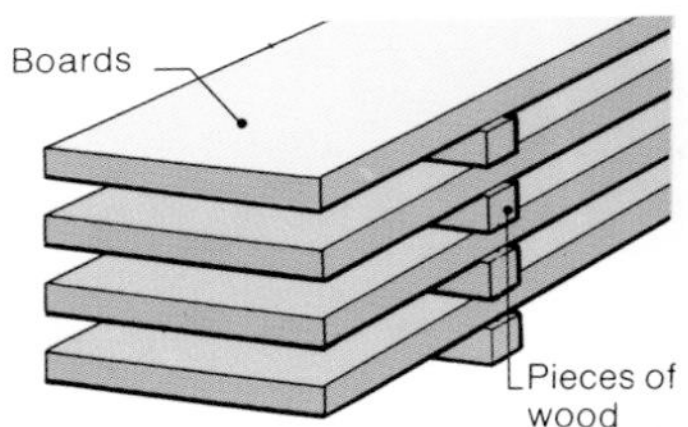

Store boards flat, one above the other, with pieces of wood between them so that air can circulate.

BOARDS FOR SHELVES AND WORKTOPS

Wide boards of solid softwood are sold for use as deep shelves, worktops or table tops. They are made from a number of boards jointed and glued together.

The timber is dry and sanded to a smooth finish, but the surface is untreated. All are finished to a thickness of 18mm (¾in). The boards range in width from 150mm (6in) to 610mm (24in). Common lengths are 1.2m (3ft 11¼in), 1.8m (5ft 10⅞in) and 2.4m (7ft 10½in).

Sheet materials for DIY

CHIPBOARD

Chipboard is a fairly coarse-grained material made of wood chips bonded together. The face of the board may be sanded or it may be coated with plastic or wood veneers.

Chipboard is widely used in DIY for making shelves, cupboards, wardrobes and doors. It is much cheaper than timber. It is also weaker, but its strength is the same either along or across the board. So if shelves are being cut from a large sheet, their strength is not affected by the direction of the cut.

Most chipboard is made for internal use. If it becomes wet, it swells quickly and the surface becomes rough. Waterproof and shuttering grades are the only ones that are not badly affected by water.

Standard grade chipboard

The cheapest type of chipboard. The face is finely sanded, ready for painting or varnishing.

The normal size of a sheet is 2440mm × 1220mm (8ft × 4ft). Thicknesses range from 3.2mm to 40mm ($\frac{1}{8}$in to 1$\frac{9}{16}$in), but the most common are 9mm, 12mm, 15mm and 18mm ($\frac{3}{8}$in, $\frac{1}{2}$in, $\frac{5}{8}$in and $\frac{3}{4}$in).

Some DIY stores also sell sheets cut to sizes 1830mm × 610mm (6ft × 2ft) and 1220mm × 610mm (4ft × 2ft).

Wood-veneered chipboard

Chipboard may be coated with wood veneers, such as pine, teak and mahogany. The boards usually also have veneered edges, and iron-on veneer is sold to cover exposed edges on cut boards.

All wood-veneered chipboard needs to be coated with varnish or Danish oil for its final finish. When buying boards, match the grain and colour.

Plastic-veneered chipboard

Wood-grain patterns are printed on plastic veneers. They are ready-finished but tend to look artificial. Iron-on veneer is sold for covering cut edges.

Pine, teak and mahogany are three common patterns, but as fashions change so do the patterns being offered.

White melamine coating

Chipboard coated with white melamine is seen in every DIY store and is used extensively in the furniture industry. The coating needs no further finishing, other than veneering raw edges after cutting or shaping, using iron-on melamine strip. Some large sheets may not have coated edges.

The material is suitable for all non-working surfaces, and is easily wiped clean with a damp cloth.

Veneered worktops

Heavyweight melamine veneers such as Formica are used to veneer worktops made of chipboard about 30mm (1$\frac{3}{16}$in) thick and 600mm (23$\frac{1}{2}$in) wide.

The veneers are available in a wide range of colours and are resistant to moderate heat, staining and short-term wetness.

Flooring grade

Chipboard sheets for flooring are available in thicknesses of 18mm and 22mm ($\frac{3}{4}$in and $\frac{7}{8}$in). They can be bought either tongued-and-grooved all round or square edged. The most common sheet sizes are 2440mm × 1220mm (8ft × 4ft) and 2440mm × 610mm (8ft × 2ft).

MEDIUM-DENSITY FIBREBOARD (MDF)

The board is made of wood fibres bonded together under high pressure to give a very fine, even textured material which can be cut and shaped more easily than any other sheet material.

The most common sheet size is 2440mm × 1220mm (8ft × 4ft). Some suppliers will cut to exact requirements at no extra charge.

The most common thicknesses are 9mm, 12mm, 15mm, and 18mm ($\frac{3}{8}$in, $\frac{1}{2}$in, $\frac{5}{8}$in, $\frac{3}{4}$in).

MDF is for internal use in dry conditions only. It is ideal for shelves and cupboards, and can be finished with paint, varnish or wall coverings.

When being cut or sanded it gives off a fine dust, so it is advisable to wear a face mask.

BLOCKBOARD

Wood strips are bonded together edge-to-edge to form a core, and are then covered on both sides with wood veneer. The core plus a single veneer on each side is called three-ply; the core plus two veneers on each side is five-ply.

The core of blockboard runs along the length of the sheet, so its resistance to bending is greater from end to end than from side to side. Check when cutting or buying for shelves that the core runs along the length.

The cut edge of blockboard should be covered with a narrow strip of wood lipping to hide the roughness (page 175).

The most common veneers are birch and mahogany-type timbers.

The standard size of a sheet is 2440mm × 1220mm (8ft × 4ft). Thicknesses include 12mm, 16mm, 18mm, 22mm, 25mm, and 32mm ($\frac{1}{2}$in, $\frac{5}{8}$in, $\frac{3}{4}$in, $\frac{7}{8}$in, 1in, 1$\frac{1}{4}$in).

Stripwood planks

Boards formed by gluing together strips of pine (redwood) to form wide boards are now a popular alternative to blockboard. They come in a wide range of sizes and are mainly used for shelves and worktops. Planks of hardwood strips are also available.

HARDBOARD

Wood-fibre pulp is heavily compressed to form sheets. There are several types of hardboard, and a variety of finishes.

For non-standard types, you should phone around to find a supplier who stocks the type you need. Suppliers can be found in *Yellow Pages* under Timber Merchants.

Standard hardboard

The face of the board has a tough, almost polished finish with a slight hammer ripple that shows up when painted. The back of the sheet is textured by the mesh on which it is made.

Hardboard has many uses, including backs and dividers in cupboards, and lining a floor before laying a covering. The most easily obtainable sheets are 3.2mm ($\frac{1}{8}$in) in thickness. They may measure 2440mm × 1220mm (8ft × 4ft), 1220mm × 1220mm (4ft × 4ft) or 1220mm × 610mm (4ft × 2ft). Also available are standard flush door panels measuring 2ft 6in × 6ft 6in, an imperial standard size.

Other thicknesses are made, and may be bought on special order.

Medium hardboard

A softer and more expensive board than standard hardboard. It is used in exhibition and display areas because it is an ideal pin board and – with lightweight support – remains fairly flat.

The normal sheet size is 2440mm × 1220mm (8ft × 4ft) and the most common thicknesses are 6.4mm ($\frac{1}{4}$ in) and 9.5mm ($\frac{3}{8}$in).

Medium hardboard should not be confused with medium density fibreboard (MDF).

Duo-faced hardboard

Polished faces on both sides make duo-faced hardboard reversible. It has the same strength and characteristics as standard hardboard.

You will probably have to phone around to find a supplier and accept the thickness he has in stock – most probably 6.4mm ($\frac{1}{4}$in). The normal sheet size is 2440mm × 1220mm (8ft × 4ft).

Perforated hardboard

The most common perforations are regularly spaced, round holes which make the board useful for mounting a display. It is also known as pegboard.

The thickness is usually 3.2mm ($\frac{1}{8}$in) and the normal sheet size is 2440mm × 1220mm (8ft × 4ft).

Plastic-faced hardboard

Standard hardboard has a plastic veneer over the polished face. There are a number of patterns.

Uses include tray and drawer bottoms. Faced hardboard needs to be fixed in a frame or firmly attached to another surface to prevent it from twisting.

Boards are usually 2440mm × 1220mm (8ft × 4ft) and 3.2mm ($\frac{1}{8}$in) thick.

Painted hardboard

Standard hardboard can be bought pre-primed ready for final painting or with a gloss finish ready for use. Uses include drawer bottoms and door panels. The hammer ripple which shows up when painting standard hardboard does not appear on these sheets.

Oil-tempered hardboard

Standard hardboard is impregnated with oil to make it water resistant. It is used as an internal lining material for sheds and outhouse walls and ceilings.

PLYWOOD

The simplest type of plywood – three-ply – consists of a central wood veneer sandwiched between two others. The grain direction of each successive veneer alternates so that in every plywood the outer veneers run in the same direction and at 90 degrees to the one in the centre. In rectangular sheets the grain direction of the outer veneers runs along the length.

A grading system is used for unfaced plywood: A/A has knot-free veneers on both sides; A/B is knot free on one side with patches replacing knots on the other; B/BB – the most common – has one face with patches and the other with the knots left in.

Standard plywood

Plywood is commonly used for drawer bottoms, low-cost furniture and flush doors. It is made with a finely sanded surface.

A great variety of thicknesses are made, ranging from 1.5mm ($\frac{1}{16}$in) to 32mm (1$\frac{1}{4}$in). The most common are 4mm ($\frac{5}{32}$in), 6mm ($\frac{1}{4}$in) and 9mm ($\frac{3}{8}$in). Sheet sizes also vary greatly. Two of the most common sizes are 2440mm × 1220mm (8ft × 4ft) and 1525mm × 1525mm (5ft × 5ft).

Many suppliers sell plywood cut to the size you want or in more handy-sized panels such as 1830mm × 610mm (6ft × 2ft) and 1220mm × 610mm (4ft × 2ft).

Wood-faced plywood

Decorative face veneers, such as oak and teak, are applied to sheets of plywood 4mm ($\frac{5}{32}$in) thick and above, for their effect and superior surface.

Sheet materials for DIY (continued)

They are available on either one or both sides of the sheet. Single-faced plywood is cheaper.

Plastic-faced plywood
Lightweight plastic veneers, including plain white and a range of printed woodgrain effects, are applied to 3.2mm (⅛in) and 4mm (5/32in) plywood. They are suitable for doors, cupboards and shelves.

Heavyweight plastic veneers – for example, Formica and Warerite – are applied mostly to 12mm (½in) plywood. They are suitable for worktops and all surfaces needing resistance to moderate heat, damp or staining.

Waterproof plywood
WBP (Weather and Boil Proof) identifies plywood which is made with waterproof adhesives.

Another waterproof type with a superior surface veneer is made for the marine industry, and is known as marine plywood. Use either WBP or marine ply for external building work. It is more expensive than ordinary plywood.

STORING SHEET MATERIALS

All sheet materials should ideally be stored flat, but where space is limited stand them on edge, as vertically as possible. If they lean, they may take on a twist which will be difficult to correct.

Thin sheets of 4mm (5/32in) or less need the support of thicker sheets on either side of them if they are stored vertically for longer than a few days.

Always store in dry conditions. Indoors is best. Alternatively, put the sheets in a dry garage or shed, slightly away from a wall, and use battens to keep them off the floor. Put battens between every sheet to provide an airflow if storing for more than a few days.

Buying secondhand timber

Cheapness is one of the great advantages of secondhand timber. It can be bought from demolition sites, friends or a secondhand materials merchant. Before you buy timber, look at it carefully for woodworm and rot. If it has been stored in a shed, it should be dried for a few days in your house before use.

SOFTWOOD

Floorboards will have had grit walked into them over the years and this wrecks cutting tools. Floor joists and rafters will contain nails. Consequently very few timber machinists will cut or plane secondhand timber. If you buy it, you must be prepared to do all the cutting yourself.

HARDWOOD

Secondhand hardwood is also likely to contain nails or screws.

In some cases, what appears to be solid hardwood is simply a softwood or chipboard covered with veneer. Look at a cut end.

Remember that, although a large piece of hardwood may be flat, cutting it to a narrower shape may release tensions that may cause it to twist.

PLYWOOD

Do not buy secondhand plywood that shows signs of mildew or has water stains.

And always search for signs of woodworm – the larvae feed on the starch-based adhesives used in early plywoods.

CHIPBOARD

If the surface is rough or if the edges are thicker than the centre, the board has soaked up moisture and expanded. This causes loss of strength. Avoid it.

HARDBOARD

Avoid warped or water-stained boards. Remember that timber takes in moisture from the atmosphere even if it is under cover.

Timber moulding and small battens

The chart on the opposite page illustrates some of the most common moulded timber sections. The sizes given are typical; other sizes may be obtainable.

For small mouldings, standard lengths are either 2m or 3m (about 7ft or 10ft). Large mouldings, such as architraves, have standard lengths ranging from 1.8m to 4.9m (about 6ft to 16ft).

Always inspect what you buy and compare one length with another. Occasionally poor machining results in incorrect shapes – quite common with dowels. The right-angled corners on square or rectangular sections are also sometimes misshapen.

Most small mouldings are made from ramin, a light-coloured, fine-grained hardwood that is usually knot-free. Ramin is inclined to split easily, so drill very fine holes before driving pins through thin pieces of moulding.

MATCHING EXISTING MOULDINGS

Architraves and skirtings are made in many shapes and sizes, and many timber merchants mould their own patterns. You may have to visit several suppliers to find the pattern you want.

Some timber merchants will make mouldings to special order – to match mouldings in an old house, for example. This usually involves making special cutters for which you have to pay. Make it plain at the time of ordering that you wish to keep the cutters so that they are ready for use if more is needed.

The measurements given in the chart are the actual, planed sizes of the timber you will buy. Most mouldings and small battens are cut to metric sizes.

GAP COVERS

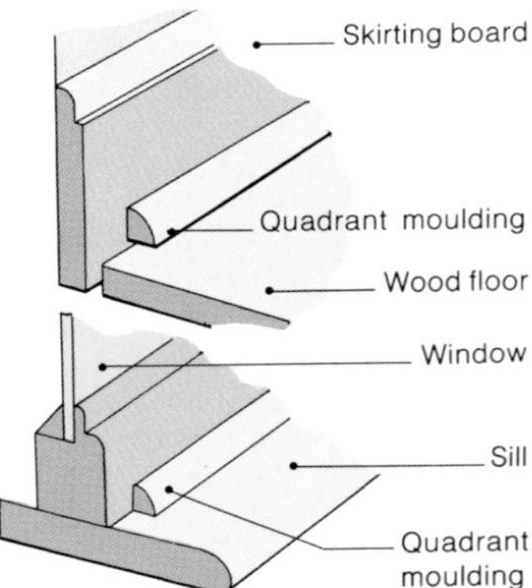

Either quadrant or scotia mouldings can be used to cover an expansion gap between a wood floor and the skirting board around the room. The moulding is pinned to the skirting board, not the floor, and allows the wood to expand and contract according to damp or dry weather conditions.

The mouldings can also be used to stop draughts at the base of a window frame.

DOOR MOULDINGS

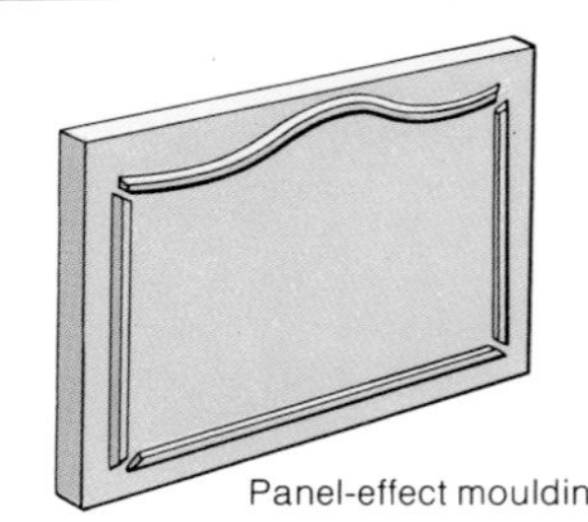
Panel-effect mouldings

Decorative mouldings can be fixed to flush doors to create a panelled effect. Sets of mouldings are available especially for the purpose, some with a curved top strip. The ends are already mitred for easy fixing to standard sized doors.

BOARD EDGINGS

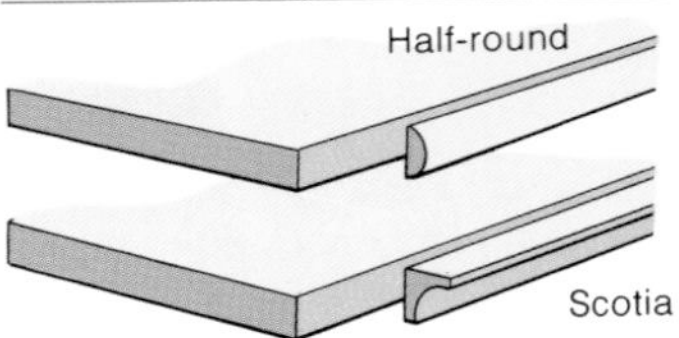

Mouldings are made as a covering for the edge of standard chipboard, blockboard and medium density fibreboard. Half-round, concave, flat and scotia mouldings can be used to give a neat appearance to the fronts of shelves.

COVERING JOINS

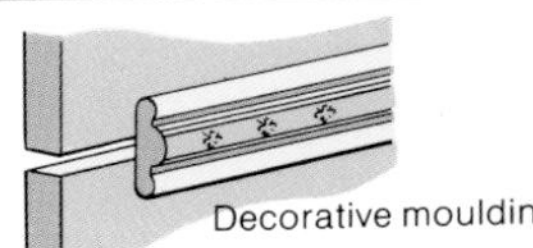
Decorative moulding

A join between two boards can be hidden by a strip of decorative moulding. Widths range from 10mm (⅜in) to 37mm (1 7/16in). There are many different patterns.

COVERING CORNERS

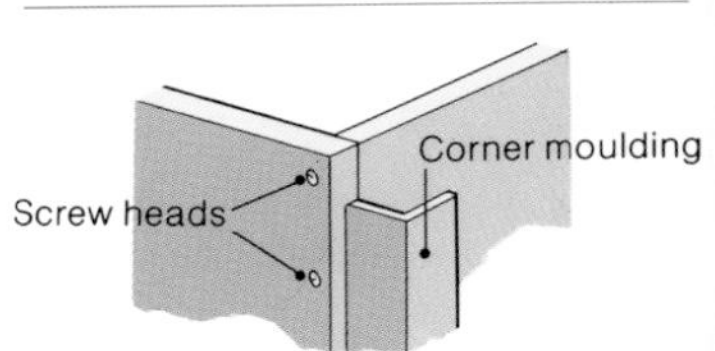

A strip of right-angled moulding, called corner moulding, can be fixed along the outside of any right-angled joint, such as the front edge of a built-in wardrobe or cupboard. It hides joins and screw heads.

MAKING UP YOUR OWN SHAPES

Composite mouldings can be made up from standard sections to fit particular situations or to create a decorative effect.

The flat surfaces of two or more mouldings are glued together to make any shape you wish. Cramp the pieces until the glue has set.

CHOOSING COMMON MOULDINGS AND BATTENS

Dowel
Used for curtain poles, towel rails, banisters, plate racks, broom handles, plugging worn screw holes.
Type of wood and sizes Hardwood. Diameters: 6mm, 9mm, 12mm, 15mm, 18mm, 25mm. Larger sizes available, some in softwood.

Square or rectangular
Used for finishing the edges of shelves made of blockboard, chipboard and plywood. Also fitted to the edge of chipboard for screwing into – when fitting butt hinges, for example.

Can be used as retaining beads for glazed doors (see also quadrant and scotia).
Type of wood and sizes Softwood. 6 × 6mm, 9 × 9mm, 9 × 15mm, 15 × 15mm, 15 × 21mm, 12 × 12mm, 12 × 18mm, 12 × 25mm, 5 × 15mm, 6 × 18mm, 6 × 22mm, 6 × 25mm.

Corner mouldings
To cover a corner where two boards join. Hides minor errors and screw fixings.
Type of wood and sizes Softwood or hardwood. 20 × 20mm, 22 × 22mm, 30 × 30mm, 40 × 40mm.

Staff and parting beads
Both types are used in wooden sash windows to hold the sashes in place. The staff bead (left) holds in the inner sash, and the parting bead (right) separates the inner from the outer sash.
Type of wood and sizes Softwood. Staff bead: 19 × 38mm, 19 × 32mm, 19 × 25mm, 12 × 19mm. Parting bead: 12 × 32mm, 12 × 25mm, 9 × 25mm.

Hockey stick and glass bead
Hockey stick moulding is used mainly for trimming decorative panelling. Glass bead secures panes of glass in rebates in door and window frames.
Types of wood and sizes Softwood and hardwood. Hockey stick: 18 x 6mm, 22 x 9mm, 35 x 12mm. Glass bead: 9 x 9mm, 16 x 9mm.

Scotia
A more decorative alternative to quadrant.
Type of wood and sizes Hardwood or softwood. 15 × 15mm, 18 × 18mm, 17 × 27mm, 15 × 21mm.

Quadrant
Used for covering gaps between floors and skirting, and between wooden windows and the windowsill.

Also to retain glass in windows and doors.
Type of wood and sizes Hardwood or softwood. 9 × 9mm, 15 × 15mm, 21 × 21mm.

Half round
Used to cover the edges of sheet material, such as chipboard and blockboard, to give a curved finish.
Type of wood and sizes Hardwood or softwood. 6 × 15mm, 6 × 18mm, 6 × 22mm, 6 × 25mm.

Triangle
For finishing internal corners. It can be used as a stair rod, and consequently is also known as stair rod moulding.
Type of wood and sizes Hardwood. Usually 25 × 25mm (1 × 1in).

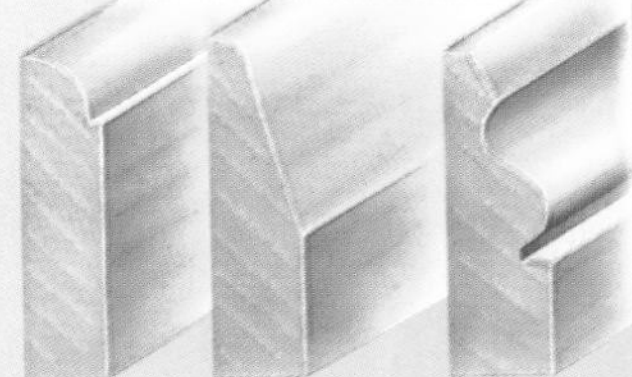

Architrave
For hiding the join between a door frame and wall.
Type of wood and sizes Softwood. Sizes range from 50 × 19mm (2 × ¾in) to 75 × 25mm (3 × 1in). Shapes and sizes vary between suppliers.

Skirting
For hiding the join between a floor and wall.
Type of wood and sizes Softwood. Sizes range from 75 × 19mm (3 × ¾in) to 225 × 25mm (8⅞ × 1in). Shapes and sizes vary.

Weathermoulding
Fits on the bottom of an exterior door to keep out rain.
Type of wood and sizes Usually softwood. 64 × 64mm (2½ × 2½in). Sold cut to the width of the door.

Tongued-and-grooved (T & G) floorboards
For repairing or replacing old floors.
Type of wood and sizes Softwood. 150 × 25mm (6 × 1in); 125 × 25mm (5 × 1in); 100 × 25mm (4 × 1in); 95 × 19mm (3¾ × ¾in) – all nominal.

Tongued, grooved and V-jointed cladding
Also called matchings. Used for cladding walls and ceilings, and making cupboards and gates.
Type of wood and sizes Softwood. 112 × 12mm (4½ × ½in); 112 × 16mm (4½ × ⅝in); 100 × 12mm (4 × ½in); 100 × 16mm (4 × ⅝in). All sizes nominal and include tongue.

Shiplap
The most common type of exterior wall cladding.
Type of wood and sizes Softwood. 150 × 25mm (6 × 1in); 150 × 22mm (6 × ⅞in); 125 × 16mm (5 × ⅝in). Sizes nominal.

Sawn featherboard
For traditional close-boarded fencing.
Type of wood and sizes Softwood or hardwood. 100 × 16mm (4 × ⅝in).

Woodwork: Tools for the job

A large amount of household woodwork can be done with a small set of tools and a workbench – which, at a pinch, can be the kitchen table.

If you buy prepared timber or sheet material, much of the work will have been done for you.

For more complicated work, such as smoothing a sawn edge on timber or cutting recesses for hinges and fittings, a few more tools will be necessary.

Workbench and holding devices

A rigid working surface, fitted with a vice or bench hook, is essential for woodwork. A portable workbench holds large pieces of timber or board in its jaws and some models can be raised to provide a work surface at two levels – one for sawing, the other for general work. It is collapsible and folds flat for easy storage.

A strong old table kept in a shed or garage can have a lightweight vice attached. Or the vice can be temporarily cramped to the kitchen table above a leg.

An alternative to a vice is a pair of G-cramps (page 191) which also have other uses.

A simple tool for holding wood while cutting is a bench hook which hooks over the edge of the table and has a second 'hook' for supporting the wood.

Drills and bits

The most useful tool for DIY work is a power drill. Mains-powered drills offer high drilling speeds, plenty of power and relatively low prices. Cordless (battery-powered) drills drill more slowly and tend to be more expensive, but can be used anywhere independent of a mains power source.

The most versatile choice for everyday use is a variable-speed mains drill with reverse gear and hammer action (for drilling holes in concrete and other masonry). Pick one with a 13mm keyless chuck, which will enable you to drill holes up to 32mm diameter in wood and 13mm in metal or masonry.

If you do a lot of work away from the workshop, add a cordless drill which will also do double duty as a cordless screwdriver. The more powerful the drill in terms of battery voltage, the heavier it is to handle, so check this before buying. Pick a model with fast battery recharge, and buy a spare battery.

You will need various drill bits. Buy high-speed steel (HSS) twist drill bits for making small holes in wood and metal, masonry bits for making holes in bricks, blocks and concrete, and flat wood bits for making larger holes in wood and man-made boards. You can buy all these in sets, but you will not use many of them. It makes more sense to buy bits in the sizes you require as and when you need them, and to replace them when they become blunt.

Hammers

A claw hammer is a dual-purpose tool – the head drives in nails and the claw pulls them out. Hammer sizes refer to their weight. The most popular is 1½(0.7kg).

Steel-handled hammers have a rubber or plastic grip to prevent slipping. A wooden handle is more comfortable and will not leave black marks on timber if the handle knocks it.

A pin hammer weighing 3½oz (0.1kg) has a cross-pein for starting small panel pins while they are held between the fingers.

Pincers

Occasionally a nail has to be removed that cannot be lifted with a claw hammer. Carpenter's pincers are the best tool, and are usually made with a claw on one handle which will remove tacks.

Saws

A panel saw 20in (510mm) long is the most useful saw for DIY jobs. If your woodwork involves cutting joints or thin sheet material, such as hardboard or plywood, a tenon saw

may be a best first buy.

Both types are available with hardpoint teeth that never need sharpening, and with a tooth configuration which makes sawing more efficient with and across the grain. Some also have a black coating which improves 'slip' and makes sewing easier. The hardpoint saw is ideal for difficult materials such as chipboard.

The general purpose saw has specially treated teeth which enable it to cut wood or metal. Use it on secondhand timber where there may be hidden nails or screws.

Screwdrivers

A cabinet screwdriver with a ¼in (6mm) wide end will fit straight-slot screws, gauge 8. A No. 2 cross-slot screwdriver will fit gauges 5 to 10 cross-slot screws. If there is a lot of work to be done, invest in a battery-powered, rechargeable, cordless screwdriver. Movement is reversible, so screws can be both driven and removed.

Bradawl

Small screws – up to gauge 6 – can be started in softwood or board with a bradawl.

Spirit level

To find a horizontal or vertical line, use a spirit level (page 479). A 3ft (900mm) model would be suitable for most jobs.

Steel tape measure

A 6ft or 10ft (2m or 3m) steel tape measure is the most useful for DIY.

Sanding block and abrasive paper

A cork sanding block should always be used to support abrasive paper when finishing surfaces.

Try square

The tool is used to mark lines across boards at a right angle before cutting. It is also used to check that one surface is at 90 degrees to another. A blade length of 9in (230mm) is useful.

Always check a new try square before using it, and an old one from time to time. Hold the square in position against a piece of timber or board with a straight edge, and draw a line across the board against the blade. Turn the stock over and check that the line still follows the blade edge exactly. If it does not, the square is out of true.

Straight-edge

Drawing lines between measured points should involve the use of a straight-edge. It can be made from a length of straight, even-grained hard or softwood between 4ft 6in and 6ft (1.4m and 1.8m) long with a cross section of about 3in x ¾in (75mm x 19mm). It should be stored flat or hanging.

Extension lead

An extension lead allows you to use power tools well away from power sockets. Buy one rated at 13 amps and fitted with an RCD for safety. Always uncoil it fully before use.

Chisels

There is no need to buy a complete set. Begin with ¼in (6mm) and ¾in (19mm) bevelled edge chisels.

Plane

A bench plane about 10in (250mm) long, with a blade about 2in (50mm) wide, is ideal for planing timber and most sheet materials.

A cheaper plane can be obtained with replaceable blades – eliminating sharpening. An extra advantage is that the blade can be moved to the front, so the wood can be planed into a corner. However the lightness of the plane makes it difficult to use on hardwood.

Oilstone and oilcan

Chisel and plane blades must be kept sharp. A combination oilstone 8in x 2in x 1in (200mm x 50 mm x 25mm) is the most useful. A can of fine oil is essential, and a honing guide is useful for holding the blade at the correct angle.

Nail and pin punches

Punches are used to drive the head of nails or panel pins below the surface of the wood. They are made in a range of sizes.

Surforms

Surforms are shaping tools for wood and come in a variety of shapes, including circular ones for enlarging holes.

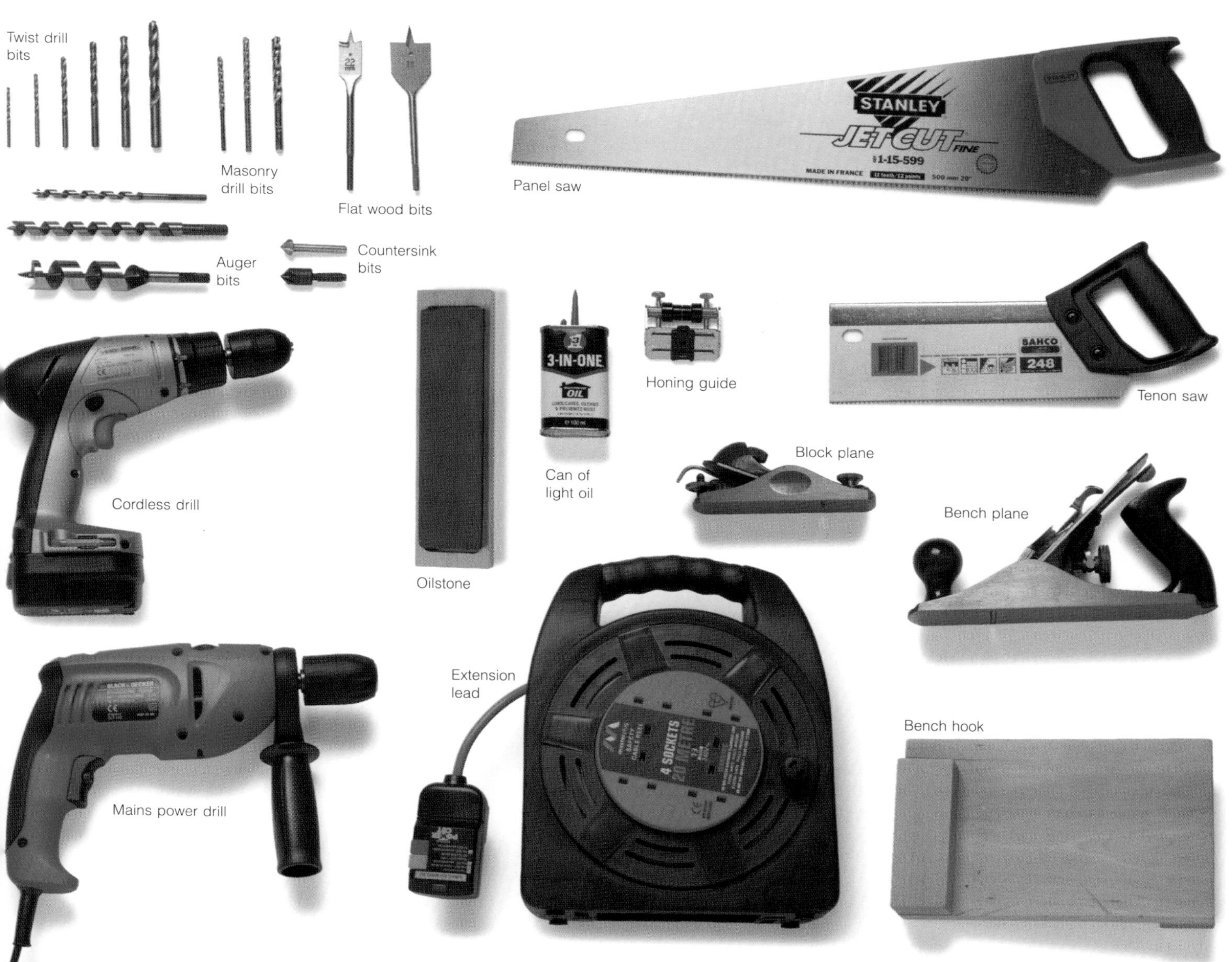

Cutting wood and board by hand

A SQUARE-CUT END

1 Hold a try square against one edge and draw a pencil line across the face. Then extend the line onto the edges, using the try square.

2 Secure the wood in a bench hook, vice or cramps.

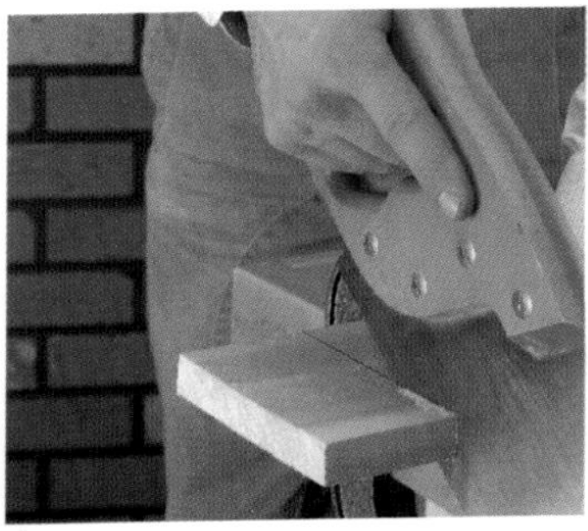

3 Grip the saw – with your index finger along the side – and begin the cut by drawing it back against the thumb of your other hand.

Make the cut on the waste side of the line. Cutting on the line will leave the wood slightly under-size.

4 Watch the lines on both the face and the edges. Use the full length of the blade, applying light pressure on the forward stroke only. Make the last few strokes gently to avoid splitting the wood.

CUTTING COATED CHIPBOARD

A melamine or wood coating will develop a chipped edge on the underside of a board which is sawn by hand. So mark the cutting line on the side that will show. Then the unseen side will have the chipped edge. (The opposite applies to a power saw – facing page.)

Score the line with a craft knife held against a straight-edge. For the best possible result, score the cutting line all around the board.

The finer the saw teeth, the better the chance of avoiding chipped edges. So use a tenon saw for short cuts and a panel saw for long ones. Hold the saw as flat as possible to the wood; if the blade is held near the vertical there is a greater danger of chipping.

TRIMMING AN END

To remove a thin slice off the end of a piece of wood, cramp a length of scrap wood to it, mark lines around both and saw through both pieces at the same time.

To remove less than ⅛in (3mm), use a plane.

CUTTING A BOARD LENGTHWAYS

1 Before cutting a long board along its length, mark the width with a pencil at several points on the side that will be seen. Join up the marks with a straight-edge.

2 Lay the board on a support about knee high from the floor. A pair of trestles is one possibility; another is a stepladder laid on its side with the two legs opened out. Or the board could be held in the jaws of a portable workbench.

Hold the board firmly with your knee and one hand, with your eye over the cut.

3 Start by drawing a panel saw back on the waste side of the line at a shallow angle, using your thumb as a guide.

4 Use the whole length of the blade, applying light pressure on the forward stroke only.

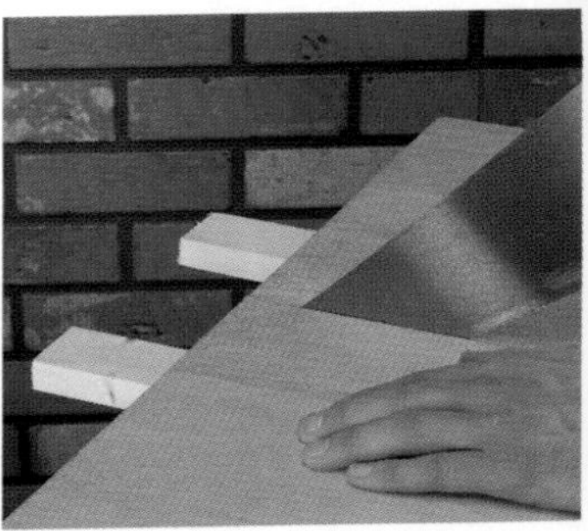

If a large board whips as you cut it, rest it on two battens on the trestles and cut between them.

If the blade wanders off the line, twist it slightly as you saw to get back on course.

HELPFUL TIP

If you are worried that you cannot cut a straight line, cramp a batten to the board and saw against it.

EDGING CHIPBOARD WITH SELF-ADHESIVE VENEER

Edging strip with a self-adhesive backing is sold in rolls to match the face veneers on 16mm chipboard. It can be bought to match either wood or plastic veneer, and can be applied to straight or curved edges.

You will need

Tools Stiff brush; trimming knife or scissors; piece of brown paper; domestic iron; flat file. Also fine abrasive paper and cork block for wood-veneer strip.

1 Brush away all dust and chips from the edges to be veneered.

2 Cut strips of veneer about ¼in (6mm) longer than the edges.

3 Place the cut length of veneer over the edge so that the ends overhang by about ⅛in (3mm) and the edges overhang the thickness of the panel by an equal amount on each side (the veneer is about 18mm wide).

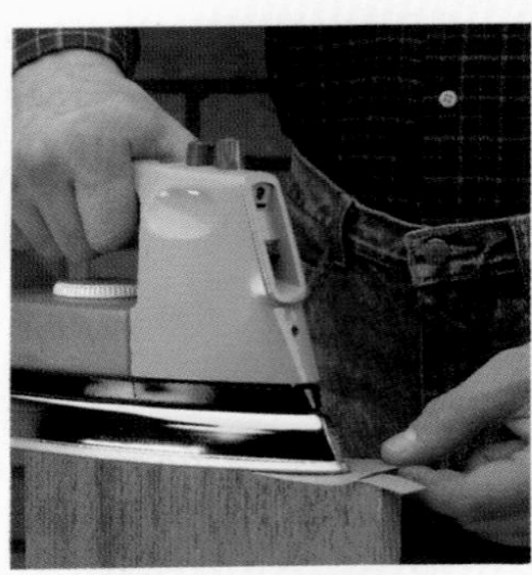

4 Hold the veneer firmly and cover it with a piece of brown paper. Apply a hot iron (if it scorches the paper it is too hot) at one end.

Use moderate pressure and keep the iron moving an inch or so forwards and backwards along the line of the veneer.

5 Gradually move along the edge, checking that the veneer is in line and is bonding.

6 Allow the veneer to cool and check that it has stuck, particularly at the ends.

7 Cut each end to the exact length of the panel.

8 Trim off the edges of the veneer with a flat file or medium abrasive paper on a sanding block. Move the file or sanding block in a direction that tends to push the veneer rather than lift it.

9 With fine abrasive paper on a cork block, finish wood veneer with long strokes over its face. Finish the edges and corners at a slight chamfer.

CUTTING HOLES IN AWKWARD SHAPES

Use a padsaw to cut a hole in the middle of a panel. If the panel has a melamine coating or wood veneer, score it first with a craft knife to avoid chipping the edges. Or put a fine-toothed hacksaw blade in the padsaw.

Circular cut-out

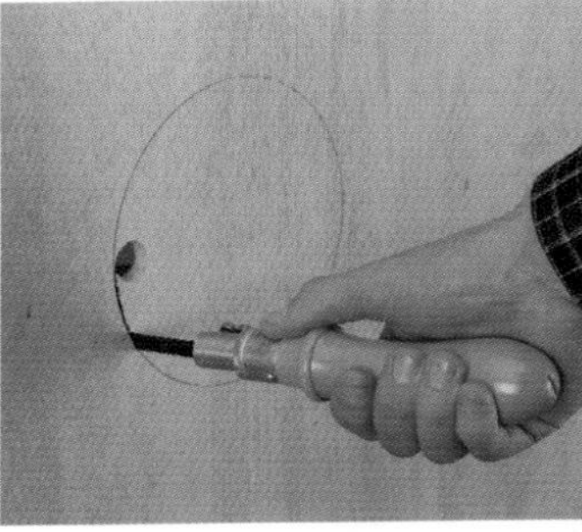

Start by drilling a hole in the waste part, large enough to take the blade. Then cut with the padsaw. The edge can be smoothed with a half-round file.

Straight cuts

Drill holes at each corner and start the cut with a padsaw. When the cut is long enough, finish with a panel saw, which is quicker and more accurate.

Keyhole

To cut a keyhole, drill a large hole and a small one below, and join them with two padsaw cuts.

Using power saws

A circular saw (left) and jigsaw (right), both have interchangeable blades for cutting different types of wood, metal or ceramics.

CUTTING WITH A PORTABLE CIRCULAR SAW

An electric circular saw will cut far more quickly and more accurately than a hand saw. Circular saws can be bought either as attachments to electric drills or as purpose-made tools.

The purpose-made saw is more expensive than the attachment but is often more powerful and does not have to be assembled every time it is used.

Blades are available to cut wood, metal, masonry and ceramics. Use a combination blade when you cut either softwood or man-made boards.

Most saw attachments will only fit the same make of drill; follow the maker's instructions when you assemble the tool and when you make any adjustments.

The blade cuts as it comes up under the wood, so coated or veneered chipboard should be laid face down on the bench. This means that the cutting line must be marked on the side of the board that will not be visible – the opposite practice from hand-sawing. It is still advisable to score the cutting line on the face of the board – the side that will show.

RECIPROCATING SAWS

A reciprocating power saw has two blades moving in opposite directions, like an electric carving knife, allowing quick and easy cutting. Blades can be changed, to cut different materials.

The saw cuts best at maximum speed, so do not force it through the wood – you will slow down the blade and may strain the motor.

HOW TO CUT WOOD OR BOARD

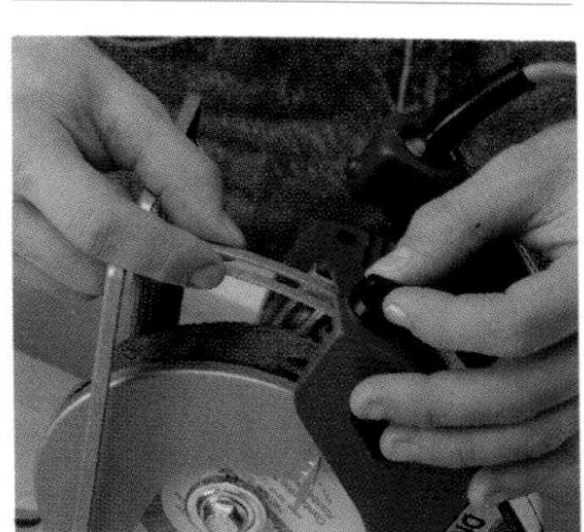

1 Adjust the height of the sole plate so that the blade will cut to a depth about $\frac{1}{8}$in (3mm) more than the thickness of the wood.

2 Before cutting, cramp the wood to a bench. Make sure there is space beneath the cutting line for the blade. A wide board can be supported with a batten at each edge and battens at each side of the cutting line.

3 Use the sighting guide to line up the blade on the waste side of the cutting line.

4 Hold the saw back from the wood and press the trigger. When the blade is turning at full speed, begin the cut.

STEERING A STRAIGHT LINE

Cutting a narrow strip

1 Adjust the fence guide on the saw to the correct distance between the edge of the wood and the cutting line. The cut will only be straight if the edge of the wood or board is also straight.

2 Make the cut with the fence guide in contact with the edge.

Cutting a wide piece

1 Cramp or nail a straight batten to the wood as a guide for the sole plate. Place it so that the blade cuts on the waste side of the cutting line. Make sure the batten is the same distance from the line at both ends.

2 Make the cut with the sole plate running against the batten.

CUTTING AT AN ANGLE

Adjust the sole plate so the blade is at the required angle to the wood. The angles are marked – from 5 to 45 degrees – on the bevel adjuster.

The adjustment will reduce the depth of the cut, so reset the blade depth as well.

Before cutting, make sure the angle will be in the right direction, keeping in mind that coated chipboard is being cut face down.

Try it out first on a piece of scrap wood.

USING A POWERED JIGSAW

A powered jigsaw is extremely useful for cutting curves and for making cuts where space is too restricted to use a wide-bladed saw. It is not as accurate on long straight cuts as a circular saw.

For cutting different materials, you can buy blades with different numbers of teeth per inch (TPI).

32 TPI: for metals and thin plastic sheet.

14 TPI: for general-purpose work – metals, plastics, plywood, hardboard and coated chipboard.

10 TPI: for solid wood, with or across the grain. Also plywood, uncoated chipboard and blockboard.

8 TPI: for cutting solid wood with the grain (ripping).

Always make sure that the blade is securely clamped, and that the roller guide is lubricated and correctly adjusted.

Using the fence

A jigsaw has a fence to guide it along a cut parallel to the edge of the timber. But this only works when the cut is taken very slowly, the blade is in perfect condition and the timber is uniform in consistency.

It is probably better to use a jigsaw freehand along carefully marked lines.

Which side to cut from?

Because the teeth point upwards the cleanest side of the cut is underneath. So cutting lines should be marked on the back of the material.

Thin material usually needs supporting when being cut to prevent the saw action whipping it about. One solution is to clamp it between two layers of old hardboard or plywood. Mark the cutting lines on the top board and cut through them all.

SAFETY TIPS

Plug the saw flex into a plug-in adapter containing an RCD (residual current device) at the socket. It will cut off the current if the saw cuts into the flex.

Check that the blade is the right way round when fitting it.

Keep the cable well away from the blade.

Do not remove the saw from the wood until it has stopped.

Pull the plug from the socket whenever the saw is not in use, even for short spells.

Keep children out of the room while you are using the saw.

Wear safety spectacles when cutting. Flying sawdust can damage the eyes.

Make sure the blade will not cut anything underneath the workpiece.

Never use blunt or bent blades.

Replace the flex if the sheathing is damaged. Check that the outer sheathing runs right into the tool and the plug.

How to use a chisel

Make sure that the wood or board you are cutting is firmly held in place so that you can use both hands to control the chisel.

The wood can usually be fixed to a work bench, either in a vice or with G-cramps.

To gain maximum control and accuracy, use only hand pressure on the chisel. If a lot of waste has to be removed, tap the handle with a wooden mallet, but finish off by hand. It is vital to ensure that the chisel is extremely sharp (see right).

Cut a series of shavings rather than chopping out large chunks.

> SAFETY TIP
> Never place one hand in front of the blade to support the wood. If the blade slips you could be badly cut.

FIVE STEPS IN CUTTING A HALVING JOINT

1 Mark the area to be removed on the top and side of the wood.

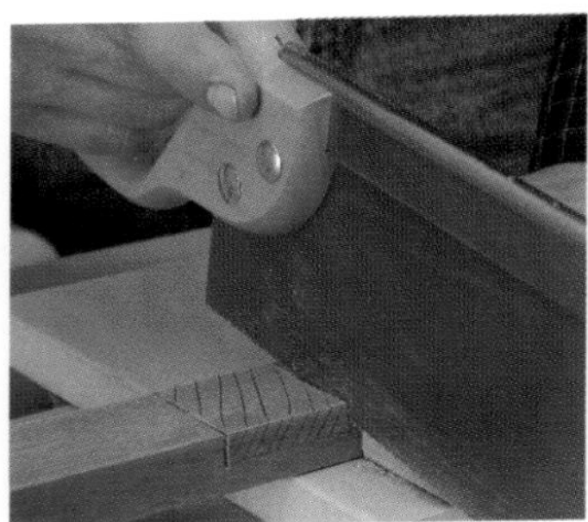

2 Saw down just inside the vertical lines as far as the depth lines. On wide areas make extra vertical cuts between the first two.

3 With the bevel of the blade upwards, chisel out the waste a little at a time from both sides, cutting upwards.

4 Pare away the centre waste until you reach the bottom of the area to be removed.

5 Shave the bottom with the chisel so that it is smooth. Check for flatness with a rule, held on its edge.

MAKING A CUT-OUT IN CHIPBOARD

1 Mark the area that you want to remove, drawing pencil lines on the top and both sides of the board.

2 Make a series of saw cuts down to the depth line, keeping the cuts close together.

3 Cramp the board to a work bench, with a piece of scrap wood under the board for protection.

4 Hold the chisel on the base line and tap the handle sharply with a mallet. Work along the line until the cut-out is complete.

MAKING A CURVED CORNER

To curve the corner of a piece of wood use a chisel and a file.

1 Mark the curve with a round object such as a lid.

2 With the wood on a piece of scrap hardboard, hold the chisel upright with your thumb on top and put your head over it. Cut off the corner at 45 degrees.

3 Pare off the corners left by the first cuts.

4 Continue cutting off corners, working in as close to the line as possible.

5 Finish off the curve with a file.

Melamine-coated chipboard

A melamine coating will blunt a chisel rapidly. To curve a corner on melamine-coated chipboard, use a fine saw to remove most of the waste and finish with a file.

KEEPING YOUR CHISEL SHARP

A chisel will only work properly if it is extremely sharp, so hone it before starting a job.

Chisel blades have two angles forming the cutting edge – the ground angle of 25 degrees and the honed angle of 30 degrees.

When buying a chisel check if it has already been honed and is ready for use. Some chisels have to be honed by the buyer, others are pre-honed.

To sharpen a chisel before a job, use a fine-grade oil stone, together with a honing guide.

Using the honing guide

1 Put oil on the fine-grade side of the stone.

2 Put the chisel in the honing guide and rub the blade to and fro at an angle of 30 degrees until a burr is raised. You can feel it with your thumb.

3 Take the blade from the honing guide, turn it over so that it is flat on its back, and rub it from side to side to reverse the burr. Repeat two or three times until the burr has gone.

Drilling holes in wood and board

HOW TO DRILL A STRAIGHT HOLE

Before starting to drill a hole, make sure that the drill is at right angles to the work surface. Various accessories are available to help with this.

Drill guide

A frame fits over an electric drill; if the frame is resting flat on the work surface the drill is vertical. It can be used for drilling horizontal holes as well. A drill guide can also be set to control the depth of the hole.

The device is cheaper but less accurate than a drill stand.

Drill stand

A drill stand will ensure total accuracy, but would only be worthwhile if you intend to do a lot of work. Before buying, make sure that your drill will fit the stand.

You can pre-set the stand so that the holes are drilled to exact depths.

A try square

Stand a try square on end beside the drill and ask someone to check that the drill lines up with it, from both the front and the side. The try square can then be removed while you drill the hole.

DRILLING HOLES IN COATED CHIPBOARD

To prevent a bit from wandering away from the mark on melamine-coated chipboard, make an indent with a nail to give it a start.

You will cause the least damage to the surface by drilling from the more important face. Use only gentle pressure.

Be careful when using a flat bit. The weak core of the board wears away rapidly and may not hold the bit on-line. If possible, sandwich the chipboard between two blocks of wood and drill through all three. Use a drill stand if you have one.

HOLDING THE WORK WHILE YOU DRILL

In a vice

Hold the work in a vice with pieces of wood protecting it from the pressure of the jaws.

With G-cramps

Cramp the work to a bench with scrap wood beneath it to prevent the bit from damaging the bench.

Alternatively, cramp the work so that it overhangs the bench.

On a portable bench the wood can be cramped to the open jaws, and the hole drilled between them.

CONTROLLING THE DEPTH

To drill holes that do not go right through – pilot holes for screws, for example – fit a depth guide to the bit. Plastic guides which fit on the bit can be bought, or you can bind a strip of coloured adhesive tape around the bit (it is less likely to move). Some power drills have an adjustable rod protruding from the front to control the depth.

MATCHING HOLES

You may wish to drill matching holes in two boards – for fitting shelf supports, for example.

Cramp them together on a bench with scrap wood beneath, making sure that the edges are flush. Drill through both and into the scrap wood. This will prevent breakthrough on the underside of the second thickness.

DRILLING LARGE HOLES

Flat bits

For holes between about $\frac{1}{4}$ and 1$\frac{1}{2}$in (6 and 38mm) in diameter, you can use a flat bit, which has a cutting head wider than the shank. (But do not use flat bits to drill holes for concealed adjustable hinges – page 183.)

To avoid splitting the wood when drilling right through with a flat bit, drill from one side until the point of the bit just breaks through on the other. Turn the wood over and complete by drilling through the centre hole.

Auger bits

An auger bit will give greater accuracy than a flat bit in both the diameter and the straightness of the hole. It is preferable for such jobs as cutting a slot in the edge of a door to take a mortise lock, where the bit must travel in a perfectly straight line.

All auger bits have a tapered screw thread at the point which draws the cutter in behind it.

Auger bits work most efficiently at slow speed, and the larger the bit the slower it should be driven.

Three types are available. The traditional pattern has a square tapered top and can be used only in a carpenter's swing brace. It is widely available in a range of sizes up to 1$\frac{1}{2}$in (38mm).

A straight-shanked type can be used in either a swing brace or a power drill at slow speeds. It is made in metric sizes only – 6mm, 9mm, 13mm, 19mm, 25mm and 32mm.

For drilling holes in fence posts where no power source is available, a hand-driven auger bit can be used. A pole fits through an eye at the top, and is turned by hand.

Holesaws

Very large holes can be cut with holesaws which are sold in sets of seven circular blades ranging in diameter from 1in (25mm) to 2$\frac{1}{2}$in (64mm).

The maximum depth of cut is about $\frac{5}{8}$in (16mm). Holes can be cut through material up to 1$\frac{1}{4}$in (32mm) thick when cutting is possible from both sides.

To drill a hole, put the workpiece on a waste board and cramp the two firmly to a workbench. Put the pilot drill on the centre mark of the hole, check that the drill is held at 90 degrees and begin drilling at a slow speed.

If you want to make a cut-out in a piece of wood – for a hand slot in a drawer front, for example – first cut holes at each end of the cut-out with a holesaw and then join them with a jigsaw.

> SAFETY TIPS
>
> Do not touch holesaw blades until a few minutes after use – they can get very hot.
>
> Do not place the drill on a workbench before it has stopped. A spinning holesaw will act as a wheel and travel rapidly across the surface.

Using a router

A router is a wood-cutting tool with a spinning bit, which can be used for joint making, to create decorative surfaces and edges, and for carving. For the serious woodworker, a power router opens up many new possibilities. The various bits and templates can be used to make channels, chamfers, a variety of joints, and to add decoration in the form of classic beading, rounding and panelling.

The tool consists of a powerful electric motor, most commonly between 400 and 800 watts, which revolves at a high speed – usually between 12,000 and 30,000 rpm. This movement is transmitted to one of a wide range of router bits, and these are used either singly or in succession to produce the desired effects. Because of their high speed, the cuts produced are accurate and smooth.

The standard HSS steel bits can need quite regular sharpening, but tungsten carbon-tipped (TCT) bits are available, which ensure long cutting life.

The standard router can be adjusted to set the depth of cut of the selected cutter and there it stays until it is reset. The plunge router is a more versatile tool, allowing the depth of cut to vary with downward pressure on the two router handles. Cutting depth can also be preset.

The tool does have a tendency to twist when it is first started up, so keep a firm grip on the handles. Take great care to keep your fingers away from the cutter projecting below the base plate.

Once it is up to full speed, ease the router into the work. Bracing yourself against the tool's natural tendency to twist. The router will then pull itself into the wood, producing a smooth and accurate cut with no vibration.

Router bits and their effects

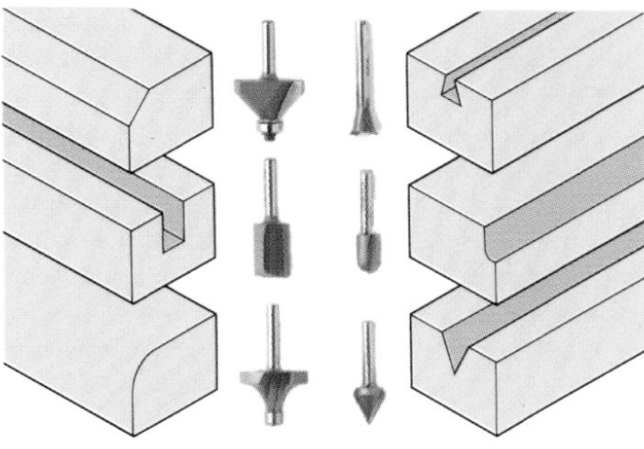

Very fine dust is produced during cutting, though many models now have a nozzle to which a vacuum-cleaner hose can be attached to remove the dust as it is produced. Although this is an effective way of keeping the work area clean, it can make the tool a little harder to control. If you do not use the dust extractor nozzle, wear a dust mask to protect your lungs. This is especially important when working with hardwoods.

The correct way to use a hammer

A slippery hammer face causes nails to bend. So keep the face clean and free of grease by occasionally rubbing it on a flat sheet of fine abrasive paper.

1 When using the hammer, hold the handle near the end and keep your eye on the nail.

2 Start the nail by tapping it into the wood.

3 Swing the hammer with a firm stroke, pivoting your arm from the elbow so that the handle is at right angles to the nail on impact. Very little wrist movement should be involved.

STARTING OFF SMALL NAILS

Very small nails – panel pins in particular – can be difficult to get started. These two techniques will help you.

Using the cross-pein

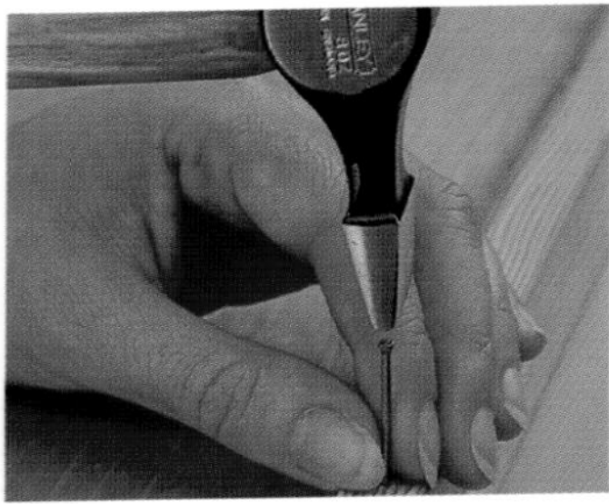

Start the nail or pin by holding it between finger and thumb and tapping gently with the cross-pein of a pin hammer. When the pin stands by itself, drive it home with the hammer face.

The paper method

When using tiny panel pins, push them through a piece of stiff paper and hold them in place as you drive them in. When the pin is almost home, tear the paper away.

MAKING NAILS INVISIBLE

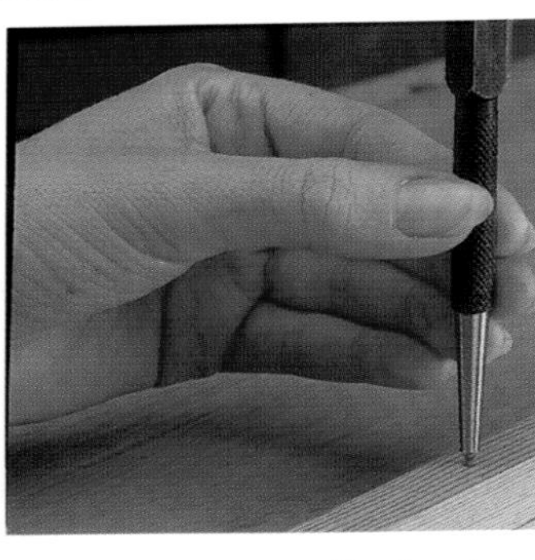

If you do not want the heads to show, use lost-head nails or panel pins. Drive the nail down almost to the surface of the wood, then punch it in with a pin punch. Fill the hole with interior filler and paint over it, or use matching wood filler.

SECRET NAILING

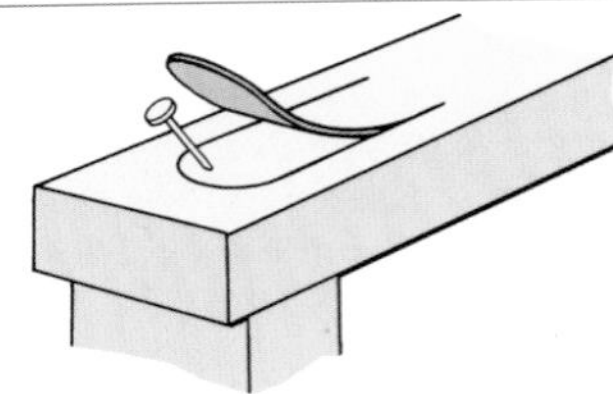

First chisel up a sliver of wood where you want the nail to go. Then drive the nail into the recess underneath. Glue the sliver back in place, holding it down with a block of wood and a G-cramp.

REMOVING UNWANTED NAILS

Once a nail has begun to bend, it will only bend again, so pull it out and start again with a new one.

1 To avoid damaging the surface of the wood, put a piece of card or thin wood under the hammer.

2 Hook the nail head in the claw and remove the nail with a series of pulls. For maximum leverage keep the handle almost upright.

3 If the nail is long, put a wood block under the hammer when the nail is partly out. Add more blocks after each pull so that the nail is removed vertically. If it curves, the hole will become lengthened, and the new nail may not go in straight.

TAKING OUT HEADLESS NAILS

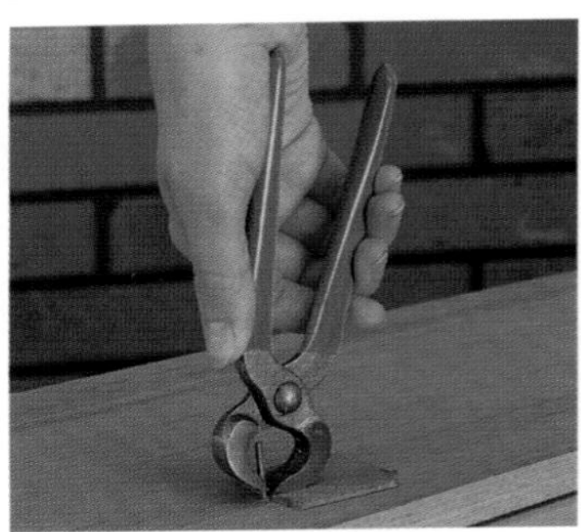

If the nail has lost its head, pull it out with carpenter's pincers. Grip it as near the wood as possible and lever with a series of movements, regripping low down each time.

If possible, use a thin piece of wood under the pincer jaws to prevent damage to the surface.

REMOVING LARGE NAILS

To remove a lot of very large nails use a wrecking bar which has a claw at its curved end and a flattened wedge at the other for levering timber away from a wall.

Put some packing under the bar to prevent surface damage.

A NAIL YOU CANNOT GRIP

If it is not possible to grip the nail with any tool, punch it below the surface and fill the hole with interior filler or matching wood filler, depending on whether the wood will be painted or varnished.

Alternatively, chisel away the wood around it until the head can be gripped with pincers.

REMOVING TACKS

One type of carpenter's pincers has a claw at the end of one of the handles which can be used to remove old tacks from wood.

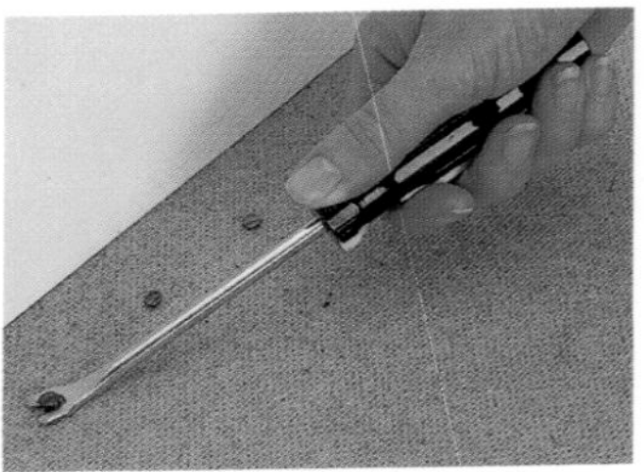

To remove a lot of tacks from a piece of wood, from an old chair for example, use a tack lifter which is designed specifically for the purpose.

NAILING INTO WOOD

Nailing is an effective way of joining pieces of softwood together, and of fixing things such as roofing slates or wall cladding to softwood battens.

Panel pins are used in the same way as nails on small-scale work, such as fixing a hardboard backing to a cupboard.

Chipboard does not take nails well; use chipboard screws, dowel joints or corner joints instead.

Fixing light to heavy

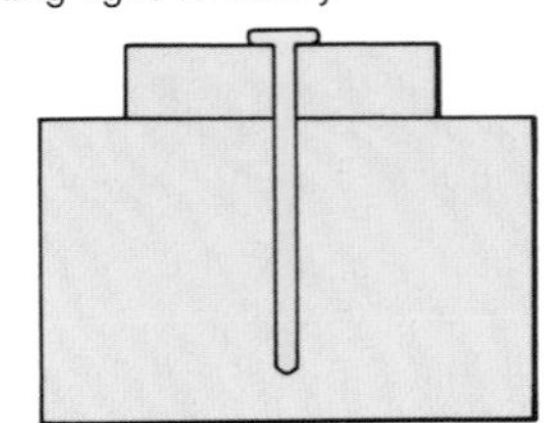

Use nails two and half to three times longer than the thickness of the timber that they must hold. Always nail the lighter piece of work to the heavier.

Fixing into end grain

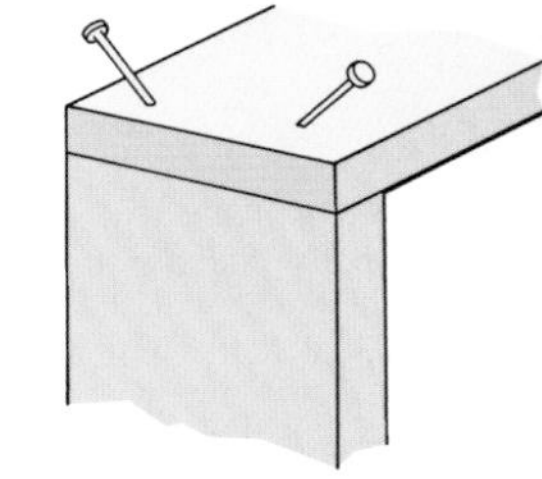

Dovetail nailing grips better when driving into the end grain of wood. Drive staggered nails at opposing angles.

Avoiding splits

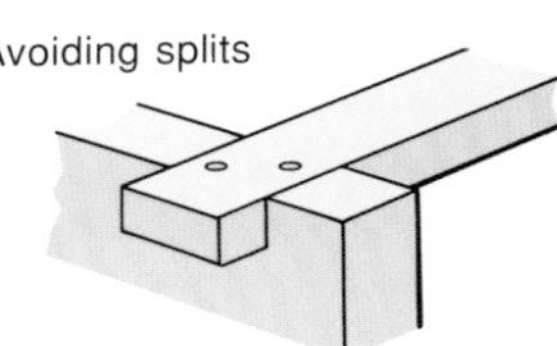

When you are nailing near the end of a piece of wood, you can usually avoid splitting it by not driving more than one nail into the same line of the grain.

Also cut the wood a little overlength and nail it in place before sawing off the excess flush with the other piece.

Fixing hardwood

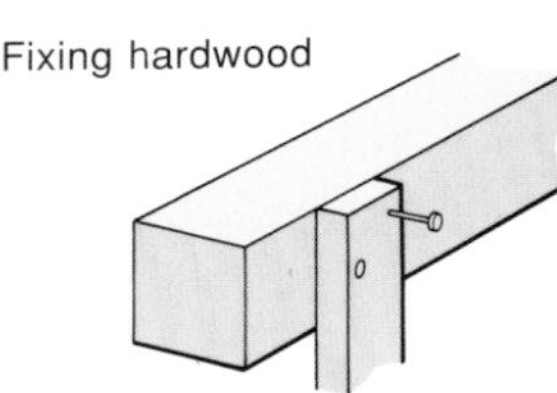

Avoid nailing into hardwood, as it will probably split. If nails must be used, bore guide holes slightly smaller than the diameter of the nail shank.

Unsupported wood

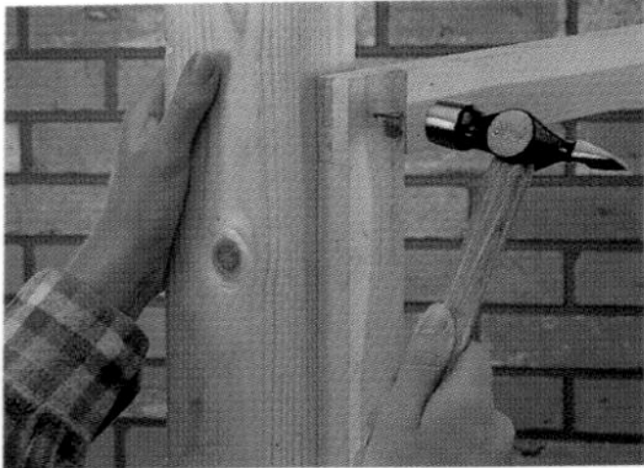

Prevent bouncing when nailing unsupported wood by holding a heavy block against the free side of the work.

NAILING WOOD TO MASONRY

If a nail penetrates more than ¾in (19mm) into masonry its grip is weakened. So use the correct length of masonry nail when fixing to brick, concrete or breeze block.

Drive the nails into the wood before fixing it to the wall.

When fixing to plastered masonry, add the thickness of plaster to the thickness of the wood when deciding on the nail length.

CHOOSING THE RIGHT TYPE OF NAIL

Nail	Description
Round wire nail	General-purpose nail, large unattractive head. Liable to split wood. Sizes ¾-6in (20-150mm).
Oval wire nail	Unlikely to split wood if driven so that long head-axis follows grain. Also available with lost heads. Sizes 1-6in (25-150mm).
Cut floor brad	Used to fix floorboards. Provides good grip; unlikely to split flooring. Sizes ½-6in (13-150mm).
Lost head nail	Carpentry and flooring nail. Head can be punched home and hole filled. Available as round or oval. Sizes 1-6in (25-150mm).
Cut clasp nail	Strong grip in wood and masonry. Difficult to remove, so twist off head and drive in shank. Sizes 1-8in (25-200mm).
Clout nail	Used for roofing felt, window sash cords, wire fencing. Galvanised for outdoor work. Sizes ¾-4in (20-100mm).
Panel pin	Used for joinery, cabinet work and mouldings; small head, fine gauge (thickness). Easily punched in. Sizes ⅝-2in (15-50mm).
Tack	For fixing carpets and fabric to wood or flooring. 'Improved tacks' are stouter and have larger heads than 'fine tacks'. Sizes ¼-1¼in (6-30mm).
Sprig	Headless tack for fixing glass in wood frames. Sizes ½-¾in (13-20mm).
Chair nail	In copper, chrome, bronze or antique finish. Used to cover tacks in upholstery work. Sizes (of head) ⅛-½in (3-13mm).
Masonry nail	Provides strong grip in soft brick, breeze block and concrete. Heavy and fine gauges. Sizes ⅝-4in (15-100mm).
Annular nail	For fixing plywood and other sheet materials. Teeth bite into wood for strong grip. Sizes ¾-4in (20-100mm).
Hardboard pin	For fixing hardboard. Diamond-shaped head is hidden in the board. Sizes ⅝-2in (15-50mm).
Galvanised roofing nail	Used on corrugated iron roofing. Head diameter ¾in (20mm), length 2½in (65mm).
Plasterboard nail	The jagged shank is designed to increase the holding power of the nail in the plasterboard. Sizes: 1¼in (30mm), 1½in (40mm).
Wire dowel	For end-to-end joints. Drive into one piece and hammer second onto nail. Scarce, but can be made by cutting the head off a round wire nail with pliers.
Corrugated fastener	For framing, battening, screening. Sizes ¼-⅞in (6-22mm) deep, ⅞-1¼in (22-30mm) long.
Staple	Quick anchorage for wire fencing, upholstery springs; often galvanised. Various designs and sizes.
Plastic-head nail	For fixing plastic to wood. The polymer head is made in white, black and shades of brown, and needs no capping. Flat or domed head. Sizes ¾in-2½in (20-65mm).

Joining wood with screws

When screwing one piece of wood or board to another, the length of screws is decided by the thickness of the top piece. Choose a length that will allow half the screw to go into the bottom piece.

1 Mark the screw positions on the top piece with a cross.

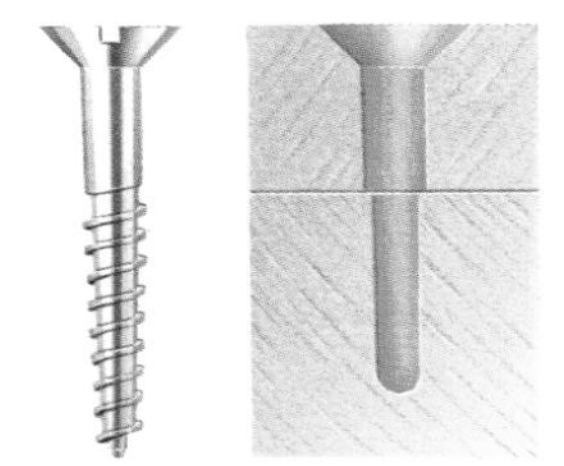

2 Drill clearance holes through the top piece, the same diameter as the screw shank (table, page 162).

3 If you are using countersunk screws, use a countersink bit to bore out space for the head. Check the depth by inserting the screw.

4 Lay the second piece in position under the first, and put a bradawl or pencil through the holes to mark the position of the pilot holes.

5 Drill the pilot holes in the second piece (table, page 162).

If you are using screws of No. 6 gauge or less, the pilot holes can be made with a fine bradawl.

6 Insert the screws and tighten them all equally.

FITTING SCREWDRIVER TO SCREW

Always use a screwdriver that fits the screw. Too narrow a blade will tend to chew up the slot; too wide a blade will slip out.

Make sure the blade is square in the slot. Driving screws does not require great pressure as the screw pulls itself in on the thread if the hole is the correct size.

HELPFUL TIPS

If you want to screw into the end grain of wood or man-made board, insert a dowel across the grain and then drive the screws into the dowel.

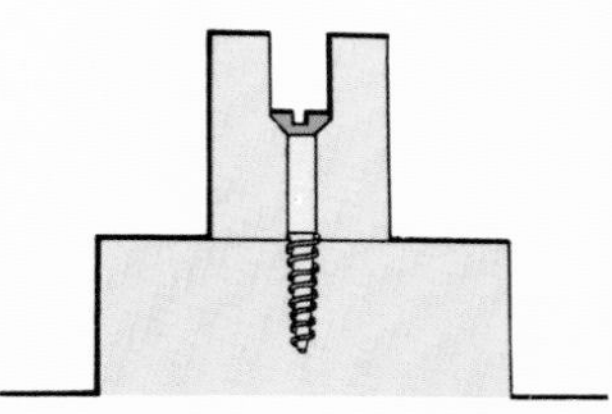

A thick piece of wood can be screwed to a thinner piece by first counterboring the thick piece with a hole the diameter of the screw head. Then drill the clearance hole in the thick piece and, finally, the pilot hole in the thinner piece.

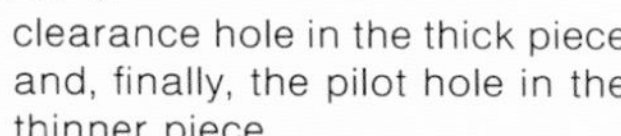

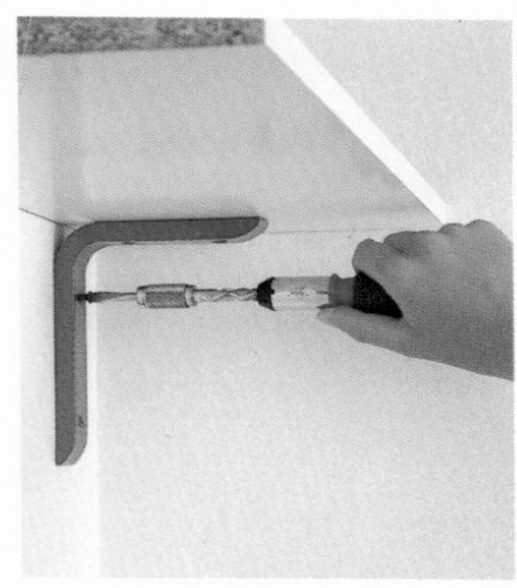

Screws in awkward corners can be turned more easily with a spiral ratchet screwdriver. Your hand is well out of the way, and is just pushing rather than turning as well.

Alternatively use an offset screwdriver, which is shaped like a crank.

The problem often occurs when shelves are fitted to walls.

Buying and using wood screws

Wood screws are made from either mild steel, stainless steel, brass or aluminium. Finishes can be black japanned, electro brassed, zinc plated, nickel plated or chrome plated.

The size of a screw is determined by the diameter of its shank (gauge), and the length from the rim of the head to the tip. Gauge numbers do not vary with screw lengths; a 1in (25mm) No. 8 gauge screw has the same size head and shank as a 3in (75mm) No. 8.

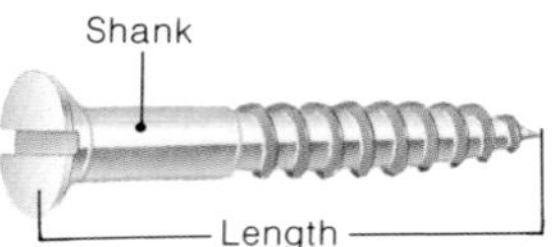

The most economical way of buying screws is by the box of 100, 200 or 500.

Two holes for shank and thread are needed before screws are driven in. A clearance hole, slightly wider than the shank, is drilled in the top piece of wood, and a pilot hole, smaller than the shank, is made in the second piece. The thread of the screw bites into the sides of the smaller hole as it is driven in.

Softwood requires smaller pilot holes than hardwood because it opens out as the screw goes in. For screws smaller in gauge than No. 7, the clearance and pilot holes can both be made with a fine bradawl.

If you are drilling a number of holes the same diameter and depth, it helps to mark the correct depth on the bit by wrapping a piece of white or coloured adhesive tape around it.

If you do not know the gauge of a screw, check it with a screw gauge – which is sometimes supplied as part of a set of plastic wallplugs.

To make driving easier, lubricate screws with wax or candlegrease.

When using brass screws in hardwood, lower the resistance by first driving in a steel screw of the same size as the brass one. This will save the brass screw from shearing off.

WHAT GAUGE – WHAT LENGTH?

Length in inches (mm)	SCREW GAUGE NUMBERS 0	1	2	3	4	5	6	7	8	9	10	12	14	16	18	20
¼ (6.5)	▽ △	▽	▽ △		▽											
⅜ (10)		▽	▽ △	▽ △	▽ ◇ △		▽ △		▽							
½ (13)			▽	▽ △	▼ ◆ ▲	▽ △	▼ ◇ ▲	▽	▽ △		▽					
⅝ (16)				▽	▼ ◇ ▲	▽ ◇ △	▼ ◇ ▲	▽	▽ ▲		▽ △					
¾ (19)				▽	▼ ◇ ▲	▽ ◇ △	▼ ◆ ▲	▽ △	▼ ◆ ▲		▽ △	▽				
⅞ (22)																
1 (25)				▽	▽ ◇	▽ ◇	▼ ◆ ▲	▼ △	▼ ◆ ▲	▽	▼ ◇ ▲	▽ △				
1¼ (32)					▽	▽	▼ ◇ △	▼ △	▼ ◇ ▲	▽	▼ ◇ ▲	▽ △	▽			
1½ (38)					▽		▼ ◇ △	▽	▼ ◇ ▲	▽	▼ ◇ ▲	▽ △	▽ △	▽		
1¾ (44)							▽	▽	▼		▼ ◇ △					
2 (50)							▽	▽	▼ ◇ ▲		▼ ◇ ▲	▼ △	▽ △	▽	▽	▽
2¼ (57)							▽		▽		▽					
2½ (65)							▽		▼ △		▼ △	▽ △	▽	▽		
2¾ (70)									▽		▽					
3 (75)									▽		▼ △	▼ △	▽	▽	▽	▽
3¼ (82)											▽					
3½ (90)									▽		▽	▽				
4 (100)											▽	▼	▽	▽	▽	▽
5 (125)												▽	▽	▽		
6 (150)													▽	▽		

KEY Easy to obtain ▼ Countersunk ▲ Round head ◆ Raised head Difficult to obtain ▽ Countersunk △ Round head ◇ Raised head

WHAT SIZE CLEARANCE AND PILOT HOLES?

	1	2	3	4	5	6	7	8	9	10	12	14	16	18	20
Hardwood															
Clearance hole in inches *(mm)*	5/64 *(2)*	3/32 *(2.5)*	7/64 *(3)*	1/8 *(3.5)*	1/8 *(3.5)*	5/32 *(4)*	5/32 *(4)*	3/16 *(5)*	3/16 *(5)*	7/32 *(5.75)*	1/4 *(6.5)*	1/4 *(6.5)*	9.32 *(7.25)*	5/16 *(8.25)*	11/32 *(9)*
Pilot hole in inches *(mm)*	3/64 *(1.2)*	1/16 *(1.6)*	1/16 *(1.6)*	5/64 *(2)*	5/64 *(2)*	5/64 *(2)*	3/32 *(2.5)*	3/32 *(2.5)*	1/8 *(3.5)*	1/8 *(3.5)*	1/8 *(3.5)*	5/32 *(4)*	3/16 *(5)*	3/16 *(5)*	7/32 *(5.75)*
Softwood															
Clearance hole in inches *(mm)*	USE BRADAWL						3/32 *(2.5)*	3/32 *(2.5)*	5/32 *(4)*	5/32 *(4)*	5/32 *(4)*	7/32 *(5.75)*	7/32 *(5.75)*	7/32 *(5.75)*	7/32 *(5.75)*
Pilot hole in inches (mm)							1/16 *(1.6)*	1/16 *(1.6)*	5/64 *(2)*	5/64 *(2)*	5/64 *(2)*	7/64 *(3)*	7/64 *(3)*	7/64 *(3)*	7/64 *(3)*

CHOOSING THE RIGHT TYPES OF SCREW

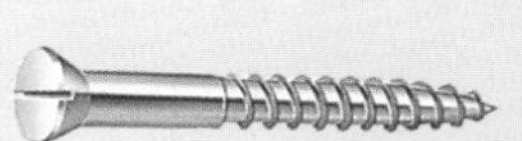

Countersunk with single-slot head
These screws are still widely used for woodwork. They can be tightened flush to the surface.

Countersunk with cross-slot head
The most popular type of screw. The cross slot driver used does not slip from the slot. Pozidriv screws (illustrated) have a choice of three screwdriver sizes. Many of these screws are hardened.

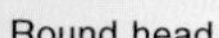

Round head
For fixing hardware fittings without countersunk holes. Head protrudes from the fitting.

Raised head
For fixing door-handle plates, decorative hardware and some hinges. Must be countersunk to the rim.

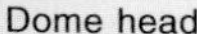

Dome head
For fixing mirrors, bath panels and splashbacks. The cap screws into the screw head for a neat appearance. Do not over-tighten the cap as it must be unscrewed by hand.

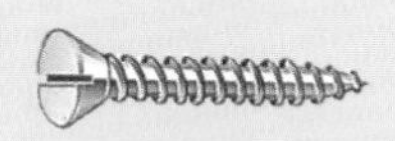

Chipboard screws
Screws with deep threads that extend right up to the head are intended for fixing into chipboard, but can also be used in solid wood.

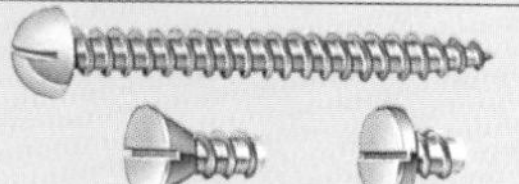

Self-tapping screws
The screw cuts a thread in the metal. First drill a hole the diameter of the screw's core (smaller than the thread).

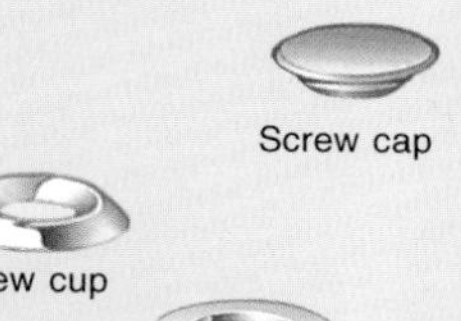

Screw cups, washers and caps
Screw cups and washers spread the pressure of the screw. Screw cups improve the appearance and are useful if the screw must be removed occasionally – on a bath panel, for example.

Plastic screw caps cover the screw heads and are commonly used when screwing into white melamine-coated chipboard.

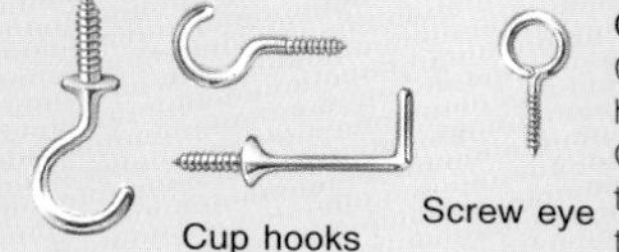

Cup hooks and screw eyes
Cup hooks and screw eyes are used for hanging things from walls and shelves. On plaster walls the short threads limit their use to only light loads. Special types can be bought.

Joining pieces of wood with a bolt

Bolts can be used for joining pieces of wood or metal that need to be dismantled occasionally.

Both sides of the assembly must be accessible so that the nut can be fitted to the threaded end of the bolt.

Bolts are tightened with a spanner, and are sold in metric and imperial sizes.

The length of the bolt must be equal to the thickness of the pieces of wood to be joined, plus the thickness of the nut and washer.

Make sure that the unthreaded part of the shank is less than the combined pieces of wood; that would prevent the nut from being tightened.

If the threaded part is too long, however, it can be trimmed off with a hacksaw after the nut has been fitted.

1 Clamp the two pieces of wood together in position.

2 Drill a hole slightly larger than the shank diameter through both pieces of wood.

3 Put the bolt through the hole, place a washer over the bolt end and tighten the nut with a spanner of the right size. Alternatively, use an adjustable spanner.

4 If necessary, cut off the protruding part of the bolt with a hacksaw, and file off the sharp edge of the thread.

A BOLTED BUTT JOINT

To bolt a vertical rail to a horizontal one, first drill the two rails to accept a machine bolt.

Then drill a large hole in the horizontal rail so that the nut can be fitted on the bolt. The hole should be centred over the end of the bolt, with at least 1¼in (32mm) of solid wood between the end of the rail and the hole.

Chisel a flat face to the hole, on the side nearer the end of the rail.

Insert the machine bolt with a washer at each end. Screw on the nut and jam it with a wedge or spanner while you tighten the bolt.

CHOOSING BOLTS FOR WOOD OR METAL

Coach bolt
The square collar under the domed head locks into the wood as the bolt is tightened, so only one spanner is needed. Use a washer under the nut to stop it sinking into the wood. Sizes: up to 20in (500mm) long; 3/16-3/4in (5-19mm) diameter.

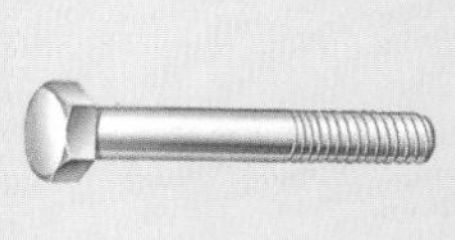

Machine bolt
The flat head does not lock into the wood, so two spanners may be needed. Use a washer under both ends. Also used for joining metal. Sizes: up to 20in (500mm) long; 3/16-3/4in (5-19mm) diameter.

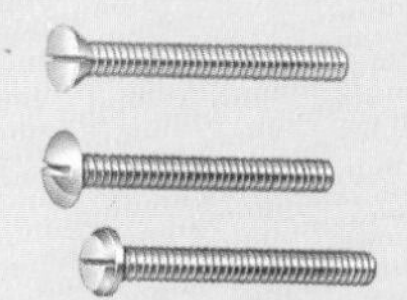

Machine screw
For smaller jobs than bolts. The slotted head is tightened with a screwdriver. A spanner will also be needed for the nut. Use a washer beneath the nut. Countersunk, round and pan heads are available. Sizes: 1/4-2in (6-50mm) long; 1/32in (1mm)-1/4in (6mm) diameter.

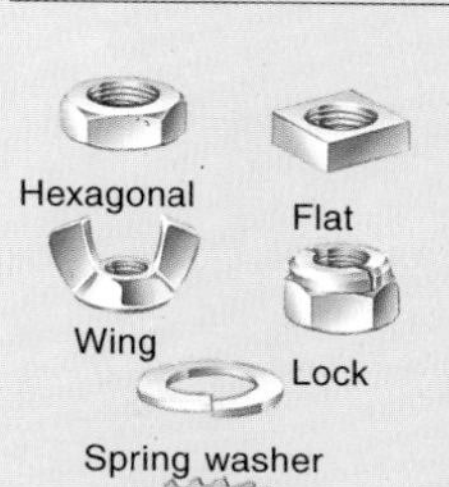

Nuts to fit the bolt
Nuts are most commonly hexagonal; wing nuts can be tightened by hand.

Make sure that a nut and bolt have matching threads. They are made with metric and five main types of imperial thread – Whitworth (BSW), British Standard Fine (BSF), British Association (BA), Unified Coarse (UNC) and Unified Fine (UNF). Spring or toothed washers prevent bolts from loosening.

If you can't find a bolt of the required length, buy a length of threaded rod and cut your own to size.

CHOOSING CORNER JOINTS FOR CONNECTING BOARDS

Corner joints are used to join boards at right angles to each other. In DIY work they have replaced traditional cabinet-making techniques such as dovetail joints which require skill or expensive equipment. Corner joints have also been made necessary by the wide use of man-made boards which cannot be dovetailed.

Particular uses include fixing shelves to wooden uprights and building cabinets.

Each type can be used to create a T-joint or right-angle joint. When joining the panels it is essential to cut the pieces accurately to length with the ends exactly square. Otherwise the final construction will be lopsided.

TYPE OF CORNER JOINT		DESCRIPTION	HOW TO FIT IT
Rigid Joint 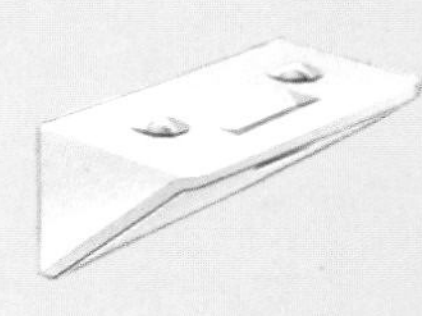	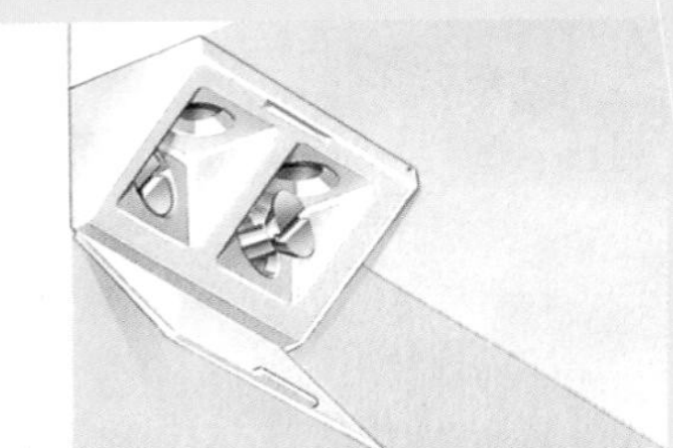	Plastic. $\frac{3}{4}$in (19mm) No. 6 countersunk chipboard screws required – four per joint.	Make two screw holes in the side panel for each block and two in the horizontal board. Screw the block in place and close the cover flap. Use two blocks for horizontal boards up to 8in (200mm) wide, and three for 9–18in (230–460mm).
Dowel joint 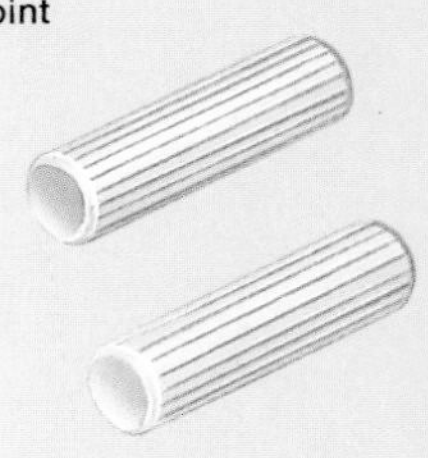		Wood. Available separately or as part of a kit also containing a wood bit, depth stop and metal centre points.	The only method which gives a completely invisible join. The joint is contained within the thickness of the shelf. For fitting sequence, see page 166.
Fixit Blocks 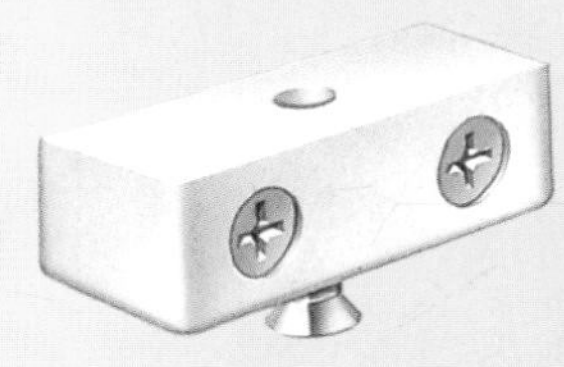		Plastic. 1in (25mm) No. 6 countersunk chipboard screws required – three per block.	Fix the block to the side panel with two screws, then screw up into the horizontal board with a single screw from underneath. Use two blocks for horizontal boards up to 8in (200mm) wide, and three for 9–18in (230–460mm).
Square-section wood batten 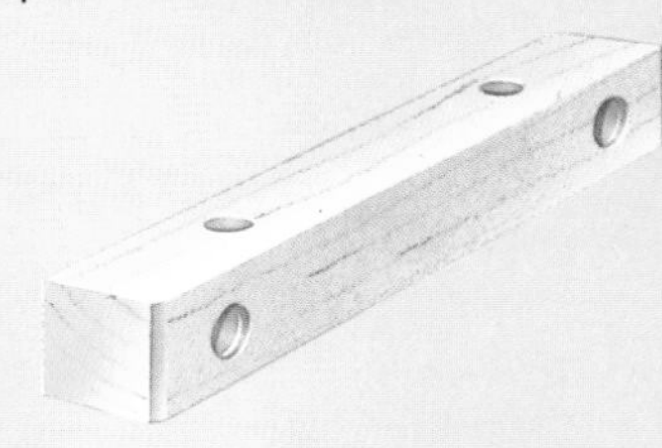	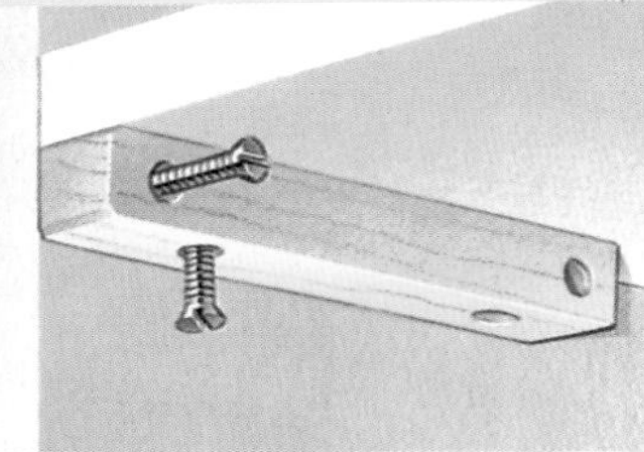	Natural wood (can be stained, varnished or painted). 1in (25mm) No. 6 countersunk chipboard screws required – four or six for each batten.	Cut $\frac{5}{16}$in (8mm) square-section battens to the width of the horizontal board. Drill and countersink the batten to fix it into the side panel and the horizontal board. A batten longer than 8in (200mm) requires extra fixings in the centre. Screw it to the side panel and then to the horizontal.
Lok-Joints 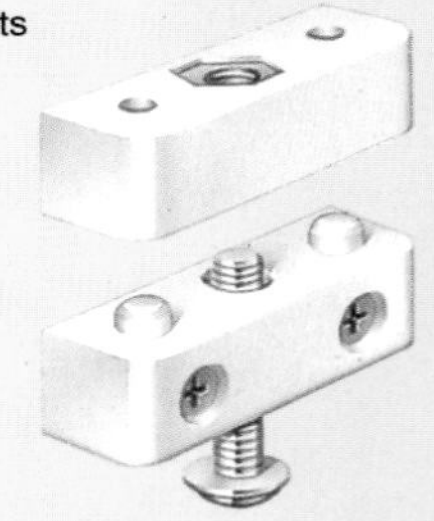	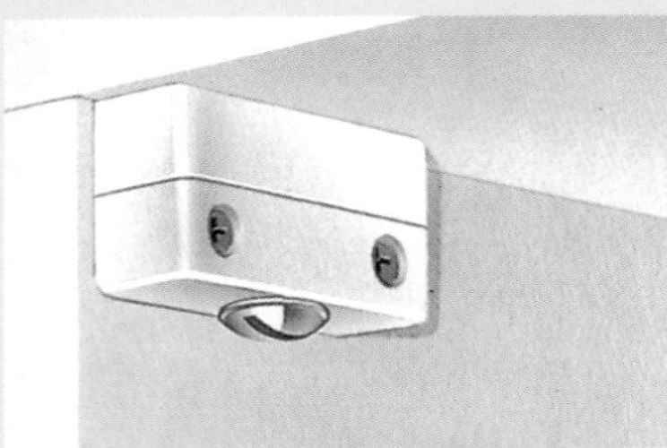	Plastic. $\frac{3}{4}$in (19mm) No. 6 countersunk chipboard screws required – four per block. Stronger and more expensive than Rigid Joints and Fixit Blocks.	They consist of two sections which are screwed to the side and horizontal boards and are then screwed together. On 15mm chipboard, use two blocks on horizontal boards up to 12in (300mm) wide, three for 18in (460mm) and four for 24in (610mm). Thicker materials need only three corner joints up to 24in (610mm).
Assembly joint 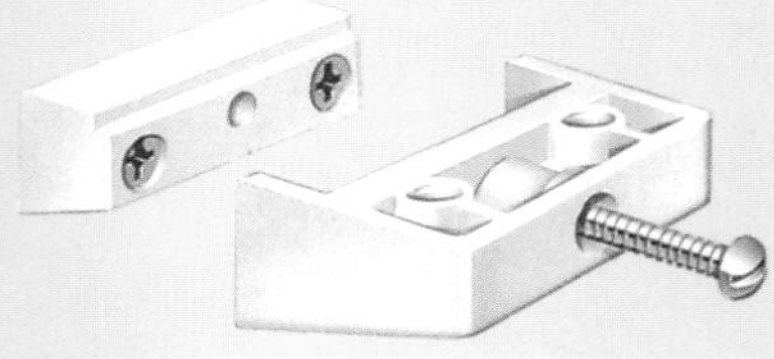	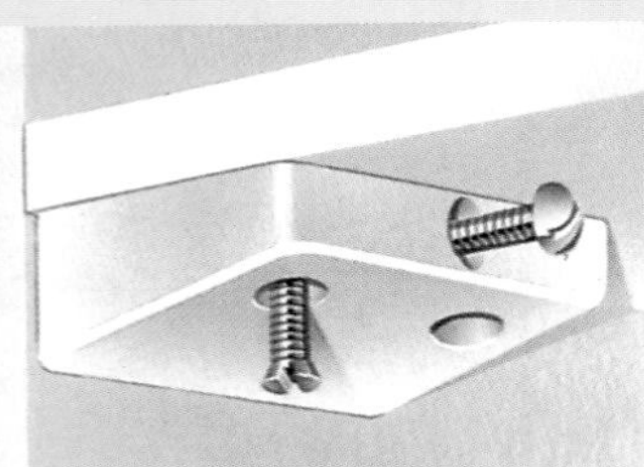	Plastic. $\frac{3}{4}$in (19mm) No. 6 countersunk chipboard screws required – four for each joint.	They consist of two sections which are screwed to the side and horizontal boards and are then screwed together. On 15mm chipboard, use two blocks on horizontal boards up to 12in (300mm) wide, three for 18in (460mm) and four for 24in (610mm). Thicker materials need only three corner joints up to 24in (610mm).

Simple ways of joining wood

NAILED T-JOINTS

Nailed joints are good enough for light frames made of softwood.

Wherever possible, drive the nails in from the outside of the frame; it makes the job much easier. Use nails with a length at least twice the thickness of the wood.

1 Cut the side piece to length.

2 Cut the cross piece to length, making sure that the ends are absolutely square, otherwise they will not make a right-angle join.

3 Hold the cross piece upright in a vice, or clamp it to the side of the bench.

4 Hold the side piece on the end of the cross piece in the correct position and drive a nail into the centre of the join.

5 Drive in two more on each side, at an angle of about 30 degrees.

SKEW NAILING FROM INSIDE THE FRAME

1 Mark the position of the join on the side piece and cramp or temporarily nail a block of wood to the side piece butting up to one line.

2 Hold the cross piece against the block, and drive the first nail in diagonally down into the cross piece about a third of the way in from one side.

3 Remove the block, and nail from the other side in the same way, holding the cross piece steady on the line.

4 Punch in the nail head to give a neat finish, and fill the holes with interior filler or matching wood filler.

BRACKETS FOR FLAT T-JOINTS

If you need strength, but appearance is not important, make T-joints with corner braces or T-plates. Screw one of the metal fixings to each side of the join; a single one will bend fairly easily.

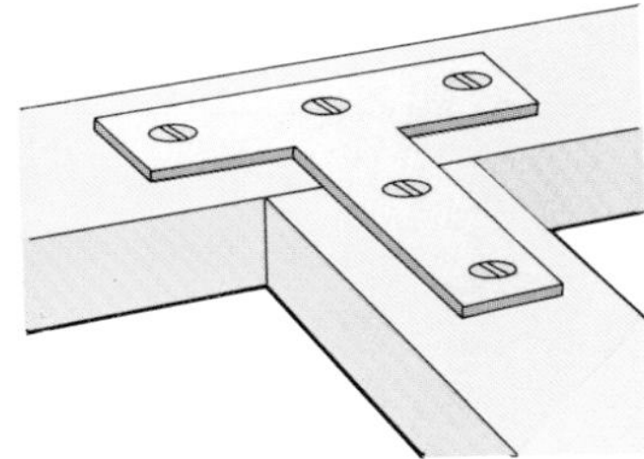

T-plates are screwed to the face of the joint.

Corner plates are screwed into the angle, leaving the face clear.

CORRUGATED FASTENERS FOR QUICK JOINTS

A light frame that needs very little strength can be made quickly with corrugated metal fasteners, which are sharp on one edge.

Push the pieces against a solid support, then place a fastener across the join well in from the edge of the cross piece to avoid splitting the wood.

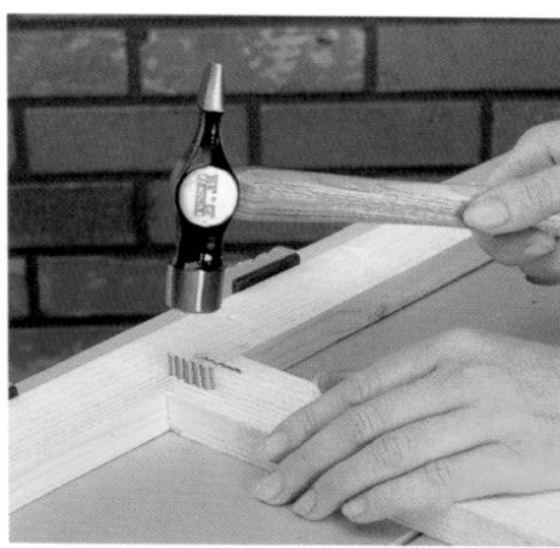

Tap it gently with a hammer, then hit it centrally until it is flush with the surface. Use two fasteners for each joint.

JOINING TWO CROSSING PIECES

The simplest way of joining two pieces of wood that cross each other is to screw one to the other, with wood glue in between. Nails can be used instead of screws but the joint will not be as strong.

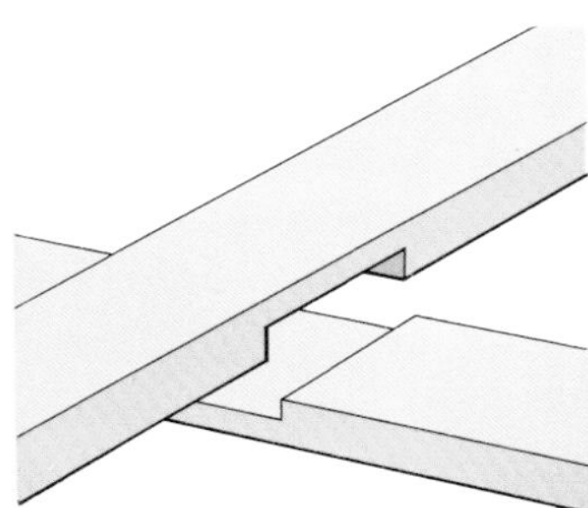

The two pieces can be made to lie flush with each other by cutting a cross-halving joint with a saw and chisel (page 158). The cut-out in each piece is half its thickness. Screws are not needed to hold the pieces; just glue and cramp them until the glue is dry.

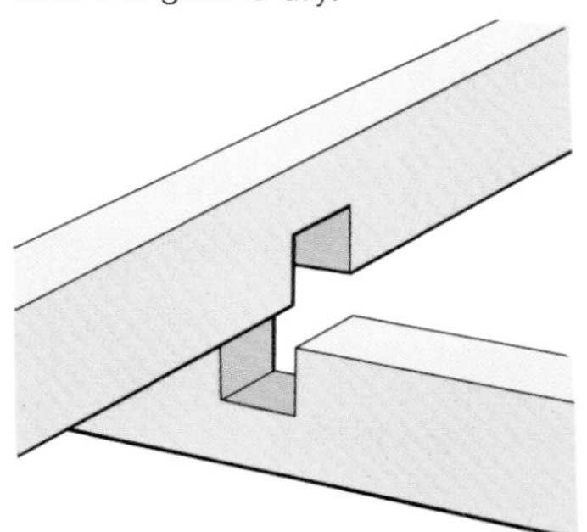

A cross-halving joint can be made with the pieces lying either flat or on edge to each other.

AN OVERLAP T-JOINT

An overlap T-joint can be used to build slatted shelves in an airing cupboard, assemble a picket fence or make general-purpose frames.

It can be fixed with screws, nails or bolts, and for maximum strength it should also be glued.

To make a screwed overlap joint, cramp both pieces of wood together with a G-cramp while you drill the holes.

Drill clearance holes through the top piece, taking care not to drill too far, and then drill smaller pilot holes in the lower piece.

Countersink the holes in the top piece, coat both inner surfaces with wood glue, and screw the joint together.

MITRE JOINTS

1 Before cutting, mark the wood to the correct length. Then draw the angle roughly on the top.

2 Cramp the wood in a mitre box, with another piece of wood underneath to raise it to the bottom of the cutting slot.

3 Cut the mitre, keeping the saw blade vertical in the slot.

4 Repeat with the matching piece.

5 Tap panel pins into one side of the joint. Hold the other piece vertically in a vice and match up the two. Start driving the pins in with the top piece slightly overlapping. As they are driven, the pins slip down a little.

MITRING A WIDE PIECE OF WOOD

If a piece of wood is too wide to fit a mitre box, mark the cutting line on the face, and a diagonal line across the edge, using a combination square or a mitre square. Follow both lines as you saw through.

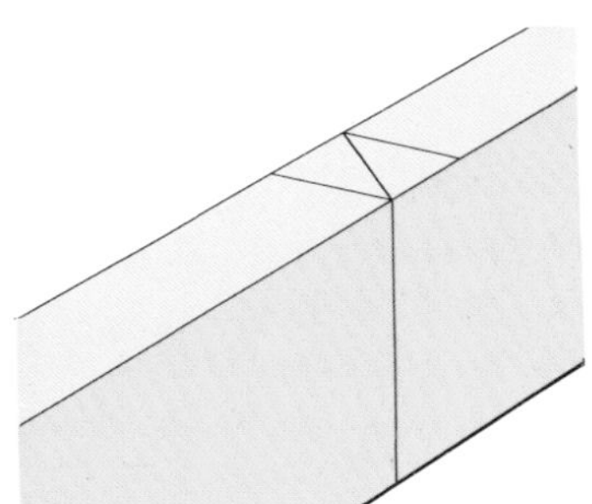

Another method is to draw a square on the edge, then draw a diagonal cutting line, continuing it down the face.

Joining wood and board with dowels

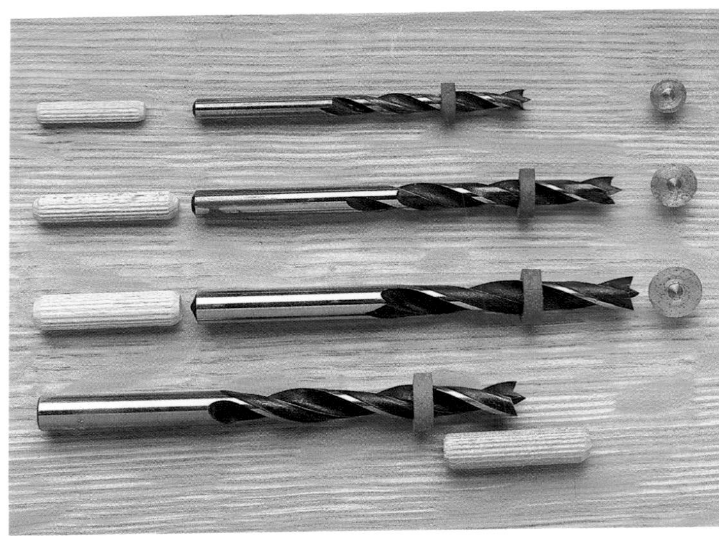

Softwood and chipboard can be joined fairly simply with glued dowels. The dowels can be bought separately or as a kit which also contains a dowel bit with a depth stop and round metal centre points. They are available in three diameters – 6mm, 8mm and 10mm. Choose dowels with a length about 1½ times the thickness of the board being joined.

MAKING A 90 DEGREE JOINT

1 Cut the pieces to length, making sure that the joining ends are square. If they are not, the joint will not be at a right angle.

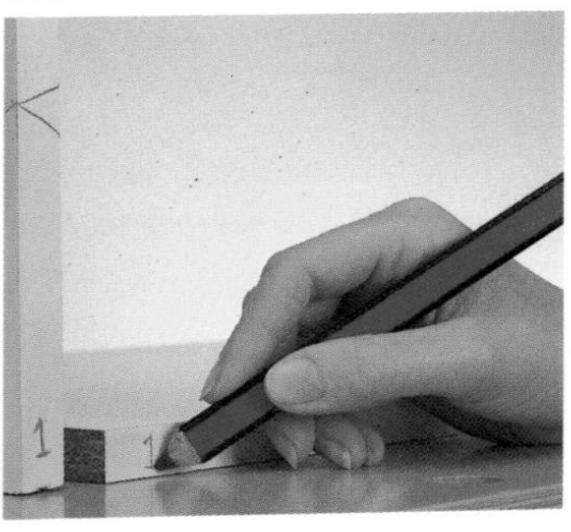

2 To guarantee that you join the correct ends the right way round, draw a pencil mark on the face of each board and run it down onto the face edge, and number the corners. This is most important if more than one joint is being made.

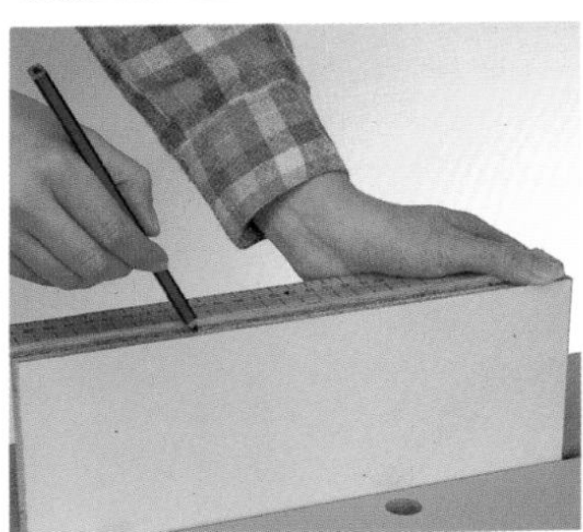

3 Mark a centre line along the end of the board that will press against the face of the other. Draw cross lines where the dowels are to go.

4 Adjust the depth stop on the bit. The depth of the hole will be the length of the dowel, less the amount that is to be let into the other board – about three-quarters of its thickness. To be on the safe side, make the drilling depth slightly more than necessary.

5 Fix the board vertically in a vice. Stand a try square on end and get a helper to check that both the board and the drill are vertically in line with each other. Check from both the side and the front.

6 Drill the holes down as far as the depth stop.

7 Push a centre point firmly into each hole, and stand the second board vertically against the board with the holes.

To be certain that the edges of the two boards are exactly in line, rest them against a straight-edge cramped to the bench.

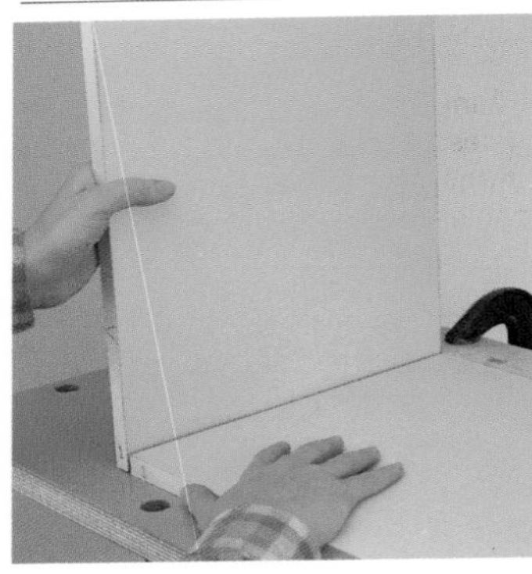

8 Press the boards together so that the points mark the end of the vertical board.

9 Reposition the depth stop to three-quarters the thickness of the second board.

10 Again check that the drill is vertical, and drill holes with the bit centred on the point marks.

Check the position of the depth stop on the bit after drilling each hole in case it slips.

11 Remove the points with pliers. Put wood glue in the holes, on the dowels and on the end grain of the first board.

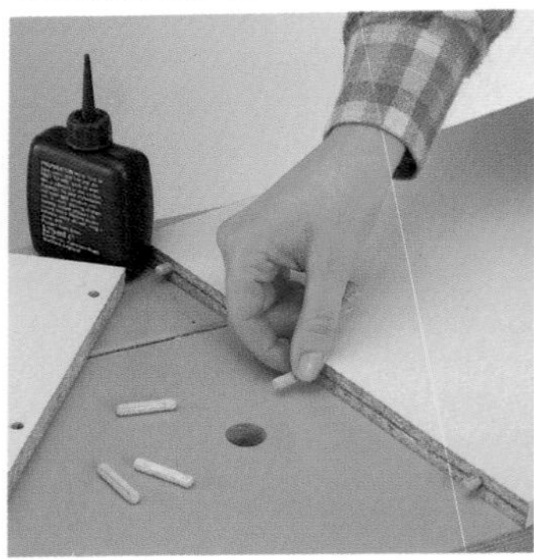

12 Put the dowels in the holes and push the joint together.

13 Cramp the joint together, and wipe away surplus glue with a damp sponge, and leave until the glue sets. For a large object you may need to hire sash cramps.

A DOWELLED T-JOINT

Use the try square to mark the position of the joint on the through-board, so it is 90 degrees across the board.

Drill the holes in the end of the board as described above. Insert the points and press the board together, using the try square to check that the drilled board is square.

A DOWELLED MITRE JOINT

The point system can also be used for mitre joints. Take care to line up the two pieces exactly when making the marks with the points. (Also see Helpful Tip below.)

EDGE-TO-EDGE JOINTS

Two or more boards – either timber or chipboard – can be joined edge to edge to make a wider or longer one. Use only boards that have been machine-cut along the meeting edges.

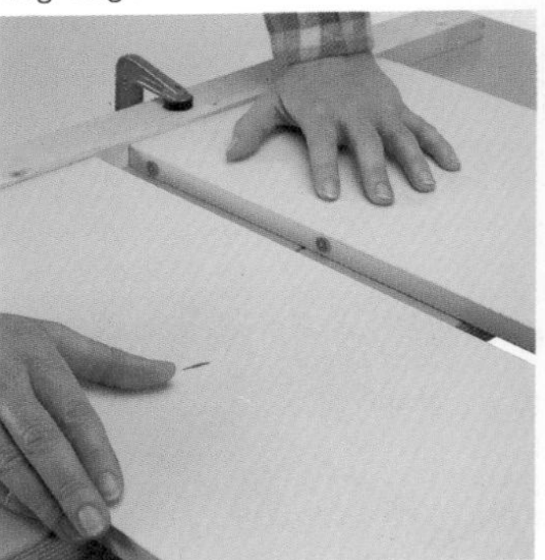

Line up the ends against a straight-edge while the point marks are made. This method can be used to lengthen a kitchen worktop.

HELPFUL TIP

The trickiest part of making a dowel joint can be deciding on the depth of the holes – particularly with mitre or T-joints.

First draw the joint to the correct size, as it will look when complete. Rest a dowel over the drawing so that it is far enough away from the faces of the panels for the bit not to penetrate. With a mitre joint this means having the dowel nearer the inner corner.

Mark the dowel position on the drawing, ensuring that its length fits in. If necessary cut it shorter.

Fit the depth stop on the bit for each hole according to the drawing, allowing $\frac{1}{16}$in (2mm) extra to allow for trapped glue.

How to use a plane

A plane must be very sharp and correctly set if it is to work properly, so check the sharpness and adjustment before each job.

Put a new blade into a replaceable-blade plane when the old one is blunt. With a conventional bench plane sharpen the blade in the same way as a chisel (page 158), but hold it at an angle to the oilstone if it is wider than the stone.

It may be possible to find a local hardware shop that will sharpen the blade for you.

Before planing old wood, check that there are no nails in it. They would ruin the blade.

Painted wood must be stripped (page 105) before planing, otherwise the blade will not bite properly and will blunt rapidly.

PARTS OF A BENCH PLANE

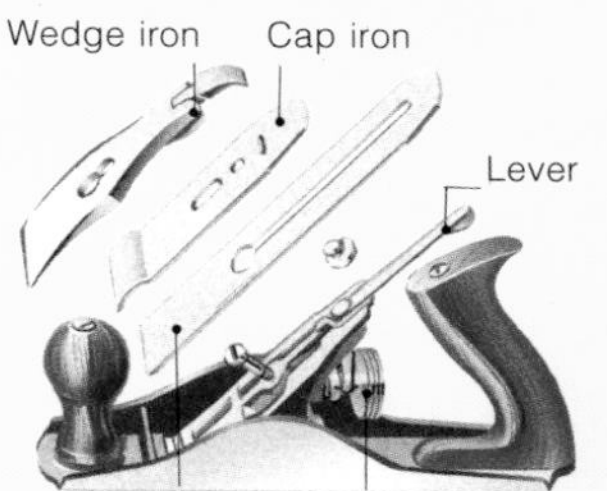

The blade and the cap iron are screwed together, with the cap iron about 1/16in (2mm) from the cutting edge. The blade is held securely in place with the wedge iron. To remove the blade, lift the wedge lever and slide the wedge out. Remove the blade and cap iron and release the screw. When replacing, put the blade's bevel face downwards. When it is not in use, protect the blade by wrapping the plane in a cloth.

ADJUSTING THE BLADE OF A PLANE

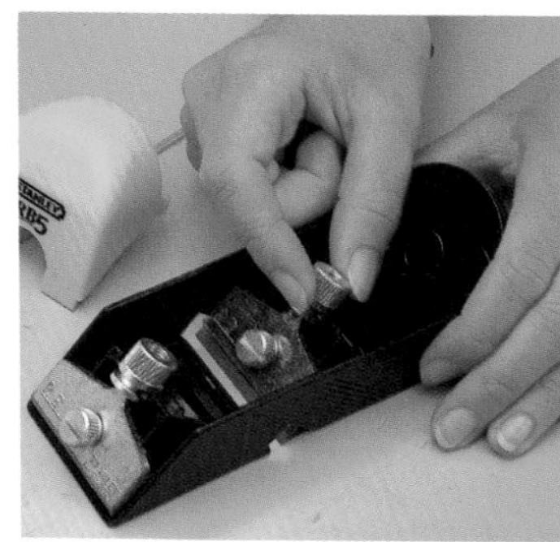

1 Turn the knurled knob to adjust the depth of the blade. Set it so that you can feel it just protruding, but be careful not to cut yourself.

2 Look along the bottom of the plane and ensure that the blade is level. On a bench plane, level it with the lever.

3 Try it out. If the cut is too fine, increase the blade depth; if too much is being cut off, retract it.

SMOOTHING A PIECE OF WOOD

1 Hold the wood firmly – in a vice if it is small or between two stops on a flat surface if it is long. The long jaws of a portable workbench are ideal.

2 Press down on the front of the plane at the start of the stroke, then keep an even pressure for the main stroke, easing the pressure towards the back as you finish. Try to produce ribbon-like shavings.

3 When planing long edges, guide the plane by pressing down with the thumb of the front hand and running the fingers along the face of the wood. Make the stroke the full length of the wood.

4 Check frequently that the edge is level by holding a straightedge along it. Use a try square to check that the edge is square.

CHAMFERING AN EDGE

Hold the wood upright in a vice, and use the fingers of the front hand as a guide, as when planing a long edge. Press the plane down with the thumb.

PLANING END GRAIN

Hold the wood in a vice, as low as possible, and plane from each end, working towards the centre. Use short strokes that do not go the full length.

Abrasive paper for a smooth surface

To get a smooth finish on softwood, hardwood or wood-veneered chipboard, wrap a piece of abrasive paper around a cork sanding block and rub it along the grain of the wood. Avoid rubbing across the grain; cross-grain scratches take a lot of effort to remove and show up sharply if left.

Abrasive papers are made to finish the surface of wood, not alter its size. On well-planed timber use two grades of fine paper – first the coarsest fine, then a medium fine.

Various abrasive grits are available, bonded to sheet materials. Glasspaper is the cheapest, but the most popular is the much tougher aluminium oxide, which will last longer than glasspaper.

Store abrasive paper where it will not get damp – not in a garage or shed. Once it is slightly damp the glue fails and the grit falls off.

SANDING VENEERED CHIPBOARD

The wood veneers used on veneered chipboard are extremely thin. When smoothing a board before final finishing, take care not to wear through the veneer, particularly at the edges and corners.

Use fine abrasive paper so that it smooths without scoring. And always wrap the paper around a cork sanding block to distribute the pressure evenly.

USING AN ELECTRIC SANDER

An orbital sander saves effort in smoothing a large flat area. Ready-cut abrasive paper strips are fixed to the bottom of the machine.

Move the sander along the grain in overlapping strips. The machine moves the paper in tiny circles so the last sanding should be done parallel to the grain by hand.

HELPFUL TIPS

For fine finishing work on furniture, you can substitute fine steel wool for abrasive papers. There are various grades available. The coarseness of the wool is indicated by a number – 4 is extra-coarse, 0 is fine and 0000 is super-fine.

The fine, chisel-like cutting action of the wool on the wood produces a very smooth, scratch-free surface.

Achieving a perfect finish

FILLING HOLES IN WOOD

Wood must have a well-prepared surface before the final finish is applied, otherwise the appearance will be disappointing. So any holes should be filled before the wood is finally sanded smooth.

If the wood is to be left its natural colour, buy a wood filler that matches. Fillers are made in a limited colour range, so look at the filler colour chart in the shop and choose the nearest. Preferably take a piece of the wood with you. Do not match the wood against wet filler. It will become paler as it dries.

If the wood is to be painted and used indoors, use an interior filler.

1 After sanding, use a fine brush to remove dust, brushing in the direction of the grain to clear all crevices.

Sunlight darkens new wood, so never leave anything standing on a freshly sanded surface; it will cause a light patch.

2 Press the filler into the holes, taking care not to spread it into the surrounding grain.

3 Wait until it has dried to the same colour all over – perhaps 15-30 minutes – then sand it flat.

4 Before starting the next stage – staining or finishing - sand off any fingermarks, and remove all dust from the bench and the floor. Cleanliness is essential.

USING WOOD STAIN ON NEW WOOD

If you want the colour of the wood to match existing furniture, either use an appropriately veneered

Achieving a perfect finish (continued)

chipboard or use a softwood and colour it with a wood stain.

Stains are available in a wide range. Look at the colour charts before buying and begin by testing the colour on an offcut of the wood. To apply the stain use a new washing-up sponge, a non-fluffy cloth, or brush.

1 Apply a liberal even coat of the stain over the whole surface of the wood, working quickly in the direction of the grain.

2 Wipe off any excess stain with a clean, non-fluffy cloth before it has dried, still working along the line of the grain.

3 If areas of wood filler do not take the stain as well as the surrounding wood, use a fine watercolour brush to touch them in with more stain until the colour is even.

4 Wait for the stain to dry. Water-based stains take half a day, spirit-based stains about an hour.

5 As some stains raise the grain, smooth the wood with very fine abrasive paper.

6 Rub on a light coating of the stain to colour any exposed grain.

7 Wipe over the surface with a clean cloth.

Applying surface finishes

Prepare the wood surface well before applying any finish. Grease, damp and dirt will spoil the final result. All finishes magnify defects in the wood. So smooth and clean the surface with fine-grade abrasive paper or steel wool, working only in the direction of the grain.

Many finishing preparations are available, but polyurethane varnish, Danish oil, silicone wax and teak oil are the easiest to use.

Polyurethane varnish and Danish oil give resistance to heat, water and staining. They also fill the grain of all but the coarsest timber. Wax and teak oil are less time-consuming to apply but do not give the same level of protection.

Applying French polish requires experience, and it is no longer used in furniture making, except for reproduction antiques. It is not recommended for DIY.

Use the following instructions in conjunction with the maker's instructions; changes in formulation may require different methods.

PREPARING A WORK SPACE

Finishing must be carried out in a well-ventilated room so that volatile fumes disperse quickly. No naked flame, such as a gas ring, pilot light or cigarette, should be allowed in the room.

The room should also be warm to allow the finish to dry. Cover floors and anything else that might get splashed.

> HELPFUL TIPS
>
> Do not rest timber on newspaper. The ink will transfer onto the wood and may not be seen until later.
>
> Before any varnishing, polishing or staining is begun, a cabinet should be completed down to the last detail.

POLYURETHANE VARNISH

Varnish with gloss, satin or matt finish can be bought in quantities from ¼ litre upwards. It is available either clear or tinted, to simulate mahogany, oak, teak, pine and other timbers. Plain colours including red, yellow, green and blue are also available. Polyurethane varnish can be applied to timber or man-made board, on either stained or natural surfaces.

Colour in varnish does not penetrate the wood but lies on top, so does not give the depth and richness of wood stain. But coloured varnish is easier to apply and gives an even colour (differences in absorption rate can make directly applied colours patchy).

1 Apply the varnish evenly over the whole surface with a brush, finishing off with long, light brush strokes in line with the grain.

2 Allow to dry overnight, then sand down to a smooth surface with a very fine abrasive paper supported on a flat sanding block, used in the direction of the grain.

3 Wipe the surface with a dry cloth and apply a second coat.

4 On areas of heavy use such as a worktop, apply a third coat.

DANISH OIL

Danish oil, which has an almost clear satin finish, is one of the easiest finishes to use. Drying time is between four and eight hours.

Brushes can be cleaned with white spirit. Rags used for oiling should be burnt or stored in a sealed metal container. In unusual circumstances they may self-ignite.

A minimum of two coats will be needed – three on worktops.

1 Apply a liberal coat over the surface with a brush or cotton cloth and leave for a few minutes.

2 When 40-50 per cent of the area looks drier than the rest, firmly wipe over the whole surface with a clean, lint-free cloth. This will redistribute surplus oil.

3 When the first coat is thoroughly dry, rub the surface lightly with very fine abrasive paper on softwood, or steel wool grade 00 on hardwood. Work in the direction of the grain.

4 Apply a second coat.

5 Wipe off any surplus oil with a clean cloth when the surface starts to feel tacky, wiping in the direction of the grain.

6 Leave to dry and finish with a final sanding down.

7 Repeat for a third coat if necessary. If the last coat has 'pips' on the surface give a light sanding down. If not, leave it alone.

SILICONE WAX

Wax by itself does not give a satisfactory finish on softwood. And on light coloured hardwoods such as ramin, a wax-only finish gives a rather dirty colour. The darker the hardwood and the closer the grain, the better a wax finish looks.

Wax, used on its own, takes years of frequent application to gather the patina that is associated with old furniture.

A good compromise is to seal the wood with Danish oil and then apply wax on top. Use a good quality silicone wax. A cream or spray wax can be applied later to maintain a good appearance.

1 Prepare the wood and apply a coat of Danish oil. On porous timber a second coat may be necessary to provide an even seal.

2 When dry, sand with a very fine abrasive paper.

3 Using a clean, lint-free cloth, apply a generous coat of silicone wax over the whole surface and rub it into an even coating.

4 Leave it for several hours to harden. Then, using a stiff, clean shoe brush, buff the wax in the direction of the grain.

5 Wrap a clean duster around the brush and give the surface a final buffing.

TEAK OIL

Developed for finishing teak, the oil gives a matt finish to hardwoods.

It is applied in the same way as Danish oil but it does not give either the shallow-grain filling or satin finish of Danish oil.

FURNITURE RESTORER

To remove a build-up of old wax and dirt from furniture, apply a furniture restorer with a clean cloth and rub gently. The old wax will dissolve and can be wiped off. Fresh wax or oil can then be applied.

THE EFFECT OF STAIN AND DIFFERENT FINISHES

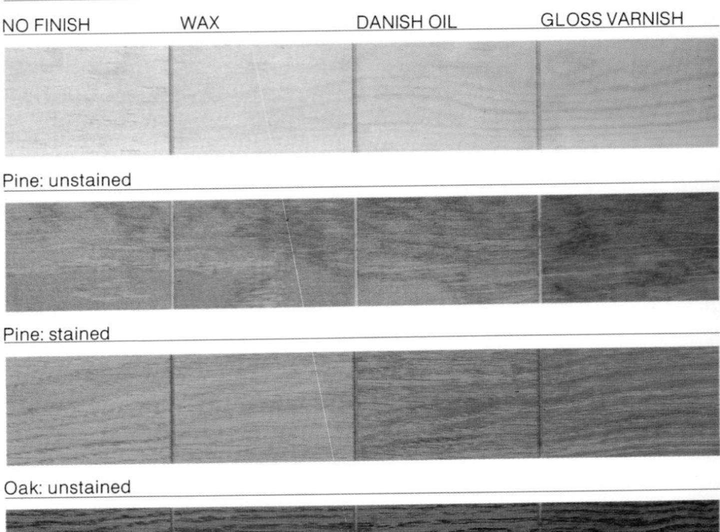

Making shelf brackets for an alcove

One of the most common situations where shelves are needed is in an alcove beside a chimney breast. But no standard brackets are easily available to fix to the side walls of the alcove.

Shelving track can be fixed on the back wall, but it is unnecessarily expensive if only fixed shelves are needed. Neat brackets (page 234) can be made cheaply and simply from either wood or metal, using the minimum of tools.

WOOD BATTENS

Wooden battens can be cut and screwed to the side walls of the alcove. Use battens that are about 2in × 1in (50mm × 25mm) nominal, and ensure that each pair lines up horizontally.

The battens are fairly unobtrusive even if left square-ended, but to make them less noticeable the ends can be angled or curved.

You may wish to screw the shelves to the brackets to prevent them from twisting or becoming dislodged. If they are made of chipboard, let mirror plates into the battens by recessing slightly with a chisel, and screw up through the single hole of the mirror plate into the shelf. If the shelves are made of solid wood you will need to allow for expansion and contraction, so use shrinkage plates, and screw through the slot into the shelf.

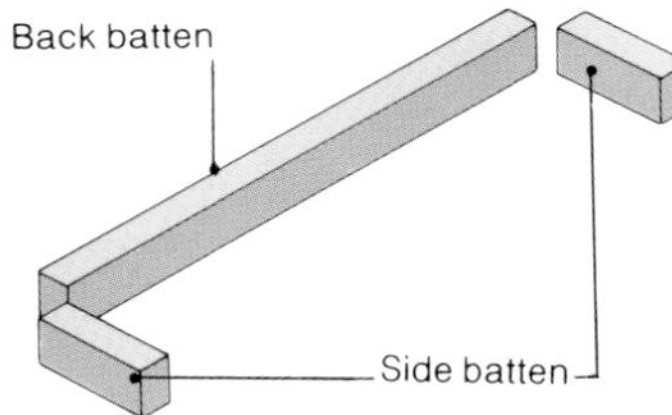

For long shelves, or where the load is heavy, a batten can also be fitted to the back wall to give extra support.

BATTENS FROM METAL BAR

Square aluminium bar about ½in × ½in (13mm × 13mm) in cross section can be drilled to give an invisible support to solid wooden shelves that are at least 1in (25mm) thick. This technique is not suitable for chipboard which would be weakened too much.

A rebate is cut in the underside of each shelf end, using a circular saw set to the correct depth of cut, and then making a series of side-by-side cuts from the underside. Smooth off the rebate with a chisel.

Aluminium bar can also be used to make small brackets for supporting glass shelves. Cover the upper surface of the bars with felt or foam plastic stuck down with contact adhesive or double-sided adhesive tape. Then lay the glass across them.

ANGLE-ALUMINIUM BATTENS

Buy angle metal from a DIY centre. The width can be either 1in × 1in (25mm × 25mm) or 1¼in × 1¼in (32mm × 32mm).

Make fixing holes with a power drill and a high-speed-steel (HSS) bit. The brackets can be fitted to the wall in either of two ways – so that the shelves drop in or stand above them. For long shelves or where heavy weights must be supported, fix a third piece of angle aluminium along the back wall.

If you wish to fix chipboard shelves to the brackets, drill a pair of screw holes in each bracket. For solid wood shelves you will need to allow for expansion and contraction, so cut slots in the brackets to take the screws. To cut slots in metal, drill two holes close together and then file out the metal between them.

WOOD BATTENS

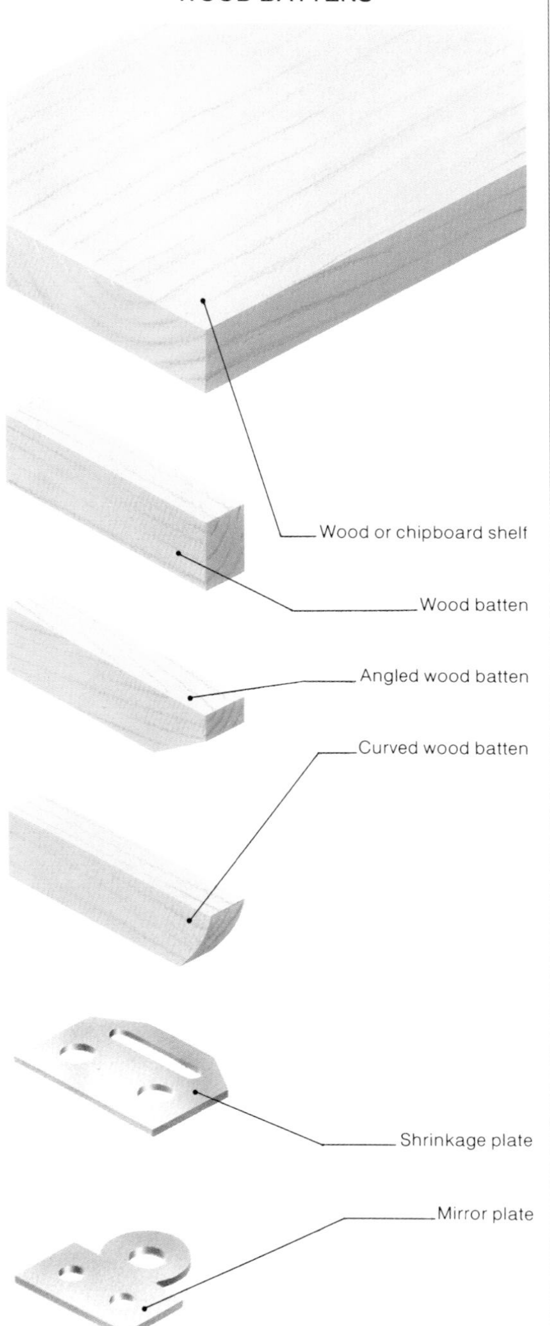

The shelf rests on a batten at each side of the alcove. The front end of the battens can be square or shaped to make them less obvious. Metal plates are used for screwing the shelf to the battens.

BATTENS FROM METAL BAR

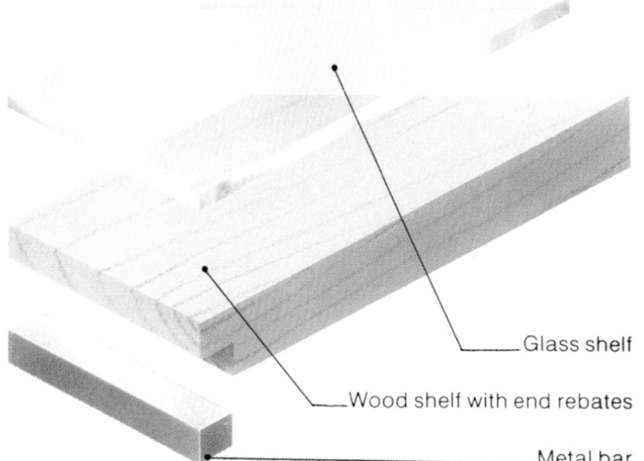

A glass shelf rests on top of drilled metal bars screwed into each side of the alcove. A shelf made of softwood or hardwood can be fitted almost invisibly, with the bars in rebates at each end.

ANGLE-ALUMINIUM BATTENS

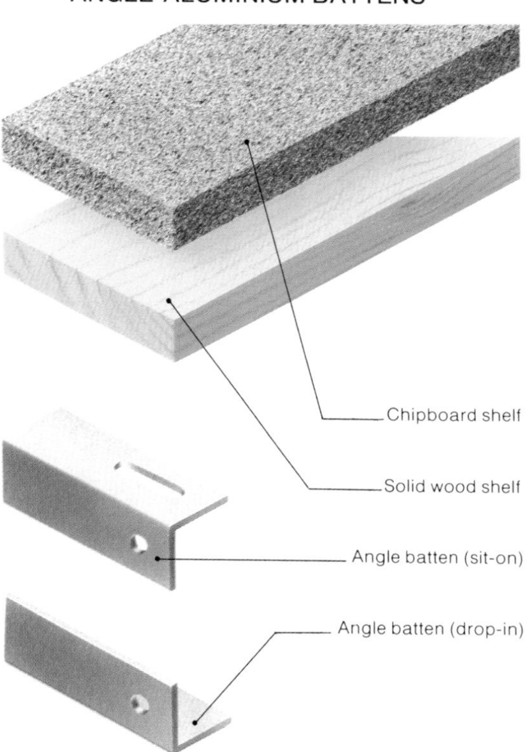

The shelf may sit on top of or drop into angle-aluminium strips at each side of the alcove. If a solid-wood shelf is screwed to the bracket, a slot needs to be cut to accommodate expansion.

Putting up a fixed shelf

Before deciding where to fix wall brackets, check with a metal detector to make sure that there are no hidden water or gas pipes, electrical or TV wires in the wall.

In the absence of a metal detector, check both sides of the wall for electrical, gas or water appliances. Most cables and pipes lie either vertically or horizontally.

Right-angled brackets will need screws about 1¾in (44mm) long to fix them to the wall. The screw must go through the plaster and at least 1in (25mm) into the brickwork or wood stud. For finding vertical posts in a stud wall, see page 230.

Avoid using winged wall plugs to fix brackets to thin hollow walls unless the shelf is only to be used to hold a light decorative object.

The screws should be the heaviest gauge that the holes in the bracket will take – usually No. 8 gauge on small ones and No. 10 or 12 on the larger ones.

You will need

Tools Pencil; spirit level; drill; masonry or wood bit to fit wall plugs; screwdriver. Possibly a straight wooden batten.

Materials Brackets; screws for fixing brackets to wall; wall plugs to fit screws; shelf; small screws for fixing shelf to brackets.

1 Mark the wall with a pencil at the height you want the bottom of the shelf. Use a spirit level to ensure the marks are horizontal. For a long shelf, rest the spirit level on a straight wooden batten.

2 Hold one bracket against the wall with the top against the mark. Use the spirit level to check that it is vertical, and mark the wall through the screw holes with the pencil.

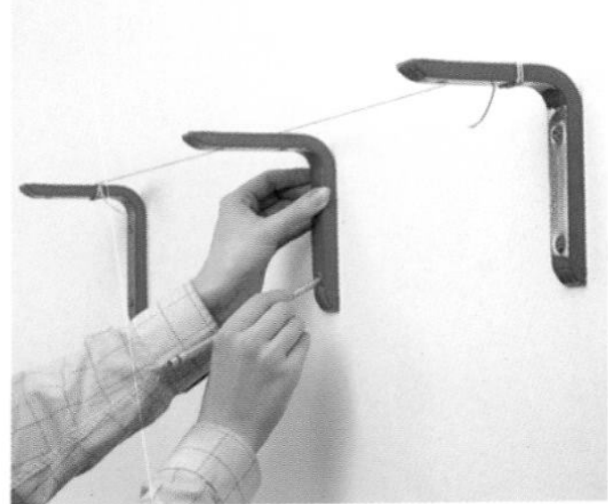

3 Repeat for the second bracket. If there are more than two brackets, it is best to fix the outside ones to the wall, and then tie a piece of string tightly between them across the tops. Then the intermediate brackets can be lined up exactly.

4 Drill holes about 1¾in (44mm) into the wall. Use a masonry bit (or a twist bit for wooden studs).

5 Insert plugs into masonry, and screw the brackets tightly to the wall. If the plug turns in the wall as you drive in the screw, remove it, insert a larger one and try again.

Do not use plugs in wood.

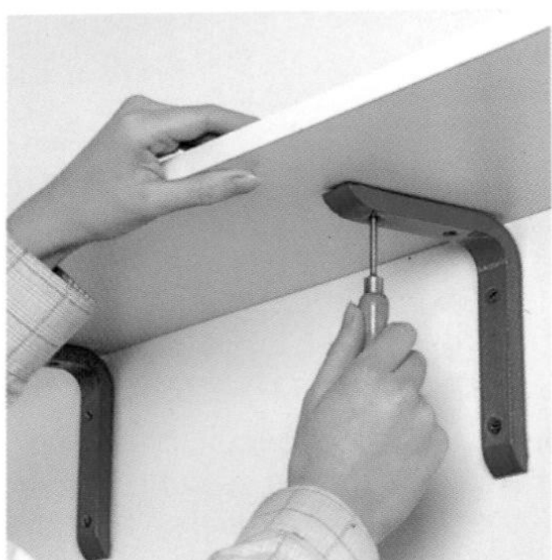

6 Lay the shelf across the bracket. Using a pencil or bradawl, mark the underside through the holes.

7 Drill pilot holes for the small screws. Do not drill right through.

8 Screw the shelf in position.

A stack of fixed shelves

Several brackets can be fitted above each other to build a stack of fixed shelving more cheaply than with track systems.

It is an advantage to fix battens to the wall first. Then the brackets can be fixed to the battens. This saves time and helps to line up the brackets accurately. It also saves the wall from becoming peppered with holes.

There is just one snag – if the backs of the shelves are required to touch the wall, the shelves will have to be cut around each batten.

Battens should be at least a nominal 1in (25mm) thick and at least 1½in (38mm) wide. That is the minimum needed for the bracket-fixing screws which should be ¾in (19mm) long.

For heavy loads, using shelves wider than 9in (230mm), use thicker battens and longer screws, and increase the number of wall-fixings.

You will need

Tools Steel tape measure; pencil; saw; try square; drill and twist bits; countersink bit; masonry bit to fit wall plugs; spirit level; bradawl; screwdriver. Perhaps a chisel.

Materials Softwood battens – at least 1in (25mm) nominal in thickness; brackets; 2½in (60mm) No. 12 gauge screws (for fixing battens to wall); wall plugs to fit No. 12 gauge screws; screws for fixing brackets; screws for fixing shelves.

1 Decide on the number of shelves and the distance between them.

2 Measure the distance from the top of the top bracket to the bottom of the bottom bracket and add about 1in (25mm) at each end.

3 Cut the battens to this length.

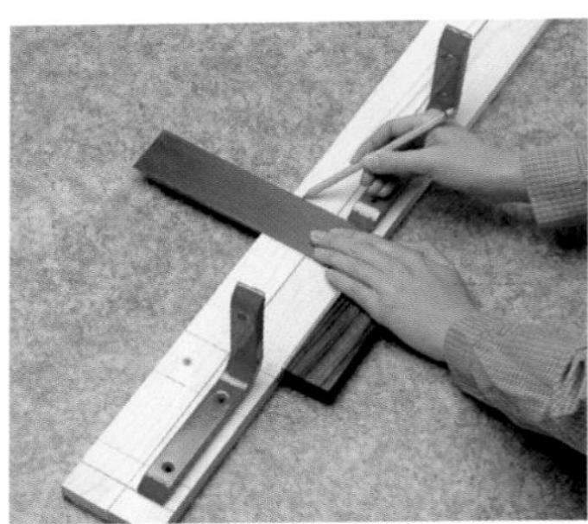

4 Using a try square, mark the positions for the brackets, and the positions for their screw holes.

5 Mark the positions for the wall-fixing screws where they will not clash with the bracket screws. Use three screws on each batten – one near the top and bottom and one in the centre – or four on a batten holding four or five brackets.

6 Drill clearance or pilot holes in the battens, using the correct size bits (page 162). Countersink those for the wall-fixing screws.

7 Sand and paint or varnish the battens.

8 Hold one batten up to the wall and check with a spirit level that it is vertical. Mark the position for the wall-fixing screws with a bradawl.

9 Drill the holes for the wall plugs, using a masonry bit for solid walls or a twist bit for wooden studs. (For finding studs see page 230.)

10 Insert the plugs and screw the batten to the wall. Drive the screws home tightly.

11 Repeat with the second batten (and any others), checking with the spirit level that the tops line up horizontally.

12 Screw the brackets in place.

13 To make the shelves touch the wall, hold them on the brackets, mark the positions of the battens and chisel out notches.

14 Mark the pilot holes for the small screws on the underside of the shelves. Drill the holes and screw the shelves to the brackets.

CUTTING AROUND THE BATTENS

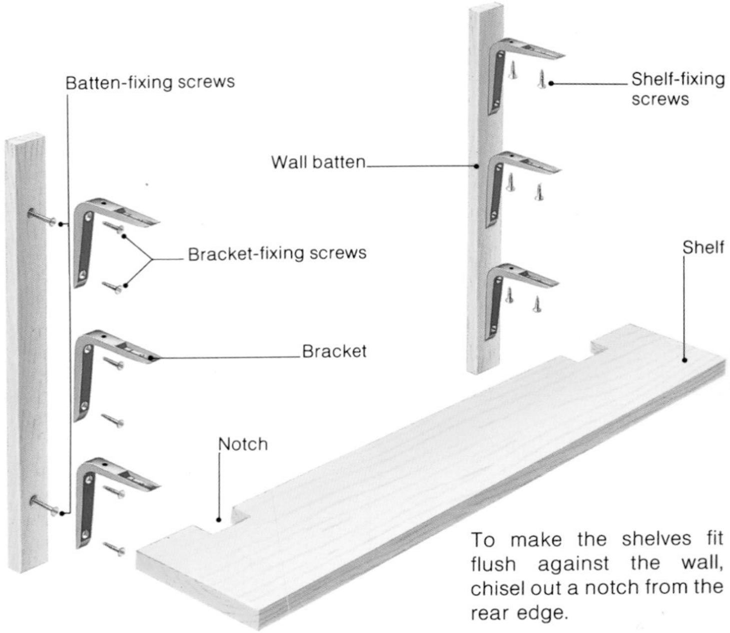

To make the shelves fit flush against the wall, chisel out a notch from the rear edge.

CHOOSING FIXED BRACKETS FOR SHELVES

Most right-angle brackets have one arm longer than the other. Fix the long arm to the wall, unless the instructions state otherwise.

The distance between brackets depends on several factors. See the table on page 174.

The width of a shelf should be only about 1in (25mm) greater than the length of the horizontal arm of the bracket. Large overhangs can lead to the shelf becoming overloaded, which may cause the brackets to fail.

Always secure shelves by screwing them to the brackets.

This chart gives examples of the different designs of fixed brackets available.

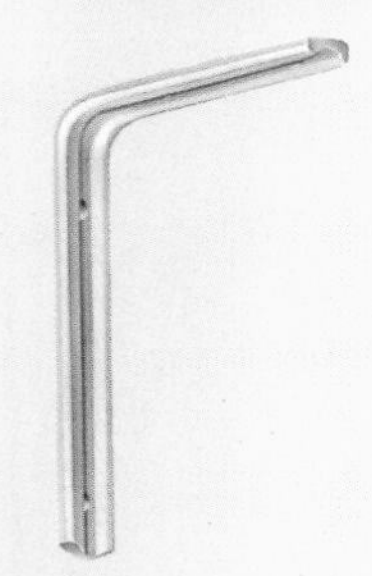

High-strength steel strip. Holes for round-head screws.

Sizes range from 3in × 2in (75mm × 50mm) to 10in × 8in (250mm × 200mm).

Galvanised finish (silvery colour).

May not be exactly 90 degrees. Bend with vice and hammer to correct. Very cheap.

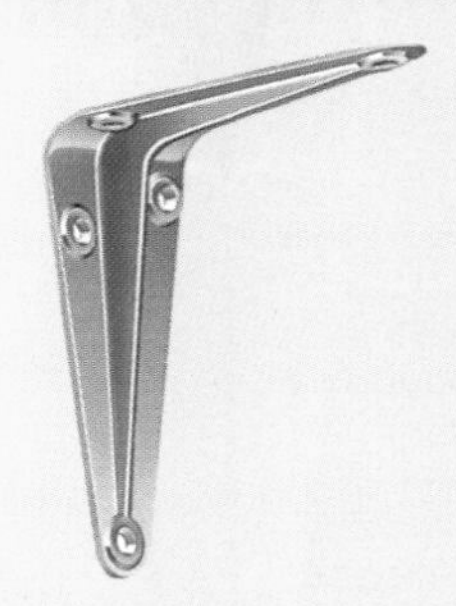

Lightweight pressed steel. Has holes for countersunk screws.

Sizes range from 4in × 3in (100mm × 75mm) to 12in × 10in (300mm × 250mm).

Dip-painted black or grey finish.

Finish rather poor, inclined to chip. Very inexpensive; useful where appearance not important, as in sheds and garages.

Heavyweight pressed steel. Has holes for countersunk screws.

One size only – 4in × 3in (100mm × 75mm).

Epoxy-coated. Red, black, white, brown.

Good finish. Inexpensive. But size suitable only for small shelves.

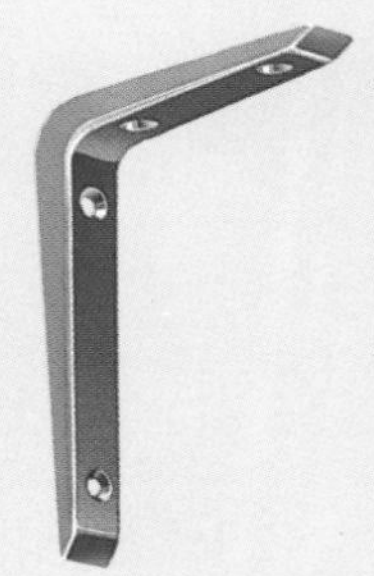

Medium/heavyweight pressed steel. Has holes for countersunk screws.

Sizes range from 4in × 3in (100mm × 75mm) to 10in × 8in (250mm × 200mm).

Epoxy-coated finish. Red, brown, gold, yellow, green, black, silver.

Good finish with attractive colours. Inexpensive.

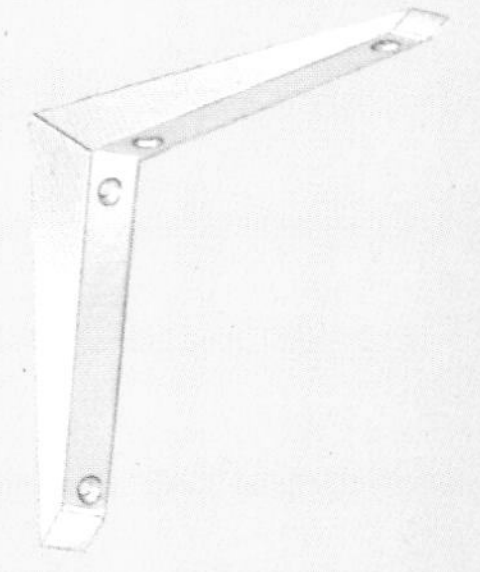

Heavyweight pressed and welded steel. Has holes for countersunk screws.

The sizes range from 8in × 8in (200mm × 200mm) to 14in × 14in (350mm × 350mm).

Epoxy-coated finish. White only.

Good finish. The manufacturers state load capacity on wrapper.

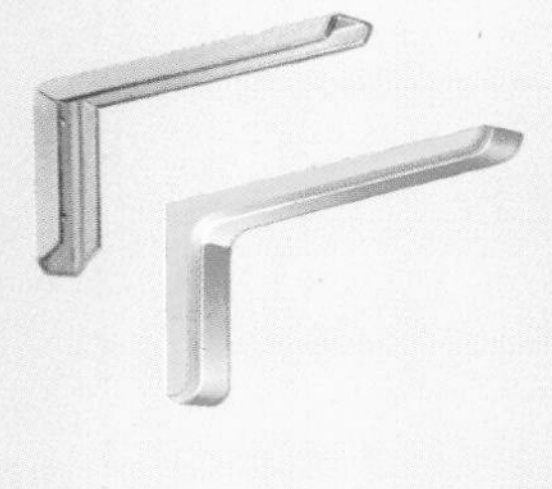

Heavyweight pressed steel with snap-on cover in coloured plastic. Has holes for round-head screws.

In one size only – 7¼in × 4½in (186mm × 115mm).

Moulded plastic covers in red, blue, yellow and green.

Screws are hidden under the plastic cover. A range of shelves is made in matching plastic veneer. Short arm of bracket is fitted to wall.

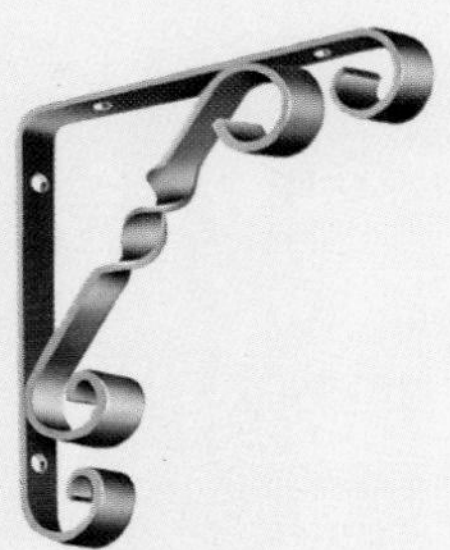

'Wrought-iron' style medium weight. Flat steel strip with brace. Holes for round-head screws.

Sizes range from 4in × 4in (100mm × 100mm) to 9½in × 9½in (240mm × 240mm).

Good finish. Two designs with slight variations. The bracing piece makes screws difficult to turn.

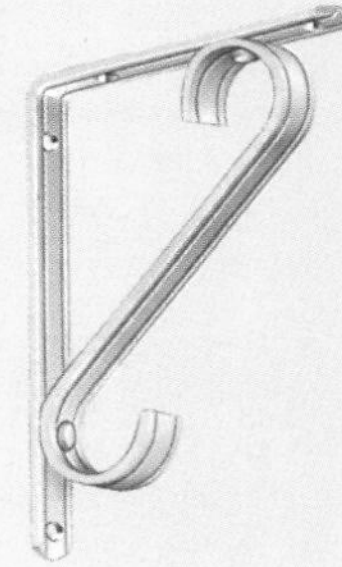

Lightweight aluminium strip with diagonal brace. Round-head screws supplied.

Sizes: 6in × 4in (150mm × 100mm) and 8in × 6in (200mm × 150mm).

Finished in anodised silver, gold and white.

Various designs available. The bracing piece makes screws difficult to turn.

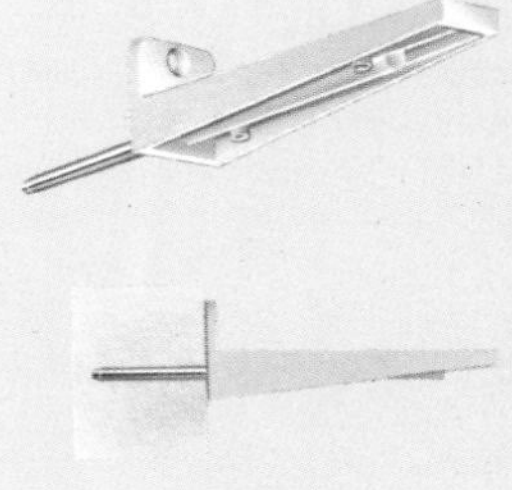

Radiator shelf bracket. Medium weight. The moulded plastic arm is supported on a steel pin.

Sizes: 4½in (115mm) and 7½in (190mm).

Finished in white or brown plastic.

The short vertical arm is fitted upwards. The steel pin fixed into the wall provides most of the support.

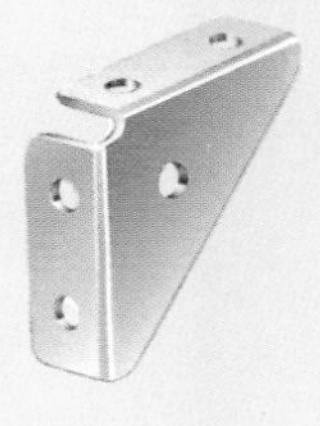

Medium/lightweight pressed-steel flange bracket suitable for narrow shelves where other brackets are too large. Holes for screws.

Size: 2in × 2in (50mm × 50mm).

Cadmium-plated finish.

Designed for reinforcing the corners of cabinets, but suitable for shelves.

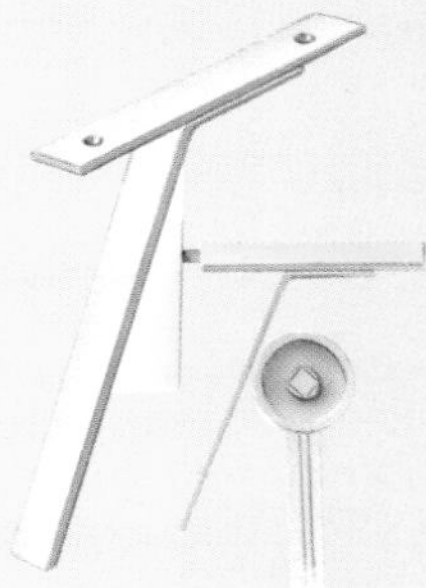

Radiator shelf bracket. Light/medium weight. No screws needed for fitting to wall.

For 5in or 6in (125mm or 150mm) shelf.

Galvanised finish (silvery colour).

For wedging behind a panel radiator. No wall fixing needed.

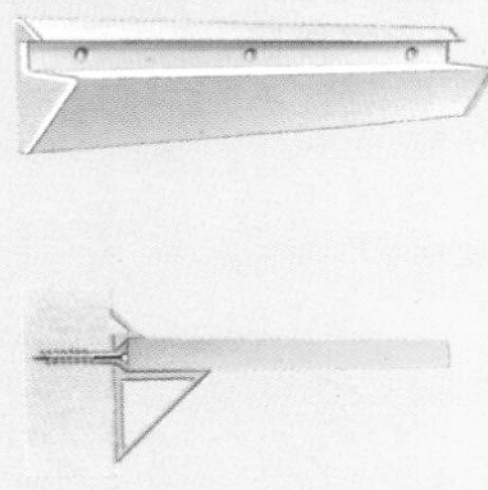

A high-strength continuous aluminium bracket to support a shelf along its full length. Screws supplied.

Takes ⅝in (15mm) or ¾in (18mm) thick board or ¼in (6mm) glass shelf. Lengths range from 2ft (610mm) to 8ft (2.4m).

Anodised-silver or epoxy-coated finish.

Neat appearance. Can be used for radiator shelves.

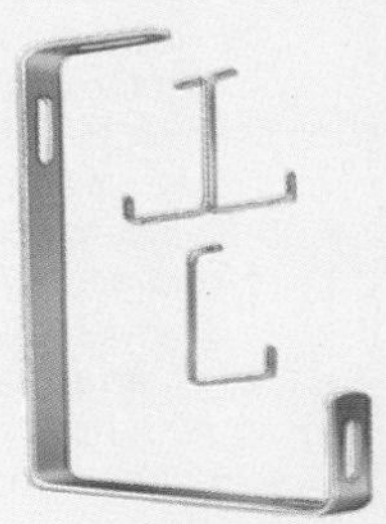

Medium weight for utility shelving in workshops and garages. Holds two shelves about 8¼in (210mm) apart. Screws supplied.

Size: 9½in × 6½in (240mm × 165mm).

Epoxy-coated finish in orange only.

Can be mounted to support two shelves; to support a single, wider shelf; or to hang from a ceiling.

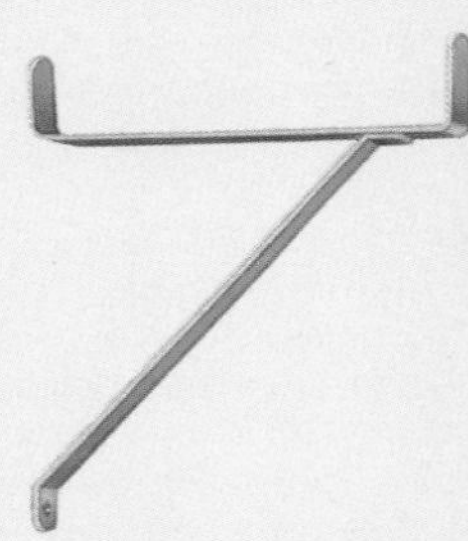

Medium/heavyweight for utility shelving in workshops or garages. Holds a single shelf. Round-head screws supplied.

Size: 12¼in (310mm) wide × 11in (280mm) deep.

Epoxy-coated finish in orange only.

Can be used to support a shelf or long lengths of timber.

Adjustable track shelving systems

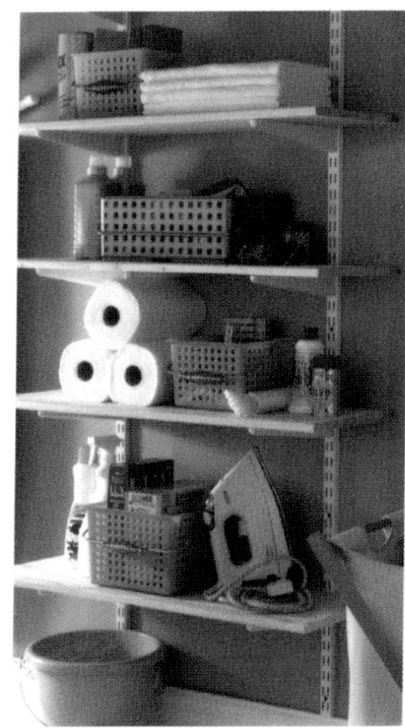

Track shelving systems consist of tracks which are fixed to a wall, plus brackets which fit on the tracks.

The shelves can be raised or lowered by changing the position of the brackets. Brackets that fit into slots are adjusted in jumps of about 1in (25mm). Consequently a pair of tracks must be fitted at exactly the same height for the shelves to be level

Shelves should be slightly wider than the brackets, but avoid wide overhangs which could tempt you to overload the system. Never put tracks farther apart than the maker recommends.

Load capacity

Lightweight systems will hold a few books or ornaments, but are not safe for a long run of books, piles of china or a television set.

Medium-weight systems are designed to support normal domestic loads, including a TV set.

Medium/heavy systems are needed for collections of hardback books or stacks of plates.

Colour and finish

The most common finish on aluminium systems is silver anodising. This is a hard metal plating which stays clean and bright. Other colours are available, but they show damage more obviously, so inspect before you buy.

Some cheaper aluminium systems have white-painted finishes which chip easily.

Steel systems are either coated with damage-resistant epoxy polyester or stove enamelled, which is less hardwearing.

PUTTING UP THE TRACK

Always ensure that the tracks are securely fixed to the wall. On a solid wall, drive the screws into wall plugs. In a hollow partition wall, screw directly into the vertical wooden studs inside the wall. For ways of locating the studs, see page 230.

The screws need to be at least 2in (50mm) long to go through the track, the plaster and well into the brickwork or stud. The diameter of the screw will probably be 8-12 gauge, depending on the design of the track.

Tracks are placed 2ft 3in (700mm) apart for shelves made of chipboard or timber at least ¾in (18mm) thick. They are placed 2ft (610mm) apart for ⅝in (15mm) chipboard. Do not put them farther apart, or there is a danger that the shelves will bend or break.

You will need

Tools Pencil; drill; masonry bit the right size for the wall plugs; screwdriver; straight wooden batten; spirit level; bradawl.

Materials Tracks and brackets; shelves; screws to fix tracks to wall; wall plugs the right size for the screws; screws to fix shelves to brackets.

1 Hold the first track to the wall and mark the position of the top screw with a pencil.

2 Using a spirit level or plumb bob, draw a vertical line down the wall equal in length to the track.

3 Measure the position of the other tracks and draw similar vertical lines for each. Once the first vertical has been set, others can be measured off with a tape measure.

4 Use a spirit level to mark the position of the top screw hole on each vertical line, level with the first screw position. It is essential that slotted tracks are fixed at exactly the same height. Otherwise the shelves will not be level.

5 Drill and plug each top screw hole. Screw the tracks temporarily in position, but do not tighten. When they are all in place, check that their tops are level.

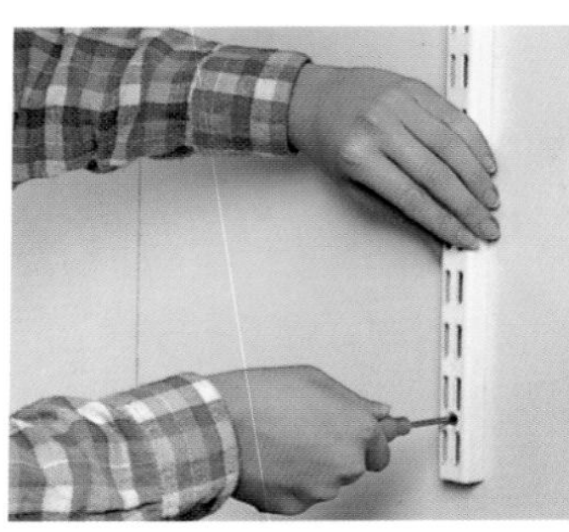

6 Use the bradawl or pencil to mark the positions of the other holes on the centre lines. Remove the tracks, or swing them sideways, and drill and plug the holes.

7 Screw the tracks in position.

8 As the screws tighten, watch the track to make certain it is not bending because of an uneven wall. Pack behind the screws with hardboard or cardboard where hollows occur.

9 Fit the brackets into the correct slots and put on the shelves. If you want the backs of the shelves to touch the wall, see *A stack of fixed shelves*, step 13 (page 170).

Line up the shelves so that their ends are above one another.

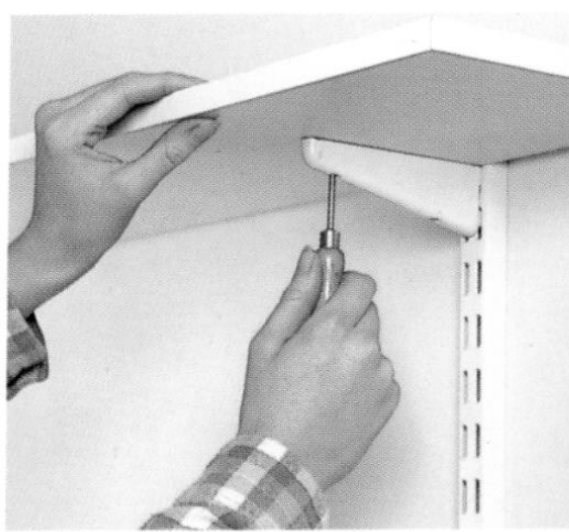

10 Mark screw holes in the underside of the shelves by pushing the bradawl through the holes in the brackets.

11 Make pilot holes for the small screws with the bradawl, and screw the shelves in place.

Screwing the shelves to the brackets improves the strength of the unit, and also prevents the shelves from tipping up if a heavy weight is put on one end. It also prevents them from sliding if they are knocked.

MORE FLEXIBILITY WITH THREE TRACKS

When only two tracks are used, the shelves can be adjusted for height, but each one must run the full width of the system.

Three or more tracks enable shelves to go halfway at one height and the other half at a different height.

This allows greater flexibility in storing objects of different sizes and can add to the appearance. Shelves of different depths can also be used.

The closeness of the shelves in height is restricted by the depth of the bracket, plus the thickness of the shelf. So shelves on large brackets normally cannot be closer than 4¾in (120mm).

If you want two adjoining shelves to be even closer, the Element shelving system has brackets designed for steel shelving which can be staggered, in slots side by side, rather than one above the other.

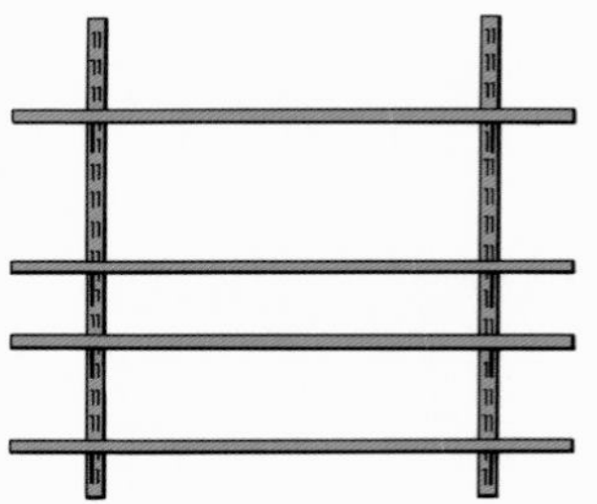

Two tracks All the shelves must extend the full width of the tracks.

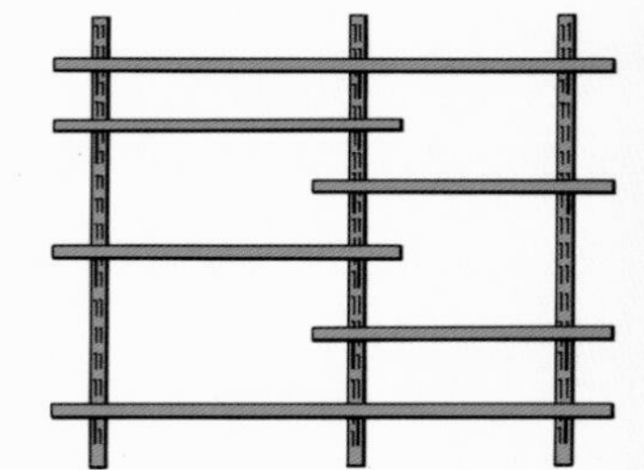

Three tracks Shelf lengths can differ, giving varied spacing.

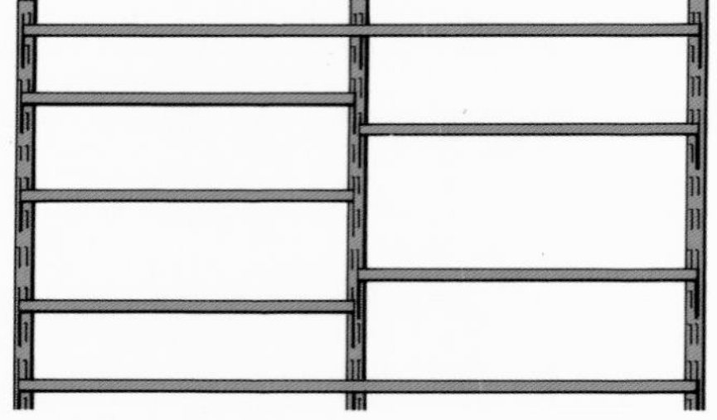

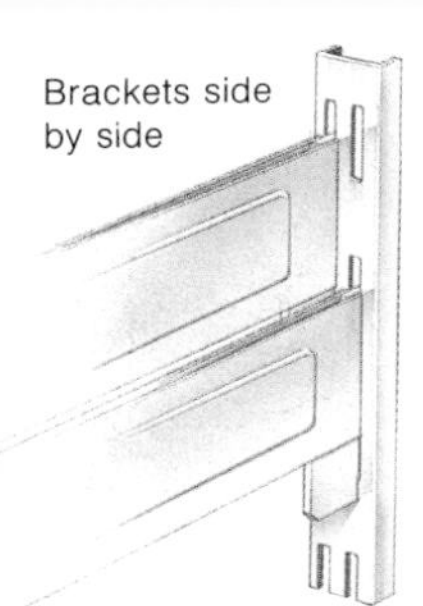

Shelf spacing Usually there must be the bracket depth between shelves. One system, however, allows closer placing with brackets side by side.

CHOOSING TRACK SHELVING

	LOAD CAPACITY	TRACK LENGTHS	BRACKET SIZES	MATERIAL	COLOURS	ACCESSORIES
Spur Budget (unnamed type also available)	Light	24, 36, 48, 72in (610, 915, 1220, 1830mm)	A range from 6–14in (150–355mm)	Aluminium	Silver, white, gold, black, magnolia	None
Tebrax	Medium	Multiples of 12in (305mm) up to 12ft (3660mm)	A range from 4–24in (100–610mm)	Aluminium	Silver, gold, black, white	Book ends
Spur Edge Slot	Medium	20, 40, 60, 80in (500,1000, 1500, 2000mm)	A range from 5-12½in (125-320mm)	Steel	White, black, magnolia	None
Element Single Slot	Medium	20, 40, 60, 80, 100in (500, 1000, 1500, 2000, 2500mm)	4, 6, 8, 10, 12, 14, 16in (100, 150, 200 250, 300, 350, 400mm)	Steel	White, black, magnolia, gold, silver	Book ends, book end shelf supports, end caps, wall plates, clip on shelving support, continuous shelving possible
Spur Steel-Lok	Heavy	17, 28, 39, 48, 63, 78, 98in (430, 710, 990, 1220, 1600, 1980, 2400mm)	A range from 5–24in (120–610mm)	Steel	White, black, magnolia, brown	Book ends, book supports, steel shelves
Element 32	Medium/heavy	8⅝, 17¾, 37½, 55, 81, 90in (220, 450, 950, 1400, 2060, 2290mm)	5, 7, 9, 10½, 12½, 14½, 18½, 22½in (120, 170, 220, 270, 320, 470, 570mm)	Steel	White, brown, black, red	Book ends, upright connectors, continuous shelving possible
Spur Inspiration	Medium/heavy	20, 27, 39in (500, 700, 990mm)	7, 10in (180, 250mm)	Wood	Light oak effect, mahogany effect, black ash effect, white ash effect	Corner shelves, infill strip
Burbidge Classic	Medium/heavy	12, 25, 43in (305, 640, 1090mm)	5, 8, 11in (120, 200, 280mm)	Wood	Mahogany effect, teak effect, antique pine	Infill strip

Shelves to go on the brackets

COATED CHIPBOARD

The easiest and cheapest material for shelves is melamine-coated chipboard. It has only to be cut to length and fixed to the brackets. No finishing is necessary.

The least expensive type is 16mm ($\frac{5}{8}$in) thick, and is coated white. The same material is also available as ready-made shelves coated in red, yellow, green and blue, in a series of lengths.

Chipboard only 16mm ($\frac{5}{8}$in) thick is not very strong, and should not be used for heavy loads such as hardback books.

Ready-made shelves in heavier-weight chipboard are available and will not bend under normal domestic loads.

TIMBER AND VENEERED BOARD

Attractive shelves can also be made from solid timber, either softwood or hardwood. Both are more expensive than chipboard – hardwood much more so.

Shelves made from timber or wood-veneered chipboard need to be sealed, otherwise they will become ingrained with dirt. For *Finishing timber*, see page 168.

Where a board, such as uncoated chipboard or medium density fibreboard, has no appearance worth retaining, it can be painted or coated with a coloured varnish.

GLASS

Do not attempt to use glass less than 6mm ($\frac{1}{4}$in) thick for shelving. Even at that thickness it should not be used for heavy loads and the brackets must not be farther apart than 16in (400mm).

Use float or cast glass 9mm ($\frac{3}{8}$in) thick for shelves to carry a normal domestic load, with bracket spacing up to 27in (690mm). For books, reduce the bracket spacing to not more than 20in (510mm).

Always get the edges of glass bevelled by the supplier, and use only medium or heavyweight brackets, as the glass is heavy.

ACRYLIC SHEET

Acrylic sheet (Perspex is one brand name), makes an unusual form of shelving. It is fairly weak in thin sheets, but can be used to hold a very light object, with a thickness of 4mm ($\frac{3}{16}$in). A thickness of 12mm ($\frac{1}{2}$in) is needed for a light/medium load. Brackets should be 16in (400mm) apart.

Acrylic sheet can be polished by cleaning a sawn edge with a fine file and then finer and finer grades of abrasive paper. Wet-and-dry paper, used wet, is very effective.

BRACKET INTERVALS FOR TIMBER AND BOARD SHELVES

Buying the cheapest shelf-and-bracket system can be a false economy if you plan to fill the shelves with heavy loads, such as books or cast-iron kitchen ware.

The cheapest shelving material is the weakest, and if it is to be heavily loaded it will require closer support.

The table below is a guide to the intervals at which typical shelf materials need to be supported under normal conditions, but also read the information provided by the manufacturer or supplier.

THICKNESS	MATERIAL	INTERVALS
16mm ($\frac{5}{8}$in)	Chipboard (coated or plain)	Heavy loads: 400mm (16in) Medium loads: 610mm (24in)
16mm ($\frac{5}{8}$in)	Softwood (FT)	
18mm ($\frac{3}{4}$in)	Coated chipboard	Heavy loads: 510mm (20in) Medium loads: 700mm (27in)
18mm ($\frac{3}{4}$in)	Medium-density fibreboard	
18mm ($\frac{3}{4}$in)	Softwood (FT)	
18mm ($\frac{3}{4}$in)	Hardwood	
25mm (1in)	Medium-density fibreboard	Heavy loads: 700mm (27in) Medium loads: 915mm (36in)
25mm (1in)	Softwood (FT)	
18mm ($\frac{3}{4}$in)	Plywood	
22mm ($\frac{7}{8}$in)	Hardwood (FT)	
32mm ($1\frac{1}{4}$in)	Veneered chipboard	915mm (36in)
32mm ($1\frac{1}{4}$in)	Softwood (FT)	
25mm (1in)	Plywood	
25mm (1in)	Hardwood	

FT = Finished thickness of timber.

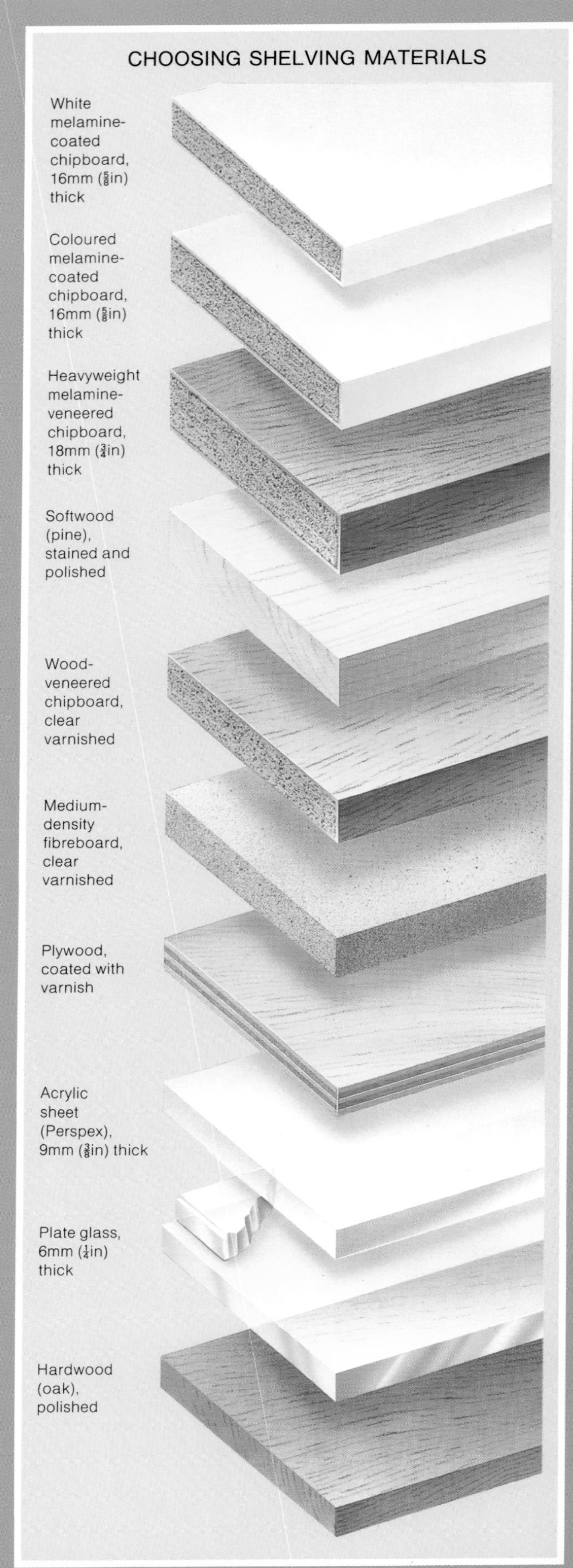

Strengthening shelves with battens and lipping

Shelves can be reinforced to improve their resistance to bending. The reinforcements can also be a decorative feature, perhaps hiding fixings or strip lights.

Apply a softwood or hardwood batten – a thick piece of wood – to the front or back edge. It should run the full length and can be either on the top or bottom. For extra strength, battens can be fixed to both front and back edges.

The deeper the batten, the greater the strength. Fix the battens to the shelf with glue and screws, screwing through the shelf.

Hardwood lipping – a thin strip of wood – can be glued and pinned along the front edge. It may be either the same depth as the shelf – giving a decorative finish but not increasing the strength – or it may be much deeper, which will strengthen as well as decorate.

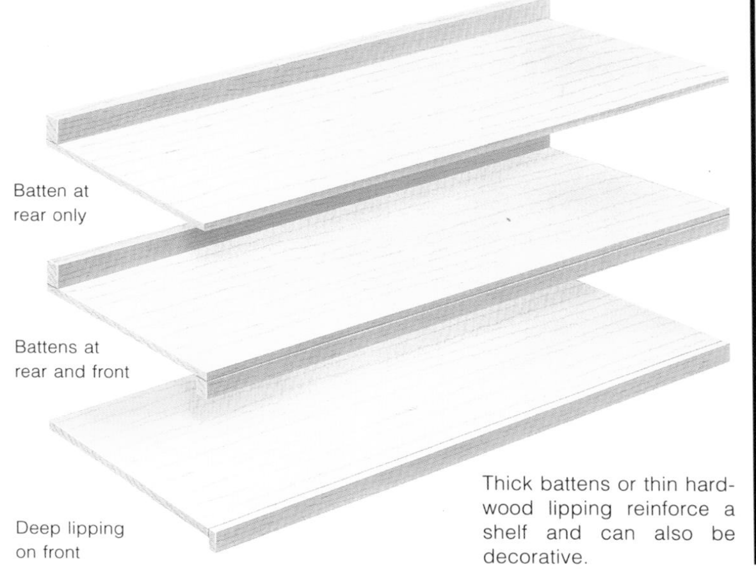

Thick battens or thin hardwood lipping reinforce a shelf and can also be decorative.

THE POSITION OF THE BRACKETS

End supports Maximum bending occurs under heavy loads.

Supports set in Loads at each end balance the central load.

The bracket positions can also give shelves greater resistance to bending.

If the shelves extend beyond the brackets they are less likely to bend in the middle. But they must be fixed to the brackets with screws, otherwise they will tip up if a weight is placed at one end – when putting up the first pile of books, for example.

Finding horizontals and verticals

USING A SPIRIT LEVEL

Whether you are fitting a sink, setting a fence post or putting up a wall, keeping surfaces level and vertical is vital, so a spirit level is a good investment. Levels are available in different lengths and designs, from miniature and pocket levels to long carpenter's levels and even digital levels which give a readout of a slope angle.

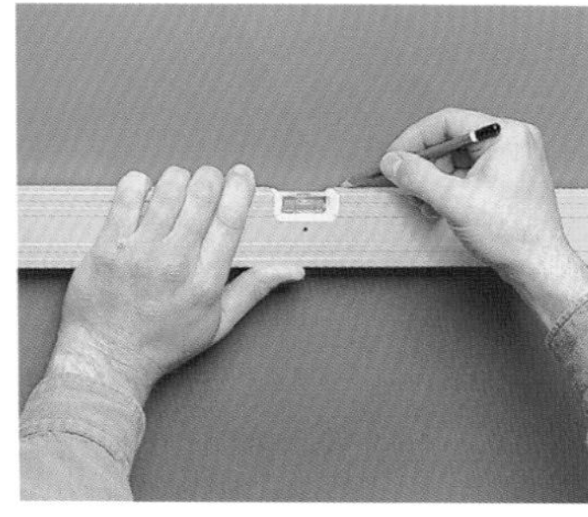

A spirit level has one or more clear vials filled with a liquid. When the level rests on a true surface a bubble in the liquid floats within an area marked on the vial to indicate that it is exactly level.

FINDING A LEVEL AROUND A CORNER

You can use a length of transparent tube to quickly and easily make a device to help you to find a level around a corner, in narrow gaps, and even between rooms. Make it as long as you like.

The tube-level is most conveniently used by two people, but with a bit of ingenuity, using string or pieces of Blu-tack, one person can work with it alone.

It only works when the bungs in the ends of the tube are removed and the water is free of bubbles.

You will need
Tools A craft knife.
Materials Transparent flexible plastic tube, with an outside diameter of $\frac{3}{8}$–$\frac{1}{2}$in (10–13mm); two bungs to fit the ends of the tube.

1 Coil the unplugged plastic tube into the bottom of a sink, and hold one end underneath a running tap.

2 When there is a steady flow from the free end of the tube and no large bubbles are left inside, keep the water running and lift the free end to join the one under the tap. Turn off the water.

3 Vibrate the tube to release any small bubbles.

4 Tip out some water until there is about 8in (200mm) of air at each end of the tube. Plug both ends. The tube level is now ready to use.

5 Mark the point from which you wish to take a level, on a wall for example.

6 Remove the bungs from the tube and hold both ends upright so that the water is level with the mark.

7 Hold one end against the mark and get a helper to move the other away from it by the distance you require. Keep the ends roughly at the same height. If one drops more than about 8in (200mm) water will spill out.

8 When the water level in the tube returns to the marked position on the wall, the water level at the distant point is at exactly the same height.

9 Mark the distant point, then insert the bungs into the tube and keep it for future use.

FINDING A VERTICAL

A weight tied to a length of string which is held firmly at the top will hang vertically, provided that the string and weight are not touching anything. Plumb bobs, with string attached, are easily bought, but it is very simple, and cheaper, to improvise your own.

You will need
Tools String 6–10ft (2–3m) long; something small but heavy for its size, such as a small screwdriver, fisherman's sinker or large nut; a hardback book; a long screw or nail; pencil; a long straightedge, such as a length of track from a shelving system.

1 When fixing shelving track, mark and drill the highest hole for a wall-fixing screw.

2 Plug the hole and partly drive the longest screw you have into it, or insert a long nail.

3 Tie the weight to the string then suspend it from the screw so that it hangs as close to the floor as possible.

4 Let the string become steady. Then place one edge of the book on the wall and slide it up to the string until they touch. Mark the wall where the corner of the book has come to rest.

5 Remove the book, string and screw. Using a track from the shelving system or a straight wooden batten, draw a line between the centre of the screw hole and the pencil mark.

This line will be the centre line for the track or brackets to be fitted.

6 Other vertical lines on the wall can be measured from the first, using a steel tape measure.

Tailor-made shelving units

Shelf units can be built to fit your own design and location, using solid timber or any of the man-made boards. Melamine-coated chipboard is the most convenient material because it needs no finishing. It is also much cheaper than solid timber. Medium density fibreboard is cheaper than timber and less fragile than chipboard, but it has to be painted or varnished.

Tailor-made units depend on vertical side panels to support the shelves and to hold the whole unit together. If these side panels move, the unit may collapse.

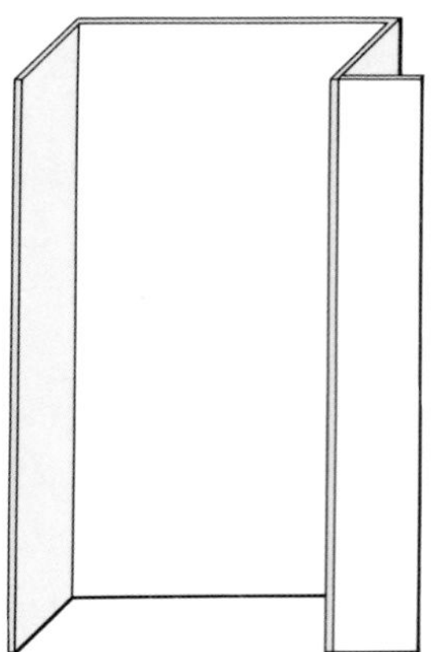

Two side walls
An alcove provides the most stable situation.

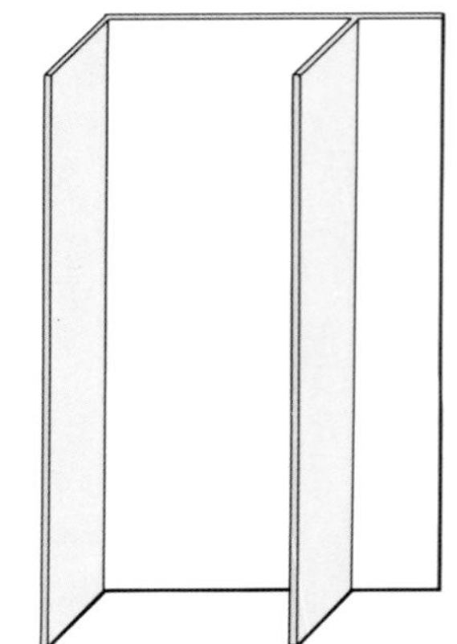

One side wall
The free-standing side panel is fixed to the wall with a batten.

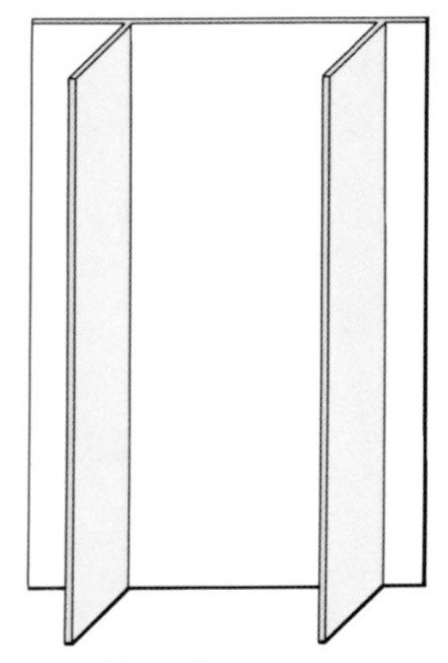

No side walls
Both side panels are fixed to wall battens.

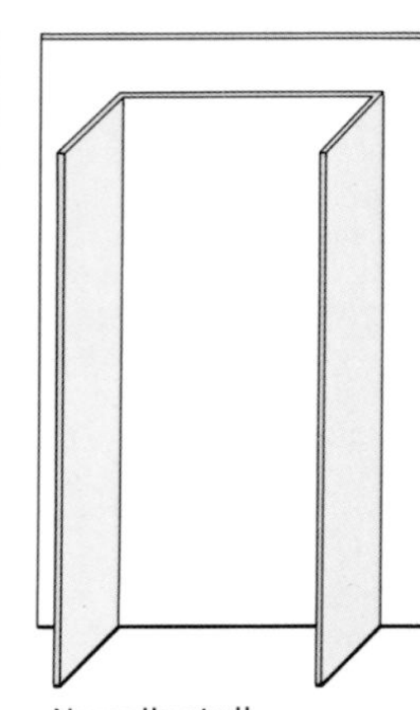

No walls at all
A free-standing unit is held together by a plywood back.

FOUR SITUATIONS FOR TAILOR-MADE UNITS

Where units are built between two side walls of an alcove, stability is assured once the side panels are secured to the walls.

Where one side panel is standing free, it must be secured along the whole length of its back edge to a batten screwed to the wall.

When both side panels are free, they should each be secured to the wall with battens.

On a free-standing shelf unit, the most efficient stabiliser is a thin plywood or hardboard sheet fixed on the back. It should be firmly pinned and glued to the back edges of the sides, top and bottom, and to any permanent shelves.

MAKING THE CORNERS RIGID

A unit with one or more free-standing side panels should be made completely rigid with plastic corner joints screwed to the top and bottom shelves and the sides. If the unit is high, one or two of the intermediate shelves should also be secured with corner joints.

Fixing side panels to the walls of an alcove

Side panels must be at right angles to the back wall. They must also be vertical and parallel to one another. This is the hardest part of making a fixed shelf unit, but it will save serious complications later.

You will need

Tools Plumb line; straight-edge; try square (or square panel of wood); tenon saw; pencil; drill and twist bits; masonry bit; countersink bit; screwdriver; spirit level; steel tape measure. Possibly a plane.

Materials Wall plugs; 2in (50mm) No. 8 countersunk screws (for fixing battens or panels to walls); side panels of man-made board or softwood; shelf supports; shelves. Possibly softwood battens and scraps of hardboard, and 1½in (38mm) No. 8 countersunk screws for fixing side panels to battens.

CHECKING THE SIDE WALLS

When planning the unit and before you get anything cut to size, begin by checking the side walls.

1 To check that they are upright and flat, drop a plumb line from the top of the wall to the bottom. Or use a long straight-edge and a spirit level with a vertical vial.

2 To check that the sides are at right angles to the back, lay a long straight-edge along the back wall and lay a try square on it against the side wall. If you do not have a try square, use a panel with right-angled corners, such as a sheet of plywood or a rectangular tray. Do not worry about the flatness of the back wall.

3 If the surfaces of the side wall are upright, flat and square, or very close to it, you can go ahead and fix the side panels directly to the wall.

> **SAFETY TIP**
> Before fixing side panels to any walls, check that you will not accidentally drill into any pipes or electrical cables. Look on both sides of the wall for electrical, gas or water appliances. Most cables and pipes lie either vertically or horizontally, so it should be safe to drill if there is no appliance directly above, below or to one side.

PUTTING UP SPACER BATTENS

If, as is normally the case, nothing is flat, square or upright, the side panels will have to be mounted on spacer battens.

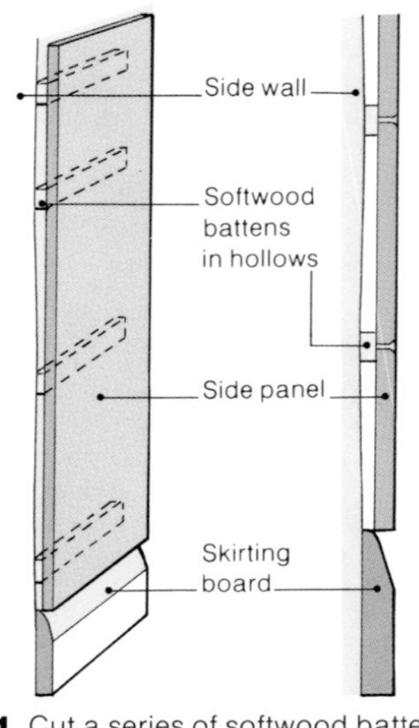

1 Cut a series of softwood battens slightly shorter than the width of the side panels. If the wall has a number of hollows, make them a little thicker than the depth of the deepest hollow.

If the wall slopes, you will need battens of graduating thickness from top to bottom.

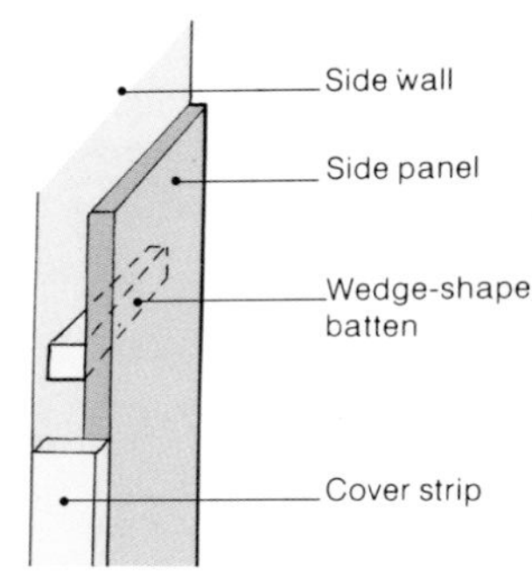

If the side wall of the alcove is not at a right angle to the rear wall, the battens need to be cut to a wedge shape to correct the angle to 90 degrees.

2 Cut and fit the top and bottom spacer battens first. Ensure that their faces end up at 90 degrees to the rear wall and are vertical with one another. Use thin packing pieces of hardboard or cardboard if necessary to make the final adjustments.

> **HELPFUL TIP**
> When drilling holes in coated chipboard, drill from the front to the back so that any breakaway in the coating will be hidden.

3 Fix intermediate battens to line up with those at the top and bottom. Put four battens on a wall 8-10ft (2.4-3m) high, three battens between 4ft and 8ft (1.2m and 2.4m) and two for anything less than 4ft.

DRILLING AND FIXING THE SIDE PANELS

1 Cut the side panels to length.

2 Lay them on the floor or on a bench, face up and side by side. Mark the faces L (left) and R (right), so there will be no confusion later. Use a pencil, which can be cleaned off afterwards.

3 Mark the position of all the shelf supports, ensuring that they are at exactly the same height on each panel, otherwise the shelves will not be horizontal. Use a try square to rule lines horizontally. Also draw vertical lines if you are using peg or block shelf supports.

4 Mark the position for the wall-fixing screws, preferably so that they will be hidden when the shelves are installed later.

If they are to be screwed to battens, this may not be possible. Hold the panels up to the wall to mark the batten positions. Also ensure that the screws will not foul the positions of anything else, such as a skirting board or a picture rail, for example.

5 When you are completely satisfied that all the positions are correctly marked, drill the holes for the shelf supports and the wall screws. This is far more easily done with the side panels flat than later when they are vertical.

6 For flat, square walls, screw the side panels directly onto the wall. For fixing into different types of wall, see page 230.

If you have put up battens, screw into them, using 1½in (38mm) screws.

FILLING GAPS BETWEEN SIDE PANELS AND WALLS

Gaps between the return walls and the side panels can be patched with cover strips of thin softwood or hardwood, which are scribed to the shape of the wall (page 188) and pinned into place.

CHOOSING SUPPORTS FOR ADJUSTABLE TAILOR-MADE SYSTEMS

If you want a shelving unit with shelves that can be moved to different positions, fit a series of supports, or support sockets, to the two side panels. They can either be regularly spaced at 1½in (38mm) intervals, or the spacing can vary to suit particular needs. There is no point in having holes too near to the top or bottom of the unit.

If the shelves are not to be moved, no extra supports are needed.

If you are using peg-type supports, two will be needed to support each end of the shelf. Set them a short distance in from the front and back edges – for example, ¾in (19mm) on shelves 8in (200mm) wide.

Remember that the top of each shelf will be higher by its thickness than the top of the supports. This may be important if the shelves are to line up with something on an adjoining wall.

Always drill holes to match exactly the diameter of peg-type supports. If the holes are too small the supports will not fit; if they are too large the supports will sag and the shelves will not be level.

Be careful to keep the drill at 90 degrees to the side panel. Wind a piece of masking tape around the bit to mark the depth of the hole. On 16mm coated chipboard a short overrun will burst through the other side.

TYPE OF SUPPORT	MATERIAL	HOW IT FITS
Socket and peg (push-fit)	Plastic (brown or white)	The peg is pushed into a plastic socket fitted into a hole in the side panel. For an adjustable system you will need one socket for every hole in the side panels, but only four pegs per shelf.
Socket and peg (push and rotate)	Plastic (brown or white)	The peg is pushed (upside down) into a plastic socket in the side panel, then turned right way up to lock in position. For an adjustable system you will need one socket for every hole in the side panels, but only four pegs per shelf.
Fixed peg (non-adjustable)	Plastic (brown or white)	The peg is tapped into the side panel with a hammer as far as it will go. Adjust with pliers so that the flat surface is horizontal. Avoid pulling pegs out of coated or veneered board as they may tear the surface.
Dowel pegs (non-adjustable)	Natural wood (can be stained, varnished or painted)	Drill holes exactly the diameter of the dowels, to about 7/16in (10mm) deep. Insert dowels 1in (25mm) long. A too-tight fit can be eased with abrasive paper.
Nail-on shelf supports	Plastic (white), nails supplied	Position the supports so they line up with the horizontal and vertical lines marked on the side panels, and drive in the nail with a pin hammer.
Slotted metal strip (also called Bookcase Strip)	Metal (brown, silver or brass)	Mark centre lines for two strips on each side panel, and a horizontal line to align the slots. Screw the strips in place and hook the shelf support into the slots, four per shelf.
Shelf bearer	Plastic (white). Chipboard screws also needed – ¾in (19mm) No. 6, six per pair	Use a single bearer for shelves 6–8in (150–200mm) wide. Use two side by side for shelves 12–18in (300–460mm) wide. Screw the bearers to the panels and close the cover strips.
Thin wooden battens	Natural wood (can be stained, varnished or painted)	Can be made from timber strip of almost any size. Tiny sections can be used for very small shelves. Sections ⅝ × ¼in (16mm × 6mm) make neat supports for normal shelves. Cut the battens as long as the shelf width. Use two screws on battens up to 6in (150mm) long, three from 6–9in (150–230mm) and four beyond that.

Free-standing units from slotted angle

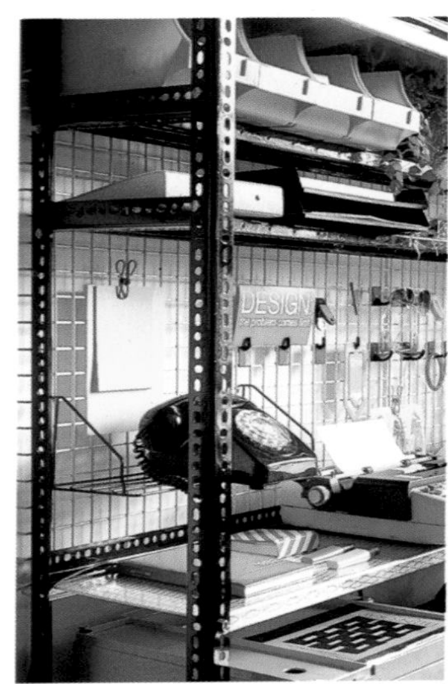

Slotted metal angle, such as Dexion, bolts together to form freestanding shelving which can take heavy loads. It is useful for a workshop, garage or home office. Painted in bright colours, it can also be used in kitchens and other rooms.

The lightest grade is more suitable for domestic use and is cheaper than the heavier grades. The metal angle is sold in long lengths which can be cut with a hacksaw. Triangular steel plates are provided to reinforce corners, and the framework is held together with nuts and bolts.

A framework of almost any dimension can be built, but a shallow unit above 3ft (1m) high should be fixed to a wall to prevent it toppling over.

The shelves can be made from chipboard or almost any other flat material.

You will need

Tools Vice or portable workbench; hacksaw; two spanners to match nuts and bolts; a wood saw for cutting the shelves. Perhaps a metal file, abrasive paper and paintbrush.

Materials Lightweight slotted angle; corner plates and nuts and bolts to match; chipboard or other material for shelves. Perhaps paint for shelves and frame.

1 Draw a rough sketch of the unit. It need not be very detailed; its purpose is to ensure that the finished unit will fit the space available, and also to help you calculate the material.

2 Use a hacksaw to cut the angle into lengths. Hold it in a vice or a portable workbench while you make the cuts.

If you intend to decorate the unit, you should remove any sharp edges with a metal file before assembling it.

3 If the unit consists of two or more 'bays', bolt together the central pairs of uprights.

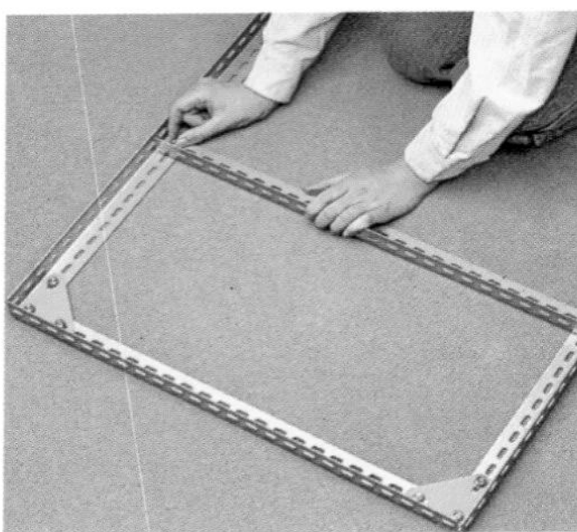

4 Make the end frames of the unit by laying the uprights on the floor and bolting on the crosspieces.

Put corner plates at the top and bottom crosspieces and at every other alternate crosspiece. These give the unit strength.

5 Bolt the horizontal pieces to the end frames, inserting corner plates.

6 Stand the unit upright and build on the next 'bay' in the same way.

7 Cut the shelves and insert them.

8 To decorate the unit, lightly rub it down with abrasive paper and paint with two coats of gloss paint.

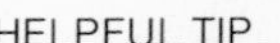

HELPFUL TIP

To save wastage, offcuts of slotted angle can be joined by butting them together, overlapping the join with an 8in (200mm) piece of slotted angle, and bolting the pieces.

Crosspiece

Corner plate

Upright

Horizontal piece

Shelf

Central pair of uprights

To protect the floor, plastic feet can be fixed to the bottom of the legs. Or the unit can be turned into a trolley by the addition of castors. Plastic drawers and bins can also be added for storage.

Displaying plates on shelves

Attractive plates can be displayed on edge on a shelf by fixing wooden beading to the shelf or by cutting a groove in it.

For most plates, the beading or groove should be ¼in (6mm) deep and ⅜in (10mm) wide. For very large or heavy objects it may need to be a little larger.

You will need

Tools Straight edge; pencil; pin hammer; small paintbrush. To cut a groove: circular saw and chisel, or router.

Materials Blu-tack or Plasticine; ½in (13mm) panel pins; beading; paint or varnish. For a groove: wood filler.

1 To decide on the position of the bead or groove, put a plate on the shelf and hold it there with Blu-tack or Plasticine. Stand back and see if the angle is right.

2 When you are satisfied with the angle, rule a line along the shelf where the base of the plate stood.

3 Fix the beading against the line with panel pins.

ALTERNATIVELY, cut a groove along it by making several passes with a circular saw, using the fence guide and readjusting it slightly for each cut. You may need a small chisel to clean out the groove.

Another solution is to hire a router, a tool for cutting grooves.

4 Finish the beading or groove with paint or varnish.

5 To prevent plates from rolling off the ends of the shelf, add an extra piece of beading behind the main one at the ends, or fill in the groove with matching beading or wood filler.

Adding a raised lip

On a narrow shelf a raised lip could be suitable for propping up large plates. Pin and glue hardwood lipping to the edges so that it stands about ¼in (6mm) above the shelf.

Fixing a shelf unit or cupboard to a straight wall

If you want to build a shelf unit or a cupboard against a straight wall, the side panels can be fixed to the wall on wooden battens. For neatness the battens are fitted inside the unit.

On a wide unit a fixed centre panel can be fitted for added stability. The batten can go on either side of the panel.

Panels must be vertical and square to the wall for both visual and practical reasons. A sloping or non-square side panel complicates the fitting of shelves.

Occasionally side panels may actually be required to be at an angle to follow the line of a sloping roof or wall. In this case they are fitted in the same way, but the angle of the panels and the shape of the shelves will have to be calculated for the particular situation.

CHECKING IF THE WALL IS VERTICAL

Before buying the materials, check whether the wall is vertical, using a long spirit level or plumb line.

If, within the height of the unit, the wall is more than ½in (13mm) off the vertical, or if it undulates to a greater extent than that, it is best to cut the rear edge of the side panel to approximately the shape of the wall before fixing it. Otherwise, the rear edge may miss the batten.

MATERIAL FOR THE PANELS

The cheapest material for side panels is ⅝in (16mm) chipboard coated with melamine or veneered with wood. It will also reduce the work as it will not need painting. Wood-veneered chipboard should be polished or varnished after it is cut to size.

Sheets ranging in size up to 8ft × 4ft (2440mm × 1220mm) are available from DIY stores.

An alternative material would be plywood of a similar thickness. It would be much more expensive but could be varnished for a natural wood finish, if its surface is good.

THE SIZE OF THE BATTENS

Small units with side panels up to 4ft (1220mm) high can be attached to walls with battens 1in × 1in (25mm × 25mm) nominal.

For taller units use battens 1in × 2in (25mm × 50mm) nominal, fixed flat to the wall.

Size of batten is not critical provided the battens are strong enough not to bend as they are fixed, and thick enough to accept the threads of the screws running into them through the side panels.

Before you buy the battens, make sure they are straight.

For fixing into different types of wall, see pages 230–233.

EXTRA SUPPORTS FOR THE PANELS

Side panels also need to be firmly held at their front edges to prevent them being forced apart. If that happens, the shelves they are supporting are likely to fall.

They can be held rigid in two ways. Shelves can be screwed to the top and bottom of the unit with corner joints, or battens can be screwed onto the floor and ceiling with the side panels screwed to the battens.

For high units, one or two intermediate shelves should be fixed to the panels with corner joints.

> HELPFUL TIP
> Have the side panels and shelves cut to length by the suppliers, particularly if they have a free cutting service. This will ensure that ends are square and that the melamine or veneer is not chipped.

You will need

Tools Spirit level; plumb line; try square; saw; screwdriver; drill and twist bits; masonry bit to fit wall plugs; pencil; hammer.

Material Side panels; battens; 2in (50mm) No. 10 countersunk woodscrews (for fixing battens to walls); wall plugs to fit; 1½in (38mm) No. 8 countersunk woodscrews (for fixing panels to battens); screw caps for No. 8 screws; shelves. Possibly scraps of plywood or hardboard and corner joints (page 164).

PUTTING UP THE WALL BATTENS

1 With a long spirit level or plumb line, mark a vertical line on the wall where the inside edge of the side panel is to be placed.

2 If the unit is to end above the floor or below the ceiling, mark the position of the top and bottom of the side panel on the line.

3 Cut one of the battens to length. For units which run down to floor level, the bottom of the batten should rest on the skirting board.

If the batten crosses a picture rail, cut the batten in two, and put one section below and the other above the rail.

4 Drill and countersink holes in the batten for the 2in (50mm) No. 10 screws that will fix it to the wall.

Drill at least two screw holes in battens up to 3ft (910mm) long, three up to 5ft (1.5m), and four above that. Make a screw hole 6in (150mm) from each end, with the others evenly spaced between.

5 Put a screw in each of the holes, and place the batten against the line on the wall so that the edge which will contact the panel follows the line. Check the height position.

6 Tap the head of each screw so that the point marks the wall.

7 Carefully drill wall-plug holes at those marks.

8 Insert the plugs and screw the batten to the wall.

If the batten follows undulations in the wall as the screws are tightened, put pieces of hardboard or plywood behind the screws. In exceptional cases longer screws may have to be substituted.

9 Put up the other batten or battens in the same way.

FITTING THE SIDE PANELS

1 Cut the side panels to length if this has not already been done.

2 On sloping or heavily undulating walls, trim the back edges of the panels to the approximate shape.

3 Cut the bottom corners of the panels to fit over the skirting board.

4 Cut out a section to fit over a picture rail, if necessary.

5 Get a helper to line up the side panels with the battens. Check that the front edges are vertical. If necessary, check the height against the positions on the wall.

Trim away any points on the back edges which prevent the side panels from going into position.

6 Mark the positions of the screws that will hold the side panels to the battens.

Any slight in-and-out wave of the batten on an undulating wall may cause the side panel to almost miss the batten edge at some points, so mark the screw positions where the screws will get an effective hold into the battens. Mark a minimum of three holes for units up to 4ft (1.2m) high and up to six for units of full room height.

Avoid a clash with the screws holding the batten to the wall.

7 Take the side panel down from the wall and drill and countersink holes for the No. 8 screws.

8 Put screws in the holes and hold the side panel back in place.

9 Tap the screws to mark their positions on the battens and drill pilot holes in the battens.

10 Screw the side panels to the battens, and cover the exposed heads with screw caps.

SECURING THE FRONT EDGES

Make the front edges of the unit rigid by either of the following methods. If the unit does not reach floor or ceiling use the first method.

Fixing a shelf unit or cupboard to a straight wall (continued)

Fixing to top and bottom shelves

1 Measure the distance between the inside faces of the side panels, taking the measurement just in front of the wall battens.

2 Cut shelves to that length, making sure that the ends are cut square.

3 Fit one shelf at the top of the unit and the other at the bottom, using strong corner joints.

Fixing to battens on the floor and ceiling

1 If the unit runs from floor to ceiling, screw battens to the floorboards at right angles to the wall, flush with the wall battens.

2 Screw the bottom of the side panels to the floor battens.

3 Fix battens to the ceiling (page 249) and screw the top of the side panels to it in the same way.

PUTTING IN THE SHELVES

If you want the back shelves to meet the wall, you will have to cut the back corners of each shelf around the battens. But in some cases a small gap at the back is not important – if the shelves are holding books or clothing, for example.

Fit the shelves in place with one of the shelf-support systems shown on page 177.

COVER STRIPS FOR UNSIGHTLY GAPS

If a gap occurs along the rear edge of the panels, make cover strips from wood about ¼in (6mm) thick and ½in (13mm) wider than the gap.

Scribe the strips to the shape of the wall (page 188) and fix them to the side panels with panel pins.

Building shelving with vertical dividers

Vertical divisions make shelves stronger, and can also provide convenient partitions to separate one area from another – books divided from hi-fi equipment on the same shelf, for example.

As the divisions prevent long shelves from bending under heavy loads, they are useful in wide shelving units.

The dividers must transfer the weight onto something solid or the shelves will still bend. So there is no advantage in fitting a divider partway up a unit if you do not put more dividers below to carry the weight down to the floor, or to some other support (see panel).

FOUR WAYS OF FIXING THE DIVIDERS IN PLACE

1 The dividers can be joined satisfactorily to the upper and lower shelves with 1½in (38mm) No. 8 chipboard screws, or 1½in oval nails or panel pins, driven down through the top shelves and up through the bottom shelves. This method is fairly simple, but requires great care to ensure that the fixings enter the centre of the dividers and do not break out to one side. So drill narrow holes through the shelves to guide nails or panel pins.

Shelves up to 6in (150mm) wide need two fixings into a divider at top and bottom; wider shelves need a further fixing for each extra 6in.

2 Fix the dividers to the shelves with dowel joints (page 166). The joints are invisible on the surfaces of the shelves and are structurally sounder than screws or nails. But they take longer to make.

3 Join the divider to the shelves with two small corner joints (page 164) top and bottom. The joints will obstruct the bottom corner on one side of the divider.

4 Shelf dividers which need no fixing can be cut from thick timber – 2in (50mm) or more.

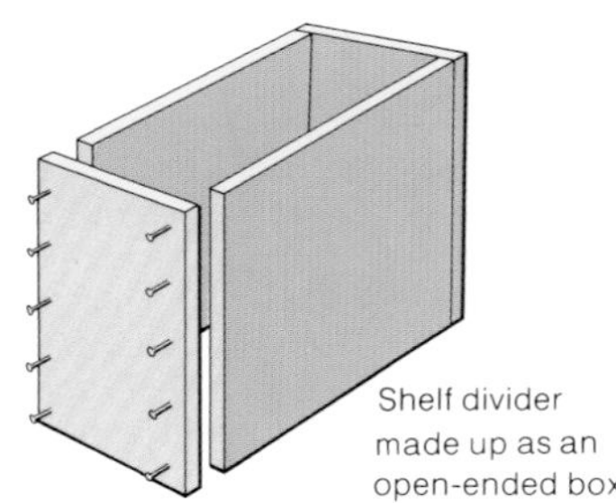

Shelf divider made up as an open-ended box

Or they can be made up as open-ended boxes of the same width. These simply stand between the shelves. Their thickness prevents them from falling over, and they are gripped by the weight of the shelf above.

FITTING THE DIVIDERS

The height of vertical dividers must be exactly the same as the distance between shelves; if they are too long or short the shelves will be out of true. They must also be cut square at the ends.

1 Plan the positions of the dividers and get them cut square and to exact size by the supplier.

2 Have all the other components cut to size and ready to assemble.

3 Number each of the shelves from top to bottom, using a soft pencil. Also mark each shelf 'top', 'bottom' and 'front', so there is no confusion as you build the unit.

4 If the gap between shelves varies from shelf to shelf, mark each divider with the numbers of the shelves it is to fit between.

5 Stand each pair of adjacent shelves on edge with the front edges uppermost, and the top face of the lower shelf against the bottom face of the upper shelf. Mark the positions of the dividers across the two edges with a pencil and try square. Mark two lines to indicate the thickness of the divider.

6 Open the boards out flat so that the inner faces are uppermost. Using a try square, mark lines across the faces from the marks on the edges. The fixings must be centred between the two lines.

7 Repeat this marking process with each pair of shelves – top and 1, 1 and 2, 2 and 3.

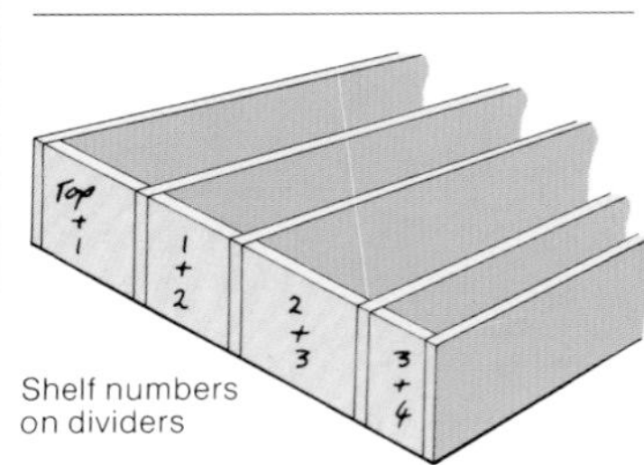

Shelf numbers on dividers

8 Before going further, double-check that the height of the dividers and the thickness of the shelves measures up to what was expected.

Stand the dividers and shelves on their back edges in numbered order. You will need help.

Move the dividers to one end of the shelves so that an accurate measurement can be taken.

A correction can be made by reducing the height of one or more dividers if the unit is over-height, or by having a larger one cut.

9 If you are making a free-standing unit, mark out the joints between the top, bottom and side panels. Assemble them and then undo the fixings.

10 Using one of the four fixing methods given on the left, assemble the shelves and dividers in their numbered order, on the floor.

11 For free-standing units, complete the construction by rejoining the side panels to the top and bottom. Line the shelves up so that they are parallel with one another and check that the front edges are flush or set back as required. Join them to the sides with corner joints.

12 For shelves and dividers which are to fit into an alcove or between sides which are already fixed, carefully lift the assembly and slide it between the uprights. Then join the shelf ends to the upright sides with shelf supports.

SUPPORTING SHELVES ON BEAMS

If you do not want to continue vertical shelf dividers down to the ground, the weight can be supported by wooden beams fixed to the bottom shelf.

Fit the beams along the full length of the underside of the shelf close to both the front and the back edges. Fix the long edge in place with corner joints or dowel joints, or by screwing through the shelf into the beam.

There is no need to fix the ends of the beam to the sides if the sides are the walls of an alcove. Otherwise, fit them to the sides with dowel joints.

Long shelves with heavy loads require wider beams than short shelves or shelves with light loads.

The following sizes of beam will carry average loads.

SHELF LENGTH	BEAM CROSS-SECTION
Up to 36in (915mm)	2in × 1in (50mm × 25mm)
36in to 60in (915-1525mm)	3in × 1in (75mm × 25mm)
Over 60in (1525mm)	4in × 1in (100mm × 25mm)

Making a basic cupboard

Any cupboard consists of a box-like carcass made up of a top, a bottom, and two sides, all jointed together. In many cases a back is also pinned and glued to the edges of the other four panels, giving extra rigidity. This basic box can be fitted with shelves and doors.

Ensure that each corner is a right angle, otherwise shelves and other fittings will not fit properly.

Chipboard – ⅝in (16mm) thick and coated with melamine or veneered with wood – is the most widely available and the cheapest material for making cupboards. If you use an alternative material which is thicker or stronger than chipboard, it will carry greater loads and the unsupported spans of shelves or tops can be longer (page 174).

MEASURING THE PANELS

If the top of the cupboard is visible, make the unit so that the top rests on the ends of the sides, but the bottom fits between the sides. This hides most of the raw ends of the panels. Only those at each end of the top can be seen and will need finishing with wood veneer or melamine strip (page 156).

On this principle, the sides will be equal in length, but the top will be longer than the bottom by the combined thickness of the two sides.

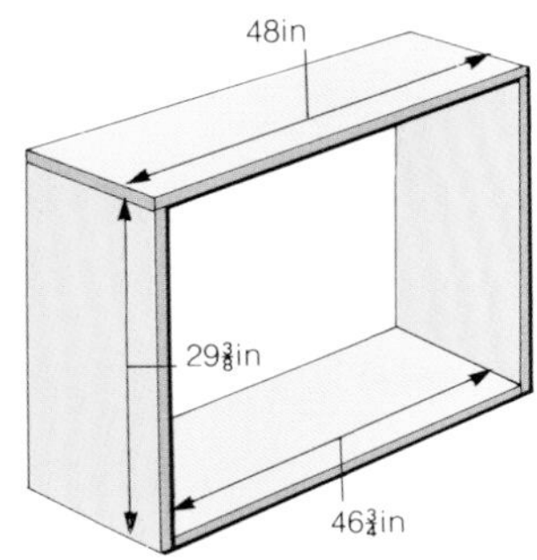

To make a cabinet of any depth, 48in (1220mm) wide and 30in (760mm) high from ⅝in (16mm) coated chipboard, you would need the following cut panels:

Top
48in (1220mm) long × depth of unit;

Bottom
46¾in (1188mm) long × depth of unit;

Sides
29⅜in (744mm) long × depth of unit.

BUYING THE MATERIAL

To get the cupboard square from front to back, it is essential that the ends of all the panels are square to start with.

The best way to get boards cut square and accurately to length is to have them cut by the supplier. His mechanical saw also normally cuts the boards without chipping the edges – a danger when cutting with DIY tools. So try to find a supplier who will do the cutting at no extra cost.

Before buying the panels, check to see that they are unmarked on both faces and that on the finished edges the melamine tape or wood veneer is firmly attached. Also check that they are flat.

Unfinished ends of standard size panels are usually rather rough and will have some surface chip damage. This has to be trimmed off to create a chip-free end that can be finished with tape or veneer.

About ½in (13mm) should be allowed for this at each end. To keep costs as low as possible allow for end trimming at the planning stage. It can save you from having to buy a panel the next size up.

Freshly cut boards are easily damaged when they are being taken home. Wrap corrugated cardboard or thick fabric around the ends to protect them.

HELPFUL TIP

To use chipboard economically, make units just short of standard panels in length. Thus for a unit about 48in (1220mm) long, make it 47in (1200mm) to allow for end-trimming of 48in sheets.

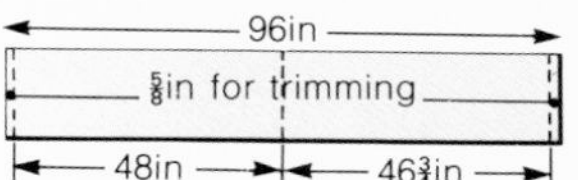

Similarly, you can make a 48in wide cupboard by cutting the top and bottom panels from a single 96in (2440mm) sheet. As the bottom is shorter than the top, there is enough waste to allow for trimming at each end.

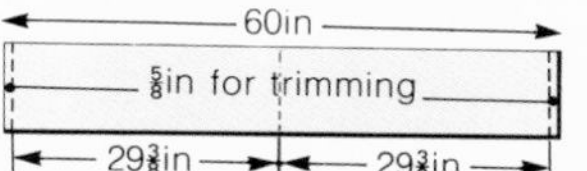

Side panels for a unit 30in (760mm) high can be cut from a 60in (1520mm) sheet.

ASSEMBLING THE UNIT

When the panels have been accurately cut, they can be assembled with strong corner joints – such as Lok-joints, assembly joints or square-section wood batten (page 164).

Ready-made corner joints, however, can cause problems if they are fitted to the inside corners of the cupboard. The joints at the bottom can prevent books, for example, from standing upright at the sides.

If you are confident that you can drill accurately, dowel joints (page 166) will overcome the problem because they give strong joints and unobstructed corners.

To achieve completely unobstructed corners there are three choices:

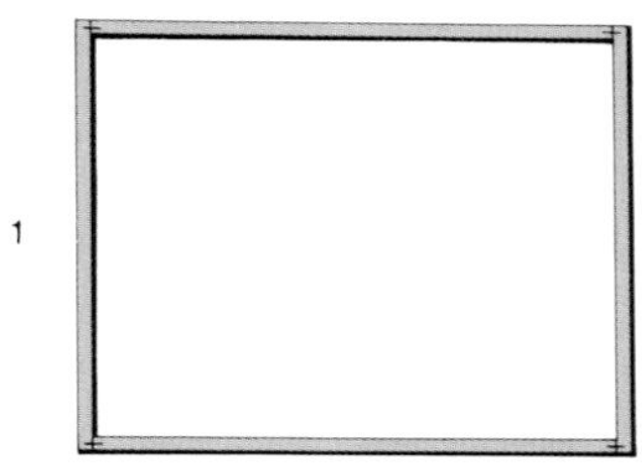

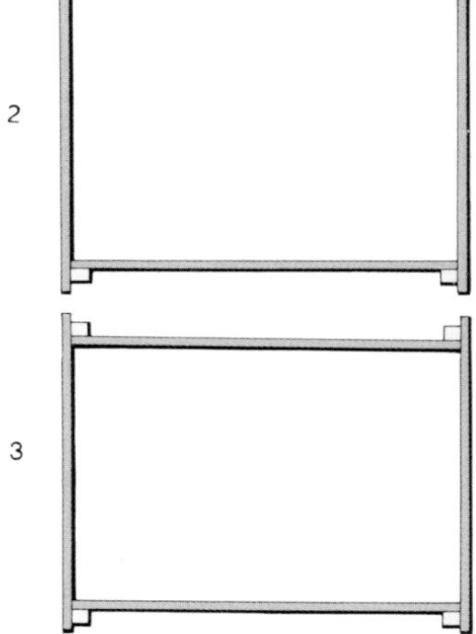

1 Dowel joints at all corners; 2 Dowel joints at the top corners and corner joints below a raised bottom; 3 Corner joints above a lowered top and below a raised bottom.

When a raised bottom or a lowered top are used, a plinth (at the bottom) and a cornice (at the top) are usually added as a cover strip to hide the fixings. These are made of the same material as the rest of the cupboard, and can be attached with small corner joints.

A raised bottom can also be used to hold hidden castors for small mobile units.

Planning drawers
If the unit is to house a bank of drawers from top to bottom, choose the drawer system at the planning stage because the style of drawer will determine the construction of the cabinet. Drawers which are not near the bottom or top of a cabinet are not affected by corner joints.

CHECKING FOR SQUARENESS

Once the unit has been assembled, turn it onto its front or back to check it for squareness.

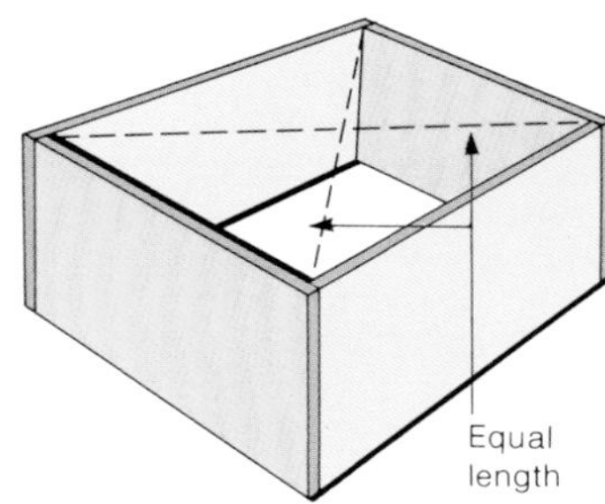

Measure the distance from one corner to the corner diagonally opposite. Then measure between the other two corners. The two measurements should be the same.

If one diagonal is longer than the other, slacken the joint screws, push the corners of the longer diagonal gently but firmly until the diagonal measurements are equal. Then retighten the joints.

For dowel joints, make this check immediately after applying the adhesive. Then cramp the unit with frame cramps or sash cramps.

FITTING ON THE BACK

When the cupboard is square, and the glue in dowel joints has dried, a back can be fitted for extra rigidity and to prevent the contents of the cupboard from being pushed through.

If you are using hardboard or plywood, lay the cupboard on the board so that two sides of the cupboard line up with two sides of the board. Mark around the other two sides, and cut the board.

Fix it to the back edges of the cupboard by running a bead of PVA wood glue along the edges of the cupboard and then pinning through the board into the chipboard edge with 1in (25mm) panel pins.

Putting a hinged door on a cupboard

DIY stores sell a wide selection of styles and sizes of doors made either of solid wood or veneered chipboard. Many sizes match the dimensions of kitchen and bedroom units. They are ideal for using when you want to fit replacement doors to give old cupboards a facelift.

If you are planning to make your own cupboards, work to these sizes, if possible. The work involved will be substantially reduced by using ready-made doors instead of designing and making your own.

Non-standard doors can be cut from melamine-coated or wood-veneered chipboard. They can also be made from plywood but plywood, especially that made from birch, tends to twist if it is less than about ½in (13mm) thick.

HOW MANY HINGES?

Hinges are usually sold and used in pairs. Those made for cupboard doors are slimmer than the type made for doors of rooms. The longer the hinge, the greater the stability it gives to the door, but as the length increases, so does the width; the hinge you choose must not be wider than the timber it is being fixed to.

Place the hinges 1½ to 2½ times their length from the ends of the door to avoid splitting the wood.

A door taller than about 43in (1100mm), made from lightweight material such as 16mm chipboard, needs a third, central hinge to keep it in line with the frame. Tall doors of heavier construction can be hinged with either two 3in (75mm) hinges or three 2½in (65mm) hinges.

MAKING HINGED DOORS FIT

Whether you are using a ready-built door or one you have made yourself, make sure it fits the opening before attaching the hinges.

A GUIDE TO HINGE AND DOOR SIZES

HEIGHT OF DOOR	NUMBER OF HINGES	SIZE OF HINGES (BUTT, FLUSH OR CRANKED)	NUMBER AND SIZE OF ADJUSTABLE CONCEALED HINGES
Up to 15in *380mm*	2	1½in *38mm*	2 × 25mm
15–30in *380–760mm*	2	2in *50mm*	2 × 25mm
40in *1020mm*	2 or 3	2in *50mm*	2 or 3 × 25mm
50in *1270mm*	2 or 3	2in *50mm*	3 × 25mm or 2 × 36mm
60in *1525mm*	3	2in or 2½in *50mm or 65mm*	3 × 25mm or 2 × 36mm
70in *1780mm*	3	2in or 2½in *50mm or 65mm*	3 × 36mm
80in *2030mm*	3	2½in *65mm*	3 × 36mm
90in *2285mm*	3 or 4	2½in *65mm*	3 × 36mm
100in *2540mm*	4	2½in *65mm*	3 or 4 × 36mm

DOORS SET INTO FRAMES

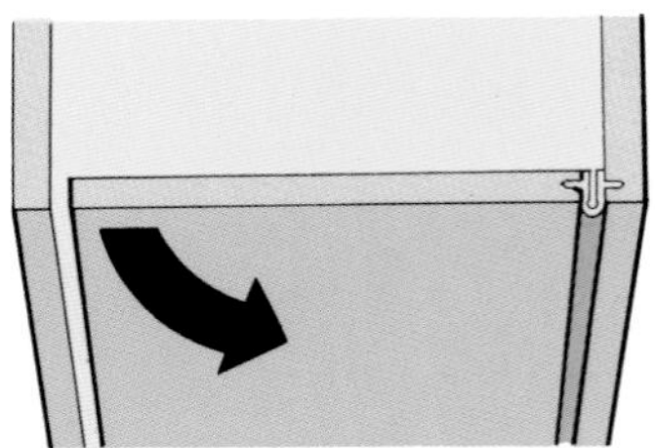

Doors that are set into the frame of the cupboard need clearance space all the way round between door and frame.

For let-in hinges, such as butt hinges, allow a $\frac{1}{16}$in (2mm) clearance on each side. This allows for the small gap created by the hinge and a similar gap at the closing edge to allow for the arc of the door as it shuts.

For hinges that are not let in but screwed onto the surface of the door and frame – flush hinges, for example – the clearance on the hinge edge must be the thickness of the hinge plus about $\frac{1}{16}$in (2mm).

The top and bottom of the cupboard door need a clearance space of $\frac{1}{16}$in (2mm).

LAY-ON DOORS

The size of a lay-on door depends on the type of hinge you are intending to use and the amount of frame you have planned for the door to cover. It may cover all or only part of the frame.

An adjustable concealed hinge demands that the door overlays the frame by about ⅝in (16mm), depending on the thickness of material from which the door is made. The amount of overlay required is shown on the table that is printed on the hinge packet.

Different patterns of cranked hinge also create size restrictions for lay-on doors. For example, a cranked hinge which is fixed to the face of the door requires the door to be set to one side sufficiently for the cranked arm to be screwed into position on the edge of the frame.

SCREWS FOR HINGES

Most hinges are drilled and countersunk to take even-number screw gauges – No. 6 or No. 8, for example. Frequently the countersink is slightly undersized with the result that the top of the screw head will not fit flush and the cupboard door would not close easily.

Instead of re-countersinking the holes, buy another set of screws that are just one gauge smaller – No. 7 screws instead of No. 8, for example.

HANGING DIFFERENT TYPES OF CUPBOARD DOORS

A hinged cupboard door has to be fixed to a vertical frame or panel. It can be fitted so that it covers the frame (a lay-on door) or so that it fits inside it (an inset door). Some hinges have to be recessed into both the door and the frame; others screw directly in place, making them easier to fit. Chipboard, plywood and medium-density fibreboard will not hold screws in their edges, so doors made of these materials must be fitted with hinges that can be fixed into the face – unless the door edges have been lipped with a strip of solid wood.

TYPE OF DOOR	TYPES OF HINGE
Lay-on doors	
Chipboard (without wood-lipped edges).	Adjustable concealed hinge.
Plywood or medium-density fibreboard (without wood-lipped edges, but where the frame faces forward).	Cranked cabinet hinge.
Solid wood door and frame (or door and frame of coated or veneered chipboard with wood-lipped edges).	Flush hinge; butt hinge; cranked cabinet hinge; adjustable concealed hinge; continuous (or piano) hinge.
Pair of lay-on doors on the same upright	
Chipboard (without wood-lipped edges).	Adjustable concealed hinge.
Plywood or medium-density fibreboard (without wood-lipped edges, but where the frame faces forward).	Cranked cabinet hinge.
Solid wood door and frame (or door and frame of chipboard with lipped edges).	Cranked hinge; adjustable concealed hinge.
Inset doors	
Chipboard (without wood-lipped edges; frame made of solid wood or lipped).	Face-fixing hinge only.
Solid wood door and frame (or door and frame of coated or veneered chipboard with lipped edges).	Flush hinge; butt hinge; face-fixing hinge; continuous (or piano) hinge.
Pair of inset doors on the same upright	
Solid wood door and frame (or door and frame of coated or veneered chipboard with lipped edges).	Flush hinge; butt hinge; face-fixing hinge (staggered so that the screws in the upright do not clash).

CHOOSING THE RIGHT CUPBOARD HINGES

TYPE OF HINGE	DESCRIPTION	HOW TO FIX	ADVANTAGES/DISADVANTAGES
Adjustable concealed hinge 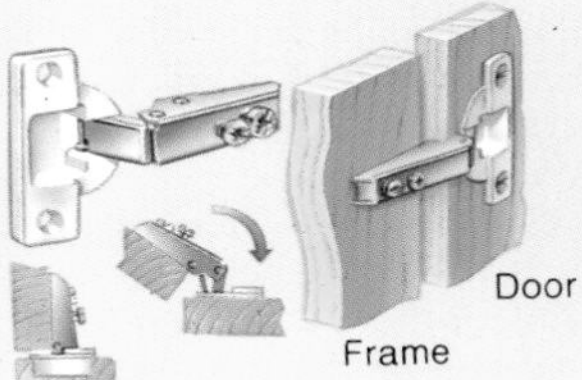	Two sizes of cylinder – 25mm and 36mm. Available with or without a catch to hold the door closed or open at 90 degrees.	Use a special bit to cut the cylinder holes in the door. Do not use a flat bit; the point is too long and the sizing inaccurate. A drill stand with depth stop, which can be hired, is essential for accuracy.	The hinge is adjustable after fitting to make the door fit the frame. Designed for chipboard and medium-density fibreboard. Supplied with template for fitting, but correct drilling equipment needed.
Butt hinge 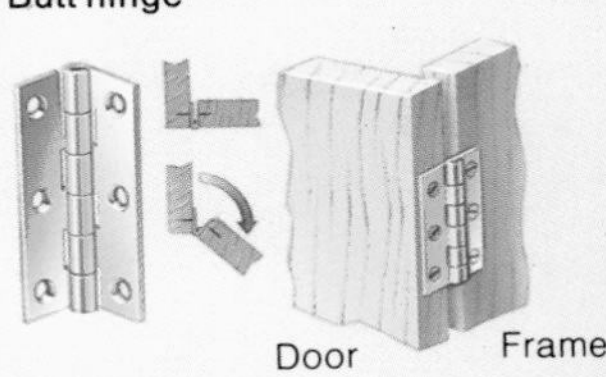	Range of sizes from ½in (13mm) to 6in (150mm). Cupboards normally take 2in (50mm).	Butt hinges have to be let into the solid timber with a chisel.	Cannot be adjusted after fitting. More difficult to fit than a flush hinge. Good for strength.
Flush hinge 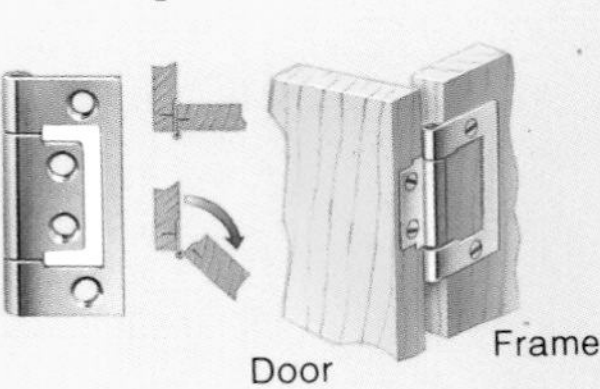	Sizes range from 1½in (38mm) to 3in (75mm). Made of steel, often zinc plated. Works in same way as butt hinge.	Screw the outer half to the frame and the inner half to the door.	Requires no recessing. Cannot be adjusted after fitting. Less strong than a butt hinge, but usually adequate for lightweight doors.
Face-fixing (butterfly) hinge 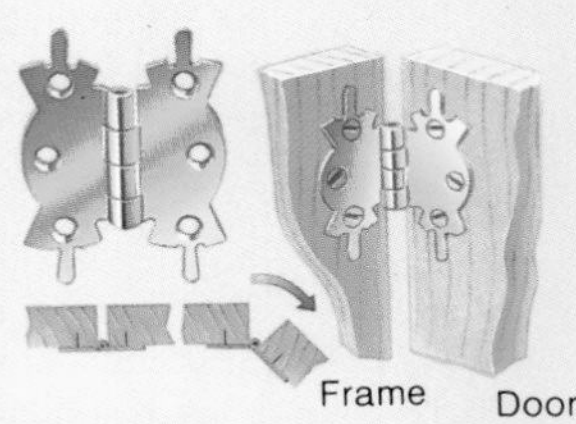	For lightweight doors. Different patterns available, in chrome or brass-plated steel.	Mount on the face of both door and frame with raised-head screws.	Easy to fit on plywood or medium-density fibreboard. Not adjustable once fitted. Not a strong fitting.
Cranked hinge 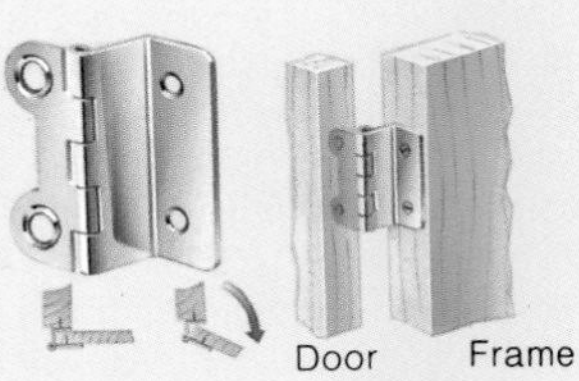 Size of crank must match thickness of door.	Sizes of crank include ¼in (6mm), ⅜in (10mm), ½in (13mm), and ⅝in (16mm). Can be obtained for decorative face-fixing or in a partly hidden version.	Fixing varies according to the design.	For lightweight doors. Cannot be adjusted after fixing. Allows the door to open through 180 degrees. Some designs are suitable for cabinets with drawers or pull-out shelves.
Continuous hinge 	Also known as a piano hinge. Supplied in 6ft (1.8m) lengths, to be cut with a hacksaw to the size of the door. Available in brass, brass-plated steel, chrome-plated steel, aluminium and plastic.	The thin, commonly available types are screwed directly to the solid wood edges of doors and frames.	Alignment is easy because of the length of the hinge which should run from top to bottom of the door. Cannot be adjusted after fitting.
Barrel hinge 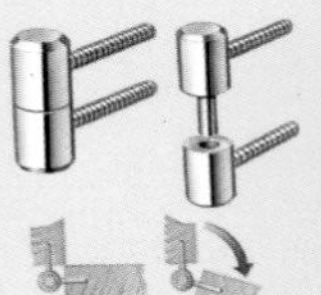 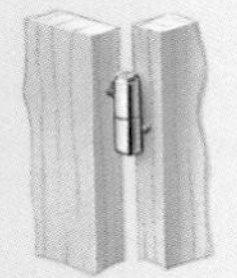 Door Frame	A simple, two-part hinge that allows the door to be removed from the cupboard without taking off the hinge.	Drill holes in the frame and the door edge to take the threaded peg snugly. Fix the part with the pin to the door (pin downwards) and the socket part to the frame. Screw in by hand.	Can be adjusted after fitting by screwing in or out. Can be used on chipboard if the holes are filled with PVA glue as the pegs are screwed in. Allow to dry before adjusting the hinge or using the door. For lightweight doors.

Making compartments of different heights

To house hi-fi and video equipment you may want compartments of several different heights. One compartment will contain records, another video tapes, another audio tapes, and other compartments will contain the equipment itself.

The same principle can be used to accommodate books of different sizes, or piles of linen.

If you put a vertical divider into the basic cupboard, the unit will be divided into two sections, each of which can then have its own shelves spaced at whatever distances you wish.

If peg supports are used to hold the shelves they will have to be staggered in the central division, otherwise the pegs on opposite sides will clash.

If every shelf in the unit is to be at

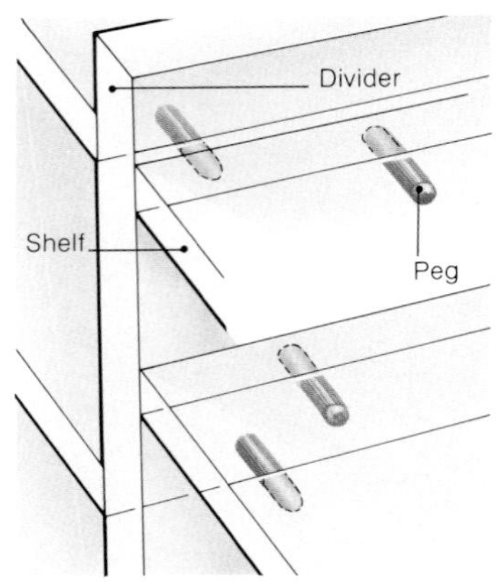

a different height, the pegs will be staggered vertically, and there is no problem. But if you want two shelves to run the full width of the unit at the same height, stagger the holes horizontally in the central division. The shelves will then align.

Fix the vertical division to the basic cupboard with either dowel joints (page 166) or corner joints (page 164).

A door can be put over the front of the cupboard, but if it is to be inset into the frame, the shelves will have to be set back far enough to accommodate it.

This technique can also be used in a shelf unit, in which case the vertical division would have to be fixed to the rear wall as shown on page 179.

Fitting a flap to a cupboard

A flap-door on a cupboard can be hinged at the top or at the bottom so that it either lifts up or drops down.

Drop-down flaps are often used to create a shelf at working height – on a drinks cupboard, for example. Lift-up flaps may be useful on a high-level cupboard to give unobstructed access.

DIY stores sell flaps made of solid wood or veneered chipboard in a range of sizes. Many sizes match the dimensions of standard kitchen or storage units. They can be used to give existing cupboards a facelift or as the basis for building a new cupboard.

If you want a non-standard flap, cut it from veneered chipboard and edge it with matching iron-on veneer or wood lipping.

Hinge the flap in the same way as a vertically hung door (page 182), but put the hinges along the top or bottom edge.

FITTING A STAY

A lift-up flap needs a pair of top-flap stays to hold it up when it is open. A drop-down flap also usually needs a stay to prevent it from falling beyond 90 degrees and breaking the hinges or damaging something else below. The stay will also allow it to be used as a light-weight work surface.

Common designs are sliding stays, in which the supporting arm slides into the cupboard when the flap is closed, and joint stays which have a hinged supporting arm that folds into the cupboard.

Friction stays are a type of sliding stay for a heavy flap, preventing it from dropping suddenly. Some friction stays can be adjusted to hold the flap open at angles other than 90 degrees.

Adjustable concealed hinges (page 183) are available with built-in catches which hold doors open.

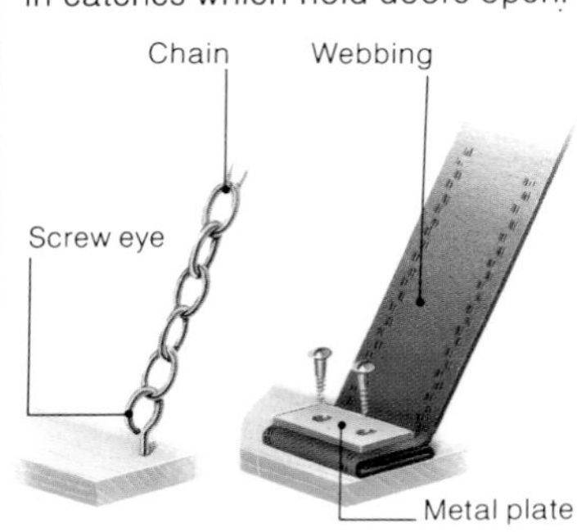

If you prefer, drop-down flaps can be restrained with lightweight chains, cords or webbing. Cords and chains can be attached with screw eyes. Webbing can be fixed with a small metal plate screwed to the flap and the cupboard.

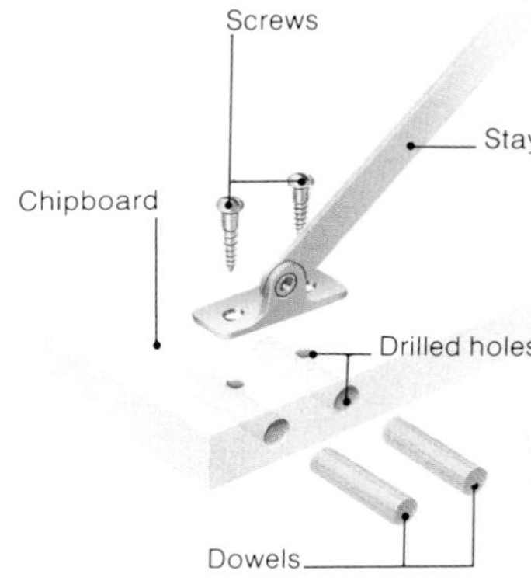

FIXING INTO CHIPBOARD

To fix screws into a chipboard flap, drill into the edge of the board where the screws are to go, and glue a piece of dowel into the hole.

When the glue is dry, drill a pilot hole through the face of the board into the dowel.

The screw will get a firmer hold, and the weight of the flap will be spread over a greater area.

Hanging utensils on pegboard

Pegboard can be fixed to a kitchen wall for hanging cooking utensils on hooks. It also makes a useful rack in a workroom for tools.

Mount the pegboard on a frame ½in (13mm) thick all round the edges to allow space behind for the hooks. Intermediate battens are only necessary if the panel measures more than 18in (460mm) from top to bottom.

A strip of hardwood moulding can be fitted to the edge of the pegboard to cover the sides of the battens and give a neat finish.

Pegboard hooks are pushed horizontally into the holes up to the cranked section, and then pushed down into their final position. They will hold quite heavy weights, such as cast-iron saucepans.

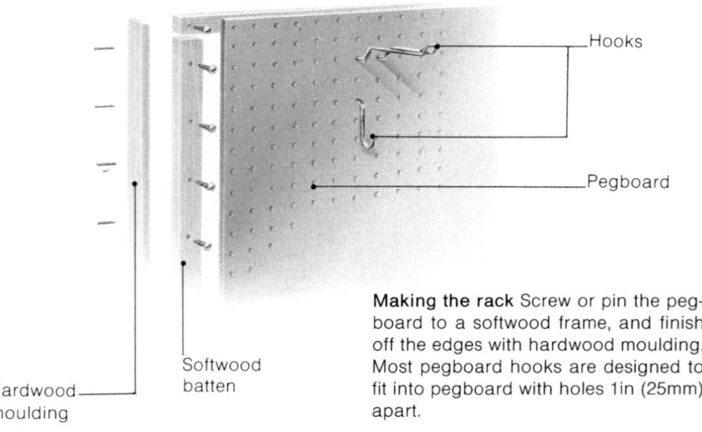

Making the rack Screw or pin the pegboard to a softwood frame, and finish off the edges with hardwood moulding. Most pegboard hooks are designed to fit into pegboard with holes 1in (25mm) apart.

Making sliding cupboard doors

Sliding doors are simpler to make and fit than hinged doors, but part of the cupboard will always be closed. Wide doors slide more smoothly than tall, narrow doors, which jam easily.

Two types of door track are available – one for small doors on wall cupboards and small bookcases, and the other for large cupboards and wardrobes.

TRACK FOR SMALL DOORS

For small, lightweight doors made from plywood or hardboard, a double track made from fibre or plastic is sold in long lengths. It has to be cut with a fine-toothed saw, such as a junior hacksaw, and fitted from side to side of the cupboard.

The system consists of a shallow-grooved bottom section and a more deeply grooved top one. It can only be fitted to cupboards where the top and bottom are parallel with one another. Buy track to match the thickness of the door.

Each section is screwed in place with the front edge flush with the front of the cabinet. Make sure that the fixing screws are well countersunk; if they project the doors will not run smoothly.

> HELPFUL TIP
> As the track stands up from the cupboard bottom, dirt collects inside it and can be difficult to get out. If you stop the track short at one or both ends, leaving a gap of about ¾in (19mm), the dirt can be brushed out.

Door width

A cupboard must have at least two sliding doors. The width of the doors must allow for an overlap of between 1½in-2in (38-50mm) where they meet.

To calculate door width, measure the distance between the inner faces of the cabinet sides. Add the overlap required, and divide by the number of doors.

Two-door example:
Overall inner width of cabinet = 48in; one overlap of 2in required. So 48 + 2 = 50 ÷ 2 doors = 25in per door.

Three-door example:
Overall inner width of cabinet = 62in; two overlaps of 2in each required. So 62 + 2 + 2 = 66 ÷ 3 doors = 22in per door.

Door height

Measure from the inside of the bottom track to the bottom edge of the top track (A). Add the inside depth of the bottom track (B). A door this height can be lifted in.

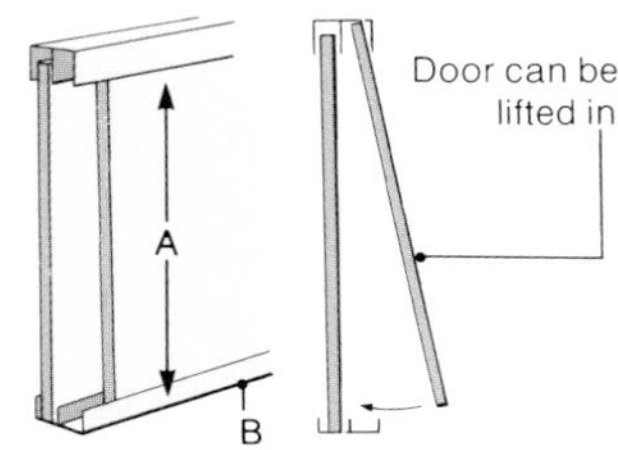

Occasionally rub a candle along the bottom edge of doors; it will keep them running smoothly.

Finger grips

Shallow grips are essential to allow the doors to pass one another. Shallow, round finger pulls can be bought.

If you prefer, holes can be drilled or rectangular cut-outs made in the edge of the doors.

OVERHEAD TRACK SYSTEMS

Large sliding doors for wardrobes and big cupboards are best fitted with an overhead system which suspends each door on rollers running in an aluminium track. The rollers are screwed to the top edge of the door. The bottom of the door is guided by a U-shaped shoe.

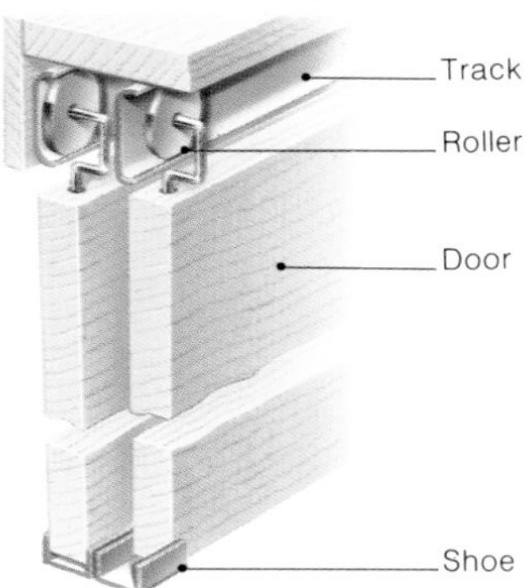

Very light, narrow doors tend to lift off the track if treated roughly, so make doors at least 15in (380mm) wide, and do not use lightweight materials for doors under about 20in (510mm) wide. Medium-density fibreboard and coated chipboard would be suitable materials.

A range of track lengths is available from DIY shops and builders' merchants.

They incorporate adjusters which enable the doors to be adjusted for height and to hang straight.

Fitting catches to a cupboard

Fix cupboard catches near the handle in order to give the most direct pull and to cause the least strain on the door and its hinges. Tall doors may need two catches spaced well apart, with the handle midway between.

MAGNETIC CATCHES

Both inset and lay-on doors can be fitted with magnetic catches.

Large catches have a powerful magnet, so match the size of the catch to the cupboard.

1 Screw the magnet to the side of the cabinet. With a lay-on door, put it flush with the front. With an inset door, set it back by the thickness of the door. It can also be fitted to a central shelf.

2 Place the flat plate squarely over the magnet bars. Close the door over the plate and gently push. The pip in the plate will make a tiny indent in the door.

3 Open the door, put the plate on the mark and make screw holes.

4 Screw the plate in place.

5 If necessary, adjust the magnet by loosening its screws, correcting the position, and retightening.

ROLLER CATCHES

Both inset and lay-on doors can be fitted with roller catches, which are made in metal or plastic in a range of sizes.

1 Screw the striker plate to the inside of the cabinet. On a lay-on door, set it flush with the front. On an inset door set it back by the thickness of the door.

2 Screw the catch to the door at the same height, and in from the edge sufficiently for the roller to strike and pass over the striker plate as the door is closed.

3 Make adjustments by loosening the screws on plate and catch.

BALL CATCHES

Plastic or solid brass ball catches are almost invisible when fitted. They are made in several sizes but can only be used on inset doors which are a close fit. They are not suitable on chipboard.

1 Mark the height of the catch centrally on the door's edge.

2 Drill a hole the exact diameter of the body and deep enough to take the whole length of the housing.

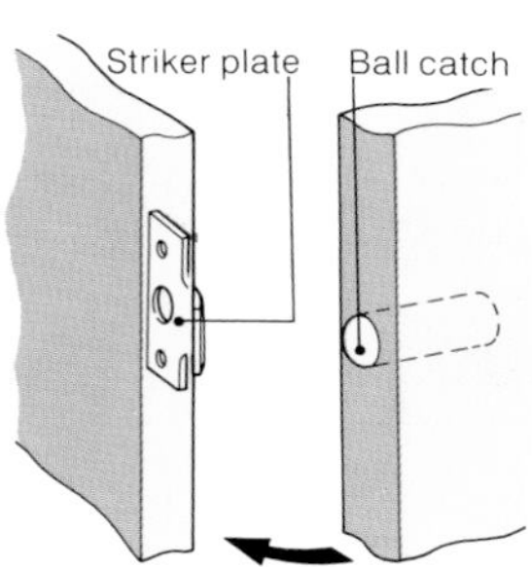

3 Drive the ball catch into the hole until the top of its rim is flush with the door. Protect the ball with a piece of wood.

4 Close the door until the ball touches the cabinet edge. Mark its centre and draw a horizontal line for a short distance.

5 Measure the distance of the ball centre from the front of the door. Transfer that onto the line. That is the point where the central hole in the striker plate must fit.

6 Place the striker plate in place, with the tab projecting, and draw around its edge.

7 Recess that area to the depth of the metal. Cut the tab position slightly deeper at its front edge. Screw the plate in place and bend the tab into its undercut wedge.

Making drawers from a plastic kit

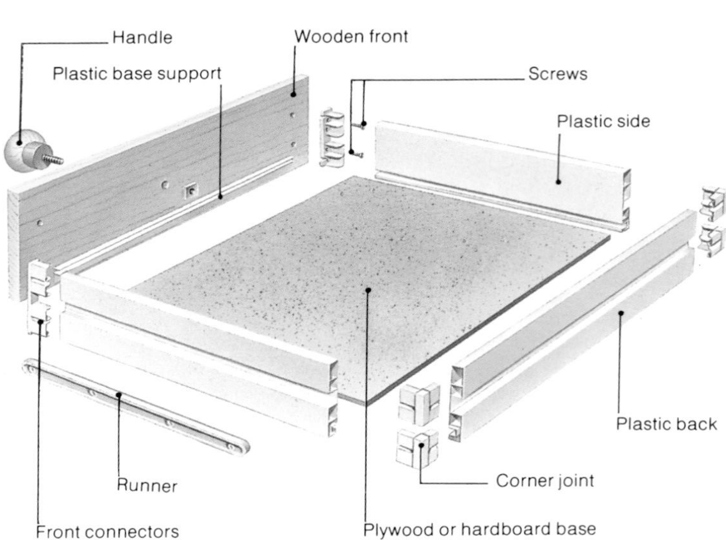

A single drawer can easily be made up and fixed inside an existing kitchen-cupboard. Several drawers can be combined as a stack.

A drawer can be made from a plastic kit, plus a wooden front and base. Lengths of extruded plastic are cut to size and connected with plastic joints to make up the sides and back.

The wooden front can be bought ready-made or can be made from softwood or wood-veneered chipboard. The drawer base can be cut to size from plywood or painted hardboard.

Plastic runners can also be bought for fixing to the cupboard.

DECIDING THE SIZE OF THE DRAWER FRONT

Using a drawer kit, any length or width of drawer can be made, but drawers will run better if they are longer from front to back than side to side.

A drawer front normally fits over the front of the cabinet, but it can also be fitted within the sides if you wish to fit a door as well.

The front of the drawer can be

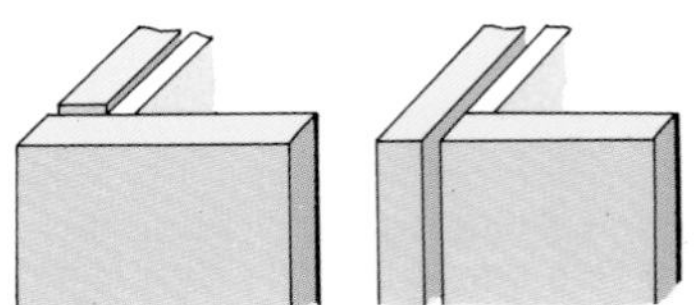

Overlapping drawer   Set-in drawer

the same height as the plastic sides, or higher. If you are installing a stack of drawers, the height may be determined by the number of drawers required in the space available. So measure out a full-size drawing of the space and the drawer sizes you want. Then the heights of drawer fronts can be checked before cutting.

A convenient method is to draw out the plan on a spare board. A gap of about ⅛in (3mm) will be needed between drawers. If you are using chipboard for the drawer front, allow for the thickness of the veneer edging – about $\frac{1}{16}$in (2mm) per front.

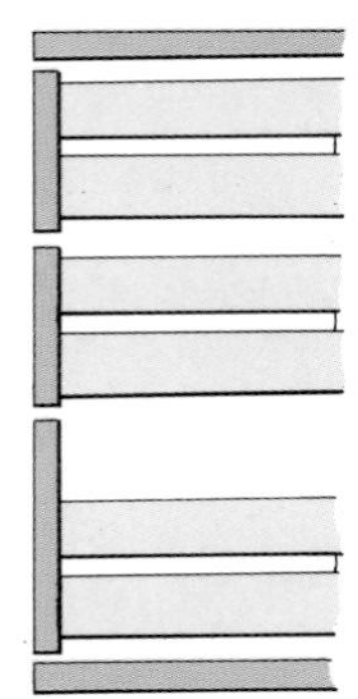

Drawer fronts can vary in height to make several drawers fit a particular space.

You will need

Tools Try square; pencil; tenon saw; screwdriver; steel tape measure; spirit level; length of wood batten.
Materials See diagram.

ASSEMBLING THE DRAWER

1 When your plan is complete, buy all the component parts (see the diagram at the top left of the page), and follow the instructions given with the kit.

The sides and back must have square ends, so mark the cutting line carefully with a try square and pencil. Use a fine-toothed saw, such as a tenon saw or hacksaw. If the ends are slightly out of square after cutting, trim them with a plane or file.

2 Cut the fronts to size and veneer any raw edges (page 156). Then screw on the plastic front connectors and base support.

3 Measure the width and length of the base so that it fits into the channels all round. Make sure that all four corners are right angles, because the base holds the drawer square. Cut the base to size.

4 When everything goes together correctly, take it apart, apply glue to all the corner joints and reassemble the drawer. Press the joints tightly together, and leave for the glue to dry.

FITTING THE DRAWER RUNNERS

Fitting drawers to runners is straightforward if the inside of the cabinet is flush from front to back. However, if there are framing pieces at the front and back, wooden packing strips will have to be fitted before the runners can be screwed in place.

1 Get someone to hold the drawer in the cupboard at the correct height. Push the drawer to one side and draw a line along the side of the cupboard where either the top or the bottom of the drawer rests against it.

2 Check with a spirit level that the line is horizontal.

3 Take the drawer out. Hold an offcut of the plastic drawer side, end on, against the line and mark the exact position of the runner.

4 Cut a batten to fit between the bottom of the cupboard and the lower of those two marks. This provides a prop to support the runner as it is fitted in place.

If you are fitting several drawers, start at the top. The batten can be cut down to fit each runner.

Connecting one cabinet to another

Sometimes you may need to join one shelf unit or cupboard to another, perhaps to extend an existing unit by adding an extra section. Standing one unit beside the other is often satisfactory if it is low. But as units become higher they tend to separate and leave a gap.

Plastic connection screws can be used to lock the two firmly together. They are made to join two ⅝in (16mm) panels, but they can be used up to a maximum width of 40mm or to a minimum of 26mm.

You will need

Tools Pair of G-cramps; pencil; drill and twist bit slightly larger than the diameter of the connecting screw; two 2p pieces.
Materials Two plastic connecting screws.

1 Place the cabinets together exactly as required. Alternatively, at the time of building two units which are to be joined, place the joining sides together.

2 Hold them together firmly with G-cramps.

3 Mark the position of the bolts on the face of one panel.

4 With a piece of scrap wood held against the far side, drill a hole slightly larger than the diameter of the screws.

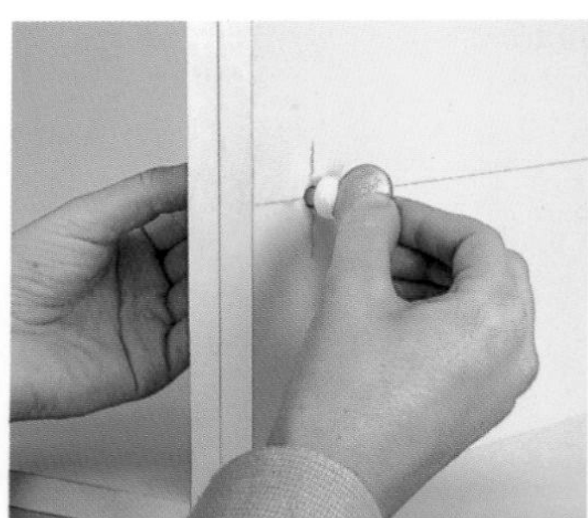

5 Insert the two halves of the connecting screw and tighten with coins (a screwdriver may damage the slots).

Planning worktops for a kitchen or workroom

There are two types of worktops – solid wood and chipboard veneered with wood or plastic.

Solid wood worktops – usually in pine – are made from a series of narrow boards jointed together to a width of 24in (610mm) and thickness of $\frac{3}{4}$in (19mm).

Veneered boards, mostly imported, are in metric sizes. The width is 600mm (23$\frac{5}{8}$in) and lengths range from 2 to 5 metres (6ft 6$\frac{3}{4}$in-16ft 5in). The thickness is usually 30mm (1$\frac{3}{16}$in). The front edge may be rounded or square. The ends may not be veneered and matching veneers are not usually available. So if one end of a worktop will be visible, try to find one that has a veneered end.

Because worktops are made in such a variety of lengths it is usually possible to span from wall to wall with a single piece.

MAKING THEM WATERPROOF

All worktops that are likely to get wet must be thoroughly sealed. Coat solid wood or wood-veneered tops with varnish or Danish oil.

Plastic veneered tops need careful sealing around edges and ends where the chipboard core is exposed.

If the sink or hob is not an inset model, with overhanging flanges, worktops will have to butt up to it. Cut the worktop ends as close as possible to it. Coat the cut ends with several coats of varnish until they are totally sealed. Fill the fine join between the sink and worktop with a waterproof sealant.

JOINING TWO WORKTOPS

When right-angled turns have to be made in a worktop a join is inevitable. The job is complicated by the fact that few corners in houses are at 90 degrees. Another problem that often arises is that the other end of a worktop may be pressed against a wall or the side of a tall fixed unit. So measurements have to be exact.

A join can sometimes be hidden under the overhanging flange of a sinktop or hob.

1 First deal with a worktop which will have no cut-out. Scribe (overleaf) and fix it in place the full length of the wall (see drawing below).

2 The exact angle of the end of the second worktop will only be found after the back has been scribed to the wall. So cut the second worktop overlength by about 1in (25mm).

3 Use offcuts to prop the far end level with the end that is resting over the fixed worktop. Carefully adjust the far end so that – apart from being propped up – it is in line with its final position.

4 Scribe the back edge to the wall (overleaf) and cut it to fit.

5 Put it back in place and draw a line on the underside of the second worktop along the edge of the first.

Use a try square to mark from the line on the underside, up the back and front edges. Draw a straight line across the top to join exactly with the marks on the edges. With a sharp blade, score down the top and edge marks to reduce the chance of chipping when cutting the top to length. Cut on the waste side of the line.

6 Trim the cut with a sharp plane until the joint fits exactly. Seal the open grain of the cut end with a liberal coat of varnish.

7 The joint should be supported and held together permanently, perhaps with three or four dowel joints (page 166).

ALTERNATIVELY, use a batten 3in (75mm) wide screwed to both tops. Use at least three screws on each side of the join.

JOINING SQUARE EDGE TO ROUND EDGE

If worktops have rounded front edges, use plastic jointing strip where two lengths meet at a corner. The strip is sold for the purpose.

Cut it to the width of the top and screw it to the square edge.

Run some silicone sealant along the curve of the strip and press it firmly against the curved edge of the other worktop.

FIXING WORKTOPS IN PLACE

Before fixing the worktops, cut away any vertical divisions in the cupboards which would prevent appliances from fitting into cutouts that are to be made later.

Supporting the back edge

The back edge of a worktop should be supported all along its length.

The cabinets beneath it may have a rail running along the top back edge. Screw through the rail into the wall and also up into the underside of the top.

If a rail does not exist, you will have to fit a piece of 2in × 1in (50mm × 25mm) softwood. The top back corners of each vertical divider of the cabinet will have to be cut away to allow space for the rail. Attach each divider to the rail with corner joints (page 164).

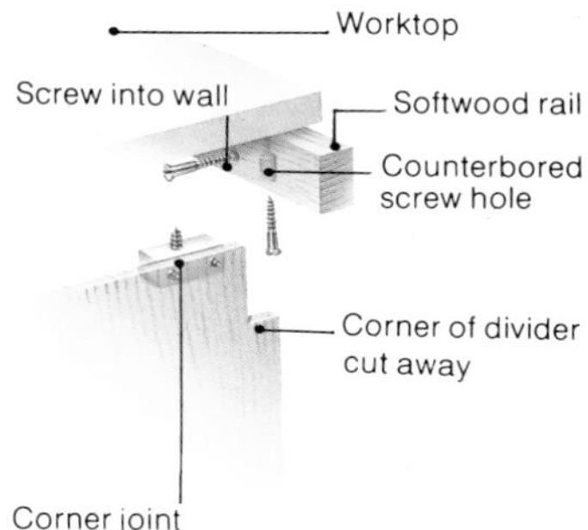

Insert screws through the rail into the wall and the worktop near each end and at about 24in (610mm) intervals along the length. To screw into the worktop, counterbore the rail to a depth of about 1in (25mm) (page 161).

The rail may have to be stopped each side of pipes.

Supporting the front edge

The front of the worktop also has to be supported. The method will depend on the construction of the cabinets. If a front rail is fitted, screw through it into the underside of the top. If there is no rail, use plastic corner joints or a small right-angled steel bracket to connect each of the front verticals of the cabinet to the worktop.

Worktops which span between units to leave space for a washing machine or dishwasher need no support; this would prevent the machine from fitting in the space.

If you intend spanning a worktop over a boiler or flue, get advice from a heating engineer. Special ventilation or heat-resistant materials may have to be incorporated.

MAKING A CUT-OUT FOR A SINK OR HOB

To prevent the worktop from breaking across the narrow strips left at the front and back of the cut-out, it is essential to centre the cut-out on the worktop. Use the paper template supplied with the sink or hob to mark the position of the cut-out on the worktop surface.

Drill a hole within the waste area big enough to admit the blade of the jigsaw. Use the type that cuts on the downstroke to minimise chipping of the laminate. Start the cut and drive the blade out to the cutting line. Then follow it round, taking care not to force it or the blade will deform and leave an angled cut. Support the cut-out as you complete the cut to prevent it breaking away.

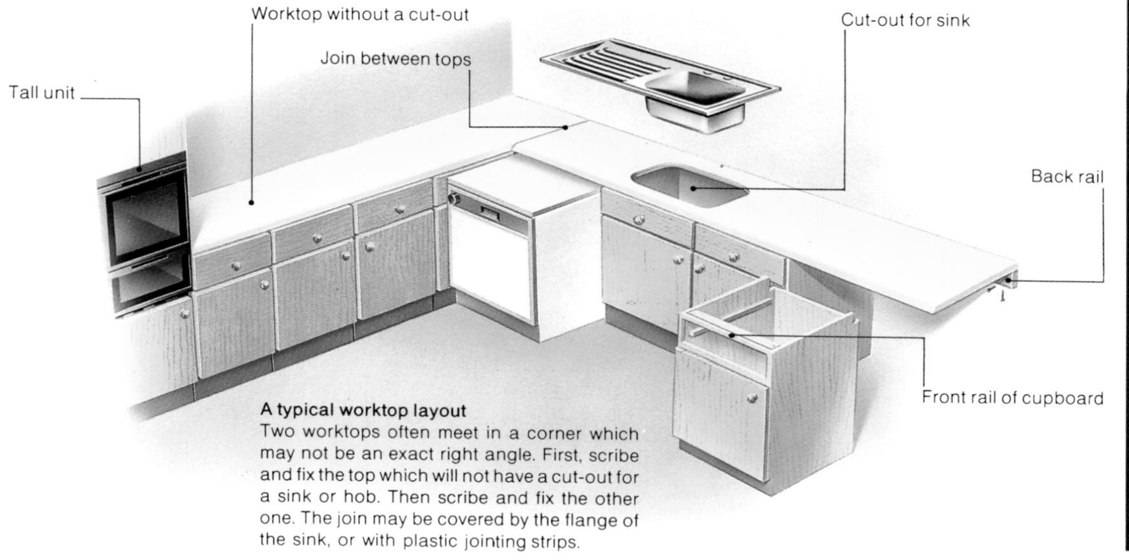

A typical worktop layout
Two worktops often meet in a corner which may not be an exact right angle. First, scribe and fix the top which will not have a cut-out for a sink or hob. Then scribe and fix the other one. The join may be covered by the flange of the sink, or with plastic jointing strips.

Fitting worktops to a wall

A worktop spanning a number of kitchen units will rarely fit the shape of the wall exactly. Before cutting it to shape, fit the base units to the walls with the blocks or metal plates that are usually provided. First, however, the side panels of the units may have to be cut to fit over skirting boards, and sometimes piping.

When the units are in place, push the worktop back until it touches the wall. There will probably be gaps and if the worktop fits into a corner any variations from 90 degrees will also show up.

Gaps of up to about ⅜in (10mm) can often be adjusted to a closer fit by cutting away high spots in the plasterwork. Use a cold chisel, or an abrasive disc on an electric drill, or an old wood chisel that is not wanted again for wood. Then finish the patches with DIY plaster (page 239).

If final decoration includes wall tiling, the thickness of the tiles is usually enough to cover the minor gaps that remain. If you are not fitting tiles, fill minor gaps with bath or frame sealant or with cover fillets.

If gaps exceed ⅜in (10mm), you will have to scribe the back edge of the worktop to the wall shape.

THE TECHNIQUE OF SCRIBING

The scribing process is identical for horizontal or vertical panels. It is essential to hold the panel as near to its final position as the wall allows while you scribe it.

The front edge of an upright panel must be vertical before scribing starts. You will need someone to hold the panel steady while the scribing is done.

You will need
Tools Block of wood about 1in × ½in (25mm × 13mm) and as long as the widest point of the gap; pencil; electric jigsaw or panel saw.

1 Measure the distance between the wall and the worktop or panel where the gap is greatest. Cut the block of wood to that length.

2 Starting at one end of the worktop or panel, place one end of the block firmly against the wall with its face on the worktop.

3 Put the point of a pencil at the centre of the other end of the block so that the lead is touching both the block and the worktop.

4 Move the block along the wall so that the pencil draws an outline of the wall onto the worktop for its whole length. Avoid tipping either the block or the pencil; you will cause the line to be inaccurate.

5 Using an electric jigsaw or panel saw, cut exactly to the line, on the waste side. The worktop will now fit the shape of the wall.

6 Any small gaps that still remain can be hidden with cover fillets (below), or they can be filled with bath or frame sealant applied with a sealant gun.

FITTING COVER FILLETS TO A WORKTOP

Small gaps or unsightly chipped edges can be covered with small wooden mouldings either square, rectangular or quadrant in shape. Buy the smallest size that will cover the gap. They can be pinned to the worktop to cover the gaps, following the undulations of the wall.

You will need
Tools Tenon saw; benchhook or vice; hand drill and $\frac{1}{32}$in (1mm) twist bit; hammer; pin punch.
Materials Small wood moulding the length of the worktop; ¾in (19mm) panel pins; waterproof wood filler.

1 Cut the wood moulding to the length of the worktop, and paint or polish before fixing.

2 Since most small wood mouldings are made of hardwood, drill fine holes through it, at about 12in (300mm) intervals. This will prevent it from splitting and will reduce the chance of the pins bending. Drill holes of the same size through melamine veneer on the worktop, but not through wood veneer. Hold the moulding against the wall as you drill into a melamine surface.

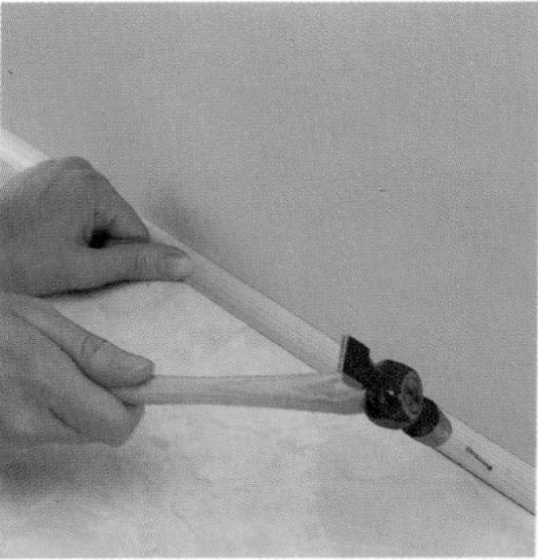

3 Hold the moulding firmly in place against the wall so that it follows any undulations, and pin it to the worktop.

4 If you wish, punch the pin heads below the surface with a pin punch and fill the holes with matching waterproof wood filler.

Filling gaps between built-in cupboards

The width of kitchen or wardrobe units seldom adds up to the dimensions of the room where they are being installed. The gap that is left can sometimes be used to create extra storage space.

A narrow gap can be left between two units and used for trays or a pull-out towel rail. The worktop simply passes across the top.

A wider space could be distributed equally between two narrow gaps at different places, or it could be used to install an extra cupboard that is narrower than the others. This is something that you could make partly or entirely yourself.

The information on making cupboards and wardrobes on pages 181-183 will provide construction details for most problems. The greatest difficulty will be matching manufactured units which are made from materials that are not available in the DIY market.

ADAPTING A MATCHING UNIT

When filling a gap with an undersized unit, the visible faces should match – worktop, door drawer front and external fittings. The inside is not important.

If the units are assembled in the factory, buy an extra door or drawer front and fit it to a framework that you make yourself.

If the units are for self-assembly buy an extra one the nearest size larger than the gap. Then cut it down to size.

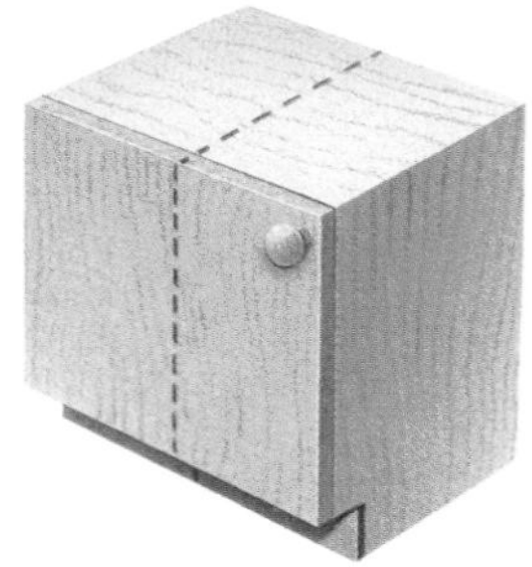

To cut down a self-assembly unit, carefully study the construction system so that you are able to relocate the fittings in their new positions when the panels are cut down to the new size. Only the cabinet sections that span the width will normally have to be cut.

If doors are flat, cut off the closing rather than the hinged side. This will save you from having to re-hinge and possibly re-lip the door.

If the door is coated with a melamine or wood veneer take extra care to score the cutting line with a sharp knife before sawing, otherwise you will get a chipped edge. When cutting with a hand saw, place the face of the door uppermost; for a power saw place it downwards because a power saw cuts upwards.

You may be able to strip the edging veneer from the offcut with a chisel or knife and re-glue it to the new edge. If this is not possible, buy a veneer strip of the nearest match, or fill and stain the edge. Alternatively, cover the edge with a thin strip of hardwood lipping, pinned and glued.

Decorative panelled doors cannot usually be reduced in width by a total of more than about 2in (50mm), depending on the width of the side rails and the joints used. So take advice before buying them. If you reduce a panelled door by a small amount, take equal slices from each side.

If the gap is too narrow to take a reduced door, a specially ordered one will have to be made, either by the manufacturer or by a woodworker. Or you could make a non-matching door with a flat front instead.

DRAWER FRONTS

Plain drawer fronts can be cut down in the same way as doors but decorative fronts provide the same problems as doors.

EXTENDING A WORKTOP

If you are planning a new installation, buy a top long enough to span the total length and, if necessary, cut it down to fit (page 187).

If the worktop is already fitted to the units it may be possible to buy a short length to match, and then join it on with dowel joints (page 166).

An alternative is to change materials completely for the area that has been extended, and make a section out of hardwood. Or you could buy a teak chopping board and cut it to fit. Or make a tiled section, which could be used for pastry making.

4 Glues for household use

Working with glue

PREPARING THE SURFACE

The surfaces to be joined should be clean and grease-free. You cannot expect a good bond if you are merely gluing dirt to dirt. Unless the instructions on the container say otherwise, the surfaces should also be dry.

Wood

Clean the wood by rubbing it with abrasive paper, and then dusting off. This will also roughen the surface slightly to provide a key for the glue. Remove any paint and other old finishes by scraping or by using a chemical paint stripper (page 105). Any old glue should also be scraped off the wood.

CHOOSING THE RIGHT GLUE FOR THE JOB

A basic glue kit will cope with most household jobs. All-purpose glue will deal with small repairs where strength is not too important. Epoxy and 'super' glues will stick pottery and metal. PVA woodworking glue is suitable for general carpentry.

Manufacturers' charts, available in shops or on the reverse of glue packaging, will tell you the right glue to use for sticking a large selection of different materials to each other. The following is a general guide for most common situations, together with the appropriate cleaner to remove excess glue before it dries. Some makers also produce solvents that will remove glue after it has dried.

TYPES OF MATERIAL	BRAND NAME AND CLEANER
General household materials All-purpose glues are sold in tubes or glue guns for sticking most household materials, such as paper, card, wood and leather and some soft plastics. Easy to use where strength is not too important.	*BRAND NAMES:* Bostik All Purpose; Evo-Stik Multi-Purpose Clear; Loctite All Purpose Adhesive; UHU All Purpose. *CLEANER:* Acetone (nail-varnish remover).
Wood and boards Modern chemical glues have largely replaced the traditional animal glues that joiners used to heat up in a kettle. They will stick hardwood and softwood, and man-made boards such as plywood, hardboard, blockboard and chipboard.	*BRAND NAMES:* Bostik Wood Adhesive Rapide; Evo-Stik Resin 'W' Extra Fast Wood Adhesive; Humbrol Extrabond; Humbrol Extrarez; Humbrol Cascamite; Unibond Woodworker. *Out of doors:* Bostik 6; Evo-Stik Resin 'W' Weatherproof Wood Adhesive; Unibond Waterproof Woodworker. *CLEANER:* See container.
Plastic laminates, foam, leather Plastic laminates and flexible sheets, such as foam or leather, can be stuck with a contact adhesive. It is spread on both surfaces and allowed to dry before the two pieces are joined. They stick immediately they come in contact, so cramps are not necessary. But you must position them accurately before pressing them together. Some contact adhesives have a short 'slip' period when the surfaces first meet so that you can move the materials as long as you do not apply pressure. Most contact adhesives are solvent-based, so never smoke or have a naked flame nearby as you work. Water-based types, which are not flammable, are also available.	*BRAND NAMES: Solvent-based:* Bostik Contact; Evo-Stik Impact Adhesive; UHU Power Stic; UHU Spray; UHU Power. *Solvent-based with 'slip' period:* Dunlop Thixofix; Evo-Stik Time Bond. *Water-based:* Evo-Stik Impact 2; PVA Unibond adhesive and sealer. *CLEANER:* Special solvents are sold for solvent-based contact adhesives. You can also try nail-varnish remover (acetone). Water-based types can be cleaned up with a damp cloth.
Flexible plastic Flexible PVC (also called vinyl) can be repaired by gluing another piece of the same material over it with PVC cement. Nylon and polythene cannot be glued, so experiment first with some spare material.	*BRAND NAMES:* Loctite Soft Plastic Adhesive. *CLEANER:* Acetone (nail-varnish remover), but use sparingly or it will damage the plastic.
Hard plastic Rigid polystyrene, which is used for some kitchen equipment and plastic models, can be glued with polystyrene cement. (It is not suitable for expanded polystyrene.)	*BRAND NAMES:* Evo-Stik Hard Plastic Adhesive; Humbrol Polystyrene Cement; UHU Plastic Glue. *CLEANER:* See container
Pottery, glass, metal Three types of glue can be used – epoxy resin, two-part acrylic, and cyanoacrylate ('super glue'). Epoxy resins consist of two parts – resin and hardener. They are mixed together and applied to both surfaces. They are totally waterproof when set, but leave a glue line. With two-part acrylic types the glue is applied to one surface and the hardener to the other. Cyanoacrylate glues are easier to use, as no mixing is needed, and they leave hardly any glue line. But they will not stand up to immersion in water. For glass and crockery which must contain liquids, use Glass Bond which also gives an invisible join. Usually surfaces to be joined with cyanoacrylate must be a perfect fit; as most types of this glue will not fill gaps. Do not get the glue on your skin. It dries extremely quickly. If your fingers become stuck to each other, soak them for a few minutes in hot soapy water and prise the fingers apart with a blunt instrument, never tear. Keep glue away from children; clean up any spilled glue immediately, using the solvent if one is supplied.	*BRAND NAMES: Epoxy resin:* Araldite Rapid; Araldite Precision; Araldite Instant Clear; Bostik Epoxy; Humbrol Selfmix Epoxy; Permabond E; Plastic Padding Super Epoxy. *Two-part acrylic:* Loctite Multi-Bond. *Cyanoacrylate:* Bostik Super Glue 4; Evo-Stik Super Glue; Humbrol Superglue; Loctite Super Glue; Loctite Supergluematic; UHU Super Power; UHU Super Power Gel. *CLEANER: Epoxy resin:* Wipe with white spirit before adhesive sets. *Two-part acrylic:* Wipe with cloth or tissue. When dry, glue can be trimmed with a craft knife. *Cyanoacrylate:* Acetone (nail-varnish remover), or release agent which may be supplied with the glue. Also hot, soapy water.
Expanded polystyrene To stick expanded polystyrene to walls or ceilings, either as tiles or sheets, use an adhesive made for the purpose.	*BRAND NAMES:* Evo-Stik Ceiling, Tile and Coving Adhesive; Unibond polystyrene and plaster cove adhesive. *CLEANER:* Damp cloth.
Paper and card Liquid pastes and gums are the traditional way of sticking paper and card, but tend to wrinkle the surface. Rubber solutions are sold in a tin and are put on with a plastic spatula. They are useful for large areas, and surplus glue can be peeled off when dry. Stick glue is sold in a plastic dispenser like a large lipstick. Reusable adhesives are used in lumps to fix card and paper to notice boards. Do not use it on a papered wall. Other glues are designed especially for children to use.	*BRAND NAMES: Pastes and gums:* Bostik Paper Glue; Evo-Stik Paper Pen; Gloy Gum; UHU Gluepen; UHU Stylo. *Stick glue:* Pritt Stick; UHU Stic. *Reusable adhesives:* Bostik Blu-Tack; Pritt Tak; UHU Tac. *Children's glue:* Copydex; Gloy Patch; UHU Magic Stic; UHU Glitter Glue; UHU Kid. *CLEANER:* Wipe up liquid paste or gum, stick glue or children's glue with damp cloth. Soap and water will wash it off fabrics.
Carpet and fabrics Use a latex-based fabric adhesive, which is white when first applied, but is less obvious when dry.	*BRAND NAMES:* Copydex; Evo-Stik Fabric Adhesive; UHU Fabric Glue. *CLEANER:* Damp cloth while wet.

Paper and card
Clean with a rubber eraser. Superficial grease can be removed with fabric cleaner (carbon tetrachloride) or pieces of bread rolled into pellets.

Crockery, ceramics, plastics
Wash with detergent in water. Stubborn marks can be scrubbed with neat washing-up liquid or abrasive powder. An old toothbrush or a nail brush are useful on small surfaces. Rinse thoroughly and allow to dry. If you are in a hurry, dry with a lint-free cloth or a hair dryer.

Metals
Wash with detergent in water but dry iron or steel immediately to avoid rust. Any rust already there can be removed with a fine wire brush or emery cloth. Or use a chemical rust inhibitor.

APPLYING THE GLUE

Liquid glues are spread on the surface by brush, more solid ones with a notched spreader. A disposable spreader is usually provided with the glue, although more substantial spreaders can be bought as permanent tools.

The spreader combs the glue into ridges, spreading it to the correct depth. Small tubes of glue often have a spreader that you screw onto the tube's nozzle in place of the cap.

A glue gun is used with a stick of glue that looks like a small candle. It is melted by a heating element in the gun and is fed onto the work through a nozzle. The gun is useful where thin ribbons, or small dabs, of glue are needed and is economical if you will be doing a lot of gluing jobs.

CLEANING UP

Try to avoid spillages, or excess glue oozing out, whenever you use an adhesive. Some glues can cause stains that are difficult to remove; woodworking adhesives, for example, can cause marks that will show through any clear finish. Have a cloth ready to clean up glue before it dries. Some glues can be removed with water, others need special cleaners.

Once a glue has hardened, it usually must be scraped off.

Cramps for holding the work

With most adhesives, the items to be stuck must be held firmly together until the glue has set. This process is known as cramping or clamping – the two terms are interchangeable. The pieces can be held in a vice, between protective pieces of wood, or they can be held with cramps.

G-CRAMPS

The most common tool for the job is the G-cramp, a metal frame shaped like the letter G. The work is gripped between two 'shoes', one of which is adjustable.

G-cramps are sold in a large number of jaw sizes, ranging from 1in (25mm) to 8in (200mm). The shoes are usually fixed to a ball joint and will adjust to grip objects of different shapes.

To get the best from G-cramps, you need more than one. For example, if you are gluing two lengths of timber together use one G-cramp at each end.

EDGE CRAMP

A third shoe on the edge cramp enters from the back of the G. It is used for holding lipping onto the edge of a board.

QUICK-RELEASE CRAMPS

Also called F-cramps, these are similar to G-cramps, but have two jaws fixed to a metal bar. One of the jaws moves along the bar, and you operate the clamping screw for the final tightening. The work can be clamped and released much more quickly than with a G-cramp.

CRAMPS FOR LARGE JOBS

Various types are used for holding large objects, such as sash windows or door frames. They are expensive but can be hired by the day from tool hire shops – found in *Yellow Pages* under Hire Services – Tools and Equipment.

Web cramp

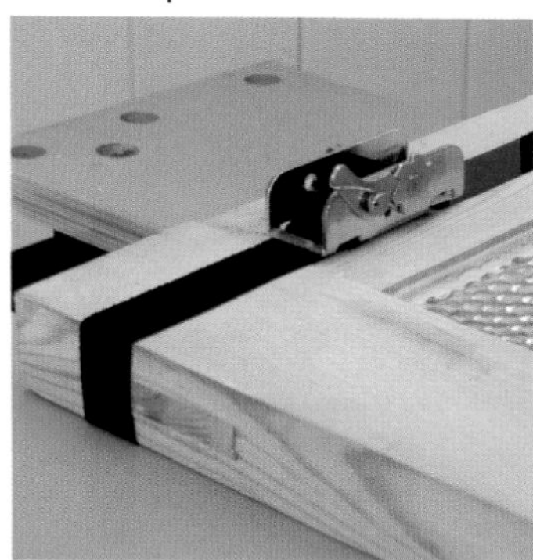

A long belt is wrapped around the objects you wish to cramp, passed through a buckle, and tightened. Web cramps are normally used for large items such as cupboards. They can also be used to hold things on a car roof rack.

Sash cramp

The long bar has two jaws. One jaw can move along the bar, and is locked in place by a metal peg. Final adjustment is made by turning the threaded shaft that moves the other jaw.

Speed cramp

The bar has two movable jaws, for speed of operation. Final tightening is done with a clamping screw.

IMPROVISING YOUR OWN CRAMPS

Heavy weights
Large, flat items can be sandwiched between two pieces of plywood with a weight placed on top. Heavy books or a bucket of water make good weights.

Cord and blocks

To tighten a picture frame or tea tray, take eight small blocks of wood and put two of them on each edge of the frame in the centre.

Put protective material, such as pieces of cardboard or leather, at the corners of the frame, and tie a cord as tightly as you can around the edge.

Push the blocks outwards towards the corners, and they will tighten the cord fully. Make sure not to disturb the corner joints as you do it.

Spanish windlass

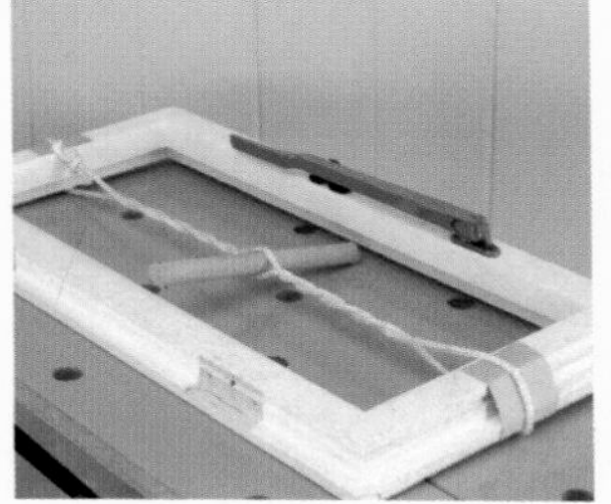

Large wooden objects, such as a window frame or chairs, can be held together with a Spanish windlass, which consists of a short stick and a length of cord or rope. Tie the cord loosely around the object. Put a stick through the cord and twist it round and round until the cord has tightened, pulling the frame together. Be sure to protect the wood from damage where the cord pulls tightly against it.

When cramping is finished, manoeuvre the stick into a position where it will not come undone until the glue dries.

Supporting awkward shapes

The most difficult part of gluing broken crockery, glasses or plastic objects can be holding them firmly in place long enough for the glue to dry.

This page gives several suggestions which can be adapted to objects of different sizes that are awkwardly shaped and consequently difficult to support.

A BOX OF SAND

1 Fill a container, such as a plastic sandwich box or a bowl, with silver sand.

The sand can be bought from builders' merchants or in small amounts from some pet shops.

2 Push the object into the sand so that the broken piece will stand upright in the correct position.

3 Apply a thin layer of epoxy resin – or other appropriate glue – to both surfaces. Take care not to put on too much glue or sand will stick to the object.

4 Press the broken piece in place and run your fingernail across the join to check that it is absolutely accurate.

5 Leave for the appropriate time until the glue has set.

GLUING A BROKEN TILE

A broken ceramic tile can easily be glued together on a flat working surface. The job is only really worthwhile for old tiles that are no longer replaceable.

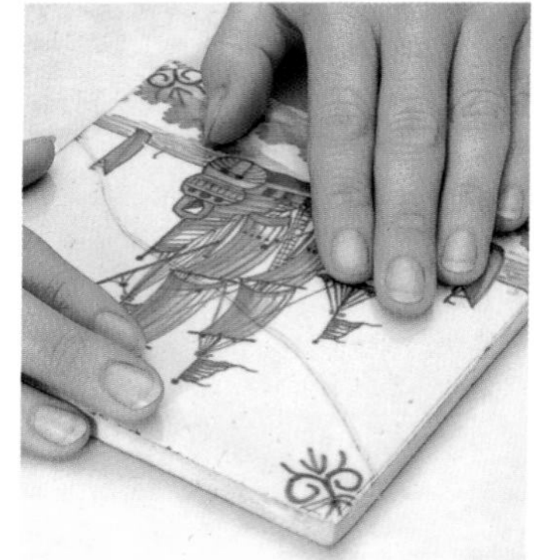

1 Put a piece of paper under the broken pieces of tile. Apply a thin coating of epoxy resin glue on both the broken surfaces and press them together. Run your fingernail across the join to check that it is accurate.

2 Wipe excess glue off the upper surface with solvent or with white spirit.

3 Tape the glass or tile to the work surface to hold the two pieces together. Leave overnight for the glue to dry.

4 Remove surplus glue from the underside of the tile with a razor blade.

PUTTY OR PLASTICINE TO HOLD A GLASS STEM

1 Rest the bowl of the glass upside down on a work surface. Press a piece of putty or Plasticine firmly against the bowl at the point of the break so that it will support the glass stem.

2 Spread a thin coating of Glass Bond on both broken surfaces, and press them together. Run your fingernail over the join to make sure it is accurate.

3 Push the putty firmly against (not around) the stem to support it. The putty must not prevent light from getting to the adhesive as Glass Bond is set by daylight.

4 Leave the glass for about ten minutes for the glue to set, then remove the putty.

TAPING A HANDLE IN PLACE

1 To glue a broken handle onto a large jug or pot, spread a thin layer of epoxy resin or Glass Bond on both surfaces and put them carefully together. Do not repair handles of vessels that contain boiling liquids. Throw them out.

2 Run your fingernail across the join to check its accuracy.

3 Place a piece of adhesive tape across the handle and onto both sides of the jug, making sure that the tension is the same on both sides. Adjust it until you have a perfect join.

4 Put more pieces of tape diagonally across the handle to hold it securely in place, and leave it for the glue to set according to the maker's instructions.

AN OPEN DRAWER TO HOLD A PLATE

1 If a plate has broken cleanly in two, stand the larger piece upright, with the broken side up, in a partly open drawer.

2 Put a thin layer of epoxy resin glue or Glass Bond on both broken surfaces and balance the top piece of plate in position. Check with your fingernail that the join is accurately aligned.

3 Leave the plate standing upright for the glue to dry. When it has set, you can trim off any surplus glue with a razor blade or a craft knife with a new blade.

USING BANDS OF ELASTIC OR RUBBER

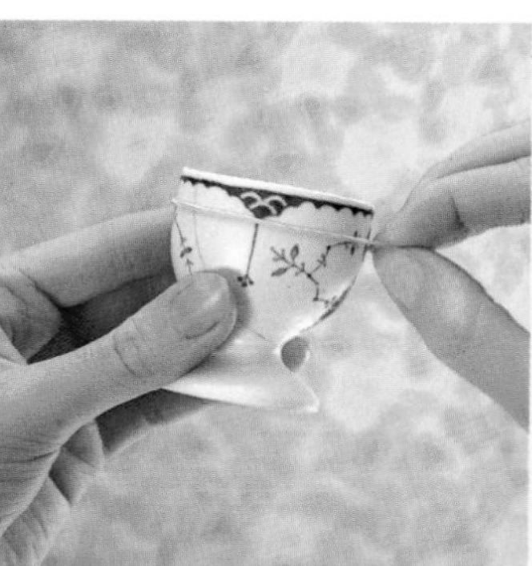

Small, awkwardly shaped objects can be held under light but steady pressure with elastic bands of different sizes and strengths.

Strips of old cycle inner tube, cut from the length of the tube, can be used in a similar way for large things.

5 Doors & windows

Doors

Windows

How doors are made

There are two main types of door – panelled and flush. Both types are available in exterior and interior grades. Exterior doors are thicker and stronger to withstand weather and intruders.

Panelled doors have a timber framework consisting of two vertical stiles and two or more horizontal rails. These enclose panels made of plywood, solid timber, or glass.

Standard sizes of panelled doors are 6ft 8in × 2ft 8in (2032mm × 813mm), 6ft 6in × 2ft 9in (1981mm × 838mm), and 6ft 6in × 2ft 6in (1981mm × 762mm). Most panelled doors can be reduced by up to ¾in (19mm) all round. Non-standard sizes have to be made to order.

Flush doors have a fairly light wooden framework faced on both sides with a sheet material. The lightest doors have a hollow core filled with a strong paper honeycomb. The best quality fire-resisting types have a solid core of timber.

Facing material ranges from plain hardboard to wood veneers on plywood. Flush doors can be reduced very little on the width.

External flush doors usually have a built-in centre rail to take a letterbox. All flush doors have built-in blocks for fitting hinges and locks. They are made in the same sizes as panelled doors, and also in widths as narrow as 12in (305mm).

The frame onto which a door is hung is screwed into the walls on both sides. The line where frame and wall meet is covered with a decorative architrave. The door closes against a door stop which is usually a separate piece of wood on an interior door but is part of the frame on an exterior door.

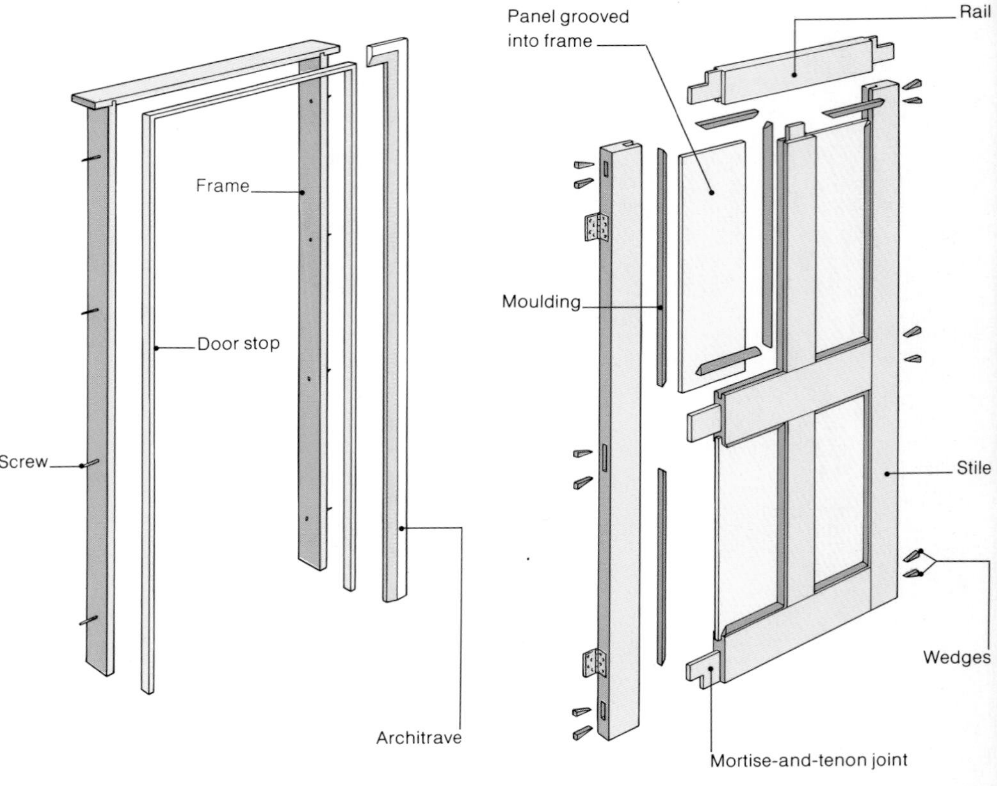

FLUSH DOORS OF DIFFERENT TYPES

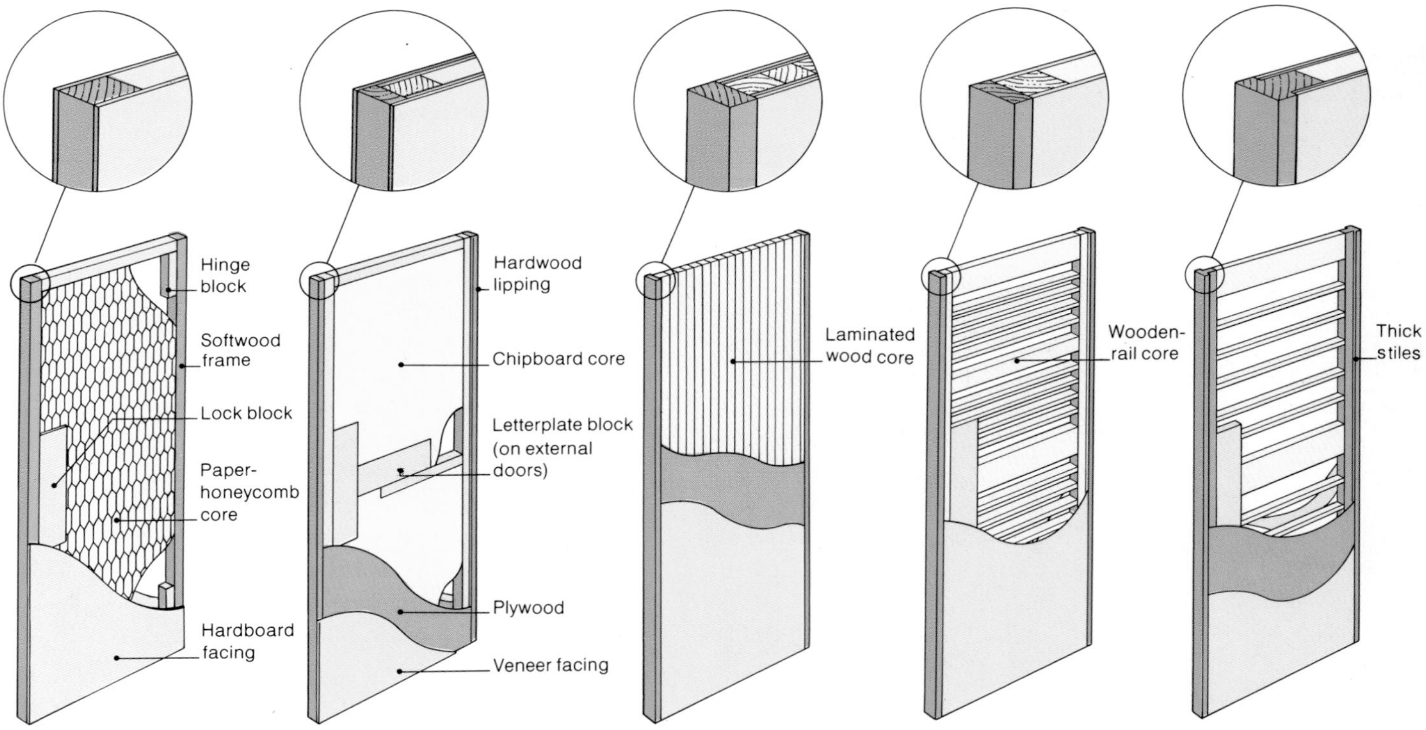

Hinge block
Softwood frame
Lock block
Paper-honeycomb core
Hardboard facing

Lightweight
A paper-honeycomb core is framed with softwood, and covered with hardboard.

Hardwood lipping
Chipboard core
Letterplate block (on external doors)
Plywood
Veneer facing

Solid core
A chipboard core gives greater weight and improved fire resistance. The plywood covering is faced with decorative veneer.

Laminated wood core

Laminated core
Strips of timber are laminated together for good fire resistance.

Wooden-rail core

Multi-rail
The core is made up of a large number of wooden rails from side to side.

Thick stiles

Hardwood stiles
Another variation of a wooden-rail core, with thick hardwood stiles.

CHOOSING A NEW DOOR FOR YOUR HOUSE

When you are thinking of buying a new door, take account of the style of your house and the type of doors already fitted, and try to match them. If the house was built before the Second World War, they will probably be panelled; modern houses are more likely to have flush doors. Try not to mix the two, as the new one will look out of keeping with the originals.

If the door is to be fitted at an entrance, where it will be exposed to the weather (and possibly burglars), you must choose an exterior grade door for greater strength and durability. For use inside the house, buy an interior grade door.

Interior grade doors are lighter and cheaper than exterior grade doors, and flush doors are generally cheaper than panelled doors.

When calculating cost remember that doors are not supplied with hinges, locks or bolts. They all have to be bought separately and then fitted. So too do other items of door furniture, such as a knocker, a letterplate, and of course the street number of your house.

Boarded doors

Tongued-and-grooved boards are nailed vertically to three horizontal struts (or 'ledgers'). Diagonal braces prevent the door from sagging, consequently this design is also called a 'ledged and braced' door. The most sturdy versions have an external frame as well. The style is popular in cottage-type houses for both exterior and interior use. A two-part 'stable' door is also available.

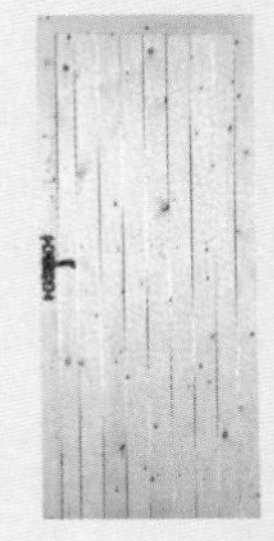

Exterior panelled doors

The most expensive types are made of hardwood, such as mahogany, sapele, iroko and teak. They can be coated with clear varnish to keep the natural appearance.

Softwood exterior doors are made of either prime quality wood, which may be varnished, or lower quality ('paint-grade') wood which must be painted. Some are solid wood, others are laminated and veneered. Laminated doors are less prone to expansion and contraction in wet or dry weather.

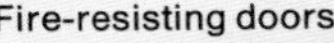

Fire-resisting doors

If a room has been built in the loft, or a garage is attached to the house, Building Regulations require fire-resisting doors. They are usually flush or moulded doors with a heavy core of fire-resisting compressed straw or heavy grade chipboard to give either half-hour or one-hour fire resistance. The doors should be fitted in fire-check frames, and an automatic door closer is usually required. A glass panel must be glazed with Georgian wired glass.

High-security doors

Steel-clad doors can be fitted to the front and back of a house to deter burglars. The doors are made to size to existing frames or to a new frame. The locking action secures the door on all four edges for maximum security.

Ultrasecure

Exterior flush doors

Mostly cheaper than exterior panelled doors. They are faced with exterior quality plywood, but must be painted to give adequate protection from the weather.

Some designs have glass panels of various sizes; others are solid.

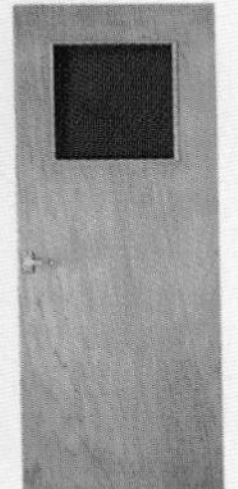

Louvre doors

Rows of angled overlapping louvres are fixed between full-length stiles, with top and bottom rails and sometimes a centre rail.

Louvre doors are always used inside the house, often on cupboards or wardrobes. They may be made from hardwood or softwood.

There is a wide range of sizes, including narrow versions for bi-fold or multi-fold doors.

Tilt-and-turn doors

This style of door can be hinged in the normal way or, by closing the door and turning the handle, it can be tilted inwards from the top for ventilation without a security risk. It is usually made of UPVC and glass.

Astraseal

Interior panelled doors

Hardwood doors may be coated with clear varnish to preserve the appearance of the wood. Prime quality softwood may be varnished, but paint-grade softwood should be painted to hide imperfections.

Interior panelled doors are much cheaper than exterior versions. They are available in many styles – from all wood to practically all glass.

Sliding standard doors

Where there is no room for a hinged door to open properly, the door can be fitted to a track at top and bottom to slide along one wall. Some types of track can be angled so that the door comes to rest against the frame to give a draught-proof seal when closed.

Any standard door can be used. Remember that the wall to one side of the opening must be kept clear.

French windows

Glazed panel doors which are sold in pairs to open outwards. The edges are rebated to close together in the middle of the opening. They are available with fixed windows of the same height, called sidelights, which are installed on each side of the doors.

Interior flush doors

The cheapest doors of all. Finishes range from plain hardboard to plastic laminate and wood veneer. Some models can be obtained with a glass section.

Sliding patio doors

A glass panel with aluminium edging slides on rollers alongside a fixed panel. The two panels are usually set in a hardwood frame. This style is usually used as a doorway to a garden or patio, and is double or triple glazed.

Bi-fold doors

Where there is no room for the swing of a conventional door, bi-fold doors can be fitted instead. They are like normal doors that have been cut in half vertically with the two halves hinged together. They can be fitted singly or in pairs, so that you have four leaves. The doors are usually made of wood, wood veneer or steel.

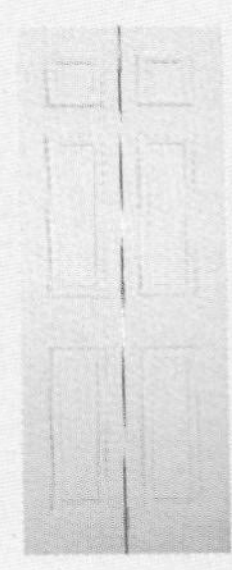

Moulded doors

This style is made like a flush door, but the facings – usually hardboard or fibreboard – are embossed to look like a panel door. Alternatively, wood mouldings are fixed to the face of the door to give the panelled effect. Moulded doors are usually for interior use only.

Aluminium frame glass doors

Aluminium-and-glass doors can be fitted at the front or back entrance of a house in a standard wooden frame. The glass is double-glazed and non see-through. The central aluminium rail contains a letter flap, but doors with a single glass panel taking up the whole area are available.

Multi-fold doors

Concertina-type doors are excellent space savers and can be used as room dividers. They are hung from a metal track, and some models have a channel set in the floor to guide the bottom edge. The panels may be made of wood, veneered chipboard, plastic, mirrored glass or steel.

Pella Doors

All photographs by Magnet and Southerns unless stated

How to hang a front or back door

Before buying a new door, measure the height and width of the frame. Get a door that is either the right size or slightly too big. A panelled door should be $\frac{1}{8}$in (3mm) smaller all round than the opening; flush doors $\frac{1}{16}$in (2mm) smaller all round.

Panelled doors can have up to $\frac{3}{4}$in (19mm) removed all round, but most flush doors should have no more than about $\frac{3}{8}$in (10mm) planed away, otherwise they can be seriously weakened.

Flush doors contain wooden blocks for fitting hinges and locks; their positions are marked on the edges of the door. When fitting the hinges and locks, note where the blocks are, as they will affect the way round that the door is placed in the frame. If you want to reverse the face of the door, most are reversible top to bottom.

You will need three butt hinges – either 3in (75mm) or 4in (100mm) long. The job will be simpler if you choose a size to fit the existing hinge recesses on the frame.

If a flush door is being fitted, buy pressed-steel cranked butt hinges. A panelled door, which is heavier, requires cast-iron butt hinges.

An exterior door is heavy, so get someone to help you if you can.

Take care to fit the door closely in the frame to prevent water from getting in, especially at the bottom.

A door which is directly exposed to rain, without the protection of a porch, will need to have a weather moulding fitted, and a water bar (see panel).

Once the door has been hung, a lock will have to be fitted (page 201), and perhaps a letter slot and other door furniture (page 203).

You will need

Tools Pencil; tape measure; try square; marking gauge; chisel – $\frac{3}{4}$in or 1in (19mm or 25mm); mallet; plane; panel or tenon saw; craft knife; drill and twist bits; screwdriver; folding workbench.

Materials Exterior quality door; three hinges; screws to fit (check that the heads fit fully into the countersunk holes on the hinge).

REMOVING STUBBORN SCREWS

When you remove your old door, the hinge screws may be difficult to get out. Scrape off any paint, particularly out of the slots. If a screw still will not shift, put a screwdriver in the slot and hit it with a mallet.

1 Remove the old door carefully, without damaging the hinge recesses on the frame. Put pieces of wood under the door to take the weight while you remove the screws, and get someone to hold it.

2 Remove any plastic wrapping from the new door. Panelled doors are sometimes protected with strips of timber at the edges; remove these by prising them off with a broad scraper blade. Panelled doors usually have 'horns' which are overlength stiles to protect the corners of the door before it is hung.

3 To remove the horns, lay the door flat over a workbench or on trestles.

4 Use a try square and pencil to mark the cutting lines on the horns in line with the edge of the top and bottom rails. Square off the line across the edge of the door.

5 Make the cut with a sharp panel saw, or tenon saw, and be careful to ensure that the edge of the door is not splintered.

6 Hold the door against the frame so it can be marked for trimming. A glass-panelled door is usually fitted with the glass putty on the outside and decorative wood beading on the inside.

7 When the door is centrally positioned, get someone to steady it, and put wedges underneath to hold it at the correct height.

CUTTING A REBATE FOR A WATER BAR

If the door sill has a water bar fitted, a rebate must be cut into the bottom of the new door to fit over it. Some external doors are supplied with the rebate already removed. (See also page 262.)

If you have to do it yourself, draw a line across the front of the door at the bottom, a little higher than the water bar.

Set the circular saw to the depth of the rebate (about half the thickness of the door) and cut right along the line.

Holding a chisel end-on to the door, chisel away the waste to form the rebate.

Door
Weather moulding
Water bar
Sill

8 Lightly mark the face with a soft pencil to give the correct gap round the perimeter. A panelled door should have a gap of $\frac{1}{8}$in (3mm) all round to allow the wood to swell in wet weather. A flush door should have a gap of $\frac{1}{16}$in (2mm). If the frame is straight you may not have to trim all the edges of the door. However, if the frame is out of true, or if there is a fair amount of trimming to do, it will be necessary to trim all the edges.

9 If there is more than about $\frac{3}{16}$in (5mm) of wood to remove, lay the door flat on boxes or trestles and saw it close to the trimming line, then finish off with a plane.

10 For planing, hold the door on its edge in the jaws of a folding adjustable workbench. Protect the bottom edge on scrap timber and then plane the top edge down to the pencilled trimming line.

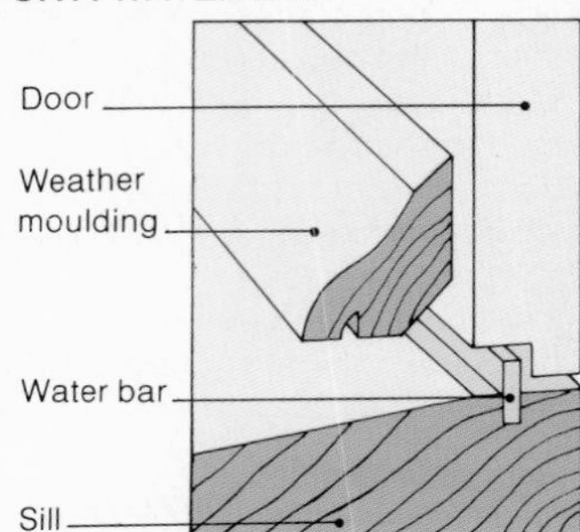

11 Plane the long edges of the door in the direction of the grain. The shavings will be removed smoothly, whereas if you plane against the grain the blade will tend to dig into the wood.

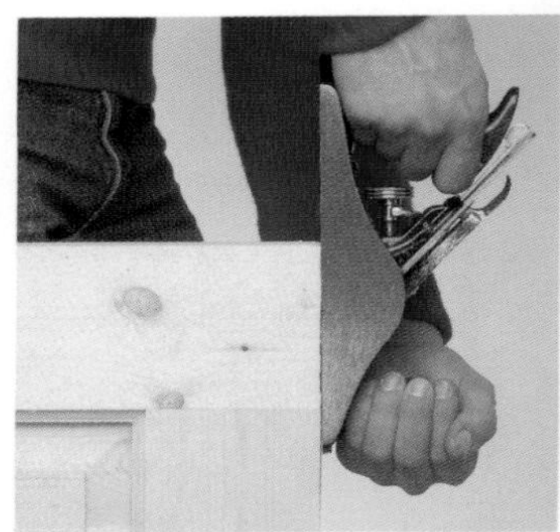

12 Plane the top and bottom edges of the door from each side towards the centre. This will avoid splitting wood at the edge of the stiles where you will be planing across the grain.

13 Stand the door in the frame on wedges and check there is the right gap all round.

14 When the fit is correct, plane a slight slope on the edges of both door stiles towards the doorstop on the frame. This will ensure that the door will close easily without binding against the frame.

15 Hold the door in the frame to mark the hinge positions. If the hinge recesses in the frame are already cut to the right size, mark the top and bottom of the recesses on the edge of the door. If not, increase the size with a chisel as explained below, and then mark the top and bottom of the hinge positions on the door.

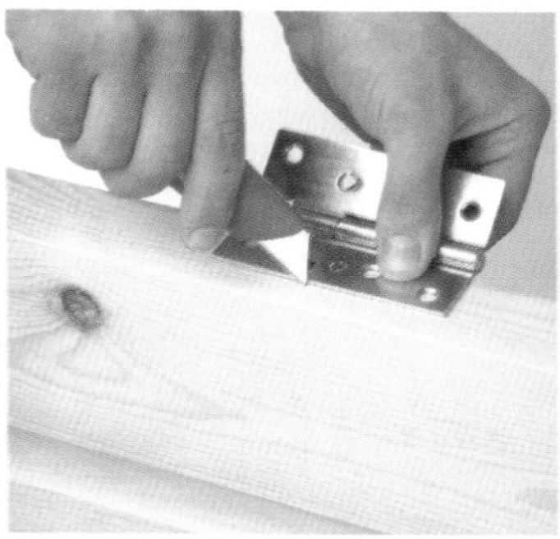

16 Hold the hinge in place on the door and mark round the edge of each hinge flap with a craft knife. With a pressed-steel cranked butt hinge the whole knuckle of the hinge should project from the face of the door and from the frame. With a cast-iron butt hinge the centre of the knuckle should be level with the face of the door and frame.

17 Mark the thickness of the flap with a marking gauge.

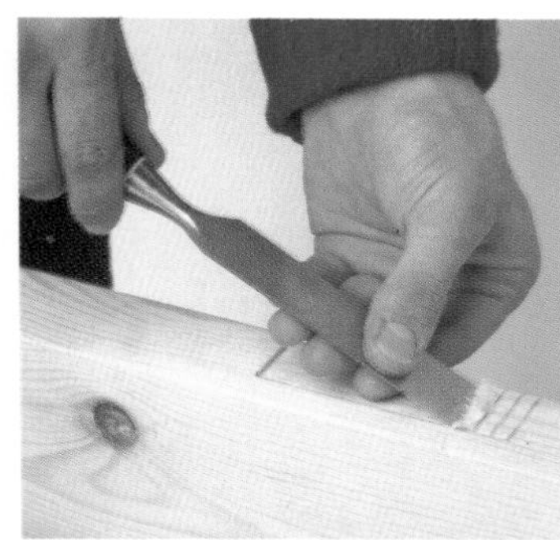

18 Cut around the perimeter of the flap with a sharp chisel. Then make a series of cuts about ¼in (6mm) apart across the grain of the wood, and carefully pare away the waste using the flat side of the chisel downwards.

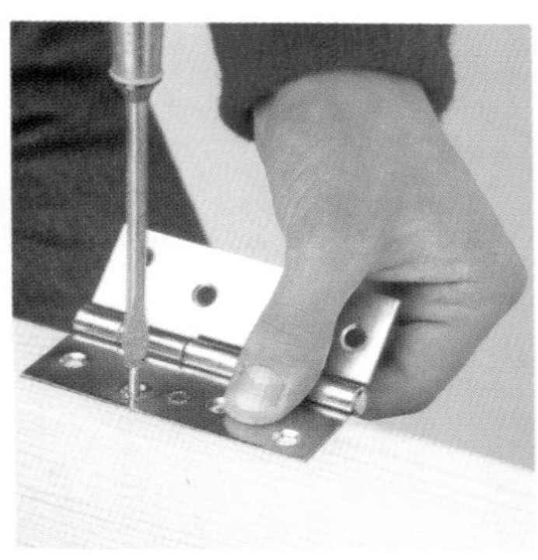

19 Screw the hinge flaps into the recesses in the door, putting only one screw in each hinge for the time being.

20 Hold the door open on wedges and screw the hinges to the frame – again with one screw each. Each screw head should lie flush with the surface of the hinge flap.

If the screw heads protrude, they will bind and prevent the door from closing. You can either deepen the countersinks in the hinge with a high-speed-steel twist bit in a power drill, or else buy screws one gauge size smaller – No. 9s instead of No. 10s, for example.

If the screws do not fit firmly into the frame, glue pieces of dowel in the old screw holes.

21 Check that the door swings open and shut easily. If it does not close properly, the hinge positions may have to be adjusted. (See *Curing door faults*, page 204.)

22 When the door moves correctly, insert the remaining screws.

Hanging an interior door

CONVENTIONAL HINGED DOORS

Normal interior doors are hung in the same way as exterior doors (see preceding pages), with the following differences.

As interior doors are not likely to swell because of moisture, a $\frac{1}{16}$in (2mm) gap between door and frame will be enough.

When cutting the door to fit, make sure that it will open over a carpet without rubbing. It should just brush the top of the carpet.

Alternatively, fit rising-butt hinges (see panel).

If you need to trim more than ⅜in (10mm) off each edge of a standard-size door, buy an interior quality panel door. The internal support-frame of a flush door is too narrow to be substantially cut down.

Alternatively, buy a slightly undersize flush door and add timber lipping all round to make up the height and width – no more than ⅜in (10mm) on each edge.

Two hinges will be enough for hanging an interior door. Use 3in (75mm) pressed-steel cranked butt hinges (next page).

HANGING BI-FOLD DOORS

Hang a bi-fold door in the same way as a conventional door, with the following exceptions.

1 If the pair of doors is not already hinged together, join them with three brass butt hinges (chart on next page).

2 Fix the door to the frame with two parliament hinges. They have projecting knuckles that allow the door to fold right back, clear of the architrave around the opening.

3 Where two pairs of bi-fold doors join together at the centre of the opening, glue and pin a full-height batten about 1½in × ½in (38mm × 13mm) to one door to overlap the closing edge and serve as a door stop.

If the meeting edges are stepped, there will be no need for the batten.

4 Fit a mortise latch and handle to the adjacent door of the other pair.

HANGING MULTI-FOLD DOORS

Some multi-fold doors are designed to hang from the opening between two rooms, possibly where two large doors were originally installed. They may have no floor channel, but simply hang from an overhead track. They take up far less room when open than conventional doors.

Door kits are normally supplied with fitting instructions.

Before embarking on the job, check that the four edges of the door frame are square (the diagonal measurements should be equal). If they are not, it may be best to call in a builder.

You will need

Tools Steel tape measure; spirit level; straight-edge; pencil; bradawl; drill and twist bits; screwdriver; hacksaw.

Materials Multi-fold door kit.

1 Measure the height and width of the opening, and order the door. The supplier will allow clearance for the track and hinges.

2 Draw a centre line along the top of the opening.

3 Hold the track on the line and mark the screw positions.

4 Remove the track and drill the screw holes. If the opening is lined with timber thinner than ¾in (19mm) you will have to drill and plug the wall above as well to take the weight.

5 Slide the track over the nylon rollers at the tops of the doors.

6 Get a helper to lift the track and door in place, and screw the track to the underside of the opening.

7 Cut the track cover moulds to length (if supplied) and screw them in place.

8 Screw the door to the side of the opening and fit the stops and catches in place, following the manufacturer's instructions.

HANGING A SLIDING DOOR

To save space in a corridor or a small room, it may be possible to hang a sliding door over the door opening. But there must be space

FITTING RISING-BUTT HINGES

Rising butts are available for right-hand and left-hand hanging, so make sure you buy the right type. Stand so the door will open away from you; if it is to be hinged on the left, buy left-hand hinges, if it is hinged on the right buy right-hand hinges.

The part of the hinge with the pin is fitted (pin upwards) to the door frame, and the open spiral section is screwed to the door.

Fit them in the same way as ordinary butt hinges. It will also be necessary to plane a small slope on the inner top corner of the door on the hinge side.This prevents the door from catching on the top of the door frame as it swings open.

Hanging an interior door (continued)

on the adjacent wall for it to slide back when open. Consequently, furniture cannot be placed against the wall.

Various designs of sliding door gear are available. The job will be easier if you choose one that fits on the wall above the door opening rather than to the ceiling.

If you do not buy gear with a built-in pelmet to hide the hangers, make a pelmet with softwood battens and a plywood or hardboard fascia, and paint it.

You will need

Tools Screwdriver; tenon saw; plane; chisel; mallet; filling knife; drill and twist bits; countersink bit; masonry bit; spirit level.

Materials Glue; interior filler; two pieces of 3in (75mm) wide softwood, the thickness of your skirting boards and the height of the door opening; one piece of 3in (75mm) wide softwood, the thickness of the skirting and a little longer than twice the width of the door; 2in (50mm) No. 8 countersunk screws; perhaps wall plugs; sliding door gear; lightweight flush door; bow handles or door knobs.

HELPFUL TIP
Buy a new, light, flush door rather than using the old one; otherwise you will have to patch the recesses where the old hinges and lock were fitted. Flush doors can be obtained quite cheaply.

CHOOSING HINGES TO HANG A DOOR

Cast butt hinge
Doors are usually hung with butt hinges – two rectangular leaves joined by a pin running through an interlocking knuckle. Butt hinges for heavy exterior doors are made of cast iron, and are either 3in (75mm) or 4in (100mm) long.

The centre of the knuckle is fitted in line with the face of door and frame.

Cranked butt hinge
A version of the cast butt hinge made of pressed steel. It is cheaper but not so strong, so should not be used to fix heavy exterior doors. When fitted, the whole of the large knuckle projects from the face of the door and the frame.

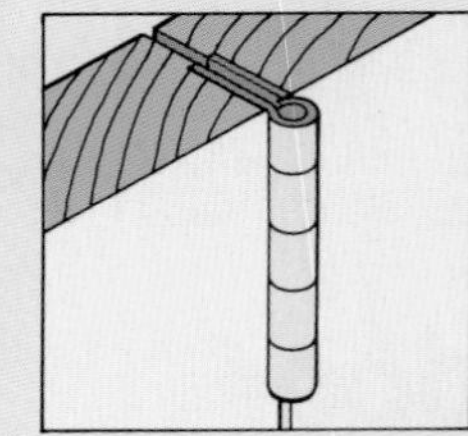

T-hinge
This old-fashioned type of hinge is used mainly for garage and shed doors, but is sometimes fitted to cottage-style house doors. It is screwed to the surface of the back of the door and the frame.

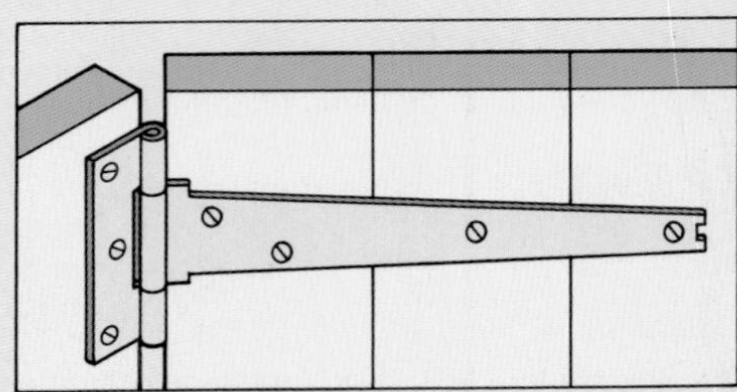

Rising butt hinge
When a door opens onto a carpet, rising butt hinges are an alternative to cutting a strip off the bottom of the door. The spiral in the knuckle of the hinge lifts the door as it opens, and also tends to close it. And the door can easily be lifted off the hinges.

The usual sizes are 3in (75mm) and 4in (100mm). The hinges are sold for both right-hand and left-hand hanging.

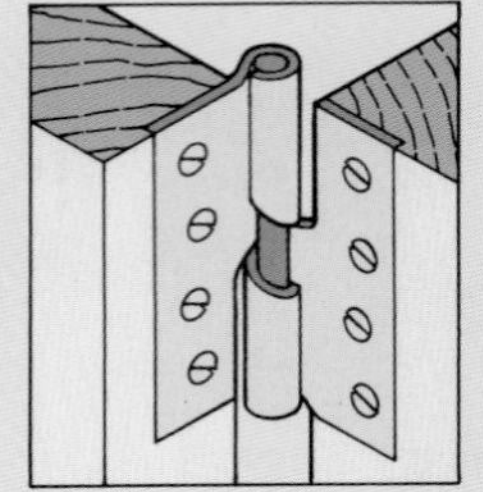

Parliament hinge
These are butt hinges with projecting knuckles, which enable an open door to swing clear of the surrounding frame.

They are made of steel or brass, in sizes (when they are open) of 4in × 4in (100mm × 100mm), 4in × 5in (100mm × 125mm), and 4in × 6in (100mm × 150mm).

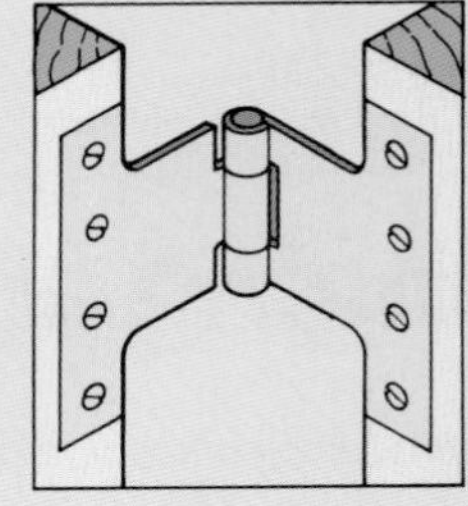

Loose-pin butt hinge
The pin can be withdrawn to separate the leaves, and remove the door easily – perhaps when laying a floor covering. Decorative finials may be fitted at the top and bottom, and are unscrewed to release the pin. The hinges are usually made of brass.

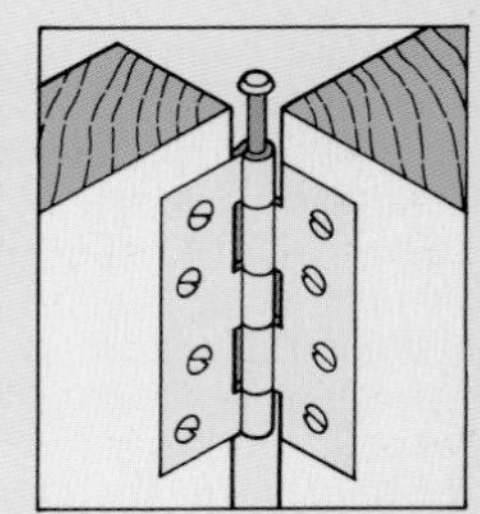

1 Unscrew the hinges and remove the old door.

2 Fill the hinge recesses in the frame with scraps of softwood cut to size and glued in place. Make them slightly proud of the surface, and secure them with partly knocked-in panel pins until the glue has dried. Then remove the pins and plane the wood down.

3 Lever off the architrave around the door with an old chisel or other lever. Wooden wedges driven between the wall and the architrave can be effective.

4 Fill any holes in the plaster, using interior filler.

5 Screw a length of 3in (75mm) softwood – the same thickness as the skirting board – on each side of the door frame between the skirting board and the top of the opening.

6 Screw the remaining piece of softwood to the frame above the door and along the wall as far as the width of the new door. It will be used to support the new door, so use a spirit level to make sure it is horizontal. Put the screws about 12in (300mm) apart.

If the wall is made of masonry, use wall plugs. If it is made of plasterboard or lath-and-plaster, you will have to locate the wall studs (page 230) and drill pilot holes for the screws.

7 Screw the sliding door track to the wood strip. Use the spirit level again to check that the track is horizontal.

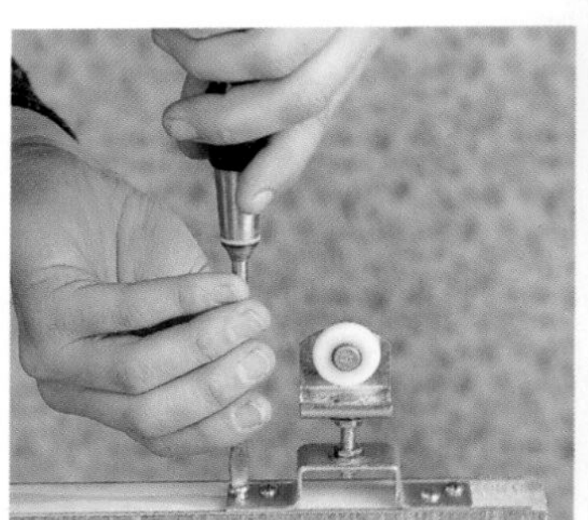

8 Screw the hangers to the top of the door.

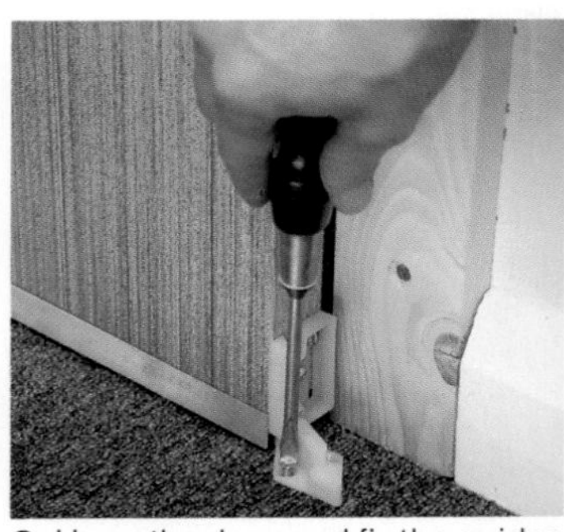

9 Hang the door and fix the guides to the floor, following the manufacturer's instructions.

10 Fit bow handles or door knobs to the door on each side, in a convenient position for opening and closing.

SLIDING DOORS IN A WIDE GAP

Where there is a wide gap in the wall between rooms, two sliding doors can be hung to fill it – perhaps for occasional use.

If each door has space to slide back along the wall at the side of the opening, they can be mounted on a single ceiling track so they meet in the middle.

Often, however, there is not enough space along the walls; the doors then have to be hung on double track, allowing them to slide past each other when open.

HAVING DOORS STRIPPED

Many firms strip doors in a bath of hot caustic soda, which saves a lot of time and laborious work.

Dip-stripping removes all the traces of paint from intricate mouldings and avoids the risk of scorching the door. However, it is possible for joints to become loose and for doors to warp after dip-stripping, so check with the company that your doors are suitable for treatment.

Firms that dip-strip doors can be found in *Yellow Pages*, listed under Furniture Repairs and Restoration.

Not all doors are worth stripping, so have one done first to assess the quality of the timber before committing yourself to paying for several.

You will need to replace the doors in the frames from which they were taken, so mark each one with chiselled Roman numerals on the top edge, and keep a note of how they have been numbered.

Re-hanging a door on the other side of the frame

To make better use of space in a room, it is sometimes necessary to re-hang a door on the opposite side of the frame. It may then open against a wall rather than into the room.

You will need

Tools Wedges; screwdriver; tenon saw; vice or bench hook; plane; hammer; abrasive paper; pencil; chisel; try square; mallet; craft knife; drill and twist bits.

Materials Scrap softwood, or pieces of timber to match the door; wood glue; panel pins; new screws for hinges – probably 2in (50mm) No. 10 gauge.

1 Open the door and put wooden wedges under it to take the weight.

2 Unscrew the hinges from the frame, take down the door, and remove the hinges completely.

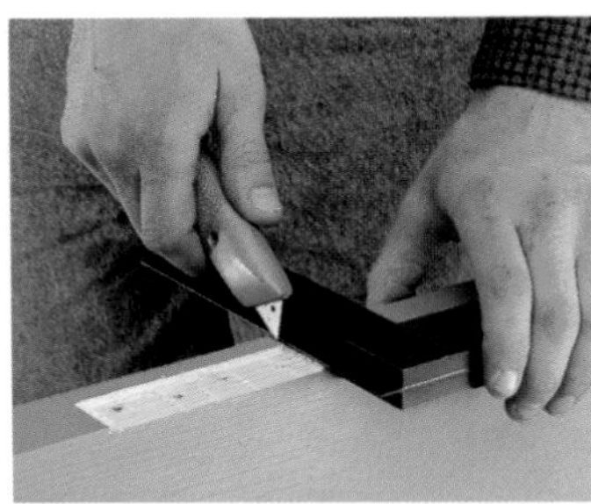

3 Use a craft knife and try square to cut through the raised wood at the ends of the hinge recesses on the door.

4 Remove the raised sections with a chisel, so that the recesses extend right across the door edge.

5 Hold a hinge against each recess on the opposite side from where it was originally, and cut strips of wood to fit along the other edge to fill the gaps. Use softwood if the door is painted, or matching timber if it is varnished. Cut the pieces to stand slightly raised.

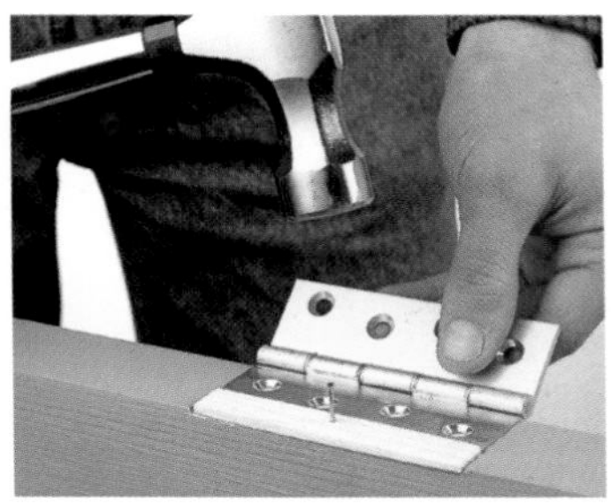

6 Glue the strips in place and temporarily hold them with panel pins that are not driven right in. If necessary, fill the screw holes with glued dowels.

7 Unscrew the lock striking plate from the door frame. Cut a thin piece of wood to fill the recess, and fix it in place in the same way.

8 When the glue has set, remove the pins and plane the filling pieces flush with the surface. Finish with abrasive paper.

9 Turn the door around so that the side that faced out of the room now faces inwards, and the lock is on the desired side. The catch will be facing the wrong way to engage when the striking plate is refitted.

10 Remove the lock and reverse the catch, either by turning the lock over or by unscrewing the side of the lock and turning the catch over.

SAFETY WITH GLASS DOORS

Any glass fitted into a door must be either laminated or toughened safety glass. This is particularly important for large panes, for low-level glass, and for any glass in a hazardous position such as at the bottom of a staircase.

Many door suppliers stock safety glass in standard sizes to fit their doors.

Laminated glass is easier to obtain and can be cut to size by many glass merchants while you wait. Toughened (also called tempered) glass is cheaper, but must be ordered to size if not stocked in a size to suit the door.

When broken, toughened glass shatters into thousands of pieces, like a car windscreen. Laminated glass can be cracked, but a plastic interlayer holds the pieces together. Consequently it also has security advantages.

11 Hold the door in the frame with wedges under it to support it the right height off the floor. Check that the gap between the door and the frame is equal all the way round, and that the bottom of the door will not catch on the carpet.

12 Mark the top and bottom of the hinge positions on the edge of the frame. Remove the door.

13 Hold each hinge in place on the frame and mark around its edge with a craft knife. If it is a standard cast-iron butt hinge (facing page), the centre of the knuckle should be level with the face of the frame (and the face of the door). A pressed-steel cranked butt hinge should have the whole knuckle projecting.

14 Mark the thickness of the hinge flap on the edge of the frame.

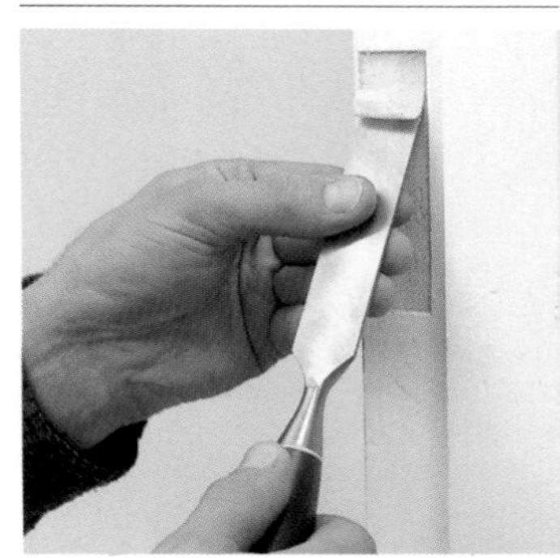

15 Cut around the scored outline with a sharp chisel. Then make a series of cuts about ¼in (6mm) apart across the grain with the chisel and carefully pare away the waste.

16 Repeat at the other hinge positions on the frame.

SAFETY TIP

Never hang a door so that it opens onto a passageway or landing if there is a danger of walking into it.

Re-hanging a door on the other side of the frame (continued)

17 Drill pilot holes for one screw in each hinge on the door, and fix the hinges into the recesses, using one screw only.

18 Hold the door open on wedges, and screw the hinges to the frame – again with one screw in each hinge. Make sure that each screw head is flush with the surface of the hinge. If the screws protrude beyond the surface of the hinge the door may not close correctly.

19 Check that the door swings open and shut easily. If it does not, the hinge positions may have to be adjusted (page 205).

20 When the movement is correct, drill the remaining pilot holes and put in the screws.

21 Close the door and turn the handle and key to indent the frame where the lock striking plate will be fitted.
ALTERNATIVELY, insert a piece of carbon paper to leave a mark.

22 Mark the frame around the striking plate, and chisel out a recess. Screw the plate in place.

RE-HANGING A DOOR TO OPEN OUTWARDS

Altering a door so that it opens outwards rather than inwards is very similar to re-hanging it to hinge on the other side of the frame (previous page). You will need the same tools and materials to do the job.

After removing the door, prise away the stop bead – the strip of wood on the frame that the door rests against when it is closed. To do this, use an old chisel together with a couple of wooden wedges or a bolster chisel.

When you have re-hung the door in its new position, pin the stop bead back on the frame so that it fits snugly against the inside face of the door.

Fitting latches and locks

FITTING A CYLINDER NIGHT LATCH

You will need
Tools Pencil; drill and large bit (size given on maker's instructions); screwdriver and a steel tape measure. Perhaps twist bits.
Materials Cylinder night latch.

1 Mark the position of the key cylinder at a convenient height on the door stile, using the dimensions or paper template usually supplied with the lock. Alternatively, use the lock mounting plate. The shape of the hole for the cylinder depends on the make of lock; some need a large round hole, others need a shaped hole made by drilling two smaller holes through what will be the circumference of a larger hole, which is drilled afterwards.

2 Drill the hole for the cylinder.

3 Position the cylinder at the front of the door and place the mounting plate on the inside face. Temporarily fix the two together with the screws provided. The cylinder connecting bar will protrude through the mounting plate to engage in the body of the lock.

4 Cut the connecting bar to a suitable length, depending on the thickness of the door, following the manufacturer's instructions.

5 If the lock has a fore-end that screws to the edge of the door, temporarily place the lock assembly on the mounting plate and mark where it will be necessary to cut a recess.

6 Remove the lock and cut the fore-end recess; if necessary, also remove the lock mounting plate.

7 Refit the mounting plate to the cylinder.

8 Put the body of the lock on the mounting plate, ensuring that the cylinder connecting bar engages in the lock.

9 Screw the body of the lock to the door.

10 Check that the bolt works, using the key and the internal knob.

11 Close the door and mark the position of the striking plate on the door jamb.

12 Cut a recess for the striking plate and screw it to the door jamb.

Check that the door closes properly and that the lock operates.

13 If not, recess the striking plate slightly deeper into the door jamb.

FITTING A MORTISE LOCK

You will need
Tools Pencil; try square; carpenter's brace and auger bit – the width of the lock body; adhesive tape; mallet; two chisels (one the width of the lock body and a wider one); pliers; bradawl; power drill or wheel handbrace and twist bits; padsaw; screwdriver.
Materials Mortise lock.

1 Hold the lock in position against the face of the door. Ideally it should line up with the centre rail of the door. On flush doors fixing points are often marked on the edge.

2 Mark the dimensions of the lock casing on the door and with the try square transfer the height marks to the edge of the door.

3 Mark the centre line of the mortise on the edge of the door between the height marks.

CHOOSING LOCKS AND LATCHES FOR YOUR DOORS

Locks and latches are available in two main types. Rim locks are screwed to the inside of the door; they are easy to install but not so secure as they are only held by screws, and could be forced off the door. Mortise locks are fitted (mortised) into the edge of the door; they are more difficult to install, but also more secure because the door frame has to be smashed to get past them.

CYLINDER NIGHTLATCH

The lock is fitted to the rim of the door. The latch is turned back by a key from the outside and by a handle from the inside. A 'snib' (knob) holds the latch in place – either out or in. Less secure than a deadlocking cylinder nightlatch.
WHERE SUITABLE On the front door, together with a mortise deadlock for extra security.

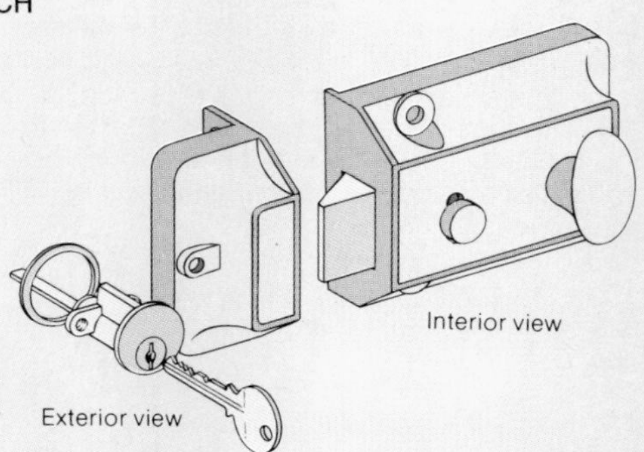

DEADLOCKING CYLINDER NIGHTLATCH

The lock is fixed to the rim of the door. When the key is turned after the door is closed, the bolt cannot be forced back. Even if a burglar breaks a nearby glass panel, the handle cannot be turned. On some models the key can be turned from inside as well as outside. They may also incorporate a door restraint.
WHERE SUITABLE On the front door, together with a mortise deadlock.

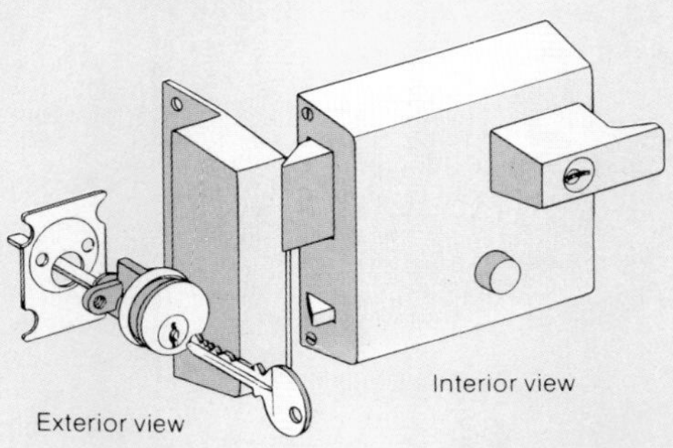

Use only locks manufactured to British Standard BS3621.

MORTISE DEADLOCK

The bolt cannot be turned back without using the key. The key operates levers, and the more levers the harder the lock is to pick. Best security comes from a five-lever lock with a box-type striking plate.
WHERE SUITABLE On the front door, together with a nightlatch for frequent coming and going.

Use only locks manufactured to British Standard BS3621.

MORTISE LATCH

Only for keeping doors closed; cannot be locked. A small model can be inserted in a circular hole. Bathroom or lavatory doors normally require a 'snib', a simple locking device that can be turned from the inside. A screw slot on the outside of the door can be used to open the latch in an emergency.
WHERE SUITABLE For interior doors, which may be best left unlocked (burglars can kick open modern interior-weight doors, causing a lot of damage).

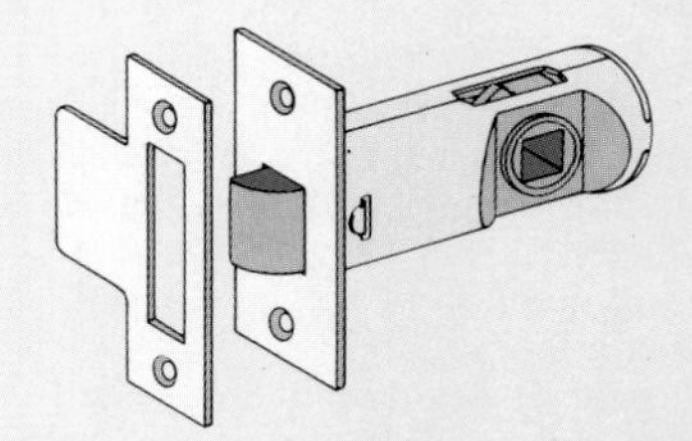

TWO-BOLT MORTISE LOCK

The lock is also called a mortise sashlock. The bolt is operated by a handle; the latch can be operated only by the key. Should have five levers for good security. Narrow models are available for doors with narrow stiles.
WHERE SUITABLE On a side or back door, together with rack bolts at top and bottom of the door.

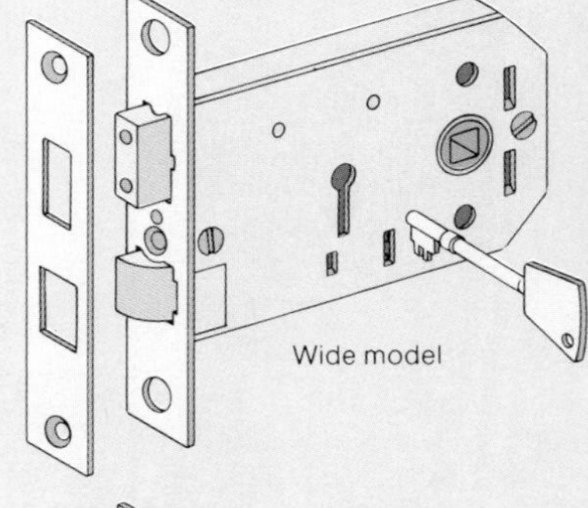

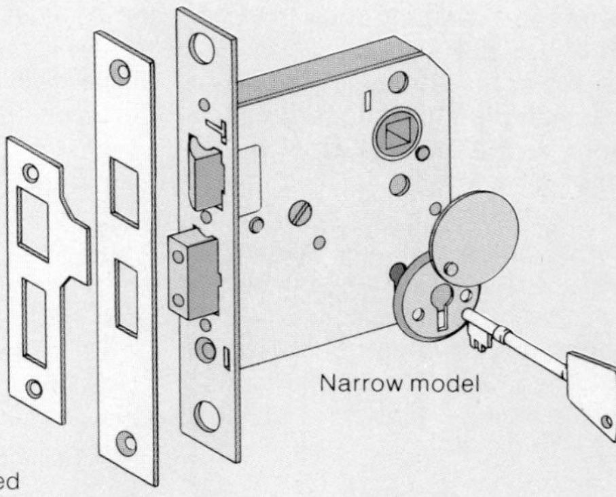

Use only locks manufactured to British Standard BS3621.

TWO-BOLT RIM LOCK

Screws to the inside face of the door. Simple to install but easy to tamper with. One, two and three-lever actions are unsuitable for external doors.
WHERE SUITABLE On a side or back door, together with bolts at top and bottom. Cheap models for interior doors (for privacy only).

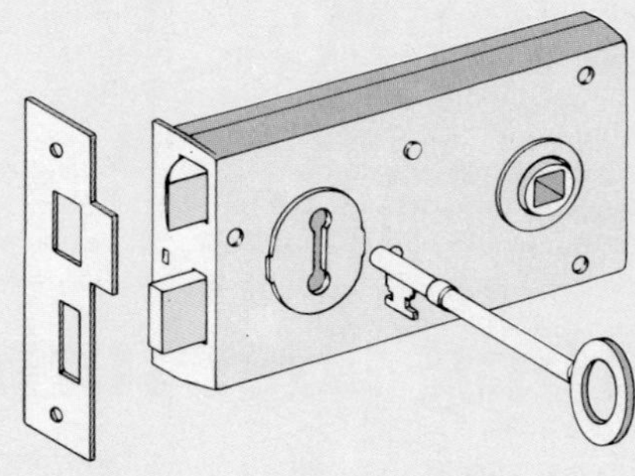

CLAWBOLT DEADLOCK

A pair of claws lock into the striking plate, and can only be operated by a key. The lock is mortised into the door stile.
WHERE SUITABLE For sliding patio doors made of wood. Metal patio doors usually come with their own lock.

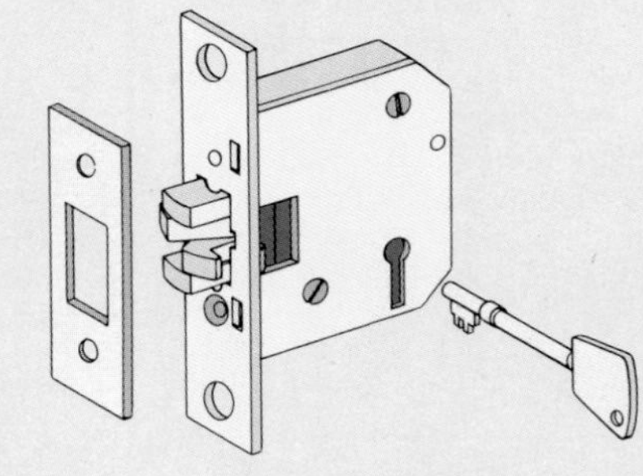

CASEMENT BOLT (espagnolette bolt)

The traditional way to lock French windows. A full length bolt, operated by a central handle, shoots into the frame at top and bottom. For security it should be used in conjunction with rack bolts at the top and bottom (page 222).
WHERE SUITABLE For French windows.

Fitting locks and latches (continued)

4 Mark the depth of the lock body on the auger bit with a strip of tape, and drill an overlapping line of holes through the centre line to the depth of the lock body.

Get someone to check that the bit is horizontal and square-on to the door, so that the hole does not go off at an angle.

5 Use a mallet and the narrow chisel to square up the top and bottom of the mortise slot.

Then use the wider chisel to smooth the sides of the mortise slot so that the lock body will slide snugly into the door.

6 Turn out the bolt of the lock with the key, then push it into the mortise slot and mark the shape of the fore-end (rectangular plate) on the edge of the door. Grip the bolt with pliers to withdraw the lock.

7 Chisel out a recess for the fore-end so that when the lock is in place it will lie flush with the edge of the door.

8 Hold the lock in position against the face of the door, and with a bradawl mark the centre point of the keyhole and the handle spindle (if there is one).

9 Using a drill and twist bit, make holes through the door the same diameter as the handle spindle and the keyhole, at the positions you have marked with the bradawl.

Make the keyhole the correct shape by enlarging the lower part with a padsaw. Or drill a smaller hole below the first and join them with a padsaw.

10 With the bolt of the lock sticking out, push the lock into the slot and check that the key and handle spindle will fit.

11 Insert screws through the fore-end of the lock into the edge of the door.

12 Push the handle spindle through the lock, and screw the handle plates on each side of the door.

13 Screw the keyhole plates on each side of the door.

14 Almost close the door and mark the positions of the deadbolt and latch on the edge of the frame. Continue the mark around onto the jamb.

15 Measure the distance from the outside of the door to the centre of the bolt, and mark that distance on the jamb – measuring from the doorstop.

16 Use the narrow chisel and mallet to cut mortises for the bolts at this position.

Check that the door closes properly. If not, enlarge the mortises as much as necessary.

17 Hold the lock striker plate over the two mortises and mark the outline of the plate on the door jamb with a pencil.

18 Cut a recess for the plate, check that the door still closes properly, and screw the striker plate in place.

Fitting door furniture

The front door of a house usually needs a letterplate, a handle to close the door (which may be built into the letterplate), either a knocker or bellpush, and probably a street number.

All are simple to install, but a power jigsaw makes the job of cutting the letter opening much quicker than doing it by hand with a padsaw.

LETTERPLATE

You will need

Tools Pencil; ruler; drill and twist bits; ½in (13mm) flat bit; power jigsaw or padsaw; chisel; abrasive paper; screwdriver; small adjustable spanner; hacksaw.
Materials Letterplate and fittings.

1 Decide where you want the letterplate. On a panel door it can be fitted horizontally in the middle rail or vertically on the lock stile. On a flush door, fit it horizontally in the middle to coincide with the rail position that is marked on the edge of the door.

2 Hold the letterplate in position on the door and lightly mark its outline with a pencil.

3 Measure the size of the flap and spring mechanism and mark the outline of the required cut-out within the larger outline.

The cut-out may have to be off centre to allow room for the flap mechanism.

4 Using the flat bit, drill a ½in (13mm) hole at each corner of the cut-out position and saw along the cut-out line. Preferably use a power jigsaw with a long enough blade. Alternatively, you can make the cut-out with a padsaw, but it will be slow work.

5 At each side of the cut-out, mark the positions of the holes for the fixing bolts.

6 Working from the front of the door, drill ½in (13mm) diameter holes to a depth of ½in (13mm) to accommodate the fixing lugs of the letterplate.

7 Using a twist bit the same diameter as the fixing bolts, drill from the centre of the holes right through the door.

Smooth the edges of the holes with abrasive paper.

8 Fit the letterplate to the door and tighten the fixing nuts with an adjustable spanner.

9 If the bolts protrude, use a hacksaw to cut them off flush with the face of the nuts.

DOOR KNOCKER

1 Hold the knocker in position and press it hard against the door so that the lugs leave light marks.

2 At these positions, drill holes for the lugs and the bolts.

3 Screw the bolts into the lugs on the back of the knocker, and push them through the holes.

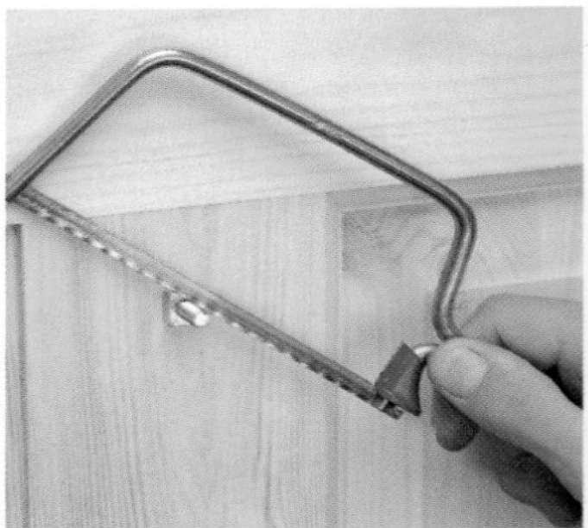

4 Tighten the fixing nuts, and if the bolts protrude cut them off flush with the face of the nuts.

CHOOSING HANDLES, KNOBS, LETTERPLATES AND OTHER DOOR FURNITURE

Door furniture is available in a multitude of designs, from ornate reproductions to simple modern styles. It may be made of cast iron, brass, aluminium, steel, ceramics, glass or plastic. But whatever the design or material, each piece of door furniture has a particular function.

HANDLES FOR A MORTISE LOCK

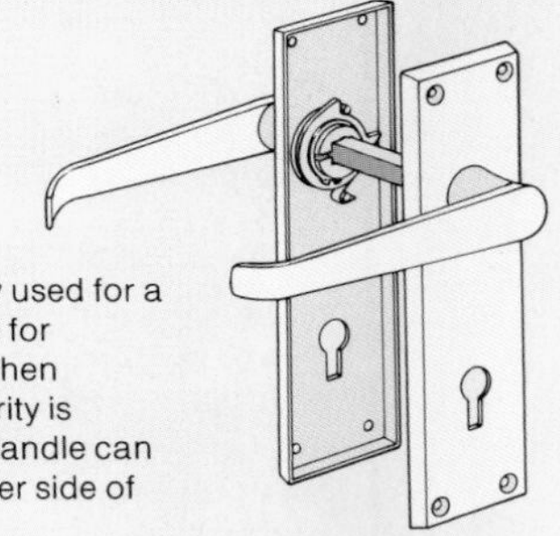

Most commonly used for a back door. Also for interior doors when privacy or security is wanted. Each handle can be used on either side of the door.

HANDLES FOR A MORTISE LATCH

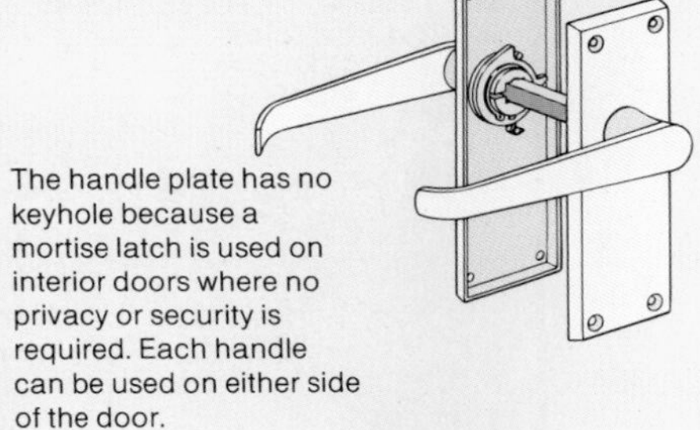

The handle plate has no keyhole because a mortise latch is used on interior doors where no privacy or security is required. Each handle can be used on either side of the door.

HANDLES FOR BATHROOM OR LAVATORY

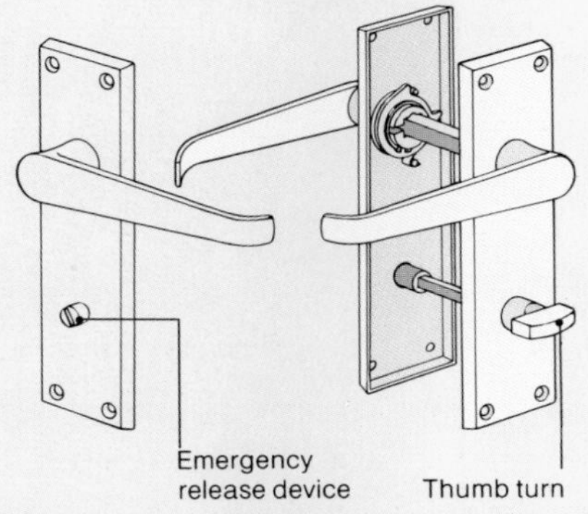

A thumb-turn on the inside of the door prevents it from being opened. The outside of the door has an emergency release device. Buy either a right-hand or left-hand opening set, as the handles are not interchangeable.

DOOR KNOBS

Can be used on a mortise lock or latch, provided the spindle is far enough from the edge of the door to allow you to open the door without scraping your knuckles. Can be used for bathroom or lavatory doors with a privacy adaptor kit.

DOOR KNOBS FOR RIM LOCKS

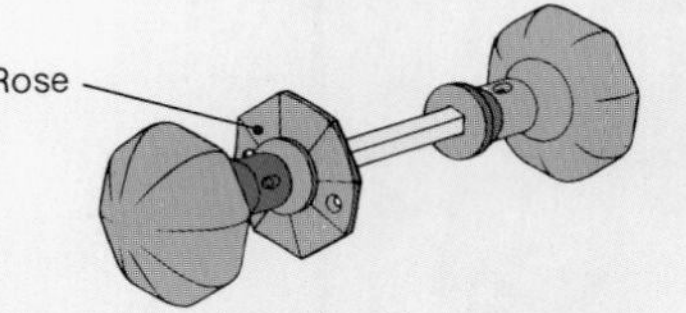

Designed to fit on a rim lock, with a rose on the outside of the door but no rose on the lock side.

DOOR KNOB FOR BATHROOM OR LAVATORY

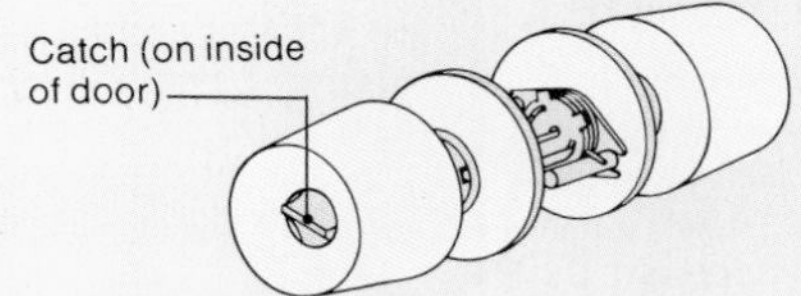

The knob has a catch that prevents the door from being opened from the outside.

LETTERPLATE AND INNER FLAP

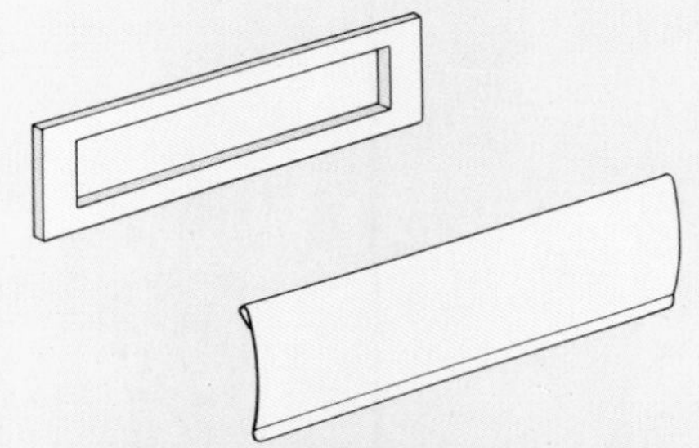

A standard letterplate fits on the middle of the front door. An inner flap fitted on the inside of the door gives a neat finish and helps to prevent draughts.

POSTAL KNOCKERS

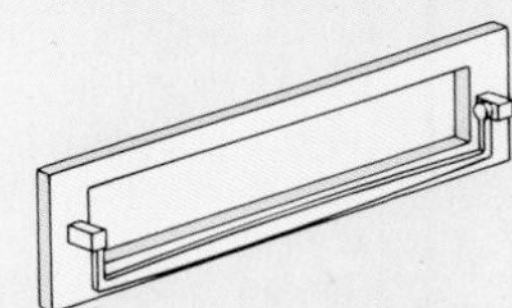

HORIZONTAL The letterplate incorporates a handle for pulling the door closed, which can also be used as a door knocker.

VERTICAL Fits on the lock stile of the door. The hole allows a nightlatch cylinder plate to be set into the knocker.

CENTRE KNOB

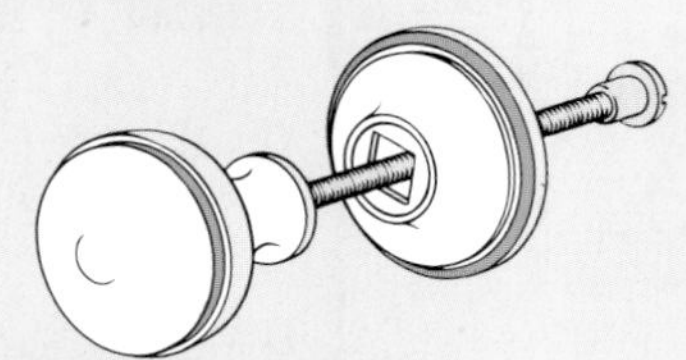

For closing the front door as you leave the house. It is often fitted to the door above a central letter-plate.

DOOR KNOCKER

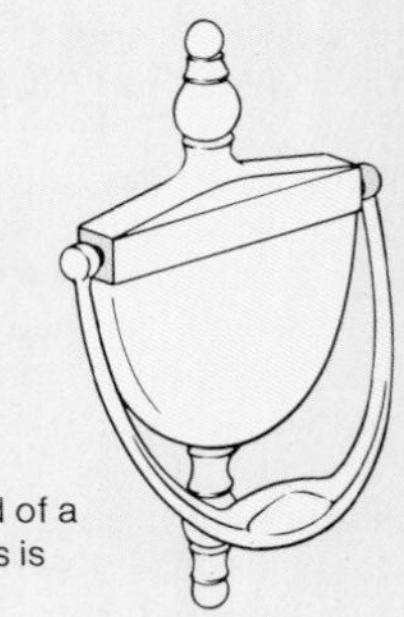

Fits to the front door instead of a bell. A wide range of designs is available.

FINGERPLATE

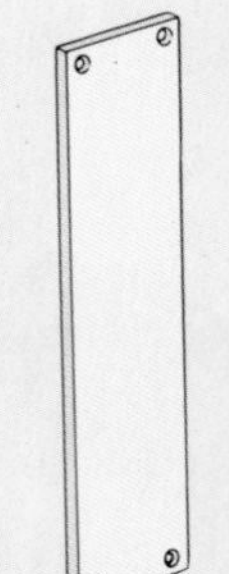

Decorative plate to protect interior doors from becoming grubby with frequent use. Ceramic, brass and plastic are the most common types.

ESCUTCHEON (OPEN OR COVERED)

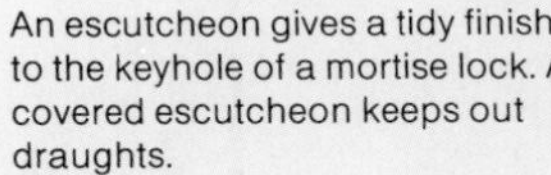

An escutcheon gives a tidy finish to the keyhole of a mortise lock. A covered escutcheon keeps out draughts.

CYLINDER PULL

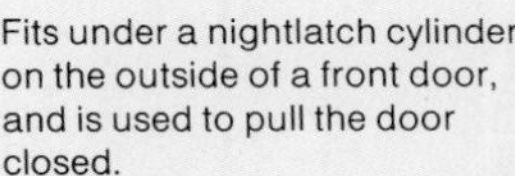

Fits under a nightlatch cylinder on the outside of a front door, and is used to pull the door closed.

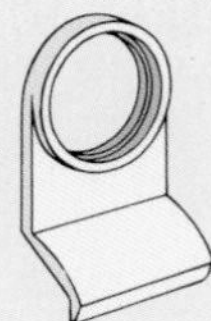

BELL PUSH

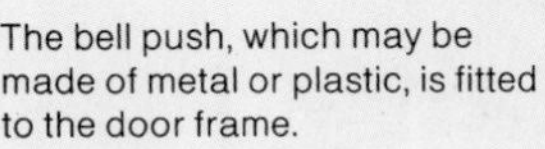

The bell push, which may be made of metal or plastic, is fitted to the door frame.

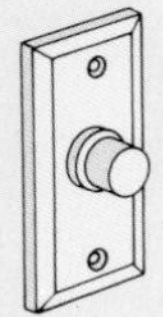

PULL HANDLE

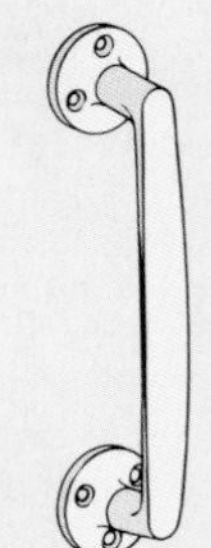

Can be fitted to either the inside or outside of a front door to provide a grip while opening or closing it.

NUMBERS

The street number of the house can be indicated with brass, iron, plastic or porcelain numbers screwed to the front door.

Curing faults in doors

STICKING ALONG ONE SIDE

Sticking is usually caused by a build-up of paint on the edge of the door and the frame. The problem is often worse in wet weather when the wood swells. If the trouble is not severe, simply rub the edge of the door with a candle or with dry powder lubricant.

If that is not enough, you will have to strip the door edge and frame.

1 Wait for a warm dry spell, and strip off the paint (page 105).

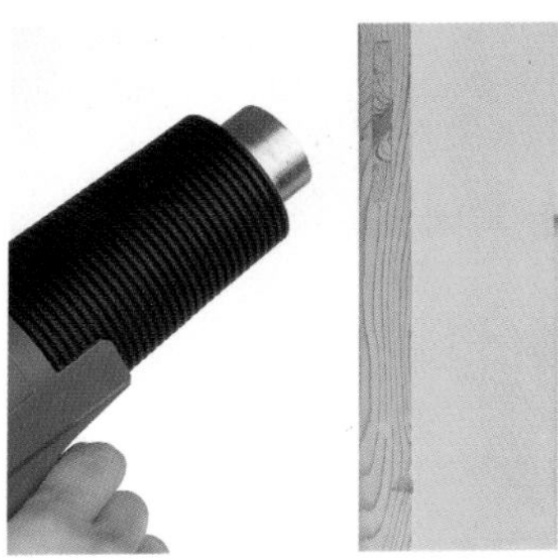

2 It is a good idea to dry out the surface with a hot-air gun before repainting.

3 Rub the stripped surfaces with glasspaper and check that the door opens and closes easily.

4 There should be a slight gap between the edge of the door and the frame, so run a thin knife blade all round the edge of the door when it is closed. Where the gap is insufficient, plane the edge of the door. It may be necessary to take the door off its hinges, and perhaps remove locks and bolts.

5 Sand, prime and paint the edge of the door. Let the paint dry before closing the door.

STICKING AT THE BOTTOM

If an external door sticks along its bottom edge, the problem is often caused by moisture being absorbed by the unpainted edge.

1 Wait for dry weather, then take the door off its hinges and thoroughly dry the bare edges with a hot-air gun.

2 If the binding is severe, hold the door on one of its long edges in a portable workbench. Mark a line to work to, then plane downwards from the edge of the door to the centre; this will avoid splintering the edge.

3 Prime and paint to match the rest of the door.

STICKING AT THE TOP

You may be able to plane the top edge of a door without taking it off its hinges. It will have to be propped open firmly while you work from a stepladder.

Doors stick at the top much less frequently than at the bottom or side.

A SQUEAKING DOOR

Oil the hinge pins with an aerosol lubricant. Work the door backwards and forwards a few times to get the lubricant into the hinge, then wipe away surplus oil with a clean rag.

With rising butt hinges, lift the open door off the hinge pins and lightly smear them with grease or petroleum jelly. Wipe away the surplus after re-hanging the door.

A DOOR THAT SLAMS

The only solution is to fit a surface-mounted hydraulic door-closer.

They are often supplied with a paper template which acts as a guide for the fixing holes to be marked at the top of the door and on the architrave above.

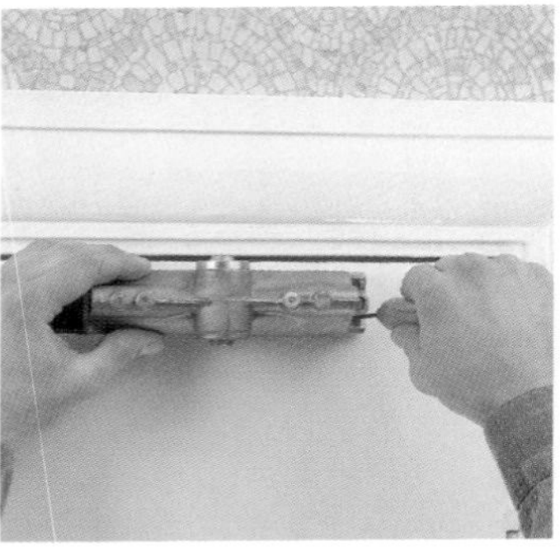

1 If a template is not supplied, hold the door-closer in position on the top edge of the door on the hinge side, and use a long bradawl to mark the screw positions.

2 Drill pilot holes, and screw on the closer. Chisel out a flat recess for the pivot arm fixing plate in the architrave, and screw it on.

3 Fix the pivot arm to the body of the closer, and turn the adjusting screws on the closer so that the door closes smoothly and slowly without slamming.

SPLIT DOOR PANELS

Sometimes splits develop in the panels of old doors. The solution varies according to whether the door is painted or natural wood.

Painted door

On a painted door, fill the crack with a two-part epoxy filler and paint over it.

Natural wood door

On a door where the filler will show, you must drive dowels into the edge of the door to press against the edges of the panel and close the crack.

1 First clean out any old paint and filler from the crack.

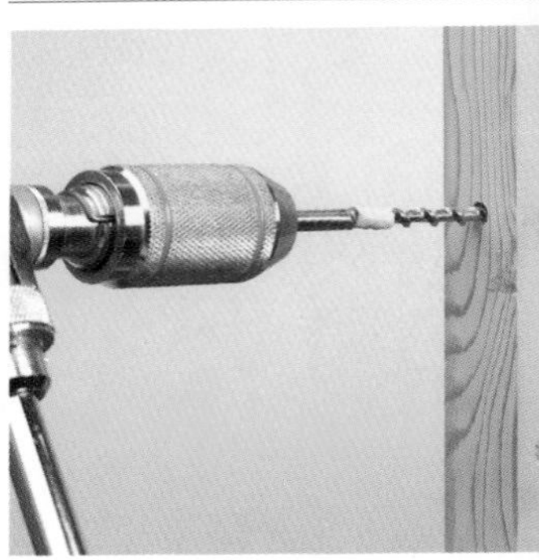

2 Using an auger bit, drill two or three ¼in (6mm) diameter holes through the edge of the door stile to line up with the edge of the panel. Measure the thickness of the stile and mark the auger bit with a piece of tape to avoid drilling too far.

3 Cut some ¼in (6mm) dowels about ¾in (19mm) longer than the width of the stiles.

4 Inject PVA wood glue into the crack in the panel and into the holes in the stile. Drive the dowels into the holes so they press against the edge of the panel and close the crack. Sash cramps can be used to squeeze the dowels inwards.

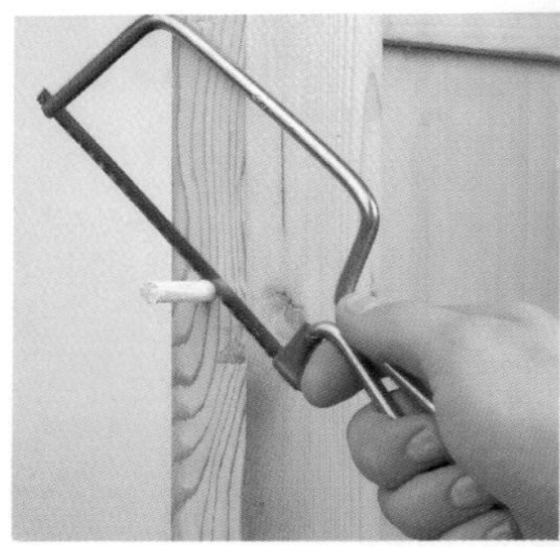

5 Clean off surface adhesive with a damp cloth, and leave the protruding dowel until the glue has set, then trim it off flush with the door.

WHEN THE LATCH WILL NOT ENGAGE

If a door sags a little or becomes slightly swollen, the latch bolt will be out of alignment with the striking plate. A small mis-alignment can be corrected by enlarging the cutout in the striking plate with a file.

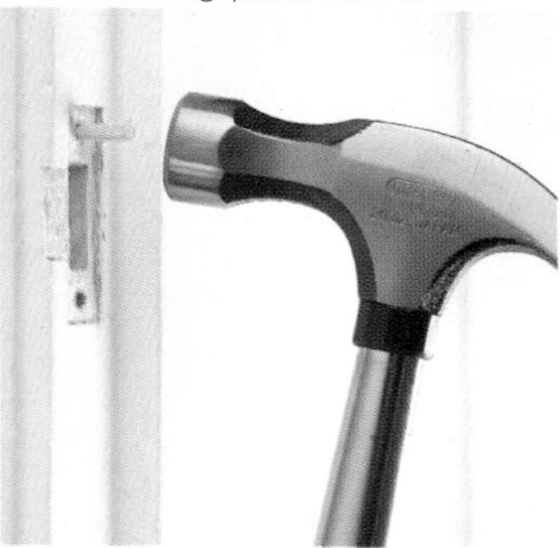

Otherwise, remove the striking plate and refix it in the correct position. If the plate has to be moved only a small distance, plug the old screw holes with small wooden pegs and drill new pilot holes for the fixing screws.

LOCK DIFFICULT TO TURN

Spray an aerosol lubricant into the lock using the narrow flexible applicator tube usually provided. Squirt the lubricant through the latch and bolt apertures and through the keyhole.

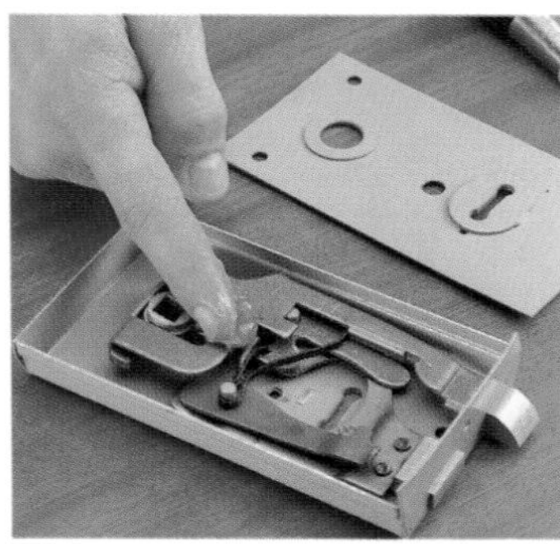

If this is not sufficient, remove the lock from the door, take off one side of the case, and lightly grease the mechanism.

Before starting work, note the positions of the components so they can be put back if they become displaced.

Do not use oil in Yale-type front-door locks. It attracts grit. Use graphite powder or PTFE dry powder lubricant.

LOOSE DOOR FRAME

Slamming a door often leads to the frame becoming loose.

Make new fixings with three large screws and wall plugs on each side of the frame. Long fixing screws, part-fitted into a plastic wall plug, are sold for the purpose. The length should be the thickness of the frame plus at least 2½in (60mm).

1 Using a masonry bit, drill through the frame and into the supporting masonry, ideally to coincide with the mid-point of a whole brick rather than a mortar joint.

2 Hammer the screw and plug into the hole so that the plug is fully into the wall, then tighten the screw to hold the frame secure.

A HINGE-BOUND DOOR

A door that is difficult to close, and tends to spring open, is said to be hinge-bound.

The problem is usually caused by hinge recesses being too deep in either the door edge or in the frame. When correctly fitted the hinge flaps should be flush with, or slightly below, the surface of the wood.

1 Open the door and push a piece of wood under the lock stile to take the weight.

2 Clear any paint from the slots in the hinge screws, and remove the screws.

3 Get someone to steady the door while you lever the hinge flap out of its recess.

Pack out the recess with pieces of cardboard, and then replace the screws.

Protruding screw heads

Occasionally the hinges may bind because the screw heads are too large, or have been put in askew, and come into contact with each other when the hinge flaps come together.

Remove the screws and replace them with screws with heads that fit the countersinks in the hinges. One gauge size smaller should be sufficient. If they will not tighten, pack out the holes with matches.

ALTERNATIVELY, deepen the countersinks in the hinge flaps so that the screw head will be flush with the surface. Use a high-speed-steel countersink bit.

If the screws were originally set in askew, plug the screw holes with pieces of scrap wood dipped in wood glue and then re-drill straight pilot holes.

Badly placed hinge flaps

Binding can also be caused by hinge flaps that are set into the frame too near to the door stop. As the door is closed, the face of the door presses against the stop, preventing it from going farther.

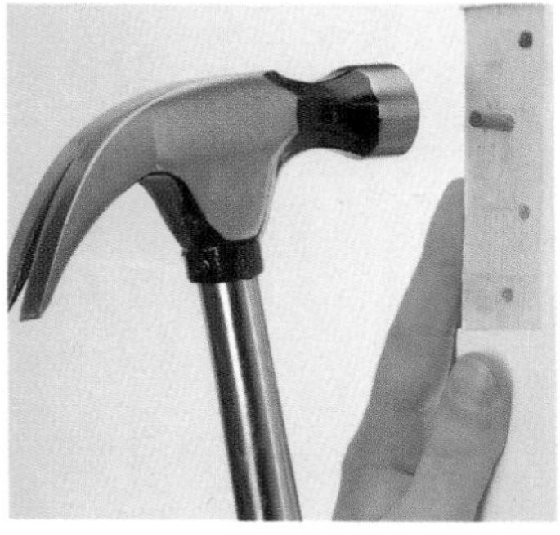

1 Remove the hinges and plug the fixing holes with pegs of scrap wood dipped in wood glue.

2 Re-drill the hinge fixing holes so that they are farther away from the door stop.

When the door is closed the hinge pin should protrude an equal distance from the face of the door and the edge of the frame.

On an internal door it may be possible to move the door stop as it is probably made from a separate piece of wood.

A ROTTEN DOOR

If exterior doors have not been protected with paint or varnish, rot may set in, especially near the bottom and at joints.

If you catch it early, you can patch it with a high-performance filler, such as Ronseal Wood Repair System.

1 On a warm, dry day, dig out the rotten wood and if possible allow the remaining wood to dry thoroughly. Warming with a hot-air gun can help.

2 Treat the area with a wood hardener, and when this has dried fill the cavity with a two-part epoxy

Curing faults in doors (continued)

filler. Build it up slightly above the surface, and sand it flat when it has hardened; hardening will take about 30 minutes.

3 Drill holes in the surrounding wood at intervals of about 6in (150mm).

4 Insert wood preservative pellets in the holes and then fill the holes with more filler.

5 Repaint the door to disguise the repair.

A ROTTEN FRAME

External door frames often rot near the sill. The only satisfactory repair is to insert a new piece of timber. Use an all-purpose saw; the teeth will not be affected by the masonry.

1 Make a sloping cut into the frame about 3in (75mm) above the rotted section. Probing with a screwdriver will reveal where the soft, rotten section ends. Make the cut at about 45 degrees.

2 Prise the rotted part away from the wall, including the base which was probably tenoned into the hardwood sill.

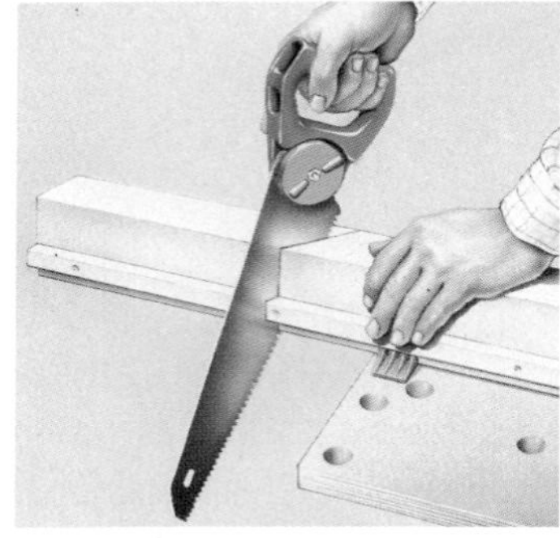

3 Cut a length of new timber to fit into the space, cutting the top at an angle to align with the saw cut.

The old frame was probably a one-piece section, but the matching repair can be made from two or more pieces of wood glued and screwed together. Make up the correct shape and add a door stop.

4 When the new section is a good fit, treat all the new wood and the cut edges with wood preservative, and fix the repair in place with $3\frac{1}{2}$in (90mm) No. 12 screws countersunk into the wood, and wall plugs.

5 Where the old and new frame sections join, drill $\frac{1}{4}$in (6mm) holes through the joint at right angles to it. Smear glue on $\frac{1}{4}$in (6mm) hardwood dowels and hammer them into the holes.

6 Trim them level with the surface when the glue has dried.

A SAGGING DOOR

When the bottom corner of the door rubs on the floor, the cause is either faulty hinges or loose joints in the door. Partly open the door and lift the handle or knob to see if there is movement at the hinges or joints.

Faulty hinges

If the hinges are loose, remove them and plug the holes with dowels. Refit the screws, or fit thicker screws. If necessary enlarge the countersunk holes in the hinge to take the larger screw heads. Use a high-speed steel bit.

If the movement is in the knuckle of the hinge due to a worn hinge pin the only cure is to fit new hinges (pages 196–197). It may be that the hinges are not big enough to support the weight of the door. In this case fit larger, heavier hinges and perhaps a third hinge midway between them.

Loose door joints

If the door joints are loose, glue and cramp them back into place.

1 Take the door off its hinges, and try to dismantle it by gently prising the loose joints apart.

2 Re-glue the joints and put them together again. If they will not come apart, inject woodworking glue into the joints.

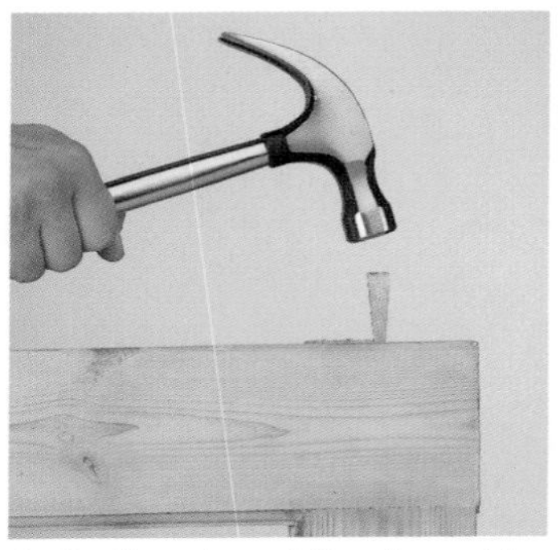

3 On the edge of the door, drive small wooden wedges into the ends of the tenons to prevent the joints from opening up again.

4 Drill through the face of the door and through the tenon and drive a dowel smeared with woodworking glue into the hole. This will lock the tenon in place. On an exterior door use waterproof glue.

5 Cramp the door with a sash cramp or Spanish windlass (page 191) while the glue sets.

6 Trim off the dowels flush with the door.

A WARPED DOOR

A cure with the door in place

It may be possible to cure a warp, with the door in place – but it will be out of action for at least 24 hours.

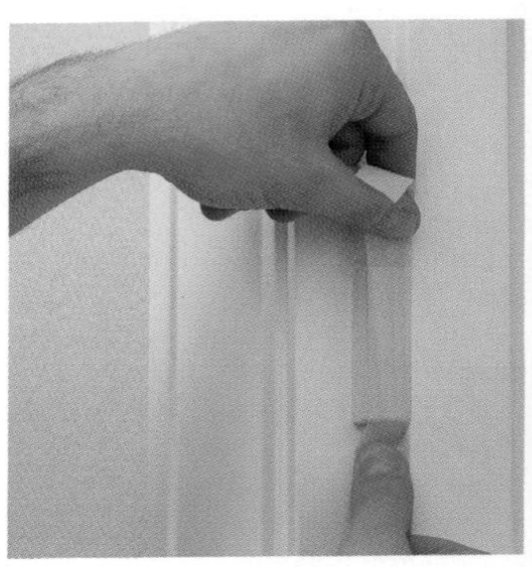

1 Close the door, putting blocks of timber behind that part that normally rests against the frame. You will probably need to tape the blocks to the frame while you close the door.

2 Push the part that bows outwards back into place by screwing a length of timber across the frame. You will have to fill the screw holes later.

3 If the door bows out in the middle, put the blocks at the top and bottom of the door and screw the length of timber across the middle.

Taking the door off its hinges

If the correction cannot be done in place, take the door off its hinges and lay it on a flat wooden floor.

Put blocks under the door in the places where the door normally rests against the frame, and correct the warp by forcing the door down to the floor with a length of timber screwed to the floor.

Adjusting the door stop

With internal doors, if the warp is not severe and is merely letting in draughts, a fairly simple cure is available. Prise the door stop away from the frame and re-fix it so that it rests against the face of the door.

This will not work with exterior doors because the door stop is an integral part of the frame.

CHOOSING THE STYLE AND MAKE OF A NEW WINDOW

When replacing a window, choose one that maintains the style of the house and is sympathetic to the building materials in the house and the neighbourhood.

All windows consist of fixed panes and opening casements or sashes. The basic styles on this page are available in a number of materials (see next page).

CASEMENT WINDOWS

Casements open on hinges. They usually open outwards and may be hinged at the side or the top. There may also be one or more fixed panes. Side-hinged casements are usually large, while top-hinged casements are often small, for gentle ventilation.

Fixed panes and opening casements can be combined in many ways and many styles.

Standard sizes range from 1ft 5¼in (438mm) wide by 2ft 6¼in (768mm) high to 7ft 10¼in (2394mm) wide by 5ft 0¼in (1530mm) high. They can also be specially made.

BOW WINDOWS

Usually multiple casements made to form a shallow curve. They are often in the Georgian style.

Standard sizes range from 5ft 0½in (1537mm) wide by 4ft 6¼in (1378mm) high to 9ft 10½in (3010mm) wide by 4ft 6¼in (1378mm) high.

LOUVRE WINDOWS

Horizontal slats of glass attached to the frame at each side can be adjusted to control ventilation. Louvres are often combined with a fixed pane, and are used in kitchens and bathrooms. They tend to let in draughts if the glass is not precisely matched to the thickness of the metal clips at the sides.

Security can be a problem because in some types the slats can be easily lifted out of the clips. But kits are available for locking louvres in frames.

When narrow louvres are combined with a large fixed light there may be no escape route from a room in case of fire. There should also be an opening window in the room as well.

Louvre windows are made to measure.

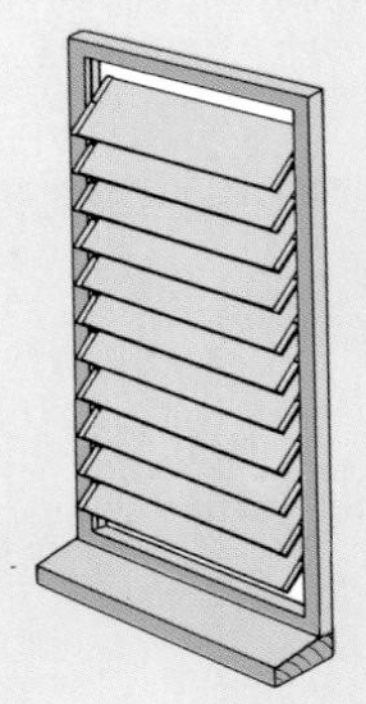

SASH WINDOWS

The windows, also called sliding sashes, usually slide up and down, but more modern types (particularly with metal frames) slide from side to side. The traditional timber type is prone to draughts, but modern sash windows can be bought fully weatherproofed.

Traditional sash windows are operated by weights attached to sash cords. Modern designs have spring-action spiral sash balances which are easier to maintain, and form a better weather seal. Some also tilt inwards for easy cleaning.

Standard sizes range from 2ft 1¼in (641mm) wide by 3ft 6¼in (1073mm) high to 3ft 5⅜in (1051mm) wide by 5ft 6¾in (1694mm) high.

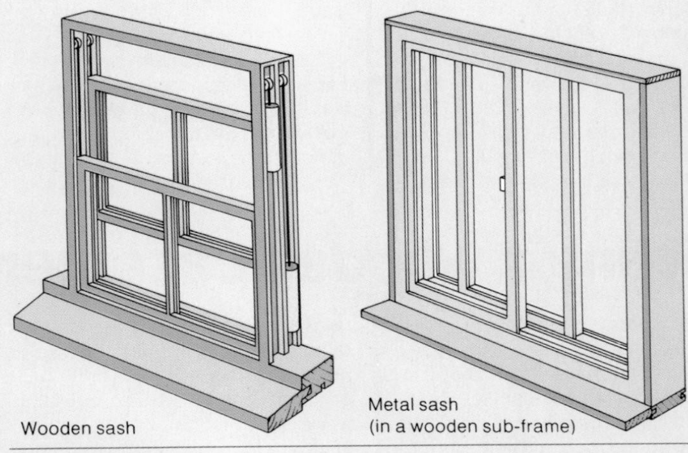

Wooden sash

Metal sash (in a wooden sub-frame)

BAY WINDOWS

Most bay windows are made with stone or brick piers projecting beyond the line of the wall, and fitted with sliding sashes. But a bay window can also be made with a series of casement windows joined together to form the projecting bay. It has angled corners rather than the curve of a bow window.

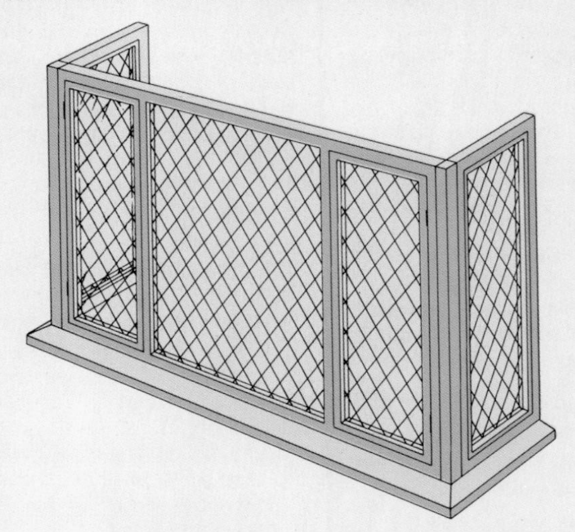

PIVOT WINDOWS

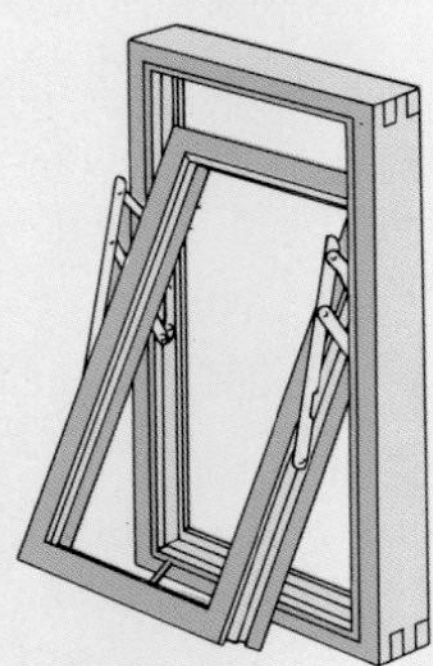

Projected windows

A sliding action moves the bottom of the window outwards while the top rail slides down in channels in each side of the frame. This allows the outside of the glass to be cleaned from the inside.

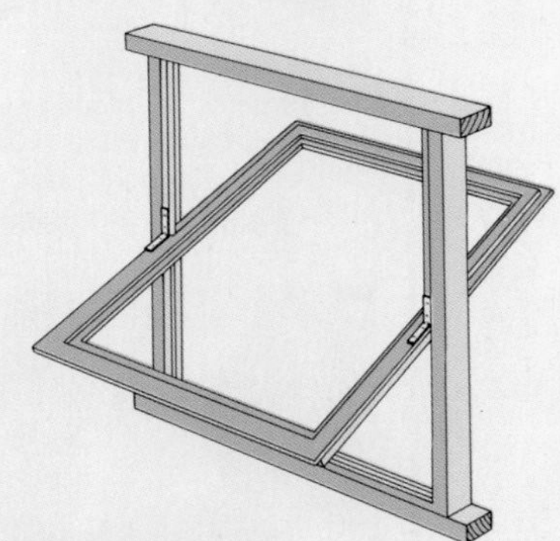

Standard model

The window pivots at its mid-point, and may also have a fixed pane. Some types are reversible for cleaning and maintenance – particularly useful for dormer windows.

Fully weather-sealed pivot windows are made for installing in pitched roofs – when a loft has been converted into a room, for example.

Tilt-and-turn

Some casements open inwards at the top, for ventilation without a security risk, and also open from one side for cleaning and maximum ventilation. Most types are made to measure.

What windows are made of

Timber
Windows made of timber look attractive and give good insulation. The cheaper types are made from paint-grade softwood which must be painted, but better quality windows are made of high grade softwood, such as Douglas fir, or of hardwood, and may be either painted or stained.

Standard size windows from reputable manufacturers are treated with preservative to meet the requirements of the NHBC (National House Building Council). Make sure that made-to-measure windows are similarly treated.

Many modern timber windows – both hardwood and softwood – are 'high-performance double-glazed windows' which means they are fully weather-sealed and made to reduce heat loss.

Steel
The metal is protected by hot-dipped galvanising, then covered with a primer, undercoat and gloss paint. Older steel windows are not galvanised and may rust.

Steel windows are strong and have a slim appearance. They are available in a wide range of types, but are not well insulated and often suffer from excessive condensation. Regular painting is needed, and they are often set in timber sub-frames which also need painting.

Aluminium
Most aluminium windows are made to measure in a wide range of types. They have a slim appearance and need little maintenance apart from washing down. Usually they are set in timber sub-frames which do need regular treatment with paint, preservative or varnish.

Like steel windows, they can suffer from condensation, although this is less on 'thermal break' types which have a central hidden insulating foam core to separate each face of the frame. Aluminium windows are usually double glazed.

Plastic
UPVC windows are attractive, practical and durable, with a chunky appearance, similar to wood, but without the maintenance requirements. They will not corrode, warp or rot and need only regular washing to keep clean. They are usually fitted in a UPVC frame containing a foam filling that gives good insulation and eliminates condensation. Ensure, however, that plastic windows have adequate security fittings when you buy them, as there are few strong points in which screws would hold.

Fitting a wooden casement window

Replacement wooden windows are usually needed because the existing windows have rotted beyond repair. Buy a replacement that matches the style of the other windows in the house, but take the opportunity to upgrade it by making sure it is double-glazed and completely weather-sealed so that it is draught-free.

Wooden casement windows are easily fitted provided they can be bought to fit the size of the existing openings.

The most important part of the job is measuring the opening in the wall. Take measurements in several positions. Check that the diagonals are equal, which means that the opening has right-angled corners. With a spirit level, check that the sill and top of the frame are both level, and that the sides are vertical. If they are not, it may be best to call in a builder, or a replacement window company.

Buy a standard size window and frame to fit the space. If that is not possible you can have one made to measure, but it will be much more expensive.

Before you fit the new frame, give it an extra coat of primer or wood preservative, depending on whether it is to be painted or varnished.

Do not start to remove the old window until you have taken delivery of the new one.

New windows are usually supplied without glass, which is installed after the window has been fitted.

The job is likely to last more than a day, so cover the wall opening – or unglazed window – with polythene or hardboard overnight to keep out the weather.

You will need
Tools Spirit level with horizontal and vertical vials; steel tape measure; screwdriver; leather work gloves; safety spectacles or goggles; claw hammer; metal container for broken glass; hacksaw blade; old wood saw; wrecking bar or lever; bolster chisel; builder's trowel; electric drill; twist bits; countersink bit; masonry bit to match wall plugs; sealant gun. Possibly a plane and Mole self-grip wrench.
Materials New wooden window, with frame; mortar (page 479); wooden wedges; 4in (100mm) No. 14 countersunk zinc-plated screws; wall plugs for screws; strip of damp-proof course the width of the window; frame sealant. Possibly also: strips of hardwood as wide as the frame's thickness; panel pins; wood mouldings to go around frame; plaster.

REMOVING STUBBORN SCREWS

While taking out an old window you are likely to encounter screws that are extremely difficult to remove. First clear the slots of paint with an old screwdriver. Then put a well-fitting screwdriver blade in the screw slot and strike the handle with a hammer. Press hard while turning the screwdriver anticlockwise.

For really stubborn screws, use an impact driver – a type of screwdriver that turns automatically when struck with a hammer. Or try heating the screw head with a large soldering iron to expand the screw temporarily and break the seal between screw and frame.

As a last resort, drill off the head.

REMOVING THE EXISTING WINDOW

1 Remove hinged windows by unscrewing the hinges. If the window is a big one, you will need a helper.

2 Remove the glass from any fixed windows. Wearing the gloves and goggles, break the glass with a hammer. Remove all the pieces from the frame and put them into a metal container for safe disposal.

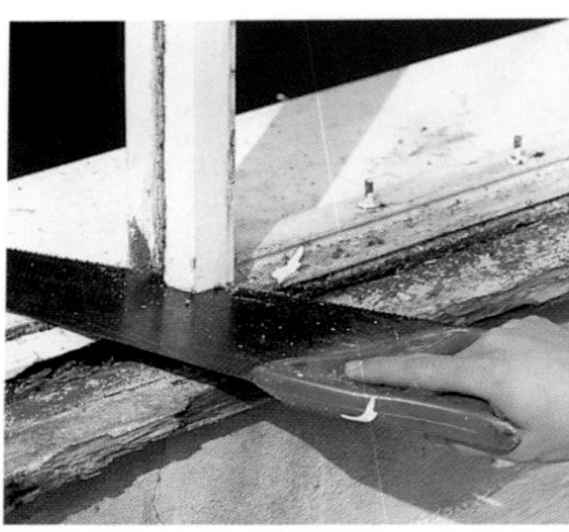

3 You will probably have to take the frame out in pieces. Use an old saw to cut through the vertical and horizontal timbers close to the sides, top and bottom of the frame.

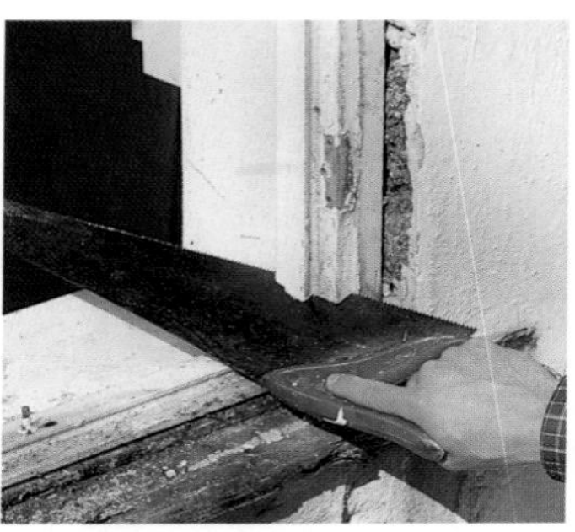

4 Saw at an angle through the jamb at one side of the frame.

5 With a strong lever, such as a wrecking bar, prise the jamb that

TAKING OUT THE FRAME IN ONE PIECE

It just might be possible to remove the old window frame in one piece.

1 Locate the screws or nails fixing the frame to the wall and clear them of mortar.

2 Cut through the screws with a hacksaw blade. Fit a handle on whichever end of the blade will allow you to cut by pulling, not pushing.

3 Try lifting out the frame.

you have sawn through until it comes away from the brickwork.

This will allow you to lever out the other parts of the frame – the top, the sill and finally the jamb at the other side.

If an internal window board is fitted inside the windowsill, keep it in one piece, as you will need it when you fit the new window.

Try also to keep the sides of the opening intact, as you do not want to damage the wall plaster or the damp-proof strip that is in the wall cavity.

6 Clean up the sides, top and bottom of the opening with a bolster chisel to leave the bricks as smooth as possible and free from old mortar.

7 Remove any protruding screws (with a Mole self-grip wrench) or nails (with a claw hammer). Also remove any bits of timber 'horns' from the old frame that might have been built into the top corners of the opening.

8 Fill any large cavities neatly with pieces of bricks and mortar and wait for the repairs to dry.

INSTALLING THE NEW WINDOW FRAME

The new window normally comes with a new exterior sill; if a separate sill is required it should be hardwood or moulded plastic.

Normally the frame is fitted up against the existing inside window board.

1 Hold the new frame up to the opening to see if it fits. (You will probably need a helper.) There should be a clearance of about ¼in (6mm) all round.

2 If the frame is slightly too big, plane a little off it. Then treat the bare wood with clear preservative followed by primer, or with water-repellent wood stain.

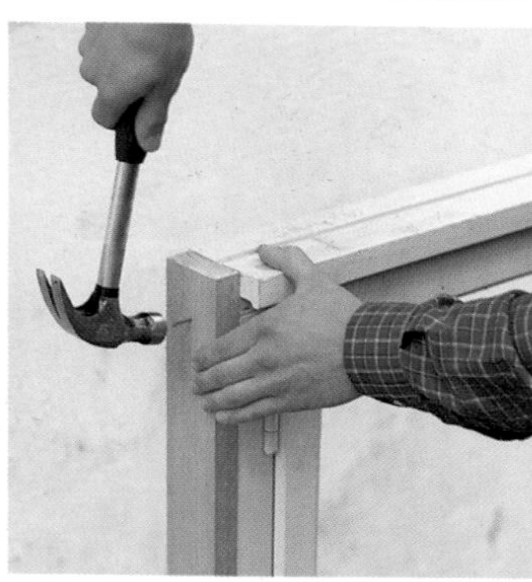

ALTERNATIVELY, if the new frame is too small, pack it out by nailing strips of hardwood up to ¾in (19mm) thick to the sides. After the window has been installed, moulding can be tacked around the edges of the frame to cover the packing strips.

3 Lift the frame into place and temporarily hold it with wedges. If the window is a large one, you will need a helper at this stage. Wedge it to within ¼in (6mm) of the lintel to allow space for mortar at the bottom.

The frame must be vertical, and must be pushed right back against the plaster inside the room. Use a spirit level to check that it is vertical and that both the top and bottom of the frame are horizontal.

4 Drill holes through the jambs (side pieces) at suitable intervals. Position the holes where they will coincide with the mid-points of bricks, not the mortar joints. Allow the drill to penetrate far enough to mark the bricks.

On most windows four fixings – at the top and bottom of each jamb – are sufficient. On windows more than 4ft (1.2m) from top to bottom, put a third fixing about midway up each jamb.

5 Carefully remove the frame from the opening and check that you can see the drilling marks.

6 Using a masonry bit, drill the bricks at the marked points and insert the wall plugs.

7 Countersink the screw holes in the frame.

8 Lay a thin bed of mortar (page 481) on the sill brickwork.

9 Lay a strip of damp-proof course along the sill and cover it with another layer of mortar.

10 Replace the frame and wedges at the sides and top, and check with a spirit level that it is level and the sides are upright.

11 Fix the frame by screwing into the wall plugs in the bricks.

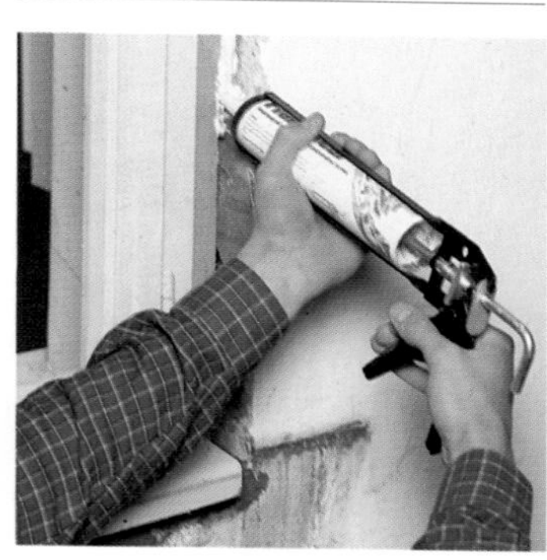

12 Use a frame sealant to fill any gaps around the frame. Inject the sealant from a cartridge with a sealant gun. Do not use mortar; it cannot accommodate movement in the wood.

13 If necessary, repair damage to rendering around the outside of the opening with mortar, and make good inside with plaster.

14 The window is then ready for glazing (page 217) and final decoration if necessary.

FITTING A SEPARATE SILL

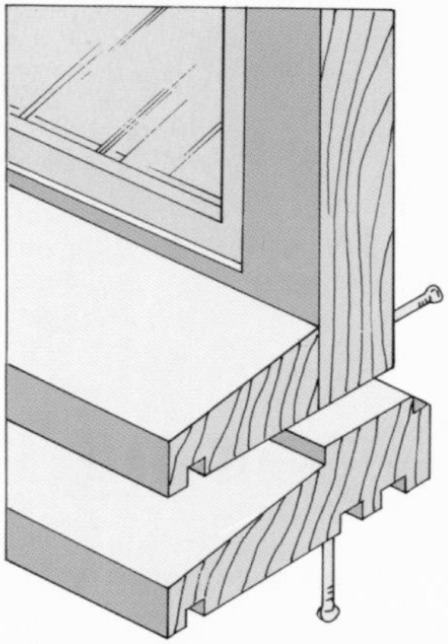

Some windows are supplied without a built-in sill and you will have to fit a separate one.

If the window opening is deep enough, fit the sill to the underside of the frame. Buy a hardwood sill, with a drip groove, measuring 7in × 3in (180mm × 75mm) in cross-section. Stand the frame upside down and run sealant along the underside close to the outside face. Put the sill (also upside down) in position on the frame, drill pilot holes and nail through from the underside using nails or screws 4½in (115mm) long. The sealant will prevent rain from getting between sill and frame.

If there is not enough depth in the opening for a sill under the frame, buy a sill with a cross-section of 5in × 3in (125mm × 75mm). Spread waterproof woodworking adhesive on the outer face of the frame, and nail or screw through from the inside of the frame into the back of the sill, using sealant between the sill and the frame.

Finally, trim the sill to length, either flush with the sides of the frame, or protruding, if the old frame had 'horns'.

Fitting a handle and stay to a casement window

Wooden casement windows are occasionally supplied without handles or stays, which have to be fitted separately.

If you wish to fit a replacement handle to an old window, the fixing method is the same.

You will need
Tools Drill and twist bits; bradawl; screwdriver.
Materials Handle and wedge plate; window stay; screws.

1 Hold the handle in place against the inside face of the window edge at about its mid-point, and use the bradawl to mark the positions of each of the screw holes.

2 Drill pilot holes for the screws at the positions you have marked, then screw the handle securely to the window.

3 Hold the wedge plate against the window frame in the correct position for the handle you have fitted to engage with it.

Mark the screw-hole positions with the bradawl.

4 Drill the pilot holes for the screws into the frame.

5 Screw the wedge plate securely to the frame.

6 Position the mounting plate for the window stay at the bottom of the window about 4in (100mm) from the hinge side of the frame and screw it in place. If necessary, fit the stay to the mounting plate.

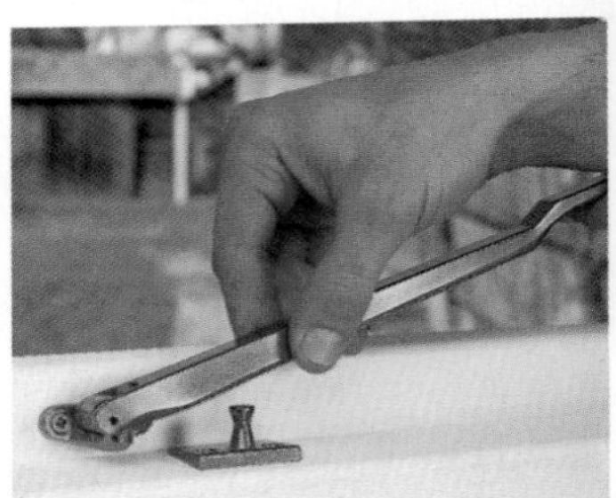

7 Position one locking peg on the base of the frame, close to the mounting plate. Check that the stay will fit over the peg with the window closed. The peg may have to fit into a hole in the stay.

8 When you have correctly positioned the locking peg, screw it to the frame.

9 Press the stay forwards to hold the window firmly closed, and fit the second fixing near to the free end of the stay.

Repairing rot with wood-repair products

The easiest way to repair rot in a wooden window is to use a combination of wood repairing products, such as a liquid wood hardener, high-performance wood filler and wood preservative pellets.

Naturally this method is suitable only for painted wood, because the repair would show up on stained or varnished wood.

You will need
Tools Old chisel, about ½in (13mm) wide; paint scraper; hot-air gun; ½in (13mm) paintbrush for applying wood hardener; filling knife; electric drill; ⅜in (10mm) bit; disc sander; paintbrush for applying finishing coats to the window.
Materials Wood-repair products (as above); clear wood preservative; primer, undercoat and gloss paint.

1 Use a hot-air gun or chemical paint stripper to loosen old paint, then scrape it off to reveal the extent of the rotted area.

> HELPFUL TIP
> If the rot is close to a joint in the window, strengthen it with a flat steel L-shaped corner plate. Recess the corner plate to lie flush with the surface of the wood so that it is not noticeable after it is painted. (See *Fixing loose joints on windows*, page 212.)

2 Dig away the worst of the rot with an old chisel. There is no need to cut back right into sound timber.

3 If the timber is wet it must be dried out. Saturated wood can be covered with a flap of plastic, taped along the top, so that it dries out naturally over a couple of weeks. If it is only damp, dry it rapidly with a hot-air gun fitted with a nozzle to keep the heat away from the glass.

4 When the wood is thoroughly dry, flood the rotted area with brush-loads of wood hardener. The liquid penetrates into the wood, and hardens it as it dries, to give a firm base for the filler. Pay particular attention to exposed end grain. Keep flooding on the hardener until it stops soaking rapidly into the wood and begins to stay on the surface. Let it harden overnight.

5 Mix a small amount of the high-performance wood filler according to the instructions on the container and apply it as quickly as you can to the hole.

The filler will start to harden in about five minutes – even quicker in hot weather.

6 Build up deep cavities in a succession of layers.

Because the filler hardens so quickly, even deep holes can be filled in a very short time.

7 Leave the surface of the filled hole as level as you can.

After about 30 minutes it can finally be smoothed level with the surrounding wood with a disc sander in an electric drill.

This will show up any areas where the filler is low.

8 Wipe away the dust and apply more filler, sanding down again afterwards so that the surface is level and smooth.

9 In the wood surrounding the repair, drill ⅜in (10mm) holes about ¾in (19mm) deep, and spaced 2in (50mm) apart.

Whenever possible, it is a good idea to position all the holes (which are for preservative pellets) along vulnerable areas, such as sills.

10 Push one of the wood-preservative pellets into each hole and then seal with the wood filler.

While the wood is dry the pellets will remain inactive, but as soon as it becomes wet the pellets will release a fungicide which will prevent wood rot.

11 Coat the frame with clear wood preservative.

12 Paint with primer, undercoat and at least two coats of exterior gloss paint. Or apply two coats of microporous (also called acrylic) paint. Microporous is a paint designed particularly for exterior use. It allows the timber to breathe, but at the same time keeps out damp. This reduces the risk of blistering and flaking.

PREVENTING WET ROT

Woodwork both indoors and outdoors is likely to suffer from wet rot (page 464). The wood darkens and starts to crumble as a result of damp.

The best way to prevent it is to ensure that any new timber used is treated with wood preservative (page 473), and to keep wood protected with regular applications of wood preservative, varnish or paint.

Seal round frames with a frame sealant (page 106) to stop moisture seeping in from walls. Make sure there is plenty of ventilation indoors.

Repairing rot with new wood

The traditional way of repairing rot in a window is to cut back the rotted part to sound wood and insert a new piece. This method is still necessary on varnished or stained windows which cannot be repaired with filler without spoiling the finish. It is also necessary if a frame has been weakened by rot damage.

The timber used for the repair should match the original timber in the window.

REPLACING A SECTION OF SILL OR FRAME

You will need

Tools Pencil; combination square; tenon saw or general purpose saw; chisel, about ¾in (19mm) wide; mallet; vice; electric drill and twist bits; paintbrush; plane.

Materials Timber to suit size of rotted section; clear wood preservative; zinc-plated No. 10 screws, about 2in (50mm) long; wood dowels (same diameter as screw heads); waterproof wood glue; paint, varnish or preservative wood stain.

1 Mark cutting lines on the frame about 2in (50mm) beyond obvious signs of rot. Draw two right-angled lines on the face of the frame and then mark two more lines at about 45 degrees to the face to form a wedge shape.

2 Using the tenon saw or general purpose saw, cut along the lines as far as possible. Brickwork may prevent you from sawing too far into a sill.

3 Complete the cut with a sharp chisel. Try to leave straight flat sides which will form a tight joint with the new timber.

4 Hold a piece of new timber against the cut-out and mark the edges of the cut-out on it with a pencil to give a cutting line.

5 Cut out the new piece with a saw and trim it with the saw or a plane until it is a good fit in the cut-out. It is better if its faces stand proud of the surrounding surface.

6 Treat the cut surfaces of the frame and the new timber with clear wood preservative and allow to dry.

7 Glue the timber in place, holding it with G-cramps until the glue is quite dry.

8 Drill pilot and clearance holes for fixing screws, about 5in (125mm) apart.

9 Drill out the holes about ½in (13mm) deep to the same diameter as the screw heads so that the heads will go well below the wood surface.

10 Insert the screws and plug the holes with pieces of glued wood dowel. Drive them firmly home with the mallet.

11 Plane the faces of the timber insert so they are flush with the surrounding surface. Smooth with abrasive paper, and fill any gaps with exterior grade filler.

12 Finish the repair by applying paint, varnish or a preservative wood stain.

HELPFUL TIP

If the frame is to be finished with paint, it is a good idea to drill the repaired area at 2in (50mm) intervals so that wood-preservative pellets can be inserted (see *Repairing rot with a wood-repair system*, facing page).

REPAIRING A ROTTEN WINDOW EDGE

You will need

Tools Screwdriver; panel saw; portable workbench; plane; drill and ¼in (6mm) twist bit; depth stop; paintbrush.

Materials Piece of timber to suit the size of the rotted section; clear wood preservative; waterproof wood glue; Spanish windlasses (page 191); dowels, ¼in (6mm) in diameter; paint, varnish or preservative wood stain.

1 If the rot is on the edge of a window, remove the window. A casement window is taken off by unscrewing the hinges from the frame. For removing a sliding sash window, see page 214.

2 Saw off the rotted part by cutting right along the edge.

Repairing a rotten window edge (continued)

3 Cut a replacement length of timber that is slightly oversize.

4 Treat the new timber and the cut surface of the window with clear wood preservative and allow to dry. Put newspaper on the bench, and ventilate the room.

5 Apply glue to the new piece of timber and fix it in position. Hold the timber together with a pair of sash cramps until the glue has set. Wipe away any excess adhesive.

6 Reinforce the repair by drilling through the new and old timber, and driving in glued dowels. Use a $\frac{1}{4}$in (6mm) twist bit and dowels of the same size.

Before drilling, mark the correct depth of the hole on the bit with a depth stop, or wrap a piece of coloured adhesive tape round the twist bit.

7 When the glue has set, cut off the protruding lengths of dowel and plane the timber to the exact width and thickness.

8 Fill any minor gaps that remain with exterior wood filler.

9 Finish the bare timber with paint, varnish or preservative wood stain, depending on how the rest of the window is treated.

Wooden windows that stick

If a window will not open or close easily, examine it carefully to discover the cause.

BUILD-UP OF PAINT

Layers of paint that have built up over the years are a common cause of sticking windows.

1 Use a hot-air gun or chemical paint stripper to strip the edge of the window and the frame back to bare wood.

2 Check that there is a clearance gap of about $\frac{1}{16}$in (2mm) between the edge of the window and the frame before repainting.

3 If necessary, plane the edge of the window to give enough clearance. A casement window can be removed by unscrewing the hinges from the frame. For removing a sliding-sash window, see page 214.

SWOLLEN TIMBER

Damp that has made the timber swell is also a cause of sticking windows.

1 Strip off the paint and either let the timber dry out during dry weather, or dry it quickly with a hot-air gun.

2 When it is dry make sure there is a clearance gap of about $\frac{1}{16}$in (2mm) between window and frame. If necessary, plane the edge of the window.

3 Repaint the window, ensuring that the putty around the glass is well covered with paint.

STAFF BEADS TOO TIGHT

On a sliding-sash window, the staff beads might have been nailed too close to the sashes.

1 Prise off the staff beads (see *Replacing broken sash cords*, page 214) and re-nail them so they lightly touch the edges of the sash. Before driving the nails right in, test that the sash will slide easily.

2 Rub the inside face of the staff bead with a candle to help improve the sliding action.

3 Check that there is not a build-up of paint on the inside edge of the staff beads.

4 If necessary, loosen the old paint with a chemical paint stripper and then scrape it off. Re-coat with new paint.

LOOSE OR BROKEN HINGES

If the hinges are loose or broken, either retighten them or replace them, using the same technique as for door hinges (pages 197, 205).

Fixing loose joints on windows

The corner joints on both sliding-sash and casement windows often work loose. A painted window can be repaired with a steel corner plate. A window finished with varnish or wood stain must be repaired with glued dowels, or the repair will show.

A CORNER-PLATE REPAIR

Flat steel L-shaped corner plates are available in various sizes. Choose one large enough to bridge the damaged area and give a secure fixing into sound wood. Before putting it on, repair any damage with epoxy filler.

You will need

Tools Small timber wedges; trimming knife; chisel; small paintbrush; abrasive paper.

Materials Steel corner plates; 1in (25mm) No. 10 countersunk zinc-plated screws; metal primer; exterior filler; paint.

1 Drive small timber wedges between the frame and the window to close the joint. On a sliding-sash window, first remove the staff beads (see *Replacing broken sash cords*, page 214).

ALTERNATIVELY, remove the window and hold the joint closed with a sash cramp.

HOW TO MAKE WOODEN WEDGES

Wooden wedges are useful for various DIY jobs when you want to hold something securely in position while you glue it or fix it in some other way.

Take a piece of softwood about 4in (100mm) long, $\frac{3}{4}$in (19mm) wide and $\frac{1}{2}$in (13mm) thick, and rule a pencil line across diagonally from one corner to another.

Hold the wood securely with cramps or in a vice while you saw along the line to produce two wedges.

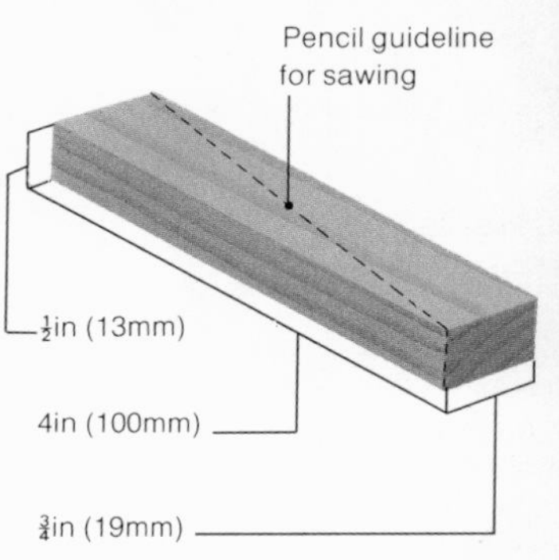

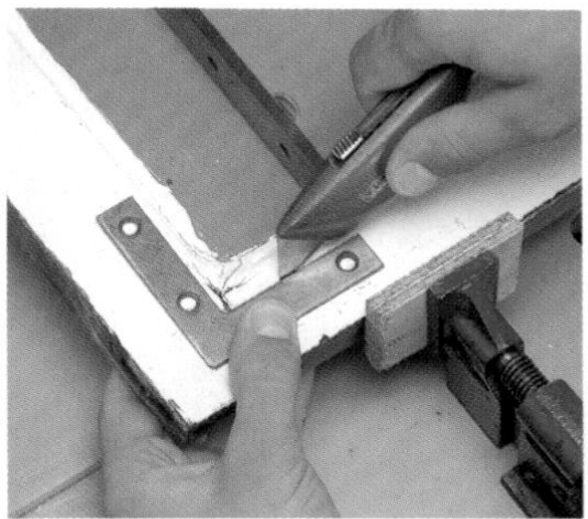

2 Put a plate over the joint on the inside or outside of the window – or both if it is very weak – and mark around it with a knife.

3 Cut a recess for the plate into the surface of the timber, deep enough for the plate to rest slightly below the surface.

4 Fix the plate with the screws, and paint it with metal primer.

5 Cover the repair with exterior filler, sand smooth, and paint with undercoat and two coats of gloss.

A DOWELLED JOINT

Glued dowels driven through the joint give an invisible and very strong repair.

You will need
Tools Screwdriver; G-cramps or portable workbench; sash cramp, web cramp or Spanish windlass (page 191); drill and ¼in (6mm) twist bit; chisel; hammer; panel saw; abrasive paper; paintbrush.
Materials ¼in (6mm) dowels; waterproof wood glue; varnish or preservative wood stain.

1 Take out a casement window by unscrewing the hinges. To remove a sash window, see page 214.

2 Close the loose joints with a sash cramp or web cramp, then cramp the window to a workbench.

3 Drill holes for three ¼in (6mm) dowels per joint. One goes through the face of the vertical stile to pin the tenon that protrudes from the end of the horizontal rail.

Two go through the side of the vertical stile into the end of the horizontal rail to reinforce both sides of the tenon.

4 Using a chisel, cut one or two grooves lengthwise down each dowel to let glue escape. Smear the dowels and the holes with wood glue, and drive in the dowels with a hammer.

5 When the glue has set, cut the surplus dowel off flush with the surface of the wood.

6 Sand the repair smooth, and coat it with varnish or preservative wood stain.

Gaps around a window frame

Gaps around the outside of the window frames will cause the frames to rot. They will also result in damp appearing on the internal walls around the window.

SEALING WITH MASTIC

Cracks up to about ⅜in (10mm) wide can be sealed with frame sealant (see panel).

You will need
Tools Craft knife; thin screwdriver; clean rag.
Materials Frame sealant and applicator. Perhaps a jar of water.

1 With a craft knife, cut the nozzle off the sealant cartridge at an angle to give the necessary width of sealant. Push a thin screwdriver blade through the nozzle and into the cartridge to break the foil seal.

2 Wipe around the frame with a clean rag, and inject a bead of sealant into the crack all round. The sealant should be placed in the angle between the window frame and the wall.

For neatness, try to inject the sealant in a single run without stopping, except at corners.

3 If it is necessary to smooth the sealant, use a wet finger.

4 Sealant can be painted once a skin has formed (one to three weeks), but it is not necessary.

SEALING WITH MORTAR

If the gap is more than about ⅜in (10mm) wide it should be filled with mortar. Use bagged dry-mix bricklaying mortar, or mix your own with 1 part cement, 1 part lime, and 6 parts builder's sand (page 481).

Your will need
Tools Plant sprayer; small trowel or filling knife; craft knife; clean rag.
Materials Water; mortar; sealant and applicator.

1 Dampen the crack with water. A plant sprayer is ideal.

2 Press the mortar in place with a small trowel or filling knife, so that it is level with the surface of the brickwork.

3 When the mortar has hardened, which will take two or three days, seal all round the frame with frame sealant in the manner described above.

EXPANDING FOAM FILLER

For large, irregular gaps that are hard to reach, use a can of expanding foam filler. This adheres to most building materials. It is injected by nozzle at any angle, after which it expands in volume, effectively sealing even hidden areas. Once hardened, the foam is heat, cold and water resistant and rot-proof. It can be cut, sanded, plastered or painted.

CHOOSING FRAME SEALANT

Frame sealant is commonly available from hardware shops and DIY stores in three colours – white, brown and transparent, but other colours are sometimes available.

The sealant is sold in a cartridge which may either have a screw-down applicator or need to be fitted into a trigger-operated sealant gun. The gun is not expensive to buy and will last indefinitely.

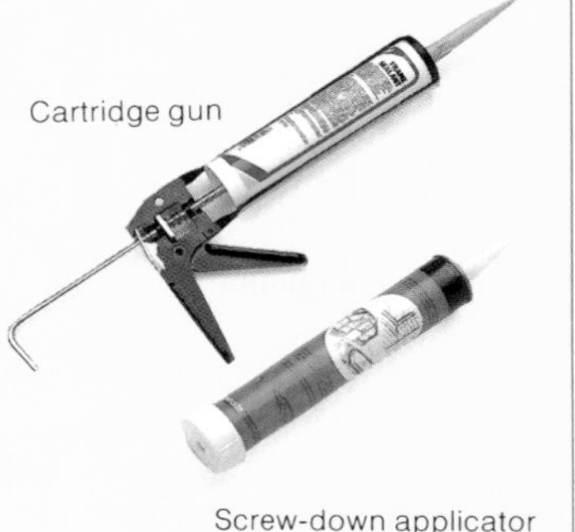

Problems with metal windows

RUST IN OLD FRAMES

Old steel windows often rust. If the putty has been dislodged or the glass cracked, first carefully chip out the putty with an old chisel or hacking knife (page 217) and remove the glass. Whether or not the glass has to be removed, the renovation process is the same.

You will need
Tools Paint scraper or small brush, for paint stripper; small cold chisel; hammer; wire brush; safety goggles; small paintbrush; gloves.
Materials Rust remover; zinc-based primer; undercoat; gloss paint; white spirit. Possibly paint stripper and epoxy filler.

1 Scrape off the paint, or remove it with a chemical paint stripper.

2 Using a small cold chisel, chip off as many of the rust flakes as possible. Then wire-brush the frame by hand, or use a wire wheel or wire-cup brush in an electric drill. Wear safety goggles and gloves during this part of the job.

3 Brush over the frame to remove dust and loose particles, then fill any holes with epoxy-based filler and allow it to dry.

4 Paint the frame with a coat of rust remover.

5 When the rust remover is dry, apply a zinc-based metal primer, then an undercoat and two coats of gloss paint.

6 If necessary, re-glaze the window, using metal casement putty (page 217).

WARPED FRAMES

Check if a build-up of paint or rust on the frame is distorting it. If so, clean it off and repaint the frame.

If the frame is warped for no apparent reason, nothing can be done to straighten it. Seal the gap between window and frame with silicone rubber sealant. First clean both frames with soap and water and dry thoroughly. Then put a bead of sealant on the fixed frame, deep enough to fill the gap.

Cover the closing frame with soapy water, shut it tight to compress the sealant, then open it at once. Leave the sealant to set, and it will form a perfect seal. Trim off excess sealant with a knife.

PAINT NOT STICKING TO GALVANISING

On new steel frames paint will sometimes flake off the galvanised surface soon after being applied.

1 Remove existing paint with paint stripper to get right back to the galvanising.

2 Rub the frame lightly with fine wet-and-dry abrasive paper used wet. Wipe it with a clean damp cloth.

3 When it is dry, wipe it with a clean rag soaked in white spirit, then prime with metal primer.

4 Repaint the window frame with an undercoat and gloss paint.

CONDENSATION ON METAL

Condensation is quite a common problem with metal windows. The best solution is to fit a replacement window and frame made of timber or plastic – or even aluminium as long as it is fitted with a thermal break to insulate the outside face from the inner face.
ALTERNATIVELY, fit a secondary double-glazing system (page 269) to isolate the metal from the warm air in the room.

Installing an extractor fan will also help.

Replacing broken sash cords

When a sash cord breaks, replace all four cords on the window. The other three are probably failing.

You will need
Tools Old chisel; string; trimming knife; pincers; screwdriver; hammer; small weight (a screw will do); matches. Perhaps machine oil.
Materials Sash cords (preferably Terylene); 1in (25mm) galvanised clout (large head) nails; 1in (25mm) oval nails; filler.

TAKING OUT THE SASHES

1 Working from inside the room, prise off the staff beads from the front of the window frame on each side. An old chisel or a large screwdriver is a suitable tool for the job.

Start at the centre of the staff bead to avoid damaging the mitre joints at the top and bottom. Once they have been lifted at the centre, the staff beads can be sprung out of place.

2 Lift the bottom sash into the room and rest it on a table or a portable workbench. Tie the end of a ball of string to the upper part of each cord (if the cords are not already broken).

THE ANATOMY OF A SASH WINDOW

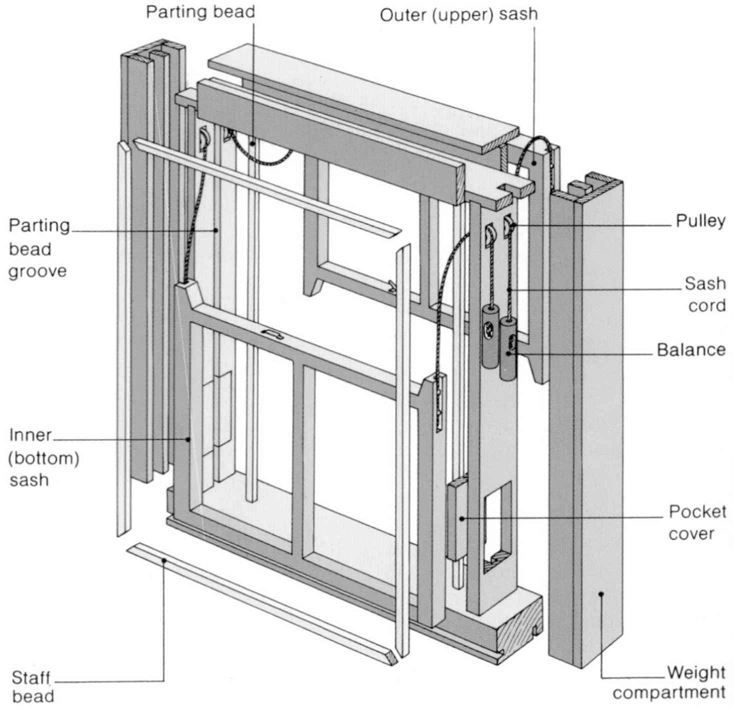

3 Hold each cord in turn, and cut through it with a trimming knife. Release it gently to lower the balance weight to the bottom of the box. This will draw the string over the pulley. The string will be used to thread the new cord.

4 With the bottom sash released, prise the narrow parting beads out of their grooves. They should be merely wedged in place. If they have been nailed (incorrectly) in the past, remove the nail with pincers, taking care not to split the beads.

If they are already split, buy new beads and cut them to length.

5 Lift the top sash into the room. If the cords are unbroken, tie string to the upper part and then cut the cords in the same way as before.

FIXING THE CORDS TO THE WEIGHTS

1 When measuring up for new cords, measure from the top of the window down to the sill, and add two-thirds again. This will allow enough spare cord for fixing at each end. Cut four pieces of cord to this length – one for each weight.

2 With the chisel, carefully prise the pocket covers from the weight channel at each side of the frame, towards the bottom. Usually they are just pushed in place, but sometimes they are screwed.

RE-TENSIONING A SPRING-LIFT SASH

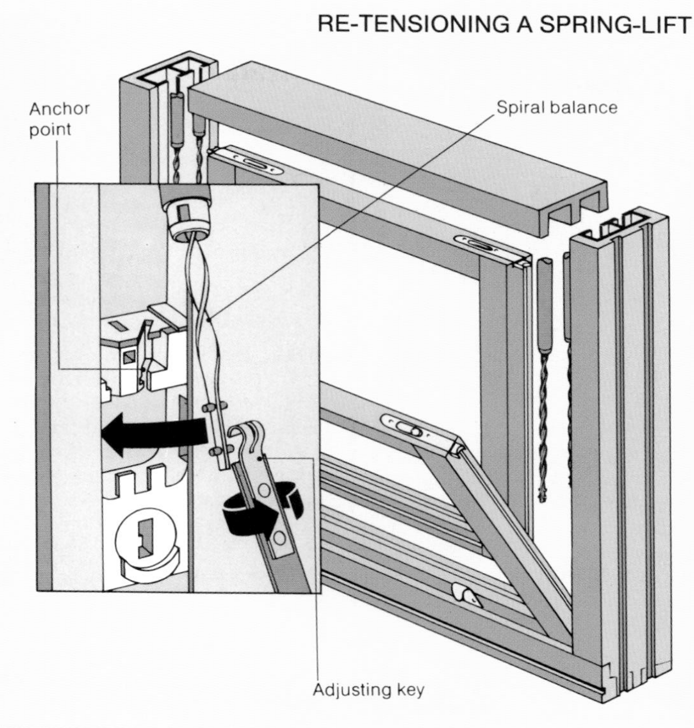

The spiral spring-lift mechanism of modern sash windows eventually loses its tension and needs adjusting. The following instructions are for one well-known make of sash window.

1 Slide the bottom sash up and pull in the finger bolts. Tilt the sash towards you until it is horizontal, then push it up on the right and down on the left and remove it from the frame.

2 Do the same for the upper sash. You can see the spiral balances set into the side of the frame.

3 A key is provided with the window. Hook it over the bottom pin of the balance and pull down to release the upper pin.

4 Turn key to the right two or three times and replace the balance in its anchor point. Test the window: repeat if necessary.

3 Reach into the pockets and lift the weights (two on each side) into the room. Leave the strings in place over the pulleys, ready to pull the new cords through.

4 Where cords have broken, tie a 'mouse' (any small weight) to a length of string and push it into the hole above the pulley, so that it lies over the pulley and drops down into the weight compartment and can be drawn out through the pocket.

5 Use a screwdriver to push the old pieces of cord out of the sash weights.

6 Remove the old cords from the grooves in the side of the window sashes. They are held with large-head nails which can be extracted with pincers.

7 Tie the end of the new cord to the string coming from one of the rear pulleys. Pull it over the pulley, into the weight compartment, and out through the pocket.

8 Untie the string, and thread the end of the cord through the hole in the top of the balance weight and out through the side hole. Tie a double knot in the end of the cord to prevent it from pulling back through the hole. To prevent Terylene cord from fraying, heat the end with a match to melt the fibres into a solid lump. Tuck the knot neatly into the cavity at the top of the weight.

9 Replace the weight into the pocket. Repeat the process for all four weights, then fit the pocket covers in place; they are not nailed or glued.

FIXING THE CORDS TO THE SASHES

1 Rest the top (outer) sash on the inside window ledge.

2 Get a helper to pull down one of the cords so that the weight is at the top of its compartment and just touching the pulley.

HELPFUL TIP

If you have no one to help you nail the cord to the side of the sash, pull the weight up to the top of its compartment and wind the cord around a screwdriver. It will hold the weight in place while you nail the other end of the cord in place.

ALTERNATIVELY, jam a wedge, such as a pencil, between the cord and the top of the pulley aperture.

3 Nail the cord into the groove at the side of the sash, using galvanised clout (large-head) nails. Do not fit the nails close to the top of

Replacing broken sash cords (continued)

the groove; they will prevent the sash sliding all the way up. The top nail must be no higher than the distance from the mid-point of the pulley to the top of the frame.

4 Repeat the same procedure with the second cord.

5 Put the sash in place and check that it operates smoothly before you reassemble the window.

HELPFUL TIP
To make sash windows slide up and down more smoothly and easily, rub a candle on all the sliding surfaces and lightly oil the pulleys. Do it at any time to ease running but make a point of doing it when the window is dismantled for repair.

REASSEMBLING THE WINDOW

1 Refit the parting beads between the runners on each side, tapping them into the grooves so they will not move.

2 Fit the lower (inner) sash in its position in the same way as the upper sash.

3 Refit the staff beads on each side of the frame, checking that the mitred ends match up neatly with the beads at the top and bottom.

Fix them without glue, using two or three oval nails so that they will be easy to remove in the future. Do not drive the nails fully home yet.

4 Check that the lower sash operates easily. If it rattles in its runners move the beads slightly closer to the sash. If not, drive the nails home.

If the staff beads are damaged, replace them with lengths of new beading mitred at each end.

5 Repair any damaged areas around the frame with wood filler. When it is dry, sand down and touch up the repairs with paint.

Renewing parting beads and staff beads

Remove damaged beads as described under *Replacing broken sash cords* (taking out the sashes) on page 214.

RENEWING PARTING BEADS

1 Buy new parting beads the same dimensions as the old ones. If identical-size beads are not available, buy slightly larger ones and plane them down to the correct thickness. Cut the beads to the height of the inner frame.

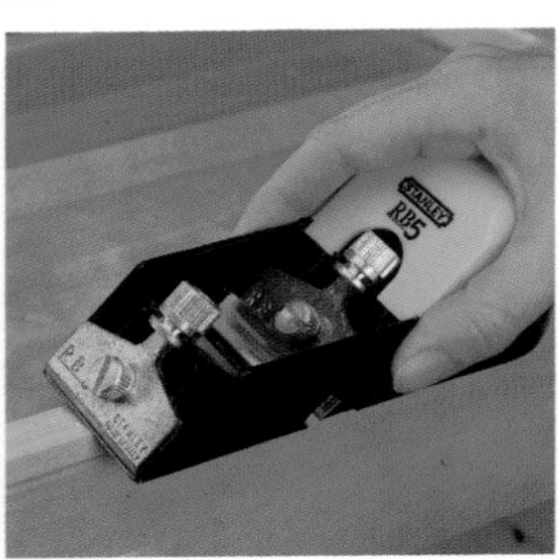

2 With a plane, take a few shavings off the length of the bead on each side, towards the edge that will fit into the groove. This slight taper will ensure that the bead is a tight fit.

3 Tap the beads into the grooves; there is no need to nail them.

RENEWING STAFF BEADS

Buy new staff beads the same dimensions as the old ones. Alternatively, buy new ones as close as possible in shape, and long enough to go all round the frame. You will need slightly more than the measurement of the frame to allow a little wastage for mitres to be cut at each corner.

1 Cut a 45 degree mitre at one end of a length of bead, using a mitre box to ensure an accurate cut.

2 Hold the bead against the frame with the mitre pressed into a corner and mark with a pencil where the other mitre is to be cut.

3 Cut a second mitre, and repeat for each length of beading all round the frame.

4 When all the lengths have been cut, wedge them in place and examine the corner joints for fit.

5 Fix each bead in place with two or three 1in (25mm) oval nails.

FIXING A SASH WINDOW THAT RATTLES

Sash windows will rattle if there is too much space around each sash. The problem occurs more often with the lower (inner) sash and is caused by the staff bead not being close enough to the sash. The remedy is to remove and re-fix the staff beads (see left).

If a top (outer) sash rattles, there is no way of reducing the width of the sliding track. But you can make the sash wider by gluing and pinning strips of hardwood to it all the way round. Rub a candle on all the sliding surfaces.

FITTING A FITCH CATCH

Another possible cure is to change the window lock for a fitch catch – a cam-shaped sash fastener which draws the sashes together when closed and often stops the rattle. The catches are screwed to the upper surfaces of the meeting rails of each sash.

Small plastic wedges can be bought for pushing between the sashes and the beads. They stop rattles, but must be removed whenever the window is raised or lowered.

FITTING A DRAUGHT EXCLUDER

To cure draughts and rattles in one operation, fit a nylon brush pile or sprung strip draught excluder to the inside face of the staff beads – both inner and outer – so that the sashes run along it.

ALTERNATIVELY, fit the draught excluder to the inner face of one of the meeting rails. This is simpler, but is only effective in reducing rattles when the window is fully closed.

Replacing a broken window pane

When buying glass, tell the supplier the size of the panes. He will cut them to fit.

Use 3mm glass in very small panes, such as Georgian-style windows. For windows up to about 12sq ft (1sq m) use 4mm glass. For anything larger, use 6mm glass.

When glass is to be used over a very large area such as a picture window, or where it may be mistaken for an opening as in a patio door, or where it will be fitted within 31in (800mm) of the floor, use safety glass (page 199).

For wooden windows use linseed oil, universal or acrylic putty; for metal windows use metal casement, universal or acrylic putty. You will need about 2¼lb (1kg) of putty for 12ft (3.7m) of frame. Brown putty is available for windows that are to be finished with preservative stain.

Broken glass in doors is replaced in the same way as for wooden windows, unless the door has been glazed with beads which are replaced as for square-edged double-glazing units (page 218).

You will need

Tools Leather gloves; safety spectacles or goggles; glass cutter; hammer; hacking knife or old chisel; pincers; dustpan and brush; paintbrush; putty knife.

Materials Primer paint; putty; glazing sprigs; glass to fit the window.

HELPFUL TIP

Disposing of broken glass can be difficult. The best way is to take it to your local bottle bank. Otherwise, wrap it thickly in newspaper and put it either beside or in your dustbin, clearly labelled 'Broken glass'.

REMOVING THE BROKEN GLASS

1 Lay newspapers on the ground on both sides of the window to catch the fragments of old glass.

2 Put on leather gloves and safety spectacles. Also wear thick leather shoes in case jagged pieces of glass fall to the ground.

3 Using a glass cutter, score the glass all round the window, close to the putty.

4 Working from the outside, tap the glass with a hammer to break it, starting from the top. Try to keep the pieces as large as possible.

5 After breaking out as much of the old glass as possible, remove the remaining putty and glass with a hacking knife or old chisel. Hold a hacking knife in one hand with the point against the putty and tap it on the blunt edge with the hammer.

Look out for old glazing sprigs embedded in the putty – or metal clips in metal frames. Pull them out with pincers.

Leave the rebate in the window as clean as possible, before putting in the new glass.

6 Brush all the dust from the frame and paint a wooden frame with primer, which should be allowed to dry. This is not necessary on a metal window unless it is rusty (page 214).

If the window has to be left overnight, cover it with a sheet of polythene or a piece of plywood (see panel below).

EMERGENCY COVER FOR A BROKEN WINDOW

It is often impossible to repair a broken window immediately, so carry out an emergency repair to keep out the weather while you arrange to get the new glass.

A cracked pane can be temporarily sealed with waterproof glazing tape, which is transparent.

If the panel is smashed, cover the window with heavy-gauge polythene, secured with timber battens nailed around the edge of the frame. The battens will prevent the sheet from tearing.

If security is important, cut a sheet of plywood to cover the window frame and fix it with either nails or screws.

REPLACING DAMAGED PUTTY

As putty hardens it tends to crack and eventually sections fall out. It is best to replace all the putty rather than re-putty the missing sections.

Remove the old putty with a hacking knife or old chisel as shown on this page. If the glazing sprigs have corroded pull them out if possible, and then drive in some new ones as described below. Brush away dust, prime the rebate and then apply and smooth in new putty.

PUTTING IN THE NEW GLASS

1 Mould the putty in your hands to get it soft and pliable. If it sticks to your hands, try wetting them, or take some of the oil out by rolling the putty on newspaper.

2 Hold the pliable putty in the palm of your hand and squeeze it out between the thumb and forefinger to form a layer about ⅛in (3mm) thick in the rebate all the way round the window.

3 Press the glass carefully into the rebate so it is well bedded on the putty. Press it round the edges only, taking care not to push too hard in one place – and never in the middle of the glass. It could break and cause a nasty injury.

4 Fix the glass in place with glazing sprigs inserted into the window about 10in (250mm) apart. Knock them in with the edge of the chisel or with the back of the hacking knife, sliding it along the face of the glass.

The heads of the sprigs should protrude about $\frac{3}{16}$in (5mm) from the frame.

5 Apply more putty to the front of the glass to fill the rebate, and smooth it off with a putty knife to form a neat triangular line of putty which covers the heads of the sprigs and lines up with the putty on the inside edge. Try to achieve neat mitres at the corners.

6 Leave the putty for about two weeks to harden slightly before painting it. When you do paint it, allow the paint to spread onto the glass by ⅛in (3mm) to keep out the rain.

Replacing double-glazed panes

There are three main ways of replacing broken double-glazed panes, depending on whether they are sealed stepped units, square-edge units, or are in aluminium or plastic windows.

Double-glazing units must be bought ready-made to the size of your window from a glass merchant or double-glazing supplier.

SEALED STEPPED UNITS

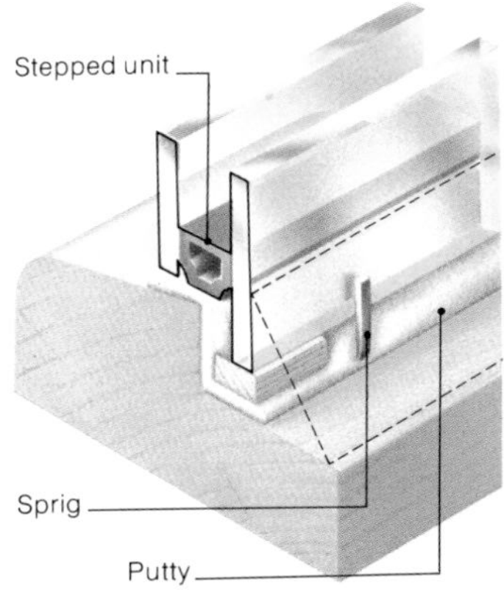

Replacing sealed stepped double glazing is similar to fitting a single sheet of glass, except that spacer blocks are fitted in the rebate of the window to keep the stepped part of the double-glazed unit clear of the frame.

Retain the old spacer blocks so they can be re-used, or buy new ones from your glass merchant. Window companies are unlikely to sell them.

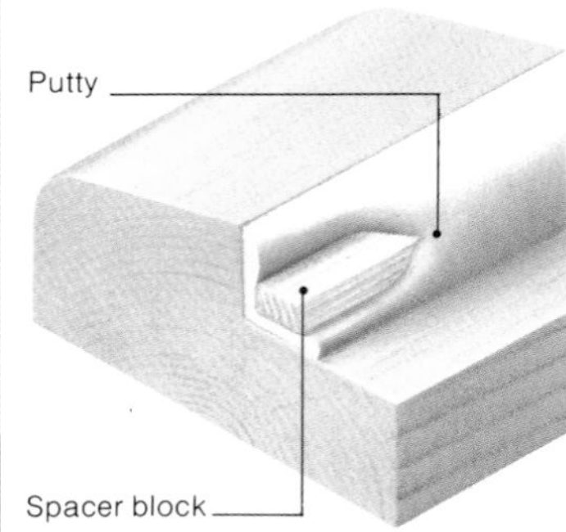

1 Place the spacer blocks in a bed of putty about 12in (300mm) apart along the bottom of the rebate.

2 Stand the double-glazed pane on the blocks and fix it in place with sprigs all round. Apply putty to the outside of the window in the normal way.

SQUARE-EDGED UNITS

Glazing beads are usually screwed into the outside of the window to hold square-edged double glazing in place.

1 Unscrew the glazing beads before removing the broken glass.

2 Put a bed of non-setting putty (available from glass merchants) around the rebate. Press spacer blocks into the putty (two blocks spaced well apart on each of the four sides).

3 Lift the sealed unit into place on the spacers and press it well back into the rebate.

4 Coat the glazing beads with non-setting putty on the inside face and press them tightly in place against the glazing units.

5 Fix the beads in place with brass screws.

ALUMINIUM OR PLASTIC WINDOWS

The glass is often in rubber gaskets, making replacement difficult. Call in a glazier, or ask the manufacturer for details on glass replacement for your particular model of window.

> DAMAGED SEALED UNITS
> If condensation appears in between the panes of a sealed unit, the seal has failed. This seal cannot be repaired. Units more than 10 years old are at risk.

Repairing leaded lights

Doors and windows may have leaded-light panels, consisting of small panes of glass held together with lead strips that are H-shaped in cross section.

DEALING WITH LEAKS

Using polyurethane varnish

1 Mark the leaks with a wax crayon so that repairs can be undertaken in fine weather.

2 Carefully scrape any dirt away from the edges of the lead strips.

3 With a small artist's brush, paint clear, exterior grade polyurethane varnish liberally along the flanges of the strips. Take great care to seal the outside of the glass.

ALTERNATIVELY, inject a bead of the clear sealant used to seal leaks around car windscreens.

4 Press the flanges down, supporting them firmly from the other side. Wipe varnish off the lead and the glass with a cloth moistened with white spirit.

Using putty

If the varnish does not work, the putty in which the glass is set must be replaced. Use soft glazier's metal casement putty. You can colour the putty grey with a little black powder paint.

1 Open up the lead strips slightly on the outside of the window by levering up the edges with a chisel. To do this it may be necessary to cut through the corner joints with a trimming knife or some side-cutting nippers.

2 Scrape out as much of the old putty as possible and clean out the dirt.

3 Press in the new putty.

4 Press the lead strip back in place, with a helper supporting the glass from the inside.

5 If it was necessary to cut the corner joints, glue them back together with two-part acrylic glue (page 190).

6 Wipe the excess putty off the lead and the glass.

Repairing cracked glass

It may not be necessary to fit new glass if the crack is only a minor one. You can try running a few drops of Glass Bond adhesive into the crack.

Replacing broken panes in a leaded-light panel is a difficult job. It would be best if you called in a glazier to do it.

Curing bulges and buckles

Take the complete panel out of the door. It may be held with putty, like an ordinary sheet of glass (page 217), or it may be held with both putty and an outer wood beading. You can remove the beading by unscrewing it or, if it is nailed, by prising it out very gently.

Lay the panel on a flat surface and press the lead strips flat. Be very careful not to press too hard or you are likely to break the glass panes.

If this does not work, it may be necessary to take the panel to a glazier to have it rebuilt. While this is being done, cover the opening in the door or window as explained on page 217.

Home security

6

Ten easy ways to avoid a burglary

Most break-ins are carried out by casual thieves looking for easy pickings. A thief is unlikely to persist if he encounters locked doors and windows. Rapid entry and exit are vital for him, and he will not climb in and out of the house through broken glass.

The tips on this page will all help to keep your home secure.

GETTING HELP FROM THE POLICE

If you want specific advice on how to protect your home, telephone the Crime Prevention Officer at your local police station. He will visit the house if necessary, point out weak spots in your defences and suggest the most appropriate security devices for your circumstances.

If you see anyone loitering in your street or acting suspiciously, do not disturb them. Call the police, then continue to watch unseen until they arrive.

Neighbourhood Watch groups, run in collaboration with the local police, are intended to encourage neighbours to work together by watching for anything suspicious in the area. They also stress the importance of protecting property, and marking valuables. If you are interested in getting involved in a group, contact your local Crime Prevention Officer.

1 Deliveries
Cancel milk and newspapers when you go away. Arrange for a neighbour to push in unexpected items like leaflets and free newspapers. If you have a glazed porch, ask the neighbour to gather up post so it is not visible from outside.

2 Garage
Add extra security to a back door inside a garage where an intruder could work totally hidden. Ensure that the garage itself is fitted with secure locks. An electronically operated, metal up-and-over door will provide the most security.

3 Ladders
Keep ladders locked away. If they must be stored outside, padlock them to a wall with special brackets.

4 Sheds
Make sure sheds are securely padlocked. Tools stored there could be used for a break-in. A garden spade, for example, makes a powerful lever for opening windows.

5 Security lights
Outside lights which switch on automatically when a sensor picks up movement outside the house can be a real deterrent to crime. Site them in areas of the house where a burglar may try to gain access, for example high above French windows at the back or over a garage door. One fitted above a front door will also help you to see who is calling at night. Site the sensor well out of reach of intruders. Bear in mind that most domestic situations do not require high power floodlights, which can be a real nuisance to neighbours.

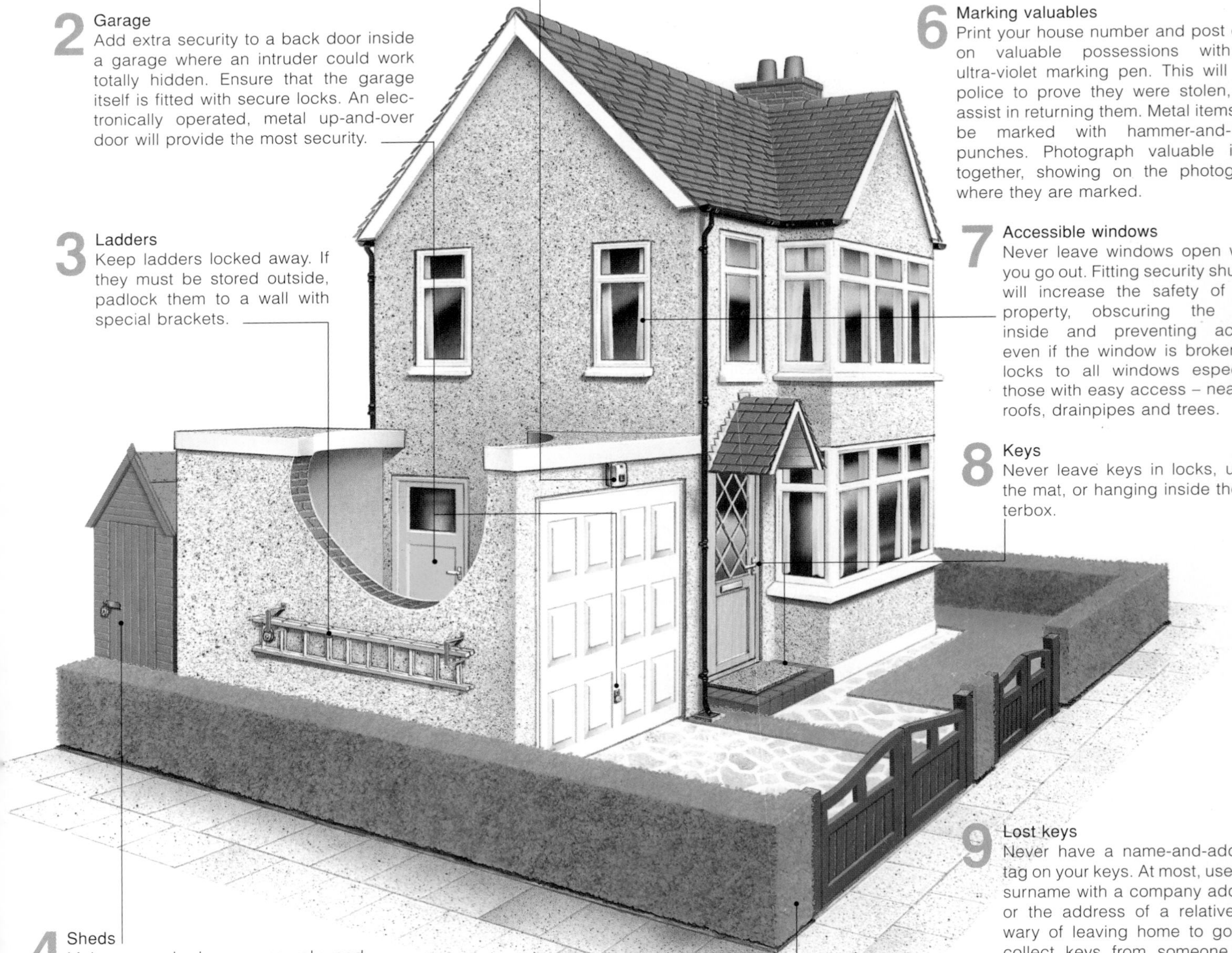

6 Marking valuables
Print your house number and post code on valuable possessions with an ultra-violet marking pen. This will help police to prove they were stolen, and assist in returning them. Metal items can be marked with hammer-and-letter punches. Photograph valuable items together, showing on the photograph where they are marked.

7 Accessible windows
Never leave windows open when you go out. Fitting security shutters will increase the safety of your property, obscuring the view inside and preventing access even if the window is broken. Fit locks to all windows especially those with easy access – near flat roofs, drainpipes and trees.

8 Keys
Never leave keys in locks, under the mat, or hanging inside the letterbox.

9 Lost keys
Never have a name-and-address tag on your keys. At most, use your surname with a company address or the address of a relative. Be wary of leaving home to go and collect keys from someone who says they have found them. It may be a ruse to get you out of the house while the keys are used for entry.

10 Hedges and shrubs
Avoid having high hedges and shrubs that will screen a thief from the road or from neighbours.

CHECKING THE SECURITY OF YOUR HOUSE DOORS

Any lock or bolt, however thief-proof, is only as strong as the door and frame to which it is fitted. A heavy boot applied to a door will often splinter the frame or even rip the lock from the door, allowing easy entry with no sign of damage on the outside. So ensure that exterior doors are tough; if necessary, have a new door frame installed. Or a metal reinforcement, called a London bar, can be fitted to the frame beside a mortise lock. It has to be ordered to size.

All surface-mounted locks and bolts are only as strong as the screws anchoring them in place. Be sure to use the length and gauge recommended for the fitting; never use anything smaller.

SECURITY LOCKS FOR FRONT DOORS

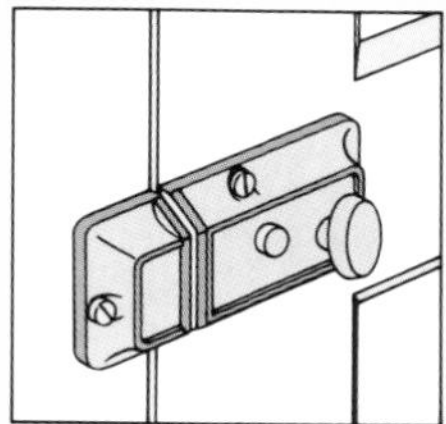

Cylinder nightlatch

Cylinder nightlatch

Many front doors are fitted with a cheap cylinder nightlatch (see also page 201), which is easy for a burglar to open. If you want no more than one lock on the door, it can be replaced with a more secure model. Often this will fit in place of the old one with little alteration to the door or frame. When choosing the lock, look for the British Standards Institution kitemark and the number BS 3621, which ensures that the lock is made to a reasonable standard.

A problem with the standard nightlatch is that if a burglar breaks the glass in the door, he can reach in and turn the latch. This can be prevented by fitting a deadlocking cylinder nightlatch, also called a deadlatch (see also page 201). When you turn the key as you leave the house, the lock becomes immovable.

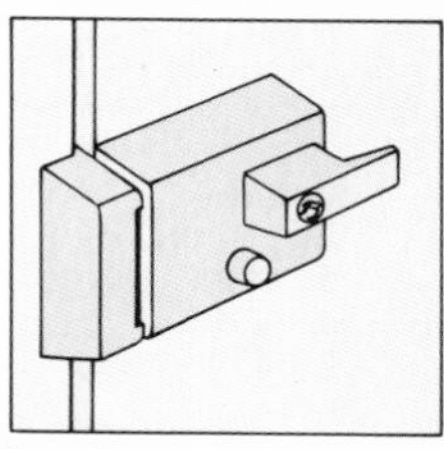

Deadlocking cylinder nightlatch

To keep the door locked when you are indoors as well, choose a model with knob locking, so that it can be locked from the inside as well as the outside. But make sure that a key is kept near the door in case of fire.

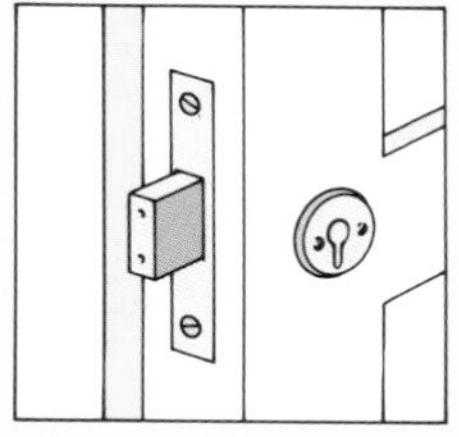

Mortise deadlock

Rather than replacing an existing nightlatch, you can add additional security by fitting a mortise deadlock (see also page 201) lower down the door. The lock, which has a single bolt, is inserted into a hole, called a mortise, cut in the edge of the door. If the door already has a cheap, two-lever mortise deadlock, it can be removed and replaced with a new five-lever model of the same size.

Use only locks manufactured to British Standard BS3621.

Latchbolt

If the nightlatch is to be removed, choose a latchbolt (also called a locking latch) which has both a bolt and a latch. The latch is operated by a handle on the inside while the bolt is key-operated. Do not put both a nightlatch and a latchbolt on one door or you will have to turn two knobs every time the door is opened.

Cutting a mortise in a door weakens it to some extent, so if you have a front door less than 1¾in (44mm) wide ask for a thin-pattern mortise lock.

BOLTS FOR FRENCH WINDOWS

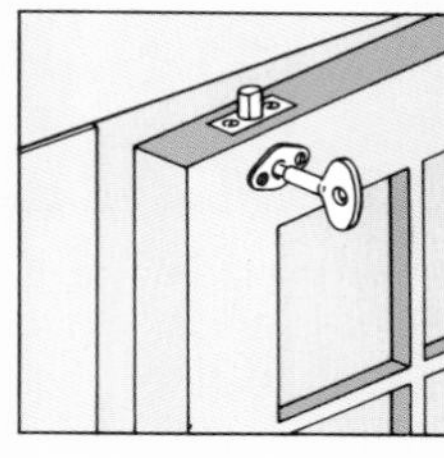

In timber frames, fit rack bolts in the doors, shooting up into the frame at the top and down into the sill or floor at the bottom. Fit the bolts on the overlapping door. Hinge bolts also give added security (see overleaf).

On metal doors, fit surface-mounted self-locking bolts in the same way (see overleaf).

SECURITY LOCKS FOR BACK AND SIDE DOORS

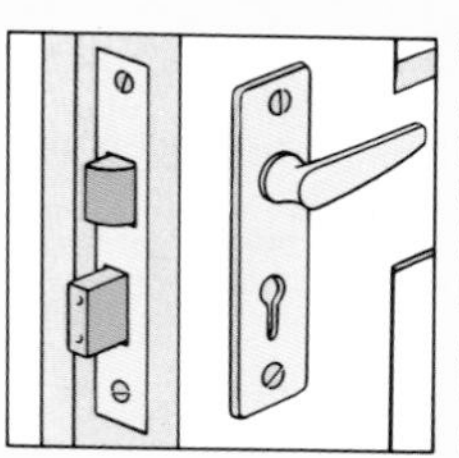

Sashlock

A sashlock – combining latch and bolt and with a handle on both sides of the door – is usually fitted to a back or side door. An existing sashlock often has only two or three levers, giving poor security. It can be removed and replaced with an 'up-grader' unit which has five levers and a dead-locking action. Take the exact dimensions of the old lock when buying a new one, as sizes vary according to make.

Deadlocking is even more important on side and back doors, as they are often glazed and in secluded positions. Burglars often break the glass and turn the latch from the inside.

Use only locks manufactured to British Standard BS3621.

SECURITY LOCKS FOR PATIO DOORS

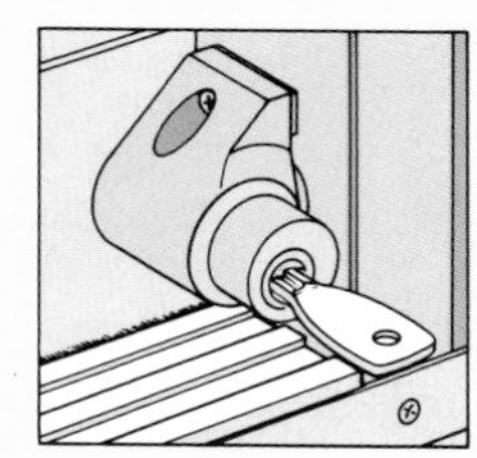

Small security locks are mounted on the inside door. A bolt engages in a hole in the other door.

The locks can be fitted to either wood or metal-framed doors, provided they come with the correct screws – either wood screws or self-tapping screws.

For maximum security, fit locks at both top and bottom of the door.This is particularly advisable for old aluminium-framed patio doors which can sometimes be jemmied out of the sliding track and lifted out of the frame.

A MULTI-LOCKING SYSTEM FOR FLATS

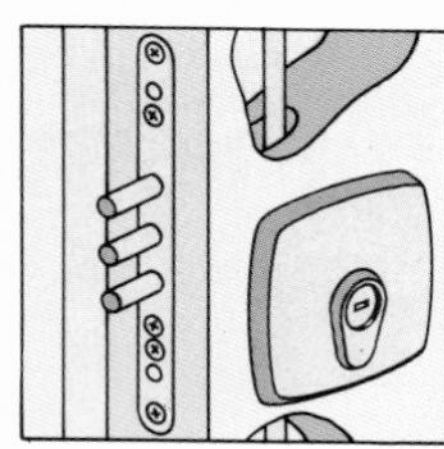

External doors in flats above ground level are often in secluded positions where an intruder is unlikely to be seen. To counter this, a multi-locking system is available. Turning the key engages a lock on the opening face of the door, and also moves bars to engage in the top, bottom and hinge-side frames. Once locked, the door becomes part of the wall and is almost impossible to break down. The system may either be surface-mounted or installed within the door itself.

With a multi-locked door it is important to have a spare set of keys kept with a trusted person. You would have to call a locksmith to drill out the cylinder if you locked your keys inside.

INTERNAL DOORS: TO LOCK OR NOT?

Unless a house is shared, and security between rooms is needed, internal doors are best not locked when the house is empty. Once a thief is inside he will usually not be deterred by locked doors unless they are particularly strong. He will kick or jemmy them open, causing extra damage to the house. The same applies to wardrobe doors and to drawers. Put valuables in a hidden safe (page 226), then leave all the doors and drawers unlocked.

When the house is occupied, ground floor doors could be locked at night. A burglar trying to get from, say, the living room to the rest of the house will probably make so much noise that he will wake the occupants.

For this purpose, fit a sashlock, as you would for a back or side door. Handles on both sides of the door will be necessary for normal use in the daytime.

ADDITIONAL DEVICES FOR DOOR SECURITY

Rack bolts
With every external door it is advisable to fit rack bolts to prevent forcing. The bolts are mortised into the edge of the door (see facing page). Fit two to each door – one in the closing edge and one at the top or bottom.

Rack bolts are an alternative method of locking a front door at night when the house is occupied.

If the glass is broken it is hard to see where the bolts are fitted. Even if the holes are found, a fluted key is needed to undo them.

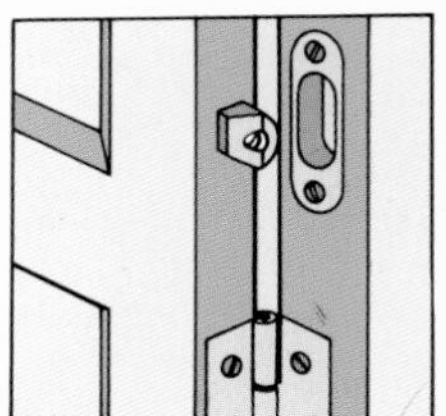

Hinge bolts
It is possible to unhinge a door by using a jemmy on the hinge side. To prevent this, fit hinge bolts – two per door – about 3in (75mm) away from the hinges (see facing page).

Self-locking bolts
Where a door is too thin to house a rack bolt without being weakened, fit a surface mounted, self-locking bolt. It is merely screwed in place; when fitted, all screws are concealed. Pushing the bolt end slides it into the locked position, where it deadlocks and cannot be moved without the use of a key.

Door chains
To prevent an intruder forcing his way in after ringing the doorbell, fit a chain to the front door. It allows the door to be opened just far enough to speak to a caller, but the door has to be shut again before the chain can be released to allow entry.

The strength of the device depends entirely on how well the chain is anchored to door and frame, so the longest and heaviest-gauge screws possible should be used.

Various patterns are available, including a simple chain, a chain combined with a sliding bolt, a chain which can be unlocked from the outside with a key, and a chain with an alarm built in which is triggered by an attempt to enter.

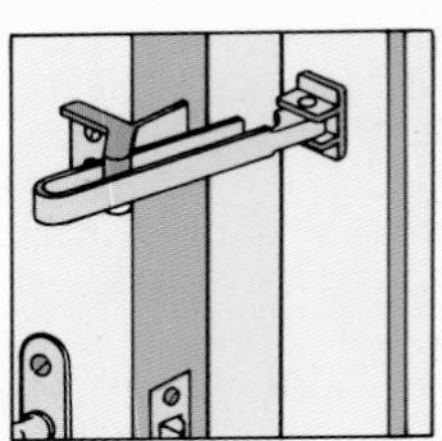

Door limiter
A more substantial version of the door chain is called a door limiter, with a sliding bar replacing the chain. When in place the bar engages with the retaining part of the unit, restricting the door's opening. The door has to be closed and the bar swung away before it can be fully opened.

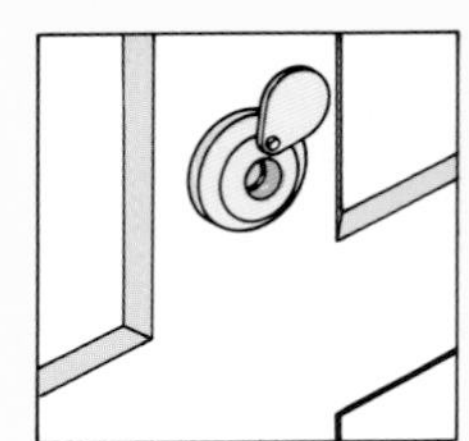

Peephole viewer
A simple lens system offers a wide-angle view of the area immediately outside the door. The occupant can look out, but a person outside cannot see in. A peephole viewer is best used in conjunction with a porch light.

Fitting a new mechanism to a lock

If the keys are lost, or if you want to be sure of security when taking over a new house, it is cheaper to replace the working part of a lock than to buy a completely new unit.

CYLINDER NIGHTLATCH

Buy a new cylinder and keys, as long as it is a straightforward lock. You cannot replace the cylinder on the type which has a locking interior handle.

You will need
Tools Screwdriver; pliers; self-grip wrench or vice. Perhaps a mini hacksaw.
Materials New cylinder and keys.

1 Unscrew the lock cover from inside the door to expose the connecting screws which hold the cylinder in place.

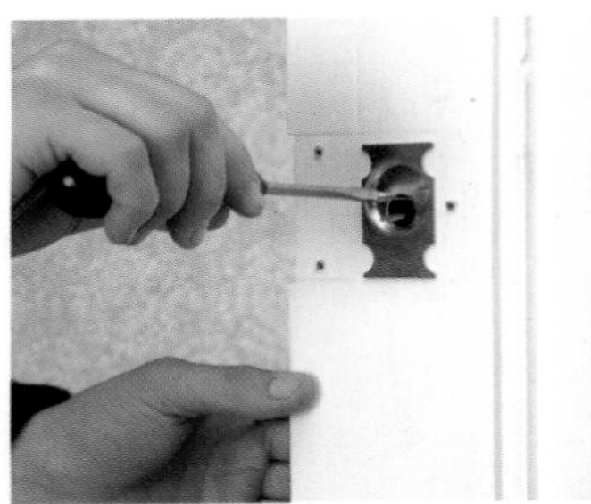

2 Unscrew the connecting screws until the cylinder can be removed. The connecting bar will come too.

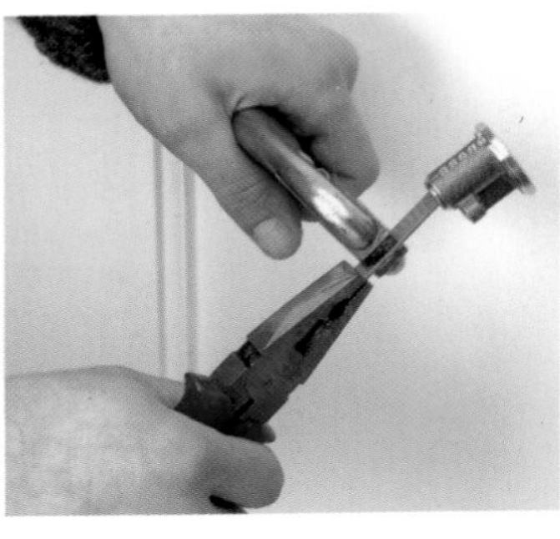

3 Hold the new connecting bar in a self-grip wrench or vice and use pliers to snap it to the same length as the old one, so it is correctly housed in the interior handle when the cylinder is in place.

The bar is divided into breakable segments along its length.

4 Make sure that the connecting screws are also the right length. They can be cut to length with a mini hacksaw.

5 Insert the new cylinder into the hole. Tighten the screws and replace the cover, making sure that the handle of the lock connects with the bar.

MORTISE LOCK

Buy a complete set of levers and keys for the right model of lock. If possible take the lock with you to the locksmith when you buy the new set.

You will need
Tools Screwdriver; hammer; small piece of wood, such as a pencil or dowel.
Materials Lever set and keys.

1 Remove the lock (see facing page).

2 Carefully unscrew the cover plate and lift out the existing set of levers.

3 Put the new ones in place. It is vital to keep the levers in the order in which they are supplied.

4 Replace the cover plate, and fix the lock back into the door.

Replacing a mortise lock

When buying a new mortise lock make sure that it is the same dimensions as the old one and that the holes for the key and the handle spindle are in the same place. If possible, take the old lock with you to the locksmith when buying the replacement.

The following technique for replacing a lock applies to any mortise lock, whether it has a bolt and latch or just a bolt.

You will need
Tools Screwdriver; hammer; small piece of thin wood (or a pencil would do).
Materials New five-lever mortise lock.

1 Unscrew the handles or knobs.

2 Unscrew the lock face on the edge of the door.

3 Tap the spindle with a hammer towards the door edge to loosen the lock. Remove the spindle.

4 Lever out the lock at the top and bottom with the screwdriver, using a small piece of wood under the screwdriver to protect the edge of the door. You can use a pencil instead of a piece of wood.

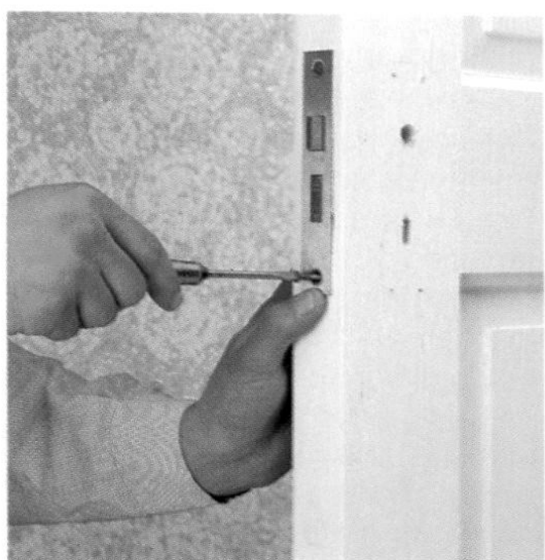

5 Insert the new lock in the slot, making sure it is the right way round. Screw it in place.

6 Replace the spindle and the handles or knobs.

Adding security bolts to doors

FITTING A RACK BOLT

You will need
Tools Pencil; drill and bits (sizes according to the manufacturer's instructions); pliers; ¾in (19mm) chisel; screwdriver; try square.
Materials Rack bolt.

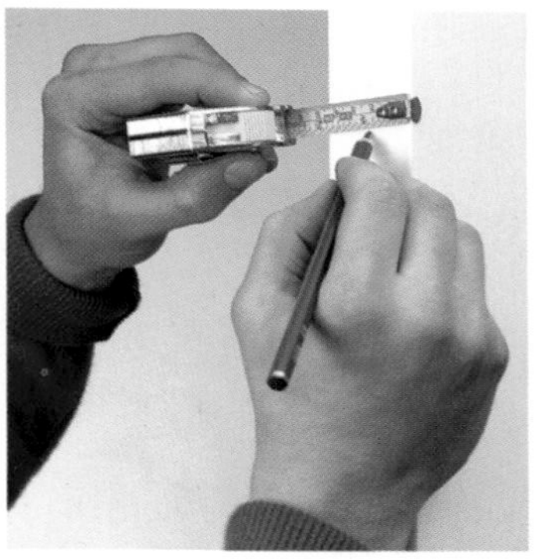

1 Mark a central point on the edge of the door where you want to fit the bolt.

2 Use a try square and pencil to continue the mark onto the inner face of the door.

3 Drill a hole into the edge of the door to the width and depth of the body of the bolt.

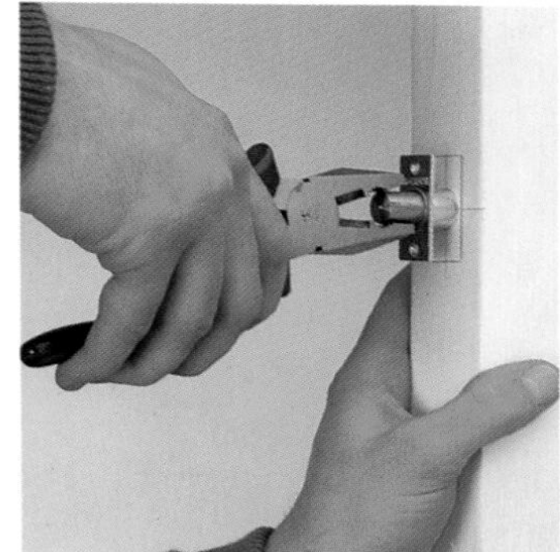

4 Wind out the bolt and push it into the hole. Mark round the faceplate, withdraw the bolt with pliers and cut a shallow recess for the faceplate with the chisel.

5 Hold the bolt flush with the face of the door, and mark the spot for the key. Drill a hole (see the manufacturer's instructions for the size) through the inside face of the door only.

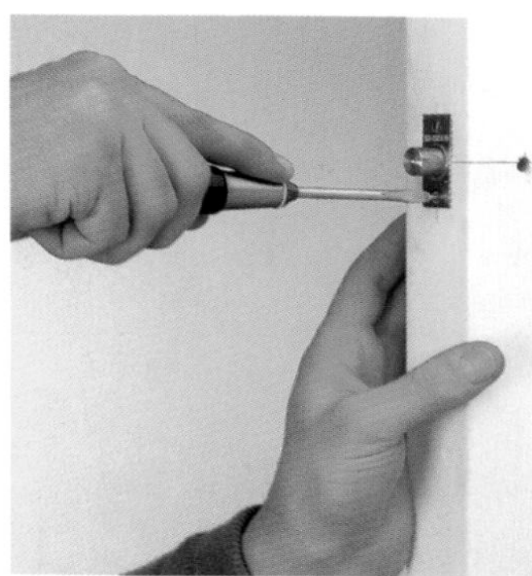

6 Push the bolt back into the door and screw the faceplate to the edge of the door. Check with the key that the bolt operates correctly. If necessary, enlarge the keyhole.

7 Screw the keyhole plate to the inside of the door.

8 Close the door and wind out the bolt to mark the door jamb. One way to make the mark is to push a piece of carbon paper between the bolt and the jamb.

9 Open the door and drill an engagement hole at the mark. Check that the bolt will go smoothly into this hole.

10 Hold the cover plate over the hole, draw around it, cut out a shallow recess, and screw the cover plate in place. Check the operation of the bolt, and make any necessary adjustments.

FITTING HINGE BOLTS

You will need
Tools Pencil; drill and bits (sizes according to the manufacturer's instructions); adhesive tape; mallet; chisel; screwdriver.
Materials A pair of hinge bolts.

1 Open the door fully and mark the centre of the door edge quite close to the two hinges at the top and the bottom.

2 Drill a hole into the door edge to the width and depth given on the maker's instructions.

Wrap a piece of coloured adhesive tape around the bit as a guide to the depth.

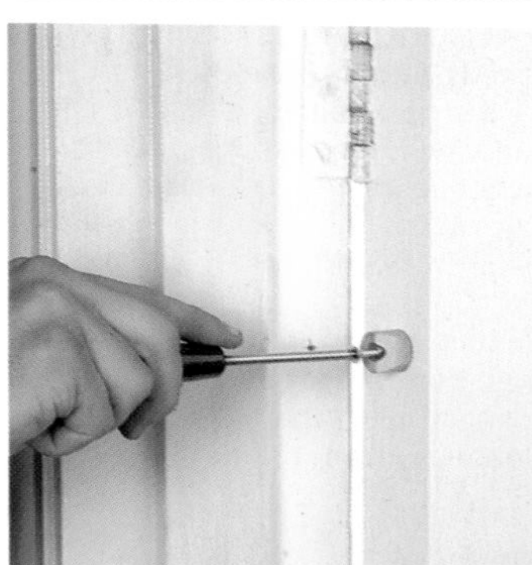

3 Fit the bolt into the hole. Partially close the door so that the bolt marks the frame.

4 At this spot, drill a hole into the frame to the depth of the protruding bolt, plus a little more for clearance. Close the door to test that it shuts easily. If necessary, enlarge the width or depth of the hole.

5 Open the door and hold a cover plate over the hole. Mark the edge of the plate with a pencil, and chisel out a recess so the plate lies flush with the frame.

Fix the plate in place with the screws provided.

Protecting outbuildings

SHEDS AND WORKSHOPS

The hasp and staple fitted to many prefabricated buildings have little security value, and need to be replaced with a strong locking bar.

Where possible, choose a locking bar which leaves no screw or bolt heads visible when it is closed. The hinged section should have a totally enclosed pin.

Buy a five-lever padlock to give a large number of key combinations. Raised shoulders on the padlock will protect it from attack by hacksaw, bolt cutters or crowbar.

Ideally the locking bar and staple should bolt right through the frame of the building.

If screws are used, buy clutch-head ones which can be tightened with a screwdriver but cannot be undone.

GARAGES

Securing hinged doors

Garages with hinged doors can be padlocked in the same way as sheds and workshops.

If a garage with hinged doors is attached to the house and there is a door leading inside, extra security is needed; once in the garage a thief can work unseen. A beam can be dropped into brackets fixed to the garage door and frame, ensuring that the doors can only be opened from the inside while you are away from the house.

You can make your own brackets by bending one arm of a large angle bracket into a U-shape.

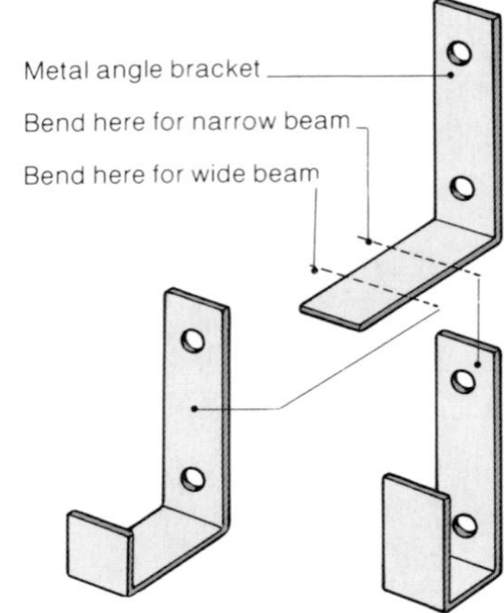

Securing up-and-over doors

Up-and-over doors are normally fitted with a cylinder lock which forms part of the door handle. If the keys are lost, a replacement handle unit should be available from the door manufacturers.

If a garage with up-and-over doors is attached to the house and there is access from the garage into the house, put a locking bar on the inside of the door about 4in (100mm) down from the top, so that the door can be locked to the vertical frame member with a padlock. This ensures that the door could only be opened from inside. Fit the hasp to the frame and the staple to the door.

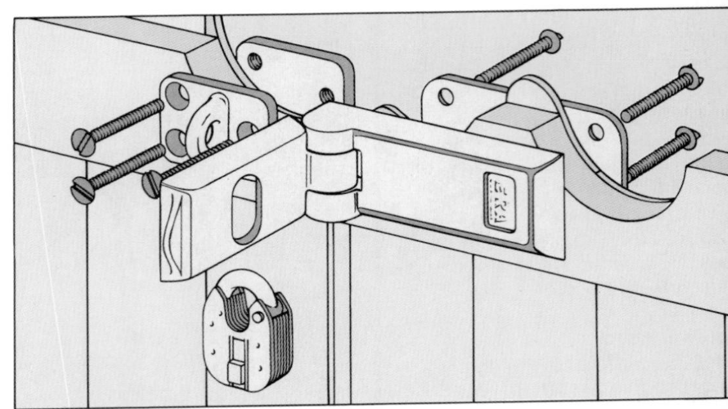

Locking bar and padlock To provide maximum security for a shed or garage, a heavy-duty locking bar, bolted through the frame, is locked with a high-shouldered, five-lever padlock.

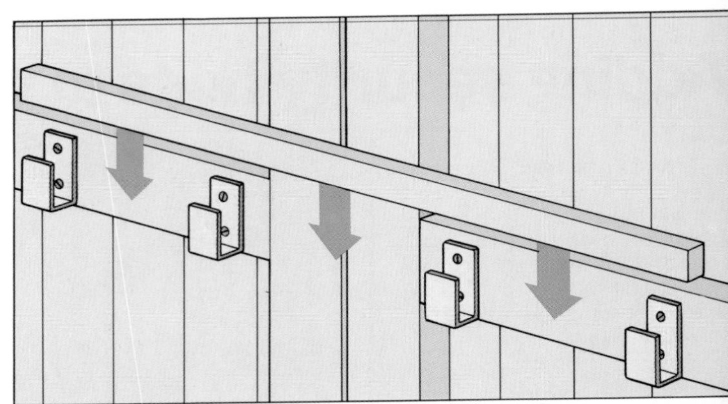

Garage-door beam A strong beam, made of either wood or metal, can be dropped into brackets fixed with stout screws to the inside of the garage door and the frame around the door.

Fitting a lock to a casement window

Surface-mounted locks are easy to fit to casement windows, provided that the fixed frame and the opening frame are at right angles to each other. If the fixed frame is tapered, wood may have to be chiselled away so that the lock fits against the opening frame. Some locks are supplied with a wedge to get over this problem.

For large windows, or for extra security, fit two locks on each frame, at top and bottom. They will withstand a jemmy attack better than a single lock.

The technique shown here is for a particular model of surface-mounted lock, but other models are installed in a similar way.

You will need

Tools Pencil; drill and twist bits; bradawl; screwdriver. Perhaps a small chisel.

Materials One or two window locks, depending on size of window.

1 Close the window firmly, and hold the body and lockplate on the opening edge. The lockplate goes against the opening frame and the body against the fixed frame.

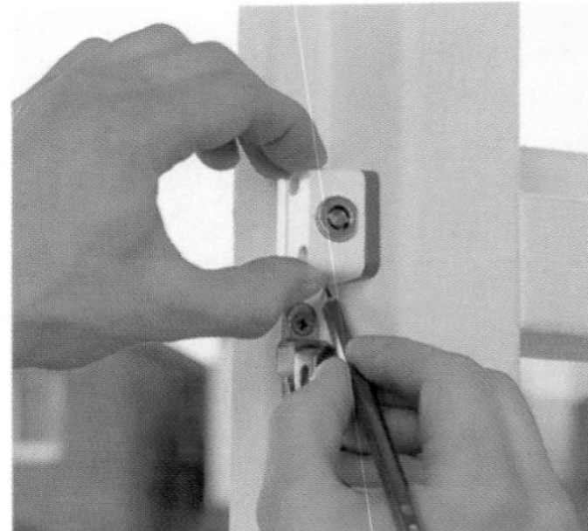

2 Mark the shape of the lockplate with a pencil, and the screw positions for the body with a bradawl.

3 Remove the lockplate from the body. Put it in position, mark the screw positions, drill pilot holes and screw it in place.

4 Drill the pilot holes for the body into the edge of the fixed frame.

5 Lock the body to the plate and screw it to the frame.

SECURITY FOR PLASTIC WINDOWS

An increasing number of plastic windows are being used in houses, and they can pose a security problem. Most manufacturers of security devices do not recommend them for plastic windows because a thin plastic section offers no grip for screws.

If a plastic window frame is known to have a timber inner frame, security devices suitable for wooden frames could be used.

If there are steel inserts within the plastic section, self-tapping screws could be used, as for metal frames.

But locks cannot be fitted to hollow sections of windows filled with rigid foam.

The ideal solution is to consult the installer of your windows at the time they are being made.

LAMINATED GLASS TO THWART BURGLARS

Particular windows in a house may be at risk from burglars. They may be ground-floor windows hidden from the neighbours, or they may be upstairs windows which are accessible from an extension roof, a tree or a drainpipe.

Fitting laminated glass would greatly add to the security. It consists of a sandwich of glass with a clear plastic film between. Although the glass may be cracked by a blow, the plastic will resist efforts to break through.

Do not use wired glass; it has little security value.

CHOOSING SECURITY LOCKS FOR YOUR WINDOWS

Windows are main points of entry for burglars. The most common method of breaking in is to smash the glass and release the catch.

Most window locks will either lock the frames together, make the handle immovable, or lock the stay arm. Locking the frames together gives the best result.

Before buying window locks, make sure they are suitable for your windows. A lock for timber frames will come with woodscrews. Locks for metal windows will have self-tapping screws. Make sure the frames are thick enough to accommodate the device.

When choosing security devices, consider how often the window is used. Some locks, such as a dual-screw, can be a nuisance if the window is in constant use. On the other hand, windows that are rarely opened can be screwed together.

SAFETY WARNING
When locks are used on windows, make sure there are keys in each room so a window can be opened in an emergency.

Do not permanently screw down windows that may be needed as an escape route in time of fire.

WOODEN SLIDING SASH WINDOWS

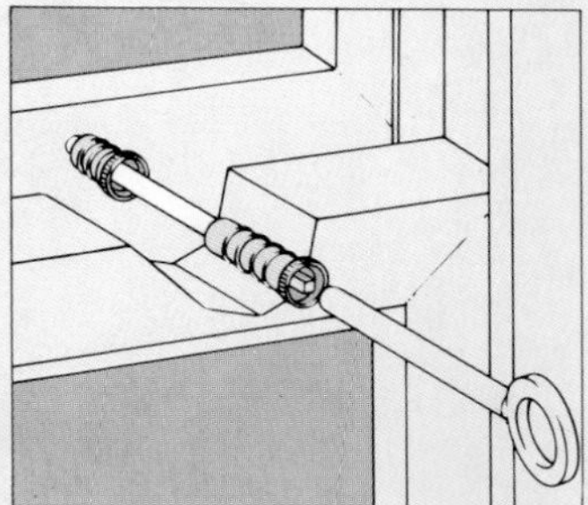

DUAL SCREW A bolt goes through a barrel in the inner frame into the outer frame. Fit two dual screws if the window is large.

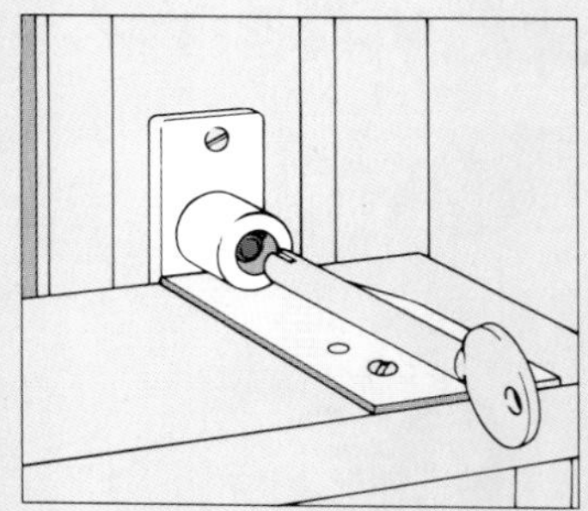

SURFACE-FITTED BOLT A bolt on the upper sash allows the window to be opened a little for ventilation. Fit two to large windows.

METAL WINDOWS

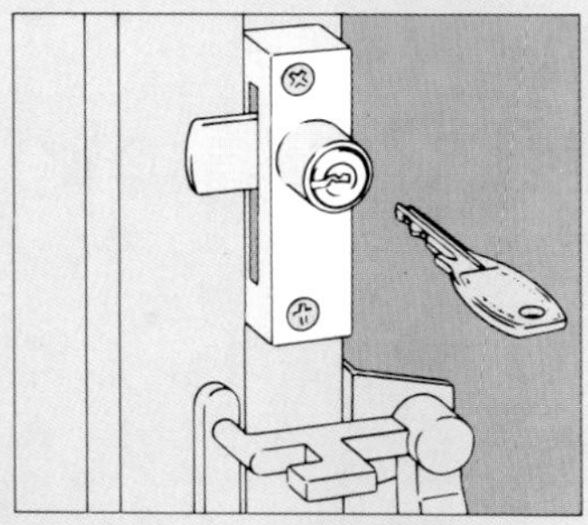

SURFACE-FITTED LOCK Fitted with self-tapping screws near the centre of the opening edge of the window. The bolt locks against the fixed frame.

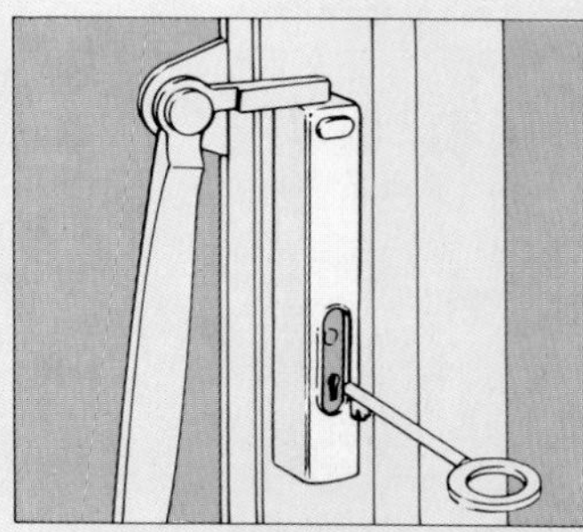

COCKSPUR BOLT When the cockspur handle is closed, the case of the bolt is moved up on the fixed frame and locked, preventing the cockspur from opening.

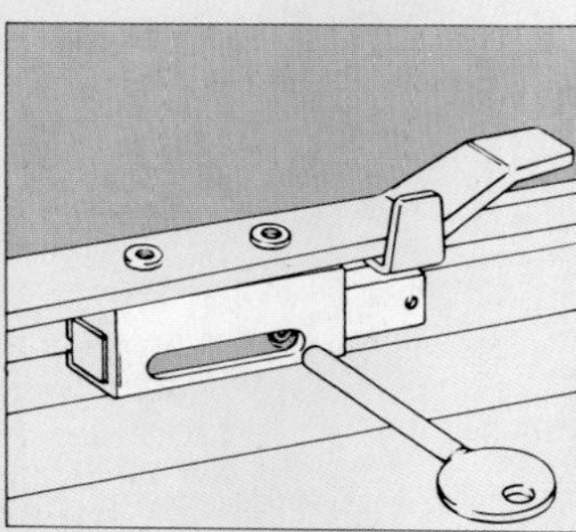

STAY BOLT Fits underneath the stay arm. A bolt slides under the stay retainer, preventing the arm from being lifted.

LOUVRE LOCK Metal inserts for Beta Naco windows lock the glass in the bladeholders. A blocking bolt can lock the handle.

WOODEN CASEMENT WINDOWS

For locking frames together

MORTISE BOLT The lock is mortised into the opening frame, and the bolt slides into a hole in the fixed frame. May be too large for narrow frames. More difficult to install than a surface-fitting lock, but gives excellent security. Fit close to the centre of the opening edge. On large windows, fit a mortise bolt at each end of the opening edge.

SURFACE-FITTED LOCK The catch is screwed to the fixed frame and the lock plate to the frame that opens. It is locked by a push-button action, and unlocked with a key. Suitable for narrow frames that may not accommodate a mortise bolt. Fit it close to the centre of the opening edge. On large windows, fit one at each end of the opening edge.

For locking the handle

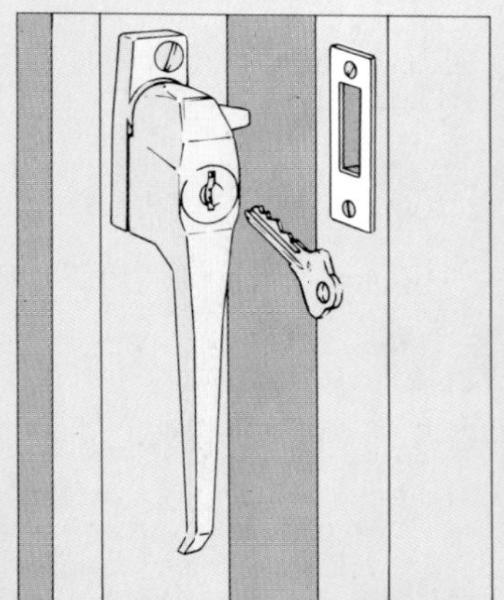

LOCKING HANDLE A new handle with a lock replaces the existing cockspur handle. Once locked, it cannot be opened without the key. Make sure you buy the correct right-hand or left-hand type for your window.

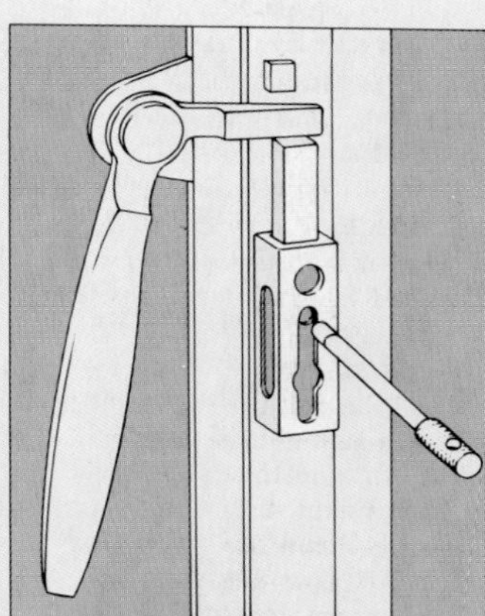

BLOCKING BOLT The lock is fitted to the fixed frame and prevents the cockspur handle from being moved. The bolt is retracted with the key. Only suitable when the cockspur is on the surface of the frame.

For locking the window stay

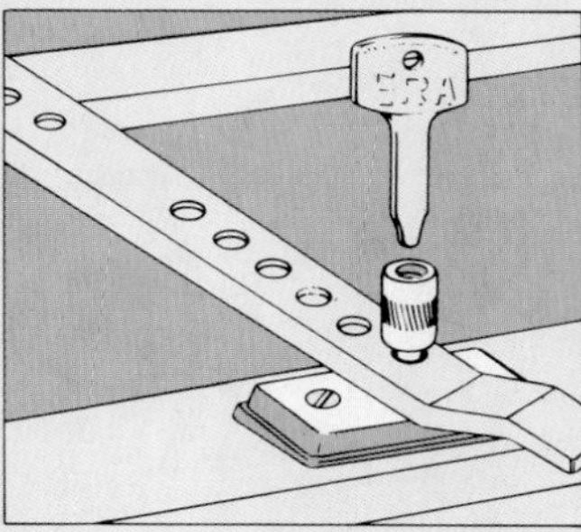

THREADED STAY PEG The lock replaces the stay peg nearer the hinge. It can secure the window in the closed position or in an open position. The device is only suitable for window stays that are pierced by holes. Locked and unlocked with a key.

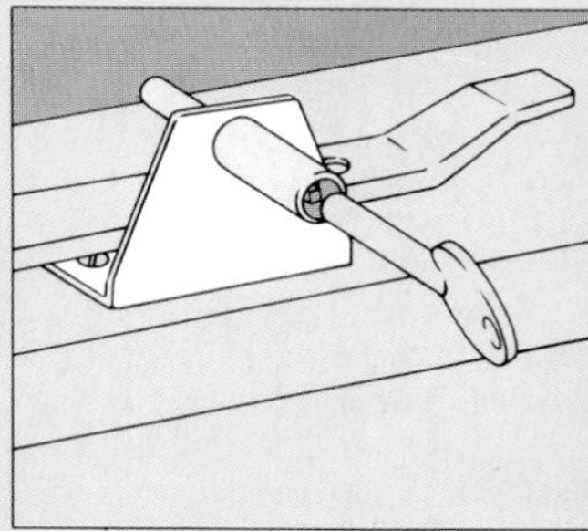

STAYBOLT A plate is screwed to the fixed frame, and a bolt passes through it to hold the stay in the closed position. The bolt can be used for stays without (or with) holes. It is fitted in place of the original stay peg which is first removed and discarded.

Fitting a lock to a metal frame

Locks are fitted to a steel or aluminium window frame with self-tapping screws, which should be supplied with the lock.

To drill a pilot hole in the frame, use a high-speed-steel (HSS) twist bit. Most locks come with instructions giving the drill size.

If in doubt, make the hole the same diameter as the 'core' of the screw, not the shank. Use a bit that is too small rather than too big.

You will need
Tools Bradawl or ball-point refill; electric drill; HSS twist bits; screwdriver.
Materials Window lock with self-tapping screws.

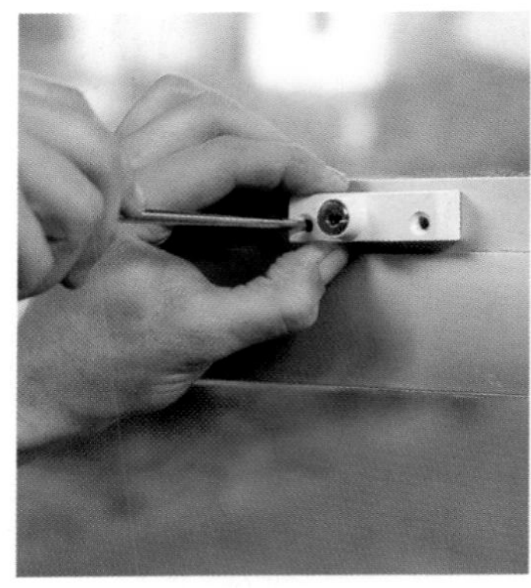

1 Hold the lock in position and mark the screw hole with a bradawl or ball-point refill.

2 Drill a pilot hole just through the metal. Provided the bit is sharp, it should not skid on the metal.

3 Screw the lock to the frame. If the screw hole is too tight, re-drill the hole one size bigger.

Fitting a dual screw to a sash window

A dual screw is a highly secure device for locking a sash window, but it is not convenient if the window is frequently opened. In that case, use a surface-fitted bolt (see chart, page 225).

For large windows, fit two locks, one at each end of the centre meeting rail.

Dual screws vary in design. Some have barrels for both inner and outer frames; others have a lock-plate for the outer frame.

You will need
Tools Drill and flat bit the width of the lock barrel; hammer and piece of wood, or a large screwdriver (depending on the model). Perhaps a small screwdriver, small twist bit and chisel (depending on model).
Materials One or two dual screws.

1 Ensure that the window is fully closed.

2 Use the flat bit to drill through the inner meeting rail and into the outer meeting rail to a depth of ⅝in (16mm). Wind some coloured insulating tape around the bit as a guide to the depth of the hole.

3 Tap the longer barrel into the inner meeting rail, using a hammer and a piece of wood to protect it from being damaged.
ALTERNATIVELY, if the barrel has a slot, use a large screwdriver to screw it into the rail until it is flush with the wood.

4 Reverse the sashes. Tap the shorter barrel into the outer meeting rail.
ALTERNATIVELY, fit the locking plate to the outer meeting rail. If the sashes clash as they pass, recess the plate with a chisel.

5 Close the window and screw the bolt into the barrel with the key.

Installing a small home safe

Locked drawers and cupboards offer no protection against a thief who has entered an empty house. The best protection you can provide for small objects inside your house is to install a domestic model safe.

Some models are designed to be installed in the floor, others in a wall, others inside a cupboard. Some are key operated, others have combination locks.

With any type of safe, it is vital that the fitting instructions are followed exactly so that it cannot be jemmied out. Each model comes with its own instructions, and can be obtained from a locksmith or from a shop specialising in home security.

The alternative to a safe is to deposit valuables with your bank when you are away from home. Hide small valuables in special 'safes' identical to normal cans of food, which can be 'lost' in a larder.

THREE MODELS OF HOME SAFE

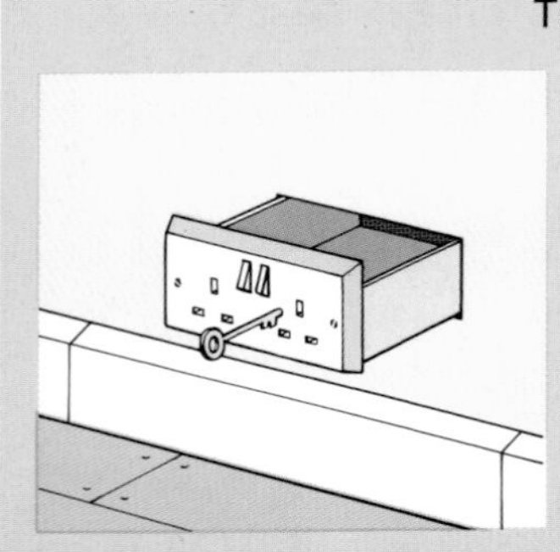

POWER-POINT SAFE The steel box has a front designed like a power socket. The drawer is opened with a key inserted into one of the pin holes. There is no electrical wiring.
The safe is big enough to hold cash and jewellery.

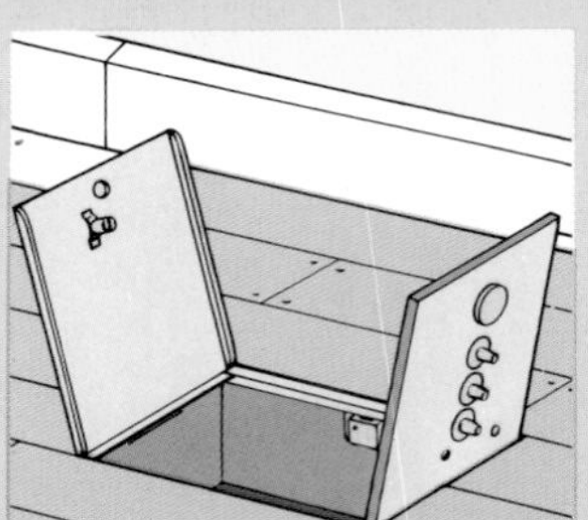

UNDER-FLOOR SAFE Designed to fit between the joists of a suspended wooden floor, and then be covered with carpet. It is screwed to the joists from inside. The combination lock is operated by three dials, each with the letters of the alphabet.

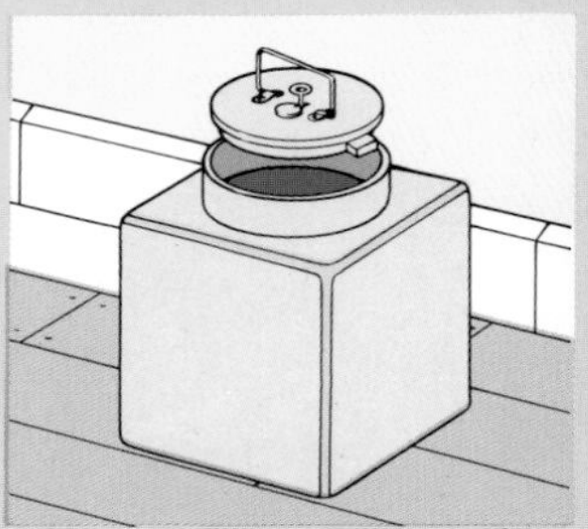

ABOVE-FLOOR SAFE A strong steel safe can be fixed on top of a suspended timber floor inside a cupboard, loft or other inconspicuous place. It is bolted to the joists from the inside on a steel frame. It can be fitted with a seven-lever or combination lock.

CHOOSING A BURGLAR ALARM TO PROTECT YOUR HOME

Most thieves are likely to be deterred by locks on windows and doors, but you may decide to install an alarm system as a defence against a burglar who tries to force his way in. A noisy alarm may deter him from entering the house, or greatly reduce the time he stays there.

Before buying a system, check that the alarm is loud enough. Anything below 95 decibels has little effect and cannot be heard over any distance. Most alarms sound for about 20 minutes and then reset to avoid nuisance to neighbours. Notify your local police and your neighbours that an alarm has been fitted, and give a trusted neighbour a spare key.

A valuable addition to a system is a panic button which can be used to trigger off the alarm at any time. Some burglar-alarm systems are designed for DIY installation; others need to be professionally fitted.

AVOIDING FALSE ALARMS

Ninety-eight per cent of all burglar alarms that go off are false. False alarms can be a real nuisance, both to neighbours and the police. You could be blacklisted if you have too many. Get advice from your local Crime Prevention Officer on leaving keys with neighbours, or at the police station, and about notifying the police if you are to be away for long periods.

If a security firm installs your alarm, get it checked regularly. If you install your own system, make sure that it is not triggered by loose window frames or normal door movement.

WHOLE-HOUSE SYSTEMS THAT WARN OF A BREAK-IN

The most common alarm systems are designed to set off a bell or siren if a burglar tries to break in. Before buying one, ensure that the alarm has a 'closed' electrical circuit. This means that when the system is turned on the circuit is completed. If there is any interference – such as the wires being cut – the alarm will go off. Each system has three main components – the switches, the control and the alarm.

The external alarm
The alarm will comprise a loud bell or siren and should be loud enough to frighten off potential intruders and alert neighbours. Some external sirens also incorporate a bright, flashing strobe light. Some also feature flashing LEDs to indicate that the system is active and to add to the visual deterrent. The external alarm box should be tamper-proof and contain its own battery, so that it will still sound if the cable to it is cut.

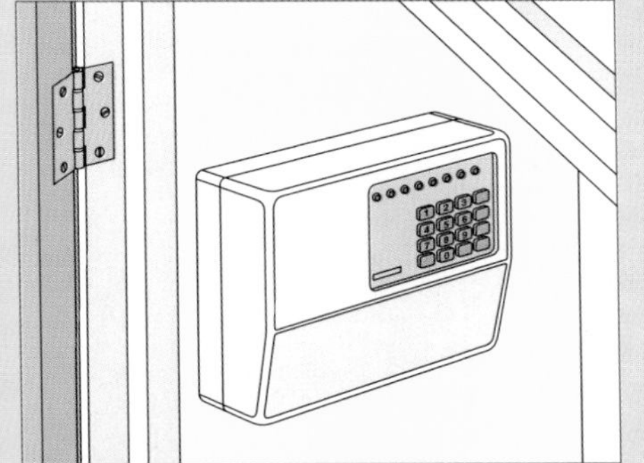

The control unit
The 'brain' of the system is the control unit which receives signals from the switches and sends an electric current to activate the alarm. The system is turned on or off with a key or a push-button panel to which a code number is first keyed in.

Connected with the control unit will be some form of power supply, either mains or batteries. In some models mains power will feed the system under normal conditions, but if the power is cut off for any reason, a battery will take over. The battery is later recharged automatically from the mains.

Panic button
A manually operated switch can be fitted as a panic button – at the bedside or by the front door. It is usually wired so that it will trigger the alarm whether or not the rest of the system is switched on. Panic buttons can be very sensitive; the slightest pressure will set off the alarm.

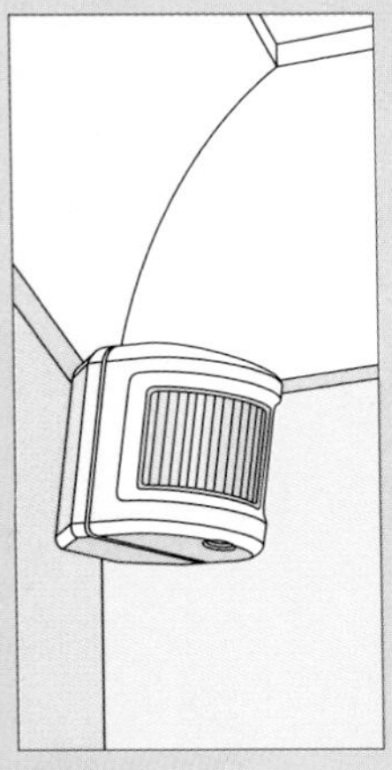

Passive infra-red (PIR) motion detectors
These are small units, fitted at ceiling height, which sense movement through changes of temperature within their field of detection.

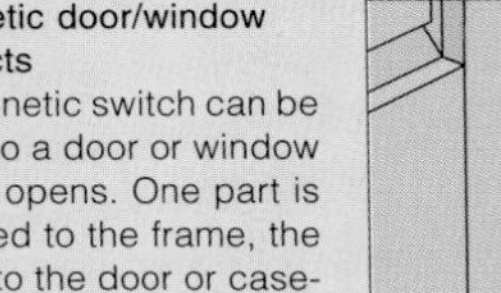

Magnetic door/window contacts
A magnetic switch can be fitted to a door or window which opens. One part is secured to the frame, the other to the door or casement. If the magnet is moved (by opening the door or window) the circuit is broken and the alarm is triggered

SELF-CONTAINED INTRUDER ALARMS

Door alarm
The unit can be fitted to an external door, and will set off an alarm if the door is opened. It is battery operated, so no wiring is needed. The alarm is turned off with a push-button code that you decide yourself, or with a key. A delay switch allows several seconds for you to enter or leave the house without triggering the alarm.

Shed alarm
This type of self-contained battery-powered alarm can be fixed quite quickly in a shed, garage, caravan or greenhouse. It will pick up movement within its field of detection and activate its own alarm.

WIRELESS ALARM SYSTEMS

The main advantage of a wireless system is that you do not need to run cables around the house to connect the switches and sensors to the control unit. Passive infra-red sensors and magnetic door contacts are independently battery powered and transmit a radio signal to the control unit when they sense movement; this in turn triggers the alarm. These 'wirefree' systems can be set using a remote key fob switch which doubles as a mobile panic alarm. Because the kits remove the need to run cables, they are much quicker to install. Some systems offer a repeater unit which increases the transmission range so that outbuildings may also be protected. One disadvantage of this system is that you must remember to replace the batteries in the sensors on a regular basis.

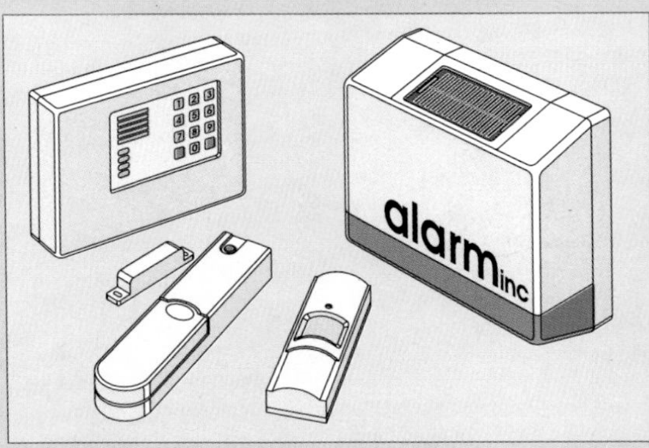

CLOSED-CIRCUIT TELEVISION (CCTV) SYSTEMS

CCTV systems have come down in price in recent years, bringing them within the reach of most ordinary householders. Cameras are now very compact and systems that you can install yourself are widely available through DIY stores. You can choose whether to have the camera connected to its own dedicated monitor, or to utilise your own TV and video set-up. Some cameras incorporate passive infra-red detectors (PIRs) enabling the video to start recording when movement is detected. When used to see who is calling at the front door, the sensor will automatically switch from the television channel you are watching, to the surveillance camera.

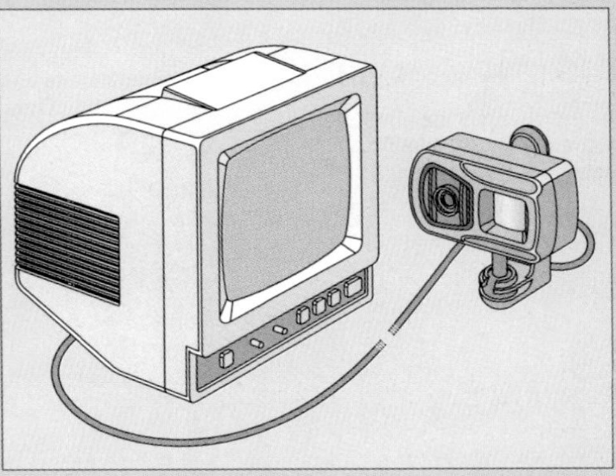

CHOOSING TIME CONTROLS FOR SECURITY

A dark, silent house can arouse the interest of burglars. If you make the house appear occupied, by day or night, a prowler is likely to move on to an easier target.

Voices, music and lights after dark can suggest you are in – but only if used with discretion; a single light in the hall left on all evening, or a radio playing all day are more likely to betray that you are out. The illusion that you are there is given by a change in the house – music stopping, or a light going off in one room and on in another.

Sockets and switches operated by timers help to create the illusion. Some sophisticated controls will memorise your schedule of switching lights on and off and reproduce it.

LIGHT-SWITCH TIMERS

Time-controlled light switches are connected to the lighting circuit in place of normal switches and are wired in the same way (page 386). Some will switch on and off many times. Others switch on only once – at dusk – so there is no danger of the light shining in the daytime because a power cut has interfered with the setting.

Sunset switch

Switching on is controlled by a light-sensitive eye that activates the switch when daylight fades. The lower part of the switch has a cover that slides down to reveal a knob for setting the switch-off time between 2 and 8 hours after the light comes on.

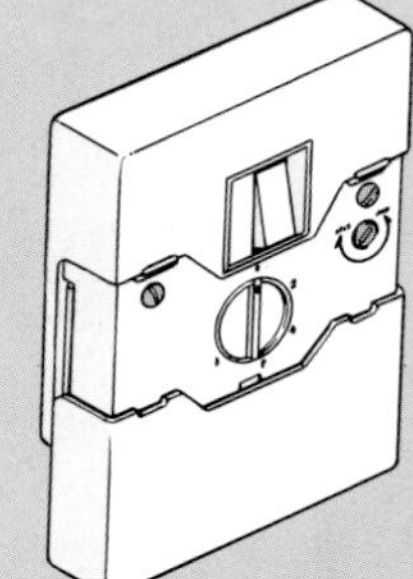

Programmable switch (tungsten lighting)

The timing is set by turning the knob until the switch-on time shows in the window and then pressing the knob. The switch is set in the same way to turn off. It will switch on and off up to 48 times a day and operate manually at any time. It can also memorise times when you switch the light on and off, and repeat the pattern.

AUTOMATIC OUTDOOR LIGHT

An infra-red sensor activates the light when anyone – visitor or burglar – comes within its field of vision. The sensor can be incorporated in either the light or a separate unit operating a number of lights. Once on, the light shines for a period chosen by the user.

SOCKET TIMERS

A plug-in timer will control any appliance that plugs into a 13amp socket – a radio or a lamp for security, to give the impression that the house is occupied, or a heater or electric blanket for convenience.

Set the required programme on the timer, plug it into a switched-on socket, plug the appliance into the timer and switch on the appliance. It will not actually come on until the programmed time. You can override the set programme manually.

Timers vary in the number of times they will switch on and off, and in the shortest possible 'on' period. There are one-day and seven-day timers.

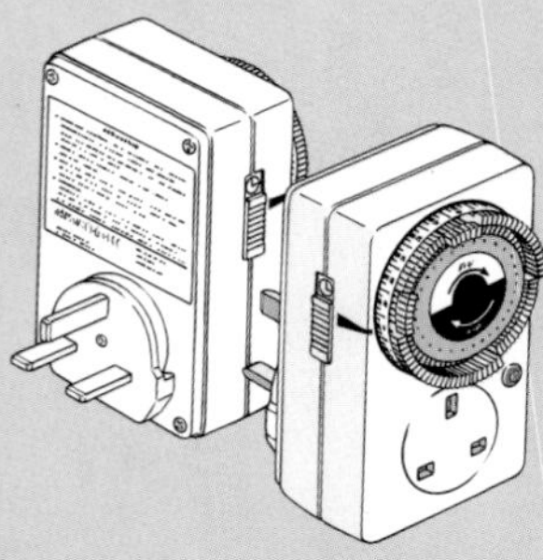

One-day timers

Some socket timers allow you to design a pattern of switching on and off a socket over a day. Some models only allow 5 changes in a day, while others allow up to 48. Markers on a dial trigger the socket as the dial turns. The shortest period for which it can be switched on is usually between 15 minutes or half an hour. The pattern will be repeated every day until it is switched off or changed.

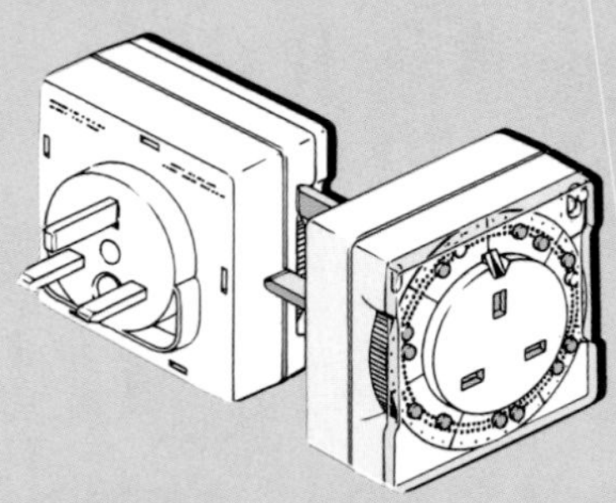

Seven-day timer

Seven-day timers allow you to set a pattern of switching on and off at different times for each day of the week. Some are clockwork, set using dials, others are digital, allowing you to adjust the setting to the minute. The on-off pattern will repeat itself each week. Digital timers can usually work on either a 24-hour cycle or a seven-day cycle.

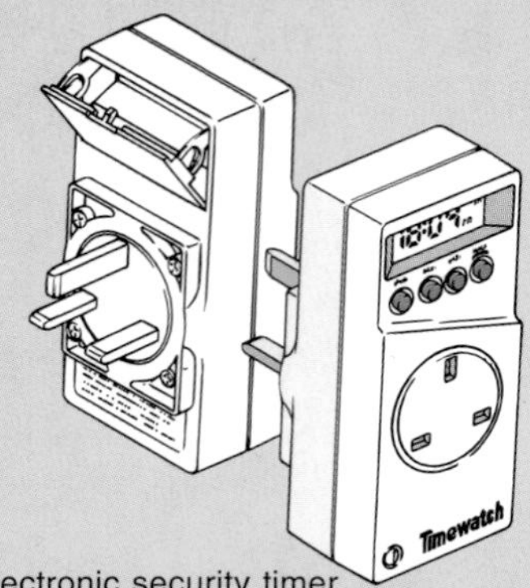

Electronic security timer

This electronic device is intended for security only. Four lighting periods can be set over 24 hours. The power is switched on and off several times at random during each programmed on period, giving the impression of people entering and leaving a room. The on-off programme is repeated daily but you can cancel or override it.

PROTECTION FROM FIRE

SMOKE ALARMS

Building Regulations state that at least one smoke alarm, wired to the mains, must be fitted in every new property. However, if your house does not have a smoke alarm, you can quite easily fit battery powered alarms yourself. Smoke alarms should comply with British Standard BS5446.

Smoke alarms should be fitted within 23ft (7m) of rooms where fires are likely to start, such as the living room or the kitchen, and also within 10ft (3m) of bedroom doors.

If the alarm is fitted to the ceiling, it should be at least 12in (30cm) away from any wall and the same distance from any ceiling light fitting. If it is to be fitted to the wall, the alarm must be between 6in (15cm) and 12in (30cm) below the ceiling.

Smoke rises and spreads out, so a central ceiling position is ideal. Alternatively, mount the alarm on a wall, but not in a corner, where the air does not move quite so easily.

There are two basic types of alarm, the ionisation model and the photoelectric. The ionisation alarm provides good general protection and works by detecting invisible smoke particles in the air. It responds quickly to fast, flaming fires, but it is not suitable in or near a kitchen because it will be set off by cooking. The photoelectric alarm 'sees' smoke and not invisible particles, so this type is far less likely to react to normal cooking in a kitchen. For good, all round protection use one of each type.

A fresh battery will last about a year. Some alarms have indicators to show that the battery is still working; others give an audible warning when the battery level is low. Check the alarm regularly.

Clean alarms regularly because dust will impair their performance. Use the upholstery brush on the end of the extension pipe on a vacuum cleaner.

FIRE EXTINGUISHERS

The simplest and most useful fire extinguisher is a fire blanket (BS EN1869) or a large, damp towel. A bucket of water is safe on some fires, but must not be used on chip pan and electrical fires.

If you are considering buying a fire extinguisher for your home, make sure it conforms to British Standards (BSEN3 and BS7863). Look for the Kitemark or the special British Approvals for Fire Equipment (BAFE) mark. All new portable fire extinguishers are coloured red, and some have a colour patch, which indicates the contents, on the front.

BLUE: *Multi-purpose dry powder* Most suitable for home use. Use on grease and fats, paint and petrol. Also safe on electrical equipment.

RED: *Water* Use on wood, paper plastics, cloth and coal. Do not use on fat or oil, or electrical fires.

BLACK *Carbon dioxide* Best for liquids such as grease, fats, oil, paint and petrol. BEWARE: gas from CO_2 extinguishers is harmful in confined spaces.

NEVER USE A FIRE EXTINGUISHER ON A CHIP PAN FIRE and never try to move a burning pan. Even small fires can spread very quickly, producing smoke and fumes which can kill in seconds. If in doubt, do not tackle the fire yourself. Get out, call the fire brigade, and stay out. Always call the fire brigade, even if you have managed to put the fire out.

7

Walls, ceilings & fireplaces

Identifying walls and ceilings for making fixings

To fix something securely to a wall, you must use a fixing screw or bolt that is both strong enough to support it and suitable for the type of wall. Screws alone cannot grip into materials such as brick or plasterboard as they do into wood, so there is a wide range of plugs and fixings for securing heavy or lightweight objects to different wall (or ceiling) materials.

On solid walls, a sufficient number of No. 8 screws plugged securely through the plaster and into the masonry at the recommended spacings (page 174) will support most household fixtures. But use No. 10 or 12 screws – or other strong fixings such as expansion bolts where convenient – for heavy items such as wall cupboards, cabinets, radiators, shelves carrying heavy items such as books or stacked plates, washbasins and lavatory cisterns.

On hollow walls and ceilings, the strength of the material limits the weight it can support. The description of a wall as load-bearing or non-load-bearing refers to whether or not it supports structural timbers such as floor or ceiling joists – it makes no difference to the ability to support fixtures.

Fix heavy objects to hollow walls with screws driven directly into the timber studs or battens of the framework (facing page). If a heavy fixture such as a wall cabinet is not wide enough to span two studs, centre it on a stud and screw it to that stud only.

If you want to fix a slim but heavy object in the space between two studs, screw a wooden batten across the wall surface between the studs to support it at the base, then use hollow fixings to hold the object to the wall.

LOCATING HIDDEN TIMBER FRAMEWORK

Consult the descriptions of types of hollow wall (facing page) to get an idea how far apart the timber studs of the framework are likely to be, and how wide they are.

One way to locate a stud – in a lath-and-plaster wall especially – is to use a metal detector (left) to find the line of nails that are securing the laths or the plasterboard. Follow the instructions to operate.

Alternatively, you can use a Rapitest joist and stud detector, which is sensitive to the differing thicknesses of the materials to which it is applied. Follow the instructions to operate.

Another method is to tap the wall surface to find the places where it sounds most solid, then probe with a bradawl to pinpoint the position of the stud or batten.

A third way is to drill a small hole into the wall and probe with a piece of wire (facing page).

RECOGNISING SOLID WALL MATERIALS

MATERIAL	WHERE IT IS FOUND	TESTING AND FIXING ADVICE
Bricks	Cavity wall Solid outer wall Solid internal wall	Brick inside the house is usually covered with a plaster layer ⅜–1in (10–25mm) thick. Test by drilling. If there is brick underneath the plaster, the dust will first be grey from the plaster, and then pinky-red or yellow as the bit cuts into brick. Use fixings suitable for solid walls (page 232).
Natural stone	Solid outer wall	The inside surface of the wall is plastered, sometimes with lath and plaster (facing page). Test by drilling. The stone is very hard and you will need a hammer drill to penetrate it, unless you strike a mortar joint, producing soft, buff-coloured dust. Use fixings for solid walls (page 232).
Concrete building blocks	The inner leaf of a cavity wall Solid internal wall	The inside surface is plastered. Test by drilling. Blocks are usually soft. Some are gritty (breeze blocks), produce black dust and cause the drill to wander a little. In houses built since the 1960s, blocks are usually easy-to-drill aerated insulation blocks, which produce grey dust. Use hammer-in fixings (page 232) or alternatively use woodscrews with either exterior-thread or helical-wing plugs (page 233).
Concrete lintel	Spanning a wall opening – usually a door, window or fireplace	Usually covered with plaster. Test by drilling. The surface is extremely hard and will need a hammer drill. Use light or heavyweight fixings for solid walls (page 232).

TYPES OF SOLID WALL CONSTRUCTION

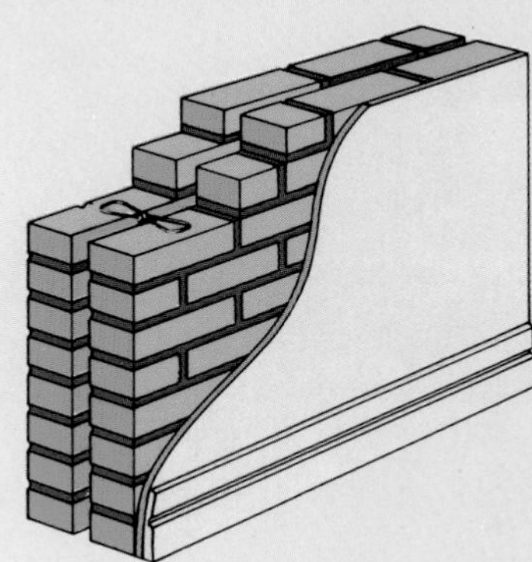

Cavity wall
A wall round the outside of a house built since the late 1920s. It is made up of two independent leaves separated by a cavity 2in (50mm) wide, and is 11in (280mm) thick overall. The outer leaf may be brick, natural stone or reconstituted stone. The inner leaf, which supports the ceiling joists and roof structure, may be built of bricks or building blocks (or could be timber-framed, facing page).

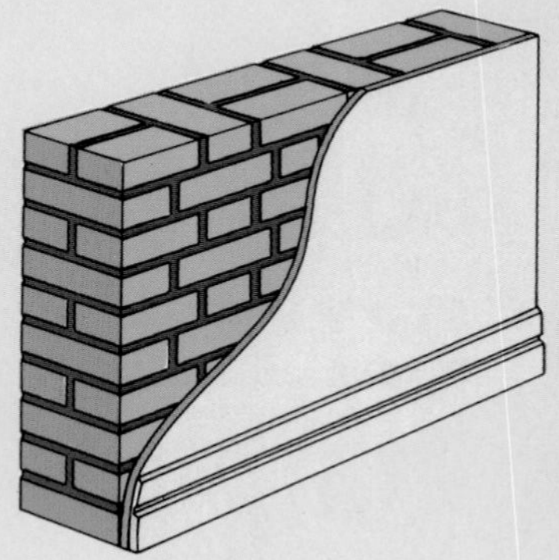

Solid outer wall
A wall round the outside of the house, built of solid brickwork or stone. Brick walls are two or three bricks thick – 9in (230mm) or 13½in (345mm) – and often have a damp-proof course of slate or engineering bricks just above soil level on the outside. Stone walls are 12in-20in (300mm-510mm) thick and rarely have a damp-proof course. Solid walls are normally found only in houses built before the 1920s.

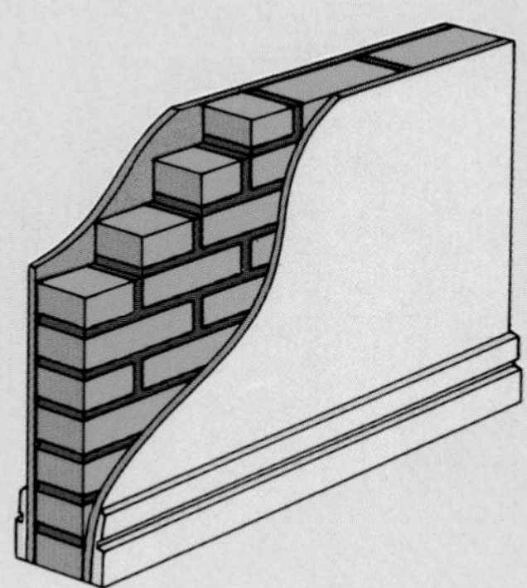

Solid internal wall
An interior dividing wall that is constructed from a single leaf of either bricks or lightweight concrete or clay building blocks. The wall is usually covered with a plaster layer ½in-1in (13mm-25mm) thick on both sides. The overall thickness of the wall is 5in-6in (125mm-150mm).

Some solid internal walls are load-bearing (that is, supporting structural joists), and some are non-load-bearing.

RECOGNISING HOLLOW WALL OR CEILING MATERIALS

MATERIAL	WHERE IT IS FOUND	TESTING AND FIXING ADVICE
Plasterboard	Timber-framed cavity wall Dry-lined wall Dry partitioning Stud partitioning Ceiling	Test by drilling – the wall does not necessarily sound hollow when tapped, especially if there is a cellular core or insulation material. There may be a skim coat of plaster on the board surface, or it may be directly painted or papered. The drill penetrates easily into a void or soft core. For lightweight fittings, use fixings for hollow walls or ceilings (page 233). For heavy fittings, screw into the timber framework (or the masonry core of a dry-lined wall).
Hardboard, plywood, chipboard, fibreboard	Hollow door Decorative wallboards (page 248)	Use the timber framework where possible. Otherwise use lightweight fixings for hollow walls (page 233).
Lath and plaster	On internal walls of houses built before the 1920s. On ceilings in houses built up to about the 1940s	Test by drilling in several places to discover the plaster thickness and the presence of laths. The plaster is soft and sometimes falls away to reveal the laths behind. For light or medium-weight fittings use spring, gravity, or nylon toggle fixings (page 233). The strength of the laths is the limiting factor. For big weights screw into timber upright.

FINDING A WALL STUD WITH A PIECE OF WIRE

You can locate the wooden studs in most hollow walls by using a drill and a piece of wire.

1 Drill a small hole horizontally into the wall with the drill slanted as far as possible, so that your hand is close to the wall.

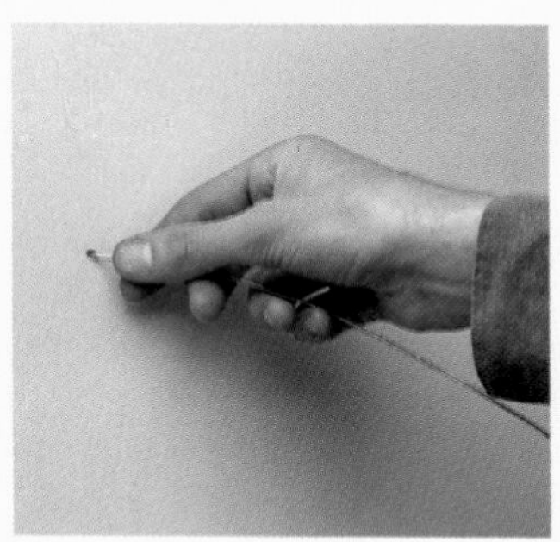

2 When the hole is through, push into it a piece of stiff wire about 20in (510mm) long until it meets an obstruction, which will be an upright timber stud.

3 Hold the wire between your finger and thumb at the entrance to the hole, withdraw it, and lay it along the wall. Where it ends, indicates the edge of the stud.

4 Drill the hole about an inch (25mm) farther on, and it should go into the centre of the stud.

TYPES OF HOLLOW WALL AND CEILING CONSTRUCTION

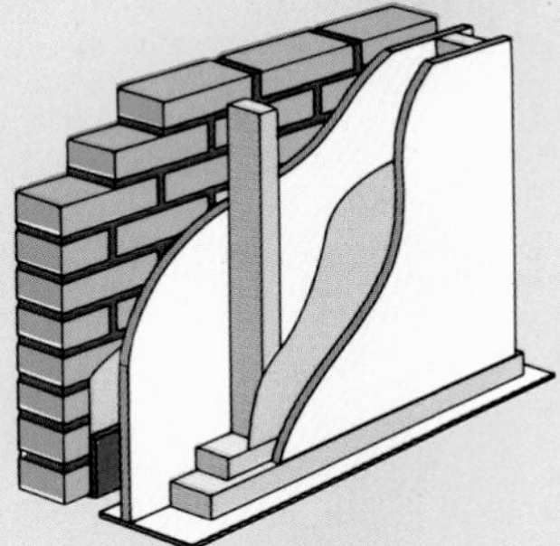

Timber-framed cavity wall
A cavity wall (facing page) with the inner, load-bearing leaf built of timber studding faced with plasterboard. Timber uprights are usually 4in (100mm) wide and 2in (50mm) thick and about 16in (400mm) apart. The side facing the cavity is sheeted with plywood. There is thermal insulation material, such as glass-fibre quilting, between the plywood and plasterboard.

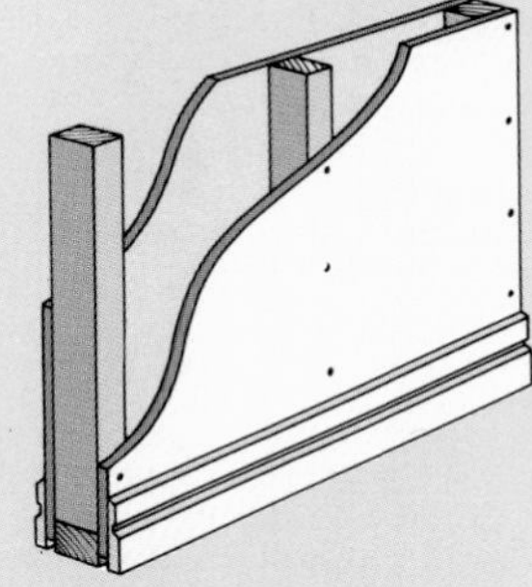

Stud partitioning
This common interior dividing wall is made from a framework of timber studding (upright posts with cross-pieces known as noggins) faced with plasterboard on each side. The posts are usually 3in (75mm) wide and 2in (50mm) thick, spaced about 24in (610mm) apart, and the wall is about 4in (100mm) thick overall. It may, or may not, be load-bearing.

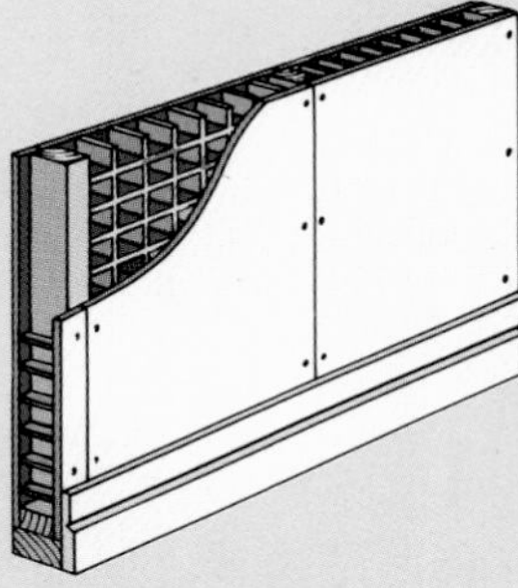

Dry partition wall
Plasterboard panels (Paramount partitioning) are slotted over timber framework. The panels consist of two wallboards bonded to a cellular core of resin-impregnated card. The timber uprights are likely to be about 3ft (910mm) or 4ft (1.2m) apart and about 1½in (38mm) wide. The wall is 2in-2½in (50-65mm) thick, lightweight and non-load-bearing.

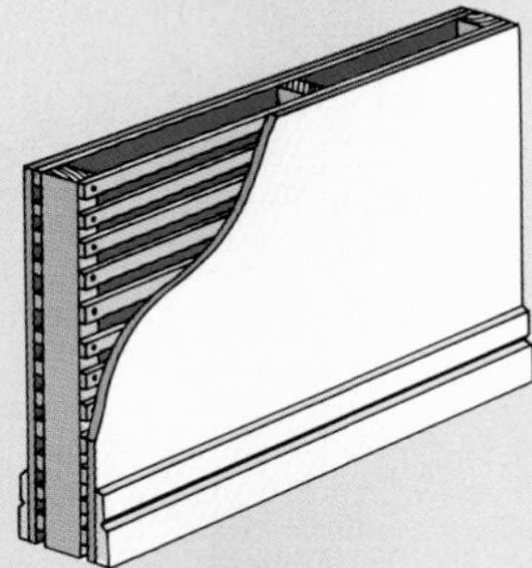

Lath-and-plaster wall
Found in houses built before the 1920s. The plaster, often about 1in (25mm) thick and mixed with horsehair to increase its strength, is bonded to horizontal laths of sawn or split timber. The laths are nailed to timber uprights, usually 4in × 2in (100mm × 50mm) at about 18in (460mm) centres. If the wall is load-bearing, it has diagonal struts between the timber uprights.

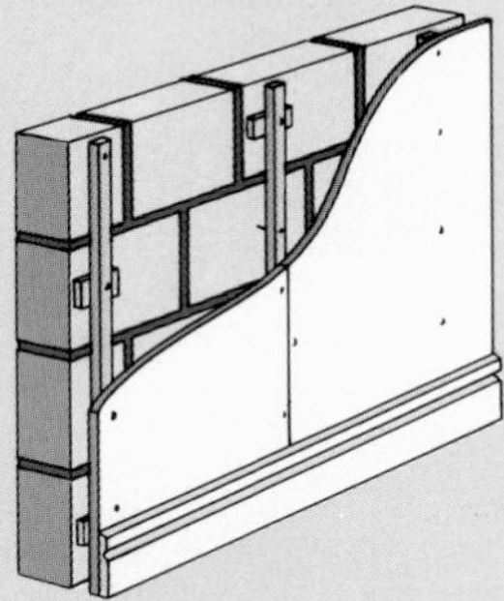

Dry-lined wall
A brick or block wall that has a surface layer of plasterboard either stuck directly to the masonry or nailed to a framework of timber battens. The battens are normally either about 16in (400mm) apart with 9.5mm (⅜in) thick plasterboard, or about 24in (610mm) apart with 12.5mm (½in) thick plasterboard. There may be insulation material between the masonry and plasterboard.

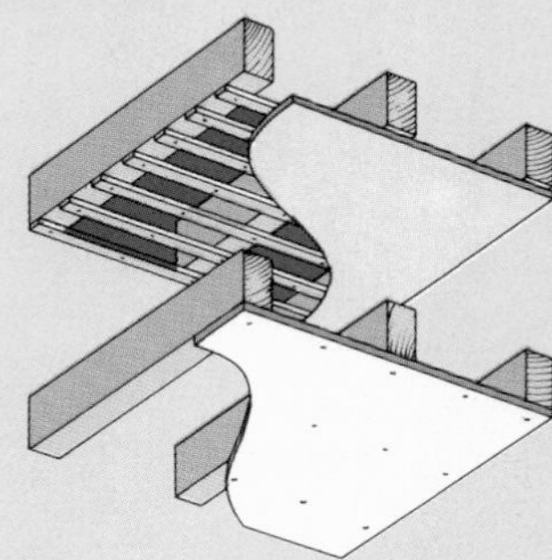

Ceilings
In houses built before the Second World War, the ceilings will probably be of lath and plaster (top). Ceilings in modern houses will probably be of plasterboard (bottom). Either type will be fixed to the joists supporting the floor above, which are spaced 16in-24in (400mm-610mm) apart. On the top storey, smaller loft joists are usually spaced about 13½in (345mm) apart.

Fixing to a masonry wall with screws and wall plugs

The commonest method of fixing an object to a masonry wall is with No. 8 screws and wall plugs.

Tapered plastic wall plugs will accommodate screws of several different gauges. To drill the hole, use a masonry bit with the same gauge number as the largest screw gauge the plug will accept – a No. 12 bit for a No. 12 screw, for example. Make the hole slightly deeper than the length of the screw.

Straight-sided plastic or fibre plugs will only accept one gauge of screw. Use a masonry bit with the same gauge number as the screw – a No. 8 bit for a No. 8 screw.

Tapered plastic wall plugs are wide enough to accept the screw shank, if necessary. Straight-sided plugs will not accept the shank.

You will need

Tools Power drill (use a hammer drill for hard masonry such as concrete or engineering bricks); masonry bit of same diameter as wall plug (use a percussion bit with a hammer drill); pencil; bradawl; safety spectacles; screwdriver. Possibly a metal detector.

Materials Suitable screws; wall plugs (or plugging compound); object to be fixed.

1 Hold the object to be fixed in the required position and mark the spot for the first plug hole with a pencil through one of its fixing holes. If the hole is very narrow, use a nail punch and tap it lightly into the wall.

2 Check that the plug hole will not go through a cable or pipe concealed under the plaster.

Most cables and pipes run either horizontally or vertically, so it should be safe to drill if there is no light fitting or appliance directly above, below or to one side of the hole. A metal detector (page 230) will reveal the positions of cables or metal pipes. The detector lights up when it passes over metal, so can be used to trace pipe and cable routes.

FIXINGS FOR SOLID WALLS

FIXING	DESCRIPTION	USE
Masonry nail	Hardened galvanised nail that will penetrate and grip when driven into bricks or blocks. Not suitable for use in concrete or hard stone. Lengths typically from ⅝in (16mm) to 4in (100mm).	A fast way of fixing timber battens to brick walls. Choose a length that will penetrate beyond the fixing by about ⅝in (16mm) into bare masonry or about 1in (25mm) into a plastered wall. Hammer with short, positive strokes. Nails will not bend, and will shatter if not struck squarely. Wear eye protection.
Woodscrew and wall plug	The fibre or plastic plug fits into a hole drilled in masonry, and the screw is fitted through the object and driven into the plug, which expands to grip the wall. Plugs are in lengths from ⅝in (16mm) to 3½in (90mm) to fit screws Nos 4-20.	For lightweight fittings, No. 8 gauge screws and matched plugs are suitable. For heavier fittings use No. 10 or No. 12 gauge screws. The screw should be long enough to extend about 1in (25mm) into the masonry after passing through the fitting and the plaster.
Hammer-in fixing or nail plug	A screw with a special thread for easy driving, ready-fitted into a nylon sleeve. It can be tapped with a hammer into a drilled hole. Lengths typically 2in-6¼in (50mm-160mm) will fix objects from about ¼in (6mm) to 4¼in (110mm) thick.	A strong, fast method for fixing a lot of timber battens to brick or concrete. Also suitable for lightweight fixings into building blocks. The hole should extend ¼in-½in (6mm-13mm) beyond the screw tip. So for a screw 2in (50mm) long fixing a ⅜in (10mm) thick object, make wall holes at least 1¾in (44mm) deep.
Frame fixing	A long screw ready-fitted into a nylon wall plug. The hole is drilled through the frame into the wall, and the fixing pushed or lightly tapped through and tightened with a screwdriver. Lengths to secure frames from about ¾in (19mm) to 4¼in (110mm) thick.	A secure and convenient method of fixing new or replacement door or window frames to walls. Useful for repairing a door frame that has worked loose. As a guide, the depth of the masonry hole should be at least five times the plug diameter. So a hole of ⅜in (10mm) diameter should extend at least 2in (50mm) into the masonry.
Expansion or anchor bolt	A bolt with a segmented metal shield. The shield fits into a drilled hole in masonry, and expands to grip the hole sides when the bolt is tightened. Bolts range from about ¼in (6mm) to 1in (25mm) in diameter, in lengths to fix objects from about ⅜in (10mm) to 4¾in (120mm) thick. The bolt head may be fixed, fitted with a nut and washer, or hook or eye shaped.	A very strong, heavy-duty fixing suitable for objects such as wall cupboards, garage doors, lean-to framework, or fence and gateposts fixed to masonry. A fixed-head bolt (known as a loose bolt) is pushed through the fixture before being screwed into the shield. A nut-head (or projecting) bolt is placed in the hole with the shield and the fitting is hung on it before the nut and washer are fitted. The masonry hole needs to be wider than the hole through the fitting – generally ¼in (6mm) wider than the bolt diameter.
Steel sleeve anchor or expansion bolt	Steel bolts with an expanding wedge at the end for gripping against the sides of a drilled hole. Bolts have screw-on nuts and washers. Sizes are available for fixing objects ranging from about ¼in (6mm) to 4¼in (110mm) thick.	Easy, quickly fitted heavy-duty fixing for things such as door and window frames, trunking, or hand rails. The hole can be drilled through the frame and masonry at the same time, and is the same diameter for both the fitting and the masonry. Bolt diameters are typically from ¼in (6mm) to ¾in (19mm).
Plugging compound 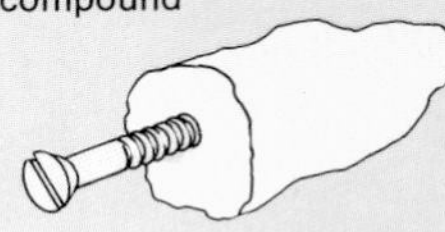	Powder based on cement and glass fibre that is mixed to a paste and packed into a masonry hole to hold a screw. Some types are resin based and are sold ready for use. Asbestos types are no longer available.	For making fixings in holes that have become enlarged because of the drill bit wandering on a hard surface. Follow the maker's instructions for using.

STANDARD TYPES OF WALL PLUG

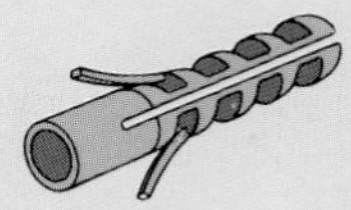

Finned plastic
Tapered plug with split end to allow expansion, and either fins or lugs to prevent it turning in the hole. A rim or flexible ears prevent it being pushed in too far. Each size will accept screws of several lengths and gauges. Can be used in damp places.

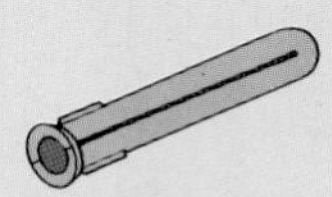

Ribbed plastic
An early type of tapered plastic plug still in use. It has no fins or lugs, but the shallow lengthways ribs prevent it turning in the hole. Sold in colour-coded sizes.

Strip plastic
Straight-sided plug with shallow lengthways ribs. Can be bought in strips and cut to length with a trimming knife. Sold in colour-coded sizes.

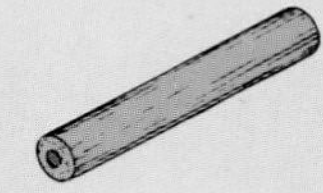

Fibre
Straight-sided plug of tough, compressed fibre. Sold in various lengths, but can be cut with a trimming knife. Not suitable for damp places.

3 On a smooth surface, such as plaster, make a small hole with a nail punch or bradawl on the marked spot to provide a start for the drill. Otherwise it can easily slip, damaging the surface as well as going off the mark. (For drilling ceramic tiles, see page 145.)

4 Mark a depth indicator on the masonry bit so that you know when the hole has reached the depth you require.

Some power drills have an extending depth gauge.

For others, use a ready-made stop that fits onto the bit. Or wrap coloured adhesive tape round the bit with the edge marking the depth.

5 Use the power drill at medium speed for boring small holes in bricks or blocks, at slow speed for large holes or in hard masonry such as concrete. If the hole is wider than about $\frac{1}{2}$in (13mm), drill a $\frac{1}{4}$in (6mm) pilot hole first.

6 Exert a steady pressure on the drill and keep it at right angles to the wall.

7 Withdraw the drill from the hole at short intervals. This not only brings out dust and debris, but allows the tip of the bit to cool. Be careful not to brush the drill tip against your skin or clothing, as it can be hot enough to burn.

FIXINGS FOR HOLLOW WALLS, CEILINGS AND LIGHTWEIGHT BLOCKS

FIXING	DESCRIPTION	USE
Woodscrew and special plug	The screw is used with a winged plastic plug (see right) that spreads out to grip the back of a wall or ceiling board. The plug can usually be re-used if the screw is withdrawn. Typical size range is 1in-$2\frac{1}{2}$in (25mm-65mm) long to fit Nos 5-16 screws.	For lightweight or medium fittings to plasterboard, hardboard, or plywood (including hollow doors) up to about 1in (25mm) thick. The cavity behind the board generally needs to be at least about $\frac{1}{2}$in (13mm) deep.
Machine screw and expanding rubber plug 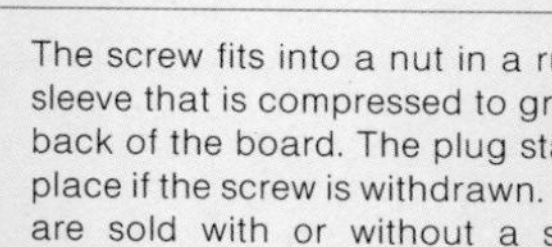	The screw fits into a nut in a rubber sleeve that is compressed to grip the back of the board. The plug stays in place if the screw is withdrawn. Plugs are sold with or without a screw. Typical size range is for screws $\frac{3}{4}$in-2in (19mm-50mm) long and $\frac{5}{16}$in-1in (8mm-25mm) diameter.	A strong fixing for plasterboard, plywood, hardboard, sheet metal, glass or plastic, up to about $1\frac{3}{4}$in (44mm) thick. The plug protects the screw from vibration, rusting, water, and electric current. It can also be used in masonry, where it shapes to the hole contours.
Machine screw and metal cavity fixing	A metal plug with a nut welded in the end. It collapses to form metal wings that grip the back of the board. Typical size range is for screws $\frac{3}{4}$in-$2\frac{1}{2}$in (19mm-65mm) long and $\frac{5}{16}$in-$\frac{1}{2}$in (8mm-13mm) diameter.	A strong fixing for heavyweight fixtures to hardboard, plasterboard, chipboard, plywood and fibreboard, up to about $1\frac{1}{4}$in (32mm) thick.
Gravity toggle 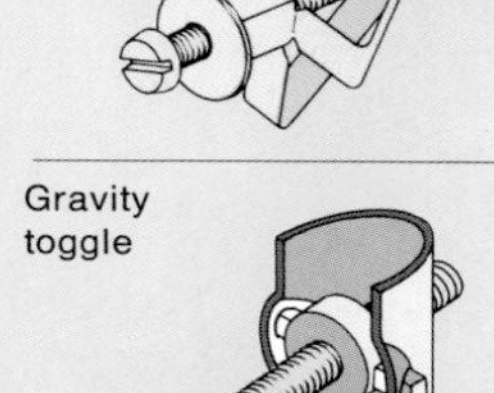	A machine screw with a swinging metal bar (toggle) attached. When the screw is inserted, the toggle swings down and grips the back of the wall. It is lost if the screw is withdrawn. Sold with or without a screw. Typical size range is suitable for screws 2in-$3\frac{1}{4}$in (50mm-80mm) long.	A strong fixing for plasterboard or lath-and-plaster walls. The cavity has to be at least $1\frac{1}{4}$in (32mm) wide, or wider for larger sizes.
Spring toggle 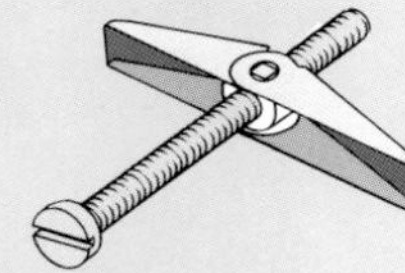	A machine screw fitted with a spring-operated toggle bar that folds back for insertion and springs open inside the cavity. The toggle is lost if the screw is withdrawn. Sold with or without a screw. Typical size range is for screws 2in-$3\frac{1}{4}$in (50mm-80mm) long.	A strong fixing for plasterboard or lath-and-plaster walls and ceilings. The cavity has to be at least $1\frac{3}{4}$in (44mm) wide – wider for larger sizes. The toggle can be used with a hook for hanging a fitting from the ceiling.
Nylon toggle and collar 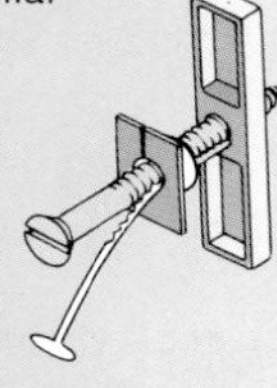	A nylon collar that takes a wood or machine screw and is linked by a notched nylon strip to a toggle. After insertion, the strip is used to draw the toggle towards the collar to take the screw tip and grip the back of the board. It is then cut off. Typical size is for No. 6 woodscrews, or machine screws $3\frac{1}{4}$in-4in (80mm-100mm) long and $\frac{1}{8}$in-$\frac{1}{4}$in (3mm-6mm) diameters.	The collar closes the drilled hole, and the adjustable fitting is useful for fixing to plasterboard, lath and plaster or suspended ceilings of different thicknesses, especially where the cavity is very narrow. In one type of fitting, the toggle is not lost if the screw is withdrawn.

SPECIAL TYPES OF WALL PLUG

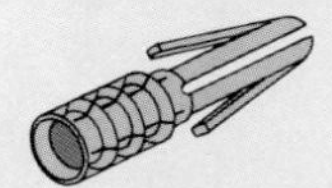

Winged-arrow type
Light plastic plug that spreads out to grip the back of plasterboard. For use with No. 8 screws and lightweight fixings. The plug can be re-used.

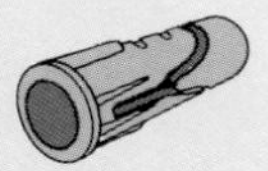

Expanding-wing type
The wings are forced apart to grip the back of the board. Small-sized plugs are for use with No. 6 screws in hollow doors. Larger-sized plugs are for use with No. 8 screws for medium-weight fixings to board. Cannot be re-used.

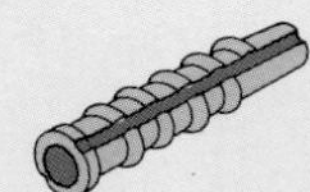

Exterior-thread type
The plastic plug cuts its own thread into the edges of a drilled hole. For use with No. 8 screws to make strong fixings into aerated (not breeze) blocks, which tend to crumble. Can be re-used.

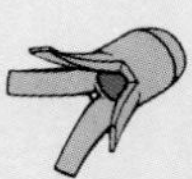

Nylon petal anchor
The wings spread out like petals to grip the back of board. For use with Nos 5-10 screws in narrow cavities such as hollow doors. Cannot be re-used.

Nylon rivet anchor
The plug is split along most of its length and is compressed into wings. For use with Nos 8-10 screws for making fixings to plasterboard, particularly partition walls. The plug can be re-used.

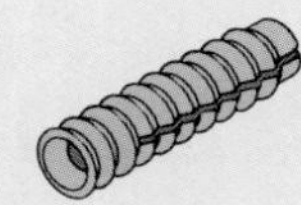

Chipboard plug
Nylon fastener with an outside thread that is hammered into a hole drilled in chipboard. It has a split end and expands to give a secure grip. For use with Nos 6, 8 and 10 screws. The plug can be re-used.

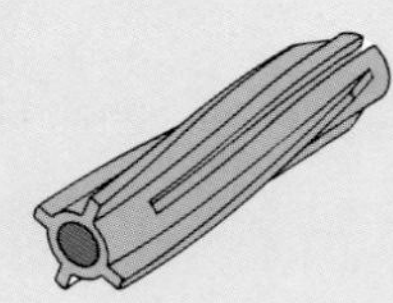

Helical wing or twist-lock type
The nylon plug has helical wings that cause it to rotate as it is tapped home with a hammer, and prevent it from coming out if the screw is ever withdrawn. For use with Nos 10, 12 and 16 screws to make strong fixings into aerated blocks. Can be re-used.

Fixing to a masonry wall with screws and wall plugs (continued)

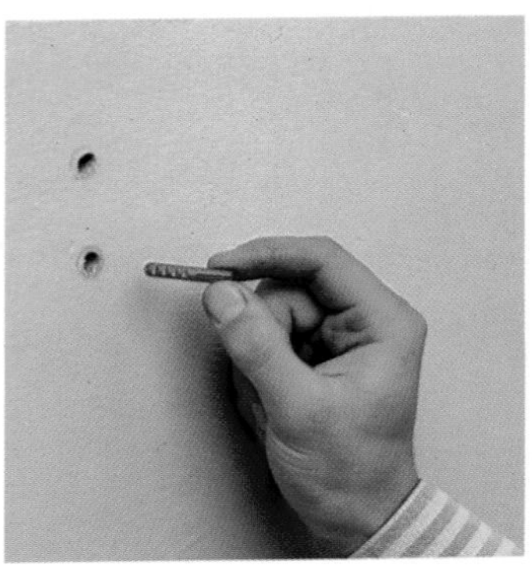

8 When the hole has been drilled to depth, push the plug in. For a straight-sided plug fit the screw one or two turns into the end first and push the plug through the plaster to range with the surface of the masonry, otherwise its expansion could crack the plaster.

Any type of plug should offer some resistance when pushed in. If it goes in too easily, the hole is too big and will have to be filled with plugging compound.

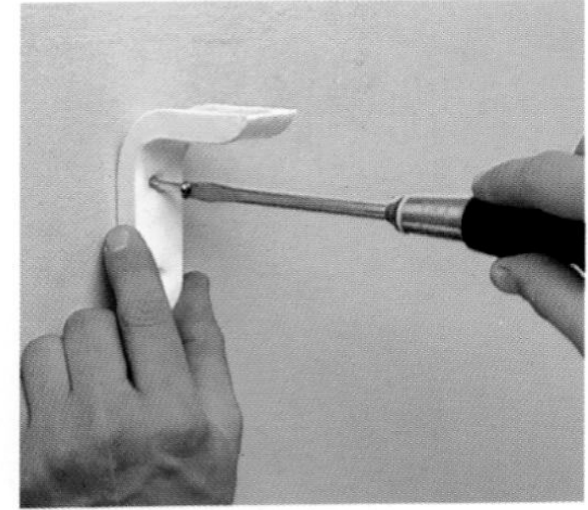

9 Pass the screw through the fitting, then screw it up tight against the hole.

FIXING A WOODEN BATTEN TO A MASONRY WALL

Use screws long enough to pass through the wooden batten (with the heads countersunk if necessary), through any plaster layer – usually about $\frac{1}{2}$in-1in (13mm-25mm) thick – and to penetrate at least 1in (25mm) into the brickwork of the wall.

1 Drill clearance holes through the batten, the same diameter as the screw shank (page 162). Countersink the hole if the screw has a countersunk head.

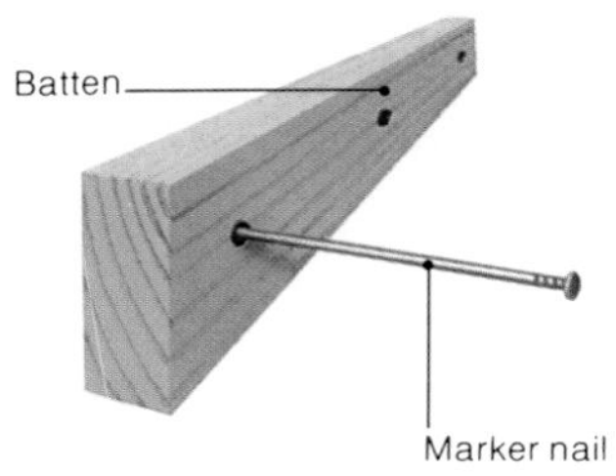

2 Hold the batten in position against the wall and make a mark at one end through the hole.

3 Using a masonry bit, drill a suitable hole for the wall plug (page 232) at the marked spot.

4 Fit the plug and temporarily fix the batten, with the screw only partly driven in.

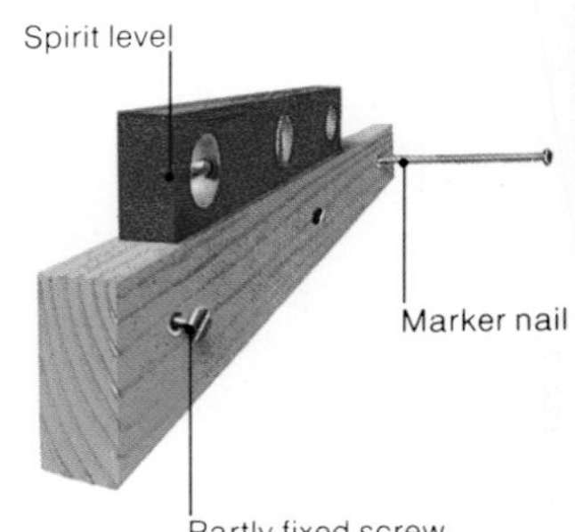

5 Rest a spirit level along a horizontal batten (or hang a plumb line down a vertical batten) to ensure that it is straight while you mark the position for the hole at the other end.

6 Drill a hole for the second plug, temporarily drive in the screw through the batten, and mark the positions of other holes, if any.

7 When all holes are prepared, screw the batten firmly to the wall.

Hanging a picture

The easiest way to hang a lightweight or medium-weight picture is with a pin-type picture hook, which can be driven into the wall with a light hammer. Such pins are strong enough to support fairly heavy pictures as long as the plaster is sound and the pin secure.

A heavy picture can be fixed with two hooks positioned near the edges of the cord rather than from one central hook. Alternatively, it can be hung from a roundhead screw fitted into a plug (page 232), or hung on battens (see right). But get professional advice if you want to hang a valuable heavy picture.

Using two hooks is advisable when hanging a wide picture, because the tension on a centrally supported cord stretched almost straight increases the load considerably, perhaps well beyond the weight of the picture.

When hanging a heavy mirror, use mirror chain rather than picture wire or cord.

POSITIONING THE PICTURE ON THE WALL

Because of the tension on a picture cord, it is difficult to judge the right spot to fix the supporting hook if you want the top of the picture to be set at a particular level and the cord out of sight.

1 Hold the picture against the wall exactly where you want it to hang, and lightly mark on the wall the positions of the top corners.

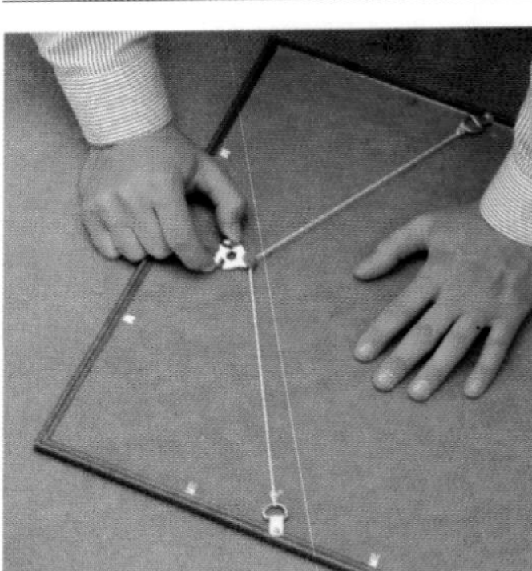

2 Lay the picture on its face, mark the top centre, and use the hook to pull the cord towards the mark until it is tight.

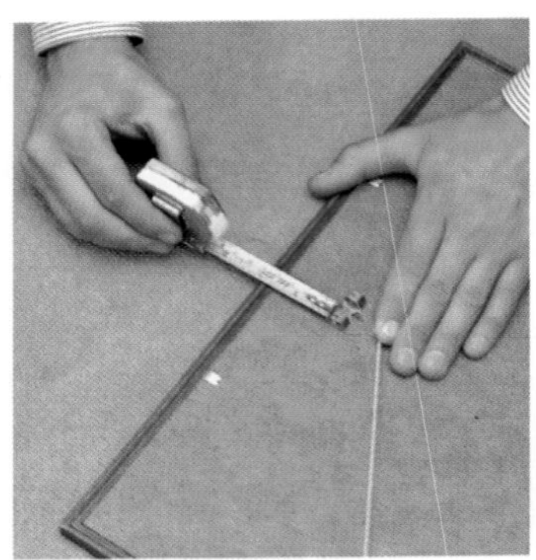

3 Measure the distance between the top of the hook and the top of the picture frame.

4 Measure the central point between the two corner marks on the wall, and then measure down the required distance between the top of the hook and the top of the frame. Mark the spot and hammer the hook into the wall with its top centre against the mark.

HANGING A HEAVY PICTURE ON BATTENS

Interlocking battens can be used to support a heavy picture. The battens are both cut from one piece of wood. One half is fixed to the wall, the other across the frame.

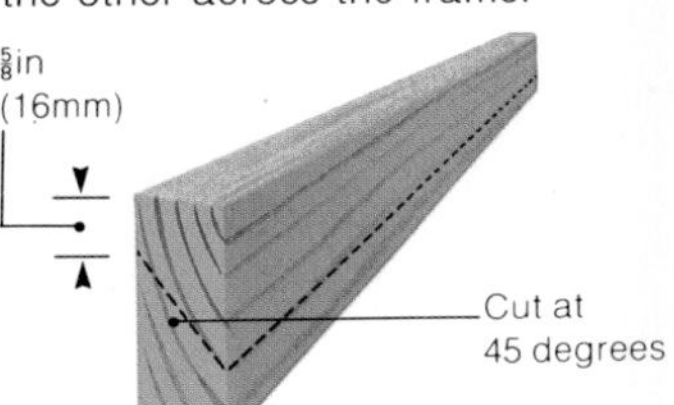

Use a piece of timber about 2in (50mm) by $\frac{3}{4}$in (19mm), and slightly shorter than the picture width. Mark a line along one face, $\frac{5}{8}$in (16mm) from the edge. Cut along the line with a circular saw at a 45 degree angle towards the batten centre.

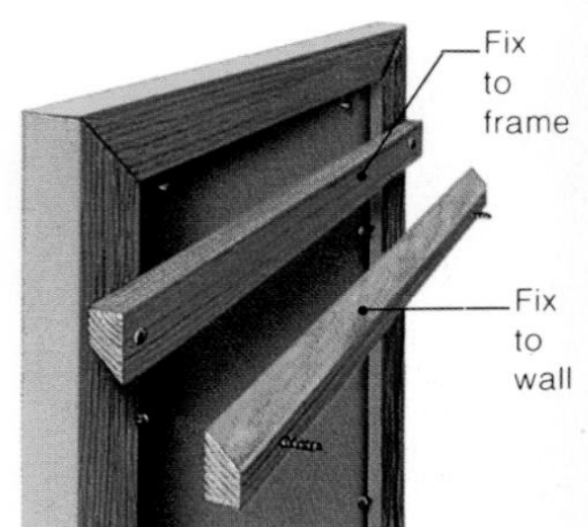

Screw one piece of batten to the back of the frame, about one-third

CHOOSING A PICTURE HOOK

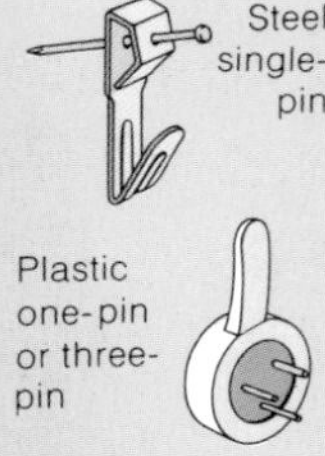

The smallest size is suitable for a light picture or mirror. A larger one can be used for a medium-sized picture or mirror.

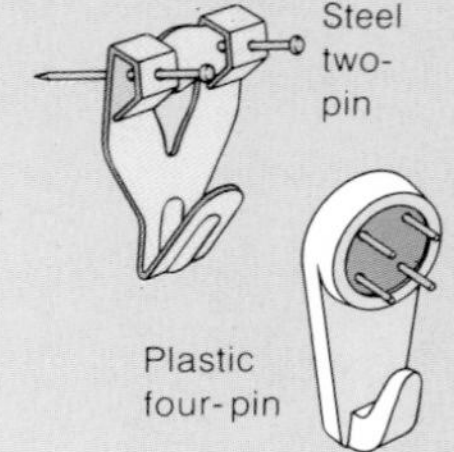

Suitable for medium-weight pictures or mirrors when used singly, or for medium to heavy types when used in pairs. The plastic hook has a long fifth pin for fixing to wood.

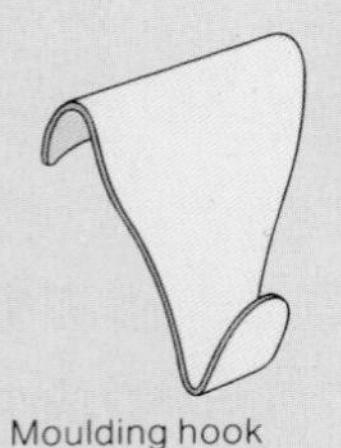

The traditional picture hook, used singly and hung from a picture rail. Suitable for light-weight or medium-weight pictures.

of its height from the top, with the point of the angle on the outside pointing downwards.

Screw the other piece of batten to the wall with the point of the angle uppermost and away from the wall.

Hook the frame batten over the batten on the wall.

FITTING A PICTURE RAIL

A picture rail is a timber moulding fixed to the wall at a suitable height for picture hanging, often level with the top of the door surround.

To fit the rail, mark a pencil line along the walls at the required height using a straight-edge and spirit level. Lengths of rail can normally be nailed direct to the wall with 2½in (65mm) cut nails. If the wall proves too hard – if the nails all bend – use 1¾in (45mm) No. 8 gauge countersunk screws and wall plugs. On a partition wall either nail the picture rail to the studs or use screws with plasterboard fixings (page 233).

Make sure screw heads are countersunk and nail heads are punched well below the surface. Cover the heads with wood filler.

At corners, shape the ends of butting rails in the same way as skirting board (page 256).

Fixing a mirror to a wall

Unframed mirrors are generally 5/32in (4mm) or ¼in (6mm) thick. Some have holes ready drilled for fixing screws. Mirrors without screw holes can be fixed with corner or sliding clips. Framed mirrors can be hung in the same way as pictures, or small, light-weight types can be hung with glass plates.

CHOOSING A MIRROR FIXING

Glass plate
For fixing to the back of the frame and the wall. Wall holes may be round or slotted.

Corner clips
Sizes are available for different mirror thicknesses. If the screws supplied are too short, enlarge holes with a drill and countersink for larger screws.

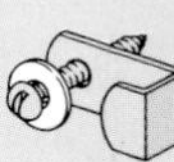

Sliding clips
The best type for fairly large, heavy mirrors. The small clips are for the mirror bottom. The slotted clips can be slid to fit snugly on the mirror, and used on the top and sides.

Adhesive pads
Generally sold with packs of mirror tiles. Suitable for mirrors up to about 12in (300mm) square. The adhesive is on both sides, and pads stick to the mirror and the wall.

FIXING WITH SLIDING CLIPS

The number of clips used depends on the size of the mirror. Use two or more bottom clips (see panel) and two or more slotted clips on the top and also along the sides of the mirror if necessary.

You will need
Tools Drill and masonry bit; spirit level; straight-edge; pencil; screwdriver. Possibly a bradawl or ballpoint refill.
Materials Bottom clips; top clips, with metal and plastic washers; wall plugs suitable for the screw length and wall material (page 232).

1 Use a spirit level and straight-edge to mark a light, horizontal pencil line where you want the bottom of the mirror to lie.

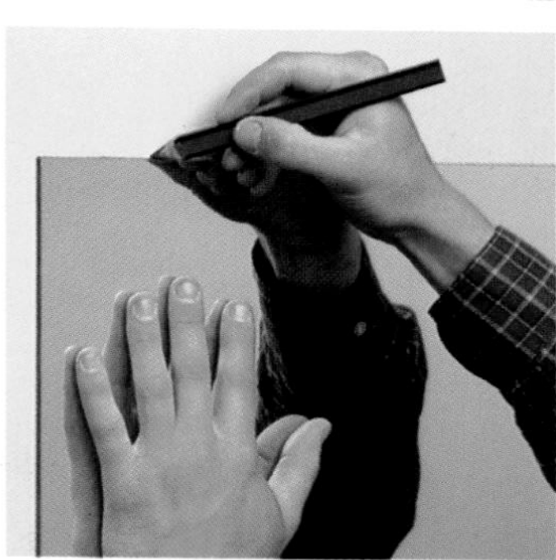

2 Hold the mirror in position against the wall, aligned at the bottom with the pencil line, and lightly mark all four corner positions and the top edge.

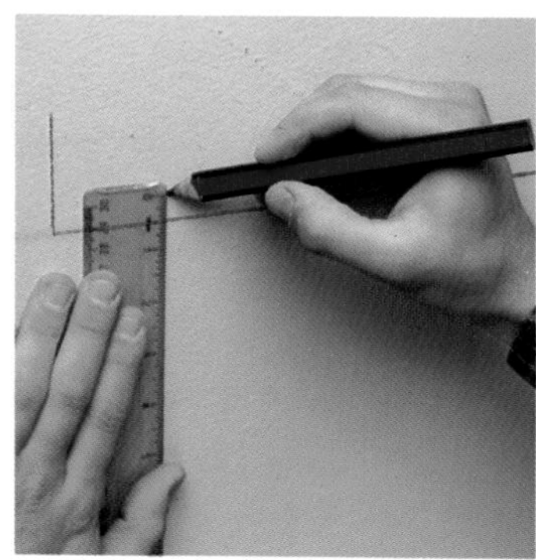

3 Measure the distance between the base of a bottom clip and its screw hole. Then mark the screw-hole position above the horizontal bottom line on the wall, about 2in (50mm) in from the edge mark.

4 Drill holes for the bottom clips and fit plugs into the holes.

5 Fit the clips firmly with the plastic washers round the screw head to cushion the back of the mirror.

6 Measure the distance from the top of the top clip to the top of the screw slot. Then mark this distance on the wall about 2in (50mm) in from each top edge of the mirror.

7 Drill holes for the clips and fit wall plugs. Then screw in each clip with its plastic washer between the clip and the screw head and the metal washer between the back of the clip and the wall.

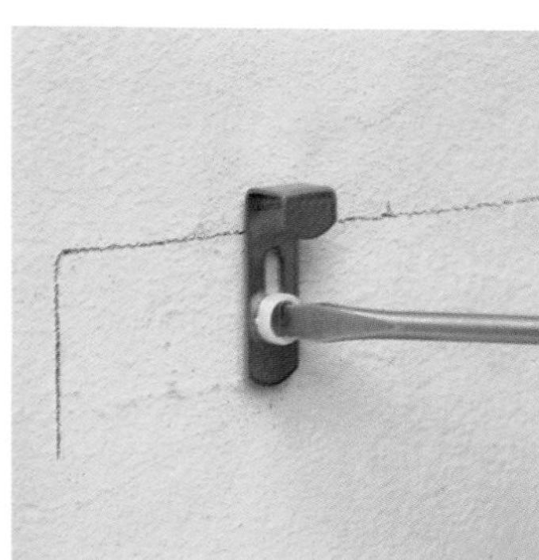

8 Secure the clip with the screw positioned at the base of the slot, with just enough play for the clip to slide when pushed.

9 Fit the mirror into the bottom clips and hold it in position while you slide the top clips into place to grip the mirror.

FIXING WITH SCREWS

Special brass mirror screws are available which have countersunk nylon washers and domed covers in various patterns and colours that screw into the head. But it is cheaper to use ordinary woodscrews fitted into plastic cup washers with white or chrome-finished snap-on head covers.

Use plastic spacer washers between the back of the mirror and the wall. This not only accommodates any slight unevenness in the wall surface, but allows some air circulation behind the mirror and so reduces the risk of damp from condensation. Tap washers are ideal. Do not use rubber washers, which perish with age and could damage the silvering on the back of the mirror.

You will need
Tools Drill and masonry bit; spirit level; straight-edge; pencil; screwdriver. Possibly a bradawl or ballpoint refill.
Materials Four mirror screws or No. 8 or 10 1½in (38mm) woodscrews (use No. 10 screws for larger or heavier mirrors); wall plugs suitable for the screws and the wall material (page 232); four tap washers; four plastic cup washers; four snap-on screw-head covers.

1 Use a straight-edge and spirit level to draw a light, horizontal pencil line on the wall to mark where you want the top of the mirror to lie.

2 Hold the mirror against the wall aligned with the pencil line and mark the position of the fixing holes on the wall. If the holes are too narrow for a pencil, use a bradawl or ballpoint refill as a marker.

3 Drill one of the top screw holes in the wall and fit the wall plug (page 232).

4 Temporarily fit the mirror with the screw partially driven in while you hold the mirror level and check the position of the other screw holes.

5 Drill the other holes and fit plugs in the same way.

6 Finally fix the mirror with a plastic washer on each screw between the mirror and the wall, and a cup washer under each screw head. Do not overtighten the screws – if the wall is uneven the mirror will crack.

7 Fit the screw covers to the screw heads to give a neat finish.

Fixing a mirror to a wall (continued)

FIXING WITH ADHESIVE PADS

Before fixing a mirror with adhesive pads, especially mirror tiles, ensure that the wall surface is flat and smooth. Otherwise tiles will lie at different angles and reflect a distorted image.

If necessary, line the wall surface with sheets of ⅜in (10mm) plasterboard or with plywood. Do not stick mirror tiles over wallpaper or badly adhering paint.

For a single mirror, mark a light, horizontal line on the wall as a guide to positioning the mirror base. For mirror tiles, start with the bottom row and use a level timber batten tacked lightly to the wall as a position guide.

Fix the self-adhesive pads a short way in from the corners of the mirror and peel off the pad backing. Carefully position the mirror and press it firmly to the wall. Positioning must be accurate first time – the mirror cannot be moved for adjustment.

DRILLING A HOLE IN A MIRROR

If you have a mirror without screw holes, it is easiest to get the holes drilled by a glass merchant. To do the job yourself, lay the mirror facedown on a flat surface and use a Chinagraph pencil to mark hole positions at least 1in (25mm) in from the edges. On a large mirror, space the screw holes at intervals of 12in-18in (300mm-460mm).

Use a spear-point glass bit in a hand brace or in a power drill set at slow speed. Start each hole to make only a dimple in the glass. Then surround each drilling point with a wall of putty or modelling clay and fill the reservoir with turpentine, white spirit or paraffin. Keep it full while drilling. Drill until the bit shows through, then turn the mirror over and finish from the front.

Making a hole in an external wall

You may have to knock a hole through a brick wall for a job such as fitting an extractor fan or an airbrick for ventilation.

With a cavity wall you will have to bridge the cavity with ducting or a sleeve liner (facing page) when fitting a fan or an airbrick. You may also have to cut through insulation material in the cavity.

Start the hole by drilling right through the wall. You can hire masonry bits long enough for this – you will need a bit at least 9in (230mm) long for a solid wall, or at least 11in (280mm) for a cavity wall.

You will need

Tools Heavy-duty hammer-action power drill; long and normal length masonry bits; club hammer; sharp cold chisel or bolster; pencil or chalk; safety spectacles. Possibly also: grinding wheel; string; knife.
Materials For a cavity wall: ducting (page 238) or sleeve liner; bagged dry-mix brick mortar.

1 Mark the outline of the hole on the inside wall in the required position. Leave enough space round the hole for the fan casing.

2 Make sure there are no pipes or cables in the way. On a timber-framed inner leaf make sure you will not cut through a stud, see *Locating hidden framework* (page 230). Adjust the outline if necessary.

HELPFUL TIP

If the hole is square, check that it coincides with as many whole bricks as possible to make removal easier – adjust the outline to do so if necessary. If the hole is circular, position it round a whole brick that can be removed from the centre of the area.

3 Transpose the outline to the outside wall. Either measure from points such as a window or soil pipe, or drill through the wall from inside at the centre, and mark from the centre point.

4 If you have not already drilled a starting hole, do so from inside. For a circular hole drill through the centre of the marked area. For a square or rectangular hole, drill through at each corner of the marked area. Withdraw the drill from time to time to cool the bit and remove dust.

5 When you excavate the hole, wear safety spectacles or goggles to protect your eyes from flying dust and debris.

Cut away plaster at the marked area inside, using a club hammer and cold chisel or bolster. Chip away the mortar between the bricks to dislodge them whole.

Work from both sides and sharpen the edge of the cutting tool whenever it begins to get blunt.

6 In a cavity wall, plug the lower section of the cavity with rags to stop debris falling down as you cut through. If the cavity is filled with foam insulation material, cut through it with a knife.

7 When the hole is complete, fit ducting or a liner (for a fan or airbrick) across the wall cavity, if there is one. Check that all parts of the ducting fit properly before fixing it in place with mortar.

HELPFUL TIP

If a wall cavity is filled with granular insulation material, it will start to fall out when you break through the wall. Keep it in place by stuffing glass-fibre insulation blanket round the cavity as you work through.

INSTALLING AN AIRBRICK

An airbrick, which is used to ventilate a wall, is usually either high up near a ceiling or low down under the floorboards. Underfloor airbricks are usually sited at least 6in (150mm) above ground level, and if possible below the level of the damp-proof course.

Some airbricks are made of brick material, others are made of galvanised steel or plastic – but all are one, two or three bricks deep.

The amount of air a brick lets through depends on the type of holes that it has. A single brick with a square grid has roughly 2½sq in (15sq cm) of opening compared with the 8½sq in (55sq cm) of a steel brick with vertical slots.

A damaged airbrick provides a way for rats and mice to get into the house under the floorboards. Replace it as soon as possible – do not block it temporarily as this will decrease ventilation under the floor, and can lead to rot in the joists and floorboards.

1 To fit a new airbrick for extra ventilation, make a hole of the required size through the wall (see left). If the brick is sited below the floorboards, you will be able to work only from the outside.

2 To replace a damaged airbrick, remove the old one by chipping out the surrounding mortar with a hammer and cold chisel.

3 Check the condition of a liner behind the airbrick in a cavity wall (see facing page), and replace it if necessary.

4 Before fitting the airbrick, damp the hole edges with water. Spread brick mortar (page 481) on the bottom brick of the hole and on the top and sides of the new airbrick. A metric-sized airbrick fitted in an old wall will need a thicker surround of mortar.

5 Push the airbrick into place, or tap it in with the brick trowel handle. Trim off excess mortar from the joint and point it (page 484) to match the surrounding mortar joints.

6 Poke a stick or a piece of wire through the openings in the new airbrick to make sure no mortar is caught inside it or is hanging at the back so that it obstructs the flow of air.

7 If the hole goes into a room, make good the inside of the hole with a filler if necessary. Then fit a plastic grille over the opening, using either a contact adhesive or screws and wall plugs.

FITTING A CAVITY-WALL LINER

In a cavity wall, there should be a liner behind the airbrick to stop the airflow being lost in the cavity. Specially made terracotta liners are available from builders' merchants.

Use a straight liner for an airbrick fitted below a damp-proof course. For an airbrick above the damp-proof course, use an inclined liner, which raises the inside hole and stops rain blowing through.

Fitting an inclined liner is a tricky job, best done by a builder.

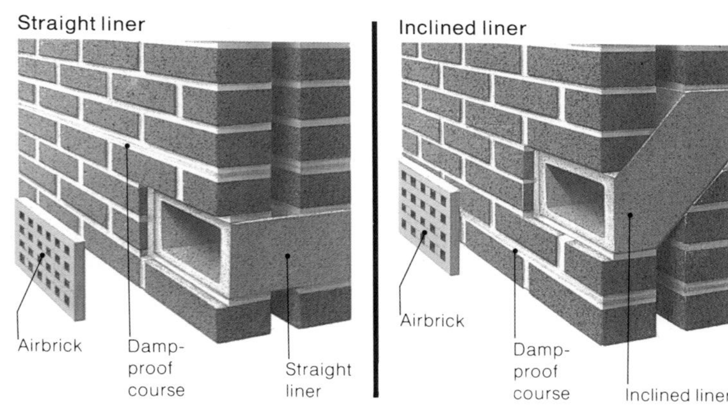

Siting and fitting an extractor fan

An extractor fan draws stale air from inside a room and discharges it to the outside (page 463). Some types are reversible and can be used to blow fresh air into the room.

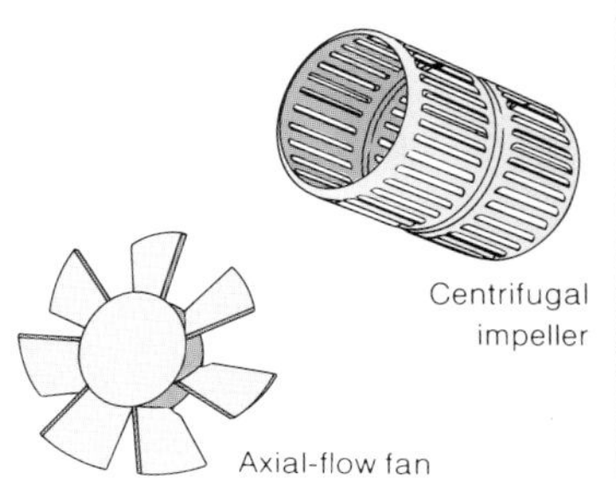

Although fans are made in a range of shapes and sizes, there are only two basic types: axial-flow fans, which contain flat, propeller-like blades, and centrifugal (or tangential) fans, which have a long, cylindrical impeller. There are models of either type designed for mounting in a wall or a ceiling. Only axial-flow types include models designed for mounting in a window.

Wall-mounted fans discharge to the outside through a hole. Ceiling-mounted fans discharge along a duct (a large tube) above the ceiling to a hole in a wall.

Window-mounted fans are normally cheaper and easier to install, but as they tend to have smaller motors, they are more likely to be affected by strong winds than wall-mounted types. This can be an advantage or a disadvantage depending on the wind direction.

All types of fan are driven electrically and controlled by either a pull-cord switch on the fan or a separate wall switch. The electrical consumption is generally low – about 40-100 watts.

A fan with a pull-cord switch is normally the best choice for a bathroom – a wall switch would have to be sited outside the room to comply with regulations for electrical bathroom fittings.

Fans with two or three speeds have complex electrical wiring. Follow the manufacturer's instructions carefully, or get the wiring done by an electrician.

FITTING A WALL OR WINDOW-MOUNTED FAN

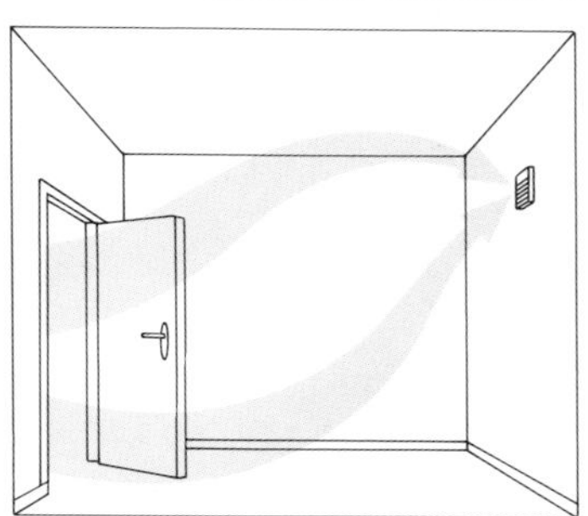

1 Position the fan as high in the wall or window as possible, opposite the door or main air entry point so that air is drawn right across the room. Do not site it where only part of the room will be ventilated – in a window close to a door, for example.

2 If there is a boiler or gas heater in the room, make sure it is independently ventilated. Otherwise, when doors and windows are shut the extractor fan could draw air and fumes from the boiler or heater flue into the room.

3 Make a hole in the wall at the chosen position (facing page), or window (next page) or ceiling, and fit any ducting necessary.

4 Fit the external clamp plate and grille and the inner clamp plate and fan assembly.

5 Prepare a cable route (page 369) to a spot within reach of the fan's flex. At the end of the route fit a mounting box for a flex outlet plate in a bathroom (page 373), or for a switched fused connection unit elsewhere (page 372).

6 Following the maker's instructions, make any electrical connections necessary to the fan assembly before fitting the internal grille and shutter. Some models are wired to a plug-in block.

Use the flex recommended by the manufacturer – usually 1.5mm^2

WALL-MOUNTED FAN

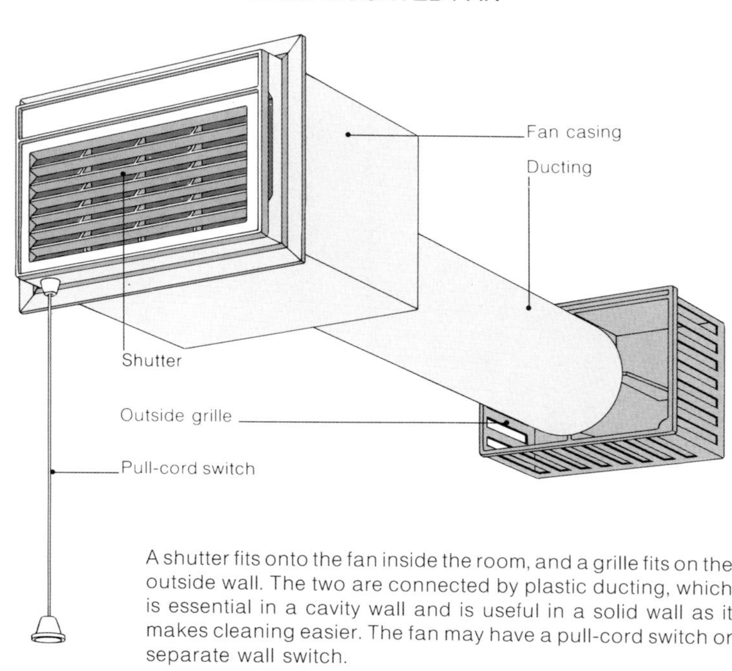

A shutter fits onto the fan inside the room, and a grille fits on the outside wall. The two are connected by plastic ducting, which is essential in a cavity wall and is useful in a solid wall as it makes cleaning easier. The fan may have a pull-cord switch or separate wall switch.

WINDOW-MOUNTED FAN

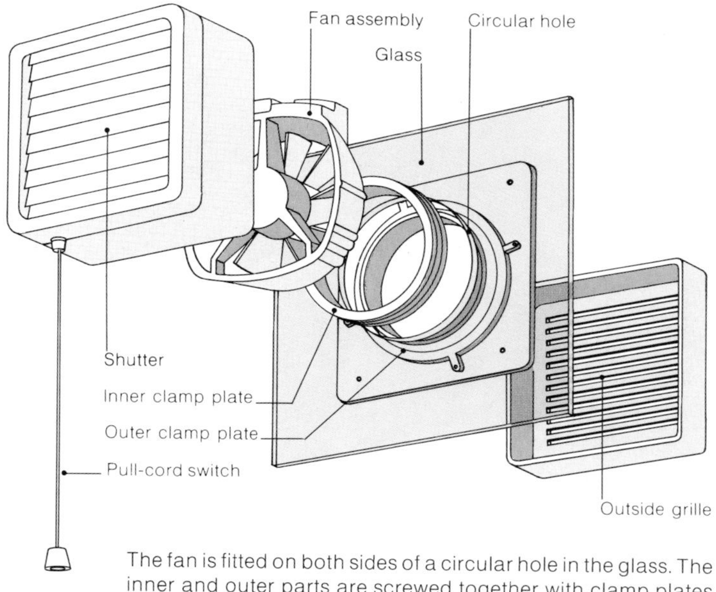

The fan is fitted on both sides of a circular hole in the glass. The inner and outer parts are screwed together with clamp plates on each side of the hole.

Siting and fitting an extractor fan (continued)

PVC insulated and sheathed flex, either two-core for a double-insulated fan or three-core for a fan that needs earthing.

7 Fit the grille and the shutter on the inside of the room.

8 Connect the fan into its electrical supply circuit.

In a bathroom, follow the method described under *Installing a heated towel rail* (page 373).

Elsewhere, follow the method described under *Fitting an FCU for a stationary appliance* (page 372).

FITTING A CEILING-MOUNTED FAN

The fan is fitted in the same way as a wall fan, except that a hole has to be made in the ceiling.

Fit a length of ducting from the ceiling intake to a wall outlet. Ducting is usually made up of slotted-together sections of metal or plastic piping. It should be ordered with the fan, together with a wall grille or roof cowl to be fixed on the outside of the wall or roof.

In an upstairs ceiling, the ducting can normally be taken through the loft space, and held by pipe clips screwed to the joists. In downstairs rooms the ducting may have to be boxed in, or concealed above a suspended ceiling.

A long length of ducting reduces the airflow capacity of the fan – probably by about 10 per cent for each 3ft 3in (1m) of run. An elbow bend will reduce it even more. Take this into account when working out the capacity of extractor fan required (page 463).

CUTTING A CIRCULAR HOLE IN A WINDOW FOR AN EXTRACTOR FAN

Some fans can be fitted in sealed double glazing but do not attempt to cut the hole yourself. The window manufacturer can usually supply a new pane with the hole prepared.

Most window-mounted fans fit into round holes. A circle glass cutter can be bought or hired.

If you do not want to cut a hole yourself (or if you break the glass), buy a new pane and have the hole cut. Then fit it to the window (page 217).

You will need

Tools Circle glass cutter; leather gloves; pincers; screwdrivers; steel tape measure; masking tape or Chinagraph pencil.

1 Use masking tape or a Chinagraph pencil to mark on the window glass the approximate position of the hole required. Make sure the glass border round the opening is wide enough to give room for the fan casing.

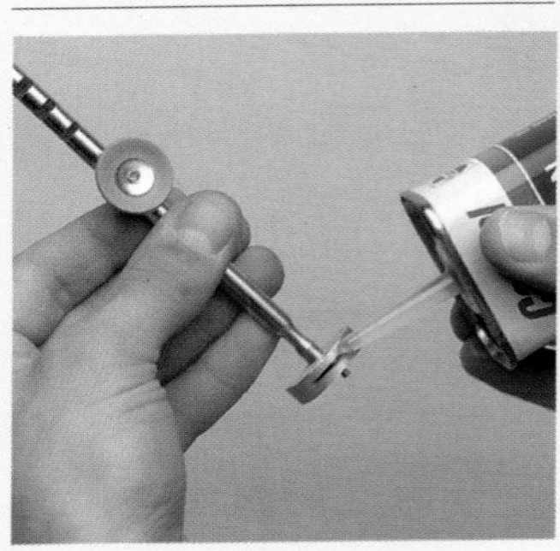

2 Oil the cutting head.

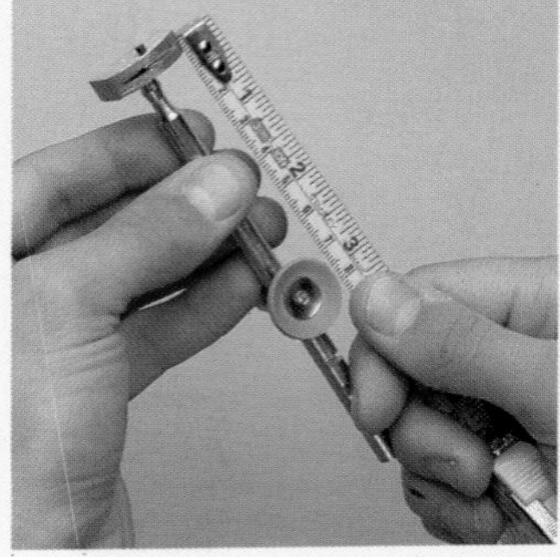

3 Set the cutter and suction pad so they are aligned and the distance between their centres is half the diameter of the hole.

4 Fit the cutter to the glass with the suction pad at the centre of the marked hole.

5 Hold the suction pad steady while you move the cutting head to score a circle on the glass.

6 Reset the cutting head about $\frac{3}{4}$in (19mm) nearer the suction pad. Score a second, inner circle.

7 Set the cutting head at right angles to the suction pad, and score a crisscross of straight lines close together within the area of the inner circle.

8 Wearing leather gloves, use the glass cutter to tap across the scored area (ideally from the back) and start a crack. Then tap out the glass within the inner circle. Lift out larger pieces with pincers.

9 Lift out the remaining pieces of glass from the outer circle.

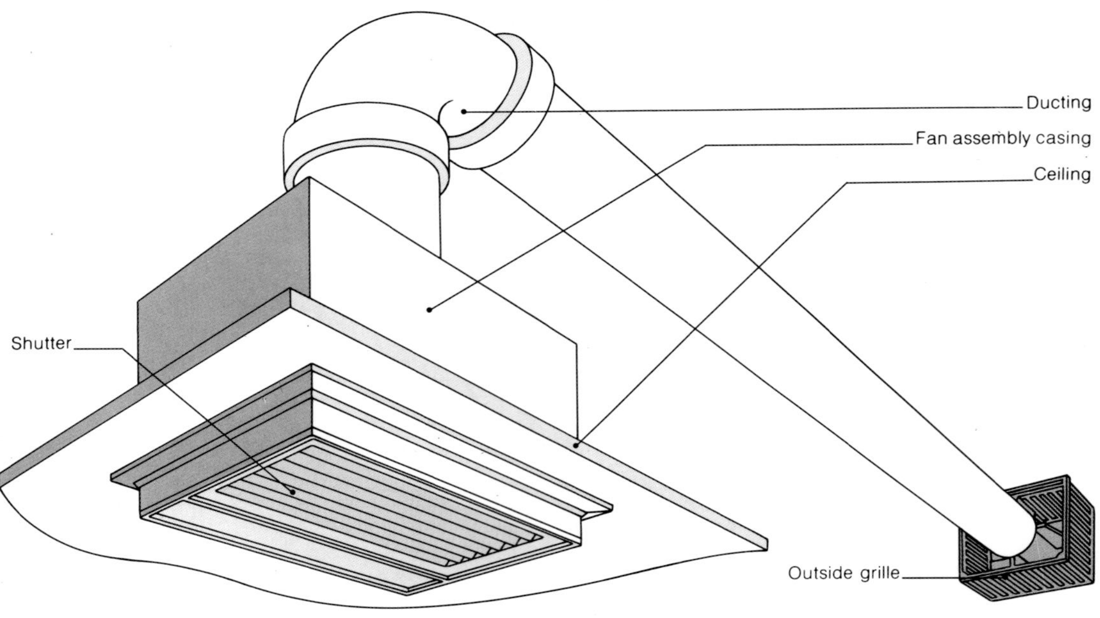

Mounting an extractor fan in a ceiling
The fan is fixed into a hole in the ceiling between joists (or into a false ceiling). The air is drawn through ducting to a hole in an outside wall or in the eaves or roof. If it goes through a wall, it terminates with a wall grille; if through the roof it is covered with a roof cowl.

Upstairs room

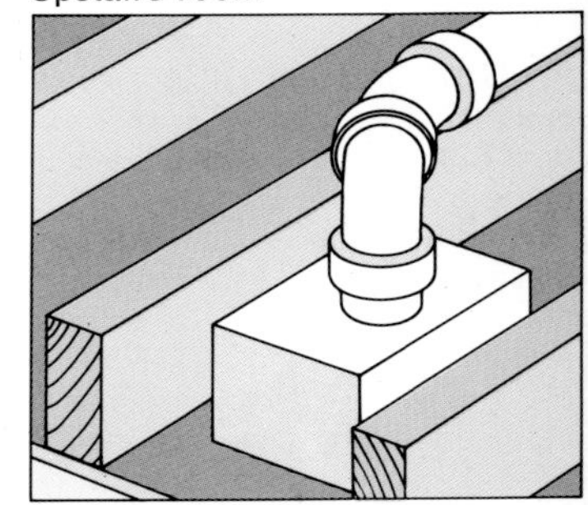

Ducting can pass through the loft.

Ground floor

A false ceiling may be necessary to hide the ducting.

Patching damaged plaster

Large cracks, holes or crumbling areas of plaster, which may result from dampness or general wear and tear, can generally be repaired quickly and cheaply with plaster. For filling small areas of damage, see page 106.

There are three types of plaster that can be used: ordinary, quick-setting lightweight gypsum plaster as used by professional plasterers (mixed with water and applied in two coats – an undercoat and a finishing coat); one-coat DIY plaster (mixed with water); and ready-mixed DIY plaster available as two coats (see chart below).

Ordinary plaster is generally the most economical, but is less convenient to use as it has to be applied fairly fast. DIY plasters allow more working time and are easier to use, but usually cost more, especially for large areas.

Do not repair damage caused by dampness until the dampness has been remedied. If large cracks re-open after repair, get the advice of a builder or surveyor, as they may be caused by structural movement of the building.

If the damage reveals a cavity underneath the plaster, the wall material is likely to be plasterboard or – in an old house – lath and plaster. These call for different types of repair (pages 240–241).

USING ORDINARY PLASTER

You will need

Tools Cold chisel; club hammer; hand brush; large paintbrush or house-plant spray; clean plastic bucket; mixing stick or wooden spoon; length of wood; plasterer's trowel; carrying board (also called a hawk, see page 479).

Materials Undercoat plaster; finishing plaster; supply of clean, cold water for mixing.

1 Chip away loose or crumbly plaster with a cold chisel until you reach firm surface all round.

2 Brush away dust and debris. If bricks or building blocks are exposed, dampen the area with water.

3 Mix the undercoat plaster with cold water in a clean bucket until its consistency is between that of stiff porridge and whipped cream. Use it as quickly as possible after mixing – within 15-30 minutes.

4 Load plaster onto a carrying board. Apply it with a plasterer's trowel held at an angle of about 45 degrees to the wall and sweep it

TYPES OF PLASTER FOR INDOOR USE

Plasters for indoor use are generally gypsum based, and sold in 50kg (1cwt) packs, but smaller packs are usually available for DIY repair work. Cement-based plasters are for outdoor use, or for damp places indoors (page 462).

Working times (the time in which the plaster must be applied before it becomes unworkable) and setting times (the time the plaster takes to become fairly hard) are given as a guide, but vary with temperature. Times are shorter in places where the temperature is high, and longer in low temperatures.

There are different types of undercoat for two-coat ordinary plasters – designed for absorbent or less-absorbent surfaces. The wall material absorbs water from the plaster, and if it is absorbed too fast the plaster will crack.

PLASTER	WHERE USED	DESCRIPTION
Browning undercoat (such as Carlite browning; Blue Hawk undercoat)	On solid, fairly absorbent surfaces indoors, such as bricks or building blocks. The layers should be about $\frac{3}{8}$in (10mm) thick.	A lightweight, quick-setting pink or grey undercoat, mixed with clean, cold water. Apply within 15–30 minutes of mixing. Sets in $1\frac{1}{2}$–2 hours. 10kg (22lb) covers about 16sq ft (1.5sq m) at $\frac{3}{8}$in (10mm) thick.
Bonding undercoat (such as Carlite bonding)	On dense, not very absorbent surfaces indoors – for example, concrete, engineering bricks, or surfaces treated with PVA adhesive, such as laths. Layers should be about $\frac{1}{3}$in (8mm) thick.	As above. 10kg (22lb) covers about 16sq ft (1.5sq m) at $\frac{1}{3}$in (8mm) thick.
Finishing coat (such as Carlite finish; Blue Hawk finish)	On browning or bonding undercoats. The layers should be about $\frac{1}{16}$in (2mm) thick.	A lightweight, quick-setting pink or grey finish plaster, mixed with clean, cold water. 10kg (22lb) covers about 48sq ft (4.5sq m) at $\frac{1}{16}$in (2mm) thick.
Plasterboard finish (such as Thistle plasterboard finish)	On a plasterboard surface (ivory side). Layers should be about $\frac{3}{16}$ in (5mm) thick.	As above. Sets in 1–$1\frac{1}{2}$ hours. 10kg (22lb) covers about 16sq ft (1.5sq m) at $\frac{3}{16}$in (5mm) thick.
One-coat plaster (such as Wonderplast, Bixmix)	On most indoor surfaces, such as bricks, blocks or plasterboard. Can be applied up to about 2in (50mm) thick into cavities.	Suitable for filling or finishing in one application. Mixed with clean, cold water; dries white or pink. Workable for 30–60 minutes. 8kg ($17\frac{1}{2}$lb) covers about $7\frac{1}{2}$sq ft (0.7 sq m) at $\frac{3}{8}$in (10mm) thick.
Renovating plaster (such as Thistle Renovating plaster and Snowplast)	For use in damp conditions (but not below ground level on an unlined background), or slow-drying places. Undercoat layers should be about $\frac{3}{8}$in (10mm) thick, finishing layers about $\frac{1}{16}$in (2mm). Some are one-coat plasters.	A lightweight plaster mixed with clean cold water. Sets in $1\frac{1}{2}$–2 hours. Treat backgrounds with low absorbency, such as concrete or dense bricks or blocks, with a water-resisting bonding aid first. 10kg (22lb) covers about $12\frac{1}{2}$sq ft (1.2sq m) at $\frac{3}{8}$in (10mm) thick.
Ready-mixed undercoat or one coat (such as Polyplasta)	On most indoor building surfaces such as bricks, blocks, plasterboard or laths. Layers can be up to about 2in (50mm) thick into cavities.	A grey paste applied straight from the container. Workable for about 4 hours after application. Slow setting – takes about 24 hours to dry. Can be used without a finishing coat if the surface is to be papered. 10kg (22lb) covers about 8sq ft (0.75sq m) at about $\frac{3}{8}$in (10mm) thick. Available in 2.5kg ($5\frac{1}{2}$lb) packs.
Ready-mixed finishing coat (such as Polyskim)	On ready-mixed undercoat or other plaster surfaces. Layers should be about $\frac{1}{8}$in (3mm) thick.	A creamy-white paste applied straight from the container. Workable for about 4 hours after application. Sets in about 24 hours. 10kg (22lb) covers about 22sq ft (2sq m) at $\frac{1}{8}$in (3mm) thick.

ACCESSORIES FOR USE WITH PLASTERBOARD

Joint compound (such as Gyproc Jointex)	On plasterboard joints and joint tape.	For filling and embedding joints on plasterboard by hand. In powder form; mixed with clean, cold water. Workable for up to 30 minutes. Sold in 10kg (22lb) or 25kg ($\frac{1}{2}$cwt) packs.
Joint tape	On plasterboard taper-edged joints before decorating (ivory side out).	A 53mm (2in) wide paper tape for reinforcing plasterboard joints. Corner tape with metal reinforcing strips for strengthening external corners is also available.
Scrim tape	On plasterboard joints before plastering (ivory side out).	Jute tape 90mm ($3\frac{1}{2}$in) wide for reinforcing plasterboard joints.
Plasterboard primer/sealer (such as Gyproc drywall topcoat)	On ivory-coloured surface of plasterboard.	For preparing plasterboard surface for decoration. Two coats will give the surface protection against moisture.
Coving adhesive	For fixing coving to walls and ceilings. Also suitable as a plaster filler in repair work.	An adhesive powder mixed with clean, cold water. Workable for about 30 minutes. Sets in 1 hour. Sold in 5kg (11lb) packs.

Patching damaged plaster (continued)

upwards to press the plaster to the surface, flattening it slightly at the end of the stroke. Be careful not to press the trowel flat against the surface, or the plaster will pull away when you lift off the trowel.

5 If necessary, build up the damaged surface in thin layers.

Wait for each successive layer to stiffen (but not to dry) before applying the next.

6 Fill the undercoat to within ⅛in (3mm) of the surface and while it is still wet knock off the high points by drawing a length of wood across it. Rest it on the edges of a firm surrounding surface and work upwards with a slight zigzag motion.

7 When the undercoat is dry (about two hours after application) mix the finishing plaster in a clean bucket to the consistency of melting ice cream.

8 Using a plasterer's trowel held at a slight angle, spread the finishing coat on top of the undercoat within about 15-30 minutes of mixing. This is a messy job, so make sure the surroundings are protected from splashes, if necessary.

9 When the finishing coat has stiffened – about 20 minutes after application – continually dampen it with a large paintbrush or houseplant spray while you smooth the surface with a plasterer's trowel held at a slight angle, using wide backwards and forwards sweeps.

USING READY-MIXED PLASTER

You will need

Tools Cold chisel; club hammer; hand brush; filling knife or plasterer's trowel. Possibly also fine abrasive paper or electric sander; face mask and safety spectacles (page 98); large paintbrush; plastic spreader (supplied with skim-coat container).

Materials Ready-mixed plaster. Possibly also: Ready-mixed skim-coat plaster.

1 Chip away loose or crumbling plaster with a cold chisel until you reach a firm surface all round.

2 Brush away dust and debris.

3 Stir the plaster and apply it to the wall with a filling knife or plasterer's trowel held at an angle.

4 Build up deep areas in layers – applied up to 2in (50mm) deep in cavities. Allow each layer to stiffen before applying the next.

USING ONE-COAT PLASTER

Mix the plaster according to the instructions on the packet – generally up to about 1pt (½ litre) per 1kg (2.2lb) of powder – until it is a smooth paste that is just stiff enough to use.

Apply it in the same way as ordinary plaster (page 239), and finish in the same way (step 9 above).

5 If the surface is to be papered, fill the undercoat to the top of the damaged area. When it is thoroughly dry, smooth it with fine abrasive paper or an electric sander (wear a mask and safety spectacles to protect you from dust).

ALTERNATIVELY, if the surface is to be painted, fill the top ⅛in (3mm) of the area with a coat of skim plaster to give a smooth finish. Apply it with a large brush, in upward strokes, then spread it with light strokes. When it begins to dry, smooth it with the plastic spreader supplied.

Filling holes in lath and plaster

Fill small holes and cracks in lath and plaster in the same way as plaster (page 106).

If the hole is large enough to reveal the laths, the method of repair depends on whether the laths are intact or broken.

IF THE LATHS ARE INTACT

1 Paint the laths with a PVA building adhesive and sealer to make the surface less absorbent.

2 Fill the hole with layers of plaster in the same way as patching damaged plaster (page 239). If you are using ordinary quick-setting plaster, use a bonding undercoat plaster rather than a browning undercoat plaster.

IF THE LATHS ARE BROKEN

Either patch the laths or – if the hole is not more than about 3in (75mm) across – plug the gap before you fill it with plaster.

1 To patch the laths, use a piece of expanded metal mesh, cut to the size you need with tinsnips. Wrap it round the laths to bridge the gap between broken edges.

ALTERNATIVELY, to plug the gap, use a ball of newspaper soaked in water and then worked round in a bowl of runny plaster.

DEALING WITH LARGE AREAS

Where a large area of plaster has crumbled away from the laths, cut back the damaged area to a regular shape and patch it with a piece of plasterboard in the same way as repairing a hole in plasterboard (facing page).

Use plasterboard (page 243) of the same thickness as the plaster, if possible. If the plasterboard is much thinner, nail an extra layer of laths across to pack it out so that only a thin layer of surface plaster will be needed. If the plasterboard is thicker, cut away the laths from the damaged area.

Nail the plasterboard patch, ivory side outwards, to the timber framework supporting the laths.

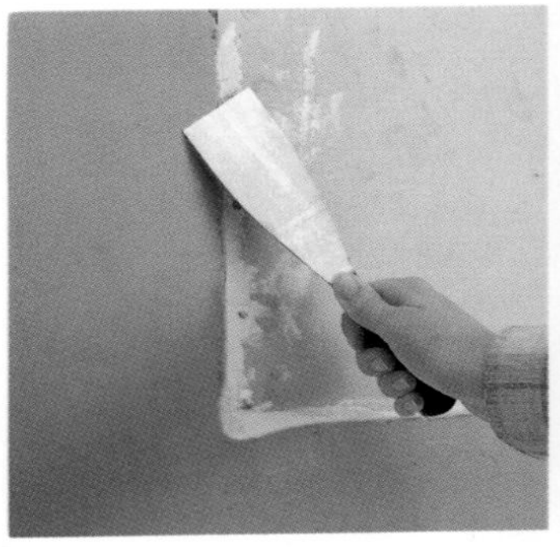

Fill the gaps round the edges with interior filler (page 106) finish the surface of the patch with a coat of skim plaster.

Repairing and reinforcing corners

When filling an external corner with plaster, it can be difficult to get a level surface and a straight edge. The job is easier if it is done in two operations using a timber batten as a guide.

You will need

Tools Cold chisel; club hammer; softwood timber batten 2in × ¾in (50mm × 19mm) and longer than the depth of the area to be filled; straight-edge; masonry nails; hammer; hand brush; plasterer's trowel. Possibly also: carrying board; large paintbrush or house-plant spray; spirit level with horizontal and vertical vials; corner trowel (see step 9); rubber gloves.

Materials Plaster (page 239). Possibly also: length of expanded metal angle beading (see panel).

1 Cut back crumbling plaster to a firm surface and brush away debris from the damaged area.

2 Drive two masonry nails through the batten, closer to one edge than the other, and position them so that they will either be driven into the mortar between bricks, or fit into firm plaster well beyond the edges of the damaged area, to avoid cracking more plaster.

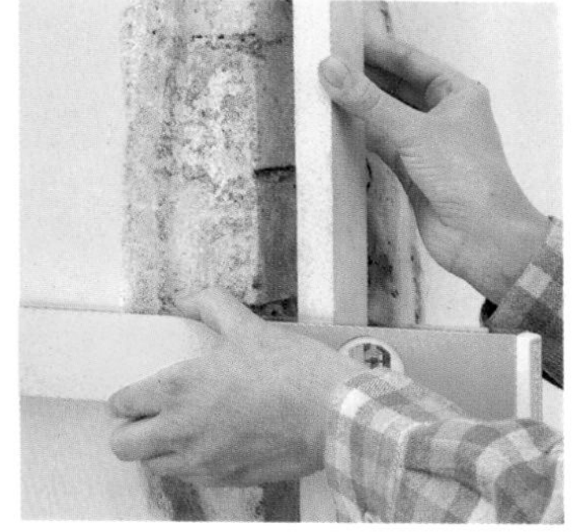

3 Hold the wood batten vertically against the damaged edge with the nails nearer to the inner side.

Use a straight-edge along the adjacent wall to align the batten with the plaster surface at the top and bottom.

4 Nail the batten gently to the wall, leaving the nail heads protruding.

5 Plaster the area with a suitable undercoat or one-coat plaster (pages 239, 240) to align with the edge of the batten.

6 When the plaster has dried, remove the nails and pull the batten carefully backwards from the wall to avoid crumbling the edge of the new plaster.

REINFORCING A DAMAGED CORNER

If an external corner is prone to damage, reinforce it with expanded metal angle beading before plastering the wall.

The beading is formed from two bands of galvanised steel mesh set at right angles to a rounded centre strip. It is sold in lengths and can be cut to the required size with tinsnips and a hacksaw. Treat the cut ends with metal primer – also any areas of the galvanised coating accidentally damaged during installation.

Fit beading against the corner with dabs of plaster about 2ft (600mm) apart on each side. Use a straight-edge and spirit level to make sure it is vertical.

Press the mesh firmly against the wall and check with a straight-edge that the centre strip will not protrude above the plaster surface.

The centre strip can be used as a guide to forming a straight edge when plastering, instead of using a timber batten.

7 Nail the batten to the other side of the corner and then plaster the remaining damaged area in the same way.

8 If using a finishing coat, use the batten in the same way to plaster both sides of the corner.

9 Finishing the edge of the corner is easier if you use a corner trowel, if one is available. Otherwise round it off with a plasterer's trowel. ALTERNATIVELY, before the plaster hardens fully, put on a rubber glove, wet it, and run your fingers down the edge to blunt it slightly.

Repairing holes in plasterboard

Small holes or dents in plasterboard can be repaired in the same way as plaster (page 239).

Medium-sized holes – up to about 5in (125mm) across – need to be fitted with a backing piece to block the cavity at the rear before they are filled with plaster filler.

Larger holes 5in (125mm) or more in diameter, or a severely damaged surface, cannot be satisfactorily repaired with a filler. The damaged section must be removed and a new piece of plasterboard patched in (see page 242).

USING A BACKING PIECE

You will need

Tools Trimming knife; drill and twist bit; filling knife.

Materials A plasterboard offcut; piece of string 6-8in (150-200mm) long; a long nail or wood sliver; interior or plaster filler (page 106) or coving adhesive (page 239). Possibly finishing plaster (page 239).

1 Trim the hole with a sharp trimming knife to give it a clean edge.

2 Cut a backing piece from a sheet of plasterboard offcut. It should be narrow enough to go through the hole, but long enough to overlap the hole by about 1in (25mm) on each side.

3 Bore a hole in the middle of the backing piece and thread the length of string through it.

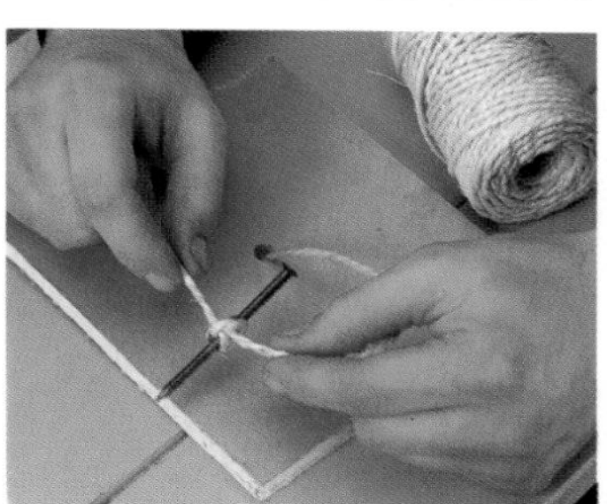

4 Knot a nail or a sliver of wood to one end of the string to anchor it against the back of the offcut. Use the grey side as the back of the backing piece, and the ivory (which will be covered with plaster filler) as the front. Make a loop in the front end of the string so that it is easy to hold.

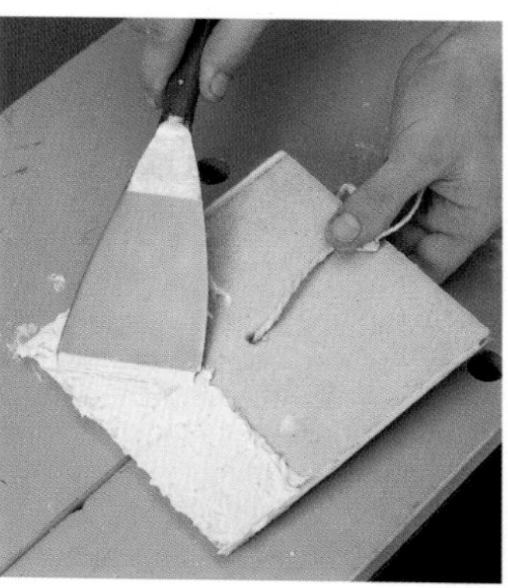

5 Apply some coving adhesive or filler to the front (the ivory side) of the backing piece.

Repairing holes in plasterboard (continued)

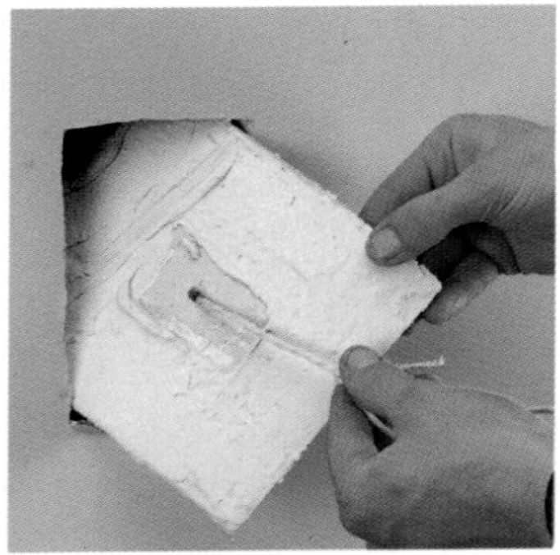

6 Guide the coated backing piece through the hole, then use the string to pull it into position against the back of the hole.

7 Hold the string taut while you fill the hole. Leave room for a finishing coat, if needed to match the surround.

8 When the filler has almost set, cut the string flush with the surface and apply a finish.

FITTING A PLASTERBOARD PATCH

You will need

Tools Trimming knife or pad saw; broad-bladed filling knife or plasterer's trowel; pencil; straight-edge; spirit level; try square; hammer; medium or fine abrasive paper; sponge; steel tape measure.

Materials Sheet of plasterboard or offcut as thick as board on wall (sizes, facing page); two lengths of timber to fit tightly between uprights (studs) – the thickness is usually 2in × 3in (50mm × 75mm) for a stud-partition wall or 2in × 1in (50mm × 25mm) for a dry-lined wall; four 3in (75mm) oval nails; large-head galvanised plasterboard nails; G-cramps; joint tape or scrim tape (page 239); joint compound or plasterboard finishing plaster (page 239).

1 Check that there are no pipes or cables behind the board (page 230). Use a trimming knife or pad saw to cut across the plasterboard from the middle of the damaged area outwards to each side until you reach the timber studs supporting the panel.

2 Use the straight edge of a spirit level to draw the edge line of the stud vertically on the plasterboard.

MENDING DAMAGED CORNERS

Damaged external corners of plasterboard can be repaired with battens and filler in the same way as plaster corners (page 241).

Reinforce the corners with joint tape bedded in joint compound (page 244). Ideally use corner tape, which is reinforced with metal strips. Crease the tape down the centre and fit it so that the metal strips lie inwards, close against the surface of the wall.

The tape gives the corner a clean, sharp edge.

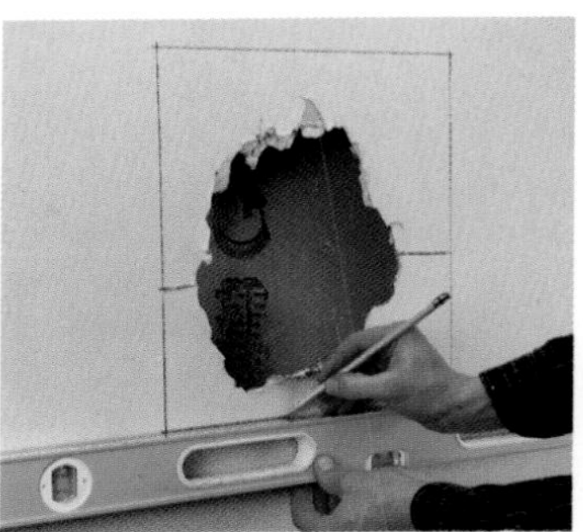

3 Draw horizontal parallel lines across the panel between the studs, about 2in (50mm) above and below the edge of the damaged area. Make sure the lines are at right angles to the studs.

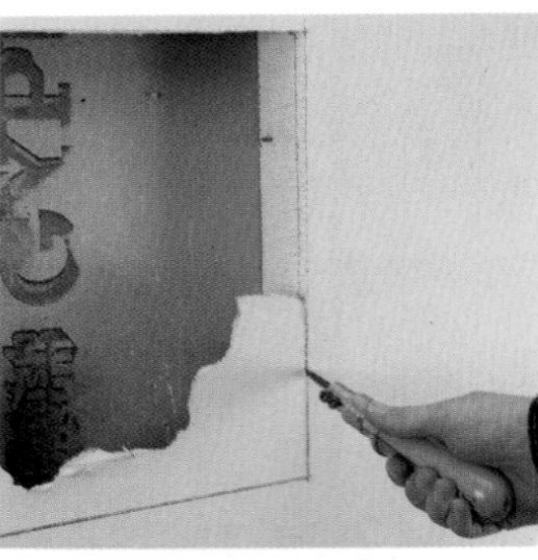

4 Cut out the squared-off section of damaged plasterboard.

5 On each side of the opening, draw a vertical line to indicate half the width – usually about 1in (25mm) of the timber stud, and score it using a straight-edge and trimming knife.

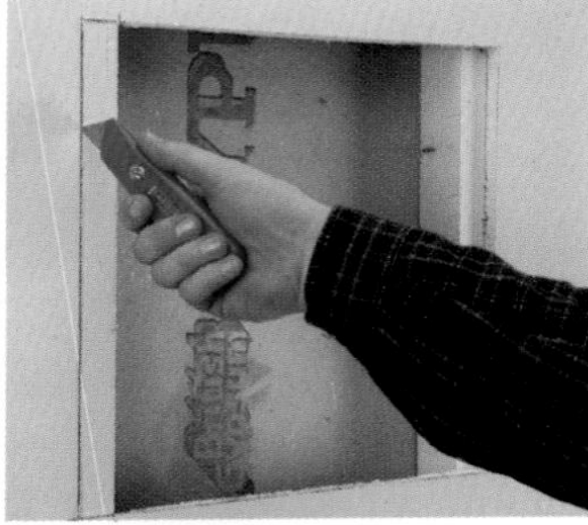

6 Cut back the sound plasterboard down the scored lines to reveal half the width of the studs.

7 Fit the two timber pieces as cross-pieces (noggins) between the studs at the top and bottom of the opening. Position them with the 2in (50mm) thick side outwards so that 1in (25mm) is under the edge of the existing plasterboard and 1in (25mm) is exposed as a nailing surface for the patch.

8 Hold the noggins in position with G-cramps while you drive 3in (75mm) oval nails through the noggins and into the studs at an angle.

9 Measure the area and cut plasterboard to fit. Insert it with the ivory side facing outwards so that it can be plastered or decorated.

10 Nail the plasterboard to the wood surround with plasterboard nails of suitable length and thickness (facing page).

Set the nails at intervals of 6in (150mm), positioned at least ½in (13mm) from the edge of the patch. Sink them into the surface of the plasterboard so they do not protrude, but take care not to damage the outer layer of paper.

11 Lightly sand the edges of the joint with abrasive paper, if necessary, to remove any burring.

12 Using a plasterboard finishing plaster or joint compound, fill the joints and sand them smooth and flat. Then decorate the surface.

DEALING WITH DAMAGE ROUND A SWITCH OR SOCKET

Switch off the mains supply at the consumer unit before patching round a switch or socket. Disconnect the fitting, noting the wiring connections, and remove it.

Whether the socket is seated in plaster or plasterboard, fill small cracks or holes with an interior filler in the same way as filling a small hole or crack (page 106), and larger holes by one of the methods described above. Wait for the plaster to dry before refitting the switch or socket.

Working with plasterboard

Plasterboard consists of a core of aerated gypsum plaster held between two sheets of tough paper. It is used mainly for lining internal walls or ceilings and for building partition walls.

It can be nailed to timber battens or joists, screwed to metal supports, or fixed directly to a masonry wall with adhesive.

There are different types of plasterboard and varying thicknesses. Common plasterboard lengths are 1800mm and 2400mm. The widths are normally 600mm, 900mm or 1200mm. Lengths may be referred to as 6ft and 8ft, and widths as 2ft, 3ft and 4ft, but these are not exact conversions – the imperial sizes are actually all about ½in (13mm) bigger than the actual metric-sized board. It is advisable to use metric measurements when calculating or fitting, as inaccuracies could cause problems.

Common types of plasterboard used for DIY are described in the chart on the right.

Other types include fire-resistant plasterboard (with vermiculite and glass fibre added to the core), and moisture-resistant plasterboard for uses such as roof boarding (sarking) – it has a bituminous wax additive in the core, which is also lined with water-repellent paper on both sides.

When patching plasterboard, take a sample to a builders' merchant to get a suitable match.

CHOOSING PLASTERBOARD FOR DIY

TYPE OF PLASTERBOARD	DESCRIPTION	THICKNESS	LENGTH OF NAIL
Standard wallboard	Has one ivory-coloured face that can be either painted, plastered or wallpapered. The board should always be fitted with the ivory face outwards. The ivory face may have tapered edges for seamless jointing, bevelled edges for a decorative V-joint, or square edges for butt joints covered with a wood or plastic strip.	9.5mm (⅜in) 12.5mm (½in)	30mm (1¼in) 40mm (1½in)
Thermal board	Standard wallboard with a backing of expanded polystyrene. Used as an insulating lining on the inner side of an external wall or on a ceiling. Vapour-check thermal board has a water-vapour resistant membrane between the plasterboard and the polystyrene. Urethane laminate board is similar to thermal board but gives better insulation for a similar thickness, and is more expensive.	25mm (1in) 32mm (1¼in) 40mm (1½in) 50mm (2in)	50mm (2in) 65mm (2½in) 65mm (2½in) 75mm (3in)
Duplex plasterboard	A grade of plasterboard that has a backing of metallised polyester to make it resistant to water vapour. The backing also acts as a reflective insulator when facing into a wall cavity. It cannot be fixed with an adhesive.	According to type	According to type
Thistle baseboard and Gyproc lath	Two types of square-edged board, grey-faced on both sides, used mainly on ceilings as a base for gypsum plaster. When fitting laths the side with continuous paper should face into the room and the side with the jointed paper lipping should go against the ceiling. Not widely available. Gyproc lath is in narrow widths only – 406mm (16in).	Both types: 9.5mm (⅜in) Lath only: 12.5mm (½in)	30mm (1¼in) 40mm (1½in)

HANDLING PLASTERBOARD

Standard plasterboard is generally supplied bound in pairs of sheets with the grey side outwards. The binding tape identifies the type of edge and the size of the boards.

Two people are needed to carry a full-length plasterboard. Carry it on edge to avoid straining the core, and handle it with care to prevent damage to the paper-covered surface or the edges.

Store boards flat. If they warp they will be difficult to fix to walls or ceilings. Stack them in a pile not more than about 3ft (1m) high, on a dry, flat surface. When removing a board from a stack, avoid dragging it, as this can scuff the surface of the board beneath.

MAKING A FOOTLIFTER

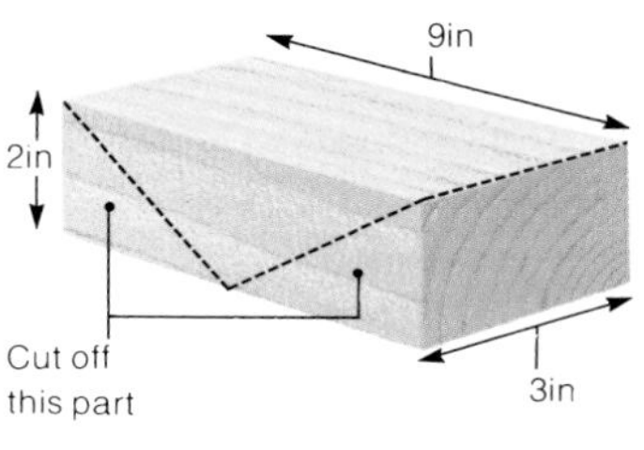

A footlifter, or rocking wedge, is needed to lift boards into position for nailing to a wall. You can make a footlifter from a piece of softwood 9in × 3in × 2in (230mm × 75mm × 50mm).

Draw lines from the top corners of the block to the centre of the base, and square them off with a try square at the ends.

Cut away the two wedge-shaped pieces of waste to create a tool that works like a see-saw. When a sheet of plasterboard is placed on one end, you lift it into place by pressing with your foot on the other end.

CUTTING PLASTERBOARD

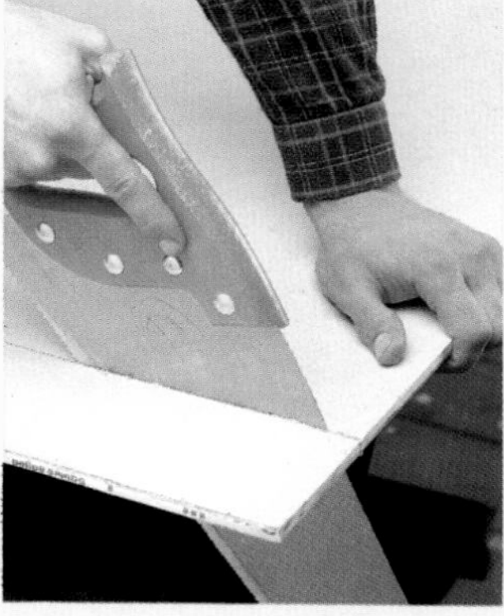

Cut plasterboard with the ivory side upwards, using either a fine-toothed saw such as a panel saw or a trimming knife. Sawing is slower and makes more mess. On a long length, support the sawn ends to prevent the board breaking.

To cut with a trimming knife, use it to score a deep line on the ivory side. Then lay a straight-edge along the back of the board and fold the board backwards to snap the cut open. Finally, cut the paper backing.

Rub sawn or cut edges lightly with medium abrasive paper.

Use a padsaw (page 156) to cut holes in plasterboard to fit switches or mounting boxes.

Filling plasterboard joints

If you are lining a whole wall that will be plastered, painted or papered, the ivory side of the plasterboard should face into the room. In the past, the grey side was used for plastering, but the makers now recommend that the ivory side is used for everything.

Use taper-edged boards to make the jointing as smooth as possible. If you have to cut ivory-faced board, joint the squared edges the same as you would the tapered edges.

Do not confuse tapered edges with bevelled edges, sometimes used as a decorative feature.

Tapered edge

Square edge

Bevelled edge

JOINTING TAPERED-EDGED BOARDS

The joint compound is workable for about 30 minutes after mixing. To begin with mix only a small amount so that you can gauge your working rate. If you mix only about a quarter of a bucketful, you can use it all up completing a number of joints up to the feathering stage.

Before you start jointing, fill any gaps more than about ⅛in (3mm) wide with a stiff mix of the jointing compound.

You will need

Tools Clean bowl or bucket; mixing stick or wooden spoon; plasterer's trowel; broad-bladed filling knife; scissors or trimming knife; sponge; large paintbrush.
Materials Joint compound (page 239); joint tape (page 239); clean, cold water; plasterboard primer/sealer (page 239).

1 To prepare the joint compound, sprinkle and stir the powder into cold water in a bowl or bucket. Measure out the quantities as advised on the packet. Then let the mixture stand for two or three minutes before stirring it to a thick, creamy consistency.

2 Use a broad-bladed filling knife or plasterer's trowel to press the compound into each joint, spreading it in a thin band just over 1in (25mm) wide on each side.

3 Cut a strip of jointing tape to length and while the compound is still wet use the knife or trowel to press it on the joint. Press out any trapped air bubbles, but make sure there is enough compound under the tape for it to stick firmly.

4 After five minutes, apply another layer of joint compound over the tape in a wide band. Smooth it flush with the board surface.

5 Before the compound begins to stiffen, moisten a sponge and use it to feather out the edges into the surrounding surface and to remove excess compound without disturbing the tape.

Rinse the sponge from time to time to prevent any joint compound setting in it.

6 Use a filling knife to cover nail heads with a stiff mix of the joint compound.

7 When the layer of compound on the joint has dried, apply another layer in a wider band – 9-12in (230-300mm) – and feather the edges smooth in the same way.

8 When the surface has dried, finish it for decoration by applying one or two coats of plasterboard primer/sealer over the whole board.

JOINTING AND FINISHING SQUARE-EDGED PLASTERBOARD

To fit square-edged plasterboard, use scrim tape and plasterboard finishing plaster, which is designed for the surface, although there is a risk of cracking at the joints.

Apply the plaster in the same way as ordinary finishing plaster. Use within 15-30 minutes of mixing, after which it is too stiff. This is a tricky job and should only be attempted over a small area – a repair in an old plaster wall, for example.

You will need

Tools Plasterer's trowel; scissors or trimming knife; large paintbrush or house-plant spray; clean plastic bucket; mixing stick or wooden spoon.
Materials Plasterboard finish (page 239); scrim tape (page 239); clean, cold water.

1 Mix the plaster in the same way as ordinary plaster (page 239).

2 Press the plaster into the joint between butted square-edged boards with a plasterer's trowel, and also spread it thinly on each side of the joint to form a band about 3½in (90mm) wide.

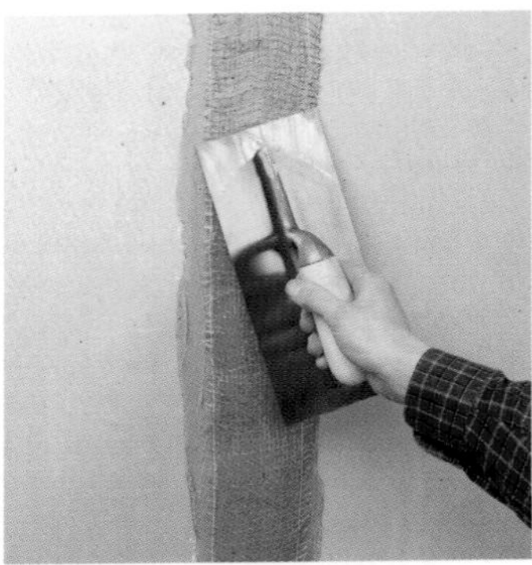

3 Cut a strip of scrim tape to length and press it into the plaster along the joint with the trowel.

4 Apply a second thin coat of the plaster along the joint.

5 When all the joints have been scrimmed, apply plaster to the boarding between the joints to cover the whole area with a thin plaster coat about $\frac{3}{16}$in (5mm) thick.

6 When the first coat has set, apply a second coat of the same thickness, and as it stiffens dampen and polish it with the trowel (page 240) to make it smooth and flat.

Building a non-load-bearing stud partition

A stud partition is made from wallboards fixed to each side of a timber frame made from uprights (studs) fitted between top and bottom rails (head and sole plates).

The board used is generally plasterboard (page 243) fixed with the ivory-coloured side outwards. The instructions given are for 12.5mm (½in) thick plasterboard on a partition no more than 8ft (2.4m) high. Thinner plasterboard would need closer-spaced studs – at 400mm (about 16in) intervals – to make it more solid. A partition higher than 8ft needs studs 4in (100mm) wide.

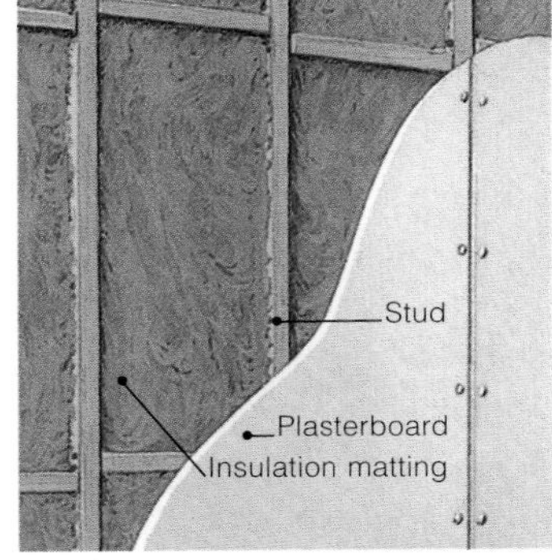

To improve the sound insulation, fit a layer of glass-fibre wool (page 264) at least 3in (75mm) thick between the lining boards. For even better insulation, build the partition with two layers of plasterboard on each side, with the joints between boards staggered. Normally this will prevent the sound of voices pitched at normal speaking level penetrating through the partition.

You will need

Tools Plumb line; a pencil; 3in (75mm) × 2in (50mm) timber offcut; bradawl; hammer; screwdriver; spirit level; power drill and twist bits; portable workbench; straight-edge; panel saw or trimming knife; foot-lifter (page 243); plasterboard jointing tools (facing page); medium abrasive paper. Possibly also: pad saw.

Materials Plasterboards 12.5mm (½in) thick and 1200mm (about 48in) wide; rolls of glass-fibre insulation at least 3in (75mm) thick; sawn timber 3in (75mm) × 2in (50mm) sufficient for head and sole plates, uprights at 600mm (about 23½in) intervals, and cross-pieces; 4in (100mm) nails; 4in (100mm) No. 10 screws; 4in (100mm) frame fixings (page 232) or screws and wall plugs; 1½in (40mm) plasterboard nails; plasterboard joint tape and compound (page 239). Possibly also: ceiling noggins 4in × 2in (100mm × 50mm); a strip of 3in (75mm) wide damp-proof membrane and either expansion bolts (page 232) or screws and wall plugs for solid floor; packing such as hardboard or vinyl tile pieces; timber door casing about 4in (100mm) × 1in (25mm); skirting board; architrave moulding and 2in (50mm) panel pins or oval nails.

FINDING SOLID FIXING POINTS

The partition must be fitted so that the head and sole plates can be securely fixed to solid floor and ceiling timbers. (Locating joists, page 249.)

If possible, position the partition in line with the floorboards so that it can be fixed across the joists supporting the floorboards. But if the partition has to be at right angles to the floorboards, try to position it along the line of a joist.

Where the partition cannot be positioned along a floor joist, fit cross-pieces (noggins) between two parallel joists to support it. Lift the floorboards (page 273) at about 3ft (1m) intervals, and skew nail (page 165) lengths of timber at least 4in (100mm) × 2in (50mm) between the joists.

Position the head plate in the same way, so that it can be fixed either across the ceiling joists or parallel with one. If the plate has to be positioned between two parallel joists, fit noggins between them in the same way as for floor joists, working from the loft or from the room above.

PLANNING WHERE TO FIX THE PARTITION

Before you build a partition wall, get approval from the local authority to make sure that the alterations planned will comply with the Building Regulations. The Building Control Officer will explain what is required.

If a room formed by the partition is, for example, a habitable room such as a bedroom, it must have sufficient window space and direct ventilation. This may mean making an extra window, because a partition cannot divide a window.

If a room formed by a partition is a non-habitable room such as a bathroom, it need not have a window but must have some form of ventilation, such as a wall-mounted extractor fan ducted to an outside wall (page 237).

PUTTING UP THE TIMBER FRAME

1 Use a 3in (75mm) offcut to mark each end of the head-plate position on the located fixing points. Place the offcut at right angles across a joist, or centred along it.

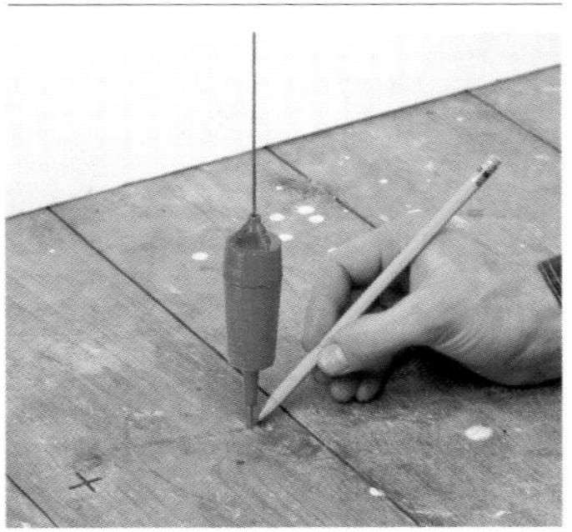

2 Drop a plumb line from each of the marked edges and get a helper to mark each point on the floor as a guide to positioning the sole plate.

THE CONSTRUCTION OF A STUD PARTITION

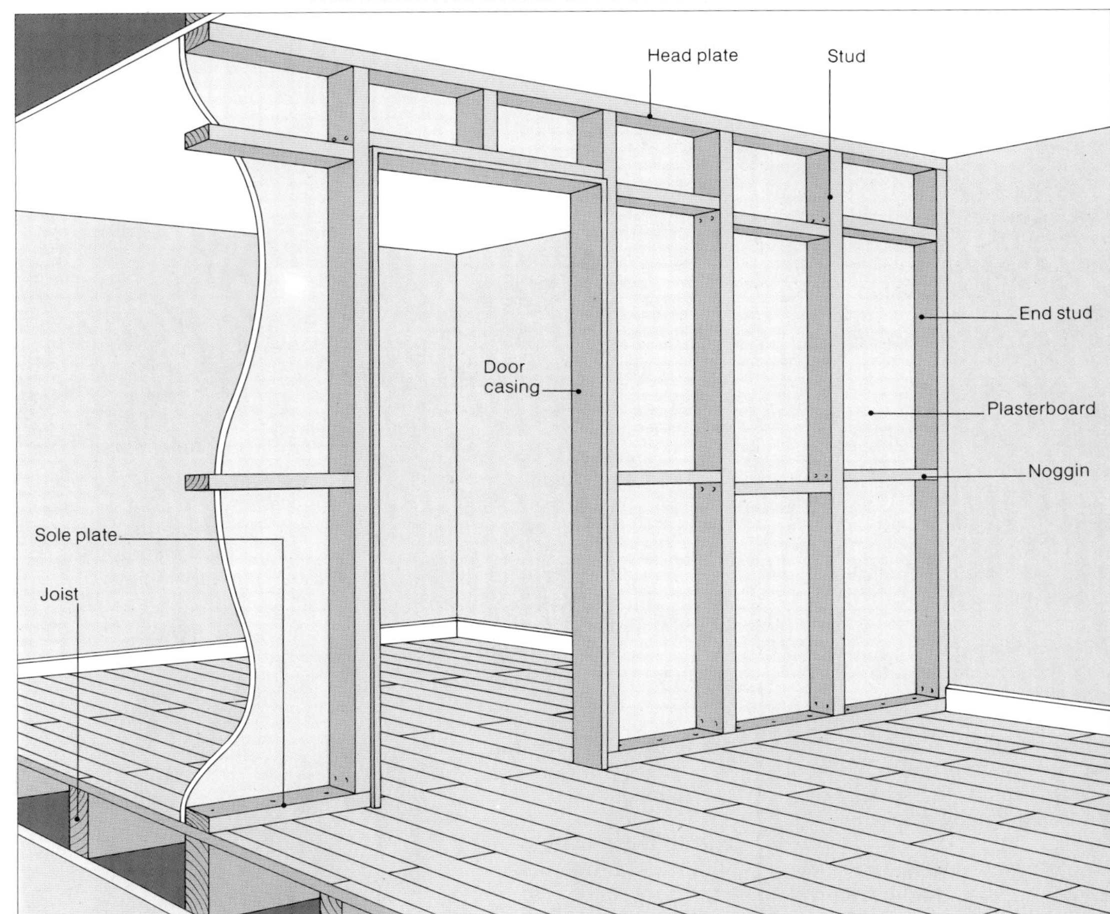

The bottom of the stud partition can be fixed along a joist, as shown in this illustration, or alternatively it can go across the joists in line with the floorboards.

Building a non-load-bearing stud partition (continued)

3 Temporarily fix the sole plate at about 600mm intervals, but do not drive the fixings fully home yet. Use 4in (100mm) nails for a wooden floor, driven into the joists where possible. Use either expansion bolts or 3½in (90mm) No. 10 screws for a solid floor.

On a solid floor, insert a damp-proof membrane between the floor and sole plate to keep the timber from getting damp.

4 Drill through the ceiling into the joists (or noggins) and screw the head plate to them temporarily using 4in (100mm) No. 10 screws.

5 Use a plumb line to check the alignment of the two plates near each end and adjust if necessary. Then drive the fixings fully home.

6 Mark one side of the sole plate with stud positions at 600mm (about 23½in) centres, taking into account the width and position of a doorway (see above).

7 Mark a centre line on the 2in (50mm) thick side of the timber offcut. Place the offcut squarely across the sole plate with the two marks aligned, and pencil in the edge positions for each stud.

8 Measure and cut the studs. They should be a tight push fit between the head and sole plates.

9 If needed, cut a recess in the skirting for each of the end studs, or recess the studs to fit over skirting (or coving) on the adjoining walls.

10 Push each end stud into place against the wall, using a spirit level to ensure each is vertical. If a wall is not true, pack gaps with hardboard or vinyl pieces.

11 Fix each end stud to the wall using either 4in (100mm) frame fixings or No. 10 screws and wall plugs (page 232).

12 Get a helper to hold each of the other studs in position, while you temporarily nail an offcut to the sole plate on one side to hold the stud in place for nailing.

13 Use a spirit level to ensure that the stud is vertical on both the 3in (75mm) and 2in (50mm) sides.

14 Nail each stud on the head and sole plates by skew nailing (page 165) with three 4in (100mm) nails – two one side and one the other.

15 Temporarily mark the stud positions on the floor as a guide when nailing the boards later.

16 Brace the studs with horizontal noggins positioned halfway between the floor and ceiling. Either skew nail them in place, or stagger the position of adjacent noggins so that you can drive the nails through the stud into the end of each noggin.

17 Fit any extra noggins needed for supporting fixtures such as wall cupboards, and mark the noggin position on the stud edges for transfer to the board.

18 Run any necessary cables through the framework. (Routing cables, page 369.)

MAKING A DOORWAY

Buy an interior door and casing before building the partition, because there are various door widths. Measure the height from the floor, not the sole plate.

If possible, avoid positioning a door right beside an adjoining wall, against an end stud.

Fit studs on each side of the doorway, far enough apart to allow $\frac{1}{16}$in-$\frac{1}{8}$in (2mm-3mm) for the hanging of the door (page 126) and for the thickness of the casing round the opening. Fix a noggin across to form the head rail of the doorway, again allowing for the casing.

The door casing should be the same width as the studs plus the thickness of the plasterboard on each side – usually 4in (100mm) over all. If fitting a window above the door, line this opening also.

To complete the doorway, saw through and remove the sole plate at the base of the opening.

LINING THE FRAME WITH PLASTERBOARD

1 Cut each board (page 243) so that it is ½in (13mm) shorter than the floor-to-ceiling height.

2 Fit whole boards first working from one side to the other. Leave narrow-width end boards, or end boards that need trimming to fit a side wall, until last.

3 Fit each board with the chosen face outwards, holding it in position resting on the footlifter.

4 Align each edge of the board midway over a stud, using a plumb line to make sure it is vertical.

5 Press the board tight against the ceiling with the footlifter while you nail it to the timber framework all round the edges and into the noggins between the studs.

6 Fix plasterboard nails at least ½in (13mm) in from the edge of the board, spaced at 6in (150mm) intervals. Drive them home until the head dimples the board surface but does not fracture the paper lining.

7 Use the floormarks and a plumb line and straight-edge to pencil in the position of the stud at the board centre. Nail the board to it.

8 Butt end boards against the wall to cover end studs and any packing. If the wall against which the board fits is out of true, scribe the board (page 188) and cut it to fit the wall contours.

9 Line the other side of the stud-partition framework with plasterboard in the same way.

10 Fill the joints between boards (page 244) according to which plasterboard face is outwards.

11 Fit skirting board round the room if required (page 256). Also fit an architrave (page 257) round the door frame, if necessary, to match other mouldings in the adjoining rooms.

Fitting a plasterboard ceiling

The simplest way to fit a new ceiling is to nail sheets of standard plasterboard (page 243) to the ceiling joists. For joists up to 16in (400mm) apart, use plasterboard 9.5mm ($\frac{3}{8}$in) thick with 30mm ($1\frac{1}{4}$in) galvanised plasterboard nails. For joists up to 24in (610mm) apart, use plasterboard 12.5mm ($\frac{1}{2}$in) thick with 40mm ($1\frac{1}{2}$in) plasterboard nails.

The plasterboard can be fitted over an existing ceiling as long as it is only cracked, not crumbling or sagging. If the ceiling is covered with polystyrene tiles, they can be left in place for extra insulation under the plasterboard. But you will have to locate and mark the joists in the ceiling (page 249), and use nails long enough to go through all the ceiling material and at least 1in (25mm) into the joists.

Take the old ceiling down, if you can (see right). You can then nail direct to the joists, and see any pipes and electric cables. It puts less weight on the joists and also enables you to treat the joists against woodworm if necessary.

It is essential to fit the plasterboard with the ivory side facing downwards, because this is the side that can be plastered, painted or papered, once you have filled the joints and applied a special primer sealer (page 239). Do not leave the grey face exposed.

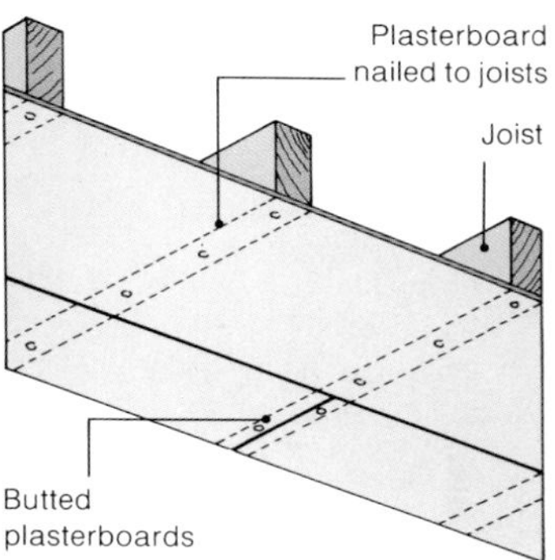

Fix boards with long edges at right angles to the joists, with board ends butted centrally on a joist. Stagger the rows so that adjacent boards do not butt on the same joist, cutting boards as necessary. Boards along the edge of the ceiling may need scribing (page 188) if the wall is not true.

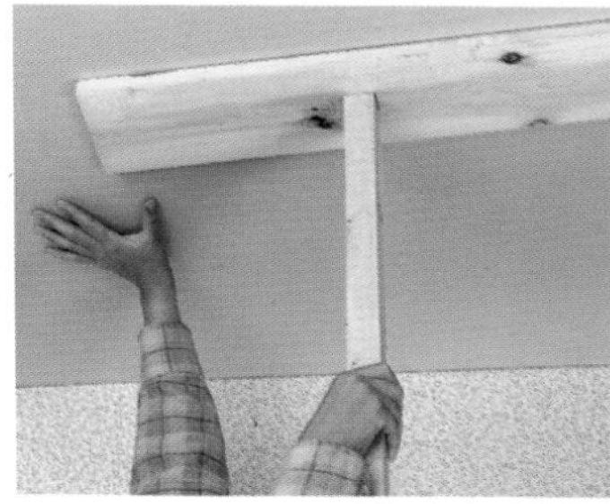

You will need a helper to lift each board into place at one end. To support the board at your end while you nail it, use a T-shaped floor-to-ceiling prop (known as a deadman). You can make it from a length of $1\frac{1}{2}$in (38mm) square timber the height of the room, with a piece of flat timber about 24in (610mm) long – such as a floorboard offcut – nailed to the ceiling end. To reach the ceiling easily and safely, with your head about 6in (150mm) from it, use either the base section of a scaffold tower, if available, or stout scaffold boards resting on two stepladders or stout wooden boxes.

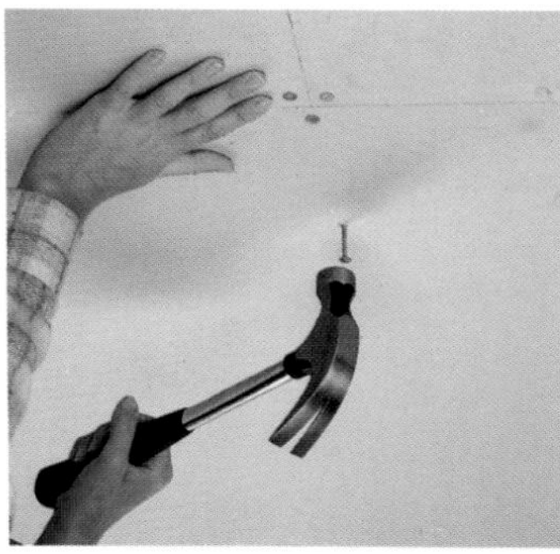

Nail the boards in the same way as for lining a stud partition wall (page 245).

When all the boards have been nailed to the joists, fill the joints between them (page 244) and finish the surface for decoration.

PULLING DOWN AN OLD CEILING

Pulling down an old ceiling is a very messy job (especially if it is lath and plaster). Before you start, clear the room and seal round door, cupboard and drawer openings with masking tape. Wear a face mask and safety spectacles as well as a hat and overalls.

Knock a hole through the ceiling with a hammer; then lever away the old board.

It is easier to break out an old lath and plaster ceiling working from above, if you can easily gain access to the ceiling void. When you have pulled away all the laths, either pull out the old nails or drive them in flush with the joists.

Repairing ceilings and cornices

Modern ceilings are generally made of plasterboard, but lath-and-plaster ceilings are still found in some older houses.

In general, cracks and holes in both plasterboard and lath and plaster can be repaired in the same way as for walls (page 239).

CRACKS WHERE WALL AND CEILING MEET

The simplest way to cover cracks between the wall and ceiling is to fit coving – decorative moulding designed for wall and ceiling joints – using an expanded polystyrene or plaster adhesive, according to the coving material. A less effective alternative is to seal the gap with mastic frame sealant.

Another method is to use plasterboard joint or scrim tape along the crack, bedded in with either joint compound (page 244) or plaster filler (page 106).

DEALING WITH A BULGE IN THE CEILING

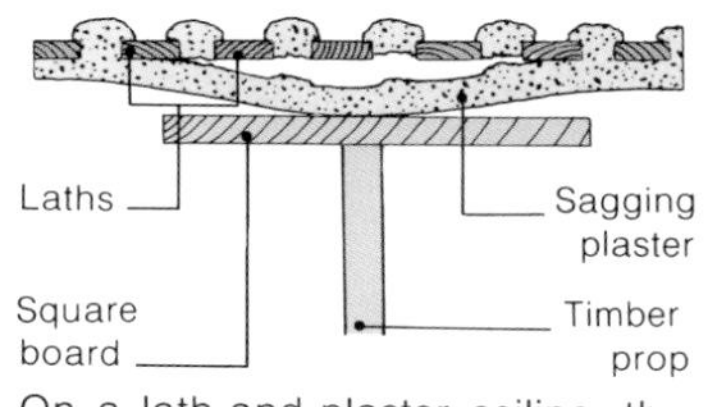

On a lath-and-plaster ceiling, the plaster sometimes sags away from the laths to form a distinct bulge.

Try to push the bulge back into position using a square of chipboard or plywood nailed to a floor-to-ceiling timber prop (a tool known as a deadman).

To re-fix the plaster, you need to reach it from above – either from the loft or by lifting the floorboards in the room above (page 273).

Vacuum clean the area between the joists at the back of the ceiling bulge.

Then pour fairly runny bonding plaster (page 239) over the area. This should bond the ceiling plaster back to the laths, replacing the 'nibs' of holding plaster that have been broken or dislodged.

Leave the supporting prop in place until the plaster has dried.

If this method does not work, or if you cannot get at the ceiling from above, remove the sagging area and patch it with plasterboard (page 241).

A ceiling that sags over a large area should be pulled down and replaced.

RESTORING A CORNICE

Old cornice (ornate decorative moulding) is often clogged with paint – usually distemper, which can be removed with water. If the cornice has been painted with a modern paint, you will have to apply paint remover.

1 Remove accumulations of distemper by soaking a small area at a time with warm water applied from a house-plant hand sprayer. Spray repeatedly for about half an hour until the distemper has been thoroughly soaked.

2 Pick out the paint carefully with an old screwdriver, taking care not to damage the plasterwork.

3 Remove loose material with a brush so that you can see the areas that still need cleaning.

REPAIRING A BROKEN CORNICE

If parts of the cornice have broken away, a repair can often be made with plaster of Paris. Mix the plaster of Paris with water to a stiff paste – only a little at a time as it sets in about three minutes.

Damp the surface of the cornice, then use the plaster of Paris to build up the moulding in layers, using a clay modelling tool or a small knife.

Traditional cornice lengths, ceiling roses and beadings made from fibrous plaster are still available from specialist firms.

CHOOSING A LINING FOR A WALL OR CEILING

Various materials can be used in place of wallpaper or ceramic tiles as a wall or ceiling lining. Some are both decorative and practical, being used to cover an insulation lining or fittings such as water pipes, or to mask a rough or uneven wall. Never use a lining material to mask damp. Get the damp remedied (page 462) and the wall or ceiling dried out before putting up the lining.

LINING MATERIAL	DESCRIPTION AND USE	TYPICAL SIZE	ADVANTAGES AND DISADVANTAGES
Plasterboard	See page 243. Used both as a building board and a substitute for plaster, and also as an insulation lining. There are several different types for different uses.	Length 2400mm (about 7ft 10in); width 1200mm (about 3ft 11in); thickness 9.5mm (⅜in), 12.5mm (½in).	The surface can be given a finishing coat of plaster, or can be papered or painted, but joints have to be taped and filled. A lining of plasterboard on battens will be about 1½in (38mm) thick, so that architraves and electrical fittings have to be remounted.
Decorative wallboards (or wall panelling sheets)	Hardboard or, more expensively, plywood with a patterned or plain face. The facing may be paper, wood veneer, vinyl or a waterproof laminate. Or a pattern may be stove-enamelled onto hardboard. Commonly used in kitchens and bathrooms. Tile patterns are popular, as patterned boards are cheaper, lighter and quicker to fix than ceramic tiles.	Length 2440mm (8ft); width 1220mm (4ft); thickness 3mm (⅛in) hardboard or 6mm (¼in) plywood.	Wallboards can be fixed to the wall with a panel adhesive if the surface is virtually flat. Or they can be stuck or nailed to timber battens, or slotted into plastic or aluminium framing. Boards need to be conditioned before fixing (page 251). Cutting boards to butt them together is difficult to do accurately. Electrical fittings may have to be remounted.
Timber cladding (or V-joint cladding)	Narrow boards interlocked along their length, usually with tongued-and-grooved or shiplap joints. Used to panel walls or ceilings. Boards may be solid timber, mostly softwood, or man-made board faced with wood veneer, plastic or patterned paper. Hardwood, which is more expensive, is also available.	Length 2400mm, 3000mm (about 7ft 10in, 9ft 10in); width 100mm (4in) or 95mm (3¾in), with cover width about 90mm (3½in); thickness 10–13mm (⅜–½in).	Boards are nailed, clipped or screwed to battens. Before fixing, they need to be conditioned to their surroundings (page 253). When fixing, allowance must be made for ventilation behind them in rooms subject to condensation. Electrical fittings may have to be remounted, but can be recessed in the panelling.
PVC cladding	Narrow white, hollow, plastic boards similar to timber cladding. Particularly suitable for walls or ceilings in kitchens or bathrooms. Can also be used outside. Matching coving is available.	Length 2330mm (7ft 6in); cover width 100mm (4in); thickness 10mm (⅜in).	Boards are fitted to timber battens with concealed clips, according to the maker's instructions. PVC profiles can be used to neaten joints and corners. Boards can be cut with a fine-toothed saw or trimmed with a sharp knife. They can be wiped clean with a damp cloth.
Brick slips 	Tiles made of fired clay, aggregate or plastic to simulate bricks. Used for decorative wall covering, laid in brick-bond patterns (page 478). L-shaped tiles are available for external corners. Can be used on outside walls but should be coated with exterior water repellent after fixing.	Length 215mm (8½in); width 65mm (2½in); thickness 13mm (½in).	Slips are stuck to the wall with the adhesive recommended by the maker, or with sand-cement mortar. Wall surfaces must be flat. Joints of even thickness must be maintained between courses, which must be kept horizontal. Clay slips can be cut with a tile cutter, other types with a hacksaw or power-drill masonry cutter.
Stone cladding 	Tiles made from reconstituted stone to simulate quarried natural stone. Used for decorative wall covering, laid in brick-bond or random-bond patterns (page 478). Irregular shapes are available for random patterns. Cladding can be used outside but should be coated with exterior water repellent after fixing.	Lengths 300mm (12in), 230mm (9in), 150mm (6in); width 150mm (6in). *OR* Lengths 200mm (8in), 150mm (6in); width 100mm (4in). Thickness 13mm (½in).	Cladding is stuck to the wall with the adhesive recommended by the makers or with sand-cement mortar (page 496). the wall surface must be flat. Courses of regular shapes must be kept horizontal when fixing. Tiles can be cut with a special grit-edge blade in a hacksaw frame, or a power-drill masonry cutter.
Cork tiles 	Thin squares of cork, available either unsealed, or sealed with a washable or steamproof finish. Used as a decorative wall covering where natural colours and texture are desired. A pack of nine covers about 1sq yd (0.8sq m).	300mm (12in) square; thickness 3mm (⅛in).	Fixed to the wall with adhesive. The wall must be virtually flat. Tiles give some sound and heat insulation. They should be left in the room for conditioning 24 hours before fixing. Not suitable for kitchens or bathrooms unless steamproof. Should not be fixed close to fireplaces.
Expanded polystyrene tiles 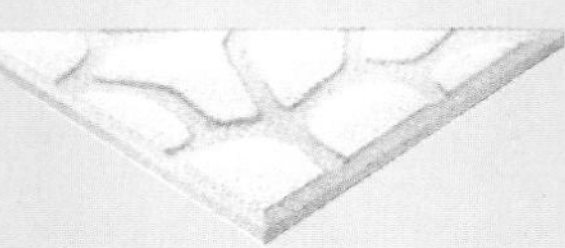	Lightweight white plastic tiles, plain or with an embossed design, used for lining ceilings. Can be over-painted with emulsion, but not gloss, paint. Modern types are self-extinguishing and less of a fire risk than old types, but avoid using where there is a lot of heat, such as less than 4ft (1.2m) above a gas water heater.	300mm (12in) or 600mm (24in) square; thickness 10mm (⅜in).	Stuck to the ceiling with ceiling-tile adhesive or as recommended by the maker. The tiles are a cheap and easy way of hiding blemishes and providing some heat and sound insulation (they cut down the noise leaving the room, but not entering).
Fibreboard tiles and plaster tiles 	White fibreboard (sometimes perforated) or fibrous or fissured gypsum plaster tiles. May be plain or embossed. Some types have interlocking tongued-and-grooved joints. They are much heavier than expanded polystyrene, and are mostly used with suspended-ceiling framing kits.	300mm (12in) or 600mm (24in) square; thickness 13mm (½in) or 19mm (¾in).	Square-edged tiles are fixed with the adhesive recommended by the maker. Interlocking types are fixed to ceiling battens with concealed staples or panel pins. Unlike plasterboard, the tiles can be put up singlehanded. They provide good sound absorption and are thicker and more expensive than polystyrene tiles.

Moving switches, sockets and ceiling lights

Where a wall lining such as plasterboard or timber cladding is fixed to a timber frame, switches or sockets on the wall often have to be moved forward and remounted. Before disconnecting and moving any electrical fitting, switch off the supply at the consumer unit (page 357).

If you have to move a socket, it is a good time to replace a single socket by double or treble fittings, if required (page 368). Or to add an extra socket on a spur of cable (page 372).

FLUSH-MOUNTED FITTINGS

Most switches or sockets are now flush mounted – with only the cover on the wall surface (page 389) and the mounting box (page 368) recessed into the wall.

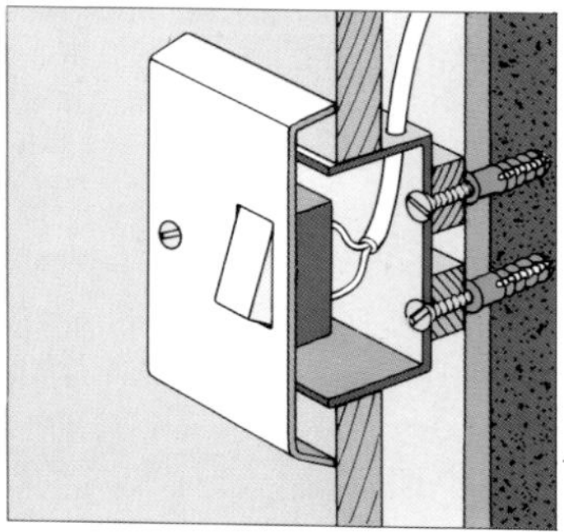

For a flush-mounted switch or socket, the mounting box must be moved forward so that it fully encases the terminal connections and the cover can be re-screwed to its lugs. If you find that a switch has no mounting box, just long screws into the back of the recess, fit a mounting box (page 368).

When moving the mounting box forward, pack the recess behind it with wood as necessary, and screw the box firmly to the wall through the packing into wall plugs in the masonry (page 232). The screws should be long enough to penetrate about 1in (25mm) into the masonry.

You may need to fit battens round the cable outlet to support the edges of the wall lining round the hole cut for the mounting box. The mounting box usually has separate lugs for fitting to plasterboard (pages 368, 370).

SURFACE-MOUNTED FITTINGS

If the switch or socket is surface-mounted with a cable-entry hole in the mounting box, fit battens round the wall outlet to support the box fixing screws. Pierce the lining for the cable.

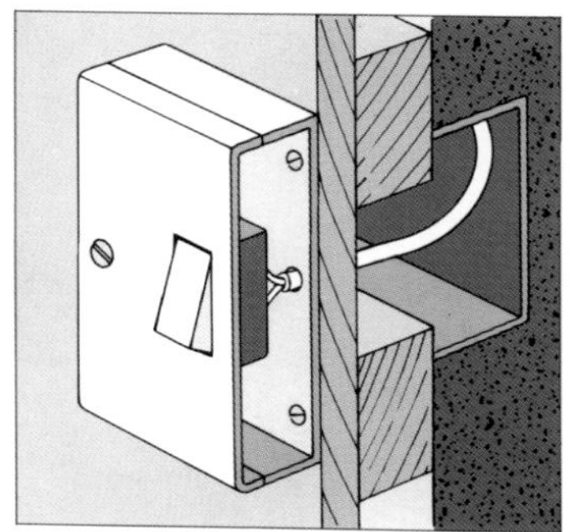

If the switch is mounted on an open frame, replace the frame with a mounting box to encase the terminal connections safely.

If the cable is too short to be pulled forward, fit new cable (page 369) of the right size (page 361). Cable can be carried in special trunking for skirting and architraves (page 371).

CEILING FITTINGS

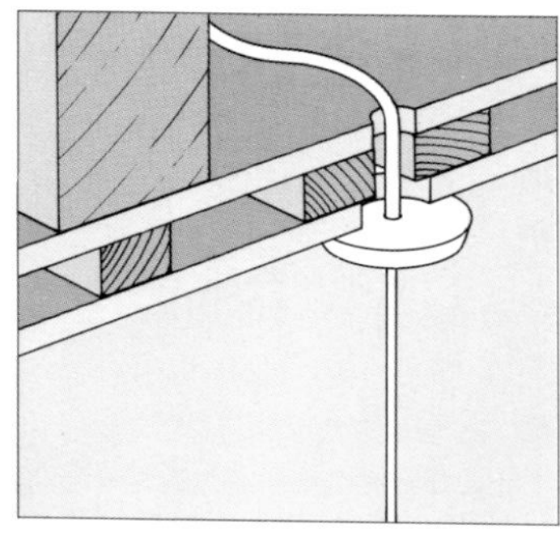

A ceiling light can be dealt with in the same way, with the rose backplate remounted on top of the panelling and screwed to battens fixed on each side of the cable outlet.

The rose position can be altered slightly as long as the cable will not be too stretched and the connections strained. If the cable will not reach the new position, fit a junction box and an extension cable as for adding a new lighting point on a spur (page 390).

RECESSING A SWITCH

With timber cladding, switches and sockets can be left in position and the panelling boxed round them so that they are in a recess.

Line the edges of the panelling with a thin timber frame.

SAFETY PRECAUTION

Do not move a switch or socket by pulling the cable forward and refitting the cover on the outside of the panelling without moving the mounting box forward.

This contravenes safe wiring practice because it leaves the terminal connections unprotected, and is a fire risk.

Locating joists in a floor or ceiling

Timber framework for supporting a partition wall or a ceiling lining must be fixed to solid timber joists in the floor or ceiling.

Joists are parallel timbers about 2in (50mm) thick stretched across from wall to wall to support the floorboards or ceiling. They are usually 16-24in (400-600mm) apart, but on a top floor ceiling joists may be 13½in (350mm) apart.

LOCATING FLOOR JOISTS

Find the positions of joists by noting the lines of nails where the floorboards are fixed to them. The joists are always at right angles to the floorboards.

LOCATING CEILING JOISTS FROM ABOVE

One way to locate the ceiling joists in an upstairs room is to get into the loft above and mark their positions through the ceiling.

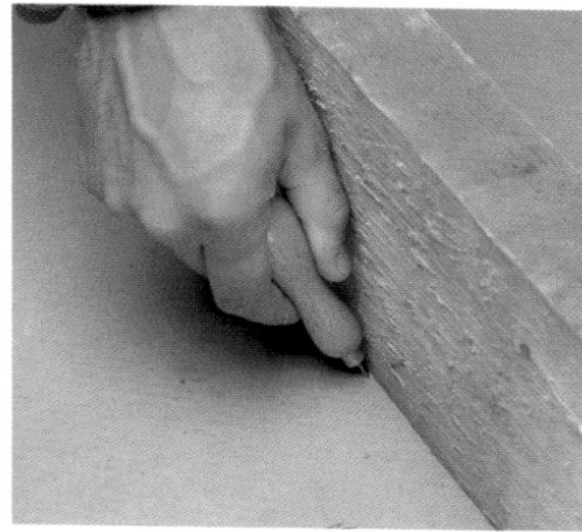

Use a bradawl to poke down through the ceiling on each side of a joist, at both ends. Measure the width of a joist and the distance between joists, and mark the position of another joist at the far side of the area through the ceiling.

From below, you can join up the marks to show the joist positions, then measure and mark the positions of the other joists.

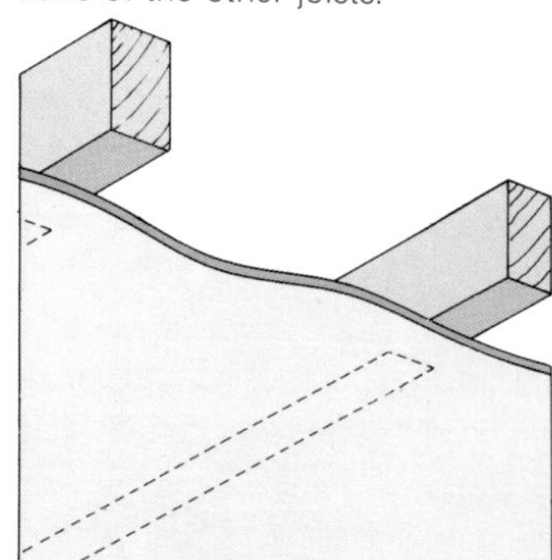

A quick method of marking the position is with a chalked string line (page 135).

LOCATING CEILING JOISTS FROM BELOW

In a downstairs room you will have to find the ceiling joists from below, unless you are prepared to lift the floorboards in the room above. You can get an idea of their positions by lifting only the floor covering and looking for the lines of nails.

On a lath-and-plaster ceiling, joists can be located from below with a metal detector (page 230), available from DIY stores. The detector lights up when it passes over metal such as a nail head, so can be used to trace the lines of nails where laths are fixed to the joists. It will also show the paths of any metal pipes or electric cables running alongside the joists.

To find the joists without the aid of a metal detector, tap the ceiling lightly to detect a solid area, then probe with a bradawl. Use the bradawl to trace the position of one joist, and mark it with a chalked string line. From this, you can measure and mark the other joists, testing each surface with the bradawl.

Dry-lining a wall with plasterboard

If a solid wall has lost its plaster, you can dry-line it with plasterboard, rather than attempt to apply wet plaster. The plasterboard is nailed to a timber frame fixed to the wall. If you wish, you can fix insulating material to the framework under the plasterboard.

A plastered wall can also be dry-lined to cover blemishes or pipe-work, or to fix insulating material.

Thermal board, which has a polystyrene backing for insulation, can be fixed direct to a plastered wall provided the wall is flat. It is held with adhesive and hammer-in fixings (page 232). Ask a builders' merchant for the correct adhesive when buying the thermal board.

Timber framework is needed for an uneven wall, and must be fixed so that its surface is level.

ESTIMATING HOW MANY BOARDS ARE NEEDED

Measure the height of the wall at each end (heights may be slightly different – use the highest figure). Also measure the width at the top and bottom.

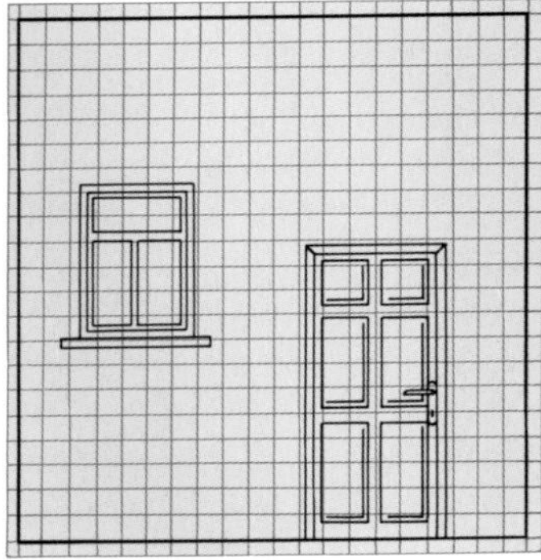

From these measurements draw a scale plan of the wall on graph paper. Then plot in the positions of any doors, windows or other openings that will not be covered by plasterboard.

Mark off the widths of the boards on the graph. Plasterboard is made in metric sizes. Preferably use metric measurements; conversions are not exact. If the widths will not fit exactly, reposition the board marks so that narrow widths fit equally at each end. Allow for separate pieces of board over door frames and above and below windows.

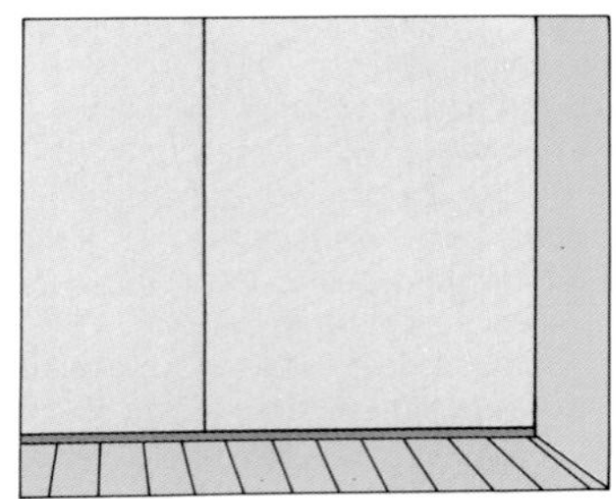

The boards do not have to fit the height of the wall exactly – a gap of about 1in (25mm) is usually left at the bottom for expansion, and may be covered by the skirting board.

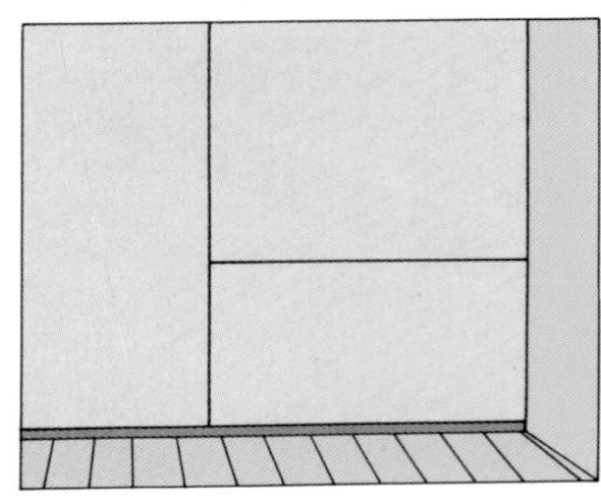

If the wall height is considerably more than the board length, fit the boards in staggered long and short upper and lower panels.

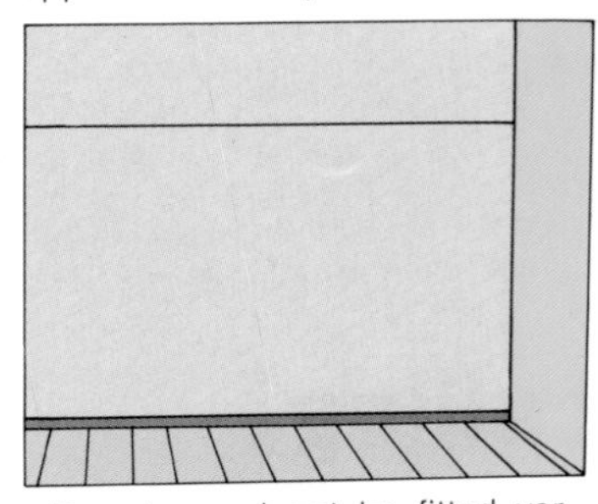

Boards need not be fitted vertically. They can be fitted horizontally if this is more convenient for the wall measurements.

When you have worked out the positions of full boards and board pieces, you can add up the number needed for the wall. Where more than one wall is being lined, estimate each one in the same way.

FIXING THE BATTENS TO THE WALL

Remove any wall fittings such as picture rails and skirting boards (page 256) for later replacement. All switches and sockets will have to be moved forward (page 249), and you will probably have to remove architraves (page 257), and refit them on the lining.

If the wall is plastered, leave the plaster in position if it is sound, but chip off any slight humps with a hammer and cold chisel. But if the plaster is broken or coming away from the wall, chip it all away.

The first job is to find the highest part of the wall surface so the timber framework can be levelled to match it.

You will need

Tools Pencil or chalk; plumb line; steel tape measure; hammer or screwdriver; hand-saw, pad saw; drill and twist bits; portable work-bench. Possibly also: trimming knife; countersink bit; masonry bit.

Materials Sawn timber battens 1in × 2in (25mm × 50mm) – all treated with wood preservative (page 471); masonry nails or hammer-in fixings (page 232) at least ⅜in (10mm) longer than the combined thickness of the batten and plaster (if any); hardboard slivers for packing pieces; plasterboard, plasterboard nails (page 243). Possibly also: Insulation material (page 264) and tacks, drawing pins or adhesive.

1 Lay a framing batten on its side flat against the base of the wall and mark its thickness, with pencil or chalk, along the floor for the whole length of the wall to be lined.

2 Take a batten of the same height as the wall and hold it vertical with its width flat against one end of the wall to be lined.

3 Using a spirit level or plumb line to keep the batten vertical, move it along the wall and mark any position where its base is outside the line marked on the floor.

On a plastered wall, avoid any obvious plaster humps, which can be chipped away.

4 At the outermost floor mark, draw a second line along the floor parallel with the first.

5 Using a plumb line and a timber batten, mark a line along the ceiling in line with the second floor line.

FINDING THE HIGHEST POINT ON THE WALL SURFACE

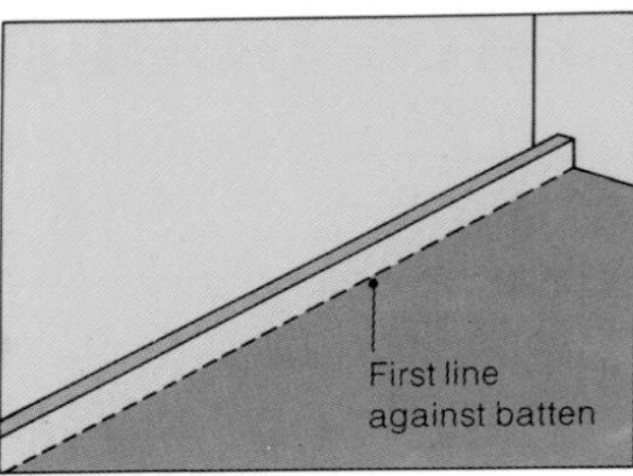

The first line Hold a batten flat against the wall, and draw a line along it on the floor.

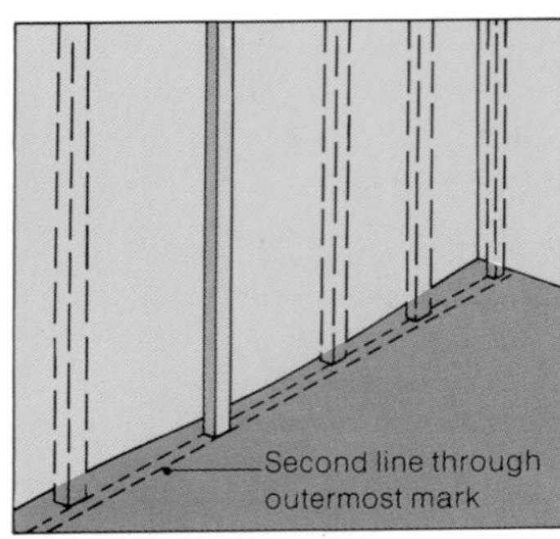

The second line Move a vertical batten along the wall – keeping it absolutely upright – and put a mark on the floor at any place where its bottom end falls outside the first line. Draw a second line, parallel to the first, through the outermost mark. The difference between the two parallel floor lines will probably be only a fraction of an inch (a few millimetres).

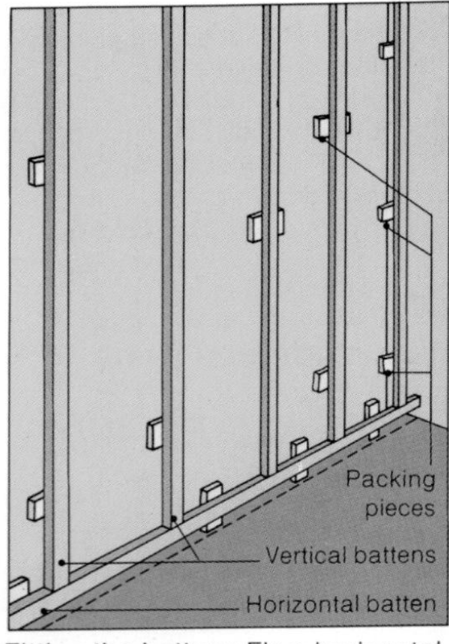

Fitting the battens Fix a horizontal batten to the wall, just above the floor, using packing pieces to align it with the second floor line.

Use a plumb line to draw a line on the ceiling above the second line, and fix a horizontal batten at the top of the wall. Then fix vertical battens to the wall in line with the top and bottom battens. Use packing pieces where necessary.

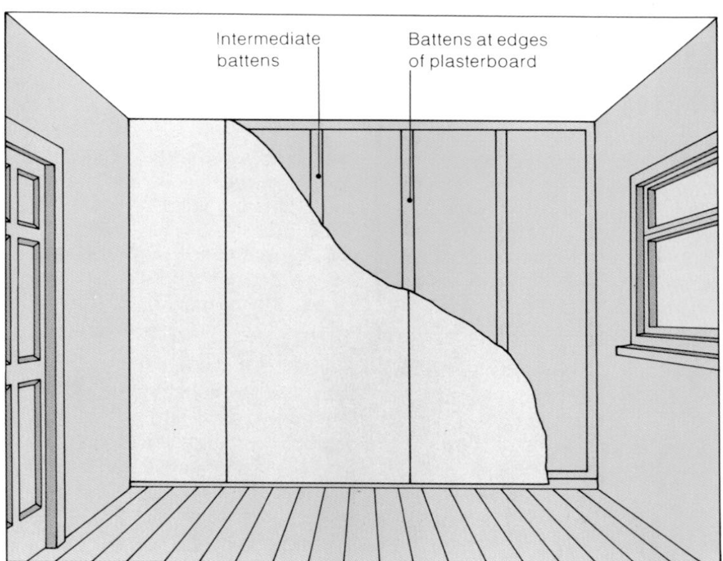

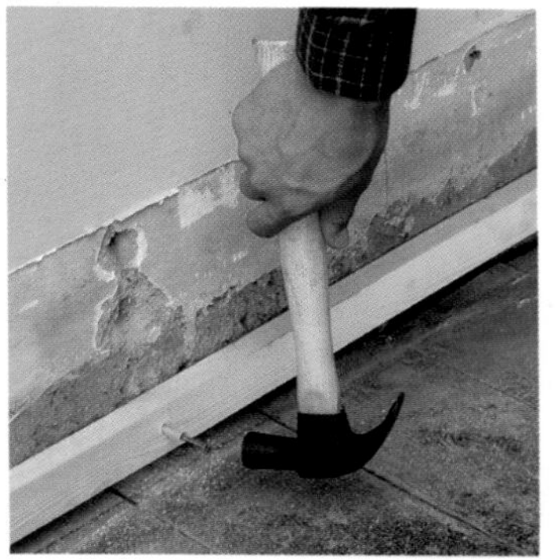

6 Use masonry nails or countersunk hammer-in fixings at about 24in (610mm) intervals to fix a horizontal batten to the base of the wall 1in (25mm) above the level of the floor.

Align the outer edge of the batten with the second floor line, placing hardboard packing pieces between the batten and the wall where necessary.

7 Fit a horizontal batten to the top of the wall, against the ceiling, in the same way.

8 Use a plumb line to check that the two horizontal battens are in line. Adjust the position of the top batten if necessary.

FIXING THE VERTICAL BATTENS

1 Working from your scale plan, draw lines down the wall where the edges of boards will meet. Vertical battens will be fixed centrally on these lines.

2 Mark the positions of the intermediate vertical battens (which will lie at board centres) midway between the edge battens.

3 Cut vertical battens to length to fit snugly between the two horizontal battens.

4 Fit the vertical battens for the plasterboard edges in the positions marked. Before driving the fixings fully home, use a plumb line to check that each batten is vertical and in line with the horizontal top and bottom battens. Pack behind the batten where necessary.

5 When you are satisfied, drive the fixings fully home.

6 Fit the intermediate vertical battens in the same way as the board-edge battens, using packing wherever necessary.

7 Fix battens all round window and door openings. Make sure they align horizontally and vertically with the other battens.

8 If necessary, put short lengths of batten round electrical outlets to support board edges (see *Moving switches and sockets*, page 249).

9 If there are to be any fixtures such as wall cupboards, fix extra battens at anchor points in the required positions. Mark a horizontal line along the centre of the batten and the adjoining studs as a guide for fixings. Transfer it to the plasterboard when fitting.

10 If insulation material is being fitted, tack it in position along the inside edges of battens (use card under the tack if there is no paper lining). Alternatively, use an adhesive as instructed by the manufacturer.

FIXING THE PLASTERBOARD TO THE FRAME

Cut the plasterboard (page 243) to leave a gap of ½in (13mm) between the base and the floor – the board will hang ½in (13mm) below the horizontal batten.

Nail the board to the battens with plasterboard nails in the same way as for building a stud partition (page 245). Then fill in the joints between boards (page 244).

Lining a wall with decorative wallboards

There are three ways of lining a wall with decorative wallboards: fixing them directly to the wall with adhesive (practicable only if the wall is virtually flat), fixing them with plastic or metal framing, or fixing them to timber framework.

A common framing system, used particularly for waterproof bathroom panels, is with PVC or aluminium profiles. The boards slot into the profiles, or channels, which are nailed, screwed or stuck to the wall. Full instructions are usually supplied with the system.

With a timber framework, the boards are normally stuck to the battens. But they can be nailed with panel pins if the board pattern conveniently allows the heads to be covered with filler – for example, in the grooves between tiles in a tiled pattern.

Prepare timber framework for the boards in the same way as for dry-lining with plasterboard (facing page), but use sawn timber battens ¾in × 1½in (20mm × 40mm). The skirting board can be left in place and the wallboard lining fitted above it.

Estimate the number of boards needed in the same way as for a plasterboard lining, but allow for a ¼in (6mm) expansion gap at the top and bottom of the lining. A gap left above the skirting board can be covered with quadrant moulding (page 153). Take up narrow widths of board at corners of the room so that any uneven edges from cut joints will be less noticeable.

PREPARING AND CUTTING DECORATIVE WALLBOARDS

Whatever method of fixing is to be used, decorative wallboards must be conditioned before they are attached to the wall.

Moisten the back of hardboard (but not plywood) wallboards with clean water, using about 2 pints (just over 1 litre) for an 8ft × 4ft (2440mm × 1220mm) sheet of board.

Stack the moist hardboard or dry plywood boards back to back on a flat surface in the room where they are to be fitted and leave them for at least 48 hours. During this time the moisture content of the boards is balanced with their surroundings. Unless you do this, they are likely to expand on the wall, causing bulges and buckling.

Before cutting boards to size, make quite sure the dimensions are correct. Where a board is butted against a ceiling or adjoining wall, you may need to scribe the contours (page 188).

Where a cut board is to be butted against another, you need to get a straight cut to ensure a true joint (although on a grooved board, a gap can be sealed with filler). Clamp a straight-edge batten to the board to act as a saw guide, and make the cut along it.

If cutting with a handsaw (page 156), work with the board face up and cut on the downstroke to avoid damaging the surface. If cutting with a power saw (page 157), work with the board face down, but make sure the surface on which it is laid is clean and smooth. After cutting, use fine abrasive paper wrapped round a sanding block to smooth the cut edges of the board.

FIXING DECORATIVE BOARDS TO THE WALL WITH ADHESIVE

The wall surface should be flat. If it is slightly uneven, the method described should give good adhesion as long as there are no gaps wider than about $\frac{3}{16}$in (5mm) between

Lining a wall with decorative wallboards (continued)

the wall surface and the board.

Remove old wallpaper and paint (pages 103-105) and ensure that the wall is clean and dry. If the plaster is new, wait at least two months until it is thoroughly dry and mature. Seal absorbent surfaces such as bricks by brushing on a solution of building adhesive as a primer according to the maker's instructions – usually a coat of 1 part adhesive to 5 parts water.

You will need

Tools Chinagraph pencil; chalk; plumb line; steel tape measure; straight-edge; timber batten ¼in (6mm) thick; cartridge mastic gun; fine-toothed saw; fine abrasive paper and sanding block. Possibly also: drill and twist bit; pad saw. *Materials* Decorative wallboards; panel adhesive in cartridge gun.

1 Working from your scale plan (see under *Estimating*, page 250), measure and mark the board positions on the wall. Use a plumb line as a guide to dot in the vertical line, then join up the dots using a straight-edge. Allow a gap of ¼in (6mm) along the top and bottom of the lining.

2 Mark each board position on the wall with a number.

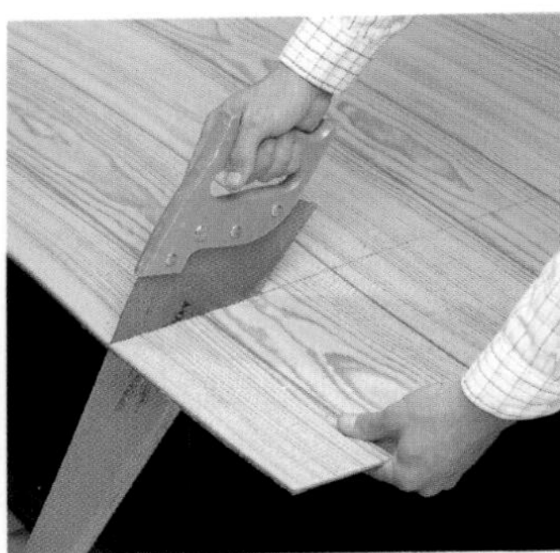

3 Cut boards to size (page 156), marking each with its position number, front and back, using a Chinagraph pencil.

4 If any boards need holes or cutouts for switches and sockets, measure and mark the positions carefully on the board and cut out the hole (page 156). For a shaped hole, cut out a pattern using a piece of card. Make sure it fits before transferring it to the board.

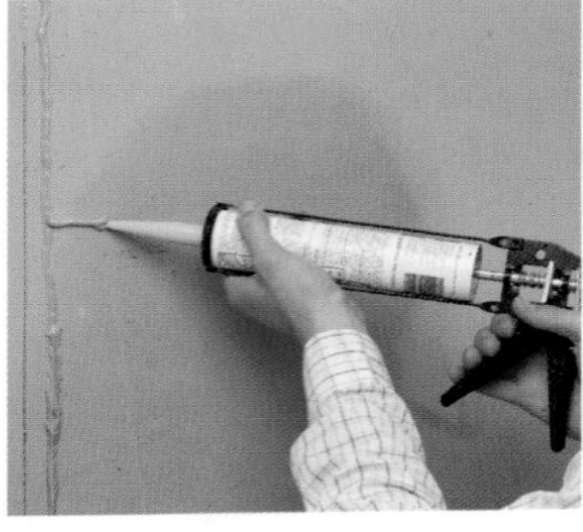

5 Choose the position of the first board to be fixed (either a full-width board butted against a door or window frame if there is one, or a full-width board butted at a corner and ready scribed) and apply adhesive to the wall. Use a cartridge gun and apply in generous strips down the long edges of the board area. Then put broken horizontal strips – with gaps about 6in (150mm) wide – between the vertical strips at intervals of about 16in (400mm) from top to bottom. Work fast, as the adhesive soon sets.

6 Hang a plumb line from the top of the wall as a guide to keeping the board vertical.

7 To allow for a ¼in (6mm) bottom gap, lay a ¼in thick wood batten on the floor against the wall if there is no skirting board – or get a helper to hold it in position on top of the skirting board. Rest each board on the batten as you fit it in place.

8 Press the board firmly to the wall in the marked position, tapping it with the ball of your fist (take care not to get adhesive on the front of the board).

9 Immediately pull the board away from the wall. Some of the adhesive will then have adhered to the board – this will aid firm, fast bonding.

10 Lay the board carefully face down on a clean, smooth surface and leave it for 10-20 minutes until the adhesive feels dry.

11 When it is ready, rest it on the batten again and reposition it carefully. Once it is bonded the position cannot be adjusted. Press it firmly into place in the same way as before.

12 After about 15 minutes, press all over the board surface again in case any part has lifted.

13 Continue hanging boards in the same way to cover the whole of the wall being lined.

14 Fit moulding (page 152–153) over a gap left above the skirting board, if necessary.

NAILING BOARDS TO A TIMBER FRAME

Set panel pins ½in (13mm) from the edges of boards. Pin the board in the middle of a long edge first, then check with a plumb line that it is vertical before pinning the opposite edge.

Drive in the pins working from the centre of each edge to avoid buckling. Use a small nail punch to drive the pin heads just below the board surface. Cover the heads with a spot of matching wood filler.

LINING A WALL WITH BRICK SLIPS

Brick slips (or stone cladding) are stuck to an internal wall in rows in a brick-bond pattern, and the joints between filled in with mortar and pointed in the same way as for brick walls, or left open and painted later.

Remove the skirting board and prepare the wall surface as for decorating. Prime the wall with a mixture of 1 part building PVA adhesive to 5 parts water, following the maker's instructions on the container.

Once you have decided on the bond pattern, lay two or three rows of slips on the floor and check the colour blend. To avoid patchiness, mix tiles from different boxes, as shades can vary.

To check how many brick slips will fit across the wall, mark a timber batten with lines 8¾in (222mm) apart – this allows for a ⅜in (10mm) joint between each slip. Hold the batten horizontally across the wall.

Decide how to arrange any part bricks needed in the first row of the bond, and mark their positions on the wall.

Mark another batten with lines 3in (75mm) apart to show slip heights (including a mortar joint). Hold it vertically against the wall, using a plumb line, to check how many rows can be fitted.

If the height fit is not exact, you can allow a small gap at the bottom of the wall. To do this, lay a flat timber batten as a base for the first row, packing under it as necessary to level it.

Alternatively, allow a deeper bottom row, such as part slips in a soldier course (fitted upright).

Carefully measure and draw a horizontal line near the bottom of the wall as a guide to the top of the first row.

Some slips will have to be cut. Use the cutting method recommended by the slip manufacturer.

Fixing to the wall

Keep separate tools for applying adhesive and mortar. Use a filling knife or pointing trowel for the adhesive, and apply it according to the maker's instructions.

You can use wooden spacers ⅜in (10mm) thick between the slips and fill in mortar joints afterwards. Alternatively, add the mortar beside the slips as you go along, then fill it in along the top of a row before starting the next one.

Check frequently with a spirit level that rows are horizontal. Use the marked batten to check that the top of each row is at the correct height.

If using mortar, point the joints (page 484) as they begin to stiffen. When the mortar has dried, brush the surface to remove any that is loose.

Preparing an inside wall or ceiling for timber cladding

HOW BOARDS FIT TOGETHER

Tongued-and-grooved with narrow V
The commonest type generally 95-100mm (3¾-4in) wide. When the tongue is fitted into the groove of the adjoining board, a narrow V-shaped channel is visible between boards. The cover width is about 90mm (3½in).

Tongued-and-grooved with wide V
The channel formed between the boards is slightly wider than for the narrow V type, but the size and cover width of the board is generally the same.

Tongued-and-grooved with double V
The board has a wide V joint and an extra V groove cut down its centre to give the appearance of narrower panelling. The board is wider than other tongued-and-grooved types – generally 120mm (4¾in) with a cover width of 110mm (4¼in).

Shiplap
Each board has an L-shaped edge and a curved edge. The boards fit together with the overlap over the curve, forming a channel curved along one side. When fitting boards horizontally, place the curved edge at the top. Some boards are wider than average, being 120mm (4¾in) with a cover width of 110mm (4¼in).

Square edges
Square-edged boards can be overlapped either louvre fashion or to form wide recesses. Or they can be spaced to form narrow channels that reveal the background. Thick boards are normally used and they can be fitted to a level surface without using a batten framework.

Boards for timber cladding (page 248) are long and narrow, and are mostly jointed together on their long edges. A number of different types are available (see left).

The boards are fixed to battens, which are fitted to the wall or ceiling at right angles to the board direction. Complete framing round the edges, as used for fitting plasterboard, is not necessary.

Solid timber cladding is usually coated with a clear surface finish or decorative stain (page 167) to protect it from dirt and darkening.

Think carefully before completely lining a small room with cladding – the effect could be overpowering. If you plan to line the ceiling and one or more walls, line the ceiling first.

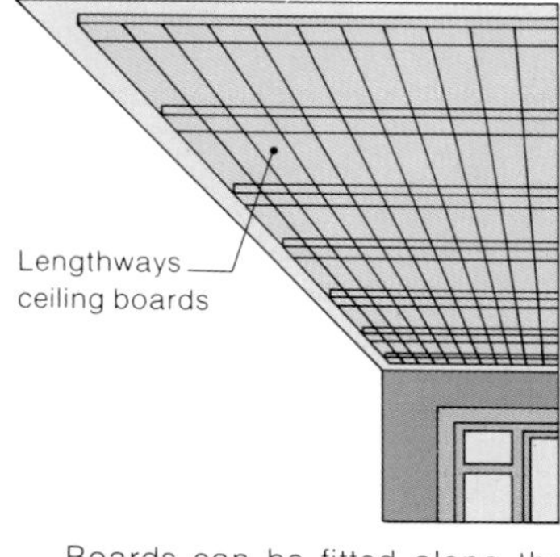

Boards can be fitted along the length of a ceiling, which makes the room appear longer, or they can be fitted across the width, which tends to make the room look wider.

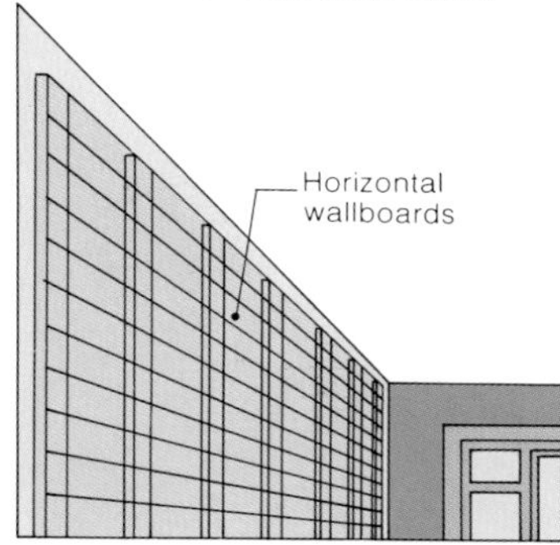

Similarly, boards fitted to a wall horizontally tend to make a room look longer, and boards fitted vertically tend to make it look higher.

BUYING AND PREPARING BOARDS

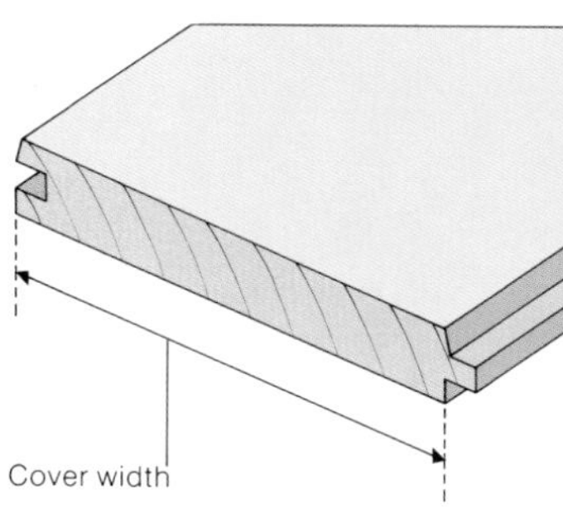

Estimate the number of boards required in the same way as for plasterboard, but remember that because the boards interlock, the actual width of a board is greater than the width it will cover.

When buying boards for cladding the same room, buy them all at the same time and ensure that they are of a similar appearance – characteristics such as knots and grain pattern can vary from pack to pack.

Buy boards about three weeks before you intend to put them up, and stack them flat in the room to be lined. This allows the moisture content to be balanced with the surroundings and lessens the risk of joints being pulled apart by boards shrinking.

FIXING BATTENS TO THE CEILING

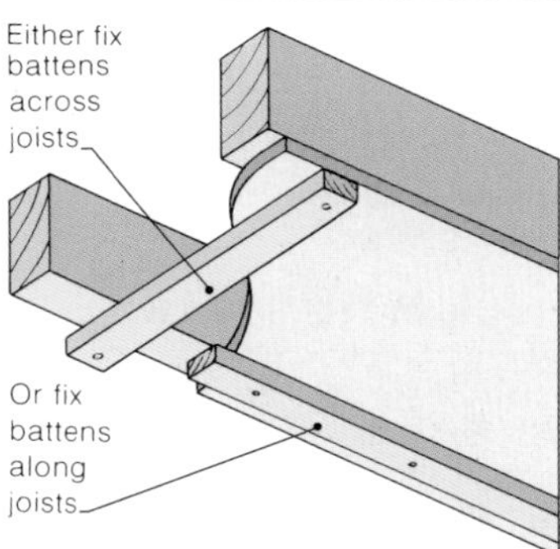

Use sawn timber battens 1½in (38mm) wide and 1in (25mm) thick, treated with wood preservative (page 473). Screw them flat against the ceiling, into the ceiling joists using countersunk screws. The fixings should be long enough to penetrate at least 1in (25mm) into the joist.

If, however, you want the boards to fit at right angles to the joists, position the battens along the centres of the joists.

Fit the battens at 16in-24in (400mm-610mm) intervals. Use a builder's square (page 479) to check whether the ceiling corners are true.

If they are not, use a chalked string line to mark true lines across the ceiling as a guide to positioning the end battens.

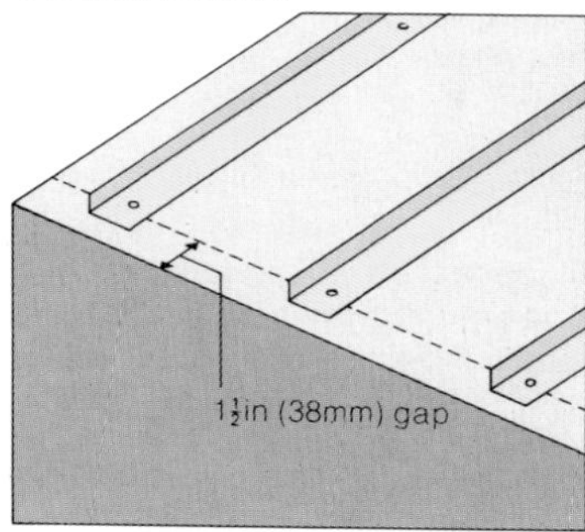

Do not position the end battens right against the wall, as it makes nailing the boards to them difficult. Leave a gap of about 1½in (38mm).

After fitting the first batten, hold a spirit level along it to check that it is

Preparing an inside wall or ceiling for timber cladding (continued)

horizontal. If necessary, pack hardboard pieces behind to level it.

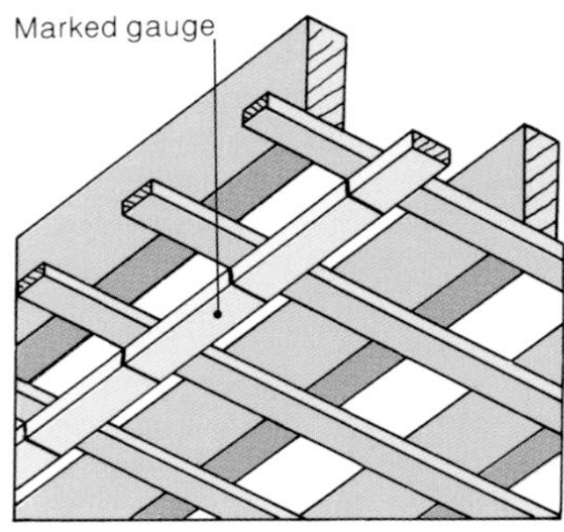

When fitting succeeding battens, use a tape measure (or make a marked gauge) to check that each batten is parallel with the adjoining batten. Hold a spirit level across the two battens to check that they are level with each other, and pack out to level as necessary.

If a batten hangs too deep because of a low point in the ceiling, you will have to plane it down to make its surface level with the adjoining batten.

FIXING BATTENS TO A WALL

Use sawn timber battens 1½in (38mm) wide and ¾in (19mm) thick, treated with wood preservative (page 473). Fix them to the wall with hammer-in fixings or countersunk screws and wall plugs (page 232).

Position battens at intervals of 16in-20in (400mm-510mm) for 9mm (⅜in) thick board, or at 20in-24in (510mm-610mm) intervals for 12mm (½in) thick board.

The fixings should be long enough to penetrate at least 1in (25mm) into the wall.

For vertical boarding, fix the battens horizontally. For horizontal boarding, fix the battens vertically. Skirting board can be left in place unless you want to remove it.

To ensure a flat, level surface for the cladding, find the highest point of the wall (page 250), and mark a guideline on the floor or skirting board for the batten surface.

Fit vertical battens in the same way as for dry-lining (page 250). When fitting battens horizontally, use a spirit level to ensure that each is horizontal.

Check that the batten surfaces are all level with each other using either a spirit level or a plumb line dropped to the marked guideline. Pack behind battens with hardboard pieces where necessary to maintain the surface level.

ALLOWING FOR VENTILATION

In kitchens and bathrooms (and other rooms where condensation is likely) allow for an airflow behind the cladding.

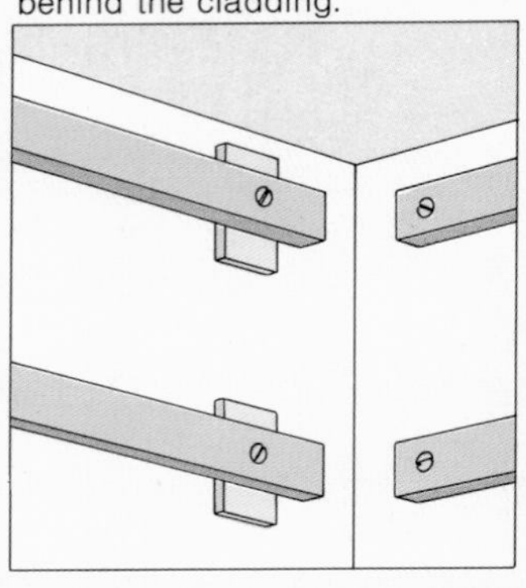

Pack behind horizontal battens with hardboard or thin plywood to lift them away from the wall. Also leave a gap at the top and bottom of the cladding. With vertical battens there is automatically an airflow if a ⅛in (3mm) gap is left at the top and bottom of the cladding.

Use vertical cladding on horizontal battens in kitchens and bathrooms because water can collect in the channelling of horizontal boards.

Stop the cladding slightly clear of a kitchen work surface to prevent it getting wet and 1in (25mm) or more clear of the top of a bath.

Ceiling cladding can be stopped short to give a small gap on all edges, allowing for board expansion and ventilation. Or leave a gap at the long edges of the cladding only to give an airflow between battens.

Lining a wall or ceiling with timber cladding

Do not fit boards right up to wall or ceiling edges. Leave a small gap of about ⅛in (3mm). This allows for board expansion, as well as being necessary where ventilation is needed (see above). If ventilation is not required, gaps can be covered with a strip of scotia or quadrant moulding (page 153) if desired.

Move electrical fittings forward if necessary (page 249), or leave them in position and line round them so that they are recessed within the cladding.

Stop cladding several inches short of a fireplace or a boiler, if you can, and use tiles or plasterboard as a surround. If you cannot stop the cladding short, protect the board edges in some way, such as with a metal edging strip.

When fitting cladding to the wall horizontally, start at the bottom.

You will need

Tools Spirit level; steel straightedge; steel tape measure; hammer; tongued-and-grooved board offcut; mallet. Possibly also: power saw; screwdriver; nail punch with square or thin tip; plane; gauge made from a batten marked with the widths of two or three fitted boards; try-square; push-pin magnetic nail holder.

Materials Cladding boards; nails, clips, screws or panel adhesive (see right). Possibly moulding (page 153); wood filler.

WAYS OF FIXING BOARDS TO BATTENS

Screwing

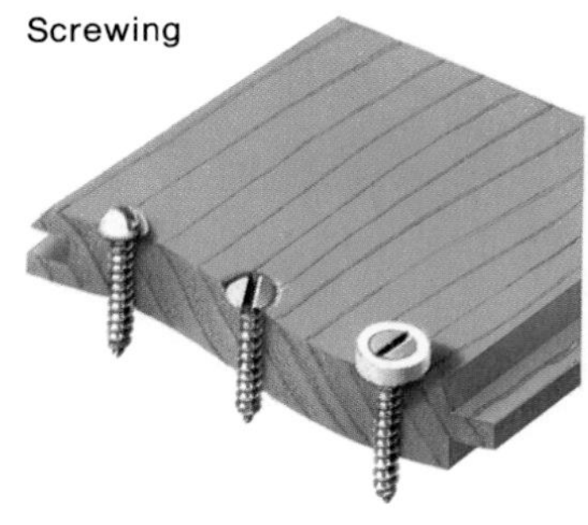

Usually used only for fixing square-edged boards, but advisable where any type of board may have to be removed to get at a covered-in fitting. Use 1¼in (30mm) roundhead or countersunk screws. Drill holes through boards before screwing.

Face-nailing

Suitable for all types of board. Use thin lost-head or oval nails or panel pins 1¼in (30mm) long. Position them at least ½in (13mm) in from the board edge. Drive them straight in, using a nail punch. Leave the head either flush with the surface or just below it.

Nails with heads left exposed should be arranged in a uniform pattern. Where nails are punched just below the surface, fill the holes with wood filler.

Secret nailing

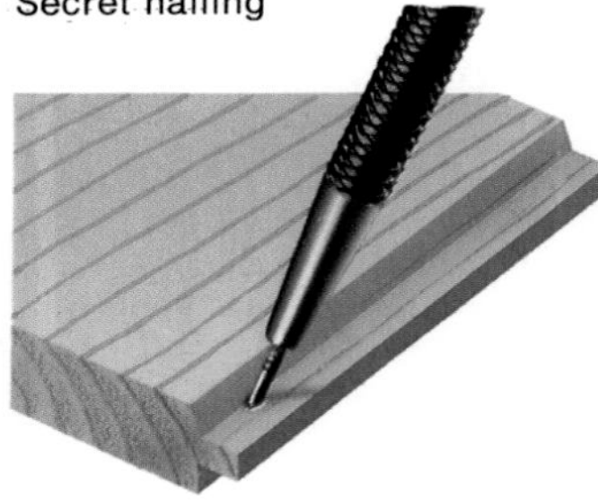

A method of nailing so that nails holding the cladding cannot be seen. Suitable for tongued-and-grooved boards only.

Use thin lost-head or oval nails or panel pins 1¼in (30mm) long. Hammer the nails in at an angle through the tongue of the board.

Use a thin nail punch when the head gets near to the board, and drive the nail in until the corner of the head just protrudes. If the nail is driven in too far, the tongue is likely to split. The nail head is hidden when the groove of the next board is fitted over the tongue.

Nail vertical boards with the tongue on the right if you are right-handed, on the left if left-handed. Nail horizontal boards with the tongue upwards. Some face nailing (left) is needed for boards fitted at the edge of the panelling.

Clip fixing

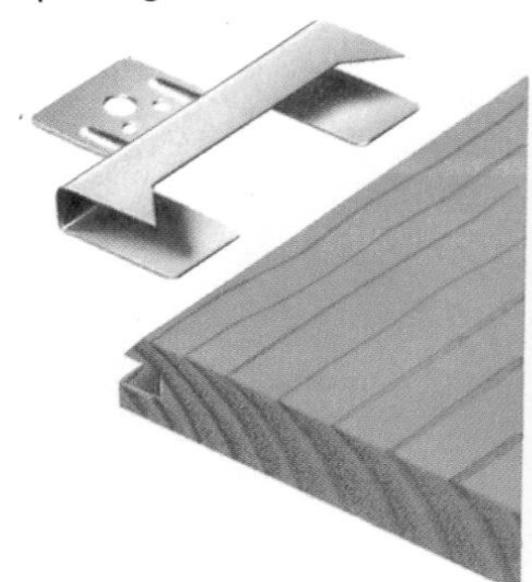

Suitable for tongued-and-grooved boards only. Specially made metal clips fit into the groove of a board and are nailed to the battens. The adjoining board hides the clips when its tongue is slotted into the groove. The last board of a run has to be face nailed or stuck down.

There are several different types of clip. Some makes have separate starter clips for end boards. Use rustproof clips and nails where condensation is likely.

HELPFUL TIPS

When secret nailing thin, dry boards such as pine, drill a pilot hole right through the board to avoid splitting the tongue.

A magnetic nail holder (pin-push), available from some hardware shops, is a useful aid to nailing, especially when working on a ceiling.

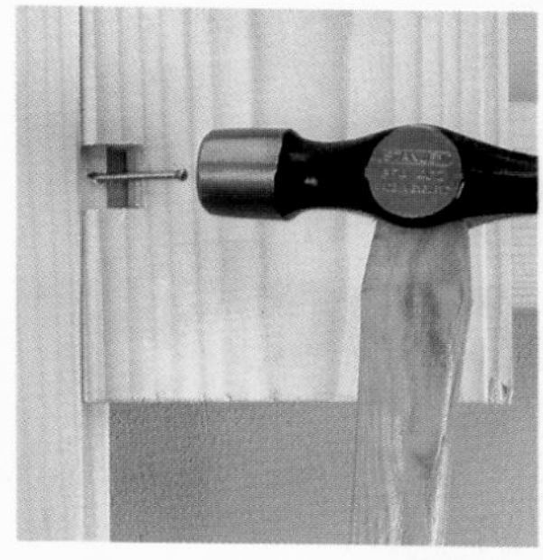

Once you have started an angled nail into the tongue, use a steadying board round it while you drive it through, to lessen the risk of splitting the tongue. Make the steadying board from a tongued-and-grooved offcut. Cut out an area about ½in (13mm) square from the grooved edge of the offcut. Fit the steadying board over the tongue with the cut out round the nail you are driving.

FITTING BOARDS ROUND DOORS AND WINDOWS

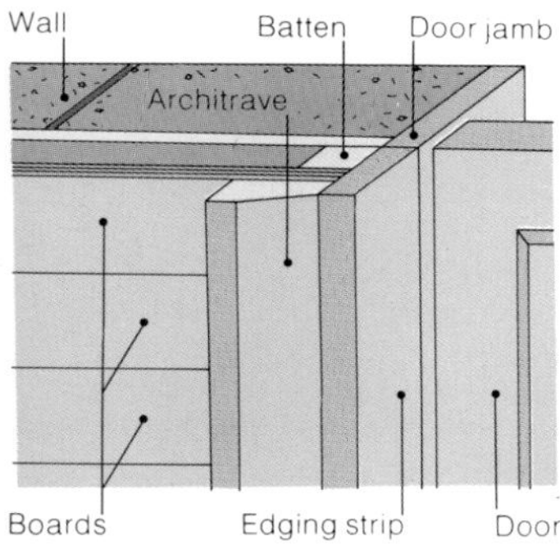

At doors and windows, remove any architraves (page 257). Fit vertical battens alongside a door jamb, leaving enough room for an edging strip to cover the batten and the edge of the end board.

If desired, the edging strip can project in front of the cladding and give an edge to which the architrave can be refitted.

You can fit edging strip round windows in the same way.

Line a deep window recess with cladding boards, with the external corners joined in one of the methods described (see right).

Windowsill boards are difficult to remove. If the edges of a sill project, it is best to cut the cladding to shape to fit round them.

FIXING BOARDS TO WALL OR CEILING BATTENS

1 Position the first board at right angles to the wall or ceiling battens and about ⅛in (3mm) from the edge of the adjoining wall. If using starter clips, plane off the tongue and fit the planed edge towards the wall. Otherwise fit the grooved edge, or the straight lip of a shiplap board, to the wall.

2 For a board fitted vertically to a wall, hold a spirit level against the free edge to check that it is vertical. For a board fitted horizontally to a wall, use a spirit level along the top to ensure that it is level. For a board fitted to a ceiling, use a try-square to ensure that it is at right angles to the batten.

3 Fix the board to the battens using the chosen method (see facing page).

4 Fix the second board, using a straight-edge to check the ends are aligned with the first board.

5 Check that the board edge is straight in the same way as before. On a ceiling, use a gauge marked with fitted-board widths to check near each end that the first and second boards are parallel.

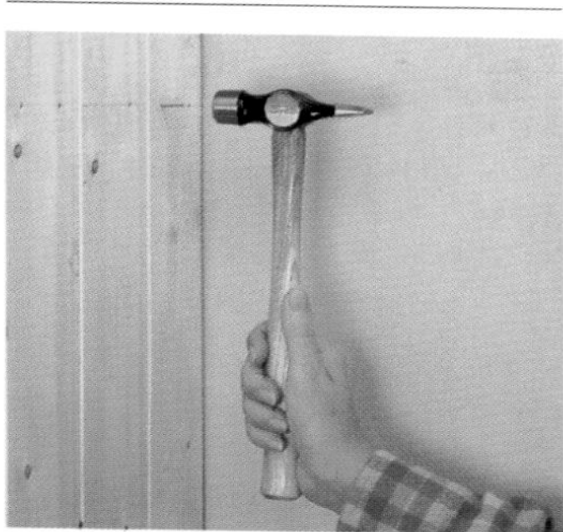

6 Continue fitting boards in the same way. The last board may have to be trimmed to fit the remaining space. When trimming, allow for a ⅛in (3mm) gap against the wall. If using clips or secret nailing, secure the last board with either panel adhesive or by face nailing.

JOINING BOARDS LENGTHWAYS

Boards are usually long enough to be used in one length for vertical panelling on walls. When fitted lengthways on a ceiling or horizontally on walls, however, two boards may have to be butted against one another end to end.

When butting boards end to end, cut the ends square if necessary, and make the joint over a batten. Joints will be less noticeable if they are staggered at random rather than fitted to a regular pattern.

JOINING BOARDS AT CORNERS

Where boards meet at corners, they have to be arranged to form a neat joint. There are several ways this can be done, depending whether the corner is internal or external (at a chimney breast, for example).

Internal corners

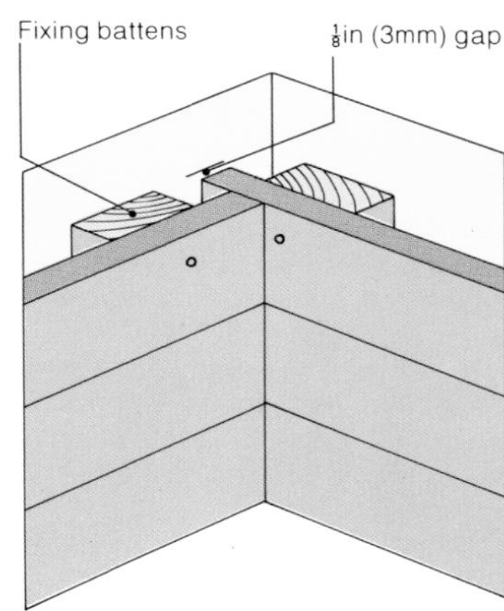

For horizontal boarding, fit one line of cladding into the corner, leaving a gap of about ⅛in (3mm) at the wall. Butt the cladding on the adjoining wall against it. Joints can be covered with quadrant moulding (page 153) if desired.

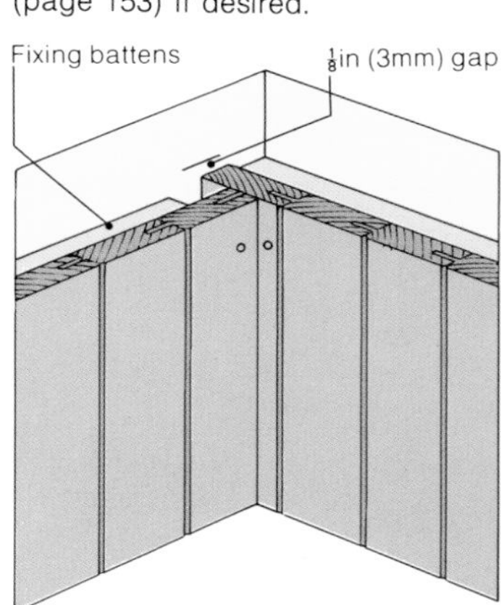

Vertical boarding is fitted into the corner in the same way as horizontal, with the cladding butted.

External corners

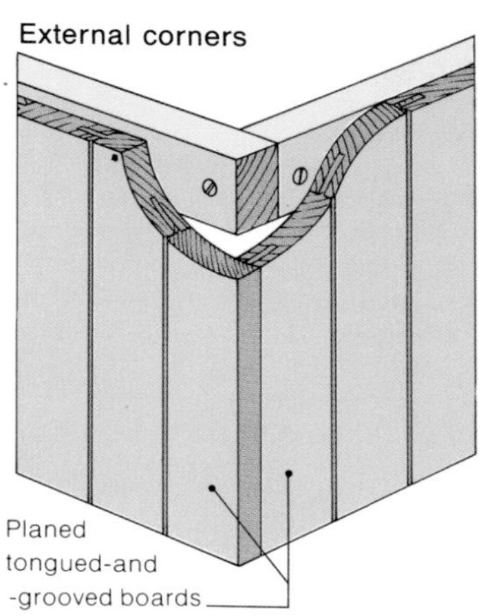

For vertical boards, one way of joining is to plane them to remove tongues or grooves and then butt them at right angles.

Another method is to butt the grooved edges of two boards and cover the joint with right-angled corner moulding.

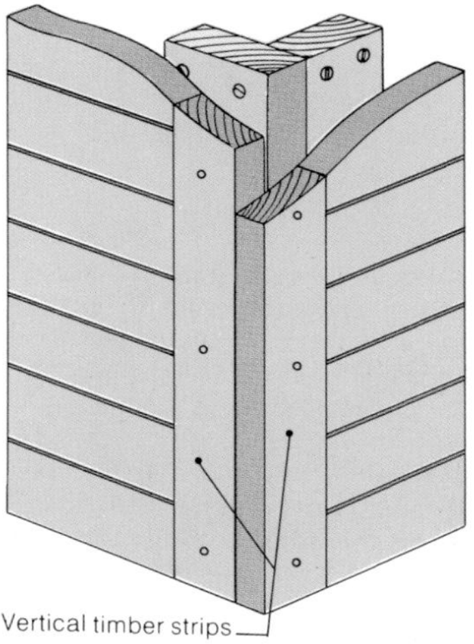

For horizontal boards, fit vertical timber strips at the corner and butt the cladding boards against them.

HELPFUL TIPS

If a tongued-and-grooved board is difficult to slot in straight, hammer it lightly with a mallet, using a board offcut between the board and the mallet. Slot the offcut groove over the tongue of the board you are fitting.

Avoid fitting boards together too tightly in kitchens and bathrooms, because humidity will cause the wood to swell and expand.

Removing and refitting skirting boards

Wooden skirting board is normally levered away from the wall, but levering can be difficult if it has been screwed or nailed directly into the masonry. If you are going to refit the same skirting board, lever it off with more care than if you intend to fit new board.

REMOVING A SKIRTING BOARD

You will need
Tools Wrecking bar; thin softwood pieces for wedging. Possibly also: Hammer and cold chisel or bolster; torch; hacksaw blade; screwdriver.

1 If plaster juts onto the top of board, chip it away only at the place where you want to lever. The board should pull clear without damaging the jutting plaster.

2 When removing only part of the skirting, note whether the board to be removed is overlapped by another at an internal corner. If it is, remove the overlapping board first. Otherwise, start levering at an external corner or where skirting butts against a door frame.

3 Hold the wrecking bar near its hooked end and insert the blade behind the skirting, then put a thin piece of wood behind the top of the blade to protect the wall.

4 Prise the board away from the wall and wedge it with a piece of wood. Move to a new position about 3ft (1m) or so away and continue in the same way until the whole board is loosened.

5 If a board is difficult to loosen, wedge a gap open to look behind and check the fixing.

6 If the fixing is a screw, gently probe the front of the board to find the head (probably covered with filler). Unscrew it if you can, otherwise cut through from behind with a hammer and cold chisel or hacksaw blade.

7 If the fixing is a large nail, you can usually lever it off but will probably damage the board. If you want to refit the board, cut through it in the same way as a screw.

8 If you want to refit the same skirting board, pull out the nails from behind to avoid damaging the face of the board.

REFITTING A SKIRTING BOARD

Plaster is rarely taken far down the wall behind skirting. When you fit new skirting, buy board of the same height as the old to avoid patching the plaster. Or raise the height of the new board by nailing moulding (page 153) to the top.

If new skirting board is narrower than the plaster or lining above it, pack behind with an extra piece of timber to bring it out to the required thickness.

If the plaster does reach to the floor, fix the skirting board through it into the brickwork with screws and wall plugs.

Coat the back of new skirting board with clear or green wood preservative to guard against rot. Shape the corners as necessary (see right).

Before refitting skirting board, lay it flat along the floor and mark on the front the positions of the fixing points so that you can nail through the marks.

Refit skirting board to existing fixing points wherever possible.

DIFFERENT TYPES OF FIXING POINT

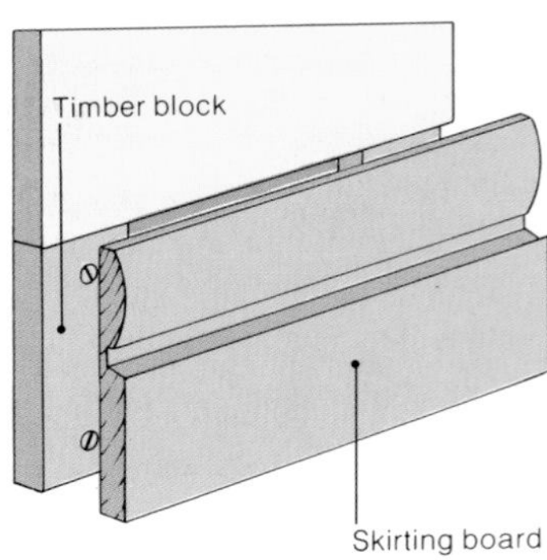

The commonest type of fixing point is a timber block called a ground. Grounds are nailed or screwed to the wall at 18-24in (460-610mm) intervals.

Fit new grounds if necessary, using timber treated with wood preservative. Fix them with masonry nails or screws and wall plugs.

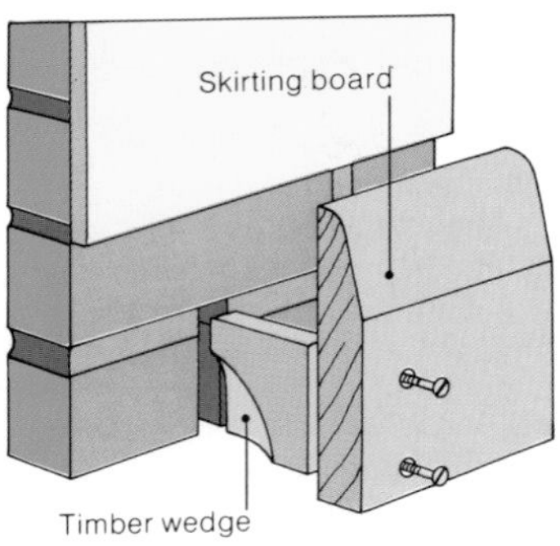

An alternative type of fixing point is a timber wedge, called a plug. They are inserted into the mortar joints between bricks. If a timber wedge is damaged, remove it by partially driving in a large screw, then pulling it out, together with the wedge, using a wrecking bar claw or claw hammer. You will have to make a new wedge to replace the damaged one.

GLUING A SKIRTING BOARD

Modern sealants and adhesives are so strong that it is now practical to secure skirting boards and other mouldings with adhesive rather than using screws or masonry nails. Some glues are made specifically for attaching coving and wooden mouldings to walls.

There are two methods of fixing items with panel adhesive.

Using the wet-bond method, the adhesive is applied in strips to the board, which is then pressed firmly against the wall and held in place while the adhesive sets.

Using a contact-bond adhesive, the glue is applied to the board, which is then pressed briefly against the wall to leave a residue behind. Once the glue is touch dry, the board can be pressed in place and will bond immediately.

SHAPING CORNERS ON NEW BOARDS

Before new skirting is fitted, shape the ends where there are external or internal corners. If a board butts against a door frame that is out of true, measure and mark the angle of the cut with a sliding bevel.

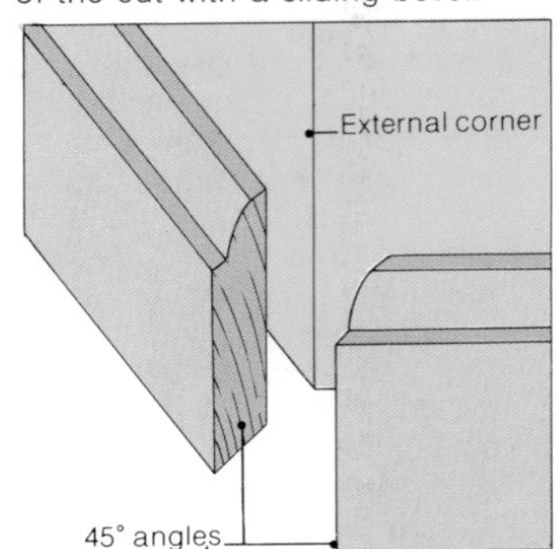

On an external corner, mitre the two boards to meet each other at an angle of 45 degrees (page 165).

On an internal corner, one board is shaped to overlap the other, in the manner described below.

1 Fit a board right against the internal corner and temporarily nail it in position.

2 Hold the second board butted at right angles to the first and pencil its profile onto the end of the first board.

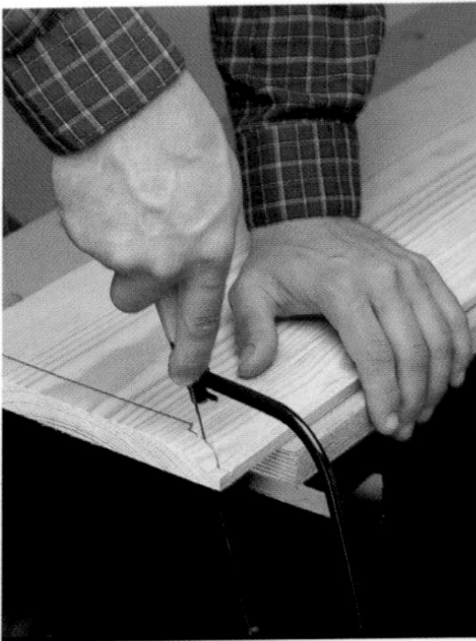

3 Remove the first board and cut away the end along the pencilled mark with a coping saw.

4 Refit the boards with the second, uncut board pushed into the corner and the first board lapped over it.

GAPS BELOW THE SKIRTING

A gap of about ¼in (6mm) between the skirting board and the floor can be useful if you want to push fitted carpet or vinyl flooring beneath it.

But if gaps occur below newly fitted skirting because the floor is not true, the simplest remedy is to nail quadrant or scotia moulding (page 153) to the bottom of the skirting against the floor.

Do not nail moulding to the floorboards, as they expand and contract more than the skirting, and another gap could open up.

JOINING STRAIGHT LENGTHS

When joining two straight lengths of skirting board, do not make straight butt joints, which are impossible to hide.

Instead, make each joint with matching 45 degree cuts using a mitre board (page 165).

REFITTING SKIRTING TO A HOLLOW WALL

Skirting board fitted to a hollow wall – a partition or a dry-lined wall – is fixed to the vertical studs and floor rail (sole plate) of the framing. Locate the studs with a metal detector (page 230) or as shown on page 231. Refit the board using 2½in (65mm) oval nails.

REPAIRING MOULDING ON A SKIRTING BOARD

It may be impossible to buy matching moulding to repair a damaged section of skirting board (or picture rail) in an old house.

Getting a similar moulding cut to order by a timber merchant can be expensive. You can do the job yourself by cutting a matching piece with a power router, which can be hired.

Another method possible for replacing a short length is to shape a simple cutter – which is known as a scratch stock – from hard steel such as an old hacksaw blade.

Grind the end of the hacksaw blade to the required profile and clamp it between two pieces of hardwood that are cut to an L shape to form an anchor for keeping a straight line.

Scrape the scratch stock slowly along a suitable piece of board to form the shape you want.

Where a small section of ornate moulding is damaged or missing, take an impression from a sound piece by pressing model-casting rubber against it. Or use dental-impression compound. Tack the hardened pressing to a piece of wood to form a mould, and fill it with glass-fibre resin. Smooth the set casting and glue in place.

DEALING WITH ARCHITRAVES AND PICTURE RAILS

Architraves are strips of moulding used to cover a joint between woodwork and a wall – such as round a door frame.

Remove an architrave or picture rail by prising it away from its backing using a mallet and wide wood chisel or bolster.

Start at the centre of the longest length and ease it gently out, working from both sides. Wedge between the backing and the moulding with a scrap of wood or hardboard as soon as possible.

When removing a picture rail, make good any damage done to the plaster.

The gap left by the rail can be difficult to disguise if the plaster is at different levels because the wall has been skim plastered since the rail was fitted.

Refit new or old architrave with thin wire nails. Punch the heads below the surface with a nail punch and fill the holes with wood filler. (See *Fitting a picture rail*, page 235.)

Removing an old fireplace

There are three main steps in removing an old fireplace – removing the surround (which may be one of several types), removing a raised hearth if there is one, and sealing off the grate opening.

Old fireplace surrounds can be quite valuable – particularly old cast-iron or timber surrounds. Remove them carefully to maintain their resale value. Modern tile or brick surrounds that have been built since the 1940s are not usually worth preserving.

An unwanted fireplace opening can be permanently bricked up, or it can be boarded up in case you want to reopen it later.

Alternatively, you can keep the fireplace opening as a wall recess by sealing off the top of the grate only. Shelves could then be added, or it could be used to display a vase of flowers.

Before sealing off a fireplace, get the chimney swept and then have it capped by a builder.

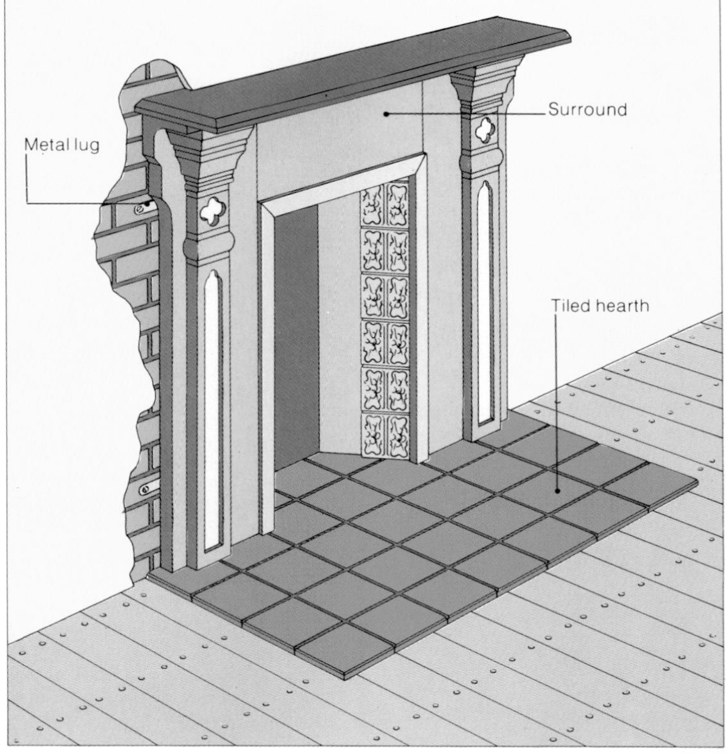

Cast-iron surround Old cast-iron surrounds can be valuable. They are usually fixed to the wall through lugs hidden under the plaster. Sometimes there is an inner surround of tiles.

A CAST-IRON SURROUND

1 The fireplace surround is normally screwed to the wall through metal lugs positioned at the sides near the top, and hidden under the plaster. Remove the wall covering and carefully chip away the plaster to expose the lugs.

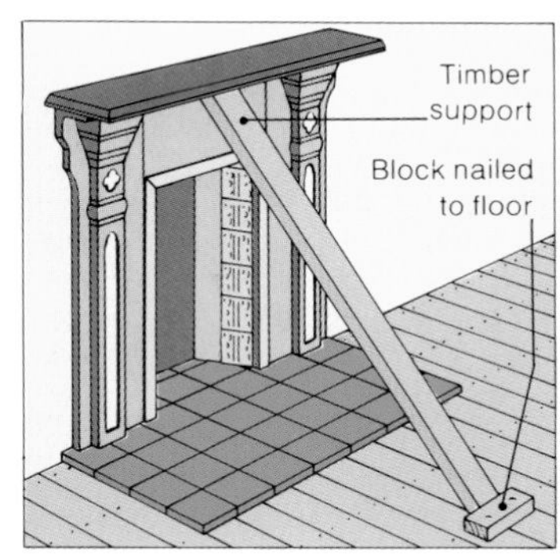

2 Support the surround by wedging a length of timber between the top and the floor. Cast-iron surrounds, particularly, are often top heavy. Without support the surround may fall forward when you undo the fixing screws.

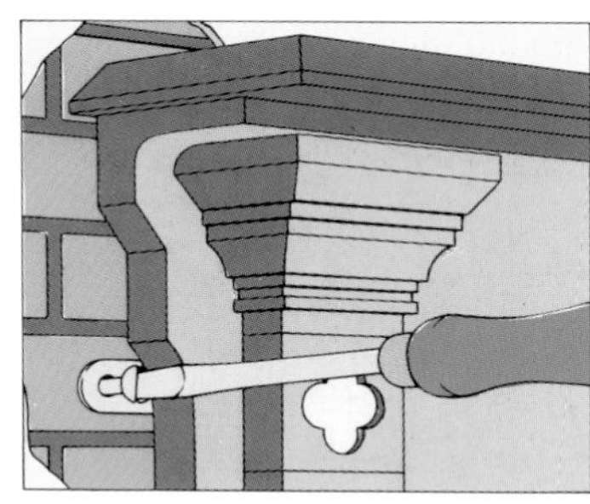

3 Remove the fixing screws if possible. Otherwise, prise the lugs away from the wall, but be very careful as they are brittle and will break easily (this lowers the value of the surround).

4 The grate may be fixed to the surround with screws or bolts, and will come away with it. There is no need to separate them unless you are planning to sell the fireplace surround only.

REMOVING OLD BOLTS OR SCREWS

If you want to separate a cast-iron surround from its grate, you may have to soak the bolts or screws with penetrating oil before you can undo them. Make several applications of oil over about 24 hours, if necessary.

If they are still difficult to undo, use a nut splitter, which can be hired, to cut through the nuts. The splitter clamps round the nut or the bolt head and cuts it off as it is tightened.

Drill out screw heads with a high-speed-steel twist bit of about the same diameter as the screw shank (compare the screw head with loose screws to estimate the size). If necessary for resale, drill screw or bolt stubs from the surround and use a tap wrench to cut new threads.

Removing an old fireplace (continued)

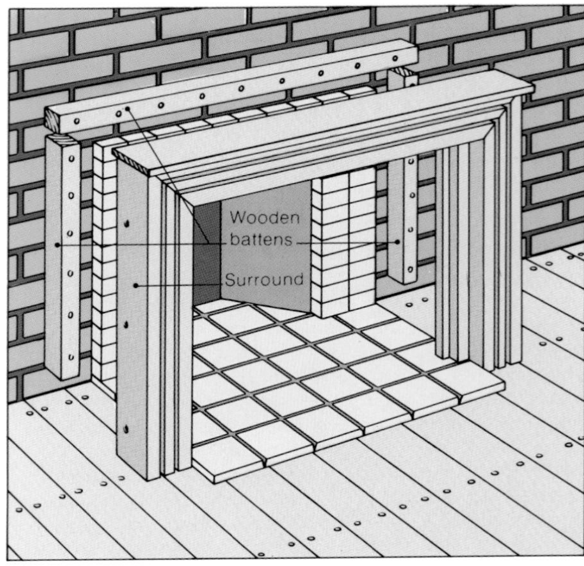

Timber surround The surround is usually screwed to wooden battens fixed to the brickwork.

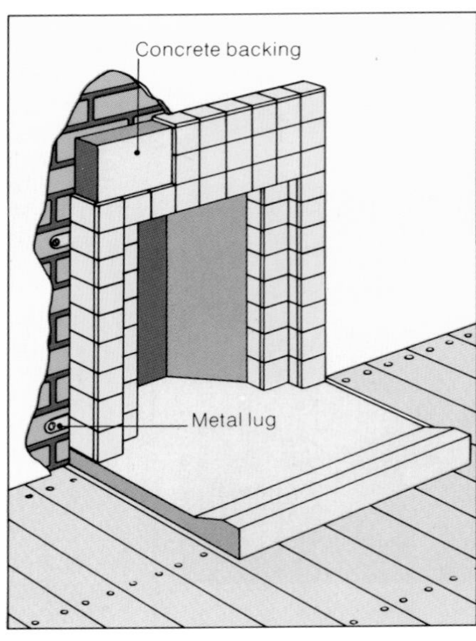

Tiled surround There is usually a concrete backing, making the surround very heavy.

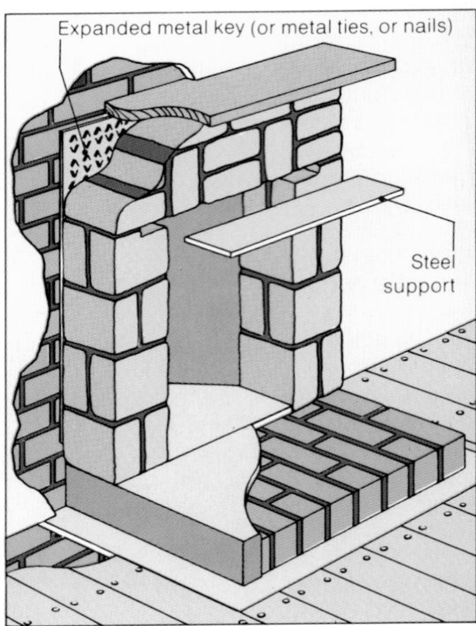

Stone surround The stones (or bricks) over the opening stand on a steel support.

A TIMBER SURROUND

A timber fireplace surround is usually screwed to battens fixed to the wall behind. There may be a tiled inner surround, which has to be removed separately.

1 Scan the timber surface to find filler covering the screw heads. If necessary strip off the surface with paint or varnish remover to reveal the screw heads.

2 Dig out the filler to clear the screw slots, and undo the screws.

3 Lift away the surround and remove from the wall the battens used for fixing points.

4 Remove an inner tiled surround in the same way as a tiled surround (below). It is usually much lighter, however, and can be handled by one person.

A TILED SURROUND

A tiled surround normally has a concrete backing that is screwed to the chimney breast through metal lugs, in the same way as a cast-iron surround.

It is normally very heavy, and you will need a helper to hold it steady and help lift it away.

If a raised hearth is resting against the front of the surround, move the hearth first (see right).

1 Remove the wall covering and plaster at the sides, near the top, to reveal the lugs. Either undo the fixings or prise the lugs away from the wall with a wrecking bar.

2 Get a helper to steady the surround as it comes away from the wall. If it does not come away easily, there may be another set of lugs lower down on each side.

3 Lower the surround with the aid of a helper. If possible, take it outside for breaking up.

4 Lay the surround face downwards and cover it with sacking. Put on safety spectacles and protective gloves before breaking it up with a sledgehammer.

A BRICK OR STONE SURROUND

Before you start, check that the surround is not imitation brick or stone with facings bonded to a concrete backing. If it is, remove in the same way as a tiled surround.

Begin removing bricks or stones at the top course, loosening them by chipping away the mortar with a hammer and cold chisel.

There may be metal ties or nails in the mortar joints, linked in to the wall behind. Chip into the wall to remove them, and make good with filler afterwards. Alternatively, an expanded metal key may link the bricks to the wall.

REMOVING A RAISED HEARTH

A raised hearth may be a tiled slab of concrete or a number of stone slabs or bricks. The raised hearth is bonded to a concrete layer flush with the floor (known as the constructional hearth) with mortar.

1 Chip away the mortar with a hammer and cold chisel and prise out stones or bricks individually. ALTERNATIVELY, use a wrecking bar to prise up a solid slab hearth.

2 Leave the constructional hearth in place. Smooth it with self-levelling compound before laying the floor covering (page 276).

BRICKING UP A GRATE

Use bricks or blocks and mortar (page 483) to block the opening, building them up in courses. The face should be level with the surrounding brickwork – that is, set back slightly from a layer of plaster. Unless the opening is wider than about 4ft (1.2m), there is no need to tooth-in the bricks (that is, remove surrounding half bricks so that new bricks can be linked in).

Insert an airbrick (page 236) in the centre of the second or third course, to keep the chimney dry.

If you are left with a gap about 1in (25mm) or more deep at the top of the opening, fill it in with a course of slates or part tiles.

Cover the brickwork with plaster (page 239) to bring the surface flush with the surrounding wall.

BOARDING UP THE GRATE

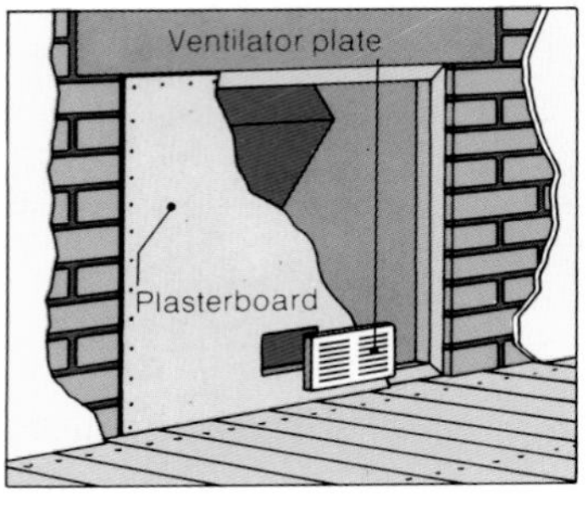

Use plasterboard or incombustible building board such as Masterboard, and cut it to fit flush into the opening. Fit a frame of 2in × 2in (50mm × 50mm) timber battens all round the edge of the opening, set back to allow for the thickness of the board. If the opening is more than about 24in (610mm) wide, fit a central vertical batten to give extra rigidity.

Nail or screw the board to the battens so that it lies flush with the surrounding wall. Cut a hole near the bottom at the centre and fit in a ventilator plate.

Cover top and side joints with scrim tape to reinforce them (page 239). Cover the board with ready-mixed skim-coat plaster, if necessary, to match the surrounding wall.

> **SAFETY PRECAUTION**
>
> If the grate to be blocked is linked to a common flue serving a grate still in use, do not fit a ventilator plate, through which hot soot may fall. When boarding up such a grate, you should use incombustible building board.

CREATING A WALL RECESS

Screw a framework of 2in × 2in (50mm × 50mm) timber battens to the inside of the chimney, just above the crosspiece supporting the front of the chimney.

Cut a panel of incombustible building board to fit to the frame. Make a hole in the centre, and fit through it a length of 2½in (65mm) diameter rainwater pipe with a bend of about 90 degrees at the top. The pipe keeps the flue ventilated, and the panel prevents soot and debris falling into the recess.

8

Draughtproofing, insulation & double glazing

Draughtproofing

Insulation

Double glazing

Draughtproofing and ventilation

A simple, inexpensive way to reduce the heat loss from your house is to draughtproof the windows and doors. Draughts are caused by cold air forcing its way into the house – through gaps in the roof, up through floors, through vents or cracks around windows and doors – and then forcing its way out through other gaps. Draughts may also occur when air is sucked in from outside to replace air used by boilers and fires.

If you block the gaps where the air is coming in you will stop the draught. Although the house will be more comfortable if you prevent streams of cold air moving through it, you must have controlled ventilation to keep the air fresh and remove excessive moisture.

Fires and boilers need air to burn efficiently and safely. Vents should be as close as possible to the appliance so that air passing to it does not cause a draught. They must never be blocked off or fumes may be sucked down a chimney, with possible lethal results. If the air has to pass across a room, fit the vent above a door or high in a wall so that air entering is mixed with the warmed air in the room before it moves to the fire.

HOW COST EFFECTIVE ARE HEAT SAVING METHODS?

Heating bills can be reduced by 60 pence in the pound by installing draughtproofing and insulation. But how much you actually save depends on the cost of the work compared to the saving in fuel.

For example, the estimated heat loss through windows can be reduced by half if you install draughtproofing and double glazing. It might take 40 years to recover the cost of custom-made double glazing but only two or three years for a DIY system.

Insulating the loft and draughtproofing doors, windows and floors are the most cost-effective forms of insulation.

Similarly, it is worth paying for cavity wall insulation – the cost will soon be recovered from savings in fuel.

Before insulation

25%

35%

10%

15%

15%

After insulation

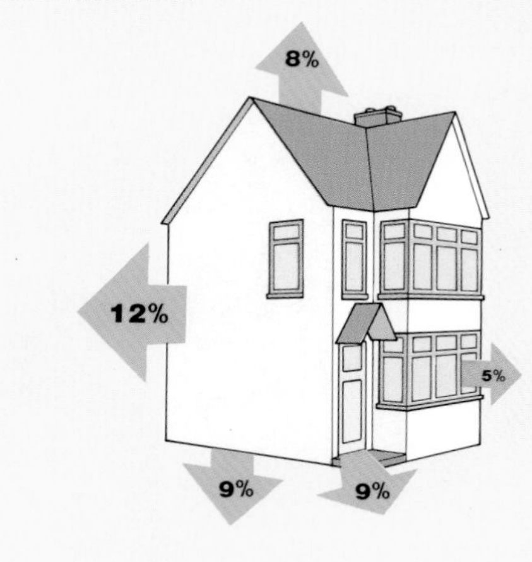

Never block out the draught designed to pass under the house – dry rot may develop if the timber is not well ventilated. You can keep cold air out of the house by draughtproofing the floor from inside.

Similarly, there must be some form of ventilation in the loft to prevent condensation.

Draughtproofing a window

A CASEMENT WINDOW

Most of the draughtproofing strips shown in the chart on the opposite page are suitable for use on a wooden casement window; but only the strips with an adhesive backing can be used on a metal casement window.

Rubber sealant for large gaps

For large or uneven gaps, a silicone rubber sealant (also called a frame sealant) is particularly useful.

Both wooden and metal casement windows can be draughtproofed with sealant, and it can be used on doors – interior or exterior. But it cannot be used on sash windows.

Read any advice on the container before you begin.

HELPFUL TIPS

If you cannot find the source of a draught, light a candle and hold it in front of the door or window. Move around the edge of the frame – the frame will flicker at the point where the draught is coming in. Take care not to set curtains alight.

If leaded lights have become draughty, seal any gaps in the lead cames (page 218).

1 Clean the fixed frame thoroughly with soapy water and a cloth so that the surface is free from dirt. Rinse and wait for it to dry.

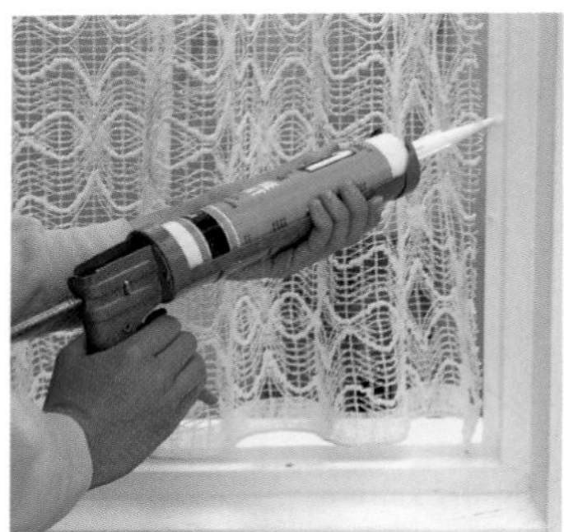

2 Apply a bead of sealant to the rebate of the fixed frame. It should be slightly larger than the gap which needs to be filled.

3 With a clean paintbrush or a cloth, cover the closing edge of the window or door with soapy water which will act as a release agent.

4 Pull the window or door tight shut to compress the sealant and immediately open it again.

5 Leave the sealant to set – this will take about 2 hours if the weather is warm, but longer if it is cold. The sealant will harden on the surface but will remain flexible underneath, forming a perfect seal when the window or door is closed.

A SASH WINDOW

Sprung strip is the most suitable material for sealing the sides of a sash window, as the sashes slide over it easily.

1 Remove the staff beads and the parting beads from the window so that both sashes swing free (page 214) and clean the frame.

2 Measure the height of the sliding sashes and cut four pieces of the sprung strip – two pieces for each sash.

3 Fix the strip to the pulley stiles which run vertically each side of the sliding sashes. Use pre-holed strip, fixing it with the pins provided and a hammer. Take the strip right into the top and bottom corners so the sashes cannot catch on any sharp edges. Unless the window is not opened very often, self-adhesive strip is not suitable because it is unlikely to withstand the friction from the sashes.

4 Replace the sashes and beading (page 216).

5 Seal the gap at the top and bottom of the sashes with any of the more durable foam strips fixed to the frame or the sash.

6 If there is a draught between the top and bottom sashes, fix nylon brush pile strip to the bottom sash at the meeting point.

CHOOSING A DRAUGHT EXCLUDER FOR DOORS AND WINDOWS

Before you buy a draught excluder, measure the width of the gaps which need to be blocked. The packaging on most draught excluders indicates how big a gap the product is intended to fill and where it can be used. Measure the height and width of the door or window you plan to draughtproof as well, so that you know how long the excluder should be.

You may need to use more than one type – a foam strip around the sides and top of a door and a threshold excluder (page 262) at the bottom, for example. If you are fitting one of the foam, rubber or flexible strips for the first time – or are unsure which excluder is most suitable – experiment on one door or window before you buy all the material you need.

Even after draughtproofing doors and windows, you may have draughts in an open-plan house as warmed air moves up the stairs. Heating the upstairs rooms will reduce air currents. Otherwise keep all the upstairs doors closed.

HELPFUL TIP

To improve the adhesion of self-adhesive strips, apply a thin coating of clear all-purpose adhesive over the surface to which the excluder is to be fixed. Let the glue dry before pressing on the strips.

TYPE OF EXCLUDER — DESCRIPTION AND FIXING INSTRUCTIONS

Self-adhesive foam strip

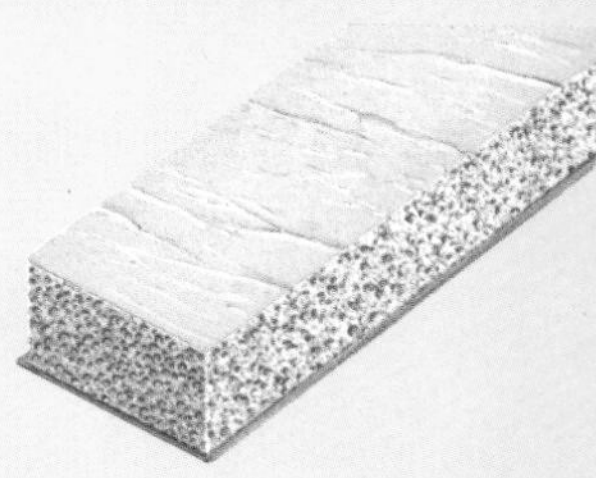

Use on casement windows and interior doors. Quality varies considerably. Some strips perish after only one or two seasons; more expensive types will last for five years or more. Cheaper versions are made of polyurethane which hardens with age. Sizes vary according to the manufacturer but strips are usually about $\frac{1}{4}$in (6mm) thick and $\frac{3}{8}$in (10mm) wide. Most strips are only supplied in white. Avoid getting paint on the foam – it will harden with age, unless the manufacturer of the strip states otherwise.

Before fixing, clean the window frame or door frame with water and a little washing-up liquid to remove all grease and dirt. Rinse and wait for the surface to dry. Cut lengths to fit with scissors or a trimming knife. Peel away the protective backing as you stick down each length on the rebate. Make sure that one piece of excluder goes right into each corner.

Self-adhesive rubber strip

E profile

P profile

Use on casement windows and interior doors. Available in a limited colour range and profiles including P and E. This type of excluder is tough and will last longer than foam.

Fix to the frame as for self-adhesive foam strip (above).

Brush strips

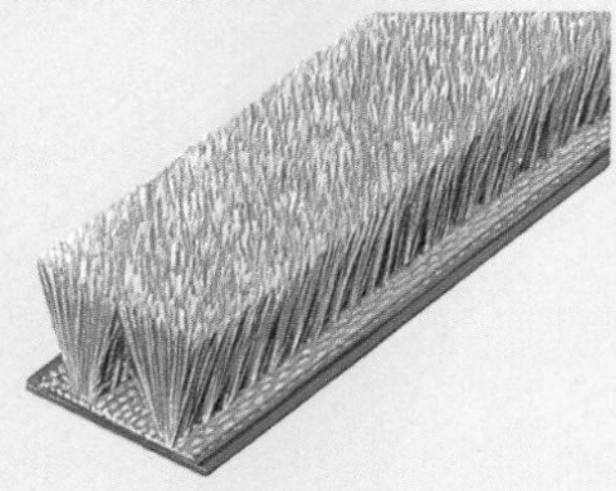

Use on interior, exterior and patio doors, and on sash and casement windows. The strips consist of siliconised nylon pile in self-adhesive strips or in a metal or plastic holder which should be tacked to the frame, not the door or window. The strip is particularly designed for surfaces which move against each other, as on sash windows and patio doors.

TYPE OF EXCLUDER — DESCRIPTION AND FIXING INSTRUCTIONS

Silicone rubber sealant

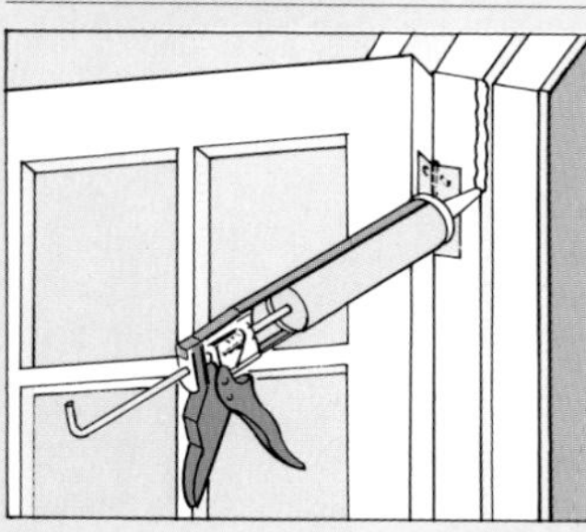

Use on interior and exterior doors and casement windows. Useful for draughtproofing frames which have irregular gaps. Available in a limited colour range and supplied in cartridges. Apply it to the fixed section of the frame so that the door or window beds onto it.

Clean the frame thoroughly before applying the sealant. Follow the manufacturer's instructions and see facing page.

Sprung strip

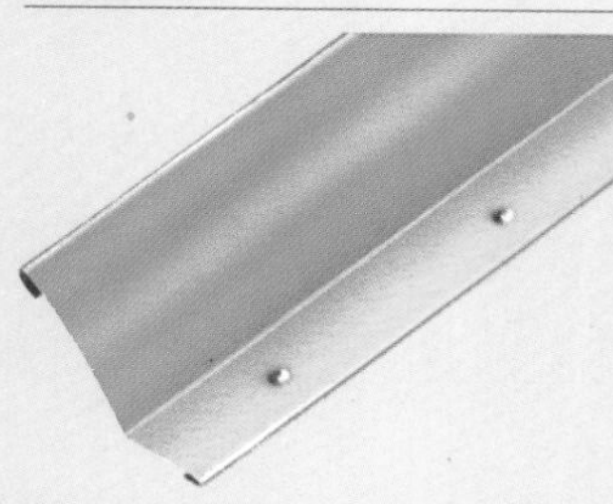

Bronze strip

Nylon strip

Use on interior and exterior doors, sash windows and wooden casement windows. Useful for sealing around frames when the gap is uneven. Made in phosphor bronze or nylon. The strip springs to form a flexible seal between two surfaces. Sprung strip is more durable than foam or rubber strip. It is usually pre-holed and supplied with small fixing pins.

Self-adhesive sprung strip is also available. Only fix it to doors and windows which are not frequently opened. It is easier to fix around a sash window than pre-holed strip but is not as durable.

Apply the strip to clean window or door frames with the raised edge facing away from the window or door. Do not use the strip for small gaps – it will make the door or window difficult to open and close. Cut metal lengths to fit with tinsnips or dual-purpose scissors; cut nylon strip with scissors. If the strip does not flex quite enough to seal a large gap, run the back edge of a penknife blade down the indent on the strip to give it a little extra spring.

Flexible tube

Use on interior doors and wooden casement windows. Made of rubber in a limited colour range including white and brown. The tube section is compressed to form a seal when the door or window shuts onto it.

Cut lengths of the tube to size with a trimming knife or scissors. Fix to the rebate of the frame with tacks spaced at about 3in (75mm) intervals.

Draughtproofing a door

Draught excluders can be fitted all round a door, both to the frame and to the threshold – although this should only be necessary on a front or back door.

Draught excluders suitable for doors range from simple foam strip, which is compressed between the frame and the door when it is closed, to weatherbar-and-threshold units which are attached to the bottom of the door and the sill.

Some threshold excluders are designed to deflect in-blown rain as well as to stop draughts.

Threshold excluders are made specifically for internal or external doors and to standard lengths, so choose the appropriate type and size for your doors.

Door edge seals may be self-adhesive or attached by screws; threshold excluders may be in two parts, one section should be screwed to the floor close to the door, the other to the base of the door.

ADDING AN ENCLOSED PORCH TO A DOOR

If you put an enclosed porch around an outside door – especially if it is exposed to prevailing winds – you will greatly reduce the draughts entering the house. You will also help to reduce condensation inside if you can leave wet umbrellas and coats in a porch.

There are regulations that govern extending outside the house building line, but porches are exempt, providing you keep your existing front door, the floor area is not more than 30sq m, and no part is higher than 3m above ground level. You must also ensure that no part of the porch is less than 2m from the boundary between the garden and a road or public footpath.

HOW DRAUGHT EXCLUDERS ARE FITTED

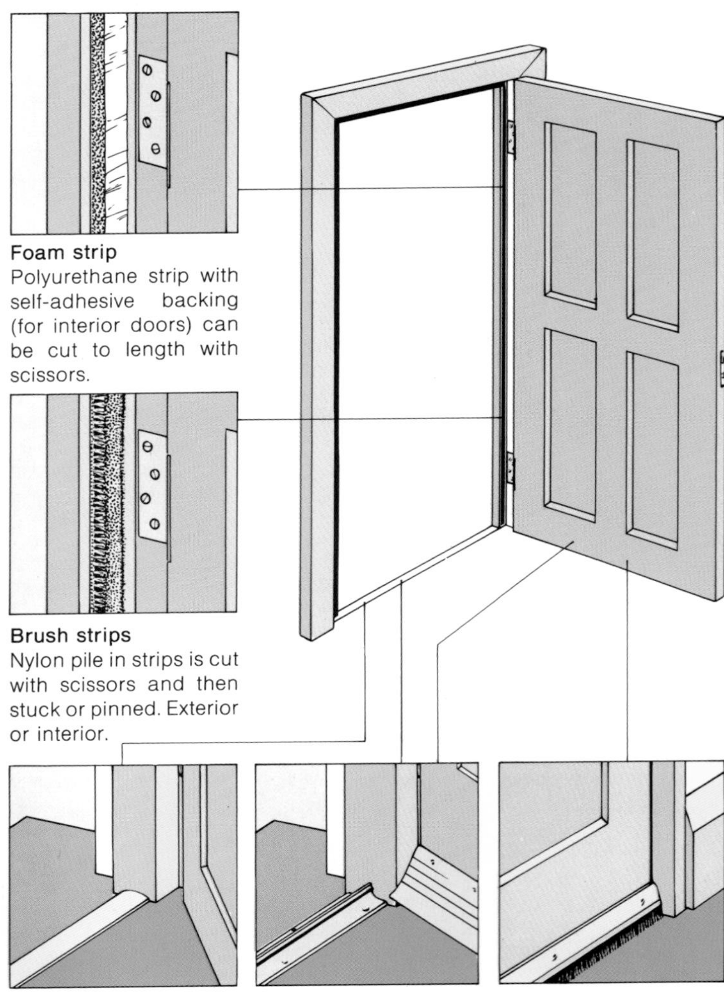

Foam strip
Polyurethane strip with self-adhesive backing (for interior doors) can be cut to length with scissors.

Brush strips
Nylon pile in strips is cut with scissors and then stuck or pinned. Exterior or interior.

Sill excluder
A plastic or metal-and-plastic bar that is fitted to the sill and seals the gap when the door is closed.

Two-piece excluder
One part is fitted to the door, the other to the sill, and a seal is made between them when the door is closed.

Brush excluder
A rubber, plastic or brush seal attached to the base of the door. Usually adjustable for height.

THRESHOLD AND OTHER EXCLUDERS

Excluders fixed to the door

NYLON BRUSH Nylon bristle mounted in aluminium. The excluder is fitted to the base of the door – on the inside if it is an exterior door.

AUTOMATIC FLAP A spring-loaded hinged flap closes when an attachment on one end of the flap strikes an attachment mounted to the door frame.

Excluders fitted to the sill

PLASTIC SEAL The plastic strip has a flexible section which compresses under the door when it is closed.

METAL/RUBBER SEAL The metal bar has a rubber insert which seals the gap under the door.

Excluders fitted to the door and sill

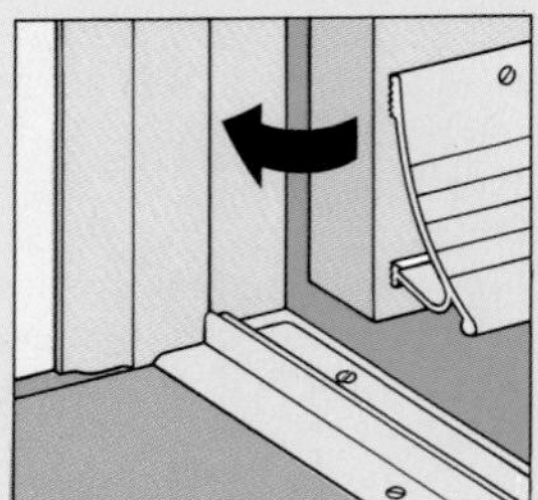

WEATHERBAR AND DEFLECTOR The weatherbar is attached to the sill. The deflector is attached to the door base and is shaped to deflect rainwater.

STORM BARRIER Interlocking sill and weatherbar sections, with a rubber seal on the weatherbar, give extra protection in exposed areas.

Keyhole cover and letterbox excluder

KEYHOLE COVER Suitable for the keyhole of a mortise lock, the pivoted cover hangs in front of the hole.

LETTERBOX EXCLUDER A plastic frame with two rows of nylon bristle fits over the inside of a letterbox.

Draughtproofing a timber floor

A well laid tongued-and-grooved floor or one covered with flooring-grade chipboard should not be draughty. But a considerable amount of air can come up into the house if the boards are merely butted together. In older properties particularly, boards may have shrunk so there are gaps between them.

There is no danger that rot will set in after you have sealed gaps in a floor, provided that air can still move freely underneath the floor through airbricks.

The way you choose to draughtproof a floor depends on the size of the gaps. Fill large gaps wider than ¼in (6mm) with wood. For smaller gaps, use a sealant applied with a sealant gun or papier-mâché.

LARGE GAPS

You will need

Tools Mallet; plane; medium-grade abrasive paper and sanding block, or a flapwheel or drum sander in a power tool.

Materials Thin strips of softwood planed to a wedge section (page 167); waterproof wood adhesive.

1 Apply adhesive to the two long sides of a wedged strip of wood.

2 Tap the wood into place with the mallet, far enough to fill the gap but leaving the strip a little proud of the floor.

3 When the adhesive has set – this will take about six hours, but it depends on the conditions – plane away the surplus wood.

4 Smooth any rough pieces of wood with a flap wheel or drum sander in a power tool, working only with the grain of the wood. Or do it by hand with medium-grade abrasive paper wrapped around a wood block.

SMALL GAPS

Fill the gaps between floorboards with a flexible acrylic flooring filler applied with a sealant gun. The colour you choose does not matter if you will be laying a new floor covering over the boards. If you intend to sand the boards and seal them with varnish, use a ready-mixed tub filler that can be stained to match the board colour.

You will need

Tools Sealant gun to take standard 310ml sealant cartridges; sharp knife for trimming nozzle to required size; filling knife for removing excess filler.

Materials Flooring filler cartridges; tubs of ready-mixed joiners' wood filler; lining paper or similar for wiping excess filler from knife (newspaper will cause black stains).

1 Check the width of the largest gap between the boards, and cut the cartridge nozzle off at an angle to give a bead of the correct width.

2 Load the cartridge into the sealant gun and squeeze the trigger to start the flow of filler.

3 Draw the nozzle steadily along each joint in turn, allowing the filler to sink into the joint.

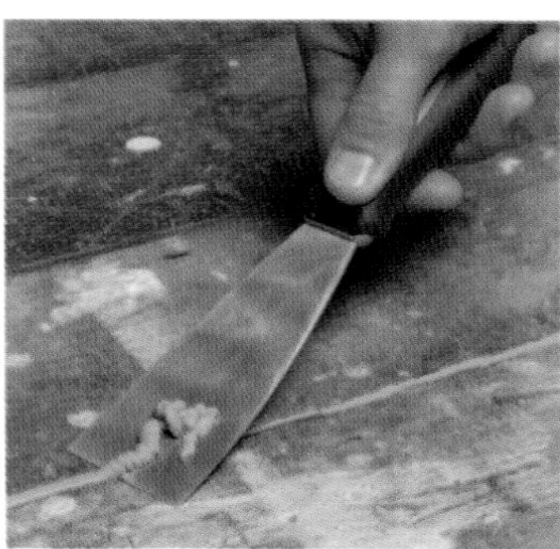

4 As you complete each joint, use the filling knife to remove excess filler and wipe the blade on some lining paper or similar material. Repeat the process to fill each joint in turn.

SEALING THE GAP BELOW A SKIRTING BOARD

A skirting board is often fitted so that there is a gap between it and the floor. If carpet has not been pushed into this gap to form a neat edge, draughts may come up from below the timber floor.

To seal the gap, use panel pins to fix quadrant beading (page 153) to the base of the skirting board, pressing it tight to the floor. Do not pin it to the floor, or the boards will not be able to expand and contract, as they normally do when the weather varies from damp to dry.

Alternatively, pin or glue a preformed skirting board made of moulded plywood over the original skirting board. It will seal any gap between skirting board and floor, and also provide a channel for new wiring.

Expect the new skirting board to add a little extra to the width of the original, and slightly more to the height.

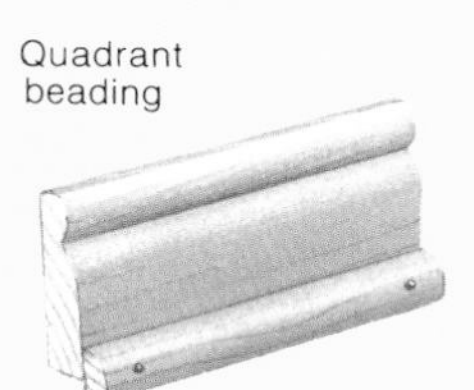

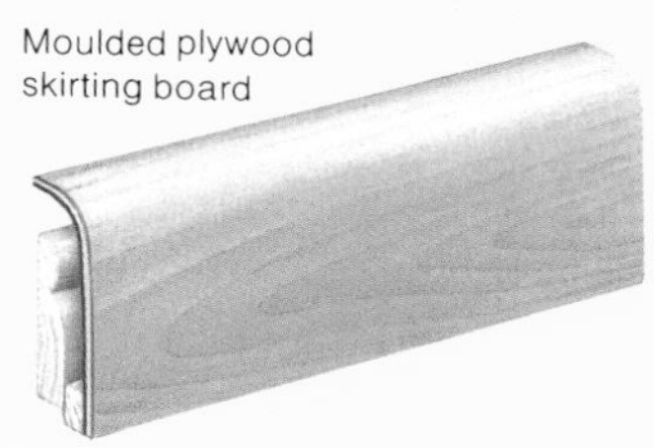

WHEN THE FLOOR IS TO BE COVERED

If you are laying carpet or tiles over a floor, you do not need to fill any of the gaps between the floorboards. A quicker technique, which will provide both draughtproofing and a flat surface for laying the new floor covering, is to put down sheets of hardboard over the whole floor (page 275).

If the cracks are small and the floorboards are level, use reflective foil building paper beneath a carpet. It is cheaper than hardboard. Lay the paper foil side up and fix it with double-sided carpet tape at the edges. The paper will stop draughts and will also reflect a certain amount of warmth back into the room.

Hardboard covering

Building paper covering

INSULATING TIMBER FLOORS

If the floorboards in a downstairs room have to be lifted (see page 274), take the chance to increase warmth and reduce heating bills by fitting underfloor insulation. There are two types available.

Staple nylon garden netting across the joists and place lengths of loft insulation blanket between them. Draw the netting up tight so the blanket does not sag between the joists.

Cut rigid polystyrene foam insulation boards into strips to match the joist spacing and support them between the joists on battens nailed to the joist sides.

Blanket insulation

Rigid insulation

CHOOSING INSULATION MATERIAL FOR A LOFT

Whichever type you decide to install, plan to lay at least 4in (100mm) of insulation. If you put down a thicker layer you will prevent more heat loss but the savings are proportionately less.

You may be able to reduce the cost if you buy insulation material in the summer when there is less demand for it and there are often special offers. You may also be eligible for a grant so that you can reclaim some of the money you spend. Contact your local council or Citizens Advice Bureau for details.

Before you buy, find out whether your supplier will deliver the insulation. Blanket rolls and sacks of loose-fill are very bulky for their weight. Even a car with a hatchback will only hold about a quarter of the amount you need to insulate the average loft.

You can insulate a loft yourself with blanket, loose-fill or sheet insulation. Alternatively, you can pay a specialist company to blow loose-fill insulation between the joists. The advantage with blowing is that the insulation can be directed into areas close to the eaves which are otherwise difficult to reach.

In addition to the more usual DIY loose-fill types of insulation, companies use other specialist materials.

BLANKET ROLLS

Mineral-fibre or glass-fibre blanket is supplied in rolls 4in or 6in (100mm or 150mm) thick. It is 16in (400mm) wide and from 17½ft to 26ft (5.3m to 8m) long. If the space between the joists in the loft is narrow and you need to cut the blanket, use a panel saw to cut through the roll while it is still in its wrapper, or you can cut through single widths with sharp scissors. Fibre blanket is cheap and effective, but it tends to compress as it gets older.

Insulation is not effective if water condenses in the material. For this reason, some rolls of blanket are backed with foil or polythene which acts as a vapour barrier – warm, moist air cannot pass into the material and condense. If you are using paper-backed or unbacked blanket, install a vapour barrier before you insulate.

HOW MUCH MATERIAL DO YOU NEED?

Calculate the size of your loft before buying the insulation material. Measure the overall length and width of your house and multiply the two figures.

If you are going to lay loose-fill, you will have to go into the loft to measure the joists. Unless you deduct the amount of space the joists take up you will have sacks left over.

Most suppliers will advise on how much material is needed for a given area. Information is often supplied on the packaging. Check how much it costs for each square metre or square foot – sometimes prices are misleading. For example, rolls of 150mm blanket may appear to be cheaper than rolls 100mm thick, but it is sold in shorter lengths and works out more expensive.

MINERAL-FIBRE SLABS

Multipurpose insulation slabs can be used instead of fibre blanket in any insulation job. They are supplied to a standard thickness of 2in (50mm) so two slabs are needed to meet the minimum depth required for insulating a loft floor. The slabs measure about 45in × 18in (1140mm × 465mm), which makes them much less bulky and easier to handle than blanket rolls – but they are more expensive.

EXPANDED POLYSTYRENE SHEETS

Sheets of expanded polystyrene are particularly useful for sliding into areas which have been boarded over or which are difficult to reach – the flat roof over an extension, for example – but it can cost up to twice as much as insulating with glass fibre. You can also use expanded polystyrene to insulate between rafters and to insulate a cold water cistern, but it is too expensive for a whole loft.

Expanded polystyrene is most commonly available in sheets 6ft × 2ft (1800mm × 610mm) and sometimes 8ft × 4ft (2400mm × 1200mm). Sheets are usually 1½in (38mm) thick, but they are also made in sizes up to 4in (100mm). Thick sheets cost more but provide the best insulation. When buying polystyrene sheets for insulation, ask for fire retardant sheets for domestic use. They are likely to be labelled Type A or FRA. Non-fire retardant sheets are Type N or Normal.

LOOSE-FILL

The material is poured out to a depth of about 4in (100mm). It is supplied in paper sacks each sufficient to insulate 12sq ft (1sq m).

The most common loose-fill materials are vermiculite granules, such as Micafil, and loose mineral wool. Vermiculite is more expensive than mineral wool but it holds its bulk better. It can also be used to top up old blanket insulation.

Polystyrene granules are a third type of loose-fill insulation, but they will blow about in a draughty loft, so pin building paper to the joists over the granules, but leave the top of the joists visible so you can walk safely.

REFLECTIVE FOIL BUILDING PAPER

Supplied in rolls just over 82ft × 3ft (25m × 900mm) and stocked by some builders' merchants. Lay the foil between joists or drape it over them. Acts as a vapour barrier so that moisture cannot condense in the insulation material. Heat also reflects off the shiny surface – either back into the house in winter or back into the loft in summer. If using it between rafters, pin the paper in position, but there is no need to pin it if it is laid on the floor beneath insulation material.

Insulating a loft

Insulate the loft floor, if the space is only used for storage. But if the loft has been turned into a room – or if you plan to convert it into a room – insulate the roof. You can make it easier to store things on the floor if you put down flooring-grade chipboard after you have insulated between the joists, and this also adds an extra insulating layer.

You cannot use the area as a room just because there is chipboard on the floor, although it is safe to walk on the chipboard for short periods of time. Loft conversions involve more complicated work which must be done by professionals and which must conform with building regulations. The joists in the floor, which are in fact only ceiling joists for the room below, must be strengthened, or new floor joists must be inserted. For this reason it is unwise to store too many heavy things, like furniture and piles of books, in the loft.

Before you start work, clear the floor space as much as possible and spring clean the loft to remove accumulated dust – use a vacuum cleaner, if possible. It may be worth hiring an industrial one. At the same time, look for signs of woodworm and rot, and if necessary call in a specialist contractor.

Also, check whether the wiring needs to be replaced. If you find any rubber-covered cables, they should be replaced at the earliest opportunity. Call in an electrician to check their safety.

If the loft does not have a boarded floor, you must keep your weight on the joists. Do not step on the plaster or plasterboard – your leg will probably go through and you could injure yourself as well as having to repair the ceiling below. Find a stout board which is thick enough to take your weight and long enough to be laid across at least two joists. It may be easier if you have two or three similar boards so that you do not have to keep moving the one you are on.

If the loft has no lighting, connect a safety light to a socket downstairs or run a table lamp off an extension cable. A torch will not give adequate light.

Opinions vary as to whether gloves are necessary when handling glass fibre and mineral wool products. If the fibre does not cause too much irritation, use bare hands and rinse them with cold water when you stop work. If you decide to wear gloves, tuck them into an old long-sleeved shirt to prevent fibres from getting inside. If they do get into the gloves, loose fibres will cause more irritation than if you wore no gloves at all.

Wear a face mask to keep dust out of your lungs if you are handling mineral wool or glass fibre, or if the surroundings are very dusty. It is also a good idea to wear a safety helmet to protect your head against the rafters – it is easy to forget that you have little headroom when you are working under the eaves.

FIXING A VAPOUR BARRIER ON THE FLOOR

You will need
Tools Scissors.
Materials Rolls of reflective foil building paper or sheets of polythene; masking tape.

1 Cut the material with scissors so that it is about 2-3in (50-75mm) wider than the gap between the joists.

2 Lay the material in the gap, taking care to keep your weight only on the joists. Reflective foil paper must be laid foil-side down.

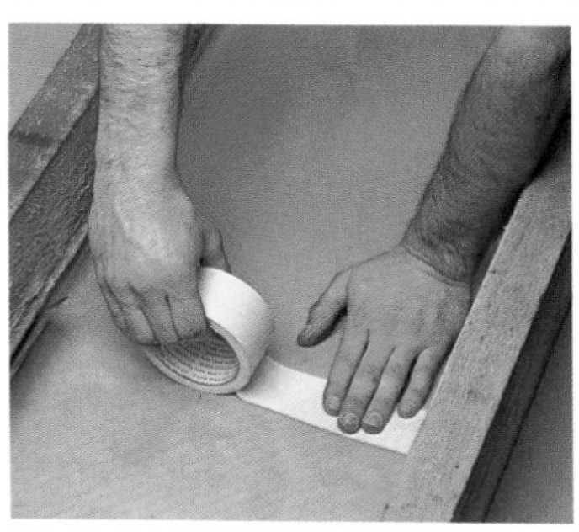

3 Seal any overlaps in the material with 2in (50mm) masking tape.

LAYING INSULATION BLANKET ON THE FLOOR

The spacing between joists varies but 13½in (350mm) is about average. Do not cut the excess off 400mm blanket – let it curl up on each side to make a snug fit.

You will need
Tools Scissors; face mask. Possibly also protective gloves.
Materials Rolls of glass fibre or mineral fibre blanket.

1 Start unrolling the blanket between two joists at the eaves at one end of the loft.

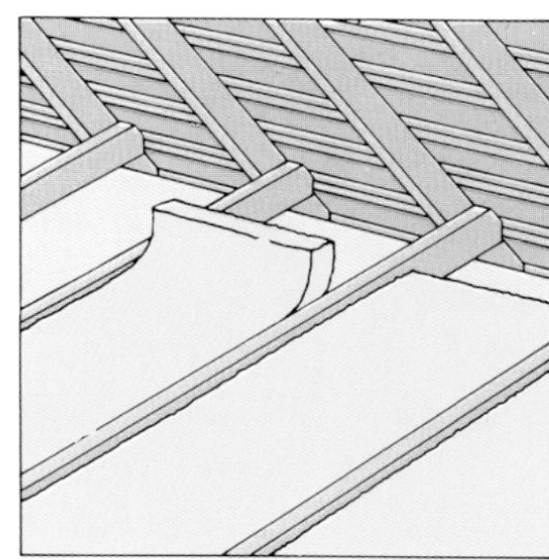

2 Do not take the material right into the eaves; you must leave a gap of about 2in (50mm) so that air can come in through the soffit and flow through the loft. If the air cannot circulate, condensation may form.

3 Press the blanket down lightly as you unroll it so that it lies flat but do not squash it so that it becomes compressed.

4 When you reach the other side of the loft, cut the blanket with scissors, again taking care not to block where the necessary ventilation comes in under the eaves.

5 Continue to lay the insulation between the other joists.

6 When joining two rolls, make a butt join, pressing the ends close to each other.

7 Cut the insulation so that it fits tight around pipes.

8 Try to place insulation under loose electric cables so that there is no danger of them becoming overheated. Where practicable, fix cables to the sides of the joists to keep them out of the way.

9 Never insulate under the cold water cistern. Leave a gap in the insulation so that warm air from below will keep the chill off the base of the cistern and help to prevent the water from freezing.

> **HELPFUL TIP**
> Use a broom to push the blanket into areas which are hard to reach.

INSULATING WITH LOOSE-FILL

It is easy to insulate with loose-fill granules – you pour the material between the joists and level it out. Make a simple levelling gauge so that the granules are at an even depth. Decide how deep the insulation layer is to be – it must be at least 4in (100mm) – and deduct this measurement from the depth of the joists.

Cut a piece of hardboard, chipboard or wood to a wide T-shape which will fit the gap above the loose-fill. The 'arms' should rest on top of the joists, so that when you run the gauge between two joists the granules are spread to a consistent depth.

PROBLEMS WITH CONDENSATION

Warm air is moist and if it meets cold air it condenses. Condensation can be a problem in a loft if you insulate the floor. No heat will escape into the loft but moisture will pass upwards and condense in the insulation material, which becomes ineffective if it is damp.

Foil-faced plasterboard is impervious to moisture so if the ceilings have been constructed of this material you do not need to take additional protective measures. If not, make sure that insulation material is protected by some form of vapour barrier below it so that the risk of condensation is reduced.

Sometimes blanket is supplied with a plastic or foil backing which moist air cannot pass through. But if you are using paper-backed or unbacked blanket or loose-fill insulation, you need to install a vapour barrier first.

LAGGING A LOFT HATCH DOOR

Cut a piece of glass-fibre or mineral-fibre blanket or thick expanded polystyrene sheet to fit above the loft hatch.

To fix the blanket, hammer about two nails along each edge of the door, depending on its size. Tie string over the top of the material and loop it around the nails to hold it in place. Do not pull the string so tight that it squashes the blanket.

Alternatively, cut a piece of tough brown paper large enough to cover the blanket. Fix the paper over the blanket, holding the edges in place with drawing pins.

If you are using expanded polystyrene sheet, stick it to the door with adhesive designed for the purpose, such as Evo-Stik ceiling tile adhesive or Unibond polystyrene adhesive.

Make sure that the hatch door is a tight fit. Fix a foam, rubber or flexible draught excluder (see chart, page 261) to the rebate so that damp air cannot pass through into the cold loft and cause condensation.

Insulating hot and cold water pipes

Hot and cold water pipes that are exposed to the cold should be lagged to prevent winter freeze-ups. Pipes in particular danger are those that run across a loft above an insulated floor, and those running along outside walls in unheated rooms.

Overflow and vent pipes that are exposed to the cold should also be well lagged.

To lag pipes that are boxed in, unscrew the box and stuff pieces of glass fibre or mineral fibre all round the pipes.

CHOOSING PIPE INSULATION MATERIAL

Plastic foam tubes
Easy-to-fit plastic foam tubes will bend round pipe curves. The tubing is split down one side and has to be eased open to wrap around the pipe. It is secured with adhesive tape wrapped round at intervals, or placed along the slit; or with purpose-made clips; or with a special adhesive. Some types are secured by integral mouldings that interlock. Tubes are available to fit 15mm, 22mm and 28mm pipes. Plastic foam tube is slightly more expensive than glass fibre and mineral fibre or felt, but it is extremely convenient to use.

Self-adhesive pipe-wrap
Thin foam insulating wrap, 2in (50mm) wide, is supplied in rolls usually 15ft (4.6m) or 32ft (10m) long. Some types have a metallic finish.

There is no formula for estimating how much wrap to buy – it depends on the size of the pipes and how large you make the overlaps. Buy one or two packs, use the material, and then work out how much more you need to complete the job.

To fix the lagging, peel off the backing paper and wind the material round the pipes. It is self-adhesive. Overlap the tape as you wind it, especially at bends.

Glass fibre and mineral fibre bandage
An inexpensive form of lagging but not widely available in bandage form. You can make your own bandage from loft insulating blanket by tearing or cutting the blanket into strips 3in (75mm) wide.

Use a panel saw to cut the blanket while it is still in its wrapping, or use use a large pair of sharp scissors on the unrolled blanket. It can be difficult to wrap around pipes that lie close to a wall.

To prevent the fibres from irritating your skin, wear gloves while using the material, or wash your hands in cold water after handling.

Sleeved felt lagging
For plumbing in new pipes, sleeved felt lagging can be slipped over a pipe before installation. It is available in packs of about 72ft (22m), in a size that will fit both 15mm and 22mm diameter pipes, and the material is easy to cut to length with scissors.

To fit sleeved felt lagging to existing pipes, run scissors along the sleeve seam to undo the stitches. Wrap the lengths of felt round the pipes and tie them in place with string. This method provides very cheap insulation for pipework.

LAGGING PIPES WITH SELF-ADHESIVE FOAM WRAP

You will need
Tools Damp rag; scissors.
Materials Rolls of self-adhesive foam wrap.

Self-adhesive foam wrap is useful where there are many bends in the pipes and it would be difficult to use flexible foam tubes.

1 Clean the pipes with a damp rag and allow to dry.

2 For pipes in the loft, begin lagging at the cistern.

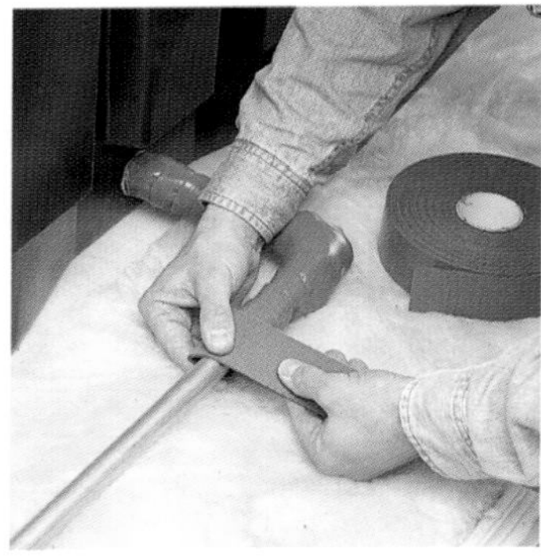

3 Continue to wrap the foam round the pipe, making generous overlaps of about one-third of the width of the bandage. Take care to cover the pipe well at bends – these are the vulnerable areas most likely to freeze. In an uninsulated loft, you can double the wrap along particularly vulnerable pipes which are near outside walls and airbricks, where cold winds can blow in.

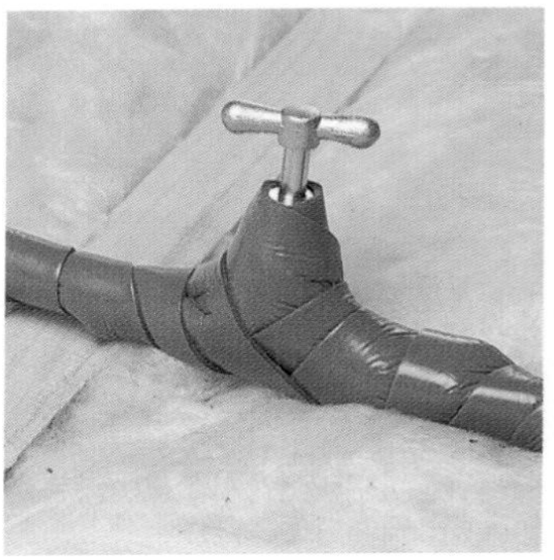

4 Take the wrap around any valves or stopcocks as you meet them, leaving only the handle exposed.

LAGGING PIPES WITH FLEXIBLE FOAM TUBE

You will need
Tools Damp rag; scissors.
Materials Foam tube of right size; adhesive tape; clips or adhesive.

1 Wipe over the pipes with the rag to remove dirt and allow to dry.

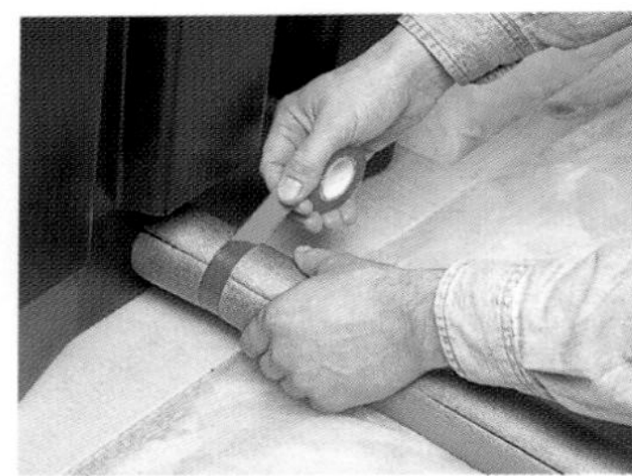

2 Lag the pipes leading from the cistern first, if you are insulating pipes in the loft. Wrap plastic adhesive tape round the first tube to hold it in place, even if the tube is one of the moulded, self-locking types. Push it up tight against the tank, so that the tank connector joint is covered.

3 Butt-join the tubes where they meet and wrap around the join to hold them tight. Also secure a tube with tape, clips or adhesive wherever it seems to want to open.

4 Cut the tube to fit around the body of a gate valve or stopcock as far as it will reach. Make sure the whole of the pipe is covered.

5 If you want to change the colour of the foam – which is only available in grey – coat it with emulsion paint. Never use oil-based paints or cellulose lacquers – they will affect the plastic.

Lagging a cold-water cistern

Never lay insulation under the cold-water cistern. Heat rising through the ceiling will help to prevent the water in the cistern from freezing. Purpose-made jackets can be used to insulate most cisterns. Measure the cistern's height and diameter if the cistern is round. If the cistern is square or rectangular, measure its height, width and length. It will not matter if the jacket you buy is too big, since the sections can be overlapped. If the cistern is an odd size or shape, or you want to provide extra insulation, use textile-wrapped glass fibre blankets. These are easier to handle and will not release fibres into the air if you disturb them in order to service the plumbing.

USING GLASS FIBRE BLANKET

You will need
Tools Steel tape measure; scissors.
Materials 150mm thick wrapped glass fibre blanket; sewing elastic; paper stapler or staple gun.

1 Wrap the cistern in a continuous length of blanket and cut it with scissors so that the edges meet. Close the open end by stapling the edges of the textile cover together.

2 Tie a length of elastic round the tank, slightly tensioning it.

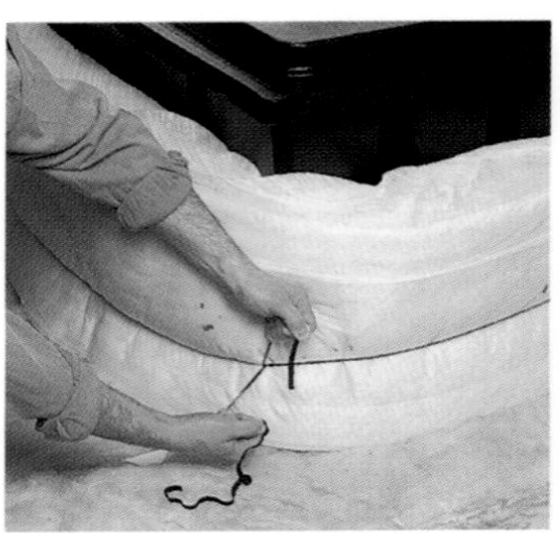

3 If necessary, wrap a second length of blanket round the tank, overlapping the first like a roof tile. Cut to length, close the end and tie

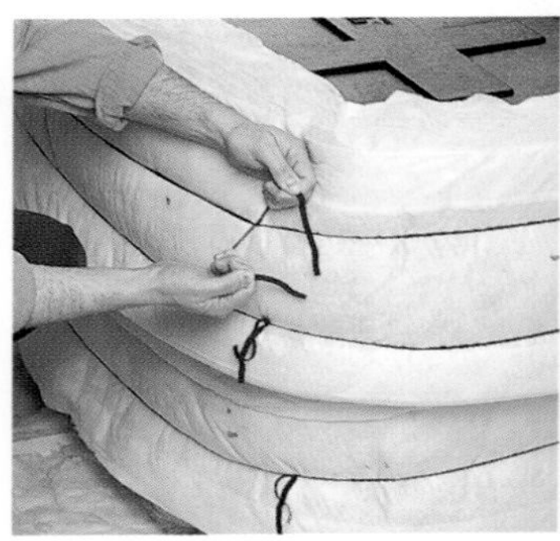

in the same way as the first layer. Extend the top layer beyond the top of the tank, to create a small rim to hold the tank's lid in place.

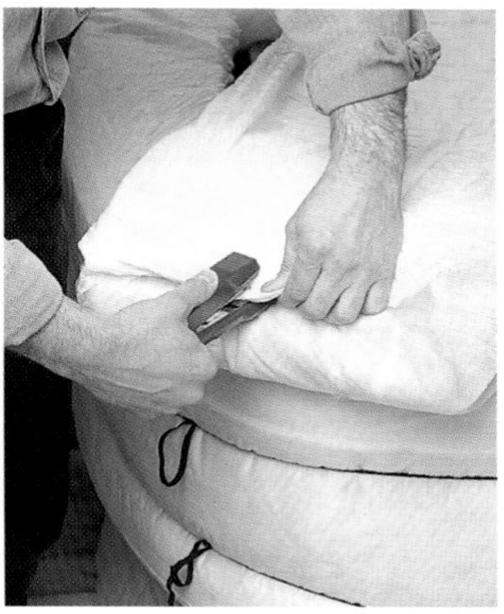

4 Measure the space inside the parapet on the tank lid. Cut lengths of blanket to match. Staple the ends closed. If the blanket is too wide, squeeze it up slightly to fit. Do not cut the blanket along its length.

COLD WEATHER CHECKS

Make sure no tap is left dripping. If that is not possible, put a plug in the basin or bath overnight. Drips cause ice to block waste pipes.

Never allow cisterns to overfill. Water in overflow pipes can freeze, causing the cistern to spill over the sides.

In a long cold spell, open the loft hatch occasionally to let in warmth from the house.

If you leave the house for short periods, keep the central heating turned on, turned down to the minimum. For long periods, drain the system by closing the main stopcock and opening all the taps. When water stops running, open the draincock near the stopcock. For central heating see page 351.

Insulating a high-level cistern

High level tanks in roof spaces are more at risk from freezing than tanks sitting on the loft floor. This is simply because the heat rising from the house is not trapped under the tank. For the same reason, the pipes leading up to the tanks are also at risk. If these pipes freeze, then there is a chance that the central heating boiler could explode. The most vulnerable pipe to freezing and bursting is the cold mains supply to the central heating tank, because the water in this pipe rarely moves so it has plenty of time to freeze.

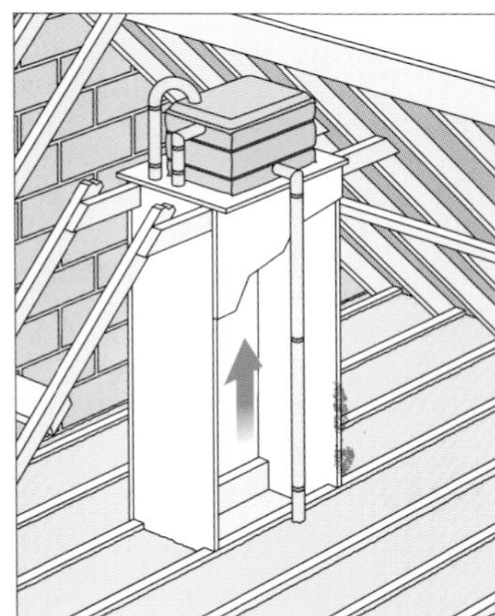

The best way to solve this problem is to build an enclosure directly under the tank in order to funnel heat upward from the house and give added protection to the pipes. You can do this from any insulation material but the easiest to work with is fire-retardant polystyrene. It is lightweight, easy to cut and self-supporting. You can buy sheets of it very cheaply from builders' merchants. You may find even cheaper sheets with corners broken off.

You will need

Tools Fine-tooth saw, hacksaw blade or serrated bread knife; tape measure; plumbline or spirit level.
Materials Sheets of polystyrene; polystyrene tile adhesive; 4-inch wire nails or wooden meat skewers; adhesive tape.

1 Use a plumbline to drop a vertical position from the edges of the high level tank down to the ceiling. Cut and peel back the insulation at this point so you have a clear piece of ceiling corresponding to the shape of the cylinder.

2 Lay a piece of polythene over the ceiling at this point, cut to the same size as the base of the enclosure. This is to stop vapour from the house, which evaporates through the ceiling, from entering the new enclosure and condensing on the underside of the tank.

3 Using the saw blade or knife cut the polystyrene sheet to form walls from the ceiling to the tank sides. Stick the sides together with a small amount of tile adhesive and push the nails or skewers through the corners to hold the sheets in place while the adhesive dries.

4 Use a little adhesive on the ceiling around the polystyrene to seal any gaps and hold the sheets in place. Remember that lofts can be quite draughty in high winds and polystyrene can be blown around if it is not fixed.

5 Bring the polystyrene right up to the underside of the tank. The tank must be supported on an independent structure. Tape the top of the polystyrene to the sides of the tank support.

6 The tank or tanks must be very well insulated. A thin jacket is not sufficient if the tank is near the slope of the roof. Use glass fibre blanket over the top of existing insulation to increase protection.

7 Make sure that the vent pipe, which goes over the tank, has an open passage to the tank to discharge any water. The vent pipe outlet must be above the water line.

Insulating a roof

If you want to use your loft for storing items which need to be kept warm and dry it is better to insulate the underside of the roof rather than leave the loft to suffer the same extremes of temperature as the outside. Remember that insulating the roof space will also keep the loft cooler in summer. This is often important because temperatures of over 35°C (95°F) can be reached throughout the summer.

THE IMPORTANCE OF VENTILATION

Airborne moisture that drifts up from the rooms below will condense on the first cold surface it meets. A good flow of air across the loft is the best way to clear the moisture and keep the roof timbers dry.

In old lofts without roofing felt under the tiles or slates, a great deal of air blows in and out through the gaps between the roof covering. If the roof has been protected against wind-blown rain by the layer of felt under the battens, then this prevents air coming in. Modern roofs therefore have ventilation around the eaves and also often at high level.

Any insulation that is laid under the felt on the underside of the roof pitch must allow ventilation to continue in order to clear any moisture from the surface of the felt. A gap of 2in (50mm) behind the insulation is usually enough to ensure good ventilation, provided there is room at the top for the air to escape and room at the bottom for it to enter. If you are in any doubt about this in relation to your roof, consult your local building control officer at your Town Hall.

If your roof is built from 4in x 2in rafters use a 2in thick insulation slab.

Do not use ordinary blanket insulation because it is impossible to control the air gap. Glass fibre cavity batts, which are semi-rigid, are perfect for this job because they are largely self supporting if cut very slightly wider than the space between the rafters.

Alternatively you can use expanded foam with a silver foil face for extra heat insulation.

INSULATING THE UNDERSIDE OF A ROOF

You will need

Tools Knife or large pair of scissors; staple gun. Possibly electric drill.
Materials Glass fibre cavity batts; garden netting. Building paper, hardboard sheets or foil-faced plasterboard and drywall screws.

1 Hold a length of insulation up to the underside of the roof and mark the width of the rafter gaps on the insulation.

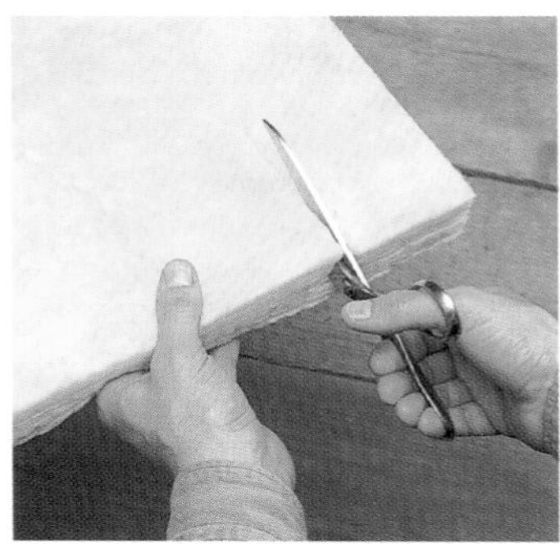

2 Using scissors or saw blade cut the insulation to fit between the rafters. Small off-cuts can be placed in the rafters first, to provide a spacing to maintain the air gap.

Insulating a roof (continued)

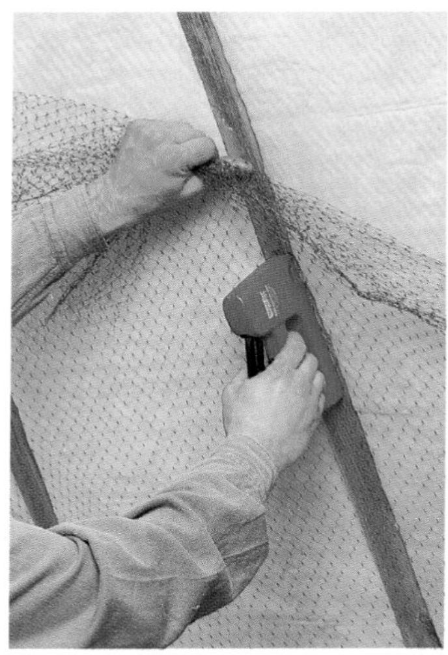

3 Do not hammer anything into the rafter because you could dislodge a tile or slate. Use a staple gun and nylon garden netting to hold the insulation in place. You may need a helper with this part of the task.

4 For a quick, simple finish, staple sheets of building paper to the rafters. Where two strips of building paper join, make sure they overlap by at least 4in (100mm) and tape along the join with waterproof adhesive tape. Alternatively, screw hardboard sheets to the rafters.

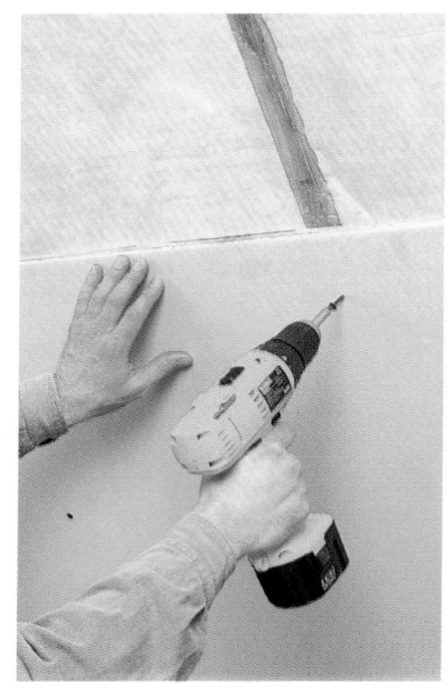

5 For an even better finish, you can screw foil-faced plasterboard to the rafters, as shown on the left. The foil should face the roof. Use plasterboard drywall screws, which can be put in with an electric drill.

COPING WITH A FLAT ROOF

Flat roofs should be insulated at the time they are built; but if you are having an extension added to your house, make sure that insulation is incorporated when the roof is constructed.

If an existing roof lacks insulation, remove a fascia board so that you can see into the space between the roof lining and ceiling.

The fascia board will either be nailed or screwed to the ends of the ceiling joists. Slide sheets of expanded polystyrene – preferably 3in (75mm) thick – into the gap.

If you cannot take off a fascia board, line the ceiling below, preferably with thermal board (page 243).

Alternatively, you can glue sheets of expanded polystyrene direct to the ceiling and perhaps stick a layer of expanded polystyrene ceiling tiles to the surface.

The thicker the layers of expanded polystyrene, the more effective the insulation will be.

Expanded polystyrene tiles by themselves will not be as effective as sheets of expanded polystyrene, but they are cheap and easy to fix.

VENTILATION OF FLAT ROOFS

Flat roofs should be ventilated above the insulation to prevent condensation on the timbers. You can do this by drilling small holes in the fascia or soffit board to take ventilator insect screens.

Insulating the walls of a house

TREATING CAVITY WALLS

It is good practice to insulate cavity walls because it saves heat loss from a house, but it is not a DIY job. To check if the cavities have already been filled, you can drill a hole into the cavity from the outside and feel with a probe. If it is empty, call in a contractor specialising in cavity insulation.

Since it is impossible to check how well the work has been done or how long the insulation will last, you have to rely on the contractor's integrity. You can get advice from the National Cavity Insulation Association, PO Box 12, Haslemere, Surrey GU27 3AH.

First, check that the walls show no sign of penetrating damp. Walls should not be filled while damp is present, so you must eliminate the cause of the damp and wait for the walls to dry out.

There are two main insulation systems to choose between, with similar installation methods. The dry system consists of mineral-wool fibres or expanded polystyrene beads being blown through holes drilled in the outer leaf of the wall until the cavity is filled.

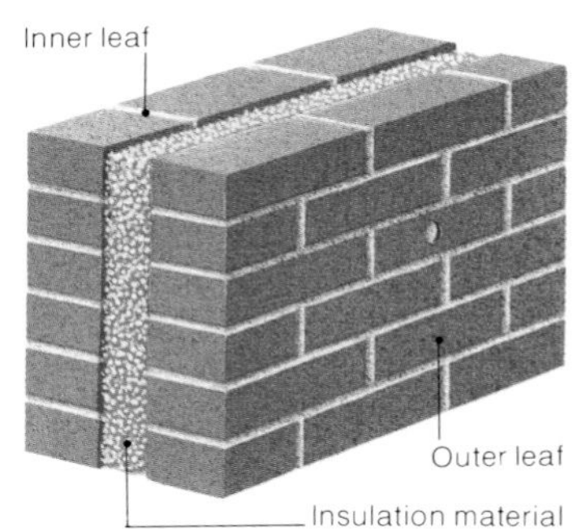

With the second system, the cavities are filled with foam. This is produced on site and pumped through holes drilled in the outer leaf. The foam normally dries after a few days and becomes firm. This system is not suitable for timber-framed houses.

PREVENTING HEAT LOSS FROM A RADIATOR

A reflector behind a radiator on an outside wall will reduce the amount of heat loss into the wall by about a quarter. It will also reflect some of the heat back into the room.

Rolls of heat-reflecting aluminium foil – easily cut with scissors – are sold with self-adhesive pads.

A cheap way of testing that the job is worth the expense is to make your own reflectors.

Cut one or more pieces of cardboard to fit behind the radiator and glue aluminium kitchen foil to one side. Slide the cardboard behind the radiator with the foil facing into the room. After about a year, the kitchen foil may oxidise and turn black so that it no longer reflects. You can then decide whether to replace it with the special heat-reflecting foil, which does not oxidise. It can also be positioned behind the radiator by sticking it to cardboard.

TREATING SOLID WALLS

Insulating the outside

Putting insulation on the outside of the house is another job that is usually done by a specialist company. The walls are clad with insulating slabs which then need decorating. This is an elaborate process because downpipes, windows and doors are affected by the extra thickness of the wall, and pipes will have to be repositioned.

It is an expensive job, only worthwhile in extreme conditions.

Insulating the inside

The extra width of insulation on the inside may bring the wall out beyond skirting boards, picture rails and architraves. Often lights, wall sockets, light switches and radiators will have to be repositioned.

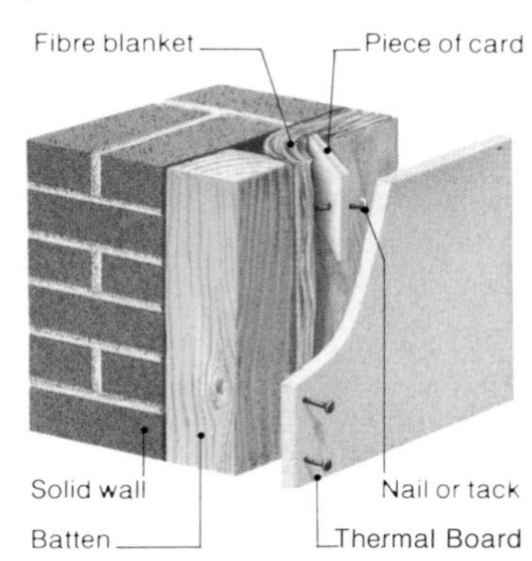

Insulate the walls with Thermal Board fixed to battens (page 250). Before nailing on the boards, pin fibre blanket to the battens.

ALTERNATIVELY, fix the Thermal Board direct to the walls with the adhesive recommended by the board manufacturer, and a secondary fixing of hammer-in fixings (page 232) or screws.

THE PROBLEM OF NOISE

It is impossible to prevent noise coming through a party wall. This is because the noise travels through adjoining walls, floor and ceiling as well as the shared wall. And once it gets into the fabric of the house nothing can stop it.

Far more can be achieved from the other side. The resiting of hi-fi equipment or TV to the far side of the room will achieve much more than spending a lot of money on insulation.

Another way to prevent noise from leaving a room is to fix insulating board, cork or polystyrene sheet to the wall, but this will not stop noise coming in.

On floors, a thick carpet and underlay will prevent most noise from travelling to the room below.

On windows, normal double glazing has little effect on noise from outside. The space between panes needs to be increased to about 4in or 6in (100-150mm). And the weight of glass for the secondary glazing must be heavier so that the two sheets do not vibrate in sympathy.

How double glazing works

Adding a second sheet of glass or plastic to a window traps a layer of air which acts as an insulator and also reduces draughts and condensation. Only about 5 per cent of the heat loss from a house is prevented by installing double glazing. It will not save much on fuel bills, but it will increase comfort near windows.

There are two main types of domestic double glazing – sealed and secondary.

Sealed double glazing consists of two panes of glass separated by a spacing strip, bonded together, and hermetically sealed all round at the factory before being fitted into the window frame. Inert gases that give extra sound and heat insulation may be sealed inside the gap, or the moisture may be removed from it during manufacture.

With secondary double glazing, a pane of glass or plastic is installed in a frame, then fixed over the existing window frame, leaving an air gap between. The size of the gap that is left between the two panes of glass is crucial. If it is too small there will be little insulation effect.

On the other hand, if the gap is too large convection currents will conduct cold air from the outer pane to the inner pane of glass, giving no more insulation than a single sheet.

The best air gap for the two panes is ¾in (19mm) – it can be a little smaller but not much larger.

SECONDARY GLAZING KITS

Simple secondary glazing kits are available at most DIY stores. They are sold in a range of sizes in packs which fit the width or height of a window. Aluminium and plastic are the main materials used.

Some of the more expensive systems are made of aluminium for strength, with a plastic insulating barrier within the aluminium to prevent condensation.

Each window needs a width pack and a height pack which match its measurements or which are slightly larger. Glass is not supplied with the kit. Get this from your local glazier, DIY store or builders' merchant once the frame is made.

With most kits, plastic channelling must be fitted together to make a frame which is fixed to the existing window frame.

> **SAFETY TIP**
> If you are putting up secondary glazing that is difficult to open quickly, consider the consequences of fire in the house. In an upstairs room it is advisable to leave one window without the secondary glazing as an escape route.

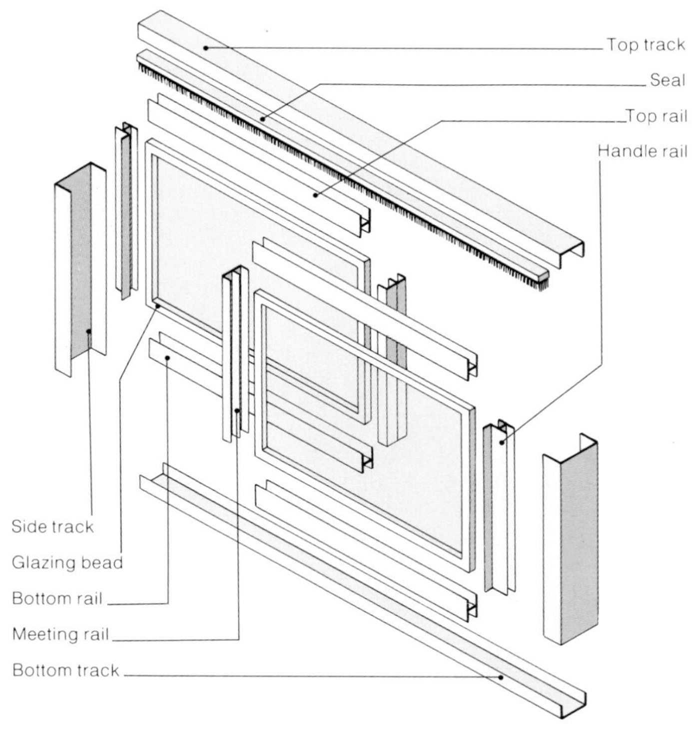

Fitting a kit The track is fitted around the window recess which needs to be at least 1¾in (45mm) deep to accommodate it. Two, three or four panels fit side by side and slide open horizontally.

CUSTOM-MADE DOUBLE GLAZING

Many double-glazing companies do the complete installation themselves, taking full responsibility for what the windows look like and for the effectiveness of the system. The cost of custom-made double glazing can run into thousands of pounds so get at least two or three quotations. If you are doubtful about a company, ask for names of customers living in your area who have had the system installed.

Some manufacturers rely on the customer to measure the windows and fill in the details on a form. If you choose to use a company which operates in this way, get all your measurements double-checked by another person.

SEALED UNITS

If you are replacing a window, you may consider installing sealed units instead of ordinary glass. A unit consists of two sheets of glass spaced between ¼in (6mm) and 1$\frac{1}{16}$in (28mm) apart. You cannot cut a hole for fan fitting after installation – a new unit is needed. If the seal is broken the unit is no more effective than a single sheet of glass, and if condensation forms between the panes it is impossible to remove. Most units are only guaranteed for 10 to 15 years and 10 years is considered a good average life.

Five cheap systems of double glazing

A house can be double-glazed very cheaply with materials that give effective results, but which usually have to be removed each summer and may have unattractive fittings. Nevertheless, the saving in cost this affords over a conventional system is considerable.

Rigid plastic sheet is cheaper, lighter and safer than glass, but is easily scratched. The cheapest plastic sheet discolours in a few years; more expensive plastic, such as acrylic (Perspex), remains clear for longer.

Study the fitting instructions supplied with the system and follow them carefully. Double-check your measurements before you order the glass or plastic sheet. Mistakes can be expensive.

Clean the windows, inside and out, before you start to install double glazing.

If you are using a system that involves adhesive tape, make sure the window frame is clean and dry. The tape will not stick to surfaces that are dirty or damp, or to surfaces that are newly painted.

Wait at least a week after painting before putting up this type of double glazing on windows.

POLYTHENE SHEETING

For really cheap double glazing, where appearance does not matter, fix a sheet of polythene over the window frame.

Polythene is not transparent and it tends to sag, but it is adequate on windows which are not opened and which are hidden from view. Or it could be used on the windows of a garden work shed.

You will need
Tools Scissors.
Materials Sheet of polythene; roll of double-sided adhesive tape.

1 Cut the polythene a little larger than the window so that it overlaps the frame by about 2in (50mm).

2 Stick the double-sided adhesive tape all around the window frame with the backing still in place.

3 Remove the backing from the tape to expose the sticky surface.

4 Press the polythene against the tape, starting at the top of the window frame and working downwards. Keep it as taut as possible as you work.

5 Trim off the excess polythene to make the finish as neat as possible. Be careful not to press against the polythene once it has been fitted in place.

Five cheap systems of double glazing (continued)

INSULATING FILM

A clear plastic film is stuck to the window frame and then shrunk with gentle heat from a hair dryer to remove wrinkles.

Although it is not a permanent system, you could extend its life by attaching the plastic film to a frame of timber battens. The framework could be taken down when not required and kept for later use.

You will need
Tools Scissors; hair dryer.
Materials Kit containing clear film and double-sided adhesive tape.

1 Cut a sheet of film a little larger than the window, so that it overlaps all round the window frame by about 2in (50mm).

2 Stick the double-sided adhesive tape around the frame.

3 Remove the backing from the tape and press the film against it, working from the top downwards and keeping it as taut as possible.

4 Warm the film with a hair dryer to remove wrinkles.

5 Trim off the excess film.

PLASTIC CHANNELLING

Strips of plastic channelling are fitted along the edges of a sheet of glass or rigid plastic. They are then fixed to the window frame with screws and fixing clips.

Some systems have hinged channelling that allows the secondary glazing to be opened.

Other types are fixed to the window frame all round and cannot be opened. They have to be taken down completely in summer before any windows can be opened.

Measure the window to allow for the glass or rigid plastic to overlap onto the frame, leaving enough space for the fixing clips to be screwed to the frame.

You will need
Tools Trimming knife or tenon saw (depending on the type of channelling); pencil; bradawl; screwdriver. Perhaps a mitre box.
Materials Sheet of 4mm glass or 2mm-4mm rigid plastic; plastic channelling; screws; fixing clips.

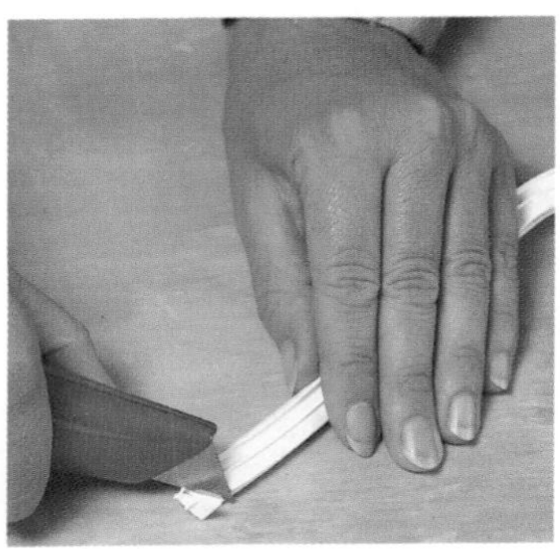

1 Cut the channelling to fit the four edges of the glass or plastic sheet. Mitre the ends to give a neat fit. If the channelling is rigid you will need a tenon saw or hacksaw and a mitre box.

2 Push the channelling onto the glass or plastic sheet.

3 Hold the glazing over the window while a helper marks positions for the fixing holes, following the maker's instructions for spacing.

4 Deepen the marked spots with the bradawl to provide pilot holes, and screw the fixing clips and glazing in place.

FIXING WITH VELCRO TAPE

Rigid plastic sheet can be fixed with self-adhesive touch-and-close fastening tape, such as Velcro.

When buying the plastic, measure it to overlap ½in (13mm) on all sides of the window frame.

Do not use glass; it is too heavy for the system.

The double glazing can be removed when necessary but the loop part of the tape will have to remain in place and may look unsightly.

You will need
Tools Scissors.
Materials Self-adhesive touch-and-close fastening tape; 2mm-4mm thick clear rigid plastic; foam-strip draught excluder.

1 Cut several pieces of tape about 1½in (38mm) long. It is too expensive to use in long strips.

2 Peel the backing paper off the loop (soft) side of the tape and fix it in place at intervals around the window frame.

3 Leave the backing paper on the hook side of the tape, and press the pieces onto the loop strips.

4 Stick foam-strip draught excluder between the patches to prevent draughts.

5 Peel off the remaining backing paper and press the pane in place.

MAGNETIC FIXING STRIP

Rigid plastic sheets can be fitted as secondary glazing using magnetic fixing strip. The strip has two self-adhesive parts, a magnetic strip that adheres to the plastic and a metal strip to go on the frame.

The system is designed for use with plastic up to 4mm thick. Never use it with glass because it is not strong enough to hold the weight.

Have the plastic cut slightly larger than the window so that it overlaps onto the frame by about 1in (25mm).

You will need
Tools Scissors or trimming knife.
Materials Magnetic fixing strip; 2mm-4mm thick clear rigid plastic.

1 Cut the strip to fit around the plastic, mitring the corners with sharp scissors or a trimming knife.

2 Stick the strip to the plastic, with the metal half upwards.

3 Press sheet to frame. The metal strip will stay on the frame when the plastic is removed.

4 The metal strip can be covered with a thin coat of paint to match the window frame. This makes it less noticeable when the sheet is removed. When redecorating, rub the surface with fine abrasive paper to prevent a build-up of paint.

HELPFUL TIP
Even the best-installed secondary double glazing may steam up slightly during the winter months. When one of your windows becomes misty, open up the frame and wipe away the moisture with a clean chamois leather.

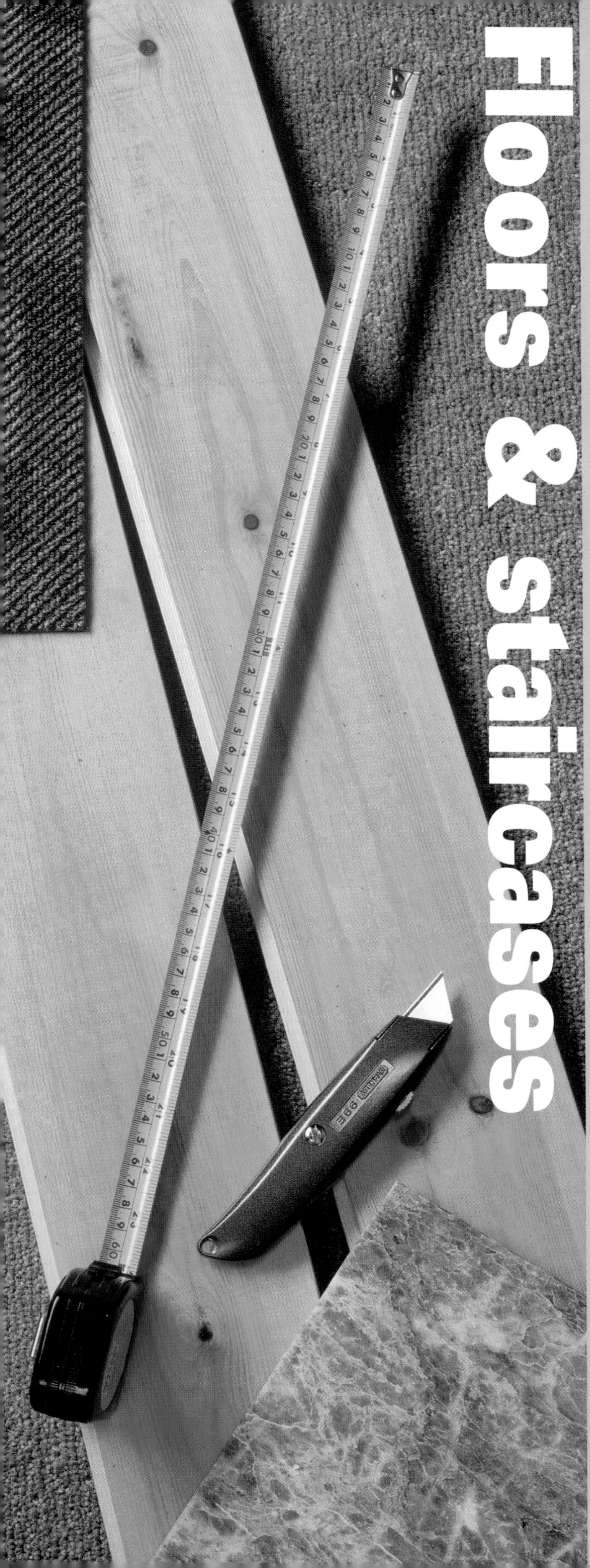

9 Floors & staircases

Floors

Staircases

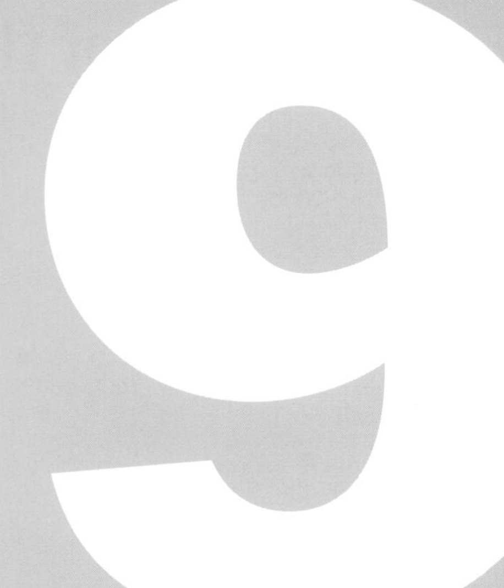

What type of floor do you have?

There are two kinds of floor, each with its own set of problems. Suspended floors are fixed some distance above the ground; direct-to-earth floors actually rest on the ground. Upper-storey floors must obviously be suspended, but ground-level floors can be either suspended or direct-to-earth. Basement floors are always direct-to-earth.

SUSPENDED TIMBER FLOORS

Suspended floors normally consist of floorboards supported on timber joists. The joists are usually at least 4in × 2in (100mm × 50mm) thick and are spaced between 16in and 24in (400mm and 610mm) apart, according to their width and thickness.

Ground-floor joists are supported either in sockets in the external walls, created by omitting bricks, or on a low wall (known as a sleeper wall) built just inside the main one.

Joist sockets are higher than the damp-proof course to prevent rising damp from reaching the timber. A sleeper wall has a damp-proof course on top of it, and usually there is a length of timber (the timber wall plate) on top of the damp-proof course. The joists are fixed to the wall plate.

Upper-floor joists can also be supported in sockets, but often rest in joist hangers – galvanised metal holders mortared into the brickwork.

Long joists also need support in the middle. On the ground floor this is provided by an intermediate sleeper wall. For upper floors the partition wall between two rooms below will often support the joists of the floor above.

The floorboards lie across the joists and are fixed to them with floorboard nails – two for each joist.

In most 20th-century houses, floorboards are usually ¾in (19mm) thick, and are tongued-and-grooved to prevent gaps developing between them as they shrink. Houses built before the First World War often have thicker boards which may be square edged (not tongued-and-grooved).

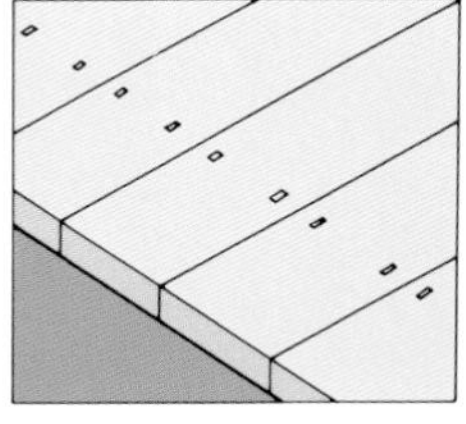
Square-edged boards

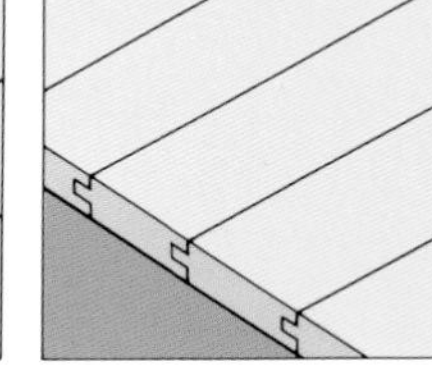
Tongued-and-grooved boards

Chipboard floors

Houses built since the 1960s may have chipboard sheets instead of floorboards. Flooring-grade chipboard comes in two main thicknesses – ¾in and ⅞in (19mm and 22mm). The main sizes are 8ft × 4ft (2440mm × 1220mm) and 8ft × 2ft (2440mm × 600mm). The sheets may have either tongued-and-grooved or square edges.

Chipboard floors are also nailed to joists, which are spaced between 16in and 24in (400mm and 610mm) apart according to the size and thickness of the board.

Ventilation

The underside of ground-storey floors must be well ventilated to keep them dry, otherwise rot may form. Grilles or air bricks are let into the walls below floor level, and gaps are left in intermediate sleeper walls so air can circulate. These openings should never be blocked up – as a draught-proofing measure, for example.

HOW A SUSPENDED FLOOR IS BUILT

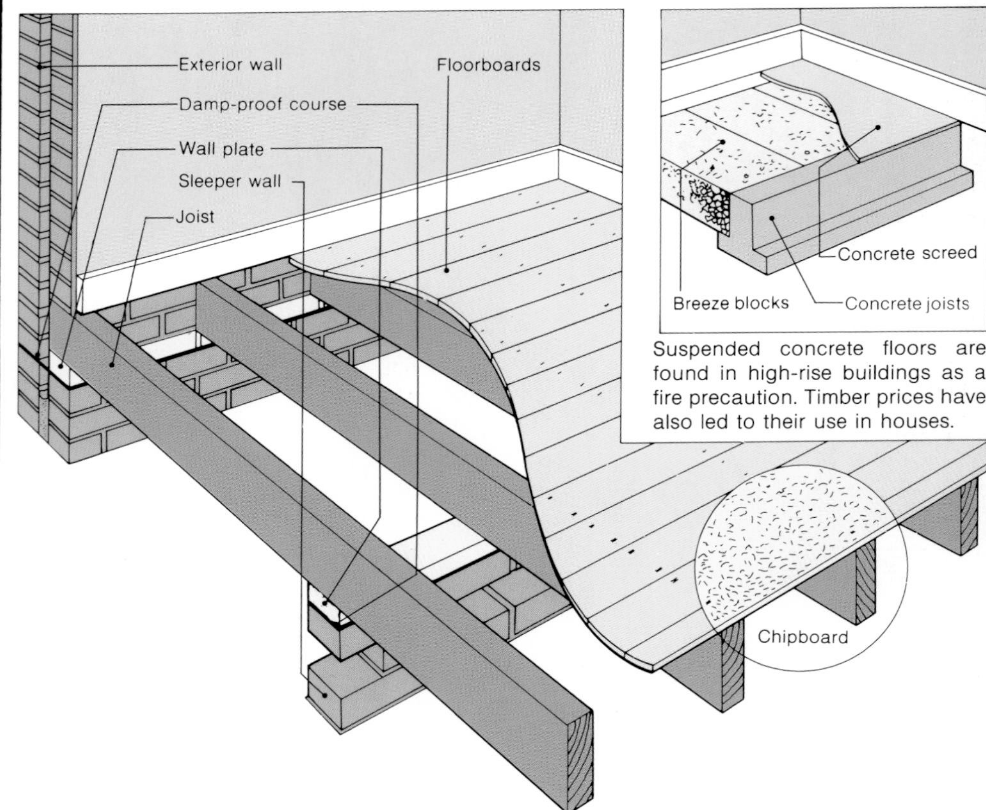

Suspended concrete floors are found in high-rise buildings as a fire precaution. Timber prices have also led to their use in houses.

HOW A MODERN DIRECT-TO-EARTH FLOOR IS BUILT

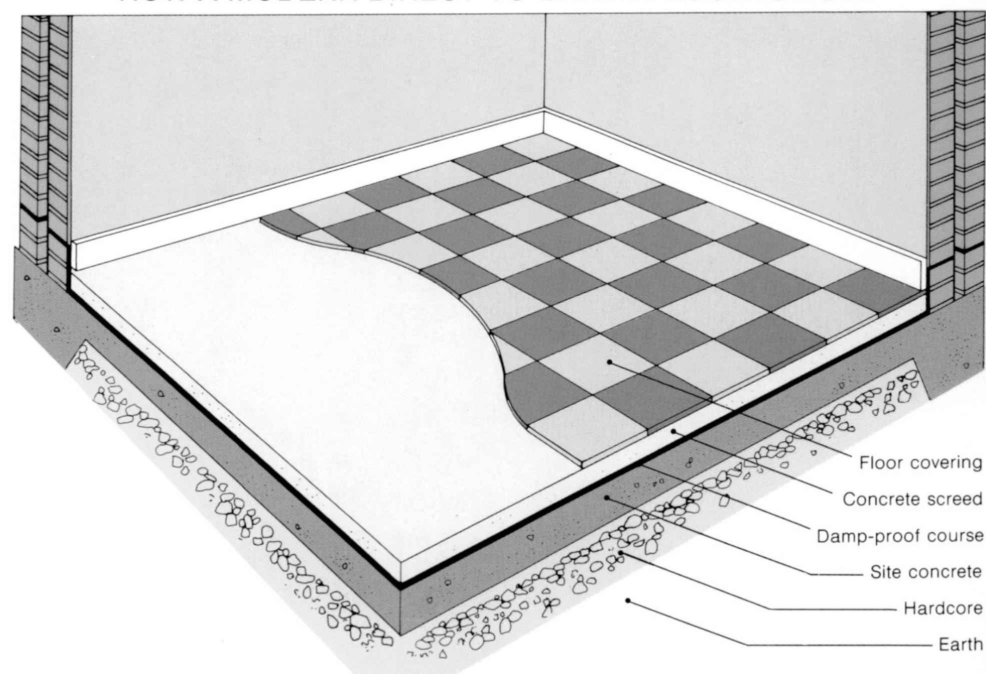

DIRECT-TO-EARTH FLOORS

Old houses may have floors of flagstones, quarry tiles or other material embedded directly into the ground, with or without mortar.

Direct-to-earth floors less than 50 years old will probably be of concrete, and if they were built since 1945 they should incorporate a damp-proof membrane linking up to the damp-proof course of the wall. The membrane may consist of asphalt, bituminous emulsion or polythene.

DANGER BELOW

The space beneath a suspended timber floor is ideal for running electric cables, water pipes and gas pipes. Before driving in nails, locate pipes or cables under the boards with a metal detector (page 230).

Pipes and cables may also be embedded in a concrete floor. They should be sunk out of harm's way, but when making fixings use nails that are no longer than necessary.

Lifting and replacing a floorboard

First find out whether the boards are tongued-and-grooved or square edged by poking a thin-bladed knife between them. If they are square edged, the blade will pass right through.

You will need

Tools Thin-bladed knife; drill and twist bits; padsaw; bolster chisel or car tyre lever; hammer; screwdriver. Also for tongued-and-grooved boards: hand-held circular saw (or wide-blade chisel and mallet, or panel saw, or flooring saw).
Materials 2in or 3in (50mm or 75mm) floorboard nails; 3in (75mm) No. 8 screws; pieces of timber about 1½in (38mm) square and 4in (100mm) longer than the width of the boards.

> SAFETY TIP
> Whenever you do not require immediate access below the floor, put the board back loosely in position, even if only for a few minutes. That will eliminate the risk of someone stepping into the hole.

REMOVING SQUARE-EDGED BOARDS

Before lifting the board, you must cut across it at each end just before it meets a joist. Lines of nails indicate joist centres.

1 Drill a ⅜in (10mm) starting hole near the edge, and complete the cut with a padsaw.

2 Starting at one end, prise out the fixing nails by inserting a bolster chisel or car tyre lever under the board and levering up.

3 Once you have loosened one or two sets of nails, push the handle of a hammer under the board as far from the loose end as possible, and press hard on the end. This sends a shock wave along the whole length, loosening nails farther along which you can remove.

4 Push the hammer farther forward, and repeat the process, until the board is free.

HOW TO REMOVE TONGUES

On tongued-and-grooved boards, the tongues on each side of the board must be removed. If adjoining boards are to be lifted, only the tongues at the outer edges of the group need cutting.

1 The best tool is a hand-held circular saw. Adjust its depth of cut so that the blade just protrudes below the underside of the tongue. Since floorboards are usually ¾in (19mm) thick, the underside of the tongue will be about ½in (13mm) below the surface. This depth of cut will avoid pipes and cables.

2 Place the blade between the boards, switch on the power, and move the saw along the length of the board.

ALTERNATIVELY, chop off the tongues with your widest-blade chisel and a mallet.

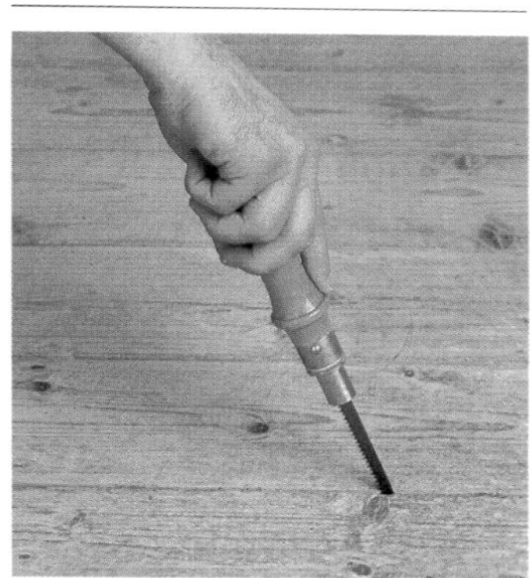

ALTERNATIVELY, try sawing them off, having drilled a starting hole; but this is not easy.

ALTERNATIVELY, special flooring saws are available and can sometimes be hired.

> CURING LOOSE AND SQUEAKING BOARDS
>
> A floorboard squeaks because it is not firmly held to its joist. When someone steps on it, it springs under the weight, rubbing against a neighbouring board.
>
> A squeak can be temporarily cured by dusting talc down the side of the board.
>
> Not all loose boards squeak – there may be too big a gap around them – but even so they should be properly secured before a floor covering is laid, otherwise you will feel the movement under new flooring.
>
> A board becomes loose when one or more of its fixing nails is shaken free – by vibration or the movement of the joist below. Prise out the nail if it is still there, starting if necessary with pincers.
>
> Refix the board with a screw big enough to fill the hole left by the nail. A No. 8 screw, 2in (50mm) long, should be suitable.
>
> The screw will hold the board securely in place, and as it goes exactly into the same hole as the nail there should be no danger of striking a cable or pipe.

3 With the tongues removed you should be able to see the joists between the boards. Now remove the board in the same way as a square-edged board.

REPLACING THE BOARD

Buy new nails (old ones may be rusty, or may be damaged during the lifting process), and use the proper floorboard type.

You will not be able to nail the board to a joist at its ends – as it has been sawn off before the joists.

1 Screw a short batten to the side of the joist, its top edge jammed hard up against the underside of adjacent floorboards still in position.

2 Nail the board to the batten.

ALTERNATIVELY, if you have old ceilings, it may be wise to screw the boards down. Vibration from heavy hammering can cause ceiling damage. Screws are also useful if access may be needed to pipes or cables in future.

Repairing a damaged floor

Floorboards may be so badly damaged that they have to be removed (page 273) and replaced with fresh ones.

The new floorboards should be exactly the same thickness and width as the old ones. Modern floorboards are usually 4in (100mm) wide and ¾in (19mm) thick, but older ones can be much larger.

You may find it impossible to buy wood of exactly the right thickness (width should be easier to match). If the floor is to be sanded (page 278) it will not matter too much if the new boards are slightly thicker than the existing ones. A heavy-duty floor sander will easily remove the excess thickness.

In all other cases use slightly thinner timber and raise it by laying scraps of hardboard or plywood on the joists, holding them in place with panel pins and nailing the board on top.

If you are replacing only one or two boards, buy square-edged floorboards.

If you have a floor made of tongued-and-grooved boards, and several of them side by side are defective, buy new boards of the same type.

However, do not confuse floorboards with the tongued-and-grooved cladding sold for decorative use on walls and ceilings. It is a much lighter material and not suitable for flooring.

You will need

Tools Saw; hammer; perhaps a chisel; perhaps an electric drill and $\frac{1}{16}$in (2mm) twist bit.

Materials Floorboards; 2in (50mm) or 3in (75mm) floorboard nails; perhaps scraps of hardboard or plywood and panel pins.

LAYING SQUARE-EDGED BOARDS

1 Cut the timber to the same length as the old boards.

2 Lay the new boards in place and nail them to each joist with floorboard nails.

LAYING TONGUED-AND-GROOVED BOARDS

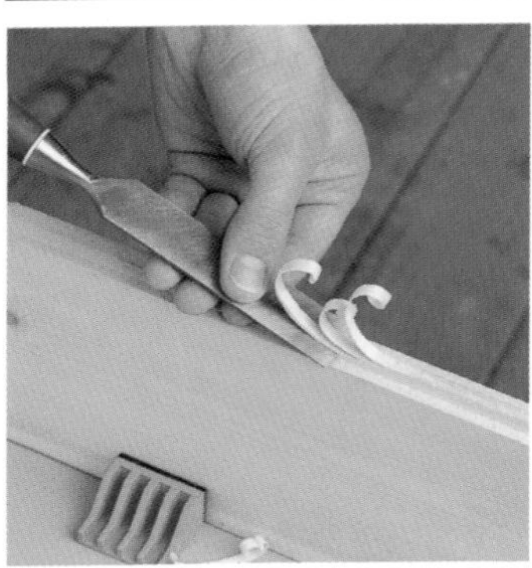

1 Cut the first board to length, and shave off its tongue with a chisel or plane.

2 Lay it in position, butting its former tongued edge to the groove edge of an existing board. This groove will be filled with the tongue of the old board, which you have removed (page 273).

3 Cut the second board to length, lay it on the joists and tap it into place so that its tongue locates in the groove of the first new board. Continue with the other boards.

4 When you come to the final board, you will probably have to shave off its tongue, as it will be too difficult to manoeuvre into place with the tongue attached.

ALTERNATIVELY there is a dodge that sometimes works. Shave off the underside of the groove of the second to last board. It may be possible to tap the last board into place with tongue intact.

5 Fix the boards to the joists with floorboard nails. You will be able to see the positions of the joists from the lines of nails in the existing floorboards.

6 If nails have to be driven in near the end of a board, first drill pilot holes smaller than the nails to avoid splitting the wood.

Replacing a floor with chipboard

If a floor is beyond repair, it can be replaced with chipboard more cheaply than with softwood floorboards.

Flooring-grade chipboard is sold in two thicknesses – ¾in (19mm) and ⅞in (22mm). If the centres of your joists are no farther apart than 18in (460mm), use ¾in (19mm) sheets.

The most common sheet sizes are 8ft × 4ft (2440mm × 1220mm) and 8ft × 2ft (2440mm × 600mm). As chipboard is heavy, use the smallest sheets available, unless you have got a friend to help you.

Flooring chipboard can be bought with either tongued-and-grooved edges – for simpler installation – or with square edges for a saving in cost.

Fix the sheets to the joists with No.10 gauge annular ring nails. Use 2¼in (55mm) nails for ¾in (19mm) sheets and 2½in (60mm) for ⅞in (22mm) sheets.

Before starting the job, find the position of the joists in the floor. The floorboard nails should reveal them, but it is advisable to take up a board to confirm.

Work out the thickness of the sheets to suit the joist spacing, and the number you will need.

You must be ready to receive the boards when they are delivered; bad storage can distort them. Lay them flat in a pile inside the house. At least 24 hours before you begin work, loose-lay them in the room where they are to be laid so they can adjust to the moisture content.

HELPFUL TIPS

If access may be needed in future to a cable junction or central heating pipe, fix the sheet above it with screws, which are much easier to remove than nails.

If you are flooring an upstairs room or loft, and are worried that the ceiling below is weak, drill pilot holes in the chipboard for the nails. This will avoid unnecessary vibration when you hammer them in.

A WARNING BEFORE YOU START

The wall on one side of the room may be a hollow partition erected after the floor was installed. It is likely to cover the top of a joist. If so, you must nail a length of 2in (50mm) square timber to the side of the joist to provide a fixing point for the chipboard.

If the partition wall has been built between joists, no fixing point for the chipboard will be available and a new joist would have to be installed. This is a job for a builder.

Before you start work, you can see the position of the joists by the rows of nails in the floorboards. Joists are usually spaced at regular intervals, so you will be able to judge whether the partition lies on top of one. If it does not, it may be wise not to proceed – or to get a new joist put in before you lay the chipboard.

You will need

Tools Circular saw, panel saw or flooring saw; hammer; brush for applying adhesive; rag. Perhaps a pencil.

Materials Chipboard; annular ring nails; lengths of 2in (50mm) square timber; 3in (75mm) oval nails; PVA wood adhesive.

1 Start by taking up enough floorboards to give space for the first row of chipboard.

2 If there is not enough space between skirting board and joist to push in the chipboard, the skirting board will have to be removed from the wall.

3 Begin laying the chipboard in one corner.

4 A gap of ⅜in (10mm) must be left around the edge of the room to allow the chipboard to expand in damp weather. If you have removed the skirting, you can see that the correct gap is maintained as you lay the chipboard.

Otherwise push the sheet of chipboard against the wall under the skirting board, draw a pencil line where it meets the skirting and then pull it away by the correct distance.

SQUARE-EDGED SHEETS

1 Lay square-edged sheets with the long edge parallel to the joists. They must be supported on every edge, so the long sides should rest on the centre of a joist, and the ends should rest on a nogging.

2 Make the nogging from a piece of 2in (50mm) square-section wood placed between the joists and fixed with 3in (75mm) oval nails driven down at an angle through the nogging and into the joist.

3 If the width of the sheets does not suit your joists, cut them to fit. However, if this involves too much waste it may be a better idea to use tongued-and-grooved sheets which are laid across the joists and so do not have to be cut to width.

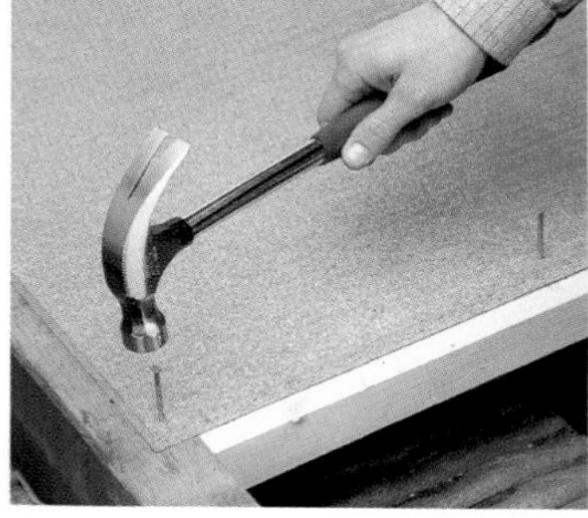

4 Nail the sheets at 12in (300mm) intervals all the way round, putting the nails ⅜in (10mm) in from the edge. On intermediate joists put nails 24in (610mm) apart.

TONGUE-AND-GROOVE SHEETS

1 Position tongued-and-grooved sheets with the long edge across the joists and nail them down. Drive in four nails to each joist, one ⅜in (10mm) from each edge and the others at equal distances.

2 The sheet must be supported at the ends, so saw off any overhang close to the side of the joist.

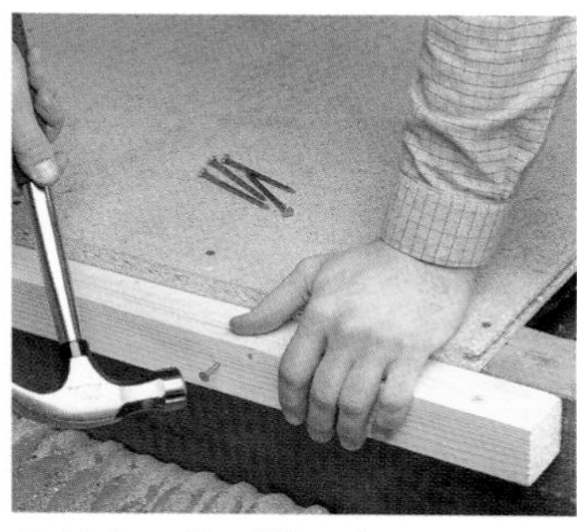

3 Nail a 2in (50mm) square-section batten to the side of the joist, flush with the top, and fix the next board to it.

COMPLETING THE JOB

Smear the meeting edges of all boards with PVA wood adhesive, then push them firmly together. The adhesive will prevent the floor from squeaking.

Wipe off any glue from the surface with a damp cloth.

If you need to hammer tongued-and-grooved sheets together, use a block of wood to protect the edge from damage.

When you come to the end of a row, cut the sheet to fit.

Use the offcut to begin the next row so that the joins do not coincide.

Finally, replace the skirting, if you have removed it.

Preparing a wooden floor to lay a covering

Most people know that preparation is needed before they paint a room or hang wallpaper, but tend to think that a floor covering can go down on any old surface.

In fact, preparation is probably more important for floor laying than any other decorative process.

Vinyl or cork flooring will show any ridges in the sub-floor, and will wear unevenly. Even carpet will wear more quickly on the ridges.

Material laid on a properly prepared floor will look far better and will last longer.

Is the structure right?

First, make sure that the floor is in good structural condition.

If it feels unstable as you walk across it, there may be a defective joist, and you should call in a builder. If there is a feeling of sponginess, there could be an outbreak of woodworm or rot below the surface. Take up a board and check, and treat or replace as necessary.

Any damp in the floor must be cured or it will attack the new covering.

Loose boards must be fixed, and badly damaged boards replaced.

Removing old tacks

Most floors are already perfectly sound, but there may be tacks left behind from a previous covering.

Prise them up with a claw hammer, pincers or tack lifter. When using a hammer, put a piece of card or thin wood under its head to protect the floor.

The best tool, however, is the tack lifter. It has a handle and blade rather like a screwdriver, but the blade tip is wider, slightly curved and has a V cut. You slip the V under the head of a tack and give a twist of the handle.

The perfect surface

Now you can create a perfect surface for any sort of covering by lining the floor with hardboard.

This may seem like unnecessary bother and expense. But it is not difficult and does not add much to the overall cost. And it ensures an excellent result.

Hardboard will level off boards that are curling at the edges; it will cover small gaps between boards, and even mask minor damage. It also covers old stains and polishes.

LINING A WOOD FLOOR WITH HARDBOARD

Use ⅛in (3mm) thick hardboard for lining a floor. The largest sheets are cumbersome, so buy boards 4ft (1220mm) square, 3ft (915mm) square, or 4ft×2ft (1220mm×610mm).

Lay the hardboard with the mesh side up. This forms a better key for adhesives than the smooth side. And when you nail down the sheets the nail heads will sink below the mesh and not create pimple marks in the final floor covering.

The fixing is best done with annular nails – they have ringed shafts for extra grip. Use nails ¾in (19mm) long so that they will not burst through the floorboards with the risk of causing damage to cables or pipes.

After laying the boards, leave them at least overnight before laying the floor covering.

You will need

Tools Hammer; panel saw; large paintbrush; measuring jug; bowl or paint kettle.

Materials Sheets of hardboard ⅛in (3mm) thick; water; ¾in (19mm) annular nails – probably about ½lb (¼ kilo).

1 The boards must be given a moisture content suitable for the room – a process known as conditioning. Otherwise they may become distorted. Brush ¾ pint (½ litre) of water into the mesh side

TAKING UP OLD FLOORINGS

It is not always necessary to take up an old floor covering before you lay the new one. Old tiles and parquet that are firmly stuck can form the basis of a new floor.

But carpets and sheet vinyls – and any other flooring that is not well stuck down – must be removed.

A garden spade is an excellent tool for lifting floorings when the glue is not holding well – vinyl tiles or old lino for example. Its blade has a sharp edge that you can push under the material (file it sharper if necessary).

The long handle allows plenty of leverage for lifting. And you can work standing up, which puts rather less strain on your back.

For a large area, a floor-stripping machine can be obtained from some hire shops.

Old quarry tiles are difficult to remove, and may only reveal an unsatisfactory sub-floor underneath. It is probably best to leave them in place.

If just a few tiles are damaged or missing, remove damaged pieces with a bolster and club hammer – wearing safety goggles. Then replace them with new tiles (page 281). Alternatively, fill the gaps with sand and cement. You can buy a bag of dry-mix.

If a quarry-tiled floor is in a really bad state, call in a builder.

Preparing a wooden floor to lay a covering (continued)

of 4ft (1220mm) square boards, and leave them stacked mesh to mesh perfectly flat on the floor of the room they will occupy for 48 hours (not much more or less) before laying.

They will adjust gradually to the humidity of the room, and dry out further when nailed down, tightening up like a drum skin to form a perfect surface for the final floor covering.

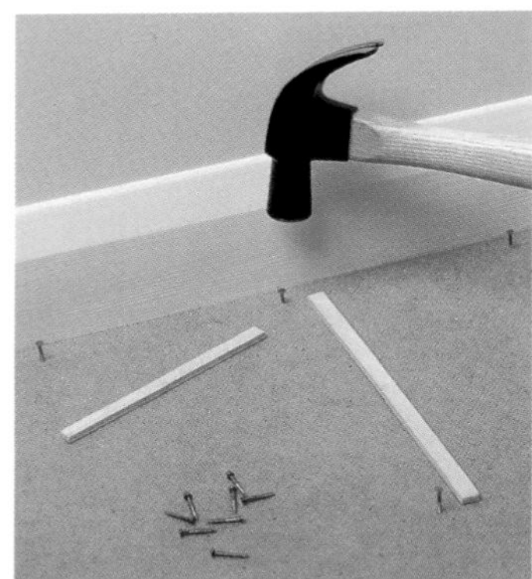

2 Begin laying the boards in a corner of the room, and start nailing along one edge of a sheet, ½in (13mm) in from the edge.

Work sideways and forwards, pyramid fashion (see the diagram). The nails should be 6in (150mm) apart along the edges of the board and 9in (230mm) apart in the middle of the board.

It helps to cut pieces of wood the appropriate length, and use them as guides to get the nails correctly spaced out.

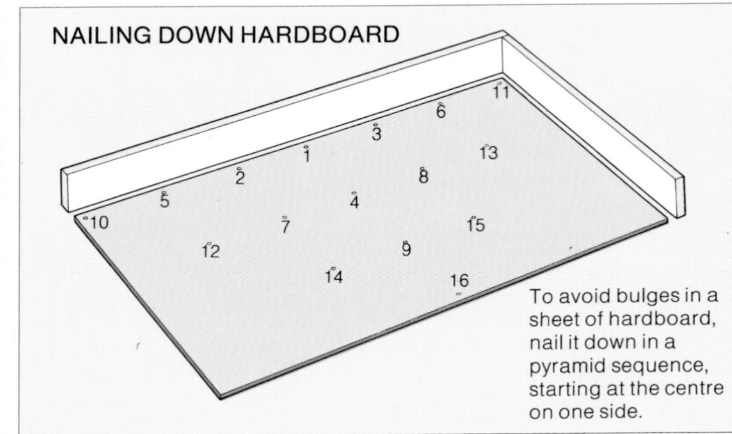

To avoid bulges in a sheet of hardboard, nail it down in a pyramid sequence, starting at the centre on one side.

3 Butt the second board firmly against the first, and begin nailing along the meeting edge.

4 Continue in this way until at the end of the row you will have to cut a board to fit.

You do not need to cut the boards to a perfect fit to the skirting board. Gaps up to ¼in (6mm) do not matter. They would be covered anyway by tiles or the gripper rod that holds a carpet.

Use the offcut from the previous board to start the next row. This not only avoids waste, but also prevents the joins from lining up across the room.

5 When you reach the end of the room you will have to cut each sheet in the final row to width to fit the remaining space.

HARDBOARD AS A FINAL FLOOR COVERING

Hardboard is an attractive floor covering in its own right – ideal for young couples starting off in a first home that has poor floorboards.

For this use, lay the hardboard smooth side up.

Oil-tempered hardboard is more durable than the standard type. Buy ⅛in (3mm) thick sheets, 3ft (915mm) square or 2ft (610mm) square and treat them like large tiles (page 279), beginning in the middle of the room and working towards the edges.

If you cannot get square sheets, buy 4ft × 2ft (1220mm × 610mm) sheets and ask the supplier to cut them in half.

After they have been laid, apply two or three coats of flooring-grade varnish. Rub on the first with a lint-free rag to spread it. The floor can be given fresh coats as it shows scuff marks.

Preparing a solid floor to lay a covering

A direct-to-earth floor can suffer from three faults that make it unsuitable for a floor covering to be laid. It can be damp; a concrete floor can suffer from a condition called 'dusting'; or the floor could be uneven.

Is the floor damp?

If a floor is damp there is no point in laying a covering. The moisture will eventually destroy the covering itself and any adhesive that was used to hold it down.

Damp in a floor is not always obvious, but if a direct-to-earth floor was laid before the Second World War it is unlikely to have a damp-proof membrane, and will have to be treated.

Ways of dealing with damp in floors are given on page 462.

A cure for 'dusting'

A concrete floor may suffer from a condition known as dusting, in which dust continually forms on the surface, no matter how often you sweep it.

This can be cured by putting on a concrete-floor sealer sold by builders' merchants. Apply it following the manufacturer's instructions. Alternatively, you can use diluted PVA adhesive.

LEVELLING A SOLID FLOOR

A solid floor with fairly small holes or ridges can be evened out with a floor-levelling compound.

A water-based compound is the easiest to apply, and can be used on terrazzo and quarry tiles, as well as on concrete.

You will need

Tools Bucket; scrubbing brush; steel float; perhaps a trowel.

Materials Water-based levelling compound; sugar soap; water; perhaps sand-and-cement mix and PVA adhesive.

1 Clean the floor by scrubbing with a solution of sugar soap in water. Rinse and allow the floor to dry thoroughly.

2 Any holes deeper than $\frac{3}{16}$in (5mm) must first be filled with a sand-and-cement mix; bags of mortar to which you merely add water are ideal.

To ensure a good bond, first brush a priming coat of PVA adhesive on the patch to be filled, and add a little of it to the mortar. Trowel the surface of the mortar patch as smooth as possible.

3 Fill small dents with a little levelling compound, and allow it to dry thoroughly before applying the main coat. Dampen – but do not saturate – the floor before spreading the water-based compound.

4 In a bucket, mix the powder with water to form a slurry. Pour it onto the floor, and smooth with a steel float. Work on a fairly small area of floor at a time; if too much compound is mixed it will stiffen up after about a quarter of an hour.

5 Trowel the compound as flat as you can. The trowelling marks will disappear as it dries out. You can usually walk on the floor two hours after the compound has been laid. It will be ready to receive the floor covering in eight to ten hours.

HELPFUL TIP

If you do not obtain a good, smooth finish after trowelling the levelling compound, sprinkle water on the surface and try again.

CHOOSING FLOORINGS FOR DIFFERENT PARTS OF THE HOUSE

TYPE OF FINISH		PLUS-POINTS	DRAWBACKS	HOW TO CARE FOR IT
Varnished hardboard Pleasantly coloured surface, achieved by laying hardboard with the smooth surface uppermost, and coating with flooring-grade varnish.		Cheap and simple to do yourself. Durable surface for children's rooms. Oil-tempered grade wears best.	Less sympathetic 'feel' than wood. Some people also think it looks a bit makeshift.	Sweep or vacuum clean frequently to remove grit. Wash with damp mop and mild detergent solution. Lightly sand worn areas and re-varnish when necessary.
Sanded and varnished floorboards Suitable finish for boards in good condition and without gaps. The floor is sanded with a heavy-duty sanding machine that can be hired for a day or weekend.	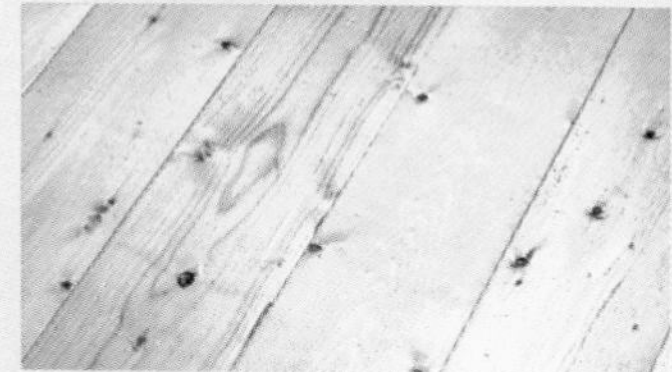	Cheap, and fairly simple to do yourself. An attractive surface that can be covered with scatter rugs.	Sanding a floor is noisy and dusty work. The finished surface is noisy underfoot. Can be draughty on a ground floor if boards are not tongued-and-grooved.	Sweep or vacuum clean frequently to remove grit which can scratch the surface. Wipe up spillages with damp cloth. Polish regularly. Lightly sand worn areas and re-varnish. Rugs advisable to reduce scuffing.
Vinyl tiles Huge range of colours, patterns and price. Available in imitation ceramic, wood or stone as well as cheaper smooth vinyl.	 Plain; Patterned	Hygienic, easily cleaned. Resistant to spillages. Good for kitchens, bathrooms, and perhaps nurseries.	Cold clinical 'feel'. Smooth vinyl is slippery when wet. Cushion-backed types – available in a limited colour range – are warmer, safer and quieter.	As for sheet vinyl (below), but beware of using too much water when you wash; it could get under the joins.
Cork tiles Pleasantly coloured natural material, available in various finishes, depending on price. Sold as strips as well as squares.		More sympathetic and warmer material than vinyl. Easily cleaned when varnished or bought factory sealed. PVC-coated cork best but more expensive.	Can become worn in heavy traffic areas, unless PVC coated.	Vacuum clean or sweep regularly to remove surface dirt, and wash with solution of mild detergent. Avoid swamping with water, and do not use abrasive cleaners.
Ceramic tiles The range runs from conventional square quarry tiles to special-purpose ceramics of various shapes. Can be obtained with anti-slip surface.	 Quarries 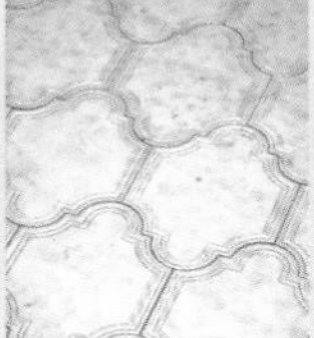 Provençal	Long lasting, easily cleaned and highly resistant to stains and spillages. Wide choice of patterns and colours.	Very expensive. Timber sub-floor needs strengthening before laying. Noisy underfoot. Cold if walked on in bare feet. Crockery breaks if dropped on it.	Remove surface grit by sweeping or vacuum cleaning, then wash with non-abrasive detergent in water. Keep water to minimum to prevent seepage under tiles. Scrub stubborn marks, and ingrained dirt round edges of tiles.
Sheet vinyl Two main types available. Smooth vinyl is cheaper; cushioned vinyl is more pleasant underfoot. Wide range of patterns and colours.	 Smooth  Cushioned	Hygienic, easily cleaned. Resistant to spillages. Inexpensive flooring for kitchens, bathrooms and perhaps nurseries.	Cold, clinical 'feel'. Smooth vinyl slippery when wet. Cushion-backed varieties are warmer, safer and quieter underfoot than ordinary vinyls.	Vacuum clean or sweep frequently in a kitchen to remove grit, which can scratch. Wash weekly with mop and detergent solution. Apply floor polish when first laid: re-polish regularly. Scuff marks can be removed by gentle rubbing with fine steel wool lubricated with white spirit. Take care not to rub through top surface. Follow with local re-polish.
Carpet Wide range of colour and price. Available as fitted carpet, carpet squares or carpet tiles.		Gives feeling of warmth and luxurious comfort. Graded according to use – from heavily used stairs to under-used spare bedrooms.	Good quality carpet is expensive. Spillages troublesome.	Vacuum clean frequently to remove grit which can harm fibres. Remove stains with proprietary cleaner. Or shampoo the carpet – powered shampoo machines can be hired. Carpet tiles can be rearranged to even out wear
Wood strip and mosaic Thick wood strip is laid in place of a damaged floor; thin wood strip goes over an existing floor. Mosaic consists of small pieces laid in patterns.	 Wood strip  Wood mosaic	Luxurious and long-lasting in living rooms, dining rooms and halls.	Natural wood is expensive. Laminated wood strip is cheaper, but the cheapest printed types do not wear well. Noisy underfoot.	Remove surface dirt with vacuum cleaner to minimise scratching. Varnished floors can be wiped over with damp cloth. Waxed floors need repeated re-polishing – an electric polisher makes this easier. Best protected with rugs.

Sanding and varnishing a wooden floor

An attractive floor can be created cheaply by sanding floorboards with a heavy-duty sander, and applying a flooring-grade varnish. Rugs can be laid where people walk most often.

Sanding a floor is a fairly simple job, but it is hard work and usually creates a lot of dust, so wear a face mask (they can be bought in DIY shops). Otherwise the dust will get into your lungs and nose.

Sanding is also extremely noisy, so do it at a time that is least likely to disturb the neighbours, and wear earmuffs, which can also be bought in DIY shops.

The sanding is done with a floor sanding machine, which uses abrasive belts, and an edging sander. They can be hired from a tool hire company – found in *Yellow Pages* under Hire Services, Tools and Equipment. A weekend's hire should be sufficient.

There are various grades of sanding belt. Begin with coarse (you can sometimes skip this if the boards are not in bad condition), then follow with medium, and finish off with fine.

New and damaged boards

On fairly new boards that have not been stained or become too dirty, sanding may not be necessary before applying the varnish. Get rid of surface dirt by scrubbing with detergent in hot water. Pay particular attention to removing dirt from nail holes. When the floor has dried, inspect it to see if it is clean enough.

Any damaged boards will have to be replaced (page 274), but new boards are unlikely to match exactly the colour of the old. For a first-class job, replace a defective board in a prominent position with an existing board from a less obvious spot (one that will be hidden by furniture or a rug, for example). This board can be replaced with a new one.

A sealed floor should be swept regularly, as floor dust contains abrasive grit that scratches the surface. Spillages can be wiped up with a damp cloth. The seal will last longer if it is polished thoroughly once a year, with a light polishing once a month.

If the seal starts to show signs of wear in some areas, lightly sand the affected places by hand, using fine abrasive paper, dust off and apply one new coat of varnish.

You will need

Tools Face mask; nail punch and claw hammer; floor sanding machine; earmuffs; sanding belts (coarse, medium and fine); edging sander; paint roller and wide paintbrush; fine steel wool.

Materials Flooring-grade varnish (gloss, satin or matt).

HELPFUL TIP

When a floor sander is switched on, the sanding belt starts to move, but does not come into contact with the floor until you lower the drum. Never let a moving belt touch the floor while the machine is stationary, or it will gouge holes in the wood. The moment the belt starts to bite into the wood – and there will be enough noise to indicate this – make sure that the machine moves forwards. It will begin to do so anyway, but inexperienced people tend to hold it back.

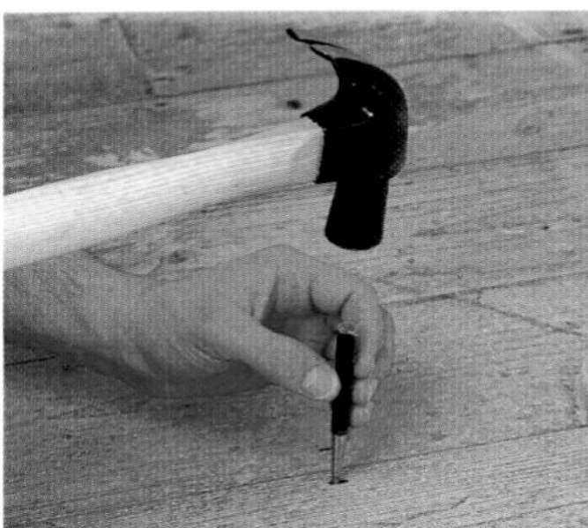

1 First, punch in all the nails in the floor, otherwise they will tear the sanding belts.

Any tacks left from previous floor coverings should also be removed.

2 If there are any traces of old polish remove them with steel wool dipped in white spirit. Otherwise the polish will clog up the sanding belt. Wear protective gloves.

3 Start at the edge of the room with your back against the wall. Keep the sander slightly away from the skirting board at the side, otherwise you may damage it.

4 It is normal to work along the length of the boards, as sanding across them causes scratches. But if the boards curl up at the edges, make the first runs diagonally across them with a coarse belt. Finish with medium and fine belts along the length of the boards.

5 On a floor where not very much stripping is needed, let the machine go forwards at a slow steady pace to the far end of the room, lifting up the drum as soon as you reach the skirting board.

6 If the boards are badly soiled, wheel the sander backwards to your start point, lower the drum and make a second pass over the first one. Never pull the sander backwards when the drum is rotating, or the machine may pull sideways out of control and score the floor surface badly.

7 When the strip looks clean, move on to the next one, and continue to the end of the room. Raise the belt as you change direction, otherwise it may damage the boards.

8 You will have started each run about a yard out from the wall behind you. When you have covered the room, turn the machine round, and deal with that area.

SANDING THE EDGES

Eventually, you will be left with a narrow border all round the room that the sander cannot reach. This must be stripped with an edging sander. Do not try to use a disc on an electric drill; it is not powerful enough. The edging tool is a much more powerful disc sander.

1 Use the edging sander all round the edges of the room, taking care not to damage the paint on the skirting boards.

2 When the sanding is finished, vacuum clean the floor to get rid of all the wood dust. Do not damp down the floor as the water may leave marks.

3 Finally, mop the floor with a clean, dry, lint-free cloth – be sure to shake it frequently outdoors – to get rid of the last particles.

APPLYING THE VARNISH

The quickest way of sealing a newly stripped floor is to use a paint roller to apply the varnish. Thin the first coat as recommended on the container to aid penetration, and apply full-strength coats for the second and third coats. Use a power sander fitted with fine abrasive paper to sand the surface lightly between coats, and wipe it with a damp cloth to remove dust before re-coating it.

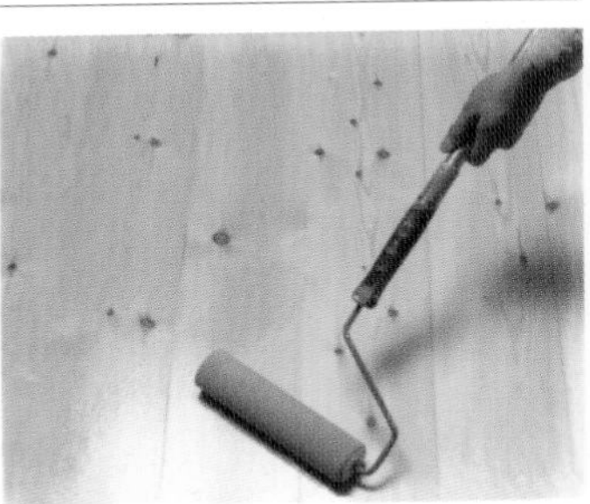

1 Apply the varnish with criss-cross passes of the roller, then finish off by running it parallel with the boards.

2 Use a paintbrush to finish the floor edges and to cut in round obstacles such as central heating pipes.

SANDING PARQUET

Parquet (also called woodblock) and wood mosaic floors can also be sanded. These floors are usually laid in patterns, so the grain lies in two directions. Consequently the floor has to be sanded twice, the second direction at right angles to the first.

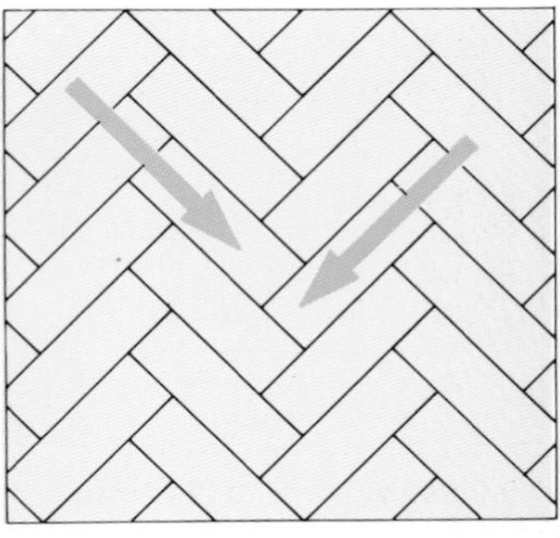

A final sanding with a very fine belt – also in two directions – is needed to remove all scratch marks.

Laying vinyl or cork tiles

Vinyl and cork tiles take longer to lay than sheet material, but they have many advantages. They are less cumbersome to handle; there is less wastage in cutting around awkward obstacles like chimney breasts; they are easier to cut to fit; and, if you make a mistake, ruining one tile is not nearly as serious as damaging a large sheet.

Vinyl tiles are available in a great range of colours, styles and price – from imitation slate to conventional smooth vinyl.

Cork tiles have different surface finishes according to price. The finishes range from transparent PVC coating to no coating at all. Uncoated cork needs to be finished with at least three coats of flooring-grade varnish.

To calculate the number of tiles you need, measure the room and multiply the width by the length to give the area. If the room has a bay or chimney breast, calculate it separately and add or subtract it from the main area.

Each pack of tiles gives the area it will cover, usually a square yard or square metre. Divide the area of the room by the area a pack will cover. The answer – rounded up to the nearest whole number – is the number of packs you need to buy.

Vinyl and cork tiles are both laid in the same way, using the adhesive recommended by the manufacturer. Some vinyl tiles are self-adhesive.

You will need

Tools Tape measure; string longer than the room; chalk; adhesive spreader; rag; pencil; trimming knife; perhaps some scrap hardboard and a metal straight-edge. *Materials* Tiles; adhesive (if tiles are not self-adhesive); perhaps white spirit for cleaning up adhesive.

WHERE TO START LAYING

Tile laying always begins in the middle of the room.

Finding the centre point

Measure two opposite walls and mark their centres. Snap a chalk line between these points.

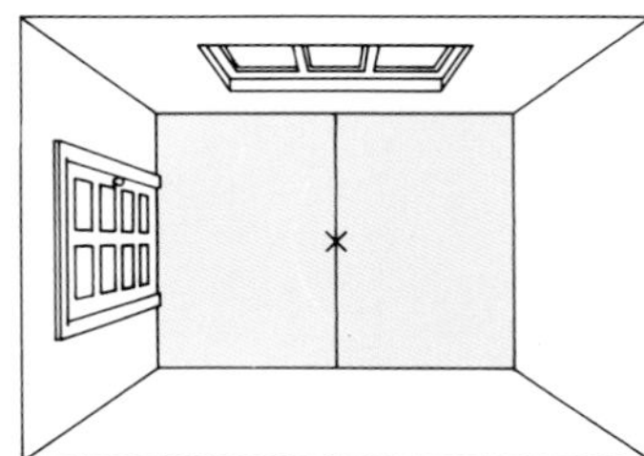

Measure the line and mark its centre. That is the middle of the room.

If the room has a chimney breast, snap the chalk line parallel to that wall.

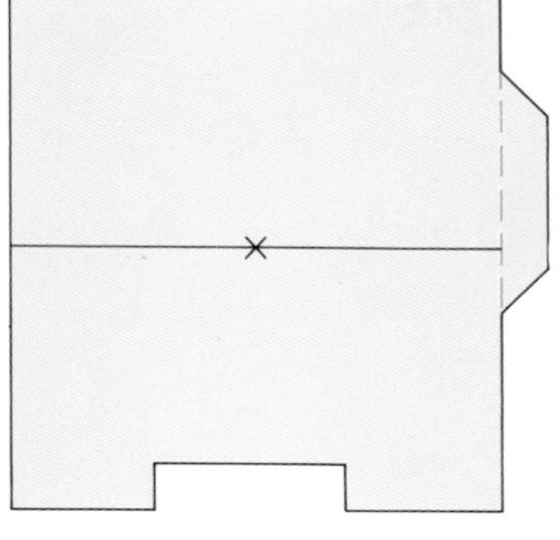

If the room also has a bay, square it off with a line between the ends of the bay and measure along this false wall line.

If the room is even more irregular in shape, choose one wall as the base wall. Snap a chalk line parallel to it, about 3in (75mm) away, and mark its centre point.

Draw a short chalk line at right angles to this base line. To obtain the right angle, use a few tiles as a guide.

Extend this line the full length of the room by snapping a chalk line. Measure this line and mark the centre.

Marking the cross-line

Once the main chalk line has been laid, a second line needs to be drawn across it at right angles. To do this, place two tiles on the floor, each with one side along the centre line and one corner on the centre point. Then snap a chalk line across the room, passing through the centre point and following the edge of the tiles.

PLACING THE KEY TILE

You must now decide the position of the first (or key) tile, which will determine the position of all other tiles in the room.

The last tile in each row all the way round the room will have to be cut to size. So site the key tile to ensure that this border of cut tiles is as neat as possible.

Ideally, all the tiles in the border should be equal in size, and at least a half tile width. Avoid very narrow slivers of tile, as they may not stick properly.

To determine the best position for the key tile, make a series of 'dry' test runs. Without using glue, or peeling off the backing of self-adhesive tiles, lay a row of tiles outwards from the centre to all edges of the room.

The key tile can be placed in any of several positions made up in the following ways:

1 Centrally on the middle point of the room.
2 In an angle formed by the two chalk lines.
3 Centrally on the main chalk line, and on one side of the line that crosses it.
4 Centrally on the crossing line, and on one side of the main one.

SNAPPING A CHALK LINE

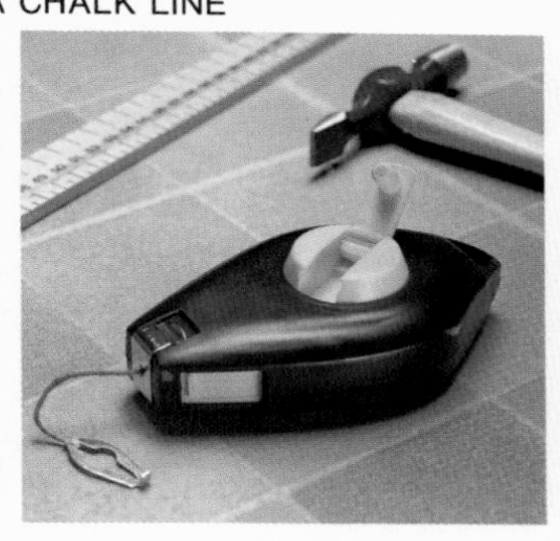

For many jobs, you need a line across the room. Rub chalk along a length of string or buy a chalk-line reel (right) which chalks the string for you. Tie one end to a nail in the floor and hold the other end at the far side of the room. Pull the string straight up and let go. It will mark a straight line on the floor.

Sometimes it is possible to lay tiles alongside a string stretched across the floor.

THE FOUR POSITIONS FOR LAYING THE KEY TILE

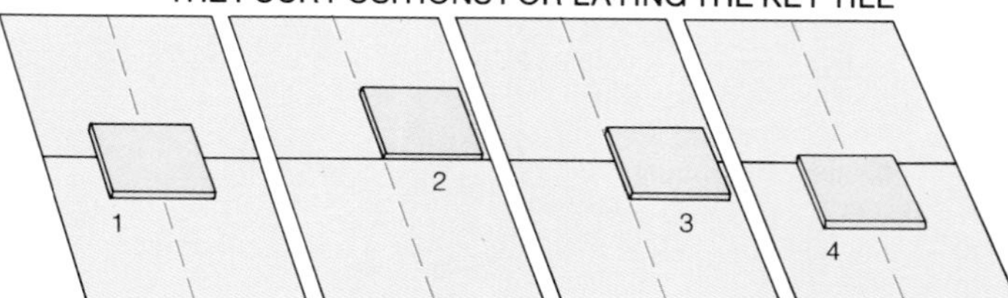

CENTRING THE TILES ON A FEATURE

1 Some rooms have a dominant feature such as a fireplace, or bay window. To get an attractive result, adjust the appropriate base line – keeping it parallel to the original line – to ensure that the tiles are centred on the feature.

Once again, ensure that you get the biggest possible cut tiles at the edges.

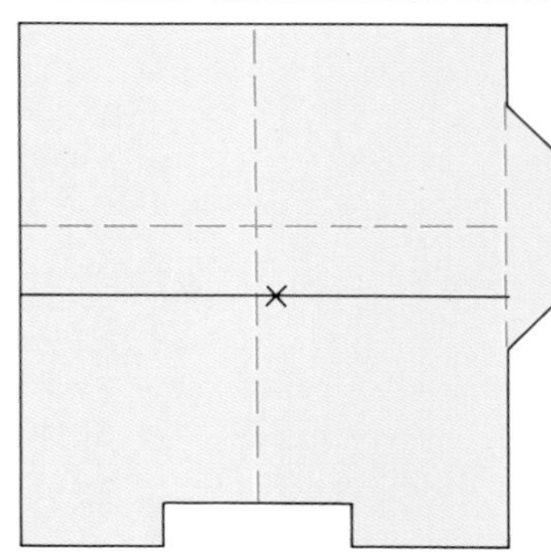

2 A room may have two features. In that case adjust both base lines, so the tiles can be centred on both features.

It is not possible to centre tiles on more than two features, except by accident.

HELPFUL TIP

Sometimes the twin aims of centring the tiles on one or two features, and getting tiles of at least half width round the edges, will conflict.

In that case, go for correct centring.

STICKING DOWN THE TILES

1 Once you have found the best arrangement of tiles, hold the key tile accurately in place, and draw a square around it with a pencil.

2 Give the floor a final dust over, then remove the backing if the tile is self-adhesive. Alternatively, spread a tile-size patch of adhesive on the floor with a plastic spreader.

3 Place one edge of the tile along one edge of the square, and roll it down flat. If you find it is not fitting exactly, pull it up immediately and start again.

HELPFUL TIP

If the tiles have any decorative markings, lay them with the lines of adjacent tiles at right angles to each other.

Laying vinyl or cork tiles (continued)

FIRE HAZARD WITH ADHESIVES

Solvent (or spirit) based adhesives are highly flammable, and give off volatile fumes which may ignite if they come in contact with a naked flame.

When laying a floor with a solvent-based adhesive, open all the windows and doors in the room to get maximum ventilation. Make sure that any pilot lights in the room are turned off, including the pilot lights in a gas stove, gas fire or a central-heating boiler.

Fumes penetrate clothing and remain there for some time. So do not go into a room with a fire or heater to warm yourself in the middle of a job. When you have finished, remove your clothes and hang them up outdoors.

Water-based adhesives are not flammable, however they take longer to dry, which slows a job down in cold weather.

4 With the first tile stuck down, work outwards from it to the walls. Where adhesive has to be spread on the floor, spread a square yard at a time.

The tiles must be positioned very accurately, each one butted up squarely to its neighbour. Take great care that the joins create a straight line, or you will need to trim tiles later to avoid gaps.

5 If any adhesive oozes up through the joins, wipe it up immediately, using a cloth damped with either water or white spirit depending on the manufacturer's instructions.

CUTTING TILES TO FIT THE BORDER

The cut tiles around the edge can be dealt with in two ways. Method 1 is likely to give the better result if adhesive is being used, but Method 2 will have to be used in small areas such as lavatories and narrow corridors.

Method 1
Lay all the tiles except for a border of one whole tile and one part tile all the way round the room.

1 Place the tile to be cut against the last one in the row, and place another tile on top of it, pressed against the wall.

2 Draw a pencil line across the face of the tile to be cut. With some vinyl and cork tiles you do not even need to draw a line; use a knife instead of a pencil, then snap the tile in two.

3 If the tile will not break, cut it on a piece of scrap hardboard, using a metal straight-edge as a guide.

4 The two tiles now change places with the part tile against the wall. Leave the whole and part tile on the end of the row until you have cut the entire border, and are ready to stick it all at once.

Method 2
With this method, you lay all the whole tiles, then deal with the border of part tiles. The disadvantage of the method is that it leaves only a narrow band of floor which may not get adequately covered with glue.

1 Place the tile to be cut squarely on the last tile in the row. Put a third on top, pressed against the wall.

2 Draw a pencil line across the face of the tile to be cut. With some vinyl and cork tiles you do not even need to draw a line; use a knife instead of a pencil, then snap the tile in two.

3 If the tile will not break, cut it on a piece of scrap hardboard, using a metal straight-edge as a guide.

4 The part of the cut tile closer to the centre of the room will fit the empty space perfectly. Leave the cut tile on the end of the row and go on to cut all the other border tiles.

Corner tiles Tiles in a corner will have to be cut to length as well as width, using the same method.

In doorways Around a doorway architrave, you will have to draw three or four lines to create the correct pattern.

CUTTING ROUND A CURVE

In bathrooms and kitchens you may have to cut round an irregular shaped object; a washbasin, for example.

1 To determine the shape of the tiles round the washbasin pedestal, take a sheet of paper a bit larger than a tile. Place it over the area the cut tile will occupy, and fold it along the line of the adjacent tiles, and the pedestal.

You may have to make cuts inwards in the paper if the obstruction is very irregular.

2 Place the completed template on the tile, mark round it, and cut.

CUTTING ROUND A PIPE

A pipe rising from the floor will normally be at the edge of a room, so cut a tile to fit the border.

1 Place the cut tile square on the last whole tile and push it against the pipe. Make a pencil mark where it touches.

2 Put the cut tile against the wall and push it against the pipe. Make another mark where it touches.

3 With a try square, draw a line across the tile from the mark on the side. Then put the try square on the uncut long edge and draw a line through the other mark. (Do not put the try square on the cut edge as it will not be square.)

4 Where the lines cross is the point where the pipe will go. Bore a hole with a brace and bit (with the tile on a piece of scrap wood), or draw round a coin of the appropriate size, and cut with a knife.

5 Make a knife cut from the hole to the wall edge of the tile, and ease it into position.

TILES ON THE DIAGONAL

1 To lay tiles in a diagonal pattern, first make a scriber from a thin piece of batten about 3ft (910mm) long with a nail in each end. A length of softwood or plywood would be ideal. Drill pilot holes, smaller than the diameter of the nails, to avoid splitting the wood.

2 Mark the cross-lines in the middle of the room in the normal way. (See *Where to start laying*, page 279.)

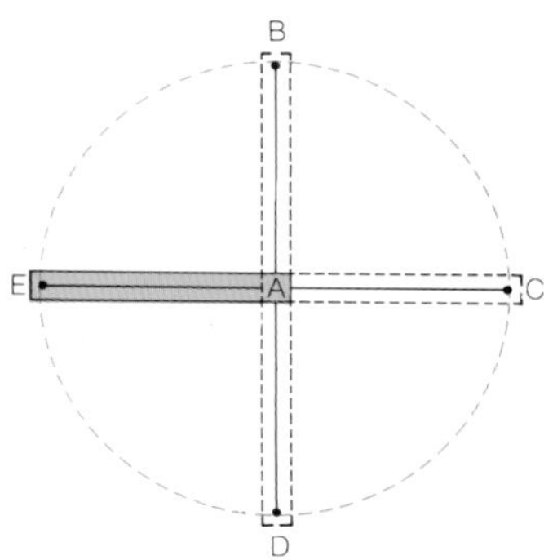

3 Put one nail of the scriber on the point where the lines cross (A), and mark four points on the cross-lines – at B, C, D and E.

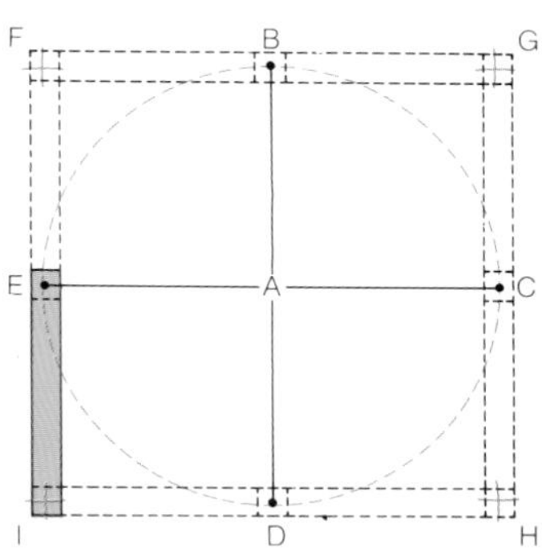

4 Put one nail of your scriber on B and scribe arcs at F and G. Move the scriber to C and scribe arcs at G and H. From D make arcs at H and I, and from E at I and F.

5 Snap diagonal chalk lines on the floor through the points where the arcs meet at G and I and at F and H.

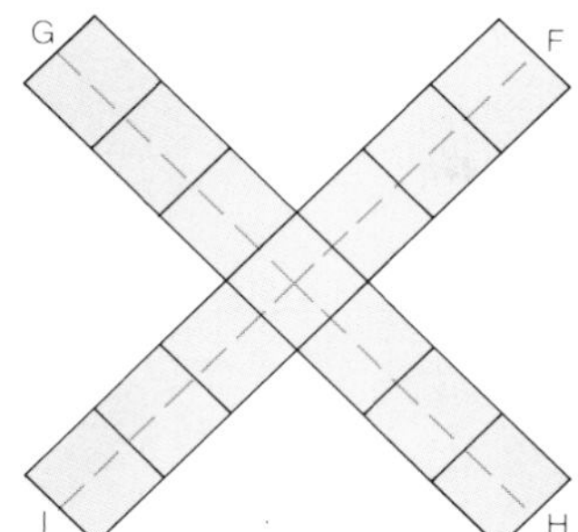

6 Lay out rows of unglued tiles along the diagonal lines to get the largest cut tiles round the border.

7 Glue down all the whole tiles.

Border tiles: Method 1
To cut the border tiles, first make a template.

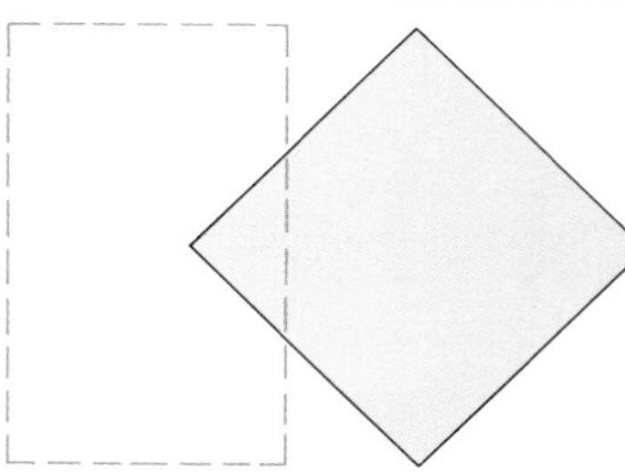

1 Cut a piece of hardboard or card with two opposite edges parallel. The distance between these edges must be the same as the distance across the tiles from corner to corner.

2 Place the tile to be cut on the whole tile nearest to the wall.

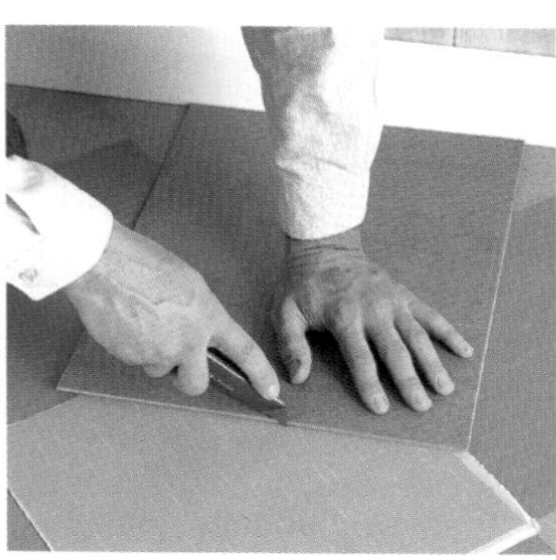

3 Place one parallel edge of your template against the skirting board, and draw or cut along the opposite edge across the face of the tile.

The piece of tile farthest from the skirting board will now fit the empty space.

Border tiles: Method 2
Diagonal tiles can also be finished off with a border of part tiles laid square to the wall.

1 When you are setting out the tiles initially, place the first tile in the centre of the room to ensure a border wider than half a tile.

2 Lay all the whole tiles.

3 Cut some tiles in half from corner to corner and lay them to square off the diagonal pattern.

4 Finally, cut the border tiles square to the wall, measuring each one individually, but sticking them down all at the same time.

HOW TO LIFT A DAMAGED VINYL TILE

To remove a damaged vinyl tile without disturbing the rest of the floor, put a piece of aluminium kitchen foil over it and press with a hot iron.

Wait until the heat penetrates the tile (this will take longer on concrete than wood), then lever up a corner with a filling knife or wallpaper stripper, and pull the tile away.

Lift the remaining adhesive with a filling knife heated with a blow torch or hot-air gun, or over a gas stove.

Lay a new tile with fresh adhesive. Do not slide it in place, or adhesive may be forced up at the edges.

A larger area can be softened with a hot-air gun. The technique will not work on cork tiles, which insulate too effectively against the heat.

PATTERNS IN TILES

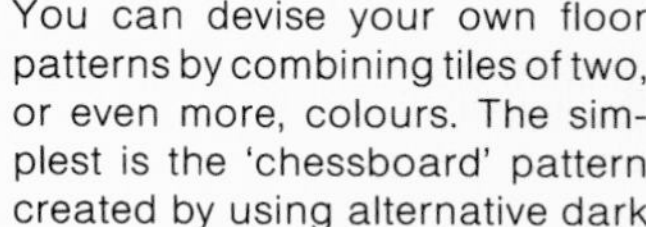

You can devise your own floor patterns by combining tiles of two, or even more, colours. The simplest is the 'chessboard' pattern created by using alternative dark and light colours. But many others are possible.

To guard against mistakes in laying the floor, draw a scale plan of the pattern on paper.

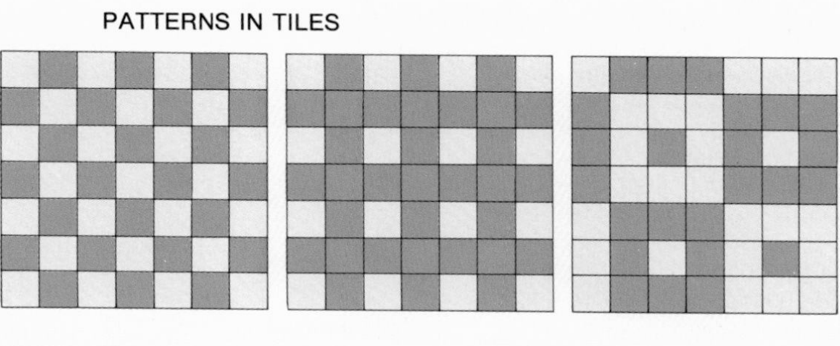

Laying ceramic tiles

Ceramic tiles and quarry tiles are much heavier than other types of floor covering. This is not a problem on direct-to-earth or suspended concrete floors, but a timber floor should be strengthened first.

HELPFUL TIP

Tiles must not be walked on for 24 hours after laying. As few homes can afford to have a kitchen or bathroom out of action for so long, tile only part of the floor at one time.

Special quick-set adhesive is also available for awkward situations.

Strengthening a timber floor
Overlay the existing floor with $\frac{1}{2}$in (13mm) thick exterior grade plywood. This grade of plywood will be capable of standing up to the moisture in the adhesive.

The plywood is laid in the same way as hardboard (page 275), but fix it with screws, not nails, at 12in (300mm) intervals. Use 1in (25mm) No.8 screws countersunk below the surface of the plywood.

Exterior grade plywood of this thickness is expensive, and that may make you decide to choose other forms of floor covering on a suspended timber floor.

Preparing a solid floor
Concrete floors should be thoroughly cleaned, using household detergent in water, and levelled if necessary (page 276).

Ceramic tiles can be laid on old quarry and vinyl tiles, provided these are stuck down properly, but vinyl needs to be treated first with a special primer, available from the shop that supplies the ceramic tiles.

Calculating the quantity
To estimate the number of tiles, measure the room and multiply the width by the length to give the area. If the room has a bay or chimney breast, calculate it separately and add or subtract it from the main area.

Each pack of tiles gives the area they will cover. Divide the area of the room by the area a pack will cover. The answer – rounded up to the next whole number – is the number of packs you need.

Cutter for floor tiles
Ceramic floor tiles are at least $\frac{1}{4}$in (6mm) thick, compared to the $\frac{5}{32}$in (4mm) thickness of the ceramic wall tiles sold for DIY use, so you will need a heavy-duty cutter. The tool can be bought or hired. Power-driven tile saws can also be hired. (See *Yellow Pages* under Hire Services – Tools and Equipment.)

PUTTING DOWN THE TILES

You will need
Tools Bucket; trowel; notched spreader; rags; tile spacers or $\frac{1}{4}$in (6mm) dowel; tile cutter.
Materials Tiles; adhesive (see *Fire warning*, page 280); grout.

1 Set out the tiles in the same way as for vinyl tiles (page 279).

2 Beginning at the centre of the room, pour adhesive on a square yard of floor and spread it evenly with the trowel.

Laying ceramic tiles (continued)

3 Go over it with the notched spreader. This creates a ribbed effect acting as a gauge to leave the right depth of adhesive.

4 Place the tiles in position one at a time, giving a slight twist. This ensures that the whole of the tile is in contact with the adhesive, and no air is trapped underneath.

5 Few ceramic floor tiles are self spacing, yet it is essential to space them out evenly to get a good appearance. Plastic spacers ⅛in (3mm) wide are sold for this purpose. If you want to make a special feature of wide grouting, take some ¼in (6mm) dowel, cut it into small lengths and use them as spacer guides.

6 Wipe off any adhesive on the face of the tiles. Dampen a cloth with either white spirit or water, depending on the adhesive.

7 To avoid walking over the tiles in the 24 hours before the glue sets, work first on the part of the room farthest from the door. Always leave a passageway of bare floor to allow an exit.

8 Once you have laid all the whole tiles, leave them for 24 hours before laying the cut tiles around the edge of the room. The cut tiles can be laid in either of the two methods shown on page 280.

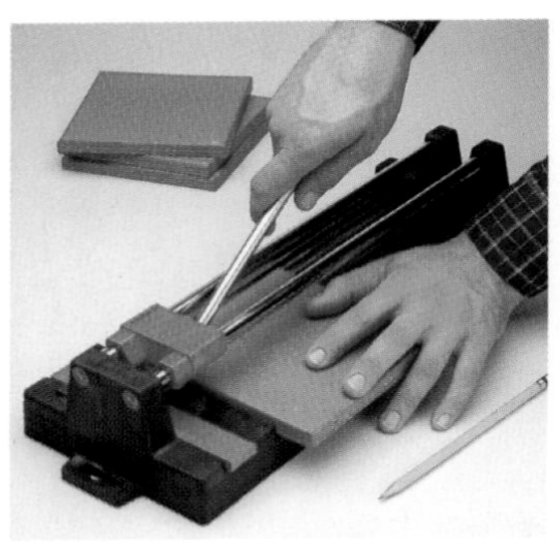

9 Mark the face of the tile to be cut in pencil, place it on the tile cutter, and operate the cutter.

10 When all the glue has set, mix the grout into a paste and tip it on the tiles. Work it into the joins with the straight edge of the spreader.

11 Run one corner of the spreader along the joins to give a neat finish. Alternatively use a piece of dowel or the handle of a wooden spoon.

12 Clean off any surplus from the tiles with a damp cloth, then polish with a dry one. Leave the grout to harden for about an hour, then give a final wipe with a damp cloth. Do not put the floor into full use for 48 hours after grouting.

Laying carpet tiles

Carpet tiles are not firmly fixed to the floor – you can take them up and move them at any time. They can be rearranged to equalise wear, or removed while the skirting board is repainted, or lifted for cleaning.

The laying method varies slightly from make to make, so follow the manufacturer's instructions.

Because carpet tiles are not rigid like other tiles, it is not easy to butt them tightly together, and if you are not careful gaps will develop between them as the tiles bed down.

You can use a knee-kicker (page 288), with just hand rather than knee pressure, to push the tiles together.

Or you can improvise a substitute (see panel)

You will need
Tools Tape measure; string longer than the room; chalk; knee-kicker (or substitute); steel rule; craft knife.
Materials Carpet tiles; normal carpet adhesive; metal threshold (page 287).

1 If you begin laying the tiles against one wall, there is a danger that when you reach the far wall only a narrow strip will be left to fill. Slivers of tile are not stable so start the job by snapping a chalk line down the centre of the room and setting out the tiles in the same way as for laying vinyl tiles (page 279).

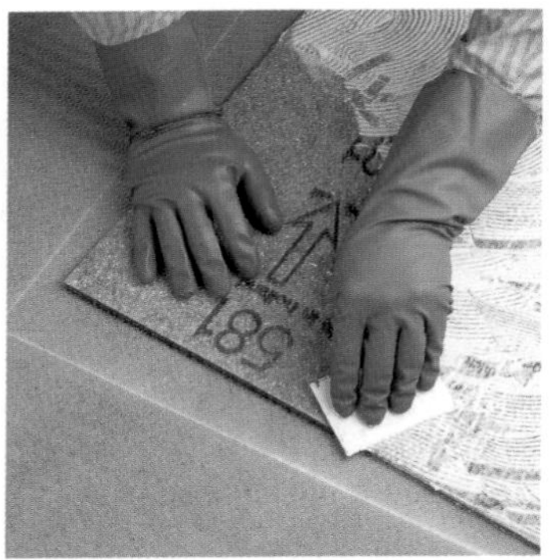

2 Whatever the method of laying down, apply a carpet adhesive to the first tile in the centre of the room. This will ensure that it is not pushed out of place during the laying process – which would ruin the final effect.

3 Lay subsequent tiles with the pile running at right angles to one another. This gives a chequerboard effect, even though the same colour is used throughout. Some tiles have an arrow on the back to show the direction of the pile, but sometimes you have to 'feel' for the pile – the surface will be smooth when you run your hand across it with the pile, rough when your hand goes against.

ALTERNATIVELY, lay all the tiles with the pile running in the same direction to give the effect of a fitted carpet.

Do not mix the two methods.

4 Put the knee-kicker or improvised tool on top of a tile so that its teeth grip, then push the tile forwards into position.

5 When all the whole tiles have been laid, measure the border tiles for cutting by one of the methods described for cutting vinyl tiles on page 280.

6 Mark the cutting line on the face of the tile by making a nick with a craft knife on each edge. Turn the tile upside down, lay a steel rule across the two nicks, and cut with the knife. Take great care not to cut your fingers.

MAKING A TILE 'KICKER'

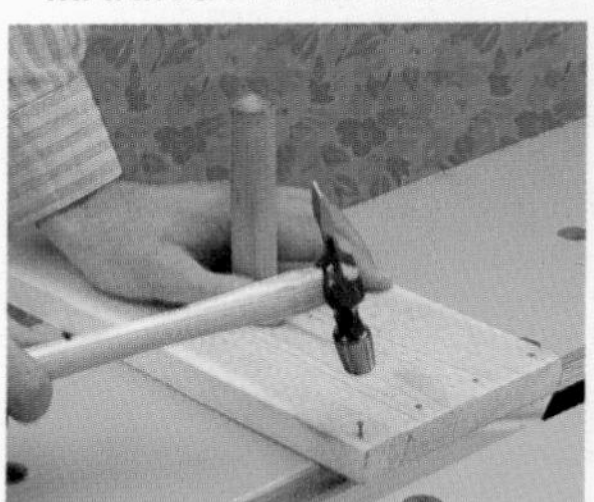

Cut a piece of 6in × 1in (150mm × 25mm) wood to 12in (300mm) long. Drill a hole in the centre ½in (13mm) deep and glue in a piece of broom handle. Drive a nail through the wood into the handle. Drive four nails through the front, projecting ⅛in (3mm) to act as teeth.

7 In a doorway, protect the edge of the tiles by fitting a metal threshold, of the kind used for normal carpet.

IF TILES SHIFT IN USE

Should movement dislodge any of the tiles in use – this can happen under chairs – lift the tile, and apply carpet adhesive to the backing.

Laying sheet vinyl in strips

Sheet vinyl is made in several widths, the most common being 2m, 3m, and 4m (about 6ft, 10ft and 13ft).

Covering a room with two or more 2m strips is the easiest technique as each strip is lighter and more manoeuvrable than a width that covers the entire room. But there will be a join which may detract from the appearance, and which could let water seep through when the floor is cleaned.

'Stay-flat' varieties of cushioned vinyl are the easiest of all to lay as they hug the floor and do not need to be glued. If you have to glue sheet vinyl, take care to follow the safety advice on page 280.

Before ordering the vinyl, decide how it will be set out. Ideally, it should run away from the window (or the main window if there is more than one). The joins will be less obvious than if the light strikes them at the side.

It is best to line the floor with hardboard (page 275) before laying the vinyl, but if you decide that your floor is in sufficiently good condition, lay the vinyl at right angles to the floorboards.

If these two recommendations conflict, it is more important that the material should run away from the window. When laying it parallel to the boards, make sure that an edge of the vinyl is not over a gap.

Avoid having a join running into a doorway; this is an area of heavy traffic, and scuffing could occur.

You will need

Tools Steel tape measure; soft pencil; string longer than the room; chalk; small block of wood, or compasses; a second piece of wood about 4in (100 mm) long; scissors or trimming knife; ruler; screwdriver; hammer.

Materials Vinyl to cover the floor; perhaps adhesive and notched spreader; metal cover strip and screws.

MARKING THE BASE LINE

1 Snap a chalk line (page 279) between the middle of the two walls that will be at the ends of the strips. This provides a base line to work from, as the walls will almost certainly be out of true.

2 If the first length of vinyl will cover the line, snap a second line parallel to the first where it can be seen.

3 Cut the first strip to length – the distance across the room plus 3in (75mm) for trimming.

4 Put it on the floor about 1in (25mm) away from the wall on the long side and parallel to the chalk line. Let each end ride up the wall by an equal amount.

SCRIBING THE WALL ON THE LONG SIDE

1 At two or three points, draw a pencil line across the floor and the vinyl. These are crosschecks that will allow you to bring the vinyl back to its original position later.

2 Find out where the gap between the wall on the long side and the vinyl is greatest. Cut a small block of wood slightly longer than that measurement. This will be used for scribing the wall to make the vinyl fit exactly.

Alternatively, use a pair of compasses and set them to the same measurement.

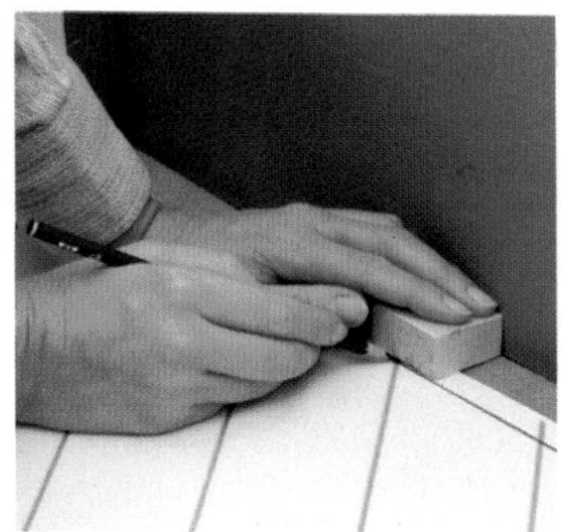

3 Place the wood against the wall, hold a pencil hard against it and move them along the wall, tracing its contours on the vinyl. If you are using compasses, place the point against the wall, and the pencil on the vinyl, keeping the compasses at right angles to the wall.

4 Cut the vinyl along the pencil line with scissors or knife.

5 Put the vinyl back in place – using the check marks for accurate positioning.

SCRIBING THE END WALLS

1 Check that the scribed edge is correctly positioned against the side wall, then draw a chalk line on the floor along the opposite edge. Make a crosscheck on the edge and the floor.

2 Pull the vinyl back from the crosscheck by the length of the second piece of wood.

3 Keeping the outer edge of the vinyl on the chalk line, use the piece of wood and a pencil to trace the contours of the wall onto the vinyl sheet.

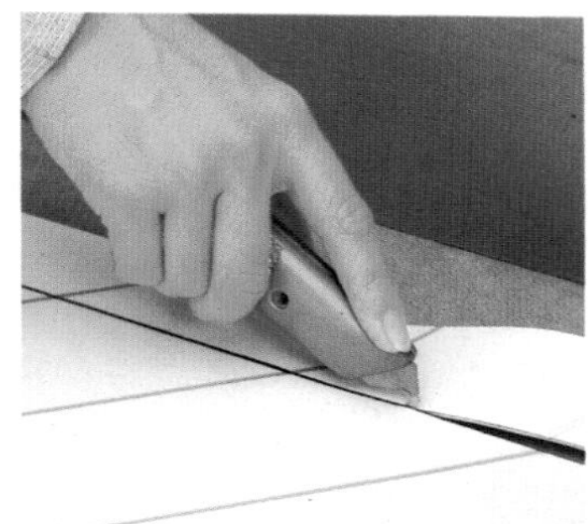

4 Cut to this line, then use chalk line and crosscheck to position the vinyl accurately, and it should fit against the end wall.

CUTTING THE SECOND STRIP

1 The second strip will almost certainly have to be cut to width. If the excess is more than about 10in (250mm) cut it back to that to give yourself a workable width. Make the cut on the wall side, not the side to be joined.

2 Put it on the floor with one edge touching the wall where the wall comes nearest to the first sheet. The other edge will be overlapping the first sheet; make sure that this overlap is exactly the same all the way along. Adjust it so that the pattern matches.

3 Cut it at each end, to leave the trimming allowance of 3in (75mm).

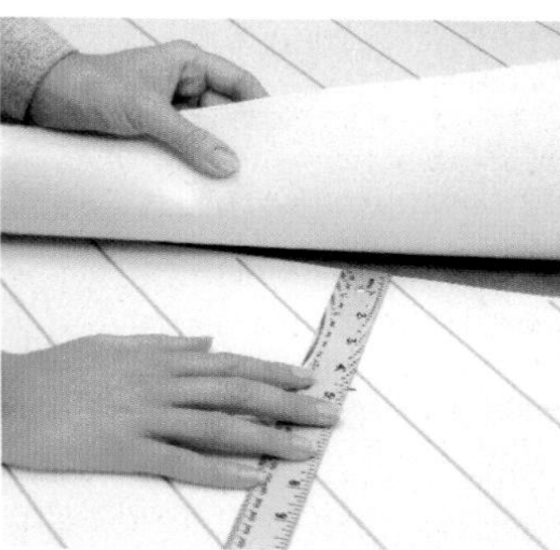

4 Make a pencil mark where the second sheet rests on the first. Lift up the second sheet and measure the amount of the overlap.

5 Place the vinyl flat on the floor again and use the ruler and pencil to scribe a line on the vinyl parallel to the wall, and the width of the overlap away from it.

6 Cut to this line.

7 Place the vinyl in position, and scribe the ends.

HOW MUCH TO BUY

Measure the room at right angles to the direction of laying to decide how many strips you will need. (As sheet vinyl is made in metric sizes, make your measurements in metric.) Measure right into any alcoves and to the halfway point under a door.

For every 2m, or portion of 2m, you will need one strip of 2m wide vinyl. So if the distance is 3.5m, you need two strips – 0.5m will be waste (in fact, a little less because of trimming).

Then measure in the other direction and multiply by the number of strips. If the length is 3.3m you will need 6.6m (2 × 3.3m), plus 75mm trimming allowance on each strip – a total of 6.75m. Since the shop probably sells to the nearest metre or half metre, you will have to order 7m. Some shops sell in metric widths but imperial lengths. So you may be able to buy to the nearest foot.

If there is a pattern you will also need an allowance for matching up. The exact amount will vary according to the pattern 'repeat', so give the shop your measurements and ask their advice.

Order the flooring well in advance. It can then be stood upright (still tied in a roll) for at least two days in the room where it will be laid in order to reach room temperature. In winter the room should be heated. The vinyl will then be flexible and easy to lay; cold vinyl tends to be rigid.

Laying sheet vinyl in strips (continued)

DEALING WITH DOORWAYS

1 Scribe the vinyl around the door frame and to a line under the door. If a threshold strip has already been laid, scribe up to it.

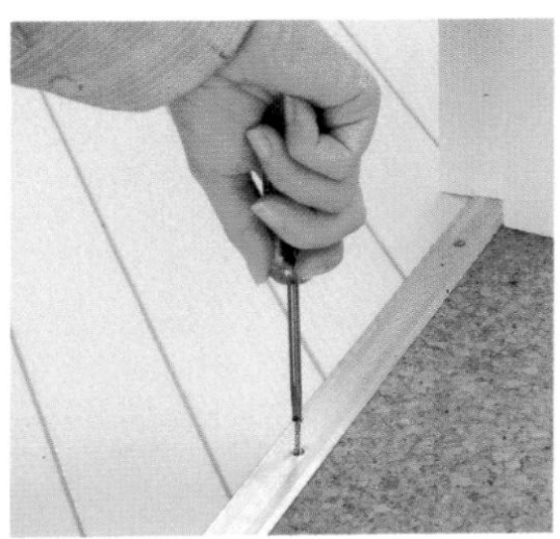

2 If no threshold strip exists, screw a metal cover strip over the vinyl and the covering beyond the door. If the floor beyond has no covering, use metal lino edging.

CUTTING AROUND ALCOVES

1 Measure and cut the vinyl to fit the full depth of the alcove, plus the trimming allowance of 3in (75mm).

2 Put it on the floor and allow it to ride up the fireplace wall.

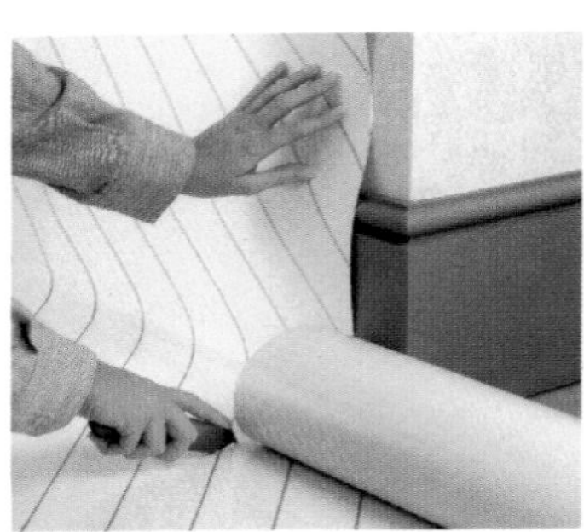

3 Make a cut parallel to the side of the chimney breast, leaving enough for final trimming. Allow the material to lie on the alcove floor.

4 Cut off the excess material riding up the fireplace, leaving a trimming allowance of 3in (75mm).

5 Trim the edges in the normal way so that the vinyl fits the alcove, and around the chimney breast. If there is a working fireplace, trim the vinyl around the hearth.

STICKING DOWN VINYL

'Stay-flat' vinyl sheeting does not need to be stuck down to the floor, because it hugs the floor closely and does not shrink once it has been laid.

Other types should be glued immediately after laying. If left for any length of time – even overnight – they may shrink slightly and gaps could develop between the strips of vinyl and around the walls.

Use the adhesive supplied, or recommended, by the manufacturer of the sheet vinyl, and apply it to the floor with a notched spreader which can be obtained with the adhesive.

For ordinary vinyl the floor should be glued all over.

Cushioned vinyl needs only to be glued in a 2in (50mm) band around the room and along joins where sheets butt against each other.

Covering a small area with sheet vinyl

A very small room, such as a lavatory or pantry, can be covered by one piece of even the narrowest sheet vinyl. The best way of cutting it is to use a paper template.

You will need

Tools Enough stiff paper (such as paper underlay) to cover the floor; perhaps adhesive tape or stapler; pencil; drawing pins or weights; scissors or knife; block of wood 1½in (38mm) wide; pencil; ruler.

Materials Sheet vinyl; perhaps adhesive and spreader.

1 If the paper is not big enough to cover the room, fasten two pieces together with adhesive tape or staples, but draw a line across both at several points so you can check later that they have not moved out of position.

2 Put the paper on the floor with the edges folded underneath. Fix it in place with drawing pins. On a solid floor use weights.

3 To fit it around obstacles such as a lavatory or a pipe, cut the paper from the wall inwards.

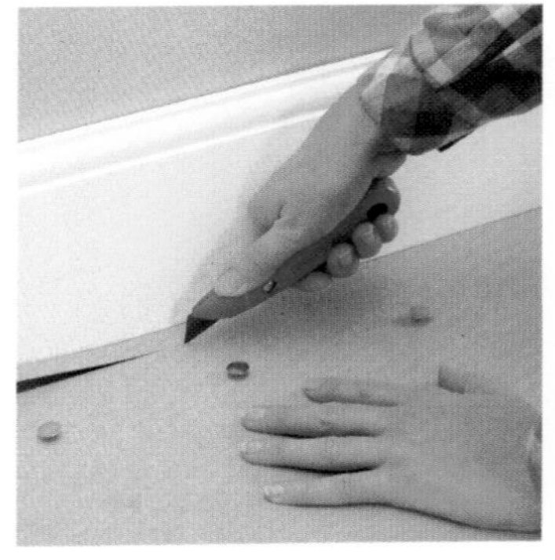

4 When the paper is laid, use scissors or a knife to trim it all the way round the room so that its edge is about ½in (13mm) from the wall or skirting board. Trim it around obstacles as well.

5 Cut a small block of wood about 1½in (38mm) wide, and mark the width on it so there is no confusion later.

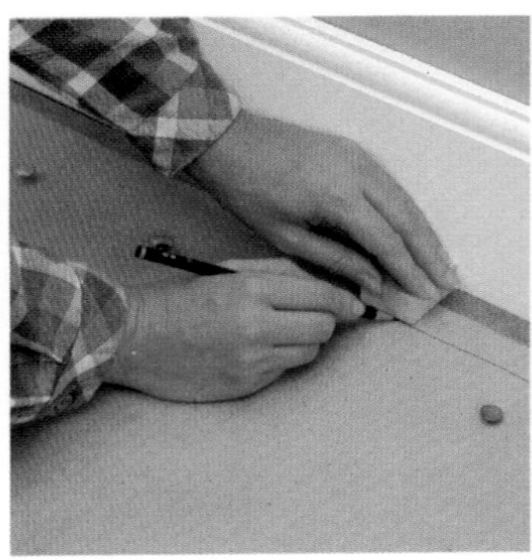

6 Put one edge against the wall and hold the pencil against the other edge. Move the block and pencil all the way around the room, tracing an outline of the room onto the paper.

7 Also trace around larger obstacles, such as the bottom of a wash basin.

8 If a pipe comes up through the floor, put a ruler against it on four opposite faces and draw a pencil line along the outside edge of the ruler to make a square.

CUTTING OUT THE VINYL

1 Lay a piece of the flooring material – right side up – on the floor of a larger room and put the template on top, fixing it in place with adhesive tape.

2 Put one edge of the wood block on the pencil line on the template. Put the pencil against the other edge and draw it along, tracing the shape of the room onto the vinyl. Do the same for large obstacles.

3 Cut the vinyl along the pencil line, using a ruler as a guide on straight lines. Put a piece of scrap vinyl or hardboard underneath to avoid damaging the floor.

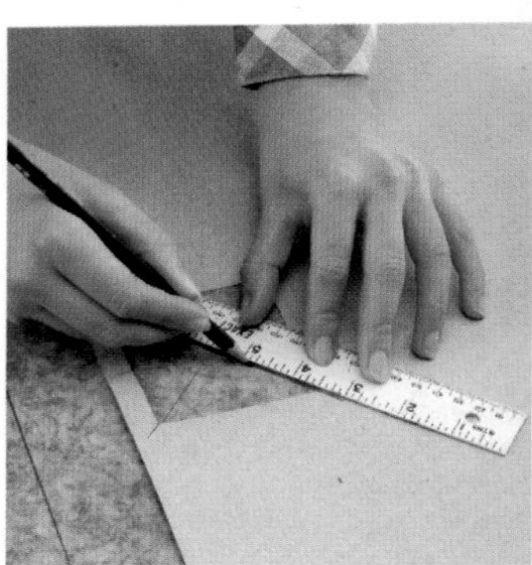

4 If you have marked a square for a pipe, draw diagonal lines from the corners of the square. Where they cross will be the middle.

5 Use a coin or other round object to draw a circle the diameter of the pipe. Cut out the circle with the knife.

6 The piece of flooring will now fit the room exactly. To fit it around obstacles, make a cut from the hole to the nearest edge. If you follow the lines of any pattern – for example, the 'grout' lines of imitation tiles – the cut will not be noticeable.

7 Stick down the vinyl in the normal way (above) unless it is a 'stay-flat' variety of cushioned vinyl which does not need to be glued.

Fitting sheet vinyl without a seam

Most rooms can be covered with a single, seamless sheet of vinyl if you use a 4m (13ft) or even a 3m (10ft) width.

Seamless laying gives a neater finish, and will probably last longer because there is no join to come apart and get damaged.

A seamless floor is, however, more difficult to lay. The size of the material makes it cumbersome and very heavy, and you will almost certainly need a helper. Trimming it to the wall also requires greater skill.

Estimate the amount of floor covering in the same way as for narrow vinyl (page 283), except that only one length will be needed. Take the measurements right into any alcoves, and to the halfway point under the door.

To make laying as easy as possible, the sheet should be about 4in (100mm) wider than the floor on every edge – that is, 8in (200mm) wider than the room in both directions. Your supplier should cut it to the required length, even if you have to pay to the next full metre or half metre.

He may also cut it to width. If you have to do it yourself, try to find a large area where it can be laid flat. As a last resort the lawn would do – on a dry day. Make the cut with a trimming knife or scissors.

Re-roll the sheet so the shorter dimension becomes the length of the roll. This makes it easier to get into the room.

Roll it with the decorative side inwards, which is the way you will need it when laying starts.

Keep the roll in the room where it will be laid for two days to reach room temperature. Have the heating on in the room in cold weather or the vinyl will be hard and brittle.

You will need

Tools Soft broom; scissors; trimming knife; small block of wood and perhaps a metal straight-edge.
Materials Sheet vinyl to cover the floor in one piece; adhesive and spreader (except for 'stay-flat' vinyl); cover strip for doorways.

1 The first job is to unroll the vinyl. This is hard work, and you will almost certainly need someone to help you. Make sure that the longer side of the vinyl runs along the longer wall.

2 If the flooring has a pronounced pattern, adjust it so that the pattern lines look to be at right angles to the wall containing the doorway by which you will most often enter the room.

Sight it by eye. If it looks right, it is right.

3 As trimming the edges is quite difficult, put the sheet up against the longest wall – then against the other walls in turn, if necessary – to see if there is one wall that is so true that the edge does not have to be cut to fit.

Do not disturb the setting-out so that the pattern is no longer at right angles to the door.

> HELPFUL TIP
>
> Trimming vinyl that is bent up a wall is not easy and takes practice. But practising is the last thing you want to do on a large piece of expensive material.
>
> Obtain some offcuts and work on these until you get the knack. After pressing the vinyl against the wall with your block of wood, it may help to hold a metal straight-edge as close to the wall as possible while you cut.
>
> Make sure that the knife cuts away from the hand holding the straight-edge, so that if it slips you will not injure yourself.

4 For laying, the vinyl must be absolutely flat on the floor. You can ensure this by sweeping over it with a soft broom.

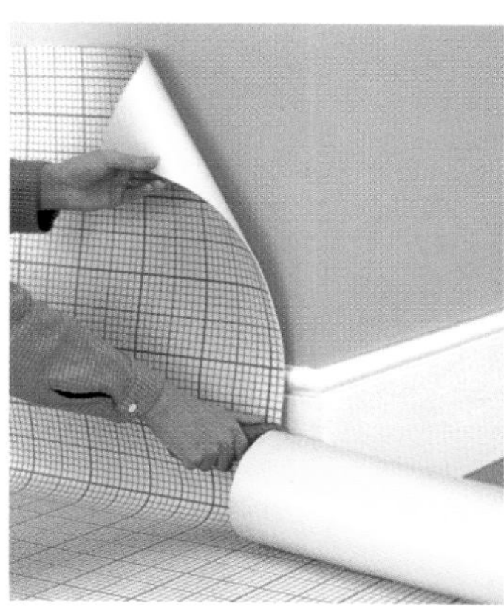

5 To fit the vinyl into an alcove beside a fireplace get your helper to hold it while you make a cut running parallel to the side of the chimney breast.

Take care to leave about 2in (50mm) surplus against each wall for final trimming.

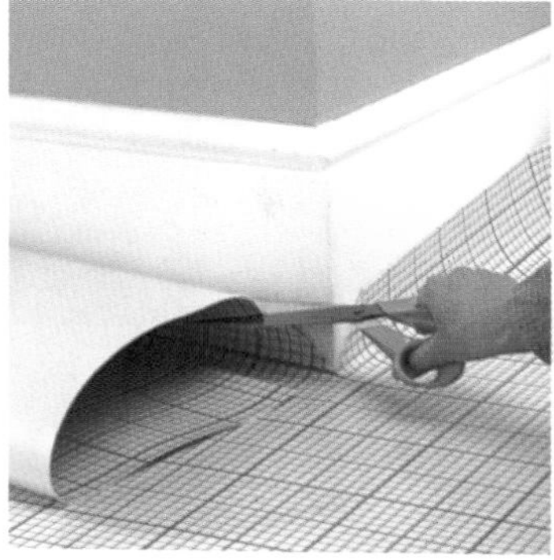

6 Lay the material on the alcove floor, lapping up against the three sides, then cut off the excess riding up the fireplace. Again, leave about 2in (50mm) surplus against the wall for trimming.

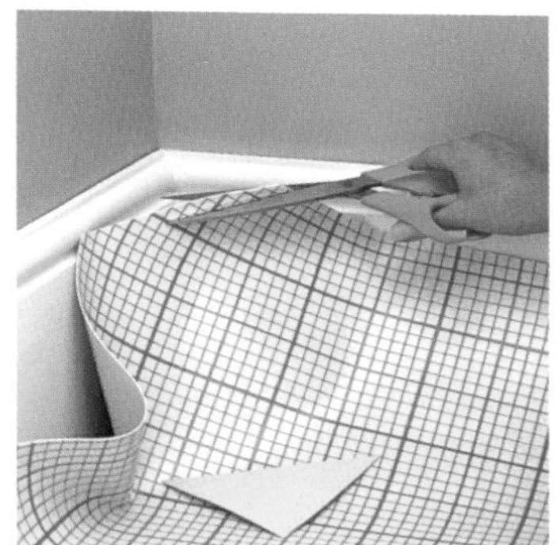

7 To fit into corners, cut off a small triangle at the corner of the vinyl, using scissors. When you push it down to the floor it will form a V, allowing it to hug the skirting. But you must cut off exactly the right amount, so first remove a triangle that is obviously too small. Then take off more small strips until it is just right.

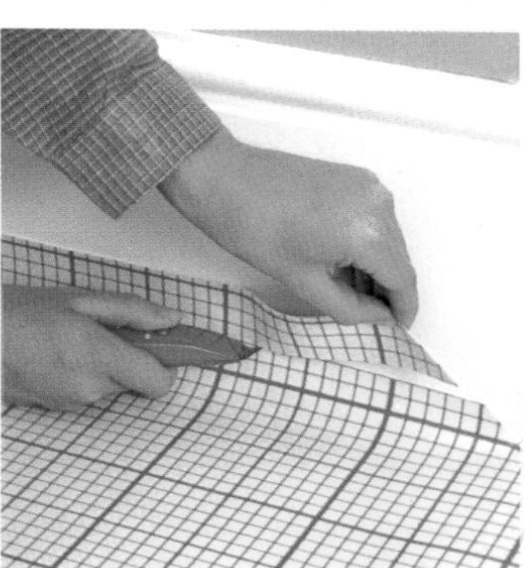

8 To trim to the wall, first run your knife along the vinyl lapping up the wall, taking off the excess so that about 1in (25mm) remains.

9 Push the vinyl firmly against the skirting board with a small block of wood.

10 Place the point of the knife on the vinyl exactly where the skirting board meets the floor, and run it along the skirting with the blade at 45 degrees to the wall. This will trim the material to fit snugly against the skirting, without leaving gaps.

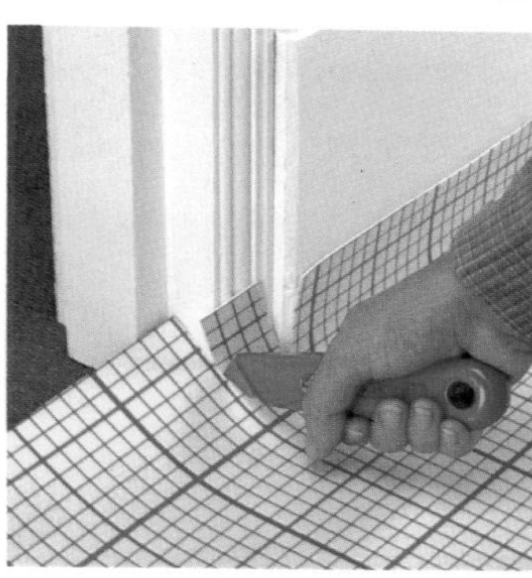

11 To cut around a door frame, make a series of vertical cuts to the point where the vinyl meets the floor, then press it into the angle between door frame and floor. Trim off the excess. In the doorway itself, cut the vinyl so that it ends halfway under the door.

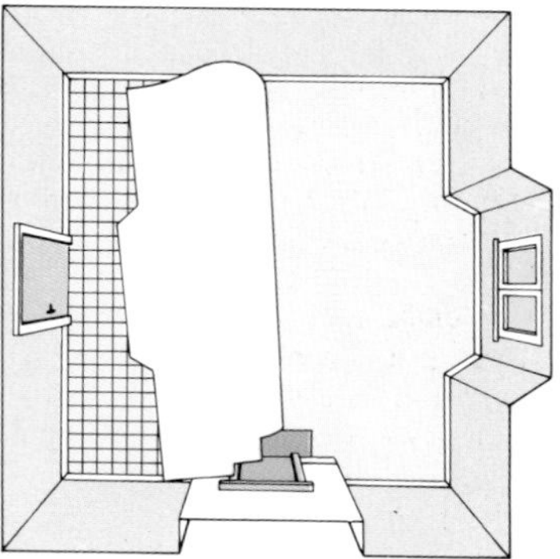

12 When the vinyl has been laid, stick it to the floor, unless it is the 'stay-flat' type which does not need sticking. Glue cushioned vinyls round the edges only. Non-cushioned types should be stuck down all over.

Roll back the sheet over half the room, and put the glue on the floor. (See fire warning, page 280.)

13 Replace the sheet and press it down with the broom. Then glue the other half of the room.

14 Finish off the doorway with metal cover strip.

COVERING LARGE ROOMS

A seamless floor cannot be laid in a room whose width is greater than 13ft (4m). The room will have to be covered with two or more lengths of 2m, 3m or 4m vinyl, depending on which size gives the least wastage of material.

Do not mix different widths on the same floor; they will have been manufactured on different machines, and there will be slight differences in the colours.

Only lengths bought from the same roll should be used on one floor.

Laying foam-backed carpet

Carpet with a foam underlay attached is much easier to lay than hessian-backed carpet, which needs a separate underlay. Not only do carpet and underlay go down in one operation, but foam-backed carpet does not have to be stretched.

Another advantage is that foam-backed carpet is held to the floor with double-sided carpet tape, eliminating the need to install gripper strip around the room.

Carpet tape can be stuck to either wood or concrete floors. It can be bought in two widths – 1in (25mm) and 2in (50mm). When you are covering a floor with a single piece of carpet, the narrow tape will do.

The laying technique for foam-backed carpet differs according to whether the carpet is in one or two pieces. The job will be easiest if you can use a single piece of carpet, a few inches bigger all round than the floor.

If you are laying carpet on floorboards that have not been overlaid with hardboard, it is advisable to fit a paper underlay to stop dust and grit from blowing up between the boards and harming the carpet.

You will need
Tools Trimming knife; clean bolster chisel or wooden kitchen spatula.
Materials Enough carpet to cover the room; double-sided carpet tape; perhaps carpet adhesive.

HELPFUL TIP
When cutting the carpet to fit exactly against the skirting board, there is a danger that a gap will be created between the carpet and the wall. For maximum accuracy, hold the knife at an angle, with the point of the blade against the skirting and the handle leaning away from the wall.

A ONE-PIECE CARPET

1 If you are using a paper underlay, put it down first (see panel). It must stop short of the walls by the width of the carpet tape so that the tape will stick to the floor, not to the paper.

2 Place the carpet loosely in position. If possible, have its pile running away from the window (or away from the main window if there is more than one). The surface should feel smooth when you run your hand away from the window (with the pile); if you feel resistance, you are going against the pile.

3 If the carpet has a pattern, adjust it so that it looks true when seen from the door.

4 To lay the carpet into an alcove, make a cut at a right angle to the back of the alcove. Take care not to cut too far, and to leave a 1in (25mm) trimming allowance. Cut off the flap riding up the fireplace.

5 Trim off the excess all round the room, so that the carpet is the size of the floor plus a trimming allowance of at least 1in (25mm) on each wall.

The surplus is cut away later to give an exact fit.

6 Re-roll the carpet and lay it diagonally across the room, so that the space all round the wall is clear for laying the tape.

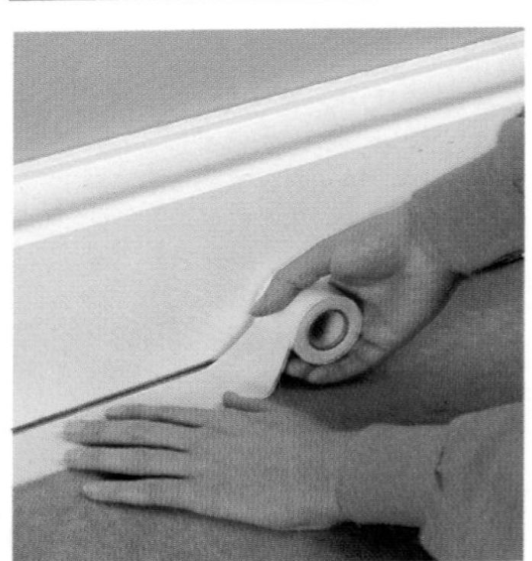

7 Fix the tape round the perimeter of the room.

Some manufacturers also recommend additional tapes across the middle of the room. Follow their instructions.

8 Unroll the carpet to its correct position.

9 Peel off the tape's backing paper, and press the carpet firmly in place all round the room.

10 Push it well into the join between floor and skirting board with a clean bolster chisel or a wooden kitchen spatula so you can see where the knife blade should go.

11 When the carpet is fixed all round, trim off the surplus with the knife.

12 Finally go all round the room making quite sure that the carpet is still adhering firmly to the tape, and pressing it back into place wherever necessary.

PAPER UNDERLAY FOR CARPET

On smooth floorboards, paper underlay can be substituted for hardboard. It will prevent dirt from blowing up between the boards and harming the carpet.

Paper underlay is sold in rolls by carpet shops.

You will need
Tools Knife or scissors; stapling hammer or electric staple gun (from a hire shop) or a hammer.
Materials Paper underlay; staples or large-headed tacks.

1 If gripper strip is being used, lay it first (facing page).

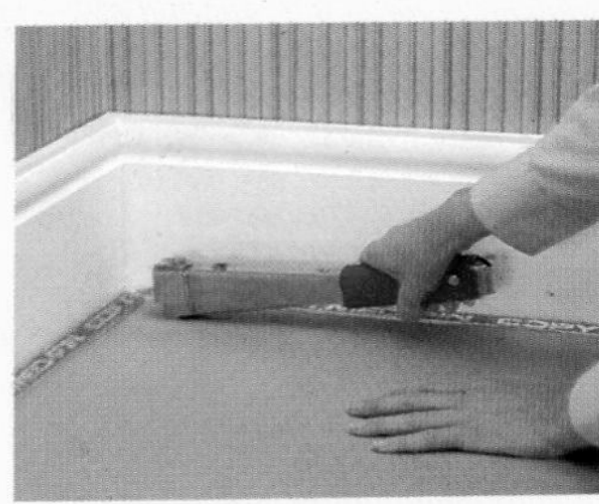

2 Beginning in a corner of the room, unroll about a yard of the paper so that it lies against the side wall (or the gripper strip) and fix it in place with a stapling hammer, staple gun or hammer.

3 Trim the end of the paper to the end wall (or gripper strip) and fix it in place.

4 Roll the paper out to the far end of the room, smoothing it as you go, and fix it along both edges, making sure it stays perfectly flat. Fix and trim it at the other end.

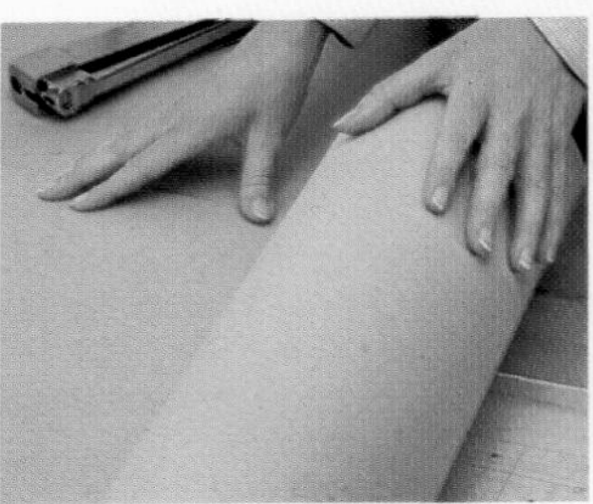

5 Fix parallel strips of paper to cover the entire room, overlapping each length by about 1in (25mm). The last length will have to be cut to width as well as length.

FOAM-BACKED CARPET IN TWO PIECES

A wide room can be carpeted with two lengths of foam-backed carpet, joined together with carpet tape. The strip of floor where the two pieces of carpet will meet must be left clear of paper underlay so that the tape can be stuck down directly to the floor.

Make sure that the pile of both pieces lies in the same direction, and – if possible – away from the main source of light. The surface should feel smooth when you run your hand with the pile; if you feel resistance, you are going against the pile.

1 Cut the first piece of carpet to length, leaving a trimming allowance of at least 1in (25mm) against all three walls for the final fitting.

2 Cut the second piece of carpet – to width this time as well as length – leaving a similar allowance for final trimming.

3 Butt the two pieces of carpet together on the floor at the meeting point.

If they fit together without any gaps, go ahead with laying the carpet (step 7).

4 If the edges of the two pieces are not straight, and gaps occur between them, snap a chalk line across the room at the meeting place (page 279).

5 Place the wider length of carpet along the chalk line, and trim it to the line with the knife.

If you have a metal straight-edge you can use it as an extra guide to get a perfect cut.

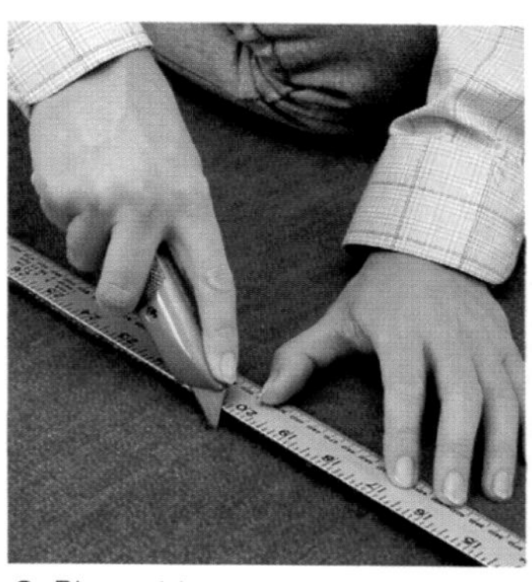

6 Place this trimmed edge on the meeting edge of the second length of carpet, and use it as a guide to trimming so that you get the best possible join.

7 Turn back the edges, and place the carpet tape on the floor, centrally along the meeting place of the two pieces. Use 2in (50mm) tape positioned centrally on the join, or two pieces of 1in (25mm) tape side by side. Peel off the backing.

8 Lay the larger piece of carpet down first, and press it into place on the tape.

9 Apply a continuous bead of carpet adhesive all along its edge.

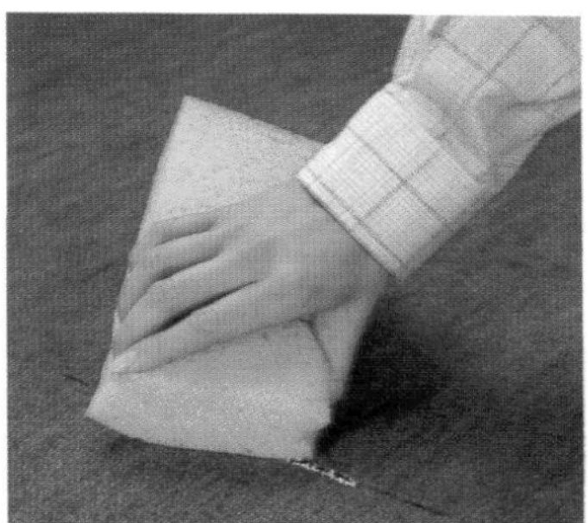

10 Place the second length in position and press it onto the tape, and against the edge of the first. Wipe up any adhesive.

11 Deal with the edges as for *A one-piece carpet* (steps 7-12).

Laying carpet with separate underlay

Carpet with a separate underlay is much more difficult to lay than foam-backed carpet. If it is to lie flat and to wear well, it must be stretched during the laying.

The stretching is done with a tool called a carpet stretcher (or 'knee-kicker').

Achieving the correct tension is the trickiest part of the job. If you stretch the carpet too much you risk tearing it; if you stretch it too little it will not lie flat and will ruck up when furniture is pushed over it. And a bumpy carpet not only looks bad, but may also become worn on the high spots.

It is probably not worthwhile laying a new carpet yourself. The price of good-quality carpet is so high that a fitting fee adds little to the overall cost. And carpet shops often include free fitting.

Used carpet, however, is easier to lay as it has already been stretched once. So if you obtain some second-hand carpet, or move house and take the carpet with you, the job is worth trying.

But it is only possible if the carpet is wide enough to cover the room without joins. Joining a carpet that has to be stretched is skilled work.

For best results, line the floorboards with hardboard (page 275), or with paper underlay (facing page), before laying the carpet.

You will need

Tools Hammer and nail punch (or carpet-layer's hammer); tenon saw or hacksaw; vice or bench hook; protective gloves; trimming knife (preferably with a hooked blade) or scissors; perhaps an electric staple gun (from a hire shop); carpet stretcher (from a hire shop); clean bolster chisel or wooden kitchen spatula.

Materials Gripper strip and nails or adhesive; threshold strip and screws or adhesive; underlay (felt or foam rubber); staples or tacks; carpet to cover the room in one piece.

HELPFUL TIP

If you are laying carpet on a concrete floor, test first to make sure that central heating pipes are not lying too close to the surface. Switch the heating full on until the radiators are hot, and then walk over the floor in bare feet. If you feel heat, do not nail gripper strip; glue it.

FIXING THE GRIPPER STRIPS

1 Measure the perimeter of the room to work out how many gripper strips you will need. The gripper strips are usually sold in 30in (760mm) lengths.

2 Put down the grippers with the pins pointing towards the wall. Leave a space slightly less than the thickness of the carpet between the gripper and the wall. This is for the trimmed carpet to be tucked into later.

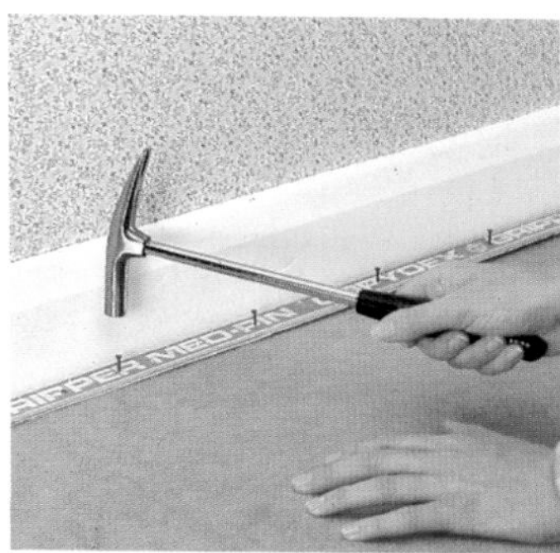

3 Nail them to the floor, using a small-headed carpet-layer's hammer. This will enable you to drive in the nails without hitting the pins. Alternatively, start off with a claw hammer, then use a nail punch when the nails get close to the pins.

CHOOSING CARPET FIXINGS

The old way of laying a carpet was to fold it under by about 2in (50mm) all round the edge of the room and tack it in place. The method can still be used, but it has been superseded by the smooth-edged method. The carpet is held by gripper strips – thin lengths of wood or metal containing two rows of angled pins.

Grippers
Some grippers come with nails ready to be hammered into the floor. Wood or concrete nails are available. Or they can be stuck to solid floors with glue sold by the makers.

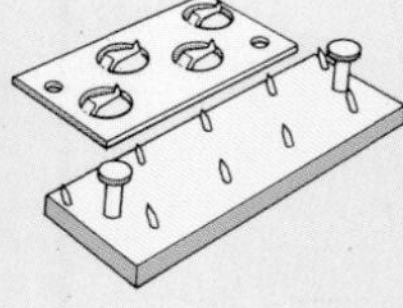

Threshold strips
In doorways, threshold strips (also called carpet edgings) are screwed, nailed or glued to the floor. They grip the carpet with spikes and fold down over the edge to protect it.

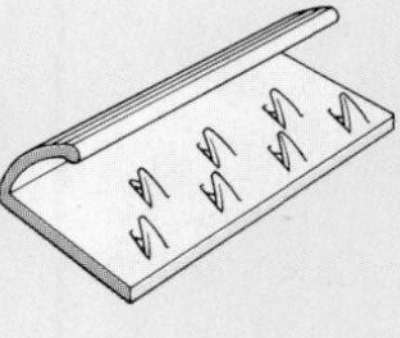

Double threshold strips
To cover the edges of two carpets laid in a room and an adjoining hall, double threshold strips can be used.

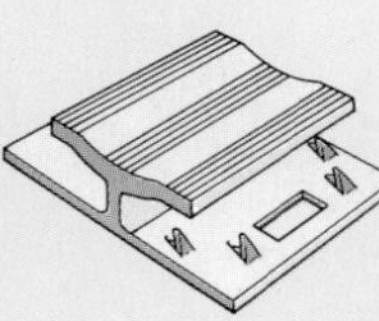

Angled grippers
For staircases, angled grippers are fitted at the junction between tread and riser. They can be bought to fit standard-width stair carpet.

Stair rods
Stair rods are again being made, and old ones can be found in secondhand shops. Make sure you have enough for your stairs. The method of fixing is usually obvious.

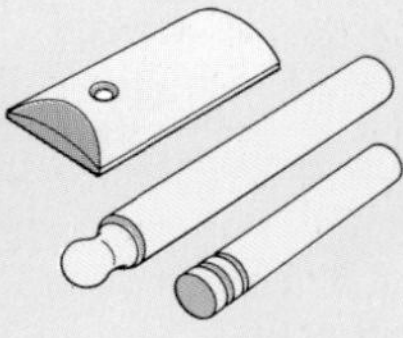

Laying carpet with a separate underlay (continued)

CARPET-LAYING TOOLS

The carpet layer's main tool is called a carpet stretcher or 'knee-kicker'. It has a flat sole with teeth at one end, which grips the carpet. At the other, there is a large pad which the layer 'kicks' with his knee.

Carpet stretchers are expensive to buy, but they can be hired quite cheaply by the day from tool-hire shops, found in *Yellow Pages* under Hire Services – Tools and Equipment.

A staple gun is needed for fixing underlay to a timber floor. Both manual and electrically operated types can be hired from tool hire shops. Use double-sided carpet tape to fix underlay to a solid floor.

A carpet-layer's hammer, which has a narrow heavy head, is useful for fixing gripper strip to a floor or stairs, as it will drive in the nails without hitting the pins on the gripper. It will probably have to be bought from a carpet shop. Alternatively, use a hammer and nail punch.

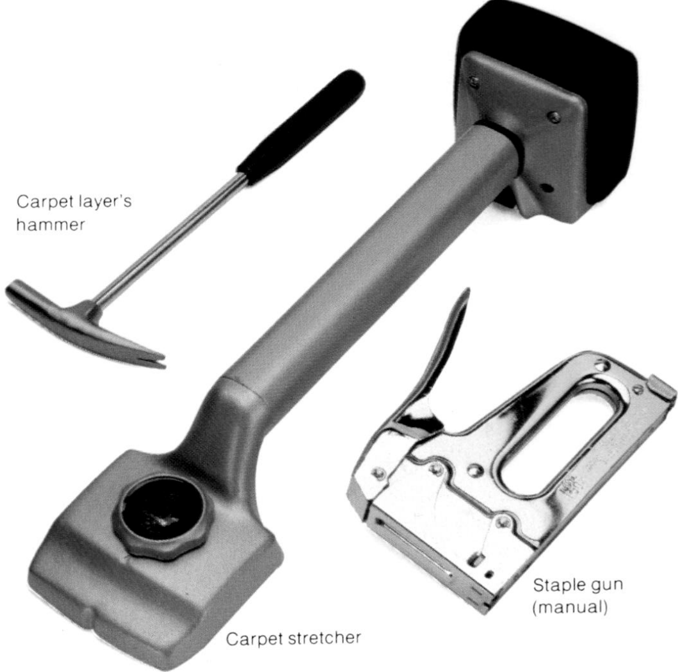

4 When a radiator prevents you from getting close to the wall, fit the gripper as close as the radiator will allow.

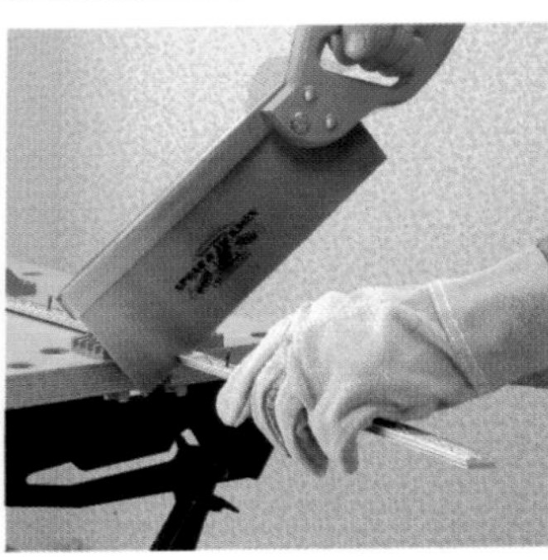

5 When you reach a corner of the room, cut the strip to length, using a tenon saw on wood or a hacksaw on metal. Hold the strip in a vice or bench hook and be careful not to hurt yourself on the pins. Heavy gloves will help to protect your hands.

6 When you come to a corner, simply butt-join two pieces of gripper. There is no need to cut mitre joints at the ends.

7 In a curved area, such as a bay window, cut the gripper into short pieces to follow the curve.

8 At a doorway, fit a metal or plastic threshold strip (also called carpet edging) midway under the door.

PUTTING DOWN THE UNDERLAY

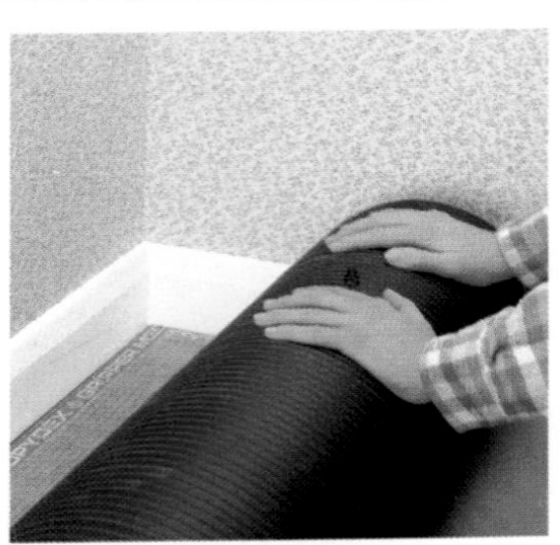

1 Unroll a short length of underlay in a corner of the room so that the end and the side lie against the gripper strip.

2 Fix the edges of the underlay to the floor with the staple gun, or with hammer and tacks. On a concrete floor, use double-sided carpet tape.

3 Roll out the underlay along the edge of the room, smoothing as you go, and fixing along both edges. Make sure it is perfectly flat on the floor.

4 It is not necessary to stretch the underlay, but it helps to push it in position with the carpet stretcher.

5 Where a radiator is fixed to the wall, lay the underlay up to the edge of the gripper, even if the gripper has been fitted a little way out from the wall.

6 At the end of the room, trim the underlay against the gripper strip with a trimming knife or scissors.

7 When you have almost covered the room, you will have to cut the last length of underlay to width as well as to length.

LAYING THE CARPET

1 In a larger room – or on the lawn if it is a dry day – cut the carpet to the size of the room to be covered. Add a trimming allowance of 6in (150mm) on all sides – even more if the carpet has a pattern.

Keep the waste; it may come in handy for patching later.

If possible the carpet should lie with the pile running away from the main or only window; this stops uneven shading in the daylight. The surface should feel smooth when you run your hand away from the window, but give some resistance when you run your hand towards the window.

2 Put the carpet in place on the floor of the room where it is to be laid. If it has a pattern, adjust it so that the pattern looks true, and does not run off when seen from the doorway.

3 Make release cuts to allow the carpet to lie flat in any alcove. Cut the carpet at a right angle to the back of the alcove and take care not to cut too far. Leave some excess for trimming around the alcove.

4 Cut off the surplus riding up the fireplace, leaving some excess for trimming.

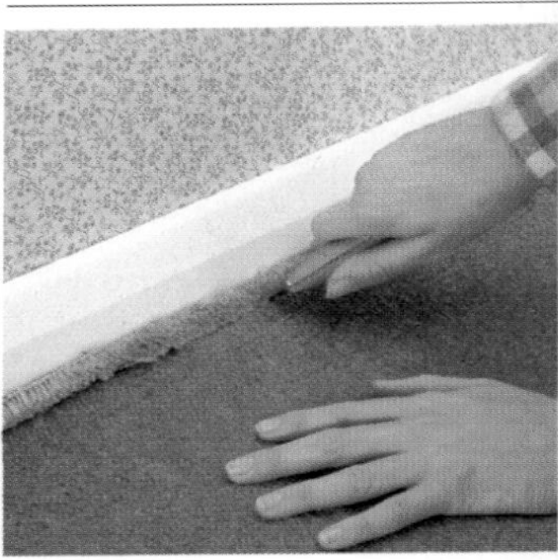

5 Trim off the excess all round the room, leaving an allowance of about $\frac{3}{8}$in (10mm) along two adjacent walls, and an allowance of about $1\frac{1}{2}$in (38mm) along the other two.

HELPFUL TIP

When trimming into an alcove it helps if you make vertical cuts at the corners. You can then press the carpet down onto the floor before cutting off the excess. This makes it easier to judge the appropriate allowance to be pushed down later.

6 Start the fixing in the corner of the room with the smaller allowance. Working along one wall, run your fingers along the top of the carpet so that it engages on the gripper pins farthest from the wall. Take care not to injure your fingers on the spikes.

7 Do the same along the second wall with the smaller allowance.

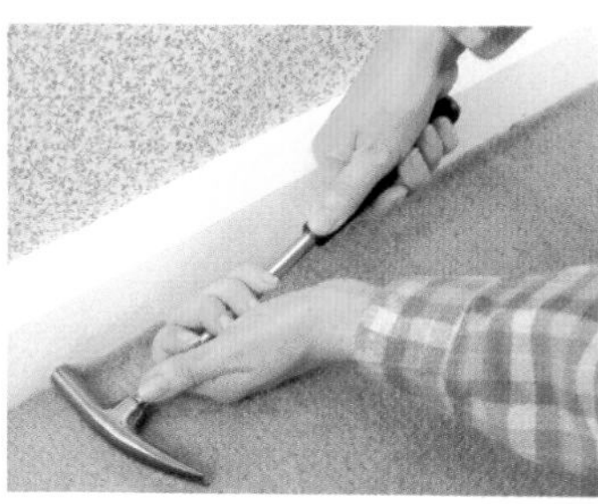

8 Run the head of your hammer flat along the top of the carpet, pushing it onto the other row of pins and forcing the excess carpet into the space between the gripper strip and the skirting board.

9 When the first two edges have been fixed, kneel on the carpet with your back to one of the completed walls.

Push the teeth of the carpet stretcher into the carpet ahead of you and 'kick' the padded end with your knee to force the carpet forwards.

Move forwards and repeat once or twice until you are close to the opposite wall.

10 Stretch the carpet again, and hook it onto the gripping pins with your hand. It will immediately contract and be firmly fixed in place. Carpet fitters know from experience when the maximum stretch has been reached. You will just have to experiment until you get the tension of the carpet firm and even all across the room.

11 Repeat this process three or four more times across the room until the carpet is fixed all along one wall.

Then turn 90 degrees and fix it along the fourth wall.

12 When the hooking is complete, excess carpet will be left lapping up the walls. Trim this off to about ⅜in (10mm).

13 Push the remainder into the space between the gripper and skirting, using a clean bolster chisel or a wooden kitchen spatula. Take care not to scratch the paintwork if you are using a bolster.

14 Check that the excess carpet on the other two walls of the room is properly pushed down, and use the bolster or spatula where necessary.

15 Finally, tap down the cover of the threshold strip at the doorway, using a piece of waste wood or carpet to protect the metal from becoming dented.

CUTTING A DOOR TO CLEAR A CARPET

After fitting a carpet, the base of the door may drag on the surface. One cure is to change the hinges for rising butts (page 198).

Alternatively, the bottom of the door can be trimmed off. With the door in place use a thin block of wood as thick as the amount of wood to be removed. Put it on the floor with a pencil on top and run it along the door to mark the cutting line.

Take off the door and either saw or plane off the base. If you use a hand saw, work slowly to avoid splintering the face.

If you use a plane, hold the door upright on its long edge in a portable work bench and plane downwards. Work inwards from each side to avoid splintering the stiles at the end. Sand the bottom of the door so that it will not damage the carpet.

It is also possible to hire a door trimming saw from tool hire shops, and trim the door without removing it from its hinges.

Patching a damaged carpet

To repair a hole or a frayed patch in a carpet, you need a piece of the same carpet slightly bigger than the damaged area.

The piece may have been left over when the carpet was laid, or you can cut it from under a large piece of furniture where it will not show. That hole could then be filled with different carpet.

The joins of the repair should not be visible. At first, there will be a colour difference between the patch and the rest of the carpet, but in time this will become less obvious.

You will need
Tools Trimming knife; hammer.
Materials Carpet patch; latex-based carpet adhesive; 2in (50mm) self-adhesive carpet tape (possibly double-sided); a piece of hessian larger than the patch (except for foam-backed carpet).

CUTTING THE NEW PIECE

1 Place the new piece over the damaged portion, ensuring that the pile runs in the same direction. (Run your hand over both carpets to find the direction in which they feel smoothest.)

2 Hold the patch firmly on the carpet and cut through both at the same time with a sharp knife. This ensures that the patch and hole are exactly the same size.

Take care not to cut through a separate underlay as well.

LOOSE-LAID CARPET

1 In the case of a loose-laid carpet, roll it back and apply a carpet adhesive round the edge of the hole and the edge of the patch to about halfway up the pile. This prevents fraying.

2 Leave the adhesive to dry, then insert the patch in position.

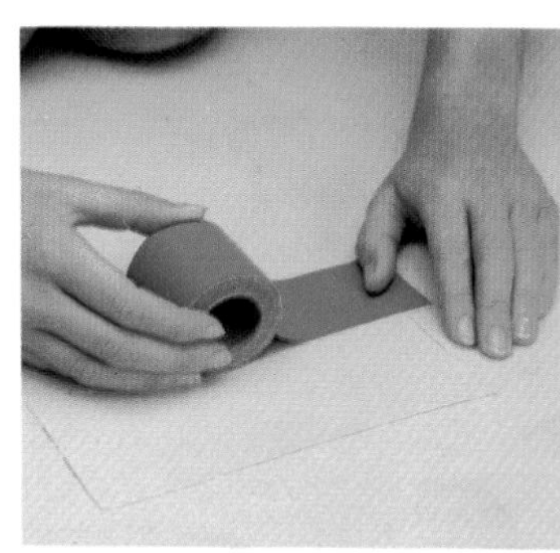

3 On a foam-backed carpet, fix the patch in place with 2in (50mm) self-adhesive carpet tape on all the edges.

With other carpets, spread carpet adhesive on a piece of hessian 2in (50mm) bigger all round than the patch. Stick it over the back of the patch and over the surrounding carpet.

4 Turn the carpet right side up and pinch the edges of the patch and the carpet between your fingers to make quite sure they stick well together.

5 Finally, tap the join all over lightly with a hammer to disguise the join as much as possible, although the colour difference will probably still be visible.

FITTED CARPET

1 Apply a carpet adhesive round the edges of the hole and the edge of the patch to about halfway up the pile, working from the back, and leave it to dry.

2 Take four lengths of double-sided carpet tape, push them through the hole, and stick them to the floor or the underlay where the patch will join onto the main carpet. Remove the backing from the tape.

3 Place the patch in position and press it firmly down.

4 Push the joins together, and tap lightly with a hammer.

Fitting a stair carpet

Staircases are often covered with a central strip of carpet, with the wood on each side either painted or varnished. The carpet is sold ready made to width – normally 27in (690mm).

Take care when laying a stair carpet; if it is not done properly the carpet can work loose, creating a risk of injury. Laying a central strip is fairly easy, but laying fitted carpet on stairs should be left to a carpet layer.

The carpet wears very unevenly because people walk on just a small part of it – near the front of the tread. You can prolong its life considerably by laying it with stair grippers or stair rods so that it can be repositioned regularly, and leaving some surplus at the bottom.

Stair carpets need an underlay, like room carpets, and it is normal to use stair pads, not a continuous roll. The pads, which you can cut from the roll, need to be slightly bigger from front to back than the depth of the tread, so that they overhang the nose of the tread.

You will need

Tools Tape measure; pencil; hammer and nail punch, or carpet layer's hammer; trimming knife or scissors; wooden spatula or spoon.

Materials Carpet to cover the stairs; carpet adhesive; carpet tacks; stair pads; narrow strips of hardboard or plywood; metal stair grippers the width of the carpet; and nails for fixing.

> SAFETY TIP
>
> Walking up a staircase with only pads in position can be dangerous, as the pads hang loosely over the edge of the tread. Also the pins on the grippers are very sharp. In a house that is occupied, carpet should be fitted over the pads as quickly as possible. Anyone who has to use the stairs in the meantime should take care.

ESTIMATING THE CARPET

1 To decide the length of the carpet, first measure from the front to the back of one tread (the part you walk on) and multiply the figure by the number of treads in the staircase.

2 Where a curving staircase has treads deeper at one end than the other, take the larger measurement. In some cases, the bottom tread may be deeper than the rest; also allow for this.

3 If the stairs turn a corner on a half-landing, measure the length of the half-landing and add it to the total. If you wish the carpet to run to the far end of any landing at the top of the stairs, add this measurement as well.

4 Now measure the height of the riser (the vertical part of each step) and multiply the figure by the number of risers.

5 Add this to the figure you already have. The total is the length of carpet needed to cover the stairs. But an allowance for moving the carpet to even out the wear is also needed, so add the depth of the bottom tread and the height of the bottom riser.

You will probably have to buy to the next metre or half metre.

ESTIMATING LENGTH OF CARPET

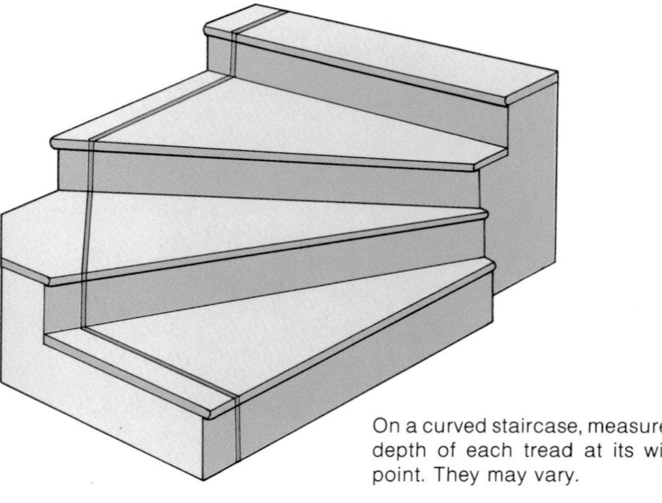

On a curved staircase, measure the depth of each tread at its widest point. They may vary.

PREPARING THE STAIRCASE

1 If an old carpet has just been removed, inspect the staircase for defects, and carry out any necessary repairs.

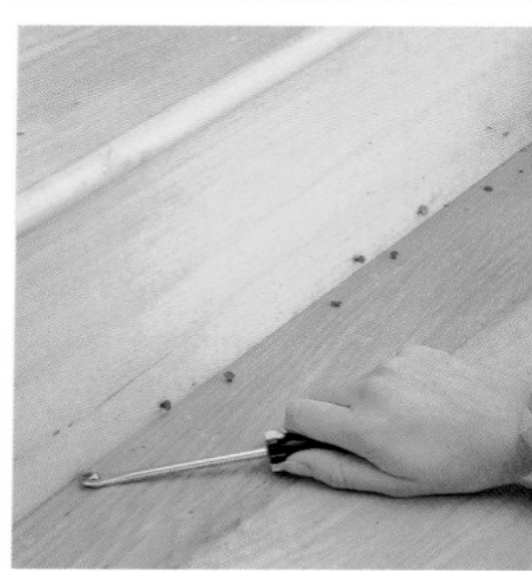

2 Remove old nails or tacks left over from the old carpet. A tack lifter is the best tool.

3 Put a pad centrally on the top tread (the one below the landing) with one edge resting against the riser and the other overhanging the front of the tread.

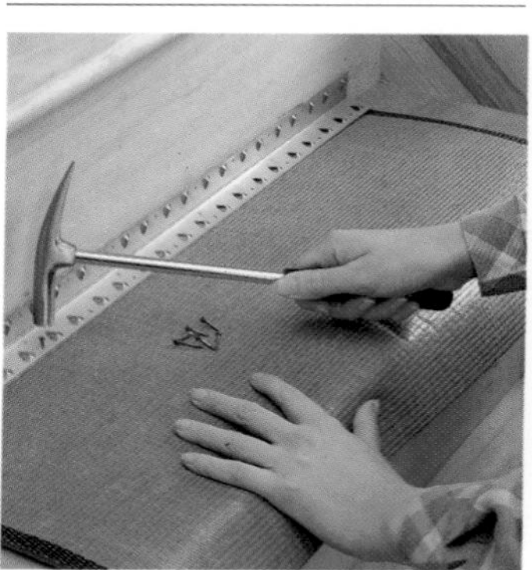

4 Place a stair gripper where the tread and the riser meet. Nail it to the tread through the pad. A carpet-layer's hammer, which has a small head, will drive in the nails without hitting the teeth of the gripper. Alternatively, use an ordinary hammer and finish off the nails with a nail punch. Nail the gripper to the riser as well.

Repeat on the other stairs, except for the bottom one. And do not fit a gripper where the bottom riser meets the floor.

LAYING THE CARPET

1 Unroll the carpet and run your hand over it. It will wear better if the direction which feels smooth runs from the top to the bottom of the stairs.

2 Re-roll it from the top, with the decorative side inwards.

3 Working from the bottom of the stairs, unroll a little of the carpet. If the end is starting to fray, spread a little carpet adhesive on the edge, taking care not to get any on the top of the carpet.

4 Cover the bottom tread with carpet, laid face down. Make sure to keep the carpet parallel to the sides of the tread.

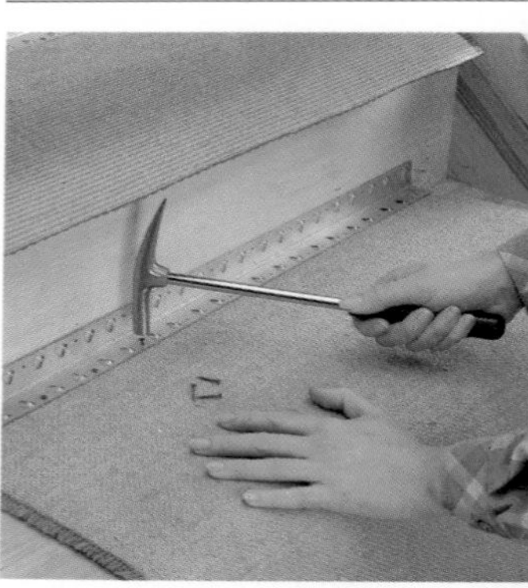

5 Fix the stair gripper on the tread, trapping the carpet in place with the nails.

6 Bring the carpet over the nose of the tread and down the riser.

7 Fix it at the bottom of the riser with a strip of hardboard or plywood nailed in place through the carpet.

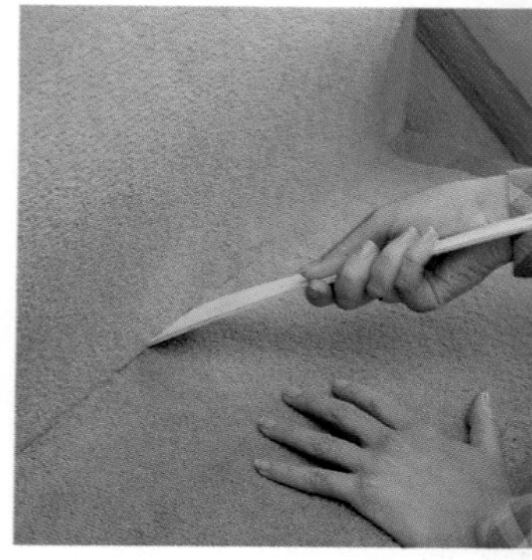

8 Bring the carpet back up the bottom riser to the starting point so the decorative surface is uppermost. Fix it to the gripper by pushing with a wooden spatula, or even a wooden spoon, onto both rows of spikes. Make sure the carpet is firmly fixed.

9 Continue up the stairs, fixing the carpet to each gripper.

A CURVED STAIRCASE

Laying carpet on a curved staircase is difficult unless you use a woven carpet such as Wilton or Axminster. Other types are extremely stiff.

1 Nail wooden gripper strip to both the rise and the tread.

2 Cut the stair pads to shape; they will have to be wider at one end than the other. Staple or tack them in place, butted up against the gripper on the tread.

3 Begin laying the carpet at the bottom of the staircase. (See Laying the carpet, facing page.)

4 Push the carpet onto the grippers with a spatula or a piece of wood ¼in (6mm) thick. Professionals use a blunted brick bolster.

5 On the first curved stair bring the carpet up the riser and nail it with 1in (25mm) tacks.

6 Fold it down so that it meets the tread below and tack it in place.

FIXING A CARPET ON A CURVED STAIRCASE

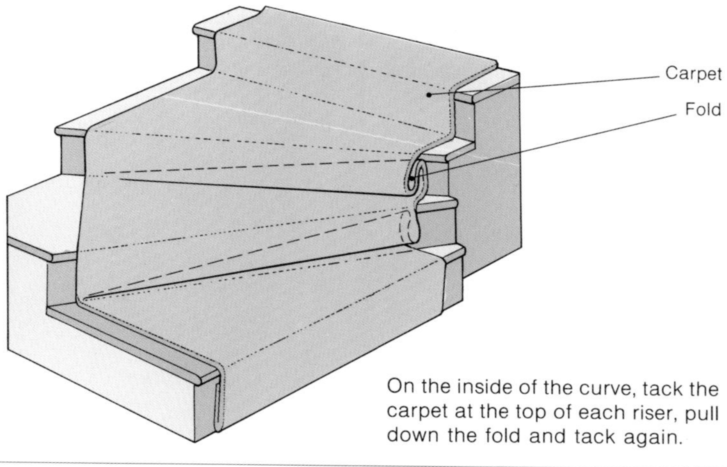

On the inside of the curve, tack the carpet at the top of each riser, pull down the fold and tack again.

7 If the curve is sharp, you may have to lay the carpet in pieces – two or three stairs for each piece.

USING STAIR RODS

1 When buying a set of stair rods, make sure there will be enough for the staircase.

2 Rods do not alter the principles of fixing stair carpet, but their fixing clips will probably not be able to hold the underlay pads, which will need to be fixed with tacks.

Put the clips for the rods at the edge of the carpet to prevent it moving sideways.

3 For the sake of appearance, fix rods on curved stairs and perhaps between the hall floor and the bottom riser, although the carpet will actually be held by the tacks.

Dealing with landings

WALL-TO-WALL CARPET

If the landing is to have wall-to-wall carpet, finish the stair carpet at the top of the last riser. Cut off any surplus, leaving about 1in (25mm) to fold under. Fix it with tacks along its top edge.

Lay the landing carpet in the same way as a room carpet, but take it over the top step and tack it to the top riser.

A HALF-LANDING

Where a staircase makes a 90 degree turn, treat it as two flights of stairs. Cover the half-landing with one of the stair carpets. Butt the other one up to it, turn under the end and tack it down.

If the staircase makes a dog-leg (180 degree) turn, there may be a wide landing to be covered with a separate strip of stair carpet laid at right angles to the two flights of stairs.

Carry both stair carpets to what will be the far edge of the landing carpet, cut them off and tack them in place without putting underlay beneath them. This surplus can be used for moving the carpet to avoid wear in future years.

Lay a third strip of carpet across them to cover the landing.

There will be a gap under the landing carpet in the middle between the two strips of stair carpet. So fit underlay – perhaps some stair pads tacked in place and trimmed to fit the space.

Tack down the landing carpet all the way round, folding under the two ends.

A FULL LANDING

On a full landing that is not to have wall-to-wall carpet, you can simply run the stair carpet to the far end without a break.

Cut it off and seal the edge with adhesive.

Put underlay beneath the carpet, overlapping the top riser. Finish off the end of the carpet with a metal threshold strip. Tack down along the edges.

FULL LANDING WITH WALL-TO-WALL CARPET

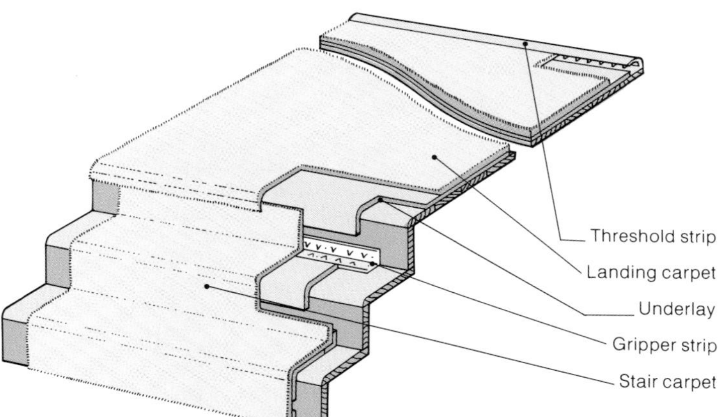

CARPET ON A DOG-LEG TURN

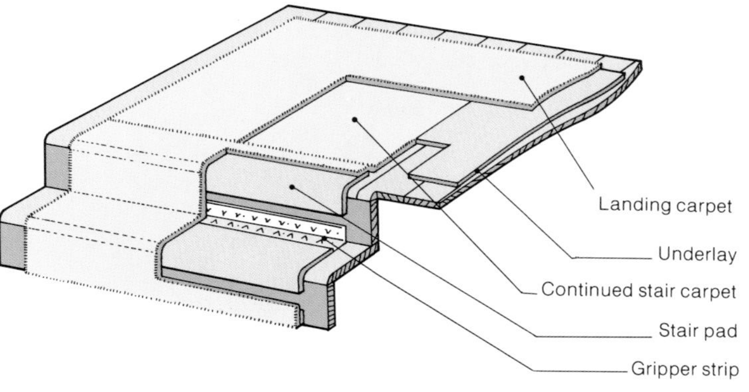

Moving stair carpet to avoid wear

People walking up a staircase tread on the front of each step, so that the carpet on the edge of the steps can become worn very quickly, particularly if it is not a heavy-duty grade.

Wear can be equalised by moving the carpet up the stairs by about 3in (75mm) every year, so that all parts of the carpet get the same amount of wear over a period of several years. The job is easiest if the carpet is held with stair rods rather than grippers.

You will need
Tools Tack lifter; hammer; wooden spatula.
Materials Narrow strip of underlay; carpet tacks.

1 Release the carpet from the tacks or metal strip holding it in place at the top, using a tack lifter.

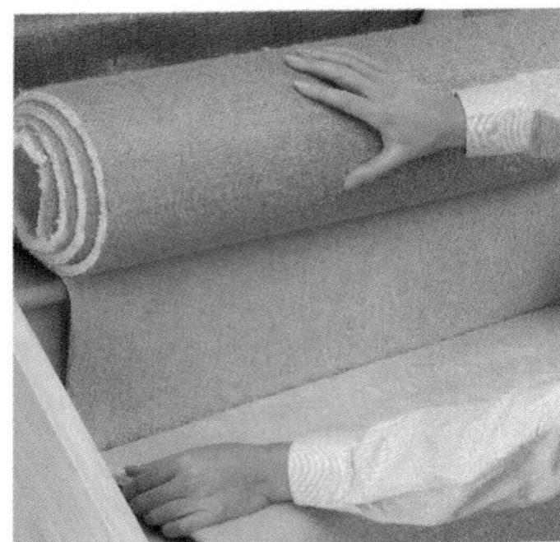

2 Fold the end into a roll, and work down the stairs, rolling as you go. This should free the carpet from the top teeth of the grippers, but you may have to lift it from the bottom teeth. Do not just drag the carpet away from the teeth, as it may get damaged.

If the carpet is held with stair rods, simply remove them.

3 With the carpet rolled up, start to re-lay it in the same way as laying it originally (page 290), except that on the bottom tread begin about 3in (75mm) away from the riser, and tack it down.

4 Fill the gap that is created with a strip of carpet underlay fixed under the gripper.

5 Where the carpet ends at the top, turn under the excess of 3in (75mm) and tack it.

6 Year by year, the surplus carpet at the bottom will become shorter, until it will all be transferred to the top, where a double pocket may be needed. At the foot of the stairs it will be tacked to the bottom of the lowest riser.

If the carpet is still in good condition the following year, start off as you began – with a double layer of carpet on the bottom tread and bottom riser.

NEWLY LAID CARPET

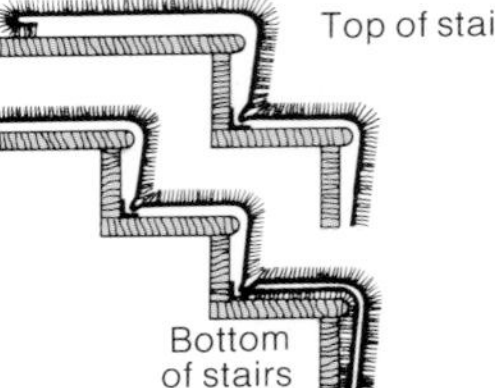

AFTER SEVERAL MOVES

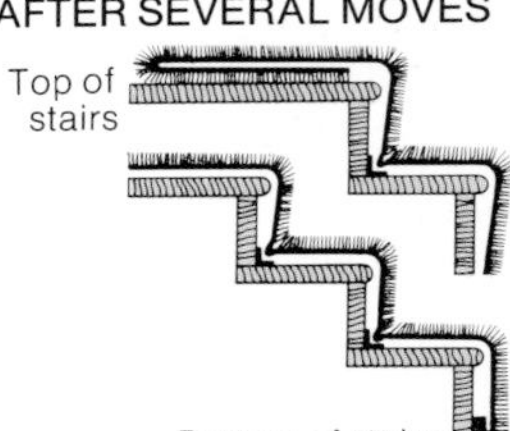

REMOVING STAINS FROM CARPETS

Try to treat stains immediately they occur. The longer they are left, the more difficult they will become.

You should not add extra liquid of any sort and do not rub the carpet. If you do so, you will only drive the stain deeper, or spread it.

First scrape off any solid matter with a spoon or blunt knife. Mop up liquid by pressing on it with a dry towel or wad of tissues. Use different areas of the towel or tissues until no more moisture can be lifted.

If a stain still remains, treat it according to whether it is water-based or grease-based. A water-based stain – a drink, for example – can be removed with a carpet shampoo; a grease-based stain, such as gravy or fat, can be removed with a dry-cleaning solvent. Brand names of dry-cleaning solvents include Dabit-off and Carpet Devils.

When applying the shampoo or solvent use just enough on a cloth to moisten the area. If you use a saturated cloth you are likely to drive the stain deeper. Turn the cloth to a dry side as soon as it becomes dirty. Work from the outside of the stain towards the middle to avoid spreading it.

Finally, cover the area with a thick wad of tissues weighed down with something flat and heavy, such as a phone book. The remaining moisture will be absorbed by the tissues, further reducing the risk of a permanent stain.

When the treated patch has dried out, it may be necessary to shampoo the entire carpet to ensure uniform colour. Carpet-cleaning firms will do the job for you, or you can hire carpet-cleaning equipment by the day from firms listed in *Yellow Pages* under Hire Services – Tools and Equipment.

Be careful not to over-wet the carpet, and never allow the back of the carpet to get wet. Do not try to dry carpets artificially, as heat may damage the pile.

Smooth the carpet pile in its natural direction and keep it well ventilated until dry.

Proprietary carpet spot-removing kits containing chemicals for treating a wide variety of stains are available from local Service-Master outlets or by post from the company's head office (call 0116 2364646 for details).

Getting professional help
The National Carpet Cleaners' Association will provide lists of member companies in your area who will advise on stain removal and carry out cleaning work. The contact address is 62c London Road, Oadby, Leicester LE2 5DH (telephone 0116 2719950).

SAFETY TIPS

Many solvents are potentially harmful. Some are flammable; many give off poisonous fumes. So treat all stain-removing solvents with extreme care.

Work in a well ventilated room.

Never smoke or work near a naked flame while using a solvent.

Remove children and pets from the room.

Never pour dry-cleaner solvent into a second container. It may later be mistaken by another member of the family for some sort of drink.

Always wear rubber gloves to protect your hands when using solvents.

Keep all solvents locked away from children.

Switch off warm-air ducted heating.

Alcoholic spirits
Mop up with a dry towel or wad of tissues. Sponge with warm water. Allow to dry. Then clean with carpet shampoo. Treat any remaining stain with methylated spirit.

Animal stains (excreta, vomit, urine)
Remove loose solids with paper. Scrape the residue with a blunt knife or spoon. Blot dry with a cloth or wad of tissues. Lightly sponge with a carpet shampoo (add acetic acid for urine). If the stain is serious call a professional carpet cleaner. The most serious stains penetrate the back of the carpet and the underlay.

Ball-point pen
Speedy action is essential. Dab with methylated spirit on a cotton wool bud. Take care not to spread the stain.

On vinyl upholstery or wall coverings, immediately scrub with a nail brush and warm soapy water (the ink will cause a permanent mark if left).

Beer
Mop up with a towel and leave to dry. If there is still a mark, treat with carpet shampoo.

Blood
FRESH STAINS Sponge with cold water. Blot dry. Clean with carpet shampoo if necessary.
DRIED STAINS May not clean completely.

Candlewax
Scrape off as much as possible. Cover remainder with blotting paper or brown paper. Apply the point of a warm iron. Do not allow the iron to touch the carpet; it may cause it to melt. Move the paper about until the wax is absorbed into it.

Clear any remaining traces with a dry-cleaning solvent.

Chewing gum
Freeze the chewing gum with blocks of ice wrapped in a plastic bag, or a proprietary chewing gum remover.

Then break it up into pieces and brush up the bits by hand – chewing gum clogs up vacuum cleaners.

Chocolate
Scrape off the chocolate with a knife, and clean the area with carpet shampoo.

Treat stubborn stains with dry-cleaning solvent when the shampoo has dried.

Cocoa
Mop up the worst and dry off with a towel or wad of tissues. Clean with carpet shampoo. Treat any remaining stain with a dry-cleaning solvent when the shampoo has dried.

Coffee
Mop up the worst of the liquid. Blot dry. Treat any remaining stain with a carpet shampoo. When dry use dry-cleaning solvent to remove grease from milk or cream.

Curry
An extremely difficult stain. Large marks should be treated professionally. With small marks, scrape off the deposit and rub lightly with borax solution (15ml borax to 500ml water). Stubborn stains can sometimes be helped with a little neat glycerine rubbed into the carpet and left for about 10 minutes. Then sponge out with warm water, and blot dry.

Dyes
Have the stain treated by a carpet-cleaning firm.

Egg
Scrape off the deposit. Treat with dry-cleaning solvent or with a proprietary carpet spot-removing kit.

Eye make-up
Moisten the area, then treat with a drop of liquid detergent on a cotton wool bud. Rinse. Treat stubborn stains with dry-cleaning solvent.

Fats, grease and oil
Mop up the worst. Scrape off any deposit. Apply dry-cleaning solvent.

Heavy deposits often respond to the blotting-paper-and-iron technique (see Candlewax).

Felt-tip pen
Some felt-tip pens have spirit-based ink, some have water-based ink. Methylated spirit on a cotton wool bud will remove spirit-based ink, which has a pungent smell. But do not allow it to penetrate to a foam backing. The methylated spirit may stain a light coloured carpet. For water-based ink, use carpet shampoo.

Foundation cream
FRESH WET STAINS Mop up any deposit and apply dry-cleaning solvent. Allow to dry, and treat with carpet shampoo. Stubborn stains can be treated with a proprietary carpet spot-removing kit.
DRY STAINS Brush off powder, then use a proprietary carpet spot-removing kit.

Fruit juice
Mop up with a clean cloth or paper towels. Clean with carpet shampoo.

Gravy
Mop up with paper towels. Treat with dry-cleaning solvent. Clean with carpet shampoo.

Hair oil
Mop up as much as possible and then apply a dry-cleaning solvent.

Ice cream
Scrape up and wipe with paper towels. Treat with a dry-cleaning solvent when dry. Clean with carpet shampoo.

Ink (fountain pen)
Must be tackled immediately. Blot with absorbent paper. Sponge with warm water to remove further ink. You may need more than one application. Blot well each time.

Treat remaining small stains with a proprietary carpet spot-removing kit.

Jam/marmalade
Spoon up deposits. Wipe area with cloth wrung out in warm water. Clean with carpet shampoo. Remove any remaining stains with a proprietary carpet spot-removing kit.

Ketchup
Scoop up or wipe away excess deposits. Take care not to spread the stain. Gently rub with lather made up from carpet shampoo. Wipe with cloth wrung out in warm water. Work in direction of the pile. Treat any remaining stain with a dry-cleaning solvent.

Lipstick
Scrape off with a knife, and use a dry-cleaning solvent. Alternatively, use a proprietary carpet spot-removing kit or a little Polyclens Plus paintbrush cleaner.

Metal polish
Scrape or blot up any deposit. Treat with carpet shampoo containing a few drops of household ammonia.

Milk
Immediate action is essential to prevent milk penetrating down into the carpet where it will give off a smell indefinitely. Blot dry. Clean with carpet shampoo. If a stain remains use a dry-cleaning solvent. May need professional attention to prevent smell recurring each time room warms up.

Mud
Allow to dry. Brush, then vacuum. Clean with carpet shampoo if necessary.

Mustard
Scrape off deposits. Sponge with damp cloth. Treat with carpet shampoo.

Nail varnish
Spoon up deposit; avoid spreading the stain. Moisten a pad of cotton wool with amyl acetate or acetone (non-oily nail varnish remover), and dab on affected area. Use it only in a well-ventilated room, and do not smoke. Do not use oily nail varnish removers – usually the more expensive brands. First test on a hidden corner of the carpet as the acetone may damage man-made fibres. Use as little as possible, as over-soaking can damage the backing. Remaining traces of colour can be removed with methylated spirit. Apply a dry-cleaning solvent if necessary.

On a carpet made of man-made fibres, use the least possible amount of the solvent, and dab dry frequently.

Paint
All paint must be dealt with immediately. Once it has dried it is almost impossible to remove. Scrape up and wipe off as much as possible, then treat according to the type of paint.
EMULSION Mop with cold water, working from the edges inwards. Large areas of dried-on emulsion should be left to professional carpet cleaners.
ACRYLIC Mop up with tissues. Sponge with warm water. Finish with methylated spirit or dry-cleaning solvent.
GLOSS OR OIL-BASED PAINT Sponge with white spirit or a dry-cleaning solvent. If dry, soften with paintbrush cleaner.

Large areas need professional attention.

Paraffin
Mop up spillage immediately. Treat the area with a dry-cleaning solvent.

Paraffin stains are very difficult to remove. Get help from a professional.

Perfume
Clean with carpet shampoo, and allow to dry. Use more shampoo if the stain persists.

Plasticine
Scrape off as much as possible, then treat the remainder with a dry-cleaning solvent.

Scorch marks
Bad scorch marks are impossible to remove as the fibres are damaged. For repairing a carpet, see page 289. For slight marks trim the pile with scissors, or lightly shave with a disposable razor. Or remove loose fibres with a stiff brush, then make circular movements with a wire brush or abrasive paper to disguise the area.

Shoe polish
Scrape off and dab with dry-cleaning solvent. Finish with methylated spirit. Clean with carpet shampoo if necessary.

Soft drinks
Mop up. Treat with carpet shampoo. Stubborn marks often respond to methylated spirit.

Soot
Vacuum the area with a suction-only type cleaner, not a brush type. Or shake a rug outside. Do not brush or the mark will spread. Use a dry-cleaning solvent to remove any small marks. Get professionals to treat large areas.

Tar
Very hard to remove. Scrape away any loose deposit. Treat with a dry-cleaning solvent. If the surface is hard, scratch it to allow the solvent to penetrate.

On stubborn stains try dabbing with eucalyptus oil or Polyclens Plus paintbrush cleaner.

Tea
Mop up as much as possible. Treat with carpet shampoo. Treat any left-over stain when dry with dry-cleaning solvent which will remove the grease from milk.

Toothpaste
Scrape up any deposit and treat with carpet shampoo.

Treacle
Scrape off, then treat with carpet shampoo.

Wine
FRESH SPILLS Blot dry, then clean with carpet shampoo. Do not put salt on the carpet; it may affect the colour.
OLD STAINS May respond to glycerine solution (equal parts of water and glycerine) left for an hour, then rinsed off. Sponging with methylated spirit may reduce very old stains.

STAINS ON UPHOLSTERY
Speed is vital in removing all stains, so there is a great advantage in having a proprietary spot-removing kit in the house (see details of manufacturers on the opposite page).

Specific stains on upholstery can be given much the same treatment as described for carpets.

Where possible, treat stains from the back of the fabric. Loose covers, for example, should be removed before treatment. Lay the fabric on a clean cloth face down and apply the solvent on the reverse side.

All velvet, except acrylic velvet such as Dralon, should be treated by a cleaning firm.

Do not dry the fabric artificially. The heat may shrink the fabric or damage some fibres.

Laying a laminate floor

A laminate floor consists of lengths of man-made board, tongued and grooved on all four edges and fitted together to form an overlay on an existing timber or concrete floor. The boards generally have a core of high-density fibreboard (HDF).

The least expensive type of laminate floor has a wood-effect surface layer that is a photographic copy of genuine wood grain. This is bonded to one face of the board and is protected by a tough, clear plastic coating. The boards are usually 6 to 8mm thick. Because they have a fibreboard core, they are not suitable for use in wet areas such as bathrooms.

More expensive types have a real wood surface veneer, again under a plastic wear layer, and a cheaper, balancing back veneer, and are up to 14mm thick. Types with a core of solid wood can be used in bathrooms. The board surface can be sanded and re-finished if it is scratched or stained.

Solid wood flooring is the most expensive of all. It is available in a wide range of woods such as oak, beech, maple and mahogany, in boards up to 19mm thick. Some are supplied unfinished; others have a factory-applied clear surface coating. Because of their thickness, these boards can be laid directly onto floor joists in place of existing floorboards if you have to renew an old suspended timber floor.

Laminate flooring is generally sold in packs containing several boards. The pack will state the floor area it covers, so to estimate the amount you need, multiply the length of the room by the width to give the area, then divide this by the coverage given on the pack. Buy one or two extra packs to allow for wastage in cutting boards to size.

LAYING METHODS

Laminate flooring is laid as a floating floor; it is not fixed to the sub-floor, and is kept in place by the skirting boards. It is laid on an underlay to cushion it and take up any slight irregularities in the sub-floor. The underlay may be a roll of foamed plastic or a layer of thicker felt boards laid edge to edge to provide greater thermal and acoustic insulation.

Some laminated boards have to be glued together edge to edge. Others have shaped tongues and grooves that interlock positively to lock the boards to their neighbours. This type has the advantage that boards can be lifted if access is needed to the sub-floor – to cope with an under-floor plumbing emergency, for example.

Solid flooring is generally fixed to the floor joists or to a timber sub-floor by a technique known as secret nailing (see Laying solid wood flooring, facing page).

Prepare timber sub-floors for laying all types of wood flooring by punching in any floorboard nails that project above the board surface with a nail punch.

You will need

Tools Tape measure; pencil; scissors or trimming knife; tenon saw; panel saw or power jigsaw; hammer; plastic or wooden edge spacers; tamping block or board offcut; edging tool; power drill with flat wood bit.

Materials Enough underlay and laminate flooring to cover the room; adhesive tape; PVA woodworking adhesive (for standard boards); quadrant beading; panel pins; expansion strip (optional).

COVERING THE EXPANSION GAP

Various shapes of wood moulding can be bought to cover an expansion gap around the walls. Two possible shapes are quadrant and scotia (page 153). Buy the moulding about ¾in (19mm) wide to cover the gap comfortably.

Press it firmly against the skirting board and fix it with panel pins about ½in (13mm) longer than the width of the moulding. Do not nail it to the floor.

At the corners of the room, cut the moulding at 45 degrees, using a mitre block.

An alternative treatment is to buy narrow strips of cork from the wood-floor supplier. The cork is used to fill the expansion gap, and must be the same thickness as the wood-strip.

LAYING THE BOARDS

1 Start by placing the underlay over the sub-floor. Unroll foam underlay, cut it to length and tape the edges and joins. Place felt underlay sheets edge to edge.

2 Start laying the first board parallel to the longest wall in the room, with its tongued edge facing the wall. Insert spacers at intervals between the skirting board and the long edge and end of the board to create an expansion gap.

3 If the boards you are laying have to be stuck together, squirt some adhesive into the grooved end of the second board. Butt it up closely against the end of the first board, and check that the two boards align precisely. Add spacers as before.

4 When you have laid as many whole boards as possible in the first row, measure the length of the cut piece needed to complete the row and cut it to size. Remember to allow for the expansion gap at the end of the row. Test its fit.

5 Apply adhesive to the grooved end of the cut piece and butt it up against its predecessor. Use the edging tool to close up the joint by hooking it over the end of the board and tapping the upstand with a hammer. Wipe away any excess adhesive with a damp cloth.

6 Start the second row of boards by fitting the offcut from the end of the first row. This ensures that the joints will be staggered between the rows. Fit spacers at the end and apply adhesive to the grooved edge of the board before fitting it.

7 Carry on placing the boards row by row. As you work across the room, tap the boards closely together by using a proprietary tamping block or a board offcut to protect the tongued edge. Wipe off excess adhesive as before.

8 To fit a board round a radiator pipe, first align the board with its neighbour and slide it up against the pipe. Mark the pipe centre on the board end. Then remove the board, butt it up against the skirting board and mark the pipe centre on the board edge. Join up the marks to indicate the pipe centre.

9 Use a 16mm flat wood bit to drill a hole through the board at the mark. Cut across the board and fit the two sections round the pipe.

10 At door openings, cut away a small amount of the architrave and door stop to allow the board to fit beneath it. Mark the board thickness on the frame and cut away the wood with a tenon saw. Trim the board to shape and slot it into position.

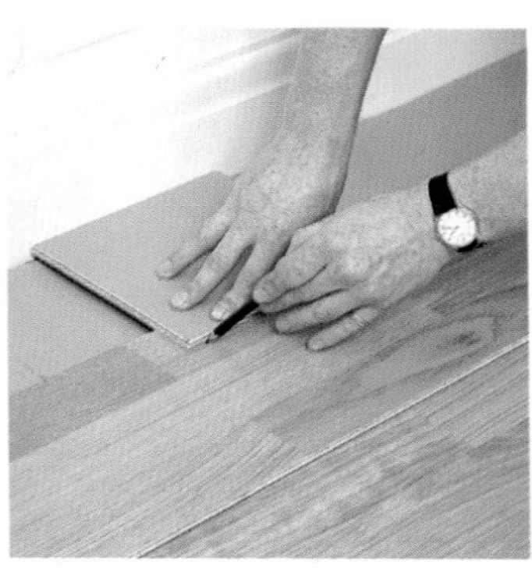

11 When you reach the opposite side of the room, you will probably have to cut the final boards down in width. Lay each board in turn over the last whole board laid, and mark the width required on it by using a pencil and a board offcut held against the skirting board to scribe the wall profile on it. Redraw the line 5mm nearer the exposed edge of the board to recreate the expansion gap. Cut each board to width with a jigsaw or panel saw and fit it in place. Use the edging tool to pull all the joints tightly together.

12 Remove the wedges from the edge of the flooring and conceal the expansion gap with strips of wood or cork (see facing page). Fit a tapered edge strip across the door threshold to conceal and protect the edge of the flooring.

SOLID FLOORS

Before laying laminate flooring on a solid concrete floor, cover it with a layer of heavy-duty polythene sheeting to protect the flooring from any dampness within the floor.

LAYING SOLID WOOD FLOORING

Solid wood flooring can be laid over a timber sub-floor, or directly onto floor joists if the existing timber floor is being replaced.

On a timber sub-floor, the boards are laid in a similar way to laminate flooring, with an expansion gap around the perimeter of the floor area. Instead of gluing the boards together, each one is fixed to the sub-floor using a technique known as secret nailing.

1 Drive panel pins down through the tongue of each board at an angle to the floor so it passes through the body of the strip and into the sub-floor. Use 32mm pins for boards up to 19mm thick, and 50mm pins for thicker boards.

2 Start the pins with the hammer. Use a nail punch to finish driving each pin so its head finishes flush with the top edge of the tongue. You can then slot the grooved edge of the next board over the tongue and repeat the fixing to secure it to the sub-floor.

Laying a wood mosaic floor

Wood mosaic is made up of small 'fingers' of wood prearranged in a pattern on a backing. It is sometimes known as finger parquet.

It provides an easy way for amateurs to lay a parquet floor. Full-size parquet blocks are not available for DIY laying.

The pieces of wood mosaic are about ⅜in (10mm) thick and are arranged in square or oblong panels. Square panels are most common, ranging from 12in (300mm) square to 24in (610mm). Oblong panels are usually 24in × 6in (610mm × 150mm).

The individual pieces are usually glued to a felt, paper or netting base, but some makes are wired and glued together. Both types are flexible, and can compensate for any slight unevenness in the sub-floor. If the sub-floor is very uneven, cover it with hardboard before laying the mosaic (page 275).

Try to examine mosaics carefully before buying (this is easiest in a self-service store). Reject any with black marks on the face. This occurs if they are stacked with the felt backing of one against the face of the other, instead of face to face, and marks can be difficult to remove.

Check, too, that the panels have been cut to the same size, otherwise you will get unsightly gaps in the finished floor which will collect dirt. Take one panel and hold all the others to it in turn, back to back. Rotate each panel through 90 degrees for a further check of squareness. Inspect the surface for chips or scratches.

Prepacked panels usually have transparent wrapping, so you can see if the panels are face to face, and you should be able to see if they are all the same size.

As wood absorbs moisture from the atmosphere, buy the panels at least two days before laying, and leave them unwrapped in the room where they are to be laid. This should prevent sudden expansion or contraction.

You will need

Tools Steel tape measure; chalk line; workbench; fine-toothed tenon saw; trimming knife; pencil; rag. Possibly also an orbital sander or sanding block; abrasive paper (medium and fine grades); hammer; paintbrush.

Materials Wood mosaic; adhesive (with spreader); wood moulding or cork strip for the edges. Possibly also panel pins for wood moulding; varnish.

1 Mosaic panels are laid in the same way as vinyl tiles (page 279). First set them out, unglued, to ensure the widest border of cut tiles all around the room. As with most wood floors, a border of ½in (13mm) must be left between the edge of the mosaic and the skirting board to allow for expansion.

2 Where possible, arrange the laying so that the panels can be cut between 'fingers' of wood, which only involves cutting the backing with a trimming knife.

3 When you have to cut through wood, hold the panel firmly on a workbench and use a tenon saw.

4 When you have laid the floor, cover the gap around the edges with wood moulding or fill it with strips of cork (facing page).

5 Some mosaic panels are prefinished and are ready for use immediately after laying. Others will need to be sanded – either with an orbital electric sander or by hand with a sanding block, using medium and fine grades of abrasive paper. Do not use a heavy floor sander. Finally, treat them with three thin coats of floor-grade varnish.

HOW TO REPAIR A DAMAGED MOSAIC FLOOR

If a wood mosaic floor becomes damaged, repair it by replacing a complete square of strips.

It is useful to keep any panels left over from the original laying as a source of repair pieces.

1 If possible, cut around the damaged square with a trimming knife. Cut right through the felt or paper backing.

2 Lever out the damaged square, strip by strip, using an old chisel. Be careful not to damage the adjoining piece. If the damaged section is large enough, begin from inside it.

3 Scrape off the old backing and adhesive from the sub-floor.

4 Cut a new square from a spare panel, together with its backing, and glue it in place.

How a staircase is built

Stairs consist of treads (the part you walk on) and risers (the vertical pieces in between).

The treads may be nailed to the risers, or the risers may have tongues slotted into a groove in the treads.

At each side, the stair is fixed to a piece of timber called a string. A closed string has its top and bottom edges parallel, and the tread and riser slot into grooves. A cut string has a zigzag profile with the risers resting on the horizontal sections.

A wall-side string is always closed, but the outer string may be either type. Cut strings are easier to repair than closed strings.

On the open side of the staircase vertical balusters are attached to the string at the bottom and the handrail at the top.

Many houses have a cupboard below the staircase, with the underside of the stairs left exposed. This is very convenient if repairs have to be carried out. However, the underside may be covered with plaster, which would have to be removed before repairs could be done.

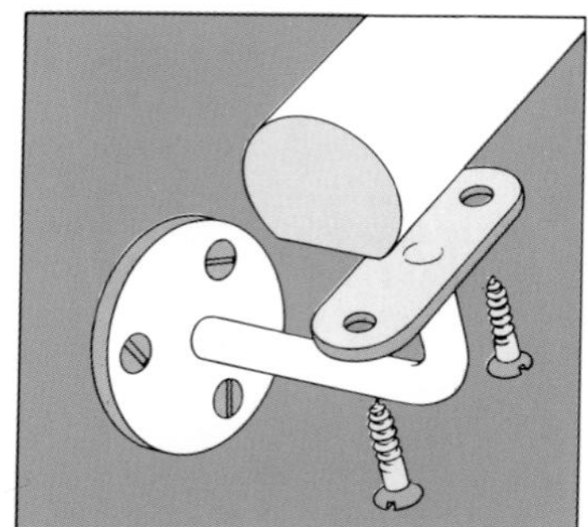

WALL HANDRAIL A handrail can be fixed to a wall on a bracket (above), or a specially shaped rail can be screwed directly to the wall (below).

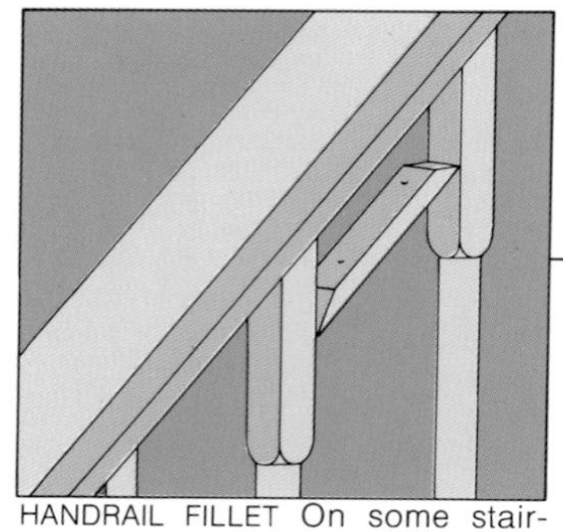

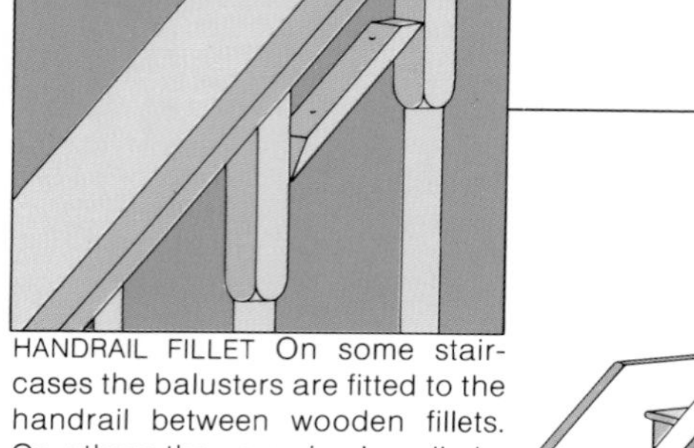

HANDRAIL FILLET On some staircases the balusters are fitted to the handrail between wooden fillets. On others they are simply nailed.

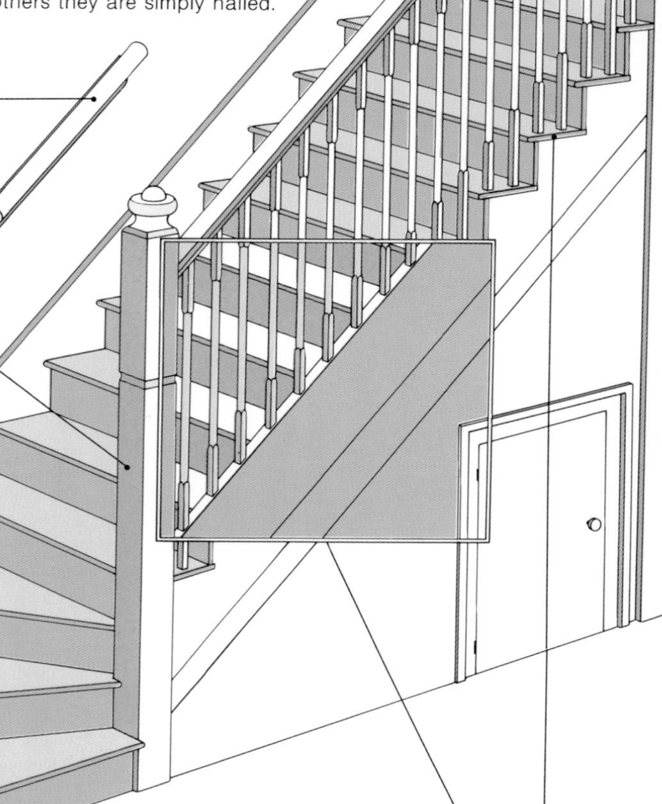

Fixing creaking stairs

Stairs creak when a tread or riser is not securely fixed and rubs against an adjacent piece of wood. The cure is reasonably easy when the underside of the staircase is accessible. This is often the case in a house with a cupboard under the stairs because the underside of the stairs might not be covered.

WORKING FROM UNDERNEATH

The best remedy is to add extra wood blocks, screwed and glued to the tread and riser from underneath. Blocks might not have been fixed there in the first place, or they might have been shaken loose by vibration.

You will need

Tools Saw; vice or G-cramp; bradawl; drill and twist bits; screwdriver; hammer.

Materials Blocks of wood about $1\frac{1}{2}$in (38mm) triangular or square in section and about 3in (75mm) long; wood glue; four No. 8 screws per block (choose a length that will not break through the face of the stair); $1\frac{1}{2}$in (38mm) nails.

1 Drill four clearance holes in each block – one pair at right angles to the other pair.

2 Hold the block at the junction of the tread and riser and make pilot holes in the stair.

3 Smear wood glue on the meeting surfaces of both stair and block.

4 Put the screws in the holes and screw the blocks to the stair.

5 If possible, strengthen the join between the riser and the tread below by squirting wood glue from a tube into the join, and driving nails through the back of the riser and into the back edge of the tread.

TREATING COVERED STAIRS

It is hardly worth interfering with the plaster covering on the underside of the stairs because of a squeak. Try forcing French chalk or talcum powder into the join that is causing the trouble. They will act as a lubricant.

If the squeak continues, try screwing down the front of the tread onto the riser.

You will need
Tools Old chisel; drill and twist bits; countersink bit; screwdriver; filling knife; abrasive paper.
Materials Wood glue; 1½in (38mm) No. 8 countersunk screws; filler.

1 Put an old chisel or screwdriver between the top of the riser and the tread above, forcing them apart far enough to insert the glue. This is only possible on a staircase on which the treads and risers are not jointed together.

2 Squirt wood glue into the join across the stair.

3 At intervals of about 10in (250mm), drill clearance holes through the tread and pilot holes into the top of the riser. Countersink the clearance holes so that the screws will sit below surface level. Insert the screws, and screw them down tight.

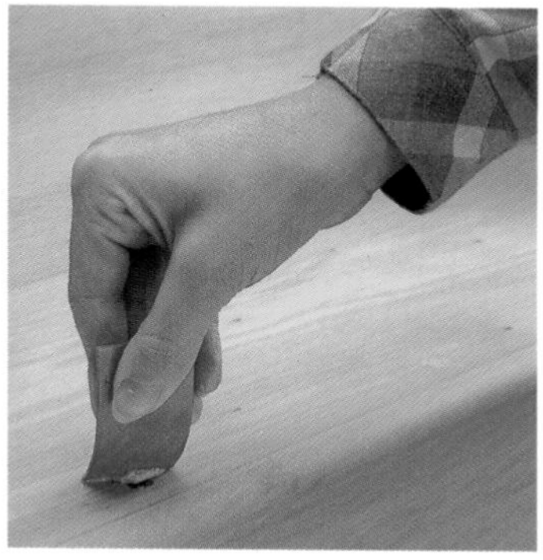

4 Cover the screw heads with filler, and sand smooth. The patches will probably be covered by stair carpet.

If the stairs are varnished, use an appropriately coloured wood filler.

Repairing broken balusters

Depending on the nature of the damage, it may be possible to retain a damaged baluster. If the baluster has split, or a piece has broken off and you still have the pieces, smear wood glue on the two surfaces and cramp them together.

If a baluster is badly damaged, it may have to be replaced.

Square-section balusters are easy to match, but turned balusters may have to be made especially for you. Remove an undamaged baluster and take it to a wood turner who will copy it for you.

You will need
Tools Mallet; an old chisel; hand saw or electric jigsaw; hammer; vice.
Materials New baluster; nails (same length as the old ones).

1 Free the baluster at the bottom.

On a cut string (see diagram, opposite), it is set into a notch in the tread, often held in place by a piece of moulding. If necessary, lever the moulding away with an old chisel. Knock the baluster out of its notch with a mallet.

On a closed string, a baluster on an old staircase may be held in a mortise or it may be pinned. Scrape away the paint to check. If it is mortised use a hand saw or electric jigsaw to cut through it at the bottom following the line of the string. If it is pinned, knock it out with the mallet.

ALTERNATIVELY, on a modern staircase it may be held at the bottom between fillets of wood. Lift out the broken baluster, and lever out the lower fillet.

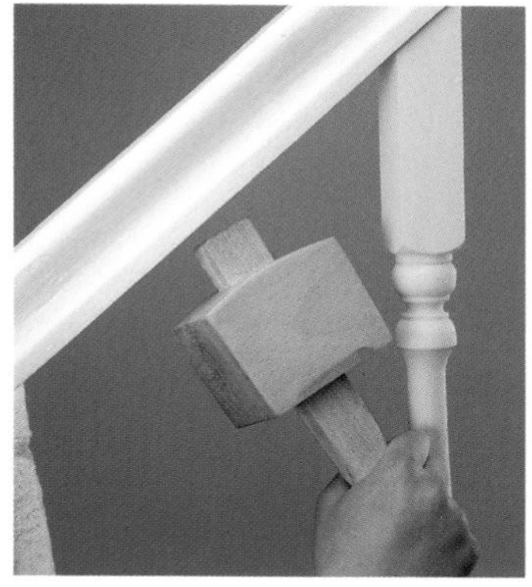

2 Remove the broken baluster at the top by tapping it with a mallet so that it is freed from the rail. If there is no space between the balusters to wield the mallet, place the end of a piece of wood against the baluster and tap the other end with the mallet.

Or perhaps pull out the baluster by hand.

ALTERNATIVELY, remove it from between the fillets of wood under the handrail, if the staircase is made that way. It should not be nailed in place, and should pull out.

3 Use the broken baluster as a pattern to mark the correct slope on the top of the new one.

Before you cut it to length, make quite sure that you have got the measurement right.

4 Hold the new baluster in a vice and cut along the marked line.

5 On a cut string, nail the baluster to the handrail at the top, and fit it back in place in its notch on the tread.

On a closed string, use the old baluster to cut the angle at the bottom and fit the new one in place, top and bottom. If the baluster was originally mortised into the string, it will have to be nailed in place. The repair will not be as strong as the original, and should only be done with one or two balusters; otherwise you will weaken the staircase.

If you have to replace a fillet, tack it in place. A nail punch will help in an awkward space.

FIXING LOOSE BALUSTERS

Balusters are usually fixed to the handrail by nails driven through them at an angle, and into the underside of the rail. Sometimes they are fitted between fillets of wood.

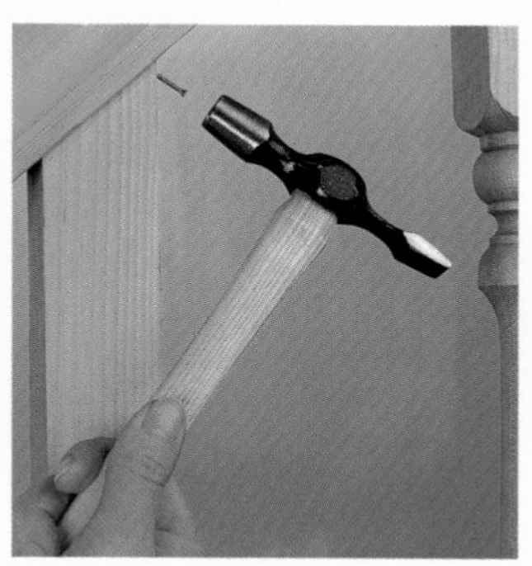

Nailing the baluster
If a nail works loose, try to remove it with pincers, and insert a longer, slightly thicker nail in its place.

If you cannot remove it, drive another one in at a different place. On slender balusters drill a fine pilot hole first.

Do not use glue. The baluster may have to be removed at some time in the future.

Replacing a fillet
The balusters may be fitted into a groove in the underside of the rail, with the spaces between balusters filled with fillets of wood.

If one of the fillets has dropped out, cut a new piece of wood to the right size, and nail it in place. Do not use glue. A nail punch will help to drive the nail in.

Baluster fillets can be bought at some DIY stores, but they may not fit your particular staircase.

Re-fixing and installing wall-mounted handrails

RE-FIXING THE HANDRAIL

A stairway with a wall on both sides usually has a wall-mounted handrail instead of a baluster rail. It may be screwed to the wall directly, or be fixed on brackets, and sometimes the fixings come loose. It must be re-fixed to the wall strongly enough to support a person who stumbles on the stairs.

1 Take the rail down from the wall and find out why it is loose.

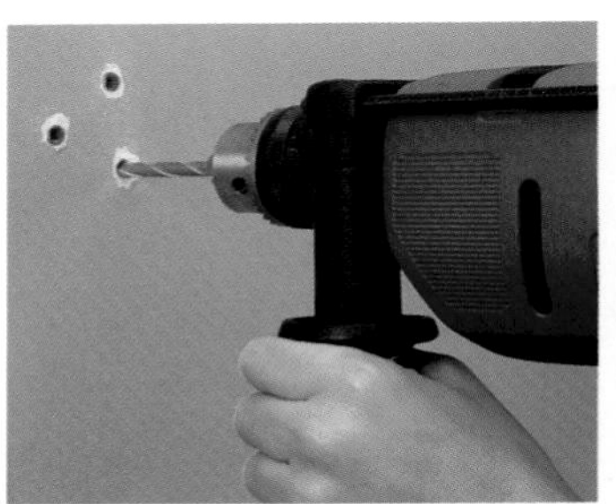

2 If the handrail is on a metal bracket, fill the existing screw holes with a plugging compound such as Plug-It. Re-drill the holes, insert a wall plug and refit the handrail with screws the same size as the old ones.

Make sure the fixing is absolutely secure; if not it is dangerous, so reposition the bracket and make new holes.

ALTERNATIVELY, if the rail is screwed directly to the wall, try using a thicker screw than the original. You may have to drill a slightly larger hole in the rail.

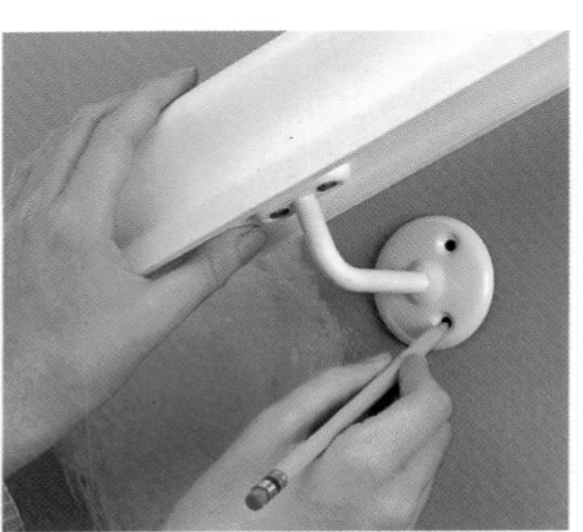

3 If the wall around the plug has become damaged, make a new fixing in a slightly different place. Brackets will also have to be repositioned on the rail.

Fill any visible holes with interior filler.

FITTING A NEW HANDRAIL

If you are putting up a new wall-mounted handrail – perhaps as an extra safety precaution – remember that it must run parallel to the string. Otherwise it will vary in height from the stairs at different points on the staircase.

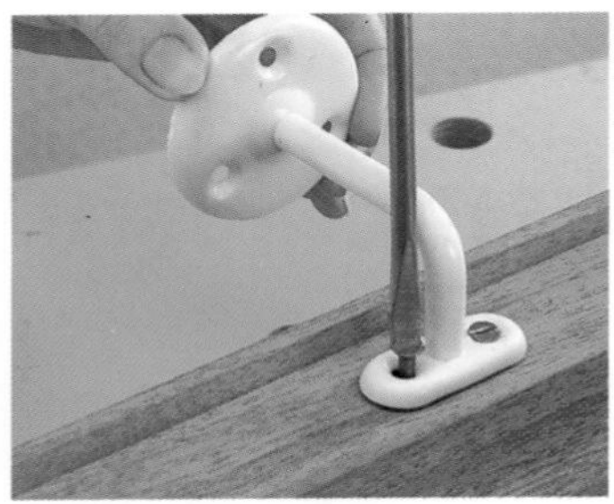

1 If you are installing a rail on brackets, fit the brackets to the rail, not the wall. Otherwise they are unlikely to line up with the rail.

2 Measure up from the treads at top and bottom of the staircase to establish the correct height. Get a helper to hold the rail while you mark the top fixings. Drill and plug the wall and fix the top bracket with one screw only. Hold the bottom of the rail at the correct height and mark the other fixings.

Let the rail swing down and drill and plug the holes. Then put in the remaining screws.

Fitting a loft ladder

Most loft ladders are made in two or three sections that slide together and lie flat on the loft floor when not in use.

The ladders are made of wood or light-weight aluminium alloy, and are raised and lowered with a pole. They vary greatly in price, depending on construction.

Some ladders are supplied with a handrail – a useful safety feature if you use the ladder regularly. This type often reaches above ceiling level when the ladder is extended.

A ladder may be supplied with a new loft door; if not, you may have to make one out of blockboard, or modify the existing hatch cover.

MEASURING UP FOR A LADDER

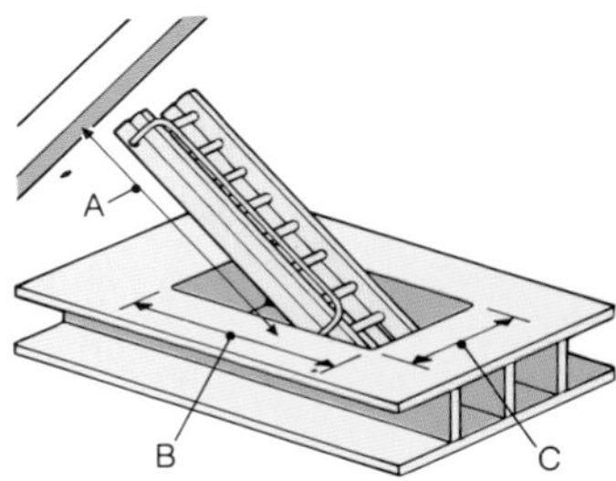

Before buying a ladder, you will need to take several measurements. It is advisable to get makers' leaflets which show the pivoting height needed by the ladder inside the loft (marked A on the diagram above). This is usually 3ft 6in (1.1m) above the loft floor. If there is not enough room, collapsible ladders are available.

The leaflets will also show the minimum length of the hatch (B) and the minimum width (C).

For easy access to the loft, the hatch should be about 2ft 6in (760mm) long and 1ft 8in (510mm) wide. Ladders can be installed in smaller openings, but you may have difficulty carrying anything into the loft.

A standard loft ladder will fit a height of up to 8ft 9in (2.6m), measured from the floor of the room or landing below to the top of the loft joists.

FITTING THE LADDER

Loft ladders are hinged in some way to the trimmer which forms part of the hatch opening.

Fitting instructions are supplied by the makers.

When working in the loft you will need a good light. An inspection lamp hung from a rafter should do, but preferably have a permanent light installed in the loft, near the hatch. Put the switch on the landing below, with a pilot light to show if it is on or off.

If the loft joists have not already been covered with flooring, put down sheets of chipboard around the hatch so there is no risk of stepping through the ceiling.

ENLARGING THE LOFT HATCH

If the loft opening is too small, it can be lengthened. The width should not be a problem. Pre-war houses will probably have an opening across three joists – about 32in (810mm). Some postwar houses have joists 24in (610mm) apart, which gives an adequate width.

To lengthen the hatch you must reposition one of the trimmers.

1 The trimmer is probably nailed at each end to a joist, so begin by cutting through the trimmer in the middle. A general-purpose saw with an adjustable blade angle is ideal. Take care not to cut into electric cables.

2 Lever out the two pieces with either an old chisel, a claw hammer or a wrecking bar.

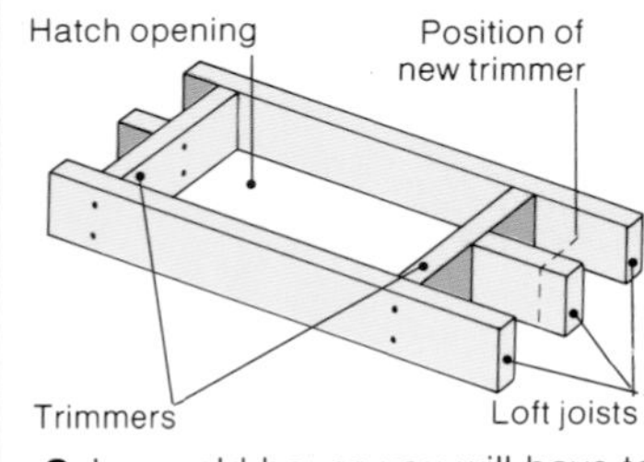

3 In an old house you will have to cut back the middle joist to make an opening of the right length. In a house with joists 24in (610mm) apart this is not necessary.

4 Prepare a new trimmer from 4in × 2in (100mm × 50mm) timber to fit between the joists.

5 Nail the trimmer in its new position. Drive 6in (150mm) nails into the two or three joists that it rests against, but check first with a try square that the trimmer is at right angles to the joists.

6 Nail a plasterboard ceiling to the new trimmer with plasterboard nails so that it is properly supported. Use thinner nails when fixing lath and plaster to avoid splitting the laths.

Cover the nails with filler.

7 Cut the ceiling back to the new trimmer, using either an electric jigsaw or a padsaw and panel saw.

REPOSITIONING THE HATCH DOOR

If a new hatch door is not supplied with the ladder you may have to replace the old door with a stronger one, as some ladders are partly supported by a hook on the door.

If the existing door rests on beading around the opening, prise the beading off with an old chisel.

Cut a new door from ¾in (19mm) blockboard, but make it ⅛in (3mm) smaller all round than the old one to provide clearance when it opens.

Screw two 2in (50mm) flush hinges to one end of the door and fix it to the frame at the end where the ladder is to be hinged, so that it opens downwards.

Fix the catches, supplied with the kit, to the opposite end of the frame and close the door.

Re-fix the beading above the door.

10 Plumbing

Plumbing emergencies: What to do

WATER POURS FROM THE ROOF SPACE

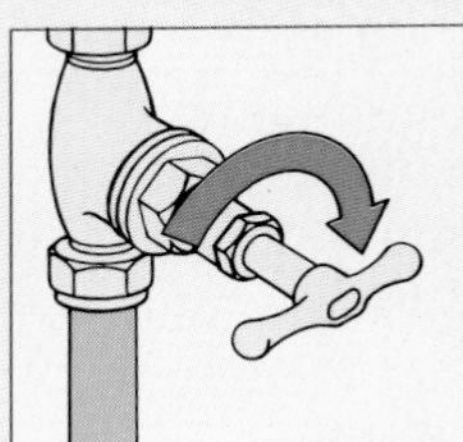

1 Turn off (clockwise) the main stopcock. It is usually under the kitchen sink (if it is jammed or broken, see below right). Put buckets under the leaks, then turn on all the taps in the house and flush all the toilets to drain the cold-water storage cistern.

2 Find the cause of the trouble. It may be a burst pipe in the loft, or a cistern overflow caused by a failed ball-valve or float and a blocked over-flow pipe.

Repairing a burst pipe, page 315
Adjusting the cistern water level, page 338

NO WATER COMING FROM A TAP

1 Check the kitchen sink cold tap. If no water flows from it, make sure the main stopcock has not been turned off by accident. If the stopcock is on, call the regional water company.

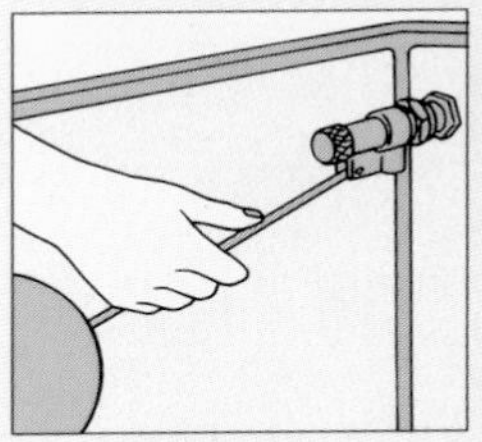

2 If the kitchen tap is working, check the cold-water cistern. It may have drained because of a jammed ball-valve. If it is drained, move the float arm sharply up and down to free the valve, then clean the valve (page 336).
ALTERNATIVELY, in frosty weather there may be an ice plug blocking a supply pipe. If the kitchen cold tap is working, check the flow into the cold-water cistern by pressing down the ball-valve. If there is no inflow, the rising main is blocked, probably between the ceiling and the cistern inlet.

3 If the cistern is filling, check the bathroom taps. If there is no flow from one tap, a supply pipe from the cistern (either hot or cold) is blocked, probably in the roof-space section.

4 To thaw a pipe, strip off any lagging from the affected part and apply hot water bottles, or cloths soaked in boiling water and then wrung out. If a pipe is difficult to get at, blow warm air onto it from an electric hair dryer.

WARNING Do not use a blowtorch to defrost a pipe. It may set the roof on fire. Also, water in the heated section of the pipe will expand and if the pipe is frozen on either side, it may burst, spraying boiling water.

LEAKING HOT-WATER CYLINDER

1 Turn off (clockwise) the gate valve, if there is one, in the feed pipe from the cold-water cistern to the hot-water cylinder.
ALTERNATIVELY, turn off the main stopcock and turn on all the taps in the house to drain the cistern. (This will not drain the hot-water cylinder, but will stop water flowing into it.)

2 Switch off the immersion heater, if there is one.

3 Switch off the boiler, or put out the boiler fire.

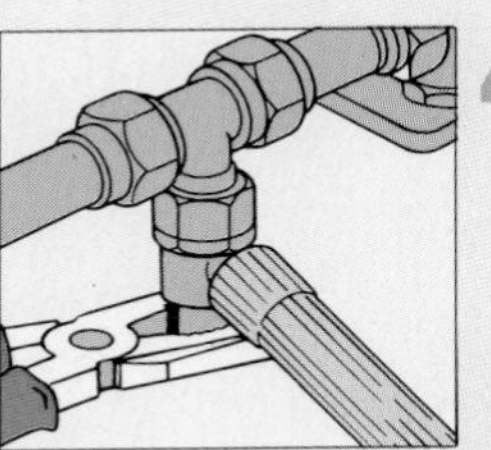

4 Connect a hose to the cylinder drain cock, if there is one (it will be on the supply pipe from the cold-water cistern). Put the other end of the hose into an outside drain.
ALTERNATIVELY, connect the hose to the boiler drain cock (on the return pipe near the bottom of the boiler) and direct the other end of the hose to an outside drain.

5 Open up the drain cock with a drain-cock key or pliers.

6 Get the hot-water cylinder repaired or replaced by a plumber.

YOU CANNOT TURN OFF THE WATER

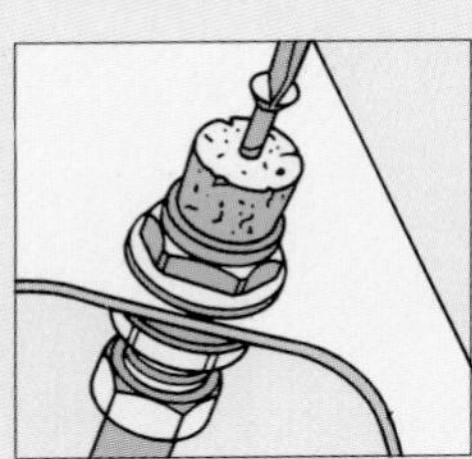

1 If you cannot turn off the water from the stopcock, tie up the float arm to stop the cistern filling, open up all the taps and flush the toilet. Then from inside the cistern, insert a cork of the correct size, or a carrot, into the inlet of the pipe that has burst or is leaking. Screw a wood screw partly into the cork to aid removal.

Allow the cistern to refill, restoring water to all fittings except those served by the burst pipe.

Alternatively, if the pipe is made of copper or lead, flatten it with a G-cramp or a hammer.

OTHER PROBLEMS WITH WATER

Tap flow poor, page 311 (Airlocks)
Tap dripping, page 308
Sink blocked or slow to empty, page 322
Lavatory cistern not flushing, page 333
Lavatory pan will not empty, page 334
Roof leaking, page 438
Overflow pipe drips or runs, page 338
Gutter overflowing, page 454
Drain or gulley blocked, page 459
Waste downpipe blocked, page 456
Walls/ceiling damp, page 462
Central-heating radiator leak, page 350

How water is supplied to the home

Most British homes have a mains water supply. This is provided by the regional water company, which distributes the water through iron or heavy plastic water mains.

From these mains, a pipe known as a communication pipe takes the water to the water company's stopcock – a control valve about 3ft (1m) below the ground at or near the boundary of each property. The stopcock, which is turned with a long key, is at the bottom of a stoneware guard pipe under a small metal cover, set into the surface of the garden or the public footpath outside. This is where the householder's pipe begins.

From the water company's stopcock, a service pipe carries water into the home. The pipe should meander slightly in the trench to allow for ground movement, which would otherwise pull on the fittings at each end. To avoid frost damage it should be at least 2ft 6in (750mm) and not more than 4ft 5in (1.35m) below ground. The pipe enters the house, usually under the kitchen sink, and from there is usually called the rising main. Another stopcock for cutting off the water supply (page 306) should be provided where the pipe enters the house.

Make sure that you know where the main stopcock is in your house. In a well-appointed house, there will be a drain cock (page 306) immediately above the stopcock, for draining the rising main.

The layout within the house depends upon whether the cold-water system is direct or indirect.

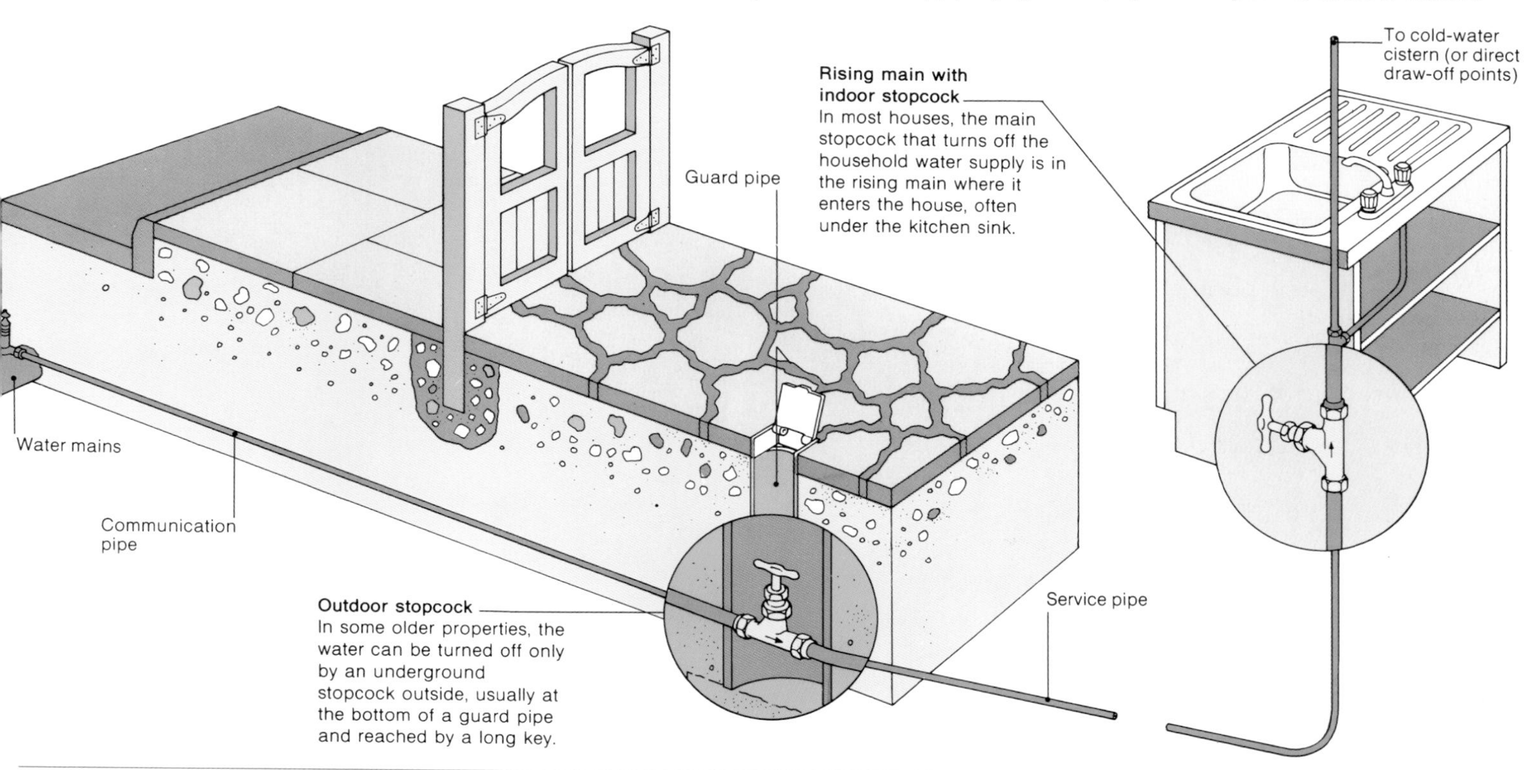

What type of water system do you have?

The cold-water supply

There are two types of water supply in British homes, direct and indirect. A direct cold-water supply has all the cold-water taps and toilets in the house fed directly from the rising main.

With an indirect system, only the drinking water in the cold tap over the kitchen sink (and possibly pipes to a washing machine and an outside tap) are branched directly from the rising main.

The rising main then goes upwards, preferably against an inside wall, to discharge into a cold-water storage cistern, normally in the roof space. The cistern has distribution pipes that supply the bathroom cold taps and lavatory cistern and feed the hot-water system.

A direct cold-water system is simpler and cheaper to install than an indirect system. It can avoid having pipes or other plumbing fittings in the roof space, where they are vulnerable to frost damage.

Despite the fact that Britain is alone in having indirect cold systems with stored water, there are some arguments in its favour. One advantage is that the cold-water storage cistern gives an even water pressure, which produces quieter plumbing with less wear and tear on washers and valves.

Leaks are also less likely on cistern-fed low pressure supplies and any leak that does occur will be less damaging because less water will escape from the leak.

It is possible to install pump-boosted power showers from an indirect cold-water system, but not from direct supplies.

Water that is stored in a cistern will be warmer than that supplied direct from the mains and this has the advantage of reducing the amount of condensation on the outside of toilet cisterns.

And on occasions when the water supply is temporarily cut off – for work on the mains for example – the householder with an indirect system still has plenty of stored water for essential uses.

The original water regulations required an indirect water system to have one drinking tap supplied with mains water. However, the law has now changed and requires cold-water cisterns to supply drinkable water. Special kits are available for modern cold-water cisterns to protect the contents from contamination.

The hot-water supply

There are two systems for providing hot water. All hot taps may be supplied from a hot-water storage cylinder, fed from the cold-water cistern and heated by a boiler or immersion heater.

Alternatively, hot taps may be supplied from an instantaneous gas multipoint water heater, or a cistern-type electric heater (page 339) connected directly to the rising main. This is the usual method of obtaining hot water when all the cold water is supplied direct from the rising main.

A gas heater has the advantage that it heats only water actually needed, and an unlimited amount of hot water can be drawn at one time.

Back boilers and separate kitchen boilers have largely been replaced by high performance boilers designed for both water heating and central heating. These heat the hot water indirectly through a separate water circuit that acts as a heat exchanger.

Combined units supplying hot and cold water

Some homes have two-in-one plumbing systems, with a cold-water cistern and hot-water cylinder fitted together in one unit. Because they are easy to install and do not need much space, they are often used in self-contained flats where a large house has been converted.

Because of their compact design, two-in-one units can be fitted into a cupboard on the landing or in the bathroom. However, with the cistern at such a low level they cannot usually provide enough pressure for a conventional shower, and there may also be poor pressure to taps and lavatory cisterns on the same floor. Lavatory cisterns need to have full-way ball valves to speed up refilling (page 336).

How a typical water system works

The cold-water storage cistern, which is normally in the roof space, is fed from the rising main, and the inflow of water is controlled by a ball valve. The rising main is usually a 15mm diameter pipe, but in areas where mains pressure is low, a 22mm diameter pipe is used. The capacity of the average household cistern is 50 gallons (227 litres), and it has an overflow pipe to carry water out if the cistern overfills through a failure of the ball valve.

Water from the cistern is distributed by at least two 22mm (or 28mm) diameter pipes fitted about 3in (75mm) from the bottom. One of them supplies lavatories and cold taps – except for the kitchen cold tap, which is fed by a branch off the rising main before it rises to the storage cistern. Normally the 22mm pipe goes direct to the bath cold tap, and 15mm branches feed washbasins and lavatory cisterns.

The other distribution pipe feeds cold water to the bottom of the hot-water cylinder – usually a copper cylinder of about 30 gallons (136 litres) capacity. In a typical modern house with a central-heating boiler, there are two water circuits through the hot-water cylinder – the primary circuit that heats the water, and the secondary circuit that distributes it.

The water-heating circuit

The primary circuit is kept supplied by a small feed-and-expansion cistern, usually in the roof near the cold-water cistern, and also supplied from the rising main through a ball valve. Once the primary circuit is in operation, the cistern is needed only as a top-up for losses caused by evaporation.

New cold-water storage cisterns and feed-and-expansion cisterns must have dust-proof and insect-proof, but not airtight, covers and must be insulated against frost.

A 28mm feed pipe from the feed-and-expansion cistern goes to the bottom of the cylinder and then the boiler. When the boiler is heated, the water in it expands as it gets hotter and, pint for pint, becomes lighter than the cold water entering. Hot water therefore rises up another pipe from the top of the boiler – a 28mm pipe known as the flow pipe. A branch from the flow pipe enters the top of the cylinder and the pipe continues as a vent pipe to hang open-ended over the feed-and-expansion cistern, allowing the escape of air bubbles.

The pipe entering the cylinder does not discharge its hot water. It carries it right through in a sealed coil, imparting heat to the stored water in the cylinder. This primary circuit water has cooled by the time it leaves the bottom of the cylinder where the pipe branches into the cold-feed pipe from the feed-and-expansion cistern and returns to the boiler. In this way, the primary circuit water constantly recirculates while the boiler is heated.

TWO-CIRCUIT SYSTEM

Cold-water cistern
Feed-and-expansion cistern
Ball valve
Ball valve
Overflow
Overflow
Hot-water cylinder with sealed primary circuit
Rising main
Boiler
Drain cock
To central heating

Indirect heat
Hot water stored in the cylinder is heated indirectly by a separate water circuit through the boiler, sometimes by an immersion heater as well. The system can supply central-heating radiators.

ONE-CIRCUIT SYSTEMS

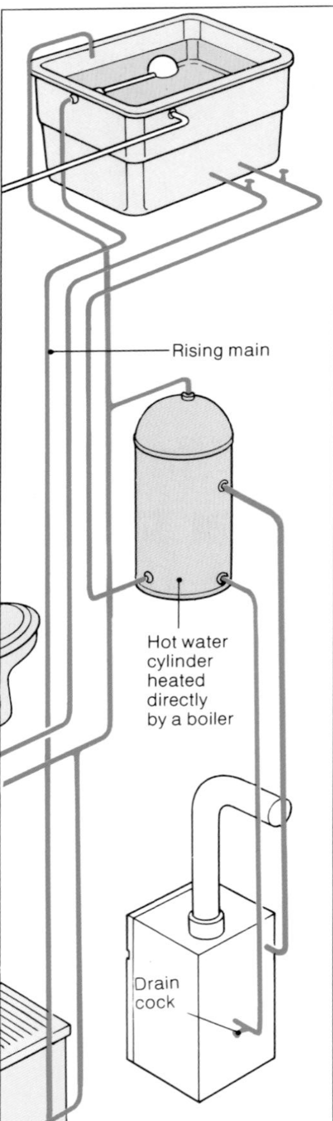

Direct heat
Hot water in the cylinder is heated by circulation through the boiler, and sometimes by an immersion heater as well. The system cannot be used to supply central-heating radiators.

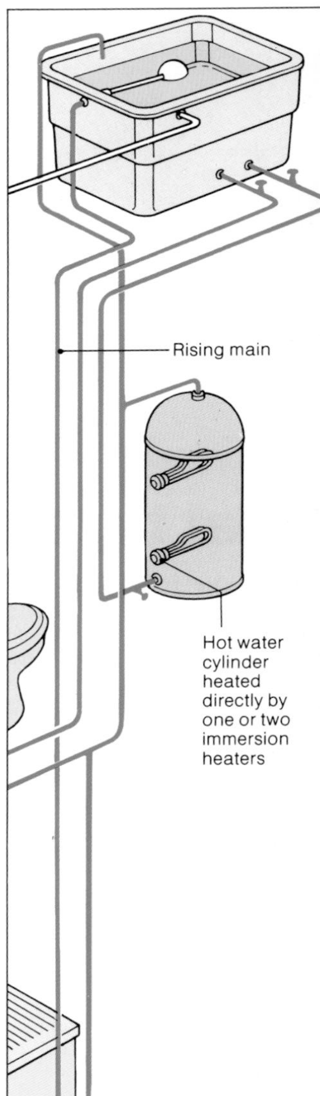

Immersion heater
Hot water stored in the cylinder is heated directly by one or two immersion heaters only. There is no boiler connected to it. The system cannot be used to supply central heating radiators.

The water-supply circuit

The water stored in the hot-water cylinder is supplied from the cold-water cistern, which keeps it constantly topped up as hot water is drawn off for use.

A 22mm vent pipe from the top of the cylinder rises to hang open-ended over the cold-water cistern, allowing for the escape of air bubbles driven off as the stored water is heated. Distribution pipes to the hot taps branch off from the vent pipe.

Because these branch pipes leave above the cylinder top, the cylinder cannot be drained through the hot taps. So there is no need to put out the boiler fire immediately if the household water supply is temporarily cut off – even if there is no supply from the taps – because the cold-water cistern has been drained and is not forcing the water through.

One-circuit hot-water cylinders

In older houses with back boilers or solid-fuel boilers, the cylinder water is usually heated directly by circulation through the boiler, not by a separate primary circuit.

There is no feed-and-expansion cistern. Water is fed from the cold-water cistern into the bottom of the cylinder and then to the boiler. The flow pipe from the top of the boiler discharges hot water directly into the top of the cylinder, forcing colder, denser water at the bottom through the return pipe back to the boiler. The hottest water, being the lightest, is always at the top ready to be drawn off.

The main disadvantage of a directly heated (one-circuit) cylinder is that – in a hard-water area especially – the cylinder, the boiler and the connecting pipes eventually become scaled or furred, causing the system to gradually become clogged up and less efficient.

Another disadvantage is that the constant circulation of fresh, aerated water through the system leads to corrosion which causes leaks. Corrosion inhibitors cannot (and must not) be used because the water is continually being drawn off for use.

In an indirectly heated (two-circuit) cylinder, scale and corrosion are less of a problem. Water in the primary circuit forms only a small amount of scale when it is first heated and after that is constantly recirculated. Some scale may be formed in the secondary circuit, which is constantly using a fresh supply, but not enough to affect circulation.

Corrosion is also less likely because air is driven off when the boiler is first brought into operation, and in any case corrosion inhibitors can be added to the primary system since the water is never drawn off for use.

Where a boiler is used for central heating as well as water heating, there must be a two-circuit system. Leaks or inefficiency caused by corrosion or boiler scale would seriously affect the central-heating system. Also, if the cylinder was directly heated, the radiators would all run cold when a lot of water had to be drawn off – for a bath, for instance. Central-heating radiators are always fed from the primary circuit through the boiler, so are virtually unaffected by water drawn off from the cylinder.

Immersion heaters

The hot-water cylinder can also be heated by an electric immersion heater. Roughly 1kW of heat is needed for every 10 gallons (45 litres) of water, so a 30 gallon (136 litre) hot-water cylinder needs a 3kW heater.

Immersion heaters may be used to supplement a boiler system, supplying extra heat as needed or the sole heat in summer when a boiler fire or central heating is not wanted. In some houses, the cylinder is heated solely by one or two immersion heaters all year round.

Whether fitted in a two-circuit or one-circuit cylinder, an immersion heater should be set no higher than 60°C (140°F) in a hard-water area. This is the temperature at which scale starts to be deposited. In soft-water areas, the setting can be up to 70°C (158°F).

Unventilated hot-water systems

These systems are supplied with water under mains pressure. No cold-water storage cistern or plumbing in the roof space is needed. Unventilated systems are not suited to DIY. Water companies are likely to insist on professional installation and Water and Building Regulation approval will be needed.

Where the water goes after use

Most houses built before the mid-1960s have what is known as a two-pipe drainage system for waste water disposal. A soil-and-vent pipe fastened upright to an outside wall carries waste from upper-floor lavatories to an underground drain; the open top of the pipe, covered with a wire guard, reaches just above the eaves and allows the escape of gases. Ground-floor lavatories have an outlet direct into the underground drain.

A second, narrower, outside pipe – known as a waste pipe – carries used water from upper-floor baths, sinks and showers to discharge over a gridded drain or gully – often the same drain into which the kitchen sink discharges.

Modern houses have a single-stack drainage system whereby waste from all sinks and lavatories is carried underground by a single pipe known as a stack. This stack is often built into the wall and its top protrudes above the roof.

Whatever the drainage system, every bath, basin or sink in the house is fitted with a trap – a bend in the outlet pipe – near the plughole. This holds sufficient water to stop gases from the drain entering the house and causing a smell. The trap has some means of access for clearing blockages. All lavatory pans have traps, with no access.

Below ground, the household waste pipes or drains are channelled through an inspection chamber near the house to form the main drain, which runs into the water company's sewer.

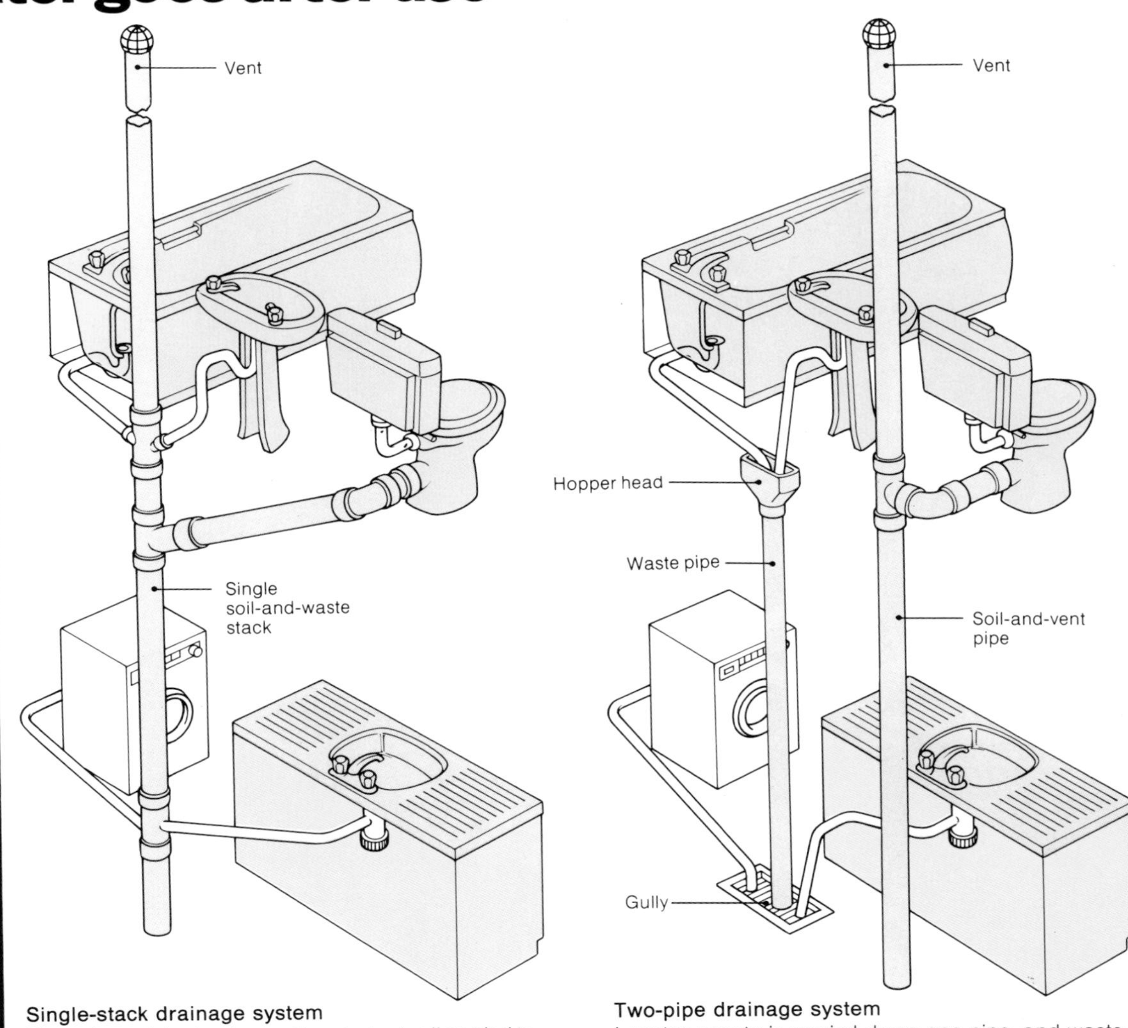

Single-stack drainage system
Waste from sinks, basins and lavatories is all carried to underground drains down one pipe.

Two-pipe drainage system
Lavatory waste is carried down one pipe, and waste from bath and basin down a separate pipe.

The tools for the job

Most of the basic tools needed for plumbing are general-purpose tools such as spanners and pliers.

For major additions or alterations, however, you will need extra tools, some of them specialised and expensive and not worth buying for occasional use. They can generally be hired from firms listed in *Yellow Pages* under Hire Services – Tools and Equipment.

A KIT FOR BASIC PLUMBING

Spanners

An average set of open-ended spanners (usually up to 1in or 22mm) can be used for many jobs. You will need both metric and imperial sizes. For larger nuts use a 12in (300mm) adjustable spanner or a pipe wrench. Use a spanner that fits the nut exactly, or it will slip and round off the edges.

Pipe wrenches

For gripping pipes, circular fittings or hexagonal nuts that have been rounded off at the edges. Two wrenches are needed for some jobs. Some pipe wrenches, such as Footprint wrenches, are operated by squeezing the handles together, but the Stillson type has an adjuster nut for altering the jaw size. Useful Stillson wrench sizes are 10in (250mm) and 14in (360mm), with jaw openings up to 1in (25mm) and 1½in (38mm) respectively. For a cistern-retaining nut you may need a wrench or adjustable spanner that will open to about 2½in (60mm).

When using a wrench, always push or pull in the direction of the jaw opening. Pad the jaws with cloth if they are likely to damage the fitting – if it is plastic, for example.

Pliers

A pair of 7in (180mm) standard combination pliers is useful for jobs such as removing split pins from cisterns, and long-nose pliers for gripping a sink or washbasin outlet grid. Mole grips will be useful, also a pair of slip-joint pliers.

Plunger (force cup)

For clearing blockages from a sink or lavatory waste pipe. A medium-sized plunger with a cup about 4in (100mm) across is usually suitable.

Sink-waste cleaner (sink auger)

Used to draw out or dislodge blockages from pipework. A 6ft or 8ft long, ⅜in or ¼in diameter tool (or a 2.4m long, 9mm diameter tool) is

BASIC HOUSEHOLD PLUMBING TOOLS

usually sufficient. A length of expanding curtain wire serves the same purpose, but use an eye end – a hook can catch in the pipe.

What you may also need

SCREWDRIVERS Two flat-bladed screwdrivers – one large, one small – are sufficient for most plumbing jobs. The large one should have a blade about 10in (250mm) long and ⅜in (10mm) wide, the small one a blade about 3in (75mm) long and $\frac{3}{16}$in (5mm) wide.

BLOWTORCH Needed for soldering capillary joints in piping. The safest and easiest type to use is a gas blowlamp fed by a butane cartridge. Use a fire-resistant mat between the torch flame and flammable material.

VICE AND WORKBENCH Not essential, but useful for some jobs, such as dismantling a ball-valve plug. An engineer's or mechanic's vice, which has serrated jaws, is best for gripping metal pipes – pad the jaws for copper, plastic or chrome fittings. Use a jaw lining on a woodworker's or lightweight portable vice. A Workmate has grooves for holding a pipe.

LADDER Plumbing emergencies usually occur in the loft. A retractable loft ladder is the best means of access. Alternatively, use a ladder that reaches right into the loft.

ELECTRIC TORCH Plumbing is often in dark places. Keep a powerful torch handy – preferably one that is square-shaped so that it will not roll away when put down, or one that is designed to strap to your head.

EXTRAS FOR MORE ADVANCED WORK

Hacksaw

For cutting metal or plastic pipes; a large or small saw is suitable. Most hacksaws are sold with medium-cut general-purpose blades with 24 tpi (teeth per inch). For copper or plastic pipes a blade of 18 tpi is best. For steel pipes use a fine blade of 32 tpi.

File

For smoothing the burred edge of a cut pipe. A half-round 8in (200mm) second-cut file is suitable.

Pipe or tube-bending springs

Hardened steel bending springs allow you to support the inside of copper tubing while bending it by hand. Separate springs are needed for 15mm and 22mm diameter tubing, the common sizes.

Pipe or tube-bending machine

A lightweight machine is useful if you have a number of bends to make in a 15mm or 22mm diameter pipe, and can be hired. It incorporates a curved former for shaping a bend, and separate guide blocks for piping of the two diameters. It can be used in a vice or in the hands.

EXTRA TOOLS FOR MAJOR JOBS

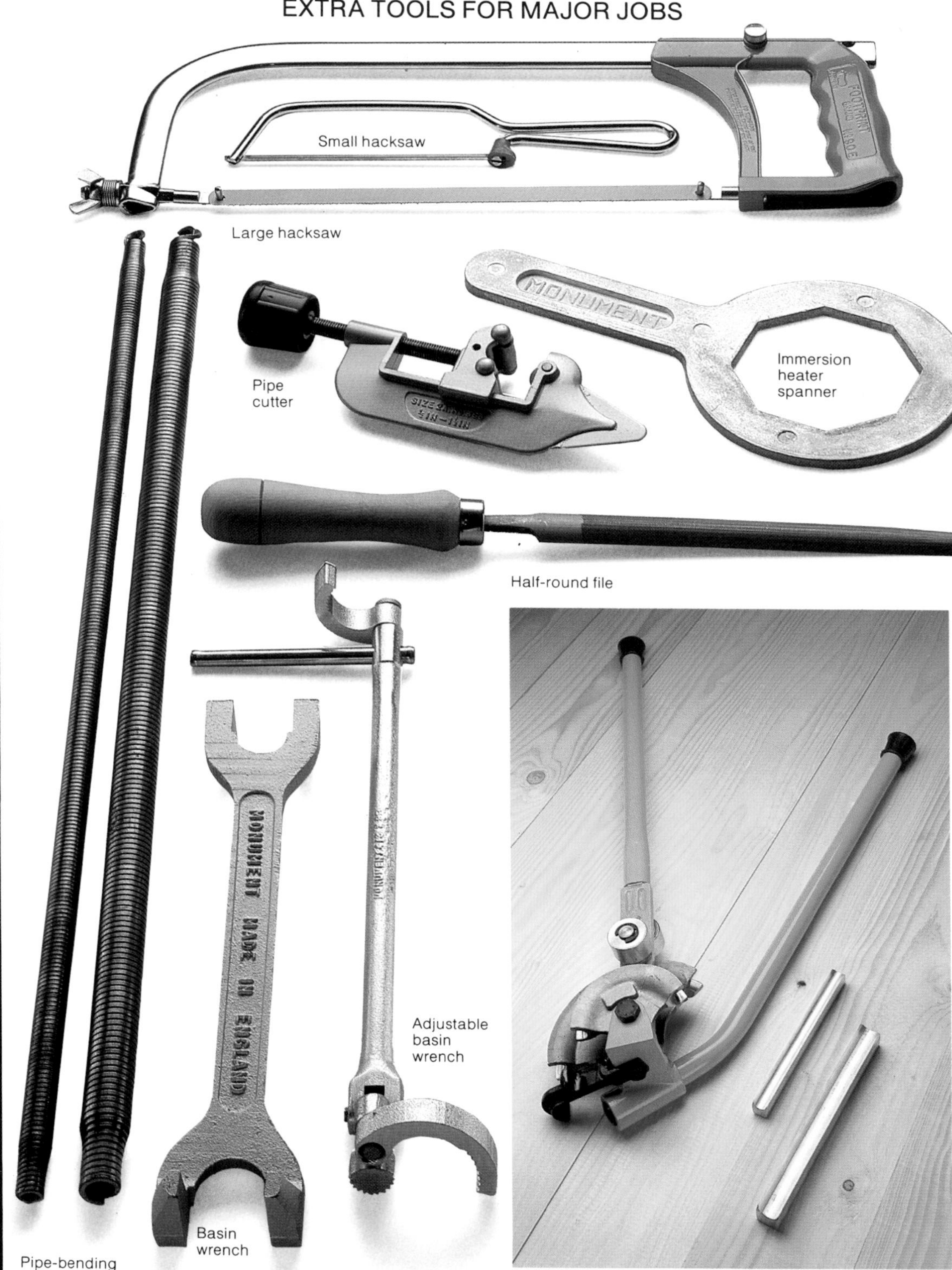

Small hacksaw

Large hacksaw

Pipe cutter

Immersion heater spanner

Half-round file

Adjustable basin wrench

Basin wrench

Pipe-bending springs

Pipe-bending machine and guide blocks

Pipe or tube cutter

Quicker and more accurate than a hacksaw for cutting copper, brass, aluminium and plastic (but not steel). It may have an adjustable slide for cutting tubes of different diameters, and a fixed cutting wheel. The tapered reamer on the front is for removing the burr from the inside of the pipe. A size 1 reamer takes pipes up to 28mm outside diameter.

Basin wrench

The basin wrench (or crowsfoot spanner) will reach the back nuts of bath and basin taps. It fits flat nuts of standard ½in and ¾in taps. The adjustable type, which can be hired, will reach nuts or fittings in awkward places. The swivel jaw is serrated for gripping uneven shapes, and is reversible for loosening or tightening. Different-sized jaws can be fitted for nuts up to 1in (25mm), 1¼in (32mm) and 2in (50mm) across.

Immersion-heater spanner

A very large spanner that will fit the securing nut of a standard immersion heater. It can be hired.

What you may also need

POWER DRILL For drilling through floorboards or walls to fix screws. A variable-speed hammer drill is best, and both wood and masonry bits are necessary. Useful attachments are a wire brush for cleaning metal, and a hole cutter for cutting metal and plastic. The diameters needed for a hole saw are 18mm and 25mm (if hiring, ask for cutters suitable for making holes for 15mm or 22mm tank connectors).

WIRE BRUSHES Useful for cleaning inside pipe ends before making joints, and for removing rust.

Cutting off the water supply

In many homes only the kitchen tap is fed from the rising main, others from the cold-water cistern. But it depends whether the plumbing system is direct or indirect (page 301).

TAPS FED FROM THE CISTERN

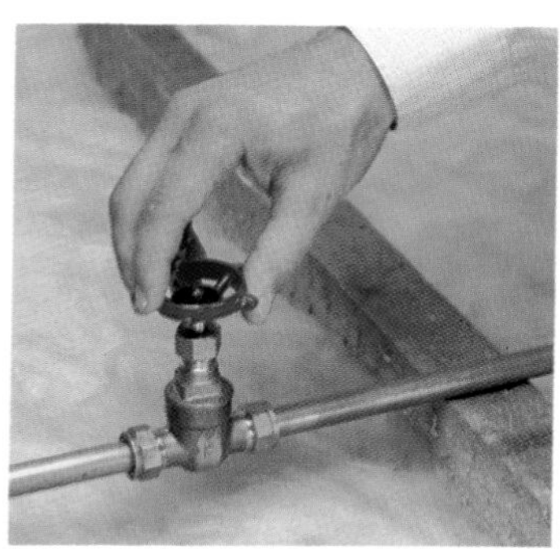

1 To isolate a hot or cold tap supplied from the cistern, turn off (clockwise), the gate valve or mini stopcock in the appropriate distribution pipe.

2 Turn on the tap until the water stops flowing.

Alternatively, if there is no gate valve or mini stopcock on the pipe, you will have to drain the cistern:

Draining the cistern

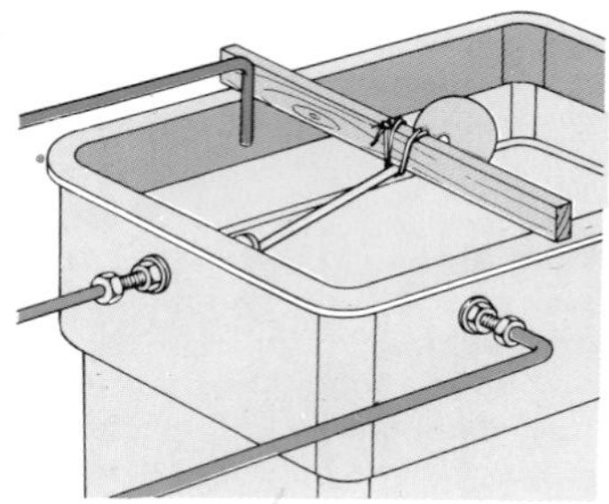

1 Tie the ball-valve arm to a piece of wood laid across the cistern. This stops the in-flow from the mains.

2 Turn on the bathroom cold taps until the water stops flowing, then turn on the hot taps – very little water will flow from them. (You need not turn off the boiler, as the hot-water cylinder will not be drained.)

TAPS FED FROM THE RISING MAIN

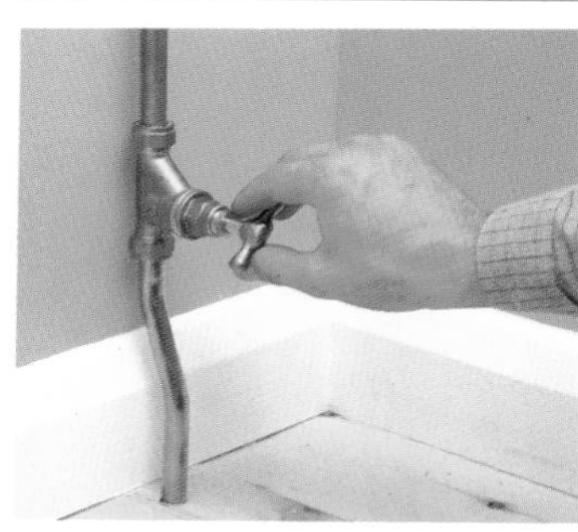

Turn off (clockwise) the main indoor stopcock, then turn on the tap until the water stops.

DRAINING THE RISING MAIN

You may want to drain the rising main to take a branch pipe from it or repair the stopcock.

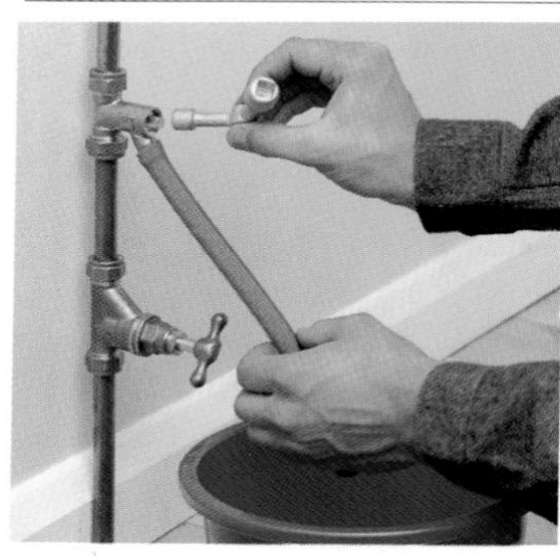

If there is a drain cock above the indoor stopcock, open it with a drain-cock key or pliers. Catch the water, usually only a pint or two, in a bucket or pan.

TURNING OFF THE OUTDOOR STOPCOCK

You may need to turn off the outdoor stopcock if the indoor one is broken, jammed, or has a leak from the spindle. Stopcock keys can usually be bought from hardware shops, but first check the type needed – the tap may have a crutch handle or tapered knob.

Alternatively, make your own.

1 Locate the stopcock, which is under a cover about 4in (100mm) across just inside or just outside the boundary of your property. (If there are two close together, test to find out which is yours, but tell your neighbour.) If you cannot find the outdoor stopcock, call the regional water company.

2 Raise the cover. This may be difficult if it has not been raised for some time.

3 Insert the stopcock key into the guard pipe and engage the stopcock handle at the bottom. Turn it clockwise.

MAKING YOUR OWN STOPCOCK KEY

If you have no stopcock key, take a piece of strong wood about 3ft (1m) long and in one end cut a V-shaped slot about 1in (25mm) wide at the opening and 3in (75mm) deep.

Securely fix a piece of wood as a cross-bar handle at the other end. Slip the V slot over the stopcock handle to turn it. This handle will not turn a stopcock with a tapered knob.

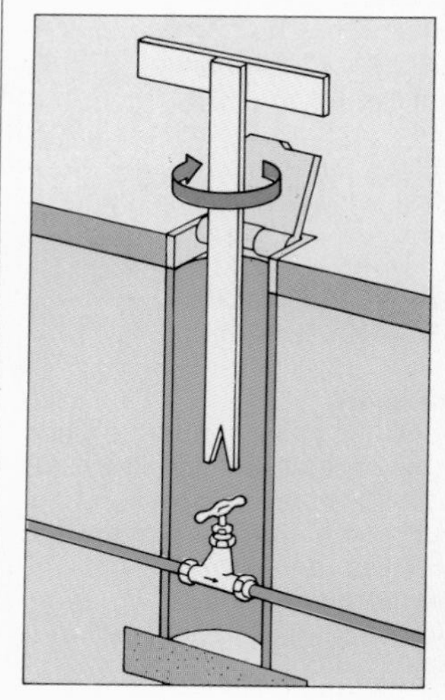

TYPES OF STOPCOCK AND VALVE

Stopcock
A tap with a valve and washer that is inserted into a run of pipe – normally mains pipe – to control the water flow through it. A stopcock is usually kept turned on, being turned off only when necessary to cut off the water. It must be fitted the right way round (an arrow mark shows the flow direction). Most stopcocks have a crutch handle.

Gate valve
A tap, usually with a wheel handle, in which the water flow is controlled by raising or lowering a metal plate (or gate). It can be fitted either way round and is normally used in low-pressure pipes such as cistern distribution pipes. With the gate open, the flow is completely unrestricted. When it is closed, the seal is not as watertight as a stopcock.

Drain cock
A tap without a handle, opened by turning the spindle with a drain-cock key. It is normally kept closed, but has a threaded outlet for attaching a hose when draining is necessary. A drain cock is fitted in those parts of the plumbing system that cannot be drained through household taps – for instance in the boiler or central-heating systems and in the rising main.

Mini stopcock (servicing valve)
A small stopcock without a handle, operated by turning a slot screw to open or close a hole to control the water flow. Normally used in a low-pressure supply pipe to a tap or ball valve to cut off the water for repairs. An in-line tap is very similar but has a lever handle and may have a threaded end. It is used to control the flow to a washing machine, for example.

HELPFUL TIP

If a stopcock is difficult to turn, do not force it – apply a few drops of penetrating oil round the base of the handle and leave at least ten minutes before trying again. Repeat as necessary.

A stopcock that has been open for a long time may be jammed. This can be disastrous in an emergency.

To guard against this, close and open a stopcock fully once or twice a year. After opening a stopcock, give the handle just a quarter turn towards closure. This will prevent jamming without affecting the water flow.

CHOOSING A TAP

Most taps work in the same way – turning the handle opens or closes a valve that fits into a valve seat. The valve – a rod and plate known as a jumper valve – is fitted with a washer that is replaced when it is worn and the tap drips.

Taps for washbasins and sinks normally have a $\frac{1}{2}$in diameter inlet that fits into a 15mm pipe. Bath taps usually have a $\frac{3}{4}$in diameter inlet that fits a 22mm pipe. The most durable finish on a tap is chrome on brass. Enamel tends to discolour in time. Some modern taps have plastic handles, others are completely plastic.

Two taps with a common spout are known as a mixer. Adjusting the hot and cold handles produces a flow at the required temperature. The taps are linked either by a deck block (flat against the surface) or a pillar block (raised). Most mixers are two-hole types that fit into a standard two-hole sink – one for the hot tap and one for the cold. Some mixers, however, need three holes (a centre hole for the spout) and some (monobloc types) only one.

TAPS WITH CERAMIC WASHERS

Some tap designs incorporate ceramic washers. The water flow is controlled by two hard-wearing ceramic discs – one fixed, one moving. When the tap is turned on, openings in the disc line up so water can flow through. The discs become smoother and more watertight with wear, so, in theory, they never need renewing.

Pillar tap
The type still often used in the home, with a vertical inlet that fits through a hole in the sink, basin or bath. The conventional tap has a bell-shaped cover – generally known as an easy-clean cover – and a capstan (cross-top) handle.

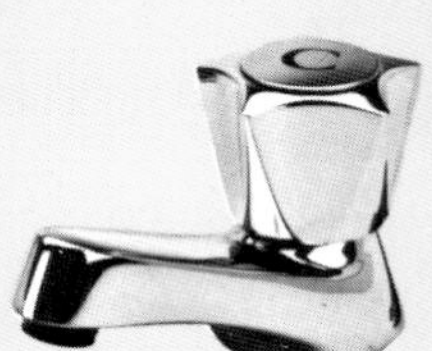

Handwheel handle
Many modern taps have the cover and handle replaced by a shrouded head that commonly forms a handwheel (a fluted knob) handle – although some shrouded heads are moulded like crosstop handles. Shrouded heads not only give a neater appearance but also prevent water from wet hands going down the spindle and allowing detergent to wash the grease out of the tap mechanism.

Lever handle
Another type of shrouded head has a lever handle, which is easy for elderly or handicapped people to use as it can be pushed rather than gripped. Lever-handle taps usually need only a quarter turn of the handle. Many, but not all, have ceramic discs in place of a valve and washer.

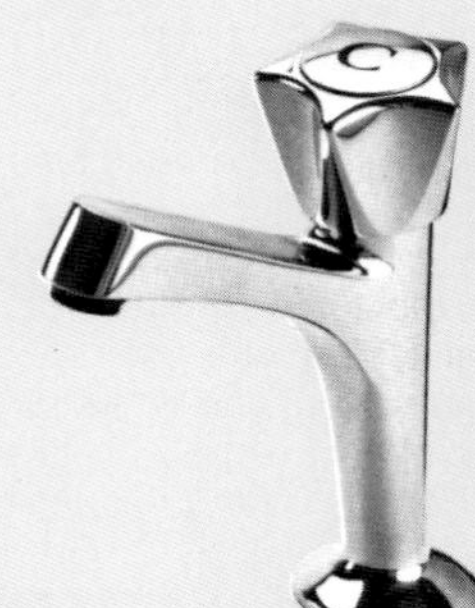

High-neck taps
Ordinary pillar taps have the spout opening about $\frac{7}{8}$in (22mm) above their base on the sink, but high-neck types stand well clear of the sink – with the spout about $3\frac{3}{4}$in (95mm) above the base. With a shallow sink this allows room for filling a bucket or rinsing a large pan under the tap. The handles may be any of the standard designs.

Bib tap
A tap with a horizontal inlet, once commonly fitted into the wall above a sink or basin. Bib taps are now used mainly outdoors, in the garden or a garage. Many are of unadorned brass with a crutch (straight) handle, but some are chromium plated with a capstan handle or shrouded head.

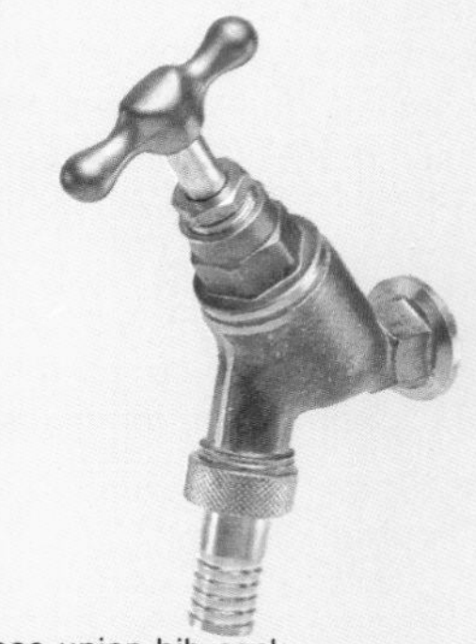

Hose union bib cock
Some bib taps have a threaded nozzle for fitting a hose. A tap installed against an outside wall should have an angled head, otherwise you will graze your knuckles when you turn the handle.

Kitchen mixer
The spout has separate channels for hot and cold water which mix only as they emerge. This is because the kitchen cold tap is fed direct from the mains, and it is illegal to mix cold water from the mains and hot water from a storage cistern in one fitting. The spout usually swivels and should be able to reach both of the bowls in a two-bowl sink.

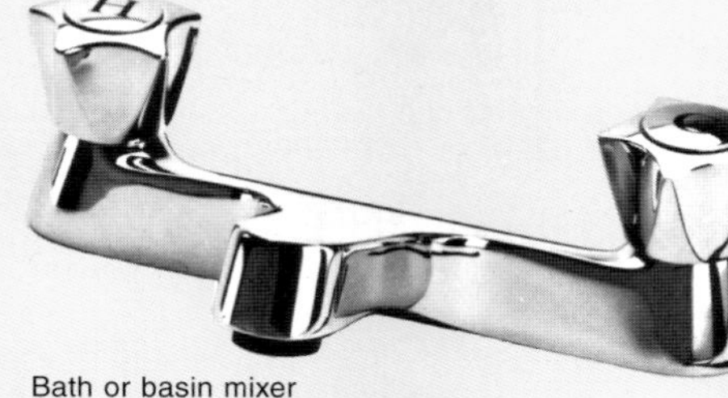

Bath or basin mixer
The hot and cold water merges within the mixer body, as both taps are usually fed from a cistern. It is against the law to fit this type of mixer in a direct system with cold water from the rising main and hot water from a cylinder. This is because mains pressure can alter and differences in pressure might cause stored – and maybe contaminated – water to be drawn back into the mains. When a mixer is used with an instantaneous gas water heater, both of the taps are fed from the rising main.

Bath/shower mixer
Bath mixers sometimes have a shower attachment with a control knob that diverts the water flow from the spout to the shower sprinkler. Do not buy a bath/shower mixer unless your storage cistern can supply adequate pressure.

Monobloc mixer
A single-hole mixer having a compact body with the handles and spout very close together. Some types have very narrow inlet pipes. There are monobloc designs for both kitchens and bathrooms. Kitchen monobloc mixers often include a hot-rinse spray and brush fed from the hot-water pipe by a flexible hose, so that the spray can be lifted from its socket for use. Some are available with ceramic washers.

ALL MIXER TAPS: IF YOU ARE MIXING MAINS WATER WITH STORED WATER, YOU MUST FIT A BACK-FLOW PREVENTION DEVICE

Repairing a dripping tap

A dripping tap usually means that the washer needs renewing, but can also result from a damaged valve seating. Unless the drip is stopped, it will eventually stain the sink or bath. In very cold weather, the constant dribble of water through the outlet pipe is likely to freeze and cause a blockage. If the drip is from a mixer spout, renew both tap washers.

You will need

Tools One large open-ended spanner, normally $\frac{13}{16}$in for a $\frac{1}{2}$in tap or $\frac{15}{16}$in for a $\frac{3}{4}$in tap (or an adjustable spanner); old screwdriver (for prising). Possibly also: one small spanner (normally $\frac{5}{16}$in); one or two pipe wrenches; cloth for padding jaws; one $\frac{3}{16}$in (5mm), one $\frac{3}{8}$in (10mm) screwdriver.

Materials Replacement washer, or a washer-and-jumper valve unit; alternatively, a washer-and-seating set (see below); petroleum jelly. Possibly also: penetrating oil.

REMOVING THE HEADGEAR

1 Cut off the water supply (page 306). Make sure the tap is turned fully on, and put the plug in the plughole to stop any small parts falling down the waste pipe.

2 Unscrew the bell-shaped cover of a conventional tap to expose the hexagonal headgear nut. This can usually be done by hand. If it is stiff, and you have to use a spanner or pipe wrench, pad the jaws with a rag to avoid damaging the surface. ALTERNATIVELY, with a shrouded head, prise off the top plate and undo the retaining screw. Then lift off the handle to expose the headgear nut. If the handle has no retaining screw, it may pull straight off, or pull off after you have given it a half turn. Or there may be a small screw in the side of the head.

3 Undo the headgear nut with a spanner. With a conventional head, the gap between the base and the lifted cover when the tap is turned fully on should be about $\frac{1}{2}$in (13mm) – not wide enough for most adjustable spanners. You will need an open-ended spanner to get at the nut. With a shrouded head you can use an adjustable or ring spanner.

4 If the nut is difficult to turn, do not force it – you may twist the base of the tap and strain the inlet pipe, and perhaps crack the basin. Instead, apply penetrating oil round the joint, wait about ten minutes to give it time to soak in, then try turning the nut again. You may have to make several applications. To guard against cracking the basin, hold the tap base steady with a padded pipe wrench, and use it to counteract the force applied to the nut by pushing in the opposite direction.

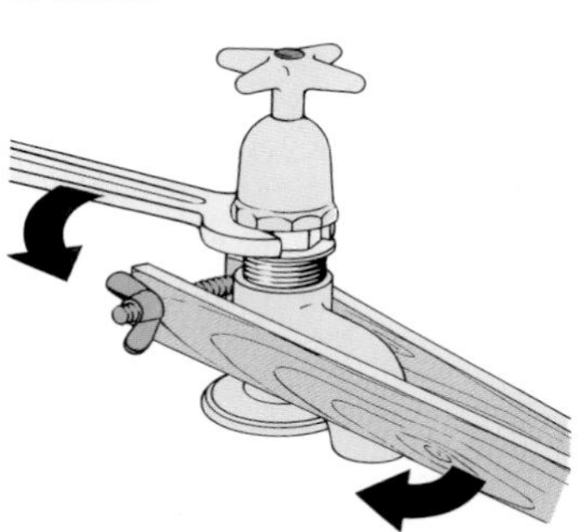

Another way is to make a gripping tool from two lengths of wood joined together at one end with a bolt; use it to hold both the body and the nozzle steady while you apply counterpressure.

FITTING THE WASHER

With a tap fed from the cistern, the jumper valve and washer will probably be fixed in the removed headgear. With a tap fed from the rising main, the jumper valve and washer will probably be resting on the valve seating when you remove the headgear.

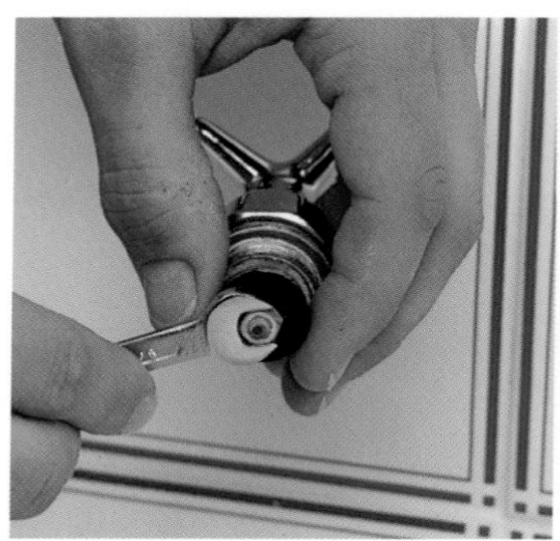

1 If there is a small nut holding the washer in place, unscrew it with a spanner (normally $\frac{5}{16}$in). If it is difficult to undo, put penetrating oil round it and try again when it has soaked in. Prise off the washer from the jumper-valve plate.

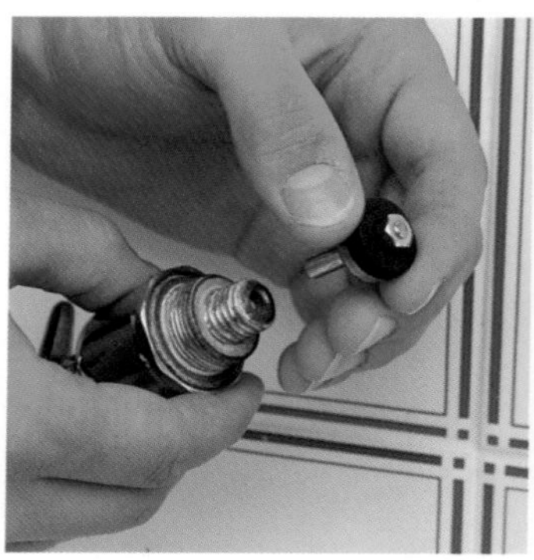

ALTERNATIVELY, if the nut is impossible to remove, you can replace

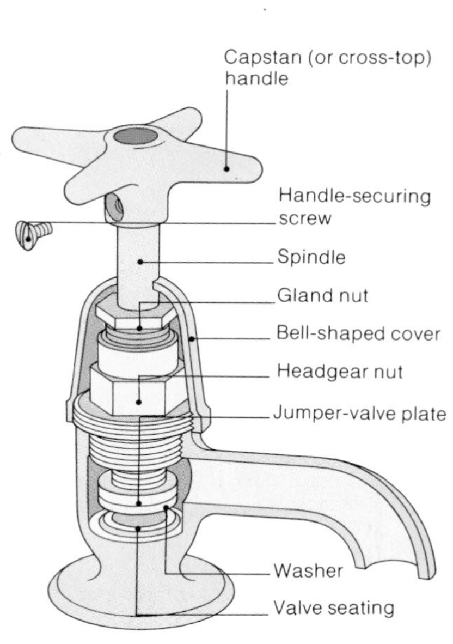

Shrouded-head tap

The valve and washer are the same as in a conventional tap (below), but the spindle is sealed by an O-ring rather than a gland. The tap handle and headgear has to be removed both to change a washer and to renew an O-ring.

Conventional tap

The jumper valve is in the shape of a rod and plate, and the washer is attached to the base of the plate. When changing a washer, the handle is lifted off with the headgear. When adjusting the gland, the handle has to be removed so that the bell-shaped cover can be pulled off out of the way.

REPAIRING THE VALVE SEATING

When renewing a washer, look at the base of the tap, in which the valve is seated. If it is scaled or scored by grit, the watertight seal will not be effective, and the tap will keep on dripping, even with a new washer.

The simplest repair is with a washer-and-seating set. This has a plastic seat to fit into the metal seat, and a washer-and-jumper unit to fit into the headgear. When the tap is turned off, the plastic seating is forced firmly in. It may take a few days for the new seating to give a watertight fit. An alternative repair is to buy or hire a tap reseating tool and grind the seat smooth.

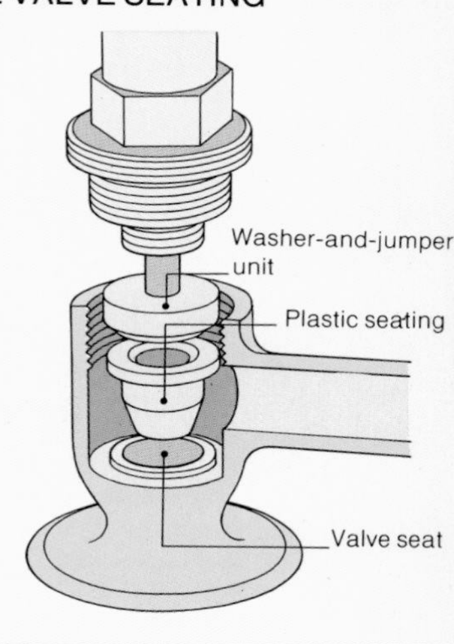

both the jumper valve and washer in one unit.

2 After fitting a new washer or washer and jumper, grease the threads on the base of the tap before reassembling. Make sure the tap is turned off before you turn on the water supply.

HELPFUL TIPS

If, after replacing the washer, you find that the tap still leaks, the valve seating is probably scored by grit. Easy-to-use reseating kits, available from DIY stores, grind the seating to a smooth surface.

If you cannot undo the peg or grub screw securing a fixed jumper valve and washer, shear it off by force. Insert a screwdriver between the base of the headgear and the washer plate and prise out the jumper. Before you fit the new jumper and washer, roughen the surface of a metal (but not a plastic) jumper rod with a coarse file. This helps it to grip when you refit the jumper.

Tap conversion kit

You can use tap conversion kits to change the style of taps and replace worn or broken mechanisms. Newer heads can be changed back to Victorian brass heads, or a tap with a crutch or capstan handle can be given a newer look. The spout and body of the tap remain in place. Some kits have bushes to fit $\frac{3}{8}$in, $\frac{1}{2}$in or $\frac{3}{4}$in taps. The kits are available from most DIY stores and fitting instructions are included.

FITTING A WASHER UNIT TO A SUPATAP

There is no need to turn off the water. The tap has a check valve that drops to stop the water flow as the nozzle is unscrewed.

1 Use a spanner to loosen the hexagonal retaining nut at the top of the nozzle by turning it anticlockwise (it has a left-hand thread).

2 Hold the loosened nut with one hand while you turn the tap on. Keep turning it to unscrew the nozzle. At first the water flow will increase, but will stop just before the nozzle comes off in your hand.

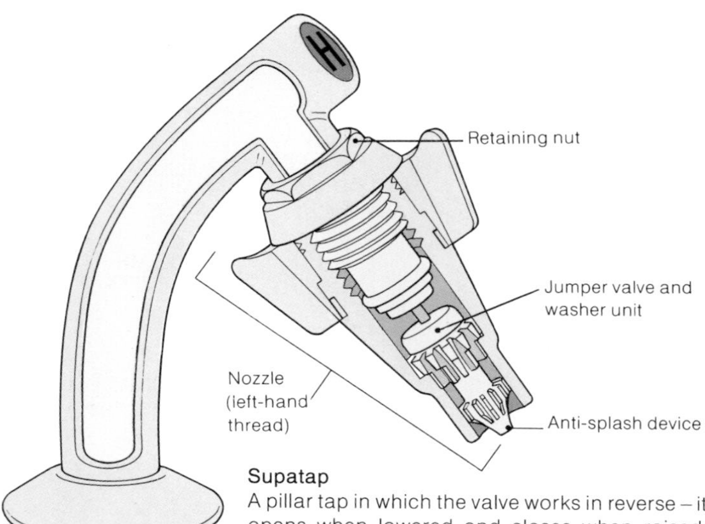

Supatap
A pillar tap in which the valve works in reverse – it opens when lowered and closes when raised, and is operated by turning the nozzle.

3 Tap the base of the nozzle against something firm – not the washbasin, or you may chip the surface. This will loosen the anti-splash device that projects slightly from the top. Then turn the nozzle upside down. The anti-splash device, which contains the jumper and washer unit, will fall out.

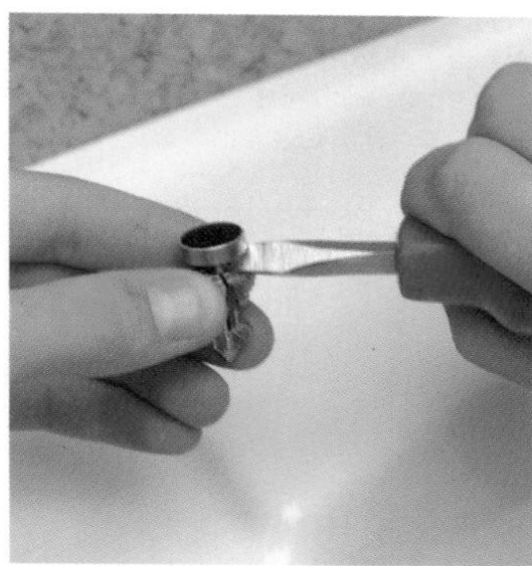

4 Prise out the jumper valve with a screwdriver blade inserted between the lip of the anti-splash device and the washer plate.

5 Snap the new washer and jumper unit into place, then reassemble the tap by screwing the nozzle anticlockwise (left-hand thread).

Curing a leak from a spindle or spout

Leakage from the body of the tap – from round the spindle, the base of a swivel spout, or the diverter knob on a shower – is caused by a faulty gland or O-ring seal.

This sort of leak is most likely to occur on a kitchen cold tap with a bell-shaped cover and visible spindle. Detergent-charged water from wet hands may have run down the spindle and washed the grease out of the gland (or stuffing box) that makes a watertight joint round the spindle. If the tap is used with a hose for filling a washing machine or watering the garden, back pressure from the hose connection will also weaken the gland.

HELPFUL TIP

If a conventional tap handle is difficult to pull off after you have removed the screw, turn the tap fully on, raise the bell-shaped cover, and put a block of wood on each side between the raised cover and the tap body. Then turn the tap off (in a clockwise direction). The pressure from the raised cover will force the handle off. Remove the blocks of wood and temporarily slip the handle on again just far enough to fully close the tap.

With a stopcock, leakage round the spindle is commoner than a worn jumper-valve washer.

On a modern tap, especially one with a shrouded head, there is an O-ring seal instead of a gland, and it rarely needs replacing. O-ring seals are also used on a mixer swivel spout or a shower/mixer diverter mechanism, and they may occasionally become worn.

You will need

Tools Small spanner (normally $\frac{11}{16}$in) or adjustable spanner. Possibly also: one $\frac{3}{16}$in (5mm) and one $\frac{3}{8}$in (10mm) screwdriver; penknife or screwdriver for prising; two small wooden blocks about $\frac{3}{8}$in (10mm) deep (such as spring clothespegs). *Materials* Packing material (either knitting wool, graphite, or O-ring). Possibly also: silicone grease; O-rings (and possibly washers) of the correct size – take the old ones with you when buying, or give the make of tap.

ADJUSTING THE GLAND

There is no need to cut off the water supply to the tap.

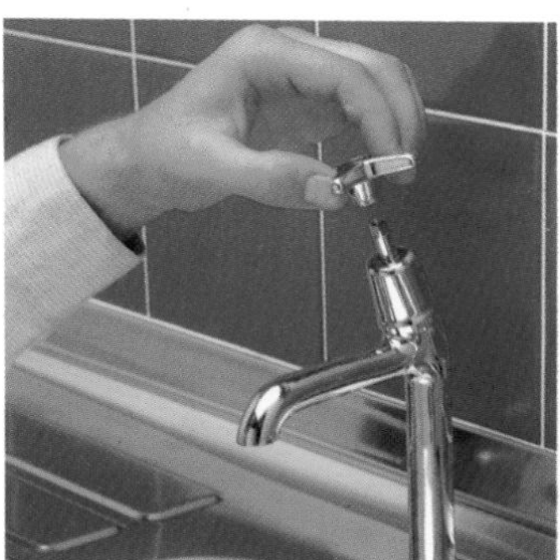

1 With the tap turned off, undo the small screw (facing page) that secures the capstan handle and put it in a safe place (it is very easily lost), then remove the handle. If there is no screw, the handle should pull off.

Curing a leak from a spindle or spout (continued)

2 Remove the bell-shaped cover to reveal the gland nut – the highest nut on the spindle. Tighten the nut about half a turn with a spanner.

3 Turn the tap on by temporarily slipping the handle back on, then check whether there is still a leak from the spindle. If there is not, turn the gland nut another quarter turn and reassemble the tap. Do not overtighten the gland nut, or the tap will be hard to turn off.

4 If there is still a leak, give another half turn and check again.

5 If the gland continues leaking after you have adjusted it as far as possible, repack the gland.

CHECKING THE PACKING

1 With the tap turned off and the handle and cover removed, use a spanner to remove the gland nut.

2 Note the type of packing used in the gland. It may be either string, hemp, graphite or a rubber O-ring. Replace the string with fibre string from a plumbers' merchant (see below). Replace other packing with the same material.

RENEWING THE O-RING ON A SHROUDED-HEAD TAP

1 Cut off the water supply to the tap (page 306) and remove the tap handle and headgear in the same way as for renewing a washer.

2 Hold the headgear between your fingers and turn the spindle clockwise to unscrew and remove the washer unit.

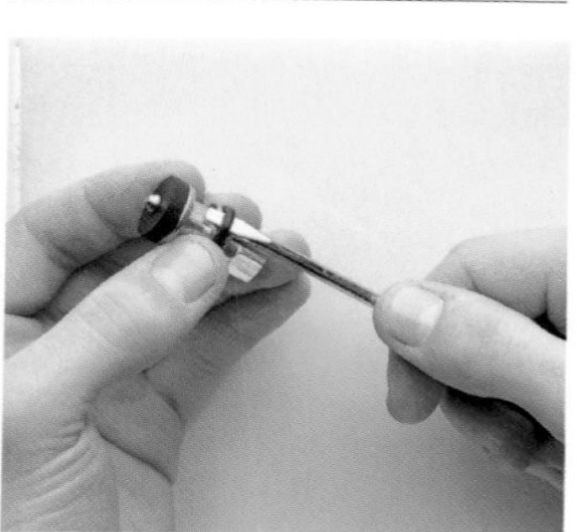

3 Prise out the O-ring at the top of the washer unit with a screwdriver.

4 Smear the new O-ring with silicone grease, fit it in position, and reassemble the tap.

RENEWING SWIVEL SPOUT O-RINGS

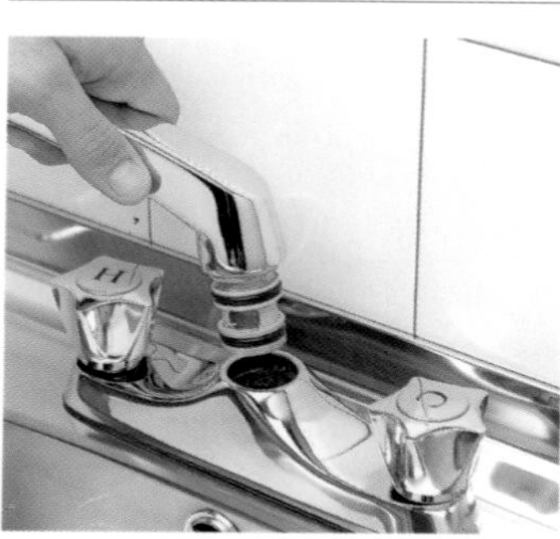

1 With both taps turned off, remove any retaining screw found behind the spout. If there is no screw, turn the spout to line up with the tap body and pull upwards sharply.

2 Note the position of the O-rings (probably two) and remove.

3 Coat new O-rings of the correct size with silicone grease and fit them in position.

4 Smear the inside of the spout end with petroleum jelly, then refit.

REPLACING SHOWER-DIVERTER O-RINGS

Although diverters vary in design, most have a sprung rod and plate attached to the diverter knob. When the knob is lifted the plate opens the shower outlet and seals the tap outlet for as long as the shower is turned on.

1 With the bath taps turned off, lift the shower-diverter knob and undo the headgear nut with a spanner (probably ½in size).

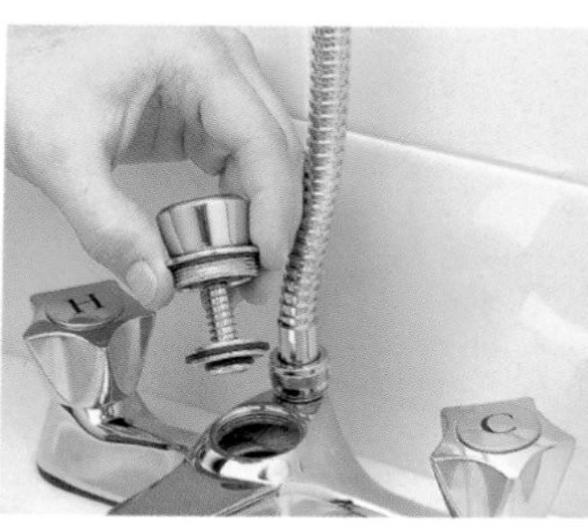

2 Lift out the diverter body and note the position of the washers and O-rings.

3 Remove the knob from the diverter body by turning it anticlockwise. You may need to grip it with a wrench.

4 Withdraw the rod and plate from the diverter body and remove the small O-ring at the top of the rod.

5 Grease a new O-ring of the correct size with silicone grease and fit it in place.

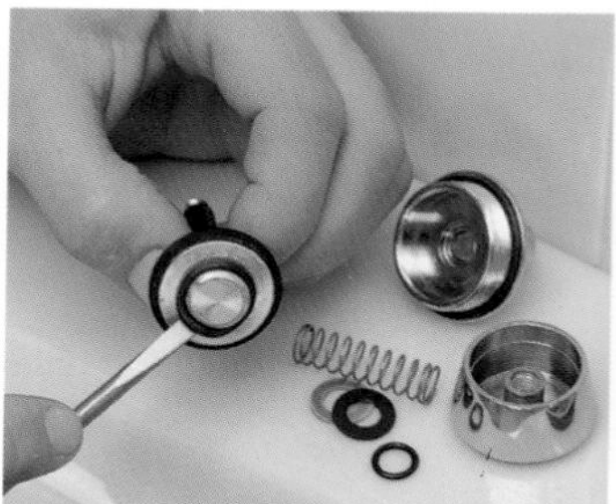

6 Replace all other rubber washers and O-rings on the base of the rod and plate. Old ones may have to be prised out.

REPACKING A STOPCOCK WITH FIBRE STRING

The gland on a capstan-handle tap or stopcock is the type likely to need repacking with fibre string (from a plumbers' merchant).

1 Turn off the stopcock. If it has a bell-shaped cover, remove the handle and cover as for adjusting the gland. Undo the gland nut and slide it up the spindle out of the way.

2 Rake out the gland packing below the nut with a penknife or similar tool.

3 To repack the gland with fibre string, steep a length in petroleum jelly and wind and stuff it into the gland with a screwdriver blade. Wind and push the string in until it is caulked down hard, then reassemble the tap.

Dealing with an airlock

If the water flow from a tap (usually a hot tap) is poor when fully turned on, then hisses and bubbles and stops altogether, air has somehow entered the system and there is an airlock in the supply pipe.

This is most likely to occur after the water system has been partially drained for repairs or improvements, or after a lot of water has been drawn off – perhaps for a bath or for washing clothes – and temporarily emptied the cistern.

You will need
Tools Length of hose with a tap adaptor at each end. Possibly also: dishcloth; screwdriver.

1 Connect one end of the hose to the tap giving the trouble. If it is a ¾in bathroom tap and the hose is difficult to fit, connect to the nearby washbasin hot tap instead.

2 Connect the other end of the hose to the kitchen cold tap or another mains-fed tap. Turn on the faulty tap first, then the mains-fed tap. The pressure of the mains water should blow the air bubble out of the pipe.

AIRLOCK IN A SUPATAP

Unscrew and remove the nozzle from the faulty tap (as for *Fitting a washer*, page 309), then connect the hose to the outlet. Do not touch the protruding, pin-like check valve, or water will spray out. Fit the other end of the hose to a mains-fed tap and turn the tap on.

AIRLOCK IN A KITCHEN MIXER

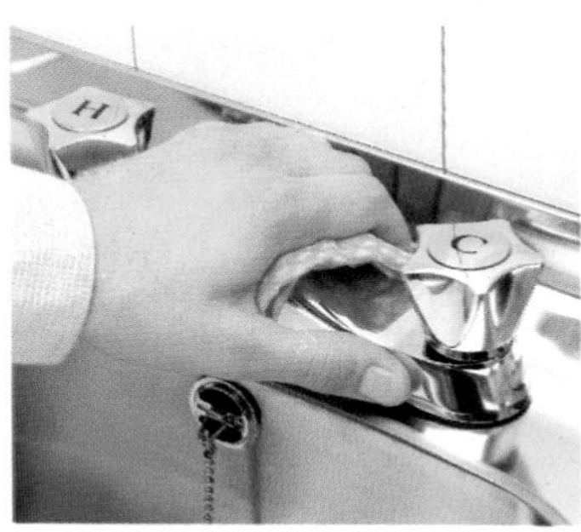

If the hot tap will not work, remove the swivel spout (page 310) and hold a cloth firmly over the spout hole while you turn on first the hot tap then the cold tap.

IF AIRLOCKS KEEP OCCURRING

There are a number of ways that air can be drawn into the water system and cause airlocks. If airlocks occur continually, check:

1 Is the cold-water cistern too small for the household's needs? If it is smaller than the standard 50 gallons (227 litres), replace it with one of standard size.

HELPFUL TIP
When additions are made to the plumbing, make sure that all horizontal lengths of distribution pipe are laid so that they fall away slightly from the main vent pipe. Any air bubbles entering the system will then be able to escape.

2 Is the ball valve in the cold-water cistern sluggish? Watch the cistern emptying while someone fills the bath. If the valve does not open wide enough as water is drawn off, there will be a slow inflow and the cistern will empty before the bath is filled, allowing air to be drawn into the distribution pipe. Dismantle and clean the ball valve (page 336).

3 Is the supply pipe from the cold-water cistern to the hot-water cylinder obstructed or too narrow? Check that any gate valve is fully open, and that the pipe is at least 22mm across. Replace it if it is narrower, as hot water drawn off for a bath is evidently not being replaced quickly enough, allowing the water level in the vent pipe to fall below the level of the hot-water distribution pipe, and air to enter.

Different ways of joining pipes

PREPARING THE PIPE ENDS

Before two pipe lengths of any material can be joined, the ends must be cut square and smooth. Copper and plastic can both be dealt with in the same way, as described here. You may be able to cut polybutylene with a sharp knife.

You will need
Tools Hacksaw or pipe cutter; half-round file. Possibly also: vice.

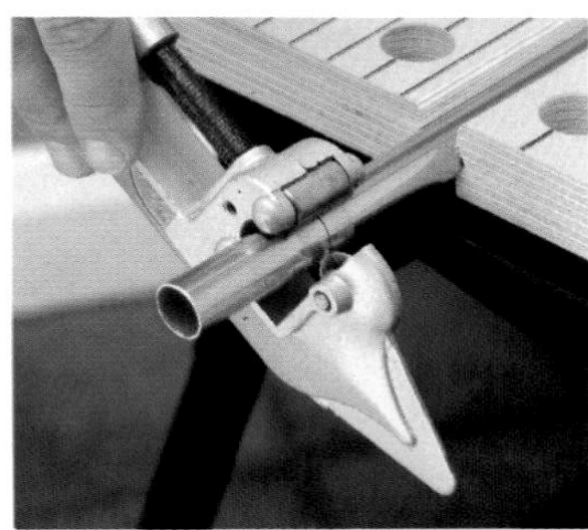

1 Cut the pipe ends square using a pipe cutter or hacksaw. Holding the pipe in a vice while sawing helps to ensure a square cut. For a plastic pipe, pad metal vice jaws to prevent damage to the pipe surface.

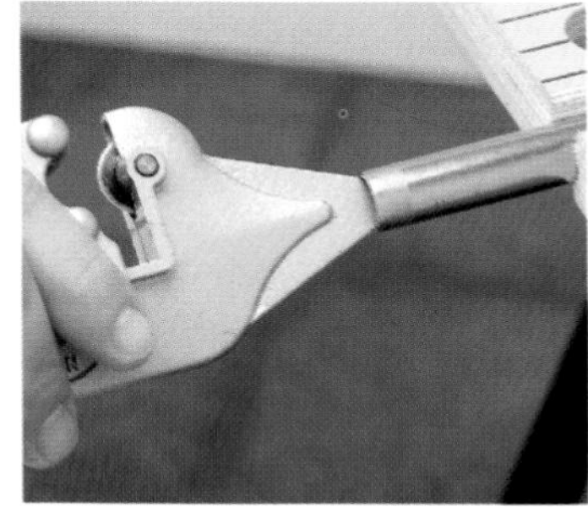

2 Smooth away burrs inside and outside the cut ends with a file or the reamer of the pipe cutter.

HELPFUL TIP
To get a square cut, join a straight-edged piece of paper round the pipe where the cut is to be made. Use the paper edge as a guide when sawing.

MAKING A COMPRESSION JOINT

A strong and easy method of joining copper piping and some plastic pipes (page 312). Tightening the nuts is critical – the joint will leak if it is loose, and also if it is strained through overtightening.

You will need
Tools Two adjustable spanners (with jaw openings up to 1½in wide for fittings on 28mm piping); OR, if you have any that fit, two open-ended spanners – cap nut sizes on different makes of fittings vary.
Materials Compression fitting; pipe jointing compound.

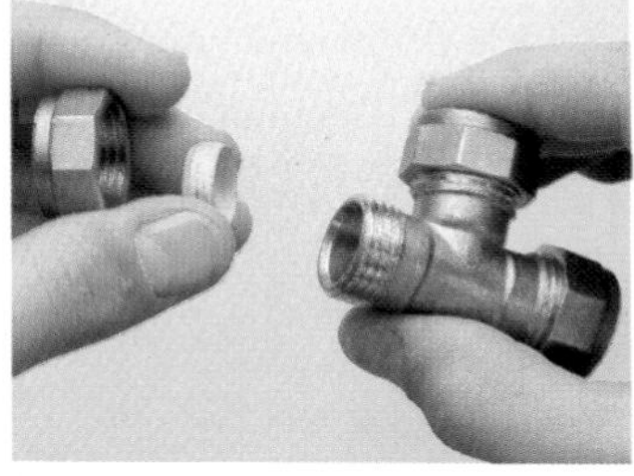

1 Unscrew and remove a cap nut of the compression fitting. Note which way round the olive is fitted, then remove it also.

2 Take one of the cut and smoothed pipe ends (see left) and slide the cap nut over it, then the olive. Make sure the olive is the same way round as it was in the fitting (with some makes this is crucial; with others it is not).

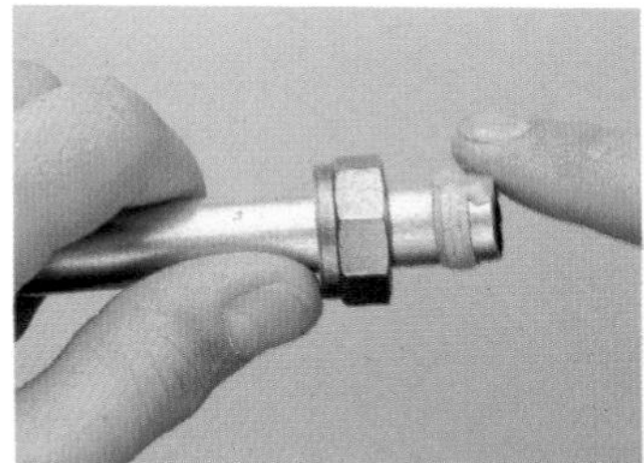

3 For a copper fitting, smear jointing compound on the pipe end and the outside of the olive.

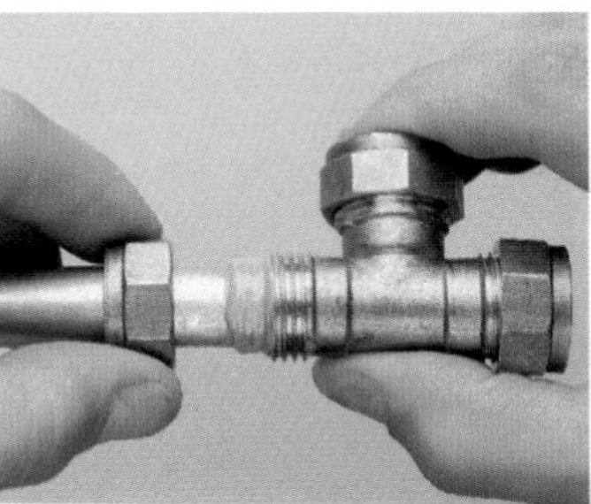

4 Push the pipe into one end of the fitting up to the internal pipe stop. Then slide the olive and nut up to the connector and hand-tighten the cap nut.

Continued on page 314

CHOOSING THE PIPE FOR THE JOB

Copper and plastic (see below) are the two commonest materials used for pipes in household plumbing. Lead pipes and galvanised steel (known as steel barrel) pipes were common before the late 1940s but are no longer used – although they may still be found in some older buildings.

Stainless steel piping can be used in the same way as copper, but is more expensive and harder to handle. It can, however, be linked to galvanised steel without the corrosive reaction that copper produces.

Domestic water supply pipes are made in metric sizes, measured by the outside diameter. Standard sizes for supply pipes are 15mm, 22mm and 28mm (waste pipes are larger, page 318). Older supply pipes were made in imperial sizes and were measured by the inside diameter; standard sizes were ½in, ¾in and 1in. Imperial and metric piping can be joined, but an adaptor is needed for some sizes, depending on the type of joint and connector used.

Plumbing and earthing

All metal pipework in the house must be joined to the same earth bonding system so that it is impossible for someone touching two pipes or metal electrical or plumbing fittings to be electrocuted. See page 360.

If you join two metal pipes or fittings with plastic pipe or plastic fittings, install an earth continuity bond between the two. When installing a sink or bath, follow the earthing instructions on page 360.

If your house earthing system relies upon a connection to the rising main for an earthing point this must be changed to a common earthing point near the meter.

PLANNING PIPE ROUTES

If you have to put in extra piping when making an installation (such as a new washbasin in a bedroom), the simplest way is often to tee into supply pipes in the roof space and bring the branch pipes down through the ceiling.

Do this either directly above the appliance, or run the pipes down the wall in a concealed spot such as a fitted cupboard, and then along the skirting board. Alternatively, use a recess, such as alongside a chimney breast, where piping can be boxed in and concealed.

Find the nearest supply pipes in the roof space and make a small hole in the ceiling to act as an indicator.

Avoid running piping under the floorboards along a joist, if possible, because of the number of boards to be taken up. But you may be able to thread flexible plastic piping under floorboards. If you decide to fix pipe supports to the side of a joist, put them at least 2in (50mm) below the top to prevent damage to the pipes from nails driven into the floorboards.

If you run piping under the floor in the same direction as the floorboards, you can drill through the joists to pass one or two 15mm pipes through. The holes should be below the depth of any nails used to fix the floorboards down. You will find it easier if you use a right-angle chuck adapter on your drill, or hire a right-angle drill.

MATERIAL	USES AND HOW SOLD	HOW JOINED AND CUT	ADVANTAGES	DISADVANTAGES	PIPE SUPPORT INTERVALS
Copper	For hot and cold-water systems indoors. Sold in rigid but bendable straight lengths for general use, or flexible coils for underground pipes or microbore central heating.	Join with compression joints, with soldered capillary joints or with pushfit joints. Cut with hacksaw or pipe cutter.	Withstands high temperatures. Durable and light in weight. Easy to bend round corners, so is neat and economic, needing few branch fittings. Can be painted. Widely available.	Pipes hot to touch. Bending neatly takes practice. May split or burst if water freezes. Brings about the corrosion of galvanised (zinc-coated) steel if joined directly to it.	For 15mm pipe: 3ft (1m) horizontal runs; 5ft (1.5m) vertical runs. For 22mm and 28mm pipe: 7ft (2m) horizontal runs; 8ft–9ft (2.5m) vertical runs.
Polybutylene (flexible plastic, such as is used in the Hep$_2$O system for hot or cold water distribution and for central heating	For hot and cold-water systems indoors, but do not link directly to a boiler (can be linked to copper piping). Sold in straight lengths of 3m or 6m (10ft or 20ft) or in long coils.	Join with either Acorn pushfit joints or with compression joints (with a metal pipe insert). Cut with a sharp knife, hacksaw, or pipe secateurs.	Easy to shape round bends. No tools or adhesive needed for pushfit joints – easy for beginner to use. Insulates well – pipes not too hot to touch. Can be painted.	Cannot withstand very high temperatures – must not be used within at least 15in (380mm) of a boiler. Runs of piping need plenty of support to avoid sagging.	For 15mm pipe: 20in (500mm) horizontal; 3ft (1m) vertical. For 22mm pipe: 32in (800mm) horizontal; 4ft (1.2m) vertical.
CPVC (rigid plastic such as beige Hunter Genova piping)	For hot and cold-water systems indoors. Do not link directly to a boiler (it can be linked to copper pipes). If used outside, protect against sunlight. The fittings can be dislodged by freezing, so lag thoroughly. Sold in straight lengths of 2m or 3m (7ft or 10ft).	Join with solvent-welded joints. Cut with a hacksaw or pipe cutter.	Light in weight and easy to handle. Can be economical for large jobs, unless being linked to copper pipe, for which connectors are more expensive. Insulates well. Pipes not too hot to touch. Not easily damaged by frost or ice.	Cannot withstand high temperatures, must not be used within 15in (380mm) of the boiler. Bends must be formed with connectors, which adds to cost. In long runs over 32ft (10m), a loop must be built in to allow for heat expansion. Water must be cut off while solvent dries.	All sizes of pipe: 20in (500mm) for horizontal runs; 3ft (1m) for vertical runs.
Cross-linked polyethylene (known as PEX).	For hot and cold-water systems indoors, but do not link directly to a boiler (can be linked to copper piping). Sold in straight lengths of 2m or 3m (7ft or 10ft).	Join with compression joints or push-fit fittings. Always use a stiffener in the pipe ends for support. Cut with knife, hacksaw or garden secateurs.	Easy to shape round bends by hand or with a former. Insulates well – pipes not too hot to touch. Not easily damaged by frost or ice. Can be painted.	Cannot withstand very high temperatures – must not be used within 15in (380mm) of a boiler.	For 15mm pipe: 20in (500mm) horizontal; 3ft (1m) vertical. For 22mm pipe: 24in (600mm) horizontal; 4ft (1.2m) vertical.

PIPE ACCESSORIES

Stop end or end cap
Used to cover a pipe end or opening not in use, such as the end of a connector fitting reserved for a future supply branch. A blanking-off disc is similar, and is used, for example, to cover an unwanted opening for an immersion heater in a hot-water cylinder.

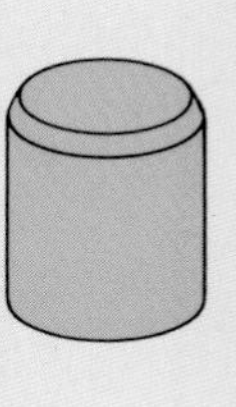

Pipe clip or strap
For fixing pipes to walls or woodwork. Position clips at the recommended intervals along a run according to the pipe material used (see above). Double-bracket clips are available for running two pipes of the same or different sizes side by side.

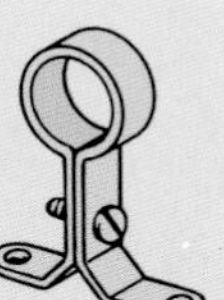

Clip-on pipe cover
Square plastic casing for boxing in pipes. Made in 10¼in (260mm) lengths in two widths to fit one, or two parallel, standard supply pipes.
The pipes are held by a tie-on clamp screwed to the wall, and the cover slides onto the clamp.

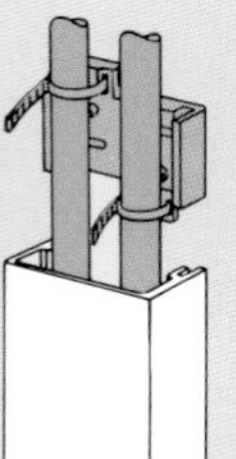

Hole plate
Plastic plate for fixing round a pipe to hide the hole where it goes through a wall. The plate is twisted over the pipe then clipped together. Made in a range of diameters. Before fitting a hole plate, check the maximum temperature it is designed to withstand.

CHOOSING THE JOINT FOR THE PIPE

All types of piping are joined with connector fittings (or sleeves). There are several different ways of securing the sleeves.

Compression joint

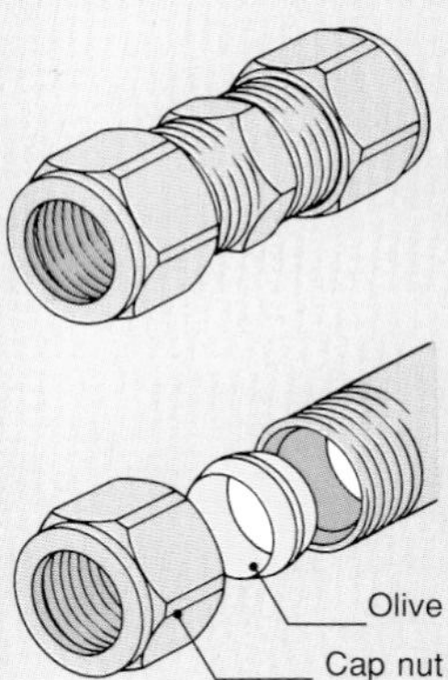

A sleeve of brass, gunmetal, or DR metal (for acid water) with screw-on cap nuts at each end. The pipe ends fit in as far as built-in pipe stops. A compression ring (or olive) fits over each pipe. When the cap nuts are tightened the olives are pressed against the pipe to form a seal. A slip coupling (page 315) has no pipe stop at one end of the sleeve.

Soldered capillary joints

A sleeve (usually copper) with built-in pipe stops in which copper pipe ends are sealed with solder heated by a blow torch (or high-heat hot-air gun). There are two types of soldered capillary joint: integral-ring joints or end-feed joints.

Integral-ring joint Has a built-in ring of solder near each sleeve end. Also known as solder-ring, pre-soldered, or Yorkshire joint.

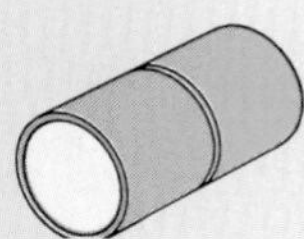

End-feed joint This is cheaper than an integral-ring joint, and needs to have solder wire applied to each sleeve opening as the joint is heated.

Speedfit joint

A plastic collet (gripper) with stainless-steel teeth and an O-ring to provide a leakproof seal. The pipe is cut to length then pushed into the fitting, where it is locked in place. Suitable for use with plastic and copper piping.

Hep$_2$O joint

A plastic sleeve in which the fully pushed-in pipe is held by a grab ring and O-ring seal. The caps at each end do not normally have to be undone. Plastic piping is supported by a stainless-steel insert before it is pushed in.

Solvent-welded joint

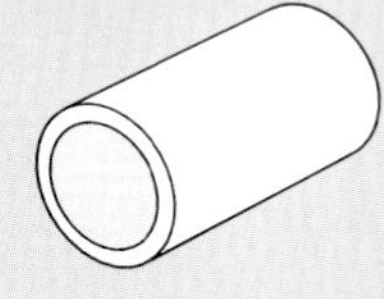

A plastic sleeve with a built-in pipe stop at each end. Used with PVC piping, which is secured in the sleeve by means of a strong adhesive recommended by the joint manufacturer.

Screwed joint

Fittings for connecting pipes to taps, cylinders and cisterns (and also to steel-barrel piping) have a screw thread at one opening.

The screw thread may be internal (female) or external (male), and threaded joints must be matched male to female.

Screwed joints are made watertight by binding PTFE thread-sealing tape three times anticlockwise round the male thread.

BRASS FITTINGS IN ACID WATER

In areas where the water supply is particularly acid, do not use brass connector fittings without first consulting the regional water company – especially if you are using copper piping.

Brass is an alloy of zinc and copper, and in highly acid water there is a reaction between the two metals that causes the zinc to gradually dissolve and the fitting to collapse. This process is known as dezincification.

Although soft water tends to be more acid than hard water, the problem is not solely confined to soft-water areas. Also, some water companies regulate the acidity of the water.

Where dezincification is likely, use connectors made of gunmetal or DR (dezincification-resistant) metal. Check whether other fittings in the house are marked with a DR symbol. If so, use similar fittings. If you decide to check the situation with a neighbour, make sure his water supply comes from the same water company.

THE JOINTS COMPARED

The jointing method must be compatible with the piping material (facing page), but some joints can be used for more than one material. Factors to be considered are cost, availability and how easy the joint is to make or dismantle, if necessary.

Compression joint
Advantages Suitable for copper and some plastic piping. Widely available. Can be re-used (with a new olive). Standard fittings will join metric and imperial pipes of 15mm and ½in or 28mm and 1in (a special fitting is used for 22mm and ¾in pipes).
Disadvantages Dearer than most other joints. Looks clumsy. Tightening can be difficult in awkward places. Special fittings needed for acid water.

Hep$_2$O joint
Advantages Used mainly for polybutylene pipes but also suitable for copper and CPVC 15mm and 22mm pipes. It can be undone and re-used if new grab ring and O-rings are fitted. Pipe can be twisted in fitting. Not affected by acid water.
Disadvantages Dearer than soldered capillary joints. Looks rather clumsy. Once pushed in, pipe cannot be pulled out for adjustment.

Soldered capillary joint
Advantages Cheaper than all the other joints. Neat appearance. Not affected by acid water.
Disadvantages Cannot be re-used if dismantled. More trouble to make than other joints, and applying heat can be a fire risk. Special fittings are needed to link metric piping and imperial piping.

Speedfit joint
Advantages No tools are needed to make the joint. Can be dismantled by pushing the collet and pulling apart. Can be re-used.
Disadvantages Expensive. Breaks the earth continuity of the pipes, so each side of the joint needs earthing.

Solvent-welded joint
Advantages Looks neat. Forms a tight seal that rarely leaks. Costs about the same as other plastic joints. Not affected by acid water.
Disadvantages Suitable for CPVC pipes only. Cannot be re-used. Solvent dries fast and gives off strong fumes. Joint cannot take water for some time after making.

CHOOSING THE CONNECTOR FOR THE JOINT

For every type of joint there is a range of sleeve connectors that allow for bends or branches in pipes or for links to fittings such as taps, as shown below. There are also sleeves for adaptations such as joining copper and lead piping, or piping of metric and imperial sizes.

Tee connector

Soldered integral-ring type

For fitting a branch pipe to a run of piping. May be an equal tee (all ends the same size) or an unequal tee (with different sizes).

Tank connector

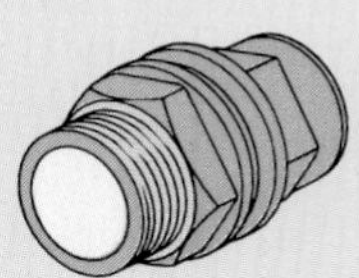

Compression type

For connecting piping to a cistern or cylinder. Has one end to fit the pipe, and one screw end with a back nut for the cistern or cylinder.

Straight connector

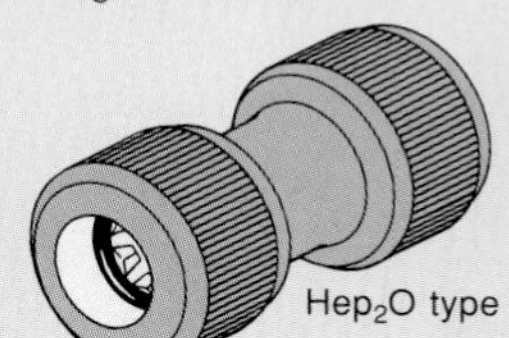

Hep$_2$O type

For joining two pipes in line. Has matched openings for pipes of the same size, or one end reduced for a pipe of different size. Some have an adaptor end.

Elbow connector

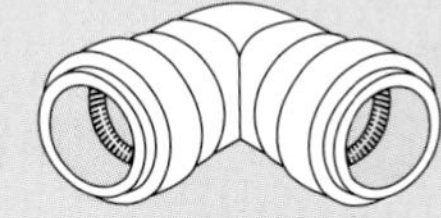

Speedfit type

For taking rigid piping round a bend. Available as right-angled or wider bends. Can have matching ends, or one end either reduced or with an adaptor.

Tap connector

For joining piping to a tap or ball-valve. May be straight or elbow. Has one end to fit to a pipe and the other with a screw joint for the tap – often a cap-and-lining joint, with a liner that fits inside the tap tail and a cap nut that screws onto it.

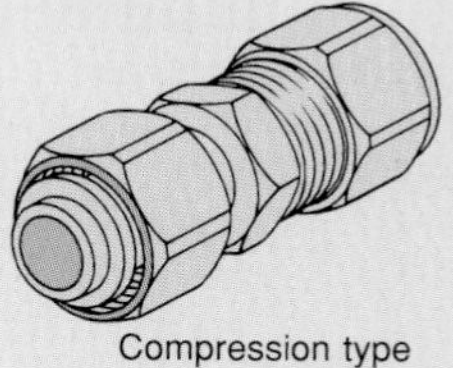

Compression type

Flexible connector

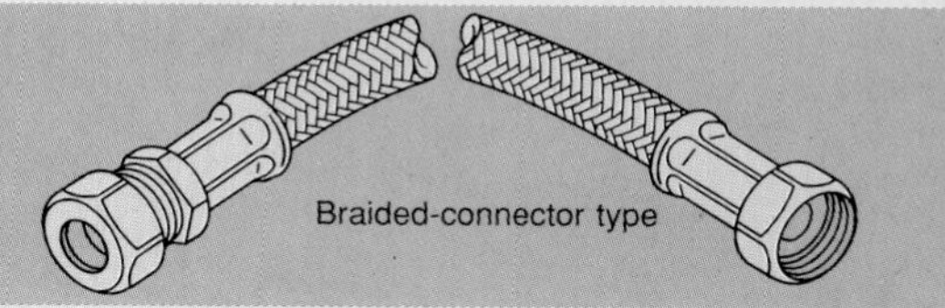

Braided-connector type

Ridged copper tubing that can be bent by hand without using springs. Has either two plain ends for fitting to compression sleeves, or a tap connector at one end. Made in both 15mm and 22mm diameters in various lengths.

Braided hose tap and ball-valve connectors are even more flexible. Some incorporate a servicing valve to allow water supply to be cut off to the tap or ball-valve.

Different ways of joining pipes (continued)

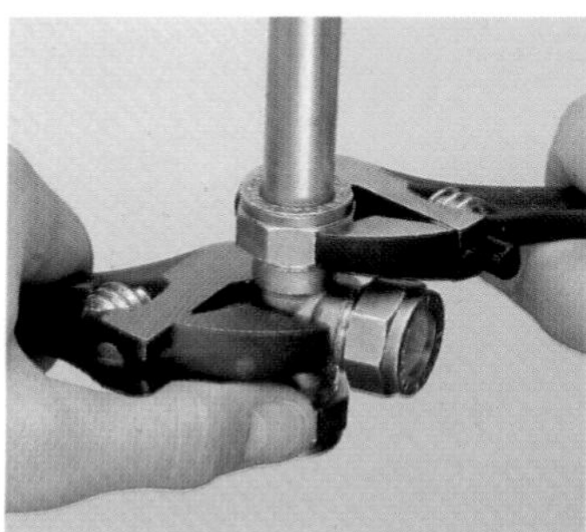

5 Hold the fitting securely with one spanner while you give the cap nut one and a quarter turns with the other. Do not overtighten.

6 Fit piping into other openings of the fitting in the same way.

HELPFUL TIPS

Until you have had some practice in making compression joints, take care not to overtighten a cap nut on copper piping. One way to do this is to make a scratch along the sleeve and cap nut before dismantling it. When you refit and tighten the nut, you will have made a complete turn when the marks meet.

When connecting a fitting to a vertical pipe, use a spring-clip clothes peg to stop the olive and cap nut slipping down the pipe while you push it in.

MAKING A SOLDERED JOINT

Lead-free solder must be used on all water supplies. Lead solder can be used on heating systems.

You will need
Tools Wire wool or fine emery paper; blow torch; clean rag.
Materials Tin of flux; soft lead-free solder wire for end-feed joints only. Possibly also; clean paint brush; sheet of glass fibre or other fireproof material for placing between the joint and woodwork while using the blow torch.

1 Clean the ends of the cut and smoothed pipes (page 311) and the inside of the fitting thoroughly with wire wool or fine emery paper. They must be completely clean to make a successful joint.

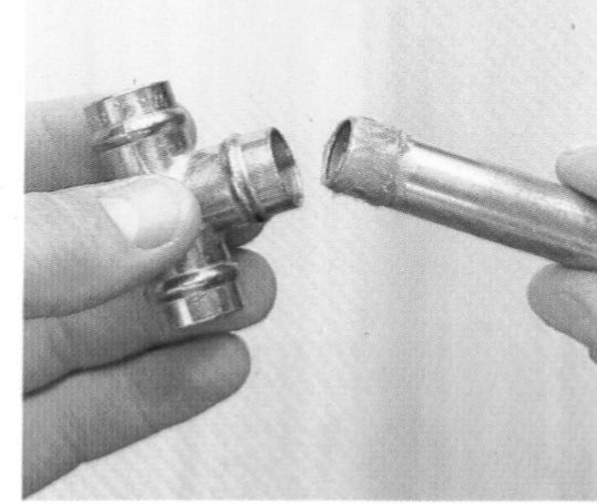

2 Smear the cleaned surfaces with flux. Use a clean brush, not a finger, for a lot of joints. Push the pipe into the fitting as far as the pipe stop. For an integral-ring fitting, push piping into all the openings because all the solder rings will melt once heat is applied.

3 Wipe off excess flux with a clean rag, otherwise the solder will spread along the pipe surface.

4 Fix the pipe securely in position with pipe clips.

5 For an integral-ring fitting, heat the joint with a blow torch until a silver ring of solder appears all round the mouth of the joint. Solder all the joints on the fitting in the same operation.

ALTERNATIVELY, for an end-feed fitting, heat the joint until you see flux vapours escaping. Then remove the heat (otherwise the solder will melt too fast and drip) and apply soft solder wire round the mouth of the fitting and heat again until a silver ring of solder appears all round. If you have to leave some joints of the fitting until later, wrap a damp cloth round those already made to stop the solder re-melting.

6 Leave the joint undisturbed for about 5 minutes while it cools.

MAKING A SPEEDFIT JOINT

A simple method that can be used to join both copper and plastic pipes. The only tools needed are those used to prepare the pipes (page 311).

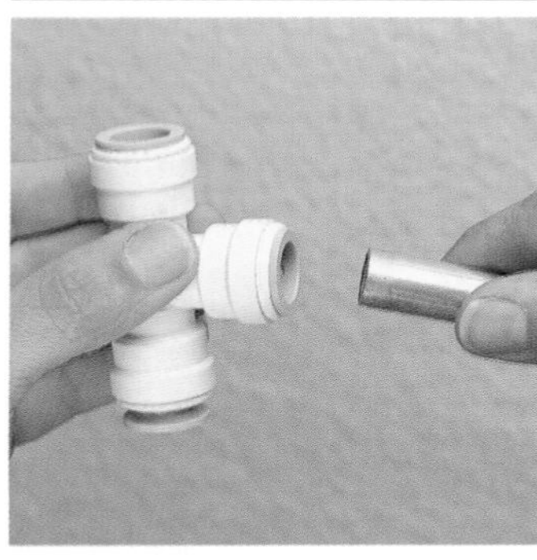

1 Take one of the cut and smoothed pipe ends and push it into the connector sleeve until it clicks into the built-in gripper.

2 Fit piping into the other end of the plastic sleeve connector in the same way.

MAKING A HEP$_2$O JOINT

This is a quick and simple method of joining polybutylene, copper or CPVC piping. In order to fit piping of Imperial size, you will have to remove the end cap and O-ring seal and replace the seal with an adapter ring. Consult the manufacturer's fitting instructions.

You will need
Tools Pencil; measuring tape.
Materials Silicone lubricant.

1 Check that the cut pipe end is well smoothed (page 311), otherwise sharp edges could damage the O-ring seal in the fitting and cause the joint to leak.

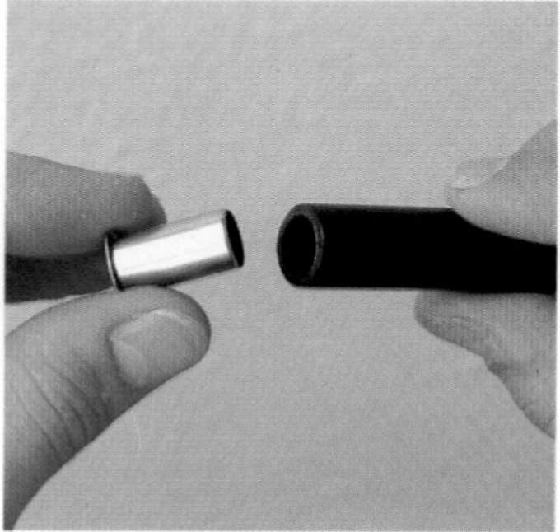

2 For plastic piping, push the support sleeve into the pipe end.

3 Make a pencil mark on the pipe 1in (25mm) from the end. This marks the insertion depth of the pipe into the fitting.

4 Smear the end of the pipe with silicone lubricant as far as the pencil mark.

5 Push the pipe into the fitting up to the insertion mark. If it is not pushed fully home the pipe will blow out under pressure.

MAKING A SOLVENT-WELDED JOINT

One of several methods for joining CPVC piping. If possible, work in a well-ventilated place because the solvent gives off strong fumes. Do not run water through the jointed pipe for at least an hour if it is to carry cold water or 4 hours if it is a hot-water pipe.

The instructions given by the pipe manufacturer may vary slightly from those given below; follow the manufacturer's instructions where available.

You will need
Tools Pencil; medium abrasive paper; clean rag; clean tissue.
Materials Degreaser or spirit cleaner recommended by the pipe manufacturer; recommended solvent cement for piping (brush usually supplied).

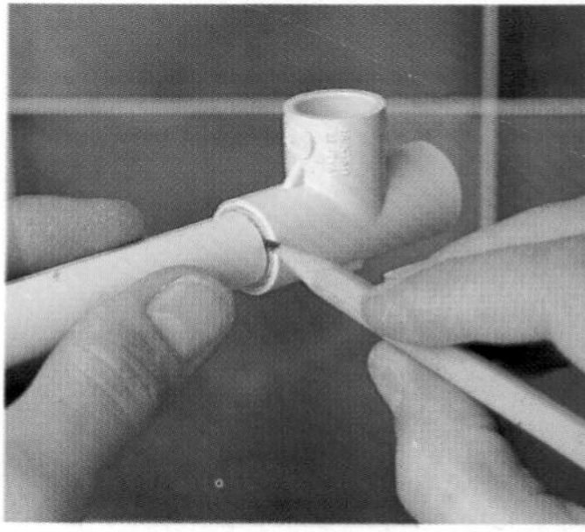

1 Insert one of the cut, smoothed pipe ends (page 311) into the opening of the fitting as far as the pipe stop (do not force it). Mark the insertion depth with a pencil.

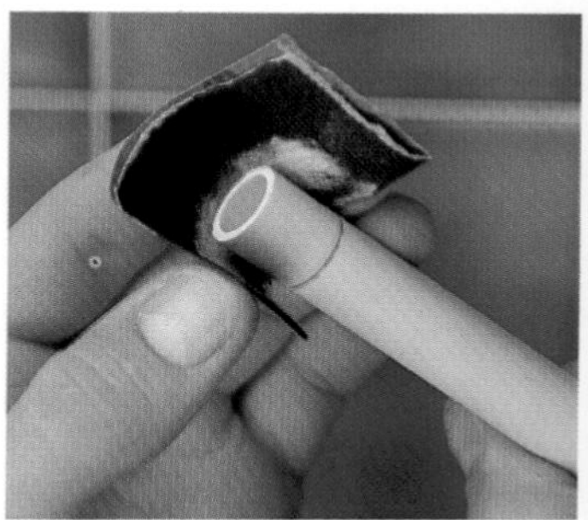

2 Withdraw the pipe and roughen the surface as far as the pencil mark with medium-grade abrasive paper. Do not use steel wool, which would polish rather than roughen.

3 Roughen the inside of the fitting in the same way.

4 Clean the pipe end and inside the fitting with rag and spirit cleaner or degreaser. Wipe dry with a clean tissue.

5 Use a brush to apply a liberal, even coat of cement to the pipe end. Apply more cement sparingly into the opening of the fitting.

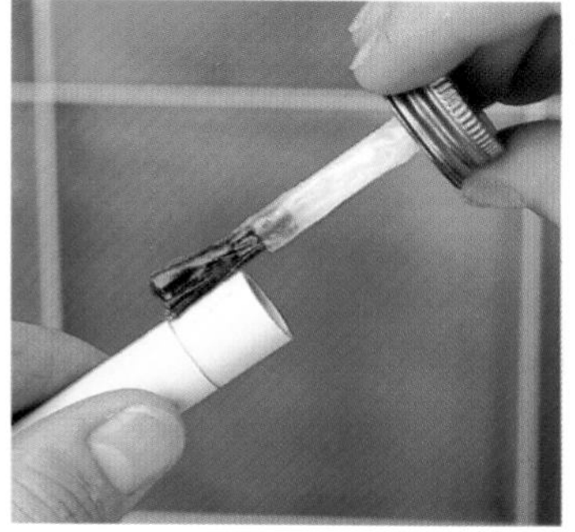

6 Stroke the cement along the surface rather than round it.

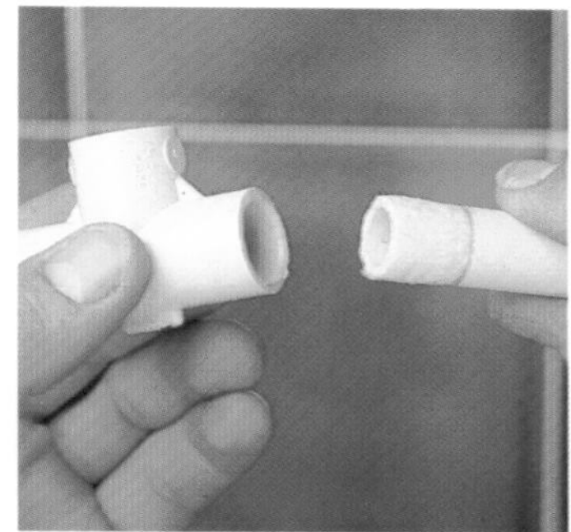

7 Push the pipe fully into the fitting with a slight twist.

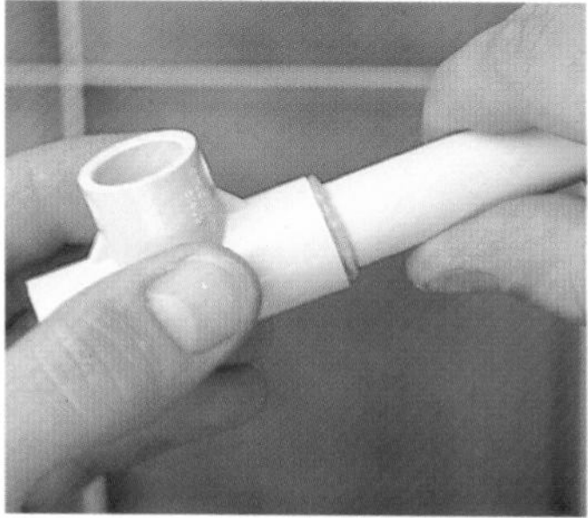

8 Hold in place for about ten seconds. Do not remove surplus cement.

Bending copper piping

Never try to bend rigid copper piping by hand without a spring to support the pipe walls – the pipe will lose its shape.

You will need

Tools Bending springs of the required diameter (15mm or 22mm); OR pipe-bending machine with 15mm and 22mm formers and guide blocks; metal bar such as screwdriver shaft; length of string. *Materials* Petroleum jelly.

BENDING WITH A SPRING

1 If the pipe is longer than the spring, tie string to the spring end.

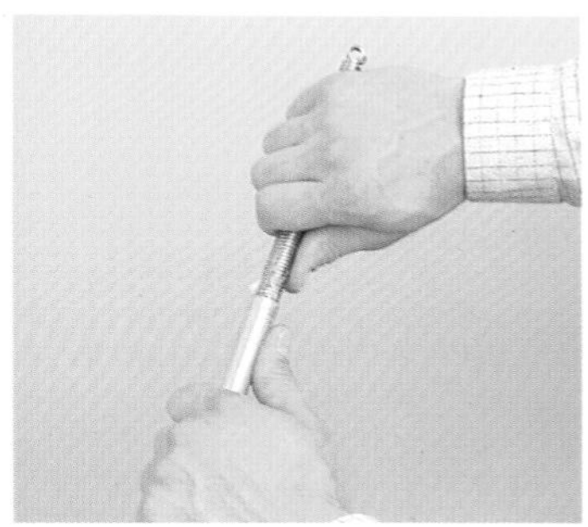

2 Grease the spring well and push it into the pipe.

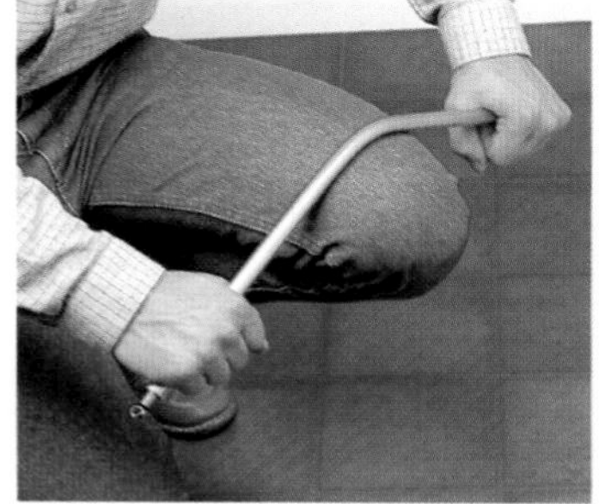

3 Bend the pipe across your knee with gentle hand pressure to the required angle.

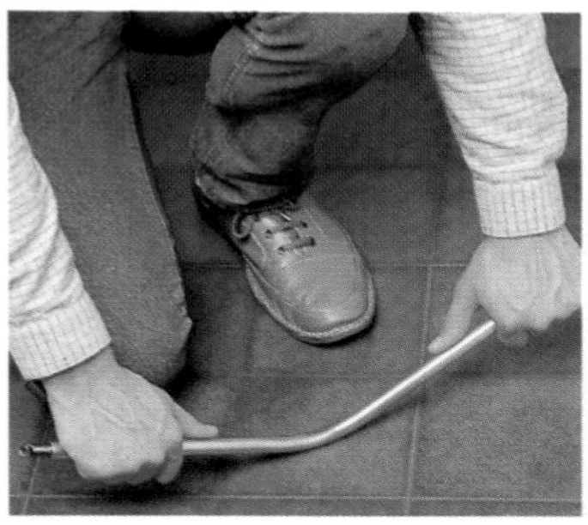

4 Overbend the pipe a little more, then ease it gently back again. This action helps to free the spring and makes it easier to withdraw.

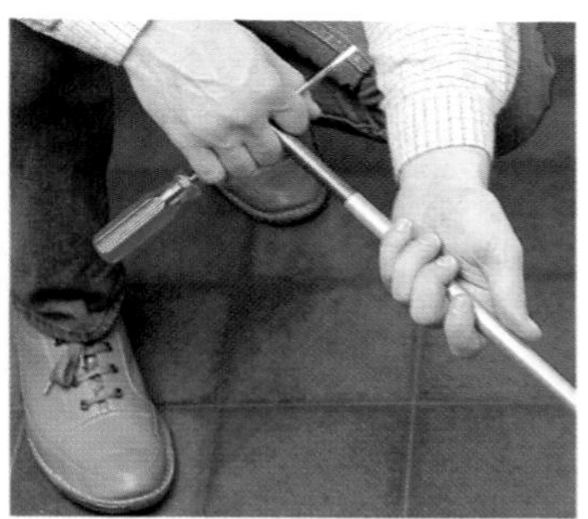

5 Insert a bar through the spring loop. Twist the spring to reduce its diameter, then pull it out.

BENDING WITH A MACHINE

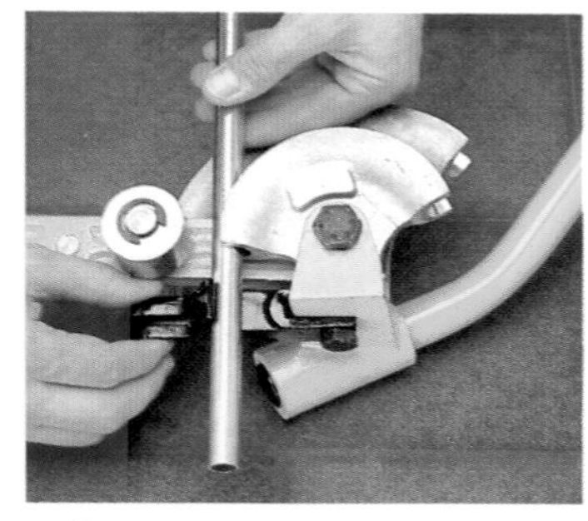

1 Clamp the pipe against the correct-sized semicircular former.

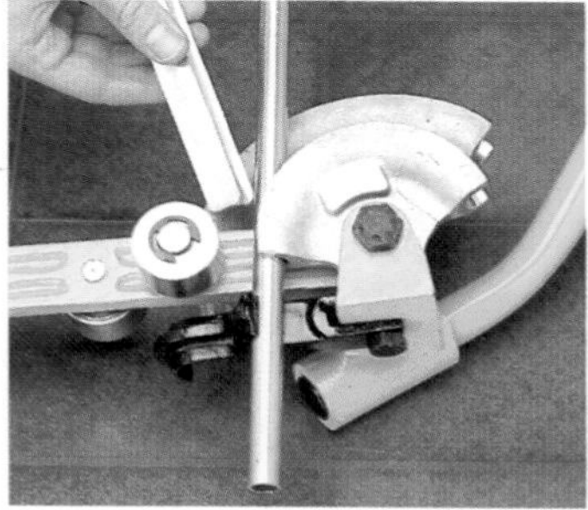

2 Place the guide block of the correct diameter between the pipe and the movable handle.

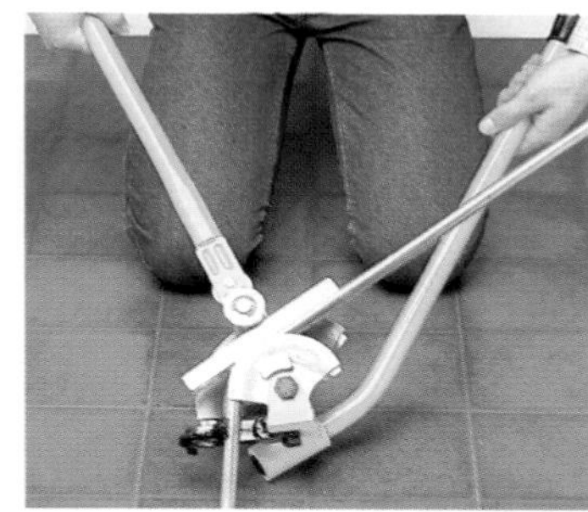

3 Squeeze the handles together until the pipe is curved to the required angle round the semicircular former.

Repairing a burst pipe

Pipes may burst in very cold weather because water expands by about 10 per cent as it changes into ice. If expansion along the pipe is prevented – perhaps by two ice plugs forming – the pressure can split the pipe or force open a joint.

Metal pipes are more likely to suffer frost damage than plastic pipes, and copper and stainless steel pipes are less vulnerable than lead.

If a copper pipe freezes it will expand and become weaker, but it might not burst in that particular spot. If you find that repair coupling olives do not fit the pipe, it is because the pipe has been frozen previously. Cut it back to an area which is undamaged and where the olives fit easily.

A split or damaged copper or plastic pipe can be temporarily repaired with a proprietary burst-pipe repair kit such as epoxy putty. Or, in an emergency, a pipe not under mains pressure can be patched with a length of hose.

Make a permanent repair as soon as possible – cut off the water supply (page 306), drain the pipe and replace the damaged length. For a split less than 3½in (90mm) long in a copper pipe, you may be able to make a permanent repair with a slip coupling (see right).

For lead piping, use a tape-repair kit for a strong temporary repair that will allow you to restore the water supply without waiting for a plumber (see next page).

USING A SLIP COUPLING

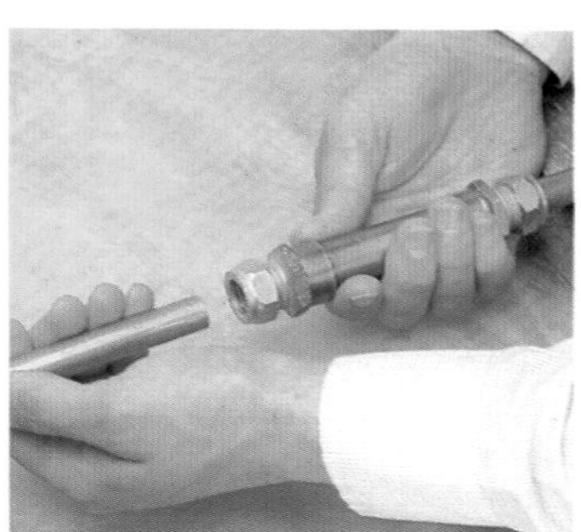

1 Cut out the damaged part and slide the slip end of the coupling (with no pipe stop) onto a pipe end. Then push it onto the other end.

2 Unscrew the compression nuts and slide the nuts and olives at each end along the pipe. Then apply pipe jointing compound.

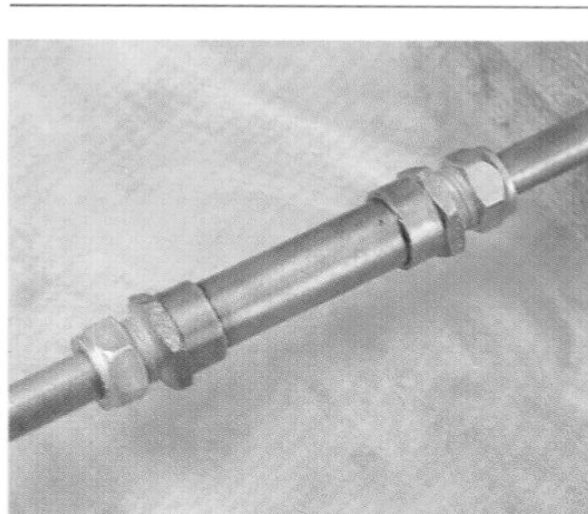

3 Refit the nuts and olives and screw finger tight. Then tighten with a spanner (facing page).

Repairing a burst pipe (continued)

PATCHING A SPLIT BRANCH PIPE

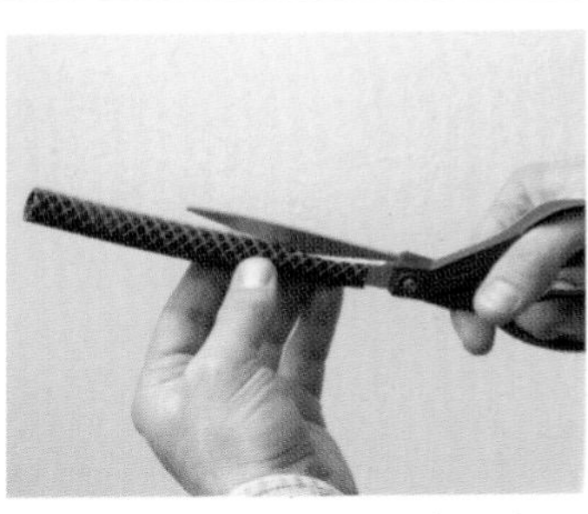

1 Cut a piece of garden hose long enough to cover the pipe for at least 50mm beyond the area of damage. Split the hose along its length.

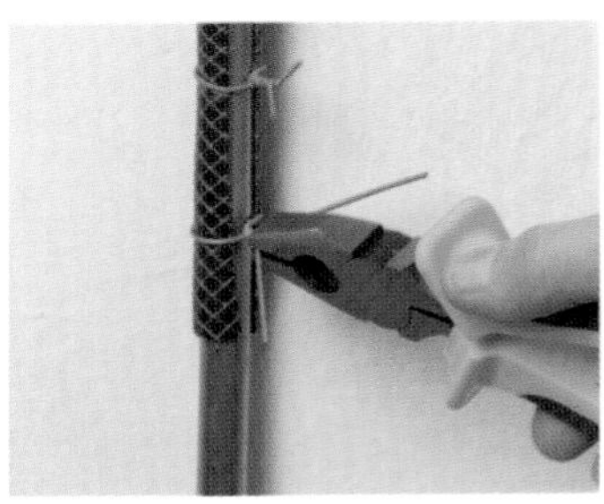

2 Wrap the hose round the pipe to cover the damage and secure it with three loops of strong wire. Twist the loops closed tightly with pliers.

3 Alternatively, fit an emergency pipe clamp and tighten the screws up fully with a screwdriver.

REPAIRING A LEAKING LEAD PIPE WITH LEAD-LOC FITTINGS

Lead piping is now prohibited on domestic plumbing for health reasons and should be replaced as soon as possible with copper or plastic. In an emergency, LEAD-LOC compression fittings can be used to connect a lead pipe to new plastic or copper pipe.

You will need

Tools Spanner; hacksaw.

Materials Lead-to-copper LEAD-LOC fitting (or similar); possibly also enough copper or plastic pipe to replace the damaged lead pipe.

1 Turn off the water supply (page 306) and drain the pipe.

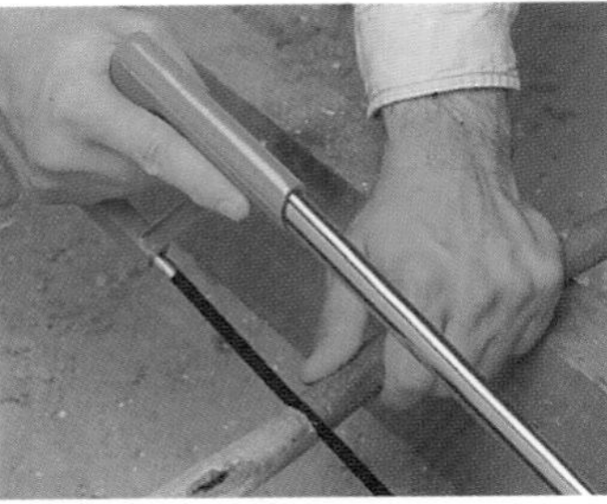

2 Cut a small section from the pipe and take it with you to the plumbers' merchant, to identify the correct LEAD-LOC fittings; lead pipes vary, even on a given size of diameter, because of the pipe's thickness.

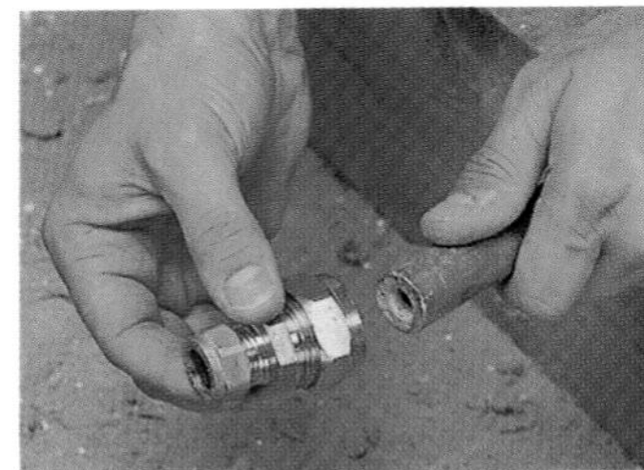

3 Slip the LEAD-LOC fitting onto the lead pipe in the same way as you would any compression fitting.

4 Connect a ½in (15mm) copper or plastic pipe to the fitting and continue the run as far as necessary.

ALTERNATIVELY, reconnect the old lead pipe to the LEAD-LOC fitting.

BANDAGING A LEAD PIPE WITH A TAPE-REPAIR KIT

In an emergency, it is possible to bandage a leaking lead pipe.

1 Turn off the water supply (see page 306) and drain the leaking pipe.

2 Hammer the split together as best you can. Clean the surrounding area with fine abrasive paper or wire wool and make sure it is dry.

3 Cover the split and 1in (25mm) each end with reinforcing tape, overlapping each layer by a half.

4 Cut a 6in (150mm) length of reinforcing tape and remove the backing. Wrap it round the pipe, covering 1in (25mm) beyond the reinforcing tape.

5 Finally wind a further layer of reinforcing tape over the entire taped area.

6 Allow two hours to pass before running any water through the pipe.

7 Get a plumber to replace all the lead pipe as soon as possible.

Installing an outside tap

A tap with a threaded nozzle against an outside wall is useful for connecting a hose. Tell your regional water company before making the installation; there may be an extra charge on your water rate for the tap. To prevent the risk of contamination by back-siphonage, you must insert a double check valve as close to the new tap as practicable. Taps incorporating check valves, and check valves to screw on to the nozzles of taps, are also available.

Installation involves running a branch pipe from the rising main through the wall to the tap. Take into account that the interior floor level could be 6-10in (150-250mm) above the damp-proof course, and that the branch pipe needs to be higher than the main stopcock and its drain cock.

The instructions given are for fitting copper piping run from a 15mm rising main with compression joints; other materials or joints could be used (pages 312-313). Make compression joints as described on page 311. You should fit a stopcock into the branch pipe, as it allows you to do the job in two stages, and in winter you can cut off the water supply to the tap and drain it to prevent frost damage. Garden plumbing kits are available containing all the necessary parts.

The best way to make a hole through the brick wall of a house is with a heavy-duty power drill and masonry bit, both of which can be hired. Choose a bit at least 13in (325mm) long and more than ¾in (20mm) in diameter to allow for a pipe sleeve – which will protect a cavity wall should a pipe burst in it.

You will need

Tools Two adjustable spanners; hacksaw; half-round file; power drill with masonry bits for fixing screws; heavy-duty power drill with masonry bits; screwdriver; two spring-clip clothes pegs; soft pencil; measuring tape; spirit level. Possibly also: shallow pan.

Materials PTFE thread-sealing tape; jointing compound; mastic wall filler; angled ½in bib tap with threaded nozzle; 15mm stopcock with compression ends; 15mm double check valve with compression ends; 15mm copper piping; plastic pipe sleeve; compression fittings as follows: 15mm equal tee (preferably with one slip end), two 15mm 90 degree elbows, one 15mm wallplate elbow (or bib-tap flange).

POSITIONING THE TAP

1 Mark the required position on the outside wall of the kitchen, as near as possible to the rising main.

2 Check that the mark is high enough for putting a bucket underneath the tap, and is at least 10in (250mm) above the damp-proof course (recognisable by a wide line of mortar in the brickwork).

3 Make another mark for the hole through the wall about 6in (150mm) above the tap mark.

4 Take measurements from the hole mark to a point such as a window, so that you can locate and check the hole position inside.

5 Mark the position of the hole on the inside of the wall. Check that it will not interfere with any inside fitting and will be above the position of the main stopcock on the rising main.

FITTING THE BRANCH PIPE INSIDE

1 Turn off (clockwise) the main stopcock, then turn on the kitchen cold tap to drain the pipe.

2 If there is a drain cock above the stopcock, turn it on to drain the rising main. A shallow pan should be sufficient to catch the amount of water (usually less than a pint) that will run out.

CHECK THE RISING MAIN

Although the rising main is normally 15mm copper piping, in some older houses it could be made of lead or galvanised steel. Get connections to a lead pipe made by a plumber. To join copper piping to galvanised steel, you will need a special tee connector.

If the rising main is 22mm, use a 22mm tee connector with a reduced 15mm branch.

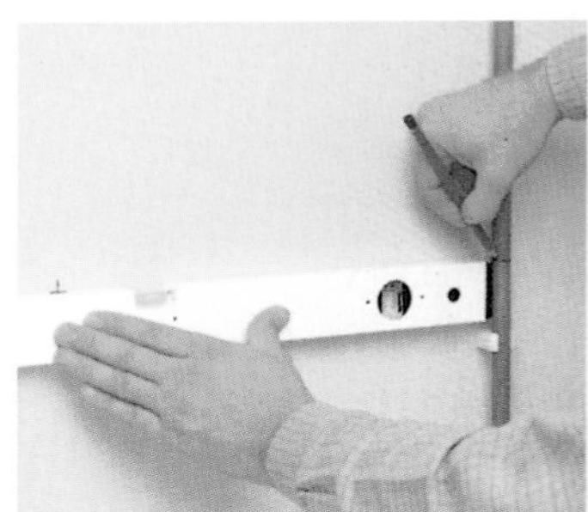

3 Mark the rising main at a point level with the hole mark on the inside wall. Make a second mark ¾in (19mm) higher.

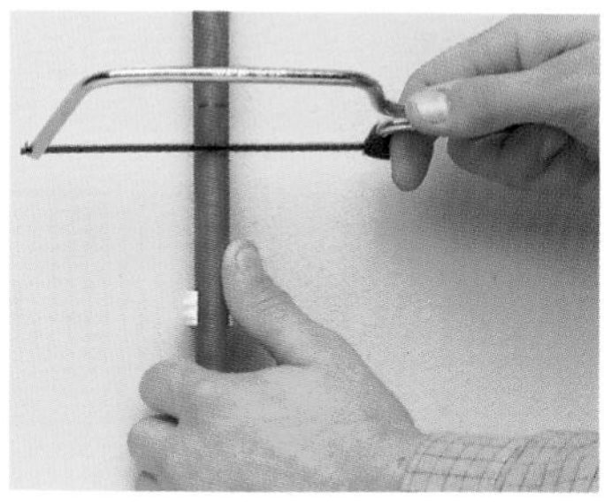

4 Cut through the rising main squarely with a hacksaw at the lowest point marked. If there was not a drain cock above the main stopcock, a small amount of water will run out as you saw through.

5 Cut through the second mark on the rising main and remove the segment of pipe.

6 Use a file to smooth the pipe ends and remove burrs, and to square the ends if necessary.

7 Using spring-clip clothes pegs to stop the caps and olives slipping down the pipe, fit the tee connector to the rising main with the branch outlet pointing towards the hole mark. Fitting will be easier if the tee has one slip end (with no pipe stop), otherwise you will have to spring the cut ends into the fitting.

8 Cut a 3in (75mm) length of piping and connect it to the branch of the tee.

9 Connect the stopcock to the piping, with its arrow mark pointing away from the rising main. Angle the stopcock with its handle leaning away from the wall.

10 Close the new stopcock by turning it clockwise. You can now turn on the main stopcock and restore the water supply.

11 Cut a 3in (75mm) length of piping and connect it to the outlet of the stopcock.

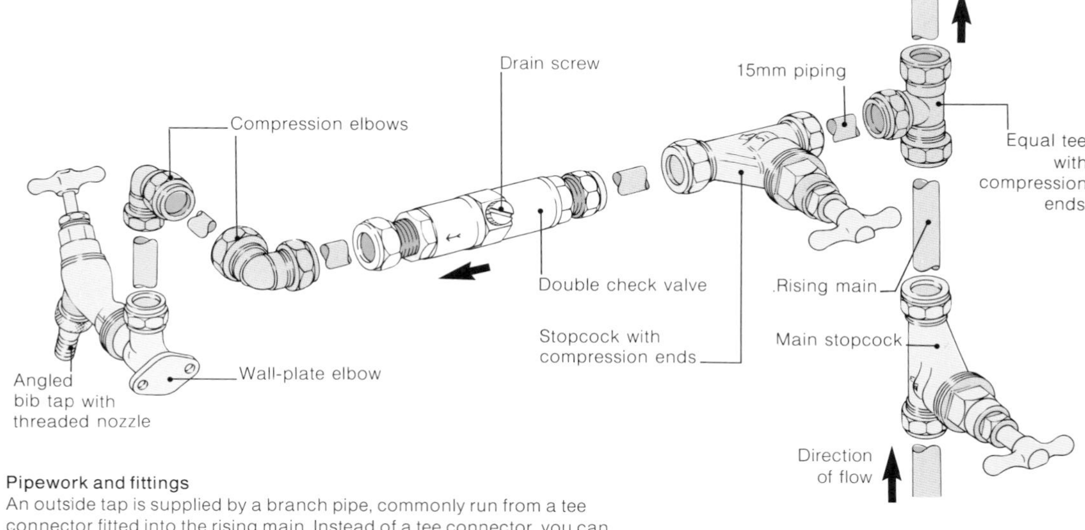

Pipework and fittings
An outside tap is supplied by a branch pipe, commonly run from a tee connector fitted into the rising main. Instead of a tee connector, you can use a self-boring tap, which can be fitted without turning off the water. No separate stopcock is then needed in the branch pipe.

12 Connect the check valve to the pipe, making sure that its arrow mark points in the same direction as the stopcock arrow.

CONNECTING THE OUTSIDE TAP

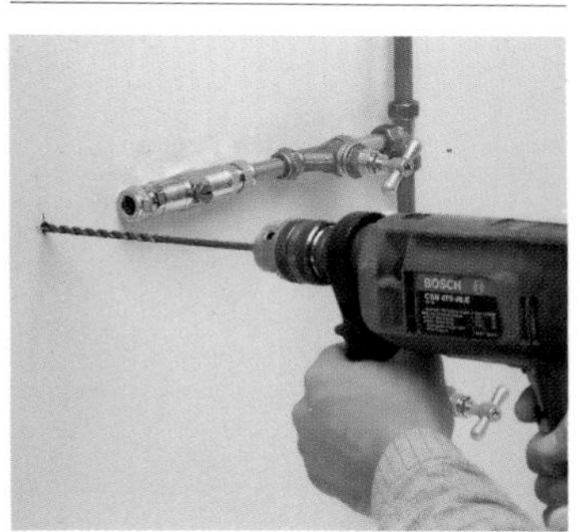

1 Use the pilot bit to drill through the wall from the inside first, making sure to keep the drill at right angles to the wall.

2 Withdraw the bit at intervals to cool it and to pull out dust.

3 Use the larger bit, working from both ends, to make a hole wide enough for the pipe sleeve to fit through easily.

4 Measure the distance from the hole to the newly fitted check valve.

5 Cut a length of pipe to reach between them, allowing extra for fitting into the check valve and an elbow connector (push the pipe into each fitting as far as it will go to check the amount). Cut a second length to go through the wall – 14in (360mm) will be long enough unless the wall is exceptionally thick.

6 Join the two lengths with an elbow connector and push the 14in (360mm) length out through the wall hole.

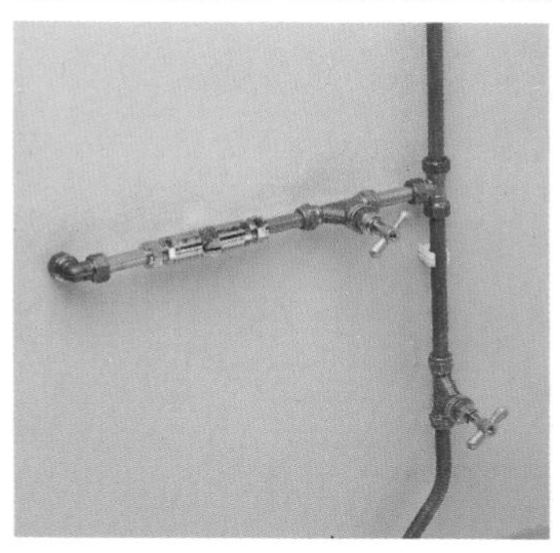

7 Connect the free end to the check valve. If this is difficult, undo the pipe at the wall hole and connect the check valve first.

8 Outside the house, cut the projecting piping to leave only 1in (25mm) sticking out from the wall.

9 Fit an elbow connector to the projecting pipe, making sure that the other end of the elbow points towards the tap position mark.

10 Measure from the elbow to the tap mark and cut another length of piping to fit the distance; again allow for fitting into the connectors.

11 Fit the pipe to the inlet of the wall-plate elbow.

12 Fit the other end of the pipe temporarily into the projecting elbow, then hold the wall plate against the wall and mark the position of the screw holes.

13 Put aside the wall-plate elbow and pipe end, and drill and plug the wall.

14 Join the pipe to the projecting elbow and fix the plate to the wall.

FITTING THE TAP

1 Bind PTFE tape several turns anti-clockwise round the tail thread.

2 Screw the tap fully into the outlet of the wall-plate elbow.

3 If the tap is not upright when screwed home, take it off again, put one or two washers over the inlet and refit. Adjust in this way until it is tight and upright.

4 Open up the new stopcock inside, and check all the pipe joints for leaks. Tighten if necessary.

5 Turn on the newly fitted outside tap and check that it is working properly.

6 Use mastic or polyurethane foam filler to seal round the pipe holes in the wall.

Fitting a waste pipe and trap

Before 1939, waste and overflow pipes for sinks, washbasins, baths and cisterns were made of lead or galvanised steel (steel-barrel). After that, copper was used until about 1960. Since then plastic has been in general use, and can be fitted as a replacement.

Plastic waste pipes are made in both metric and imperial sizes, depending on the manufacturer, and are generally 1½in or 38-42mm for sinks, 1¼in or 32-36mm for washbasins and ¾in or 21-23mm for overflow pipes from cisterns. Imperial pipes are measured by the inside diameter, metric by the outside diameter.

If you plan to fit an additional waste pipe that has to be connected to single-stack drainage (page 303), get the approval of the local authority Building Control Officer.

Connector fittings for joining waste pipes are basically the same as those for joining supply pipes (page 313); additional fittings are shown below.

CHOOSING A WASTE PIPE

MATERIAL	USES AND JOINTING METHOD	APPEARANCE AND HOW SOLD
UPVC (or PVC) (unplasticised polyvinyl chloride)	For cold-water overflow pipes from lavatory and storage cisterns. Joined by push-fit or ring-seal connectors or by solvent welding (page 314).	White, grey, brown, sometimes black. Sold in 3m (10ft) or 4m (13ft) lengths. Straight, elbow, and tee connectors available (page 313). Also adjustable elbows and straight and bent tank connectors.
MUPVC (modified unplasticised polyvinyl chloride)	For hot waste from sinks, baths, washbasins and washing machines. Joined by push-fit or ring-seal connectors, or by solvent welding (page 314). Ring seals for connection to main stack.	Grey, white, sometimes black. Sold in 4m (13ft) lengths. Connector fittings include reducers, copper and iron (steel) adaptors, and also expansion couplings, adjustable bends and stack-pipe connectors.
Polypropylene	For cold-water overflow pipes and hot waste from sinks, baths, washbasins and washing machines. Joined by push-fit or ring-seal connectors only.	White and black. Has slightly waxy surface. Sold in 3m (10ft) and 4m (13ft) lengths. Connector fittings include tank connectors, stack-pipe connectors and traps.

SPECIAL FITTINGS FOR WASTE PIPES

Locking ring-seal connector

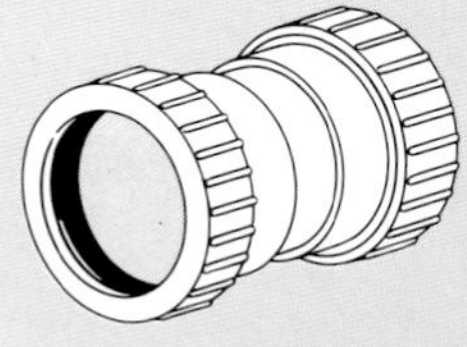

Polypropylene fitting with screw-down retaining caps, available as a rigid sleeve or a flexible connector. The sealing ring is usually ready-fitted. Can be connected to copper, plastic or steel waste pipes, but do not overtighten.

Push-fit ring-seal connector

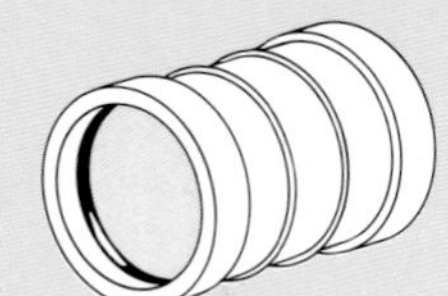

Rigid polypropylene sleeve with a slot-in push-fit connection. Cannot be connected to any existing copper, steel or plastic system unless a locking-ring fitting is interposed. The sealing ring is normally ready-fitted.

Adjustable bend

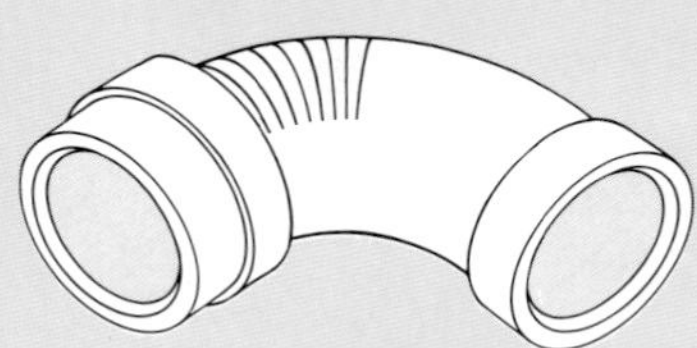

Two-piece elbow fitting made in UPVC and MUPVC. It can be adjusted to a range of angles, allowing some adjustment when fitting solvent-welded waste-pipe systems.

Expansion coupling

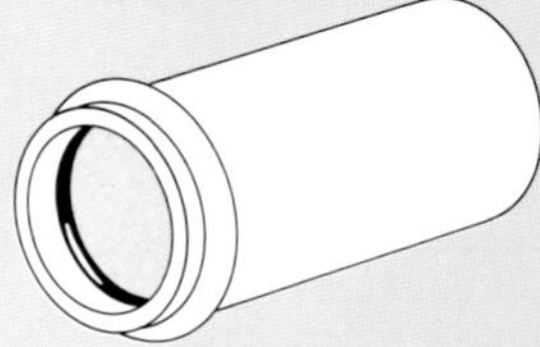

MUPVC fitting designed for a solvent-weld joint at one end and a ring-seal joint at the other. Because solvent-weld joints do not allow for heat expansion, the coupling should be inserted every 6ft (1.8m) in a long run of solvent-welded waste pipe.

Pipe strap

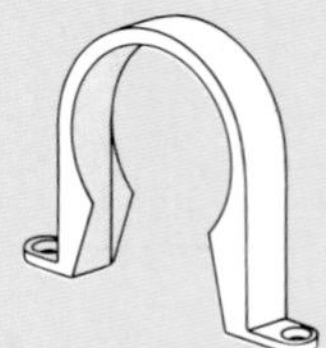

Straps or clips for supporting waste pipes are available in compatible sizes. For sloping pipes they should be fixed about every 20in (510mm). The slope must be at least ¾in (20mm) per 3ft 3in (1m) run (page 325). For vertical pipes, fix clips every 4ft (1.2m).

Stack connector

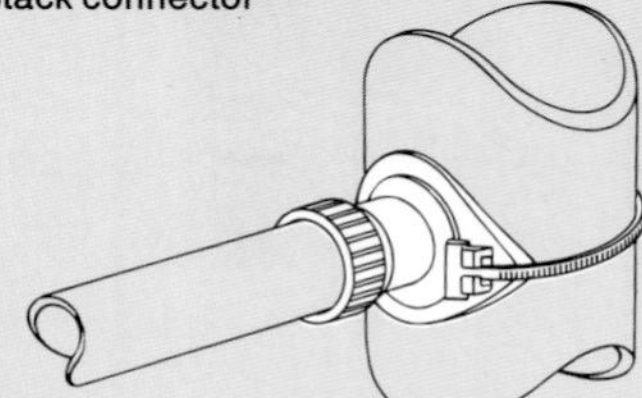

A clip-on polypropylene boss for fitting a new waste pipe into the stack, in which a hole has to be cut. For do-it-yourself use, suitable for connecting to a waste downpipe. The best method for fitting to a single stack (page 303) is to have a boss inserted by a plumber.

MAKING A RING-SEAL JOINT

Ring-seal joints are used to link polypropylene pipes. Some makers recommend chamfering the pipe ends with a special tool. Fittings can be re-used, with a new seal.

You will need

Tools Hacksaw; sharp knife; clean rag; newspaper; adhesive tape; pencil. Possibly also: manufacturer's chamfering tool.

Materials Ring-seal connector; silicone grease.

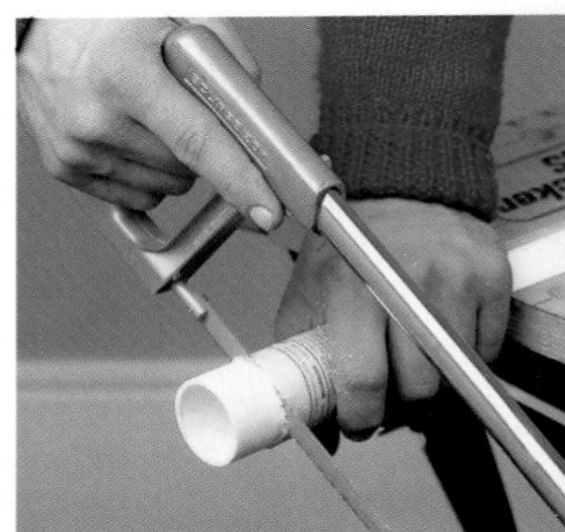

1 Wrap a sheet of newspaper round the pipe (with the ends joined flush) as a saw guide. Cut the pipe square with a hacksaw.

2 Use a sharp knife to remove fine strands of polypropylene and any rough edges from the pipe.

3 If the pipe has to be chamfered, draw a line round it about ⅜in (10mm) from the cut end. Chamfer back to the line.

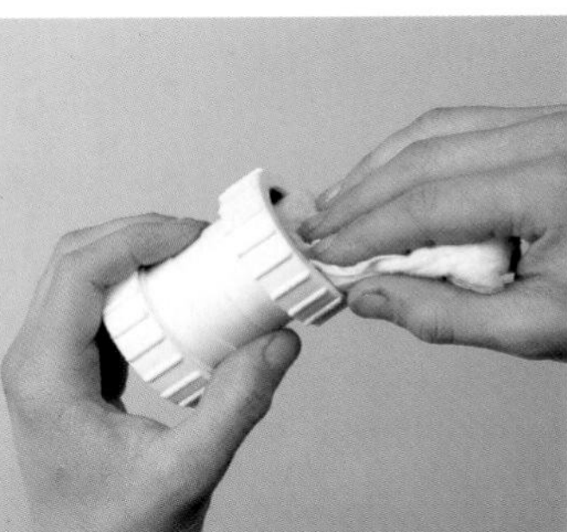

4 Wipe dust from inside the fitting and the outside of the pipe.

5 On a locking-ring connector, loosen the locking ring.

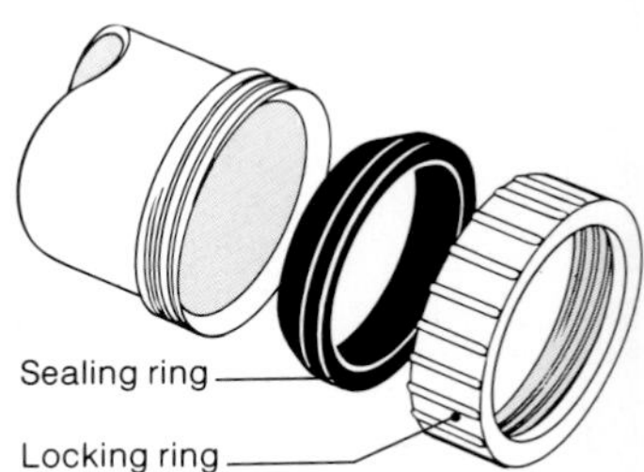

6 Make sure that the sealing ring is properly in place, with any taper pointing inwards. Remove the nut to check if necessary.

7 Lubricate the end of the pipe with silicone grease.

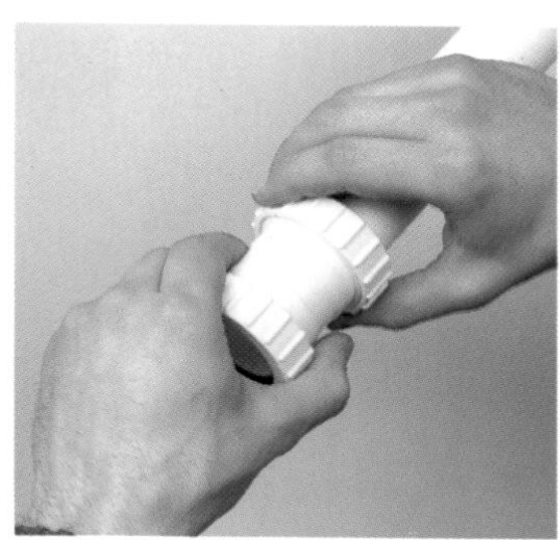

8 Push the pipe into the socket as far as the stop – a slight inner ridge about 1in (25mm) from the end. This allows a gap of about ⅜in (10mm) at the pipe end for heat expansion.

ALTERNATIVELY, if there is no stop, push the pipe in as far as it will go, mark the insertion depth with a pencil, then withdraw the pipe ⅜in (10mm) to leave an expansion gap.

9 Tighten a locking ring.

FITTING A TRAP

All waste-water outlets (from a sink, washbasin, bath, washing machine or dishwasher) are fitted with a trap – a bend in the piping that retains water and stops gas from the drain getting back into the room.

Old-style traps were simply a U-bend of lead, copper or brass with a screw-in access cap for clearing blockages. Modern traps are usually plastic, and are either tubular or bottle-shaped. They are made in suitable sizes to fit between a sink, bath or washbasin waste outlet and its waste pipe.

Tubular traps are cleaned by unscrewing the part connected to the sink waste outlet. Bottle traps have a removable lower half. They are suitable only for washbasins, not for a large-volume flow such as from a sink.

There are different types of trap for different adaptations. There may also be different outlet types (vertical or horizontal) and different seal depths. The seal – the depth of water maintained in the trap – is normally 1½in (38mm), but a trap with a deep seal of 3in (75mm) must, by law, be fitted to any appliance connected to a single-stack drainage pipe. This guards against the seal being destroyed by a heavy rush of water, allowing foul gas from the stack to enter the house.

You will need
Materials Suitable trap.

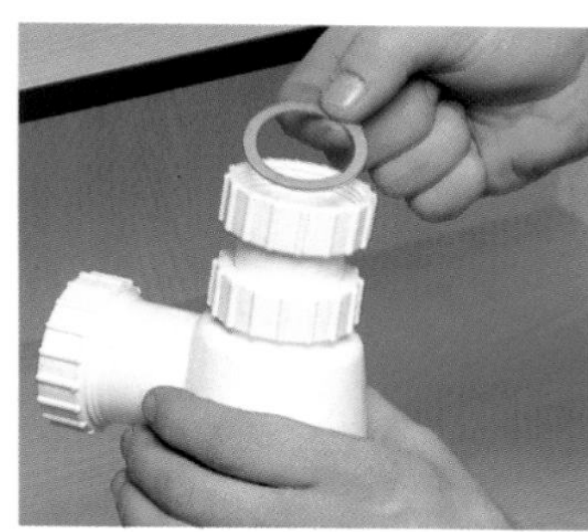

1 Check that the locking nut on the trap inlet is unscrewed and the rubber washer in position.

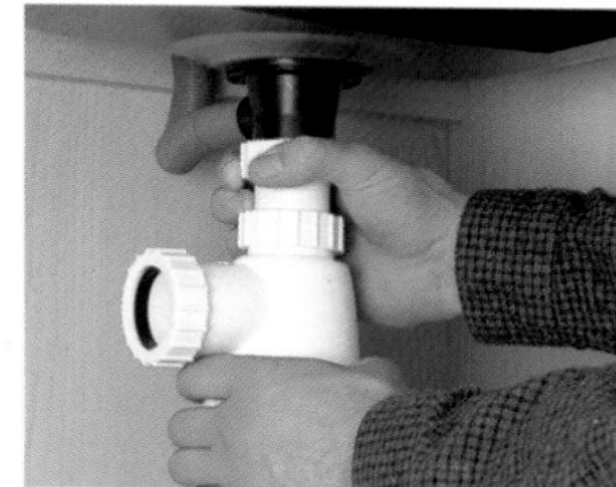

2 Push the trap inlet into the waste outlet and screw the nut onto the waste outlet thread.

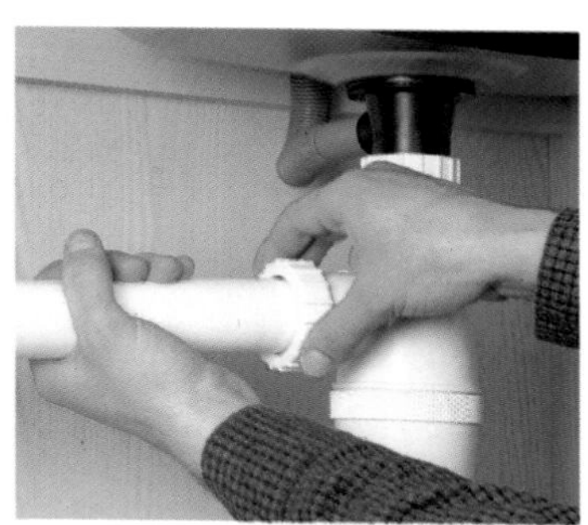

3 Connect the trap outlet to the waste pipe with a ring-seal joint.

CHOOSING A TRAP

Tubular S trap

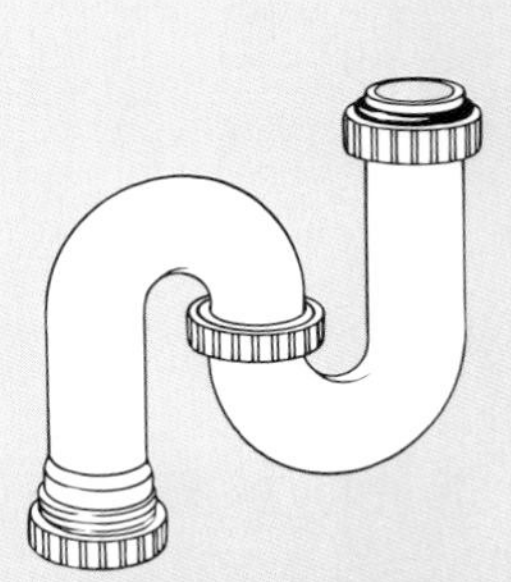

A two-piece trap for a sink or basin with an S (down-pointing) outlet. Traps are also available with a P (horizontal) outlet.

Tubular telescopic P trap

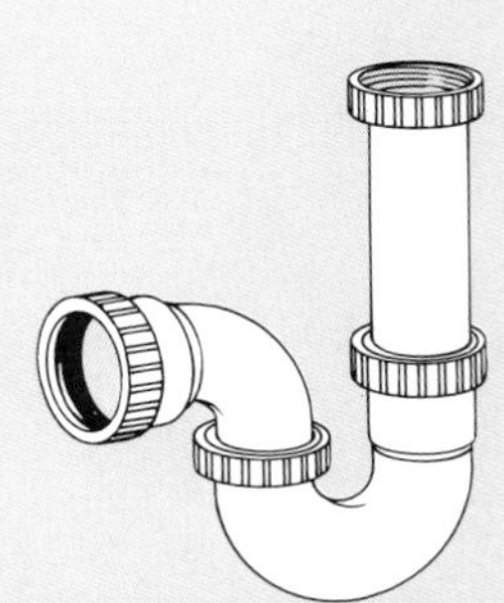

A sink or basin trap which has an adjustable inlet. Allows an existing pipe to be linked to a new sink at a different height.

Bath trap with cleaning eye and overflow pipe

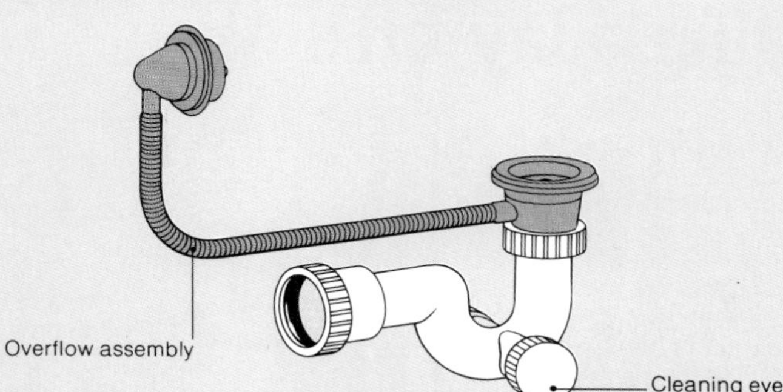

A cleaning eye can be unscrewed to clear a blockage and is useful where access is difficult. A flexible overflow pipe can be connected to a side or rear inlet on some bath traps. The overflow is a safeguard in case a tap is left running while the bath plug is in.

Washing-machine trap

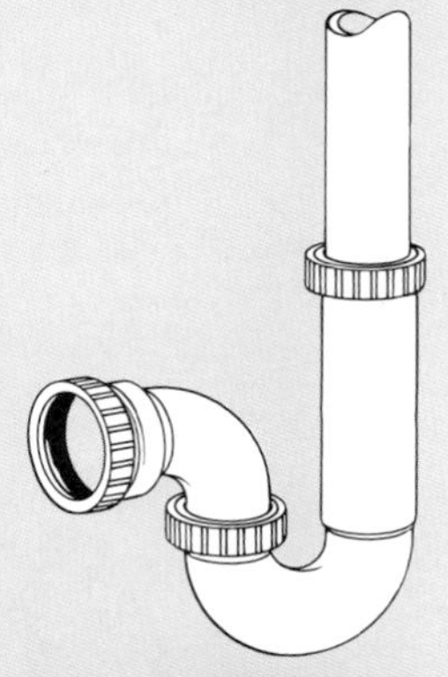

A tubular trap with a long stand-pipe for the washing-machine waste hose, and an outlet to link to the waste pipe.

Standard bottle trap

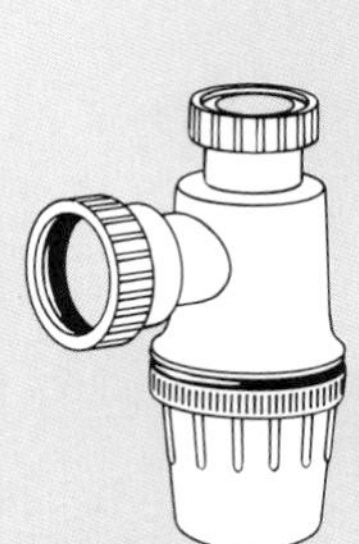

Use only for washbasins, which usually have a small outflow. Most have a P outlet, but an S converter may be available.

Telescopic bottle trap

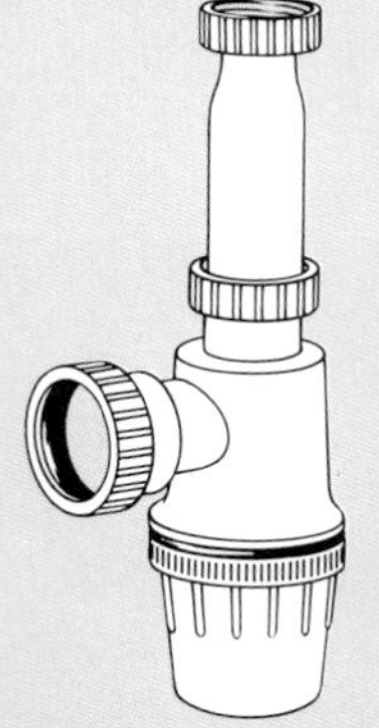

The inlet tube of the trap can be adjusted to different heights – usually up to 7in (180mm) – to make fitting to a basin easier.

Anti-siphon bottle trap

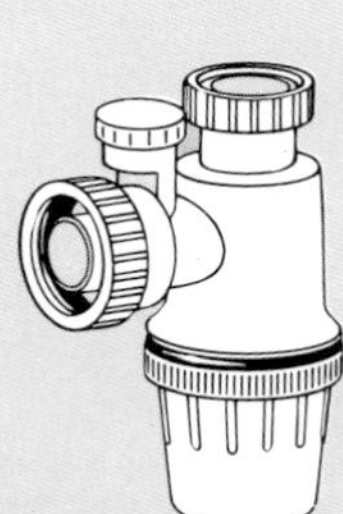

Designed to hold a water reserve to re-seal the trap if the seal is lost. Use where there is an occasional heavy flow, or long, steep pipe run.

Replacing a sink

You may want to replace a modern sink that has pillar taps with an old fashioned deep fireclay sink that has bib taps, or vice versa. Some sinks have two tap holes, or holes for a two hole mixer. Others have only one hole for a monobloc mixer (page 307). All have an outlet hole – either a $1\frac{1}{2}$in (38mm) hole for fitting a standard waste outlet or a $3\frac{1}{2}$in (90mm) hole for fitting a waste disposal unit.

There are two basic sink designs – lay-on or inset. Lay-on (or fit-on) sinks rest on a unit of the same size as the sink rim. They are being replaced by inset types, which fit into the worktop and may be one unit or a separate bowl and drainer.

Sinks are available in a range of sizes and patterns. They are typically about 20in (500mm) wide and vary in length from about 31in (780mm) to 5ft (1.5m). Patterns vary from one bowl and a drainer in one unit, to combinations of one and a half, two and two and a half bowls with a drainer, two drainers, or no drainer at all. Drainers can be to the right or left side of the unit.

Stainless steel is the commonest sink material. Enamelled pressed steel and more expensive polycarbonate are available in a range of colours. Easy-to-clean ceramic sinks are the toughest and most expensive, but china banged against them may chip.

CHANGING THE SINK HEIGHT

Before choosing a sink, check the height of the waste outlet of the existing sink. The new sink may be higher or lower depending on the bowl depth or the height of a new support unit. A typical waste-outlet height from a bowl 7in (180mm) deep in a unit $34\frac{1}{4}$in (870mm) high would be 27in (690mm).

If the new outlet will be higher than the old one, use a telescopic trap. If the new outlet will be lower, either raise the unit height (undesirable for a short person) by adding a wooden plinth, or reposition the waste pipe.

If the pipe runs into an outside drain, you may need a new exit hole in the wall. If the pipe links to a drainage or single stack, make a new connection. The downward slope should be about $\frac{3}{4}$in (19mm) for every 3ft 3in (1m) of run. Connecting the waste pipe to a single stack should be left to a plumber.

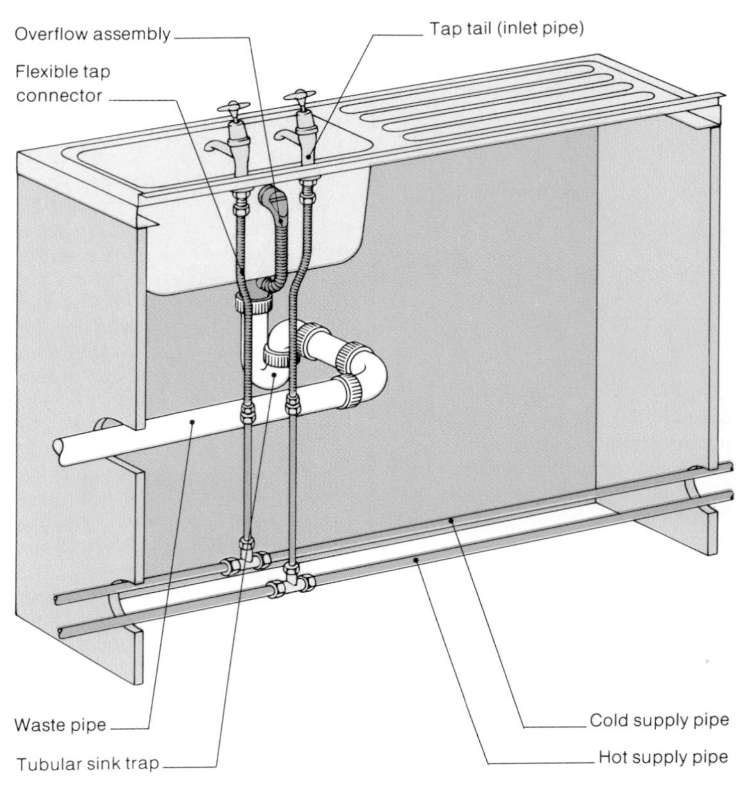

Fitting a lay-on sink

Unless you intend keeping the existing taps, fit the new taps and waste outlet to the new sink before you disconnect the old one. This gives more working room, and the water supply will not be cut off for so long.

Only one trap is needed for a unit with more than one bowl, unless one of the bowls has a waste-disposal unit. Fit the trap to the bowl nearest to the waste pipe and drain. A bowl with a waste-disposal unit must have its own separate tubular trap and waste pipe.

You will need

Tools Adjustable spanner or open-ended spanner (probably size $\frac{13}{16}$in); pair of long-nose pliers; steel tape measure; spirit level; damp cloth; bucket. Possibly also: pipe wrench; screwdriver; hacksaw; wooden batten at least 2ft (610mm) long; length of string.

Materials Sink; two $\frac{1}{2}$in pillar taps or kitchen mixer; combined waste outlet and overflow; tubular sink trap; two flat plastic washers for $\frac{1}{2}$in taps; two $\frac{1}{2}$in tap top-hat spacing washers; two $\frac{1}{2}$in tap connectors (preferably flexible ones); two $1\frac{1}{2}$in waste-outlet washers; non-setting mastic filler; thread-sealing PTFE tape.

FITTING THE TAPS

1 Remove the back nuts from each of the new tap tails (inlet pipes).

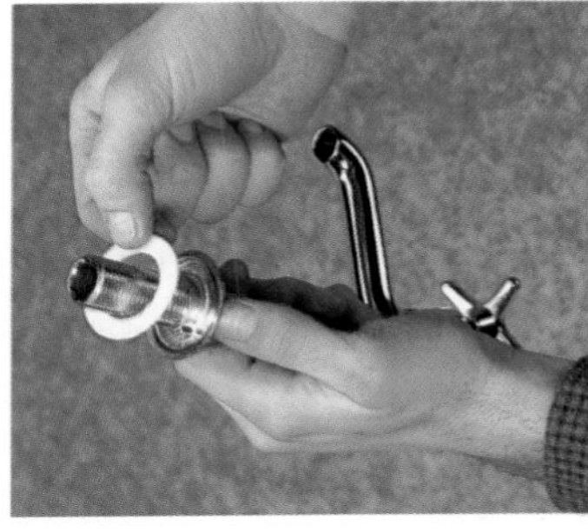

2 Slip a flat plastic washer over each tap tail.

3 Note the position of the hot and cold taps on the existing sink. The hot tap is normally on the left and the cold tap on the right as you face the sink.

4 Push the tail of each new tap through the appropriate hole (the hot or cold position) in the new sink.

5 Slip on a top-hat washer to cover the small amount of the protruding unthreaded shank. The washer will allow the nut to fully tighten against the sink.

6 Replace the back nut and tighten firmly with the adjustable spanner. Then fit a top-hat washer and back nut to the second tap.

7 Using a spanner, screw on a tap connector to each tap tail.

FITTING THE WASTE OUTLET

1 Dismantle the new waste-and-overflow unit. (If the waste outlet is a type with no tail, see step 3, page 327.)

2 Smear plenty of mastic filler round the sink outlet hole.

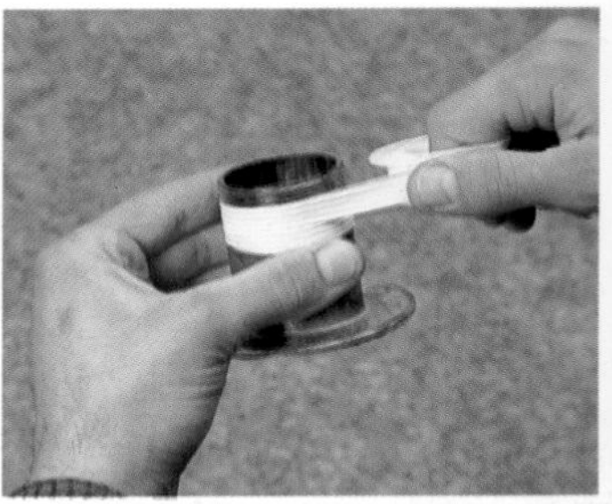

3 Bind the threaded tail of the waste-outlet fitting three times anticlockwise with PTFE tape.

4 Put the waste fitting through the waste hole with the body slots facing back and front. Bed the rim in the mastic filler.

5 Under the sink, slip a flat plastic washer over the protruding tail of the outlet. Then fix the ring (banjo) of the flexible overflow pipe over the outlet tail, covering the body slots. Finally fit another flat washer.

6 Screw on the back nut. To stop the waste outlet moving, hold the grid from above with long-nose pliers while you tighten the back nut firmly with a spanner.

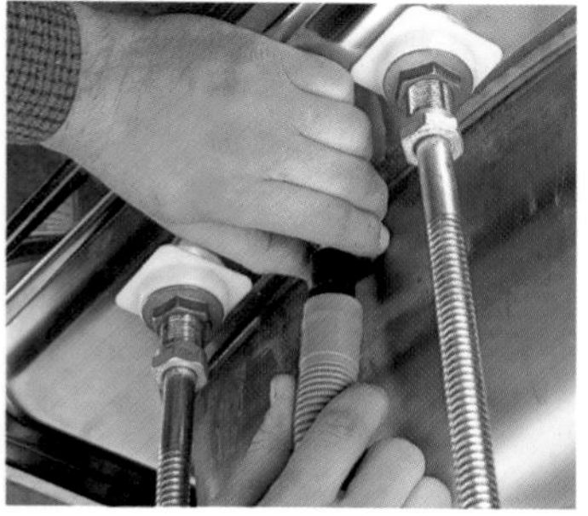

7 Connect the top of the flexible overflow pipe to the sink overflow outlet; it may screw or push on.

8 Remove surplus mastic filler from round the waste rim inside the sink with a damp cloth.

DISCONNECTING AN OLD LAY-ON SINK

1 Cut off the water supply to the taps (page 306).

2 Turn the kitchen taps fully on until the water flow stops. A few pints will be left in the pipes.

3 Get under the sink and undo the cap nut of each tap connector, then disconnect the supply pipes from the old taps. (The nuts are not usually difficult to undo, but if they do prove difficult, do not struggle with them. Use a hacksaw to cut through each supply pipe a little way below the tap connector.)

4 Unscrew the nut connecting the waste outlet to the sink trap (you may need a pipe wrench to apply sufficient force).

5 Put a bucket under the trap and disconnect the trap.

6 Check whether there are any brackets fixing the sink to the wall. If so, remove them.

7 Lift the sink off the support unit. It is not usually very heavy.

FITTING A NEW LAY-ON SINK

1 Use a spirit level on all four sides to check that the top of the support unit is horizontal. If it is off level, level it by adjusting the feet or wedging the base.

2 Place the new sink (with the taps, tap connectors and waste outlet already in position) on the support unit.

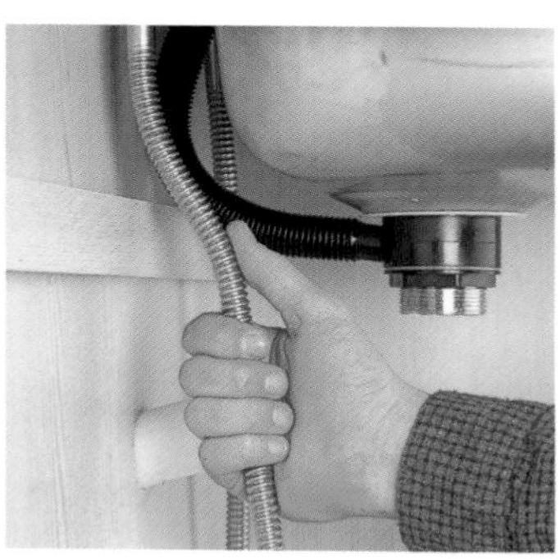

3 Fit the tap connectors to the supply pipes. Flexible connectors can be bent a little way as necessary to allow for differences in the height and alignment of the supply pipes.

4 Fit the new trap to the waste outlet and connect it to the waste pipe (page 319).

5 Restore the water supply and check for leaks, tightening joints as necessary.

Fitting an inset sink

Standard inset sinks may have two holes for hot and cold pillar taps, but many have only one 1⅜in (35mm) diameter hole for a monobloc mixer (page 307). The waste-outlet fitting (and flexible overflow pipe, if needed) is usually supplied with the sink. Ceramic sinks usually have a built-in overflow duct.

Installation is similar to a lay-on sink, but fitting to the sink unit is different. So is connecting a monobloc mixer, which has two flexible tails projecting from the back-nut tail. They are connected with reducer fittings if the tails are 12mm diameter (some are 15mm).

Mark the sink outline on the worktop and cut out the area with the worktop on the unit (pages 187, 188). You will have to get under the sink to secure the sink-fixing clips. Seal the cut out with oil-based paint or varnish to protect it from water.

You will need

Tools Two adjustable spanners for monobloc mixer reducer couplings;

Continued overleaf

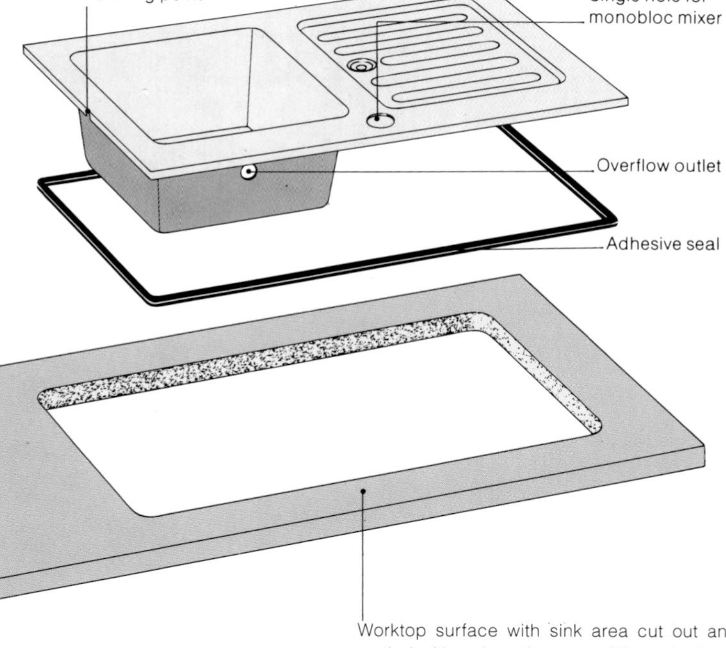

Fitting an inset sink (continued)

long-nose pliers; screwdriver; a damp cloth; two spring-clip clothes-pegs; jig saw or pad saw; power drill and wood bit, pencil. Possibly also: hacksaw.
Materials Inset sink (fixings are usually provided); monobloc kitchen mixer with top and bottom washers; two compression fittings (probably 15mm × 12mm reducers); non-setting mastic filler (silicone rubber type for plastic); PTFE thread-sealing tape.

1 Mark the required aperture on the worktop according to the sink manufacturer's instructions. Cut it out with an electric jig saw.

2 With the sink on its face, seal round the rim as instructed, and fit any earthing needed (page 359) into the slot marked E on the rim.

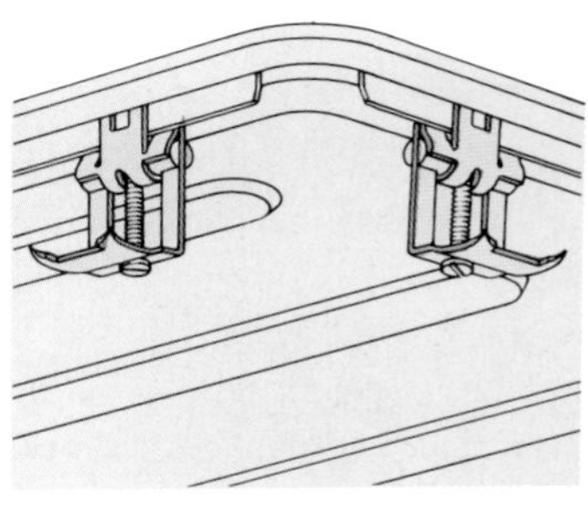

3 Fit the securing clips to the sink following the maker's instructions. They are commonly hinged clips that are screwed to the sink rim and can be adjusted to fit worktops 1in–1¾in (27mm–43mm) thick.

4 Fit the taps or mixer and also the waste outlet in the same way as for a lay-on sink, following any special instructions from the manufacturer. Do not fit the couplings to monobloc tap tails at this stage.

5 Fit the sink to the worktop as instructed, tightening the clips gradually in sequence.

6 With the sink in position, connect the trap, waste pipe and earth, and restore the water supply as for a lay-on sink.

FITTING A WASTE-DISPOSAL UNIT

A waste-disposal unit is fitted to a sink waste outlet 3½in (90mm) in diameter. A steel sink with a 1½in (38mm) hole can be enlarged with a special cutter normally on hire from unit suppliers.

The unit is screwed to the waste-outlet tail, and a tubular sink trap fits between the unit base and the waste pipe. Fitting instructions are supplied by the manufacturer.

CONNECTING A MONOBLOC MIXER

1 Check that the supply pipes are the right height for fitting the tap tails. Cut the pipes if they are too high. (They are unlikely to be too low, as the tap tails are long and flexible.)

2 Check whether the hot pipe is on the left as you face the sink.

3 Undo the cap nuts on the pipe (15mm) end of each connector, and slip each nut and olive onto the pipe. Put a spring-clip clothespeg below each to stop it slipping down the pipe.

4 Undo the tail (12mm) end of one of the reducer fittings and fit it onto a tap tail with the olive.

5 Insert the tap tail into the appropriate supply pipe and screw the fitting together until it is finger tight at both ends.

6 Hold the fitting steady with one spanner while you give each nut 1¼ turns with another spanner.

7 Fit the other tap tail to its supply pipe in the same way.

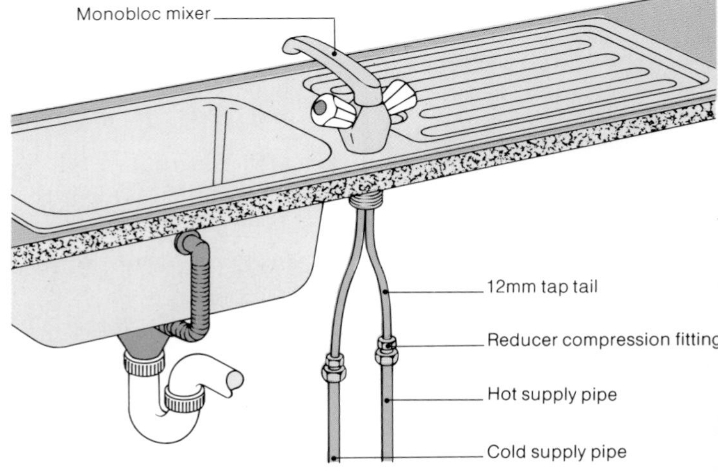

Dealing with a blocked sink

If the sink is slow to empty, there is probably a build up of grease in the trap and waste pipe. Or a tassel of accumulated hairs or cloth fibres may be clinging below the grid on the plug hole.

If the water will not run away at all, accumulated grease has built up to a complete blockage, or something such as a bone or hair grip is obstructing the waste pipe. If you cannot find an obstruction in the trap or waste pipe, clear the drain (page 459).

You will need
Tools Possibly a length of wire; sink-waste plunger; sink auger or a length of expanding curtain wire (page 304); bucket.
Materials Possibly caustic soda or proprietary chemical or enzyme cleaner; petroleum jelly.

Sink slow to empty

1 If the sink is slow to empty, smear petroleum jelly on the rim of the plug hole to protect it. Then apply caustic soda or a chemical or enzyme cleaner according to the manufacturer's instructions.

2 If necessary, clear hairs from the grid with a hook of wire, working from above.

Sink completely blocked

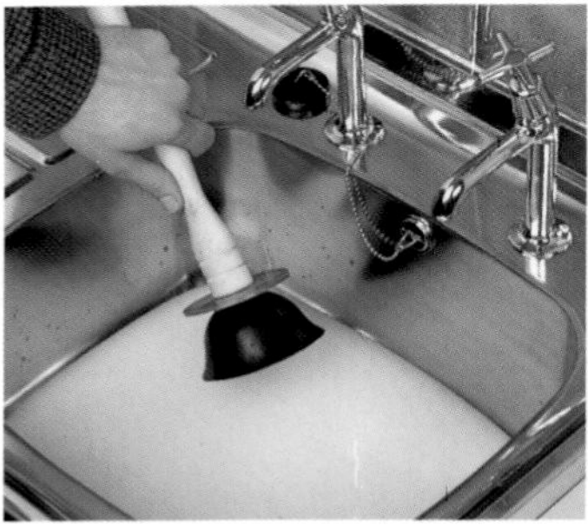

1 If the water will not run away at all, place the sink plunger cup squarely over the plug hole.

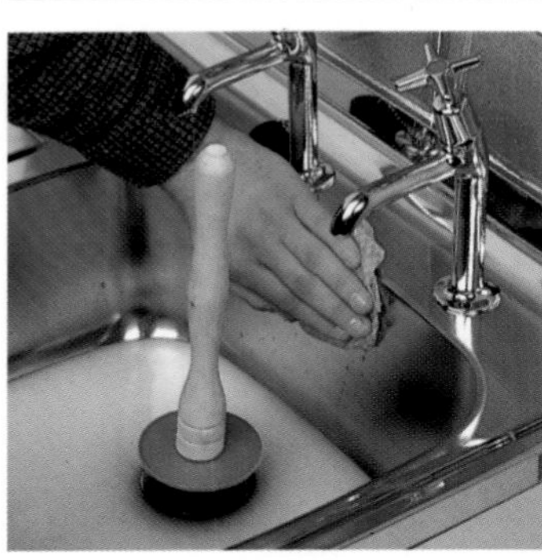

2 Stuff a damp cloth firmly into the overflow opening and hold it there. This stops air escaping through the hole and dissipating the force you build up by plunging.

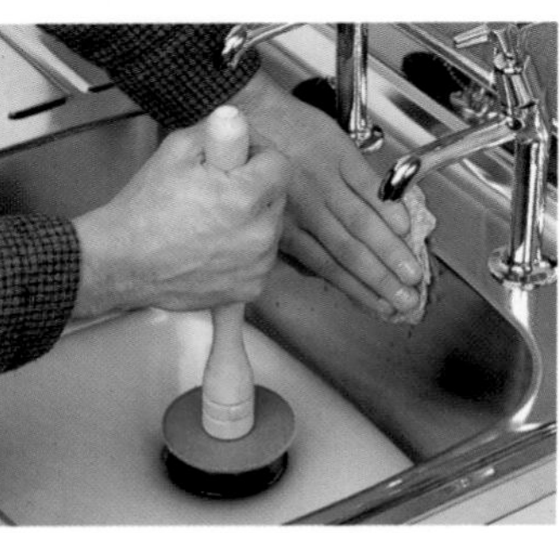

3 Pump the plunger sharply up and down. If the blockage does not clear, continue for a few minutes.

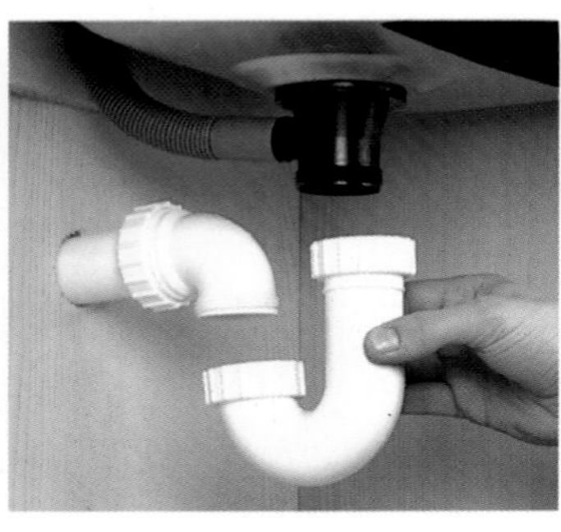

4 If plunging fails, put a bucket under the sink and open the trap.

HELPFUL TIP

If you have a vacuum cleaner that is designed to cope with liquids, you can use it to try to dislodge a blockage in a sink trap. Press a cloth over the overflow in the sink. Then place the suction tube of the vacuum over the plughole and switch on. This will probably loosen the blockage sufficiently to allow it to be carried away by the water flow through the trap.

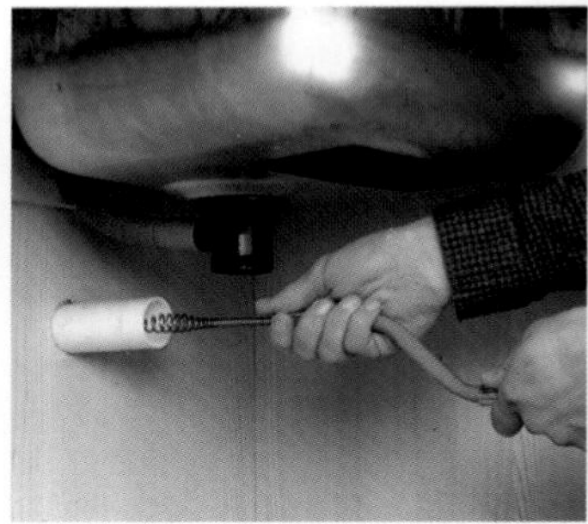

5 If the obstruction is not in the trap, use a sink auger to probe the waste pipe and dislodge the blockage.

CHOOSING A WASHBASIN OR BIDET

Vitreous china (ceramic) washbasins mounted on pedestals are the commonest type, but there are a number of other materials and methods of support available.

Order the taps or mixer and other necessary fittings at the same time as the basin. Many modern basins and bidets have only one 1$\frac{3}{8}$in (35mm) diameter tap hole for a monobloc mixer (page 307). Two-hole types with holes about 7in (180mm) apart for two separate taps or a two-hole mixer are also available, as well as three-hole mixer types with separate holes for each tap and the spout.

Some ceramic basins have a centre tap hole only, with semi-punched holes each side that can be tapped out if required. A reputable supplier should do this for you, because inexpert attempts can damage the basin.

A basin or bidet waste-outlet hole is 1$\frac{1}{4}$in (32mm) across. The waste-outlet fitting should include a plug, but a chain for the plug may be an extra. Ceramic basins usually have a built-in overflow duct. On other types, a flexible overflow pipe has to be fitted.

TYPE OF WASHBASIN OR BIDET	TYPICAL SIZE AND MATERIAL	ADVANTAGES AND DISADVANTAGES	COMMON FIXING METHOD
Pedestal basin 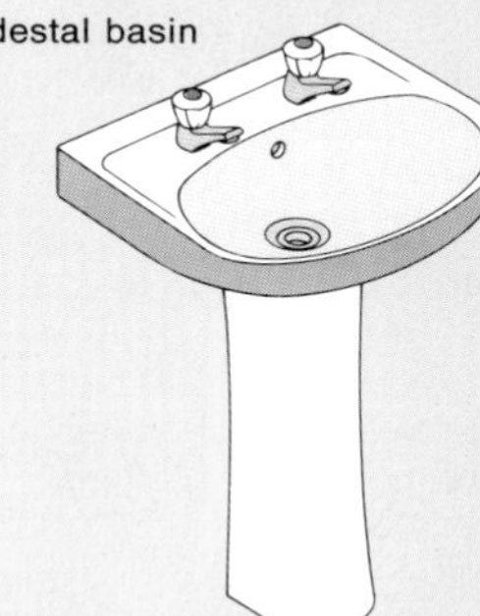	Length: 600mm (about 24in); Width (front to back): 400mm–500mm (16in–20in); Rim height from floor: about 800mm (32in); Bowl depth: about 125mm (5in). Usually made of vitreous china.	Pedestal conceals the plumbing, although connecting the pipes can be awkward. Height not adjustable. Pedestal should not be sole support for basin – other fixings needed.	Back of basin screwed or bracketed to wall through screw holes in concealed recess. Basin may be joined to pedestal with fixing clips or mastic cement. Pedestal screwed to floor through holes at rear. Fixing screws and rubber washers not usually supplied with the basin.
Wall-hung basin 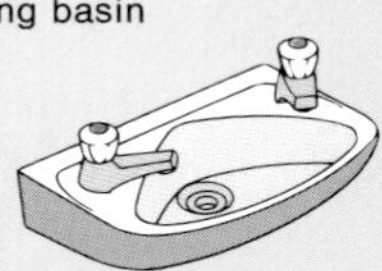	Size as above or smaller. For example, length 300mm (12in); width (front to back) 350mm (about 14in). Usually made of vitreous china.	Useful where floor space is fairly limited. Corner-fitting types are available. Can be fixed at any height (low in a nursery, for example). Waste trap is visible unless boxed in. Cheaper than pedestal types.	1. Back of basin screwed to wall with special screws through concealed holes. 2. Basin bolted to side brackets or combined wall plate/waste bracket (see right). 3. Basin hung on concealed hangers (see right).
Vanity or countertop basin 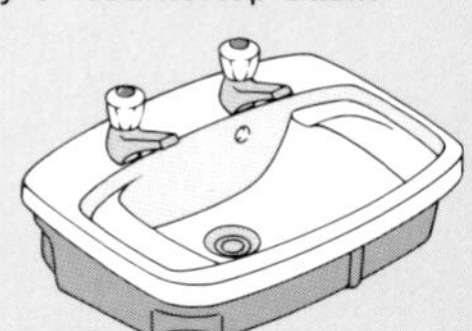	Length: 500mm–560mm (20in–22in); Width (front to back): 400mm–450mm (16in–18in). Usually enamelled pressed steel or acrylic plastic. Sometimes vitreous china.	Designed to fit into the surface of a unit with a laminated plastic or tiled top. Often used in a bedroom. Plumbing is concealed in the unit, which also provides cupboard space for toilet requisites.	Basin rim rests on edge of cut-out in unit top (or on recessed ledge). May rest on a ribbon of mastic or sealant, or have a rubber sealing ring and securing clips.
Semi-countertop basin 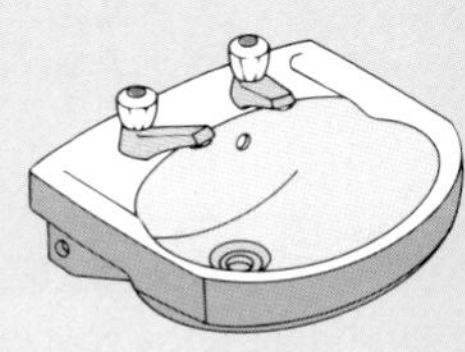	Length: 560mm (22in); Width (front to back): 450mm (18in). Usually made of vitreous china.	Designed to be partly recessed into a narrow unit fitted against a wall, with the plumbing concealed.	Securing clips screwed to the underside of the countertop on each side, fit into side slots in the basin (see right). Basin rim set on ribbon of mastic or sealant.
Over-rim supply bidet  	Length: 350mm (13$\frac{1}{2}$in); Width (front to back): 600mm (24in); Rim height from floor: 400mm (16in). Usually vitreous china.	Fitted with two taps or a mixer above the bowl, like a washbasin. May be floor standing or wall hung.	Screwed to the floor inside rear of pedestal. Wall-hung types (for concealed plumbing) are bolted at rear through wall to metal support brackets.
Rim-supply bidet with rising spray 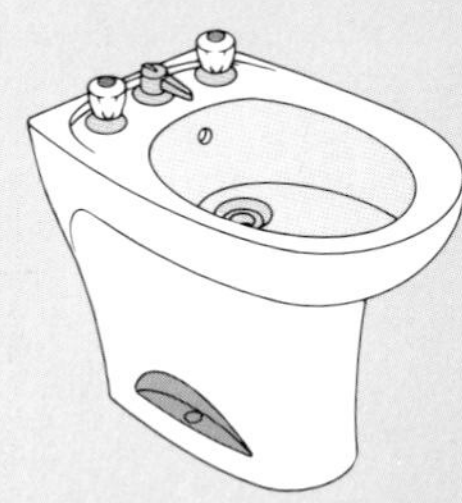	As over-rim supply type above.	Water enters under rim, so warm water warms the rim. A control knob between the taps diverts water to an ascending spray. More expensive than an over-rim bidet. Must be installed in accordance with Water Authority requirements. Not suitable for DIY.	Floor standing, as over-rim supply bidet.

TYPICAL FIXINGS FOR WALL-HUNG AND SEMI-COUNTERTOP BASINS

For a wall-hung basin, make sure the wall is solid enough for the type of fixing (page 230) and the basin weight. Special types of fixing are usually supplied with the basin, but not screws for a wall or floor.

Wall plate and waste bracket

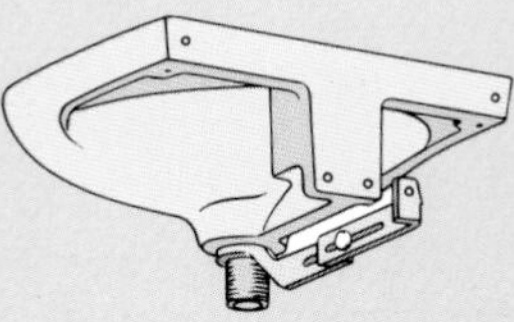

The waste outlet of the wall-hung basin fits through the bracket, with its back nut below the bracket.

Concealed wall hangers

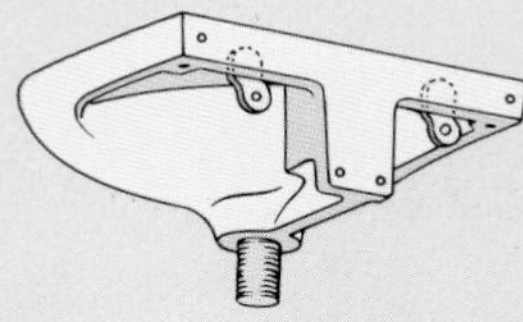

A pair of hangers for a wall-hung basin screwed to the wall. They fit into slots in the back of the basin to support it.

Towel-rail side brackets

A pair of side brackets for a wall-hung basin is screwed to the wall at the back. They bolt into the basin at the front.

Semi-countertop basin

The basin is fixed to clips screwed to the underside of the countertop. The clips fit into holes in the basin side and have a tightening screw to secure them.

Replacing a washbasin or bidet

A washbasin is fitted to the plumbing in much the same way as a kitchen sink. The main difference is in the way the basin is fixed to the wall (page 323).

There may also be slight differences in the washers needed for tap fitting, because of the different thicknesses of basin materials.

As with a sink, do as much of the plumbing as possible before you fix the basin in position. Fit an over-rim supply bidet in the same way as a washbasin.

You will need

Tools Basin wrench; spanner; long-nose pliers; steel tape measure; spirit level; damp cloth; screwdriver; bucket. Possibly also: hacksaw.

Materials Basin or bidet; two ½in taps or mixer, with washers; deep seal or anti-siphon bottle trap (page 319); waste outlet with two flat plastic washers, plug and chain; two ½in tap connectors (preferably flexible ones); non-setting mastic filler (silicone rubber type for acrylic basin); PTFE thread-sealing tape; fixing screws for wall (and floor if required) – preferably No. 12 roundhead wood screws; rubber washers to fit between screws and basin; waterproof sealer. Possibly also: flexible overflow assembly.

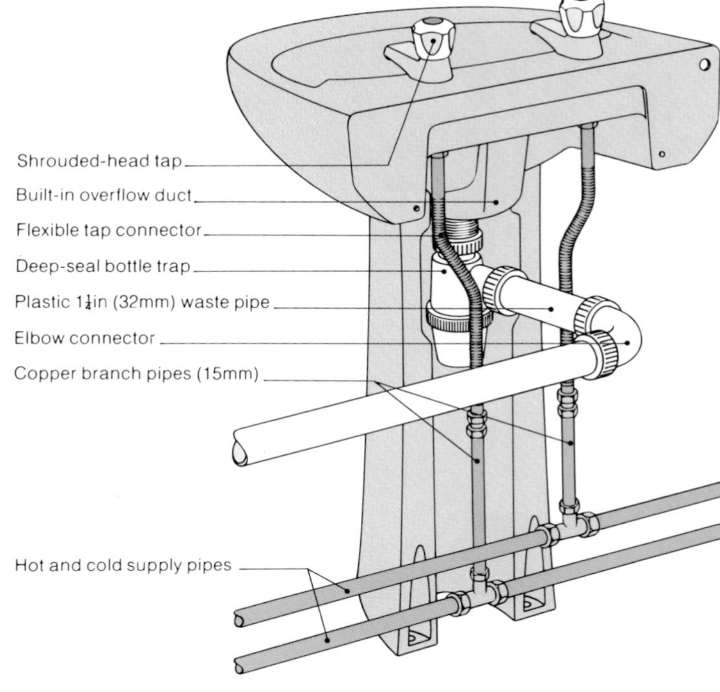

Connecting a washbasin

The connections for a washbasin are similar to the connections for a kitchen sink (page 320). Ceramic basins have a built-in overflow duct, but others usually need a flexible overflow assembly that connects to the waste outlet in the same way as for a sink (page 320), or a bath (page 327).

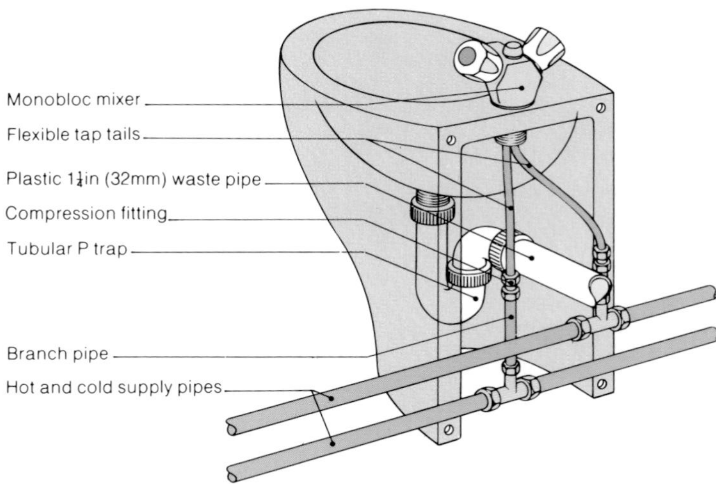

Connecting a bidet

An over-rim supply bidet is connected to the hot and cold water supply pipes in the same way as a washbasin.

1 Fit the taps or mixer unit and the tap connectors to the new basin in the same way as for a sink (page 320). Use the top-hat washer only if necessary to take up space on the tap tail and ensure a firm fixing. It is more likely to be needed on an acrylic or enamelled pressed steel basin than a ceramic basin.

2 Unless the basin is to be wall-hung on a waste bracket, fit the waste outlet to the new basin in the same way as for a sink (page 320). Ensure that the slots in the outlet tail line up with the outlet of a built-in overflow duct.

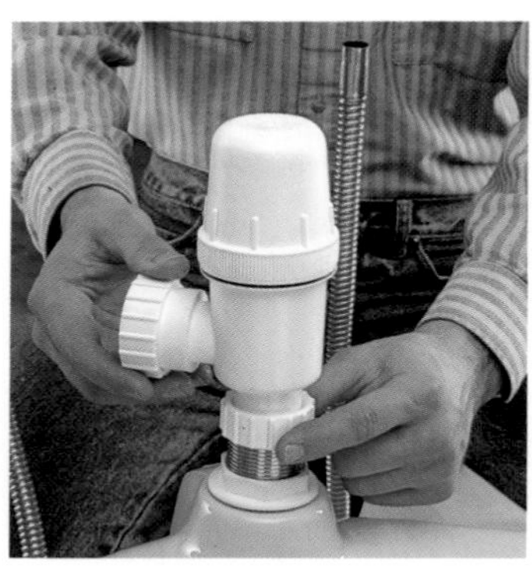

3 Fit the bottle trap to the tail of the waste outlet.

4 Cut off the water supply (page 306).

5 Disconnect or cut through the supply pipes to the taps on the old basin (page 321), and disconnect the old trap from the waste pipe.

6 Unscrew and remove the fixing screws or support brackets from the old basin and remove it.

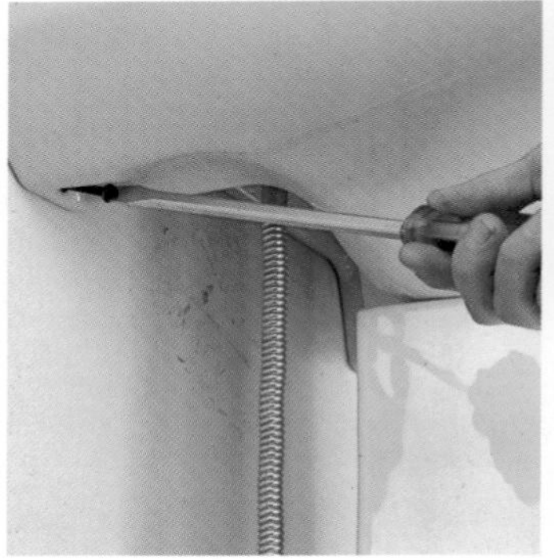

7 Plug the wall or fit any supporting brackets for the new basin, and fix it in position (page 323). For a wall-hung basin with a waste bracket, fit the waste outlet, which slots through the bracket, and then fit the bottle trap to the tail of the waste outlet.

8 Connect the taps or mixer to the supply pipes in the same way as for sink taps (page 320).

9 Connect the outlet at the base of the bottle trap to the waste pipe (page 319).

10 Restore the water supply and check all joints for leaks. If necessary, tighten them.

11 Seal the edge between the basin and the wall or countertop with a waterproof sealer.

HELPFUL TIP

If you want to renew the taps on an existing basin, it is often easier to remove the basin from its supports. Even with a basin wrench, the back nuts can be extremely difficult to undo. With the basin upside down on the floor, it is easier to apply penetrating oil, and also to exert enough force without damaging the basin.

If removing a basin is impracticable, the tap handles and headgear can be replaced with a tap conversion kit, sold in packs with fitting instructions (page 309). Some kits have bushes to fit taps of various sizes.

Installing a washbasin in a bedroom

Washbasins, particularly vanity (countertop) basins, are very often installed in a bedroom to ease the demand on a family bathroom. Get permission from the local building control officer before you start work. The chief problem when planning where to put the basin is organising the drainage.

1 Choose a site for the basin as near as possible to the bathroom drainage and supply pipes – ideally against a wall adjoining the bathroom.

2 Work out how to route the waste water from the basin to an outside drain (see below).

3 Trace the routes of existing hot and cold supply pipes and work out the shortest route possible (*Planning pipe routes*, page 312).

4 Check that the basin position will allow sufficient space for a person using it. Generally, allow at least 25in (640mm) bending room in front of the basin, and at least 3ft 7in (1090mm) elbow room centred on the basin.

5 Check that the installation of the basin will not interfere with any electric cables, gas pipes or other fittings, especially where you need to make a hole in a wall.

6 Fit the taps, waste outlet and trap to the new washbasin as described (facing page). Use a deep-seal trap (or an anti-siphon trap, if required).

7 Cut off the water supply and use tee connectors to run hot and cold-water pipes to the basin site as 15mm branch pipes from the supply pipes to the bathroom (Choosing pipes and joints, pages 312-313). Be careful not to tee into the cold supply feeding a shower, unless it has a thermostatic mixer (page 329).

If you have to tee into a 22mm distribution pipe, you will need an unequal tee connector with two 22mm ends and a 15mm branch.

8 Fit the waste pipe in position (*Waste pipes and fittings*, page 318). If you have to make a hole through the wall, do it as for installing an outside tap (page 316).

9 Fit the basin or basin unit to the wall and connect it to the supply pipes and waste pipe (facing page).

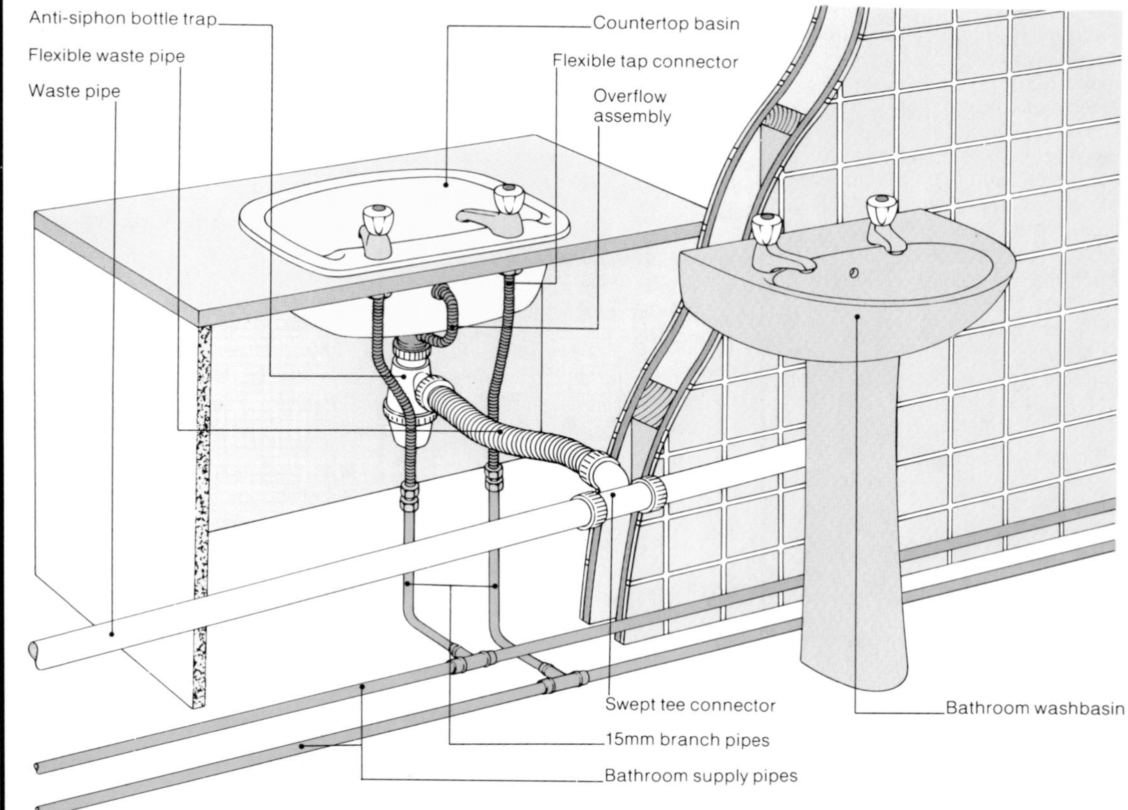

ROUTING THE WASTE PIPE

The route of a waste pipe to an outside drain should be as short and straight as possible, and not too steep. If the waste pipe is too long and steep, the rush of water emptying from the basin is likely to leave a partial vacuum behind it. This results in the water seal in the trap being sucked out, and is known as self-siphonage.

The waste pipe should not be any longer than 5ft 9in (1.75m). It must slope enough for the water to run away – not less than ¾in (19mm) for each 3ft 3in (1m) of run – but the depth of fall to the pipe outlet should be no greater than about 2in (50mm) for a pipe under 3ft 3in (1m) long, or about 1¼in (25mm) for a longer pipe.

If you cannot avoid a pipe run longer than 5ft 9in (1.75m), prevent self siphonage by fitting an anti-siphon (or self-sealing) trap (page 319), or a Hep$_2$0 waste pipe valve.

Alternatively, use a waste pipe of larger diameter – 1½in (38mm) instead of 1¼in (32mm). This should be no longer than 7ft 6in (2.3m), and you will need a reducer fitting to connect 38mm pipe to a 32mm trap outlet. If you need a run longer than 7ft 6in, ask the advice of the Building Control Officer of your local authority.

LINKING TO AN OUTSIDE DRAIN

How the waste pipe is linked to a drain depends on the household drainage system.

Where the bedroom adjoins the bathroom, you may be able to link into the waste pipe from the bathroom basin using a swept tee connector. Otherwise, fit a separate waste pipe through an outside wall to link with a household drain.

If the bedroom is on the ground floor, direct the waste pipe to an outside drain or gully, if possible, such as the kitchen drain. The pipe must go below the grid.

Where the bedroom is on an upper floor, the method of connecting the waste pipe depends on whether you have a two-pipe or single-stack system (page 303).

With a two-pipe system, you may be able to direct the waste pipe into an existing hopperhead. You must not, however, fit a new hopperhead and downpipe. Alternatively, you can connect the waste pipe to the waste downpipe (not the soil pipe) using a stack connector.

In a house with a single-stack system, the waste pipe will have to be connected to the stack. For this you need the approval of the local authority Building Control Officer. There are regulations concerning the position of the connection in relation to lavatory inlets, and the length and slope of the pipe is particularly critical. The connection is best made by fitting a new boss, a job for a plumber.

HELPFUL TIPS

If you tee into an old distribution pipe, it is likely to be an Imperial size of ¾in internal diameter. There is no way of recognising an Imperial size, except by measuring the internal diameter of the pipe once you have cut into it.

On ¾in copper pipe, you can fit 22mm compression fittings straight onto it provided that you substitute the olives for ¾in olives, available at the plumbers' merchant.

Similarly, the Hep$_2$0 type of joint can be used with Imperial O-rings.

On soldered capillary joints, use adapters, available from a plumbers' merchant, that convert ¾in piping to 22mm before inserting the tee (see below).

Flexible plastic waste pipe connectors with ring-seal joints are useful for fitting between the trap and waste pipe where alignment is difficult. For example, round a timber stud in a partition wall.

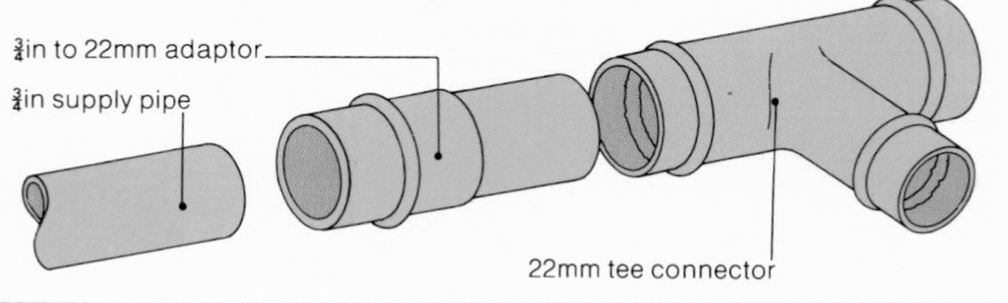

Renovating and repairing a bath

Bath renovation is best done by professional firms – listed in *Yellow Pages* under Bath Equipment. They renovate a suite in about one day – cleaning, repairing cracks or chips, and applying a thin coat of hard-wearing plastic, available in a range of colours. Use a proprietary cleaner, suitable for use on your type of bath, to remove limescale.

REPAIRING BATH ENAMEL

1 Fill small surface chips with an epoxy resin filler (such as car-body filler), then degrease the surface.

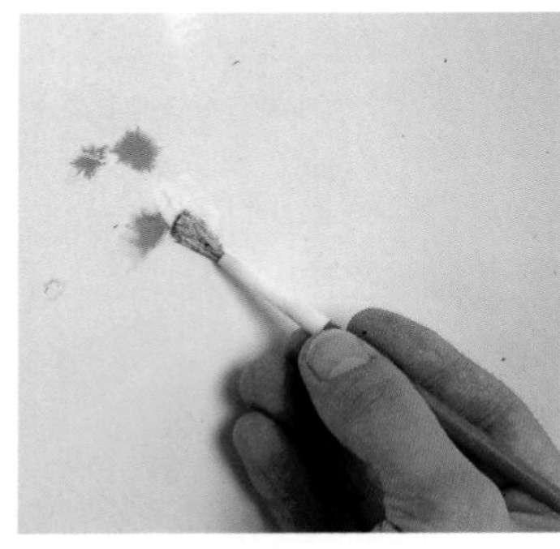

2 Rub the surface smooth with fine abrasive paper, then coat the repaired area with two coats of matching bath enamel, following the instructions on the pack.

REPAIRING A PLASTIC BATH

Burns on an acrylic surface cannot be repaired. However, chips can be filled with an acrylic paste available as a kit from Evode. Get the colour code from the bath manufacturer. You can polish out scratches with metal-polish wadding because the colour goes right through the material.

Such a repair is not possible with glass-reinforced polyester – it can be damaged by abrasive cleaners and is usually coloured in the top layer of material only.

CHANGING BATH TAPS

Because of the cramped space at the end of a bath, fitting new taps to an existing bath can be difficult. It is often easier to disconnect and pull out the bath (see below) so that you have room to apply enough force to undo the back nuts of the old taps, also to hold each tap body steady and exert counterpressure (page 308) to avoid cracking the bath.

You may have to disconnect and move the washbasin in order to pull out the bath.

The alternative to disrupting the bathroom is to fit new tap headgear only, using a tap conversion kit (page 309).

CHOOSING A BATH

Most modern baths are made from plastic in various colours, and are light and quite easy to install compared with old-style, porcelain-enamelled cast-iron baths. Vitreous-enamelled pressed-steel baths are lighter and cheaper than cast-iron baths. Some makes are meant to be cradled in a support frame to avoid distortion.

Most plastic baths are acrylic, which needs supporting with glass fibre or a tough outer shell. Cheaper baths are thinner and tend to need more support to prevent sagging and creaking. A good-quality plastic bath should be at least ¼in (6mm) thick.

Bath designs include two-person, corner-fitting and whirlpool types (with water recirculated through nozzles for underwater massage).

Removing an old cast-iron bath

A cast-iron bath may weigh around 15 stone (100kg). Unless you want to keep the bath intact and have strong helpers to assist you, it is easier to break it up after disconnecting it than to remove it whole. Be careful when you break it up, as the pieces are often jagged and very sharp.

A pressed-steel bath is lighter. With help, it can usually be moved intact.

You will need

Tools Torch; adjustable spanner; safety spectacles; ear defenders; club hammer; blanket; protective gloves. Possibly: padded pipe wrench; screwdriver; hacksaw.

1 Cut off the water supply to the bath taps (page 306).

2 Remove any bath panelling. It is often secured with dome-head screws, which have caps that are removed to reveal the screw slot.

3 With a torch, look into the space at the end of the bath to locate the supply pipes connected to the tap tails, and the overflow pipe. In older baths, the overflow pipe is rigid and leads straight out through the wall. In more modern types the overflow is flexible and connected to the waste trap.

4 Check the position of the hot supply pipe – it is normally on the left as you face the taps.

5 Use an adjustable spanner to unscrew the tap connectors from the supply pipes and pull the pipes to one side. If unscrewing is difficult, saw through the pipes near the ends of the tap tails.

6 Saw through a rigid overflow pipe flush with the wall.

7 Disconnect the waste trap from the waste outlet. For an old-style U-bend, use an adjustable spanner. A plastic trap can normally be unscrewed by hand, but use a padded pipe wrench if it proves difficult. Pull the trap to one side.

8 Disconnect a flexible overflow pipe from the overflow outlet.

9 If the bath has adjustable legs – normally brackets with adjustable screws and locking nuts – lower it to lessen the risk of damaging wall tiles when you pull it out. But if the adjusters on the far side are difficult to reach, lowering may not be worth the effort.

10 Pull the bath into the middle of the room ready for removal or break-up.

11 To break up the bath, wear safety spectacles, gloves and ear defenders (the bath will ring like a bell when hit). Drape a blanket over it to stop fragments flying out and hit the sides with a club hammer.

CONNECTIONS TO AN OLD BATH

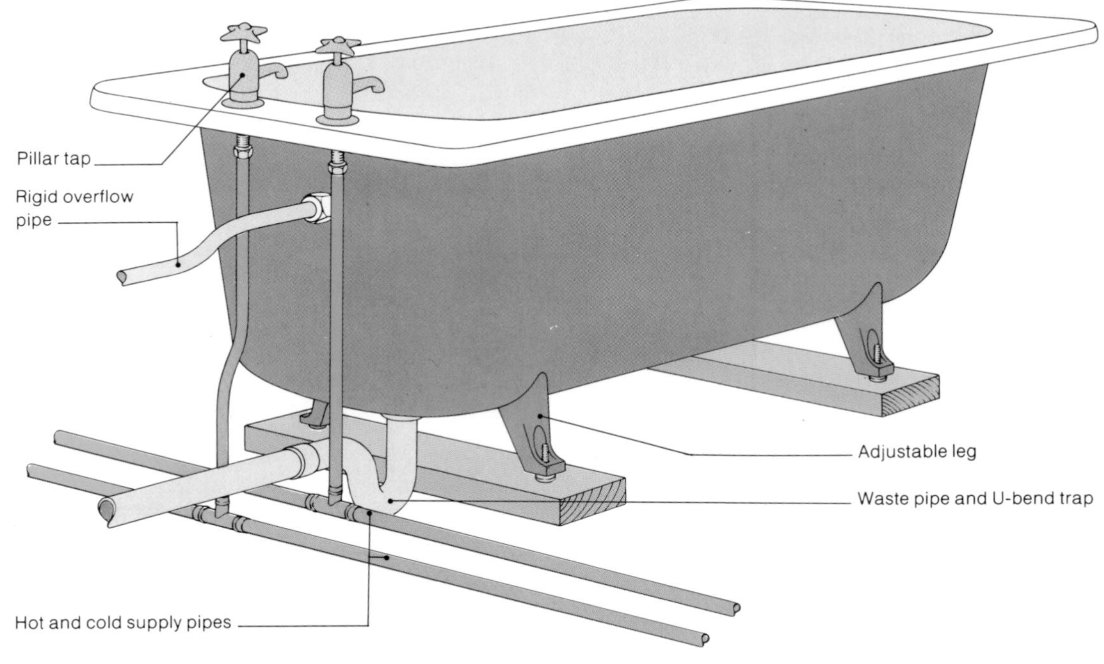

Installing a new bath

Assemble as many fittings as possible on the new bath before you remove the old one. Not only will fitting be easier before the bath is in position, but the water will not be cut off for so long.

You can fit the new bath in a slightly different position from the old one with the aid of flexible tap connectors and a flexible waste connector. But if you want to put it in a different position altogether, you will have to work out how to re-route the waste pipe and link it to the drain (page 325), as well as adapt the supply pipes.

You will need

Tools Two adjustable spanners; spirit level; damp cloth. Possibly also: long-nosed pliers; small spanner; hacksaw; screwdriver.

Materials Bath; two 1in (25mm) thick boards to support feet; two ¾in pillar taps or mixer (with washers); two 22mm flexible tap connectors; 1½in (40mm) waste outlet (unslotted) with plug and two flat plastic washers; bath trap (deep-seal if the waste pipe links to a single stack) with flexible overflow assembly; non-setting mastic filler (silicone type for a plastic bath); PTFE thread-sealing tape; bath sealant (silicone rubber type for plastic).

HELPFUL TIPS

If, on a mixer, the hot and cold indicators are on different sides from the appropriate supply pipes, reverse the discs on the tops of the taps, if possible. Or cross the flexible tap connectors to join the taps to the correct pipes.

The most effective bath seal is a waterproof strip which goes under the tiles and over the edge of the bath. Bed it in silicone and tile over the top.

1 Fit the supporting frame following the maker's instructions. It is usually done with the bath placed upside down. Some glass reinforced polyester and pressed-steel baths do not need support frames.

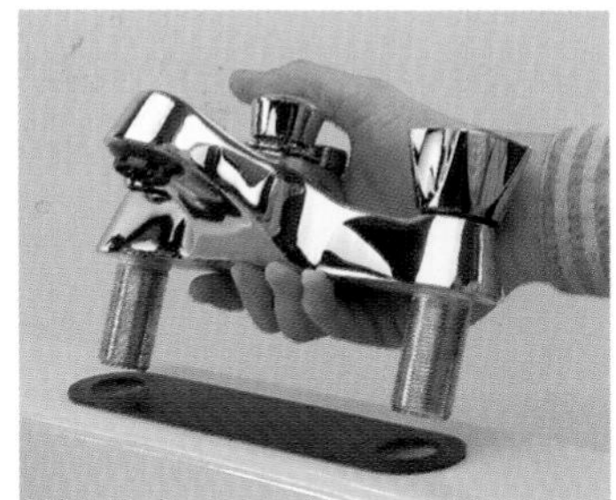

2 Fit the taps or mixer and the tap connectors in the same way as for a kitchen sink (page 320). Some deck mixers come with a plastic washer to fit between the deck and the bath. On a plastic bath, fit a reinforcing plate under the taps to prevent strain on the bath deck.

3 Fit the waste outlet. This may be a tailed grid fitted in the same way as for a sink. Or it may be a flanged grid only, fitted over the outlet hole (with washers on each side of the bath surface) and fixed with a screw to a tail formed at one end of the flexible overflow pipe.

4 Fit the top end of the overflow pipe into the back of the overflow hole and screw the overflow outlet, backed by a washer, in position.

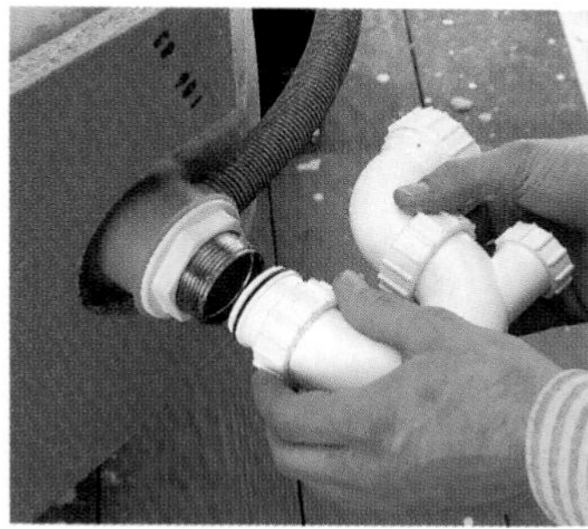

5 Slot the banjo overflow, if supplied, onto the threaded waste and then fit the bottom washer and back nut. Seal the thread with silicone mastic or PTFE tape.

6 Fit the bath into position with a flat board under each pair of feet in order to spread the load evenly.

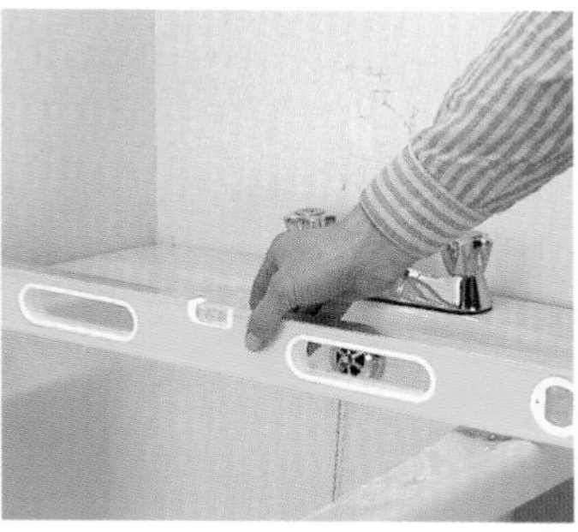

7 It is important that the bath is sitting true. Place a spirit level on each of the four sides of the bath to check that it is horizontal. If necessary, adjust the legs until the bath is perfectly level.

8 Tighten the locking nuts on the adjustable legs.

9 Fit the tap connector on the farthest tap to its supply pipe, making a compression joint (page 311). If the supply pipe is too high, cut it back to a convenient length, leaving it too long rather than too short, as the connector can be bent slightly to fit. To fit a monobloc mixer, see page 322.

10 Connect the second tap in the same way as the first.

11 Connect the trap outlet to the waste pipe (normally a locking ring-seal joint, page 318).

12 Restore the water supply and check the joints for leaks. Tighten if necessary, but not too much.

13 Fix the bath panels according to the maker's instructions. They may screw or clip to a wooden frame, or be fixed to a plywood strip held to the floor with brackets.

14 Wait until the bath has settled in position before sealing the joints between the bath sides and walls to prevent leakage over the sides. This usually means waiting until after the bath has been filled and used at least once.

15 Before sealing the joints of a plastic bath, fill the bath with warm water so that the sealer will be applied while the bath is midway between any movement occurring when in use and when empty, and the flexible sealant will have the minimum stretch each way. Use a silicone rubber sealant if the bath is plastic.

CONNECTIONS TO A NEW BATH

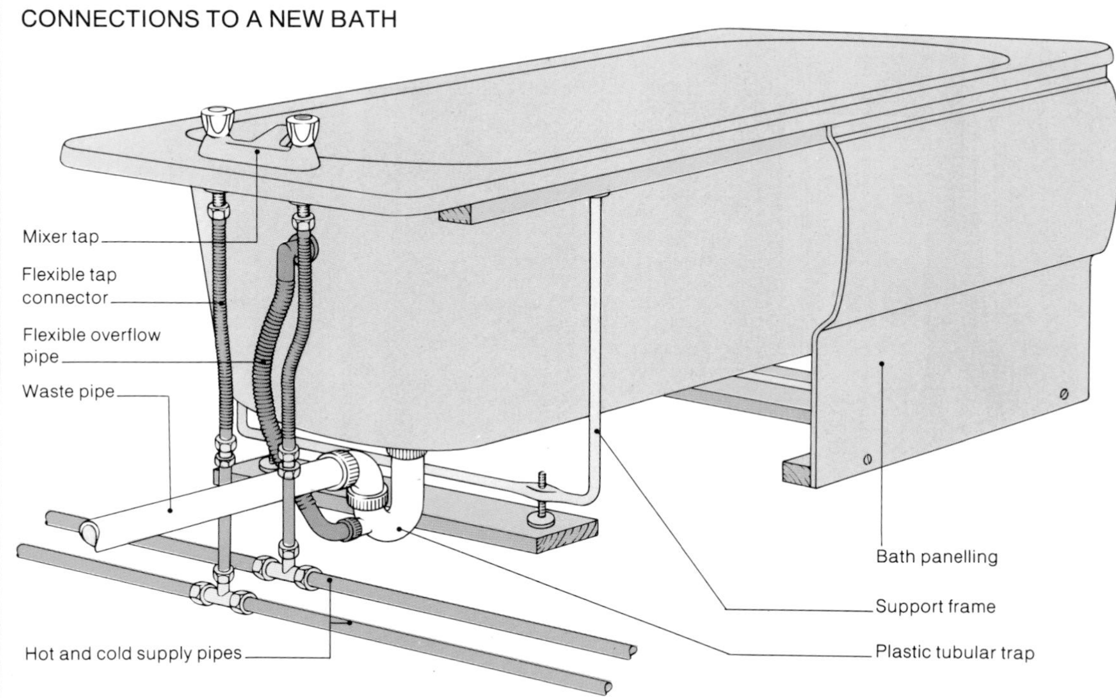

CHOOSING A SHOWER

The type of shower that can be installed depends to some extent on the household water system.

Where hot and cold water are both supplied from the household storage system at equal pressure (indirect system, page 301), a mixer is the most economical type of shower.

Many showers are now designed to cope with widely differing water pressures, such as stored hot water and cold mains. If you connect mains water to a shower, you must fit a double seal check valve on the mains supply to prevent back siphonage. Some showers incorporate check valves.

If hot water is supplied from the mains via a multipoint or combination boiler, ensure that the shower is designed to cope with this system and allows sufficient flow of water through the boiler. Check the installation requirements with the manufacturer, and get the shower fitted by a CORGI registered plumber.

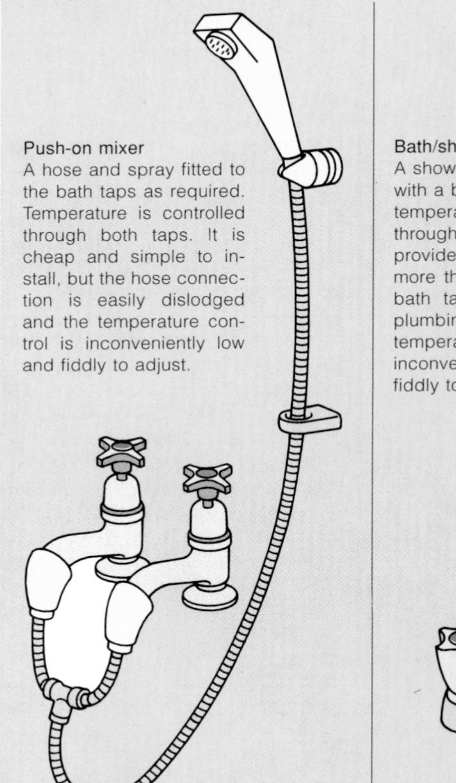

Push-on mixer
A hose and spray fitted to the bath taps as required. Temperature is controlled through both taps. It is cheap and simple to install, but the hose connection is easily dislodged and the temperature control is inconveniently low and fiddly to adjust.

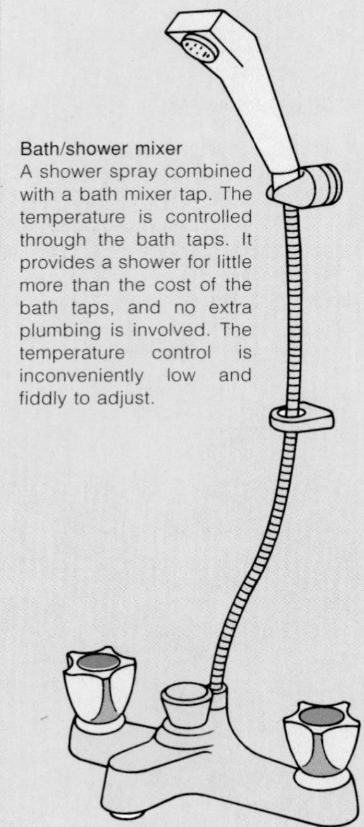

Bath/shower mixer
A shower spray combined with a bath mixer tap. The temperature is controlled through the bath taps. It provides a shower for little more than the cost of the bath taps, and no extra plumbing is involved. The temperature control is inconveniently low and fiddly to adjust.

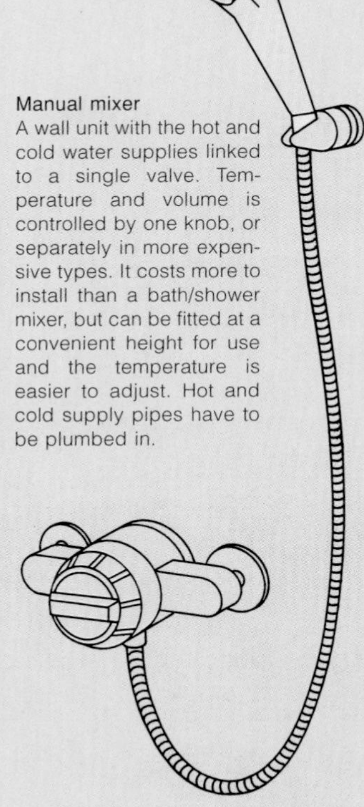

Manual mixer
A wall unit with the hot and cold water supplies linked to a single valve. Temperature and volume is controlled by one knob, or separately in more expensive types. It costs more to install than a bath/shower mixer, but can be fitted at a convenient height for use and the temperature is easier to adjust. Hot and cold supply pipes have to be plumbed in.

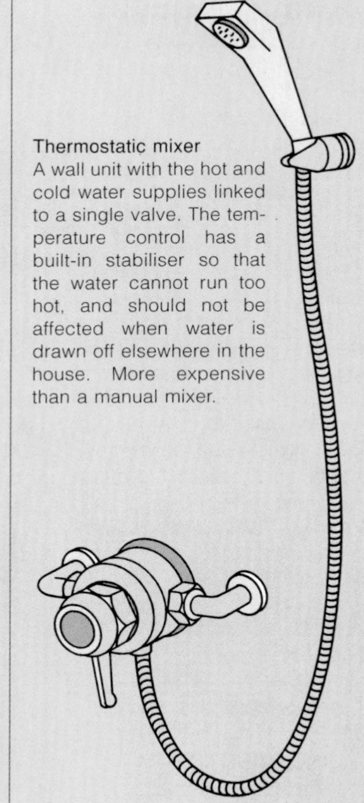

Thermostatic mixer
A wall unit with the hot and cold water supplies linked to a single valve. The temperature control has a built-in stabiliser so that the water cannot run too hot, and should not be affected when water is drawn off elsewhere in the house. More expensive than a manual mixer.

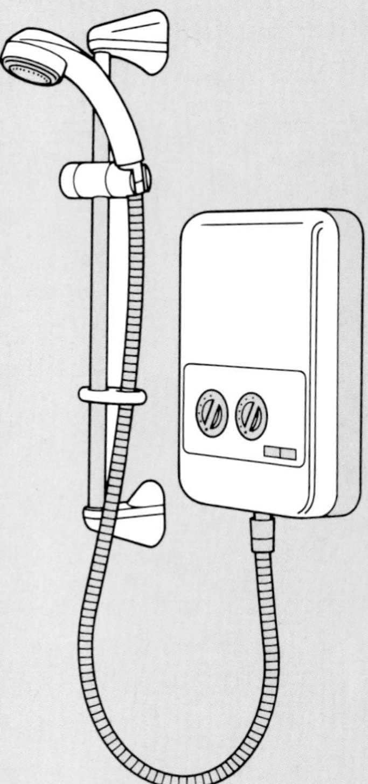

Power shower
An all-in-one shower which incorporates a small, but powerful electric pump. The pump boosts the rate that hot and cold water are supplied to the shower-head from the cold-water cistern and the hot-water cylinder. This type of shower can be installed only with a water supply from a cold-water cistern and a hot-water cylinder. A power shower is unsuitable for water heated directly by the shower, or where water is supplied to the shower from a combination boiler under mains pressure.

With a power shower, removing the waste water quickly enough can be a problem. If in doubt use a 2in (50mm) waste pipe.

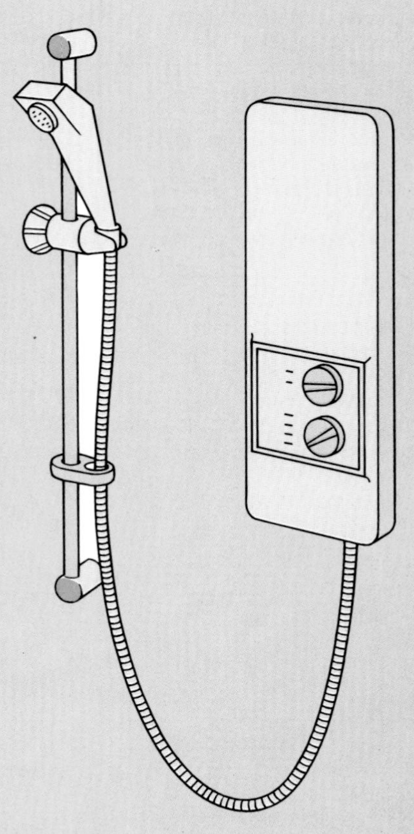

Instantaneous electric shower
A wall unit plumbed in to a mains cold water supply, which is heated by an electric element to feed the shower. It allows a shower where a mixer would be illegal, but mains pressure needs to be at a normal level – at least 10lb/sq in (0.7kg/sq cm). The control knob allows either less water at a higher temperature or more at a lower temperature, so the spray is weaker in winter when mains water is colder. Dearer models have a winter/summer setting. Some models have a temperature stabiliser and cannot run too hot or be affected by other taps in use. The unit must be wired to an electric power supply according to Electricity Board requirements (page 375).

Planning a shower

Unless the water pressure at the shower head is adequate, there will be only a dribble of water from the shower spray.

For a mixer supplied from the household's stored hot and cold supplies, the bottom of the cold-water cistern needs to be at least 3ft (910mm) – and preferably 5ft (1.5m) – above the shower head for the pressure to be adequate.

For an instantaneous shower supplied direct from the mains, the pressure requirement varies according to the model, but in most homes it is unlikely to be too low, except, perhaps, at the top of a tower block or in an old house converted into flats. Contact the local water company if in doubt.

ENSURING ADEQUATE WATER PRESSURE

If you do not have sufficient water pressure to supply a shower at the required position, there are two ways by which the pressure can be increased – you can either raise the height of the cistern or have a booster pump installed.

The cold-water cistern can be raised by fitting a strong wooden platform beneath it, constructed from timber struts and blockboard. You will also have to lengthen the rising main to reach the cistern, as well as the distribution pipes from the cistern.

A booster pump incorporates a small electric motor and must be wired into the power supply. There are two main types: a single pump, which is fitted between the mixer control and the spray and boosts the mixed supply to the spray. Or a dual or twin pump that is fitted to the supply pipes and boosts the hot and cold water supplies separately before they reach the mixer.

Depending on the model, a booster pump will provide sufficient pressure with as little as 6in (150mm) height difference between the water level in the cistern and the spray head.

Some dual pumps will provide sufficient pressure to a shower head sited higher than the cold-water storage cistern. This allows a shower to be installed in an attic, for example.

WORKING OUT THE PIPING AND DRAINAGE LINKS

Little or no pipework is involved in installing a shower over a bath, but both piping and drainage routes must be worked out for a shower in a separate cubicle.

The drainage is often more difficult to arrange than the water supply to the shower, and you may need to get approval from the local government authority. See *Linking to an outside drain*, page 325.

Use 15mm diameter supply pipes (page 312). For heating economy and to limit loss of pressure, pipe runs to the shower should be as short and straight as possible. Avoid using elbows on corners – bend pipes if possible so that there is less resistance to flow. When routing a pipe, make sure that fixings will not interfere with electric cables or gas pipes.

The two types of shower that will involve additions to the pipework over a bath are a mixer type or an instantaneous electric shower. For a mixer shower you need both hot and cold water supply pipes. For an instantaneous shower you need only a cold supply pipe direct from the rising main.

If you are installing a manual mixer, whether over a bath or in a separate cubicle, you must take the cold water supply direct from the cold-water cistern – not from a branch pipe supplying other taps or cisterns.

Taking the supply from a branch pipe is unsafe because when the other fitting is in use, the cold supply to the shower could be so reduced that the shower becomes scalding hot.

Hot water for the mixer can be taken from a branch pipe, because there is no danger if the hot supply to the shower is reduced, although it can be unpleasant. If you take the hot supply from the cylinder distribution pipe, make the connection at a point above the height of the cylinder top.

With a thermostatic shower mixer, however, both hot and cold water can be taken from the branch pipes, as the water temperature is automatically controlled.

PIPEWORK FOR A SHOWER MIXER

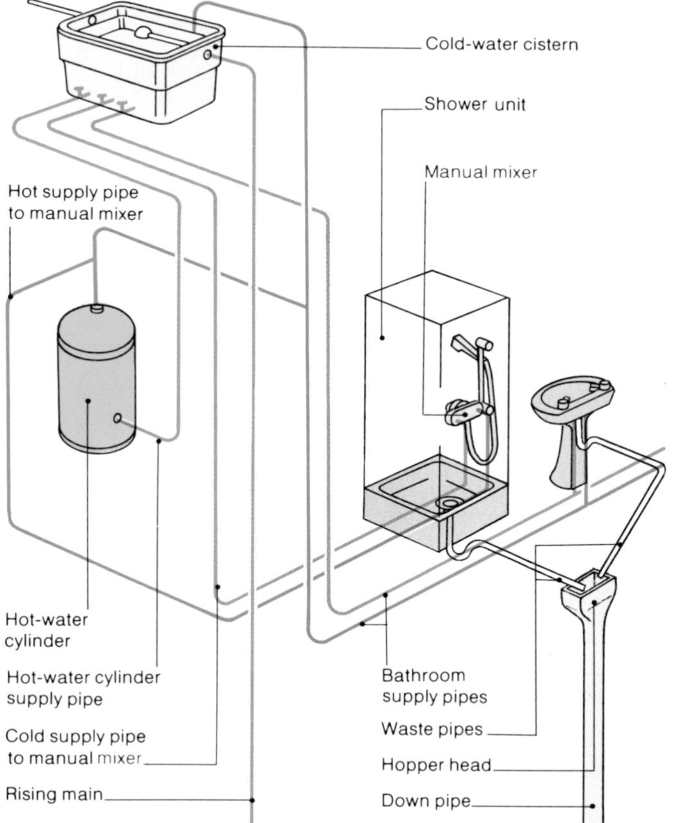

For a manual mixer, take the cold supply pipe direct from the cold-water cistern so that the flow cannot be reduced by water drawn off from other taps. If that happened, someone taking a shower could be scalded. Take the hot supply from the hot-water cylinder distribution pipe – tee in above cylinder height.

For a thermostatic mixer, which has a temperature stabiliser, you can tee into bathroom supply pipes.

INCREASING WATER PRESSURE WITH A DUAL BOOSTER PUMP

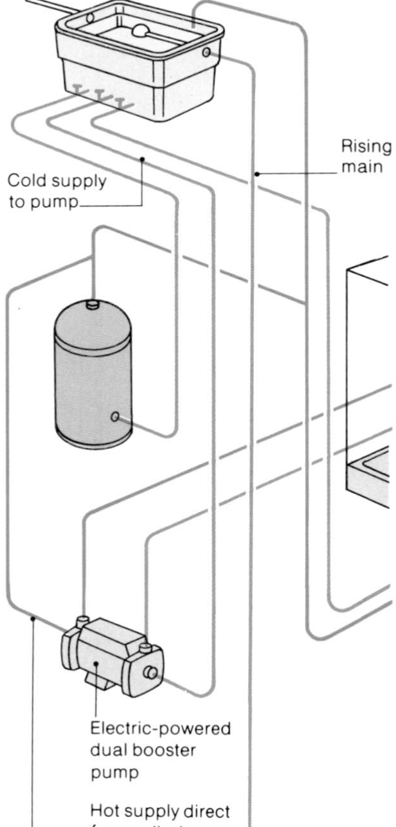

A dual pump boosts the hot and cold water supplies separately. Some types of pump have a hot supply pipe direct from the cylinder casing, some from the vent pipe. Get the dual booster pump fitted by a plumber, as installation can be quite complex.

PIPEWORK FOR AN INSTANTANEOUS SHOWER

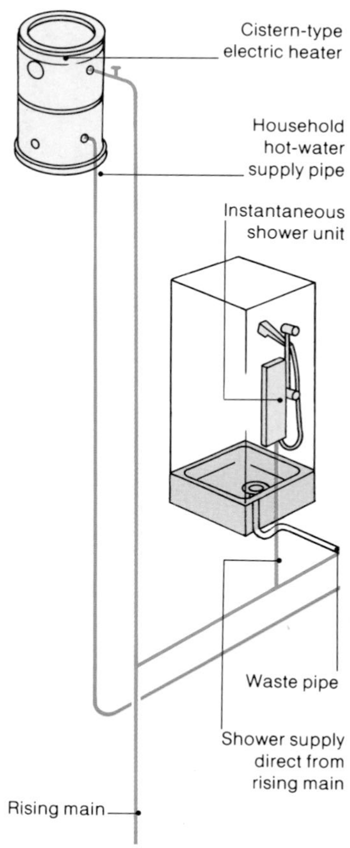

With an instantaneous electric shower, only a cold supply is needed, direct from the rising main. This is useful where there is no cold-water storage cistern, as mains cold water and stored hot water must not be mixed in one fitting.

Installing a shower

Most types of shower can be fitted either over a bath or in a cubicle. The fixings and pipe routes vary according to the shower type, the bathroom layout and the shower location, but the method of installation is basically the same.

The shower head must either be fitted so as to prevent it coming into contact with water in the bath or base tray, or it must have a check valve (non-return valve) where the hose is attached to the shower control.

1 Decide on the type of shower.

2 Mark the required positions of the spray head and shower control.

3 Plan the pipework to the shower control (see page 329) and how the waste water will be routed to the drainage system (see page 325).

4 If you are fitting an instantaneous electric shower, work out the positions of the cable route and the switch (page 375).

5 Fit the shower control. Most units are available as either surface mounted or recessed fittings and come with fixings and instructions.

When fitting a recessed mixer, if possible mount it on a removable panel flush with the wall so that you have easy access to the controls (see pages 145, 156, 232).

6 Cut off the water supply and fit the water supply pipes (*Different ways of joining pipes*, page 311). You can recess the pipes into the wall and then replaster or tile over them. However, they must be protected with a waterproof covering and have isolating valves fitted, serving only those pipes.

Alternatively, you can box the pipes in with surface-mounted casing (see page 312) or wall panelling (see page 248).

7 Fit the shower head and spray. For a separate cubicle, fit the base tray and waste fittings.

8 Connect the supply pipes to the shower control. An adaptor with a female screw thread (copper to iron) may be needed.

9 Restore the water supply and check piping for leaks. Tighten any joints as necessary.

10 For an electric shower, turn off the electric supply at the consumer unit. Make electrical connections (page 375), following any maker's instructions. Restore the supply.

11 Fit screening panels and seal the joints between the wall and screening and a cubicle tray.

A TYPICAL CUBICLE INSTALLATION

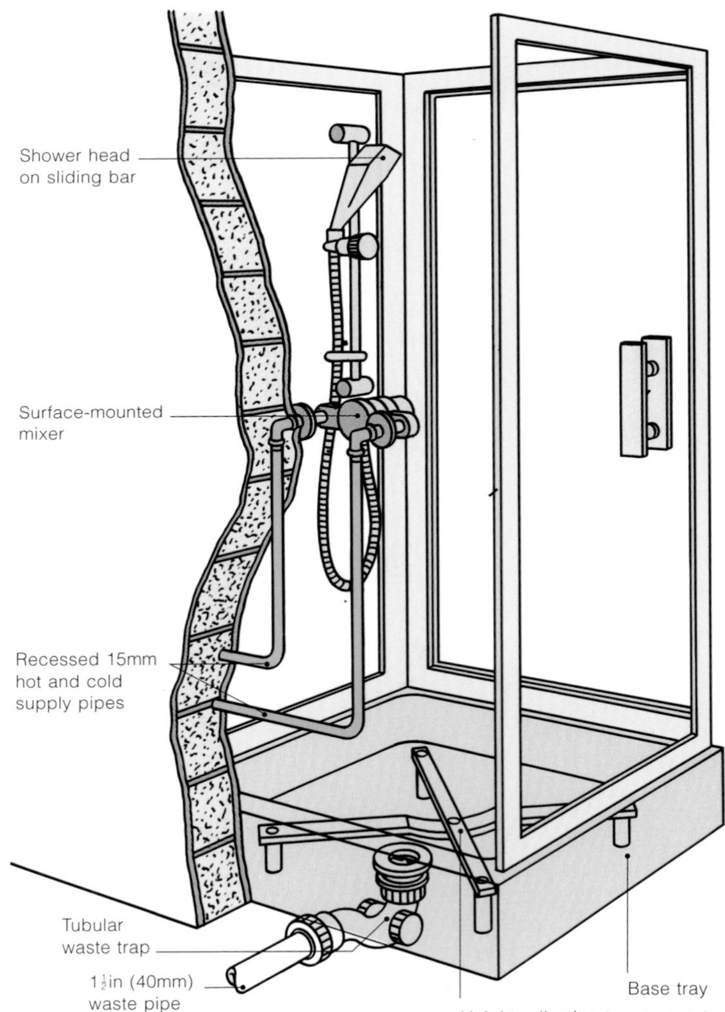

Screens are typically about 6ft (1.8m) high. Panel widths can usually be adjusted by 1in-2in (25mm-50mm) to allow for walls that are out of true. Doors may be hinged, folded (with panels shaped to keep water in), sliding with corner entry, or pivoted to give a wide entry without taking a lot of opening space. Some base trays have an adjustable support by which the height can be altered so that the waste pipe and trap can be positioned either above or below the floorboards.

SHOWER FITTINGS

With an over-bath shower, only a shower head, tap or mixer and curtain or screen are needed. With a separate cubicle, a base tray, trap and waste pipe (page 318) are also necessary.

SPRAY ROSES

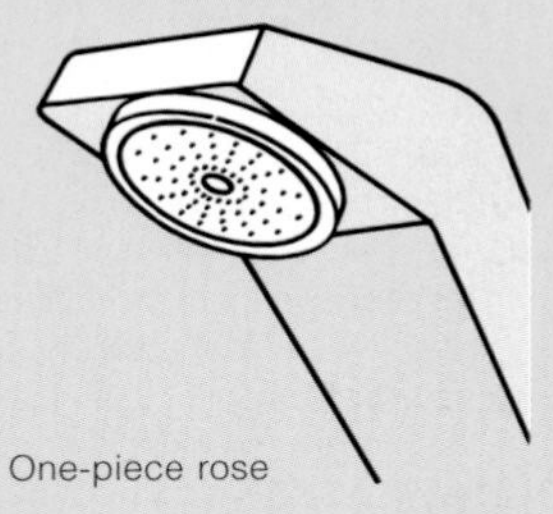
One-piece rose

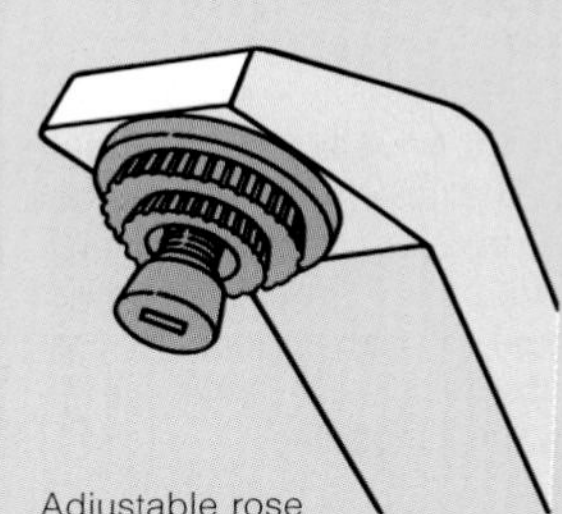
Adjustable rose

Shower heads may be fixed or adjustable, or on a flexible hose. The spray rose may be in one piece or in a series of rings that allow adjustment of the density of the spray.

TRACK FOR SHOWER CURTAINS

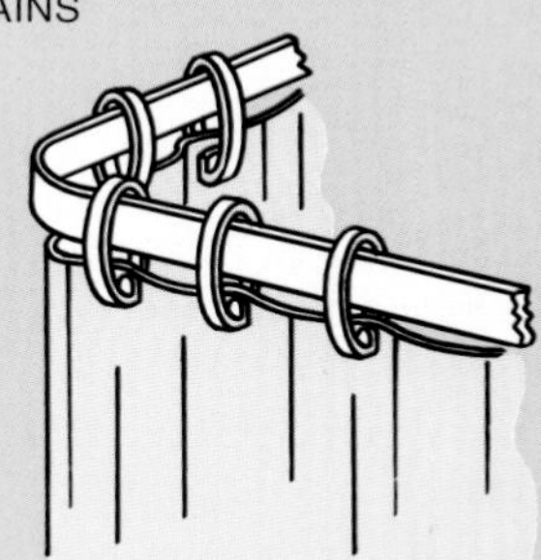

Track for shower curtains is sold in kits with instructions and all necessary fittings. Where there are ceiling brackets, they should be fixed to ceiling joists (*Locating joists*, page 249). Track is in sections and can enclose one side 6ft (1.8m) long, or two sides of an area 3ft (910mm) square. Extra straight or curved pieces allow variations such as three 3ft sides. In place of curtains there are fold-back over-bath screens that can be opened as needed.

BASE TRAYS

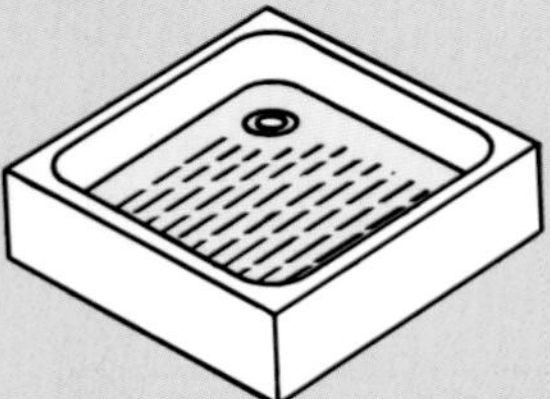

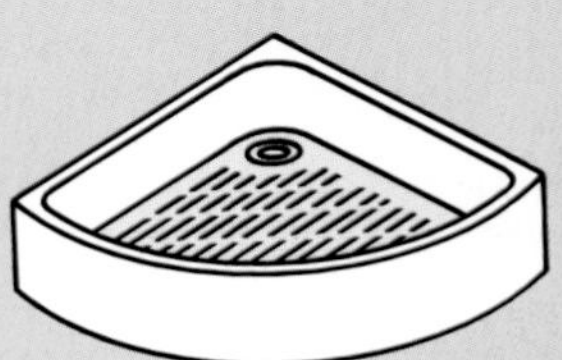

A glass-reinforced polyester tray is light to handle and not easily damaged. A reconstituted stone or resin shower tray is heavy and stable, but it may crack if placed on an uneven floor. A weak mix of sand and cement must be used to level the floor before the tray is fitted.

Base trays are typically 30in (760mm) square and 8in-12in (200mm-300mm) high. A tray with a curved front can be used to save floor space.

Types of lavatory suite

A lavatory suite consists of a cistern and a pan. The cistern can be low or high level, joined by a flush pipe to the pan, or close coupled with a direct connection. Modern pans, even though they might be old fashioned in appearance, are designed to use less water than old suites – 12 pints (7 litres) rather than 16 pints (9 litres). If you use a high-level cistern you will need to fit a restricter in the back of the pan to stop the water entering so fast that it shoots over the top of the pan rim.

When siting a lavatory suite, allow for at least 21in (530mm) of space in front of the pan, and for about 30in (760mm) overall space from side to side.

LOW-LEVEL SUITE DESIGNS

In a low-level suite, the cistern is either linked to the pan by a short flush pipe or is close-coupled, with the cistern and pan joined together in one unit.

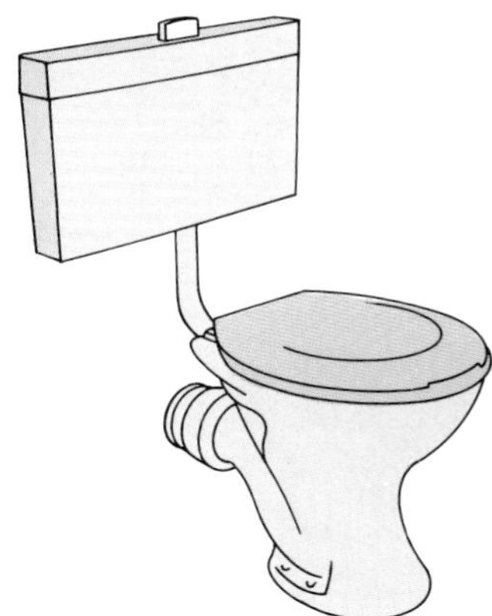

Separate low-level suite

Close-coupled suite

TYPES OF CISTERN

Cisterns may be made of enamelled cast-iron, plastic or vitreous china (ceramic), and are normally designed to be screwed to the wall from inside through the back. The flushing control may be a central push button or a side lever. Many levers can be adapted to fit either to the right or left of the cistern.

For the flushing action to be

CHOOSING A LAVATORY PAN AND CONNECTOR

Pans are normally made from vitreous china and are screwed to the floor through holes in the base of the pedestal. Some are designed to fit flush to the wall with their plumbing concealed, and some can be wall-hung.

Pans on upper floors have an almost horizontal (P-trap) outlet to fit a wall-exit pipe. Pans on ground floors often have a down-pointing (S-trap) outlet to fit to a floor-exit pipe. When you buy a new pan, a down-pointing outlet may no longer be available, but a horizontal outlet can be linked to a floor exit with an angled connector.

Flush water from the cistern enters the pan down a flush pipe (or a concealed channel in a close-coupled suite) and spreads round the pan under the rim. There are variations in the way the pan is emptied. The commonest design is the washdown pan. More expensive is the double-trap siphonic pan, which is available only with a close-coupled suite. It takes more space from front to back than a washdown pan.

A third design, the single-trap siphonic pan, is commonly used in public buildings but not very often in homes.

At one time, lavatory pans were connected to the flush pipe with a rag-and-putty joint and to the inlet branch of the soil pipe with putty or a mastic filler, sometimes with cement. Flexible plastic push-fit connectors are now commonly used instead, and are particularly suitable for DIY installation.

Washdown pan

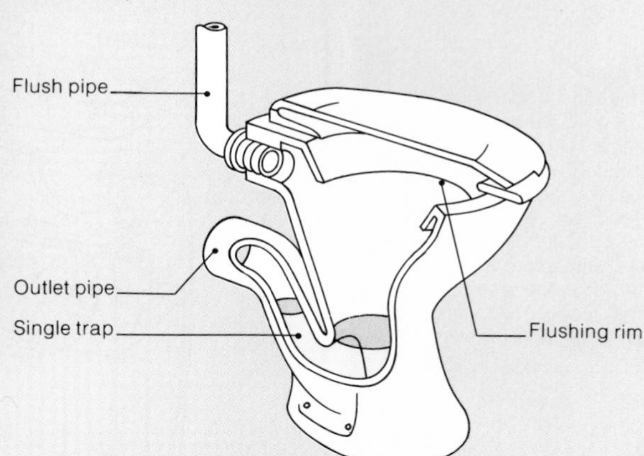

The bowl is cleaned and emptied by the force of the water released when the cistern is flushed. It is rather noisy.

Double-trap siphonic pan

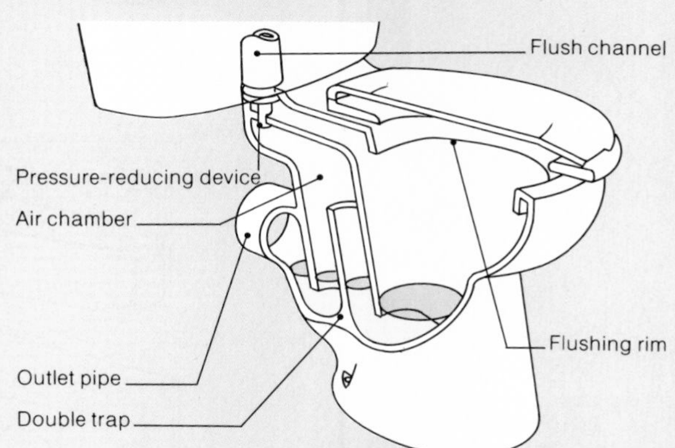

When the cistern is flushed, the pan starts to empty by suction before the flush water reaches it, making it very silent and efficient in operation.

Suction from the lavatory pan is set in motion by means of an air pipe (or pressure-reducing device) from the cistern flush channel to the air chamber between the pan's two traps. As the cistern is flushed, air is drawn up into the flush channel from the air chamber, creating a partial vacuum in the chamber. The change in air pressure causes the water in the pan to be siphoned down the outlet pipe.

Straight pushfit pan connector

For a straight link between the pan outlet and the inlet branch to the soil pipe. The cupped end fits over the pan outlet, and the narrow (spigot) end inside the soil-pipe inlet. Different diameters and lengths are made. Before buying, check the outside diameter of the pan outlet, the inside diameter of the soil-pipe inlet, and the distance to be bridged. Connectors have watertight seals at each end. Offset types can be used where the alignment is not exact.

Angled pushfit pan connector

A 90 degree connector for converting a horizontal (P-trap) pan outlet to a down-pointing (S-trap) outlet for a floor-exit pipe. It can also be used to link a horizontal outlet to a wall-exit pipe situated at right angles to the pan. Low-angle connectors – generally 2½ degrees or 14 degrees – can be used for an angled connection from a horizontal outlet to a wall-exit pipe.

Rubber cone connector

For linking the flush pipe from the lavatory cistern to the flush horn of the lavatory pan.

Flush pipe

Angled plastic pipe linking a separate cistern to the lavatory pan. Pipes for high-level suites are normally 1¼in (32mm) internal diameter, and pipes for low-level suites 1½in (38mm) diameter.

Types of lavatory cistern (continued)

correct, the cistern should be mounted at the height specified by the manufacturer – usually with the base about 24in (610mm) above the floor. The water flow into the cistern is controlled by a ball-valve (page 337). A cistern fed from a cold water storage cistern is quieter than one fed from the mains.

The standard cistern is a direct-action type. It is normally installed at a low level, but can be used at high level, and is quieter in use than the chain-pull type of cistern.

If a suite is converted from high level to low level, the standard size of cistern – about 8in (200mm) from front to back – is too deep to be fitted behind the pan, so a slimline type is necessary. Low-level suites are designed with the bowl 2in-3in (50mm-75mm) farther forward to accommodate a standard cistern.

A slimline cistern is the normal measurement from side to side but very narrow from front to back – as little as 4½in (115mm) in some designs, but it still provides a full flush. It is useful for concealed installation behind panelling.

Another variation on the direct-action cistern is the dual-flush type, which provides either a water-saving small flush, or a double-sized flush for solid waste.

Most cisterns found in the home still have a 2 gallon (9 litre) flush: the dual-flush type provides either 1 or 2 gallons. Water regulations now restrict the capacity of newly installed cisterns.

HOW A CISTERN WORKS

An inverted U-pipe in the cistern is linked to the flush pipe into the pan, and at the other end opens out into a dome (siphon). When the flush is operated, a lift-rod raises a plate in the dome and throws water into the crown of the U-bend.

Openings in the plate are covered by a plastic flap valve held flat by the weight of the water. As water falls down the flush pipe, it creates a partial vacuum, causing water to be sucked up through the plate openings and to raise the flap valve. The base of the dome is about ½in (13mm) above the cistern bottom. When the cistern water level falls below the dome base, air drawn in breaks the siphonic action and stops the flush.

On a dual-flush cistern there is a hole in the side of the dome, and if the flush control is released immediately the hole lets in air to break the siphonic action after a gallon of water has been siphoned. When the control is held down for a few seconds, it operates a device that temporarily plugs the air hole, allowing a double flush.

STANDARD CISTERN

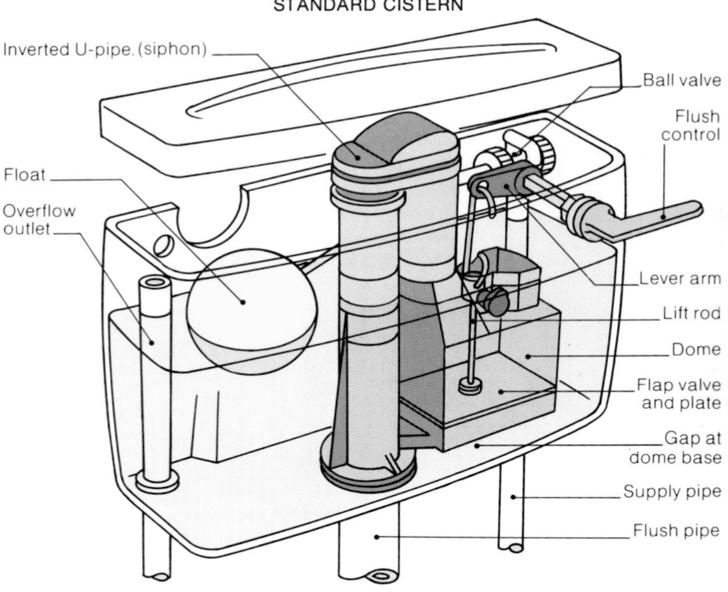

SLIMLINE CISTERN

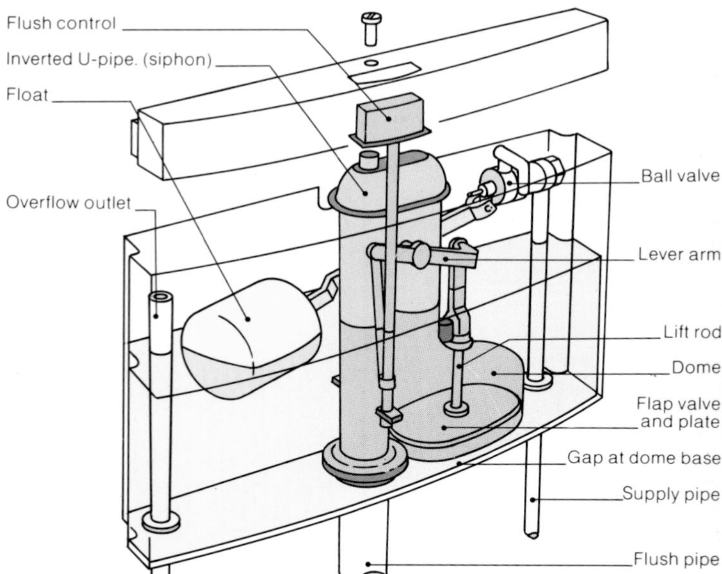

SPECIAL TYPES OF LAVATORY

Pump/shredder unit

22mm pipe leading to soil pipe or stack
Pan outlet
Pump/shredder unit

A small-bore waste system allows a lavatory to be installed where there is no direct wide-diameter connection to the soil pipe or stack, such as in a basement below the level of the underground drain. Permission must be obtained from the local authority before installation.

The lavatory pan discharges into a sealed pump/shredder unit fitted behind it, and connected to an electric power supply. The waste is shredded then pumped through a 22mm pipe to the soil pipe or single stack. Different models will pump waste through 65ft-165ft (20m-50m) of horizontal pipe, or push it up 5ft-13ft (1.5m-4m) of vertical pipe. Some models will also accept bath and basin waste.

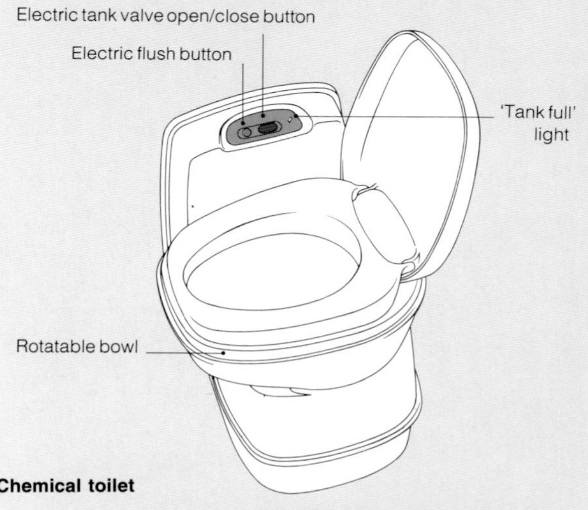

Chemical toilet

Modern chemical closets have been developed primarily for caravanning and camping use; but they are equally useful in holiday chalets and for invalids and the elderly in the home.

In the closet shown, the bowl is rotatable, to the most convenient position in a confined space. A container is filled with water and a perfumed detergent. After use, an electric push-button flush, which has a hand-pump back-up, delivers the water to cleanse the bowl. An electrically-operated valve admits the bowl's contents to a waste tank holding a perfumed liquefying agent. The water container and waste tank are isolated from the closet area, enabling all filling and emptying operations to be done through an outside hatch. In another model, the water container and waste tank detach from the bowl.

Repairing a faulty lavatory cistern

Common faults with a lavatory cistern are an overflow or failure to flush properly. A faulty ball-valve can cause either because it affects the water level. Failure to flush properly is caused by either a low water level or a worn or damaged flap valve. To determine the cause, check the water level (see below).

The plastic lever arm linking the spindle of the flush control to the siphon lift rod may eventually wear out and break. A replacement can be bought and is easily fitted.

CHECKING THE WATER LEVEL

1 Remove the cistern lid (it may lift off or be held by one or more screws). When the cistern is full, the water level should be about 1in (25mm) below the overflow outlet. Or there may be a water level marked on the inside wall of the cistern.

2 If the level is low, repair or adjust the ball-valve (page 336).

If the level is too high and the cistern is overflowing or in danger of doing so, flush it, then repair or adjust the ball-valve (page 336).

If the level is correct, renew the flap valve (see below).

RENEWING THE FLAP VALVE ON A STANDARD SUITE

A standard low-level suite has a full-sized cistern separate from the pan. The flap valve may be sold under the names siphon washer or cistern diaphragm. If you do not know the size you want, buy the largest available and cut it down.

A slimline cistern is repaired in the same way as a standard cistern, but some types are linked to the flush pipe with a locking ring-seal joint (page 318) rather than with two nuts.

You will need
Tools Screwdriver; wooden batten slightly longer than the cistern width; string; footprint pipe wrench with a jaw opening of about $2\frac{1}{2}$in (65mm); bowl or bucket. Possibly also: sharp coloured pencil; scissors; container for bailing, or tube for siphoning.
Materials Plastic flap valve. Possibly also: O-ring for ring-seal joint.

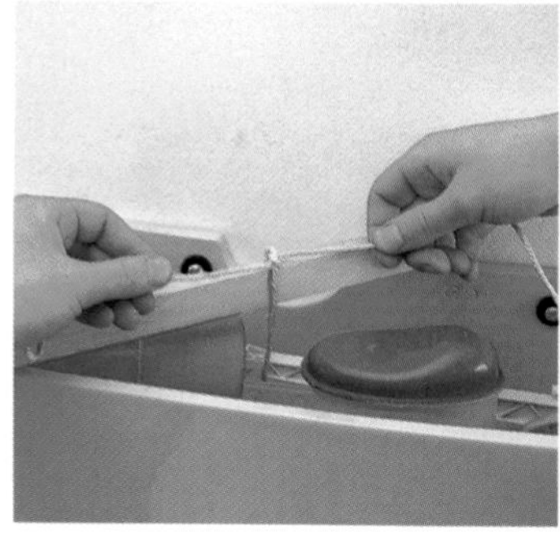

1 With the cistern lid removed, lay a batten across the cistern and tie the float arm to it to stop the inflow of water.

2 Empty the cistern. If it cannot be flushed at all, bail or siphon the water out.

3 Use a large pipe wrench to undo the lower of the two large nuts underneath the cistern, then disconnect the flush pipe and push it to one side.

4 Put a bowl or bucket underneath the cistern and undo the large nut immediately under the cistern (this is the siphon-retaining nut). A pint or two of water will flow out as you loosen the nut.

5 Unhook the lift rod from the flushing lever.

6 Lift the inverted U-pipe (the siphon) out from the cistern and lay it on its side.

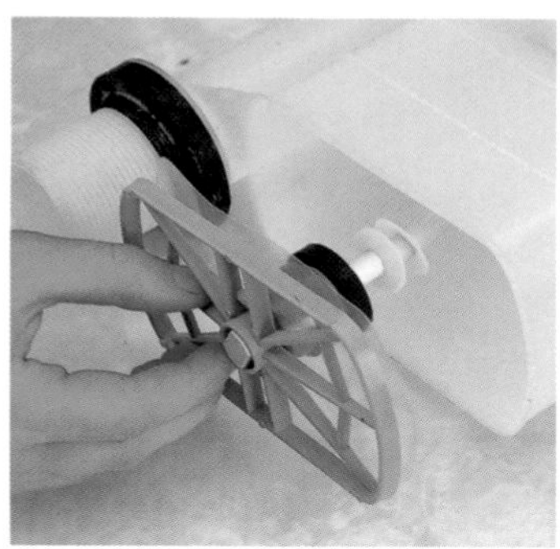

7 Pull out the lift rod and plate and remove the worn flap valve. If the new valve is too big, cut it down with scissors using the old valve as a pattern. It should touch, but not drag on, the dome sides.

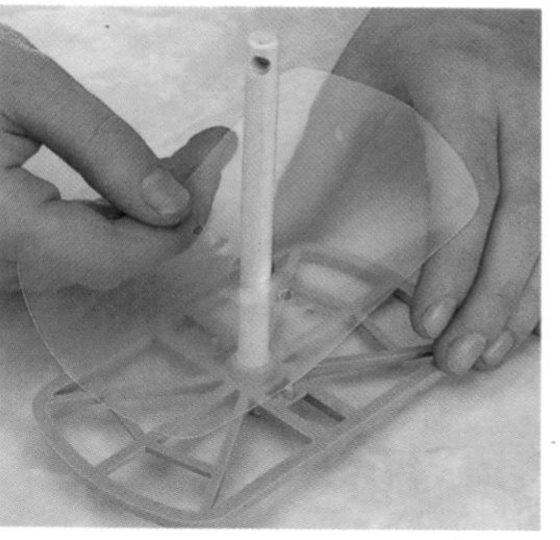

8 Fit the new valve over the lift rod and onto the plate, then reassemble the flushing mechanism.

RENEWING THE FLAP VALVE ON A CLOSE-COUPLED SUITE

On some close-coupled suites, the siphon is held by two or more bolts inside the cistern rather than by a large nut underneath. Except for this difference, the flap valve is renewed in the same way as on a standard suite.

On others, the cistern must be lifted off in order to disconnect the siphon. The flap valve can then be renewed in the same way as on a standard suite. Lift off the cistern as follows:

1 Cut off the water supply to the lavatory cistern in the same way as for a tap (page 306). Empty the cistern by flushing, bailing or siphoning out the water.

2 Disconnect the overflow pipe and water supply pipe from the cistern. They generally have screw fittings with a back nut.

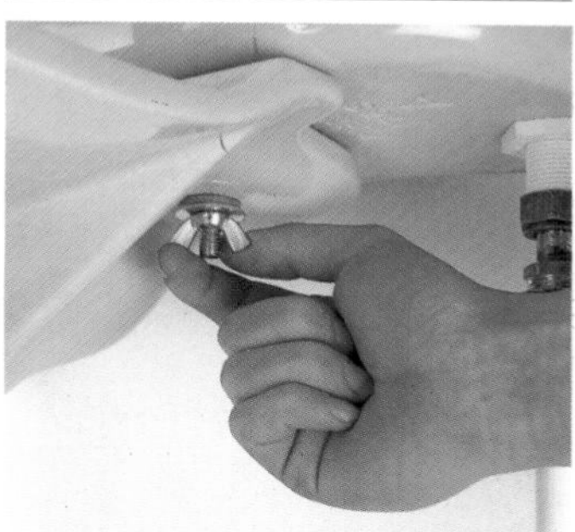

3 Undo the wall screws holding the cistern, and any bolts securing it to the rear platform of the pan.

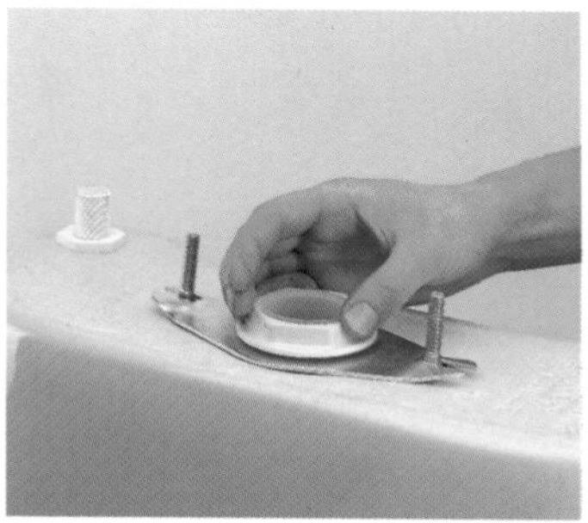

4 Lift off the cistern from the pan and unhook the lift rod. Turn the cistern over, unscrew the retaining nut, remove the siphon and plate and renew the valve as above.

RENEWING THE FLAP VALVE ON A TWO-PART SIPHON

If a cistern is fitted with a two-part plastic siphon such as a Turbo 88, there is no need to stop the inflow or, with a close-coupled suite, to remove the cistern.

A two-part siphon can be fitted to most types of lavatory cistern. The initial fitting does involve cutting off the water supply and, if necessary, lifting off the cistern (see above). After that, maintenance is as below.

You will need
Tools Screwdriver.
Materials Spares pack for size of siphon (containing flap valve; washers; possibly O-ring seal).

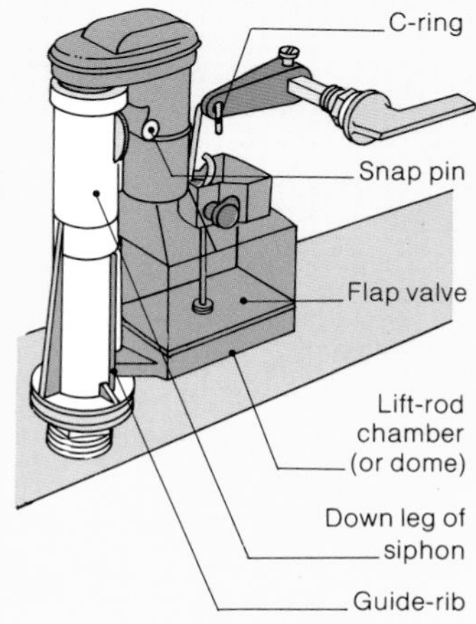

1 With the cistern lid removed, unhook the flush lever from the lift-rod C-ring. Remove a lever-type flush handle, as it may be in the way later.

2 Withdraw the yellow snap pin about $1\frac{1}{4}$in (32mm) to disconnect the lift-rod chamber from the down leg of the siphon.

3 Slide the chamber upwards to disengage it from the guide rib on the down leg.

4 Remove the C-ring and washer from the top of the lift rod and slide the lift rod from the bottom of the chamber.

5 Take off the lift-rod washers and weight so that you can remove the old flap valve and fit a new one.

6 Before reassembling, check if the O-ring seal at the top of the chamber section is worn. Renew it if necessary.

Dealing with a faulty lavatory pan

The usual faults with a lavatory pan are blockages or leaks. A leak from the pan outlet is not difficult to repair, but a cracked pan will have to be replaced (see below).

CLEARING A WASHDOWN PAN

When a washdown bowl is flushed, the two streams of water, one from each side of the rim, should flow equally to meet at the front. The water should leave the pan smoothly, not eddying like a whirlpool. If the cistern is working properly but the bowl fails to clear, something is obstructing either the flush inlet or the pan outlet.

If the flush water rises almost to the pan rim then ebbs away very slowly, there is most likely a blockage in the pan outlet or possibly in the drain it discharges into.

You will need

Tools Plunger with long handle. Possibly also: flexible drain auger; bucket; mirror; a pair of rubber gloves.

> HELPFUL TIP
> If you have no plunger, you may be able to use a mop or broom tied round with rags. Or stand on a stool and tip in a bucket of water in one go.

1 To clear the pan, take the plunger and push it sharply onto the bottom of the pan to cover the outlet. Then pump the handle up and down two or three times.

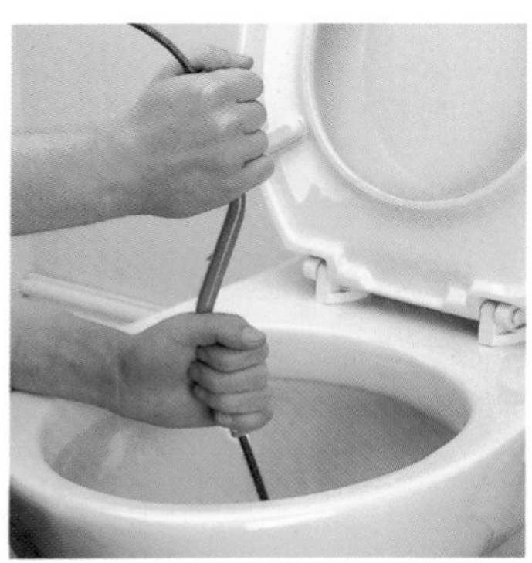

2 If this does not clear the pan, use a flexible drain auger to probe the outlet and trap.

3 If the blockage persists, clear the underground drain (page 459).

4 Flush the cistern to check that water is entering the pan properly, with streams from each side of the rim flowing equally to meet at the front.

5 If the flow into the pan is poor or uneven, use a mirror to examine the flushing rim. Probe the rim with your fingers for flakes of rust or debris from the cistern that may be obstructing the flush water.

CLEARING A SIPHONIC PAN

Blockages are more common in siphonic pans because of the double trap and the delicate pressure-reducing pipe seal (also known as the atomiser seal). Do not use a plunger on a blocked siphonic pan because this can dislodge the seal.

A blockage can usually be cleared with an auger or by pouring several buckets of warm water into the pan. But if, after clearing the blockage, the water still rises in the pan as it is flushed, renew the atomiser seal.

You will need

Tools Screwdriver; adjustable spanner; container for bailing or a tube for siphoning; silicone grease. *Materials* A new atomiser seal.

1 Remove the cistern (see page 333) and locate the pipe protruding from the bottom of the siphon.

2 Remove the rubber mushroom-shaped seal and fit a replacement.

3 Lubricate the new seal with silicone grease so that it will slide down the pipe.

4 Refit the cistern and test the flush. The water should be removed from the bowl with a sucking noise before the clean water comes in from the rim of the bowl.

REPAIRING A LEAKING PAN OUTLET

A putty joint may leak when the putty gets old and cracked.

To replace a putty joint with a push-fit connector (page 331), the pan must be moved forward then refitted. Alternatively, you can repair the joint using waterproof building tape or cord (glazing tape) and non-setting mastic filler.

Chip and rake out the old putty with an old chisel and bind two or three turns of tape round the pan outlet. Then poke more tape firmly into the rim of the soil-pipe inlet. Fill the space between the rim and pan outlet with mastic.

Bind two more turns of tape round the joint.

Replacing a lavatory pan

At one time lavatory pans were always cemented to a solid floor, but the setting of the cement often put a strain on the pan and caused the china to crack. Now they are usually screwed down to a wooden or a solid floor.

An old or cracked lavatory pan with a down-pointing outlet cemented to a floor-exit pipe is the most difficult type to remove.

You will need

Tools Screwdriver; spirit level. Possibly drill and wood or masonry bits; safety spectacles; club hammer; cold chisel; rags; old chisel; thin pen, pencil or nail; trimming knife.

Materials Lavatory pan and seat; pan fixing kit; rubber cone connector; suitable push-fit pan connector. Possibly also: wall plugs (for a solid floor); packing (to steady the pan) such as wood slivers, vinyl tile strips, or silicone sealant.

REMOVING A PAN WITH A HORIZONTAL OUTLET

1 Disconnect the flush pipe by peeling back the cone connector. ALTERNATIVELY, chip away a rag-and-putty joint with an old chisel.

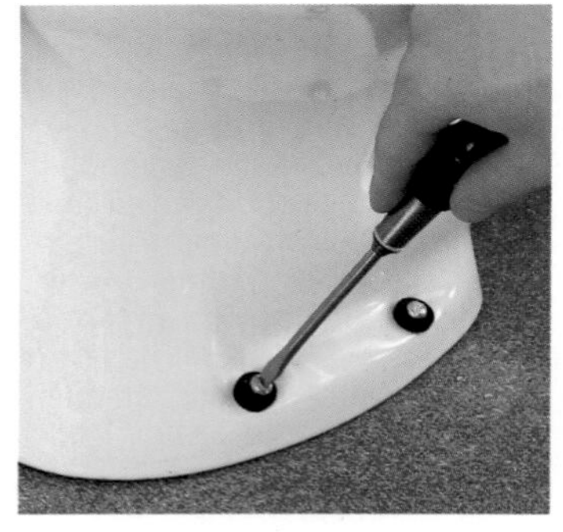

2 Undo the screws holding the pan to the floor.

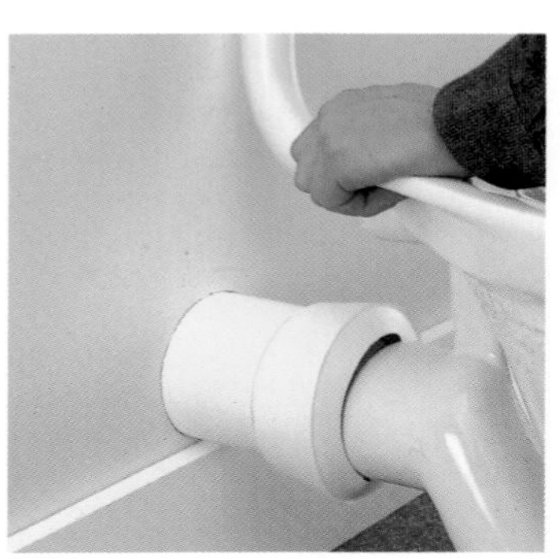

3 Pull the pan slowly forward, moving it from side to side, to free it from the soil-pipe inlet. It should come away easily. If you have any difficulty, break the pan outlet in the same way as for a down-pointing outlet (below).

4 If the outlet joint was cemented with putty or mastic filler, chip it off the metal soil-pipe inlet.

REMOVING A PAN WITH A DOWN-POINTING OUTLET

1 Disconnect the flush pipe in the same way as for a horizontal pan.

2 Undo the floor screws, or break cement with a hammer and cold chisel.

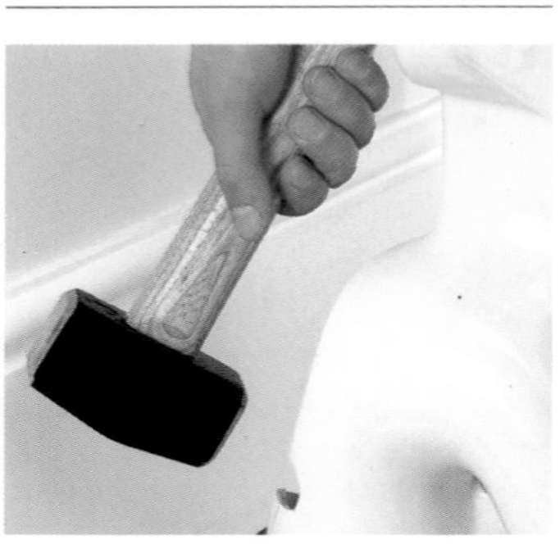

3 To free the pan outlet, put on safety spectacles and use a club hammer to break the outlet pipe just above its joint with the drain socket in the floor. Then pull the pan forward, away from the jagged remains protruding from the drain socket.

4 Stuff rags into the drain socket to stop debris falling in, then chip away the rest of the pan outlet with a hammer and cold chisel. Work with the chisel blade pointing inwards, and break the china right down to the socket at one point. The rest of the china should then come out easily.

5 Chip away any cement from round the collar of the drain socket with a hammer and cold chisel. It does not matter if you accidentally break the collar.

6 Clear away any cement left where the pan was cemented to the floor, leaving a flat base for the new lavatory pan.

FITTING A SEPARATE PAN

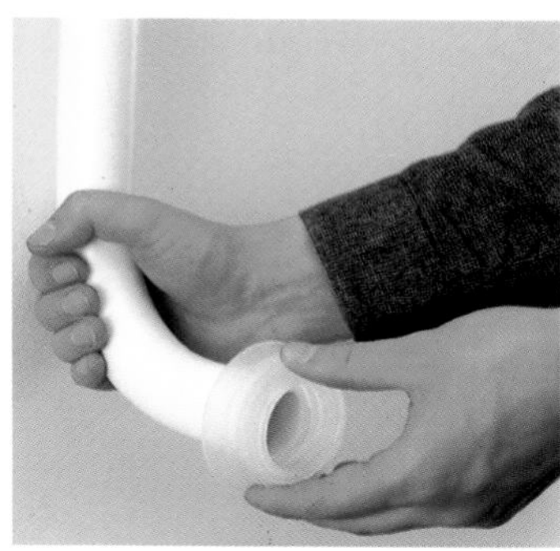

1 Fit a rubber cone connector to the flush-pipe outlet, unless one is already fitted.

2 Fit a plastic push-on connector to the pan outlet.

If the drain socket for the pan is in the floor, use an angled 90 degree connector to link a horizontal pan outlet to the vertical inlet to the soil pipe.

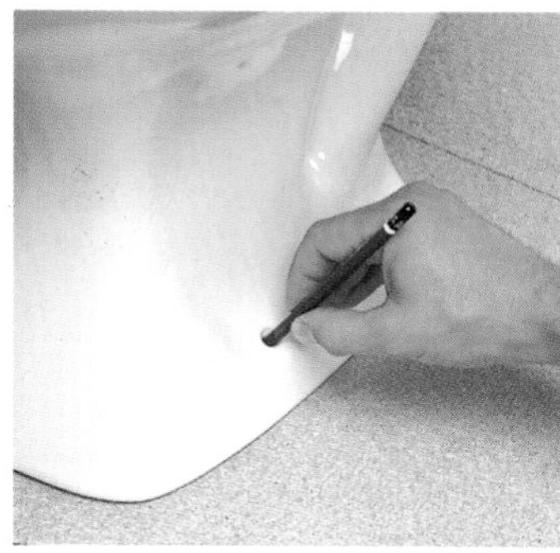

3 Mark the position of the holes in the pan onto the floor, using a slim marker such as a ballpoint pen or a pencil.

4 With the pan still in position, draw a line round its base so that it can be put back in place accurately. Then move it out of the way.

5 Cut the plastic threads on the pan-fixing brackets to length. Drill and fix the brackets so that the plastic thread lines up with the marks on the floor.

On a solid floor, such as concrete, use a masonry bit and insert wall plugs for the screws.

6 If the soil-pipe inlet is a floor socket, remove the rags, taking care not to spill any of the debris in the inlet.

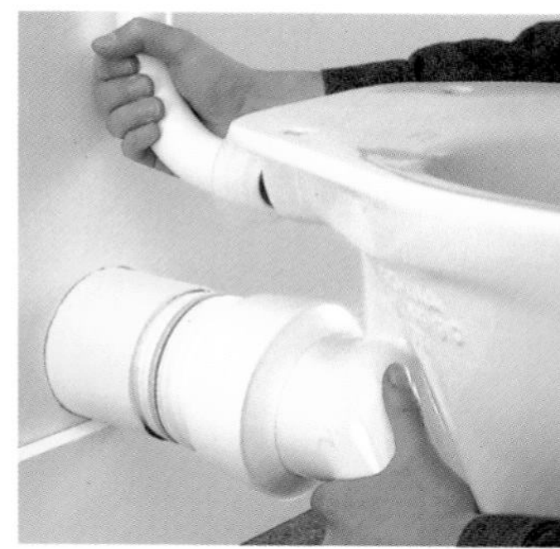

7 Carefully lift the lavatory pan into position over the plastic threads, using the previously marked outline to guide you, and at the same time positioning it so that you can push the flexible connector into the soil-pipe inlet.

8 Fold back the rubber cone connector and slip it over the flushing horn of the pan.

9 Screw on the plastic nuts to hold the pan firmly in position. Do not tighten them fully yet.

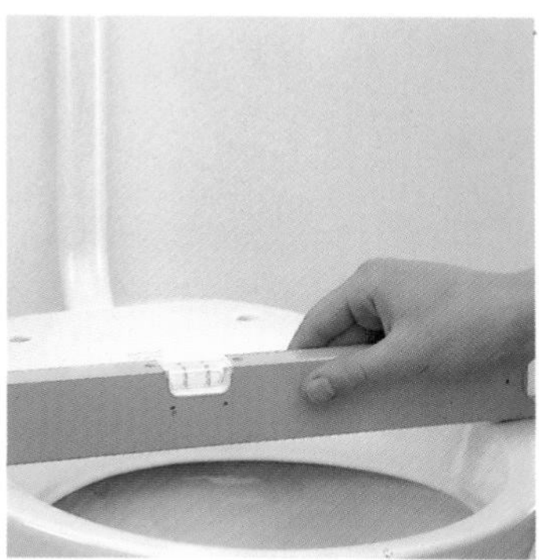

10 Use a spirit level placed across the top of the pan to check that it is level from side to side and from front to back.

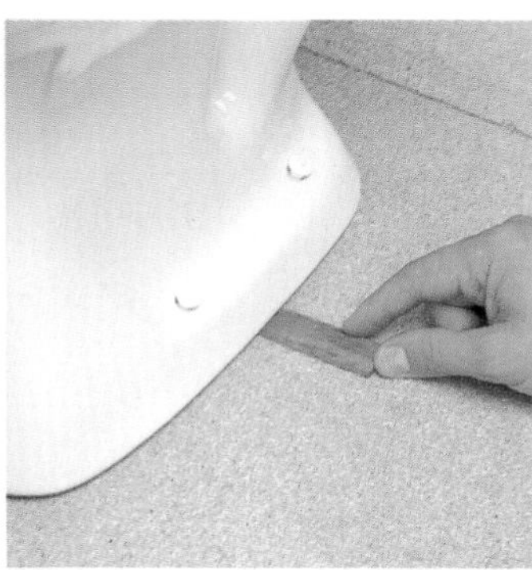

11 To level the pan, loosen the plastic nuts and pack under the pedestal with strips of vinyl tile, or use a bead of silicone sealant to steady the pan and provide an even bed. Once the pan is level, screw it down firmly.

FITTINGS FOR A SEPARATE LOW-LEVEL SUITE

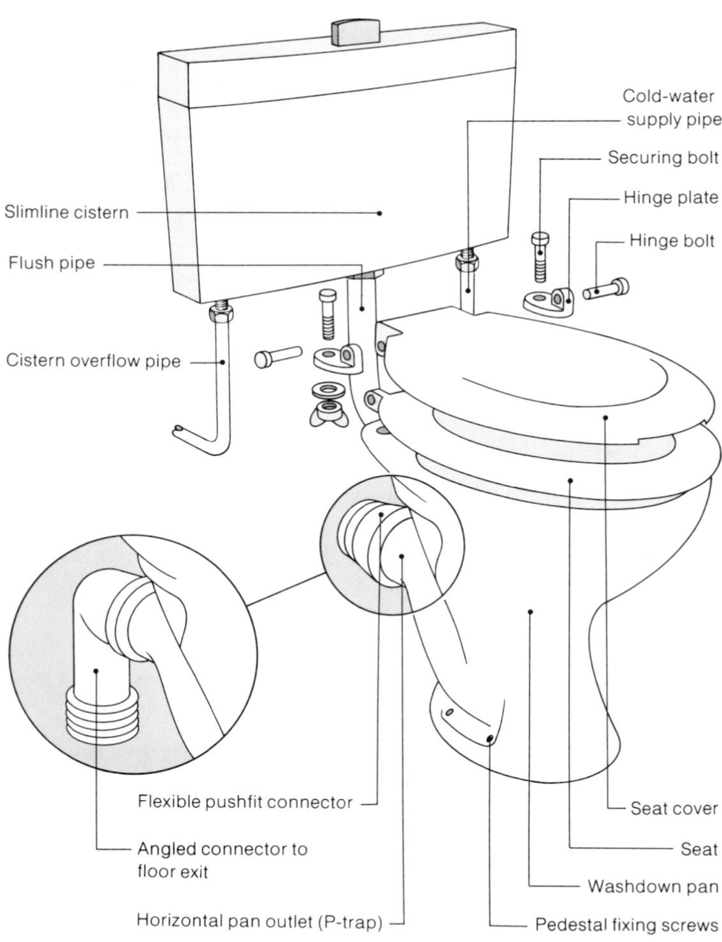

Most modern lavatory pans have a horizontal outlet. If the replacement pan has to be fitted to a soil pipe in a drain socket on a ground floor, connect the P-trap outlet of the pan to the soil-pipe inlet using an angled push-fit connector (page 331).

After fitting a lavatory suite, you may find that condensation – particularly apparent on a ceramic cistern – is a nuisance and leads to damp walls and floors. Make sure the lavatory or bathroom is properly ventilated (page 463). In a bathroom, avoid drip-drying washing over the bath, as this contributes to condensation.

FITTING A NEW SEAT

A lavatory pan seat and cover are usually hinged onto hinge bolts or a rod at the back. These fit into hinge plates or covers at each side of the pan.

Hinge plates or covers are each held in place by a securing bolt that fits through a fixing hole in the back of the pan and is secured by a wing nut.

Make sure you insert washers to shield the pan from the head of the securing bolt and the wing nut. Washers shaped to the pattern of hinge covers are often supplied. Screw the wing nuts firmly finger tight.

A lavatory seat breaks easily if misused – such as by standing on it to close a window.

CHECKING THE FITTING

When fitting a new lavatory pan, make sure that it is level and that the connections to the flush pipe and soil pipe are true. Otherwise slow pan clearance or a blockage could result.

On an existing lavatory pan with old-style joints rather than flexible connectors, blockages can occur because the openings are out of true or partially obstructed by the jointing material. Putty from an old rag-and-putty joint between the flush pipe and horn may have squeezed into the flush inlet and be impeding the inflow of water.

Putty or other jointing material could be obstructing the joint between the pan outlet and the soil-pipe inlet. This is evident if the water rises slowly in the pan before it flows away.

Make sure the lavatory pan is firmly fixed and that the fixing screws have not worked loose. Check that the pan is horizontal when fixing it in place.

How a ball-valve works

In a cold-water storage cistern or lavatory cistern, the water level is regulated by a ball-valve (or ball-cock) – that is opened and closed by a lever arm attached to a float.

When the cistern is at normal level, the float holds the arm horizontal and the valve is closed. When the water level drops, the float lowers the arm and the valve opens to let more water in. The name ball-valve is from the early type of copper ball float. Modern floats are not always balls, and valves are often called float valves.

Ball-valves may be made from brass, gunmetal or plastic, or may be metal with some plastic parts. The size is measured by the inlet shank diameter; ½in or ¾in (15mm or 22mm) sizes are usually needed for domestic cisterns.

A cold-water storage cistern or lavatory cistern where the supply is direct from the mains needs a high-pressure valve. A lavatory cistern supplied from the cold-water storage cistern needs a low-pressure valve. If the pressure is very low because the lavatory cistern is only slightly lower than the storage cistern, a full-way valve is needed.

Low-pressure valves have wider inlet nozzles than high-pressure valves. If a high-pressure valve is fitted where a low-pressure valve is needed, the cistern will fill much too slowly. If a low-pressure valve is fitted in a cistern supplied from the mains, water will leak past the valve.

Most modern valves can be changed from high-pressure to low-pressure operation either by inserting a different fitting into the inlet nozzle or by changing a detachable inlet nozzle. Some types are suitable for high or low water pressure without any alteration.

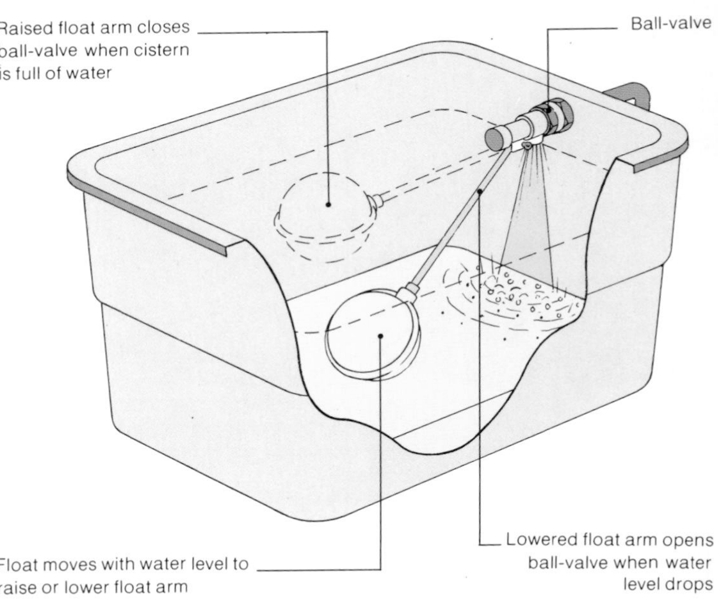

Repairing a faulty ball-valve

If a ball-valve does not open fully, the cistern (lavatory or cold-water storage) will be slow to fill. With a cold-water storage cistern this results in airlocks in the supply pipes and a poor flow from taps.

If the ball-valve does not close fully, the water level in the cistern will become too high and there will be a constant outflow from the overflow pipe.

PORTSMOUTH VALVES

The valve will not work efficiently if the washer is worn or moving parts are clogged by scale or corrosion.

You will need
Tools Combination pliers; small screwdriver; fine abrasive paper; pencil. Possibly also: penknife.
Materials Split pin (cotter-pin); washer; petroleum jelly. Possibly also: penetrating oil.

1 Turn off the main stopcock if you are working on the cold-water cistern, or the gate valve to the lavatory cistern (page 306).

2 Use a pipe wrench to loosen the ball-valve end cap, if there is one, then unscrew and remove it.

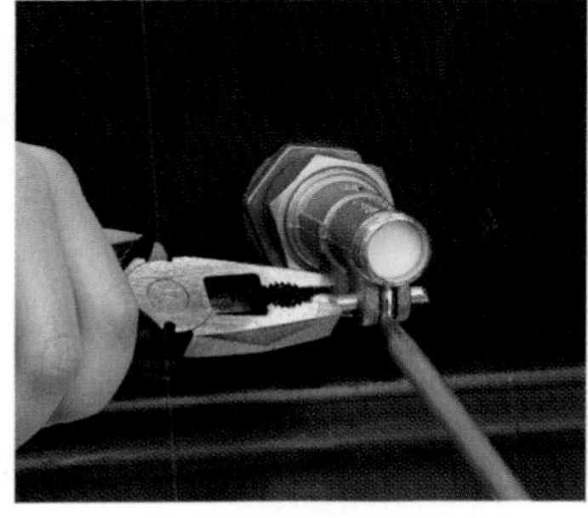

3 Use pliers to close the end of the split pin securing the float arm, then withdraw the pin.

4 Remove the float arm and put it to one side.

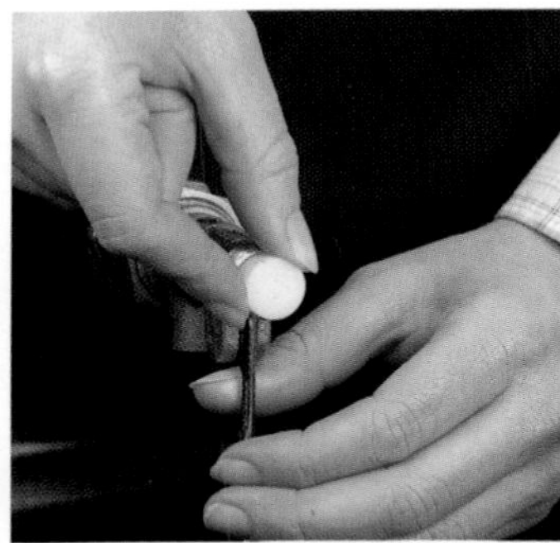

5 Insert a small screwdriver blade into the slot where the float arm was seated. Use it to push the plug from the end of the casing. Catch the plug with your other hand as it comes out.

6 Clean the outside of a metal plug (not a plastic plug) with fine abrasive paper.

7 Wrap fine abrasive paper round a pencil shaft and clean the inside of the metal valve casing.

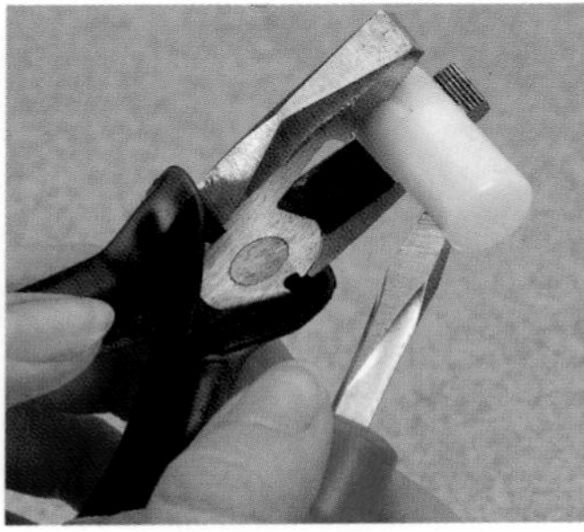

8 To renew the washer, hold the plug with a screwdriver thrust into the slot and use pliers to unscrew its washer-retaining cap. Do not force it or you may damage the plug. If a metal plug is difficult to undo, smear penetrating oil round the cap edge and try again after about ten minutes.

9 With the cap removed, use a screwdriver to prise out the washer from the inside. (If you were unable to remove the cap, try to pick out the old washer with a penknife through the cap's open centre.)

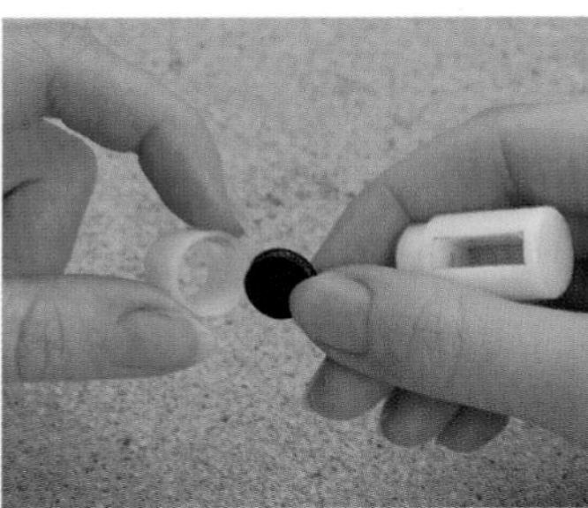

10 Fit the new washer and screw the plug cap back on. Tighten with pliers. (If the cap is still on, try to force the new washer through the centre hole and push it flat with your finger.)

11 Before refitting the plug, turn on the water supply briefly to flush out dirt from the valve casing still attached to the cistern.

12 Lightly smear the plug with petroleum jelly before reassembling the valve and float arm. Use a new split pin to secure the arm.

13 Restore the water supply.

DIAPHRAGM-TYPE VALVES

The cistern will be slow to refill if the inlet gets clogged or the diaphragm gets jammed against it.

You will need
Tools Screwdriver. Possibly also: pipe wrench; cloth for padding wrench jaws.
Materials Lint-free rag; warm soapy water in container; clear water for rinsing. Possibly also: rubber or synthetic diaphragm.

1 Turn off the main stopcock if you are working on the cold-water cistern, or the gate valve to the lavatory cistern (page 306).

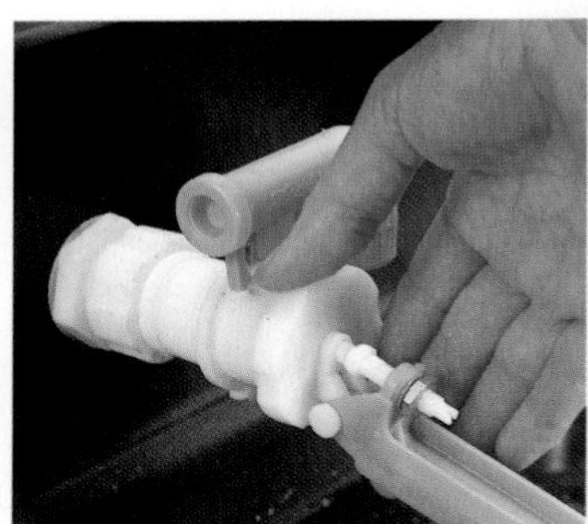

2 Unscrew the large knurled retaining nut by hand. If it is stiff, use a padded pipe wrench.

3 With the nut removed, the end of the float arm and plunger will come away. Put them to one side.

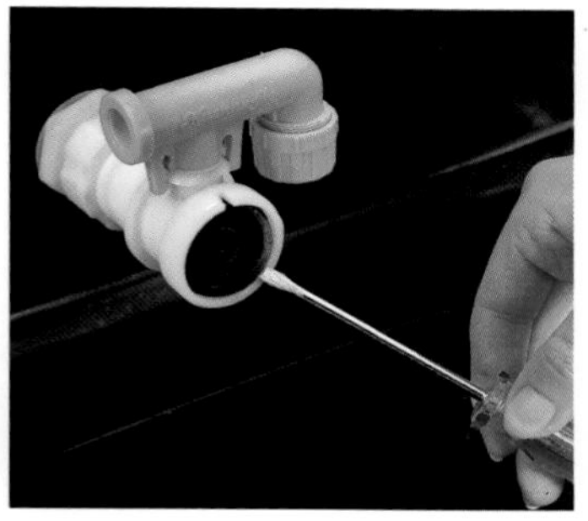

4 Use a screwdriver blade to free the diaphragm from the inlet pipe, taking care not to damage it.

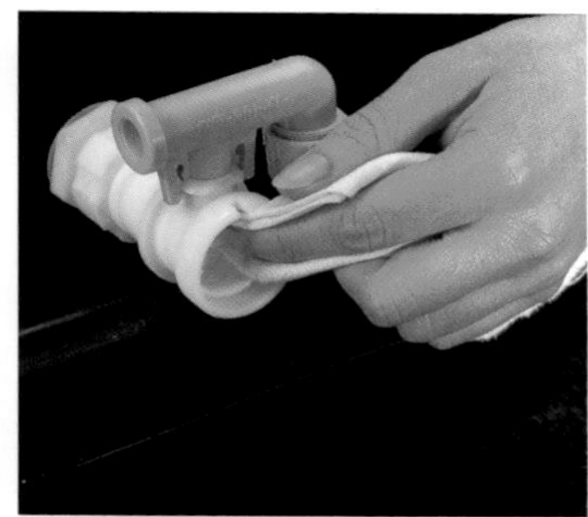

5 Use a piece of clean, lint-free rag to clean out any dirt and debris from the inlet pipe.

6 Wash the diaphragm in warm soapy water, then rinse it. If it is pitted or damaged, replace it. Fit with the rim inwards.
ALTERNATIVELY, if the valve is a servo type with a filter fitted, remove the filter and wash it in warm soapy water, then rinse it. If the servo valve has no filter, flush the part attached to the float arm under the tap.

7 Before reassembling the valve, turn on the water supply briefly to flush dirt or debris out of the casing. Then refit the parts and restore the water supply.

BALL-VALVES IN COMMON USE

TYPE OF VALVE	DESCRIPTION	ADVANTAGES AND DISADVANTAGES
Portsmouth 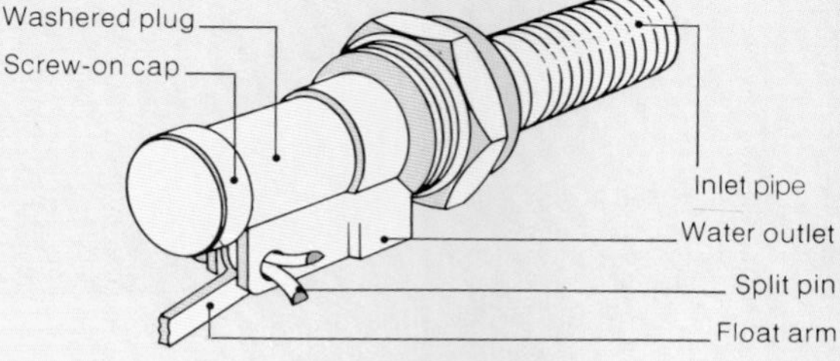 	The commonest type in British homes. The water inlet is opened and closed by a washered plug (or piston) that moves horizontally. The plug is slotted onto a float arm and secured with a split pin. Some types have a screw-on cap at the end of the plug. The water outlet is on the bottom of the valve in front of the float arm. The detachable inlet pipe can be changed to suit the water pressure.	Sturdy and long-lasting. Water hammer – vibration of the rising main – can result from the valve bouncing in its seating. The bouncing is caused by ripples on the water surface when the cistern is almost full making the float arm shake; sometimes also by the pressure of incoming water against the valve. Scale or corrosion can prevent the valve from operating properly.
Equilibrium (Portsmouth pattern) 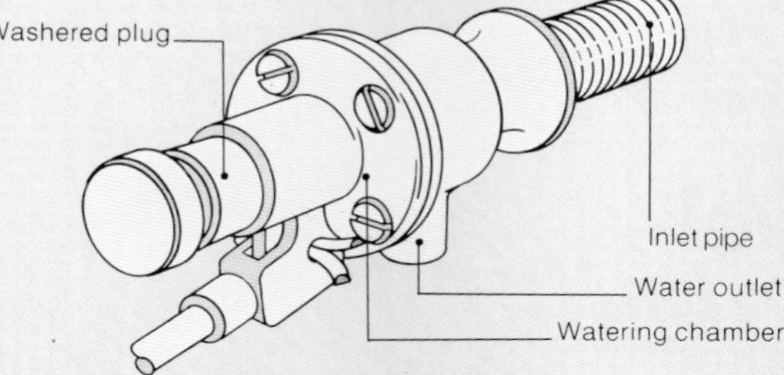 	Similar in appearance and operation to a Portsmouth valve, but there is a horizontal channel through the centre of the plug leading to a washered, watertight chamber at the rear of the valve. The inlet water fills the channel and chamber so that water pressure is the same at both ends of the plug. The large inlet pipe is suitable for all pressures.	Designed for use where mains pressure tends to fluctuate. The equal pressures on the valve make water hammer less likely than in standard Portsmouth' types, and there is also less wear on the washer, so it rarely needs changing. Scale or corrosion can affect valve operation.
Diaphragm (also known as BRE, BRS or Garston) 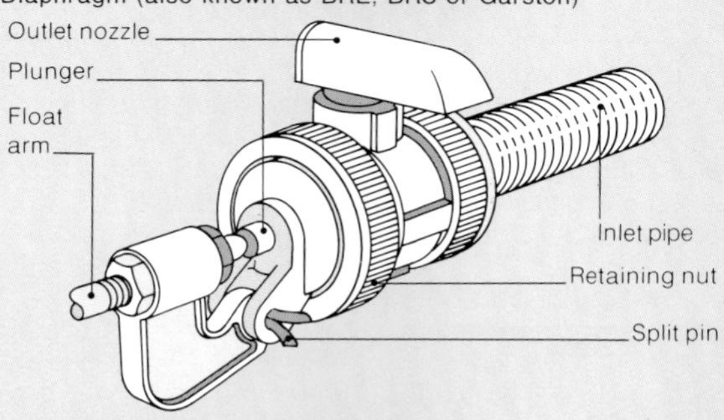 	The water inlet is closed by a large rubber or synthetic diaphragm pushed against it by a plunger attached to the float arm. A detachable nylon overhead outlet nozzle discharges water in a gentle shower. The inlet pipe can be changed to suit the water pressure.	The discharge spray cuts down filling noise and rippling, and the diaphragm keeps the plunger and float arm from contact with water, so they are not affected by scale and corrosion. The diaphragm can become jammed, and grit can block the inlet chamber. The valve can be dismantled by hand by undoing a large knurled retaining nut.
Servo-diaphragm (also known as diaphragm/equilibrium or Torbeck) 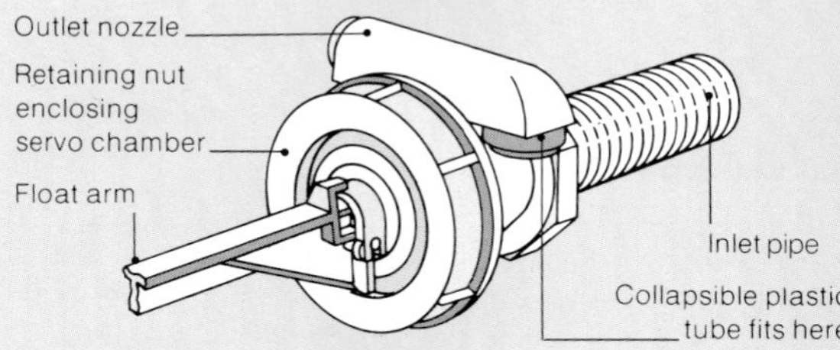 	A plastic valve with a small float and short float arm. Behind the large rubber or synthetic diaphragm covering the inlet there is a water (or servo) chamber which is fed via a metering pin. Equal water pressure on each side of the diaphragm keeps it closed. When the float arm drops, it opens a pilot hole in the back of the chamber, covered by a sealing washer. The tiny outflow through the pilot hole reduces pressure in the servo chamber, and the diaphragm opens the inlet. The outlet is overhead, but water flows to below the cistern level through a collapsible plastic tube.	The design allows very rapid and silent delivery. Because the plastic tube is collapsible, it cuts down the noise of filling without the risk of water being drawn back into the main – a risk that makes rigid silencer tubes illegal. The valve can be fitted with an optional filter, which needs regular cleaning but collects grit that might otherwise obstruct the metering pin and pilot hole. Flow restrictors are fitted into the inlet pipe to adapt it for high or low pressures. This type of valve is designed for use on a toilet only.

Fitting a new ball valve

Fit a new ball-valve if the old one gets damaged or broken, or if you decide to change the type of valve, to get rid of noise and vibration.

You will need
Tools Two adjustable spanners.
Materials Ball-valve with float (of same size as existing valve); two flat plastic washers to fit valve inlet shank ($\frac{1}{2}$in or $\frac{3}{4}$in); mini-stopcock (page 306) with compression fitting inlet and tap connector outlet.

1 Turn off the main stopcock to cut off the cistern water supply.

2 Use a spanner to undo the tap connector securing the supply pipe to the valve tail. You may need to hold the valve body or any securing nut inside the cistern steady with a second spanner.

3 Disconnect the supply pipe.

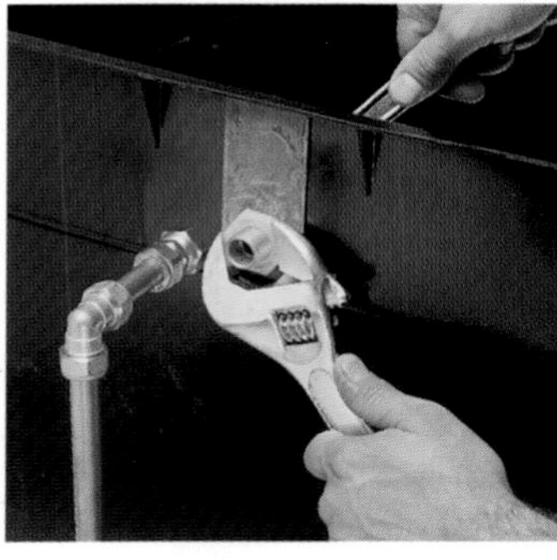

4 Undo the back nut securing the ball-valve to the cistern. Remove the valve.

5 Take off the back nut from the new ball-valve and put it aside.

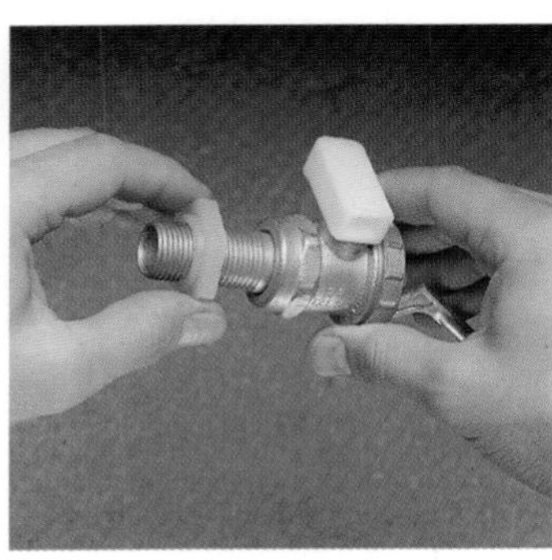

6 Slip a flat plastic washer (and an inner securing nut, if supplied) over the new valve tail and push the tail through the cistern and the bracing plate from the inside.

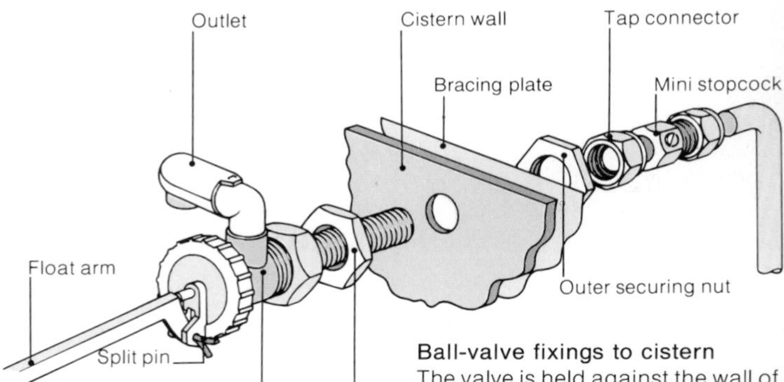

Ball-valve fixings to cistern
The valve is held against the wall of the cistern by a back nut over its threaded inlet tail.

7 Slip another plastic washer over the protruding tail and screw on the back nut by hand. Tighten it half a turn with a spanner.

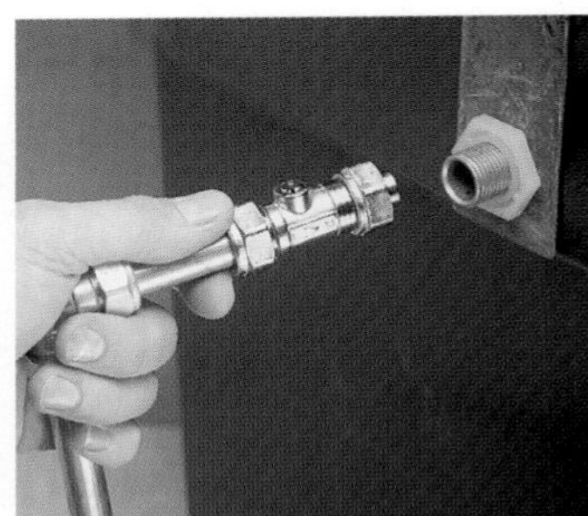

8 Remove existing tap connector and fit mini-stopcock. Screw connector nut to new valve tail.

9 Restore water supply, making sure mini-stopcock is fully open. Adjust cistern level (see below).

Adjusting the cistern water level

The normal level of a full cistern is about 1in (25mm) below the overflow outlet. The level can be raised by raising the float, or lowered by lowering the float. If the cistern overflows, the level is too high because the float either needs adjusting or is leaking and failing to rise to close the valve (or the valve may be faulty, page 336).

ADJUSTING A BALL-VALVE

You will need
Tools Possibly small spanner; vice.

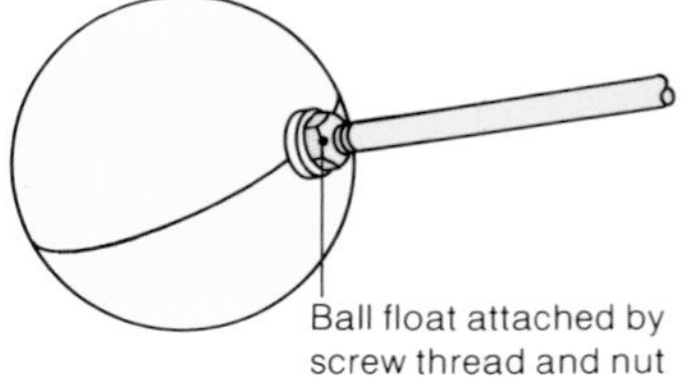

On a Portsmouth-pattern valve with a ball float, unscrew and remove the float from the arm. To lower the level, hold the arm firmly in both hands and bend it slightly downwards. Then refit the float. If the arm is too stiff to bend in position, remove it from the cistern and grip it in a vice.

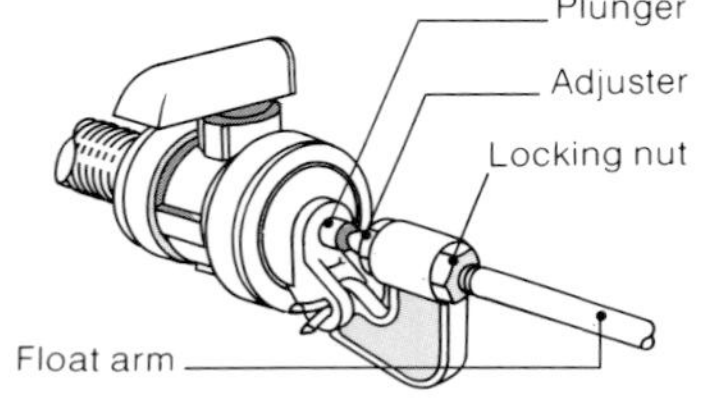

On a diaphragm valve with an adjuster at the top of the float arm, adjust the level by loosening the locking nut and screwing the adjuster forward, nearer to the plunger. ALTERNATIVELY, use an adjuster nut or clip near the float to move the float farther away from the valve along a horizontal arm, or to a lower position if it is linked to the arm by a vertical rod.

REPAIRING A LEAKING FLOAT

For a permanent repair, a new ball float must be fitted. But to get the valve back in action again until a new float is obtained, the old one can be temporarily repaired.

You will need
Tools Small spanner; sharp knife or old-fashioned tin opener; piece of wood to go across cistern.
Materials Plastic bag; string.

1 Raise the float arm to close the valve and cut off the flow of the water. Then tie the arm to a length of wood laid across the top of the cistern.

2 Unscrew and remove the ball float from the float arm.

3 Find the hole through which the water is leaking and enlarge it with either a sharp knife or tin opener.

4 Drain the water from the float, then screw it back in position on the float arm.

5 Slip the plastic bag over the float and tie it securely to the float arm.

6 Release the arm and lower it into position.

GETTING RID OF WATER HAMMER

Banging or humming from the rising main is due to the pipe vibrating when the cistern ball-valve bounces on its seating. This occurs when the float is shaken by ripples on the water as the cistern fills. Cut down the bouncing, by fitting the float with a stabiliser made from a plastic pot. Hang the pot on a loop of galvanised wire from the float arm. It should trail underwater a few inches below the float.

Ensure that the rising main is securely clipped to the roof timber near its entry to the cistern. Also, check that a metal bracing plate is fitted on a plastic cistern (see above), to reduce distortion of the cistern walls.

The surest way to reduce water hammer is to replace a Portsmouth valve with an equilibrium valve – a type less affected by water pressure.

Alternative ways of heating water

The average household uses 50-70 gallons (227-320 litres) of hot water a day. The commonest type of water-heating system is a hot-water storage cylinder heated by either a gas or solid-fuel boiler (pages 345-346), probably combined with a central-heating system. Various kinds of gas or electric heater can also be used to supplement the system, or as a complete system in themselves. They may be fed either by a low-pressure supply from the cold-water cistern, or by a high-pressure supply direct from the mains.

TYPE OF HEATER	DESCRIPTION	ADVANTAGES AND DISADVANTAGES
Immersion heater	Electric element fitted into a standard storage cylinder to heat water. May be 1kW, 2kW or 3kW. There are three types: top-entry with one element extending almost to the cylinder bottom; top-entry with two elements – a long one for cheap night electricity and a short one for heating a small amount of water as needed; side-entry – usually a pair, one at the bottom to heat the entire cylinder and one at the top for heating small amounts. All types have one or two thermostats, usually adjustable (page 341).	Can be fitted into a copper hot-water cylinder as the sole means of heating, or as a supplement to a boiler. Can be renewed if it burns out. Modern cylinders usually have 1¼in (32mm) or 2¼in (57mm) bosses in the dome or low in a side wall (or both) for heater fitting. Only water above the level of the heater bottom is heated. Expensive unless the storage cylinder is well insulated and used only as needed. (Ways of saving heat, below.)
Electric storage heater (low-pressure type)	Large-capacity, heavily insulated storage cylinder supplied from the cold-water cistern and heated by one or two immersion heaters fitted horizontally. When two heaters are used, the upper one can be kept on for a permanent hot-water supply, the lower one turned on for extra heat when a large supply is needed, such as for a bath.	Can be installed at any convenient point to supply a number of hot taps, but must have a vent pipe to the cold-water cistern. There are types for fitting under a sink or draining board (UDB), and floor-standing types. Floor-standing types are very well insulated and designed for use with off-peak meters.
Electric storage heater (cistern type)	Medium or large capacity, heavily insulated storage cylinder supplied from the rising main through its own built-in cold-water cistern. The cylinder is heated by one or two immersion heaters, in the same way as a low-pressure type (above).	Useful for supplying a number of hot taps where the water supply is direct from the mains. The built-in cistern feeds the heater only – no other cold taps. There are wall-mounted types or floor-standing types. Large, well-insulated floor-standing types are designed for use with off-peak meters.
Instantaneous gas heater	The water is heated by gas as it flows through small-bore copper tubing. When the hot tap is turned on, the gas jets are ignited by a pilot light that burns continuously. The jets go out when the tap is turned off. Large multipoint heaters can supply all household hot taps; smaller single-point types supply one tap only. The water supply is normally direct from the rising main. But a heater can be fed from a cold-water cistern if it is high enough – usually at least 6ft 6in (2m) above the highest tap – to give enough pressure.	Useful where there is no cold-water cistern. Only the water used is heated – there is no slow cooling of unused water. But the delivery rate is slower than from a cylinder, and the flow from one hot tap is interrupted if another is turned on. The heater has a flue and must be fitted against an outside wall. It is designed to raise water temperature by about 26°C (47°F), so in cold weather – when mains water can be near freezing – the heated water is either cool or slow running. In summer it may be too hot. Some have a winter/summer setting to vary the heat.
Open-outlet electric storage heater	Small-capacity storage heater – about 1–3 gallons (4–13 litres) – supplied direct from the rising main. The heater's tap is on the inlet pipe, and when it is turned on cold water from the mains forces out the stored water through an outlet spout or nozzle. The water is heated to a thermostatically controlled temperature.	Useful for supplying small, frequent amounts of water economically – there is no pipework from the cistern to lose heat in transit. Each heater supplies one point only – over-sink types from a built-in spout, under-sink types from special taps fitted to the sink. The water outlet also acts as a vent, and must not be blocked.
Instantaneous open-outlet electric heater	Small heater, supplied direct from the rising main, in which the water is heated as it passes through. Heaters with a 7kW element are designed for showers (page 328), those with a 3kW element for washing hands. The water emerges through a spray nozzle – heaters are not intended for filling basins.	Useful for providing a shower where there is no suitable cistern supply (page 329), or for hot water for washing hands in a lavatory or cloakroom that has no hot-water supply pipes. Heaters usually raise the temperature by about 26°C (47°F), so water heat varies according to mains water temperature in the same way as gas, but some types have a winter/summer setting. Also, flow may be interrupted when other taps are used, unless a compensating valve is fitted.

Ways of saving heat

Money is wasted if water is heated and then not used. Inefficiencies in the plumbing system, or inefficient use of heaters, can waste heat unnecessarily.

Insulate the hot-water cylinder

A 3in (75mm) thick lagging jacket on a hot-water cylinder cuts down weekly heat loss by about 70 per cent. A 30 gallon (136 litre) cylinder without a jacket, maintained at a temperature of 60°C (140°F), loses enough heat every week to heat about 20 baths – equivalent to the cost of about 86 units of electricity. Many modern cylinders are foam-lagged by the manufacturer. Never strip off part of a cylinder lagging jacket to warm an airing cupboard. It is cheaper to install a low-powered heater in the cupboard.

Keep hot-water pipes short

The length of pipe between the hot-water cylinder and a hot tap is known as a dead leg, because hot water left in the pipe after each use of the tap cools and is wasted. The longer the pipe, the more the waste. Water at 60°C (140°F) travelling through a 15mm copper pipe loses heat equivalent to more than 1 unit of electricity for roughly each foot (300mm) of run per week – enough to heat about 10 gallons of water.

Where a hot-supply pipe to a basin or shower would involve a dead leg of piping more than 20ft (about 6m) long, use an open-outlet storage heater or an instantaneous heater instead.

If you have an electric storage heater installed, position it as near as possible to the hot tap most often used – usually the one over the kitchen sink.

Avoid secondary hot-water circulation

At one time, if a shower or tap was some distance from the hot-water cylinder, there was a constant circulation of hot water to it by means of a return pipe back to the cylinder. This ensured that there was no delay in the arrival of hot water to the tap. Because of the heat lost, avoid such secondary circulation, particularly with electric heating.

Install a shower

Use a shower for daily bathing and keep the bath for relaxed soaking. A bath takes about six times as much water as a shower.

Heat water only as needed

Although a thermostat gives economical heating by controlling temperature, even a well-lagged cylinder will lose heat (generally the equivalent of about 6 units of electricity a week). This can add considerably to costs if the heater is left on all the time.

Savings can be made by switching on an immersion heater or boiler only about an hour before hot water is needed, and switching it off when it is not wanted.

Ways of saving heat (continued)

The most convenient way to do this is to have the heater fitted with a time switch (page 228) that is set to turn it on for times of peak household use. Time switches have a manual override to allow use of the heater at other than the set times. Take advantage also of cheaper night rates for electricity. Details of off-peak meters and tariffs are available from the local electricity board.

Avoid a wholly vertical vent pipe
The vent pipe from the top of the cylinder should run horizontally for at least 20in (about 500mm) before rising vertically to hang over the cold-water cistern. If it goes straight up, heated water rising up the middle of the pipe will cool and run back down the pipe walls to the cylinder.

Prevent scale formation in water pipes and appliances
About 65 per cent of British homes – chiefly those in the south-east and Midlands – have hard or moderately hard water. The hardness is caused by a high concentration of dissolved calcium and magnesium salts, and is evident when, for example, soap does not dissolve properly and scale forms inside the kettle and round a tap nozzle. Hard water drying on any surface leaves a crust of the salts behind, and at high temperatures the salts solidify into scale. When scale forms inside a domestic boiler or hot-water cylinder, it insulates the water from the heat and wastes fuel, and pipes gradually become blocked.

Scale can be prevented or limited by a number of methods:
1 Controlling water temperature – scale starts to form above 60°C (140°F).
2 Suspending scale-inhibiting chemicals in crystal form in the cold-water cistern. They need changing every six months.
3 More expensively, by plumbing a water softener into the rising main – beyond the kitchen tap and a branch to an outside tap. This leaves hard water, which most people prefer, for drinking. It is not worth softening the water for garden use.
4 By plumbing a magnetic water conditioner into the rising main directly above the main stopcock. In this, the water passes through a magnetic field so that the structure of the scale-forming salts is altered; they change into fine particles that flush through the pipes instead of clustering to form scale. The conditioner has a filter that needs cleaning about twice a year.

Descaling an open-outlet heater

A common fault of open-outlet water heaters is a build-up of scale around the heating element. This makes the heater slower to heat up and will lead to the heater element burning out prematurely.

It is possible to remove the heating element through the bottom of the heater, and clean it by immersing it in descaler, but it is easier to pour the descaler into the heater

You will need
Tools Adjustable spanner; pipe wrench; glass or plastic funnel (do not use a metal funnel); length of hosepipe; hose clip; bucket. Possibly also: cloth for padding pipe wrench jaws.
Materials Proprietary liquid descaler, for a large-volume vessel.

1 Switch off the electricity supply to the heater overnight to allow the water to cool.

2 Cut off the water supply to the heater by turning off an isolating stopcock or the main stopcock (page 306).

3 Place a bucket under the heater, below the tap handle – which is at the base of the heater, on the water inlet pipe – to catch stored water.

4 Hold the supply pipe to the heater steady with a pipe wrench (padded if the pipe is plastic) while you undo the cap nut of the heater inlet connection (just above the tap) and disconnect the pipe.

5 Connect the hose to the tail of the heater inlet with a hose clip.

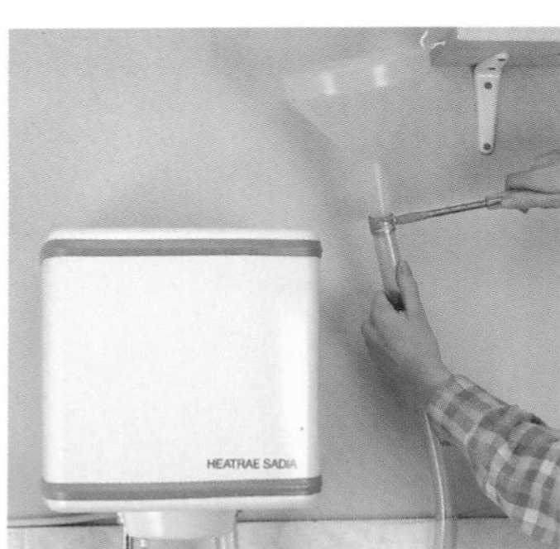

6 Push the glass or plastic funnel into the other end of the hose and raise the funnel until it is higher than the heater top. Secure it in position in some way, if possible.

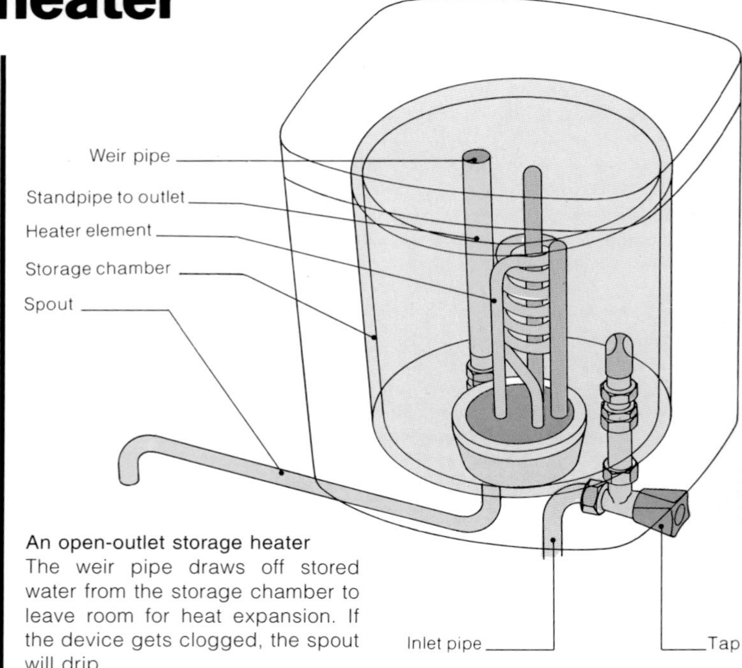

An open-outlet storage heater
The weir pipe draws off stored water from the storage chamber to leave room for heat expansion. If the device gets clogged, the spout will drip.

7 Following the maker's instructions for the amount of liquid descaler to use, slowly and carefully pour undiluted descaler into the funnel until it starts to foam back up the hosepipe.

8 Pour in water through the funnel. Continue until the water starts to drip from the outlet spout of the heater.

9 Wait for about half an hour for the chemical action to stop.

10 Remove the funnel and hose pipe and reconnect the heater supply pipe.

11 Restore the water supply at the stopcock and flush water through before switching on the electricity supply.

Renewing an immersion heater

An immersion heater can burn out after long use or if it gets clogged with scale. Water that takes longer than usual to heat up may indicate scaling. Some immersion heaters are designed for use in hard water.

Although modern heaters have a thermostat and can be prevented from heating above 60°C (140°F) – the temperature at which scale starts to form – they may be used as a supplement to a boiler that does not have the same degree of heat control.

To fit a replacement immersion heater to a low-pressure or cistern-type electric storage heater (page 339), follow the heater maker's instructions. The heater may be on a plate assembly that can be withdrawn without draining the water chamber.

You will need
Tools Immersion-heater spanner (page 305) – box-type for deep lagging; tester screwdriver (page 361); adjustable spanner; hose clip. Possibly also: light hammer.
Materials Immersion heater; PTFE thread-sealing tape. Possibly also: 1.5mm^2 three-core heat-resisting rubber electric flex (page 362); penetrating oil.

1 Switch off the boiler that heats the cylinder, if there is one.

2 Switch off the electricity at the consumer unit.

3 Stop the water supply to the cylinder. Either turn off the gate valve in the feed pipe if there is one, or drain the cold-water cistern (page 306).

4 Turn on the bathroom taps to draw off any water in the pipe.

5 Locate the cylinder drain cock. For an indirect cylinder (or a direct cylinder heated solely by an immersion heater) it is at the base of the feed pipe from the cistern.

For a direct cylinder heated by a boiler, use the boiler drain cock (page 302).

6 Drain water from the cylinder (page 300) as necessary – about 1 gallon (4.5 litres) for a top-entry or high side-entry heater, or the whole cylinder for a low side-entry heater.

7 Unscrew and remove the immersion heater cover. Note which of the three conductors is connected to which terminal, then disconnect them using a tester screwdriver. There should be no current, but if there is current, the screwdriver handle will light up as a warning.

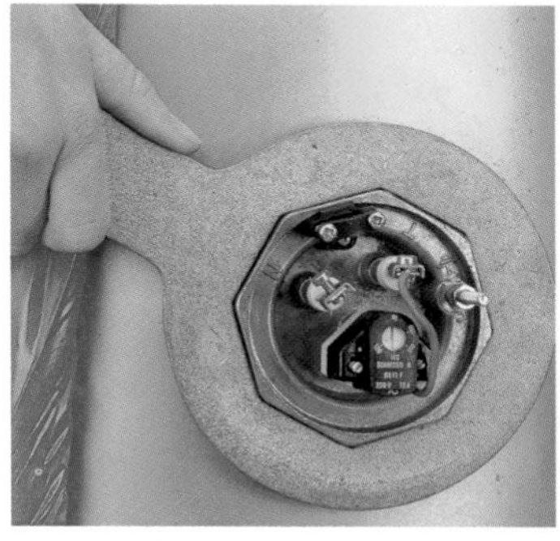

8 Use an immersion-heater spanner to unscrew the old immersion heater and withdraw it from its boss. A flat spanner is suitable if there is no deep lagging.

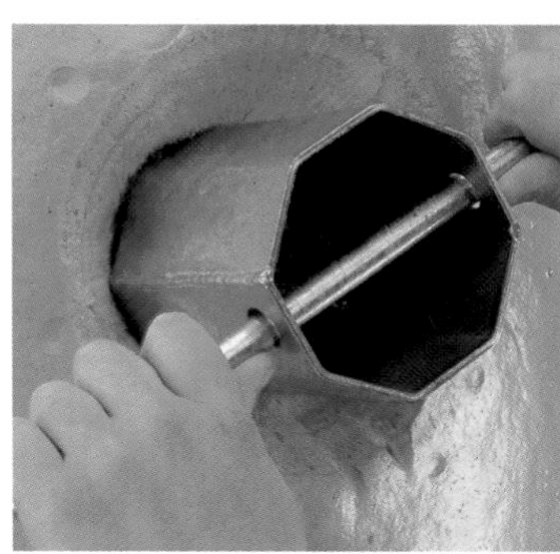

ALTERNATIVELY, for a deep-lagged cylinder, you will need a box-type immersion-heater spanner, turned with a tommy bar.

HELPFUL TIP

If the heater is difficult to remove, do not force it. Put penetrating oil round the joint and leave it overnight. Alternatively, warm the joint with a hair dryer.

Then try again with the spanner. Do not give one strong pull. Instead, loosen the thread by giving two or three sharp taps with a light hammer in the opening direction (anticlockwise).

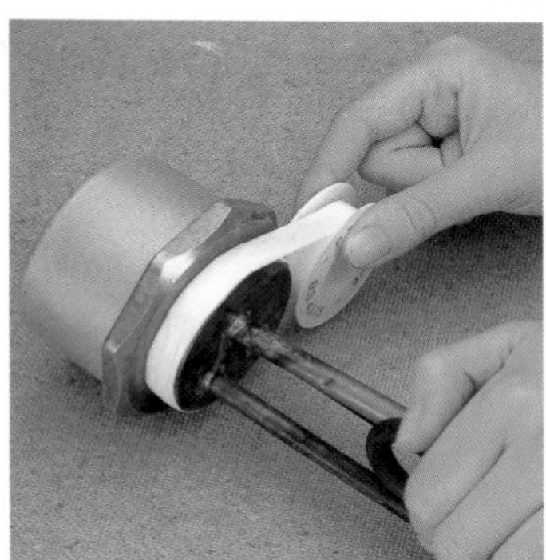

9 If there is no fibre washer, bind over the thread on the tail of the new immersion heater three times, anticlockwise with PTFE tape.

10 Insert the heater into the cylinder boss.

In an indirect cylinder, make sure the element does not foul the heat exchanger.

11 Use the immersion-heater spanner (either a flat or box type as necessary) to screw the heater firmly home.

12 Restore the water supply and check for leaks round the heater boss. If there are any, tighten the heater slightly.

13 Remove the retaining cap of the new heater and refit the three electric conductors to their correct terminals. Use new flex if necessary (page 363).

14 Set the heater thermostat (see below). Set a single thermostat (or the cheap-rate thermostat in a twin system) no higher than 60°C (140°F) in a hard-water area (to prevent scale forming), or up to 65°-70°C (149°-160°F) in a soft-water area. Where two thermostats are fitted, set the one for day-time operation to 50°-55°C (120°-130°F).

15 Refit the cap on the immersion-heater, then restore the electricity supply at the consumer unit.

SETTING THE THERMOSTAT

The temperature control can normally be adjusted with a screwdriver – the settings are marked round the screw. Some two-element heaters have one thermostat, some have two.

Dual (two-element) immersion heaters sometimes have a thermostatic switch unit that can be switched to either 'bath' or 'sink'. Their thermostats cannot normally be adjusted.

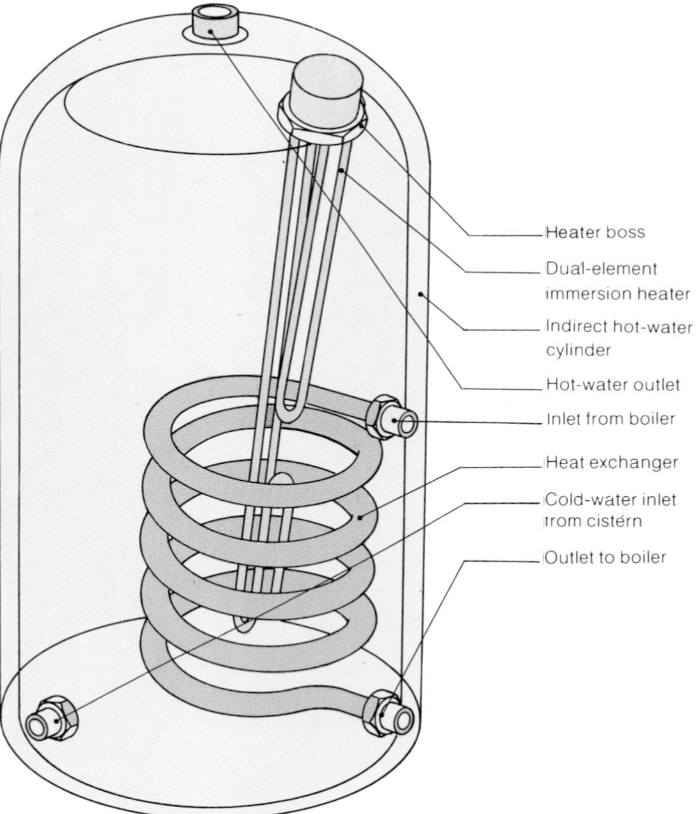

Immersion heater in a hot-water cylinder
The heater may be inserted into the top of the cylinder, and have either one or two elements. Alternatively, there may be one or two separate immersion heaters inserted through the side of the cylinder, one at the top and another at the bottom. The lower one is normally used with off-peak electricity.

Plumbing-in a washing machine or dish washer

A washing machine (or a dishwasher) is easy to install beside a kitchen sink if the existing water pipes and waste pipe are conveniently positioned for fitting a drain kit and branch pipes for the machine stopcocks. When a washing machine or dishwasher is newly plumbed-in, a single check valve (non-return valve) must be fitted to the hot and cold pipes supplying the hoses.

Drain kits will not fit every type of washing machine, so check in the manual or with the manufacturer before choosing one.

You will need

Tools Hacksaw; half-round file; two adjustable spanners; medium-sized screwdriver; measuring tape; soft pencil; two spring-clip clothes pegs; spirit level. Possibly also: shallow pan.

Materials About 24in (610mm) of 15mm copper piping; two 15mm stopcocks with compression ends; two 15mm single check valves; two 15mm equal tee compression connectors with slip ends; one drain kit; one hose clip of the diameter of the drain hose.

CONNECTING UP THE WATER

1 Check the rising main; turn off water and drain pipe (*Fitting the branch pipe inside*, page 316).

2 Mark the sink cold water supply pipe at a point convenient for connection to the machine. Make a second mark ¾in (19mm) higher.

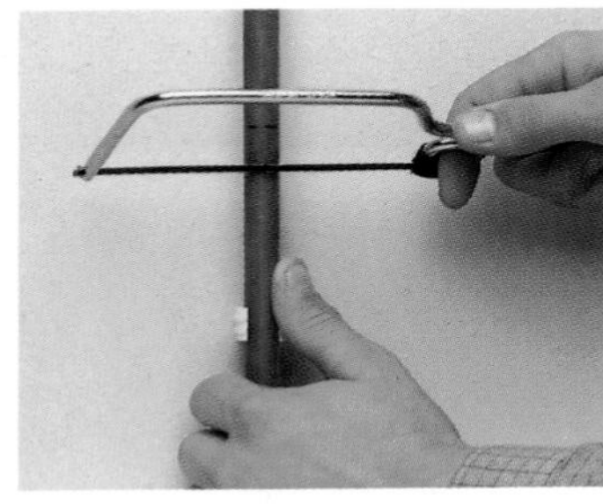

3 Cut through the cold water pipe squarely with a hacksaw at the lowest point marked. If there was not a drain cock above the main stopcock, a small amount of water will run out as you saw through. Cut through the second mark on the cold water pipe and remove the segment of pipe.

4 File the pipe ends smooth and square.

5 Using spring-clip clothes pegs to stop the caps and olives slipping down the pipe, fit a tee connector to the pipe with the branch outlet pointing towards the machine.

6 Cut a 3in (75mm) length of piping, fit it into the tee outlet and connect to a check valve, making sure that the valve's arrow mark points towards the machine.

7 Cut another 3in (75mm) length of piping (or a longer piece if necessary) and fit it to the check valve outlet.

8 Fit the other end of the pipe to compression joint inlet of a machine stopcock. Connect the machine's cold water hose to the stopcock.

9 Turn off the water supply to the hot tap over the kitchen sink (*Taps fed from the cistern*, page 306). Cut the hot water supply pipe, and fit a tee connector, piping, check valve and stopcock as above. Connect the machine's hot water hose to the stopcock and restore the hot and cold water supplies.

FITTING THE WASTE PIPE

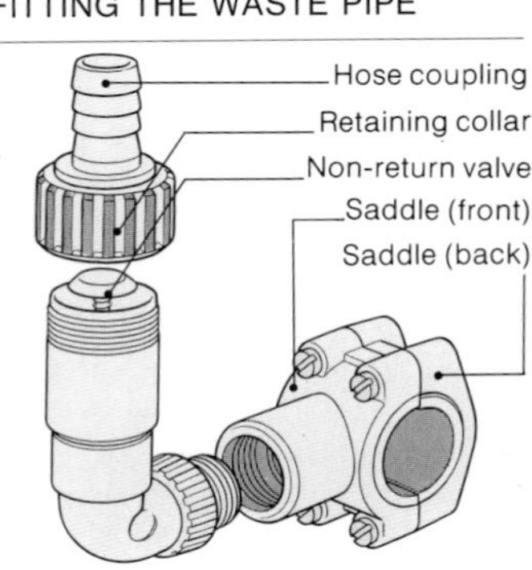

1 Unscrew the saddle from the rest of the drain kit.

2 Fit the saddle round the plastic waste pipe leading from the sink. Choose a convenient place away from joints, and well beyond the trap.

3 Screw the cutting tool into the saddle until a hole has been cut in the waste pipe.

4 Remove the cutting tool and screw on the rest of the drain kit. It includes a non-return valve to prevent water from the sink flowing into the machine.

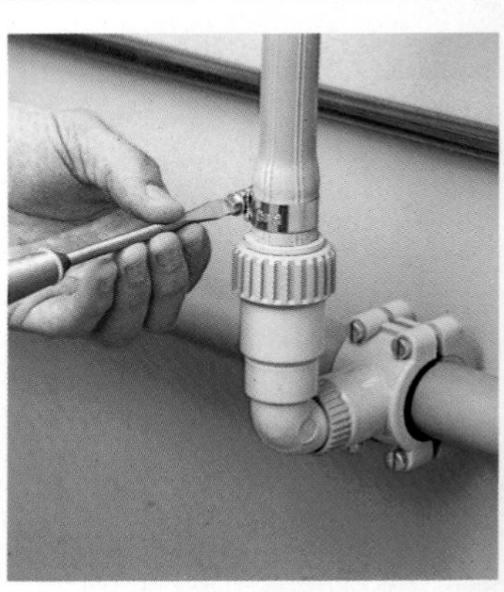

5 Push the drain hose from the machine over the coupling and fix it in position with a hose clip. The machine is now ready to use.

6 Every two or three months, unscrew the plastic retaining collar and remove any fluff that may be clogging up the non-return valve. Be sure to tighten it fully afterwards.

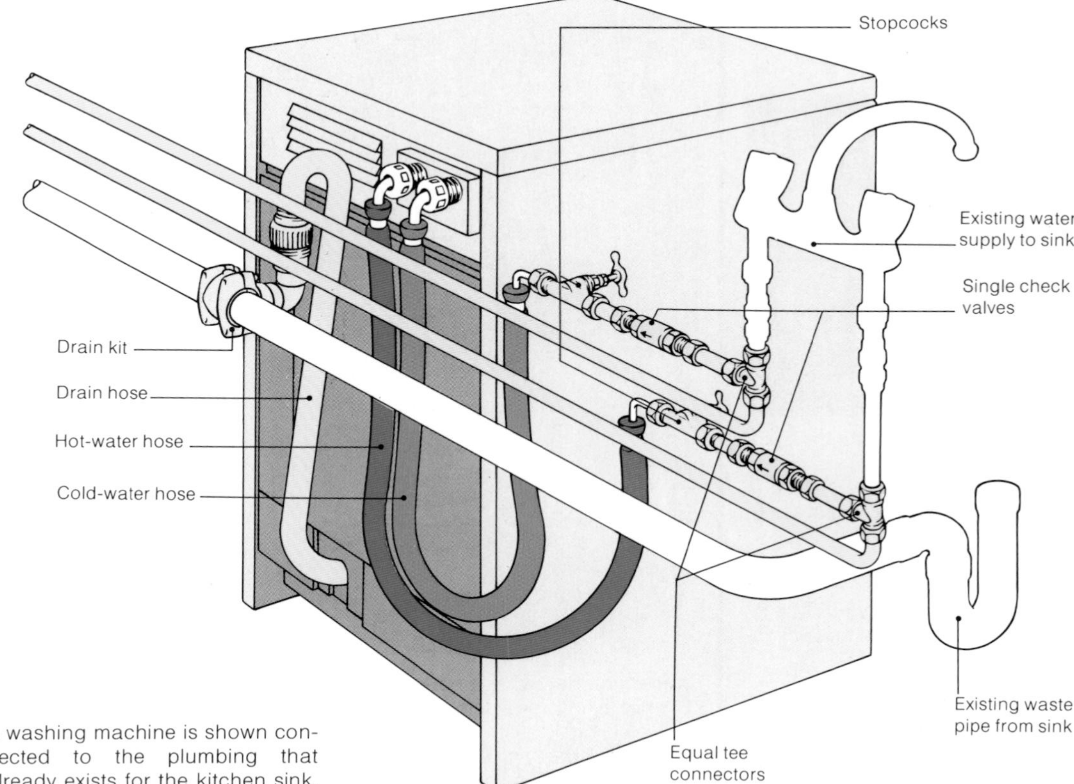

A washing machine is shown connected to the plumbing that already exists for the kitchen sink.

11 Central heating

How central heating works

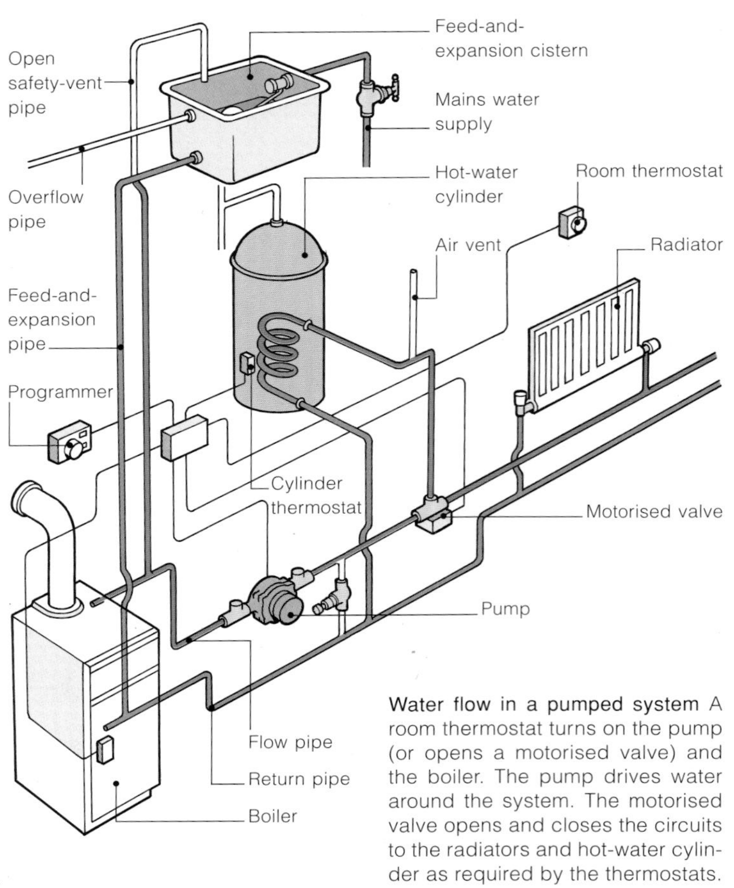

Water flow in a pumped system A room thermostat turns on the pump (or opens a motorised valve) and the boiler. The pump drives water around the system. The motorised valve opens and closes the circuits to the radiators and hot-water cylinder as required by the thermostats.

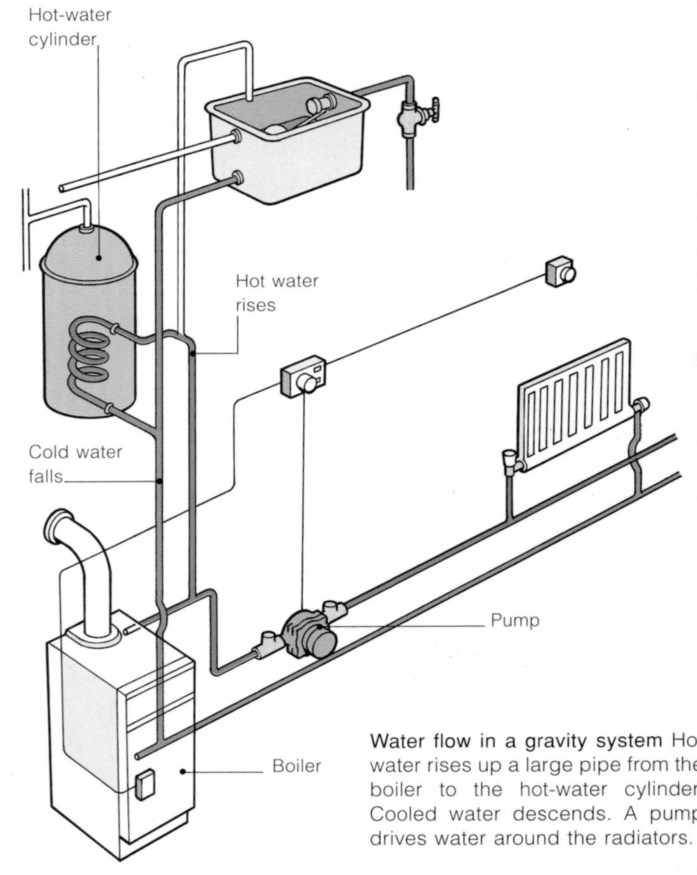

Water flow in a gravity system Hot water rises up a large pipe from the boiler to the hot-water cylinder. Cooled water descends. A pump drives water around the radiators.

A TYPICAL PUMPED SYSTEM

Most central-heating systems warm rooms by passing hot water through radiators. The water is heated by a boiler and is driven around the system by a pump. The water in the central-heating system is separate from that supplied to the hot taps.

A programmer switches on the boiler and the pump at preset times of the day. A room thermostat controls the room temperature and turns the heat on and off as the air temperature falls and rises. The thermostat either switches on the pump or opens a motorised valve. The electrical controls start up the boiler. Water is then heated by the boiler and flows through either small bore or microbore pipes to the radiators. When the air temperature reaches the required level the valve is closed or the pump is switched off.

The same water is constantly circulated around the system. In an open system, in case of leakage or evaporation the water is topped up from a feed-and-expansion cistern. This cistern also takes up expansion that occurs when the water heats up from cold.

An open-ended pipe, called the open safety-vent pipe, provides an escape route for steam and excess pressure if the boiler overheats.

GRAVITY CIRCULATION

In some older central-heating systems and in solid fuel systems, water is circulated by gravity. When water is heated it expands and, pint for pint, weighs less than cold water. The cold water descends down the return pipe pushing the lighter hot water up the flow pipe. Gravity circulation is reliable as it needs no mechanical assistance, but it requires larger 28mm pipes. The system is most efficient if the cylinder is directly over the boiler.

A SEALED SYSTEM

A sealed central-heating system has an expansion vessel instead of an expansion cistern, and instead of a safety-vent pipe it has a pressure relief valve. The valve should be of the type that is set permanently to 3bar. Any water lost over time through minor leaks is topped up from a small bottle installed in the system. Sealed systems are ideal for flats where it is difficult to find space for tanks.

The boiler has an over-heat cut-out to prevent boiling should the standard thermostat fail, and on no account must a boiler without a fail-safe be fitted to a sealed system.

It is now more common to use a combination boiler rather than to build up a sealed system from individual components. The illustration shows the essential components of a sealed system, which are now usually housed inside the boiler. As well as saving space because of the lack of a feed-and-expansion cistern, a combination boiler also has the advantage that no hot-water tank is needed as the boiler heats mains water and delivers hot water directly to the taps.

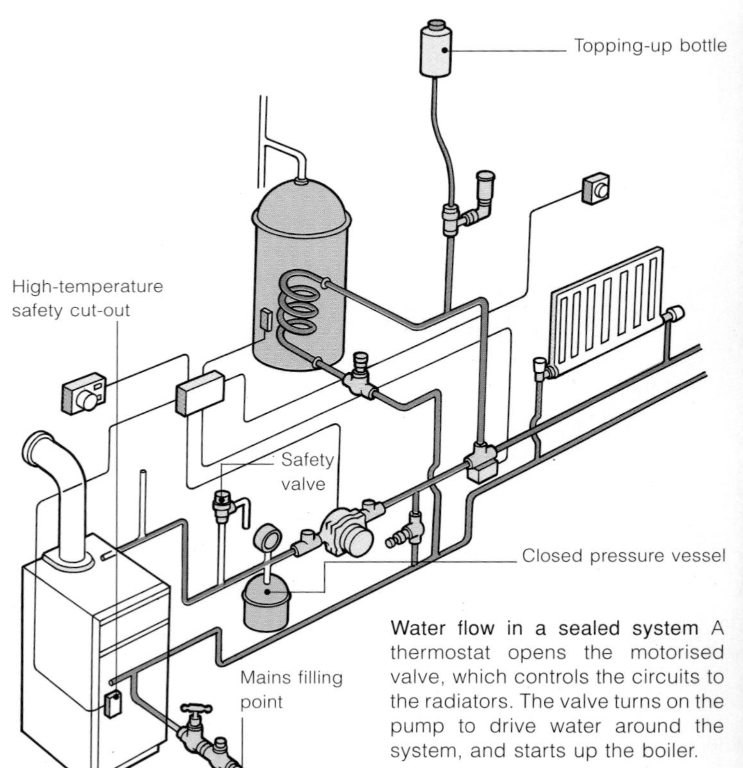

Water flow in a sealed system A thermostat opens the motorised valve, which controls the circuits to the radiators. The valve turns on the pump to drive water around the system, and starts up the boiler.

CHOOSING A BOILER

When choosing a boiler, its proposed position affects whether you need a wall-hung or floor-standing model. The boiler's distance from an outside wall or the roof will affect what type of flue you can have.

Choose the right boiler for the job. For example, must it supply heating and hot water for several bathrooms? What size of household will it cater for?

Look for energy rating labels to compare running costs. But bear in mind that some boilers need more maintenance than others.

All boilers must be serviced regularly and faults dealt with by an expert. Only installers registered by the Council for Registered Gas Installers (CORGI) should work on gas boilers. Do not alter boilers or flues without seeking expert advice and ensure that leaks are fixed immediately. In the meantime do not use the system, and drain it down if the leak is bad.

TRADITIONAL BOILER

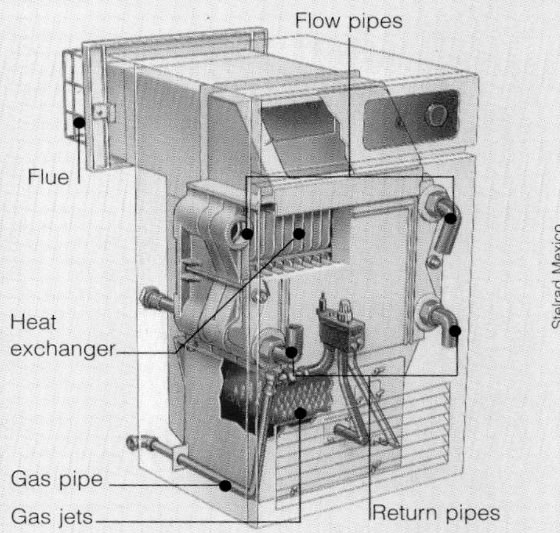

A cast-iron heat exchanger heats the water in a traditional boiler, rather like a gas burner under a kettle. This type of boiler operates quietly and has reliable controls that are easy to understand. Fuel consumption is relatively high, but this is offset by the boiler's reliability. It can be used with a fully pumped or gravity-driven hot-water system. The huge range of sizes will suit anything from a terraced house to a mansion.

COMBINATION ('COMBI') BOILER

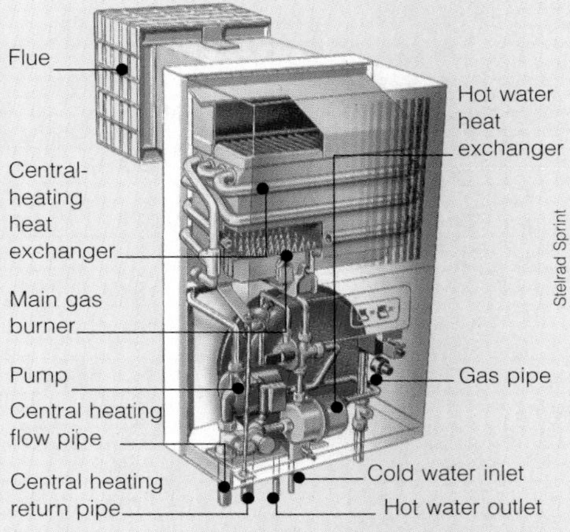

As well as providing hot water for the central heating a combination boiler also provides instant hot water to the taps. The water for the central heating is heated in a closed circuit like any other boiler. The water for the hot taps, however, is fed from the mains through the boiler and then directly to the taps, instead of being stored in a hot-water cylinder.

The internal workings are complicated and can be expensive to repair, so a maintenance contract is a good idea.

A combination boiler is ideal for a flat or a small house as the lack of tanks saves space. It is a less suitable option in a larger house where several people may require hot water at the same time. There is also the drawback that there will be no airing cupboard containing a hot-water cylinder.

CONDENSING BOILER

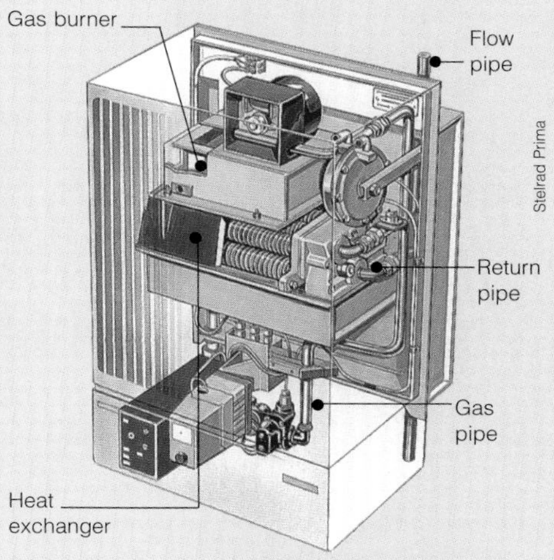

An efficient modern gas boiler, available for fully pumped systems or as a combination boiler. It uses less fuel than other boilers for the same heat output.

The condensing boiler is designed so that water returning from the heating system is used to cool the flue gases, thereby extracting heat, which is normally lost. The water vapour in the flue gases condenses in the heat exchanger and is taken away through a small drain pipe at the bottom of the boiler.

Condensing boilers work best with radiator temperatures of about 60°C (140°F), but even with higher temperatures, up to 80°C (176°F), they are significantly more efficient than other boilers.

A condensing boiler requires a fan-assisted flue.

OIL-FIRED BOILER

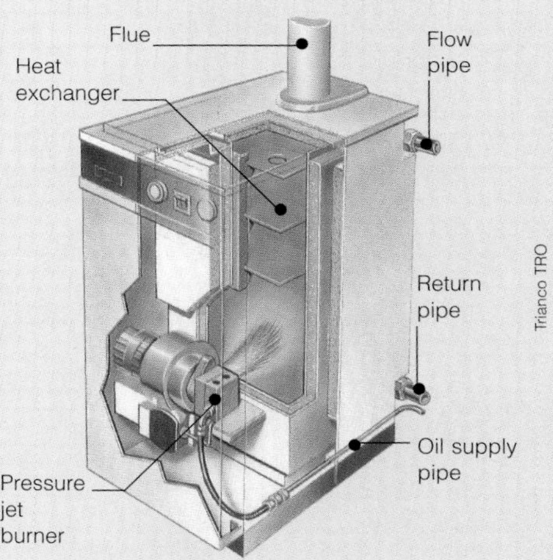

Traditional, combination and condensing boilers can be oil-fired. They are mostly floor-standing, though there are some wall-hung models.

Low level, room-sealed flues, which protrude through the wall are available (see right), but you will need to seek local authority approval before fitting one, as it can cause a nuisance to neighbours.

Oil has been the cheapest heating fuel for many years but servicing costs on oil-fired boilers are generally higher and deliveries must be planned.

A heat operated shut-off valve must be installed to cut off the oil supply if the boiler catches fire.

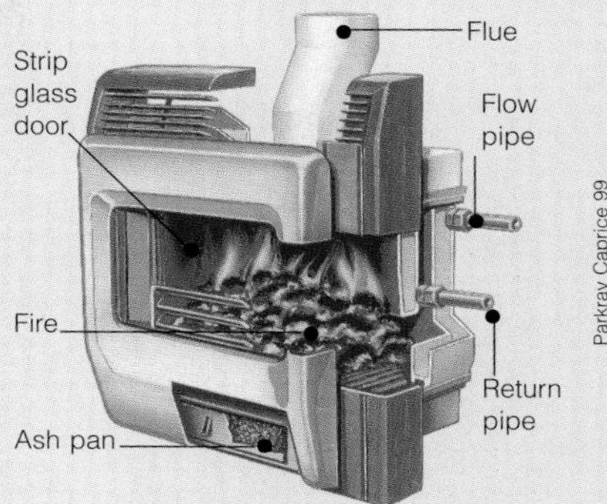

BACK BOILER

Fuelled by gas, oil or solid fuel (above). All require a lined, natural-draught open flue. Gas and oil back boilers work independently of the fire front so they can provide hot water all year round. Solid fuel back boilers work only when the fire is lit, so an electric immersion heater is needed for hot water in the summer.

THE TWO TYPES OF FLUE

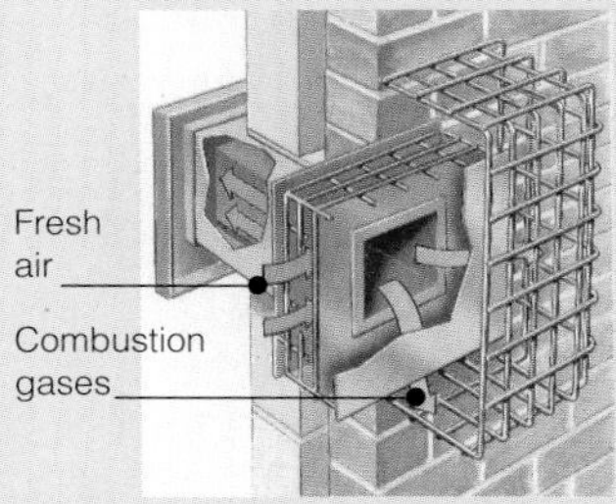

Room-sealed flue Fumes are sealed against contact with the room where the flue is mounted. There are two types.

A natural draught flue (above) must be mounted directly on an outside wall. Less efficient, but quieter than a fanned flue.

A fan-assisted flue is smaller and allows the boiler to be mounted up to13ft (4m) away from an outside wall. It can also exit through a roof. A fan assisted flue is more efficient and produces lower fuel costs.

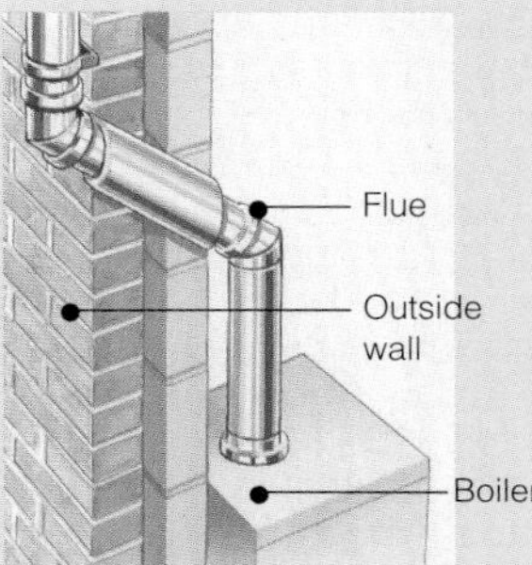

Open flue Can run up an outside wall, or incorporate a flexible, stainless-steel liner in an existing chimney. It takes air from the room in which it is sited, and if ventilation is inadequate, fumes can spill into the room. The room where the flue is installed must have an air supply from outdoors through a nonclosable grille. Never cover an air brick if you have an open-flue boiler, and before building a cupboard around a boiler check the ventilation requirements in the instructions.

Balancing a radiator circuit

A typical radiator circuit

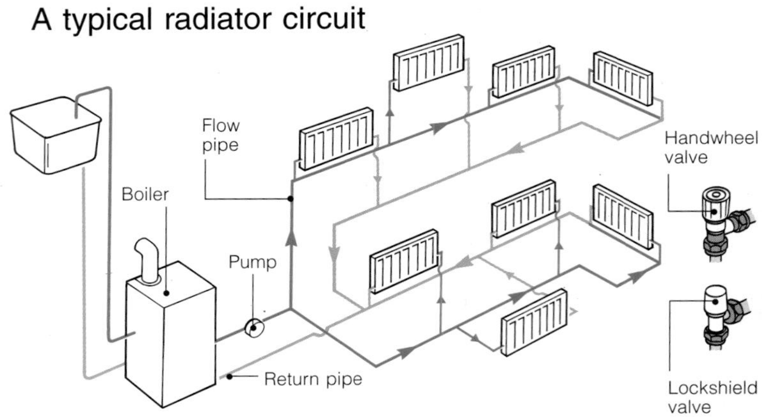

Hot water is carried from the boiler to the radiators by a flow pipe, which branches off to supply each radiator. Cool water leaves each radiator at the opposite end and joins a return pipe carrying it back to the boiler.

Water flows most readily round the radiators nearest to the pump, so the water flow through the circuit is balanced out by adjusting the lockshield valve on each radiator.

The valves are set so as to make it harder for the water to travel through the radiators nearest the boiler. If the circuit is not properly balanced, some radiators will get too hot, and others will be cool.

You will need

Pair of clip-on radiator thermometers, spanner, small screwdriver, sticky labels and a pencil.

1 Two or three hours before you intend to start work on the radiators, turn off the central-heating system in order to allow the water in the radiators to cool down.

2 Open all lockshield valves and handwheel valves fully.

3 Turn on the central-heating system and work out the order in which the radiators heat up, and label them accordingly.

4 Clip a radiator thermometer onto the flow pipe bringing water into the first radiator, and one onto the return pipe.

5 Turn down the lockshield valve until it is closed, then open it slightly. Adjust the flow until the temperature of the flow pipe is roughly 11°C (20°F) higher than that of the return pipe.

6 Repeat for all radiators in the circuit, working in the order as labelled. The valve on the last radiator will probably need to be fully open.

Choosing radiators and other heat emitters

Though most people's first choice is a radiator there are many other heat emitters that can be connected to central-heating pipes. These include, fan convectors, trench-duct heaters, skirting heaters and underfloor heaters. When mixing different types of heat emitter on the same system, fit thermostatic valves to each one in order to allow full control.

Radiators

Despite the name, only a tiny proportion of heat given off by a radiator is emitted from the front through radiation. If you put your hand just a few inches from the front the heat is negligible. Most of the heat is given out from the top by convection.

To work properly a radiator must have a good flow of air passing from the bottom on the front and back surfaces. There must be at least 4in (100mm) clearance from the floor for air to enter and 1½in (38mm) at the top.

Old style plain panel radiators have now been almost completely superseded by convector radiators, which have metal boxed fins welded to the hidden faces of the panels. The fins act as chimneys for hot air, almost doubling the heat output and making it possible to fit smaller radiators.

Fan convectors

Use a fan convector where there is not enough wall space for a radiator. Special kick-space models are made to go under kitchen base units. Low voltage versions are available for bathrooms. Air curtain models can be installed above doors and wall units, and some models sink into the floor.

An electrical fan blows air across copper fins, which are heated by hot water from the central-heating circuit. A filter in the air intake traps dirt, this should be regularly cleaned to maintain maximum performance and to prevent noise.

Trench-duct heaters

If windows go down to the floor, trench heaters can be installed. A pipe fitted with fins runs along one side of a trench in the floor. A dividing plate along the centre of the trench separates hot air rising from the pipe from the cooler air returning to be reheated.

Skirting heaters

Small metal convectors run round the room just above or in place of a skirting board. This system is good for background heating and it gives an even spread of heat, which can help to prevent condensation on walls. However, it is not usually powerful enough to heat a room in very cold weather.

Underfloor heaters

Burying pipes under concrete floors has gained in popularity. Plastic pipe is laid in a continuous loop and carries hot water under the floor. The pipes must be fitted on top of underfloor insulation and are normally covered with sand-and-cement screed which helps to spread the heat evenly. This is an ideal system for use with a condensing boiler because it works well at low temperatures.

Where to install radiators

Radiators and natural convectors should be fitted in the coldest part of the room, preferably under the windows. The heat rising from the radiator will counteract the cold air falling from the glass. This produces a mixed-temperature flow of air across the room.

Radiators placed on inside walls opposite a window can accentuate the flow of cold air down a window and can produce a cool draught across the floor.

Make sure that there is at least 4in (100mm) of space between the bottom of a radiator and the floor to allow a good circulation of air and so that the floor can be cleaned.

At least 1½in (38mm) should be left between the wall – or the skirting board – and the back of the radiator to allow air to circulate.

A shelf should not be placed any closer than 2in (50mm) to the top of a radiator for the same reason.

A radiator installed inside a decorative casing can lose a quarter or more of its output unless the casing permits a full flow of air over all of the radiator's surfaces.

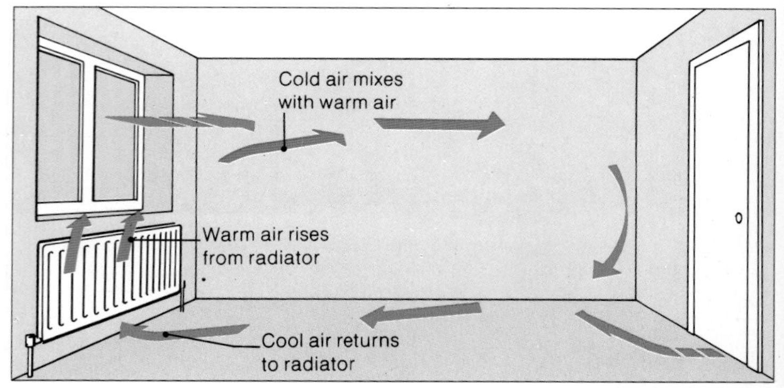

Removing and replacing a radiator

It may be necessary to remove a radiator in order to flush out sludge that has built up inside, to replace it with a new radiator or simply in order to decorate behind it. This can be done without draining the whole system.

You will need
Tools Towels or dustsheets; rags; two bowls; pliers; two large adjustable spanners; newspaper; hammer; PTFE tape; Allen key.
Materials Perhaps a radiator the same size as the old one; a new radiator air vent, and perhaps a new radiator plug.

1 Lay towels or dustsheets around the radiator and, if possible, to the nearest outside door.

2 Close off the control valve by hand. Then use pliers or a small spanner to close the lockshield valve. Count the number of turns that this takes and write it down.

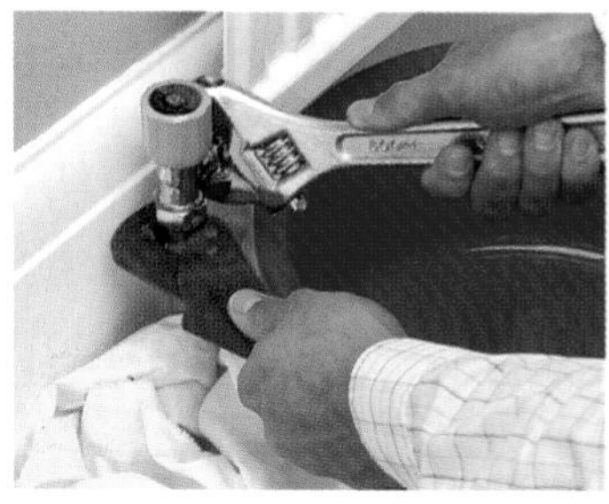

3 Put a bowl under the control valve, and disconnect the union nut. Take care not to distort the pipe (see box). Water will flow out (there may be a lot, so have bowls ready).

4 Open the air vent to increase the flow of water.

5 When it has stopped, undo the union nut on the lockshield valve. Some more water may come out.

6 Block up the open ends of the radiator with twists of paper.

7 Lift the radiator off its brackets and carry it outside. You may need help.

REPLACING THE RADIATOR

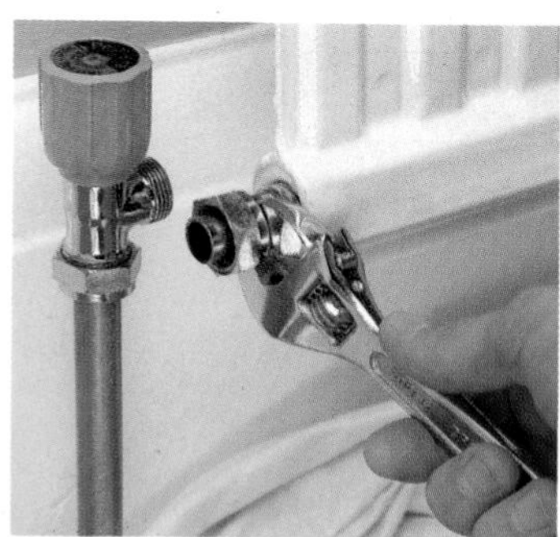

1 If you are replacing a radiator, but keeping the valves, remove the valve tail pieces from the old radiator with an adjustable spanner or a special valve Allen key. Turn the valve tail anticlockwise (when looking at the end of the radiator). If it is stiff apply penetrating oil to the thread and wait for half an hour. Alternatively, apply gentle heat with a hot-air gun to soften the jointing compound.

2 Hold the new radiator in position to check if the wall brackets need replacing (manufacturers sometimes change their design).

3 Wind PTFE tape around the thread of the valve tail pieces. Start from the end and make a 50 per cent overlap on each turn. Screw the tail pieces in place.

4 Fit a new air vent at the same end of the radiator as before, using PTFE tape as for the valve tail. The vent may be made to screw in with either a spanner or an Allen key.

Fit a new plug if there is a spare tapping in the other top end.

5 Fix the radiator on the wall brackets and reconnect the union nuts.

6 Open the valves to fill the radiator with water. Let air out through the air vent, and check for leaks. Reset the lockshield valve to its original position.

WARNING

Never leave a thermostatic radiator valve with the tail pieces disconnected while removing a radiator. If the temperature drops, the thermostatic valve will open, flooding the room.

Use the special screw-down caps, supplied with new valves, which fit in place of the sensor to shut off the valve.

HOW TO AVOID DISTORTING A PIPE

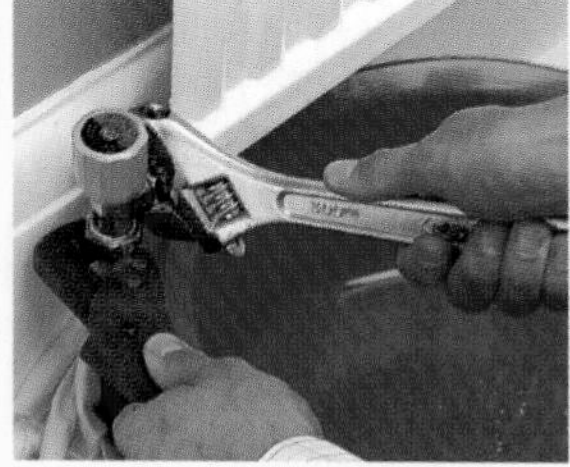

The union nut on a radiator may need force to undo it. There is then a danger of bending the pipe, causing a leak at the compression joint.

To avoid this, apply penetrating oil, and hold the nut just below the valve with a wrench to counteract the pressure as you undo the union nut.

Radiators that do not heat up correctly

RADIATOR COOL AT THE TOP

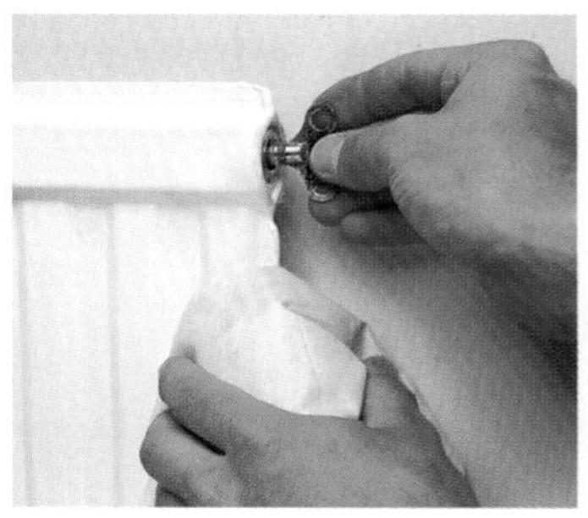

Air is trapped at the top of the radiator. Turn off the central heating. Then use a radiator bleed key to open the air vent at one end of the radiator. Hold a rag under the key and open no more than one turn anticlockwise. Air should start to hiss out. When water appears close the vent. Turn the heating on again.

If radiators need bleeding more than once a year, air is entering the system and this can cause corrosion. There may be a serious fault that needs expert attention.

Some systems have one or more extra bleed points on the pipes either upstairs or in the loft. Manual bleed points are opened with a screwdriver.

On an automatic air valve the small, red plastic cap must be loose in order for air to escape. If it is tight, unscrew it.

RADIATOR COOL AT THE BOTTOM AND HOT AT THE TOP

Sludge (black iron oxide) can build up at the bottom of a radiator and stop the circulation. Remove the radiator, take it outside and flush it through with a hose.

Alternatively, add sludge removal liquid to the feed-and-expansion cistern. Two days later drain and refill the system (page 351).

TOP-FLOOR RADIATORS COLD

Cold radiators upstairs only, often indicate that the feed-and-expansion cistern is empty. The ball-valve may be faulty (see page 336).

Refill the feed-and-expansion cistern so that there is just enough water to float the ball when the water in the system is cold. The extra space accommodates expansion of the water as it heats up.

TOP-FLOOR RADIATORS HOT, LOWER RADIATORS COLD

This is almost certainly due to pump failure (see Central Heating problems: What to do, page 352).

COOL RADIATORS THROUGHOUT THE HOUSE

Deposits of sludge caused by internal corrosion can result in poor water circulation and radiators being cooler than they should be. The system needs to be chemically cleaned out (see page 350).

RADIATORS FARTHEST FROM THE BOILER ARE COOL

The system is not properly balanced (see page 345).

TOP RADIATORS HEAT UP WHEN HOT WATER ONLY IS SELECTED ON PROGRAMMER

Hot water naturally rises above cooler water. On a gravity driven system, hot water for the hot-water cylinder is prevented from creeping into upstairs radiators when the heating is switched off by a mechanical valve, called the gravity-check valve. It is situated on the flow pipe to the upstairs radiators.

If the gravity-check valve is stuck in the open position, the pipe on either side of the valve will be warm. Call a central-heating engineer to replace it.

Controlling your central heating

Efficient temperature and time controls can save a great deal of money on fuel bills.

ROOM THERMOSTATS

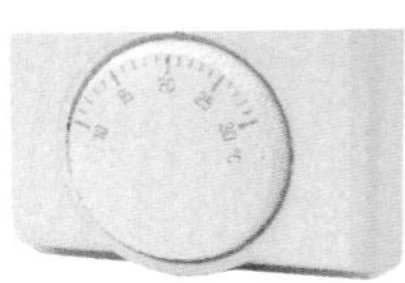

A room thermostat is a temperature sensitive switch, set to a certain level. It sends an electrical signal to switch the heating on when the air temperature around it falls below that level, and off when the temperature rises above it.

On fully pumped systems the room and hot-water cylinder thermostats operate motorised valves. When these are fully opened they in turn switch on the boiler and pump.

On gravity hot-water systems the room thermostat operates the pump and the boiler is switched on and off by the programmer.

A room thermostat is best positioned in a draught-free place on an inside wall away from direct sunlight, about 5ft (1.5m) above floor level, and away from a radiator or heat source.

THERMOSTATIC RADIATOR VALVE

The best means of controlling the temperature in each room is to fit a thermostatic radiator valve (TRV) to each radiator. The valve opens and closes according to the temperature in the room. If the room is cold, a full flow is allowed through to the radiator. Then as the room warms up, the valve closes to reduce the hot water flow through the radiator.

Rooms facing south and rooms with open fires or heat producing appliances, such as an oven, benefit most from TRVs.

Most systems are suitable for use with thermostatic radiator valves. Seek expert advice on which ones to buy.

Leave one or two radiators without TRVs to act as a bypass, in order to maintain good circulation in the system. Alternatively, a bypass pipe can be installed just after the pump. The best type of bypass is a pressure operated valve which opens progressively as the TRVs close the radiators down. This also helps eliminate surging noises.

TRVs do not control the central heating pump and boiler, so they must be combined with a room thermostat or a boiler energy manager.

PROGRAMMERS AND TIME SWITCHES

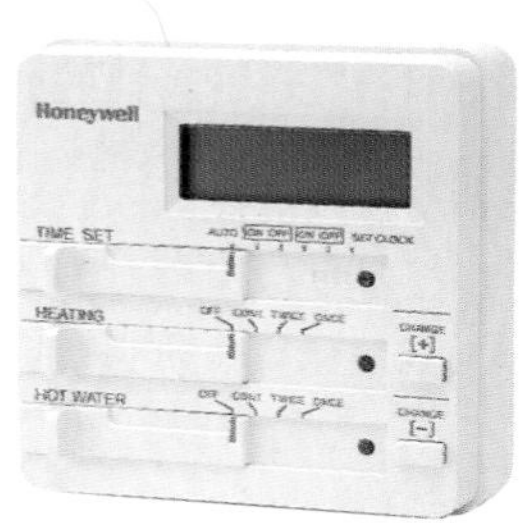

Time controls range from simple time switches to complex electronic programmers.

The most useful programmers can time space heating and domestic hot water separately. Then water heating can be turned on and off at the same times of day all year round, while space heating varies with the season.

Modern electronic programmers can give you three control periods in a day and different settings for every day of the week. Some can even be set for holidays to switch the heating or hot water on just before you return.

WATER HEATING CONTROL

The hot-water temperature is usually only controlled by the boiler thermostat. So the hot water to the taps is the same temperature as the water supplied to the radiators. This is probably hotter than necessary.

An electric thermostat fitted on the outside of the hot-water cylinder will restrict the temperature of the water inside. It switches a valve on and off to control the flow of water passing through the heating coil inside the cylinder.

BOILER ENERGY MANAGEMENT

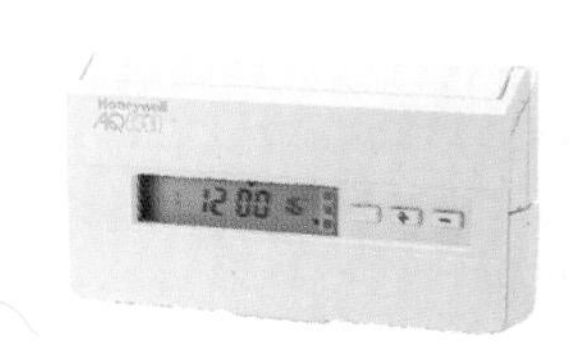

Sophisticated boiler energy management devices make sure that the boiler is working only when it needs to.

A boiler energy manager will reduce wasteful short cycling on a boiler: When 'hot water only' is selected on a conventional central-heating programmer the boiler will continually switch on and off to keep the water in the boiler at the selected temperature. It will do this even though the hot-water cylinder is already full of hot water. This 'short cycling' can add as much as 30% to fuel bills.

The boiler energy manager will also take account of outside temperatures and heat loss, and regulate the central-heating system accordingly. For example it will override the setting and delay the start time of the central heating on warmer days.

HOW THE CONTROL DEVICES LINK UP

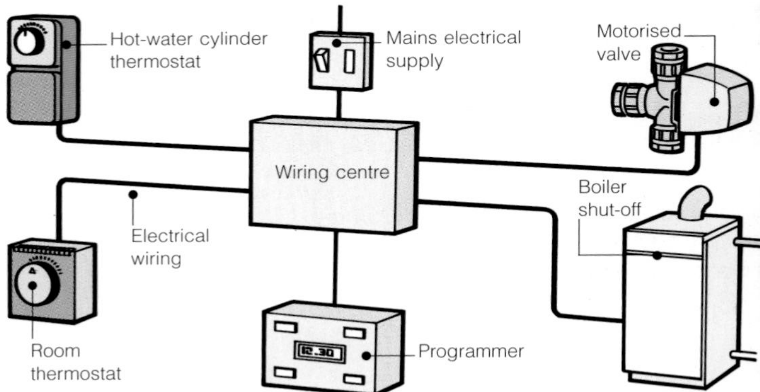

Updating your central-heating programmer

An old-style programmer can be replaced quite easily with a more modern one. If the old one has an industry-standard back-plate the programmer face plate can be changed without rewiring the backplate. If the new programmer is incompatible with the old back plate, you will have to do some rewiring. Full instructions will be supplied with the new programmer.

You will need
Tools Electrical screwdriver
Materials New central-heating programmer. Possibly: Pencil, paper and masking tape.

1 Turn off the power to the central heating and remove the fuse.

2 Undo the screw securing the face plate of the programmer. It is usually on the underside.

3 Lift the bottom of the face plate outwards. The programmer will then lift clear of the back plate that is attached to the wall.

4 Set the switch on the back of the new programmer to suit the type of system you have. For a gravity hot-water system, select '10'; for a fully pumped system, select '16'.

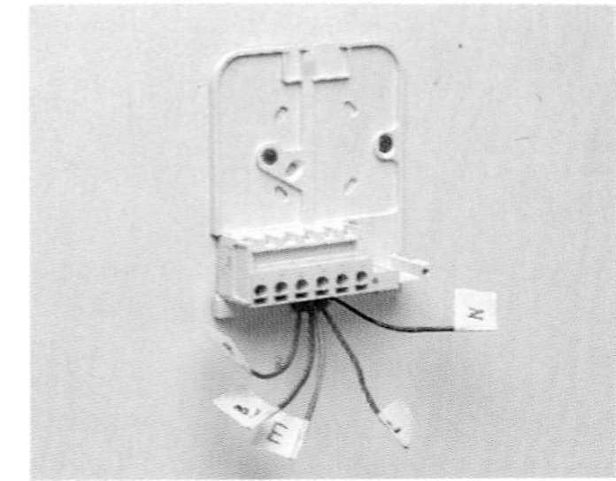

5 If the new face plate does not fit the old back plate, study the wiring carefully and label each wire clearly. Sketch the old connections then unscrew the connectors.

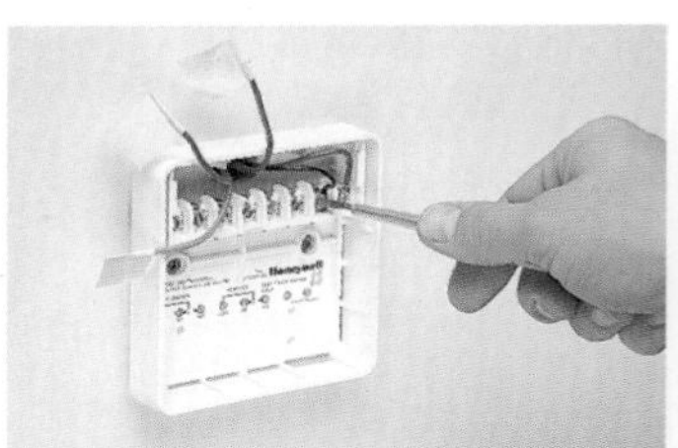

6 Remove the old back plate and attach the new one, using the manufacturer's instructions and your sketch of the old programmer to wire it up. Then push the new face plate into position and turn the central-heating system back on.

Having central heating installed – a checklist

If you are planning to have central heating installed in your house, first read as much about heating as you can so that you can discuss it with the heating contractors.

BOILERS, HEAT EMITTERS AND CONTROLS

Read pages 344 to 348 and get further information on boilers and heat emitters. You can get additional information from a number of advisory bodies and trade associations listed here.

Visit your local plumber's merchant and pick up brochures on the latest boilers and heat emitters. Bear in mind that the contractor's recommendations may be influenced by incentives from the manufacturers.

OBTAINING QUOTATIONS

Find three CORGI registered contractors in your area and ask them to quote. Give them all the same outline brief, including where you would like radiators positioned, and what temperatures you wish to achieve in the rooms. A living room temperature of 21°C (70°F) when the temperature outside is −1°C (30°F) is normal. If you need a margin built in for extra cold weather you should say so. Do you want thermostatic radiator valves fitted?

Make a list of conditions you feel are important. Most contractors will already comply with them as normal working practice:

1 Be wary of paying a deposit. The first payment should be when materials are delivered. Retain a small amount (2%) for small items that need fixing after completion.

2 Ask the contractor to give start and completion dates.

3 Consider where the pipes will go. Before the job starts, decide where pipes are to run and in what order they will be laid so that you can clear the room. If you want pipes to be concealed, state this before the work starts. It may cost more.

4 If several rooms will be affected, request that the contractor finish in one room before starting in the next one.

5 Your home should be left clean and tidy at the end of the day and be respected. For example, no loud music or smoking.

6 Work should comply with statutory requirements such as water and building regulations and relevant codes of practice. Materials must meet CEN (European) or British Standards where applicable.

7 'Making good' means filling in holes and replacing panels. Floorboards should be screwed back down to prevent creaking. Damaged boards should be replaced. Normally, making good does not include decorative work, such as replacing wallpaper.

Carpets should be refitted by the contractor, but you may need a carpet fitter to re-stretch them.

8 Establish what other contractors will be required to complete the work – electricians, for example.

9 The contractor must leave you all instructions and technical leaflets and fill out guarantee cards.

WHEN THE WORK IS FINISHED

The contractor must flush out the new central-heating system in order to remove debris which could corrode and clog it in the future.

Run the system to full heat and check that all the radiators heat up. Allow it to cool and listen for creaks and groans.

TRADE ASSOCIATIONS AND INDUSTRY BODIES

The Building Centre
26, Store St, London WC1E 7BT
tel: 020 7692 4000
www.buildingcentre.co.uk

Heating and Ventilating Contractors Association
ESCA House
34, Palace Court,
London W2 4JG
tel: 020 7313 4900
www.hvca.org.uk

CORGI
1, Elmwood
Chineham Business Park
Crockword Lane
Basingstoke, Hants RG24 8WG
tel: 01256 372200
www.corgi-gas.com

Association of Plumbing and Heating Contractors
14, Ensign House
Ensign Business Centre
Westwood Way, Coventry CV4 8JA
tel: 0800 5426060
www.licensedplumber.co.uk

The Central Heating Information Council
36, Holly Walk,
Leamington Spa,
Warwickshire CV32 4LY
tel: 0845 600 22 00
www.chic-info.org.uk

Institute of Plumbing
64, Station Lane
Hornchurch,
Essex RM12 6NB
tel: 01708 472791
www.registeredplumber.com

Noise in a central heating system

CREAKING IN THE FLOOR OR WALLS

Pipes expand as they heat up and contract as they cool. If the pipe is gripped tight by timber or a wall, or if it is in contact with another pipe, a creaking noise will occur when it gets hot or cold.

1 Pack some felt or pipe lagging around the pipes where they come up through the floorboards.

2 If that does not work, take up the floorboards around the source of the noise (page 273).

3 If one or two pipes are lying in a notch in a joist, and there is no room for movement, make the notch slightly wider by cutting down with a tenon saw and chiselling away the waste. Do not make the notch deeper; you may weaken the joist. Ease a piece of felt or pipe lagging under and between the pipes.

4 With the floorboards up, use a rasp to enlarge the holes through which the pipes rise to the radiator if they are tight. Cover the pipes with pipe lagging where they pass through the boards.

5 Where pipes run the same way as the joists, make sure they do not sag or touch. Hold up sagging pipes with pipe clips fitted on struts between the joists. Put padding between any pipes that touch.

6 If the pipes go through a wall, sleeve them with fire-resistant material, such as glass fibre matting, or pack it in around them, tamping it fairly hard with a screwdriver.

HUMMING IN THE PIPES

An annoying humming usually originates from the pump. Anti-vibration pump brackets can be fitted to reduce the problem. Pipes may vibrate if they are too small for the amount of water they have to carry, or if the pump speed is set too high. Call in an expert to find the cause.

BOILER NOISE

If scale and corrosion form in the boiler it can cause hot spots which produce loud bangs from steam bubbles. Try adding some non-acidic cleanser and de-scaler to the feed-and-expansion tank.

Noise may occur if the water flow through the boiler is insufficient. With modern, wall-hung, lightweight gas boilers, waterflow rate is particularly important.

Boiler noise is often due to air in the system, which may be caused by the open safety-vent pipe (page 344) being installed incorrectly. Get expert help.

AIR NOISE – LIKE THE SOUND OF RUSHING WATER

Air that has entered the system, or gas that has formed as a result of internal corrosion, can cause a noise in central-heating pipes like the sound of rushing water.

Try releasing the air from the air vents on the radiators, and any other venting points in the system. If the noise continues, it may be a symptom of serious faults that could eventually ruin the whole installation. Poor positioning of the open safety-vent pipe (page 344) could be the cause. Get expert help.

Leaks in a central heating system

Never ignore leaks in a central-heating system. Fresh water that is drawn in to replace the lost water contains free oxygen which causes radiators and cast iron boilers to rust.

Internal leak sealants similar to the radiator seal used in cars can be used to seal very minor leaks. Pour the sealant in through the feed-and-expansion tank. Do not use leak sealant in a sealed system.

A LEAKING PIPE JOINT

Most leaking pipe joints are compression fittings, which can be repaired with a spanner or wrench. Tighten the joint slightly, no more than a quarter turn. If this does not stop the leak, do not tighten any further as this will damage the joint.

Drain the system to below the leak (facing page), or isolate the area by closing the valves on each side of it. Undo the nut on the joint and pull the pipe out slightly. Wrap two or three turns of PTFE tape around the face of the olive where it meets the joint. Tighten the nut.

If the leaking joint is soldered, drain the system. Heat the joint with a blowtorch and take it apart, then replace it (see page 314).

A LEAKING RADIATOR VALVE

If the leak is from the compression joint below the valve, drain down the system to below the joint (facing page). Then call a plumber or repair the joint yourself (page 311). Use PTFE tape to cure a leak from the union nut connecting the valve to the radiator.

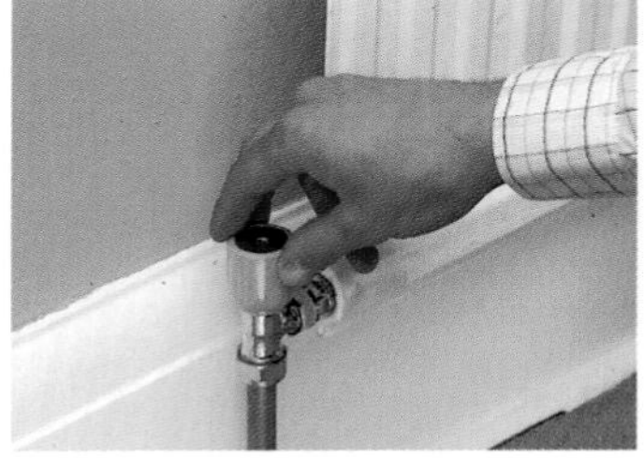

1 Turn off the valves at both ends of the radiator, counting the number of turns on the lockshield valve. Write the number down.

2 Put a towel and a bowl under the valve to catch water, and have a bucket and a second bowl ready.

3 Use an adjustable spanner to turn the union nut anticlockwise (when looking from the radiator to the valve). Some water may run out.

4 Open the air vent to allow the rest of the water to flow out.

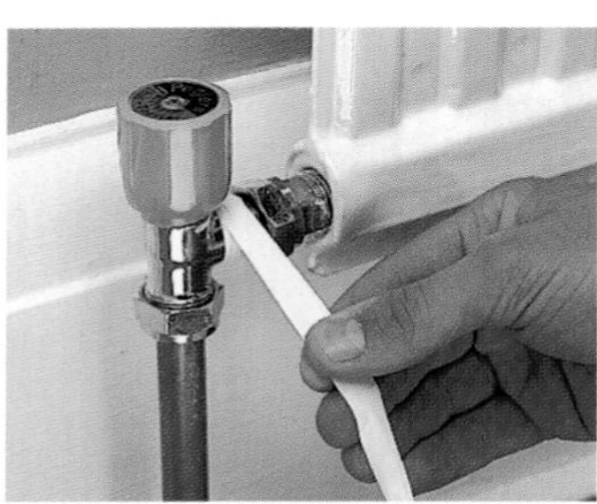

5 Wind PTFE tape tightly around the male thread on the valve tail. Start at the end and make a 50 per cent overlap on each turn.

6 Screw the nut back on, and open the valves and air vent. Open the lockshield valve by the number of turns that were necessary to close it. Check for leaks and close the air vent when water flows from it.

A LEAKING VALVE TAIL

The leak may be from the valve tail screwed into the radiator. To remove it a plumber uses a special tool, but an Allen key or a large screwdriver will usually do the job. Cover the male thread on the valve tail with PTFE tape (see left, step 5).

A LEAKING RADIATOR AIR VENT

If the radiator air vent leaks, drain the system to below the vent (facing page). Remove the air-vent fitting using a spanner or Allen key.

Bind the screw joint with PTFE tape (see left, step 5), and replace the fitting.

A LEAKING RADIATOR

A small jet of water from the body of the radiator is called a pinhole leak. It is caused by internal corrosion and can happen within a few weeks of the system being fitted if the debris that collects during installation has not been removed, or if air is being drawn in.

Turn off the valves at each end to relieve the pressure then remove the radiator and leave the rest of the system running (see page 347).

Before fitting a new radiator, flush out and clean the system using a non-acidic cleaner.

REPACKING A RADIATOR GLAND

If a radiator valve weeps water from under the cap, the packing gland is worn. You can replace the packing with PTFE or thread-sealing fibre, sold in plumbers' merchants.

'Belmont' valves cannot be repacked, instead they have renewable O-rings which can be replaced with a kit.

You will need
Small adjustable spanner, small screwdriver, PTFE tape, silicone grease.

1 Turn off the valve. If it continues to leak, close the lockshield valve at the other end of the radiator.

2 Remove the cap from the leaking valve and undo the small gland nut. Slide it up out of the way.

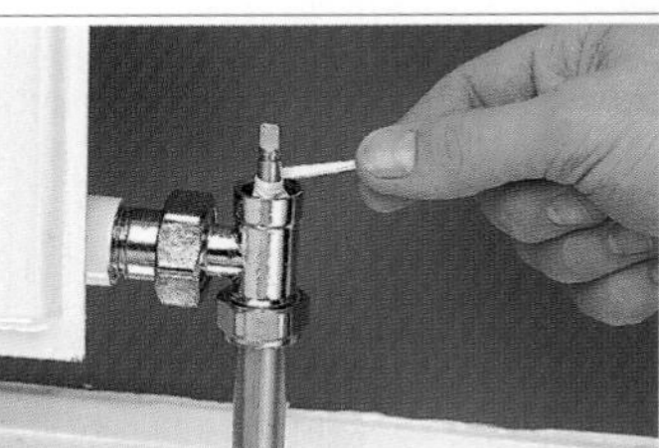

3 Pull a length of PTFE tape into a string and wrap this around the spindle four or five times.

4 Use a small screwdriver to push the tape down into the valve body. Smear on silicone grease and re-tighten the gland nut. Replace the head and turn the valve back on.

Protecting a system against corrosion

The life and efficiency of a central-heating system can be increased by adding a corrosion and scale inhibitor.

Test the water in the system every year or so for signs of internal corrosion. To do this drain a sample of the heating system water into a jar and place two bright (not galvanised) wire nails into the jar. Screw the lid on. Wait for a week.

If the nails rust and the water turns rusty orange, this indicates serious corrosion and you must eliminate the problem as soon as possible. If the water remains fairly clear and the nails do not rust, then no further action is necessary, since the water in the system has lost its free oxygen. A few black deposits are acceptable.

FINDING OUT WHERE AIR IS ENTERING THE SYSTEM

The most common cause of corrosion is air in the system. If the radiators need bleeding more than once or twice a year then too much air is being drawn into the system and this must be eliminated.

The most common areas where air gets into the system are a leaking joint on the suction side of the pump, or through the feed-and-expansion cistern.

Leaks around pumps can be repaired in the same way as other leaking joints. But if air is entering through the feed-and-expansion cistern you will need expert help.

You can find out if the feed-and-expansion cistern is the source of the problem by running the programmer through its functions and checking for any swirling movement of water in the cistern.

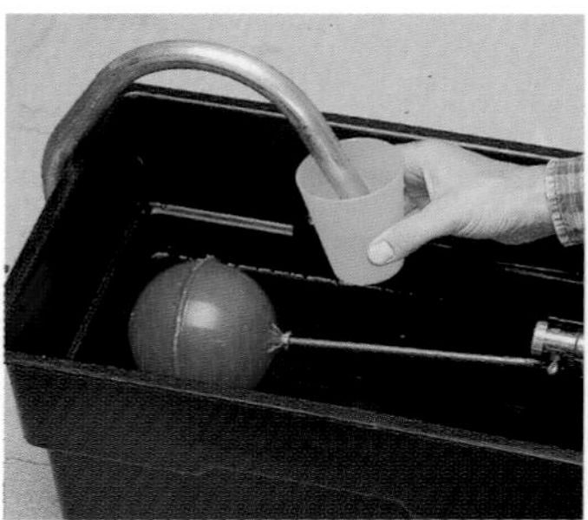

To find out whether the vent pipe is sucking in air, submerge the end of the pipe in a cup of water. If the pipe draws up water from the cup, then air is entering the system up the pipe and causing corrosion. You will need to call a central-heating engineer.

ADDING CORROSION INHIBITOR

Corrosion inhibitors are available in liquid form. In an open-vented system the liquid is added to the system through the feed-and-expansion cistern in the loft.

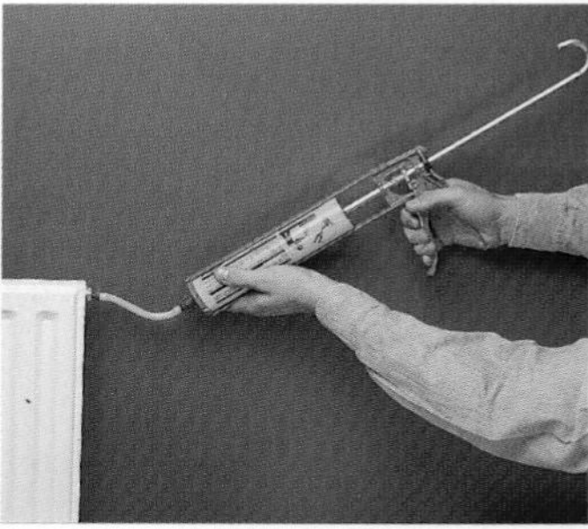

In a sealed system inject the corrosion inhibitor into a radiator through the air valve.

Draining down the system

Central-heating systems sometimes have to be drained down – to repair a leak, for example. The following method is for an open-vented system, the most common type.

1 Switch off the boiler at the programmer or time switch, and pull out the plug that provides electricity to the system, or remove the fuse.

2 Turn off the gas, either at the isolating cock near the boiler or by the meter. Or make sure that the fire in a solid-fuel boiler is out and the boiler cold. There is no need to turn off the oil in an oil-fired system.

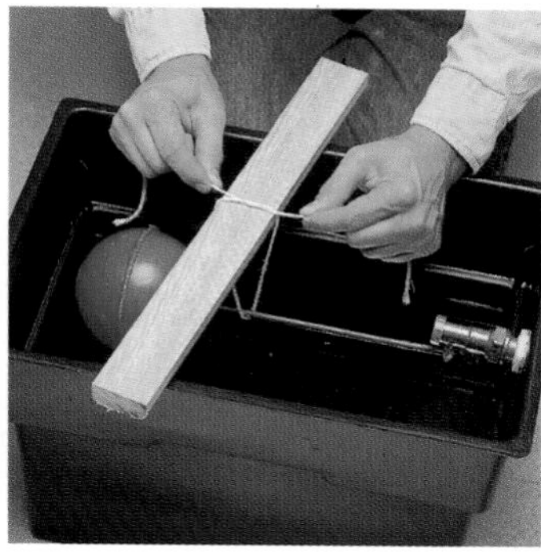

3 Shut off the water supply to the feed-and-expansion cistern. There should be a separate stopcock for this on the branch pipe from the rising main connected to the cistern's ball-valve.

If there is no separate stopcock, stop the water flow into the cistern by tying up the ball-valve to a piece of wood laid across the top of the cistern.

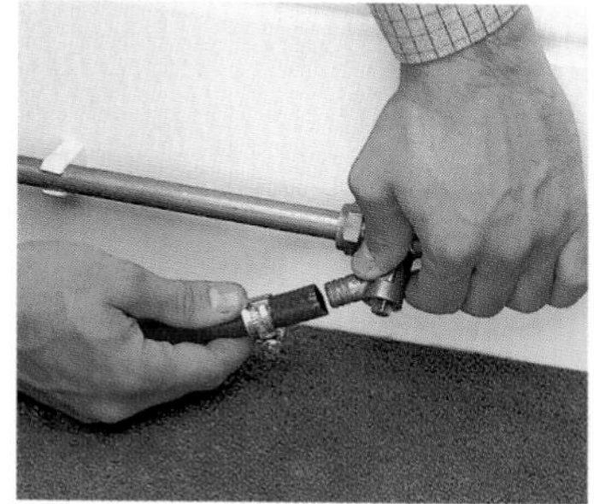

4 Locate the drain cock, which may be near the bottom of the boiler. There may be more than one drainage point on the system. Clip a garden hose onto the drain cock and run the hose to a drain outside, or into buckets.

5 Locate all the points at which air is vented from the central-heating system. These will be radiator vents, a vent on the primary flow near the hot-water cylinder in fully pumped systems, and vents in the loft if circulating pipes run there. There could be additional vents at other points as well.

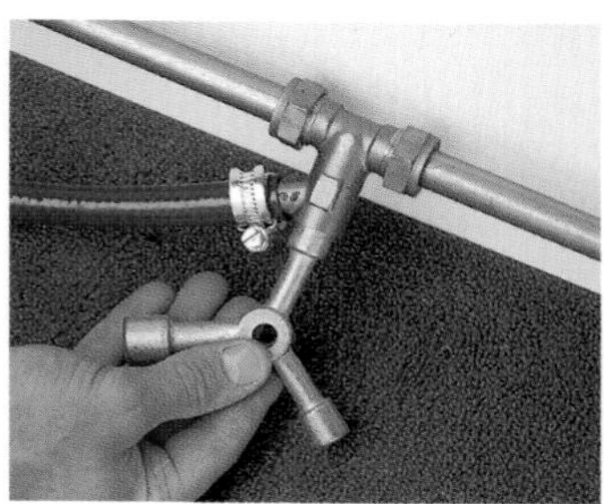

6 Open the drain cock with a spanner or pliers, turning it anticlockwise. Water will then start to flow out of the hose at a fairly slow rate.

7 Start opening the venting points at the top of the system. This will greatly speed up the flow from the drain cock. As the water level drops further, open the lower venting points until they are all open.

8 When the water stops flowing, close all vents in case the water is accidentally turned back on.

REFILLING THE SYSTEM

1 Close all the drain cocks and all the air vents in the system. Then check that all work on the system is finished.

2 Turn on the stopcock to the feed-and-expansion cistern, or untie the ball-valve, in order to let water back into the system.

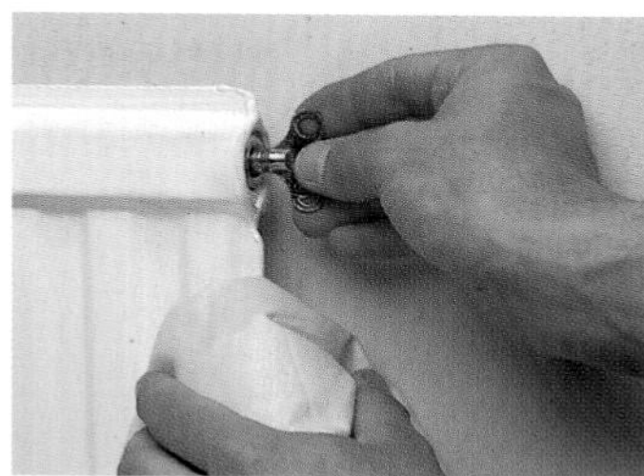

3 Open one of the lowest air vents until water starts to flow out, then close it. Repeat with the lower air vents until the bottom of the central-heating system is full of water. Then do the upper vents, and check the system for leaks.

4 Make sure that the ball-valve to the feed-and-expansion cistern has closed. The water level in the cistern should be just high enough to float the ball. The rest of the cistern space is to take up the expansion of the water in the central-heating system as it heats up.

5 If the water is too high, close off the mains water to the cistern and open the drain cock to let some out. Adjust the arm on the ball-valve so that it closes the valve at the correct water level (page 338). Check that the cistern's lid and insulating jacket are in place.

6 Switch on the electricity and turn on the gas. Re-light the pilot light in a gas boiler. Turn on the system at the programmer or timeswitch. Turn up the room thermostat.

7 Re-light the boiler, following the manufacturer's instructions.

8 As the system heats up more venting will be necessary in order to release air driven off from the water. Minor venting will be required for a few days.

9 Check for leaks again.

10 Remove the hose from the drain cock, and make sure the cock is watertight. If it is leaking, drain the system again, and remove the spindle. The washer is on the end of the spindle. Remove it and replace it with a new one. Use a fibre type in preference to a rubber one because rubber washers tend to bake on and disintegrate.

Preventing a freeze-up

If you turn off your central heating while you go on a winter holiday, there is a danger that the system will freeze and burst a pipe. Lagging only reduces the speed of heat loss, so eventually the temperature of an unused system will drop to the level of the surrounding air.

On a gas-fired or oil-fired system you could turn the room thermostat down to its minimum setting if you will only be away for a few days.

USING A FROST THERMOSTAT

For a long holiday, you could have a frost thermostat installed (it is also called a low-limit thermostat). It overrides the other controls and turns on the system when the air temperature approaches freezing point. Rising air temperature makes it turn the system off again.

ADDING ANTIFREEZE

You can also add antifreeze to the water in the central-heating system. Tie up the ball-valve arm in the feed-and-expansion cistern and pour in antifreeze according to the maker's instructions. Then drain off enough water for the antifreeze to be drawn into the system.

After restoring the water level in the cistern to the correct level, turn the central heating on for a few minutes in order to thoroughly mix the antifreeze with the water.

Solid-fuel systems can also be protected with antifreeze. But remember that if you overrun the system, water is discharged from the safety-vent pipe and fresh water is drawn in. Over time this will dilute the antifreeze.

USING TRACE HEAT TAPE

If your home is plagued by burst pipes, for example, if the main feed to the central-heating feed-and-expansion cistern keeps freezing, it may be worthwhile investing in some trace heat tape, to keep the temperature of the problem pipes

above freezing point. The trace heat tape is fixed to the outside of the pipe with flexible ties. One end is fixed to a special block which is supplied with the tape, and the other is connected to a frost thermostat. The tape is then covered with high-grade insulation.

As the temperature drops the frost thermostat switches on the tape, which warms up, just enough to prevent the pipes from freezing.

Changing a central-heating pump

It is possible to change a central-heating pump without first draining down the whole central-heating system, provided that there are isolating valves fitted on each side of the pump in order to cut off the water supply.

Domestic pumps are now a standard size, but if the old pump was longer than the new one, you may need adapters to fill the gaps.

When you go to buy a replacement from a plumber's merchant take all the details of the old pump with you. Measure the length of the old pump, and the diameter and type of the connections. Most domestic pumps have $1\frac{1}{2}$in BSP threaded connections.

Also make a note of the type of pump and the setting of its output regulator (domestic pumps are available with different strengths).

You will need
Tools Electrician's screwdriver; bowl; towels; pipe wrench/adjustable spanner; pencil and paper.
Materials New pump.

1 Switch off the electricity to the central-heating system and pull out the plug.

2 Make a note and sketch of how the electrical wiring on the old pump is connected. It may be helpful to label each wire. Then disconnect the wires with a screwdriver.

3 Close down the isolating valves on each side of the pump using the valve handle or an adjustable spanner. If there are no isolating valves, drain down the system (page 351).

4 Put a bowl and towels under the pump ready to catch any water that escapes when you remove it.

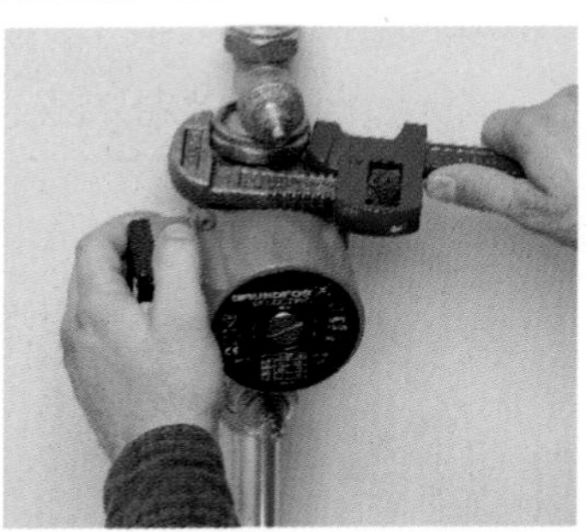

5 Unscrew the union nuts holding the pump in place. Turn them anticlockwise (facing along the pipe towards the pump).

6 Remove the old pump.

7 Fit the new pump in positon with the new sealing washers in the unions to prevent leaks.

8 Open the isolating valves (or refill the system) and check that the unions are watertight.

9 Dry the pump carefully to remove any traces of moisture; reconnect the wiring.

10 Test the newly installed pump by switching on the electricity supply and turning on the central-heating system at the programmer or time switch. You may also need to turn up the room thermostat to get the system going.

11 Once the central-heating system has started up, check that the open safety vent pipe over the feed-and-expansion cistern does not discharge water when the pump starts or stops. If it does, seek expert advice.

12 If you have had to add much fresh water to the cistern, bleed any air out of the system in order to guard against future corrosion and to protect the new pump.

HELPFUL TIPS

The central-heating pump is designed to run full of clean water. Any air or sludge that gets into the water can damage the pump, so keeping the system full of water and limiting corrosion are essential. Never run the pump unless it is full of water.

If your pump is out of use in summer, as is normally the case with a combined gravity and pump-driven system, run it for about a minute once a month in order to keep its impeller free.

Central-heating problems: What to do

If the hot water or heating stop working, there are some simple but useful checks that you can make before calling out a central-heating engineer. They could save you a call-out fee, or help you to give an engineer information about the nature of the problem.

NO CENTRAL HEATING OR HOT WATER

- Check that the programmer is set for 'on'.
- Check that the thermostats are turned up.
- Check that the electricity supply is switched on and that the fuse is in working order. If the power is switched on and the fuse is working, but the programmer is not receiving power, there may be a loose wire. Call a central-heating engineer.
- If a motorised valve is fitted, check that it is working properly. Slide the manual lever to open the valve. If there is resistance, the valve is not opening. This could indicate a burnt out motor. Call a central-heating engineer.
- If the pump is not working, you can try to start it manually. Turn off the central-heating system and wait until the pump is cold. Remove the screw in the middle of the pump and turn the impeller (the pump's manual starter). On some models this is a small screw which is turned with a screwdriver, on others there is a small 'handle' attached.

If this does not work, try tapping the pump casing sharply, but gently, with a mallet two or three times.

If this does not work, remove the pump (see above), and flush clean water through it with a hosepipe. Do not submerge it.

If this does not work, replace the pump (see above).

- If the pump is running, but the boiler does not light, check that the gas is turned on at the meter. If you have an oil boiler, check that the fuel is turned on and that there is oil in the storage tank. Check that the filter is clear.
- If the pilot light is not lit, follow the procedure in the handbook or on the boiler casing to relight it. If the flame will not stay lit, the flame failure device probably needs renewing. Call a central-heating engineer.
- If a combination boiler will not light, check on the pressure gauge that the water pressure is at least $\frac{1}{2}$bar. If it is above $\frac{1}{2}$bar, call a central-heating engineer. If it is below $\frac{1}{2}$bar, top it up from the cold-mains filling point. This could be part of the boiler, or a tap on a pipe next to the boiler (check the handbook and boiler casing).

If the mains pressure to the house as a whole has dropped (check by running the taps), call the water company for advice.

THE CENTRAL HEATING IS WORKING BUT NO HOT WATER

- Make sure that the thermostat on the hot-water cylinder is set to 60°C (140°F).
- Check that the motorised valve (if fitted) to the cylinder is open (see 'No central heating or hot water', left).
- Bleed the air-release valve beside the hot-water cylinder (if there is one). The valve is usually located on the pipe which enters the heating coil (see page 344).

UPSTAIRS RADIATORS HOT BUT THE DOWNSTAIRS ONES ARE COLD

- This is probably due to a jammed pump (see 'No central heating or hot water', left).

DOWNSTAIRS RADIATORS ARE HOT BUT THOSE UPSTAIRS ARE COLD

- Check that there is water in the feed-and-expansion cistern. If there is not, the ball valve has probably jammed (see page 336).
- Bleed the air from the system (see page 347).

Home electrics

12

Electrical emergencies: What to do

ELECTRIC SHOCK

WARNING Quick action is essential but do not touch directly a casualty who is still in contact with the faulty electrical equipment. If you do, the current will pass through you as well, giving you an electric shock.

1 Immediately turn off the electricity at the main switch on the consumer unit if you know where it is and have access to it.

2 If you cannot get to the main switch immediately, stand on a dry floor or carpet indoors, or a dry mat or wooden box out of doors. Push or pull the casualty out of contact with the source of the shock, using a wooden chair or stick, or a loop of dry rope, fabric, or even tights.

3 Dial 999 for an ambulance or call a doctor if the casualty is or has been unconscious, or is burnt or unwell. If you have no telephone, send or shout for help.

4 If the casualty is not breathing, give the kiss of life. Tilt the head back, check the airway is clear and pinch the nose shut. Blow four breaths into the mouth then let the chest fall. Continue breathing into the mouth at normal speed.

5 If the casualty has burns, cover the burns with a clean, dry cotton sheet until medical help arrives.

FIRE IN AN ELECTRICAL APPLIANCE OR FITTING

1 Do not touch any part of the burning appliance or fitting.

2 If a plug-in appliance is on fire, switch off at the socket and pull out the plug.

3 If a socket or fixed appliance with no plug is on fire, turn off at the wall switch, if you can, or at the main switch on the fuse board.

4 Do not use water. Smother the fire with a rug or blanket, or use a dry-powder fire extinguisher.

5 Have the appliance or socket checked by a qualified electrical contractor before you use it again.

SPARKS OR SMELL OF BURNING

1 If sparks or a burning smell come from an appliance, first turn off the socket switch and pull out the plug. If it is a fixed appliance with no plug, turn off the main switch at the consumer unit on the fuse-board. It is then safe to turn off the appliance switch. Check the flex connections in the appliance and renew if necessary; if they are sound, have the appliance checked by a qualified electrical contractor.

2 If the sparks or smell come from a socket or a plug, turn off the main switch at the consumer unit on the fuse board before you touch the socket or plug. If the plug is hot, check its connections including the fuse contacts, and examine the flex for damage. Renew them if necessary (page 364). If the socket is hot, check it for damage and faulty connections and renew if necessary (page 366). Check the cable for damage where it enters the socket mounting box.

NO ELECTRICITY

1 If power throughout your house fails and neighbouring houses are also without power, there is a mains supply failure. Report it, using the emergency number under 'Electricity' in your telephone directory.

2 If the neighbours have power when you have none, the fuse in the sealed unit on your fuseboard may have blown. Do not touch it. Report the power failure as described above.

MINOR EMERGENCIES

1 If one appliance fails, check its plug, fuse and flex and renew them if necessary. If the appliance still fails, try it in a different socket before taking it for repair. If the fault was in the socket, check the socket connections (page 366).

2 If several appliances on one circuit stop working at once, switch off at the consumer unit and check the circuit fuse (page 365). If it is sound, there may be a fault in the circuit cable. Call in a qualified electrical contractor to test it.

Does your wiring need replacing?

If you examine your wiring and find it needs replacing, there is at present no law to stop you doing the work yourself. The electricity companies have the right to test any wiring and to refuse to supply an unsafe connection. Any work you carry out should comply with the Wiring Regulations drawn up by the Institution for Electrical Engineers, and since made into a British Standard (BS 7671). In Scotland electrical systems are covered by the Scottish Building Regulations.

THE JOBS DESCRIBED ON THE FOLLOWING PAGES ARE SUITABLE ONLY FOR MODERN WIRING SYSTEMS

Round-pin plugs and sockets

If you have round-pin sockets, some for 15amp plugs and some for the smaller 5amp and 2amp plugs, your wiring system is likely to be 50 or more years old. The conductor wires carrying the current are insulated with rubber and sheathed with rubber or lead, or run in steel conduit.

Although the system was safe when it was installed, it is now very old. The rubber sheathing or insulation will almost certainly have deteriorated during the 50 years, and have become brittle or even be crumbling away.

Your home should be rewired as soon as possible.

Wiring with round-pin plugs and sockets may be over 50 years old. The insulation on the cable is unlikely to have remained sound.

Old switches and fuses

Look at the main fuseboard beside the meter for signs of old wiring. The cables from the meter may go to a metal box with an on/off switch for the installation; inside the box there are fuses in porcelain holders for lighting, sockets, and so on. Or there may be separate switch-fuses for each circuit.

The system is an old one which you should replace as soon as possible with a modern consumer unit which houses the main switch and the circuit fuses in one box. Replacement is especially important if each circuit has two fuses; the system could be dangerous.

Old wiring, porcelain fuse-holders in an old metal box, or a cluster of separate switch-fuses could be a danger.

Old wiring in conduits with modern sockets

You may have a system where the old rubber-insulated cables in steel conduits remain but the old sockets have been replaced by square-pin 13amp sockets.

Here again the rubber insulation may have become hard and started to crumble. Switch off the mains and unscrew the sockets so that you can see if the cables are new or old and examine the condition of the insulation.

You should plan for your home to be rewired as soon as it is convenient – perhaps when you redecorate.

Circuit wiring in conduits may be old even if modern 13amp sockets have been connected.

Old light switches on wooden blocks

Look at the light switches. Round brass or Bakelite switches mounted on wooden blocks are signs of a lighting system that is more than 50 years old.

The lighting circuits should be rewired with new cable and fittings as soon as possible.

Round brass switch

Round Bakelite switch

Radial socket circuits

Your socket circuits may have PVC-insulated and sheathed twin-core-and-earth cable and 13amp plugs, but installed as a radial system not a ring circuit. You can keep the circuits if the wiring is in good condition but you cannot add extra sockets as described in this section. Sleeve any bare earth conductors.

To find out if you have a radial circuit, turn off the main switch or switches on the fuseboard and unscrew a socket that is likely to be part of the original system, not an afterthought – in the living room, for example. Examine the terminals behind it; if only one conductor wire is connected at each terminal, the system is probably radial. Make sure by examining the two sockets nearest to the first, one on either side of it and probably in the adjoining rooms. If these also have only one conductor wire connected at each terminal, your system is a radial one.

Unscrew and look behind a living-room socket and a socket in the adjoining room on either side.

If all three sockets have only one conductor wire at each terminal, the system is radial.

HOW YOUR ELECTRICAL SYSTEM WORKS

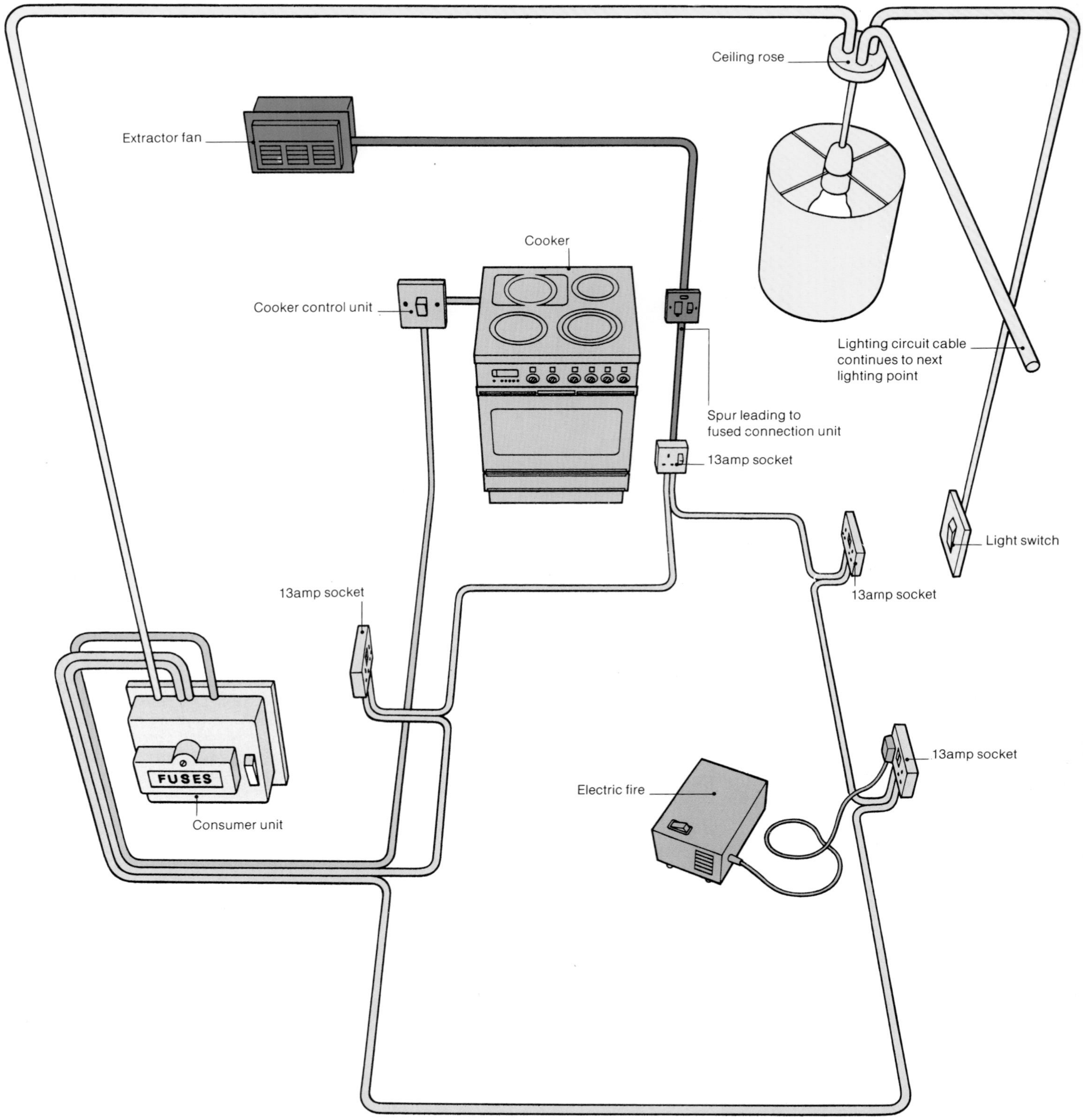

Ceiling rose
Extractor fan
Cooker
Cooker control unit
Lighting circuit cable continues to next lighting point
Spur leading to fused connection unit
13amp socket
Light switch
13amp socket
13amp socket
13amp socket
Electric fire
FUSES
Consumer unit

LIGHTING CIRCUIT

The circuit runs out from the consumer unit linking a chain of lighting points; cables branch off to switches. It is protected by a 5amp fuse. It can safely supply up to 1200 watts at one time but should not link more than ten lighting points. The circuit would be overloaded if each of the lighting points had one of the higher-wattage bulbs.

RING CIRCUIT

The circuit, which starts from the consumer unit and returns to it, can serve an area up to 120sq yds (100 sq m). It is protected by a 30amp fuse. It can have any number of sockets or fused connection units on it, but its maximum total load is 7200 watts. For larger total loads and larger floor areas, additional ring circuits are needed.

SOCKET OUTLET

The maximum permissible load on a socket outlet that takes a 13amp plug is 3000 watts. A plug is fitted with a 13amp or a 3amp fuse according to the wattage rating of the appliance connected to it. If an adaptor is plugged into the socket, the adaptor's sockets cannot supply 3000 watts each but only a total of 3000 watts together.

SPUR ON A RING CIRCUIT

Extra sockets can be added to an existing ring circuit on spurs branching off the ring at a socket. In theory, each socket on the ring could supply a spur to a single or double socket or a fused connection unit. However, the circuit including spurs must not serve an area of more than 120sq yds (100sq m) – and its maximum load is still 7200 watts.

SINGLE-APPLIANCE CIRCUIT

An appliance that is a large consumer of electricity and in constant or frequent use – a cooker, a fixed water heater, or a shower heater unit, for example – has its own circuit running from the consumer unit. It would take too large a proportion of the power available on a shared circuit and would be likely to overload the circuit.

Understanding the fuseboard

The appearance of a modern fuseboard (now usually called a consumer unit) varies from home to home. The basic items are the same; only their arrangement is different. There is a mains switch and fuses to protect the circuits that supply electricity to different parts of the home. There is also an earth terminal.

Older fuseboards use rewirable fuse carriers or cartridge fuses as protection for each circuit – upstairs lights, downstairs lights, upstairs sockets, downstairs sockets and so on. The new fuseboards have small automatic switches called miniature circuit breakers (MCBs). They also contain a residual current device (RCD) protecting some or all circuits.

THE POWER CENTRE OF YOUR HOME

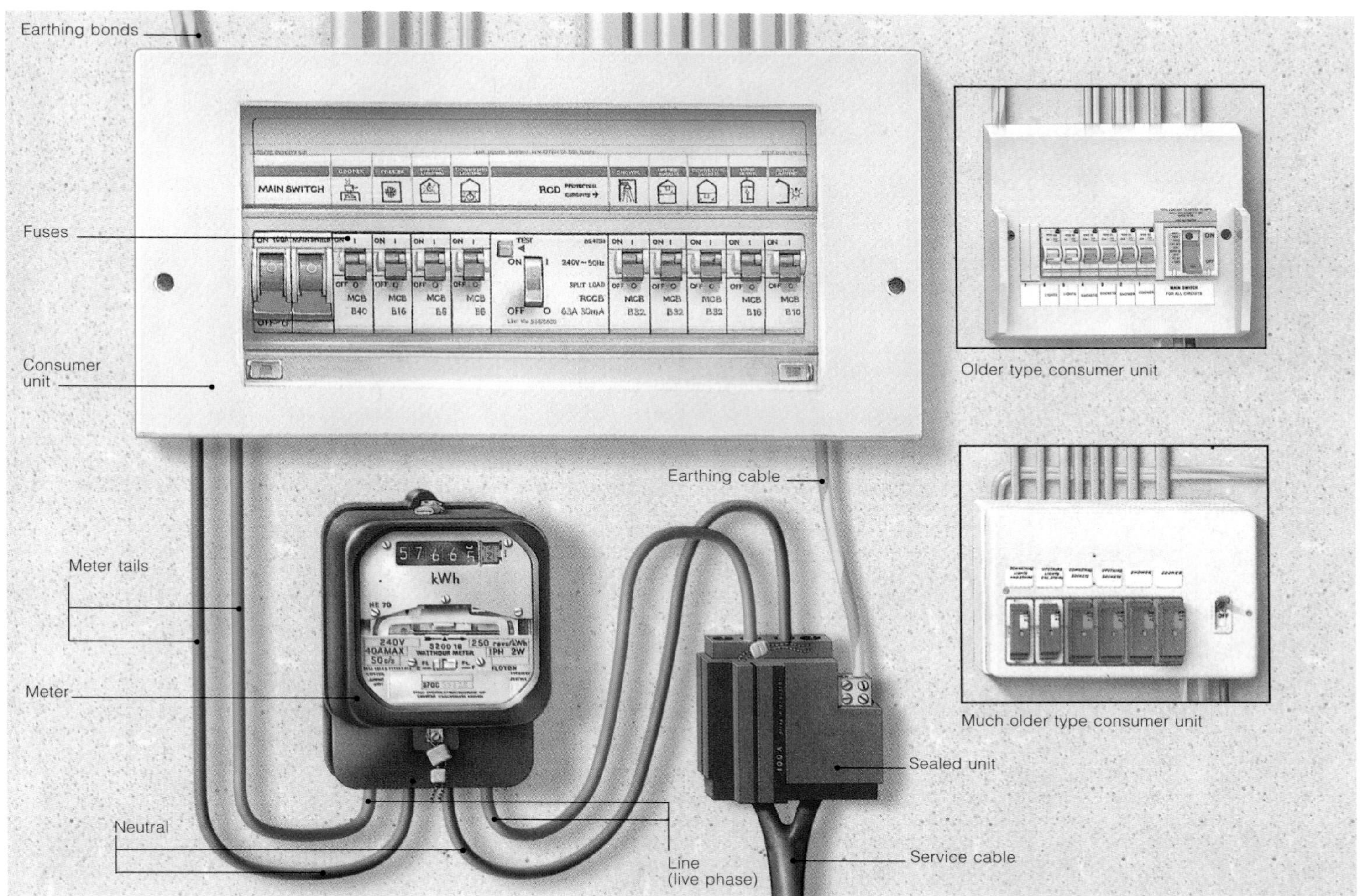

Service cable

Electricity comes into the home through the service cable, often called the main cable or mains. It carries electric current at 230 volts. The current flows along the line (also called live or phase) conductor and returns along the neutral conductor. Do not interfere with the service cable.

The term live has been replaced by line. Live implied that only one of the conductors was carrying live current, whereas the neutral conductor is also carrying live current.

Sealed unit

The service cable ends here. Its neutral conductor is connected to a solid terminal. Its line conductor is connected to a fuse, called the service cut-out, which is usually rated at 60amps or 100amps. It is a deliberate weak link which will soon melt and disconnect the system if current greater than the fuse rating reaches it. Do not tamper with the sealed unit.

Meter tails

These two cables (line and neutral) run from the sealed unit to the meter and from the meter to the consumer unit. The line cable is red-insulated and the neutral cable is black-insulated. Each tail has an outer sheath which may match the colour of the insulation or may be grey. The electricity supply company must disconnect the supply before any work can be carried out on the meter tails.

Meter

The meter records how much electricity a household uses. It belongs to the electricity supply company and the standing charge on the electricity bill includes a sum for the hire of the meter.

Older meters have a row of dials to record the amount of electricity used. Modern meters are digital – they record the amount of electricity used on a row of roll-over figures – or on two rows in a two-tariff meter.

Meter housing unit

On a new house, the builder may fit the meter in a locked steel or plastic cupboard on the outside of the building. The householder and the supply company have keys for reading the meter from outside. If the supply company agrees, an indoor meter can be moved outside at the householder's expense.

Two-tariff meter

Two-tariff meters have two rows of figures, one for registering consumption on the day rate, the other for registering consumption on the lower night rate.

Time clock

A two-tariff meter is linked to a sealed time clock that changes the meter to the day or night register.

Consumer unit

The householder's responsibility for the system starts here. A modern unit combines a main switch, the earthing terminal block for all the household circuits, and the fuses or MCBs for all the circuits. The circuits vary in number and purpose according to a household's needs, but always include separate lighting and socket circuits. Label the fuse carriers or MCBs to show which circuit each fuse protects – if the installer has not already done this. To identify the circuits, turn off the main switch and remove one fuse carrier, or switch off one MCB. Turn the main switch back on and check which lights or appliances are not working. Repeat the procedure with

CURRENT RATINGS

As part of a move towards European standardisation, some of the ratings marked on new MCBs are being changed.

IMPERIAL		REYNARD
5amp	becomes	6amp
15amp	becomes	16amp
30amp	becomes	32amp
45amp	becomes	40amp

Understanding the fuseboard (continued)

each fuse carrier or MCB.

Most modern consumer units allow for additional MCBs to be installed at a later date.

The controls of the electricity supply system, such as the meter and consumer unit, must be mounted on a fire-resistant board.

Fuses

A fuse carrier is marked with the amp rating of the fuse it needs. A lighting circuit is protected by a 5amp fuse, a ring circuit by a 30amp fuse. If current greater than these ratings reaches the fuse, the fuse blows and the circuit is disconnected. The fuse link inside a carrier may be a wire or a cartridge.

The most modern units have miniature circuit breakers (MCBs) instead of fuses. If too much current flows, the circuit is disconnected instantly and a switch moves to the off position or a button pops out to indicate the disconnection.

Circuit cables

The various household circuits are supplied by cables leading off from the consumer unit. The line conductor in each cable is connected to a terminal on a bar behind the fuse or MCB for the circuit, the neutral conductor to a neutral terminal block and the earth conductor to an earthing terminal block.

Earthing cable

This connects the earthing terminal block in the consumer unit (to which the circuit cables are connected) to the earthing point provided by the electricity supply company – usually on the sealed unit or the service cable. Bonding cables connect metal pipework to the earthing terminal block.

Residual current device (RCD)

An RCD (formerly called an RCCB – residual current circuit breaker) checks constantly whether the line and neutral currents are in balance. If it detects an imbalance, it switches off the supply in a fraction of a second. An imbalance shows that current is flowing out of the circuit because of a broken flex or cable or a faulty appliance. An RCD can protect all or part of a wiring system. An RCD may replace the main switch or protect one or more circuits. All newly wired homes now incorporate RCD protection, but only on some circuits.

An RCD in its own enclosure may have been added to an existing installation to protect new circuits.

Measuring the electricity you use

READING THE METER

The unit for measuring electricity consumption is the kilowatt-hour (kWh). The three types of meter display the number of kilowatt-hours used in different ways.

Digital meter

Modern meters are the digital (also called cyclometer) type with a row of figures rolling over to register how much electricity has been used. To read such a meter, write down the figures exactly as they appear on the meter, but ignore the one on the extreme right.

Two-tariff meter

NIGHT

10 000 1000 100 10 1 1/10

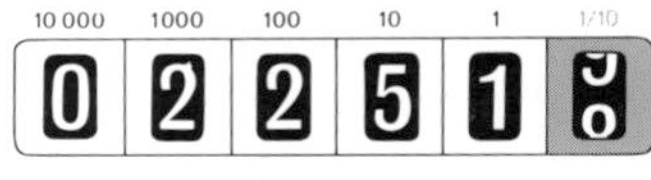

DAY kWh

10 000 1000 100 10 1 1/10

With a two-tariff meter, read and record both rows of figures (for night-time and daytime consumption) as they appear on the meter. Ignore the figure on the extreme right in each row.

Dial meter

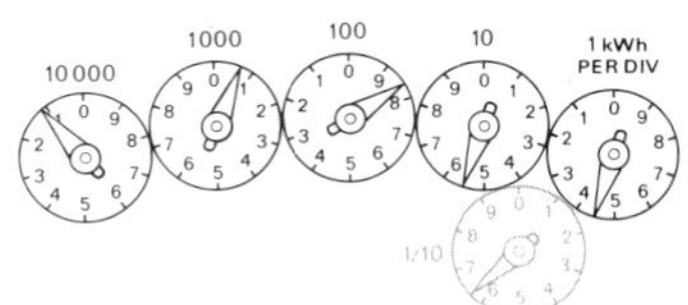

Older meters have a row of dials, with some of the hands turning clockwise and others turning anticlockwise. Record the figures from right to left. Ignore the small dials marked 1/10 and 1/100. Read the last figure that a hand has passed, not the one it is nearest to. When the hand seems to be right on a figure, record the previous figure unless the hand on the dial to the right is between 0 and 1.

WHAT IT COSTS

You pay for electricity by the unit. The price per unit changes from time to time, but is always shown on the electricity bill along with the number of units used.

A unit is equivalent to 1000 watts of electricity used for one hour (usually called a kilowatt-hour, kWh for short). A 1kW (1000 watt) electric fire will consume one unit an hour, a 500 watt appliance will consume one unit in two hours; a 100 watt light bulb will consume one unit in ten hours. From the wattage rating marked on an appliance, you can see how much electricity it will consume.

The meter records how many units the household is consuming. To check whether your electricity bill is accurate, keep a note of the reading each time the meter is read. Subtract the previous reading from the latest one; the answer is the number of units to be paid for.

IS YOUR METER ACCURATE?

If you suspect that your meter is faulty, contact your electricity supply company. They may be able to give an immediate explanation for an unusually high bill. If not, a sample check on the meter can be made by one of the company's officials. If you are still dissatisfied the company will install a second meter alongside yours to check its accuracy.

The final means of checking lies with the Department of Energy. The department certifies all meters, and all consumers are entitled to have their meter tested by the department if there are good grounds for suspecting that it is faulty. When it is decided that the department will test the meter, you have to agree to abide by the examiner's findings.

The department appoints an examiner who calls at your home by appointment, examines the meter and then tests its parts in a laboratory. There is usually no charge if the meter proves faulty. If the customer has overpaid, the supply company will make a refund.

WHAT THE TECHNICAL TERMS MEAN

Watts

Electric power (or any other form of power) is measured in watts (W for short). Every electrical appliance has a wattage rating marked on its rating plate. The higher the wattage rating, the more electricity the appliance consumes when it is in use.

Amps

The amount of current flowing in a conductor is measured in amperes (amps or A for short).

With a cable or flex, the greater the number of amps it must carry, the thicker its conductors must be. Its current-carrying capacity also depends on the length of its run and whether it is running through thermal insulation or thermal plasterboard.

Fuses and sockets are rated according to the maximum flow of amps they can carry. A 5amp fuse, for example, can normally take up to 5amps of current.

Volts

Electrical pressure is measured in volts (shown as V for short). The pressure of the public supply in Britain has been standardised at 230 volts. The supply voltage may vary by plus 10 per cent (23V) or minus 6 percent (14V) and a further drop of 6V is permitted on individual circuits.

Voltage-sensitive equipment, such as a computer or a word processor, can be protected by a voltage stabiliser.

Batteries and some portable generators and transformers supply other voltages for lighting and appliances that have been designed to operate on them.

Ac and dc

Mains electricity in Britain is alternating current (ac) It has an oscillating wave pattern, rather like waves of the sea, but the pattern is regular – the complete cycle from the crest occurs 50 times a second. This is known as the frequency of supply and is written as 50~ or 50hz.

The electricity from batteries is direct current (dc). Its continuous flow of electrons is steady in its direction, with no oscillation.

The advantage of alternating current is that it can be transformed from one voltage to another. Because of this, a power station can supply a very high voltage to substations which reduce the voltage to feed at 230V to many individual properties.

Inside the home, the voltage can be reduced again by a transformer, to make it low enough for a doorbell, for games such as miniature car circuits and for model railways, for example.

Providing a safe earthing system in your home

Safety from electric shock for everyone in your home depends not only on correct wiring connections but also on the correct earthing of the metal parts you touch on electrical equipment; some other metal items that you might touch at the same time as faulty electrical equipment should be bonded to the earthing system.

The earthing system offers an easy route along earth conductors for any 'escaped' current; the earth conductors have low resistance which allows an increase of current to pass along them if its normal route is interrupted – for example by damage to one of the live conductors. 'Escaped' current always seeks to travel to earth and will take the easiest route available. This could be through a person touching the faulty equipment if the earth conductors were not there offering an easy route.

Earth conductors are connected to the earth block in the consumer unit. The earth block is connected to a terminal provided by the electricity company – the earthing point.

Modern installations have protective multiple earthing (PME). The system is earthed via the electricity supply cable's neutral

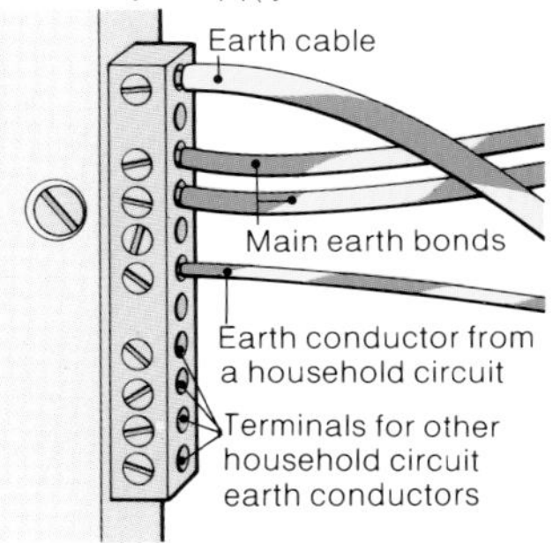

connector to the 'star point' at the local electricity supply transformer, which is connected to a permanent earth at the substation.

The earth block in the consumer unit (above) has terminals for the house circuits plus some extra. One is for the main earth cable, called the earth continuity conductor (ECC), running to the earthing point. Other terminals earth metal pipes carrying water and gas.

A house in a rural area with an overhead power supply may have no earth connection via the supply cable. The house is earthed by an earth electrode (a metal spike) driven deep into the ground close to the house. This 'TT' earthing needs additional protection, provided by a residual current device (RCD).

The wiring and sockets in a house are connected to the earthing system via the earth conductors in the cables. The casing of electrical equipment is insulated or earthed by the manufacturer. Check that any metal items which you install yourself, or have installed for you, are safely earthed (see next page).

IS YOUR EARTHING POINT CORRECTLY FITTED?

Check that your earthing point complies with one of the safe means of earthing described below. Ask the electricity supply company to remedy any defects.

AN ELECTRICITY SUPPLY COMPANY TERMINAL

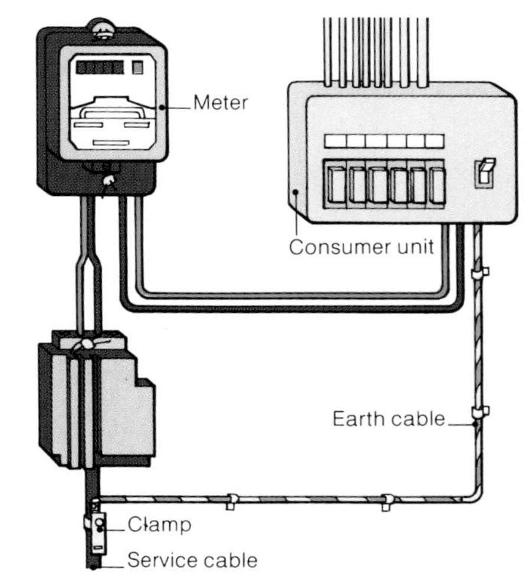

The earth cable runs from the earth terminal block in the consumer unit to a terminal provided by the electricity supply company. This may be on the metal sheath of the service cable.

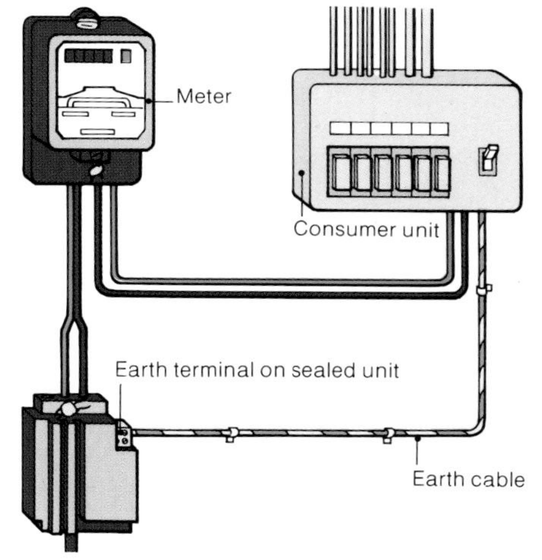

The electricity supply company terminal may be on the sealed unit instead of the service cable.

In some cases the earthing point provided is a separate terminal on the fuseboard.

The size of the earthing cable between the company's terminal and the earth block in the consumer unit should be not less that 16mm²; it should be covered with green-and-yellow insulation (green on older installations).

The connections to the earth block in the consumer unit and to the company's earthing terminal should be screwed tightly in place. Between the two connections, the cable should be held in place on the fuseboard or the wall by cable clips.

EARTHING TO A METAL STAKE

The earth cable from the earth block in the consumer unit runs to a purpose-made metal stake driven into the ground outside the house. Modern practice is to fit one or more RCDs (residual current devices) on or near the fuseboard to cut off the electricity instantly if a fault should develop. Ask for advice from the electricity supply company or some other

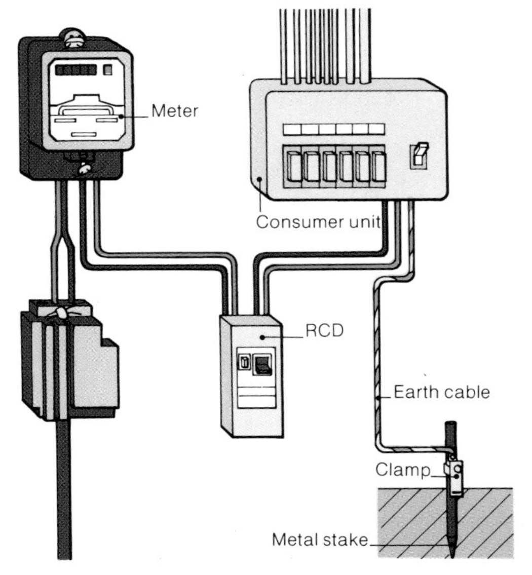

approved electrical contractor if you have a metal stake earthing point but no RCD.

The earth cable should be connected to the stake by a clamp complying with British Standard 951 and marked SAFETY ELECTRICAL CONNECTION – DO NOT REMOVE. The stake is not always easy to locate. If it is next to the outside wall, as is most usual, it will not be buried but may have a brick or similar surround protecting it. If it is some distance from the building, it will be buried and should have a paving slab or some similar protection over it.

The stake and the earth cable should be free from corrosion and be protected so that they cannot be damaged – by gardening equipment for example.

The earth cable should be green-and-yellow insulated (green on older installations). Its minimum size should be 25mm² if it has to be buried in the ground, 6mm² if it does not need to be buried.

UNSAFE EARTHING TO A WATER PIPE

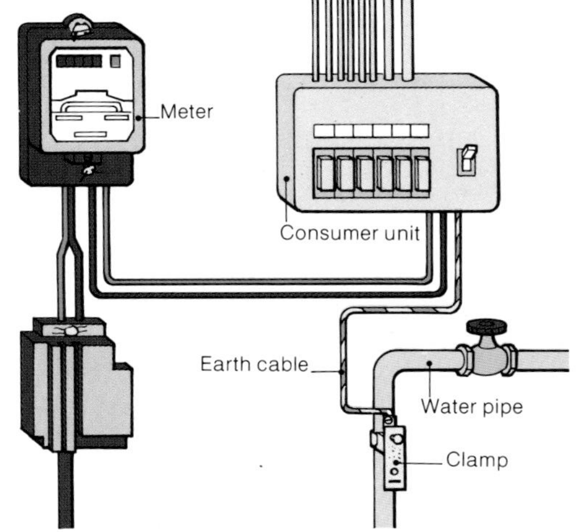

The earth cable from the consumer unit runs to a terminal fixed by a clamp to the main water pipe. Since 1966 this method of earthing has not complied with the Wiring Regulations. It is unsafe because metal water mains are being superseded by plastic and there is no continuity for the earthing system. The earthing point should be replaced as soon as possible. Ask the electricity company to provide an earthing terminal. If this is not possible, have an earth stake system installed as described above.

Bonding metal fittings to the earthing system

Check that all non-electrical metal equipment that you could touch at the same time as faulty electrical equipment is bonded to the earthing system as described below.

MAIN BONDING

One or more green-and-yellow insulated cables called main bonding conductors should run from the earth block in the consumer unit to incoming metal water, gas and oil service pipes (but not to telephone or television cables). The size of the cable should not be less than 10mm². Some electricity supply companies require the main bonds to run from their earthing point instead of from the consumer unit.

If a main bond runs to one metal pipe and then on to another, it should be one unbroken length.

CONNECTING MAIN BONDING CONDUCTORS

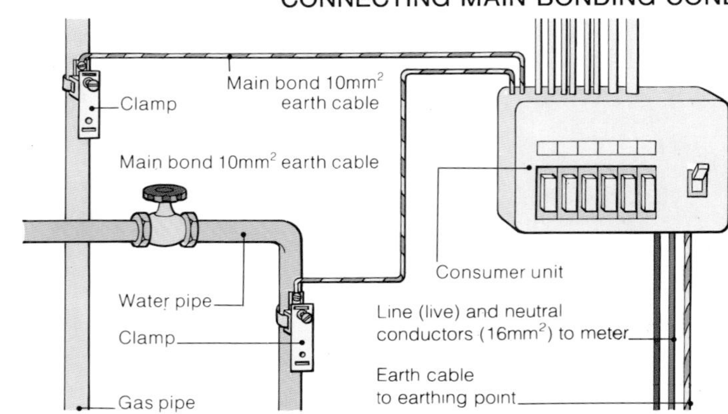

The main bonding conductors should be connected at one end to terminals on the earth block in the consumer unit and at the other to water, gas and oil pipes.

Connections to the pipes should be made with clamps complying with British Standard 951 and marked SAFETY ELECTRICAL CONNECTION – DO NOT REMOVE.

Clamps must fit tightly and be in contact with bare metal, not paint. They must be free from corrosion and should be easily accessible for inspection.

SUPPLEMENTARY BONDING

Sinks, baths, taps, radiators and towel rails are among the items of non-electrical metal equipment that could be a danger if they came into contact with a conductor carrying current or if an electrical fault occurred anywhere in the house. If you can touch any of these items at the same time as earthed metalwork of electrical equipment, you should bond them to the earthing system. An electrical contractor can test whether items already in the house are bonded. If the test result is not satisfactory, or if you are installing new metal items, you must also install supplementary bonding, using 4mm² earth cable.

In each bathroom or shower room, all metal items which you can touch must be connected together by bonding conductors and be bonded to the earthing system.

INSTALLING SUPPLEMENTARY BONDING CONDUCTORS

Use green-and-yellow insulated earth cable not less than 4mm² in size. To connect it to metal pipes, use clamps complying with British Standard 951 and marked SAFETY

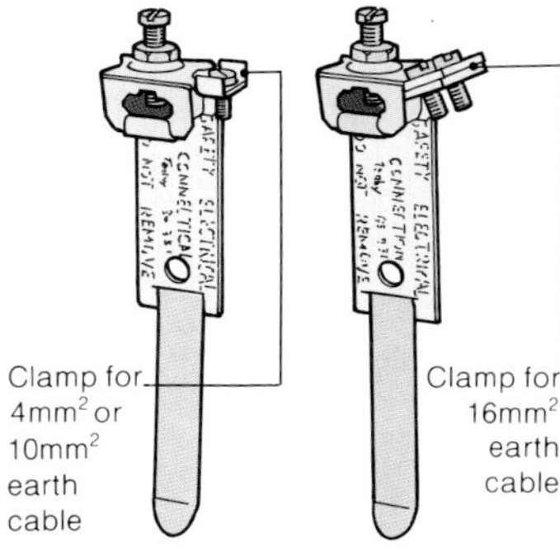

ELECTRICAL CONNECTION – DO NOT REMOVE.

For a neat appearance, plan the route of the bonding cable as for any other electrical cable – take it behind a bath panel, inside a basin pedestal, under the floor, behind a hollow wall, in plaster or in trunking. You can lead the earth cable from the metal item either to the earth terminal behind a socket or to metal pipework which will have been connected to the earth block in the consumer unit by a main bond. If you are connecting to a socket, first turn off the main switch at the consumer unit and remove the fuse for the socket circuit. If you are going to connect to pipes, make sure that there is a continuous metal route back to the consumer unit. Now that many water tanks and expansion tanks are plastic, the continuity of the metal is interrupted. You should lead a 4mm² green-and-yellow-insulated earth cable from the ingoing pipework to the outgoing pipework to bridge across the plastic interruption.

The connections of supplementary bonds should be accessible for inspection and checking. Connections to the earth terminals of sockets are easy to inspect. Connections to pipework can be made in cupboards, behind removable panels or under the floor; if they have to be made under the floor, the section of floorboard above should be fixed with screws so that it can easily be lifted if necessary.

When you are connecting an earth clamp to metal pipework, clean the pipe with wire wool first; if the pipe has been painted, strip off an area of paintwork.

Screw the tip of the earth cable tightly into the terminal.

Metal baths and sinks are made with an earth tag. Connect the bonding cable by winding the bared end of the conductor round a bolt passed through the tag. Trap it with a metal washer secured under the nut. Make sure that the tag is clean and free of paint or enamel. If you have an older bath or sink with no earth tag, it is usually possible to secure the bonding conductor to a bolt holding a bath foot, or to a screw holding the overflow grid and plug chain; otherwise drill a hole through the foot of the bath or in the rim at the back of the basin to receive the bolt.

INSTALLING SUPPLEMENTARY BONDING

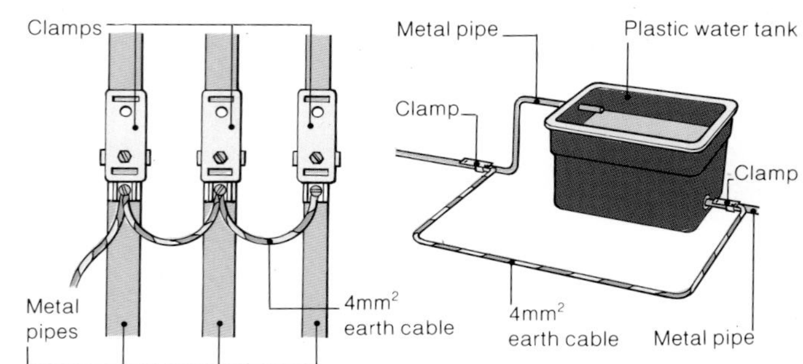

Link airing cupboard pipes to ensure the pipework offers an unbroken metal earth route.

Bridge across a plastic water tank from metal pipe to metal pipe with 4mm² earth cable.

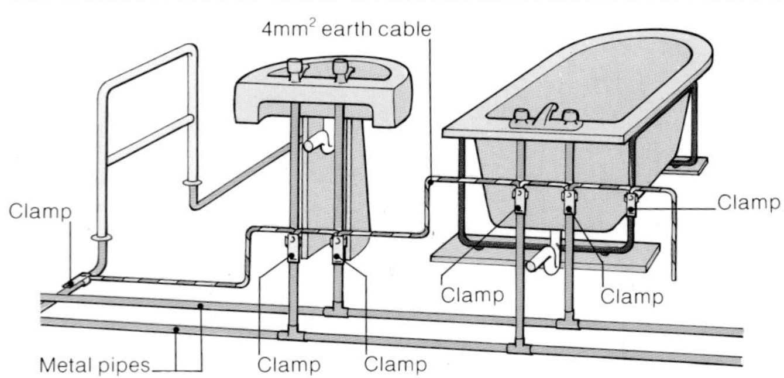

Link together non-electrical metal fittings in bathrooms or shower rooms with 4mm² earth cable. Such fittings might include inlet pipes to taps on basin, bath and bidet; towel rails; porcelain-enamelled cast-iron baths; and the metal cradles of plastic baths. Connect the earth cable to the metal with clamps. You can conceal the cable behind fittings and under the floor.

Home electrics: Tools for the job

Much of the work in modernising or extending wiring is non-electrical – cutting chases for cables, raising floorboards, drilling holes and the like. For working with the actual wiring and electrical accessories a few special tools are essential.

Pliers
A pair of 6in (150mm) electrician's pliers with cutting blades is sturdy enough for cutting conductor wires in cables. Make sure the handles are insulated – plastic-covered, for example.

Torch
A powerful torch, squat enough to stand on its own, will light up work under floors and in lofts. Make sure that it has a plastic or rubber case. Buy a spare set of batteries before beginning any electrical job for which you will need the torch on a lot, in case its batteries start to fail.

Wire cutters
A pair of 5in (125mm) or 6in (150mm) side cutters with insulated handles cuts wires in flexes and the thinner cables.

Wire strippers
These should have insulated handles and may be combined with cutters. The adjustable blades strip the insulation from different-sized flexes and cables without damaging the wire strands inside.

Tester screwdriver
An $\frac{1}{8}$in (3mm) blade, insulated screwdriver is used for screwing wires to terminals in plugs and light fittings. It has a neon lamp in the handle which lights up if the tip touches a live screw or conductor.

Insulated screwdriver
Use a $\frac{3}{16}$in (5mm) blade screwdriver with an insulating sleeve on the shaft for screws on fuse carriers, plug covers and sockets.

Knife
A sharp knife will cut through thick cable sheath and flex sheath.

Circuit continuity tester
With a simple battery-powered tester you can check the continuity of circuits and whether a socket is on a ring circuit or on a spur.

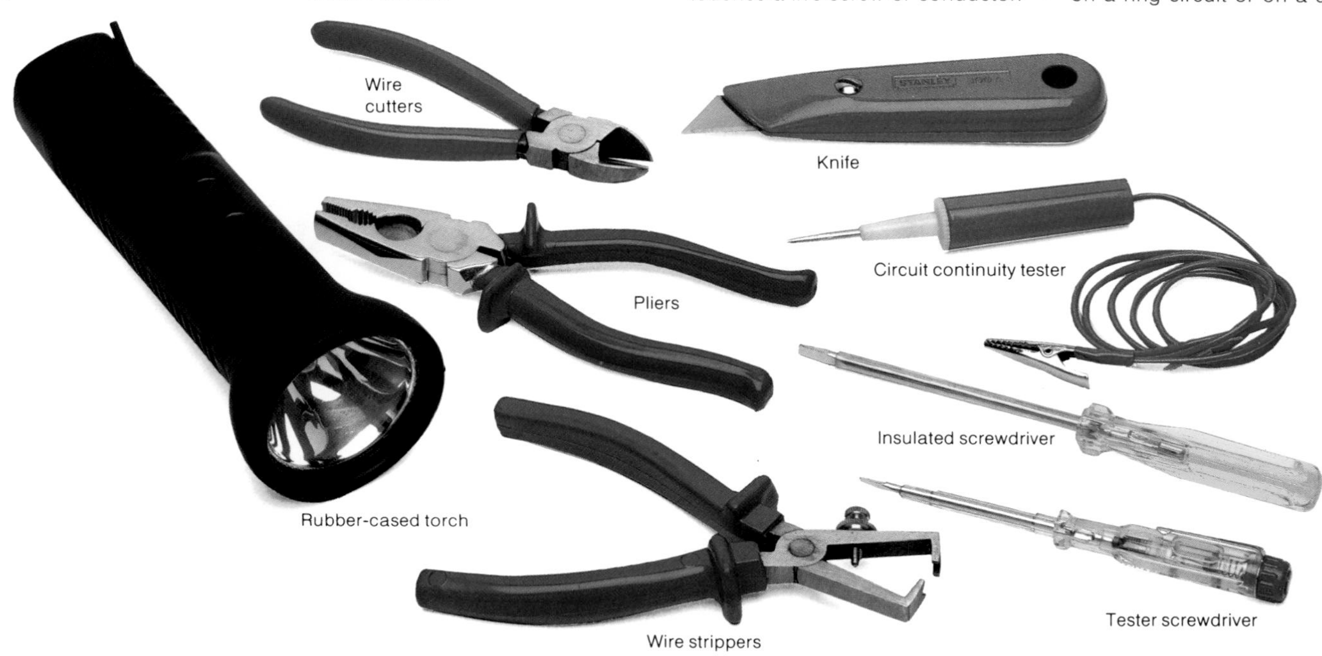

CHOOSING CABLES FOR INDOOR CIRCUITS

Cable carries electricity round the household circuits to ceiling roses, light switches, socket outlets and fused connection units. It is the permanently fixed wiring – which is not moved about as flex is.

Modern cable – known as twin-core-and-earth cable – has a grey or white oval PVC sheath with three conductors inside. The red-insulated conductor is now called the line (formerly live or phase); the black-insulated conductor is the neutral; the bare wire is the earth conductor.

The greater the current, the thicker the cable carrying it has to be. Cable size is given in square millimetres. In thermal insulation or for a very long run, cable of a larger size than usual may be needed; ask an electrician.

Sleeving for earth conductors

When you strip off the outer sheath of a cable, cover the bare wire of the earth conductor with a sleeve of green-and-yellow PVC.

KEY TO COLOUR AND CODING

L – Line, live or phase (red)

E – Earth (bare wire)

N – Neutral (black)

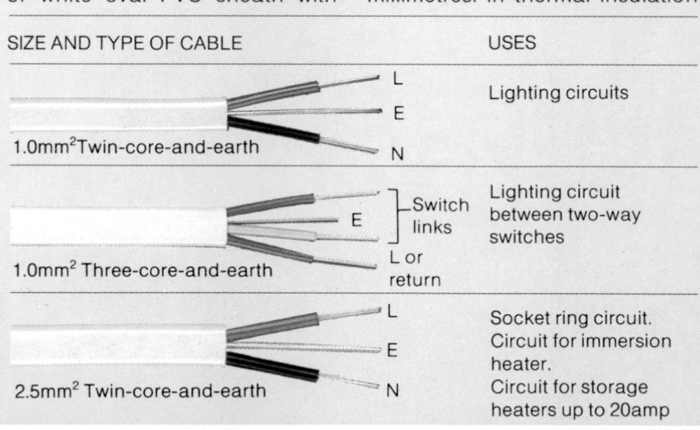

SIZE AND TYPE OF CABLE	USES
1.0mm² Twin-core-and-earth (L, E, N)	Lighting circuits
1.0mm² Three-core-and-earth (Switch links, E, L or return)	Lighting circuit between two-way switches
2.5mm² Twin-core-and-earth (L, E, N)	Socket ring circuit. Circuit for immersion heater. Circuit for storage heaters up to 20amp

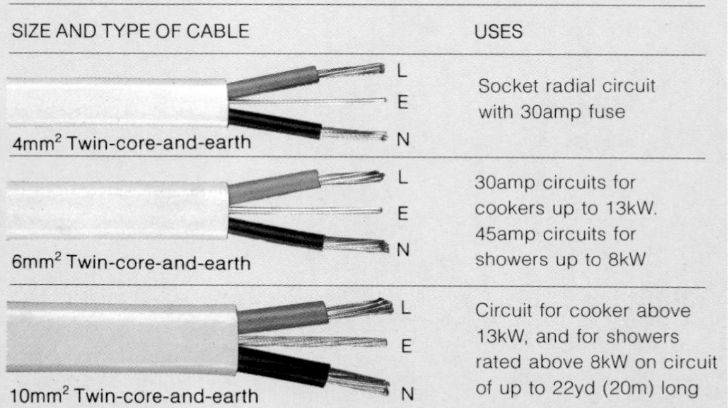

SIZE AND TYPE OF CABLE	USES
4mm² Twin-core-and-earth (L, E, N)	Socket radial circuit with 30amp fuse
6mm² Twin-core-and-earth (L, E, N)	30amp circuits for cookers up to 13kW. 45amp circuits for showers up to 8kW
10mm² Twin-core-and-earth (L, E, N)	Circuit for cooker above 13kW, and for showers rated above 8kW on circuit of up to 22yd (20m) long

CHOOSING FLEXES FOR APPLIANCES AND LIGHTS

Flexible cord, usually called flex, connects an appliance or light to a circuit supplying power. The connection may be made with a plug and socket or with a fused connection unit.

On fixed lights, the flex connects with a lighting circuit at a ceiling rose and with the light bulb at a lampholder.

Most appliances – irons, toasters, table lamps, hairdryers, for example – have the flex permanently wired into them. Others, including sewing machines, kettles and tape recorders, have flexes that connect to them by a push-in connector.

Most flex is round in cross-section. Non-sheathed figure 8 and twin-twisted flex are not now permitted and should be replaced. The sheathing depends on the temperature it must withstand. Ordinary rubber and PVC withstand temperatures up to 60°C. Heat-resistant rubber or PVC withstand up to 85°C. Rubber-sheathed flexes have an outer cover of braided fabric. Flexes that may be used out of doors should be orange-sheathed to make them easy to see.

Flex with two conductors is for double-insulated appliances (marked ⧈), or non-metal light-fittings; flex already wired into a double-insulated appliance may be oval instead of round in cross-section. Metal light fittings and most appliances need three-core flex, which has an earth conductor. A conductor in flex consists of many fine strands of wire twisted together – which is what makes it flexible. The thicker the conductor, the more strands it has; the thickness determines how much current it can carry.

Never join lengths of flex with insulating tape. Use a cable connector or fit a flex of the right length. Do not run flex under a carpet; it could fray and cause a fire. Do not trail flex across a room; somebody could trip over it and damage its connections.

Curly flex
Two and three-core curly flexes are sold in several lengths and colours. Some have connectors and plugs already fitted; others have the ends free for connecting. The flex extends when you move the appliance – a lamp, perhaps – out from the socket and contracts neatly when you put the appliance near the socket again.

KEY TO FLEX CODING

L – Line, live or phase (brown)

E – Earth (green and yellow)

N – Neutral (blue)

APPEARANCE OF FLEX	FLEX SIZE IN MM²	FOR AMPS UP TO	FOR WATTS UP TO	NUMBER OF CORES	SHEATH	EXAMPLES OF USE
L N	0.5	3	700	Two; colour coded	Heat-resisting PVC (85°C)	Non-metal lamps and pendant light fittings up to 4½lb (2kg) in weight
L N	0.75	6	1400	Two; colour coded	Ordinary PVC (60°C)	Non-metal lamps with flex more than 7ft (2m) long. Some hair dryers, food mixers and other double-insulated appliances up to 1.4kW
L N	0.75	6	1400	Two; colour coded	Heat-resisting PVC (85°C)	Pendant light fittings up to 6½lb (3kg) in weight
L E N	0.75	6	1400	Three; colour coded	Ordinary PVC (60°C)	Metal table and standard lamps. Some vacuum cleaners, hair dryers, food mixers, refrigerators, television sets
 L E N	0.75	6	1400	Three; colour coded	Heat-resisting braided rubber or PVC (85°C)	Room heaters up to 1kW. Irons, toasters, and other appliances that become hot and could damage ordinary PVC
L N	1.0	10	2300	Two; colour coded	Heat-resisting PVC (85°C)	Pendant light fittings up to 11lb (5kg) in weight
L E N	1.0	10	2300	Three; colour coded	Ordinary PVC (60°C)	Kettles or jugs up to 2kW. Slow cookers. Frying pans
 L E N	1.0	10	2300	Three; colour coded	Heat-resisting braided rubber or PVC (85°C)	Room heaters up to 2kW
L E N	1.25	13	3000	Three; colour coded	Ordinary PVC (60°C)	Kettles or jugs from 2kW to 3kW
 L E N	1.25	13	3000	Three; colour coded	Heat-resisting braided rubber or PVC (85°C)	Room heaters up to 3kW
L E N	1.5	15	3600	Three; colour coded	Ordinary PVC (60°C)	Some extension leads
L E N	1.5	15	3600	Three; colour coded	Heat-resisting rubber (85°C)	Immersion heaters up to 3kW. Storage heaters up to 3kW

Preparing flex and cable for connection

The conductor wires of a cable or flex have to be exposed before they are connected to the terminals of a plug, socket, switch or ceiling rose. With the plastic outer sheathing and inner insulation stripped away, the metal parts can touch each other and complete the circuit to conduct the electricity.

You will need
Tools Sharp knife; wire cutters and strippers; pliers.
Materials Flex, or cable and a short length of green-and-yellow plastic sleeving. Perhaps plastic insulating tape or a rubber sleeve.

STRIPPING THE OUTER SHEATH

Most cable and flex has an outer sheathing of tough plastic. Remove enough to make sure that the conductors can reach the terminals easily or they may be pulled out. Take care not to cut or nick the insulation on the conductors as you cut the outer sheath.

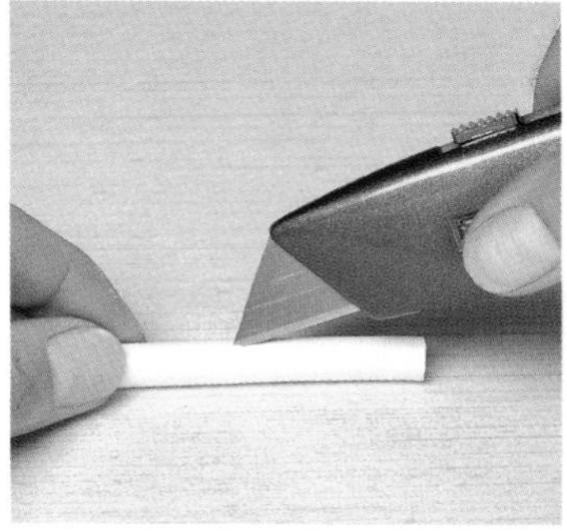

1 Lay the cable or flex on a firm surface and cut through the outer sheath with a sharp knife, making a single lengthwise cut.

2 Bend back the insulation and cut at the fold to remove the unwanted section of sheathing. For most connections you need to remove about 1½in (38mm) of the outer sheathing, but for some – a cooker control unit, a shaver socket, a consumer unit, for example – more must be removed.

CUTTING AND STRIPPING THE CONDUCTORS

1 Cut the individual conductors to the right length to reach their own terminals.

2 Adjust the hole of the wire strippers to the thickness of the conductors you are stripping. Use a spare bit of conductor to get the adjustment right. The conductor should just be able to slide into the stripper hole.

3 Press the handles firmly together to cut the conductor insulation about ⅝in (16mm) from the tip.

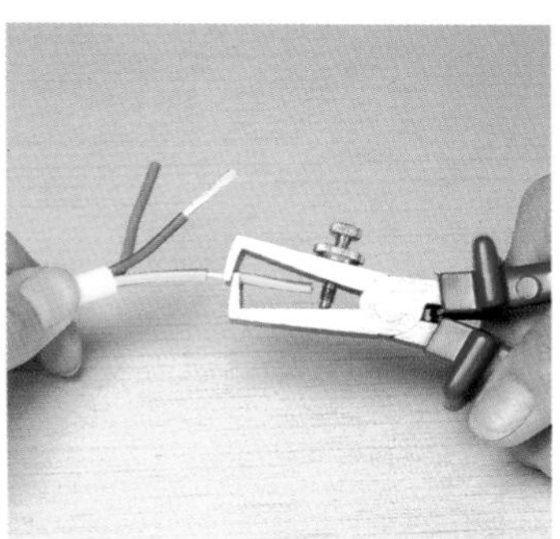

4 Rotate the strippers half a turn and pull them towards the tip of the conductor. The unwanted insulation will slide off.

INSULATING THE EARTH

In flex the earth conductor is already insulated by a green-and-yellow plastic coating.

In most sizes of twin-core-and-earth cable, however, the earth conductor is a bare wire. Before you connect it to the earth terminal, slide a green-and-yellow plastic sleeve over it to cover it from the point where you cut off the outer sheath to about ⅝in (16mm) from the tip. There is then no risk of it making contact with another conductor. Different sizes of sleeving are made for earth conductors in different sizes of cable; most fit loosely.

TIDYING THE TIPS OF THE CONDUCTORS

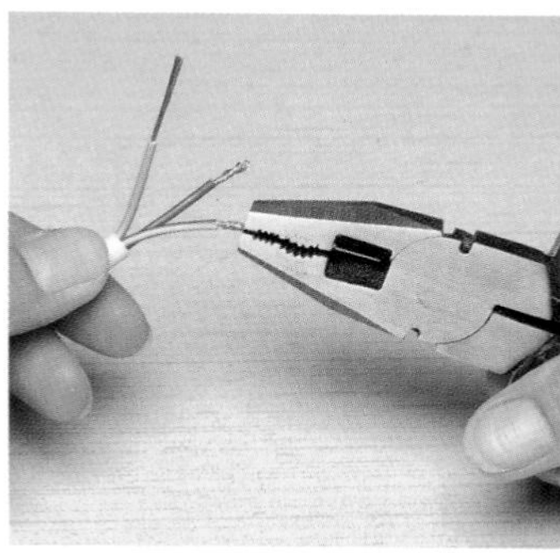

1 In a flex, which has more than one strand of wire in each conductor, tidy up the tips. Twist each conductor tip with pliers to wind the wire strands tightly together and make sure that no whiskery strands are splaying out. There is then no danger of stray strands from different conductors making contact with one another, and causing the plug fuse to blow.

Do this also with larger size cables, which have more than one strand of wire in the conductors.

2 If you are preparing very thin flex for connection, strip off 1¼in (32mm) of insulation at the tip of each conductor. Bend back the tip of each conductor and twist it with pliers to make sure that no strands of wire are splaying out. Bending and twisting the tip also gives a firmer tip which it is easier to insert into the terminal and screw down securely so that it does not slip out.

FABRIC-COVERED FLEX

An outer cover of braided fabric on a flex – as on many irons, for example – is likely to fray where it is cut.

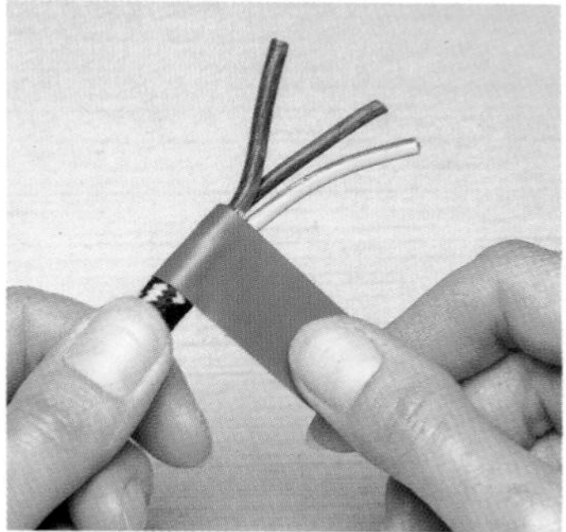

Wrap a piece of plastic insulating tape two or three times round the cut end of the fabric to seal down the loose threads.
ALTERNATIVELY, cover the cut with a purpose-made rubber sleeve. This will be held by the cord grip of the plug. Remember to put it on before inserting the flex in the plug.

Extending a flex

Never join lengths of flex by twisting together the conductors and binding over the join with insulating tape. The join may overheat and there is a risk of fire.

If you have to join lengths of flex, use a purpose-made connector, either fixed or detachable. Two-pin detachable connectors are sold but they are suitable only for non-metal table lamps, or for double-insulated appliances which are marked with the symbol ⧈.

For joining flex for any other appliance, you must use a three-pin connector to provide a connection for the earth conductor.

You will need
Tools Insulated screwdrivers; sharp knife; wire cutters and strippers; pliers.
Materials Appliance with flex already connected; flex connector; length of flex fitted with a plug.

FITTING A FIXED FLEX CONNECTOR

1 Prepare the ends of both flexes for connection (above).

2 Unscrew the connector cover and remove it. Loosen the flex grip at each end.

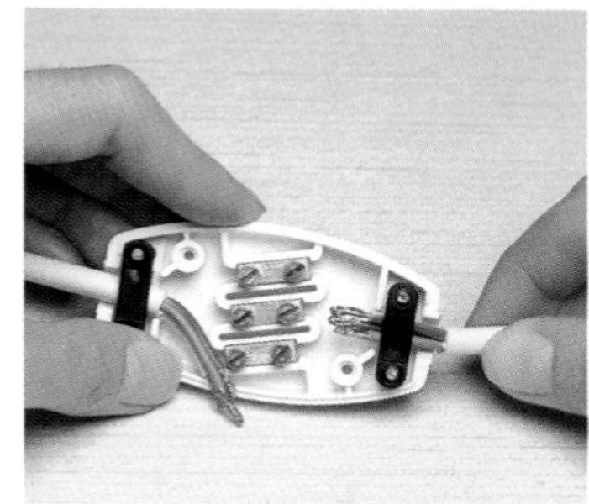

3 Fit a flex under each grip.

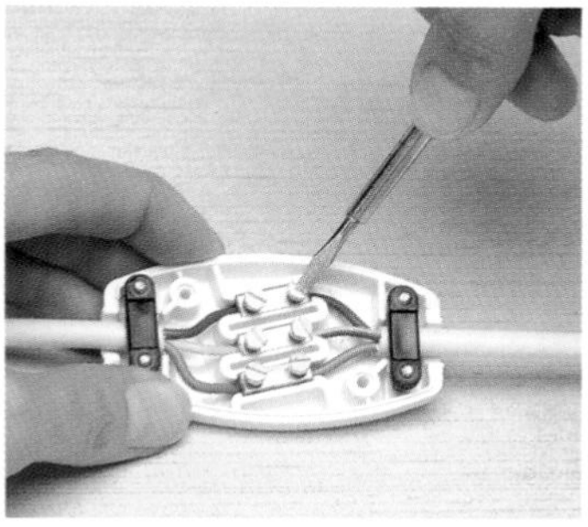

4 Screw the conductors tightly into place at the terminals so that the pairs match – brown to brown at one side, green-and-yellow to green-and-yellow at the centre, and blue to blue at the other side.

5 Tighten the grips to hold the flexes securely.

6 Replace and screw back the cover.

FITTING A DETACHABLE FLEX CONNECTOR

Because this type of connector is often fitted on an electric-powered tool that is to be used outside the house or in the garden, it is made from a tough, damp-proof rubber.

Make sure that you buy a connector suitable for the amperage of the appliance. The amperage will be marked on the connector.

You must fit the flex from the appliance to the half of the connector that has the pins, and the flex from the electricity supply point to the half of the connector that has the holes.

If you fit the two flexes to the connector the other way round, you will have live pins exposed if the two halves of the connector should become separated while the power is still switched on.

Extending a flex (continued)

1 Prepare the ends of both flexes.

2 Unscrew both halves of the connector and release the flex grip at each end.

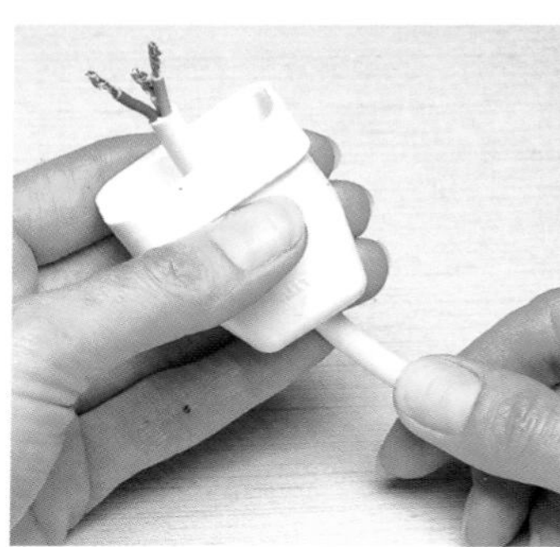

3 Slide the outer covers onto the prepared flexes.

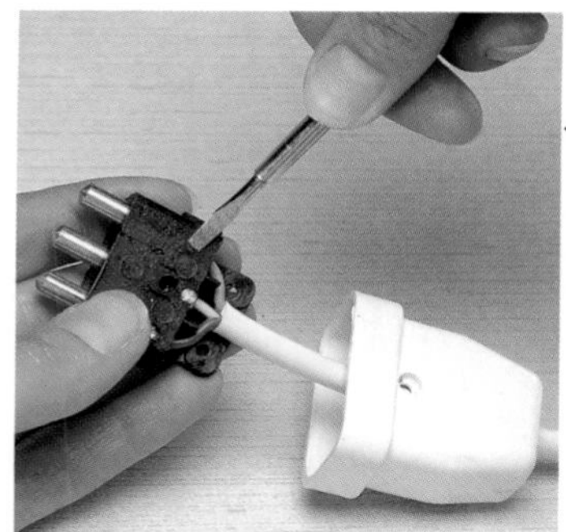

4 Connect the conductors with the green-and-yellow in the middle and the brown and blue in each half opposite each other so they connect when the halves are joined.

5 Tighten the flex grip and screw the cover on each half.

HOW TO USE AN EXTENSION FLEX SAFELY

A purpose-made extension flex with a plug at one end and a socket at the other lengthens the reach of a drill or other power tool used at varying distances from the source of power. Choose a 1.5mm^2 flex, which is suitable for high wattage tools. Use orange flex out of doors.

The flex can be stored on an open reel. Some flexes retract into a drum with a built-in socket. Unwind the flex fully for use or it will overheat.

Plug the flex into a residual current device (RCD) at the circuit socket – a 30 milliamp RCD for outdoor tools. This cuts off the power at once if damaged flex, a faulty tool or a loose connection creates a risk of electric shock.

Plug-in RCD

Wiring a plug

The colours of the plastic insulation on the conductors in flex were changed more than 25 years ago. Some of your old plugs may still be connected to old flex.

All modern plugs need a cartridge fuse. Many are fitted with a 13amp fuse when you buy them, but you should fit a fuse of the right amperage to protect the flex (see facing page).

Old colours	New colours
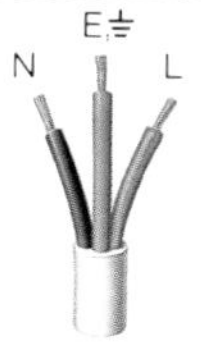 E ⏚ N L	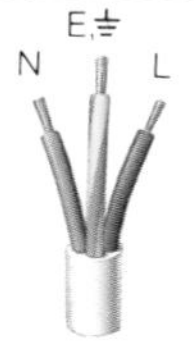 E ⏚ N L
Black to N	Blue to N
Green to earth (E or ⏚)	Green-and-yellow to earth (E or ⏚)
Red to L	Brown to L

You will need

Tools Insulated screwdrivers; sharp knife; wire cutters and strippers; pliers.

Materials Plug; flex; cartridge fuse (either 3 amp or 13 amp).

1 Unscrew or unlock the plug cover and remove it.

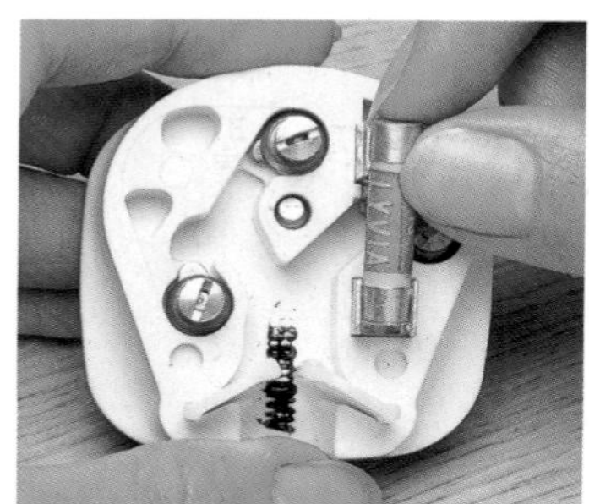

2 Gently prise out the cartridge fuse if necessary to reveal the terminal. Loosen the flex grip if necessary; plastic flanges grip the flex in some plugs; in others a bar held by screws grips it; in others one hand-turned plastic screw grips it.

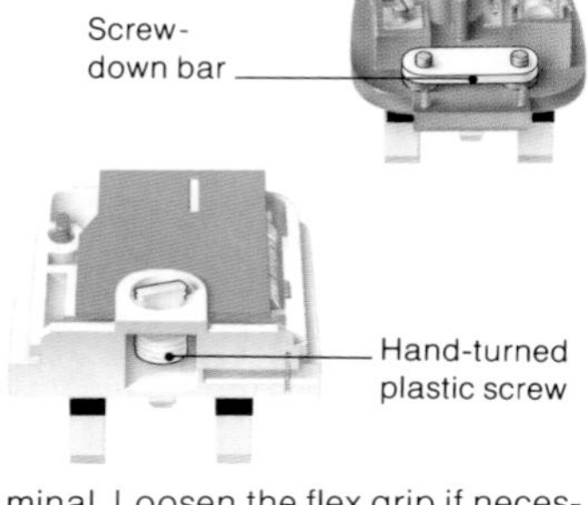

3 Prepare the end of the flex for connection (page 363). For some plugs all the conductors have to be the same length, for others they have to be different lengths.

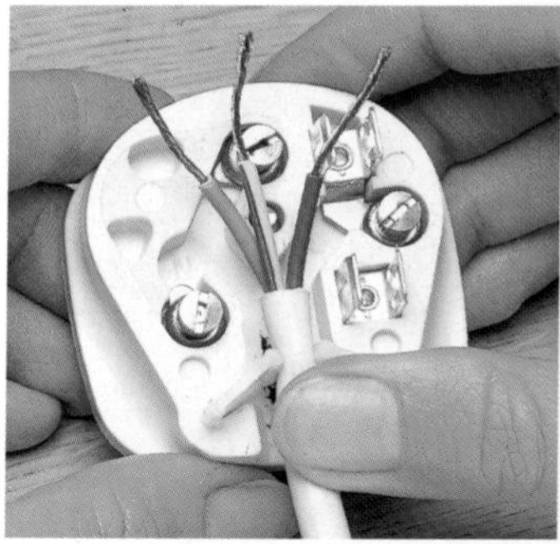

4 Fit the flex into the plug, pressing it between the flanges. If the plug is the type where the flex passes through a sleeve at the base of the

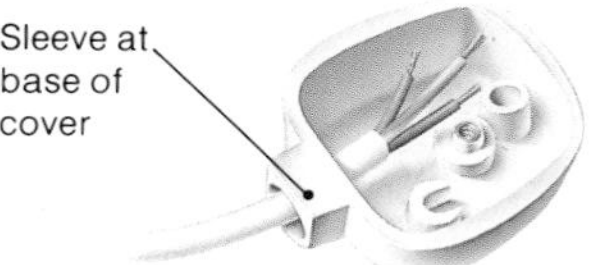

CHOOSING PLUGS FOR ELECTRICAL APPLIANCES

Coloured plug
A wrap-over resilient plastic cover gives some extra protection. Coloured covers are available to make the plug more noticeable – in outdoor use on power tools, for example – and reduce the risk of accidental knocks.

Plastic plug
Moulded plastic plugs are the commonest type. All new plugs are sold with sleeves on the pins connected to the brown and blue conductors, to prevent finger-tip contact with live metal when a plug is partly out of its socket.

Rubber plug
Tough rubber is used in place of the standard plastic to cover some plugs. Rubber will not crack if the plug is knocked – by furniture being moved or by a vacuum cleaner, for instance. The flex threads through the rubber cover.

Moulded-on plug
All major appliances are now sold with a moulded-together, one-piece plug and flex. These units are not designed for reconnection, so do not try to use a discarded but sound unit to connect other appliances. You should throw it away so that no child is tempted to plug it into a live socket. The cut end of the flex will give a shock if touched.

cover before being clamped in place, thread it through the sleeve.

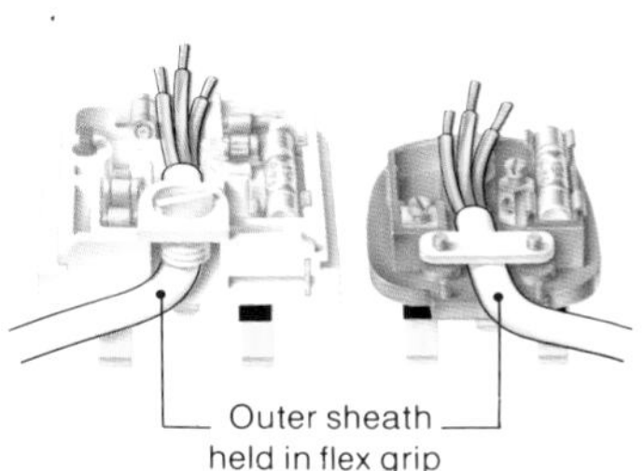

ALTERNATIVELY, screw in place the bar that grips the flex.

It is important to secure the outer sheath in the flex grip, not just the conductors. No unsheathed conductor must be visible outside the plug casing.

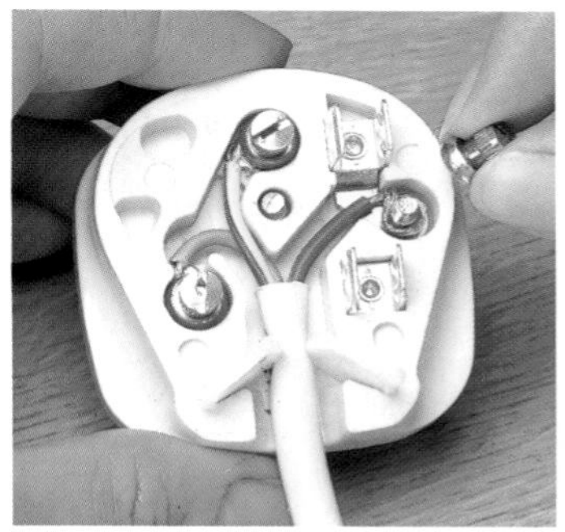

5 Connect the conductors to the correct terminals, securing them tightly in place. The brown conductor is connected to the terminal marked L, the blue conductor goes to the terminal marked N, and the earth conductor (green-and-yellow) goes to the terminal marked E or ⏚. Wind each conductor tip round the correct terminal and tighten the screw. Wind the conductor clockwise round the terminal. If you do not, it will be loosened as you tighten the screw and weaken the connection.

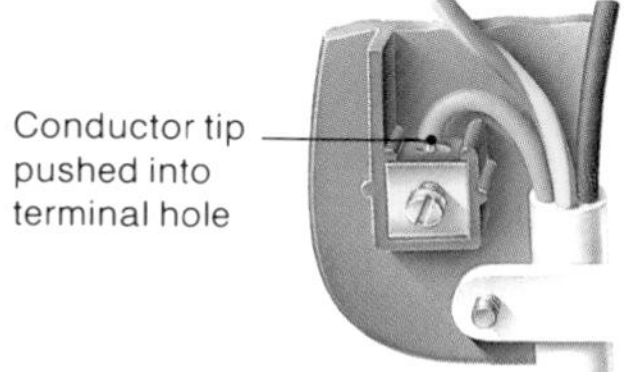

ALTERNATIVELY, if the terminal has a hole, push the conductor into the hole and tighten the screw.

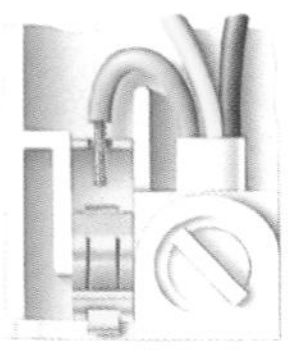

Conductor tip inserted in slot

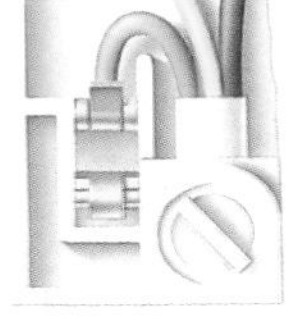

Conductor tip clamped in place

ALTERNATIVELY, if the terminal is of the no-screw type, push the conductor into the slot and swing over the clip to secure it.

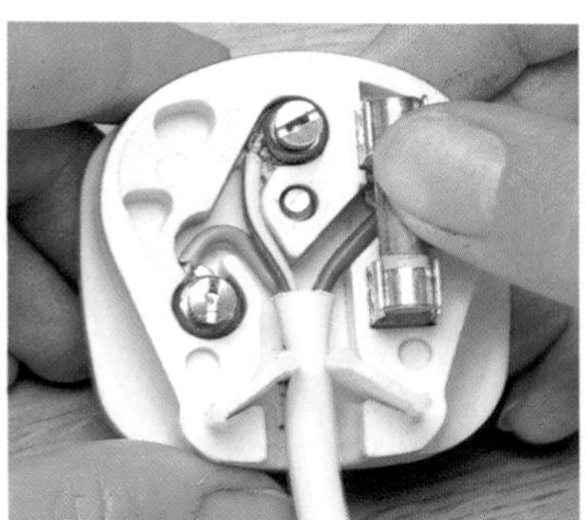

6 Replace the cartridge fuse if you had to remove it to reach the terminal. Make sure that it is of the correct amp rating.

7 Screw the plug cover back in place.
ALTERNATIVELY, slide the cover in place and turn the plastic lock to secure it.

CHOOSING THE RIGHT FUSE

Always use the correct fuse; never make do even temporarily with the wrong wire or cartridge. The circuit wiring or fuse carrier, or both, could be damaged by this – and perhaps start a fire. Do not simply replace a blown fuse with one of the same amp rating – it may have been wrong. On the consumer unit, fit one of the amperage shown on the fuse carrier.

FUSES FOR THE CONSUMER UNIT

Fuse wires

Use 5amp wire for a lighting circuit. Use 15amp wire for single appliance circuits up to 3kW. Use 30amp wire for a socket circuit and circuits for cookers up to 13kW.

Cartridge fuses

Use for a lighting circuit.

Use for a storage heater or water heater circuit.

Use for a 20amp radial power circuit.

Use for a ring circuit or 30amp radial circuit.

Use for a cooker or shower circuit.

FUSES FOR PLUGS

3amp cartridge
Use in plugs for appliances up to 700 watts. Check the wattage on the rating plate of the appliance. Low wattage appliances include table or standard lamps, hi-fi equipment, home computers and ancillaries, and electric blankets.

13amp cartridge
Use in plugs for appliances between 700 and 3000 watts. Look on the appliance's rating plate for the wattage. Appliances in this wattage range include most TV sets, vacuum cleaners, large power tools, room heaters and all domestic appliances that contain a heating element.

Changing a fuse on the consumer unit

MENDING A REWIRABLE FUSE

You will need
Tools Small insulated screwdriver; wire cutters; perhaps a torch.
Materials Fuse wire.

1 Turn off the main switch, which is on the consumer unit or on a main switch box installed near the meter.

2 If you have not previously marked the fuse carriers to show which circuit each protects, you need to find out which fuse has blown. Scorch marks round the fuse carrier often show this. If there are no marks, inspect each fuse wire in turn, removing only one fuse carrier at a time and replacing it before you remove another one for inspection.

TYPES OF REWIRABLE FUSE CARRIER

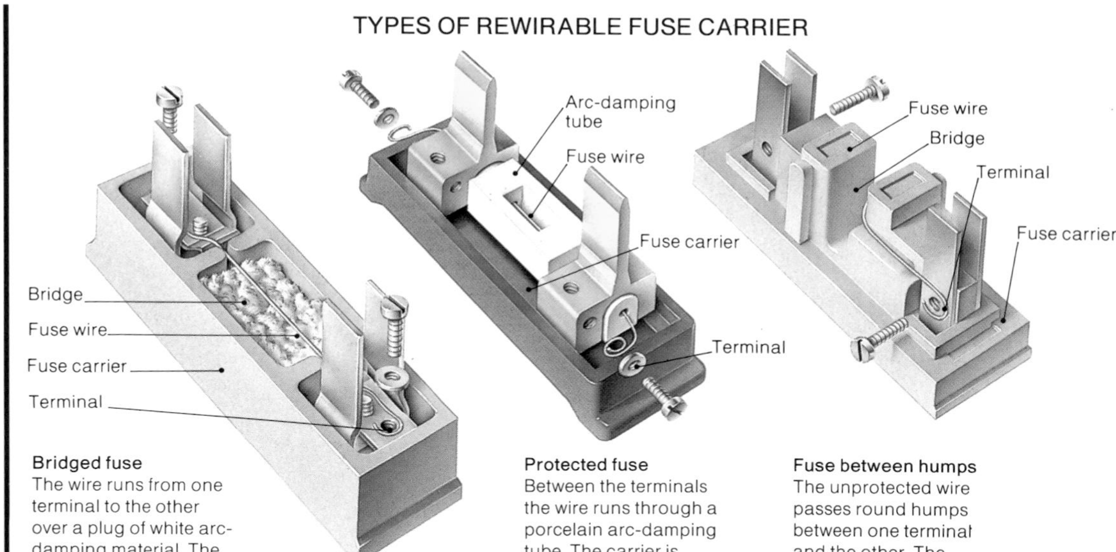

Bridged fuse
The wire runs from one terminal to the other over a plug of white arc-damping material. The carrier is ceramic.

Protected fuse
Between the terminals the wire runs through a porcelain arc-damping tube. The carrier is tough plastic.

Fuse between humps
The unprotected wire passes round humps between one terminal and the other. The carrier is ceramic.

Changing a fuse on the consumer unit (continued)

3 Switch off and unplug all the appliances on the faulty circuit; if there are switches on the sockets, turn them off. If it is a lighting circuit that has failed, the light switches should be turned off. If you do not switch everything off the fuse is likely to blow again immediately you turn on the main switch.

4 To replace the damaged wire, loosen the two fixing screws and remove any pieces of old wire. Cut a new fuse wire of the amp rating shown on the fuse carrier and long enough to cross the carrier and go round both screws. Use one strand only. Do not double it.

5 Wind the wire clockwise round one screw and tighten the screw.

6 Pass the wire across the bridge or thread it through the holder. If you are unsure about how the wire runs in the carrier, examine one of the intact fuses.

7 Wind the wire clockwise round the second screw. Make sure there is a little slack in the wire so that it will not snap as you tighten the second screw. Tighten the screw.

8 Replace the fuse carrier.

9 Close the box and turn on the main switch.

Checking the circuit
Look for damage on the appliances, lights and flexes that were in use on the circuit when it failed. Make repairs if necessary then switch on the appliances or lights one at a time. Make sure you are not overloading the circuit (page 356) before using them all at the same time. Overloading is the likeliest cause of the blown fuse.

If the fuse blows again, call an electrician.

REPLACING A CARTRIDGE FUSE

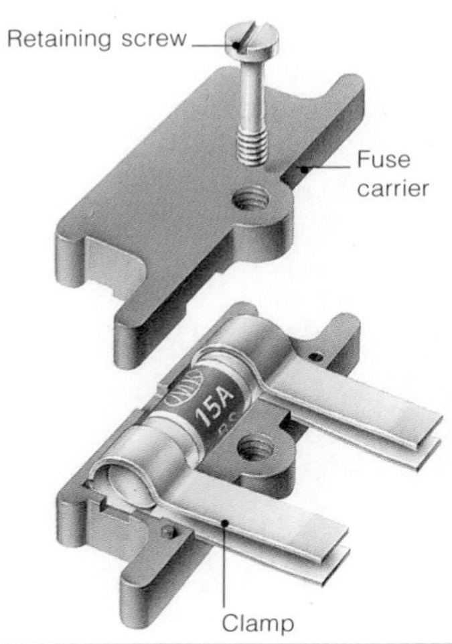

You will need
Tools Insulated screwdriver; fuse tester.
Materials Cartridge fuses.

1 Turn off the main switch on the consumer unit.

2 If you have not previously labelled the fuse carriers to show which circuit each protects, you need to find out which fuse has blown. Take out each fuse carrier in turn to test the cartridge.

3 Prise the cartridge gently from the clamps. Some carriers are in two halves and the screw holding them together has to be removed to give access to the cartridge.

4 Test the cartridge with a fuse tester (see above).

Remove only one carrier at a time. Test its cartridge and replace the carrier before removing the next one for inspection and testing.

TESTING A FUSE
It is possible to buy an inexpensive battery, bulb and fuse tester, which can tell you immediately if a fuse has blown. It can also tell you if batteries are flat, and if light bulbs have blown.

5 When you have traced the blown fuse, replace the cartridge with a new one of the amp rating shown on the carrier.

6 To avoid risk of the new fuse blowing immediately, do not replace the carrier until you have switched off and unplugged all appliances on that circuit. If there are switches on the sockets, turn them off. If it is a lighting circuit that has failed, the light switches should be turned off.

7 Replace the fuse carrier, close the box and turn on the main switch.

8 Check the circuit in the same way as for rewirable fuses (left).

CHECKING A MINIATURE CIRCUIT BREAKER

If the consumer unit is fitted with miniature circuit breakers (MCBs) instead of fuses, it is immediately clear which circuit is faulty. The operating lever will be in the off position or the button will have popped out.

MCB with push button
MCB with operating lever

1 Turn off the main switch on the consumer unit. Do not touch any of the circuit breakers until you have done so.

2 Switch off and unplug all the appliances on the circuit whose MCB has tripped. If there are switches on the sockets, turn them off. If it is a lighting circuit, the light switches should be turned off. If you do not switch them off, the circuit breaker may trip again immediately you reset it.

3 Push the operating lever to the on position or push in the button on the circuit breaker and turn on the main switch on the consumer unit.

4 Check the circuit in the same way as for a rewirable fuse (left).

Replacing a damaged socket

Electric shock or a fire could be caused by contact with the conductors in a damaged socket. Replace the socket as quickly as possible and make sure that it is not used in the meantime.

A recessed socket will need only a new socket plate but with a surface-mounted socket you may need to replace the socket, the mounting box, or both.

If the socket is a single one, you could take the opportunity to replace it with a double or a treble socket (page 368).

You will need
Tools Large and small insulated screwdriver; perhaps also a sharp knife; wire cutters and strippers; pliers.
Materials New socket, preferably switched, and complete with fixing screws. Perhaps a new plastic mounting box, with fixing screws; green-and-yellow earth sleeving.

1 Turn off the mains at the consumer unit and remove the fuse or turn off the MCB that protects the circuit you want to work on. Plug in a lamp you know to be working to check that the socket is dead.

2 Undo the two screws that hold the socket in place and remove any broken pieces of plastic. If any fragments fall into the mounting box, remember to remove them later. Keep the retaining screws. When screws became metric, the sizes changed slightly. You may find that the screws supplied with your new socket will not fit the lugs of the mounting box. In that case, use the old screws.

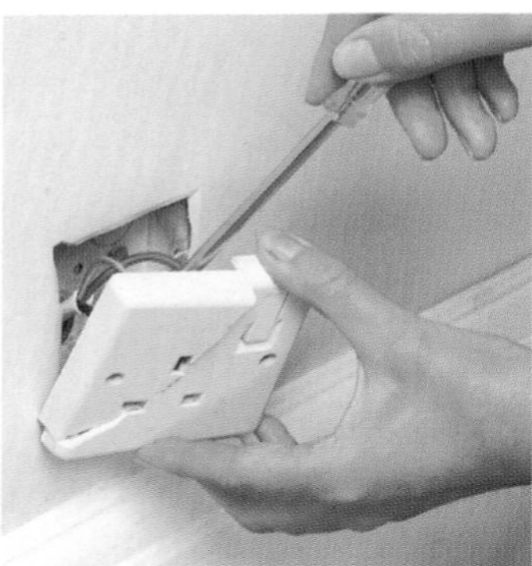

3 Ease out the socket and loosen the screws at the three terminals on the back to release the conductors. Note how many conductors are connected to each terminal; there may be one, two or three depending on whether the socket is on a spur, or is on the ring circuit or is supplying power to an extra socket on a spur. The new socket must be connected in the same way as the damaged one was.

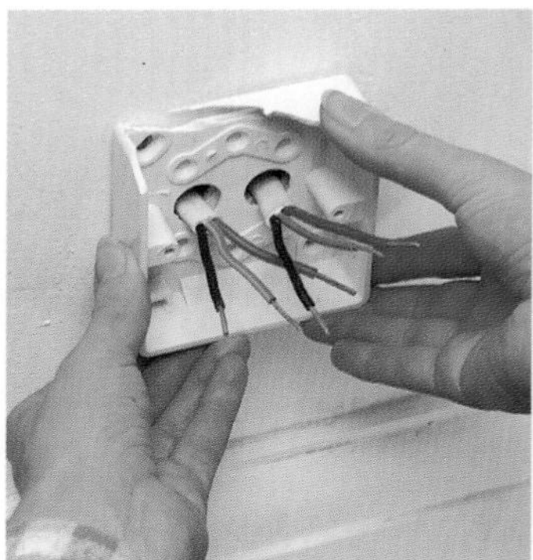

4 If there is damage to the plastic mounting box of a surface-mounted socket, take out the screws holding it to the wall or skirting and ease off the box. Check that the wall plugs or other fixing points are sound. Fill and re-plug them if necessary. Pass the cable or cables through the entry hole of a new mounting box and screw the box in place.

5 Inspect the ends of the conductors for damage. If they are blackened or broken, cut off the ends with wire cutters and prepare them afresh (page 363). If necessary, cut back the outer cable sheath with a sharp knife to free the conductors enough to reach the terminals easily. Take care not to nick the insulation of the conductors. If the earth conductors are bare, cover them with green-and-yellow plastic sleeving, leaving only the metal tips exposed.

6 Insert the conductors into the terminals and tighten the terminal screws firmly. Connect the red conductor or conductors to the terminal marked L, the black to the terminal marked N, and the earth (sleeved green-and-yellow) to the terminal marked E or ⏚. Check that the conductors are properly secured in their terminals by pulling on them lightly.

7 Place the socket on the mounting box, pressing it gently into position. Check that the conductors fit easily and will not be dislodged or pinched or twisted when the socket is in place.

8 Screw the socket into position. Drive in the screws until there is no gap between socket and mounting box, but do not over-tighten them or the plastic may crack.

9 Replace the fuse or turn on the MCB for the circuit you have been working on. Switch on the mains and check that the new socket works – by plugging in a lamp, for example. If it does not work, switch off at the mains and check and tighten the connections in the socket.

CHOOSING SOCKETS FOR INDOOR CIRCUITS

SOCKETS

Plastic sockets

The terminals are behind the socket. Holes for the plug pins have spring-loaded shutters to prevent children from poking anything into them. Single and double sockets with switches for each outlet are safest; treble sockets have a fuse to prevent overloading. Mounting boxes are 25mm or 35mm deep according to the design of the socket; a thicker socket goes with the 25mm box, a slimmer one with the 35mm box.

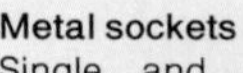

Metal sockets

Single and double brass, chrome and stainless-steel sockets are sold to match metal light switches. The sockets are made with or without switches. You need 35mm deep mounting boxes to accommodate these sockets. There are plastic inserts round the pin holes and switches.

Sockets with indicators

Both plastic and metal sockets are available with a neon indicator above each outlet. The indicator lights up to show when the socket outlet is switched on – and acts as a reminder to switch off when the socket is not in use. The wiring for the indicators is already fitted behind the socket. Take care not to dislodge the small bulb clipped behind the coloured insert.

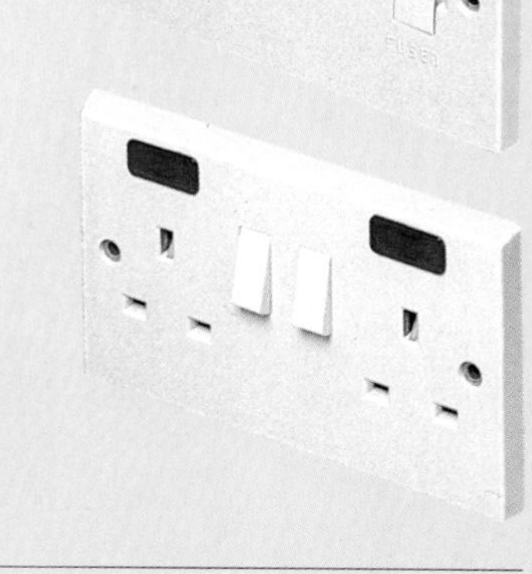

FUSED CONNECTION UNIT

Fixed appliances, such as wall-mounted heaters and fans, should be connected to a ring circuit by a fused connection unit (FCU) with a direct connection rather than by a socket. The cable or flex from the appliance can enter the FCU from behind, at the side or in front. The FCU may have a switch and a neon indicator.

FLEX-OUTLET PLATES

In bathrooms, where sockets are not permitted, a fixed appliance, such as a wall-mounted heater, is wired into a flex-outlet plate. The flex enters through the front on one type of plate and is connected at the back of it; on another type, flex enters at the edge and goes to a connector block in the mounting box.

Front-entry plate

Side-entry plate

ADAPTORS

Plug-in adaptor

Plug-in adaptors are made with two, three, even four outlets but it is unwise to use one with more than two as the cluster of plugs is often knocked. Adaptors can supply up to 3kW and should be fused.

Trailing socket adaptor

The adaptor is a four-socket panel with a fuse and neon indicator. It is plugged into an existing socket. The panel can be wall mounted to protect it from kicks. It can supply a maximum of 3kW, not 3kW at each of its sockets. Use it for low wattage appliances such as hi-fi equipment and take care not to overload it.

Wire-in adaptor

Up to four low-wattage appliances can be wired into the adaptor. It is mounted on the wall within 3ft 3in (1m) of an existing socket and plugged into the socket. Its maximum output is 3kW; take care not to overload it. It is useful only for equipment that you keep in the same place, not for items that you take from room to room.

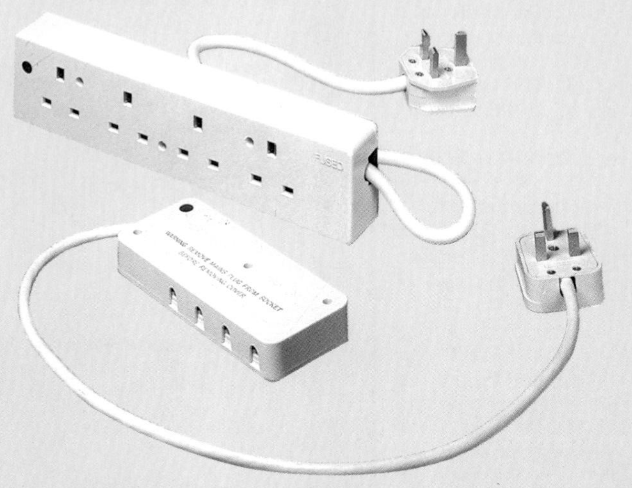

Replacing a single socket with a double or treble

If the single socket is surface mounted, use a surface-mounted replacement. If it is recessed, you can fit a plastic, surface-mounted pattress over it. The cable may be long enough to reach the terminals of the new socket easily; if not, you can add cable, using a three-way connector block. Alternatively, you can enlarge the recess for a larger metal mounting box.

Recessed fittings are neater, and safer because they are less likely to be damaged by knocks from furniture. You will have to cut into the wall to fit a new double or treble mounting box.

Each of the new sockets can supply up to 3kW.

You will need

Tools Tools for preparing the route (page 369); insulated screwdrivers; sharp knife; wire cutters and strippers; pliers.

Materials Double or treble mounting box (or pattress) and socket with fixing screws and grommets; wall plugs; 13amp fuse for a treble socket. Perhaps earth sleeving; extra cable; connector block.

REMOVING THE SINGLE SOCKET

1 Turn off the main switch on the consumer unit and remove the fuse that protects the circuit you will be working on. Check that the socket is dead by plugging in a lamp you know to be working.

2 Unscrew the socket and ease it away from the mounting box.

3 Disconnect the conductors from the terminals behind the socket.

FITTING THE MOUNTING BOX

Recessed mounting boxes

1 Take out the screw or screws holding the old box in place and ease the box out of the wall or skirting.

2 Prepare the hole for the new mounting box (page 369). If the socket is in the skirting, use a wood bit first to drill out the holes round the areas to be removed. Chisel out the wood. If the hole is not deep enough for the box, enlarge it as for a mounting box in a wall.

3 Feed the cable into the box and fix the box in place.

Surface-mounted boxes

1 If you are replacing a surface-mounted box, take out its fixing screws and remove it.

If you are fitting a pattress (see panel below) leave the old recessed mounting box in place unless it is damaged; in that case replace it.

2 Hold the mounting box or pattress in place, check with a spirit level that it is horizontal, and use a bradawl to pierce the wall or skirting through the fixing holes.

3 If you are fixing to the wall, drill holes at the marked spots and insert plugs in them. Check with a wiring detector before drilling so that you will not drill into cable.

4 Pass the cable through the hole in the back of the box or pattress. Screw the box or pattress into the plugged holes in the wall or the bradawl marks on the skirting.

CONNECTING THE SOCKET

1 If the conductor tips are blackened or broken, prepare them afresh (page 363).

2 Use pliers to straighten the tips of the conductors. Sleeve the earth conductors if this had not been done originally.

If the socket is at the end of a spur, there will be only one set of conductors. If the socket is on the ring and supplying a spur, there will be three sets of conductors.

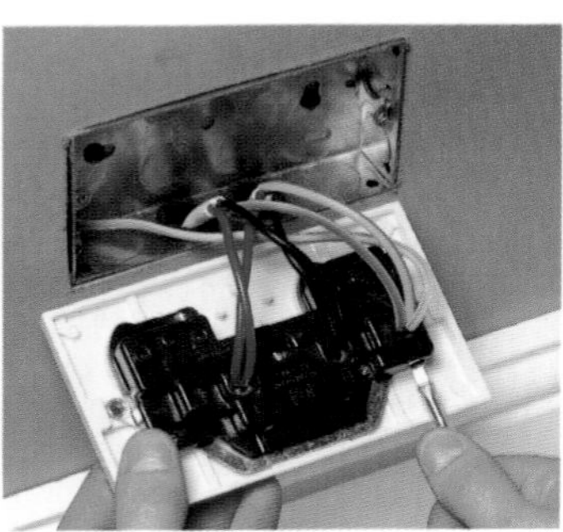

3 Screw the red conductors firmly into the terminal marked L. Screw the black conductors firmly into the terminal marked N. Connect a short length of sleeved earth cable to the terminal on the mounting box and screw the three earth conductors into the terminal marked E or ⏚. ALTERNATIVELY, if you are adding to the cable, screw the conductors into one side of the connector block with the earth in the centre. Screw the conductors of the prepared extra cable into the other side of the block with red opposite red, black opposite black and the earth in the middle. Connect to the socket as above.

4 Press the socket in place without dislodging the conductors.

5 Screw the socket in place until it meets the mounting box or pattress. Do not overtighten the screws or the plastic may crack.

6 If you are fitting a treble socket, insert a 13amp fuse inside the door on the socket front.

7 At the consumer unit, replace the fuse and switch on the mains.

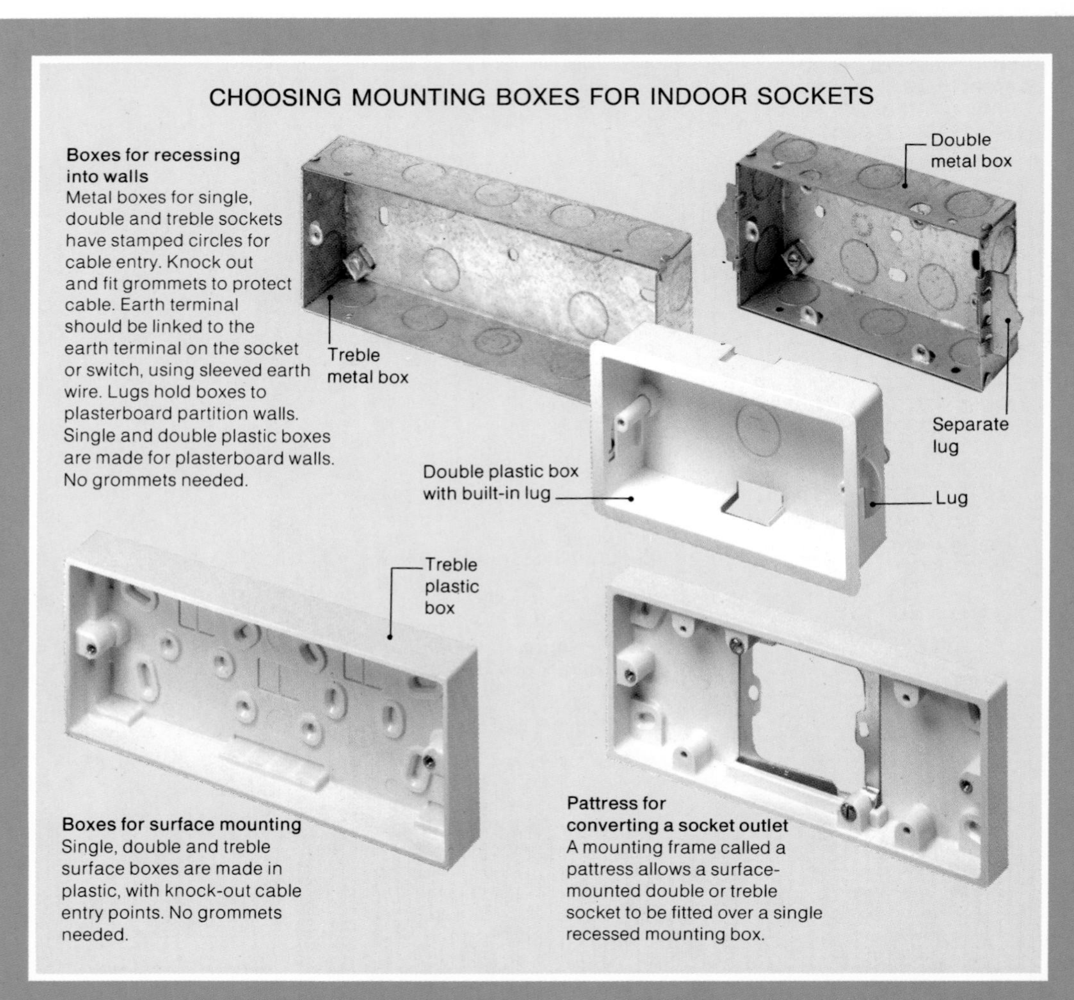

CHOOSING MOUNTING BOXES FOR INDOOR SOCKETS

Boxes for recessing into walls
Metal boxes for single, double and treble sockets have stamped circles for cable entry. Knock out and fit grommets to protect cable. Earth terminal should be linked to the earth terminal on the socket or switch, using sleeved earth wire. Lugs hold boxes to plasterboard partition walls. Single and double plastic boxes are made for plasterboard walls. No grommets needed.

Boxes for surface mounting
Single, double and treble surface boxes are made in plastic, with knock-out cable entry points. No grommets needed.

Pattress for converting a socket outlet
A mounting frame called a pattress allows a surface-mounted double or treble socket to be fitted over a single recessed mounting box.

Preparing the route

The route has to be planned for the location and will usually need preparation such as chasing in plaster, crossing or running along joists, and fitting a mounting box or ceiling rose.

Do not run cable through thermal insulation or thermal plasterboard (page 243).

A route under floorboards is often easiest to make. If the floor is solid, you can make the route in the wall plaster or run cable behind wooden skirting or inside plastic skirting. If none of these is possible, run it inside plastic trunking on the wall or ceiling (page 371).

Cable in plaster should be run in oval PVC conduit. This gives the cable extra protection from nails or screws. Oval conduit is sold in sizes from 13 × 8mm to 29 × 11mm, in 3 metre lengths.

Cable should not be drawn tight, so allow extra when you are measuring the length of cable needed.

You will need

Tools Insulated screwdrivers; hammer; masonry chisel; drill with wood bit thicker than the cable (to put cable under floor); wiring detector; masonry bit and router bit for drill (to put cable in plaster); pencil; sharp knife; saw; chisel; spirit level; bradawl; filling knife; wire cutters and strippers; pliers.

Materials Cable; cable clips; oval PVC conduit; galvanised nails for oval conduit; mounting boxes with screws; wall plugs and grommets; adhesive tape. Perhaps ceiling roses; plaster or interior filler; plasterboard.

FITTING A MOUNTING BOX

1 Hold the mounting box in position. For a socket it should be at least 6in (150mm) above floor level. A box above a work surface should be at least 6in (150mm) above it. For a light switch, the mounting box should usually be about shoulder height. Check with a spirit level that the mounting box is horizontal and draw a line round it as a guide for drilling.

2 Using a drill with masonry bit, drill holes all round the marked rectangle to the depth of the box. If the drill has no depth gauge, mark the bit with adhesive tape at the required depth and drill until the tape reaches the wall. Drill more holes over the marked area.

3 Finish knocking out the cavity with a masonry chisel and hammer.

4 Brush out the cavity, slide in the mounting box and make marks with a bradawl through the fixing holes at the back of the box.

5 Take out the box, drill holes at the marks and insert wall plugs.

6 Knock out the most convenient circle or circles stamped in the back or sides of the box for the cable or cables to enter. Fit a grommet in each entry hole.

7 Do not screw the mounting box in place until any chases to it through the plaster have been made.

LAYING CABLE UNDER A FLOOR

The cable may have to run alongside one joist and cross several others.

1 Where the cable is to be at right angles to the joists, lift one floorboard (page 273) to get access to the joists. Drill holes through the joists about halfway down them, at least 2in (50mm) from the top and the bottom and big enough for the cable to pass through easily. A right-angle adaptor fitted to the drill makes this easier, or you can drill with a long bit at a shallow angle.

2 Where the cable runs at right angles to the joists, thread it through the drilled holes.

3 Where the cable runs along a joist, lift a floorboard (or a section of one) about every 20in (510mm) along the joist. Secure the cable with clips to the side of the joist. Run it 2in (50mm) from the top and hammer in a clip about every 10in (250mm) along the cables.

BURYING A CABLE IN PLASTER

1 Plan the route for the cable. It should run vertically above or below a socket or switch. A horizontal run should be close to the ceiling or the skirting board. Never run it diagonally. Do not run it in thermal plasterboard.

2 Mark the route with two lines 1in (25mm) apart. Avoid making sharp bends wherever possible.

3 Check with a wiring detector or very fine bradawl along the route to make sure that you are not going to interfere with any cable or pipe already in the wall. If you are at all uncertain whether there is live wiring near the spot where you are working, switch off at the mains until you have made sure.

4 When you know that the route is safe, use a sharp knife to score along both edges of the chase.

5 Use a masonry chisel and hammer to chip out the plaster. Protect your eyes with safety spectacles. ALTERNATIVELY, with a drill and masonry bit, drill a series of holes about 1in (25mm) apart along the route, then use a plaster router bit to clear the chase. This creates a great deal of dust which spreads everywhere, so shut all doors.

6 Chisel out any plaster behind a skirting where you are leading a route down a plaster wall to run under the floor. You can do this without removing the skirting.

ALTERNATIVELY, use a long drill bit to make a hole behind the skirting. Enlarge it with a chisel if necessary. This may be the easiest method if the skirting board is a deep one.

7 Check that the whole length of the chase is deep enough for the cable to fit easily. If it is too near the surface, only a skim of plaster or filler will cover it when you make good and it will probably crack. A covering of ¼in (6mm) of plaster or filler over the cable should be thick enough to stay sound and prevent cracking.

Preparing the route (continued)

8 Feed the cable into the conduit before securing it into the chase with galvanised nails on each side. When the cable comes up behind a skirting, feed it into the conduit so that the end of the conduit is below the top of the skirting. Do not pull the cable tight.

9 Leave enough spare cable at each end to reach any part of the mounting box easily. Ease the end of the cable or cables through the grommet into the mounting box. Slide the box into the prepared cavity and screw it into the plugged wall behind.

ROUTES IN STUD PARTITION WALLS

Cutting the route

With walls of plasterboard fixed to both sides of a timber frame, the cable can run in the cavity between the plasterboards. You have to cut grooves in the frame.

1 Use a very fine bradawl to locate the frame, or a wiring detector to locate the rows of pins holding the plasterboard to the frame. Draw pencil lines to show where the timbers are.

2 With a sharp knife, cut away a section of plasterboard about 4½in (115mm) square wherever your planned route crosses timber.

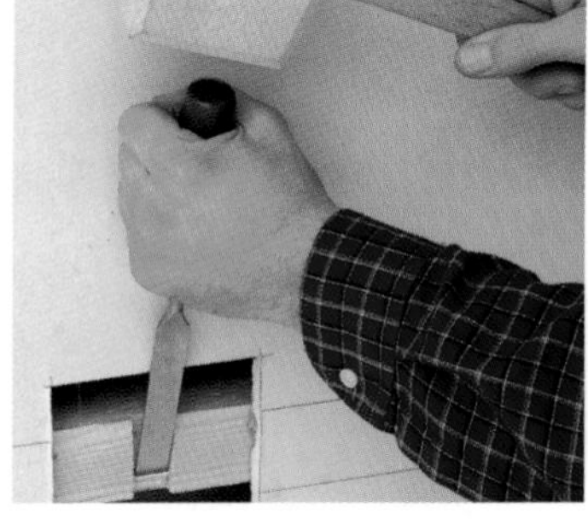

3 Chisel a groove in the exposed frame to hold the cable easily.

Feeding in cable from above

1 Cut out a square of the plasterboard to reveal the top of the timber frame and drill a hole through it large enough to hold the cable easily. You can use a long drill bit and drill at a shallow angle, or fit a right-angle adaptor and drill vertically.

2 Thread the cable down through the drilled hole. Feed it down, with a helper to ease it over each cross-piece of the frame and position it in the groove. There should be plenty of slack in the cable.

Feeding in cable from below

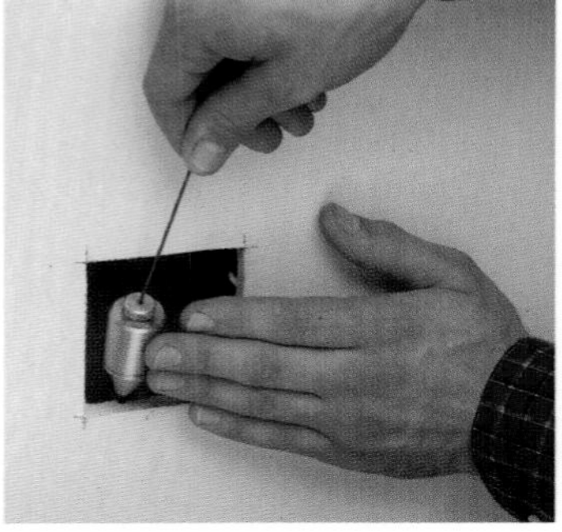

1 Cut out a square of plasterboard near floor level to reveal the base of the frame. Drill a hole through it for the cable, using a long bit and drilling at an angle or fitting a right-angle adaptor and drilling vertically. Feed a weighted cord down from the highest point the cable is to reach.

2 Tie the cord to the cable and draw it up carefully, with a helper to ease it over crosspieces of the frame and position it in the prepared grooves. Leave plenty of slack in the cable.

Feeding in cable sideways

1 Push the cable along between the plasterboard panels. At each upright, draw out a loop of cable long enough to reach the next upright. Feed it along and set it in the prepared groove. When the cable is in the required position, fix it to the timbers with clips or cover the groove with a metal plate, pinned to the wood above and below, to prevent accidental damage from a nail or picture hook.

2 Cut new squares of plasterboard to replace the sections cut away. Tack them securely to the timbers at top and bottom, keeping the tacks well clear of the cable. Fill in round the edges of the squares with interior filler.

Fitting a mounting box

1 Knock out the most convenient holes for the cable or cables to enter the mounting box and fit grommets, if using a metal box.

2 Hold the box in position, check with a spirit level that it is horizontal and draw a line round it.

3 Cut away the marked section. If the box has separate lugs, do not fit them in place yet.

4 Feed the cable or cables into the box through the grommets.

5 Rest the mounting box in the hole.

If it seems very unsteady, you can thread a string through holes in the back of the box and wind the ends round nails in the wall.

Prepare the conductors (page 363) and connect them to the terminals behind the socket (page 366).

6 Press the mounting box back through the plasterboard far enough for you to insert the separate lugs and clip one on each side of the box.

If the lugs are spring-loaded, make sure that they slot behind the plasterboard so that the board is between the lugs and the box rim.

7 Screw the socket in place. As you do so, the lugs will close up tightly behind the plasterboard and grip it firmly. If you have held the box with string, withdraw the string before the screws are tightened fully; take out the tacks that held the string.

FITTING A CEILING ROSE

A ceiling rose has to be screwed securely into wood above the plasterboard of the ceiling. It is not sufficient merely to screw it through plasterboard into winged plugs. Plasterboard (or lath and plaster) is not strong enough to bear the weight of the light fitting and lampshade. The rose must be screwed to a joist or a strut between joists.

1 Mark the spot on the ceiling where you want the light fitting to hang.

2 Drill up through the plasterboard (or lath and plaster) at the marked spot. If the drill strikes a joist, probe with a bradawl about 2in (50mm) round the hole until you find space above the plasterboard. Insert a piece of spare cable through the hole to stick up above the ceiling as a marker.

3 Examine the ceiling from above, lifting a floorboard if necessary, and locate the hole with its piece of spare cable identifying it.

4 If the hole for the cables is between joists, cut a wooden strut 3in (75mm) wide and 2in (50mm) deep to fit between the joists.

5 Lay the strut between the joists with its edge touching the hole for the cables and mark the edge just beside the hole.

6 Drill through the centre of the strut, aligning the drill bit with the mark at the edge. The hole must be large enough to hold three or four cables without chafing.
ALTERNATIVELY, if the hole for the cables is immediately below a joist, chisel out a groove in the bottom of the joist to fit the cables. You may need to nail a block of wood to the side of the joist to widen it sufficiently to screw the ceiling rose exactly where you wish. Chisel a groove down the side of the block that will fit against the joist. The groove must be large enough to hold three or four cables easily.

7 Thread the cables through the hole in the strut and then through the hole in the plasterboard.

8 Secure the strut to the joists with a nail hammered in at an angle at each end.

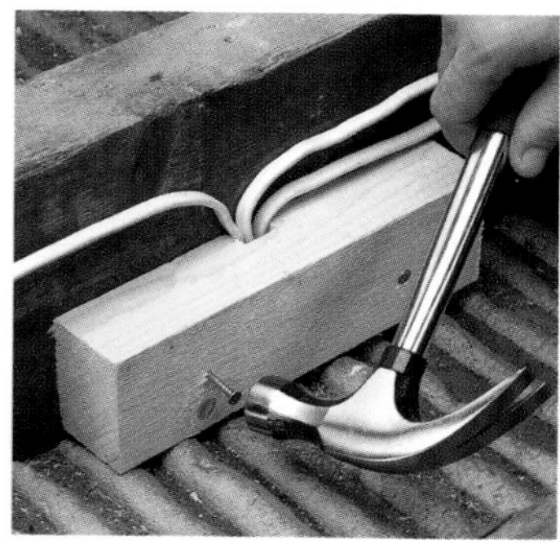

ALTERNATIVELY, thread the cables through the prepared groove at the bottom of the joist and down through the hole in the plasterboard. Fit the cables into the groove in the side of the prepared block of wood. Hold the block in position beside the joist and nail it to secure it, keeping the nails well clear of the cables.

9 Knock out the entry hole for the cables in the ceiling rose and thread the cables through the hole.

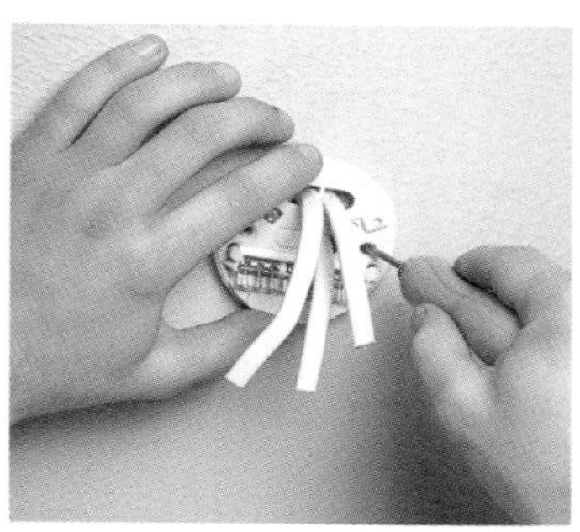

10 Hold the ceiling rose in place and insert a bradawl through the screw holes to penetrate through the plasterboard and pierce the timber above.

11 Screw the ceiling rose firmly in place.

MAKING GOOD

Do not connect any sockets or switches before the walls are made good or the connections are likely to be dislodged as you make the necessary repairs.

1 Repair all damage to the plaster with new plaster or interior filler and leave it to dry completely. For the best finish, fill in two stages; rough plaster over the cable leaving a shallow depression to be repaired with a fine filler the next day.

2 Replace any floorboards you have lifted. If any board is likely to pinch a cable where it starts to run up a wall from below the floor, cut a notch in the end of the board before you replace it. Boards, or sections of boards, that you may need to lift again in the future – to add a junction box in a lighting circuit, for example – should be screwed down, not nailed. They can then be lifted without being damaged.

CABLE IN TRUNKING

Where it is not possible to lead cable under a floor or bury it in plaster, or if you want to reduce the labour, run the cable in surface-mounted trunking or behind a hollow skirting. This protects the cable from damage as well as concealing it.

Plastic mini-trunking, skirting, architrave and cornice is screwed or glued in place; the plastic cover clips on. For hollow wooden skirting, a wooden mounting strip is nailed to the wall and the facing is glued to it.

PLASTIC SKIRTING AND ARCHITRAVE There are connectors to join them. Adaptors give access to purpose-made sockets and switches.

PLASTIC CORNICE Sections have connectors for internal and external corners and adaptor pieces to connect with mini-trunking.

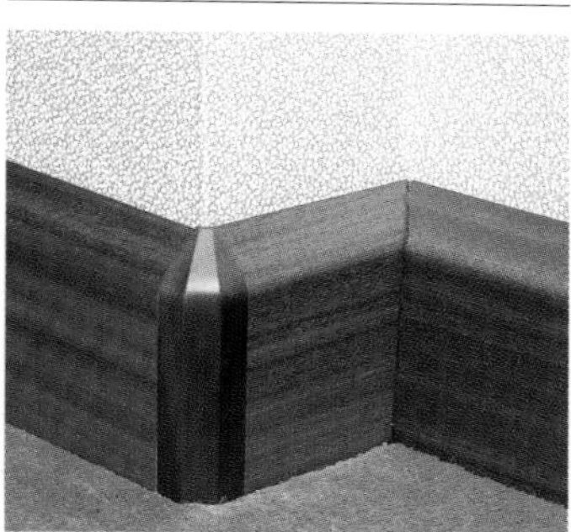

HOLLOW WOODEN SKIRTING The curved veneered plywood is cut to length and joined to connectors for internal and external corners.

CHOOSING TRUNKING AND SKIRTING FOR CABLE

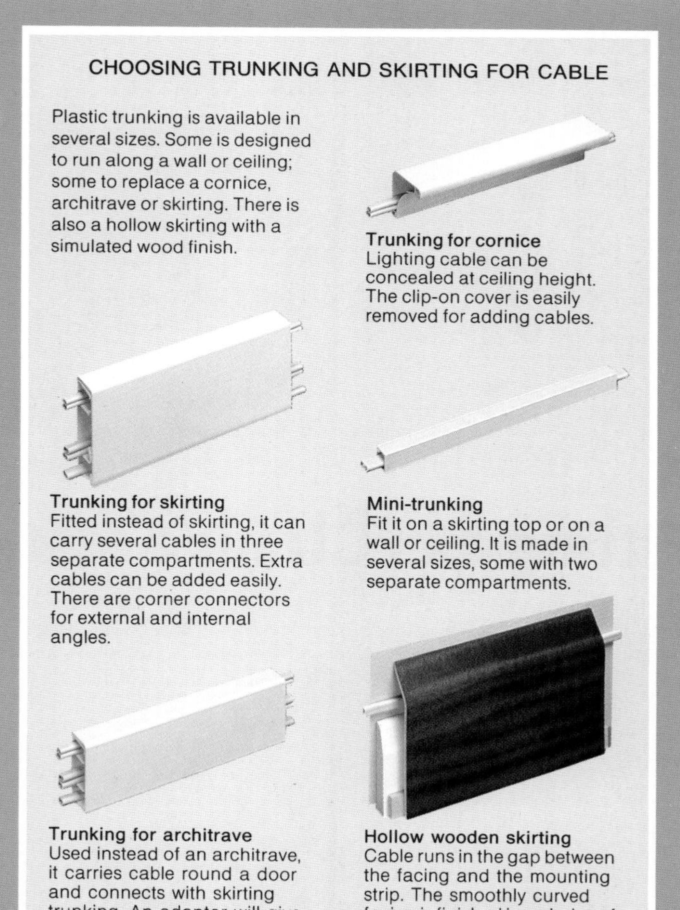

Plastic trunking is available in several sizes. Some is designed to run along a wall or ceiling; some to replace a cornice, architrave or skirting. There is also a hollow skirting with a simulated wood finish.

Trunking for cornice
Lighting cable can be concealed at ceiling height. The clip-on cover is easily removed for adding cables.

Trunking for skirting
Fitted instead of skirting, it can carry several cables in three separate compartments. Extra cables can be added easily. There are corner connectors for external and internal angles.

Mini-trunking
Fit it on a skirting top or on a wall or ceiling. It is made in several sizes, some with two separate compartments.

Trunking for architrave
Used instead of an architrave, it carries cable round a door and connects with skirting trunking. An adaptor will give access to a surface-mounted light switch.

Hollow wooden skirting
Cable runs in the gap between the facing and the mounting strip. The smoothly curved facing is finished in a choice of several wood veneers. It is permanently fixed with glue.

Adding a spur socket to a ring circuit

The easiest way of adding a socket outlet to a wiring system is to lead off a spur from the ring circuit. The spur is wired from the back of a socket and can supply only one single or double socket, or one fused connection unit. Care is needed to find a suitable supply socket. You must not use one that is already on a spur or supplying a spur.

Make sure that the spur will not increase the total area served by the ring circuit to more than 120sq yds (100sq m). Check also that the likely load on the circuit will not exceed 7.2kW.

You will need
Tools Tools for preparing the route (page 369); insulated screwdrivers; circuit tester; sharp knife; wire cutters and strippers; pliers.
Materials $2.5mm^2$ twin core-and-earth cable; cable clips; green-and-yellow earth sleeving; mounting box with grommets and fixing screws; socket with switch.

FINDING A SUITABLE SUPPLY SOCKET

1 Turn off the main switch on the consumer unit and take out the fuse for the circuit you want to work on. Check that the socket is dead – for example by plugging in a lamp that you know to be working.

2 Unscrew the socket you plan to lead the spur from and ease it off the mounting box until you can see the cables in the box. If there is only one, the socket is on a spur and you cannot use it. If there are three, the socket is supplying a spur and you cannot use it.

3 A two-cable socket may well be suitable but check with a circuit tester (see right) before you go ahead. It could be the first socket on a two-socket spur installed earlier (but not now permitted).

PREPARATIONS

1 When you have found a suitable supply socket, draw it out far enough to undo the screws at the three terminals and release the conductors so that you can remove the socket.

2 Remove the screw or screws that hold the mounting box in place and carefully draw it out of its cavity.

3 Prepare the route (page 369) for the cable from the supply socket to the new socket.

4 Feed the cable ends into the mounting boxes for the new and the supply sockets and fix the cable and the boxes in place (page 369).

5 Prepare the new cable ends for connection (page 363), remembering to put green-and-yellow sleeving on the earth conductors.

CONNECTING AT THE SUPPLY SOCKET

1 Match the new conductors with the original ones, red with red, black with black, and green-and-yellow with green-and-yellow. Use pliers to straighten the original conductor tips if necessary.

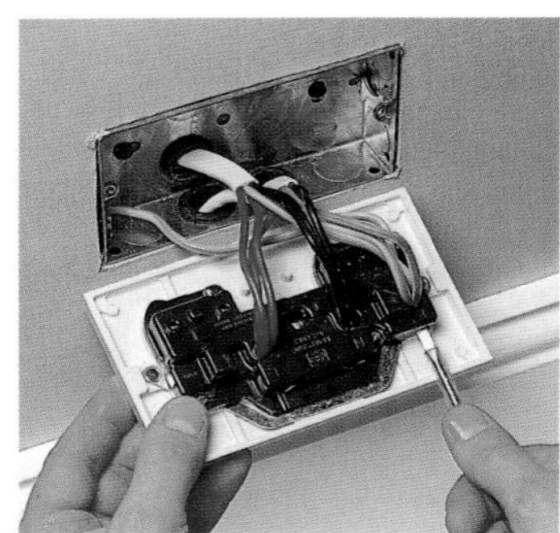

2 Screw the conductors tightly into the terminals behind the socket. The red conductors go to that marked L, the black to that marked N, and the green-and-yellow-sleeved earth conductors to that marked E or ⏚.

3 Gently press the socket into position over the mounting box, making sure that the conductors are not dislodged, pinched or twisted sharply.

4 Screw the socket over the mounting box until there is no gap between the two. Do not overtighten the screws or the plastic of the socket may crack.

CONNECTING AT THE NEW SOCKET

1 Screw the conductors firmly into the terminals – red at L, black at N and green-and-yellow at E or ⏚.

2 Press the socket over the mounting box without dislodging the conductors and screw it in place until it meets the mounting box.

3 At the consumer unit, replace the fuse for the circuit you have been working on and turn the main switch back on.

USING A CIRCUIT CONTINUITY TESTER

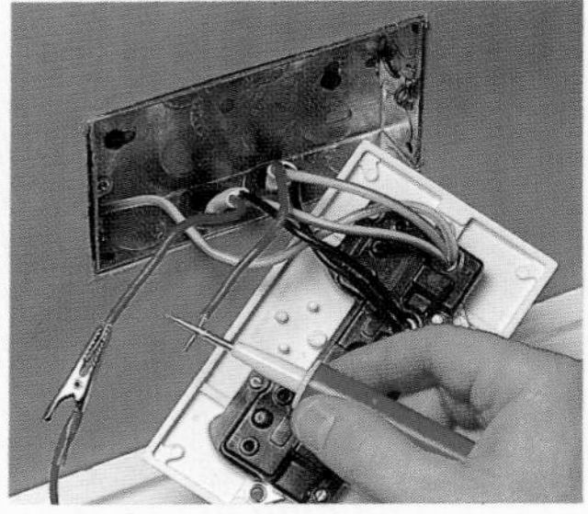

Adding a spur
When you are finding a suitable supply socket to run a spur from, first switch off the electricity at the consumer unit, remove the fuse for the circuit you will be working on and unplug all appliances and lamps on the circuit. At the socket, disconnect the two red conductors. Fasten the tester's crocodile clip on the metal tip of one conductor and touch the tester's probe to the other tip. If the socket is part of a ring circuit, the bulb on the tester will light up because you have completed the circuit; this is a suitable supply socket for a spur. If the tester does not light up, the socket is itself on a spur; this is not a suitable supply socket.

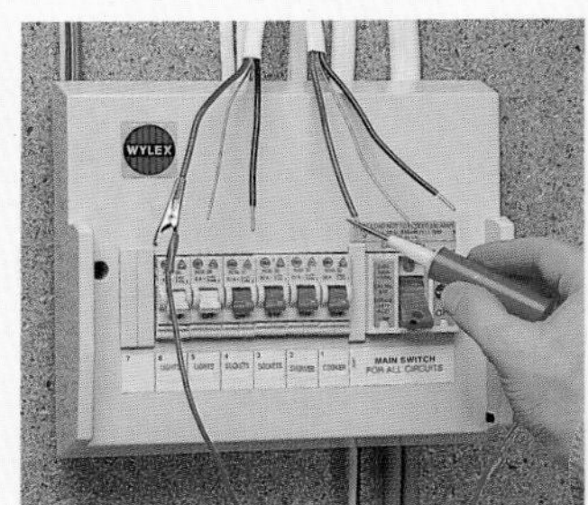

Testing a ring circuit
If you install a ring circuit, use the tester to check that all the connections are sound before you connect it at the consumer unit. Where the two cable ends approach the consumer unit, clip the tester to the tip of one red conductor and put the probe on the other. If the tester fails to light, tighten the connections all round the circuit.

Carry out the same checking procedure with the black conductors and with the earth.

If the tester lights when it is linking two different conductors – red and green, for example – there is a serious fault and you should call in a qualified electrical contractor.

Fitting an FCU for a stationary appliance

A fused connection unit (FCU) is for connecting a stationary appliance to the power supply. Wall heaters, extractor fans, cooker hoods, central-heating timers and freezers are among the many appliances that may be permanently wired to an FCU. An FCU is safe from the knocks that sometimes damage plugs in sockets – and there is no fear that someone will unthinkingly unplug the freezer, for example.

An FCU is the only kind of electric supply point (except for a shaver socket) allowed in a bathroom – for an extractor fan or a wall-mounted heater, both of which must be pull-cord operated and out of reach of a person using the bath or shower.

The FCU can be installed on a new ring circuit, or fitted as a replacement for one of the sockets on an existing circuit, or it can be installed on a spur (see above).

A cartridge fuse is housed behind a small door in the FCU plate. The door can be opened by undoing a screw or can be prised open with a screwdriver to give access to the fuse. The fuse should be 3amp for appliances rated up to 720 watts and 13amp for higher-wattage appliances.

For a wall-mounted heater, choose an FCU that has a flex outlet at the front or side. An appliance where all the wiring can be concealed in plaster does not need an entry hole from the front. Side entries are often knock-outs so that they can be left whole if all the wiring is concealed. If the wiring is concealed, you must connect twin-core-and-earth cable to the appliance, not flex. All FCUs fit a standard single mounting box. They may be switched or unswitched. An unswitched FCU is suitable only for an appliance that has its own on/off switch.

You will need
Tools Sharp knife; wire cutters and strippers; pliers; insulated screwdrivers. Perhaps tools for preparing the route (page 369).
Materials Appliance in place with flex fitted; appropriate fuse.

1 Turn off the main switch on the consumer unit and take out the fuse for the circuit you will be working on.

2 If the FCU is replacing an existing socket, no preparation is needed except for unscrewing the socket and undoing all the conductors from the terminals behind it.

3 If the FCU is on a new spur or new ring circuit, install the spur or circuit as described above or on page 379 until the mounting box and cable are in place. Remember that for many of the appliances connected to an FCU, the FCU should be above worktop height so that the switch and fuse are easily accessible.

4 Prepare the ends of the cable and the flex for connection (page 363). Remember to sleeve the earth conductor of the cable. If the FCU is replacing an existing socket, the cable will already have been prepared.

5 Feed the flex from the appliance to the back of the FCU. If there is a flex grip, release it sufficiently to let the flex through and then tighten it securely.

6 Screw the tip of the brown conductor from the appliance flex tightly into the terminal marked L and Load (or Out).

7 Screw the tip of the blue conductor from the flex to the terminal marked N and Load (or Out).

8 Screw the green-and-yellow earth conductor from the flex on the appliance into one of the terminals marked E or ⏚. If the FCU has only one earth terminal, do not connect it yet. It will share the earth terminal with the cable earth and you should insert them both together when you are connecting the cable to the FCU.

CONNECTING A SPUR CABLE TO THE FCU

1 Screw the tip of the red conductor from the cable tightly into the terminal marked L and Mains (or Feed or Supply or In).

2 Screw the tip of the black conductor from the cable tightly into the terminal marked N and Mains (or Feed or Supply or In).

3 Screw the green-and-yellow-sleeved earth conductor from the cable into the second terminal marked E or ⏚.
ALTERNATIVELY, if there is only one earth terminal, screw the earths from both flex and cable into it.

4 Fit the correct cartridge fuse (page 365) into the FCU.

5 Gently press the FCU into position over the mounting box, making sure that none of the conductors is dislodged, pinched or twisted sharply.

6 Screw the FCU into position until there is no gap between it and the mounting box, but do not overtighten the screws or the plastic may crack.

CONNECTING AN FCU ON A RING CIRCUIT

Connect the flex conductors as for an FCU on a spur.

Connect the conductors from the cables into the terminals marked Mains (or Feed or Supply or In) as for an FCU on a spur – red to L, black to N, green-and-yellow to E or ⏚ – but there will be two conductors to screw into each terminal.

Screw the FCU to the mounting box as for one on a spur.

Fitting a heated towel rail or bathroom radiator

An electrically heated towel rail or oil-filled radiator in a bathroom must be connected to a flex-outlet plate (page 367). If the appliance has not been fitted with a flex, fit the right flex following the manufacturer's instructions.

Cable runs from the back of the flex-outlet plate to a switched fused connection unit (FCU) outside the bathroom. The FCU can be fitted on a spur led from a socket on the ring circuit.

You will need

Tools Tools for preparing the route (page 369); sharp knife; pliers; insulated screwdrivers; wire cutters and strippers.

Materials Two standard single mounting boxes; 2.5mm² twin-core-and-earth cable; cable clips; green-and-yellow sleeving for the earth conductors; FCU; 13amp cartridge fuse; flex-outlet plate with terminals behind; towel rail or radiator fixed on the wall, with flex fitted.

PREPARATIONS

1 Check the earthing and bonding (page 359) and remedy defects. All the metallic parts in the room must be cross-bonded to earth (page 360).

2 Turn off the main switch at the consumer unit and remove the fuse for the circuit you want to work on.

3 Find a suitable supply socket to run the spur from (facing page). Remove the socket and unscrew the terminals to release the conductors.

4 Prepare the route (page 369). Lead it from the supply socket to the wall outside the bathroom and from there to the bathroom wall where the flex-outlet plate is to be fixed.

5 Prepare cavities for the mounting boxes for the FCU and the flex-outlet plate.

6 Fix two lengths of cable in place, one from the supply socket to the FCU, the other from the FCU to the flex-outlet plate.

7 Feed the ends of the cables into the mounting boxes and screw the boxes in place; feed the end of the appliance flex through to the back of the flex-outlet plate. Prepare the new cable and the flex for connection (page 363).

Continued on page 374

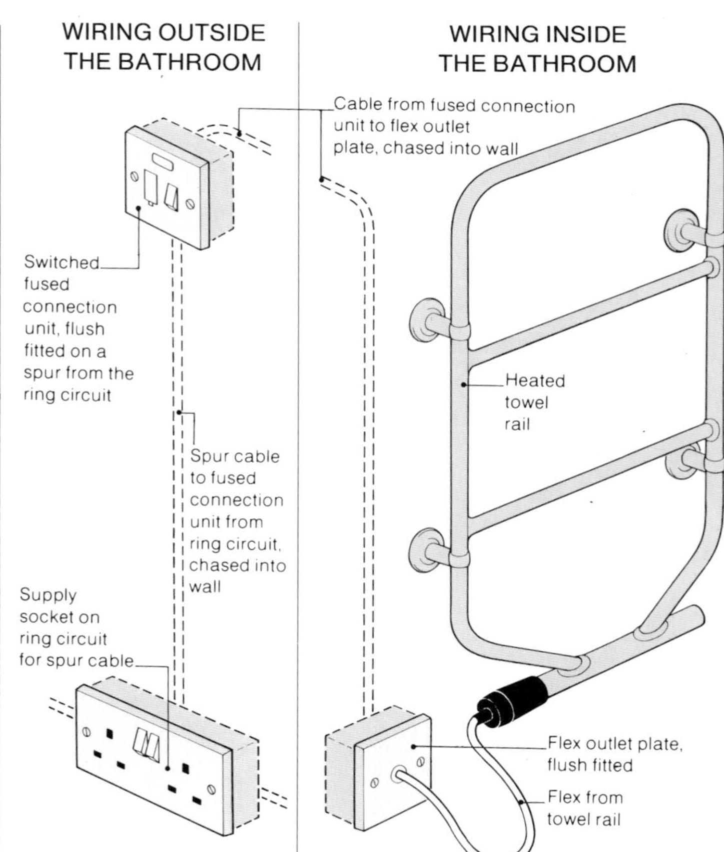

Installing a heated towel rail or bathroom radiator (continued)

CONNECTING AT THE SUPPLY SOCKET

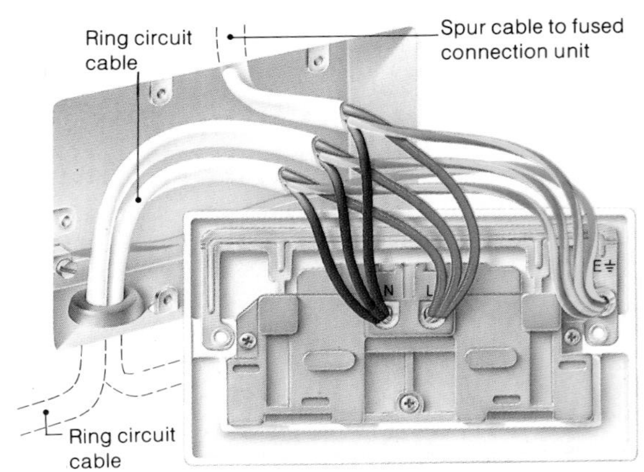

CONNECTING AT THE FCU

Cable to flex outlet plate

Spur cable from the supply socket

CONNECTING AT THE FLEX-OUTLET PLATE

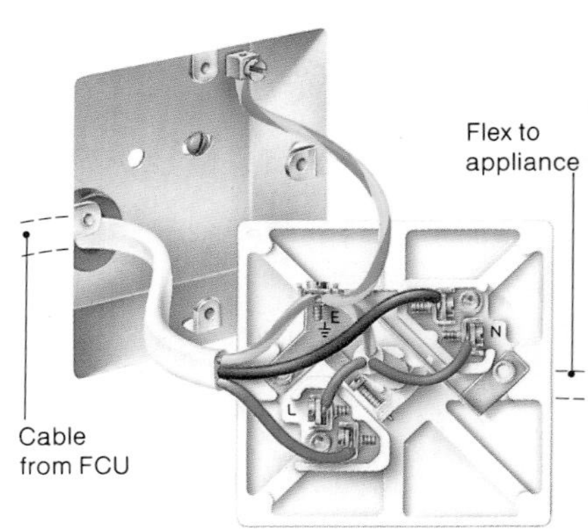

8 Repair the plaster and wait for it to dry. Replace any floorboards.

CONNECTING AT THE SUPPLY SOCKET

1 Match the conductors of the three cables – red with red, black with black and green-and-yellow with green-and-yellow.

2 Screw the sets of conductors tightly into the correct terminals – red at L, black at N, and green-and-yellow at E or ⏚.

3 Press the socket onto the mounting box without disturbing the conductors and screw it in place until it meets the mounting box.

CONNECTING AT THE FCU

1 Connect the conductors coming from the supply socket, screwing the tips tightly in place at the terminals. The red conductor goes to the terminal marked L and Mains (or Supply or Feed or In). The black conductor goes to the terminal marked N and Mains (or Supply or Feed or In). The green-and-yellow earth conductor goes to the nearer of the two terminals marked E or ⏚. If the FCU has only one earth terminal, do not connect to it yet.

2 Connect the conductors leading from the FCU to the flex-outlet plate. The red conductor goes to L and Load (or Out), the black conductor to N and Load (or Out), and the green-and-yellow-sleeved earth to the second terminal marked E or ⏚. (If there is only one earth terminal, connect both earth conductors to it).

3 Fit the 13amp fuse behind the door on the FCU.

4 Press the FCU gently over the mounting box and drive in the screws until there is no gap between mounting box and FCU.

CONNECTING AT THE FLEX-OUTLET PLATE

1 Connect the conductors from the flex to one set of terminals – brown to L, blue to N, and green-and-yellow earth to E or ⏚. Release each terminal screw enough to wind the conductor tip clockwise just below the screw head, then drive the screw in tight to secure the conductor.

2 Connect the cable conductors in the same way to the other set of terminals – red to L, black to N and green-and-yellow to E or ⏚.

Installing a shaver socket in the bathroom

The only electric socket permitted in a bathroom is a shaver socket. It has a built-in transformer which isolates the user from the mains and makes the socket safe for use in a bathroom.

When you buy the shaver socket, make sure that it bears the British Standards kitemark showing that it complies with BS 3535. This is your guarantee that the socket is safe for a bathroom. Cheaper shaver sockets without transformers (that comply with BS 4573) are sold for installing in bedrooms. Do not install this type in a bathroom.

There are purpose-made mounting boxes for shaver sockets. Surface-fixed boxes are available but it is usual – and safer – to sink a recessed box into the wall. Many bathrooms are small and a box projecting at about shoulder height is a hazard as well as being in danger from accidental knocks.

You can install the socket on a spur led from a suitable existing socket on the ring circuit to a fused connection unit (FCU) outside the bathroom and from there to the bathroom wall.

It is also very common to install the shaver socket on a spur led from a junction box inserted in the lighting circuit above the bathroom (page 391).

You will need

Tools Tools for preparing the route (page 369); sharp knife; insulated screwdrivers; wire cutters and strippers; pliers.

Materials $2.5mm^2$ twin-core-and-earth cable; $1mm^2$ twin-core-and-earth cable; cable clips; green-and-yellow sleeving for earth conductors; FCU; 3amp cartridge fuse; single mounting box with grommet and screws; shaver socket with mounting box, grommet and screws.

PREPARATIONS

1 Turn off the main switch at the consumer unit and remove the fuse for the circuit you want to work on.

WIRING OUTSIDE THE BATHROOM

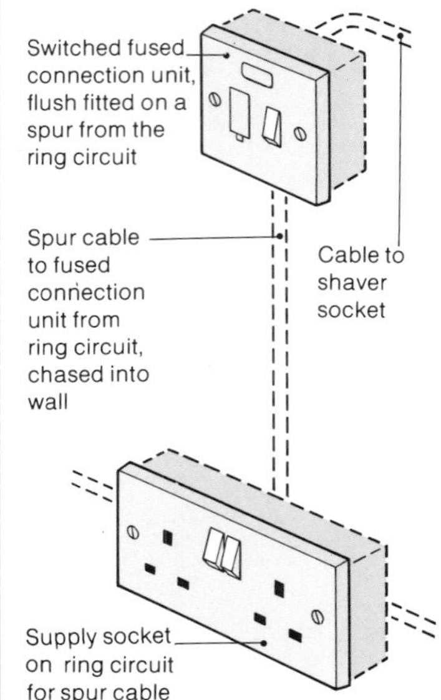

WIRING INSIDE THE BATHROOM

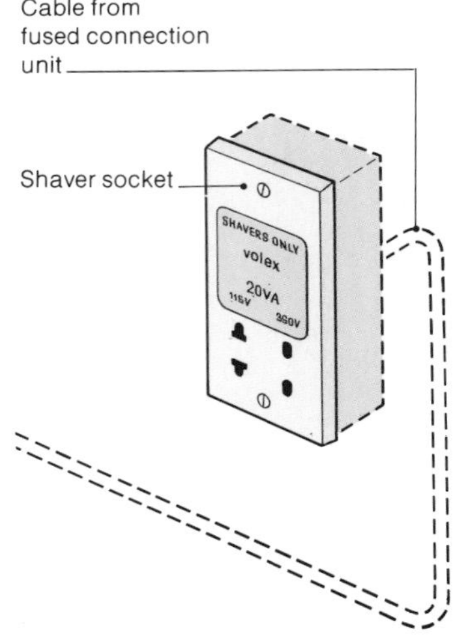

2 Find a suitable supply socket for the spur (page 372); one near the bathroom is the most convenient. Disconnect the conductors from it and unscrew and withdraw the mounting box from the cavity.

3 Prepare the route for the cable (page 369). Lead it from the supply socket to the position for the FCU outside the bathroom door. From there lead it to a spot immediately below the position for the shaver socket and then vertically up to the shaver socket position.

Prepare the cavities for the mounting boxes for the FCU and the shaver socket.

4 Fix $2.5mm^2$ cable along the route from the supply socket to the FCU position.

5 Fix $1mm^2$ cable along the route from the FCU to the shaver socket position.

6 Feed the original cables and the new cable into the mounting box at the supply socket. Screw the mounting box in place in the cavity.

7 Feed the ends of the $2.5mm^2$ and $1mm^2$ cable into the mounting box for the FCU and screw the mounting box in place in the cavity.

CONNECTING AT THE SUPPLY SOCKET

Ring circuit cable

Spur cable to fused connection unit

Ring circuit cable

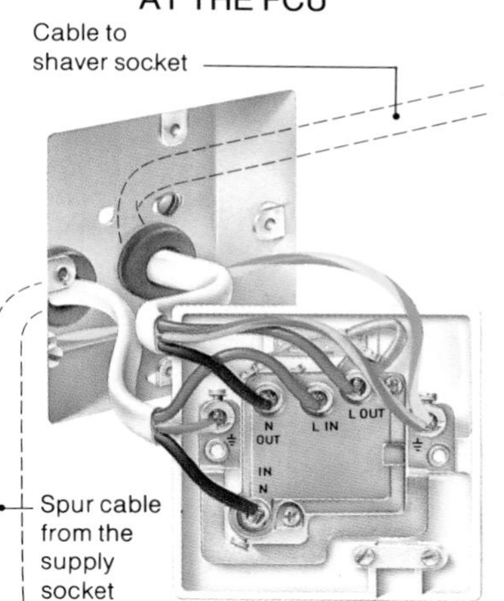

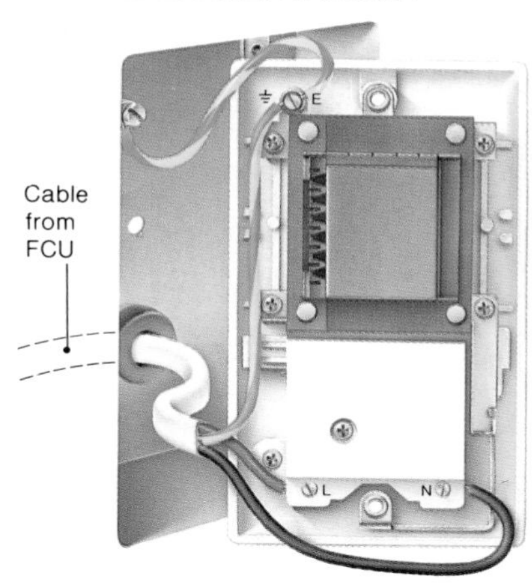

8 Feed the other end of the 1mm² cable into the mounting box for the shaver socket. Position the mounting box in the prepared cavity and screw it into the plugged hole in the wall.

9 Prepare all the ends of the new cables for connection (page 363), remembering to put green-and-yellow sleeving on the earth conductors. Sleeve the earth conductors of the original cables if this has not already been done.

10 Repair the plaster and wait for it to dry. Replace any floorboards (page 273).

CONNECTING AT THE SUPPLY SOCKET

1 Match the three sets of conductors from the cables and screw each matched set into its terminal behind the socket – reds to L, blacks to N, and green-and-yellows to E or ⏚. Connect a sleeved earth wire from the lug on the mounting box to the earth terminal on the socket.

2 Press the socket gently over the mounting box without dislodging the conductors and screw it in place until it meets the box.

CONNECTING AT THE FCU

1 Screw the conductor tips of the 2.5mm² cable into the terminals marked Supply (or Feed or In) – red to L, black to N and green-and-yellow earth to E or ⏚. If there is only one earth terminal, do not connect the earth conductor yet.

2 Screw the conductor tips of the 1mm² cable into the terminals marked Load or Out – red to L, black to N and green-and-yellow earth to E or ⏚. If there is only one earth terminal, connect both earth conductors to it.

3 Press the FCU over the mounting box and screw it in place, taking care not to trap the conductors.

CONNECTING AT THE SHAVER SOCKET

1 There is only one set of conductors to connect. Screw them tightly in place – red at L, black at N, and green-and-yellow at E or ⏚.

2 Screw the shaver socket in place until it meets the mounting box.

3 At the consumer unit, replace the circuit fuse and turn the main switch back on.

Connecting the circuit for a shower heater unit

An instantaneous shower heater (page 328) is a heavy consumer of electricity during the short periods it is in use and would be likely to overload a circuit shared with other appliances. Because of this it should have its own circuit leading from the consumer unit and protected there by its own 45amp fuse, or by an MCB which is suitable for shower heaters up to 8kW.

The circuit goes first to a 45amp double-pole, pull-cord switch on the ceiling of the bathroom or shower room. The switch disconnects both the live and neutral conductors when it is off. It must have a mechanical indicator that clicks over to the on or off position when the cord is pulled; this shows that a safe gap is separating the conductors when the switch is off.

From the switch the circuit goes to the back or base of the shower heater unit, where it enters and connects with the flex incorporated in the unit. It is best to bury the cable in the wall but, where this is impractical, you can fit it inside surface-mounted plastic trunking.

The size of the twin-core-and-earth cable needed depends on the distance between the consumer unit and the shower heater, and on the shower wattage. Use 6mm² cable for a shower rated at up to 8kW,

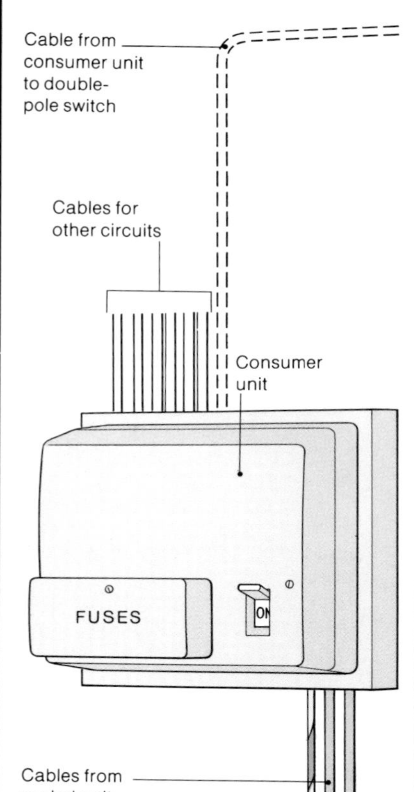

WIRING INSIDE THE BATHROOM

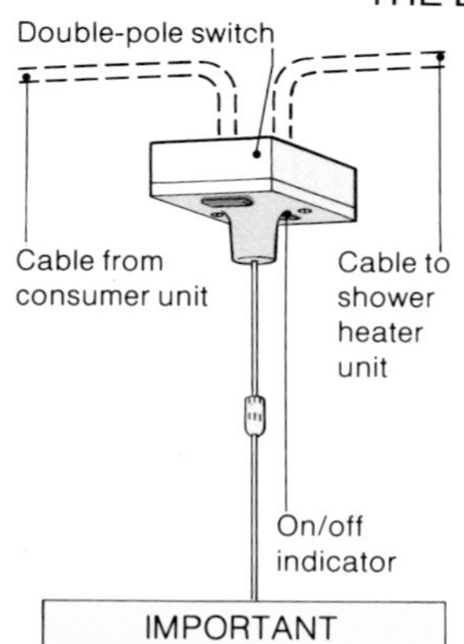

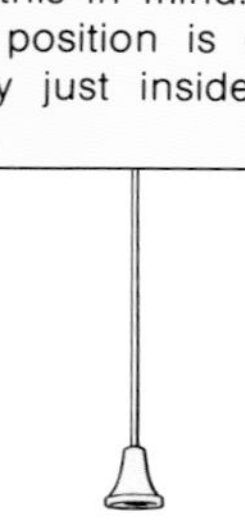

IMPORTANT
The pull-cord for the shower heater unit must not be within reach of a person using the shower or the bath. Plan the cable route with this in mind. The best position is commonly just inside the door.

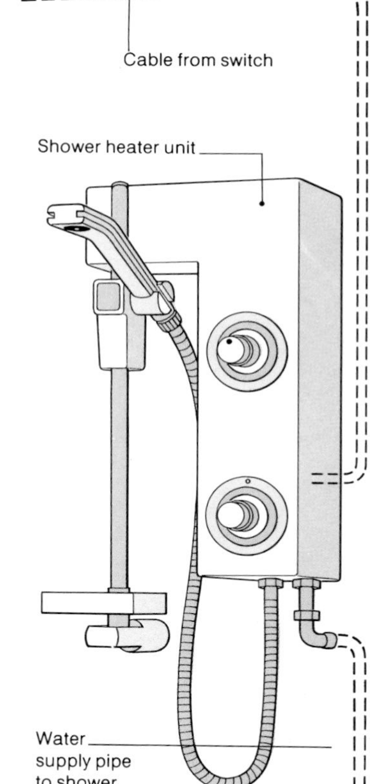

Connecting the circuit for a shower heater unit (continued)

and 10mm² cable if the circuit length is over 14 yd (13m) long or the shower is rated at more than 8kW. Where the distance is between 22 yd and 36 yd (20m and 33m) use 16mm² cable.

The cable should have a route separate from other cables. It should not pass through thermal insulation or thermal plasterboard. If this is unavoidable, use 10mm² cable even for a short run.

It is important to follow the maker's instructions on fitting the unit to the wall and plumbing it in.

You will need

Tools Tools for preparing the route (page 369); insulated screwdrivers; sharp knife; wire strippers and cutters; pliers.

Materials Twin-core-and-earth cable of appropriate size; green-and-yellow plastic sleeving for earth conductors; cable clips; 45amp double-pole pull-cord switch with mechanical on/off indicator; shower heater unit; 45amp fuse or suitable MCB.

CONNECTING AT THE CEILING SWITCH

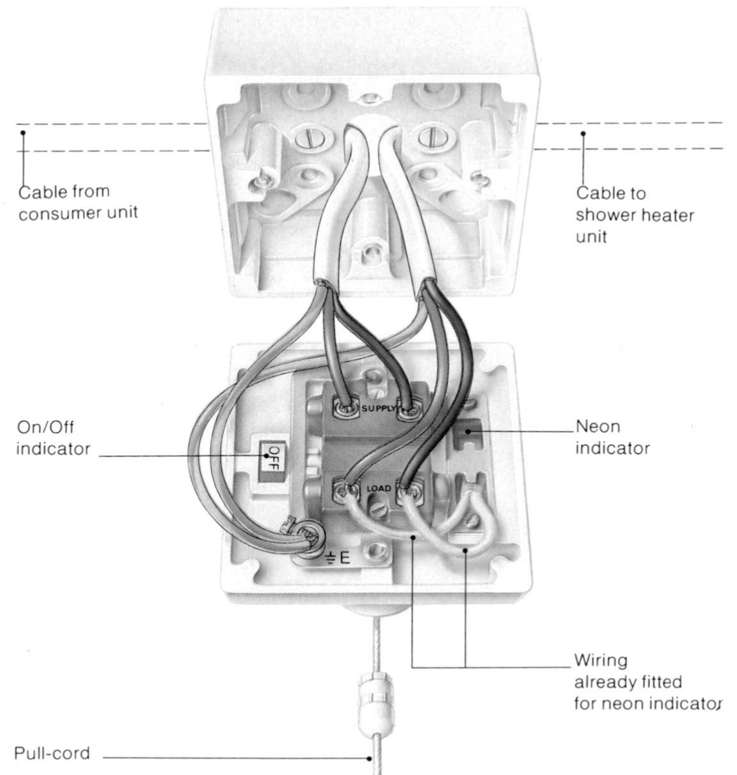

CONNECTING AT THE SHOWER HEATER UNIT

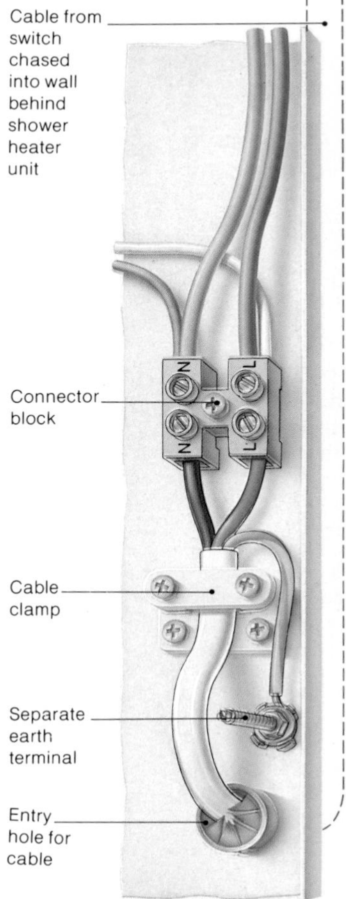

PREPARATIONS

1 Choose the position for the shower and plan the plumbing layout (page 329). You may choose to fit the shower over the bath or there may be another position where you can conveniently fit the tray and drainage and tap into the rising main.

2 Take off the front cover of the shower heater and hold the back plate against the wall. Mark the wall through the cable entry point so that you know where to lead the cable, and also through the screw fixing points. Drill and plug the screw fixing points.

3 Check the earthing and bonding (page 359) and remedy any defects.

4 Prepare the route for the cable (page 369). There is no need to switch off the electricity until you are ready to make the connection at the consumer unit. Make the route from the consumer unit to the pull-cord switch position on the ceiling of the bathroom or shower room and on from there to the position for the shower heater. The switch must be well out of reach of anyone using the shower or the bath. Make the route from the switch above the ceiling to a point immediately above the shower so that the final part of the route runs vertically to the unit.

5 Fit the base for the double-pole switch to the ceiling, following the method for fitting a ceiling rose (page 370). Before you screw it in place, knock out two of the stamped circles for the cables to enter.

6 Lay the cable along the route (page 369), one length from the consumer unit to the double-pole switch and another from the switch to the position behind or beside the cable entry point on the shower heater unit. Allow sufficient cable at each end to reach all the terminals comfortably.

> HELPFUL TIP
> At the double-pole switch, mark the cable ends 'From mains' or 'To shower' to identify them so that you connect them to the correct terminals later. Write on the outer sheath with a ballpoint pen.

7 Feed the cable ends into the double-pole switch.

8 Feed the cable through the entry hole of the shower heater unit and screw the unit to the prepared holes on the wall.

9 Prepare all the cable ends for connection (page 363). Remember to fit short lengths of green-and-yellow sleeving on all the bare earth conductors.

10 Lay the pipes and make the plumbing connections (page 330).

11 Repair the plaster. Leave it to dry out thoroughly before you start making the connections.

12 Replace floorboards that were lifted (page 273).

CONNECTING AT THE CEILING SWITCH

1 Insert the tips of the two green-and-yellow-sleeved earth conductors together into the terminal marked E or ⏚ and screw them tightly in place.

2 Connect the red and black conductors of the cable going from the ceiling switch to the shower unit, screwing them tightly into place at the terminals. The red goes to the terminal marked L and Load (or Out) and the black to the terminal marked N and Load (or Out).

If the switch is wired for a neon indicator, connect the indicator conductors at the same time, one (it does not matter which) to the same terminal as the red and the other to the same as the black. Take care not to dislodge the small bulb.

3 Connect the red and black conductors of the cable coming from the mains to the remaining terminals (marked Supply or Feed or In). Screw the red in place at the terminal marked L and the black at the terminal marked N.

4 Press the switch cover over the base without dislodging or trapping the conductors and screw the cover in place until it meets the base. Do not overtighten the screws or the plastic may crack.

CONNECTING AT THE SHOWER HEATER UNIT

Do not disturb the internal wiring already fitted in the shower. Different manufacturers may fit internal wiring with differently coloured insulation.

1 Release the screws of the cable clamp, lead the cable under the clamp and screw the clamp back in place.

2 Connect the conductors of the cable to the connector block incorporated in the shower heater unit. Conductors will already be connected at one side of the block. Screw the red conductor tightly into the terminal opposite the brown (or red) conductor, and the black conductor into the terminal opposite the blue (or black) conductor.

3 Instead of a pair of earth terminals on the connector block, there

CONNECTING THE CIRCUIT AT THE CONSUMER UNIT

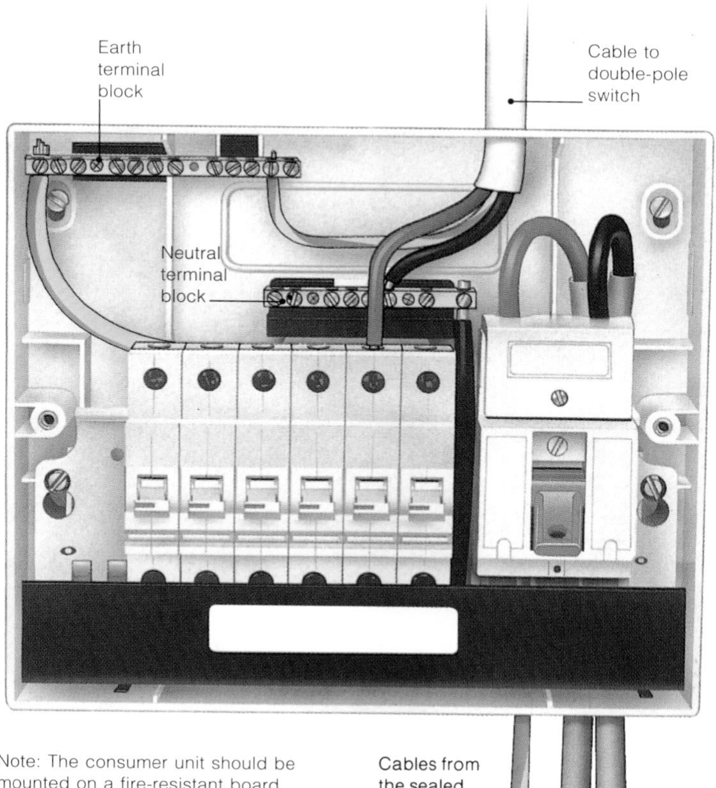

Note: The consumer unit should be mounted on a fire-resistant board

may be a single, separate earth terminal marked E or ⏚. Connect the green-and-yellow-sleeved earth conductor to this terminal.

ALTERNATIVELY, if the connector block has a third terminal for the earth conductor, screw the sleeved conductor tightly into it opposite the green-and-yellow conductor already connected there.

CONNECTING THE CIRCUIT AT THE CONSUMER UNIT

Once the new circuit is installed, connect it to the consumer unit yourself or have it connected by a qualified electrical contractor.

1 Turn off the main switch at the consumer unit and withdraw the fuse carrier or MCB from the fuseway you are going to use.

2 Remove the screws from the cover on the consumer unit and open the unit.

> WARNING
>
> The switch disconnects only the fuses or MCBs and the cables leading out from the consumer unit to the household circuits. It does not disconnect the cables entering via the meter from the service cable. You must not interfere with these cables. They are always live at mains voltage.

3 If the unit has a wooden frame, drill a hole through it and feed in the cable.

ALTERNATIVELY, on a metal unit, knock out the entry hole in the top immediately above the fuseway you will be using. Fit a grommet into the hole and feed in the cable.

4 Check that you have stripped off enough outer sheath for the conductors to reach the terminals easily.

5 Screw the conductors tightly into the terminals. The red goes to the terminal at the top of the fuseway you are using, the black to the corresponding position on the neutral terminal block, and the green-and-yellow to the corresponding position on the earth terminal block.

6 Fit the 45amp fuse in the fuse carrier and insert the carrier; or insert the correct MCB.

7 Screw the cover of the consumer unit back in place.

8 Turn the main switch back on.

If there is no spare fuseway in your consumer unit, fit beside the consumer unit a double-pole mains switch with a 45amp fuse carrier, as may be done for a cooker (see page 379). Your electricity supply company will connect this to the sealed unit. You must not tamper with the sealed unit yourself.

Installing an electric cooker circuit

An electric cooker uses so much electricity that it must have its own circuit; if it shared a circuit with other appliances the circuit would frequently be overloaded.

At the consumer unit the cooker circuit is protected by its own fuse or MCB – 30amp for a cooker up to 12kW if the control unit does not include a socket. A 45amp fuse or 50amp MCB is needed for a cooker above 12kW. A large split-level oven and hob operating on the same circuit may have a higher rating than 12kW.

The cable goes from the consumer unit to a cooker control unit mounted above worktop height on the kitchen wall – beside the cooker, not above it. The cooker control unit has a double-pole switch which disconnects both the line (live) and neutral conductors. The unit may have a neon light which glows when the unit is switched on. Many older units included a 13amp socket but these are best avoided because they take too long to disconnect in an emergency. If the control unit includes a socket, a 30amp fuse or MCB will still be suitable for a cooker up to 10kW.

For a free-standing cooker, a second length of cable runs from the control unit to a cooker connector unit fitted on the wall about 24in (610mm) above floor level behind the cooker. A 7ft (2m) length of cable runs from the connector unit to the cooker, so that the cooker can be drawn away from the wall when necessary. Use the same size of cable for this as for the rest of the circuit; the cooker is not moved often so the flexibility of flex is not needed.

Both parts of a split-level cooker can be connected to one cooker control unit provided that neither the hob nor the oven is more than 7ft (2m) away from the control unit. You can make the connection by running two cables from the control unit, one to the oven and the other to the hob. Alternatively, you can run one length of cable from the control unit to one part of the cooker and a second length of cable from there to the second part of the cooker. No connector units are needed on the wall behind split-level cookers because they are seldom moved but permanently built in. The cable from the control unit simply emerges from the wall behind the appliance and is wired into the back allowing enough cable for installation.

The size of twin-core-and-earth cable needed depends on both the wattage of the cooker and the length of the cable run. For a circuit with a 30amp fuse or MCB, use $6mm^2$ cable if the total length of the cable run is up to 23yds (21m), and use $10mm^2$ cable if the total

CIRCUIT FOR A FREE-STANDING COOKER

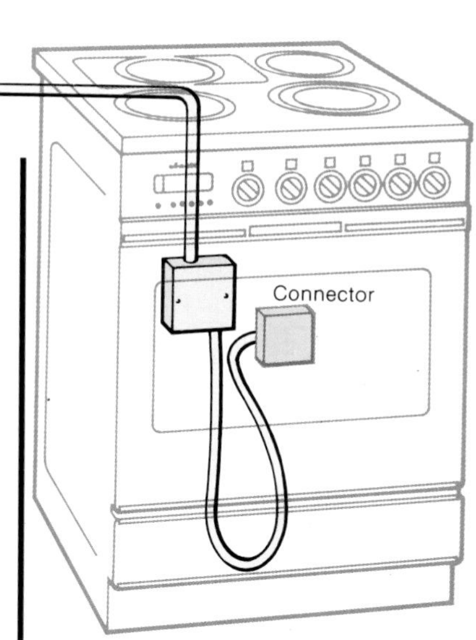

Free-standing cooker

Installing an electric cooker circuit (continued)

length of the cable run is between 23yds and 37yds (21m and 34m). For a circuit with a 45amp fuse or 50amp MCB, use 10mm² cable for a cable run of up to 12yds (11m), and 16mm² cable for a run of between 12yds and 24yds (11m and 22m).

Plan the cable route (page 369) from the cooker control unit back to the consumer unit. Do not run it through thermal insulation or thermal plasterboard. It can be chased in ordinary plaster at ceiling or floor level before approaching the control unit vertically; or the cable can run in surface-mounted white plastic trunking at ceiling, worktop or floor level. Surface-mounted control units are also available. You can run the trunking from there to a surface-mounted socket box and fit the cooker connector unit over that.

You will need

Tools Tools for preparing the route (page 369); sharp knife; insulated screwdrivers; wire cutters and strippers; pliers.

Materials Cooker control unit with mounting box; cooker connector unit with mounting box (for a free-standing cooker); fixing screws, wall plugs and grommets; twin-core-and-earth cable of the correct size; green-and-yellow plastic sleeving; cable clips; free-standing cooker or split-level cooker; fuse or MCB of the correct rating.

PUTTING IN THE CABLES

There is no need to switch off at the mains until you are ready to connect the new circuit to the consumer unit.

1 Check the earthing and bonding (pages 359 and 360) and remedy any defects.

2 Prepare the route (page 369), leading it from near the consumer unit to the cooker control unit. From there lead it to the cooker connector unit behind a free-standing cooker, or to positions behind the two parts of a split-level cooker. Do not interfere with any other cables near the consumer unit.

3 Fit the mounting box (page 369) for the cooker control unit and, if you are installing a free-standing cooker, fit the mounting box for the connector unit. Remember to knock out the necessary entry holes for the cable.

4 Fit lengths of cable along the route (page 369) from the consumer unit to the control unit, and from the control unit to the connector unit or to positions behind the parts of a split-level cooker. Do not feed the cable into the consumer unit but feed the other cable ends into the boxes. Allow enough spare cable at the ends to reach all the terminals easily.

5 Prepare the cable ends for connection (page 363), remembering to sleeve the earth conductors.

6 Repair the plaster and wait for it to dry. Replace any floorboards (page 273).

CONNECTING AT THE CONTROL UNIT

1 Connect the cable from the consumer unit to the terminals of the control unit. Screw the red conductor into that marked L and In. Screw the black conductor into that marked N and In. Screw the green-and-yellow-sleeved earth conductor into the nearer of the terminals marked E or ⏚.

2 Connect the cable leading out to the connector unit or split-level cooker into the terminals behind the control unit plate. Screw the red conductor tightly into the terminal marked L and Out. Screw the black conductor tightly into the terminal marked N and Out. Screw the green-and-yellow-sleeved earth conductor tightly into the nearer of the terminals marked E or ⏚.

If you are leading separate cables to a split-level cooker, there will be two outgoing sets of conductors. Match the conductors in pairs – red with red, black with black and green-and-yellow with green-and-yellow. Insert the pairs into the correct terminals and screw them in place.

CONNECTING AT THE CONNECTOR UNIT FOR A FREE-STANDING COOKER

1 Remove the screws holding the cover to the metal frame.

2 Unscrew and remove the cable clamp at the bottom of the frame.

3 Pair the conductors of the cables from the control unit and to the cooker – red with red, black with black, and green-and-yellow with green-and-yellow. Screw the pairs into the terminal block on the frame – red to L, black to N and green-and-yellow to E or ⏚.

ALTERNATIVE CIRCUITS FOR SPLIT-LEVEL COOKERS

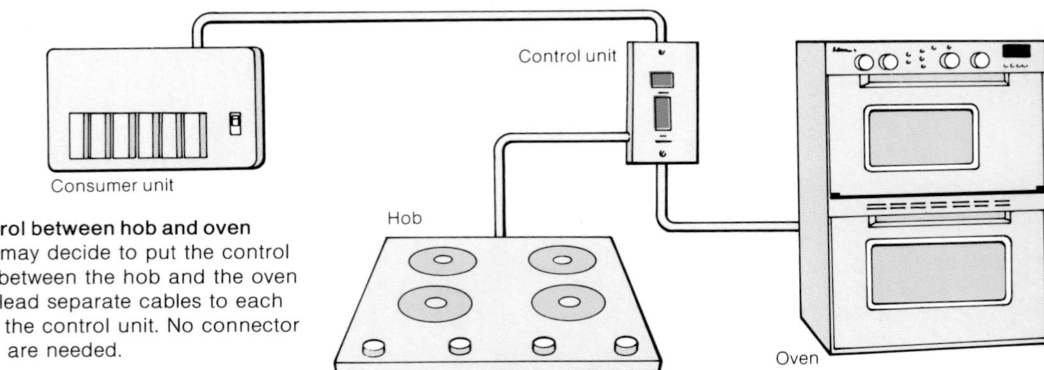

Control between hob and oven
You may decide to put the control unit between the hob and the oven and lead separate cables to each from the control unit. No connector units are needed.

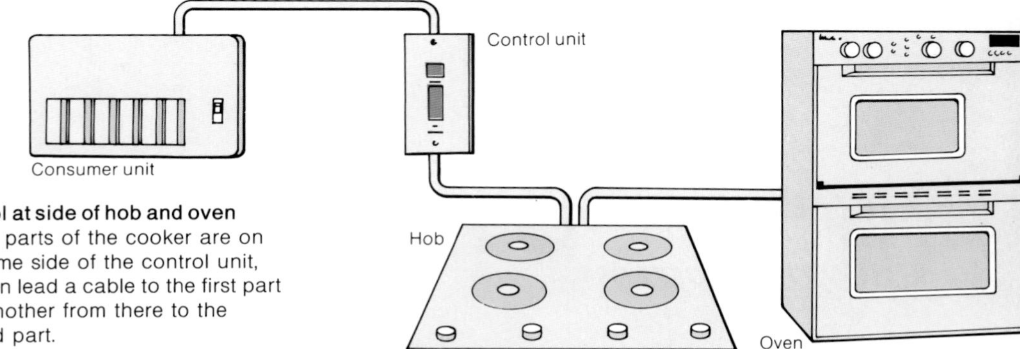

Control at side of hob and oven
If both parts of the cooker are on the same side of the control unit, you can lead a cable to the first part and another from there to the second part.

CONNECTING AT THE CONTROL UNIT

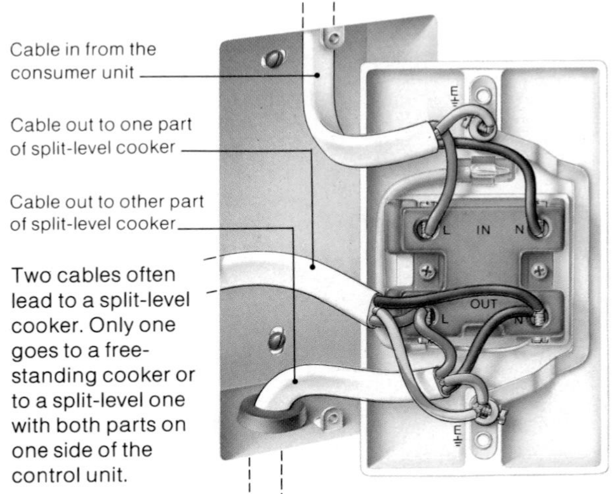

Two cables often lead to a split-level cooker. Only one goes to a free-standing cooker or to a split-level one with both parts on one side of the control unit.

FITTING THE CONNECTOR UNIT

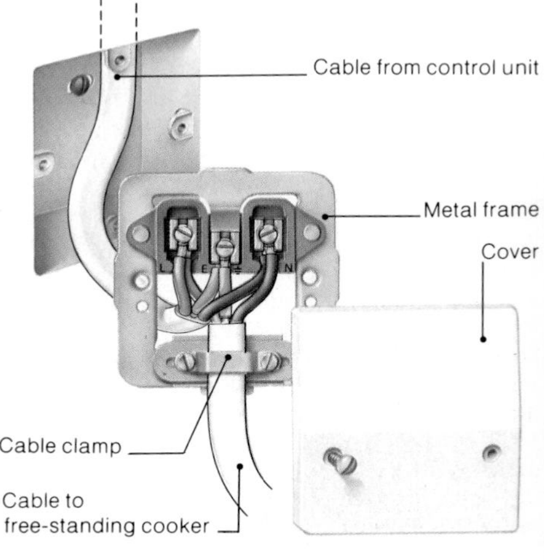

4 Screw the frame to the mounting box and screw on the cable clamp.

5 Screw the connector unit's cover in place.

CONNECTING TO A FREE-STANDING COOKER

1 Remove the metal plate covering the terminals on the back of the cooker. Release the cable clamp.

2 Connect the supply cable conductors to the terminals, red to L and black to N. Usually the conductors have to be bent round a pillar and held down with brass washers and nuts. Make sure enough insulation has been removed for bare wire to wind round the pillars. Connect the green-and-yellow-sleeved earth to E or ⏚.

3 Screw the clamp over the cable.

4 Screw the plate back over the connection point.

CONNECTING TO A SPLIT-LEVEL COOKER

If you have led two cables from the control unit, one for each part of the split-level cooker, connect each one in the same way as a free-standing cooker (above) and secure each under the clamp.

ALTERNATIVELY, if you have led one cable from the cooker control unit to the first part of the split-level cooker, you will have two cables to connect and clamp there – one from the control unit and one going to the second part of the cooker. Match the conductor tips – red with red, black with black, and green-and-yellow-sleeved with green-and-yellow-sleeved. Connect them to the terminals, red to L, black to N, and green-and-yellow to E or ⏚.

Connect the second part of the cooker as a free-standing cooker.

CONNECTING A SPLIT-LEVEL COOKER

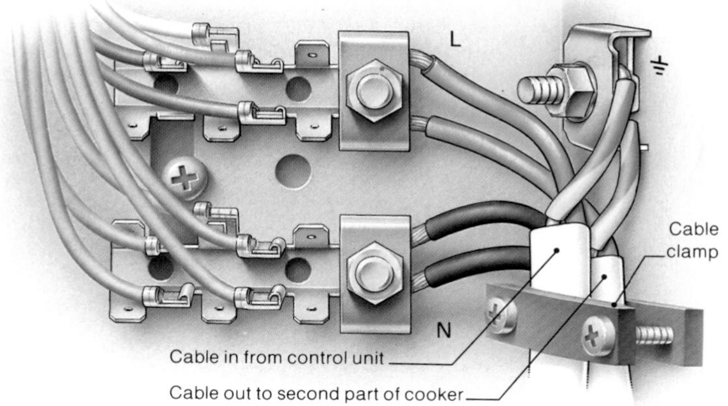

CONNECTING TO THE CONSUMER UNIT

1 Turn off the main switch at the consumer unit and take out the fuse carrier or MCB for the cooker circuit. Make sure the control unit and all cooker controls are off.

> WARNING
> The main switch disconnects only the fuses or MCBs and the cables leading out from the consumer unit to the household circuits. It does NOT disconnect the cables entering via the meter from the service cable. Do not tamper with these cables. They are always live at mains voltage.

2 Remove the screws of the consumer unit cover and take it off.

3 Drill through the frame of the consumer unit if it is wooden, or knock out an entry hole and fit a grommet if the consumer unit is a metal one. Feed in the cable. Make sure that you have removed enough outer sheath for the conductors to reach the terminals.

4 Screw the black conductor into the neutral terminal block.

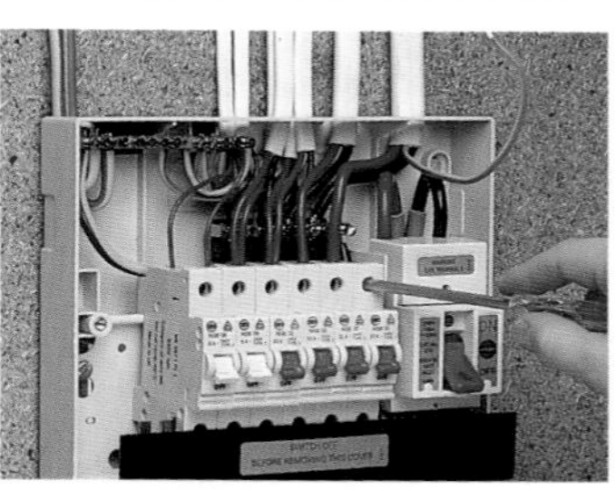

5 Screw the red conductor into the terminal at the spare fuseway.

6 Screw the green-and-yellow conductor into the earth terminal block.

7 Fit the fuse and replace the fuse carrier, or fit the MCB.

8 Screw the cover of the consumer unit back in place and turn the main switch back on.

> WHAT TO DO IF THE CONSUMER UNIT IS FULL
>
> 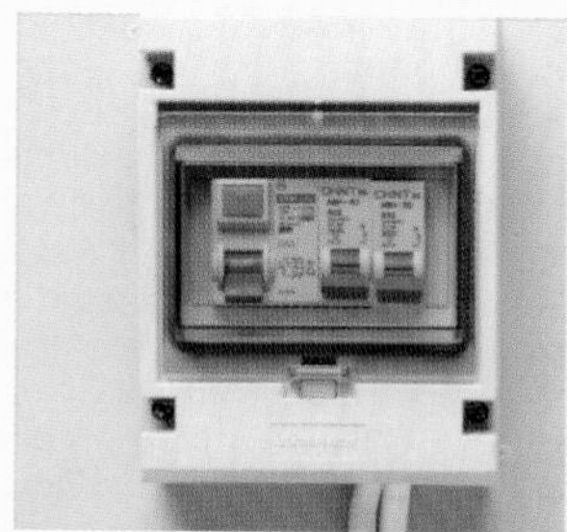
>
> If your existing fusebox has rewirable fuses, choose a new switchfuse unit containing two new fuseways and a double-pole isolating switch. If you have a modern consumer unit with MCBs, choose a two-way or four-way enclosure that can accept MCBs and an RCD if required. Mount the new unit or enclosure on the fuseboard or on the wall near to it. Connect the new circuit cables, meter tails and earth cable to the unit.
>
> Call in your electricity company to connect the new unit or enclosure to the meter.

Installing a ring circuit

A ring circuit to supply electricity to the power sockets starts at a 30amp fuseway in the consumer unit. A 2.5mm^2 twin-core-and-earth cable goes from the fuseway round the rooms supplied by the circuit, looping into each socket outlet in turn before going to the next room. Finally the cable returns to the fuseway to complete the ring.

If you have a modern consumer unit and are installing a new ring circuit – perhaps in an extension or in a part of the house that was not rewired earlier – you can connect the circuit to the consumer unit.

If you do not have a modern consumer unit, install the new circuit until it is ready for connection and arrange with your local electricity supply company to fit a consumer unit, connect it to their meter and disconnect the circuits which you have replaced. As you gradually replace other old wiring you can connect the new circuits to the modern consumer unit.

Any number of single, double or treble sockets can be installed on the new ring, but the floor area served by the ring must not be larger than 120sq yds (100sq m). This area must be reduced if the estimated load on the ring exceeds 7.2kW. If a socket is needed in a position that is not on the most convenient route for the ring circuit, you can run a non-fused spur to it from one of the sockets on the ring, but you should avoid this as much as possible because it reduces the possibility of adding spurs later. The number of non-fused spurs must not exceed the number of outlets on the ring.

PLANNING THE ROUTE

First draw a plan of the rooms that the ring circuit will supply. The length of the cable must not exceed 65yd (60m). You must not route the cable through thermal insulation or thermal plasterboard as it may over-heat.

The circuit may be for the kitchen only, for all the other ground floor rooms, or for all the upper floor rooms. Mark on the plan where socket outlets are needed – and where they might be needed in the future. Most rooms will need sockets on at least two sides. Large rooms may need them on three sides and at two places along the sides. A choice of socket position does away with flexes trailing across rooms. Install a double socket at each outlet on the new circuit – and in a kitchen or living room a treble socket at each outlet may be wiser.

At some positions you may want to fit a fused connection unit (FCU) rather than a socket for a stationary appliance such as an extractor fan or a freezer (page 372).

Very large consumers of electricity, such as cookers, instantaneous electric shower units, fixed

Installing a ring circuit (continued)

water heaters, storage heaters and some washing machines must have their own circuits.

Installing a ring circuit is a long job, especially if you can only work at weekends, so do not disconnect or remove the old sockets until the new circuit is finished. You will then be able to use power tools during the preparation. However, when you are channelling walls, lifting floorboards, or cutting into walls, take great care not to strike the old wiring. Use a metal detector to avoid accidents (page 230). If you have any doubts at all about whether there is live wiring near the spot where you are working, switch off the electricity at the mains until you have made sure either with a metal detector or by probing with a fine bradawl.

You will need

Tools Tools for preparing the route (page 369); sharp knife; insulated screwdrivers; wire strippers and cutters; pliers.

Materials Mounting boxes (with screws, wall plugs and grommets where necessary); sockets (and perhaps FCUs); 2.5mm² twin-core-and-earth cable; green-and-yellow plastic sleeving for the earth conductors; cable clips; fuses for treble sockets and FCUs; 30amp fuse or MCB for the consumer unit.

PREPARATIONS

1 Check the earthing and bonding (pages 359 and 360) and remedy any defects.

2 Prepare the route (page 369), leading it from the consumer unit to the nearest socket position on the new ring circuit, and on from there to each socket position in turn. Prepare the route for any spurs branching off the ring circuit. Lead the route back to the consumer unit.

3 Prepare recesses for the mounting boxes of the new sockets.

4 Fit the mounting boxes in position, remembering to knock out the most convenient cable entry holes, and fit grommets in metal boxes.

5 Lay the cable along the route (page 369). Start above the consumer unit, leaving plenty of spare cable for the conductors to reach the terminals in the unit easily. Do not interfere with the consumer unit at this stage. Continue along the route, taking the cable in and out of the most convenient entry holes at each mounting box. Cut the cable at each box, leaving 4in (100mm) spare at each cut. Fit cable along any spur. Again leave 4in (100mm) spare at each end of the cable. Lead the cable back from the last socket on the circuit to the consumer unit.

6 Prepare all the cable ends for connection (page 363).

7 Repair the plaster and wait for it to dry completely. Replace any floorboards (page 273). Do not fix them down if you will be removing old wiring from under them later.

PLANNING A RING CIRCUIT

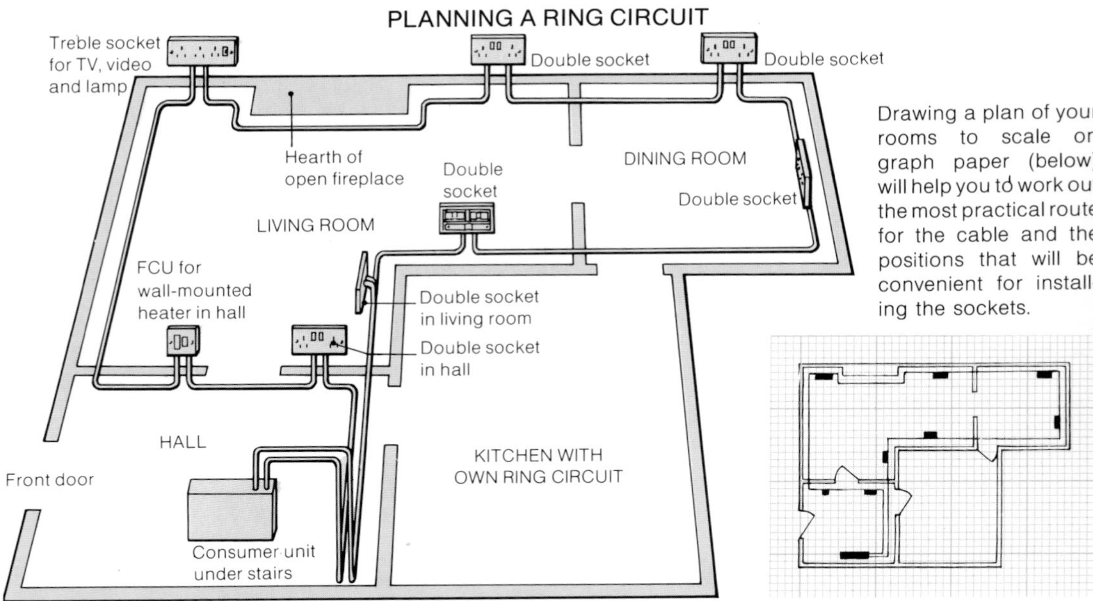

Drawing a plan of your rooms to scale on graph paper (below) will help you to work out the most practical route for the cable and the positions that will be convenient for installing the sockets.

You could save cable and some labour by running the ring only through the living room and hall and giving the dining room one double socket on a spur (page 372) taken from the socket on the right of the fireplace. However, you could not extend the spur later if you needed more sockets in the dining room. Instead of double sockets you could fit singles, but doubles need no more work and allow for future appliances.

CONNECTING THE SOCKETS

1 At each socket, pair the two sets of cable conductors – red with red, black with black, and green-and-yellow with green-and-yellow.

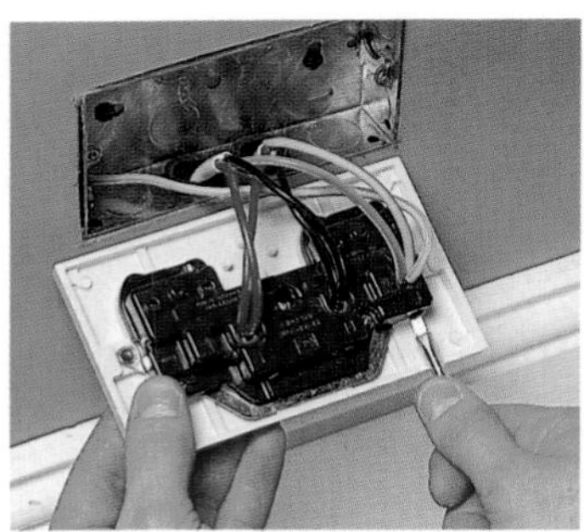

2 Screw the conductors tightly into the terminals behind the socket – red to L, black to N, and green-and-yellow to E or ⏚.

3 If the socket is a treble, fit a 13amp cartridge fuse in the fuseholder.

4 Press the socket gently over the mounting box without dislodging or trapping the conductors. Screw it in place until there is no gap between the socket and the mounting box. Do not overtighten the screws or the socket may crack.

CONNECTING SPUR SOCKETS

1 At sockets supplying spurs there are three sets of conductors, one from the previous socket on the circuit, one going to the next socket on the circuit, and one for the spur. Match the tips together in threes then follow steps **2**, **3** and **4** from the previous section.

2 A socket at the end of a spur has only one set of conductors to connect. Follow steps **2**, **3** and **4** from the previous section.

CONNECTING FCUs

The appliance should be fitted in place, complete with flex.

1 Feed the flex through the entry hole to the back of the FCU and prepare the end of the flex for connection (page 363).

2 Connect the flex conductors, screwing them tightly into place at the terminal – brown to L and Load (or Out), blue to N and Load (or Out), and green-and-yellow to the nearer of the two terminals marked E or ⏚.

3 Pair the conductors from the two cables, red with red, black with black, and green-and-yellow with green-and-yellow. (If the FCU has been fitted at the end of a spur there will be only one cable.)

4 Screw the cable conductors into the terminals behind the FCU – red goes to the one marked L and Mains (or Supply or Feed or In), black to the one marked N and Mains (or Supply or Feed or In), and green-and-yellow to the nearer of the two terminals marked E or ⏚.

5 Fit a 3amp or 13amp cartridge fuse in the fuseholder according to the wattage rating of the appliance (page 365).

6 Press the FCU into place without dislodging or pinching the conductors, and screw it in place until it meets the mounting box.

HAVING A CONSUMER UNIT INSTALLED

If you do not have a modern consumer unit, arrange with your electricity supply company (or another approved electrical contractor) to install one. The supply company will connect it to the meter. They will also disconnect the circuit you have replaced from the meter and their sealed unit. At the same time, they will connect the new circuit to the new consumer unit if you wish.

TESTING THE NEW CIRCUIT

Use a circuit tester (page 372) to test the continuity of each conductor in the circuit – red, black, green-and-yellow. Check and tighten all connections if necessary.

CONNECTING AT THE CONSUMER UNIT

1 Turn off the main switch on the consumer unit.

> WARNING
> The main switch disconnects only the fuses or MCBs and the cables leading out from the consumer unit to the household circuits. It does NOT disconnect the cables entering via the meter from the service cable. Do not interfere with these cables. They are always live at mains voltage.

2 Remove the retaining screws and the cover of the consumer unit.

3 Drill through the top of the consumer unit or knock out an entry hole and fit a grommet. Feed in the cables and make sure that enough sheathing has been removed for the conductors to reach the terminals easily.

4 Match the tips of the conductors, red with red, black with black, and green-and-yellow with green-and-yellow.

5 Screw the conductors tightly into the terminals – red to the terminal at the spare fuseway, black to the neutral terminal block, and green-and-yellow to the earth terminal.

6 Fit the 30amp fuse and insert the fuse carrier, or insert the MCB.
Screw the cover of the consumer unit back in place.

7 Turn on the main switch and test the circuit by connecting an appliance to each socket in turn.

CONNECTING AT THE CONSUMER UNIT

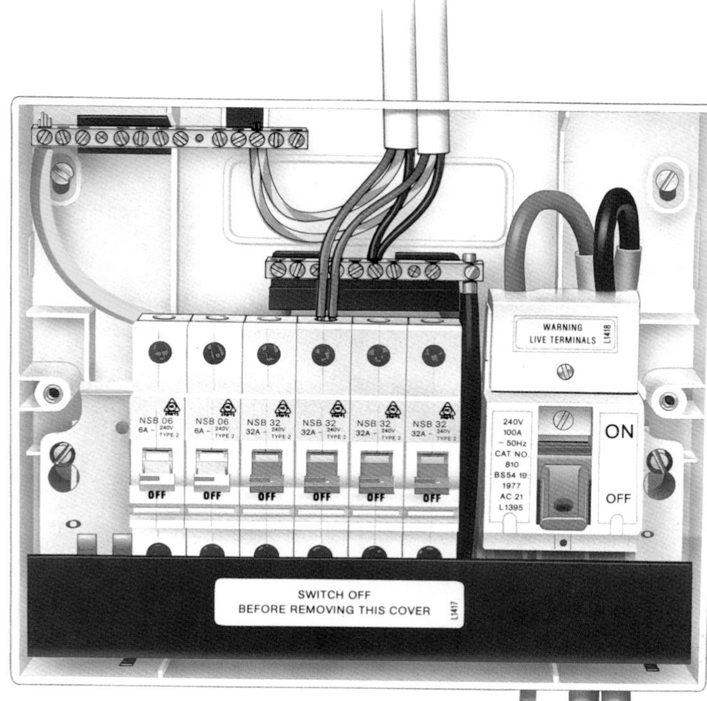

DISCONNECTING THE OLD WIRING

1 At the fuseboard turn off the main switch or switches that controlled the superseded circuits and remove any fuses. You can arrange for the electricity board to disconnect the old system from their meter. If they are connecting a new consumer unit, they can also disconnect the old system.

2 Trace the cables leading from the switch to the old sockets down to the floor or up to the ceiling. Cut them off there.

3 At each of the old sockets unscrew the cover plate and release the conductors from the terminals behind it.

4 Unscrew the retaining screws and prise out the mounting box.

5 To remove all the old wiring you may have to lift several floorboards (page 273). Remove as much as you can trace and wherever possible remove any conduits and junction boxes, but leave any conduits in the wall to reduce repairs.

6 Repair the walls and skirtings.

7 Replace the floorboards (page 273).

8 Remove the old main switch and old fuse box if they have been disconnected by the supply company. Remove the cables that lead from them. If the old system has not been disconnected, do not remove the switch or fuse box. Keep the switch off and the fuse out.

A MULTISOCKET MAINS ADAPTOR

There may be situations at home when you need to use more electrical sockets than are available. In a living room, for example, you may need power for a lamp, a television, a video, and a stereo.

Trailing flexes are a safety risk and look untidy. A neat alternative is to connect the appliances to a multi-socket mains adaptor unit. Each unit can take up to six plugs, with a maximum total load of 3000 watts (13 amps). This type of unit, however, is unsuitable for use with appliances that have heating elements, such as hairdryers, irons, and tumble-dryers, which will overload it.

Mini-plugs, wired in the same way as standard three-pin plugs slot into the top of the multi-socket unit. The unit is plugged into a wall socket with an ordinary 13amp plug. It can be mounted on the wall.

1 Remove the mini-plugs from the connector block.

2 Screw the connector block to a skirting board or a wall.

3 Unscrew a mini-plug cover and loosen the cord grip screws.

4 Remove the old plug from the first item to be connected.

5 Trim the conductor wires in the flex to the same length.

6 Thread the flex through the cord grip and connect each wire to its terminal. Brown to the right, blue to the left and green-and-yellow to the centre. Check for stray or exposed wires then screw the terminals tight.

7 Tighten the cord grip and screw down the plug cover. Insert the mini-plug into the connector block, groove-side forward. Repeat for all the appliances. Place any spare plugs into their sockets.

8 Connect the 13 amp plug to the socket and switch on.

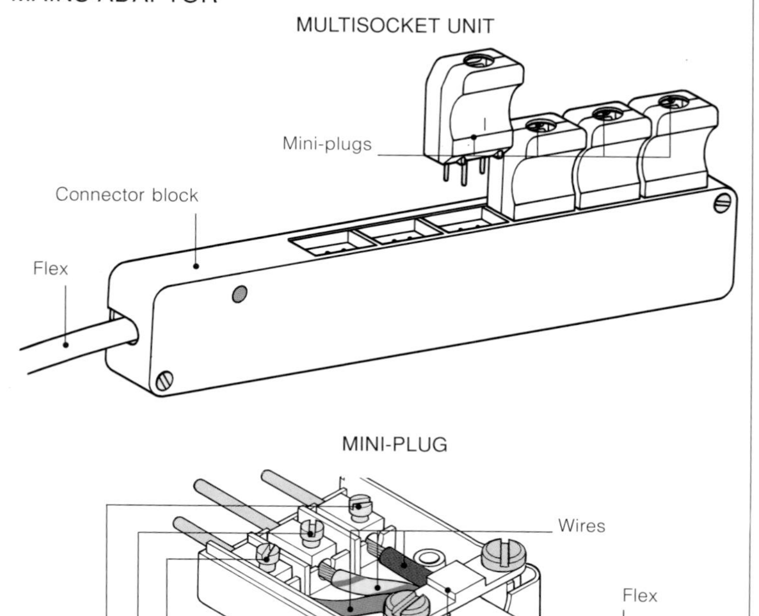

Outdoor wiring

An electricity supply to a detached garage, greenhouse, garden shed or other outbuilding should be via a permanently fixed cable run from the fuseboard in the house. A long flex run to the outbuilding from a socket inside the house is not an acceptable arrangement, and contravenes the wiring regulations.

It is best to bury the cable despite the work involved. Cable underground does not mar the view, and with careful planning the length of the underground section can be kept to a minimum. Run the cable through the house to the point nearest the outbuilding to save work. If this is difficult, run the cable along the outside wall of the house to reach the point nearest the outbuilding. You can also run it along a boundary wall, but not along a fence.

You can take the cable overhead, but it is unsightly to have such a cable hanging immediately outside the house. It should be fixed at least 11ft 6in (3.5m) above the ground, which frequently entails fitting a timber post securely to the outbuilding to achieve the clearance. If it is more than 9ft 10in (3m) long, the cable span must be supported along its length by another wire and must have a drip loop at each end.

For underground cable, make the route of the trench as short as possible but divert it well clear of obstacles such as rockeries, inspection chambers or trees. Allow some extra cable when you calculate the length needed in case you meet unexpected obstacles.

A professional electrician is likely to install MICC or armoured cable (see *Cables and fittings for outdoor wiring*, below), but these are difficult for the do-it-yourselfer to connect correctly without the use of specialist tools, and the various components are relatively expensive. It is easier to use ordinary twin-core-and-earth cable for the entire sub-circuit between house and outbuilding, but the outdoor section of the circuit cable must be run in protective PVC conduit (above) fixed to the walls of the buildings and laid in the trench. The run is made up using lengths of conduit linked with solvent-welded straight and elbow connectors.

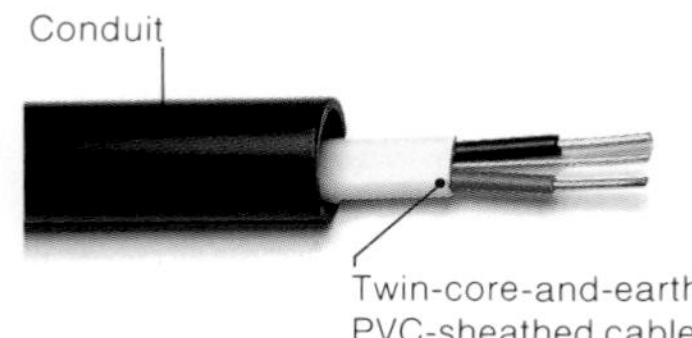

Start the new sub-circuit with an enclosure containing a 30milliamp RCD and one or two 30 or 32amp MCBs, fitted on or near the house fuseboard. This serves as the isolating switch for the sub-circuit. Call in your electricity supply company to connect this to the meter once you have installed the circuit wiring. You are not allowed to do this yourself.

Inside the outbuilding, the cable should run to a socket. A switched, fused connection unit (FCU) can be run from this to provide a starting point for lighting wiring.

CABLES AND FITTINGS FOR OUTDOOR WIRING

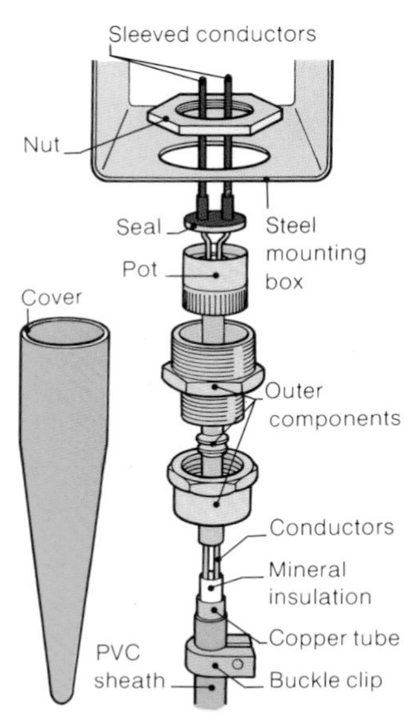

MICC cable
Mineral-insulated copper-clad cable (MICC) has two conductors set in mineral filling inside a copper tube that acts as the earth conductor. There is an orange PVC sheath. Special tools are needed to strip off the copper tube and fit the watertight seals. As soon as you buy the cable, seal its ends with tape. Leave the tape on until you are ready to connect, or the filling will absorb moisture.

A waterproof gland seals the cable into a steel mounting box 1¾in (44mm) or more deep – deeper than boxes normally used indoors – to give room to fit the gland. A blank plate covers the front. Use copper clips to hold MICC cable.

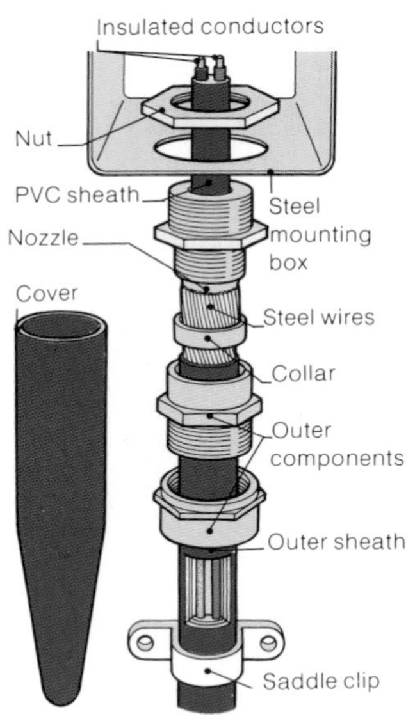

Twin-core armoured cable
Two insulated conductors are in a PVC sheath inside steel wires that serve as earth conductor. There is a PVC outer sheath.

Three-core armoured cable has a third core, in yellow plastic, for the earth. Sleeve its ends with green-and-yellow plastic.

This cable is the most suitable for an open position on a patio and for a supply to a garden pond. Armoured cables do not need special tools.

Use the right size and type of gland to seal the cable into a deep steel mounting box. On the twin-core cable, be sure to tighten the gland nut hard to complete the earth continuity. Use galvanised, copper or plastic clips to hold the cable.

You will need
Tools Tape measure; side cutters; wire strippers; mains power drill; 10mm flat wood bit; long 20mm masonry bit; hammer; spade; hacksaw; screwdrivers.
Materials 2.5mm^2 twin-core-and-earth cable; cable clips; green-and-yellow PVC earth sleeving; red PVC insulating tape; 20mm PVC conduit; wall clips; straight connectors and elbows; solvent-weld adhesive; sand; bricks; paving slabs; warning tape; enclosure with 30milliamp RCD and one/two 30 or 32amp MCBs; metalclad double socket and mounting box; metalclad FCU and mounting box; 1mm^2 twin-core-and-earth cable; batten holder; metalclad light switch and mounting box; grommets; woodscrews; wallplugs.

WORK INSIDE THE HOUSE

1 Plan and prepare the cable route from the fuseboard to the point where it will leave the house. If you have suspended timber floors, it can be run beneath the floorboards (page 369). Otherwise it is simplest to surface-mount it in plastic minitrunking (page 371).

2 At the point where the circuit cable will leave the house, locate a mortar course in the house wall at least 150mm above the level of the damp-proof course. It is easier to drill through mortar than solid brickwork. Use a long 20mm diameter masonry drill bit to drill through the wall from the outside, sloping the hole slightly upwards to discourage rainwater from entering.

3 Mount the new RCD unit on the existing fuseboard if there is room for it, or on the wall nearby otherwise. Remove knockouts from the base of the unit to admit the incoming meter tails and main earth cable, and also the cable supplying the new sub-circuit. Clip the RCD and the MCBs onto the metal busbar, ready for connection when the sub-circuit wiring is complete.

OUTSIDE WORK

1 Plan the cable route between house and outbuilding, and excavate the trench along the marked route. Avoid cultivated ground if possible; a route running close to a path or boundary wall is often the ideal choice.

2 Check the depth of the trench with a tape measure. It should be at least 500mm deep. Excavate further if it is not deep enough.

3 Remove any sharp stones from the bottom of the trench and put in a layer of dry sand about 50mm deep to protect the conduit.

4 Measure up the conduit run and work out how many lengths of conduit will be needed to make it up. Conduit is available in 2m and 3m lengths, so you should need relatively few lengths to make up the run for a typical sub-circuit.

5 At the house end of the run, feed the end of the circuit cable into the first length of conduit. Pull enough cable through the conduit to make up the run inside the house from the entry point in the house wall to the fuseboard position.

6 Start to assemble the conduit run by solvent-welding lengths of conduit together with straight connectors. Brush a little of the special adhesive onto the pipe end, taking care not to get any on the cable sheath. Push the fitting onto the pipe and rotate it slightly to ensure a waterproof joint. Feed the cable through the next length of conduit before joining it to the previous one. Continue adding lengths of conduit one by one in the same way.

7 Use a hacksaw to cut the last section of conduit to length as necessary. Smooth off any roughness with fine abrasive paper before joining it to the previous length.

8 As you join lengths of conduit together, lower the completed run into the base of the trench. Use large-radius elbow fittings and short lengths of conduit and take the run up to the point where it leaves the house and where it enters the outbuilding. Secure these sections of conduit to the house and outbuilding walls with clips.

9 Fit a standard elbow to each end of the conduit run and insert one into the hole in the house wall and one into the outbuilding wall. Feed enough cable into the outbuilding to allow it to be connected to the wiring accessories that will complete the sub-circuit.

10 When you have completed the conduit run and laid it in the trench, place a line of bricks on the sand bed at each side of the conduit and lay narrow paving slabs over the bricks. This ensures that any future digging cannot damage the conduit or the cable inside it. For extra protection, place lengths of special yellow-and-black plastic warning tape over the slabs.

11 Back-fill the trench with the soil you excavated earlier, and tamp it down firmly.

WORK IN THE OUTBUILDING

1 Decide where in the outbuilding you want to position the various wiring accessories. Because the sub-circuit is controlled and protected by the RCD and MCBs at the house end of the circuit, the simplest way of wiring up the accessories is to create a radial circuit. Run the incoming cable to the first socket, then on to any other sockets you want to install. At a convenient point in this radial circuit, include a fused connection unit (FCU) fitted with a 3amp fuse. From here a length of $1mm^2$ cable is run to supply one or more light fittings and a separate light switch.

2 Screw the metal mounting boxes for the various wall-mounted accessories to the wall of the outbuilding. Use woodscrews driven directly into timber walls or frame members, and into wallplugs in drilled holes in masonry walls.

3 Remove metal knockout discs from the mounting boxes to admit the cables, and fit a rubber grommet into each entry or exit hole to prevent the cable from chafing.

4 Feed the incoming cable into the first mounting box and cut it to leave about 150mm of cable within the box. Then run cable from this box to the next one, cutting it to length as before. Carry on adding lengths of cable one by one to connect all the wiring accessories.

5 Prepare all the cable ends for connection by stripping about 75mm of insulation from each conductor. Cover the bare earth cores with a length of green-and-yellow PVC sleeving. Fold the ends of the earth cores over the sleeving to stop it from slipping off until you are ready to connect these conductors to the earth terminals.

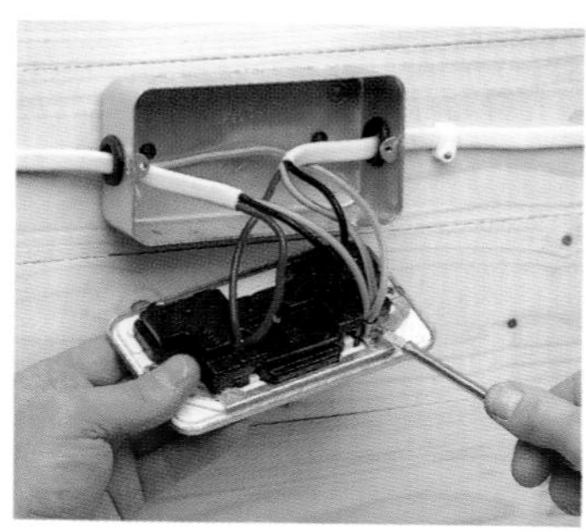

6 There will be two sets of conductors to connect to the socket faceplate at each socket (except at the last one on the circuit, which will have just one set). Connect the two red conductors to the terminal marked L and the two black conductors to the terminal marked N. Connect the sleeved earth conductors to the earth terminal on the faceplate. Add a short length of sleeved earth core (taken from a cable offcut) between this terminal and the earth terminal in the mounting box to earth the mounting box.

7 Check that all the connections are secure. Fold the conductors back into the mounting box and screw the faceplate to it. Repeat this process to connect up the other sockets on the sub-circuit.

8 At the fused connection unit (FCU), connect the conductors of the incoming cable to the terminals marked FEED or IN. The red conductor goes to the terminal marked L, the black conductor to the terminal marked N and the sleeved earth conductor to E. Add an earth link between the earth teminals on the faceplate and the mounting box as before. Connect the $1mm^2$ cable that will supply the light fitting in the same way, but to the terminals marked LOAD or OUT. Run this cable up to the position of the batten holder or light fitting you are installing. Fit a 3amp fuse in the fuseholder and screw the faceplate to the mounting box.

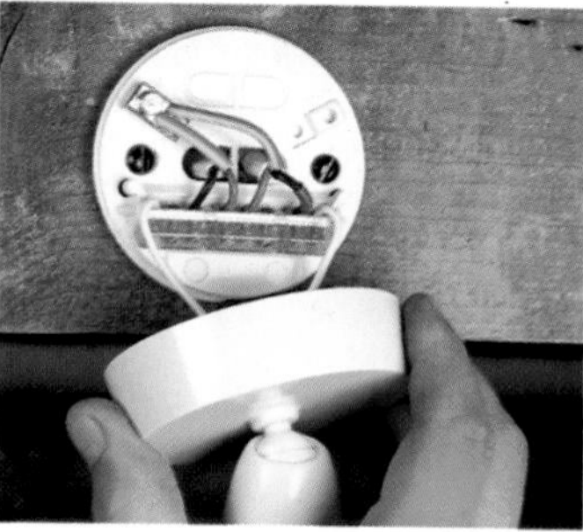

9 At the batten holder or light fitting, connect in the $1mm^2$ cable from the FCU and another $1mm^2$ cable to run on to the light switch. The two red conductors go to the centre bank of terminals, and the black conductors to the end terminals; it does not matter which way round these two are connected. Connect the two earth conductors to the earth terminal. Screw the cover onto the batten holder.

CONNECTING AT THE MCB/RCD UNIT

At the new MCB/RCD unit in the house, connect the red conductor of the circuit cable to the top terminal of one of the MCBs. Connect the neutral and earth cores to their respective terminal blocks. The second MCB shown here is already wired to supply another sub-circuit. Your electricity supply company will fit the meter tails to the RCD and add the main earth cable shown here.

WEATHERPROOF SOCKETS

Sockets and light switches fitted out of doors must be weatherproof. Sockets on the house wall can be wired as spurs from an indoor power circuit (page 372), but must include a high-sensitivity (30milliamp) RCD for user protection.

Reconnecting a flex to a lampholder

An accidental knock may dislodge a lampholder and stop the light working, but it is a simple matter to reconnect it. You will also need to reconnect if you are shortening the flex, perhaps to fit a new lampshade which needs to be higher.

If the lampholder is a metal one without an earth terminal, replace it with an earthed one – or with a plastic lampholder if the flex has no earth conductor. You must have three-core flex with a metal lampholder or metal lampshade.

If the flex is discoloured or cracked, fit a new one.

You will need

Tools Insulated screwdrivers, one with a small, fine tip; wire cutters and strippers; pliers.
Materials Heat-resisting flex. Perhaps petroleum jelly and a new ring or lampholder.

1 Turn off the switch at the consumer unit and remove the fuse for the circuit you will be working on.

2 Remove the light bulb and unscrew the ring that holds up the shade. If it sticks, rub petroleum jelly round it and leave it for half an hour. With a very old lampholder, you may have to break the ring; some shops sell the new rings separately. Remove the shade.

3 Unscrew the upper cover of the lampholder and push it up the flex to reveal the flex connections. Prise the flex conductors out of the clamping grooves which are part of the central pillar.

4 With the fine-tipped screwdriver, unscrew the terminals enough for you to draw out the flex conductors.

5 Push each terminal plunger inside the body of the holder to see if the tension is still firm. If not, or if the moulding is damaged or scorched, fit a new lampholder.

6 Prepare the ends of the flex afresh for connection (page 363).

7 If you are fitting a new lampholder, thread the cover onto the flex.

8 Screw the brown and blue conductors tightly into the terminals; it does not matter which each goes to. In a metal lampholder you must connect the green-and-yellow earth conductor to the earth terminal; it is usually on the cover.

9 Fit the flex conductors into the grooves on the central pillar.

10 Screw down the upper cover, making sure that the conductors are not disturbed. If they are, the tension will be affected on the plungers which contact the bulb.

11 Insert the lampholder into the lampshade and screw the retaining ring in place to secure the shade.

12 Fit the light bulb and shade.

13 Replace the circuit fuse and switch on at the consumer unit.

THE PARTS OF A LAMPHOLDER

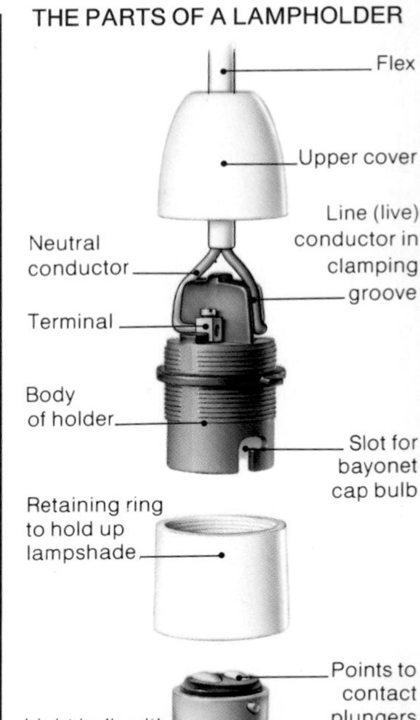

Connecting a light flex to a ceiling rose

If a light flex has discoloured or become brittle, it is easy to connect a new one between the ceiling rose and the lampholder.

Inside a modern ceiling rose on a loop-in wiring system (page 395) is a row of terminals in groups which are not always marked. A separate terminal is marked E or ⏚ for the earth conductors.

Use the right flex for the installation (page 362). If it connects with a metal lampholder or light fitting, it must have an earth conductor.

You will need

Tools Insulated screwdrivers, one with a small, fine tip; sharp knife; wire cutters and strippers.
Materials Heat-resisting flex.

JUNCTION BOX SYSTEM

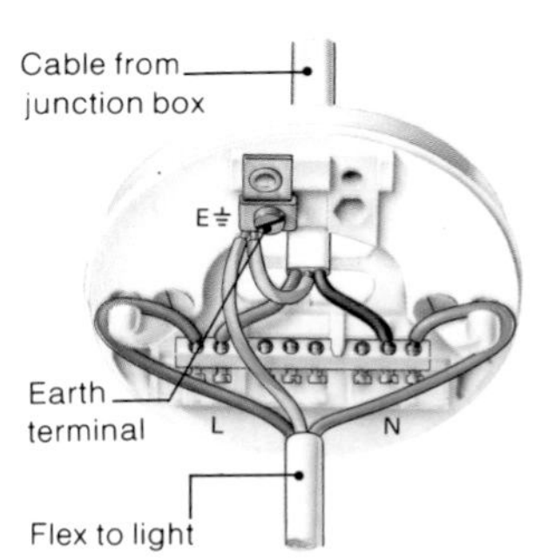

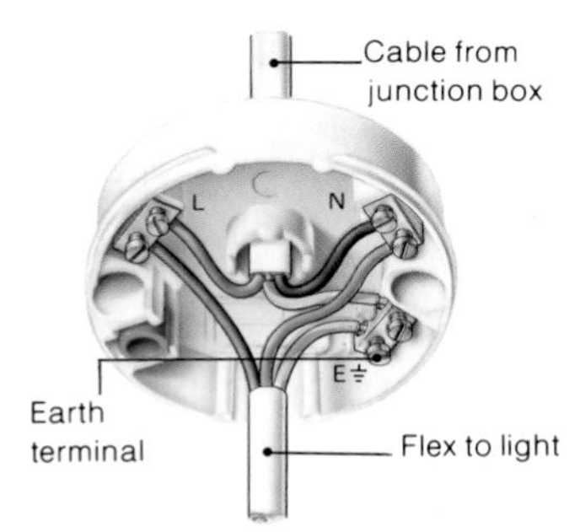

A ceiling rose for a loop-in system might have been used on a junction box system (above). There will be one cable entering the base of the rose. The flex connection is the same as for a loop-in system (instructions 5–7, facing page, top).

Another type of ceiling rose used on a junction box system (above right) has three or four sets of terminals, not in line.

1 Connect the blue flex conductor to the same set of terminals as the black cable conductor.

2 Connect the brown conductor from the flex to the same set of terminals as the red conductor from the cable.

3 Connect the green-and-yellow earth conductor from the flex to the same set of terminals as the earth conductor from the cable.

If the earth from the cable has not already been sleeved with green-and-yellow insulation, disconnect it and sleeve it before connecting it – with the flex earth – to the terminal.

DISCONNECTING THE OLD FLEX

1 At the consumer unit, turn off the main switch and remove the fuse for the circuit you will be working on. It is not enough simply to turn off the light switch.

2 Remove the light bulb and shade to avoid the risk of dropping them.

3 Unscrew the cover of the ceiling rose and slide it down the flex.

4 Using the small screwdriver, loosen the terminal at each end of the row. Withdraw the conductors.

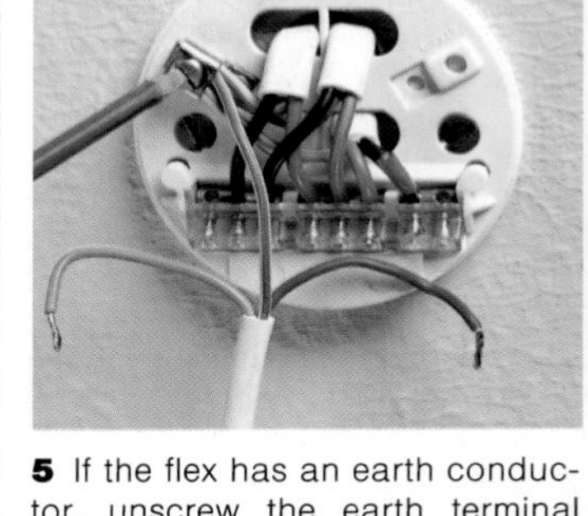

5 If the flex has an earth conductor, unscrew the earth terminal enough to withdraw it. Do not dislodge the other earth conductors.

CONNECTING THE NEW FLEX

1 Connect the new flex first to the lampholder (above).

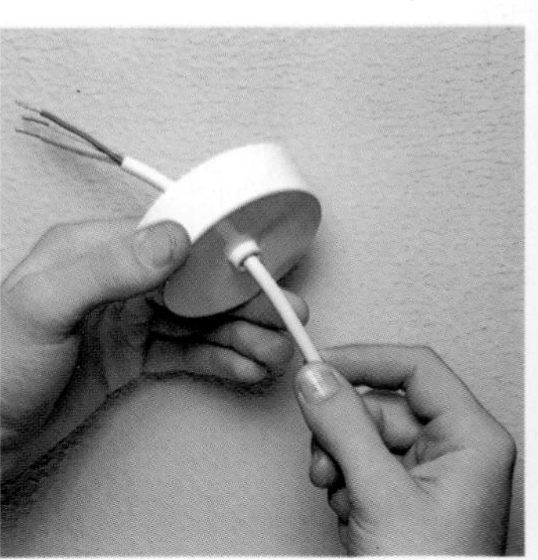

2 Thread the new flex through the cover of the ceiling rose.

3 Prepare the new flex for connection (page 363). Take care not to strip off too much of the outer sheathing. The conductors have to reach the terminals without strain, but they must not show below the ceiling-rose cover; the outer sheathing of the flex must enter the hole in the cover.

4 Slip the tip of the green-and-yellow-insulated earth conductor of the flex under the metal cover of the separate earth terminal in the ceiling rose. Make sure before you screw it down that the other earth conductors, from the cables and the switch, have not been dislodged from under the terminal. Drive the screw down tightly.

5 Connect the blue conductor at the outer hole of the outer trio.

6 Connect the brown conductor at the outer hole of the pair.

7 Press the blue and brown conductors into the notches above the knobs at the ends of the row of terminals. Slide the cover up the flex but it must stay on the outer sheath.

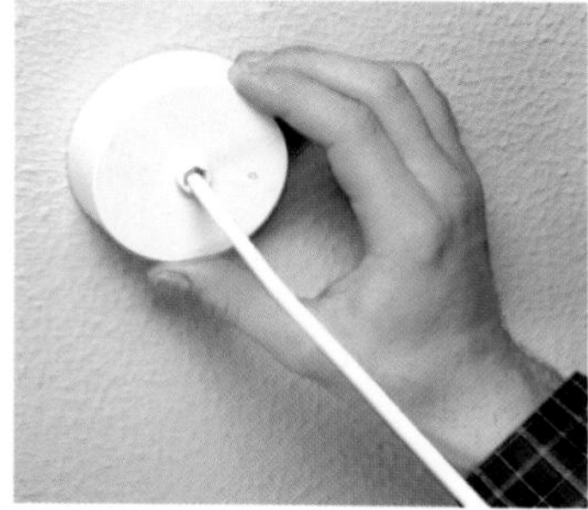

8 Screw on the ceiling-rose cover and replace the shade and bulb.

9 Replace the circuit fuse and switch the electricity back on.

Rewiring a table lamp or standard lamp

If a lamp flex is fraying or cracking, fit a new one. Heat-resisting flex is not necessary. For a table or standard lamp with no exposed metal parts, or for a double insulated lamp (marked ⧈), use a flex with no earth conductor (page 362). For a lamp with metal parts which is not double insulated, use twin-core-and-earth flex.

If the lamp is a treasured old one with a brass lampholder without an earth terminal, you must fit a new brass lampholder with an earth terminal, or a plastic lampholder. If it is not possible to fit a new lampholder, do not use the lamp.

Do not run the flex up the outside of the lamp. It must be threaded up inside the lamp base. The hole to thread it through is often on the side of the lamp near the bottom. If the hole is underneath, the lamp base should have small feet to raise it and keep its weight off the flex.

Some lamps have a push-through switch in the lampholder. Others need to have a switch fitted in the flex; otherwise they can be switched on and off at the socket, but this may be inconvenient.

You will need

Tools Insulated screwdrivers; sharp knife; wire cutters and strippers; pliers.
Materials Lamp; suitable flex. Perhaps also a flex switch.

1 Unplug the lamp and remove the light bulb.

2 Screw off the first narrow ring and lift off the lampshade.
ALTERNATIVELY, screw off the upper half of the plastic cover and remove the lampshade.

3 Unscrew and remove the second narrow ring so that you can lift out the outer lampholder section and then raise the inner section which has the flex connected beneath it.
ALTERNATIVELY, unscrew the rest of the plastic lampholder from the base, then screw down the lower cover to reveal the terminals.

4 Release the flex conductors from the terminals. Wind the wire tips securely round the end of the new flex and tape the two together.

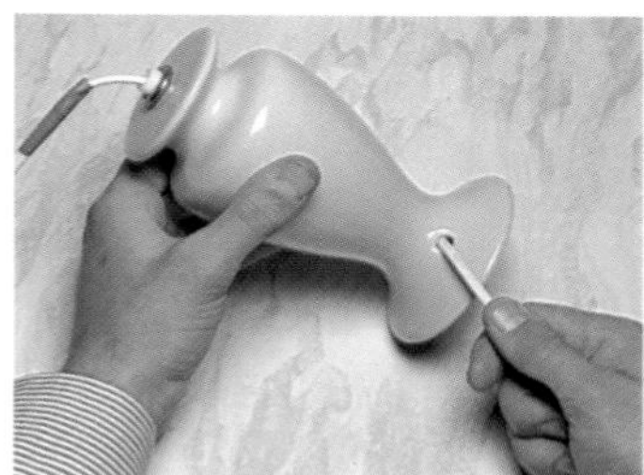

5 Gently pull out the old flex from below, using it to pull the new flex through the lamp base.

TWO TYPES OF LAMPHOLDER

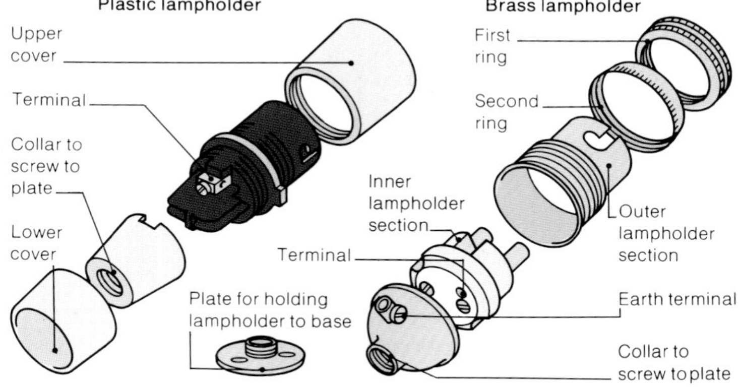

6 Prepare the flex for connection (page 363) and then finish drawing it through the lamp base until only about $1\frac{1}{2}$in (38mm) is protruding.

7 Screw the brown conductor tip into one terminal and the blue conductor tip into the other.

If the terminals are marked L and N, the brown conductor goes to L and the blue to N. If you are using twin-core-and-earth flex, connect the green-and-yellow conductor to the terminal marked E or ⏚.

8 Lower the inner section of the lampholder back into place. Fit the outer section on top and secure it with the screw-on ring.
ALTERNATIVELY, screw the plastic cover over the terminals and screw the lampholder to the lamp base. As you do so, turn the flex or it will become twisted.

9 Replace the lampshade support and secure it with the upper narrow ring or plastic cover.

10 Fit the light bulb and shade.

FITTING A SWITCH IN THE FLEX

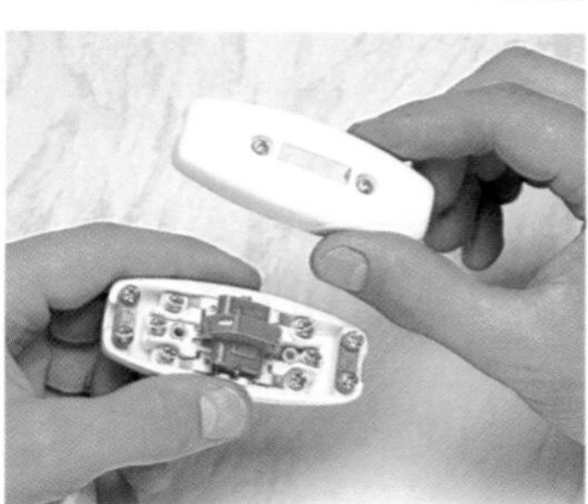

If you are using twin-core-and-earth flex, use a switch with an earth terminal. For a two-core flex on a double-insulated lamp, no earth terminal is necessary.

If you are adding a switch to a lamp already in use, switch off and unplug the lamp.

1 Cut the flex where the switch is to go and prepare the ends for connection (page 363).

2 Unscrew and remove the cover of the switch.

3 Take out a screw from the flex clamp at each end so that you can swivel the clamps aside.

4 Feed the flex ends under the clamps and screw the clamps down on the outer sheath.

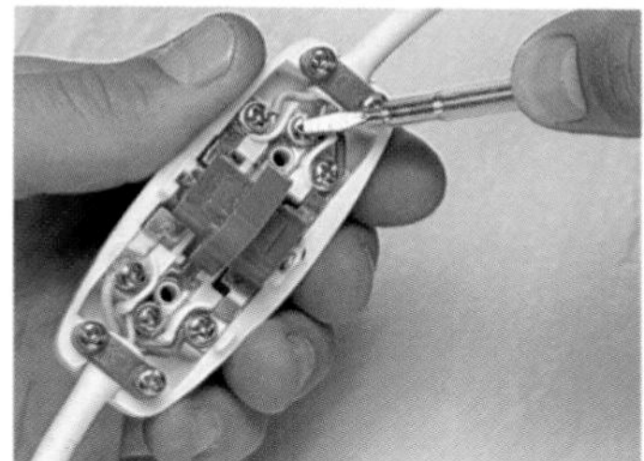

5 Release the terminal screws and wind each conductor tip clockwise round the screws – brown to the terminals marked L, blue to the terminals marked N, and green-and-yellow to the terminals marked E or ⏚. Tighten the screws.

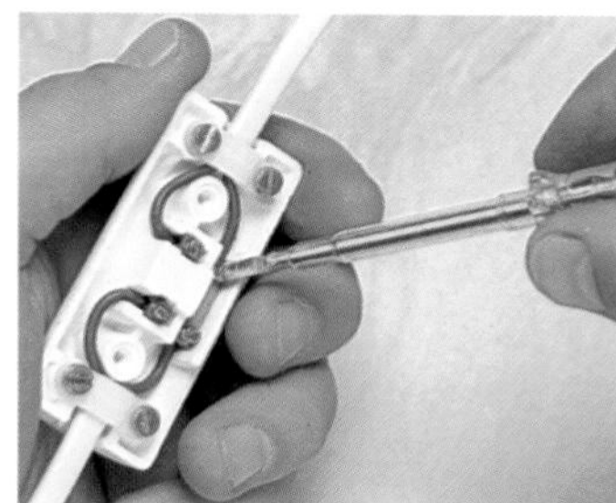

ALTERNATIVELY, in a switch with no earth terminal, connect the two brown conductors to the terminals behind the switch mechanism and the two blue conductors to each end of the through terminal block.

6 Screw the switch cover back in place.

FITTING A PLUG TO THE NEW FLEX

Connect the plug as described in *Wiring a plug*, page 364.

Replacing a one-way switch or changing to a dimmer

If a light switch is cracked, you must replace it at once to prevent any damp from reaching the conductors. You may also want to replace a light switch with one of a different style – one with a rocker switch, or with a brass plate to match other fittings. If you want to fit a brass plate, the lighting cable must have an earth conductor connected to an earth terminal screw in the mounting box for the switch.

You may want to replace a switch with a dimmer. Connect this exactly as an ordinary switch.

You will need
Tools Insulated screwdrivers (one with a small, fine tip).
Materials Light switch.

1 Turn off the main switch at the consumer unit and remove the fuse for the circuit you are working on.

2 Remove the screws in the switch cover and ease the switch away from the mounting box. Keep the screws; the ones provided with the new switch may be metric and not fit the holes of the mounting box.

3 Use the fine-tipped screwdriver to release the conductors from the terminals behind the switch.

4 Screw the conductors tightly into place at the terminals behind the new switch. It does not matter which goes to which terminal. If there is an earth conductor in the cable, it will be connected to a terminal in the mounting box and there is no need to disturb it.

5 Screw the switch back in place until there is no gap left between it and the mounting box.

6 At the consumer unit, replace the fuse and turn on the electricity.

CHOOSING LIGHT SWITCHES

A modern switch is of the rocker type; it is pushed in at the bottom to turn the light on and in at the top to turn the light off, except in a two-way switch system where the switch may be on or off in either position. A single switch plate $3\frac{3}{8}$in (85mm) square can have one, two or three switches, and a double plate $3\frac{3}{8}$in (85mm) high and $5\frac{7}{8}$in (148mm) across can have four or six switches. The switchplates fit over standard single or double flush or surface-mounted boxes.

PLASTIC SWITCHES

The most common light switches are white plastic, designed to blend with light-coloured paintwork. There is no earth terminal for the cable behind plastic light switches; it is in the mounting box.

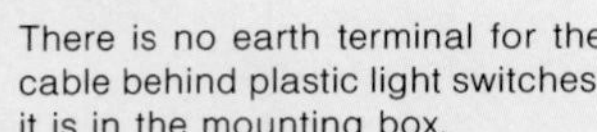

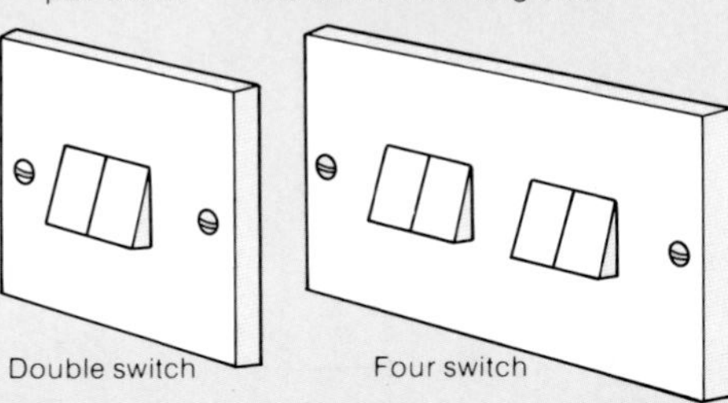

Single switch

Double switch

Four switch

METAL SWITCHES

Metal switches are made in satin finish or shiny brass or chrome; some have decorative scrolling at the edge. Be sure to choose makes of switch that have earth terminals. The switch rockers are fixed on plastic inserts.

Three switch – chrome

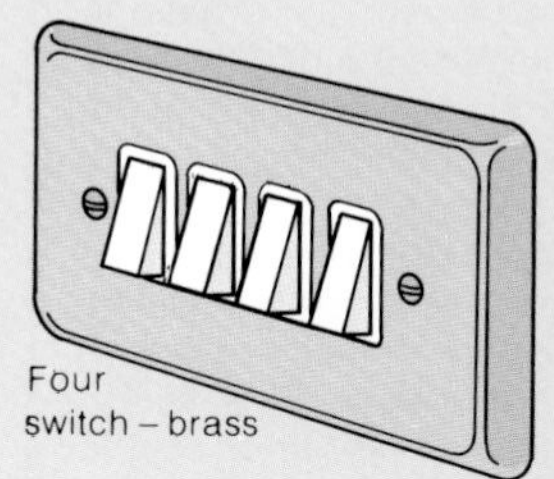

Four switch – brass

SLIM ARCHITRAVE SWITCHES

The switch can be fitted to a door architrave or in limited wall space – for example, where two door frames are so close together that there is not enough space between them for a standard switch. Mounting boxes are made to suit them.

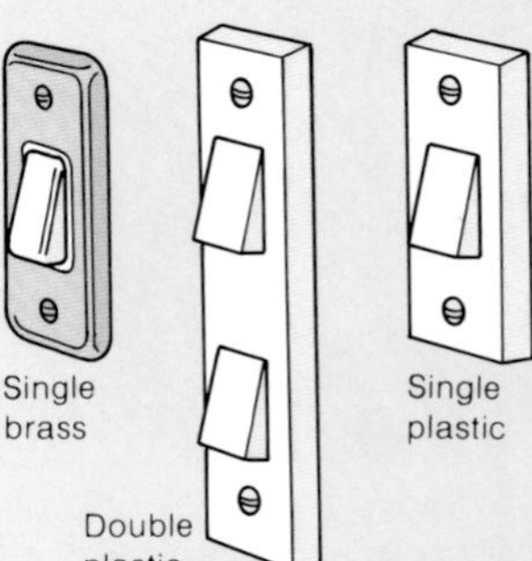

Single brass

Double plastic

Single plastic

DIMMER SWITCHES

In place of a standard rocker switch, you can fit a dimmer which controls the amount of light the bulb gives. Some dimmers have a sliding or turning switch; some have a touch switch that makes the brightness go alternately up and down when the plate is touched, while a quick touch turns it on and off. Dimmers cannot be used with fluorescent lights.

Double touch dimmer

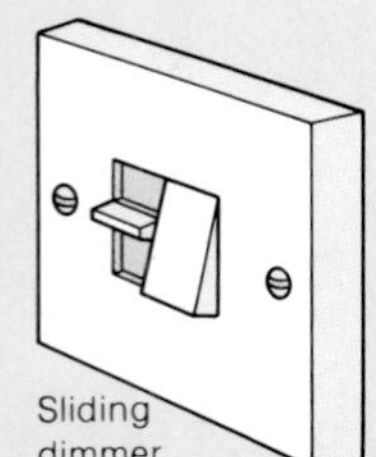

Sliding dimmer

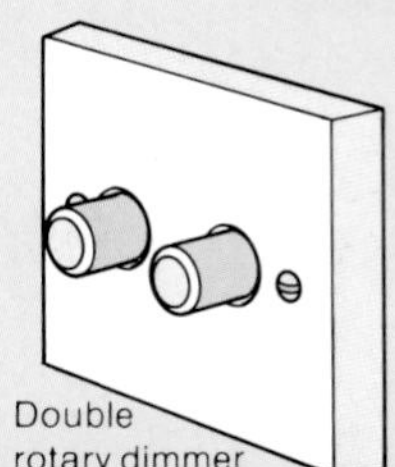

Double rotary dimmer

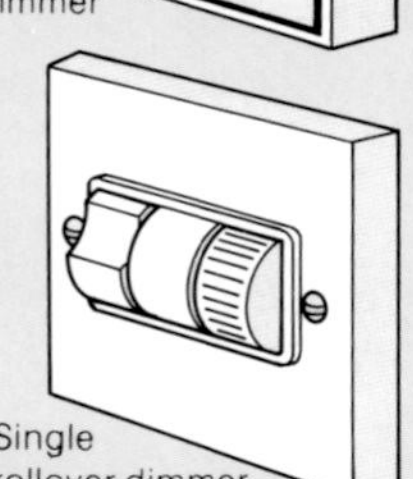

Single rollover dimmer

PULL-CORD SWITCH

A pull-cord switch is convenient over a bed and must be fitted in a bathroom to keep the mechanism well out of reach of anyone who is using the bath or shower.

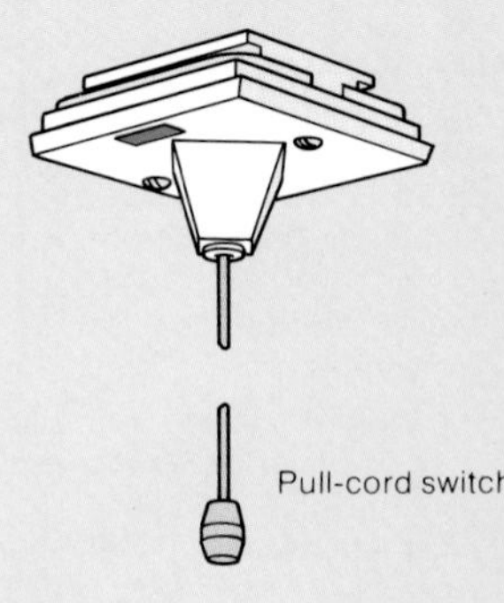

Pull-cord switch

REMOTE CONTROL SWITCHES

An infra-red signal from a control unit triggers wall-mounted receivers which act as switches. The receiver must be in sight of the control but can be up to 30ft (10m) away. The system is useful for disabled people. The control can be held in the hand or wall mounted.

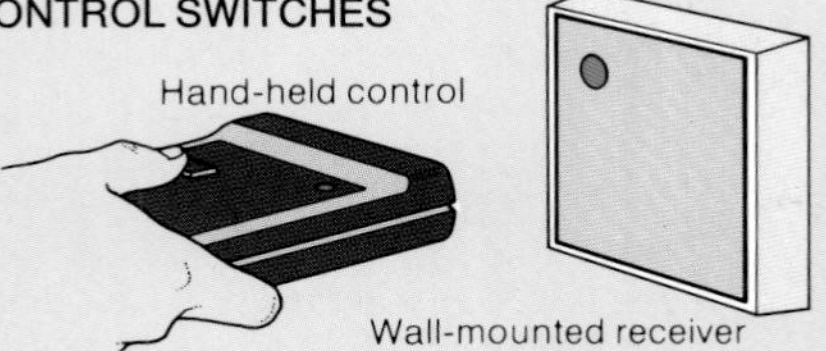

Hand-held control

Wall-mounted receiver

WEATHERPROOF SWITCH

A dustproof and moisture-proof seal fits over the switch and makes it suitable for fitting out of doors – in a porch or a greenhouse or on a patio. The switch is a rocker of the usual type but you cannot push it directly – only through the plastic 'bubble'.

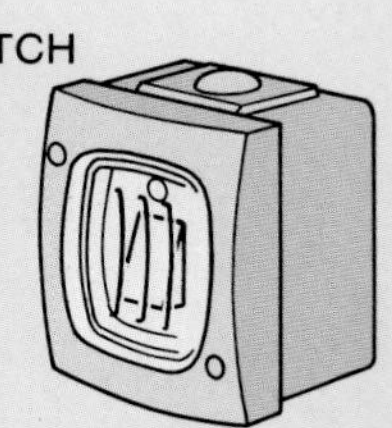

Replacing a one-way switch with a two-way system

If you fit two two-way switches, you can turn a light on and off from both switches. This is necessary for stairs and rooms with two entrances, and useful in a bedroom.

A length of three-core-and-earth cable has to be run between the two switches. A two-way switch has three terminals, usually marked L1 and L2 (or just 1 and 2) and COM (or COMMON). Occasionally, the common is marked A and the other two terminals A1 and A2. All two-gang switches are two-way, but you can use them on a one-way system (using the common terminal and either of the other two terminals).

In three-core-and-earth cable, the conductors are red, yellow and blue, and the earth bare. There are no regulations about which terminals the three colours should go to. Often the red is connected to the common, the yellow to L1 and the blue to L2. If your house already has two-way switches connected in this way, follow the same pattern. However, if this is your first two-way system, you can use an alternative, more logical, wiring pattern. It is also essential to tag the yellow and blue conductors with red sleeving because they become the line (live) conductors when the switch is on. Both methods are shown below.

You will need

Tools Tools for preparing the route (page 369); insulated screwdrivers (one with a fine tip); sharp knife; wire cutters and strippers; pliers; metal detector or fine bradawl.

Materials Two two-way switches; one single mounting box with screws and grommet; 1.0mm2 three-core-and-earth cable; green-and-yellow plastic sleeving; red plastic sleeving; oval conduit; galvanised nails (page 369).

1 Turn off the main switch at the consumer unit and remove the fuse for the circuit you are working on.

2 Unscrew the retaining screws that hold the one-way switch in place. Ease the switch away from the mounting box. Disconnect the two conductors from the terminals behind the switch and the earth conductor from the terminal in the mounting box.

If the cable has no earth conductor, use plastic switches and plastic mounting boxes. If the cable has an earth conductor, the mounting box must have an earth terminal; replace the box if necessary.

3 Prepare the route (page 369) from the new switch position, up the wall, above the ceiling and down the wall to the original switch position. Use a metal detector or fine bradawl to find the cable to the original switch. Enlarge the channel without damaging the cable.

4 Feed the cable into the conduit before securing it into the chase with galvanised nails (page 370). Fit the new mounting box into position and replaster (page 369).

5 Prepare the cable for connection (page 363); remember to sleeve the earth conductors. Use pliers to straighten the original conductors.

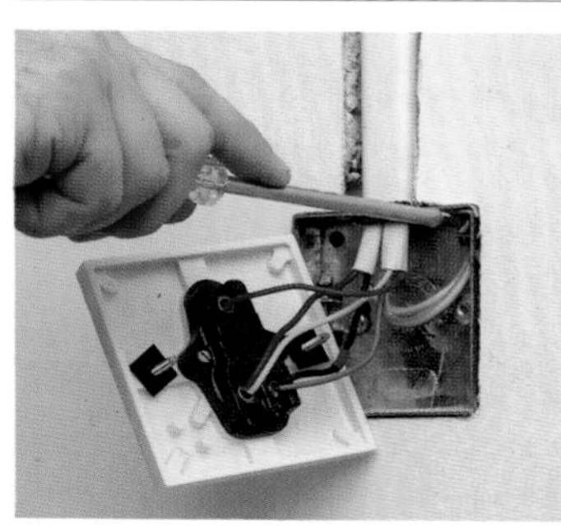

6 At the original switch position, connect the red conductor from the original cable and the new yellow conductor to the terminal marked L1 (or 1) on the new switch. Connect the red-tagged black conductor from the original cable and the new blue conductor to the terminal marked L2 (or 2). Connect the new red conductor to the terminal marked COM (or COMMON). Screw the two green-and-yellow-sleeved earth conductors into the terminal at the back of the mounting box.

7 Screw the switch in place until it meets the mounting box.

8 At the new switch, screw the red conductor in place at COM, the yellow at L1, the blue at L2, and the green-and-yellow-sleeved earth at the terminal in the mounting box.

9 Screw the new switch into place over its mounting box.

10 At the consumer unit, replace the circuit fuse, then switch the electricity back on.

SWITCHES AND MOUNTING BOXES ON TRUNKING

Trunking systems for carrying cable have mounting boxes and switches made to connect with mini-trunking or with an adaptor fitted to architrave trunking.

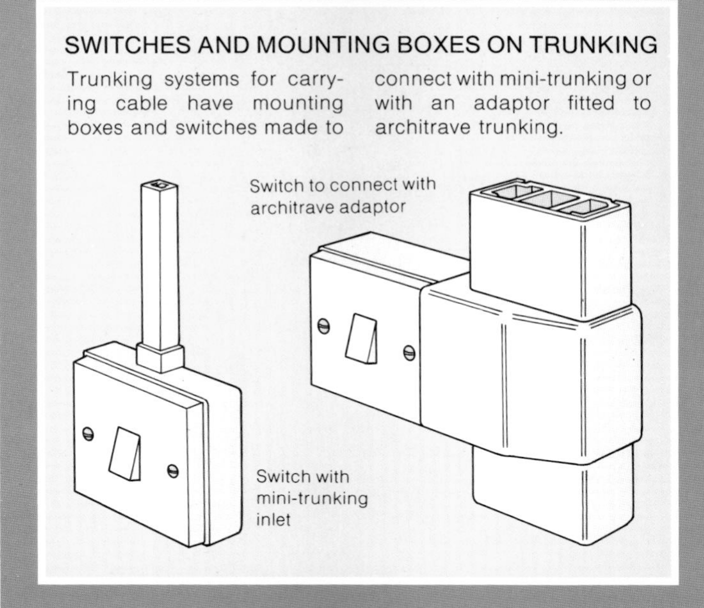

ALTERNATIVE METHOD OF CONNECTION

Follow steps 1-5 as above, then:

6 At the original switch position, connect the red conductor of the original cable and the red conductor of the three-core cable to the terminal marked L1 (or 1) on the new switch. Connect the black conductor of the original cable and the blue conductor of the three-core cable to the terminal marked L2 (or 2). Connect the yellow conductor of the three-core cable to the terminal marked COMMON. Screw both the green-and-yellow-sleeved earth conductors into the terminal at the back of the mounting box.

7 Screw the switch in place until it meets the mounting box.

8 At the new switch, connect the yellow conductor at COMMON, the red conductor at L1 and the blue conductor at L2. Connect the green-and-yellow-sleeved earth conductor to the terminal at the back of the mounting box.

Carry out steps 9 and 10 as above.

CHOOSING FITTINGS FOR YOUR LIGHTS

CONVENTIONAL LIGHT FITTINGS

A ceiling rose is the connecting point for the flex of a pendant light and the cable of the lighting circuit. The connection terminals on the base of the rose are hidden by the screw-on cover.

The body of a lampholder is concealed inside a two-part heat-resistant cover. It should be marked BS 5042 T2. The lampshade fits between the cover's two parts. Some holders have a deep shield over the bulb; they are for use where the lampholder is within reach of earthed metal.

A batten holder serves as a ceiling rose and lampholder combined. The bulb and shade are held at ceiling height – and at an angle by some batten holders.

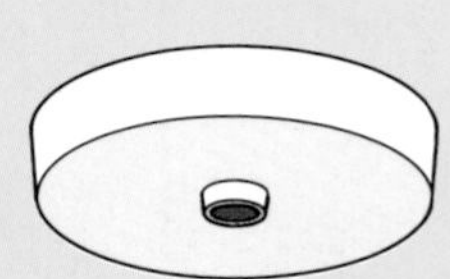
Ceiling rose

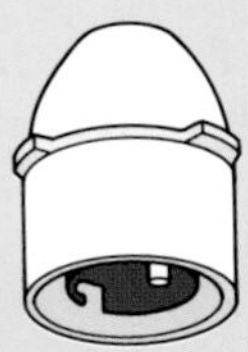
Lampholder

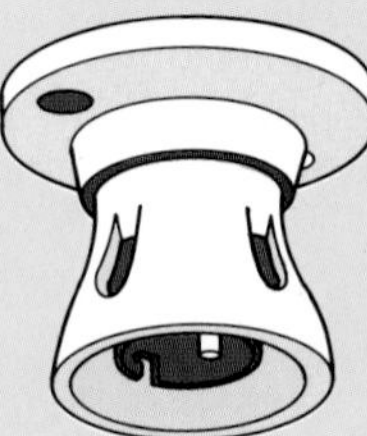
Batten holder

SPECIAL LIGHT FITTINGS

Fittings with connector blocks must have a heat-resistant cover over the terminals or be set into a heat-resistant recess above the ceiling. Covers can be obtained for most fittings. A spotlight directs light one way. It can be recessed into the ceiling, or surface mounted and angled, or mounted with others on a track. Eyeball lights are recessed and swivel to beam light at any angle. They all need about 5in (125mm) of space above the ceiling but vary in diameter. Downlighters can be fully or partly recessed; partly recessed ones are for shallow ceiling spaces. The spread of light narrows the more the fitting is recessed. Among the available covers are clear, sculpted and milky glass, a louvred baffle and a lens. Plastic baffles are made for strip lights.

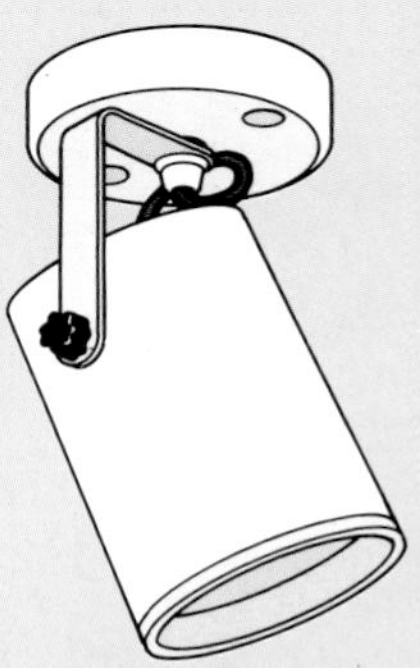
Ceiling-mounted spotlight

Recessed eyeball

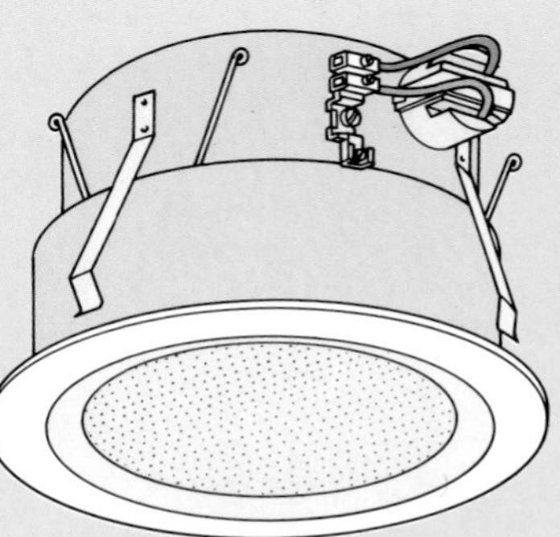
Recessed downlighter

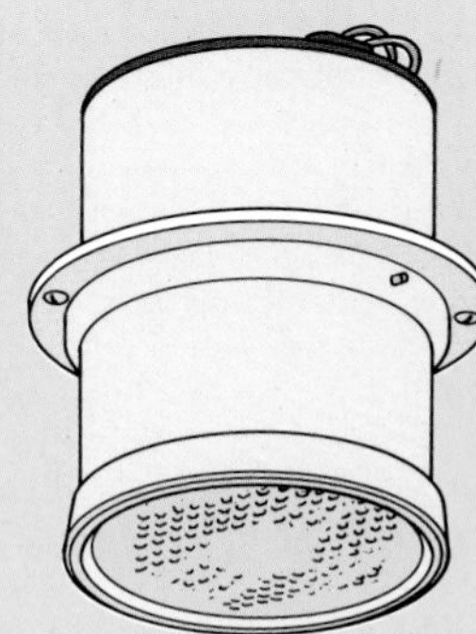
Partly recessed downlighter

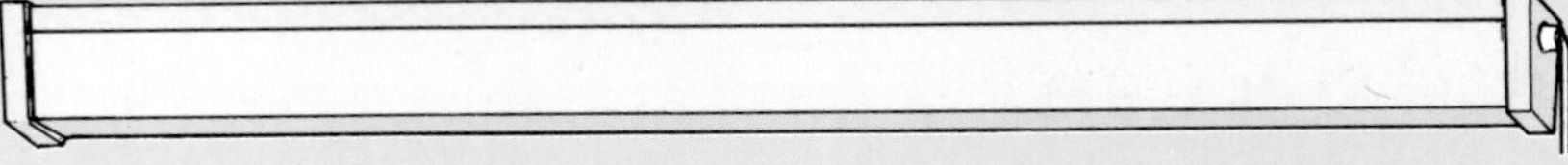
Backplate and baffle for fluorescent tube

FITTINGS FOR WALL LIGHTS

A conduit box, once called a BESA box, is recessed as a heat-resistant mounting box for a light fitting that has a wide round base to fit flush to the ceiling or wall. It will hold a terminal connector block cut from a strip. The block should be heat-resistant plastic, not the type made for electronic circuits.

Terminal connector block

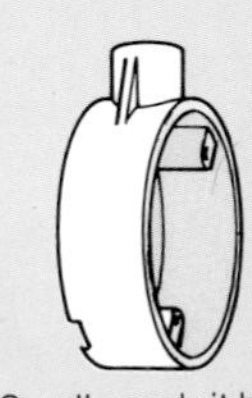
Small conduit box to use with internal wall light

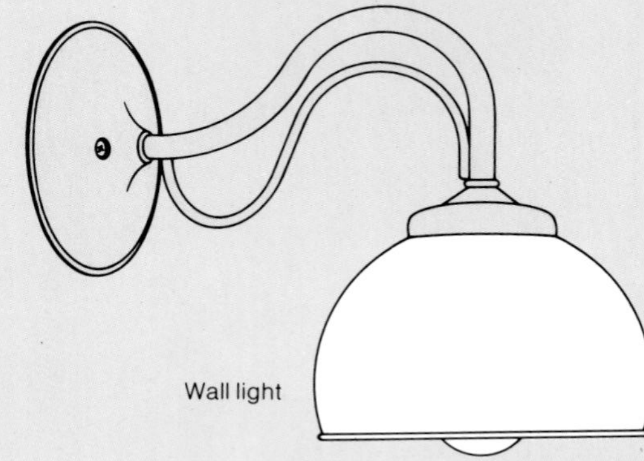
Wall light

Small conduit box to use with some external wall lights

LIGHTING TRACK

Track can be wall or ceiling mounted and lengths can be joined. Several types of small, neat light fittings are made to clip into the track. You can mount track over a lighting point or lead flex to it from a lighting point a short distance away. Make sure that you will not overload the circuit if you fit a multi-spot track.

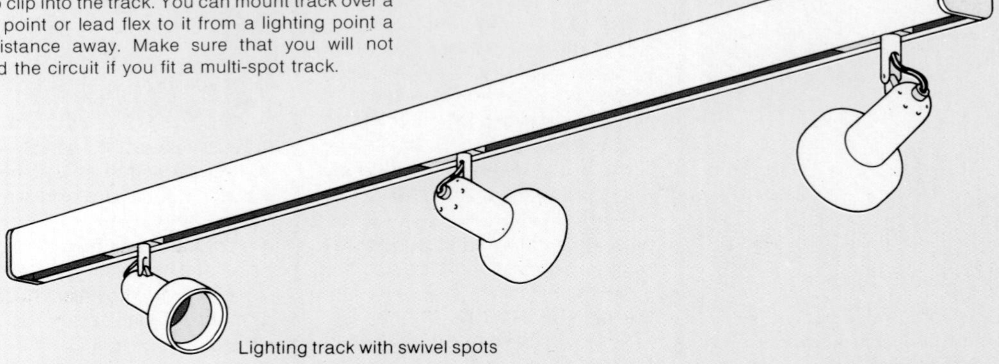
Lighting track with swivel spots

WEATHERPROOF WALL LIGHT

Outdoor fittings have seals to keep damp away from the connections.

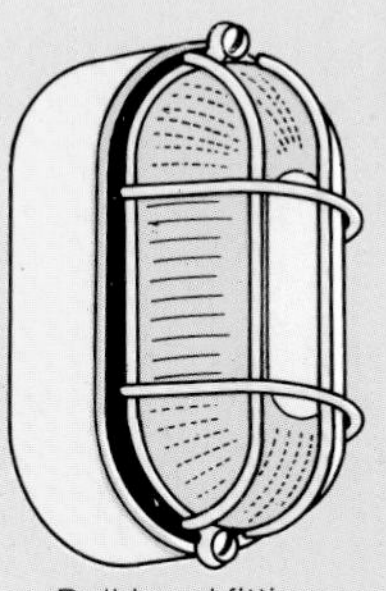
Bulkhead fitting

CHOOSING MOUNTING BOXES FOR LIGHT SWITCHES

Boxes can be metal or plastic for flush fitting, or plastic for surface mounting. A single mounting box will take a switchplate with one, two or three switches; a double box is needed for a switchplate with four or six switches. There is no earth terminal behind the switchplate, so metal boxes must have an earth terminal for the earth conductor of the lighting cable; many plastic boxes also have one. Trunking systems for cables that run along the surface of a wall have their own designs of mounting box.

FLUSH-MOUNTING METAL AND PLASTIC BOXES

A standard mounting box for a flush-fitted switch is made of metal and is 25mm deep. It is set in a cavity in the wall and screwed in place at the back. A plaster-depth box only 16mm deep is also made and can be used where it is difficult to cut into the wall enough for a standard-depth box, but the space for the conductors is more cramped.

There are also plastic boxes in both the 25mm and the 16mm depth.

Earth terminal

25mm metal box

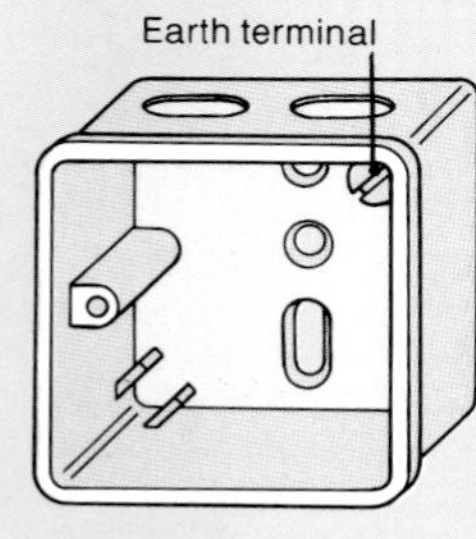

16mm plastic box

SURFACE-MOUNTING PLASTIC BOX

The mounting box and the switchplate together project about 1¼in (32mm) from the wall surface, but since no cavity is needed the work of fitting the box is much reduced. The boxes are plastic and 19mm deep.

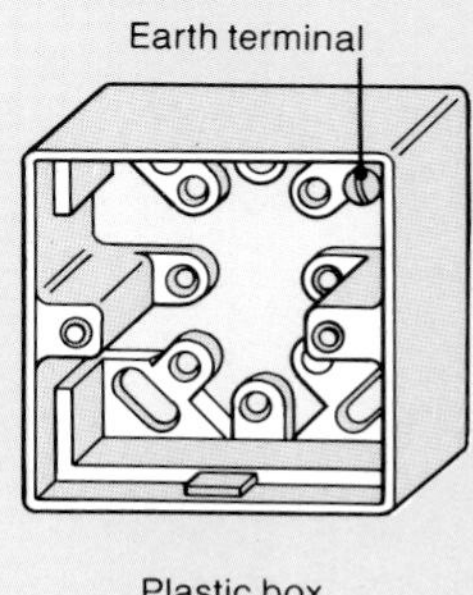

Plastic box

SLIM BOXES FOR ARCHITRAVES

Metal boxes to set in cavities for flush-mounted switches are 27mm deep; plastic boxes for surface mounting are 17mm deep. Both types are made with earth terminals and for single or double switches.

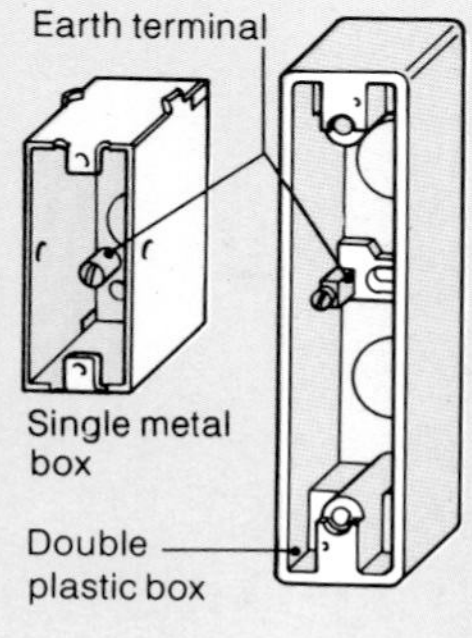

BOX FOR STUD PARTITION WALLS

Boxes for flush-fitting switches in plasterboard are made in both plastic and metal. The plasterboard is gripped between the lugs and the flange of the plastic box. Separate metal lugs are used to fix metal boxes.

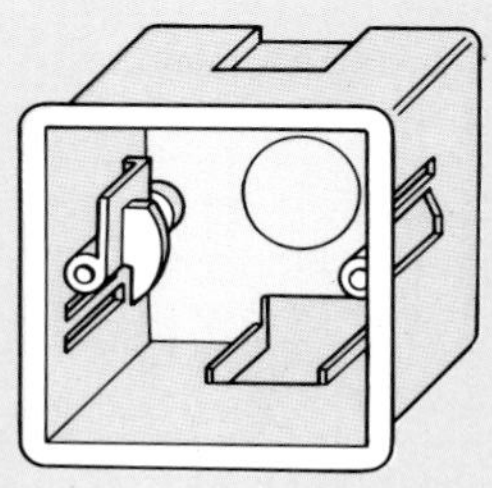

Plastic box with sprung lugs

Fitting a pull-cord switch

In a modern bathroom, the light is turned on by a pull-cord switch, but some older bathrooms still have a wall switch. It could be dangerous if a wiring fault made the switch live and it was touched by someone having a bath or shower; you should replace it.

A pull-cord switch is usually fitted also in a downstairs cloakroom and it may be convenient to have one in a store cupboard full of shelving, or over a bed.

You will need

Tools Tools for preparing the route (page 369); insulated screwdrivers, one with a fine tip; sharp knife; wire cutters and strippers; pliers.

Materials Pull-cord switch with fixing screws; perhaps green-and-yellow sleeving for earth conductor and plaster for making good.

PREPARATIONS

1 Turn off the main switch at the consumer unit and remove the fuse for the circuit you are working on.

2 Take out the screws of the old switch and ease it away from the wall so that you can disconnect the conductors of the switch cable.

3 Use a wiring detector or fine bradawl to trace the cable up the wall to ceiling level.

4 Use a hammer and chisel to knock out the plaster covering the top 6in (150mm) of the cable in the wall, then cut it off 3in (75mm) below ceiling level. Remove a floorboard above or go into the roof space and pull up the cable.

ALTERNATIVELY, if the old wiring is in a conduit, you can remove a floorboard above it or go into the roof space and pull up the cable once it has been disconnected from the switch. Cut it off, allowing 3in (75mm) to feed into the switch.

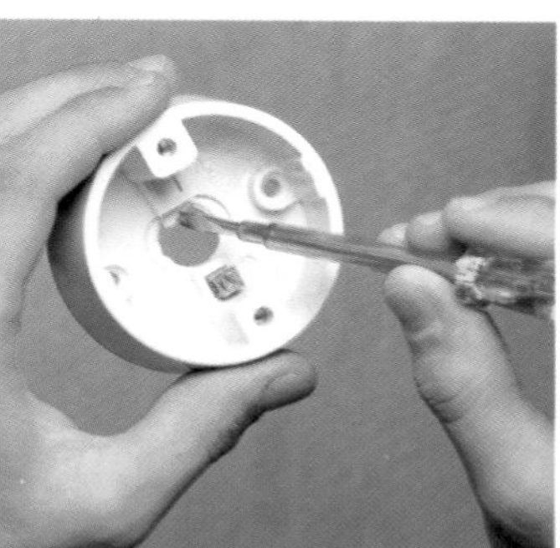

5 Undo the retaining screws that hold the pull-cord switch to its base. Push out the stamped knockout hole in the base of the box to make an entry for the cable.

6 Screw the base for the switch securely into timber above, as for a ceiling rose (page 369).

7 Feed the cable through from the back of the base.

8 Make good any plaster and wait for it to dry.

MAKING THE CONNECTIONS

1 Prepare the cable for connection (page 363). If you are using cable that was already in place, there may be no earth conductor.

2 If there is an earth conductor, slip green-and-yellow insulating sleeve over it. Screw the tip into the earth terminal, marked E or ⏚.

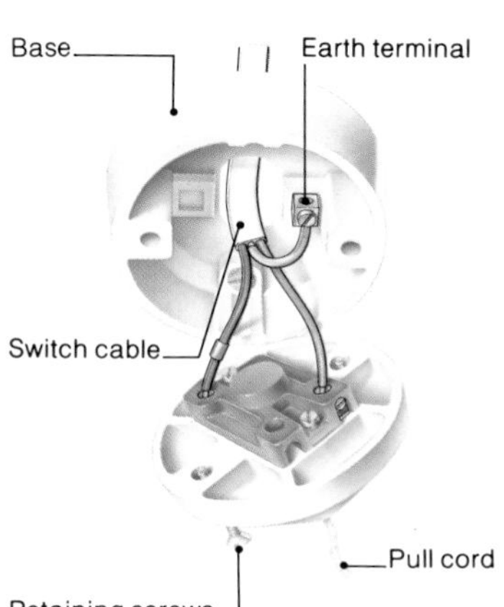

3 Screw the tips of the red and black conductors into the terminals behind the switch; it does not matter which goes to which terminal.

4 Press the switch gently over the base and screw it in place until there is no gap between the two. Do not overtighten the screws.

5 At the consumer unit, replace the fuse and turn on the main switch.

CHOOSING BULBS FOR YOUR LIGHT FITTINGS

Light bulb is the usual name for a tungsten filament lamp, which is the commonest home light source. Fluorescent tubes are used most often in kitchens.

Halogen lamps bring out natural colours and can give a softer light than most filament lamps. They are dear, but give more light and last twice as long.

Most bulbs have bayonet caps (BC) to push into a lampholder. Some have Edison screws (ES); these fit a special lampholder.

Filament light bulbs are made in a range of wattages, and last about 1000 hours. Long-life bulbs give a little less light and cost more, but last twice as long.

PEAR-SHAPED LIGHT BULBS
The most common light bulbs are General Lighting Service (GLS) bulbs. They are used in pendant lights and table and standard lamps. Some are squatter than others and described as mushroom-shaped. Clear bulbs give extra sparkle to glass lampshades while pearl bulbs diffuse the light more. White bulbs diffuse the light even more and reduce dazzle where the bulb is not covered by the lampshade. Coloured bulbs can give a soft glow, while brighter colours make special effects for parties.

HALOGEN LAMP
Halogen, a chemical additive to the gas in this lamp, gives high luminosity. It is interchangeable with normal lamps, is dimmable, gives 25 per cent more light than lamps of the same wattage, and has a 2000 hour life.

CANDLE-SHAPED AND ROUND BULBS
These bulbs for wall lights and small lamps may have small bayonet caps (SBC) or small Edison screws (SES).

INTERNALLY SILVERED LAMPS
A reflective back reduces scatter and directs light in a wide cone. ISLs are for recessed fittings.

CROWN SILVERED (CS) LAMPS
A reflective coating at the front makes the light form a narrow cone as it bounces off the reflector of a spotlight or downlight.

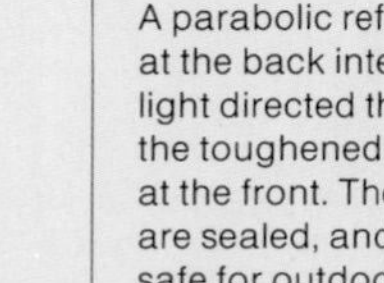

PRESSED GLASS (PAR 38) LAMPS
A parabolic reflector at the back intensifies light directed through the toughened glass at the front. The lamps are sealed, and so are safe for outdoor use. The version for floodlights has a wider beam than that for spotlights, which gives a very strong beam and is suitable only for fittings that can stand the heat it gives off.

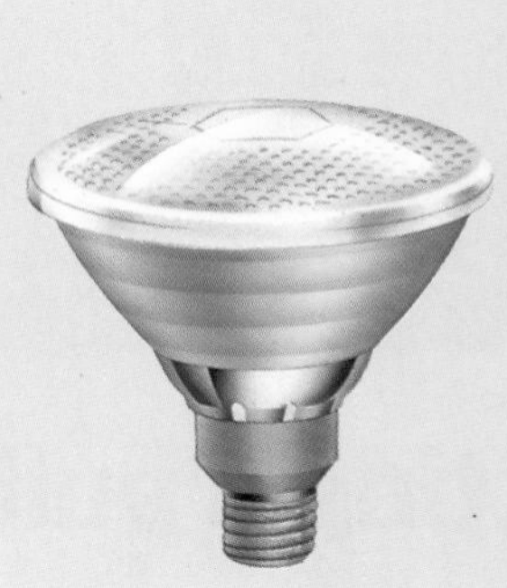

LINEAR FILAMENT LAMPS
The long, slender bulbs can have a cap at one end or at both. They are often fitted under shelves or over mirrors.

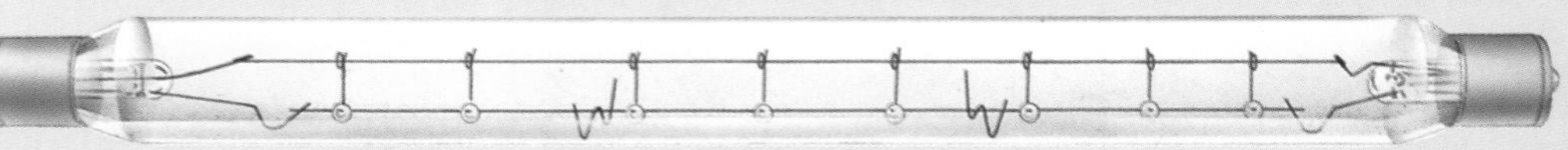

Adding a new lighting point on a spur

You can run a spur of cable from a lighting circuit to supply an extra light. Make sure the light will not take the load on the circuit above its safe limit of 1200 watts. There are three places where the spur can start: the last ceiling rose on a loop-in system (page 395); a box on a junction-box system (page 395); or a new junction box inserted into the circuit whether it is a loop-in or a junction-box system.

It is just possible to start a spur at a loop-in rose that is not last on the circuit, but there is barely room for the cable and its conductors. It is far easier to insert a junction box.

You will need
Tools Insulated screwdriver; tools for preparing the route (page 369); wire cutters and strippers; pliers.
Materials $1.0mm^2$ twin-core-and-earth cable; green-and-yellow plastic sleeving; cable clips. Perhaps a three-terminal junction box with slotted terminals; 3in × 2in (75mm × 50mm) batten.

PREPARATIONS

1 Turn off the main switch at the consumer unit and remove the fuse for the circuit you are working on.

2 Prepare a route (page 369) to the new lighting point from the spot where the spur will begin.

3 Lay the cable along the route allowing enough spare for it to reach the terminals easily.

ADDING TO THE LAST LOOP-IN CEILING ROSE

1 Unscrew the loop-in ceiling-rose cover and slide it down the flex.

2 Loosen the screws holding the rose to the ceiling. This will make it possible to work the new cable carefully through the ceiling in the same hole as the existing circuit cable and through the entry hole in the ceiling rose.

3 Prepare the new cable for connection (page 363).

4 Tighten the screws of the ceiling rose again, making sure that the new cable is not kinked between the rose and the ceiling.

5 Connect the new red conductor to the spare terminal in the central threesome, which already holds two red conductors.

6 Connect the black conductor to a terminal in the outer threesome – but not the outermost terminal which holds the blue conductor from the flex.

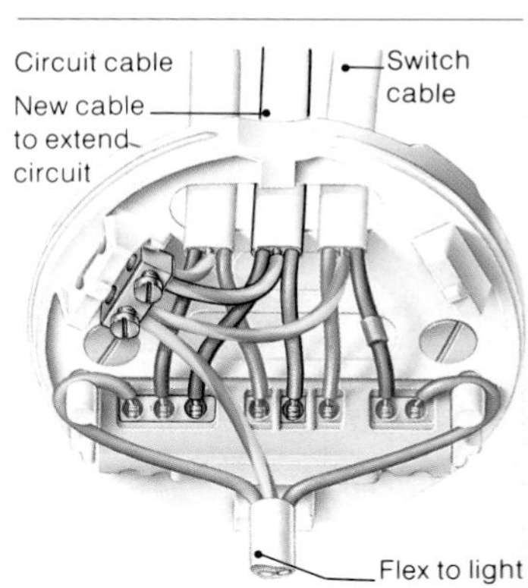

7 Connect the green-and-yellow-sleeved earth conductor to the separate earth terminal.

8 Screw the ceiling-rose cover back in place.

ADDING A SPUR TO A JUNCTION BOX WIRING SYSTEM

1 Remove the cover of the junction box where the spur will start. You can knock out an entry hole in it for the spur or let the spur share the same entry as an existing cable.

2 Prepare the spur for connection (page 363) and feed it into the box.

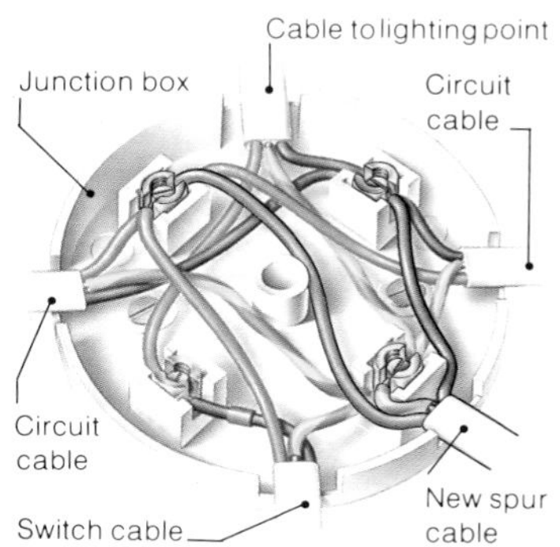

3 Connect the red conductor to the terminal where two or three red conductors are already connected. Connect the black to the terminal where two or three black conductors are already connected. Connect the green-and-yellow-sleeved earth to the terminal where the other earth conductors are already connected.

4 Screw the cover on the junction box.

LEADING A SPUR FROM A NEW JUNCTION BOX IN THE CIRCUIT

1 Trace the cable you are planning to tap into, to make sure that it is not the switch cable but the circuit cable from one loop-in rose or junction box to the next.

2 Screw the new junction box to the side of a joist, or to a batten nailed to the joist. Place the opened box so that the cable runs across it and is at least 2in (50mm) below the top of the joist.

3 Cut the cable over the centre of the box, then strip back enough of the outer sheath to allow the cores to reach their terminals with the sheath still within the box. Then strip about ½in (16mm) of the core insulation from the line (live) and neutral cores.

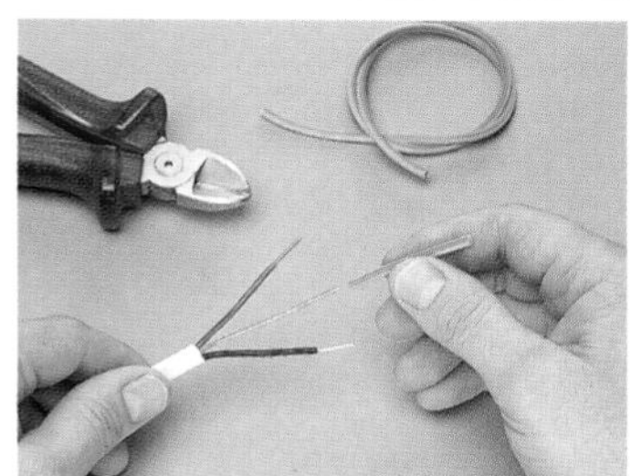

4 Sleeve the bare earth conductor with green-and-yellow-striped PVC sleeving (see page 361). Make sure you cover all of the bare conductor.

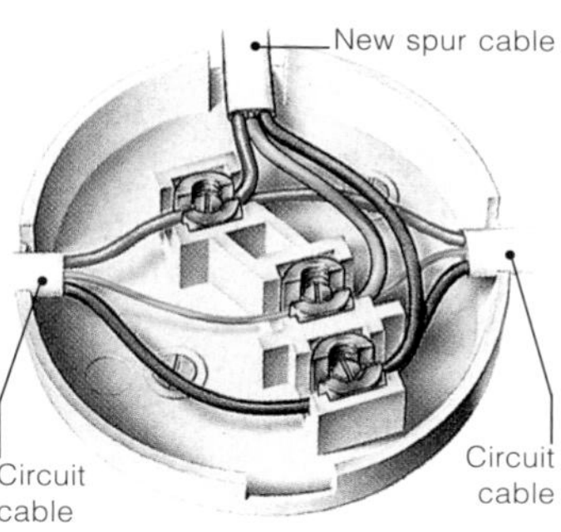

5 Prepare the ends of the spur for connection as shown on page 363.

6 Screw the spur's red, black and earth conductors into the same terminals as the circuit conductors. Then screw the cover back onto the junction box.

AT THE LIGHTING POINT

If the spur is for a pendant light, connect it as described in *Making loop-in connections at ceiling roses* (see page 396).

For a special light fitting, lead the spur to a junction box and then connect as described in *Wiring a lighting circuit* (pages 396-397) or for a wall-light as described below.

A SHAVER SOCKET ON A LIGHTING SPUR

You can add a shaver socket on a spur from the lighting circuit using one of the methods described here, provided that the circuit has an earth conductor.

1 Lead the spur from the lighting circuit to the socket position, using 1.0mm² twin-core-and-earth cable.

2 At the shaver socket position, at about shoulder height on the wall, fit a mounting box (page 374) that is purpose made for a shaver socket. Feed in the cable through the grommet.

3 Prepare the end of the cable for connection (page 363) and screw the conductors into the terminals behind the socket – red goes to L, black goes to N, and the green-and-yellow-sleeved earth goes to E or ⏚.

4 Press the socket gently over the mounting box and screw it in place until it meets the mounting box. Do not dislodge the conductors.

Adding a lighting point for a wall light

You can add a wall light by leading a spur (facing page) from an existing lighting circuit. The light may be for the wall of a room or for a porch or a patio.

The fitting for an indoor wall light may incorporate a switch; if it does not, you can take the spur in and out of a junction box and connect the switch cable to it there.

The connections at the light must be within a heat-resisting box so you may need to fit a conduit box in the wall. If the base of the lamp is too small to conceal a conduit box, use instead a slim architrave mounting box.

Choose a light that has been wired with an earth conductor or is double insulated (marked ⧈).

INDOOR WALL LIGHT

OUTDOOR WALL LIGHT

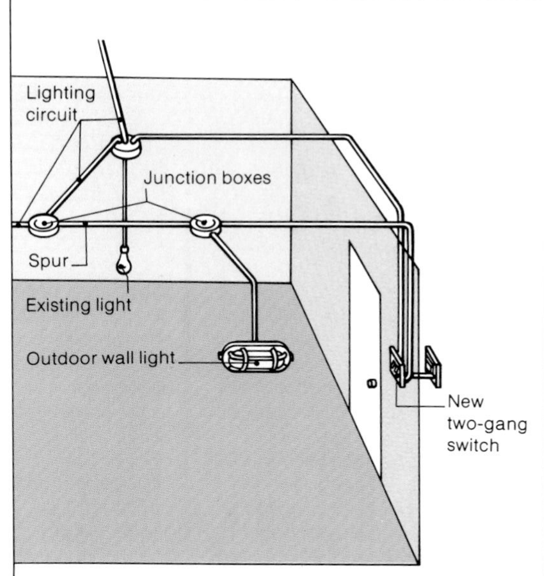

FITTING AN INDOOR WALL LIGHT

You will need

Tools Insulated screwdrivers; sharp knife; wire cutters and strippers; pliers; tools for preparing the route (page 369). Perhaps a circuit tester and fine bradawl.

Materials Wall light; 1.0mm² twin-core-and-earth cable; green-and-yellow plastic sleeving for earth conductors; conduit box with a side entry spout, or a slim architrave box and a short length of green-and-yellow-insulated earth conductor; connector block with three pairs of terminals (cut from a strip). Perhaps a three-terminal slotted junction box for connecting the spur; 3in × 2in (75mm × 50mm) softwood batten; wall plugs. For a separate switch, four-way junction box with fixing screws; red plastic sleeving; two-gang light switch.

PREPARATIONS

1 Switch off the electricity, using the main switch in the consumer unit, and withdraw the fuse for the circuit you will be working on.

2 Prepare the route (page 369) for the spur cable. You will need to lead it above the ceiling from a convenient spot on the lighting circuit to a point immediately above the wall light position, and then down the wall to the wall light position. This should be about 6ft (1.8m) above floor level. Make a recess there for the conduit box or slim architrave box.

ALTERNATIVELY, if the wall light does not incorporate a switch, lead

Adding a lighting point for a wall light (continued)

the spur cable route above the ceiling to a spot halfway between the wall light position and the switch position and fit the four-way junction box there. Continue the route from there to the wall light position and make another route from the junction box to a point directly above the switch. You will probably be able to complete the route by enlarging the recess in the plaster leading down the wall to the existing switch. Take great care not to damage the existing cable. Unscrew and disconnect the switch. You can use the single mounting box already fitted and fit a two-gang switch over it when you are ready to make the connections.

3 Lay the spur cable along the route from the circuit either to the wall light position; or to the junction box position and from there to the wall light position; and also to the switch position if necessary. Secure the cable along the route.

4 At the wall light, feed the cable into the conduit or architrave box. If you are fitting a switch, feed the switch cable into the mounting box.

5 Prepare the new cable ends for connection (page 363). If you are fitting a switch, slide a piece of red sleeving on each end of the switch cable's black conductor.

6 Connect the spur to the lighting circuit (see *Adding a new lighting point on a spur*, page 390).

7 Hold the wall light or its bracket in place and push the bradawl through its fixing holes to check that they match up with the lugs of the conduit box. If they do not align with the conduit box lugs – or if you are using an architrave box – make drilling marks with the bradawl. Drill at the marks and plug the holes.

8 Make good any plaster and wait for it to dry.

MAKING THE CONNECTIONS AT THE WALL LIGHT

1 Connect the red and black conductors from the cable that enters the conduit (or architrave) box to the two outer terminals on one side of the connector block.

2 At the central terminal on the same side, connect the green-and-yellow-sleeved earth conductor from the cable. If you are connecting within an architrave box, connect the short extra piece of insulated earth conductor also to the central terminal. Connect the other end of this short piece to the earth terminal in the box.

3 Connect the conductors from the wall light to the connector block with brown, blue, and green-and-yellow opposite red, black, and green-and-yellow respectively.

4 Screw the wall light over the conduit (or architrave) box.

MAKING THE EXTRA CONNECTIONS FOR A SEPARATE SWITCH

1 Make the connections behind the new two-gang switch. All two-gang switches are designed to operate two-way switch systems. When you use one as part of a one-way system you must use the Common terminal and one of the other two terminals. (Sometimes the terminals are marked A, A1 and A2 instead of Common, L1 and L2.) Connect the new red and red-sleeved black conductors to the two terminals marked Common and either L1 or L2.

Connect the conductors from the original cable to the second set of terminals in the same way. (These may be marked B, B1 and B2.)

Screw both the green-and-yellow-sleeved conductors into the terminal at the back of the box.

2 Screw the switch in place until it meets the mounting box.

3 At the junction box, connect the red conductors from the spur and switch cables to one terminal.

4 Connect the black conductors from the spur and the cable leading to the wall light to another terminal.

5 Connect the red conductor from the wall light cable and the red-sleeved black conductor from the switch cable to a third terminal.

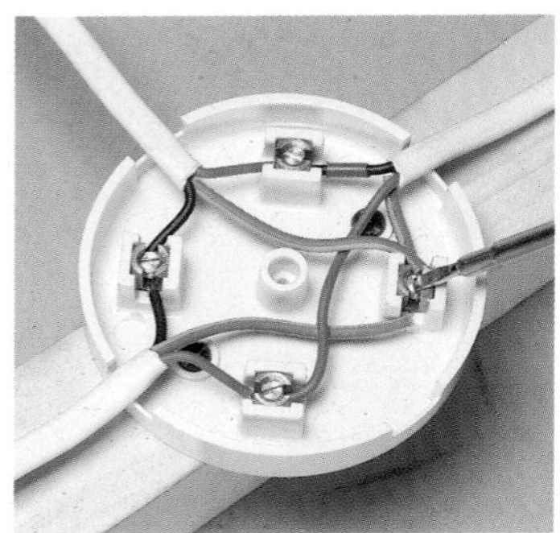

6 Connect the green-and-yellow-sleeved earth conductors to the fourth terminal.

7 Replace any floorboards (page 273).

8 Fit the light bulb and shade.

9 At the consumer unit, replace the fuse and turn the switch on.

FITTING AN OUTDOOR WALL LIGHT

To install a light on an outside wall – under a porch or on a patio – follow the same method as for an inside wall. Choose a weatherproof light fitting designed for an outside wall. If the light is on a bracket, not a flush-fitting base plate, you will need waterproof sealant or a rubber gasket to fit the bracket's base.

It is safest to have the switch indoors. You can take the cables for the light and the switch along the same route over the ceiling and down the indoor surface of the external wall where you are going to install the light. At the right height for the wall fitting – about 6ft (1.8 m) above ground level – drill from the back of the chase through the inner and outer leaves of the external wall to make a hole to lead the cable outside. Feed the light cable out through the hole.

Install and connect the junction box and the switch in the same way as for an indoor wall light.

Light on a base plate

1 Hold the base of the light against the wall and probe with a bradawl through the fixing holes to mark drilling spots on the wall. Drill holes at the marks and insert wall plugs in them.

2 Feed the cable through the base of the light fitting according to the maker's instructions and screw the base to the wall. Prepare the cable for connection (page 363).

3 Connect the red and black conductors to the terminals of the lampholder; it does not matter which the black or red goes to. Connect the green-and-yellow-sleeved earth conductor to the terminal marked E or ⏚.

Light on a bracket

1 If your light is on a bracket, not a base plate, you cannot reach the lampholder. Flex will have been connected to it already and the flex end will stick out from the bracket. Prepare the conductors and connect them to a connector block as for an indoor wall light. At the terminals on the opposite side of the block, connect the conductors of the light cable you have laid. Coat the rim of the bracket's base with sealant, or fit a rubber gasket of the right size.

2 Screw the light fitting into the drilled and plugged holes. Make sure that any sealant or gasket is squeezed tight against the wall to make a weatherproof seal.

FITTING AN OUTSIDE SWITCH

If you want a switch out of doors as well as inside for the new light, use a two-way sealed splashproof design. Put it on the outside wall back to back with a two-way indoor switch. You will need a short length of three-core-and-earth lighting cable for the connection between the two switches. Drill and chisel a cavity on the outside wall for the mounting box for the sealed switch. Drill a hole between the cavities for the indoor and outdoor switches for feeding three-core-and-earth cable through. Connect the cable as for *Replacing a one-way light switch with a two-way system*, page 387.

Replacing a pendant light with a rise-and-fall fitting

The lamp and shade of a rise-and-fall light hang on a curly flex which allows them to be lowered and raised. A tensioned control cord holds the light at the chosen height. When the fitting is raised, light spreads over the room; when the fitting is lowered, light is concentrated on one area, for example a table or desk. You will need access to the joists above the light position. The wiring is connected inside a heat-resisting plastic conduit box. This must be securely fixed to timber above the ceiling because the load on the fixing is considerable when you pull the light to lower it.

You will need

Tools Insulated screwdrivers; bradawl; pencil; sharp knife; wire cutters and strippers; pliers; claw hammer; pad saw; drill with twist bit; chisel. *Materials* Rise-and-fall fitting; small plastic conduit box with back entry, complete with fixing screws; batten of 3in × 2in (75mm × 50mm) softwood to fit between the joists; four 1in (25mm) angle brackets with ¾in (19mm) No. 8 screws for fixing; one-way connector block. Perhaps red plastic sleeving; three-way connector block if the light fitting does not include one; perhaps a screw eye about 2in (50mm) long.

REMOVING THE CEILING ROSE

1 Turn off the main switch at the consumer unit and remove the fuse for the circuit you are working on.

2 Take out the light bulb and remove the lampshade of the pendant light.

3 Unscrew the cover of the ceiling rose and slide it down the flex to reveal the terminals.

4 Identify the switch return conductor in a loop-in ceiling rose (page 384) if this has not been done. Release the conductors of what you think is the switch cable, turn on the light switch and grip the red conductor tip with the clip of a circuit continuity tester. Touch the probe to the black conductor tip. The tester should light up. Slip a red sleeve over the black insulation.

5 Unscrew the terminals holding the brown and blue conductors of the light flex. If the flex has an earth conductor, release it. Take down the flex.

6 Unscrew the remaining conductors.

7 Unscrew the ceiling-rose base from the ceiling and remove it.

FITTING THE CONDUIT BOX

1 Examine the ceiling from above, lifting one or two floorboards to give access to the joist on each side of the lighting point. If the ceiling rose has been positioned wholly or partly under a joist, you will have to set the conduit box in a slightly different position so that the joist does not prevent the box from being recessed. If you have to change the position, push a bradawl through the ceiling from above to show where the joist's edge is.

2 From below, hold the conduit box against the ceiling and draw a line all round it to show where to saw.

3 Cut round the guideline carefully with a pad saw to make the hole.

4 Withdraw the cables from the hole so that you can fit the conduit box beneath them.

5 With a helper holding the conduit box flush with the ceiling, rest the piece of batten in position between the joists. The helper can make a drilling mark on the batten through the spout of the box.

6 Still with the box held in place, rest the batten on the body of the box. Mark the fixing height for the batten on the joist at each end.

7 Drill and chisel through the batten at the marked spot to make a hole for the spout of the box.

8 Secure the batten to the joists in the marked position, using two angle brackets at each end.

9 Screw the conduit box to the batten from below through two of the holes in the back of the box.

10 For a screw eye and hook fixing, drive the eye through one of the spare holes in the back of the box into the timber above. If there is no spare hole, drill one.

MAKING THE CONNECTIONS

1 Feed the cables through the spout of the conduit box.

2 Check that the conductors will reach the connector blocks easily; strip the sheath further if necessary, but only a little; the blocks should be within the conduit box, not dangling into the cover which may not be heat-resisting.

3 If the fitting is supplied with the flex already in the connector block, disconnect it. It is easier to connect cables before flex.

TYPICAL RISE-AND-FALL FITTINGS

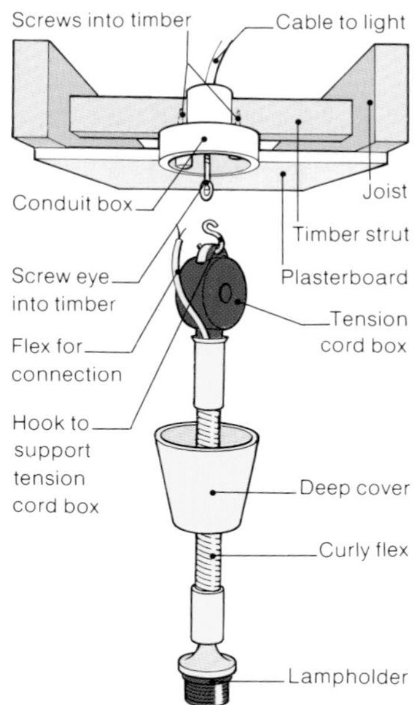

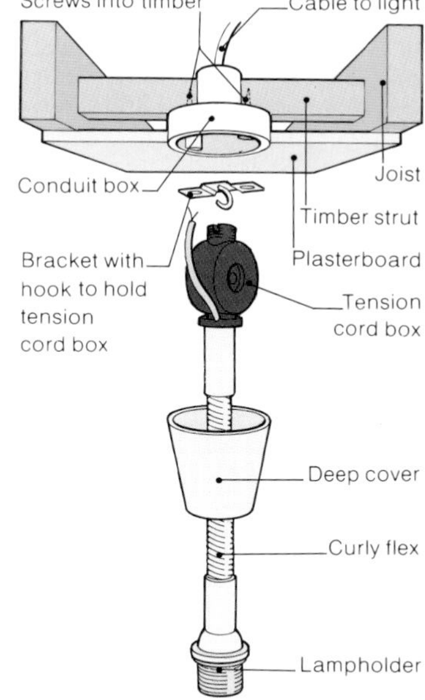

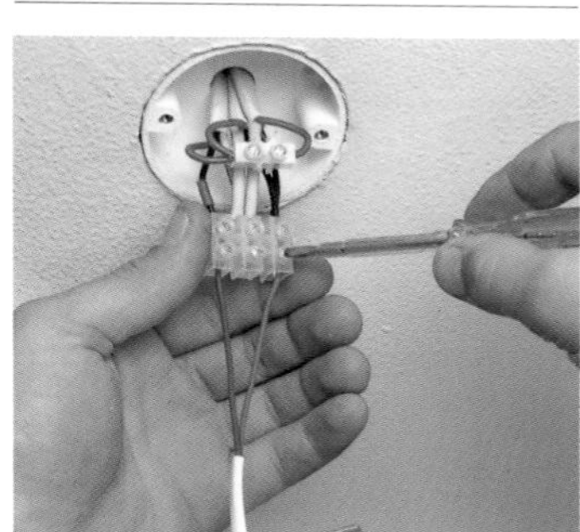

4 On a loop-in wiring system, first connect the red-sleeved black conductor to a terminal at one end of the connector block. In the central terminal on the same side screw all the earth conductors. (If they are not covered with green-and-yellow sleeving, sleeve them before connection.)

Connect the black conductors from the other two cables to the remaining terminal.

Connect the red conductors to the one-way connector block. Those from the two circuit cables go to different terminals. The red conductor from the switch cable can go to either terminal. Connect the conductors from the light flex to the terminals on the other side of the connector block. The brown goes opposite the red-tagged black conductor, the green-and-yellow in the centre, and the blue opposite the black conductors of the circuit cables. If the light fitting is double-insulated (marked ⧈), it will not have an earth conductor to connect to the block.

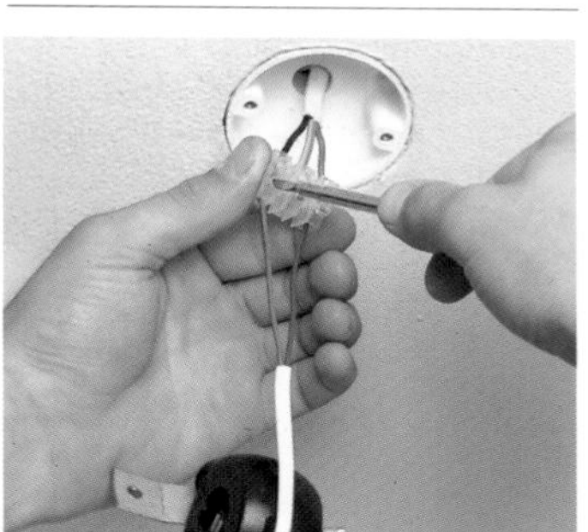

ALTERNATIVELY, with a junction box wiring system, only one cable will enter the conduit box. Use a three-way connector block and connect the red and black conductors to the outer terminals, the green-and-yellow-sleeved conductor to the central terminal. Connect the light flex as for a loop-in system.

5 Screw the bracket of the rise-and-fall fitting to the lugs of the conduit box and hook the tension cord box of the light fitting to it. ALTERNATIVELY, with a screw eye and hook fixing, slip the hook through the tension cord box and lodge the hook in the screw eye.

6 Fit the lampshade and light bulb to the rise-and-fall fitting.

7 Adjust the tension screw of the fitting according to the manufacturer's instructions to make the light balance.

8 Screw or slide the cover in place over the fixing and tension cord box of the rise-and-fall fitting.

9 At the consumer unit, replace the fuse and turn on the main switch.

Fitting a fluorescent light to a cupboard or shelf

A built-in cupboard which is dark at the back can be lit by a fluorescent strip fitted inside. Choose a slim strip, only two or three inches deep including the base plate it is mounted on; it will project very little from the wall or shelf and be safer from accidental knocks than a bulkier fitting. The smallest strip is only 12in (300mm) long.

If the cupboard is wide as well as deep, you can fit a row of two or three miniature strips that are designed to be linked by short lengths of flex supplied with pins already fitted. If you are going to put the light near the front of the cupboard, you can choose one that incorporates a pull-cord switch. If the light will be out of easy reach, at the back of the cupboard, you will need a separate switch.

You can install a miniature strip light in the same way under a permanently fixed shelf in an alcove, or under wall-hung kitchen cupboards to throw light onto a work surface beneath. A narrow trim along the front of the shelf (page 175) will conceal the strip light. Some lights have a built-in push-button switch, which is convenient under a shelf or cupboard.

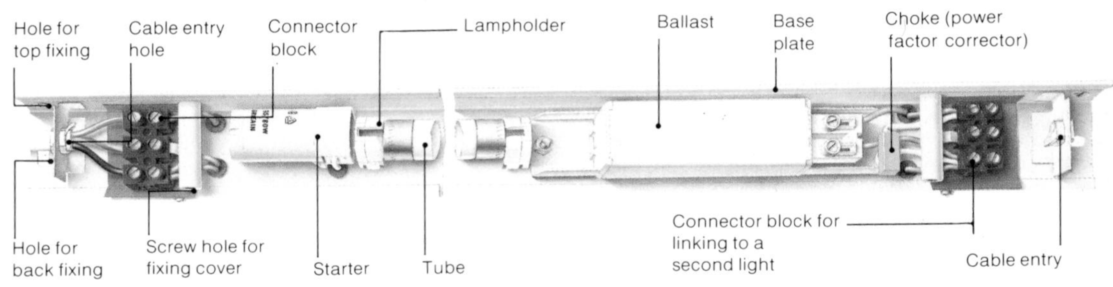

If you want to fit a very slender strip – along the back edge of a display shelf, for example – it is possible to fit the tube alone in terry clips; flex with pins already fitted leads from the clips to the ballast, starter and switch which have to be mounted elsewhere.

To connect the fitting to the electricity supply, lead a spur to it from the lighting circuit (page 390).

You will need

Tools Bradawl; tools for preparing the route (page 369); sharp knife; wire cutters and strippers; insulated screwdrivers; pliers.

Materials Miniature fluorescent strip light with built-in ballast and starter; 1.0mm^2 twin-core-and-earth cable; some green-and-yellow plastic sleeving for the earth conductors; cable clips. Perhaps also 3in × 2in (75mm × 50mm) softwood batten and nails to fix it between ceiling joists; four-way 20amp junction box; one-way light switch with mounting box, fixing screws and grommet; red plastic sleeving; insulating tape.

PREPARATIONS

1 Remove any baffle and end covers from the fitting. Hold the base plate against the ceiling, wall or shelf; make marks with a bradawl through the fixing points and, if necessary, the cable entry hole.

2 For fixing to wood, drill pilot holes at the marks.

ALTERNATIVELY, for fixing to a wall, drill and plug holes at the marks.

ALTERNATIVELY, for fixing to a ceiling, check with a fine bradawl that the fixing screws will be entering joists. If not, adjust the position of the light slightly or fix a batten between the joists to give sound timber for screwing the light into.

3 For ceiling fitting, drill a hole at the marked spot large enough for the cable to enter. If the spot is immediately below a joist, work from the loft or ceiling space to drill or chisel the underside of the joist, making a groove large enough to accommodate the cable.

4 Screw the base plate of the light fitting firmly in place.

CHOOSING FLUORESCENT LAMPS

A fluorescent tube gives almost five times as much light as a filament bulb of the same wattage. A tube costs more but its life is 7500 or more hours in use. There are now tubes that give a warm white light much closer in colour to that of filament bulbs than the rather cold white tone of earlier tubes. Coloured tubes are also made now. Slim fluorescent tubes twisted into compact shapes are beginning to replace conventional bulbs. They are dearer but give at least 5000 hours of use.

STRIPS

Fluorescent strips range from pencil-slim lamps 12in (300mm) long and only 8 watts, to the more common 1½in (38mm) diameter 5ft (1.5m) tube of 65 watts. They can be operated by an ordinary switch or by a built-in push button or pull cord.

CIRCLES

Circular lamps of three sizes are available – 8¼in (210mm) diameter and 22 watts, 12in (300mm) diameter and 32 watts, and 16in (400mm) diameter in either 40 or 60 watts. The only colour is warm white. Special fittings are available to conceal the control gear and lamp. They have circular diffusers in patterned and moulded glass or acrylic to give a sparkling or milky effect. The fittings are designed for flush mounting on the ceiling and project about 4in (100mm) down from it. The fixing point is at the centre.

SQUARES

The tube, bent into a broad flat shape 5½in-8in (140mm-200mm) across or arranged in the form of short pillars, can be used in specially designed fittings, or it can be used in most ordinary light fittings provided that an adaptor is first plugged into the lampholder. The adaptor is about 3½in (90mm) deep.

CYLINDERS

The tube is in a glass holder larger and heavier than a light bulb. One version fits a normal lampholder, another fits into a range of light fittings.

TUBES

A compact, energy-saving arrangement of small tubes. A 9-watt version gives the same light as a 40-watt bulb; an 18-watt version, the same light as a 75-watt bulb. Their life is 8000 hours.

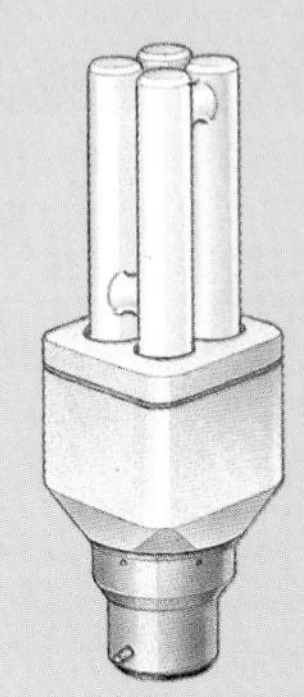

FITTING A LIGHT WITH A BUILT-IN SWITCH

1 Turn off the main switch at the consumer unit and remove the fuse for the circuit you are working on.

2 Lead a spur from the lighting circuit (page 390) right to the point where the light is fitted and thread it into the fitting through the cable entry hole.

3 Repair the plaster and let it dry. Refit any floorboards (page 273).

4 Prepare the cable for connection (page 363).

5 Connect the spur to the lighting circuit.

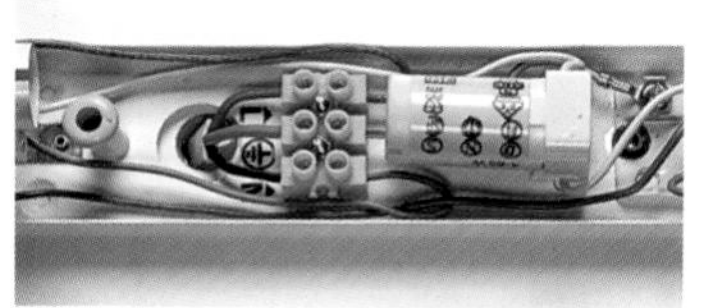

6 Connect the cable conductors to the terminals of the connector block in the light fitting, which already holds the flex conductors. Connect the red opposite the brown flex conductor, the black opposite the blue flex conductor, and the green-and-yellow-sleeved conductor to the terminal marked E or ⏚. If the fitting is double-insulated (marked ⧈) and has no earth terminal, bend back the earth conductor of the cable and seal it with insulating tape.

7 Screw the end covers in place and fit the baffle.

8 At the consumer unit, replace the fuse and turn the main switch on.

FITTING A LIGHT AND SEPARATE SWITCH

1 Turn off the main switch at the consumer unit and remove the fuse for the circuit you are working on.

2 Lead a spur from the lighting circuit (page 390) to a junction box in the ceiling space or loft above the position for the light.

3 Prepare the cable routes (page 369). You will need one from the junction box to the lighting point and another from the junction box to the switch position. Fit a mounting box (page 369) for the switch.

4 Lay cable from the junction box to the light. Feed it into the light fitting through the entry hole.

5 Lay cable from the junction box to the light switch position and feed it into the mounting box.

6 Make good any plaster and wait for the repairs to dry.

7 Prepare all the cable ends for connection (page 363). Remember to put a piece of red plastic sleeving over the black conductor of the switch cable at both ends.

8 Screw the light fitting in place and connect the cable to the terminal block as for *Fitting a light with a built-in switch* (left, step 6). Fit the end covers and baffle.

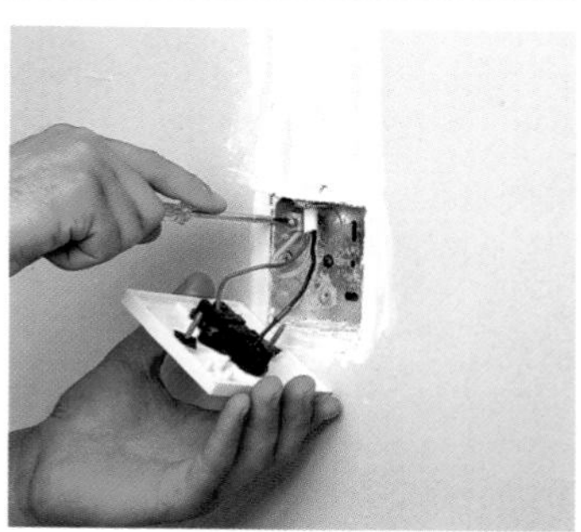

9 At the light switch connect the red conductor to one of the terminals behind the switch and the red-sleeved black conductor to the other terminal. Connect the green-and-yellow-sleeved conductor to the earth terminal screw in the mounting box. Screw the switch in place until it meets the box.

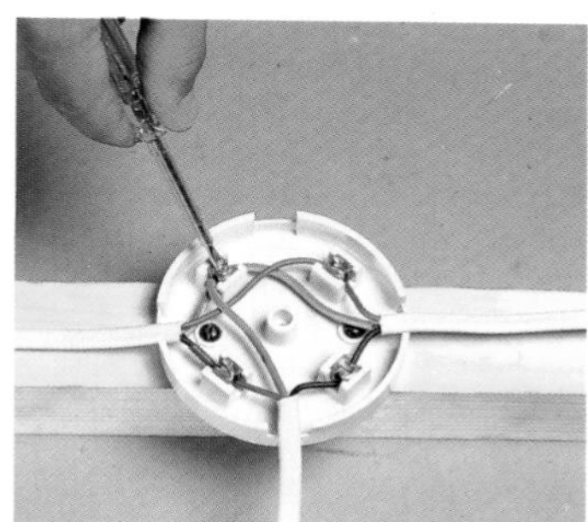

10 At one terminal in the junction box connect the red conductors of the spur cable and the switch cable. At another terminal connect the black conductors of the spur cable and the cable from the light. At a third terminal connect the red conductor of the cable from the light and the red-sleeved conductor from the switch. At the fourth terminal connect all the earth conductors. Screw the cover on the junction box.

11 At the consumer unit replace the fuse and turn on the power.

12 Refit any floorboards that were lifted (page 273).

Wiring a lighting circuit

Lighting circuits are wired with 1.0mm^2 twin-core-and-earth cable. A house usually has two lighting circuits, one serving the downstairs rooms and the other the upstairs rooms. Each circuit leads from the consumer unit to the various lighting points on the circuit, linking them in a chain and ending at the last lighting point.

A lighting circuit is protected by a 5amp fuse at the consumer unit. The maximum load that one circuit can supply is 1200 watts – that is twelve 100 watt light bulbs, or any combination of wattages adding up to 1200 – but in practice not more than ten lighting points are connected to one circuit. Bear this in mind especially when considering fitting a multi-spotlight track; it could overload the circuit and may require an extra circuit.

For each lighting point on the circuit, the cable passes through either a loop-in ceiling rose or a junction box and is connected to terminals there. From the rose or junction box, wiring leads off to the light and to the light switch. In many houses, a lighting circuit will include both loop-in ceiling roses and junction boxes.

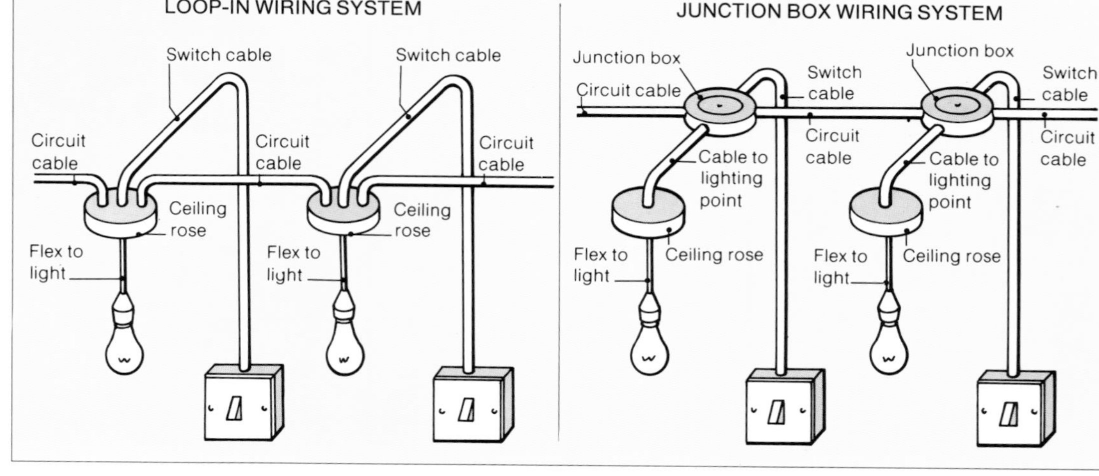

LOOP-IN SYSTEM

The modern ceiling rose has a row of terminals to receive conductors from four cables – the cable bringing in the power, the cable carrying the power on to the next lighting point on the circuit, the cable leading to the switch that will control the light, and the flexible cable (flex) that goes to the lampholder. If the rose is the last one on the circuit, there will not be a cable leading on to another lighting point.

All the connections, except the earths, are in the same row of terminals. All can be reached simply by unscrewing the cover. There is no need to lift floorboards in the room above to reach them as with junction boxes.

JUNCTION BOX SYSTEM

The circuit cable is not led to the lighting point but to a junction box between the lighting point and the switch position. The junction box has four sets of terminals for receiving the conductors of four cables – the cable bringing in the power, the cable carrying the power on to the next junction box, the cable leading to the light switch and the cable that goes to connect with the light flex at a ceiling rose or at a light fitting flush on a ceiling or wall.

This system is seldom used for a whole lighting circuit because of the extra work involved in installing a junction box for each lighting point, and the fact that once the wiring is completed the connections are not accessible without lifting a floorboard. But there are some situations where it is needed for individual lighting points. For example, strip lights, spotlight tracks, recessed lights, and some other special fittings are not designed for linking to two circuit cables as loop-in ceiling roses are; instead they incorporate a connection block or a flex for connection to a cable from a junction box.

Wiring a lighting circuit (continued)

PLANNING THE CIRCUIT

Consider whether each lighting point will be better suited by loop-in or junction box wiring. Position any junction boxes in a ceiling space or loft where you can screw them to joists. Use screws rather than nails to hold down the piece of floorboard (spanning two joists) over the junction box for easy lifting later.

You may have to run the circuit cables on the wall and ceiling surfaces. Lead them horizontally across walls, as close to the ceiling as possible. Conceal them with plastic trunking.

Cables to light switches must go from the rose or junction box to a spot directly above the switch and then be chased in plaster or led inside a stud partition wall or in trunking vertically down the wall. Never run cables diagonally across walls; there is a danger of piercing them later with fixings for pictures or built-in furniture.

INSTALLING THE CIRCUIT

You will need

Tools Tools for preparing the route (page 369); sharp knife; wire cutters and strippers; insulated screwdrivers; pliers.

Materials 1.0mm^2 twin-core-and-earth cable; green-and-yellow sleeving; red sleeving; flex of suitable type (page 362); lampholders; light switches with mounting boxes, screws and grommets; ceiling roses; 5amp fuse for consumer unit. Perhaps 1.0mm^2 three-core-and-earth cable for two-way switches; junction boxes; two-way switches; special light fittings; conduit boxes.

1 If you are replacing an existing circuit, turn off the main switch at the consumer unit and withdraw the fuse protecting the circuit you will be working on. Open the consumer unit and disconnect the red, black and green-and-yellow earth conductors of that circuit from the terminals.

Do not replace the fuse, but you can replace the cover and turn on the main switch if you wish until you are ready to connect at the consumer unit. The work will take some time and you will need to use other circuits. Make sure the disconnected conductors do not touch any other terminals.

WARNING
The main switch disconnects only the fuses or MCBs and the cables leading out from the consumer unit to the household circuits. It does NOT disconnect the cables entering via the meter from the service cable. Do not interfere with these cables. They are always live at mains voltage.

Trace the cable, lifting floorboards where necessary and removing old materials as you go.

2 Prepare the route (page 369) for the circuit cable. Lead it up from a point above the consumer unit to ceiling level and then to each lighting point in turn. If it is to go above the ceiling, you will have to lift floorboards to run it along and through joists. For surface fixing, you will have to chase into plaster or fit plastic trunking.

3 Prepare the routes for the switch cables which will run from every loop-in ceiling rose or junction box to the switch positions. If a light is to be controlled by two-way switches (page 387), prepare a route to the second switch position.

4 For lighting points that will be wired on the junction box system, prepare routes from the junction boxes to the positions for lights.

5 Fit ceiling roses (page 370) where there are to be pendant lights.

6 Fit junction boxes where necessary for special light fittings, screwing the base of each to the side of a joist. The rim of the junction box should be positioned so that no cable is less than 2in (50mm) below the top of the joist.

7 Fit mounting boxes (page 369), with grommets, for all the switches.

8 Lay lengths of cable from the consumer unit to the first ceiling rose or junction box, from there to the next rose or box, and so on. Leave enough extra at the ends of the lengths of cable for the conductors to reach all the terminals easily. Secure the cable by threading it through joists; or driving in clips to hold it to the sides of joists or in chases in plaster; or pressing the cover on trunking. Do not draw the cable tight or bend it sharply.

9 Lay and secure switch cables from each loop-in ceiling rose or junction box to each one-way switch. For any two-way switches, lay 1.0mm^2 three-core-and-earth cable to connect the two switches. Allow enough cable to reach all the terminals easily.

10 From any junction boxes lay and secure cables to the point for the special fitting.

11 Feed the cable ends into any ceiling roses or junction boxes and into the light switches. For special light fittings, make the required size of hole in the ceiling to pass the cable through.

12 Prepare the cable ends for connection (page 363). Make sure that the cable sheath enters the ceiling rose; strip off only enough sheath to allow the conductors to reach the terminals. Sleeve the earth conductors and on all switch cables put red sleeving over the black conductor at both ends.

13 For every lighting point for a pendant light, cut a length of flex that will make the lamp hang at the desired height. Prepare both ends of the flex for connection. Connect the lampholder first (page 384). Slide the cover of the ceiling rose onto the flex.

CONNECTING AT SWITCHES

1 Connect one-way switches as described on page 386.

2 Connect two-way switches as described on page 387.

LOOP-IN CONNECTIONS AT CEILING ROSES

At each ceiling rose except the last on the circuit, two circuit cables have to be connected; at the last there is only one circuit cable. There is also a switch cable and a light flex to connect at each rose.

1 In the central group of three terminals connect the red conductors from the two circuit cables and from the switch cable. Screw the conductors tightly in place.

2 In the outer group of three terminals connect the black conductors from the two circuit cables to two of the terminals. Leave the outermost one clear for connecting the flex.

3 At the outer pair of terminals, connect the red-sleeved switch conductor to the inner of the two, leaving the outer terminal clear for the flex.

4 Connect the blue flex conductor to the outer threesome of terminals, using the outermost one. Connect the brown conductor to the terminal at the other end of the row of terminals. Pass the flex conductors over the hooks to take the lampshade's weight.

5 Connect all the green-and-yellow-sleeved earth conductors to the terminal marked E or ⏚.

6 Screw on the ceiling-rose cover.

MAKING CONNECTIONS ON A JUNCTION BOX SYSTEM

At each junction box except the last on the circuit there will be two circuit cables, a switch cable and a cable to the lighting point. At the last box there will be one circuit cable instead of two.

1 At one of the terminals (it does not matter which) connect the red conductors from the two circuit cables and the switch cable.

2 At another terminal, connect the black conductors from the two circuit cables and from the cable to the lighting point.

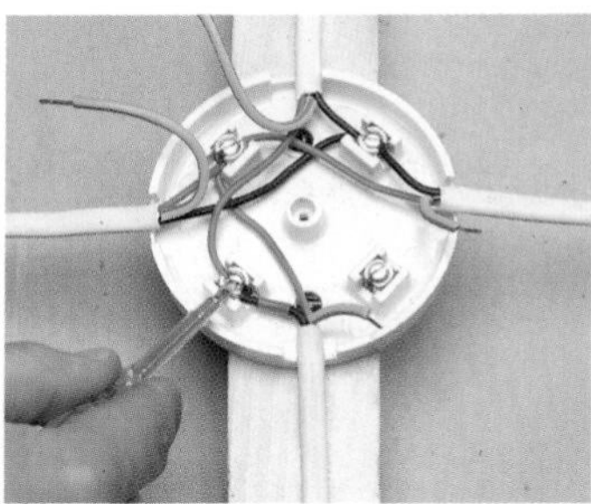

3 At a third terminal, connect the red conductor from the cable to the lighting point and the red-sleeved switch conductor.

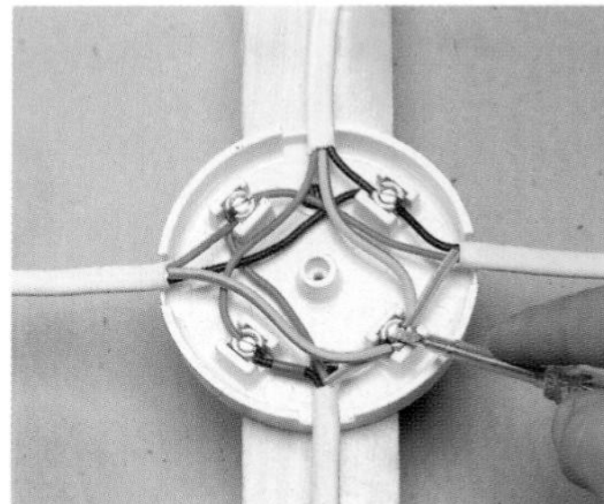

4 At the fourth terminal, connect all the (sleeved) earth conductors.

5 Screw on the junction box cover.

CONNECTING LIGHT FITTINGS TO A JUNCTION BOX SYSTEM

Single spotlights, multi-spotlight tracks, recessed lights and strip lights are among the special light fittings that are connected to a junction box system.

1 Fix the light fitting to the ceiling according to the manufacturer's instructions. The mounting plates to hold tracks and strips should be screwed through the plasterboard or plaster into joists or into struts nailed between the joists to give a secure fixing.

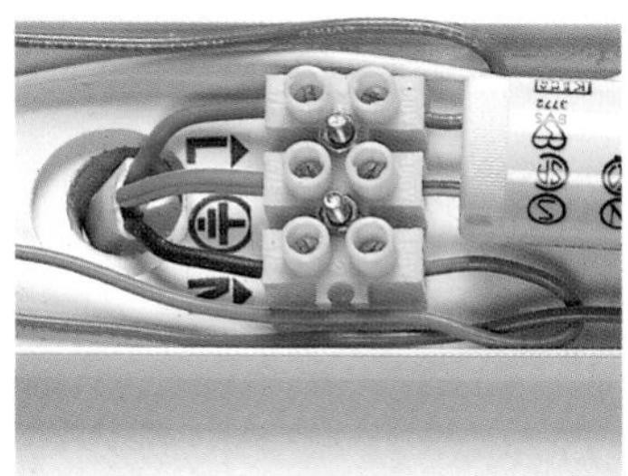

2 The track, strip or recessed light may be fitted by the manufacturer with a terminal block already holding the flex conductors and ready to receive the conductors from the light cable.

Connect the red cable conductor to the terminal opposite the brown flex conductor and marked L. Connect the black conductor to the terminal opposite the blue flex conductor and marked N. Connect the green-and-yellow-sleeved earth to the third terminal, marked E or ⏚; it may be a separate screw terminal instead of in the terminal block.

RECESSED LIGHTS

Recessed lights must be fitted between joists where there are no pipes or obstacles above the fixing spot. Draw round the inside edge of the trim to mark a cutting line on the ceiling. Cut the hole with a pad saw, first making a cut with a drill or a sharp knife to allow the saw through the plasterboard or plaster. Some recessed fittings have screw-in fixings, some are held by strips of metal bulging out from the fitting, and some have spring clips that sandwich the plasterboard between two arms. Whatever the design of fitting, make sure that you know how to reach the lampholder to replace a light bulb before you install the fitting; this varies from make to make.

If the light fitting is double-insulated (marked ⧈) there will be no earth terminal; cut short the earth conductor and seal it with insulating tape to make sure that it cannot touch any terminals.

ALTERNATIVELY, the light fitting may not have a terminal block. Instead, insulated flex conductors trail from it. Feed the flex directly into the junction box, which should have been fitted above the ceiling very close to the light fitting position. Connect the flex to the terminals described for the cable to the lighting point in *Making connections on a junction box system* (facing page).

CONNECTING AT THE CONSUMER UNIT

1 Turn off the main switch on the consumer unit, if you did not turn it off earlier.

2 Remove the screws from the consumer unit cover and open it.

WARNING

The main switch disconnects only the fuses or MCBs and the cables leading out from the consumer unit to the household circuits. It does NOT disconnect the cables entering via the meter from the service cable. Do not interfere with these cables. They are always live at mains voltage.

3 Feed the circuit cable into the top of the consumer unit. Use an existing hole if there is room in it.

ALTERNATIVELY, knock out an entry hole above the fuseway you will be using, fit a grommet in the hole and feed in the cable.

ALTERNATIVELY, drill through the wooden surround of the unit or chisel out plaster behind its frame to make an entry hole and feed in the cable.

4 Check that you have stripped off enough outer sheath for the conductors to reach the terminals easily, but make sure that the sheath enters the consumer unit.

5 Screw the new red conductor tightly into the terminal at the top of the fuseway you are using.

6 Screw the new black conductor into the corresponding position on the neutral terminal block (that is, as many places to the right as the fuseway is).

7 Screw the new green-and-yellow-sleeved conductor into the corresponding position on the earth terminal block.

8 Fit a 5amp fuse in the fuse carrier and replace the carrier. If the consumer unit has a miniature circuit breaker simply replace it and set the button to ON.

9 Screw the cover of the consumer unit back in place, refit the cover over the fuse carriers and turn the main switch back on.

TESTING AND MAKING GOOD

1 Fit bulbs or fluorescent lamps into the lampholders and fittings and turn on each light in turn to make sure that it is working. If not, check and tighten the connections, remembering to turn off the electricity at the consumer unit before you do so.

2 Replace any floorboards and finish making good.

Fitting a new flex to an iron

Frequent rubbing against the edge of an ironing table wears through the sheathing of the iron's flex. You

should not use the iron with a worn flex. Buy the correct flex (page 362) as a replacement; it must be heat-resistant and is usually sheathed with braided rubber.

If there are cracks or splits in the rubber sleeve that protects the flex where it enters the iron, replace it with a new sleeve at the same time as you fit the new flex.

You will need

Tools Insulated screwdrivers; sharp knife; wire cutters and strippers; pliers.

Materials New flex; perhaps a new rubber sleeve.

1 Make sure that the iron is unplugged before you start.

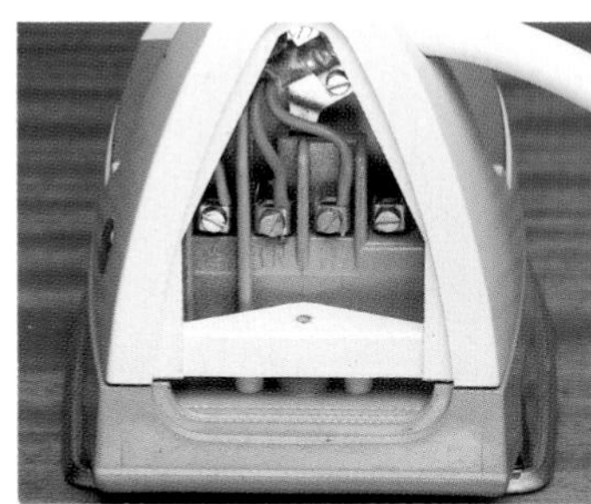

2 Undo and withdraw the retaining screw at the back of the handle and take off the cover.

3 Loosen the terminal screws, then unwind and withdraw the conductors from the screws.

4 Cut off the conductors of the old flex where they emerge from the outer sheath. You can then pull the flex out easily through the sleeve.

5 If necessary, pull out the old sleeve and fit the new one.

6 Slide the end of the new flex through the sleeve.

7 Prepare the end of the new flex for connection (page 363), remembering to twist the strands of each conductor tip with the pliers so that no strands are projecting.

8 Wind the tip of the brown conductor clockwise round the screw at the terminal marked L and drive the screw in firmly.

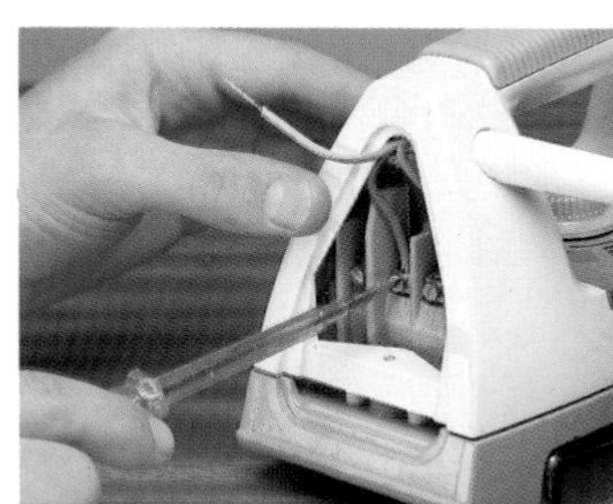

9 Wind the tip of the blue conductor clockwise round the terminal marked N and screw it in firmly.

10 Wind the tip of the green-and-yellow earth conductor clockwise round the terminal marked E or ⏚ and screw it tightly in place.

11 Replace the cover over the terminals and screw it in place.

12 Connect the plug (page 364).

Adding an aerial socket for a second TV set

You can connect more than one TV set to your aerial by leading the aerial cable into a splitter unit, which has one input and two outputs. Run coaxial cable from each output to a coaxial socket near each TV set. Link each set to a socket with coaxial cable fitted with a coaxial plug at each end. Plugs vary in design but have the same basic features. There are male and female plugs to suit different socket outlets.

In areas of poor reception, the slight loss of signal strength a splitter causes may result in a poor picture. If it does, install a TV signal amplifier.

The aerial cable may be run outside the house and brought inside through a hole drilled in a wall or window frame, but if you have unfilled cavity walls, it is neater to bring the cable inside under the eaves, drop it down the cavity and feed it through an air-brick to connect with the splitter under the floor. Position the splitter where the cable enters the house, or halfway between the two sets, or at the most convenient access point for you. The cables between splitter and sockets can be laid in the same way as other fixed cables (page 369).

You can use flush-fitting sockets over standard single mounting boxes in the wall or skirting, or surface-mounted sockets screwed to the skirting. If a flush aerial socket is directly alongside a mains socket, you can mount them both on a barriered dual mounting box.

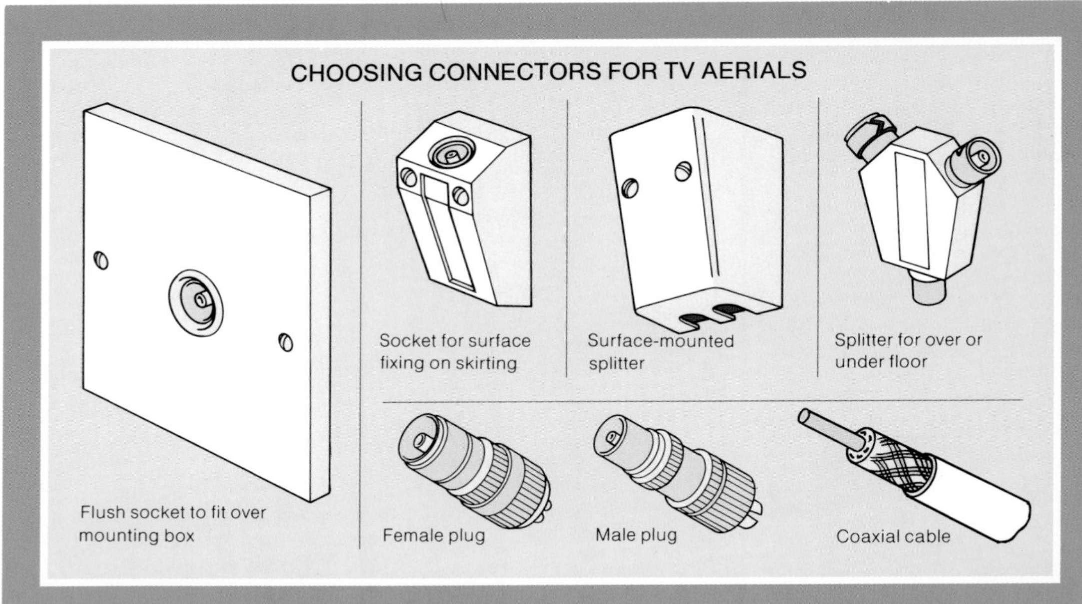

You will need

Tools Tools for preparing the route (page 369); sharp knife; wire cutters and strippers; insulated screwdrivers; pliers.

Materials Coaxial TV cable; cable clips or trunking; splitter unit; two flush-fitting coaxial sockets with mounting boxes and grommets, or two surface-mounting coaxial sockets with 1½in (38mm) screws; coaxial plugs to suit the sockets.

1 Prepare cable routes from the position for the splitter to the positions for the sockets and, if necessary, from where the cable enters the house to the splitter.

2 If you are using flush-fitting sockets, fit mounting boxes for them. Knock out a convenient entry hole in each box, fit a grommet and screw the boxes in place.

3 Feed the aerial cable to the chosen position for the splitter.

4 Lay cable along each route from the splitter position to the socket positions. Use cable clips or trunking to secure it. Do not draw it tight or bend it sharply.

5 If you are fitting flush sockets, feed the cable end for each socket through the grommet into the mounting box. Make good the plaster and wait for it to dry.

ALTERNATIVELY, for surface-mounted sockets, feed the cable end up through the floor at the base of the skirting. You will have to cut a notch or drill a hole in the floorboard to prevent it from chafing the cable. If the cable is not under the floor, feed it from the trunking to the spot where the base of the socket will be.

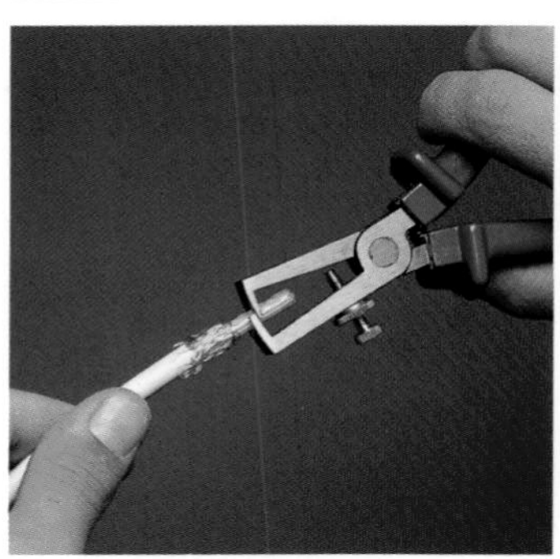

6 Prepare all the cable ends for connection. Make a 1¼in (32mm) slit with a sharp knife lengthwise at the end of the outer sheath. Fold back the sheath and trim it off. Loosen the wire mesh and press or fold it back to leave clear ¾in (19mm) of inner insulation. Use wire strippers to remove ½in (13mm) of the inner insulation.

7 To connect at a flush socket, screw the inner wire tightly in place at the terminal. Loosen the adjoining clamp, secure the wire mesh and cable under it and screw the clamp tight. The strands of the mesh must not touch the inner wire. Screw the socket over the mounting box.

ALTERNATIVELY, with a surface-mounted socket, loop the inner wire clockwise round the central screw and under any retaining plate. Screw it down and secure the clamp. Screw the socket to the skirting board.

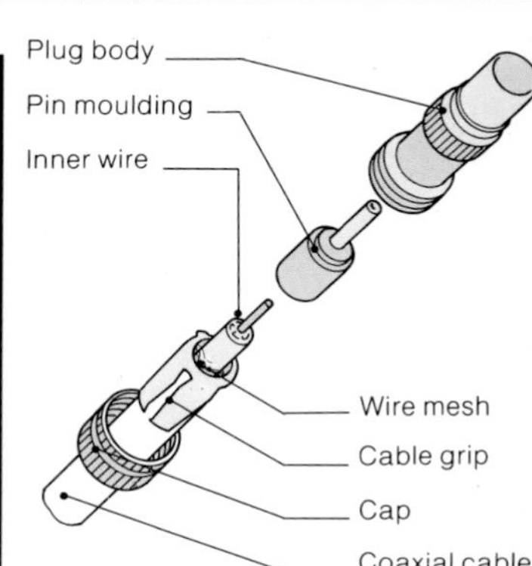

8 To connect a plug, slide the cap down the cable and fit the cable grip over the exposed mesh and cable. The strands of the mesh must not touch the inner wire. You will have to open the jaws of the grip to cover the mesh and then squeeze them together with a pair of pliers.

Feed the inner wire into the pin moulding and fit the moulding in the plug body. Slide the cap over the cable grip and screw it to the plug body.

Connect all the plugs in the same way, fitting a male or female plug as necessary to suit the connection on the socket or splitter.

9 Secure the splitter to a joist or to the skirting and push the aerial cable plug into the right socket on the splitter.

10 Push the plugs of the two cables that run to the sockets into the outlets of the splitter.

11 Refit any floorboards (page 273). Make good any damage to the plaster and wait for it to dry.

12 Plug the other two cables into the socket at one end and into the TV set at the other end.

Installing your own telephone extensions

You can install telephone extensions easily by using kits sold in electrical shops, DIY centres and phone shops.

The law requires a master socket to be fitted by the company that provides the service. You may already have one; it is a square white socket. An old-style box will not accept the new plugs.

Once you have a new master socket you can install extensions throughout the house, provided there is no more than 110yd (100m) of cable between the master socket and the farthest extension socket, and no more than 54yd (50m) between the master socket and the first extension socket. Extensions should not be fitted in damp areas such as bathrooms or toilets, or close to swimming pools.

For safety reasons, telephone wiring must be kept at least 2in (50 mm) from mains electric cables. The wiring works on a safe voltage, but it is advisable not to plug it into the master socket while doing the installation. If you need to join lengths of cable, use a joint box (see below).

These instructions use British Telecom fittings; others may vary.

You will need

Tools Electrical screwdriver; trimming knife; bradawl or pencil; drill and masonry bit to fit wall plug provided with kit; screwdriver to fit wall-fixing screw; small hammer; insertion tool (provided with kit).

Materials Telephone socket for each extension; socket converter attached to cable; cleats; two or more telephone sets fitted with plugs. Possibly extra cable (without converter) and cleats, depending on the number of extensions.

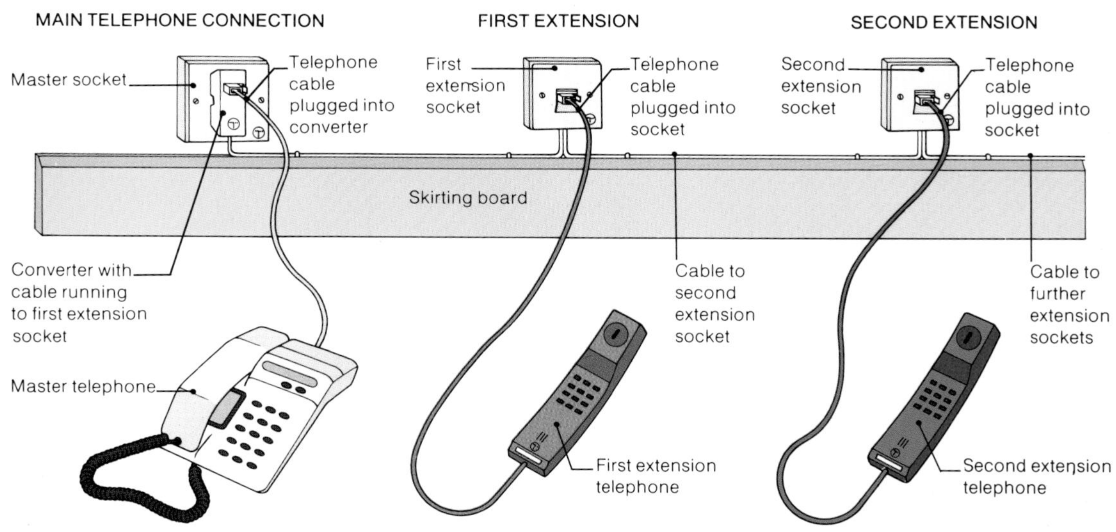

Main telephone and extensions The square white master socket must be installed by the company that provides the telephone service. This socket is the starting point for all extensions, which can be fitted anywhere in the house. A converter plugs into the master socket, and its cable runs to the first extension socket where the other end is wired in. Another cable runs to the next extension. Telephones are plugged into the converter and the sockets.

WIRING ONE EXTENSION

1 Decide where the extension socket is to be placed, and plan a route for the cable. It can be fitted along walls or skirting boards, or it can run above ceilings and under floors (see pages 369–371). Avoid laying cable across floors because there, it may cause an accident when someone trips over it or steps on it.

2 Run the cable from the master socket to the point where the extension socket will be fitted. The converter on the cable goes at the master-socket end, but do not connect it yet.

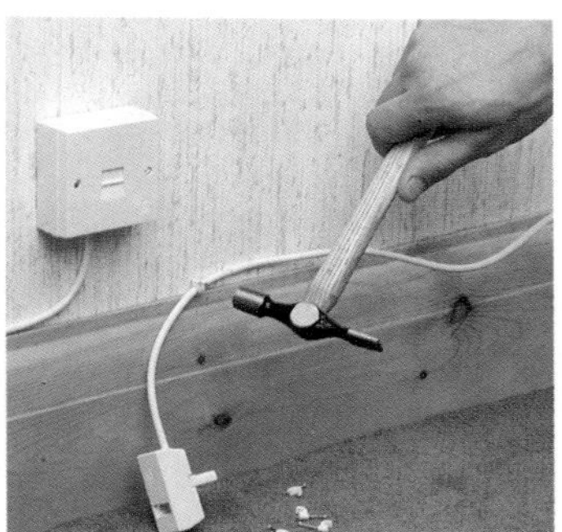

3 Fix the cable by hammering in the cleats every 12 in (300 mm), but leave the last few cleats at the extension end until later.

4 Cut the cable where it reaches the extension-socket position, leaving about 3 in (75 mm) to spare.

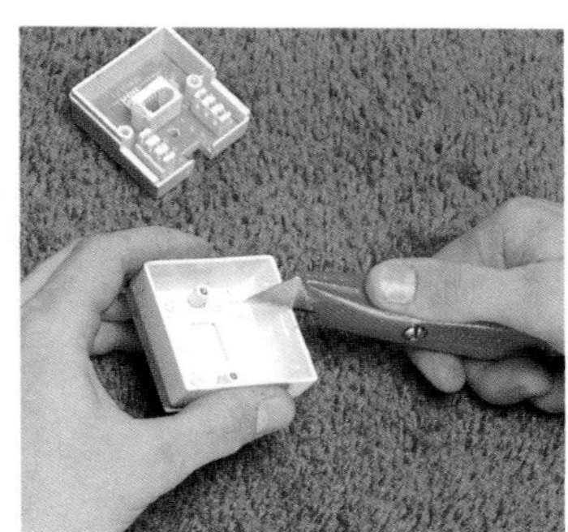

5 Unscrew the front plate from the extension socket and use a sharp knife to cut away the entrance hole

COMPONENTS FOR DIY TELEPHONE WIRING

Extension sockets look like the modern master socket which is installed by the telephone company. They are wired up with a plastic insertion tool supplied with the extension kit. A converter is supplied already attached to a long length of cable which is fixed in place with cleats. A telephone joint box can be used to take up to three extensions from one point, as well as the cable. It can also be used to join two lengths of cable together, if you need to.

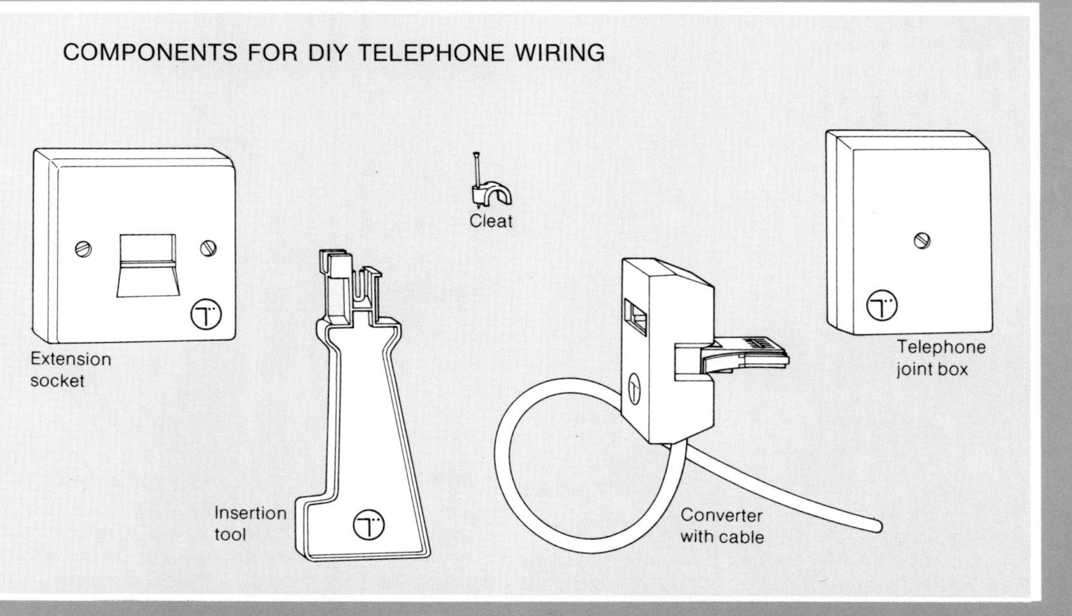

which is marked on the inside of the plate at the bottom.

6 Using the trimming knife, strip about $1\frac{1}{4}$ in (32 mm) from the cable's outer sheath.

HELPFUL TIP
You will probably find it easier to wire the socket before fixing it to the wall (as described). However, if you want the socket in an exact position, screw it to the wall before doing the wiring.

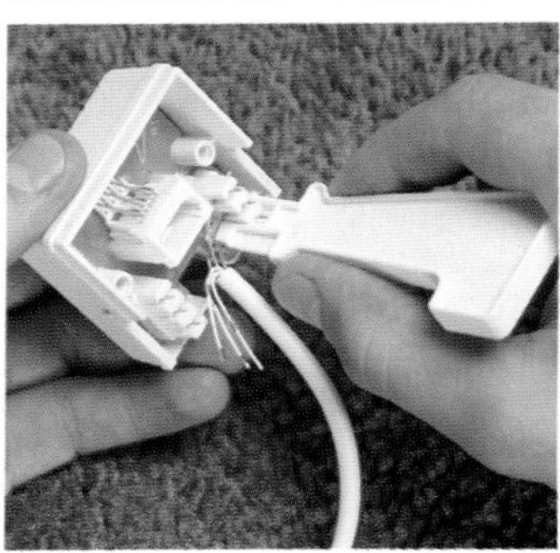

7 When there are six conductors, use the insertion tool to connect them to the socket, pushing them firmly into the grooves.

Hold the tool as shown above and push the green conductor with white rings into the connection marked 1; blue with white rings into connection 2; orange with white rings into connection 3.

Now reverse the tool to push in the others, but be careful; the numbers 4, 5 and 6 run from bottom to top. Push the white conductor with orange rings into connection 4, white with blue rings into connection 5, and white with green rings into connection 6.

8 Hold the back plate on the wall in the chosen position and mark the wall through the middle hole with a bradawl or pencil. Drill a hole in the wall to the depth of the wall plug. Insert the wall plug and screw the box to the wall.

COLOUR CODE OF TELEPHONE CABLE

TERMINAL	WIRE COLOUR CODE
1	Green/White ring
2	Blue/White ring
3	Orange/White ring
4	White/Orange ring
5	White/Blue ring
6	White/Green ring

9 Fit the front plate onto the back plate with the two screws.

10 Plug the converter into the master socket.

11 Fit the plug from the master telephone into the socket on the face of the converter.

12 Plug the extension telephone into its own socket.

FEWER CONDUCTORS

If there are fewer than six conductors, leave the connectors empty or choose a four-connector extension socket. Most telephones are sold fitted with a standard connector. If your telephone is not, consult British Telecom or Mercury Communications before connecting.

WIRING EXTRA EXTENSIONS

You can install a second extension socket by running another cable from the first extension socket. No converter is needed. A third extension socket can be installed by running cable from the second, and so on.

1 Unplug the converter from the master socket.

2 Unscrew the front plate from the first extension socket.

3 Connect the conductors of the new cable in the same order as previously, on top of the existing ones. This can be done with the socket on the wall, or – if you prefer – the socket can be temporarily removed.

4 Wire the other end of the cable to the second extension socket.

5 Continue in this way for any further extensions – always fitting the new conductors on top of those already installed.

6 Screw the front plates on the sockets and plug in the converter and the telephones.

WHAT IF IT FAILS TO WORK?

If your newly installed telephones fail to work properly, carry out this fault-finding procedure:

Unplug the converter from the master socket, plug in the telephone and make a call. Test each extension telephone by plugging it into the master socket as well.

If none of them works, the fault is in the wiring installed by the telephone company.

If one of the phones fails to work it is probably faulty. Return it to the supplier.

If they all work, the fault lies in your new wiring, so check each socket to make sure that you have wired the coloured conductors to the correct numbers. Check that you have pushed them right in. If the conductors are wrongly connected, pull them out one at a time with long-nosed pliers, cut off the used piece of cable and re-make the connection.

If the sockets are properly connected, check that the cable is not kinked, cut or squashed. If so, replace it.

If the phones still do not work, return the sockets, joint box, converter and cable to the suppliers so they can be checked for faulty manufacture.

MORE THAN ONE EXTENSION FROM A SINGLE POINT

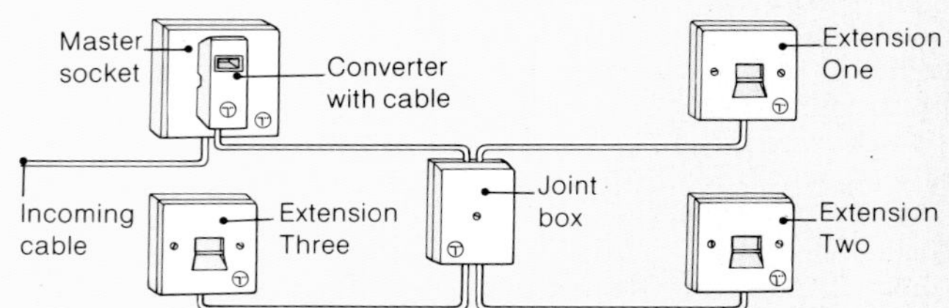

There are some situations where you may want to run more than one extension from a single point – perhaps from a landing outside three rooms. In this case, run cable from the converter at the master socket to a telephone joint box which will accommodate that cable plus as many as three extensions.

1 Fit cable between the master socket and the position for the joint box. Do not plug in the converter yet.

2 Unscrew the front plate from the joint box and cut out the plastic for the cable at the top of both plates.

3 Fit the conductors into the joint box in the same way and the same order as in an ordinary socket. The one difference is that the six connectors are in line down the sides rather than to the left and right, so strip off about $1\frac{1}{2}$ in (38 mm) of the cable sheath to fix them.

Fit one of the extension cables.

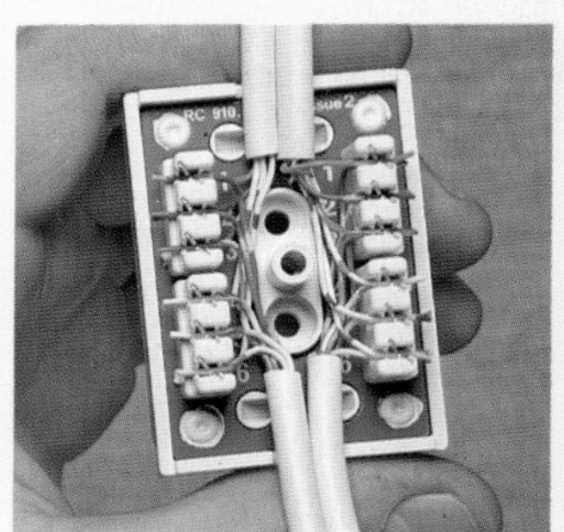

4 Fit the remaining extension cables in the same way, feeding them in from the top or bottom.

5 Push the cable straps under the pairs of cables and through the holes at the top and bottom of the back plate, and pull them tight. Then cut off the tails.

6 Fix the back plate to the wall with the two wall plugs and screws that are provided.

7 Fit the extension cables to their sockets in the normal way.

8 Screw the front plates on all the sockets, then plug in the converter and the telephones.

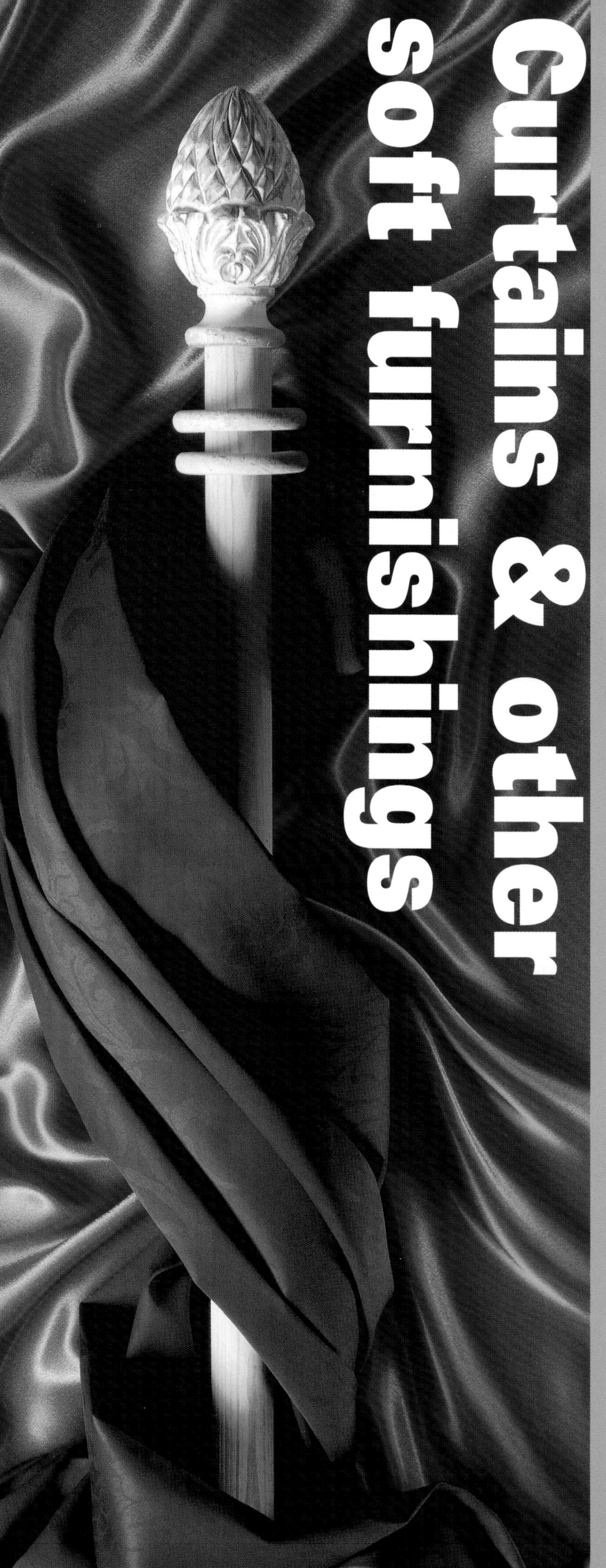

13 Curtains & other soft furnishings

Curtains

Blinds

Cushions

Upholstery

Curtains: Tools for the job

A large work surface is essential for spreading out the fabric. Clean, carpeted floor is ideal; a big table with a thick cover on it is almost as convenient and saves kneeling.

Measure
Use a metre-long wooden measure or a 10ft (3m) steel tape for measuring windows and long fabric.

Tape measure
Use a tape to measure hems. Linen or glass-fibre are best; cotton tapes shrink, and plastic ones stretch.

Chalk
Tailor's chalk is useful for marking guidelines on fabric.

Set square
Use it for ensuring that panels of curtain fabric are cut across at right angles to the sides. A length of about 8in (20cm) is adequate.

Scissors
Forged-steel dressmaking scissors with 9in (23cm) blades ease straight cutting of fabrics. Embroidery scissors will cut threads and tapes.

Pins
Use dressmaker's steel pins, which do not rust.

Needles
These must be sharp, rust-free and not worn at the eye. Keep a range for different fabrics – the finer the fabric the more slender the needle.
SHARPS are medium-length needles with small eyes.
CREWELS are often called embroidery needles, but many prefer them to sharps because the eye is larger for threading.
MACHINE needles are numbered for thickness. Your machine handbook will list the fabrics for which each needle is suitable.

Thimble
Protect the middle finger when hand-sewing with a metal thimble; plastic ones tend to split.

Quick-unpick (seam-ripper)
The point is easily slid between layers of fabric. The sharp edge within the curve cuts the stitches as the tool is pushed along.

Iron and ironing board
Both are used in curtain-making. Clean the iron frequently (with Dabitoff paste or Vilene or Sunbeam chalk stick, for example).

Sewing machine
Sewing the long seams and heading tapes on curtains takes much longer without a machine. If you buy a machine, it should be strong enough for heavy fabrics but not too heavy for you to lift. Elaborate extras are unnecessary for soft furnishings, but a zipper foot is a worthwhile extra for inserting the zips and piping in cushion covers.

Always unplug the machine from the mains when not in use. Clean and oil the machine regularly and have it serviced from time to time. Store it in its case, away from direct heat.

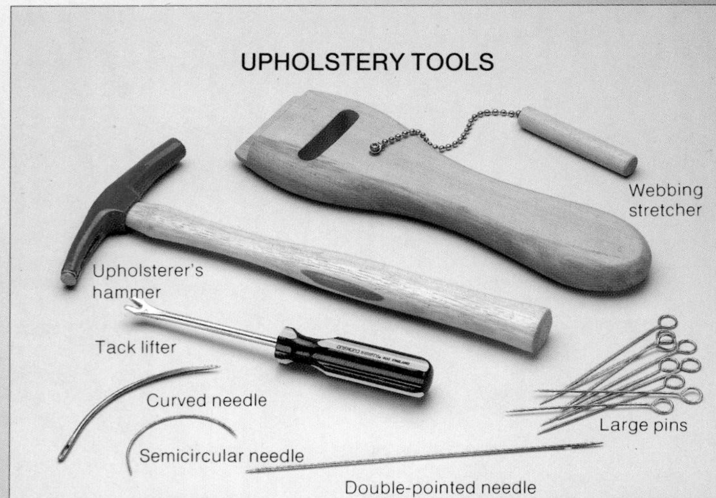

TOOLS FOR UPHOLSTERY

Needles
SEMICIRCULAR needles let you sew fabrics where you can only reach the top side.
CURVED needles are for sewing springs to webbing.
DOUBLE-POINTED needles are for sewing buttons on upholstery.

Pins
Use large-headed pins about 3in (7.5cm) long.

Tack lifter
The curved, notched claw prises out tacks from old upholstery.

Upholsterer's hammer
Upholstery tacks are hammered in with a small head to avoid damaging surrounding wood. Some upholsterer's hammers have an integral tack-lifting claw.

Webbing stretcher
Strands of upholstery webbing are drawn taut by the stretcher.

TOOLS FOR SEWING CURTAINS AND CUSHIONS

Ironing board and iron

Sewing machine

Set square

Embroidery scissors

Dressmaking scissors

Sharps

Crewels

Machine needles

Pins

Thimble

Quick-unpick

Tape measure

Chalk

Measure

The right curtains for your window

Most styles and shapes of window can be curtained in a variety of ways. You can make a narrower window seem wider, a squat one seem more elegant. A flattering but practical treatment is possible for even the most unorthodox shape.

PROBLEM WINDOWS

Windows that are overlooked or have an unattractive view can be dressed with a net curtain or a thin cotton café curtain to give privacy without much loss of light.

Large picture windows or patio doors are usually fitted where there is an attractive view, but the large curtains they require are very bulky. Curtains with a cartridge heading take up less hanging space than other pleated styles. Hang them as high above the window as possible; use tie-backs to hold them aside.

WINDOWS ON NARROW LANDINGS

On a narrow landing where people would brush against curtains, you can hang the curtains in the window recess or fit a blind.

Curve the track onto the sides of the recess so the curtains draw well back to let in maximum light. The fabric must not touch the glass or the sill; it would develop stains which will not come out. Curtains in a recess are not as draughtproof as those hung outside the recess.

DIFFERENT-SIZED WINDOWS

Give unity to different-sized windows in one wall by running one track or pole above both. Hang curtains of the same length at both windows and on the wall between. Matching wallpaper and curtains enhance the illusion of regularity.

DORMER WINDOWS

There is rarely any wall space beside dormer windows. Orthodox curtains there will cover part of the glass, and exaggerate the tunnel effect. You can fit a blind, or hang curtains on a flexible track curved onto the side walls.

WINDOWS ABOVE RADIATORS

Full-length curtains seal off a radiator from the room. Even with short curtains, much heat is lost behind them. Heating engineers recommend fitting a ledge 2in (5cm) above the radiator or extending the windowsill to deflect heat into the room, and hanging curtains to the ledge or sill. People who do not want a projecting sill make the standard short curtains to 4in (10cm) below the sill or to 2in (5cm) above the radiator – and put up with the extra cost of heat lost.

KITCHEN WINDOWS

It is dangerous to hang curtains near a cooker hob. Even a curtain that normally hangs at a safe distance may blow near the hob when a window is open. If the window is recessed, hang the curtains within the recess; secure them with tie-backs when they are open. A blind is safer if there is no recess.

Curtains hanging over a sink may be splashed by running water or brushed by wet hands reaching for the taps. You may be able to avoid this by making the curtains as short as possible. If not, hang the curtains in the window recess or fit a blind instead of curtains.

SHORT, WIDE WINDOWS

With a window at the narrow end of a room, try to give a wider look. Fit a pole or track just above the window and make it wide enough for sill-length curtains to hang entirely against the wall when open. Elsewhere, you can make a short window seem taller with long curtains hung well above the window.

ARCHED WINDOWS

Do not conceal the elegant curve of an arched window. Fit a pole or track well above the arch and make it wide enough for the curtains to draw back completely onto the wall. If privacy is not needed, you could confine the curtains to the lower part of the window.

TALL, NARROW WINDOWS

The long, slender shape of sash windows in a high-ceilinged room is emphasised by floor-to-ceiling curtains hung on a pole.

If you prefer a broader effect, fit a deep pelmet to extend well beyond the sides of the window and let the curtains pull back over a wider section of wall than usual.

A narrow window in a modern lower-ceilinged room can be used to create an illusion of height. Fit a track as high as possible and hang floor-length curtains from it.

BAY WINDOWS AND RETURNS-TO-THE-WALL

Do not diminish the spacious air a bay window gives by hanging curtains in a straight line from one side of the bay to the other. They will cut the bay off when they are closed.

At modern bays and at bow windows, fit flexible track to follow the sweep of the window, and hang one large pair of curtains to draw right back to the wall at each end. On older bays with wide uprights at the angles, you can curtain the three windows separately without losing too much light when the curtains are open.

To cover the gap between curtains and wall at each end, make the curtains with a return-to-the-wall. Carry the curtain edge beyond the track and slip the last hook into a screw eye in the wall.

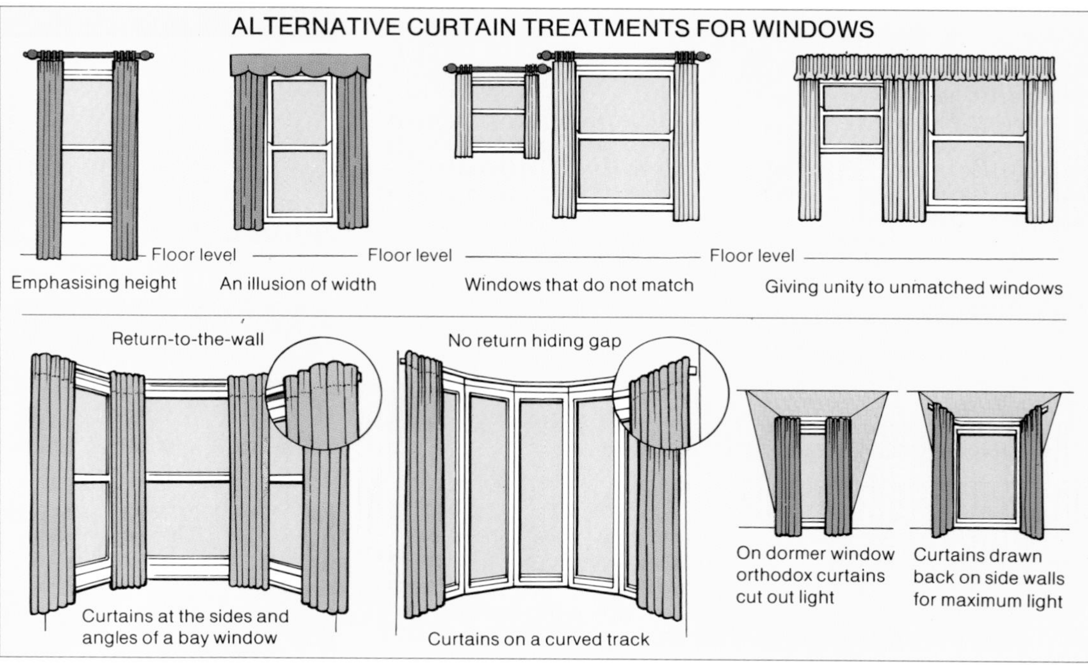

Choosing the style of heading

The style of heading determines how the curtains hang in folds – and how many widths of fabric you will need in order that the finished curtains cover the windows.

Gathered or pleated headings can be achieved by hand or by using one of several ready-made heading tapes.

On hand-pleated curtain tops, a broad tape without any draw-cords or pockets in it is sewn behind the pleats to strengthen the heading. The hooks for hanging the curtains have to be sewn on by hand, or pin-on hooks are stabbed into the back of the tape.

Pockets in the ready-made tapes hold curtain hooks for hanging on gliders, combined glider-hooks or rings on the track or pole. Some types of headings require no sewing. Some special headings designed to hang lightweight dress curtains at an arched window are also available.

Ready-made tapes are available in many styles. They can be washed or dry-cleaned, and are suitable for any curtain fabric. The gathering or pleating is created by drawing tight the cords that run along the tape. You can open the curtains out flat again for cleaning. Hand-pleated headings are held permanently in place by tape sewn on once the heading is pleated.

By hand-working a heading, you can space out the goblets, box-pleats, or other decoration to fit an individual track, with one at each end of the curtain and the others spaced symmetrically along it. Hand-made headings are not difficult but they take more time than using a ready-made tape.

A READY-MADE CURTAIN HEADING TAPE

The way the cords are threaded in a heading tape and the number of cords makes the pattern of pleats. Tapes for the more intricately pleated headings – smocking, for example – have four cords for drawing up. The pleats are sharpest when the cords are drawn up tightly. Most tapes have more than one row of pockets for the hooks to adjust the height of the heading.

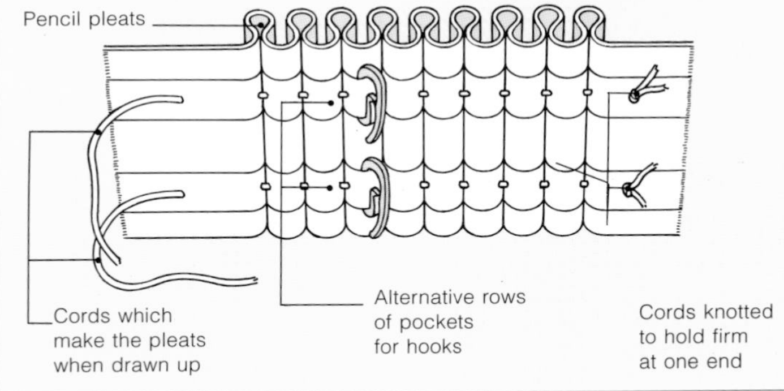

HEADINGS WITH READY-MADE TAPE

Simple gathered heading

Many shallow gathers are evenly spaced across the curtain. Use the tape for curtains whose top is behind a pelmet or valance. Multiply the track width by 1½-2 when estimating for fabric.

CLUSTER PLEATS Simple gathering tape may have a second pair of drawing cords. They create clusters of small pleats at intervals. Curtains must be twice the track width to make the cluster pleats.

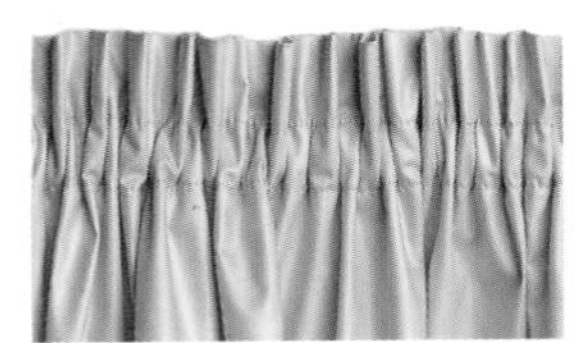

HOOKS TO USE
Plastic or metal hooks

Pencil-pleated heading

The stiffened tape is available in several depths from 2½in to 6in (6cm to 15cm). A lightweight version is suitable for net curtains. Some tapes have three rows of pockets for hooks. Use the top row if the curtain is to hang below a pole. Use a lower row to make the heading stand up the required amount to conceal a track. Multiply the track width by 2¼-2½ when estimating for fabric.

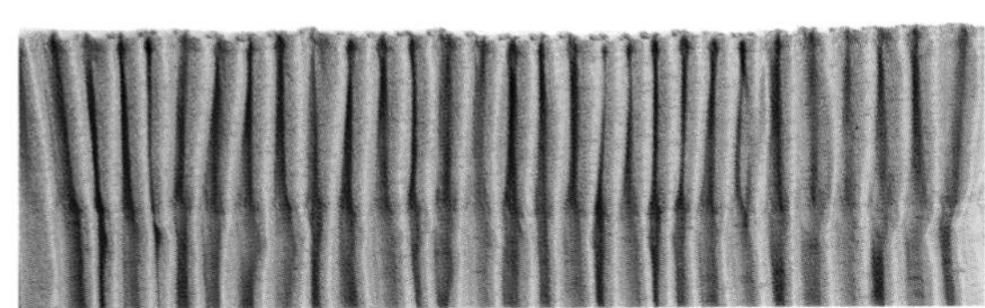

HOOKS TO USE
Plastic or metal hooks

Cartridge-pleated heading

Stuff the pleats with cotton wool or tissue paper to maintain their shape. Remove the stuffing for washing or cleaning the curtains. A lightweight tape is made for net curtains. There are two rows of pockets so that the curtains can hang below a pole or stand up to conceal a track depending on which pockets you use. Multiply the track width by 2 when estimating for fabric.

HOOKS TO USE
Split hooks

Pinch-pleated heading

Fans of pleats are made by drawing cords or by multi-pronged hooks. The synthetic tape will suit all fabrics including nets. Several depths from 1½in to 5½in (4cm to 14cm) are available. The deepest is best suited to floor-length curtains. There are two rows of pockets, one for curtains hanging below a pole, the other for headings to cover a track. Multiply the track width by 2 when estimating for fabric.

HOOKS TO USE
Multi-pronged or split hooks

Smocked heading

A diamond-shaped pattern of tucks is formed by drawing up four cords. The tape requires four rows of stitching across it. Sew it with the pockets for hooks at the top or the bottom depending whether the curtain is to hang below a pole or stand up to conceal a track. It is suitable for main or net curtains. Multiply the track width by 2 when you are estimating how much fabric is required.

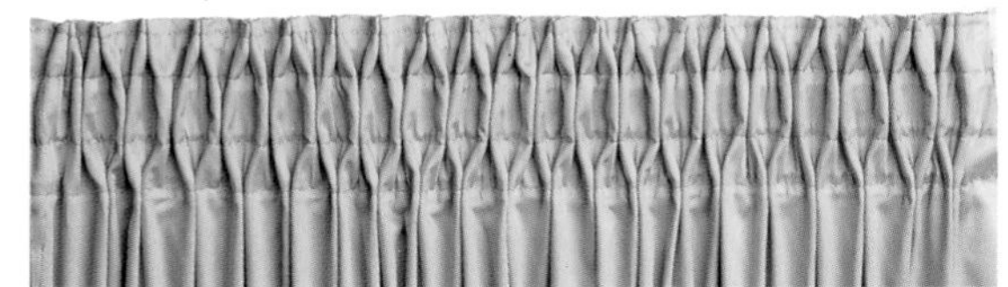

HOOKS TO USE
Plastic or metal hooks

Ruffed heading

Three overlapping rows of narrow, upright tucks form when the four cords are drawn up on the ready-made heading tape. It needs four rows of sewing across it. A choice of pockets for the hooks in the central strip of the tape allows a small adjustment on how far the curtain hangs below the track. Double the track width when estimating for fabric. The tape is suitable for main or net curtains.

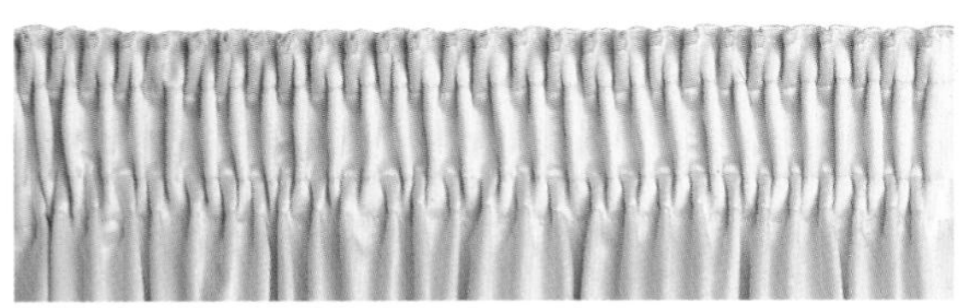

HOOKS TO USE
Plastic or metal hooks

Trellis heading

Two overlapping rows of pencil pleats are formed by drawing up three cords on the heading tape. The tape needs three rows of stitching across it. Put the pockets for hooks at the top for the curtain to hang below a track or pole. Put the pockets at the bottom to make the heading cover a track. Use the tape on net or main curtains. Double the width of the track when estimating for fabric.

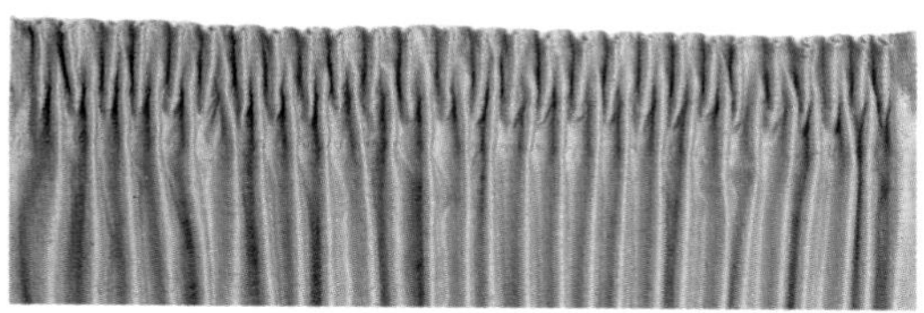

HOOKS TO USE
Plastic or metal hooks

Loose-lining heading

A tape with two flanges at the bottom sandwiches the raw top edge of the lining between its layers. Loose-lining tape allows separate linings to be hung on the same hooks and gliders as the main curtains. The linings can be unhooked and removed separately when necessary – to be washed for example. The tape is drawn up by cords in the same way as other ready-made heading tapes.

HOOKS TO USE
Same hooks as main curtains

HAND-MADE CURTAIN HEADINGS

Cased heading

A simple cased heading is used mainly for net or other curtains that are not to be opened and closed. A casing or channel sewn across the top is left open at the ends. A slender curtain rod or plastic-covered spring wire slots through the channel and fits onto hooks or into sockets at the sides of the window. Multiply the rod or wire length by at least 3 when estimating for fabric.

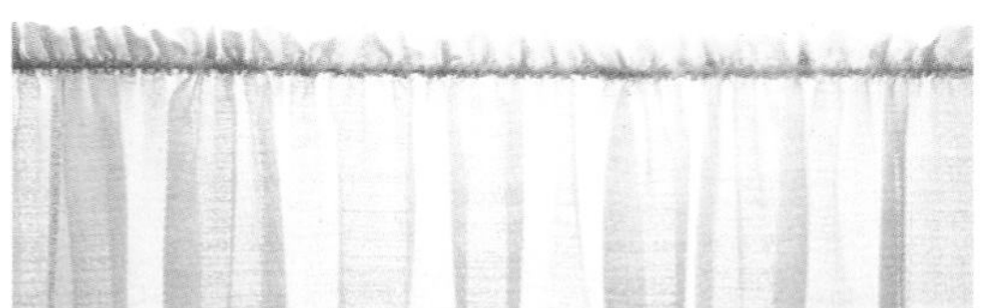

HANGING METHOD
Slender rod or spring wire

Goblet heading

A deep rounded pleat falls from each goblet. A stuffing of tissue paper or cotton wool keeps the goblets in shape. Remove the stuffing before washing or cleaning the curtains. The heading is best used on floor-length curtains because the goblets are large. A plain fabric shows off the detail of the goblets most clearly. Multiply the track width by 2½ when you are estimating how much fabric to buy.

HOOKS TO USE
Sew-on or pin-up hooks

Box-pleated heading

Flat pleats give a tailored look and drape into deep folds down the full length of the curtain. Multiply the track width by 3 when estimating for fabric. Allow only 1in (2.5cm) on one curtain for the central overlap. The pleats butt onto each other with no interval between them. Make the overlap by placing the curtain hook 1½in (4cm) in from the edge of the curtain that you want to overlap onto the other.

HOOKS TO USE
Sew-on or pin-on hooks

Scalloped café heading

The curves make a decorative top on a curtain hung permanently across the lower part of a window and not intended for opening and closing. The scallops are cut from a home-made pattern designed to fit the width of an individual window. Hang the curtain by small rings slid onto a slender rod. Allow a bare 1½ times the width of the rod when you are estimating how much curtain fabric to allow.

RINGS TO USE
Brass or plastic rings

CURTAIN HOOKS AND RINGS

Except when a track has its own combined glider-hooks (page 406), it is best to buy the hooks at the same time as the curtain heading tape; some tapes require a particular kind of hook to secure the pleats. Plastic or metal hooks are sold for ready-made tapes. Most have a double bend to hold them securely in the pockets of the tape, and will fit nearly all types of heading tape.

Pinch-pleating tapes require multi-pronged or split hooks. Cartridge-pleating heading tape requires split hooks.

For hand-pleated headings, where the tape has no pockets, you can obtain pin-on hooks or sew on brass hooks by hand.

For scalloped café headings, sew on small brass or plastic rings by hand to slot on the curtain rod.

Plastic hook

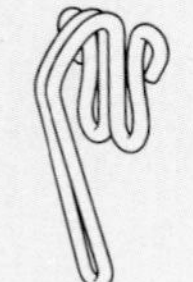

Brass sew-on hooks

Metal hook

Split hook

Pin-on hook

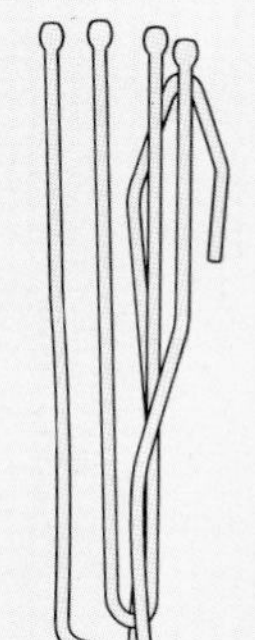

Multi-pronged hook

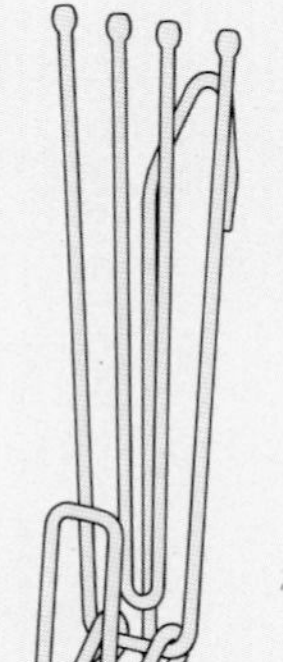

Multi-pronged hook with clasp

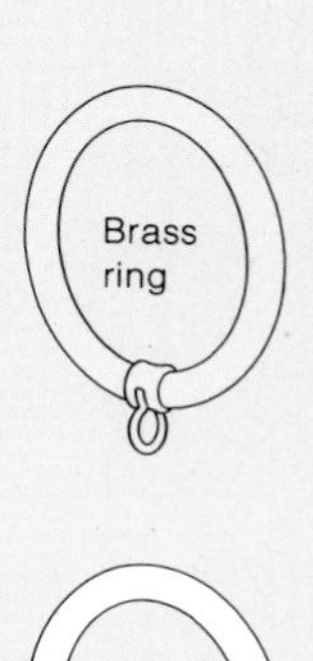

Brass ring

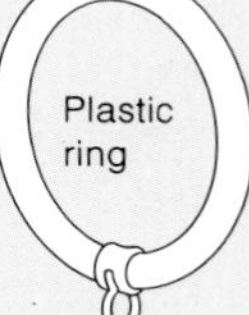

Plastic ring

CHOOSING TRACKS AND POLES FOR HANGING CURTAINS

CONTINUOUS TRACK

Buy all the brackets, gliders or rings, and endstops or finials when you buy the track; the right ones could be out of stock or discontinued later. Tracks are made of steel, aluminium or plastic, in many styles. Brackets to hold tracks in place can be screwed into either the wall or the ceiling. Some tracks will fit flush up to the ceiling. Some brackets are unobtrusive, others very noticeable. Bracketless tracks screw direct into a wall, ceiling or window recess. Gliders on the track carry the curtain hooks. Some tracks have combined glider-hooks. Endstops or finials stop the gliders running off the track ends.

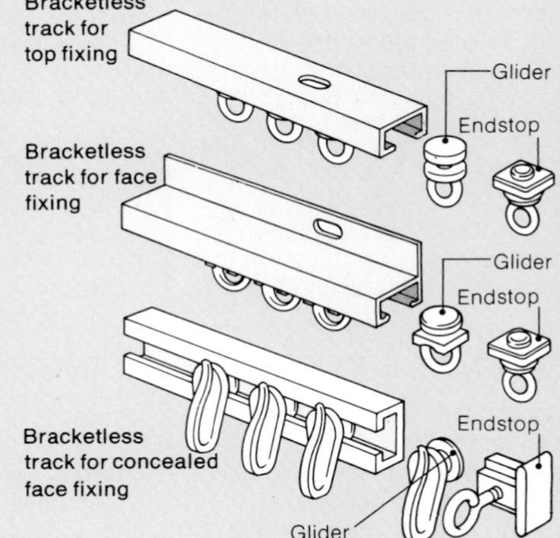

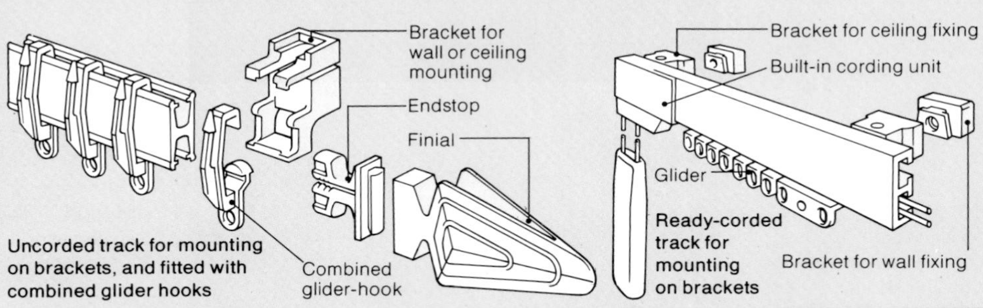

CONCEALED TRACK

A track concealed by a pelmet or valance can be cheaper and less streamlined than one that will be on view. The brackets for holding it in place can be fixed to either wall or ceiling. The track is usually fitted in two halves with a central overlap held by a bracket.

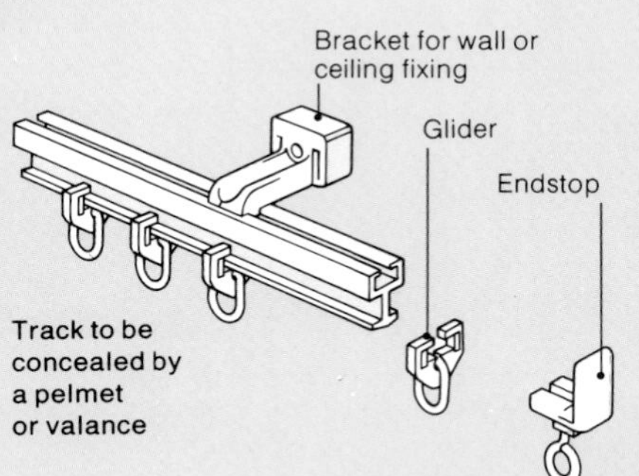

TRACK FOR BAY WINDOWS

Many tracks will bend round bay windows. The makers' instructions show how much each type will bend. Some shops will have steel track bent for you. In a right-angled bay, you can fit three straight sections of track with connector pieces at the corners. Curtain the three sides separately.

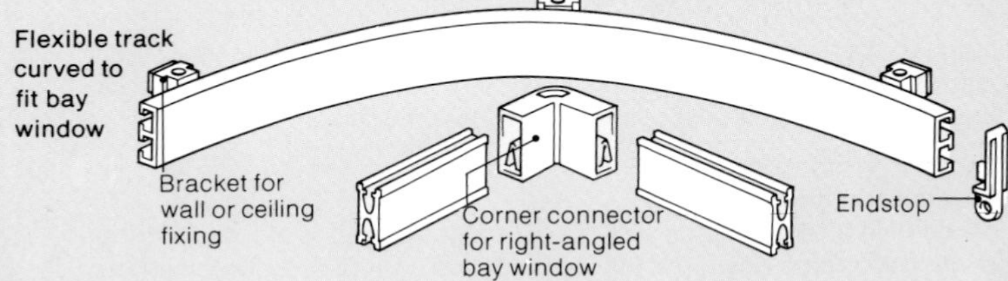

POLES

Poles can only be used for straight runs. They are made in wood, metal and plastic. Some poles have rings encircling them, others have half-rings attached to gliders in a track behind the pole. Poles with glider tracks often have a built-in central overlap. Usually brackets are needed only at the ends. A pole that is 8ft (2.4 metres) or longer will need a bracket at the centre. There is often a choice of brackets to hold the pole different distances from the wall. Some poles with glider tracks are fitted on the same kind of concealed brackets as plastic tracks; others have metal brackets. There are side-fixed brackets for some poles. Finials on the ends of the pole act as endstops.

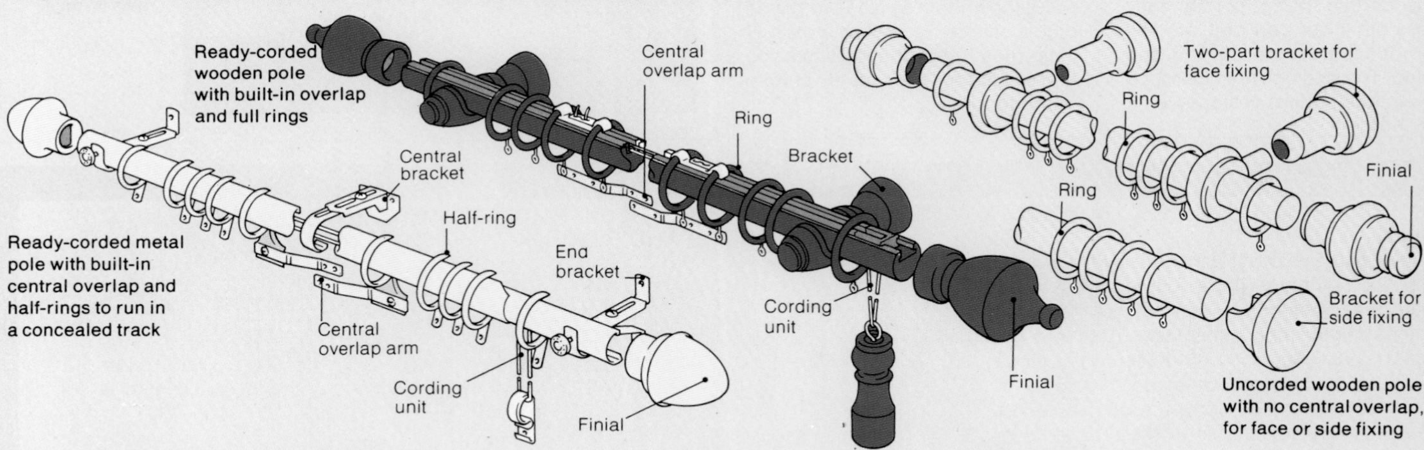

WIRES AND RODS FOR NET CURTAINS

Net and sheer curtains that are not opened and closed can be hung on a plastic-coated spring wire or on a plastic-coated extending metal rod. Café curtains can also be hung on wires or extending rods, or on slender face-fixed or side-fixed poles.

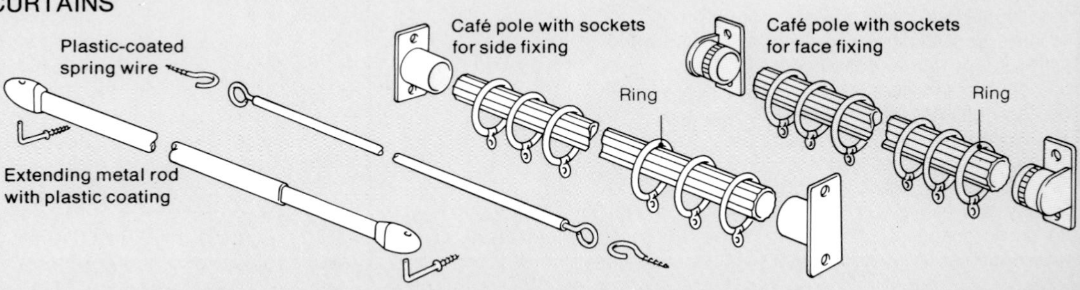

How to put up a track or pole

Tracks and poles come in many lengths. Saw off any excess length, but if possible let the track or pole extend far enough at the sides for the curtains to draw back clear of the glass. This lets in maximum light during the day. The wider and thicker the curtains are, the more wall space they will cover at the sides of the window when they are drawn back clear of the glass.

If the track will be on view, fix it directly to the wall or ceiling. The screws supplied with a track or pole when you buy it are not always long enough to make secure fixings. Replace them if necessary. Most must be screwed into sound ceiling timbers or plugs in a wall; extra brackets on ceilings may be screwed into winged plugs in plasterboard.

You will need

Tools Long wood or metal rule; pencil; bradawl; drill with wood or masonry bit; screwdriver.

Materials Track, pole, or curtain wire or rod; perhaps a length of batten; wall plugs (standard and winged if necessary); brackets or sockets, 1½in (38mm) No. 6 screws; perhaps screw eyes; gliders or rings; end stops or finials.

FIXING BRACKETS FOR A TRACK ON THE WALL

1 Mark the fixing height for the track at least 2in (5cm) above the top of the window or it will be too near the edge of the brick, masonry or timber beneath the plaster. Brackets on which a track slots down should not be within ¾in (2cm) of the ceiling or there is no access for fitting the track. Brackets for clip-on tracks can be up against the ceiling.

2 Measure up from the window top every 8in (20cm) across and make pencil marks at the right height. If the track or pole is to be nearer the ceiling than the window top, measure down from the ceiling. Neither window top nor ceiling is necessarily horizontal. The track should be parallel to whichever of the two is closer or it will always look askew.

3 Join the pencil marks with a straight line and extend it at the sides to the width of the track.

4 Mark positions for the brackets with pencil crosses on the guideline. Put one 2in (5cm) from each end. Space others about 12in (30cm) apart, or as specified in the manufacturer's instructions.

5 At each cross drill through the plaster into the lintel and insert a plug. On a concrete lintel, you will need to use a power drill with hammer action.

6 Screw a bracket into each plug.

FIXING BRACKETS FOR A TRACK ON THE CEILING

1 Draw a pencil guideline on the ceiling parallel to the top of the wall where you want the track to be.

2 Locate the joists (page 249) and make pencil lines to mark where they are. If they run at right angles to the window, mark spots for drilling where the pencil guideline and the joists cross, and also 2in (5cm) from the ends of the track if the ceiling is plasterboard; do not make such hollow fixings at the ends into a lath and plaster ceiling.

On a plasterboard ceiling you can mark extra drilling places between the joists if the curtains are heavy, or if the track is going to be curved and needs a bracket to hold the curve at a point where there is no joist. Do not do this on a lath and plaster ceiling.

FIXING TO JOISTS THAT RUN PARALLEL TO THE WINDOW

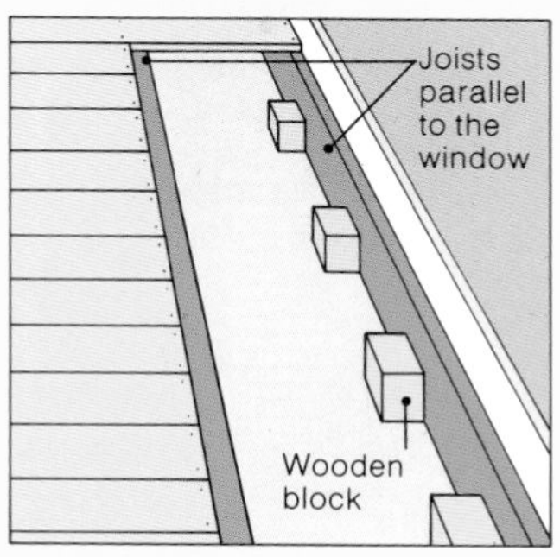

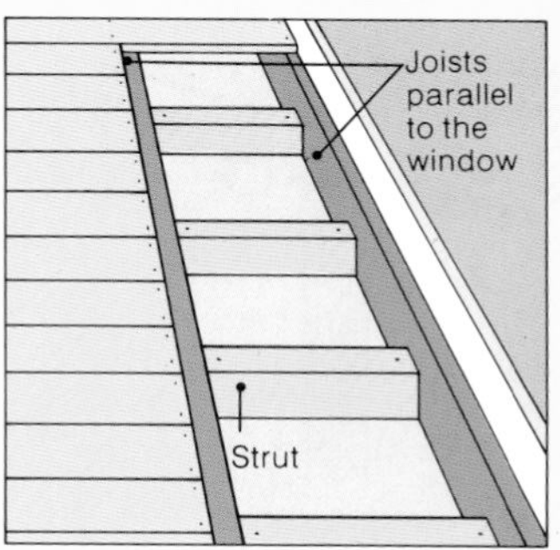

If the joists run parallel to the window and are not positioned conveniently to hold the bracket screws, you can fix wooden blocks to the side of the joist to give fixings up to 4in (10cm) away. Mark spots on the ceiling for drilling into the blocks. If the joists run parallel to the window and are more than 4in (10cm) away from the points where you need to make fixings, fit wooden struts between the joists. You can fit a strut wherever you need to fix a bracket. Mark spots for drilling into the struts.

ALTERNATIVELY, to take particularly heavy curtains, you can skew-nail wooden struts between the joists. Then mark the spots for drilling into the struts 2in (5cm) from the ends of the track and about every 12in (30cm) between them, or as recommended in the manufacturer's instructions. This method of fixing makes sure that every bracket is screwed securely into timber above the ceiling.

If you cannot gain access to the loft or the floor above the window to fix wood to the joists, a wall-fixed track is safest.

3 Drill through the plaster at the marked spots and into the timber where possible.

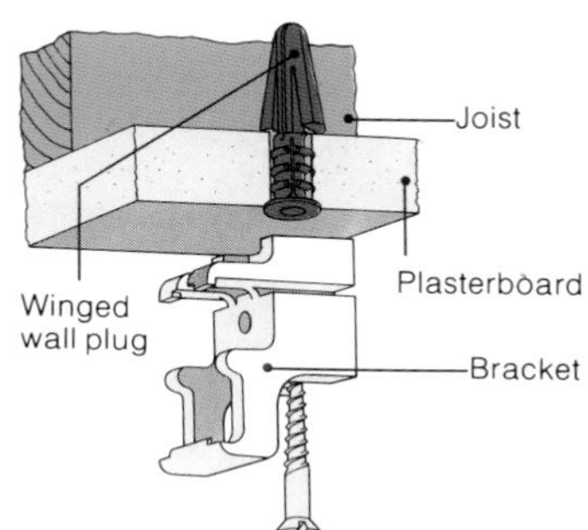

4 Where you have not drilled into timber, insert a winged wall plug through the plaster.

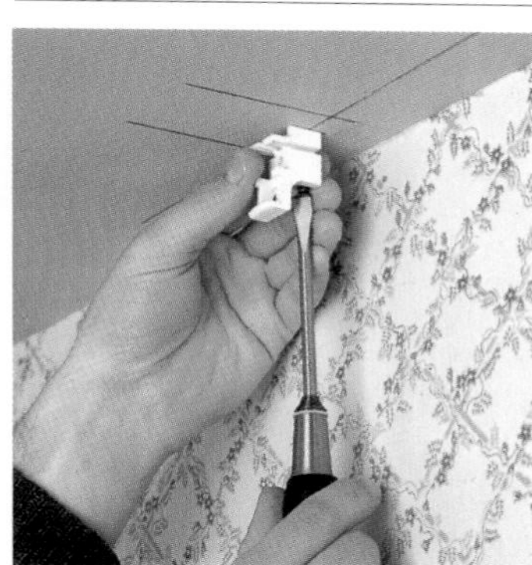

5 Screw the brackets into the timber or plugs (unless the track has slide-in brackets; see *Fitting the track*, page 409).

FIXING A BRACKETLESS TRACK

Prepare the holes in exactly the same way as for a track with brackets. Screw in the track with 1½in (38mm) No. 6 screws.

FIXING TO A WINDOW SURROUND

Windows with wooden surrounds on the wall surface may seem to offer easy fixing points for brackets. However, the track cannot extend

How to put up a track or pole (continued)

beyond the sides of the window. This excludes too much daylight because the curtains cannot be drawn back to clear the glass.

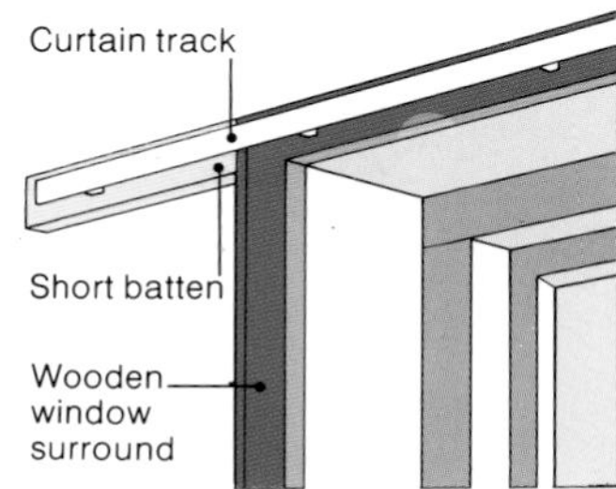

Fix a wooden batten (page 234) at each side of the window to extend the fixing width.

FIXING BRACKETS IN A RECESS

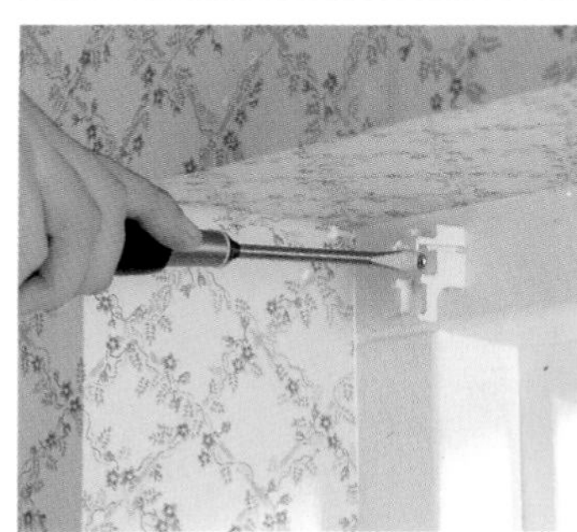

1 For tracks in a window recess, screw the brackets securely into the window frame, if it is wooden.

2 Where the frame is metal or PVC, screw the brackets upwards with 1½in (38mm) No. 6 screws into drilled, plugged holes.

FIXING A CONCEALED TRACK

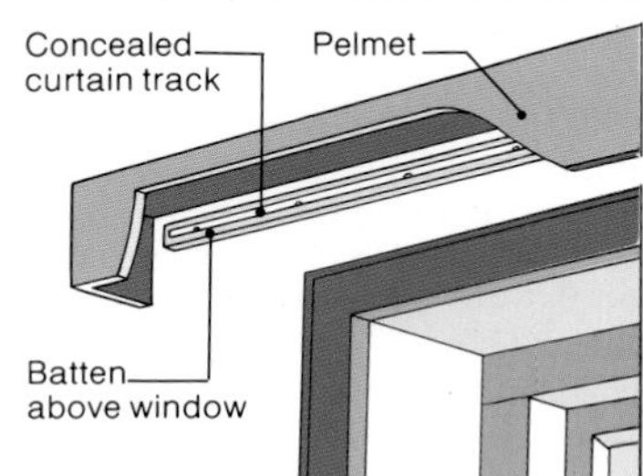

Where a pelmet or valance is going to cover the curtain track, fix a wooden batten (page 234) above the window and screw the brackets into it.

CHOOSING OPTIONAL FITTINGS FOR TRACKS AND POLES

EXTENSION BRACKETS FOR TRACKS

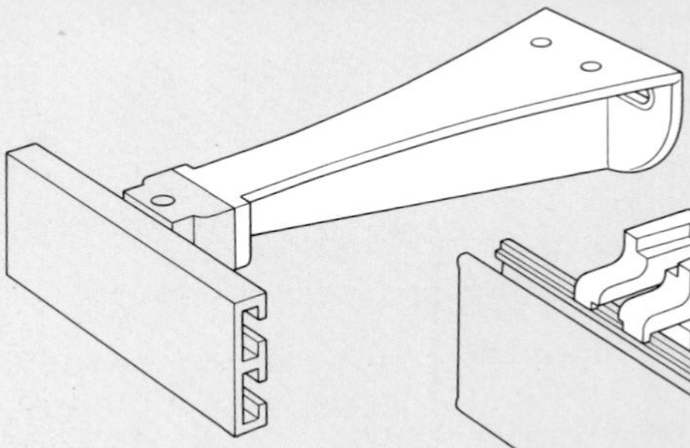

Extension bracket with fixed arm
Extension brackets fitted instead of standard brackets will hold a track farther out from the wall – so that the curtains clear a projecting sill or a wooden window surround, for example.

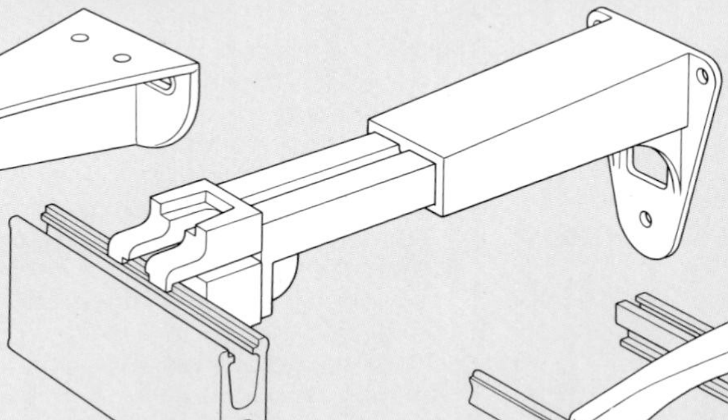

Adjustable bracket
One type of bracket has a sliding arm that you can adjust to project different amounts.

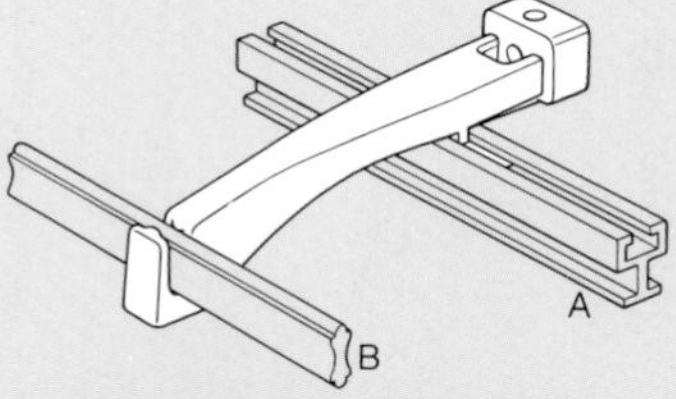

Clip-on bracket for a valance rail
Secondary brackets clipped onto the main track (A) will carry the rail for a valance (B).

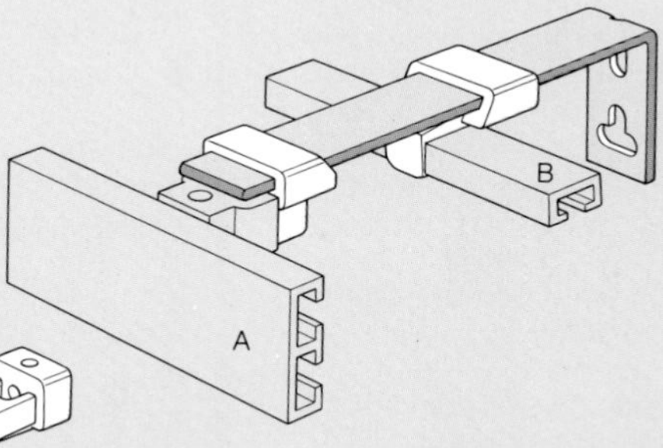

Metal bracket to hold two tracks
There are brackets to carry two tracks – one for the main curtain (A) and another for a net curtain behind it (B). You can adjust the track positions by sliding their carriers backwards or forwards.

CORDING SET AND DRAW RODS

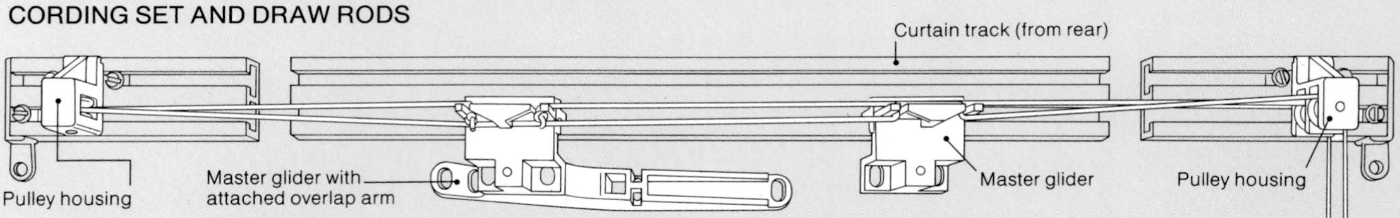

Curtain track (from rear)
Pulley housing
Master glider with attached overlap arm
Master glider
Pulley housing

A cording set can be fitted to many tracks and poles, often on straight runs only. The cords pass through master gliders and round pulleys at the track ends. They may be pulled by two weighted knobs or pass through a tension arm.

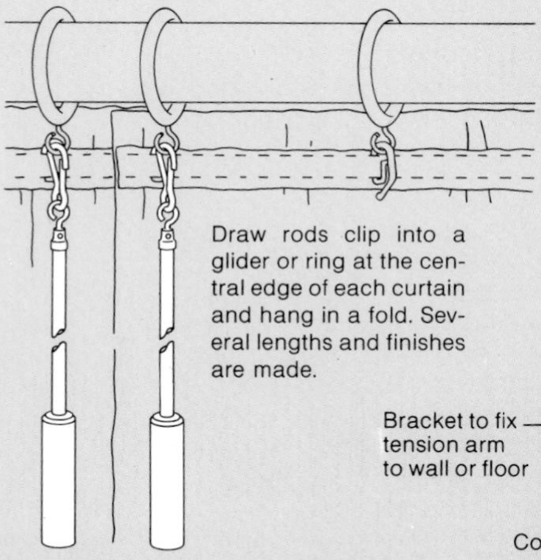

Draw rods clip into a glider or ring at the central edge of each curtain and hang in a fold. Several lengths and finishes are made.

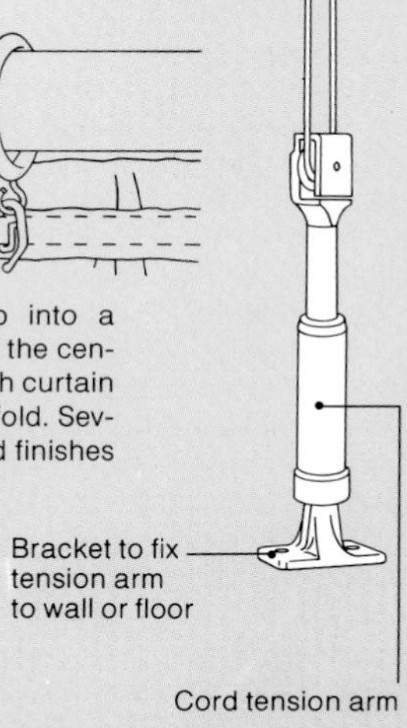

Bracket to fix tension arm to wall or floor
Cord tension arm

OVERLAP ARMS FOR TRACKS

Fixed overlap arm
A track behind a pelmet or valance is fitted in two halves and made to overlap by a bracket.

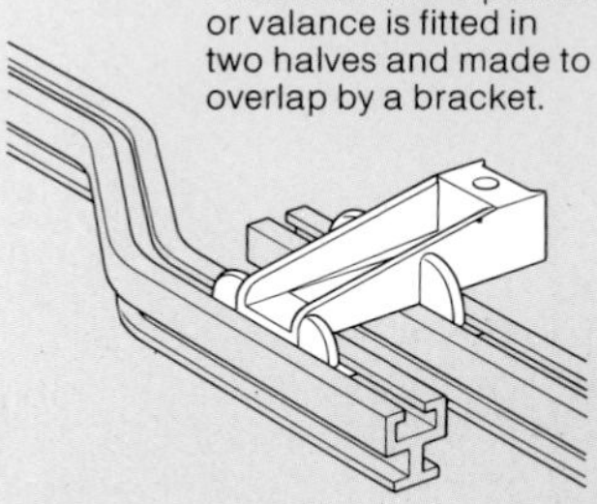

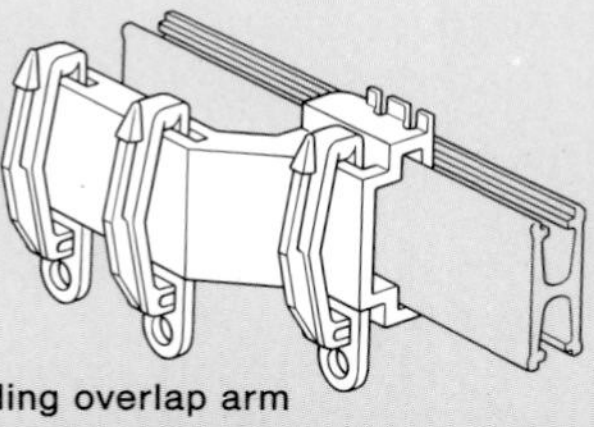

Sliding overlap arm
For most continuous tracks there are overlap arms that slide along the track like gliders. The arm carries the leading edge of one curtain over the other.

FITTING THE TRACK

With a wall-fixed track, clip or slot it onto the brackets.

With a ceiling-fixed track of the clip-on type, clip the track to the brackets. With a ceiling-fixed track which has a channel for the brackets to slide in, position the brackets on the track before screwing them in place.

Once the track is in position, slide on the gliders and fit the end stops or finials in place.

RETURN TO THE WALL

Screw eyes to support a return-to-the-wall (page 403) should be screwed into wall plugs or they will work loose.

FIXING A POLE TO THE WALL

1 Draw a guide line on the wall as for fixing brackets for a track on the wall (page 407).

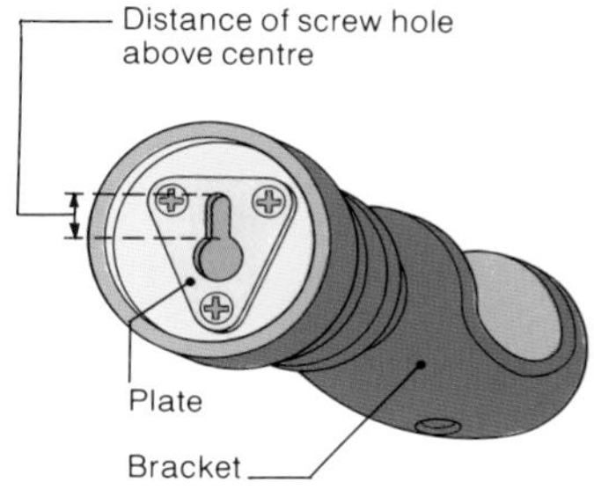

The screw hole in the bracket plate is often above centre.

2 Measure how far above centre the screw hole is and make the drilling marks that distance above the line; 4in (10cm) from each end, and in the centre if needed. ALTERNATIVELY, if the bracket is in two parts, make drilling marks on the guide line. Make them through the screw holes on the mounting plate.

3 Drill and plug the holes.

4 Drive in the screws, letting the heads project; or screw in place the plates for two-part brackets.

5 Fit the brackets in place.

6 Position the pole, centring it on the brackets, and slide on the rings. Make sure that one ring is outside each end bracket and the remainder between the brackets. Push the finials firmly into place at each end of the pole.

7 Drive the screw provided into the hole in the base of each bracket until it bites into the pole. This prevents the pole from being dislodged.

BRACKETS ENCIRCLING THE POLE

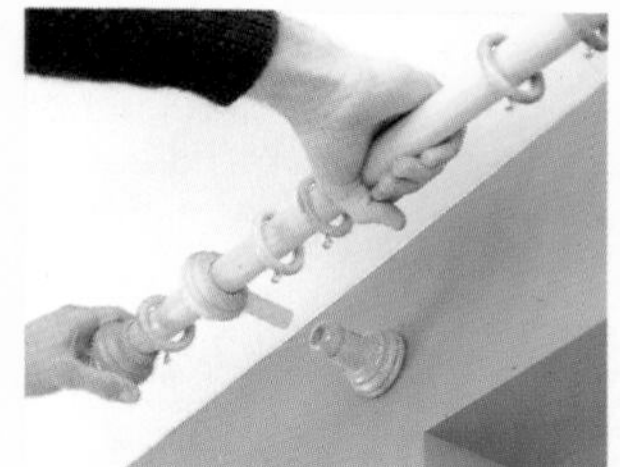

Before fitting the brackets on the screws or mounting plates that hold them in place on the wall, slide the brackets onto the pole with all but two of the rings between them.

Fit the brackets on the screws or mounting plates then slide one more ring on at each end of the pole. Finally, push on a finial at each end.

FIXING WIRES AND RODS

The wires and rods for net or café curtains are held by screw hooks. Screw them to the window frame if it is made of wood; if it is metal or PVC, screw them into drilled and plugged holes in the sides of the window recess.

Some rods are held in place by sockets. One type is face-fixed; screw the sockets into wooden window frames. Another type is side-fixed for use where a window frame is not wooden; screw these into drilled and plugged holes in the sides of the recess.

Choosing the fabric and thread

Colour and pattern may be the decisive points when you choose a furnishing fabric, but take other factors into consideration. Pay attention to manufacturers' recommendations on fabric use. Buy only curtaining fabric for making curtains and blinds; upholstery material, which is often bulkier and stiffer, may not gather or drape properly.

Most patterned fabrics involve some extra cost. A large pattern could cause considerable wastage; almost a whole pattern may have to be cut off each panel of fabric to ensure that patterns match up at the edges where the panels are sewn together. On fabrics with small patterns, panels will match with less wastage.

HELPFUL TIP
Check that the pattern is printed straight on the fabric. If it is askew – which may happen particularly near the ends of a roll – it will slant across the curtain hem which will never appear to be level.

Cost can also be kept down by avoiding the heading styles that use the greatest width of material (page 404). Sill-length or radiator-length curtains are cheaper than floor-length curtains.

Do not be tempted to cut costs by skimping on width. You will be more satisfied with a cheap fabric made up with a lining, plenty of fullness and a smart heading than with an expensive fabric unlined, sparsely gathered or with insufficient overlap at the centre or onto the walls. A cheaper, lightweight fabric will hang better if you enclose a string of small lead weights in the hem, or sew in individual wrapped weights (page 413).

SEEING THE FABRIC AT HOME

Always ask to see fabric draped before you buy. The pattern and texture rarely look the same hanging as they do lying flat. Hold the draped fabric against the light, not just facing it. Some fabrics are enhanced by strong, direct lighting but disappointing in your own room. Borrow a length of the fabric to look at beside your window.

Washable fabrics cut out costly dry-cleaning, but check that the fabric is shrink-proof and colour-fast. Some curtaining fabrics have a fade-proof guarantee – useful for unlined curtains and for those where the daylight may fall onto the face of the fabric. Fabrics that contain any wool should be moth-proof.

HELPFUL TIP
Buy sufficient material to complete the task; manufacturers discontinue patterns to bring in new ones. Beware of buying material from more than one roll. Colours may vary on different rolls.

Visit several types of fabric supplier before making a decision. Large department stores usually display a wide selection of materials. Local discount houses frequently offer the keenest prices. Small, specialist fabric shops are often a source of unusual designs.

Do not buy a cheap lining fabric. It is more likely to shrink when it is washed or dry-cleaned.

Make a sketch of your window and discuss your plans with an experienced soft-furnishing assistant who will check your estimates and advise on the suitability of fabrics.

PICKING THE RIGHT THREAD

Haberdashery counters now offer a bewildering choice of threads. One basic rule simplifies the choice: use synthetic threads on synthetic fabrics, natural threads on natural fabrics. Some synthetic threads are extremely strong and can damage natural fabrics. Polyester thread in just one thickness is suitable for all synthetic fabrics. Cotton thread looks too thick on many synthetic fabrics and, when it is washed, it may shrink and make the seams pucker. Cotton thread is made in sizes 10 to 60. The higher the number, the thinner the thread. No. 40 suits medium-weight fabrics, 60 suits fine ones. On upholstery fabric, use carpet thread made entirely of flax. To lash springs to webbing, use cord, sisal or No. 2 twine.

Choosing whether to line or interline

Lining and interlining are second and third layers of material that can be added to the main fabric for protection from dirt and sunlight, for insulation and for extra light-proofing.

LINING

A cotton sateen fabric protects the main fabric from dirt and sunlight. It makes the curtains warmer and more light-proof, and generally gives a more luxurious fullness to the draped folds.

There are three ways to make up lined curtains: as a simple bag; with detachable loose linings; and with locked-in linings.

The bag method is quick and simple but flouts several rules followed by professionals to give the perfect hang to their curtains. The linings are not attached to the main curtains except at the edges and unless the two fabrics are hanging perfectly straight, the edges of the main curtains may twist and show the linings. Much of the sewing can be done by machine.

Curtains with detachable loose linings are easy to make – and practical. The linings can be removed for washing if the main fabric is not washable, or for more frequent washing than the main curtains need. They can also be changed from one set of curtains to another. The linings have their own separate heading tape but hang on the same hooks as the main curtains. They keep out more light and cold than unlined curtains and protect the main curtains, but because their folds tend to hang separately from those of the main curtain they do not improve the body or draping of the curtains as much as locked-in linings do.

Locked-in linings lie closely against the main curtains and drape in exactly the same folds, giving a rounded fullness to all the gathers or pleats. It takes more time and care to sew them in from top to bottom at several points across the curtains.

INTERLINING

A third layer – of a thick, soft fabric sewn between the main fabric and the lining – gives extra body and insulation to curtains but adds considerably to the cost. If your windows are double-glazed or you have chosen a thick, warm curtain fabric, the extra expense may be unnecessary.

The fabrics sold for interlining are not washable, so otherwise washable curtains will require dry-cleaning if you interline them. This problem can be overcome by using flannelette sheeting as interlining. It can still be bought by the metre but if you cannot obtain it, use a pair of flannelette sheets. Wash the flannelette once or more to make it less likely to shrink later.

If you are interlining for extra warmth or to keep out light rather than to add body to the main fabric, you can attach the flannelette to separate loose linings instead of to the main fabric. Follow the instructions for making lined curtains by the bag method (page 412), using the lining as the main fabric and the flannelette as the lining. Apply the loose-lining tape in the normal way (page 413).

Estimating the amount of fabric

Always fix the track or pole in position before beginning to measure for fabric. The fixing points may not be firm enough in the spot you originally planned and the track may have to be moved, which will affect the measurements.

Choose the style of heading before you calculate how much material you need, as both width and length vary according to the heading.

CALCULATING THE LENGTH

1 Measure the 'drop' from the base of the glider or ring on the track to the required length. Measure at several spots – floors and windowsills are not always level.

Short curtains should hang to 4in (10cm) below the sill or 2in (5cm) above the radiator. Full-length curtains should end 1in (2.5cm) above the carpet or other floor covering.

Make heavy, interlined curtains 1in (2.5cm) shorter than the length you want because they will drop slightly during the first few weeks of hanging.

2 Add on 3in (7.5cm) for turning at the top of the curtain.

3 Add on 6in (15cm) for the lower hem.

4 If you are using a patterned fabric, add on the length of one extra pattern repeat to ensure that you will be able to make the pattern match across the whole curtain.

5 If the pleated heading is going to stand up above the glider to conceal the track, add on the depth of the heading tape. This varies from about 2in to 6in (5cm to 15cm) in different styles.

CALCULATING THE WIDTH

1 Measure the full width of the track or pole, not just the width of the window.

2 Multiply this by 1½-2 for a simple gathered heading, more for a style with heavier gathering or pleating (page 404).

3 Add on 12in (30cm) for side turnings and central overlap.

4 Add on the width of any return to the wall (page 403) at each end of the track.

5 Most curtain fabrics are 48in (122cm) wide, but other widths are available. Divide the total width needed by 48in (122cm), or by the width of your chosen fabric. Round up the answer to the nearest whole number. This is the number of panels you need to make up the curtain width.

FABRIC NEEDED

To estimate the total amount of fabric required, multiply the length by the number of panels.

LINING

Estimate for a lining in the same way as for the main fabric. Remember that the lining may be made in a different width from the curtain fabric and you must make a fresh calculation to find the number of panels needed. No allowance is needed for pattern matches.

Cutting out

As soon as you have cut out each panel of fabric, mark the top with a stitch of bright thread as a guide for when you join the panels. Even plain panels look different if they hang in opposite directions.

You will need

Tools Measure; tailor's chalk; scissors; set square; needle; large working surface.
Materials Curtain fabric; bright thread.

CUTTING FABRICS WITH A STRAIGHT WEAVE

If curtain panels are not cut straight across the fabric, they may hang in uneven folds, especially at seams.

On straight-weave fabrics you can draw out a thread to make a straight cutting guide.

1 Make a small snip at an angle through the selvedge into the body of the fabric so that you can catch hold of a cross thread.

2 Draw the thread out carefully, easing the fabric back from it.

CUTTING FABRICS WITHOUT A STRAIGHT WEAVE

Many fabrics, however, including most satin-finish cottons, chintzes and lining fabrics, have no straight thread running across which you can use as a cutting guide.

To ensure you cut these fabrics straight, chalk a cutting line across the fabric. Use a set square and ruler to make sure that the chalked line is at right angles to the selvedges of the fabric.

> **HELPFUL TIP**
> An easy way to square up fabric for cutting is to lay it along a rectangular table with the selvedge running exactly down the long side. Run chalk across the fabric where it bends over the end of the table. Cut along the chalk line.

CUTTING FLOOR-LENGTH CURTAINS

For floor-length curtains, where the top is more noticeable than the hem, cut the fabric panels so that a complete pattern will start just below the gathered heading.

CUTTING SILL-LENGTH CURTAINS

Because the lower edge is more noticeable on sill-length curtains than it is on floor-length curtains, cut the fabric panels so that the finished curtain (with hem turned up) will show a complete pattern at the bottom.

CUTTING OUT AN ODD NUMBER OF PANELS

When using an odd number of panels to make up the width for a pair of curtains, cut one panel in half from top to bottom. Use the half panels at the outer edges of the curtains and complete panels at the centre.

CUTTING VELVETS AND VELOURS

With velvets and velours, run your hand to and fro over the pile to find which way it lies sleek and smooth. It should lie sleek from top to bottom of the curtain. Make sure the fabric is running the right way on every panel.

TRIMMING THE EDGES

Cut away selvedges from both main fabric and lining. The selvedge is the tightly woven strip at each edge, not the whole of the unprinted strip. The tighter weave will cause seams to pucker. There is enough surplus width to allow for trimming and seams without losing any pattern.

What stitches and seams to use

In all hand sewing except tacking, secure the end of the thread in the fabric with a couple of small stitches made one on top of the other. Finish off the stitching also by making two or three stitches over one another before cutting off the thread.

For tacking, knot the end of the thread to secure it. In machine sewing, secure the beginning and the end of a seam with ½in (1.3cm) of reverse stitching before cutting off the threads.

The stitches are shown in black for clarity. Use thread in the colour of the curtains or the lining, as appropriate; when you are sewing a lining to the main curtain, use thread to match the main curtain. For tacking, cheaper thread is made with a reverse twist for easy unpicking.

HAND STITCHES

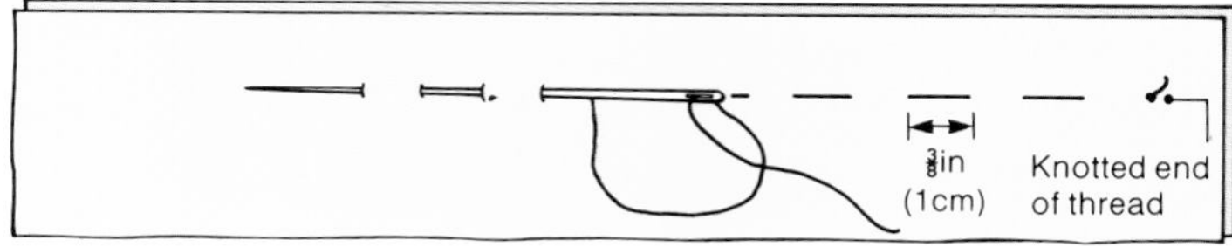

Tacking or basting Temporary stitching holds fabrics together.

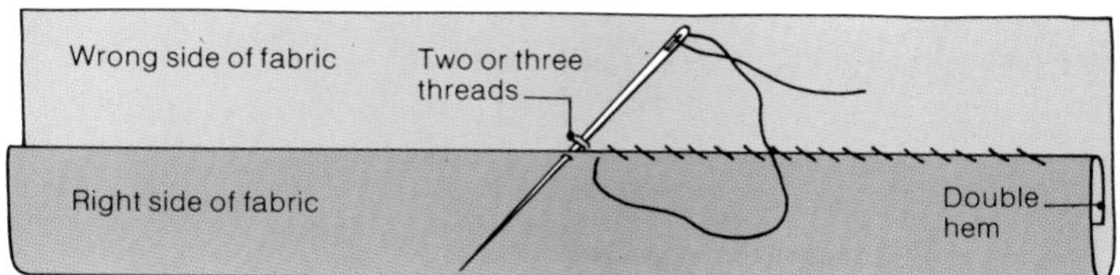

Hemstitch Small slanted stitching secures a folded fabric edge.

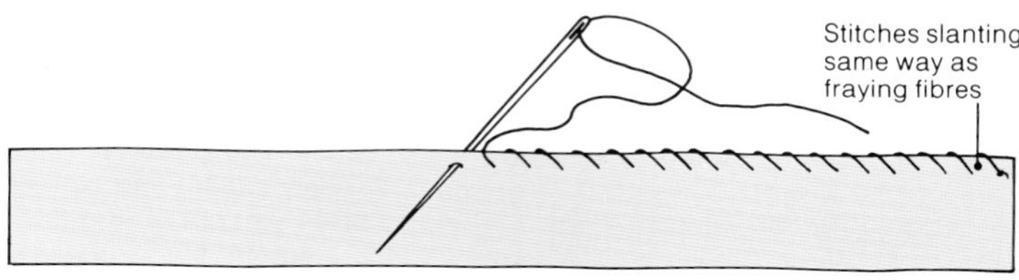

Oversewing Slanting stitches neaten raw edges and hold down cut fibres.

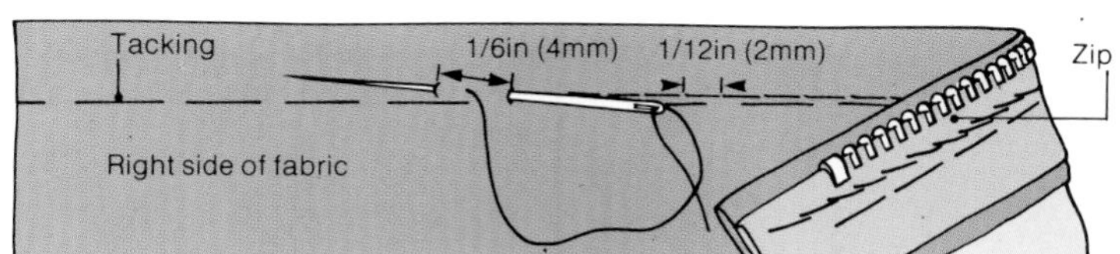

Prickstitch or backstitch Small even stitches are used to put a zip in by hand.

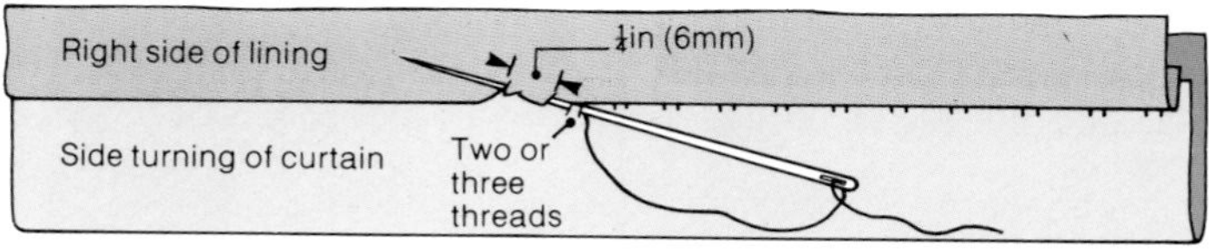

Slipstitch Invisible sewing holds a turning to another piece of fabric.

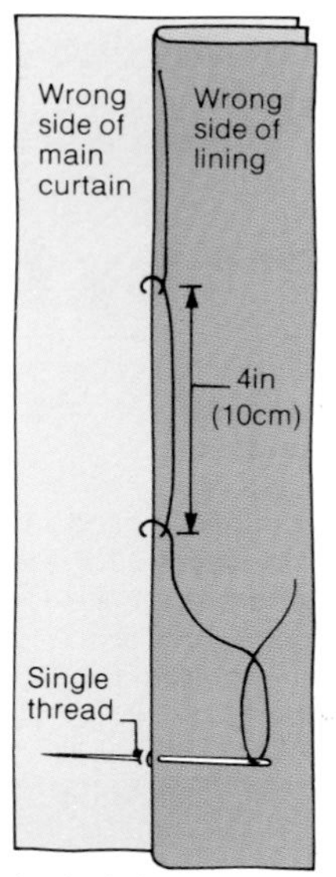

Lockstitch Long stitches hold locked-in linings or interlinings to the main curtain fabric.

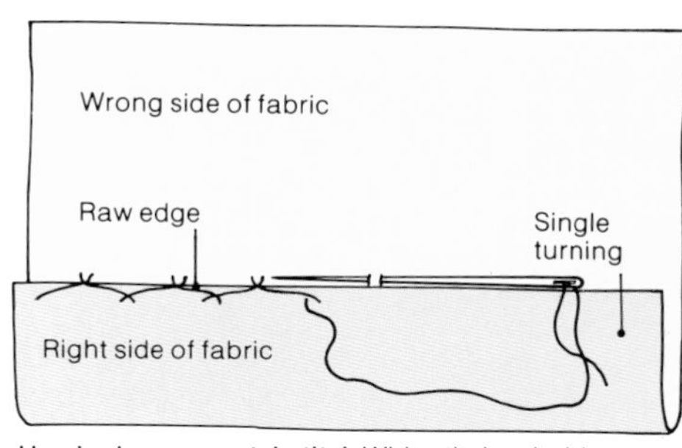

Herringbone or catchstitch Wide stitches hold an interlining, a heavy hem or a side turning.

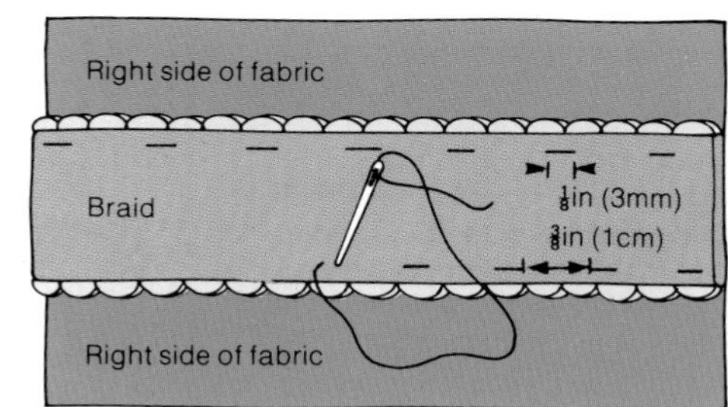

Stabstitch Small stitches sew braids in place on thick fabrics or pelmets.

MACHINE-STITCHED SEAMS

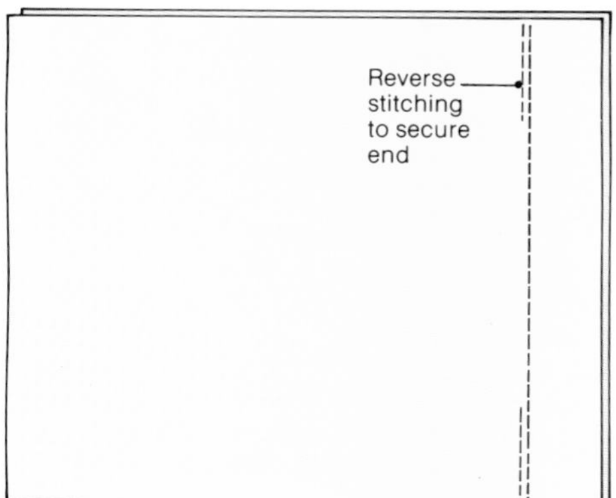

Plain open seam

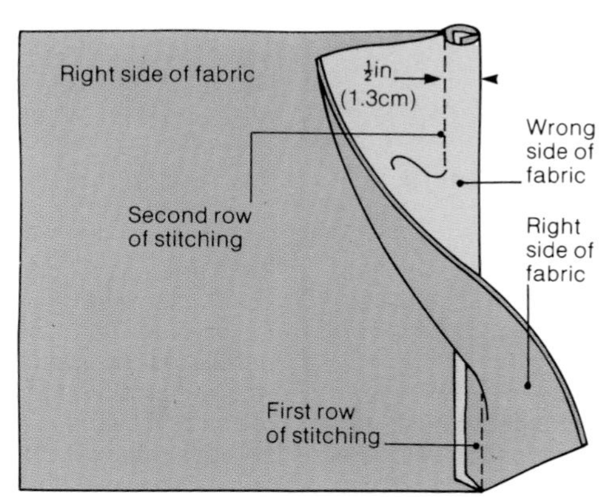

French seam

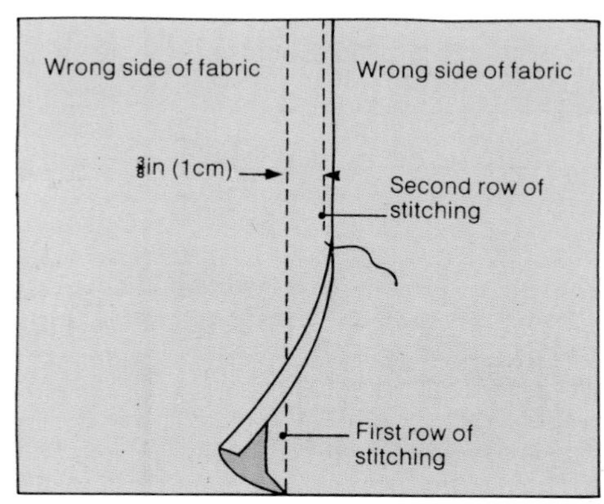

Run-and-fell seam

Making unlined curtains

You will need
Tools Measure; tailor's chalk; scissors; pins; needles; sewing machine; iron; large working surface.
Materials Fabric; heading tape; thread; perhaps weights; curtain hooks.

1 Cut out the panels of fabric (page 410).

2 If panels have to be joined to make up the required width, pin together the edges to be joined with the right sides of the panels together. Join on any half panels so that they will be at the outer edges of the curtains.

3 Open out the panels to check that any pattern matches are accurate and adjust the pins if necessary.

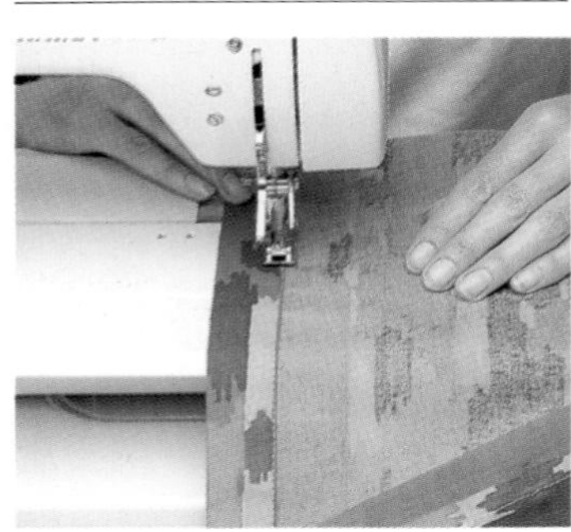

4 Tack the joins (page 411) and sew with a run-and-fell machine seam (page 411). Remove the tacking before stitching the second seam.

5 Remove the tackings from the second part of the run-and-fell seams and press the seams.

6 Place each curtain in turn right side down on the working surface. Pin 1¼in (3cm) double turnings down each side and sew them in place with hemstitch (page 411). Stop sewing 12in (30cm) from the bottom to allow for folding the mitre.

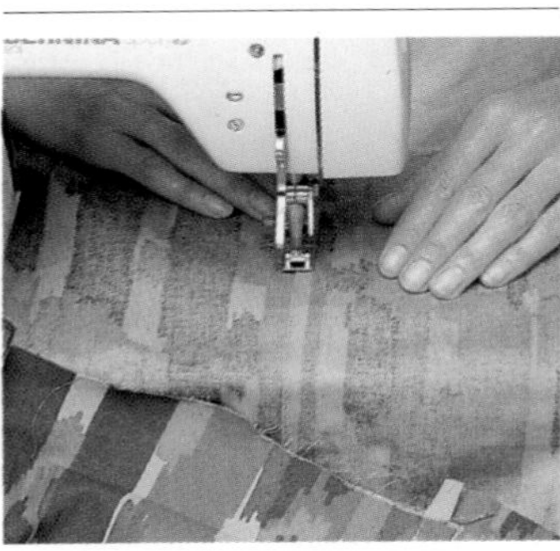

ALTERNATIVELY, if you do not mind the stitching showing, you can save time by machine stitching the side turnings instead of hemming them.

On velvet and other thick fabrics, make single side turnings and hems. Sew them with herringbone stitch (page 411).

7 Turn up and pin into place a 3in (7.5cm) double hem along the bottom. As you do so, check that any pattern is finishing where you planned. If you are using weights, stitch them in place (opposite page) as you pin the hem.

8 Hemstitch the hem, mitre the corners (opposite) and finish off the side turnings with hemstitch.

9 The curtain is now ready for its heading (pages 415–416).

Making lined curtains by the bag method

You will need
Tools Measure; tailor's chalk; scissors; pins; needles; sewing machine; iron; large work surface.
Materials Main fabric; lining fabric; heading tape; thread; perhaps weights; curtain hooks.

1 Cut out the main fabric panels (page 410).

2 If you have to join panels to make up the width required, pin together the edges with the right sides of the panels together.

3 Open out the panels to check that any pattern matches are accurate. Adjust the pins if necessary. Half panels should hang at the outer edges of the curtains.

4 Tack the joins (page 411). Machine with a plain seam (page 411).

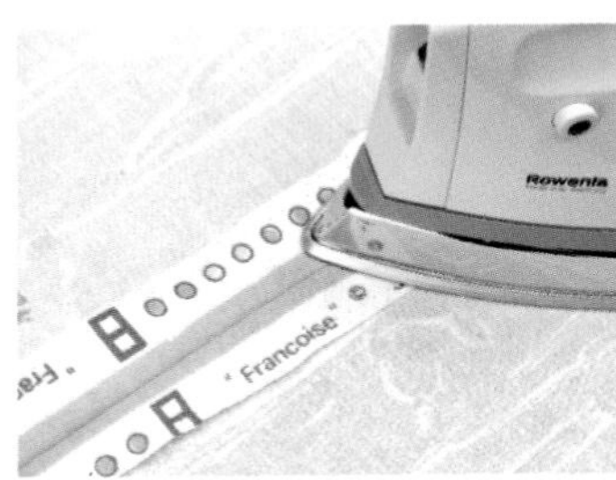

5 Remove the tacking and press the seams open.

6 Cut out the lining fabric (page 410), making it 4½in (11.5cm) shorter than the main fabric.

7 Join together panels for the linings in the same way as for the main curtains, and press them.

8 Trim off 1½in (4cm) from the two sides of each lining.

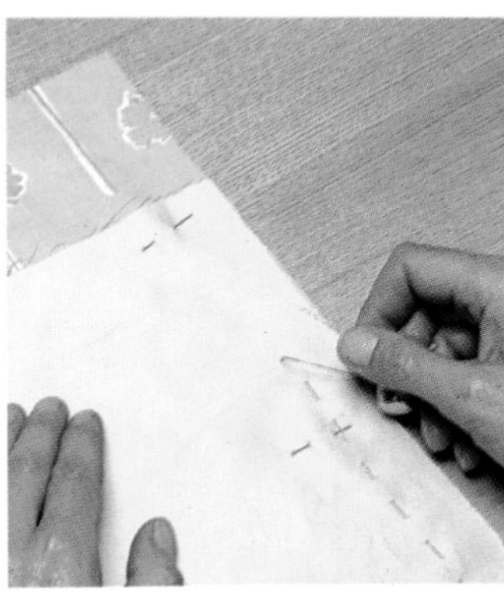

9 Spread out each curtain in turn, right side up. Lay the lining over it right side down with the top 2½in (6.5cm) below the main curtain top. Align the fabrics at the right and pin and tack them together ¾in (2cm) from the edge.

10 Draw the lining to the left and align it with the main fabric. Pin and tack the fabrics together ¾in (2cm) from the left edge.

11 Machine the two tacked seams from top to bottom, stopping 12in (30cm) from the bottom of the lining to allow for folding the mitres at the corners. Remove the tacking.

12 Fold up and pin the bottom of the lining to make a double 3in (7.5cm) hem.

13 Tack and machine the hem. Remove the tacking.

14 Turn each curtain right side out. Spread it out lining side up and make sure that the lining runs parallel to the curtain top all the way across it. Smooth out the lining to centre it over the curtain so that an equal amount of the main curtain is showing down each side. Press the side turnings.

15 Fold up and pin the bottom of the main curtain to make a double 3in (7.5cm) hem. Check on the right side that any pattern is finishing where you planned. If you are using weights, sew them in place (opposite) as you pin up the hem. Tack the hem in place, making mitres (opposite) at the corners.

16 Sew the bottom of the curtain in place with hemstitch (page 411) and slipstitch the diagonal folds of the mitres.

17 Use slipstitch to finish joining the sides of the lining to the curtain.

18 The curtain is now ready for a ready-made heading tape (page 415) or for a hand-pleated heading (pages 416–417).

Making curtains with loose linings

You will need
Tools Measure; tailor's chalk; scissors; pins; needles; sewing machine; iron; large working surface.
Materials Main fabric; main heading tape; perhaps weights; lining fabric, loose-lining heading tape; thread; touch-and-close fastening tape; curtain hooks.

1 Make the main curtains exactly as unlined curtains (opposite).

2 Sew on the chosen heading tape (page 415).

3 Cut the lining fabric (page 410) to the same width as the main curtains but shorter. Measure it from the bottom of the glider or ring, but do not add any turning allowance at the top. Reduce the turning allowance at the bottom to 4¾in (12cm).

4 Join the panels of fabric with a run-and-fell seam; remember to remove the tacking before sewing the second part of the seam. Sew the side turnings as for the main curtains. If you need to use half panels to make up the required width, remember to put them at the outer edges.

5 Turn up, pin and tack a double 3in (7.5cm) hem across the bottom. It is not necessary to mitre the corners but you can do so if you wish. Machine the turning in place and remove the tacking.

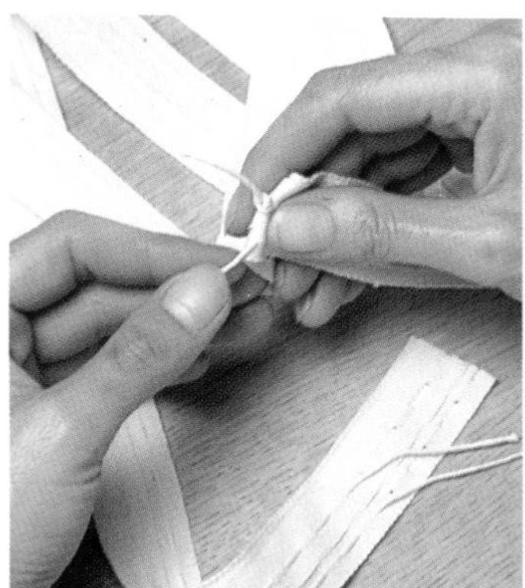

6 To fit the loose-lining heading tape, cut the tape to the width of the lining with an extra 1¼in (3cm) extending at each end. Pull the cords free from the last 1½in (4cm) at each end. Knot the cord ends that will be at the centre of the window on the finished lining; knot them separately so that the tape does not buckle when they are drawn up. Leave the other cord ends free for drawing up later.

MITRED CORNERS ON HEMS

Mitred corners give a neat finish, reduce bulky overlaps of fabric and allow the sides to hang well.

1 Fold in and press the turning allowance at each edge of the fabric in turn.

2 Fold over the corner of the fabric at the point where the pressed lines cross. Make the fold so that the sections of the pressed lines match up exactly.

3 Press the corner fold lightly in place.

4 Refold the hems. If they are to be double hems, fold under half the fabric. On finer fabrics you can leave the corner uncut in case you wish to alter the curtain in the future – for a different window, perhaps.

ALTERNATIVELY, on thick fabric, cut the corner off ¼in (6mm) from the fold; then refold the turnings.

5 Slipstitch (page 411) the diagonal folds together. The two will not be the same length unless the turning allowances are the same.

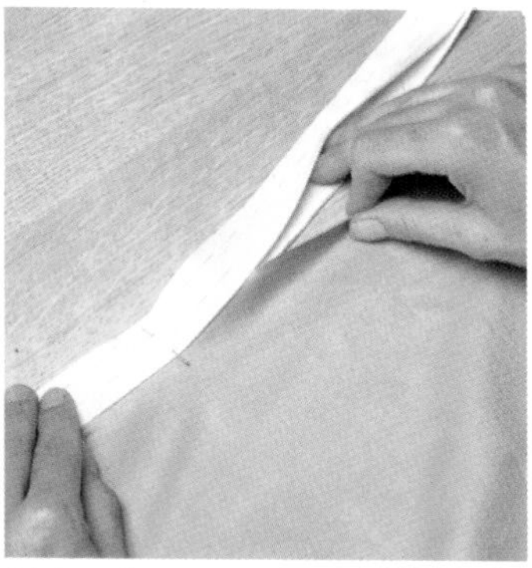

7 Lay the tape, corded side up, on a table and feed the raw top edge of the lining right side up between the two layers of the tape, pinning it in place as you work along the lining. Let the tape extend 1¼in (3cm) beyond each side turning.

8 Tack the tape in place. Fold the surplus tape under at each end and tack it in place.

9 Machine stitch the ends and along the lower edge of the tape through all three thicknesses – tape, lining, tape. The plain lower layer of the tape is slightly deeper than the corded upper layer so that you will not miss it as you machine. Remove all tacking and press.

10 Pull up the free cord ends to make the lining 2in (5cm) narrower than the main curtain and knot the cords firmly.

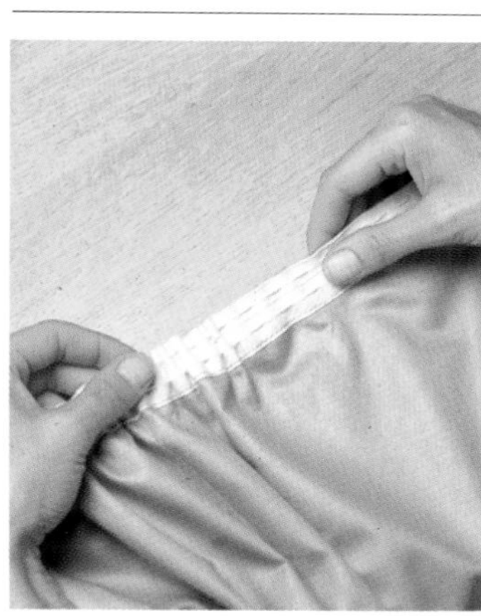

11 Slide the heading tape along the cord to distribute the gathers evenly along the lining.

SEWING WEIGHTS IN A HEM

Curtains with weighted hems hang well. Choose weights of a size and heaviness to suit the thickness of the fabric.

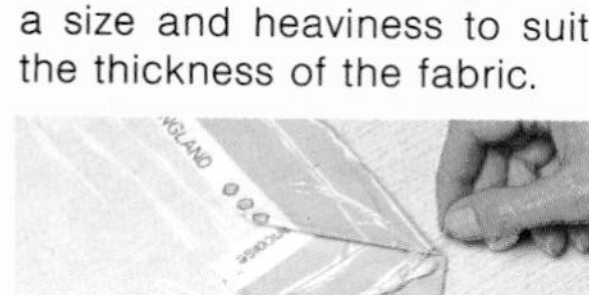

Lay a strip of weights on the hem fold. Sew it in place at each end.

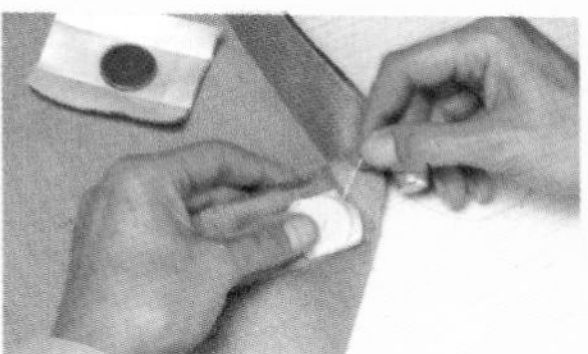

Wrap round weights in fabric. Sew them at the corners and where panels are joined.

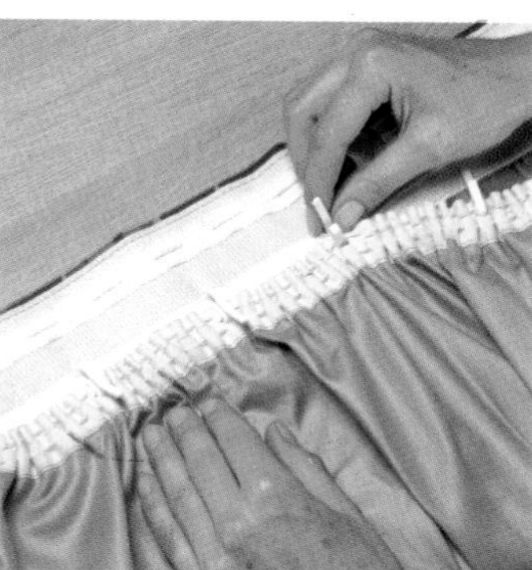

12 Slip the hooks first into the slots at the top of the lining tape and then into the pockets of the main curtain tape. Twist the hooks over into their final position.

13 If the track has combined glider-hooks, use ordinary curtain hooks in the lining and slip them into the holes at the bottom of the glider-hooks.

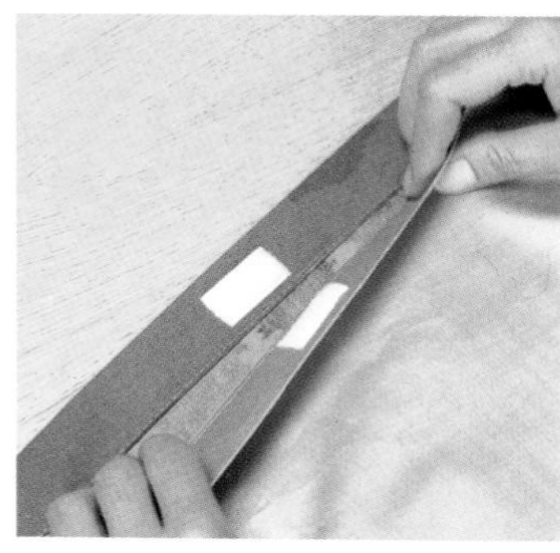

14 Hand-sew short strips of a touch-and-close fastening tape, such as Velcro, to the lining and main fabric at two or three places down each side turning to prevent the lining from showing.

Making curtains with locked-in linings

You will need
Tools Measure; tailor's chalk; scissors; pins; needles; sewing machine; iron; large working surface.
Materials Main fabric; lining fabric; thread; curtain hooks. Perhaps also curtain weights.

1 Cut out the main fabric (page 410).

2 If you need to join panels of fabric to make up the width required, pin together the edges to be joined with the right sides of the panels together.

3 Open out the panels to check that any patterns are matching accurately; adjust the pins if necessary. Half panels should hang at the outer edges of the finished curtains.

4 Tack the joins (page 411) and machine them with a plain seam (page 411). Remove the tacking and press the seams open.

5 Fold in 2½in (6.5cm) single side turnings and pin them in position.

6 Sew the side turnings by hand with hemstitches (page 411) spaced well apart, taking care not to let the stitches show on the right side of the curtain. Stop sewing 12in (30cm) from the bottom to allow for folding the mitre at the corner.

7 Pin up a 3in (7.5cm) double hem across the bottom, mitring the corners (page 413). Make sure the pattern is finishing where you planned. If you are using weights (page 413), stitch them into place as you pin the hem. Stitch the hem by hand, again taking care that the hemstitch does not show on the right side of the curtain. Slipstitch (page 411) the diagonal folds of the mitre together and finish sewing the side turnings with hemstitch.

8 Cut out the lining fabric (page 410) to make up the same width as the main curtains, but 6in (15cm) shorter. Join any panels together in the same way as for the main curtains and press.

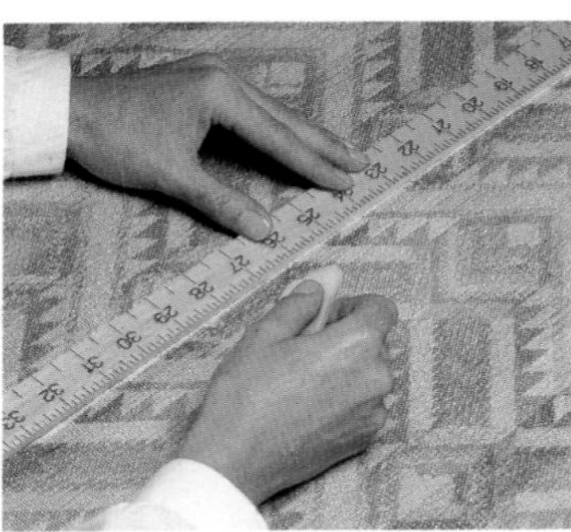

9 To join the lining and main fabric together, spread the main fabric out flat, wrong side up. Using a measure and tailor's chalk, mark guidelines from top to bottom of the curtain, making them at 12in (30cm) intervals across the whole curtain width.

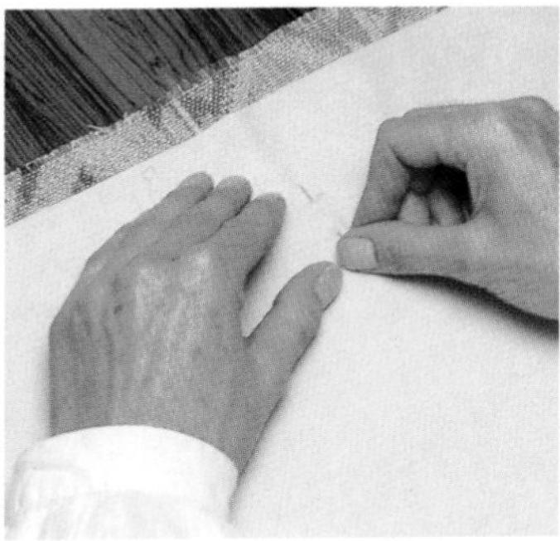

10 Lay the lining, right side up, carefully over the main fabric. Position it ¾in (2cm) from the top of the curtain, with 2½in (6.5cm) overlapping at each side. Smooth it out and make sure that any seams are straight, not sloping across the curtain. Pin the lining to the curtain from top to bottom almost 12in (30cm) from the right-hand edge.

11 Carefully fold back the lining from the left until you can see the chalked guideline nearest to the right edge of the curtain.

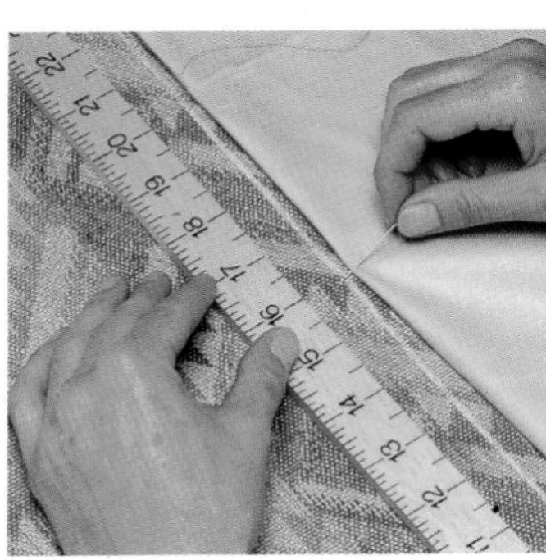

12 Starting 6in (15cm) from the top of the curtain, lockstitch (page 411) the lining to the guideline. Use thread that matches the main fabric, not the lining.

13 Make the stitches 4in (10cm) apart and do not pull the thread too tight or the main fabric will pucker. Pick up only one thread of the fabric with each stitch.

14 When the row of lockstitch is completed, unfold the lining towards the left until it reaches the next guideline. Repeat the sewing and continue across the curtain until the lining is in place.

15 Trim away any lining extending beyond the curtain down the sides and along the bottom.

16 Fold under and pin 1in (2.5cm) of the lining down each side and across the bottom. Make the corners of the lining meet the mitre joins of the curtain.

17 Tack the curtain and lining together across the top, 2in (5cm) down from the curtain's raw edge, to keep the fabrics in position.

18 Slipstitch the lining to the main curtain down the sides and across the bottom; begin stitching 6in (15cm) from the top to allow for the heading.

19 The curtain is now ready for the heading (pages 415–416).

Making interlined curtains

You will need
Tools Measure; tailor's chalk; scissors; pins; needles; sewing machine; iron; large working surface.
Materials Main fabric; lining fabric; interlining fabric; heading tape; thread; curtain hooks. Perhaps also curtain weights.

1 Cut out the main fabric (page 410).

2 If necessary, join panels together to make up the required width. First pin together the edges to be joined with the right sides of the panels together.

3 Open out the panels to check whether any pattern matches are accurate and adjust the pins if necessary. Remember to join on any half panels so that they will be hanging at the outer edges of the finished curtains.

4 Tack the joins (page 411) and sew them with a plain machine seam (page 411). Remove the tackings and press the seams open.

5 Cut out the lining fabric (page 410) to make up the same width as the main curtains, but make the panels 6in (15cm) shorter.

6 Join panels of lining fabric together in the same way as the main fabric and press the seams open.

7 Cut the interlining fabric to the size of the finished curtain. No allowance for turnings is needed but add ½in (1.3cm) for any joins.

8 Join panels if necessary to make up the width you need. Spread out the panels with the edge of one overlapping ½in (1.3cm) onto the edge of the next. Tack them and machine two rows of stitching down the overlap. Remove the tacking. Interlining fabrics tend to stretch and machine stitching will prevent this.

9 Spread out the curtain wrong side up. Use a measure and tailor's chalk to mark guide lines from top to bottom, making the first 8in (20cm) from the right-hand edge and others 16in (40cm) apart.

10 Lay the interlining over the curtain 6in (15cm) from the bottom and smooth it out. Pin it in place at the right-hand end then fold it back carefully from the left until you can see the chalk line nearest the right-hand edge of the main curtain.

11 Sew the interlining in place following the same method as for a lining when making a curtain with locked-in lining (facing page). Check that the interlining is 6in (15cm) from the bottom before you sew each row of lockstitching.

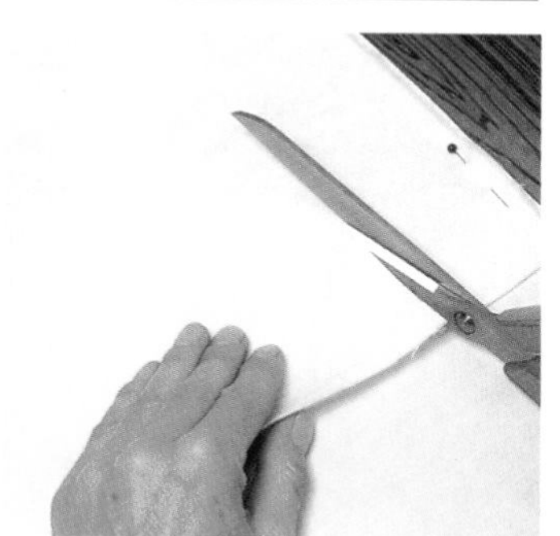

12 Trim the interlining at both sides to end 2½in (6.5cm) within the main curtain.

13 Pin the edges of the main fabric over the interlining down the sides. Pin up a 3in (7.5cm) double hem onto the interlining across the bottom, making mitres (page 413) at the corners and checking that the pattern is finishing where you planned. If you are using weights, stitch them into place (page 413) as you pin the hem.

14 Sew the side turnings and hem of the main fabric onto the interlining using a herringbone stitch (page 411). Slipstitch (page 411) the diagonal folds of the mitre together.

15 Place the lining right side up over the interlining ¾in (2cm) below the raw top edge of the curtain. Smooth it out carefully and trim the sides and bottom so that no lining fabric is extending beyond the main curtain.

16 Fold under 1in (2.5cm) of the lining at the sides and bottom and pin it in place, making the corners meet the mitre joins of the main curtain. Tack the lining in place down the sides and across the bottom, then run a line of tacking across the top to hold the curtain and lining in position.

HELPFUL TIP
If you prick your finger and a drop of blood falls on the fabric, chew a length of cotton thread and dab it on the stain to clean it off without leaving a mark.

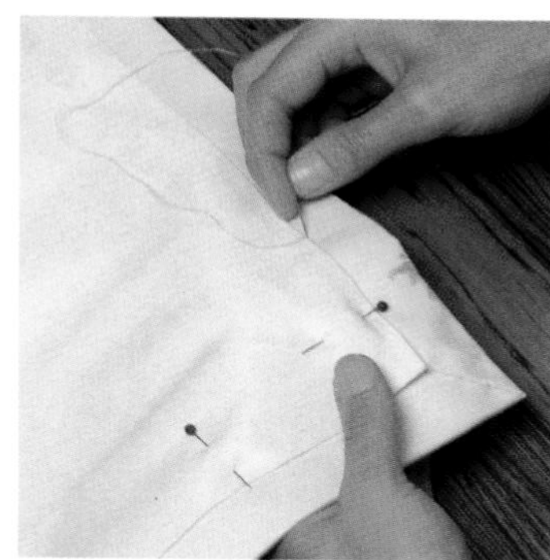

17 Sew the lining to the main curtain, using slipstitch. Remove the tacking from the sides and bottom of the curtain.

18 The curtain is now ready for its heading (pages 415–416).

Applying ready-made heading tape

Keep as much as possible of the surplus fabric allowed at the top of the curtain; fold it behind the tape. If the curtain shrinks, you can refit the tape on the surplus instead of lengthening at the hem, where a line may show.

Make sure that there is a pocket right at each end of the tape. You can do this easily by stretching it or easing it up as you fit it.

Loose lining tape is fitted in a different way (page 413).

You will need
Tools Measure; tailor's chalk; scissors; pins; needles; sewing machine; iron; large working surface.
Materials Heading tape; thread; made-up curtain; curtain hooks.

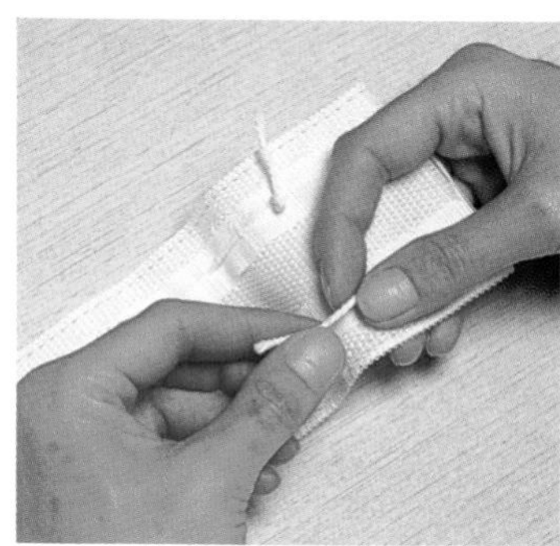

1 Cut the tape the width of the curtain plus 1¼in (3cm) at each end. Free the cords from the tape for 1in (2.5cm) at the end that will be at the centre of the track; knot each cord – separately so the tape does not buckle. At the other end, free the cords from the tape for 1½in (4cm).

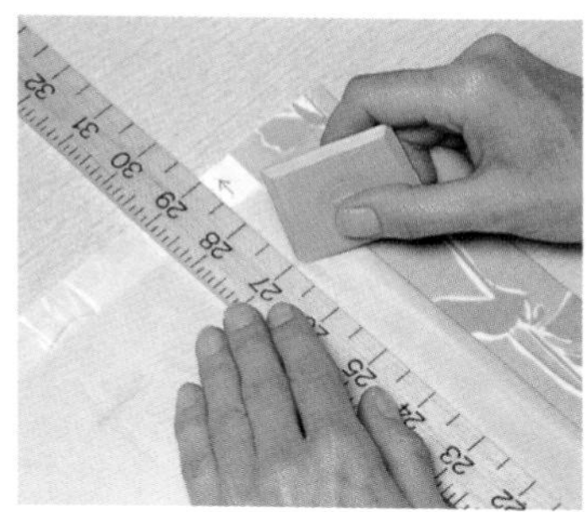

2 Spread out the curtain right side down. If it is lined, make sure that the lining and main fabric are both smoothed out fully. Every 4in (10cm) across the curtain measure from the hem upwards and use tailor's chalk to mark the required length – that is, the length you originally measured when estimating for fabric, from the base of the glider or ring to the bottom of your curtains.

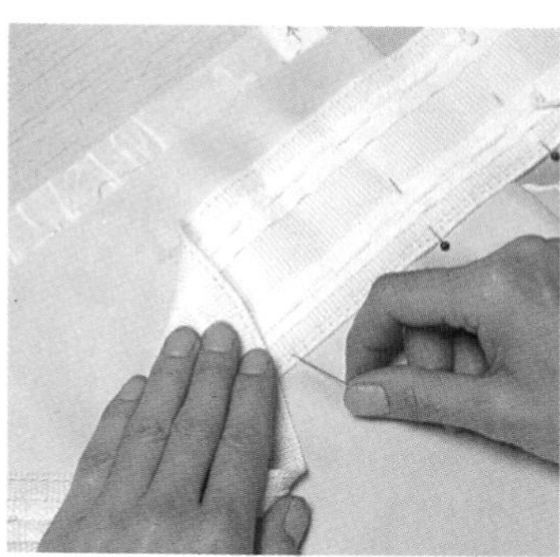

3 Start laying tape on the curtain with cord side up and the 1¼in (3cm) surplus extending at the end. Align the top of the pockets that will take the hooks, with the row of chalk marks you have made. Some tapes have more than one row of pockets (page 404). As you work across the curtain, pin the bottom edge of the tape in place.

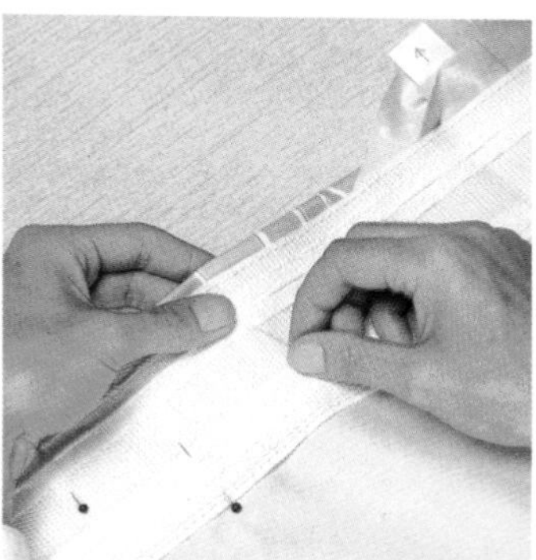

4 Fold the raw top edge of the curtain, and lining if fitted, towards you. Tuck it neatly behind the tape and pin it in place.

5 When you are using simple gathering tape the folded top will be too big to tuck behind the tape. Let the fold stand up above the tape as a top frill. If the frill would rub against a pelmet top board, trim the material back but keep as much of it as possible.

ALTERNATIVELY, when you are using a deep heading tape, most of the top fold will tuck behind the tape. Leave only ¼in (6mm) of it showing above the tape, unless you want the heading to stand up particularly high to conceal the track. In this case adjust the top turning to give the height you want.

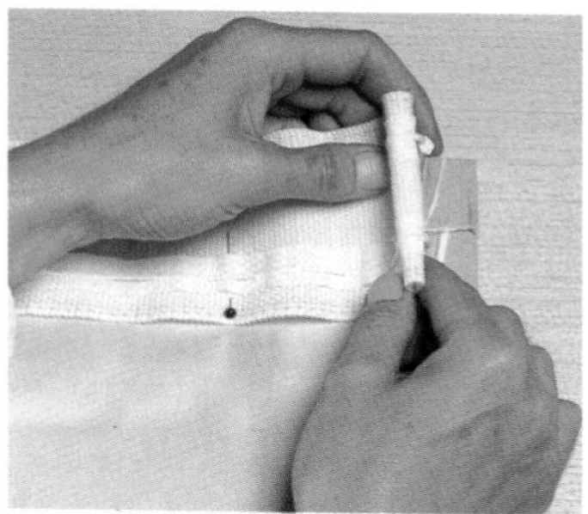

6 Tuck under the spare 1¼in (3cm) of tape at each end. Make sure the unknotted cords are free.

7 Tack the tape firmly in place round all four sides.

8 Insert a few hooks and hang the curtains to check the length and see if the heading either covers or reveals the track as planned.

9 If you have doubts, draw up the cords, insert all the hooks and hang the curtains. Moving tape at this stage is much easier than making adjustments later.

10 Machine the top of the tape in place. Machine across the bottom in the same direction to ensure that the tape does not get pulled askew. On tapes which need three or four rows of stitching, sew all the rows in the same direction. Sew the ends by hand or machine.

11 Remove all tacking and press the curtains before hanging and draping (page 418).

Making a handmade goblet-pleated heading

Buttoned goblet pleats (page 405) make an elegant formal heading on full-length curtains.

You will need
Tools Measure; tailor's chalk; scissors; pins; needles; sewing machine; iron; large working surface.
Materials Stiffener; made-up curtain; non-drawing curtain tape; thread; tissue paper or cotton wool; self-covered buttons; curtain hooks.

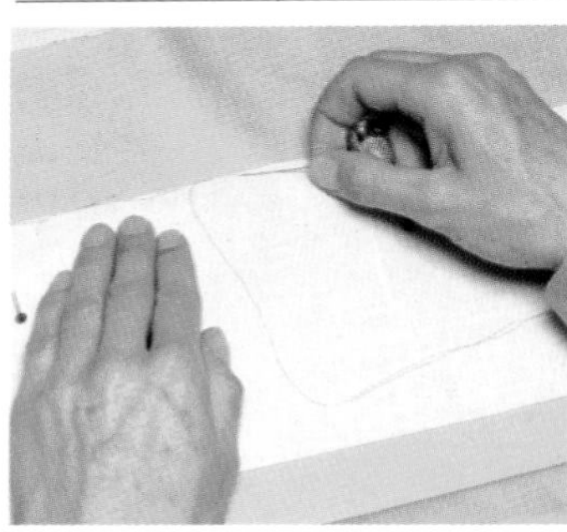

1 Stiffen the top of the curtain on the wrong side by catch-stitching (page 411) a strip of buckram across the top, or applying a strip of iron-on stiffener. Make it the depth the finished heading is to be. Apply it 3in (7.5cm) below the raw edge of the main curtain.

2 Measure the width of the track and add on any return-to-the-wall (page 403) and the central overlap. Subtract this total from the width of your pair of curtains. The amount left over is the spare fabric for the pleats.

3 To work out how much spare fabric to use in each pleat, divide the amount of spare fabric by the number of pleats – four pleats to every 48in (122cm) panel of fabric in the curtains is usual.

4 Next work out the width of the intervals between pleats. A pair of curtains made from three panels of fabric (one and a half in each curtain) will have 12 pleats with 11 intervals between them; a pair made from five panels (two and a half in each curtain) will have 20 pleats with 19 intervals between them. From the width of the track subtract the overlap and divide the amount left by the number of intervals required.

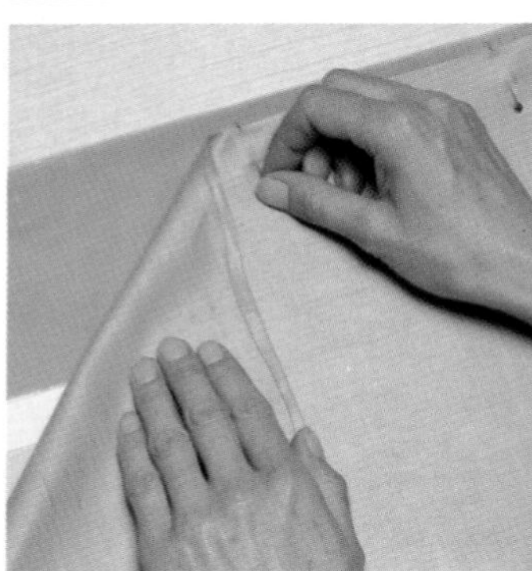

5 To make the heading ready for pleating, fold the turning allowance at the top of the main curtain over the stiffener. Fold in the lining and hemstitch it (page 411) by hand across the top.

6 Spread the curtain out flat. Measure and mark the pleats on the lining with tailor's chalk. Starting at the outer edge, mark any return-to-the-wall, then mark the width you have calculated for one pleat, then the width for one interval between pleats. Continue marking off pleats and intervals across the curtain.

7 Line up together the chalk marks for one pleat, lining side inside. Tack and then machine stitch them together on the right side of the curtain. Do this for each pleat, machining from top to bottom of the heading. Remove the tacking.

8 Round out each pleat to make a cylindrical shape and stuff it with tissue paper or cotton wool.

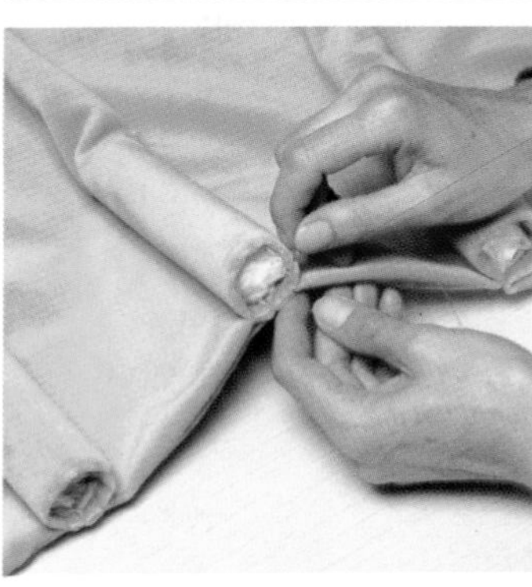

9 At each side of the vertical row of machine stitching, oversew (page 411) the top rim of the goblet for ⅜in (1cm) to the interval between pleats along the edge of the curtain. This helps the goblet hold its shape. Do this with each goblet.

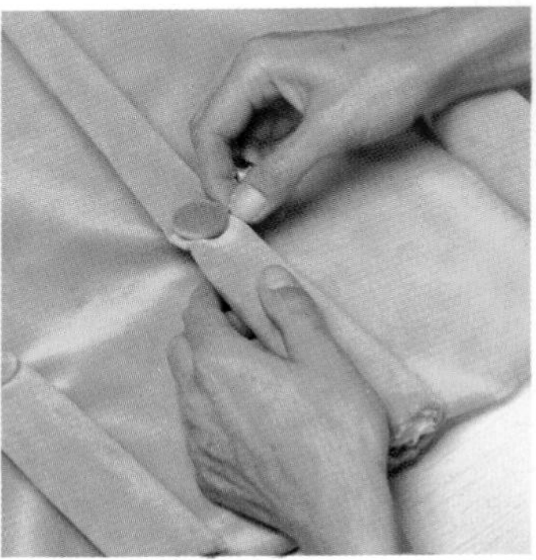

10 Finish the goblets with buttons covered with curtain fabric. Sew a button at the base of each goblet to pinch its sides together.

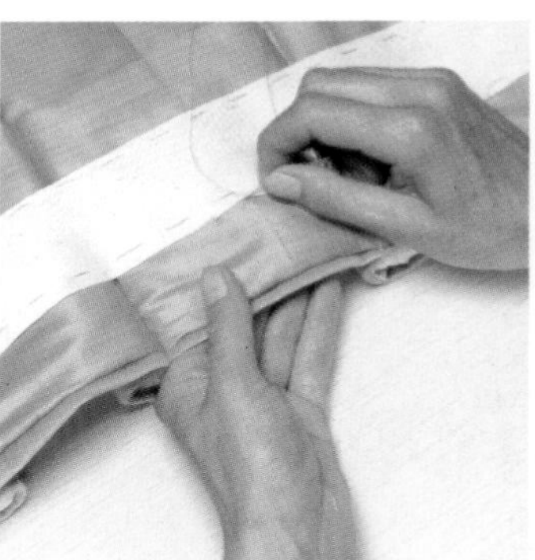

11 Pin non-drawing curtain tape along the back of the heading, turning the ends under neatly. Pin its top edge ½in (1.3cm) higher than where the base of the gliders will be. Its distance from the curtain top will depend on the height of heading allowed for. Hemstitch all round the tape.

12 Fix a hook (page 405) behind each goblet and at each end.

The curtain is now ready for hanging and draping (page 418).

Making a handmade box-pleated heading

Box pleats give curtains a crisp, tailored look and ample fullness.

You will need
Tools Measure; tailor's chalk; scissors; pins; needles; sewing machine; iron; large work-surface.
Materials Stiffener; made-up curtain; non-drawing curtain tape; thread; curtain hooks.

1 Stiffen the curtain top and make it ready for pleating as for a goblet heading (instructions 1 and 5 above).

2 To work out the pleating, subtract any return-to-the-wall (page 403) and central overlap (page 405) from the width of the curtain. Divide the remainder by 12in (30cm) for each pleat; share what is left between the pleats.

EXAMPLE 1 Take a curtain made from three 48in (122cm) panels of fabric. After allowing for any return-to-the-wall and any central overlap, it will be about 140in (350cm) wide.

Dividing 140in or 350cm by 12in or 30cm gives 11 pleats and there is 8in or 20cm left over. This 8in or 20cm is then shared equally between the 11 pleats and gives an extra ¾in or 1.8cm to each pleat.

So each pleat allowance is 12¾in or 31.8cm of material.

EXAMPLE 2 A curtain made from two 48in (122cm) panels of fabric will be about 91in (231cm) after allowing for any return-to-the-wall and any central overlap. Dividing 91in or 231cm by 12in or 30cm gives 7 pleats and there is 7in or 21cm left over to share between the 7 pleats. So each pleat allowance is 13in or 33cm of material.

EXAMPLE 1

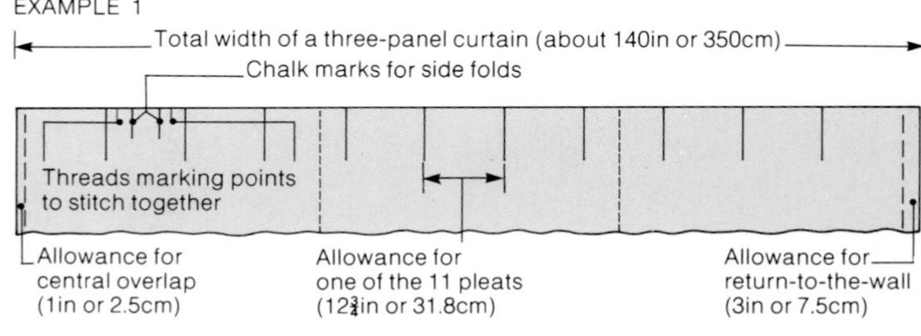

Curtain fabrics vary in width and the number of panels needed varies, so that your curtain will have its own specific width. These examples show you the steps to follow for pleating.

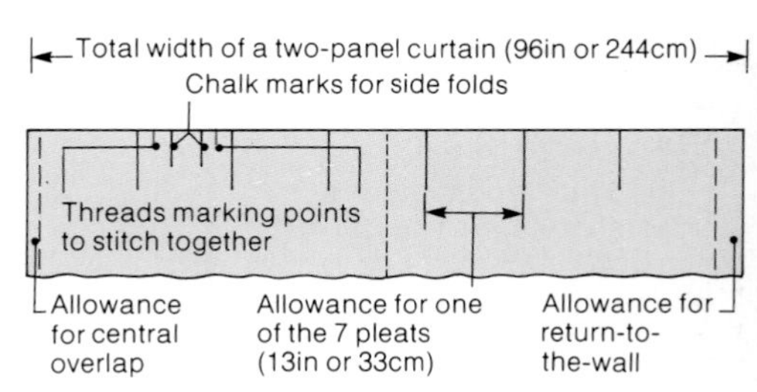

3 Measure and chalk the guide marks for pleating on the back of the curtain top. Start at the edge that will be at the centre of the window. Mark off the 1in (2.5cm) overlap allowance at the centre of one curtain. Then mark off the allowance for each pleat, leaving any return-to-the-wall at the outer edge of the curtain.

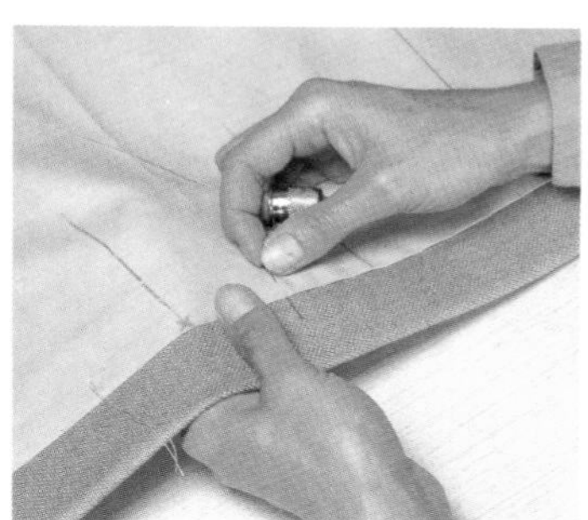

4 Divide each pleat allowance into three equal parts, marking the divisions with chalk. Then halve each of the two outer parts, and mark each halfway point with a stitch of coloured thread.

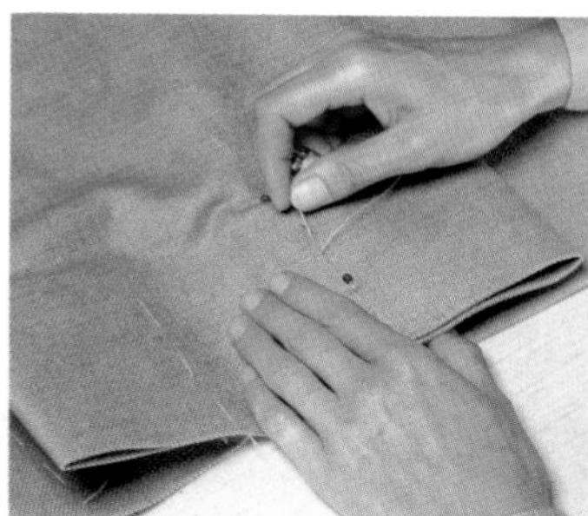

5 To form a pleat, bring the coloured threads together with the lined side of the curtain inside. Working on the right side of the fabric, tack through both thicknesses of curtain. Start tacking at the top and continue down for about $3\frac{1}{2}$in (9cm).

6 Machine the seam in place and remove the tacking. Do this for each pleat.

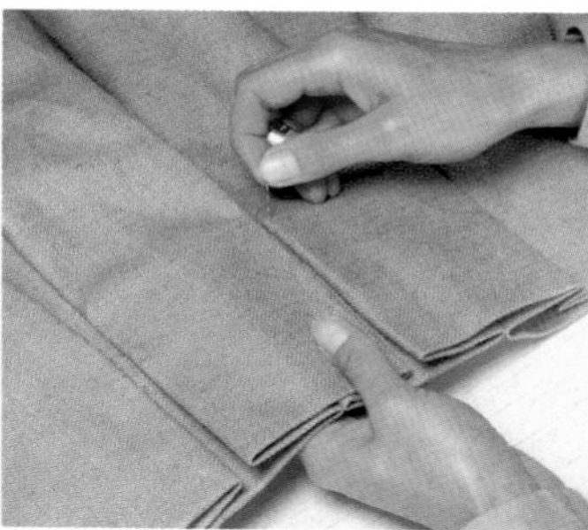

7 Flatten the pleats, forming the side folds on the chalk marks. Hemstitch the side folds for 1in (2.5cm) at the bottom of the heading to hold them in place.

8 Pin non-drawing curtain tape along the back of the heading, turning the ends under neatly. Pin its top edge $\frac{1}{2}$in (1.3cm) higher than where the base of the gliders will be Its distance from the curtain top will depend on the height of heading allowed for. Hemstitch all round the curtain tape.

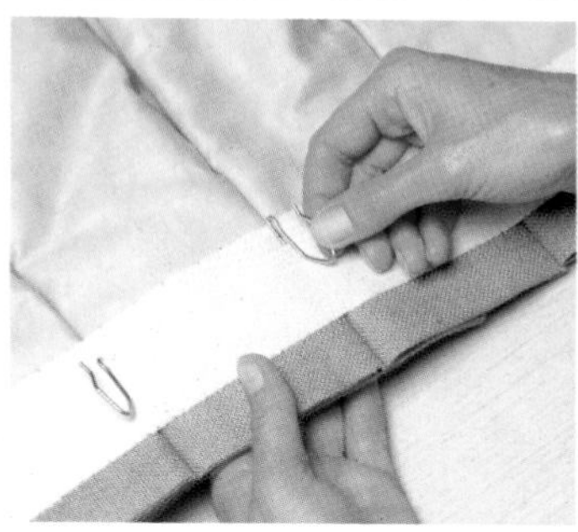

9 Fix a hook (page 405) behind each pleat and at each end. Place the hook $1\frac{1}{2}$in (4cm) from the edge that is to overlap.

The curtain is now ready for hanging and draping (page 418).

Making a handmade scalloped café heading

A café curtain (page 405) at a window's lower half gives privacy without excluding too much light.

You will need

Tools Measure; tailor's chalk; scissors; pins; needles; sewing machine; pencil; saucer or round lid; iron; large working surface.
Materials Stiffener; made-up curtain; paper for pattern; thread; curtain rings.

1 Make up an unlined curtain (page 412), a bare $1\frac{1}{2}$ times the width of the track. Allow for a $4\frac{3}{4}$in (12cm) turning at the top.

2 Sew a strip of buckram behind the curtain, using herringbone stitch (page 411) and sewing round all four sides. Position it $4\frac{3}{4}$in (12cm) down from the raw top edge of the curtain.

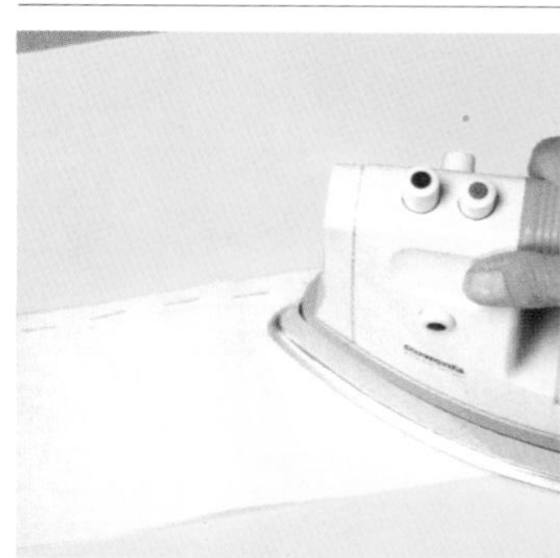

ALTERNATIVELY, apply a 4in (10cm) deep strip of iron-on stiffener to the back of the curtain if the fabric is suitable for a hot iron.

3 Cut a strip of paper about 4in (10cm) deep and the width of the made-up curtain. Fold the strip into equal sections, $1\frac{1}{4}$in (3cm) wider than you want the scallops to be.

4 Make a pencil mark on the top section of the folded strip $\frac{5}{8}$in (1.5cm) in from each side. Using an upturned saucer or a round lid as a guide, pencil a curve across the top of the section of paper, making it extend from one pencil mark to the other.

5 Cut along the pencilled curve, cutting through all the thicknesses of paper together. This will ensure that all the scallops are identical.

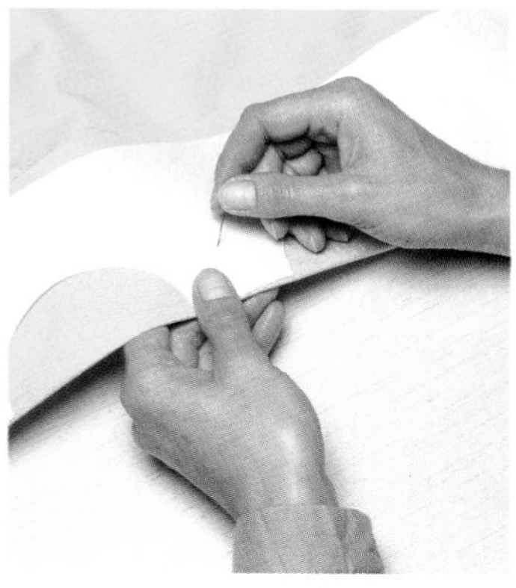

6 At the top of the curtain, fold the $4\frac{3}{4}$in (12cm) turning allowance over to the right side. Pin the paper pattern in place at the top of the curtain with the scalloped edge along the fold. Tack the pattern round all the curves of the scalloped top.

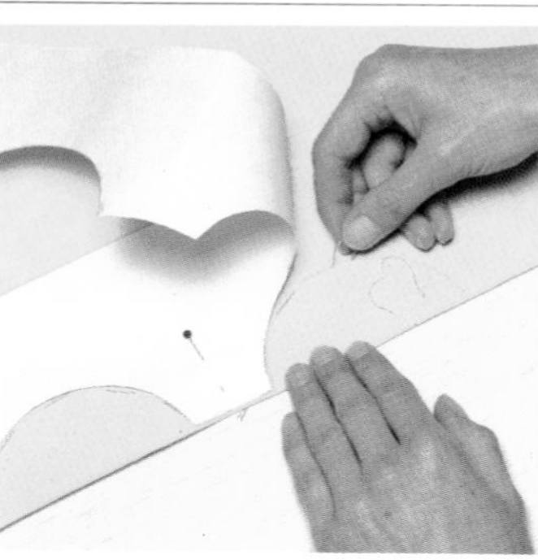

7 Machine round the outline of each scallop, stitching on the fabric as closely as possible to the edge of the paper. Remove the tacking and pattern.

8 Trim the surplus fabric away to make the scallops, cutting $\frac{1}{4}$in (6mm) above the stitching.

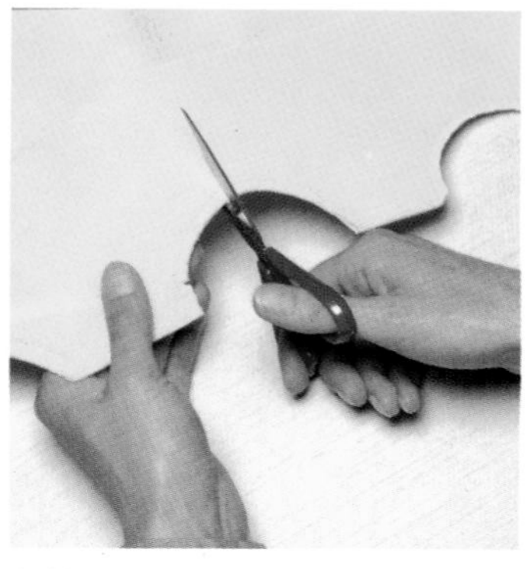

9 Make small snips into this $\frac{1}{4}$in (6mm) allowance round all the curves and cut off the points at the tops of the scallops to prevent puckering.

10 Turn the scalloped top right side out.

HELPFUL TIP
To help turn the tabs between scallops right side out, use a spoon handle or nail file. Slide the tip between the two layers of fabric and push it well into the corners to ease them out.

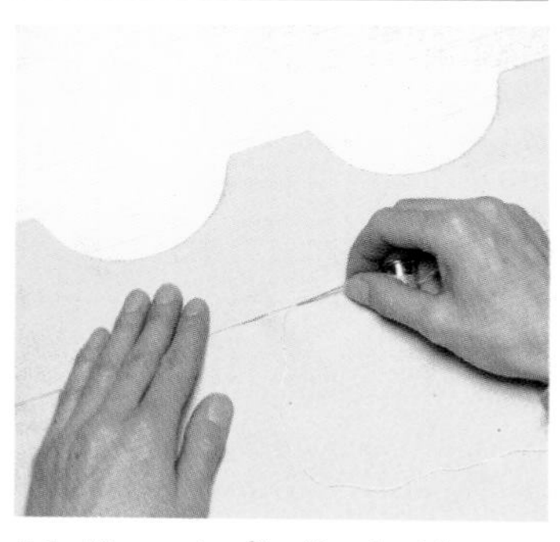

11 Pin under $\frac{3}{4}$in (2cm) of the raw edge of the heading and hemstitch (page 411) it to the back of the curtain. Press the curtain.

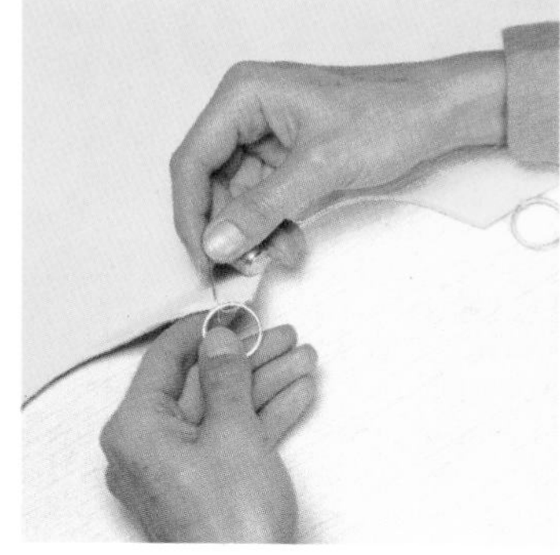

12 Sew a curtain ring to each straight tab along the top, ready for slotting on a curtain rod.

Making sheer curtains

Sheer or net curtains give a room privacy and screen off an unpleasant view. They need plenty of fullness to look their best so multiply the track width by at least 3 when estimating the fabric required for a cased heading.

Finished decorative hems are already made on some sheer fabrics. They are available on fabrics 36in-108in (91cm-270cm) from top to bottom.

> HELPFUL TIP
> Many sheer fabrics are made much wider than other curtain fabrics. Look for one that will need few joins or, if possible, none at all. Joins will always show against the daylight coming through the curtain.

MAKING A NET CURTAIN WITH A CASED HEADING

Allow 4¾in (12cm) for the top turning and 6in (15cm) for the hem. You will need a rod or wire for hanging the curtain.

You will need
Tools Measure; pins; scissors; needles; sewing machine fitted with its finest needle; iron; large working surface.
Materials Sheer fabric; synthetic thread; tissue paper if panels have to be joined to make the required width.

1 If you are joining panels of fabric together, machine them with a French seam (page 411). Remember to remove the tacking before machining the second row of stitching.

> HELPFUL TIP
> Put a strip of tissue paper between the two layers of fabric while you machine the first side of the French seam to prevent it from slipping. Remove it before you machine the second seam or it will not come out.

2 No side turnings are needed if the fabric selvedges are at the sides. If the sides are cut, turn in, pin and machine a ¾in (2cm) single turning at each side.

3 Turn up, pin and machine a double 3in (7.5cm) hem across the bottom.

4 Fold over and pin a double 2½in (6.5cm) turning at the top of the curtain. Tack the fold in place along its bottom edge and make another tacking line 1in (2.5cm) higher up.

5 Slot the rod or wire through the channel between the two tacked lines and check that the curtain length is right.

6 Remove the rod or wire, and machine as closely as possible to the two lines of tacking. Machine in the same direction for both seams to avoid any risk of puckering. A frill about 1¼in (3cm) deep will stand up at the top of the curtain when it is gathered onto the rod or wire.

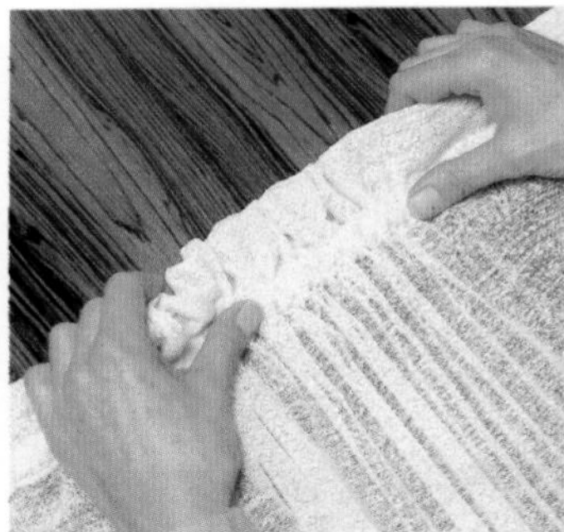

7 Remove all pins and tacking and press the curtain lightly. Slot the rod or wire into place and hang the curtain.

NET CURTAINS WITH A READY-MADE HEADING TAPE

Lightweight ready-made tapes are available for sheer curtains (page 404). Estimate for length and width as you would for a main curtain with the same heading.

A track, gliders and hooks will be needed to hang the curtain.

Make up the curtain as for a cased heading until it is ready for the heading, then follow the instructions for applying heading tape (page 415).

Hanging and draping

Once the sewing is finished and the curtains are ready to put up, take care over hanging them and in training them to drape in the way you wish to show the fabric and the pleating to best advantage.

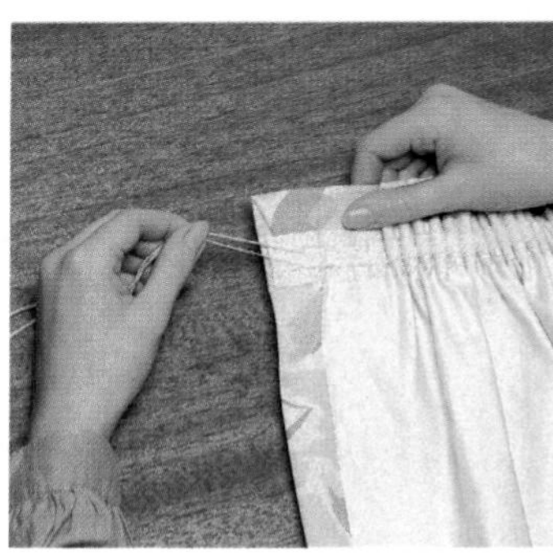

1 If you have headed the curtains with ready-made tape, pull on the free end of the cords and push the material along the cords towards the end where they are knotted.

> HELPFUL TIP
> Drawing up the cord of bulky curtains can be hard work. Make it easier by hooking the cords over a door handle at the knotted end. Grasp the cord ends at the other edge of the curtain and work the curtain along bit by bit towards the door.

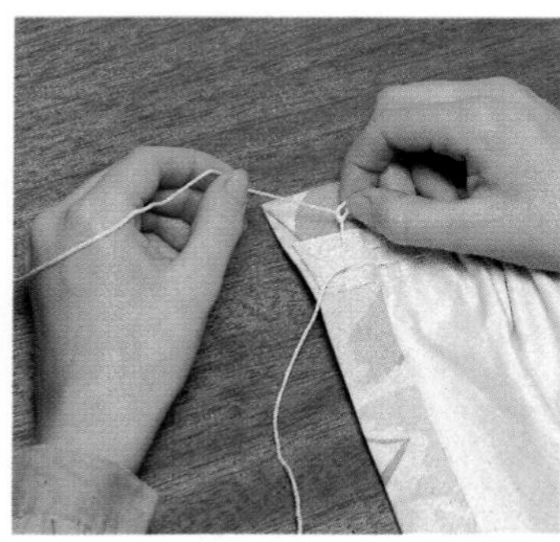

2 When the curtain is the required width for the track, knot each cord firmly. Knot the cords separately. If you do not, the tape is likely to buckle when you draw up the cords, especially if the tape is a deep one.

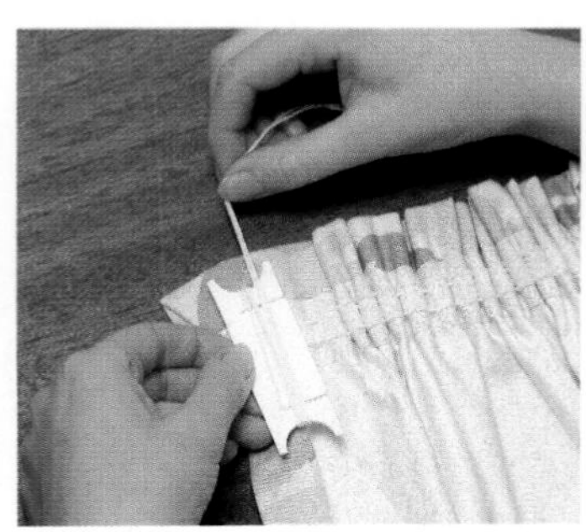

3 Wind the surplus cord round a cord tidy and lodge it in the last pocket of the tape.

Do not be tempted to cut off the surplus cord for the sake of neatness. The surplus is needed so that you can open the curtain fabric out flat again for washing or dry-cleaning satisfactorily.

4 Distribute the fullness evenly along the curtain top if the heading is simple gathered, pencil-pleated, smocked, trellised or ruffed. If the heading has cluster pleats, pinch pleats or cartridge pleats, make sure that the fabric is perfectly smooth in the intervals between pleats. Time spent arranging the fullness properly shows off the heading style and helps the curtains to drape well.

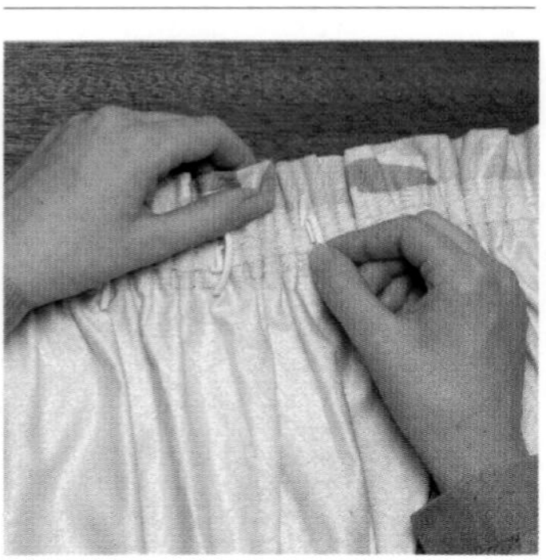

5 Insert a hook at each end of a curtain and behind each pleat or at 3in (7.5cm) intervals across evenly gathered headings.

On curtains finished with hand-pleated headings, which do not have pocketed heading tape for slip-in hooks, you will already have sewn on or pinned on the curtain hooks behind the pleats and at the ends of the curtains.

6 Once the hooks are in place, hang and drape all curtains in the same way, whether they have a hand-pleated heading or have a ready-made heading tape.

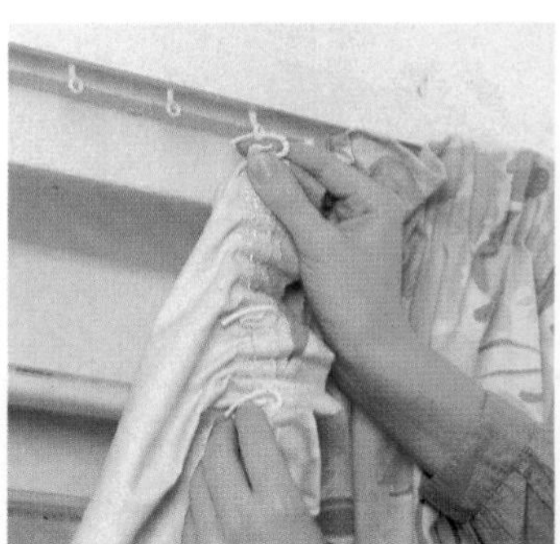

7 Start at the edge of the curtain that will hang at the centre of the window. Slip the curtain hooks into the gliders or rings.

If the track that the curtain is to hang from takes combined glider-hooks, slip the tips of the hooks upwards into the pockets of the curtain tape and clip the glider-hooks onto the track.

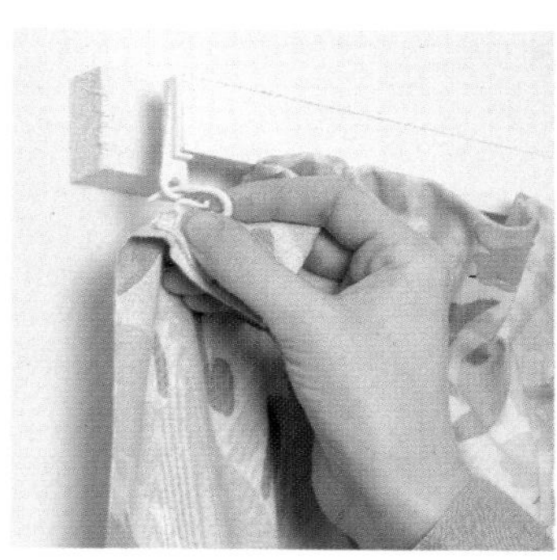

8 Slip the hook at the outer edge of the curtain into the end stop or into the screw eye fixed for a return-to-the-wall (page 403). On ready-corded tracks, the cording unit acts as end stop and has a hole for the last curtain hook. On poles, the end ring beyond the bracket acts as end stop.

9 Draw back the curtains as far as possible.

Where the curtain is hanging below a pole or track, push back the fabric between the hooks.

Where a curtain heading stands up to cover a track, pull the fabric between hooks forwards.

10 With simple gathered, pencil-pleated and some other headings, you can emphasise certain parts of the pattern by making sure they come forward on a fold rather than being pushed back; adjust the hook positions slightly if necessary to achieve this. You cannot do this if the hook itself holds the pleat in place – as in a cartridge heading, for example – or if the hooks have to be at absolutely regular intervals – to support handmade goblets, for example.

11 To train the curtain to fall into the folds you wish, take hold of a fold at the top between finger and thumb and run down it for about 12in (30cm). Do this several times with each fold.

12 Tie a thin strip of material or tape loosely round the curtain to hold the folds in place. For a full-length curtain, tie at two or three points down the length.

13 Leave the ties in place for a few days. After that the folds fall into position naturally.

14 Hang and drape the curtains in the same way after they have been dry-cleaned or washed each year. Between cleaning times, brush them with a hand brush or with a vacuum cleaner at least once a month.

HELPFUL TIP

If a curtain's outer edge hangs away from the wall, anchor it in place with two or three short strips of a touch-and-close fastening – sewn to the curtain and stuck to the wall.

Making pelmets

A pelmet is usually made of heavily stiffened fabric. It is fixed to a board, which must be in place before you design the pelmet. The board rests on a batten (page 234) and is held to it by angle brackets. The track is screwed to the batten. The board must project far enough over the track for the pelmet to hang clear of the open curtains. Using pre-cut lengths of MDF can greatly simplify this job.

FITTING THE PELMET HEAD

You will need

Tools Tenon saw; rasp; abrasive paper; drill with twist bit; screwdriver; bradawl.

Materials Pre-cut MDF lengths or plywood or hardwood ⅜in (1cm) thick and 4-6in (10-15cm) wide; 2½in (6.5cm) angle brackets; ½in (1.3cm) countersunk No. 6 woodscrews; ¾in (2cm) countersunk No. 8 woodscrews.

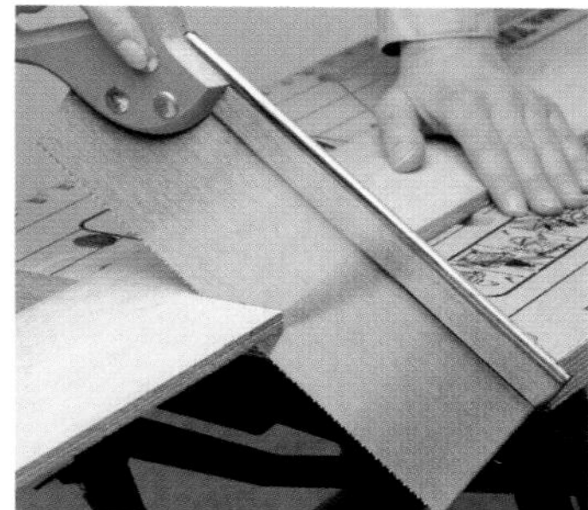

1 Cut the wood to length for the top and the ends of the board. The top should be the length of the track plus 2in (5cm). Cut the end pieces about an eighth of the depth of the curtain drop. Smooth the edges.

2 Drill two clearance holes through each of the end pieces. Position the holes 3/16in (5mm) from the top of an end piece and 1in (2.5cm) from the sides.

3 Lay the top board flat and hold each end piece in turn in position against it. Push a bradawl through the clearance holes to mark spots for drilling on the board.

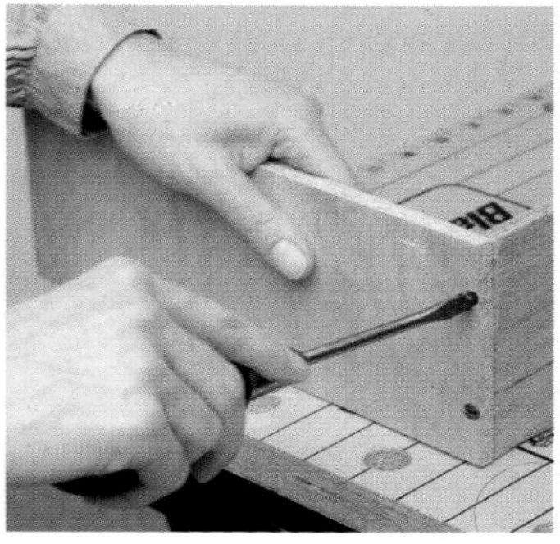

4 Drill pilot holes at the marked spots in the ends of the board and screw the end pieces in place with the ¾in (2cm) countersunk screws. Make sure that the screwheads do not project; they have very sharp edges that would wear and cut through the pelmet fabric.

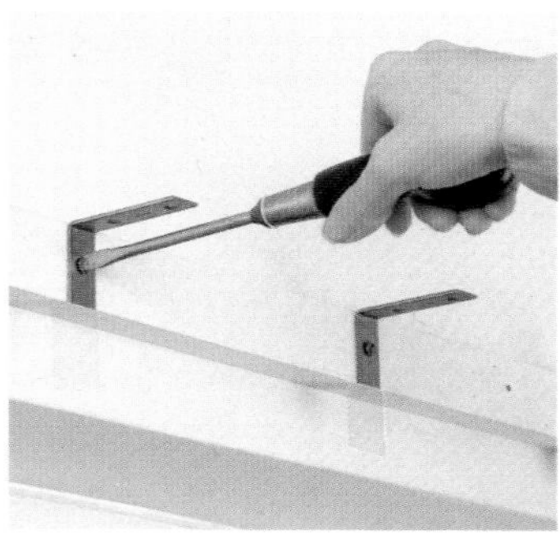

5 Screw the angle brackets to the batten with ½in (1.3cm) screws. Fit a bracket about 3in (7.5cm) from each end and others at intervals of about 8in (20cm). Make sure the bracket tops are level with the top of the batten.

6 Rest the board on the angle brackets and centre it over the window. Make sure that its back edge is against the wall. Use a bradawl to mark drilling spots on the board through the holes in the angle brackets.

7 Take down the board and drill pilot holes at the marked spots.

8 Put the board back on the angle brackets and screw it in place.

9 Once the board has been fixed in place, you can design the pelmet.

CHOOSING THE FABRIC

A pelmet is often made from the same fabric as the curtains, but it need not be. Velvet or heavy satin may be too expensive or mark too easily for you to choose it for the curtains, but it gives a luxurious finish as a pelmet over curtains made from dupion, polyester or satin-finished cotton.

When the curtains are patterned, you may choose to emphasise one of the colours and make the pelmet in a plain fabric of that colour. You can dress up a plain curtain with a pelmet in a contrasting colour and put a border on the curtain to match the pelmet.

If the pelmet fabric has a pattern, design the pelmet with its bottom edge straight. A shaped edge will not show up well and is hard to cut out symmetrically on the pattern of the fabric.

With a plain fabric, you can design a scalloped or scrolled edge to fit exactly across the width of the pelmet.

The depth of the pelmet must be in proportion to the length of the curtains; if it is too shallow it looks cheap, and if it is too deep the window looks top-heavy. Measure the drop from track to curtain hem and allow 1½in (4cm) pelmet depth for every 12in (30cm) of the drop.

DESIGNING THE PATTERN FOR THE PELMET FRONT

Use wallpaper lining, brown paper or shelf paper for making the pattern. Cut and join strips to make up the exact width across the pelmet board – including the thickness of the end pieces. Make the depth of the strips exactly the same as the measurement from top to bottom of the end pieces.

For a pelmet shaped along the

Making pelmets (continued)

CUTTING OUT THE PATTERN

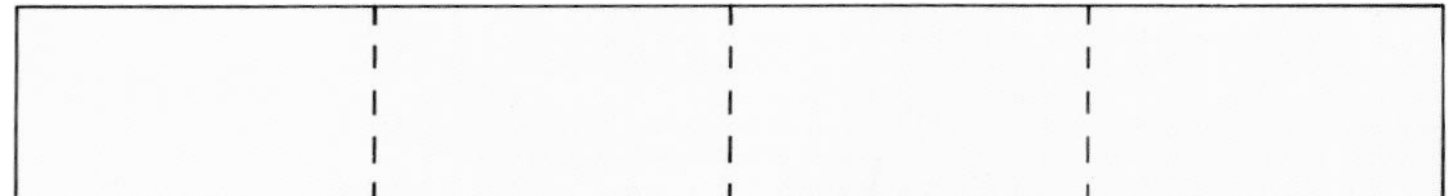

Make up the paper for the pattern to the exact width and depth needed for the pelmet front. Fold the paper in half and then in half again.

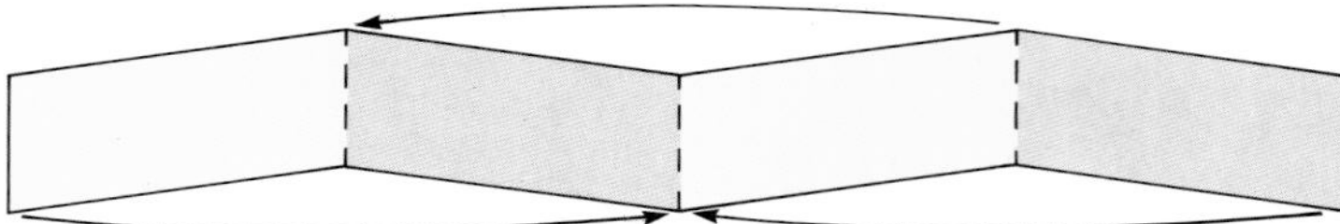

Open out the paper and refold it concertina-fashion using the earlier folds as guides to keep the sections equal. Press the folds down firmly.

Draw a shallow curve; start at the cut edge and sweep up to the fold. Cut on the line through all sections at once.

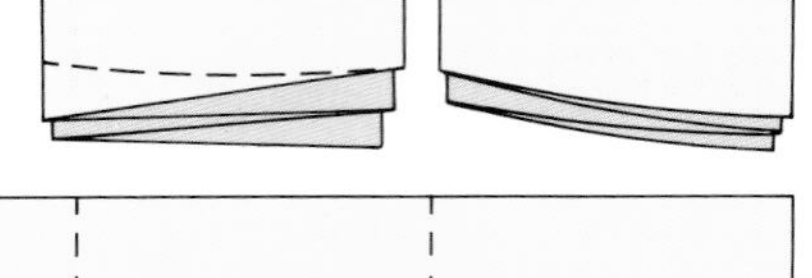

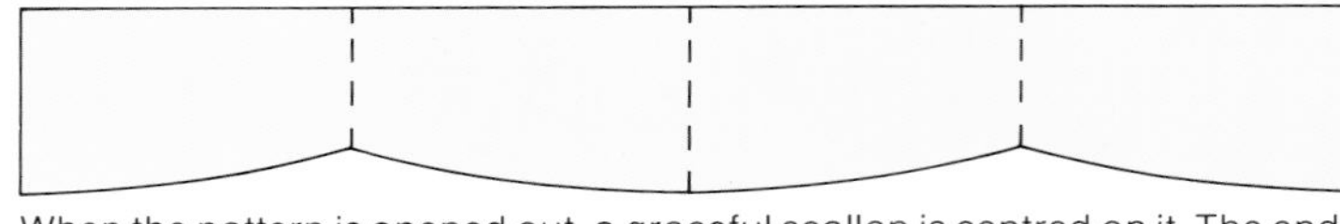

When the pattern is opened out, a graceful scallop is centred on it. The ends are full depth so that they conceal the ends of the pelmet board.

bottom, fold and cut the pattern (see diagram above). Open out the pattern and pin it to the board. Check that even at its shallowest point the pattern conceals the track.

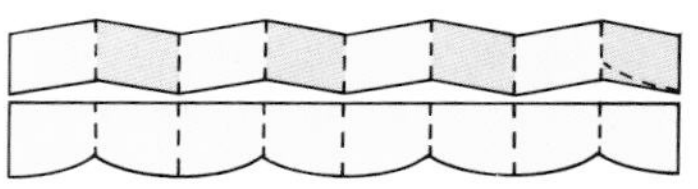

For more scallops, fold the paper in 8 or 12 sections.

CUTTING OUT AND MAKING UP THE PELMET

You will need
Tools Ruler; pencil; tailor's chalk; scissors; pins, needles; sewing machine; iron; large working surface; clothespegs; ironing table; hammer or staple gun.
Materials Paper; sticky tape; pelmet fabric; lining fabric; interlining fabric; buckram of furnishing weight; thread; perhaps fabric glue; touch-and-close fastening tape; gimp pins or staples.

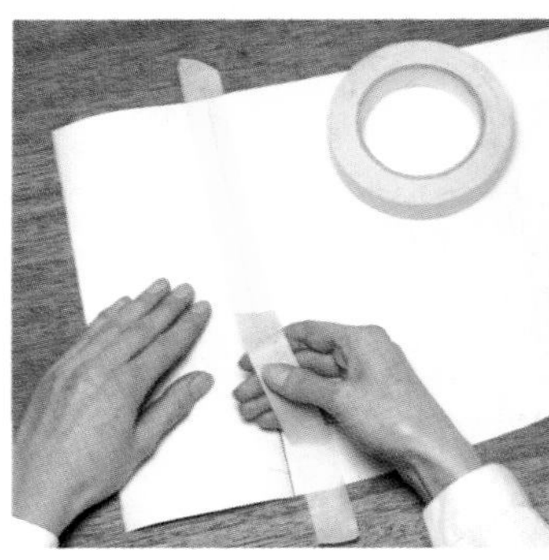

1 Take down the paper pattern and at each end tape on a section of paper cut to exactly the same size as the end pieces of the pelmet board.

2 Estimate the requirement for the main fabric, lining, interlining and buckram. Measure the total width for fabrics, at the top of the pelmet board from wall to wall round the three sides of the board, then add on 4in (10cm) at each end for turnings. You will need to join short panels of fabric together to make up the width; if the fabric is patterned, there may be considerable wastage. Each panel should be the depth of the paper pattern at its deepest point plus 4in (10cm) at both top and bottom for turnings.

3 Cut out the panels of the main fabric, trim off the selvedges and join the panels together with an open machine seam. Do not have a join at the centre of the pelmet; instead, centre one panel at the middle of the pelmet and join panels as necessary at each side. Make sure that the pattern matches are accurate. Press open the seams.

4 Cut out and join the lining in the same way and press the seams.

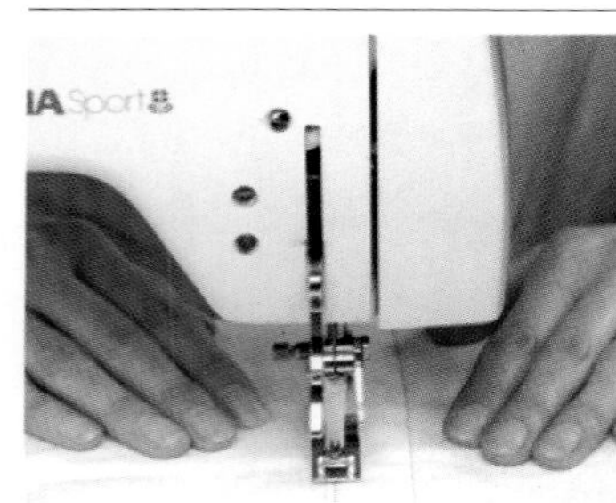

5 Cut out the interlining and join together panels if necessary by lapping one panel 1in (2.5cm) onto the next and sewing two plain machine seams down the overlap. Trim the fabric edges as close as possible to the machine stitching.

> HELPFUL TIP
> You can buy thick, sticky-backed stiffening material for pelmets. Use it in place of the interlining and buckram. The peel-off backing is squared to make accurate cutting out easier, and has some pelmet designs ready printed.

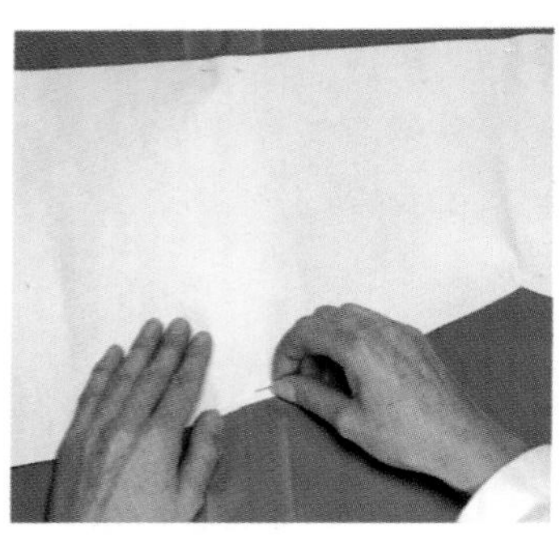

6 Spread out the main fabric, wrong side up, and pin the pattern over it, making sure that it runs level across the fabric. Cut the fabric 4in (10cm) larger than the pattern all round; mark a guideline first with a ruler and tailor's chalk.

7 Cut out the lining to the same size as the main fabric, using the main fabric as your pattern.

8 Cut out the interlining 2in (5cm) larger than the pattern on all four sides.

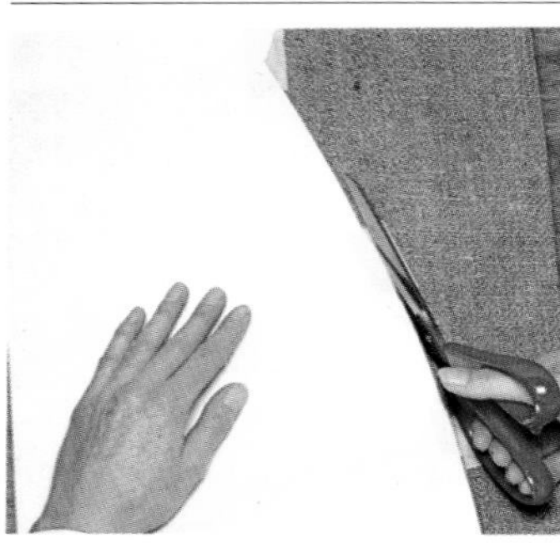

9 Cut out the buckram the same size as the paper pattern. Use sticky tape to hold the pattern in place.

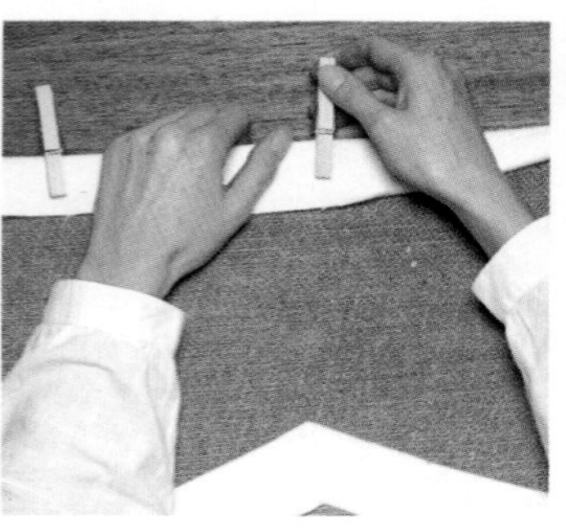

10 Lay the interlining on the ironing board or a work surface well protected against damp heat. Lay the buckram on top and centre it. Damp a ¾in (2cm) rim of the buckram all round. Fold the edge of the interlining over the damp buckram and hold it in place with clothespegs. It is too stiff to push pins through it.

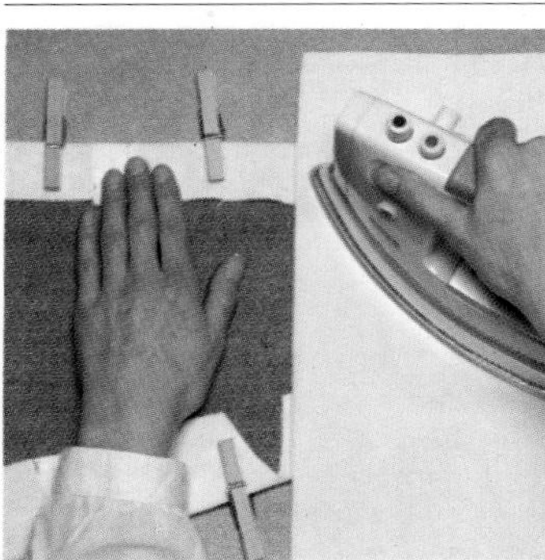

11 Press the edge with a hot iron and damp cotton cloth to bond the two fabrics together; remove the clothespegs as necessary as you work. Damp heat releases the glue which is incorporated as stiffener in the buckram. If the fabric and buckram do not bond at some points, use a dab of glue. Work along the top edge of the pelmet first. Where there are curves along the bottom edge, make snips into the edge of the interlining so that it folds over without pulling. Make the snips V-shaped on convex curves to avoid overlaps in the folded edge and give a smooth finish.

12 Place the main fabric, wrong side up, on the ironing table or protected work surface. Lay the interlining and buckram over it with the interlining against the main fabric. Make sure the interlining is centred. Damp a ¾in (2cm) rim of buckram all round, next to the edge of the interlining. Fold the edge of the main fabric onto the buckram and hold it with clothespegs. Form mitres (page 413) at the corners. Steam-press the main fabric in place, removing the clothespegs as necessary.

13 Slipstitch (page 411) the mitres to secure them.

14 Measure the length of braid or cord trimming needed for the edge. You may apply it only to the bottom edge, or all round the face of the pelmet, or continue it round the end pieces to the wall. Buy the trimming in one length, allowing ¾in (2cm) for the join.

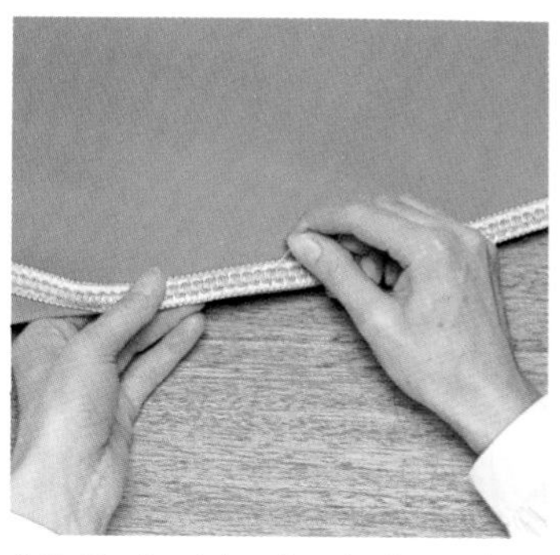

15 Fix the trimming to the pelmet with stab stitches (page 411) from the front of the pelmet through the buckram to the wrong side. Make the stitches ¼in (6mm) long and about 1in (2.5cm) apart.

16 Lay the lining, right side up, on the buckram. Fold in the turning and slipstitch (page 411) all round.

17 Hemstitch (page 411) one strip of touch-and-close fastening along the back of the pelmet at the top.

18 Fix the other strip to the top of the pelmet board with gimp pins or staples 3in (7.5cm) apart.

19 To fix the pelmet to the board, press the two strips of touch-and-close fastening tape together. Start at the centre and work towards the ends, smoothing out the pelmet firmly sideways so that it hangs without wrinkles.

Making tie-backs

Straight or shaped tie-backs are easy and inexpensive to make. They can match the curtains or match a pelmet made in a different fabric from the curtains. If the wall space beside a window is rather narrow, a tie-back will hold the curtain aside to let in more light.

For an informal window treatment there is no need to stiffen the tie-back. When the curtains are more elegant, make a firmer tie-back. Cut a strip of buckram to the same size as the interlining and oversew them together all round. Put the buckram side to the main fabric when assembling the tie-back.

You will need

Tools Pencil; drill and masonry bit; screwdriver; measuring tape; scissors; pins; needles; iron. Perhaps clothespegs.

Materials Two decorative hooks for the tie-backs; screws and wall plugs of the appropriate size for the tie-back hooks; paper; main fabric; lining fabric; interlining; thread; four small curtain rings. Perhaps also buckram of furnishing weight.

1 Hold the hooks in the positions where you want the tie-backs to be anchored and make drilling marks through the screw holes. Drill at the marked spots, insert plugs in the drilled holes and screw the hooks firmly in place.

2 Open the curtains fully. Slip a measuring tape round a curtain, drawing in the fullness as much as you wish. Measure the distance from the tie-back hook round the gathered-in curtain and back to the hook to find the required length for the tie-back. The usual depth for a tie-back is 4in (10cm), but you can make it deeper if you want to.

3 Draw a pattern on wallpaper lining or brown paper, making it the length you have measured and the depth you have chosen. Leave the ends square, or taper them to points, or round them off.

4 If you want to make the tie-back a curved shape, fold the paper in half and draw half a crescent on it with the wider part of the crescent on the fold. Cut through both thicknesses of paper together to make sure that the crescent is symmetrical.

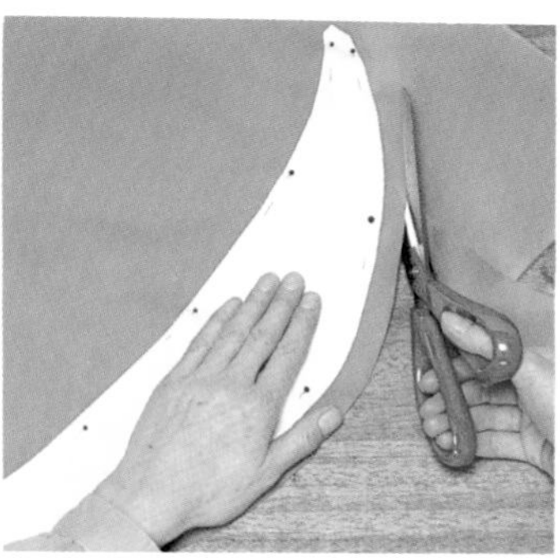

5 Pin the paper pattern on the main fabric, making sure that it is set straight on any design on the fabric. Cut out the fabric, making it ¾in (2cm) larger than the paper pattern all round.

6 Cut out the lining the same size as the main fabric.

7 Cut out the interlining exactly the size of the paper pattern. No turning allowance is needed. Cut the buckram if you are using it.

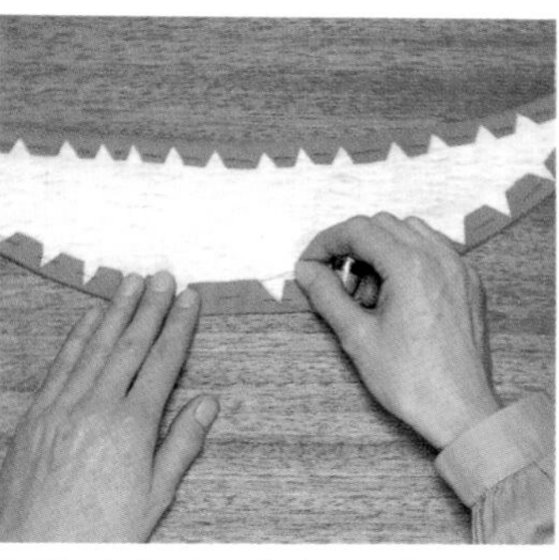

8 Tack the interlining to the wrong side of the main fabric. Fold the turning allowance of the main fabric over the interlining and pin it in place. If the interlining is too stiff to take pins, because buckram is sewn to it, hold the turning allowance in place with clothespegs. Cut V-shaped notches in the allowance along any curved edges and snip off any corners. Tack and press the turning and sew it in place with herringbone stitch (page 411). Remove all tacking.

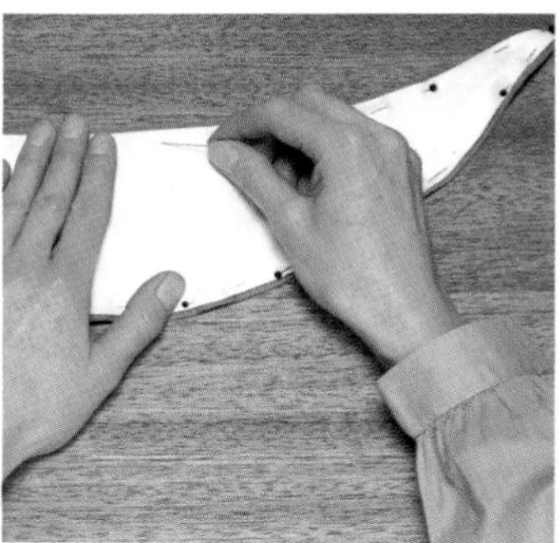

9 Place the lining over the interlining, right side up, and centre it carefully. Snip the edges of the lining where necessary or cut V-shaped notches to prevent any bulky overlaps. Turn in the edges to finish ¼in (6mm) from the edge of the tie-back. Press and pin the lining in position or secure it with clothespegs if the tie-back is too stiff for pins. Sew the lining in place with slipstitch (page 411).

10 Sew a ring at each end of the tie-back.

11 Make the second tie-back in the same way as the first. When you pin the pattern on the main fabric, check to make sure that any design on it will fall in the same place as it does on the first tie-back.

Making valances

A valance is a very short curtain and is made in almost the same way. Its gathers or pleats make a softer, less formal window treatment than a pelmet. The valance is usually in the same fabric as the curtains. Because the valance conceals the track, the simplest and least expensive track can be used. Clip a valance rail to the track with the brackets made for the purpose.

If the curtains are in a recess, you can hang the valance at the front edge of the recess. Make the valance like an unlined curtain (page 412), give it a cased heading (page 418) and hang it on a wire or rod (page 406) held by screwhooks at the sides of the recess.

For a more elaborate style, make the valance as an interlined curtain and use a ready-made heading tape on it or make a hand-pleated heading (page 416). You will need main fabric, lining, interlining and perhaps heading tape.

1 Estimate the amounts of fabric needed. For the main fabric allow 1½in (4cm) of valance depth for every 12in (30cm) of curtain drop and add on 3in (7.5cm) for the hem and 3in (7.5cm) for the top turning. Calculate the width according to the style of heading you choose; add on the width of any return-to-the-wall (page 403) at each end and 2½in (6.5cm) at each end for turning allowances.

Allow the same amount for the lining, but for the interlining you need no turning allowances at all.

2 Make up the valance as an interlined curtain (page 414), but with a 1½in (4cm) double hem.

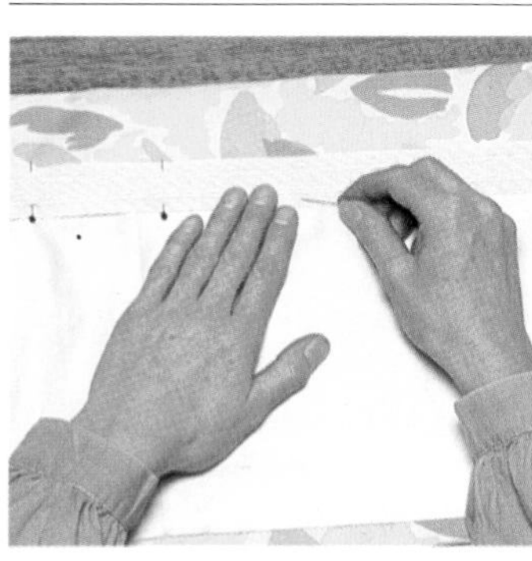

3 Apply the ready-made heading tape (page 415) or make the hand-pleated heading. Plan the heading so that the curtain hooks will be 2in (5cm) from the top of the finished valance; the top of the valance will then conceal the rail.

4 Draw up the cords of a ready-made heading tape to make the valance the right width. Distribute the fullness evenly across the valance unless it has cluster pleats, pinch pleats or cartridge pleats. For these, make sure that the intervals between the pleats are perfectly smooth.

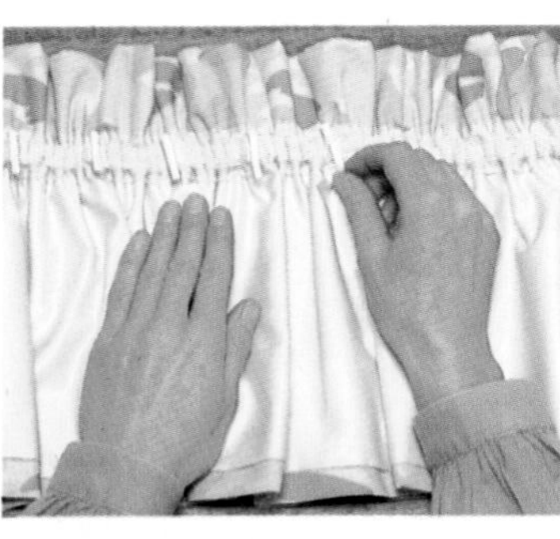

5 Insert curtain hooks into the pockets of ready-made heading tape, placing them at the ends and at intervals of not more than 3in (7.5cm) across the valance. On handmade headings, pin or sew the hooks in place. Pin-on hooks fit the valance rail easily. Some sew-on hooks are a very tight fit.

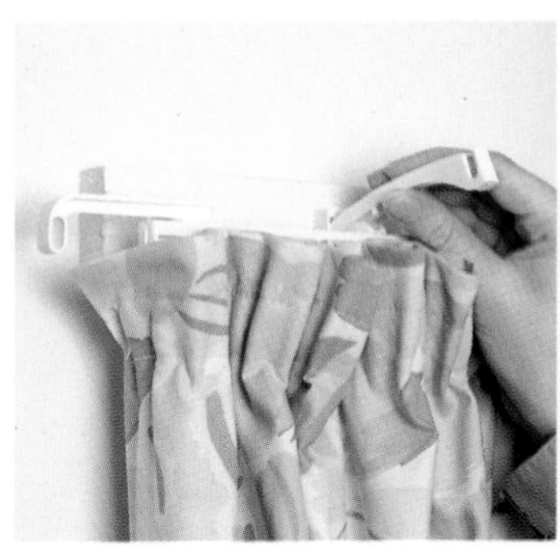

6 Fit the brackets and valance rail.

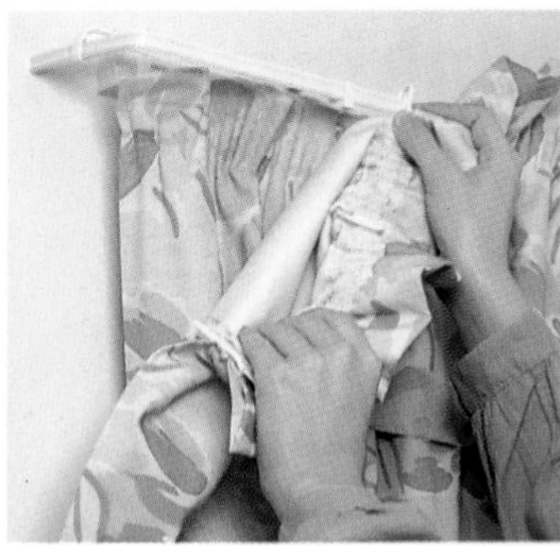

7 Attach the valance to its rail. The hooks simply push down on the top of the valance rail.

Making curtains without sewing

Curtains sewn together in the traditional way are sturdiest and last longest, but you can make serviceable sill-length curtains in unlined lightweight fabrics such as cotton without any sewing at all.

A modern material called bonding web, which is applied with a hot iron over a damp cloth, takes the place of needle and thread. Follow the instructions on pages 409-411, then replace sewing with the techniques described below.

MAKING CURTAINS WITH HEADING TAPE

Cords hold the curtains open; the heading is stiffer than a sewn one.

Joining the panels of fabric

1 On one of the panels, turn over the edge that is to be joined onto the right side of the fabric. Make the turning ½in (1.3cm) wide. Press it firmly with the iron so that it lies flat all down the edge of the panel.

2 On the other panel, turn over the edge to be joined ½in (1.3cm) onto the wrong side of the fabric. Press it firmly with the iron so that it lies flat.

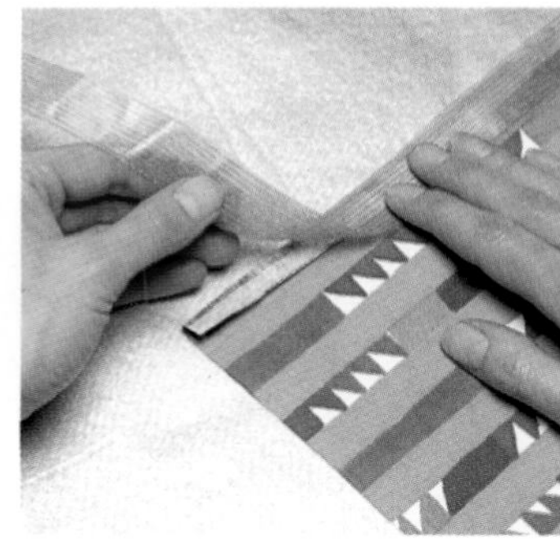

3 Spread out the first panel with the turning uppermost. Lay a strip of 1in (2.5cm) wide bonding web all along the tape, arranging it carefully so that half is covering the turning and half covering the main fabric. Check that the bonding web is not projecting over the folded edge at any point.

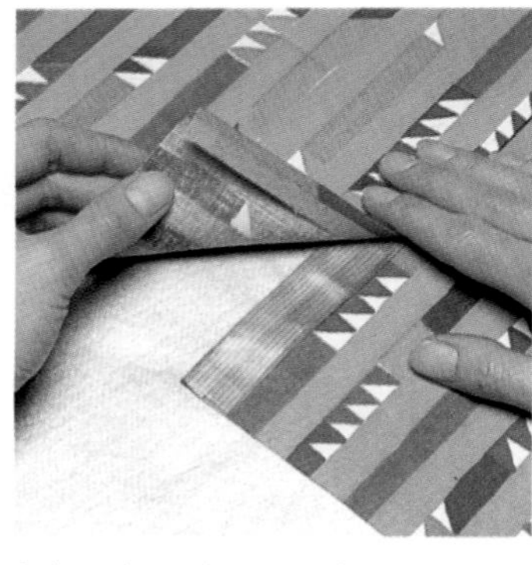

4 Lay the other panel over it, with the turning down, so that it just covers the bonding web. Lay it in place gently; the web is very light and easily dislodged.

5 Press the join with a hot, dry iron over a damp cloth to seal the web in place. Press until the damp cloth is dry.

6 Join on other panels in the same way if necessary.

Making a side turning or hem

1 Fold up and press in place the turning allowance.

2 Fold under ½in (1.3cm) of the raw edge and press it in place all along the turning.

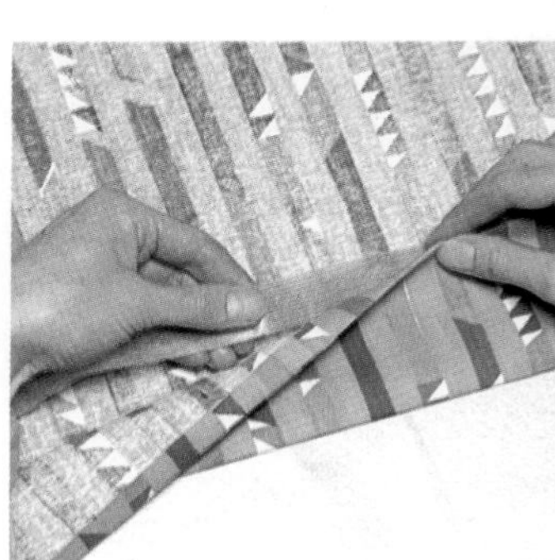

3 Slip a 1in (2.5cm) wide strip of bonding web under the turning so that the web is just covered by the curtain fabric.

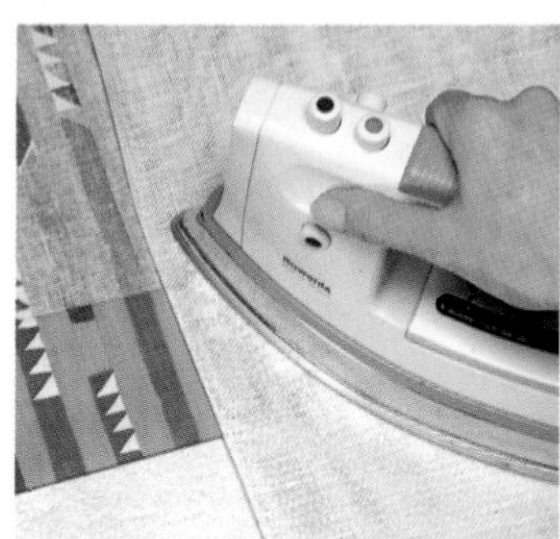

4 Press all along the turning with a hot, dry iron over a damp cloth until the pressing cloth is dry.

Mitring a corner

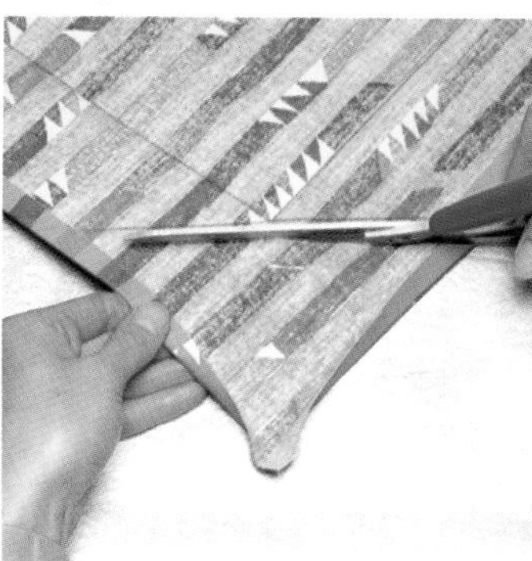

1 Fold and press the turnings as for a sewn mitre (page 413). Cut off the excess fabric across the corner to reduce the bulk and to ensure that the web will make a firm bond.

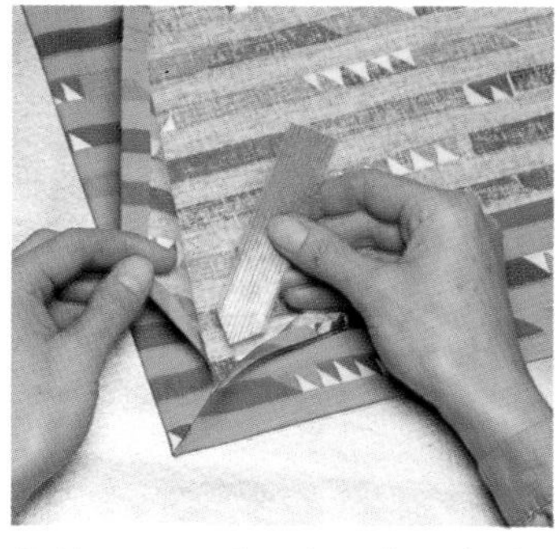

2 Measure the length of the diagonal fold and cut a strip of bonding web to that length. At one end of the strip, trim off the corners to make an arrowhead shape.

3 Slip the bonding web under the turnings, making sure that it is centred under the diagonal folds. Press it in place with a hot, dry iron over a damp cloth.

Applying the heading tape

Use simple gathering tape. Choose a make that is free of pockets and cords for at least ¼in (6mm) along each edge so that you can bond the edge in place without sealing down any pockets or cords.

1 Fold over the top of the curtain onto the wrong side. Make the turning at least the depth of the heading tape and press it in place.

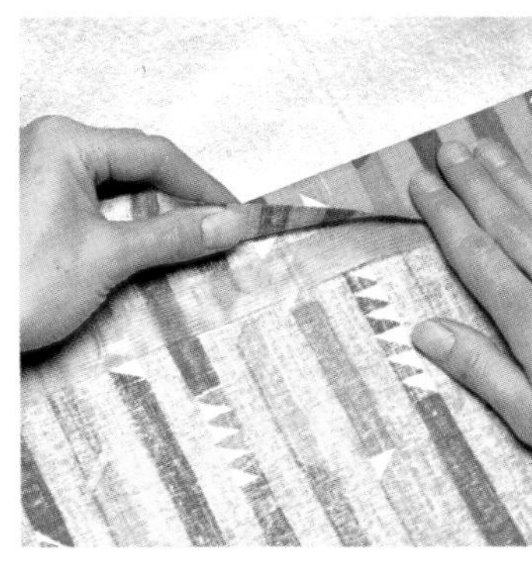

2 Lay a 1in (2.5cm) wide strip of bonding web under the turning. Lay it in place carefully so that ¼in (6mm) projects below the raw edge.

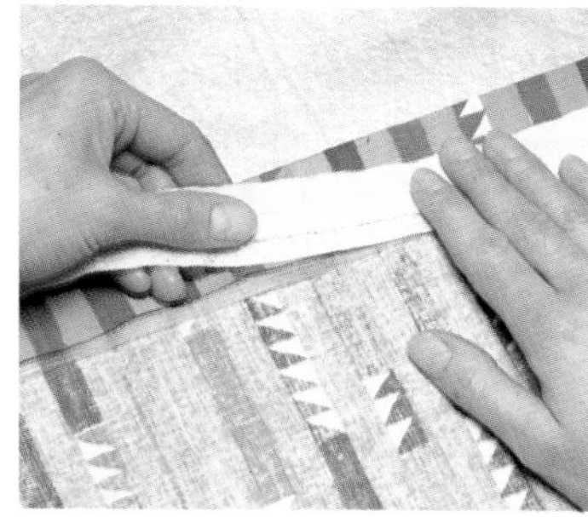

3 Lay the heading tape in place just covering the projecting bonding web. Turn under the ends of the heading tape to give a neat finish. Press firmly over the bonding web with a hot, dry iron and a damp cloth to seal both the turning and the tape in place.

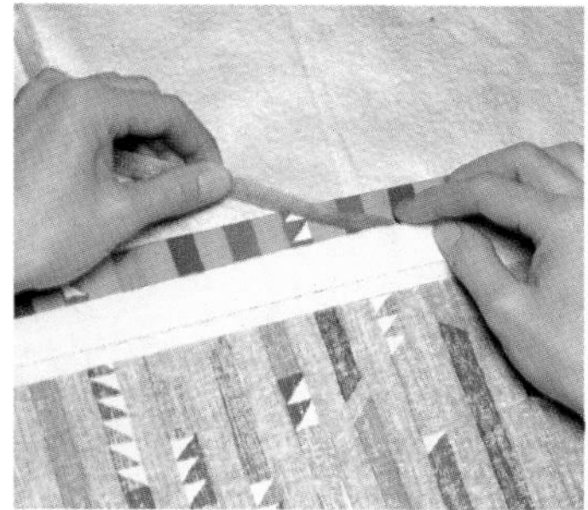

4 Under the top edge of the heading tape, slip a strip of the narrow bonding web made for sealing trims and braids. Arrange it carefully; it must not lie under the pockets or cords or it would seal them down and prevent the heading from gathering. Press with a hot, dry iron over a damp cloth to seal the tape edge down.

5 Hang and drape the curtains (page 418).

MAKING CURTAINS WITH A CASED HEADING

The curtains hang on a slender rod which is pushed through a channel made across the curtain tops. Hold the curtains open with cords looped round hooks on the wall.

1 Join the panels of fabric together, make the side turnings and hems, and mitre the bottom corners as for curtains with a heading tape (facing page).

2 Across the top of the curtain, fold over and press a 3in (7.5cm) turning onto the wrong side.

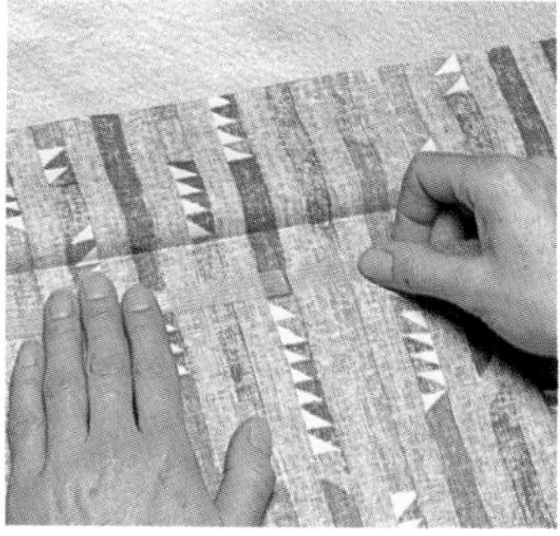

3 Lay a strip of narrow bonding web (for fixing trims and braids) under the fold. Place it 1in (2.5cm) below the fold and press it in place between the layers of fabric with a hot, dry iron over a damp cloth.

4 Fold the raw edge of the curtain top under by ¼in (6mm) and press it in place.

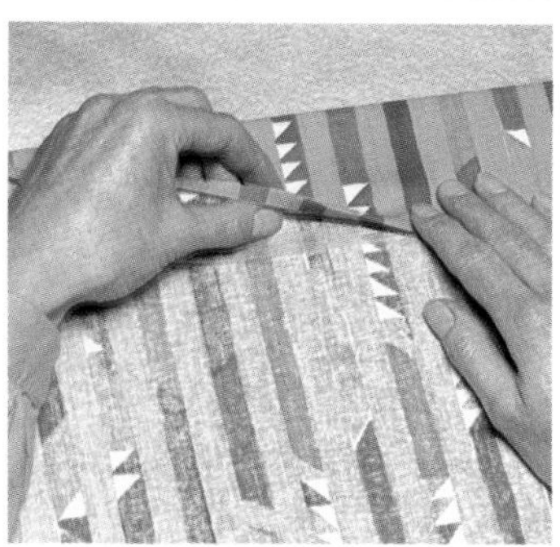

5 Lay another strip of the narrow bonding web under the turning and press it in place with a hot, dry iron over a damp cloth.

6 Hang the curtains on an extending rod slid through the channel between the two strips of bonding web.

MAKING CURTAINS WITH A SLOTTED HEADING

A slender brass pole is slotted in and out through slits cut in the curtain tops. Cords or tie-backs will help to keep the curtains open.

1 Join the panels of fabric together, make the side turnings and hems, and mitre the bottom corners as described for making curtains with a heading tape (facing page).

2 Across the top of the curtain, fold over a 3in (7.5cm) turning onto the wrong side of the fabric and press it flat.

3 Turn under the raw edge for ½in (1.3cm) and press it flat.

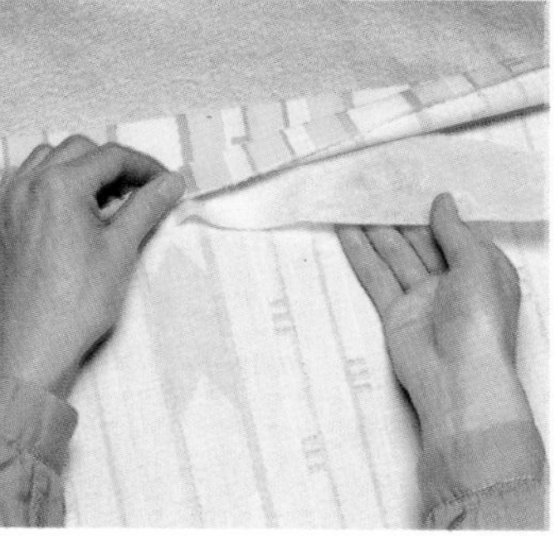

4 Cut 2½in (6.5cm) deep strips from a sheet of bonding web to make the width required to go all across the curtain tops. Slip the strips under the fold so that they are just covered. Bond them in place with a hot, dry iron over a damp cloth.

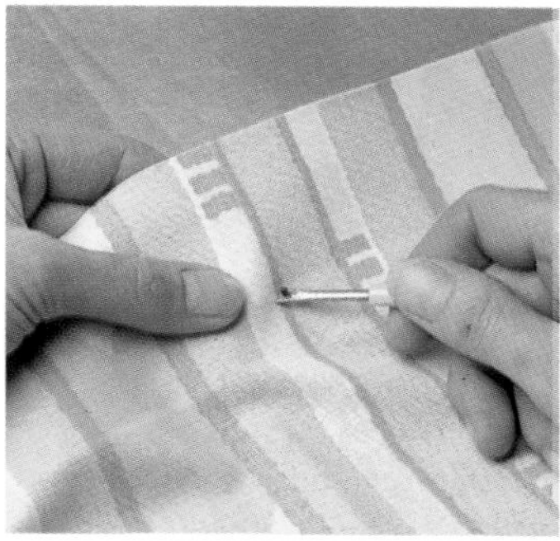

5 Cut 1½in (4cm) long vertical slits 1in (2.5cm) from the top of the curtain and 3in (7.5cm) apart. Use a seam ripper to start off the slits and complete them with small, sharp scissors.

6 Slide the pole in and out through the slits to hang the curtains.

MAKING CURTAINS WITH A VALANCED HEADING

Make the curtains in a fabric with no noticeable right and wrong side – a gingham or a woven stripe, for example – and allow an extra 9in (23cm) for folding over a pole to make the valance. Cords or tie-backs looped round hooks on the wall will hold the curtains open.

1 Join the panels of fabric together, make the side turnings and hems, and mitre the bottom corners by the methods described for making curtains with heading tape (facing page).

2 Across the top of the curtains, fold a ½in (1.3cm) turning onto the right side of the fabric. Lay a strip of the narrow bonding web made for trims and braids inside the fold and

Making curtains without sewing (continued)

seal it with a hot, dry iron over a damp cloth. Hold the iron in place until the damp cloth is dry.

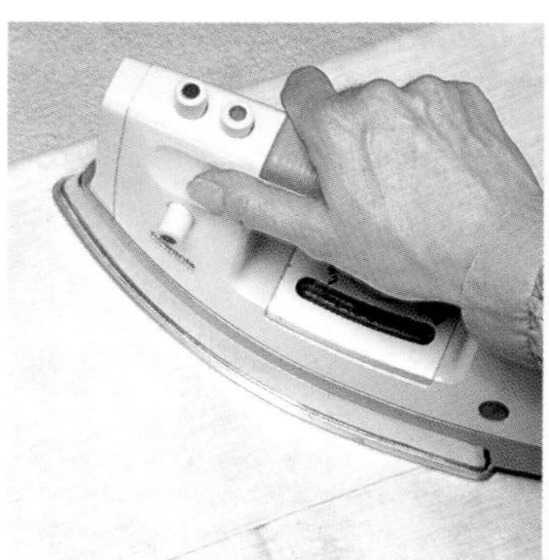

3 Fold over an 8in (20cm) turning onto the right side of the fabric all across the top of the curtains to form the valance. Press lightly along the fold.

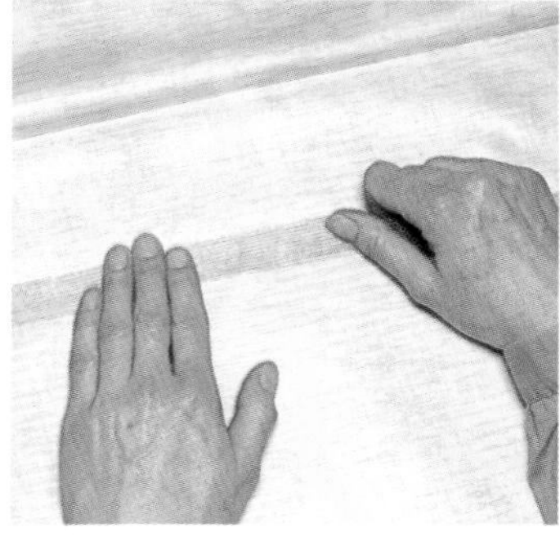

4 Lay a strip of 1in (2.5cm) wide bonding web inside the fold, placing it 3in (7.5cm) from the top. Press over the web with a hot, dry iron and a damp cloth to seal it between the layers of fabric.

5 Slide the curtain pole along the channel formed above the strip of bonding web.

MAKING CROSS-DRAPED CURTAINS

Extra-wide semi-sheer fabric, needing no joins and without a right or wrong side, drapes softly over a pole to make translucent curtains. Hold them aside with cords.

Buy fabric twice the length of the curtain drop plus 6in (15cm).

1 Use bonding web to seal up a 3in (7.5cm) turning at each end of the fabric. Make the first turning onto one face of the fabric and the second turning onto the other face.

2 Hang the fabric over a wooden pole with the turnings level.

3 Use a staple gun to staple the edges of the fabric to the ends of the pole. Distribute the fullness evenly along the pole. Drive in staples about 3in (7.5cm) apart.

4 Fit decorative hooks at the sides of the window to hold cords that draw the curtains apart in the daytime. The higher you fix the hooks, the more daylight the curtains will let in.

How to make a roller blind

Roller blinds can be made quickly and cheaply at home by combining ready-made aids with your own fabric and labour. The blinds are simple and functional. If you want to soften their rather bare look, hang narrow, gathered, non-drawing curtains beside the window.

MEASURING FOR THE ROLLER

If the window is in a recess, first decide whether to fix the blind inside or outside the recess. If the blind is to be inside the recess, measure the full width from one side of the recess to the other. This will be the size of the roller blind kit you require. For a blind to go outside the recess, add 2in (5cm) onto the measurement.

If the exact size of roller you need is not made, buy the nearest size above. You can cut it to the required measurement with a saw; some stores will cut one of their rollers to the exact size you need.

A roller blind kit will contain: the roller with a spring, cap and square pin fitted at one end; a cap with rounded pin for the other end; two brackets with screws, for side or face fixing; tacks or adhesive tape for fixing the fabric to the roller; a lath to weight the blind's hem; and a cord with holder and knob.

FABRIC REQUIREMENT

The fabric must be exactly the same width as the roller excluding the caps. For a blind in a recess, the fabric must be the length from the top of the recess to the sill plus 12in (30cm) for turnings. For a blind outside a recess add another 2in (5cm) to the length.

CHOOSING THE FABRIC

Ready-stiffened roller blind fabrics are sold in various widths up to 72in (183cm). They have a finish that resists fading, repels dust and wipes clean. PVC and plastic-backed fabrics are also wipe-clean and need no stiffening.

If you cannot find a colour or design you like among the special blind fabrics, you can prepare your own fabric. Strengthen the cloth with coats of stiffening liquid; you can buy it in a bottle or in an aerosol can.

HELPFUL TIP

Apply stiffening liquid to both sides of the blind fabric. This doubles the strengthening effect – and also prevents the fabric edges from fraying or curling.

You will need

Tools Measure; pencil; power drill with masonry bit; saw; bench hook or vice; screwdriver; set square; tailor's chalk; scissors; hammer; iron; sewing machine; needle; large working surface.

Materials Roller blind kit; wall plugs; prepared fabric; adhesive tape; thread; perhaps fringe or braid for trimming, and fabric glue.

1 Hold each bracket in turn in its position inside the recess as near the top as possible and make marks through the screw holes for drilling. Make sure the brackets will be level and the same distance from the front of the recess. For a blind outside the recess, make the drilling marks 2in (5cm) above the top of the recess and again make sure that the brackets will be level.

2 Drill and plug the holes.

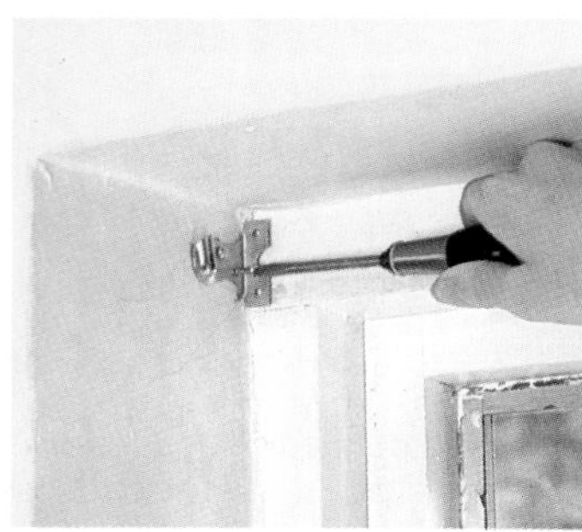

3 Screw the brackets in place. Be sure to put the bracket for the ready-fitted cap at the left of the window.

4 Saw off any excess length from the roller to make it fit exactly between the brackets.

HELPFUL TIP

To make a guide line to help you saw straight across the roller, wind a strip of straight-sided paper round it, overlapping the ends and securing them with sticky tape.

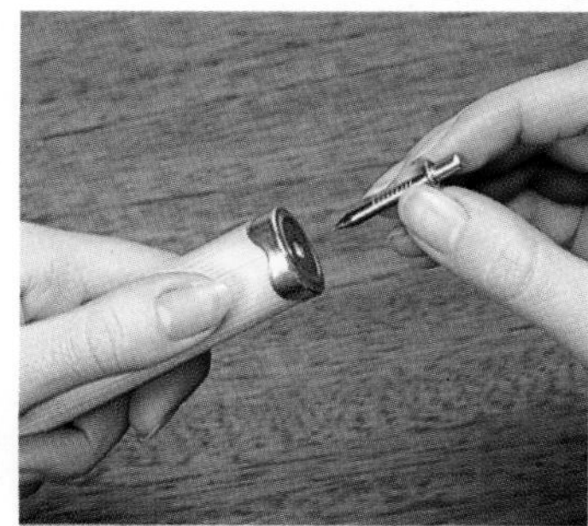

5 Fit the metal cap and round pin to the bare end of the roller and hammer it home.

6 Measure the fabric with care, making sure that any pattern will fall centrally or symmetrically on the blind. Mark cutting lines with tailor's chalk to the exact width of the roller. Use a set square or a table corner to make sure that you mark the top and bottom cutting lines at right angles to the sides. Cut out the fabric.

7 Fold up a ⅜in (1cm) turning onto the wrong side of the fabric across the bottom of the blind and press it lightly in place. Use a warm iron for pressing ordinary woven fabrics. If the blind is being made from PVC or a plastic-coated fabric, do the pressing simply with your fingers or with a cool iron over a dry cloth.

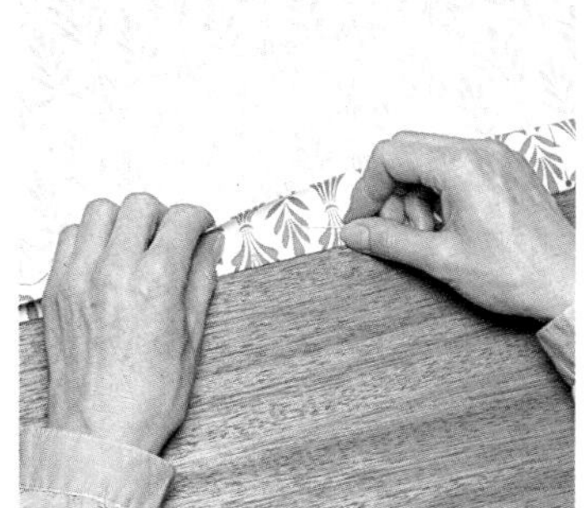

8 Fold up and press a further turning of 1½in (4cm) onto the wrong side of the fabric across the bottom of the blind. Pin and tack it in place if you are using an ordinary woven fabric. You can hold PVC or plastic-coated fabric in place with pieces of adhesive tape.

9 Machine stitch the turning in place; adjust the stitch length setting to give long stitches for a PVC or a plastic-coated fabric. Remove any tacking or adhesive tape.

10 Lay the lath against the bottom of the blind, aligning one end of it with the edge of the fabric. At the other end, make a mark on the lath ¾in (2cm) in from the edge of the fabric. Saw through the lath at the marked spot.

11 Slide the lath into the channel along the bottom of the blind. Hand sew the ends with hemstitch (page 411) to hold the lath in place and conceal its ends.

12 Spread out the blind right side up. Lay the roller across it near the top. Place it so that the square pin will be at the left of the blind when you are hanging it. Fold under ¾in (2cm), then pull the fold over the roller and align it with the guideline marked on the roller. The blind will hang askew if it is not aligned exactly. Use small pieces of adhesive tape to hold it in place temporarily.

13 Hammer the tacks into the folded fabric to secure it to the roller. Remove the temporary pieces of adhesive tape as you work along the roller.

ALTERNATIVELY, if the roller blind kit is of the type where the fabric is stuck to the roller, not held with tacks, follow the maker's instructions for fixing the blind to the roller.

14 Thread the blind cord through the hole of the holder and make a double or treble knot at the end. Measure along the bottom of the blind at the wrong side and make a mark at the middle. Centre the cord holder on the mark and screw it firmly to the lath.

15 Thread the loose end of the cord through the cord knob and tie a double or treble knot at the end.

16 Roll the roller carefully and evenly down the right side of the blind fabric.

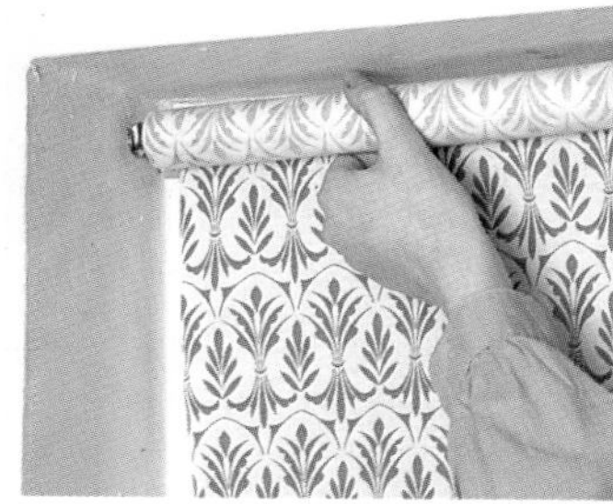

17 Insert the pins of the roller into the brackets, with the square pin to the left.

18 Pull down the blind as far as it will go and then let it roll itself up, to adjust the spring tension.

19 If the bottom of the blind is to be trimmed, fix the trimming in place with fabric glue.

HELPFUL TIP

Never oil the roller spring. Oil will clog the mechanism and may stain the fabric. Instead, use a dry powder lubricant.

To keep the blind straight, always use the cord to pull it down and to activate it to roll up; pull directly down on the cord, not at an angle.

How to make a festoon blind

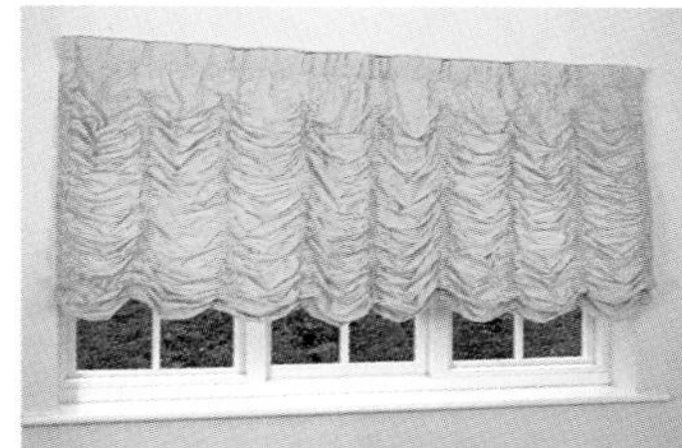

A lightweight silky or fine cotton fabric which will fall in graceful, puffy folds is needed for this style of blind.

The full, scalloped draping is made by gathering both the width and the length of the blind. The width is gathered by a curtain heading tape across the top of the blind. The length is gathered by strips of curtain tape of the simple gathering type sewn from top to bottom of the blind at intervals across it.

Fit the blind just under the lip of the window recess or wooden surround so that it will hang flush with the wall and not leave draughty gaps at the sides.

FABRIC REQUIREMENT

To calculate the width to make the blind, double the width of the window recess (or of the inside of the wooden surround of an unrecessed sash window) and add on 1½in (4cm) for side turnings. You will need to join panels of fabric together to make up the required width. If possible, plan the joins where one of the vertical tapes will come so that the join does not show up as a dark line against the light coming through the blind.

Each panel should be at least 1½ times the length of the window plus 8in (20cm) for turnings. This will allow light horizontal gathers to form when the blind is down. They become heavier from the bottom as the blind is raised. For heavier horizontal gathering, over the whole blind when it is down, each panel of fabric should be 2½ times the length of the window plus 8in (20cm) for the turnings.

If the fabric is patterned, you must also add the length of one pattern repeat to each panel except the first.

A non-stretch cord for drawing up the blind runs behind each vertical row of tape. For each cord allow twice the length of the window plus the width of the window.

You will need

Tools Measure; pencil; bradawl; power drill with twist bit and masonry bit (and hammer action if the lintel is concrete); screwdriver; scissors; tailor's chalk; pins; needles; sewing machine; large working surface.

Materials Strip of 1½in × 1½in (4cm × 4cm) softwood batten the width of the window recess or of the inside of a wooden surround; a 1½in (4cm) angle bracket for each end and about every 18in (46cm) across the batten; wall plugs and 1in (25mm) No. 8 screws for the brackets; simplest curtain track in one piece the same length as the batten, complete with brackets, screws, gliders and end stops; fabric for the blind; thread; curtain heading tape of the simple gathering type; small split curtain rings; curtain hooks; screw eyes; non-stretch cord; brass cleat with wall plugs and screws.

PREPARING FOR THE BATTEN

1 Mark spots at several points along the top of the recess or under the lip of a wooden surround. Make them 2in (5cm) back from the lip of the recess or surround.

On a sash window with beading projecting down from the inner lip of the wooden surround, butt the angle brackets up to the back of the beading. Use brackets on which the vertical arm will show two screw holes below the beading.

Draw a line through the marks.

2 Make marks on the line where the angle brackets are to be fixed. One should go at each end, and others be spaced equally between them about 18in (46cm) apart along the line.

How to make a festoon blind (continued)

3 Use a bradawl to mark drilling spots for the bracket screws. Hold a bracket in place at each mark with the angle on the line and push the bradawl through the screw holes.

4 In a recess, drill a hole at each mark and insert a wall plug in each hole. If you are fitting the blind under the wooden surround of a sash window, drill pilot holes at the marked spots.

5 Screw the brackets in place.

6 Hold the batten against the brackets; push a bradawl through the holes to mark the batten.

7 Drill pilot holes in the back of the batten.

PREPARING THE BLIND

1 Cut out the panels of fabric as for curtains (page 410).

2 Pin and tack the panels together with wrong sides facing and any patterns accurately matched.

3 Join the fabric panels together with machine-sewn French seams (page 411), remembering to remove the tacking before sewing the second row of stitching:

4 Fold in, pin and tack a double $\frac{3}{8}$in (1cm) turning onto the wrong side of the fabric down each side of the blind, and a double $2\frac{1}{2}$in (6.5cm) turning across the bottom.

5 Hemstitch (page 411) the turnings or machine them in place. Remove the tacking. Slipstitch (page 411) the open ends of the bottom turning so that they do not gape open when the blind has been gathered.

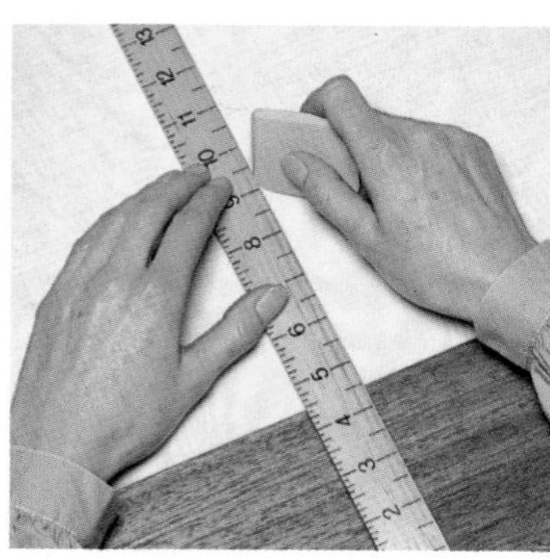

6 Spread the blind out, wrong side up. Measure and chalk in lines where the vertical tapes are to go. Put one at the very edge at each side and others at equal intervals of 8in (20cm) or more across the blind.

7 Pin and tack rows of tape down the chalk lines, starting 6in (15cm) from the top and ending about $2\frac{1}{2}$in (6.5cm) from the bottom. Make sure each row has a pocket at the very top and bottom. Free the cords from the last $1\frac{1}{2}$in (4cm) at each end of each tape and tuck in the ends of the tapes neatly. Knot the cords at the bottom of the blind.

8 Machine the tapes in place down each side. Sew all the rows from top to bottom to prevent wrinkles. Remove the tacking.

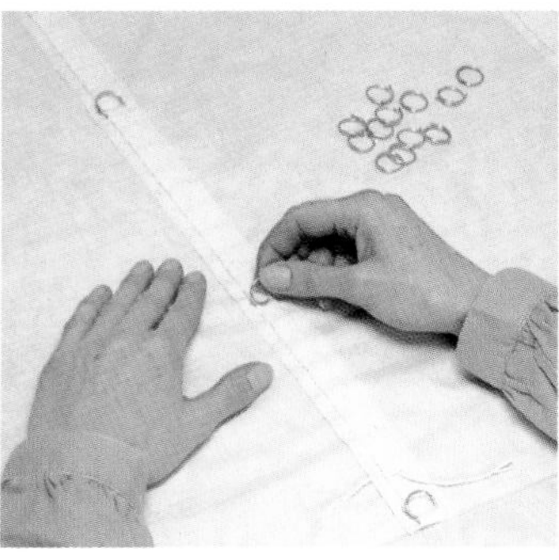

9 Attach the rings to each tape, inserting them through the pockets or sewing them in place by hand. Put a ring at the top of the tape, one at the bottom, and space out others equally between these two at intervals of about 8in (20cm). Make sure that the rings are exactly aligned across the blind.

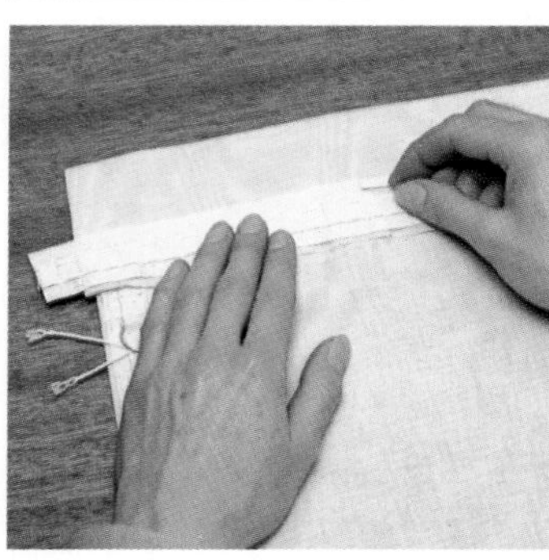

10 Fold over and press in place a 3in (7.5cm) turning across the top of the blind and pin the top edge of the heading tape across it $1\frac{1}{2}$in (4cm) from the fold. Leave 1in (2.5cm) of tape jutting beyond each side of the blind.

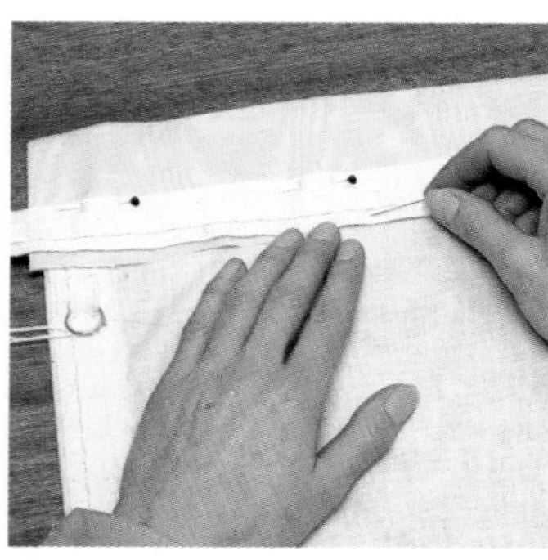

11 Fold the raw edge of the fabric under and pin the bottom edge of the tape in place across the fold. Free the cords from the last $1\frac{1}{2}$in (4cm) at each end of the tape. Knot the cords at one end; knot them separately so that the tape does not buckle when they are drawn up.

12 Tack the tape in place, folding the ends under neatly.

13 Machine the tape in place. Sew across the top of the tape and then sew across the bottom in the same direction to prevent puckering. Remove the tacking. Leave the ends of the tape open.

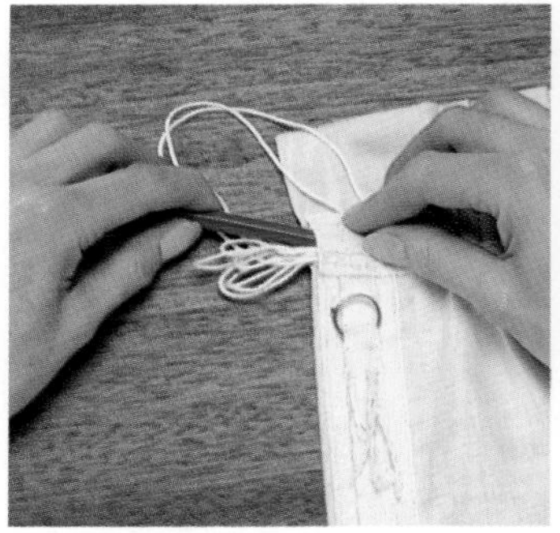

14 Draw up the cords of the heading tape to make the blind exactly the same width as the batten and knot the cords separately. Wind up the spare cord into a neat bundle. Tuck the bundle behind the tape.

15 Distribute the gathers evenly across the blind.

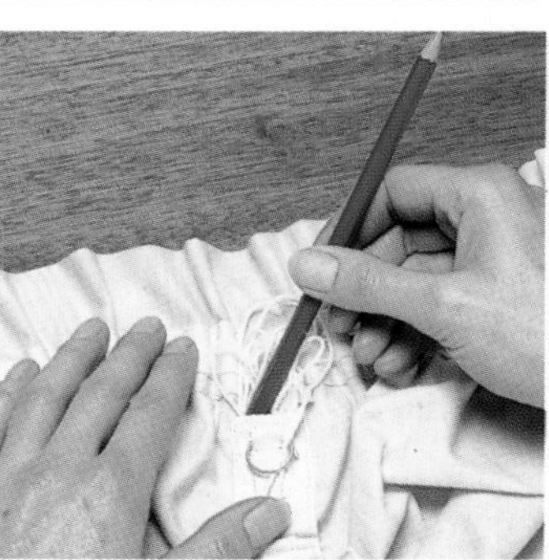

16 Draw the vertical tapes up from the top to make the blind the required length for the window. Knot the cords separately and tuck the spare cord neatly behind the tape. Distribute the gathers evenly down the length of the blind.

17 Insert curtain hooks in the pockets of the heading tape at the top of the blind. Put a hook at each end and space out others equally at intervals of about 3in (7.5cm).

ASSEMBLING AND FITTING THE BLIND

1 Cut a length of non-stretch cord for each vertical row of rings. Each cord should be the width of the window recess plus twice the length of the blind.

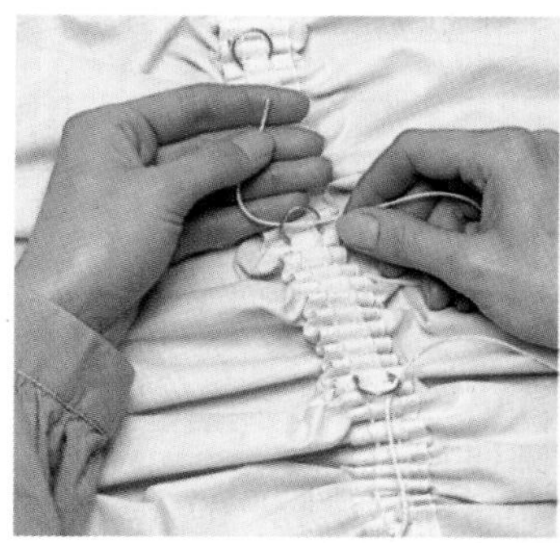

2 Spread the blind out flat, with its wrong side up, on a large working surface – a clean floor is the most convenient. Tie a cord securely to the bottom ring of each row. Thread each cord up through the line of rings above it in the tape.

3 Screw the brackets for holding the curtain track onto the front of the batten, spacing them out according to the manufacturer's instructions. Push the curtain track into place through the brackets. Slide the gliders onto the track and screw an end stop in place at each end of the track.

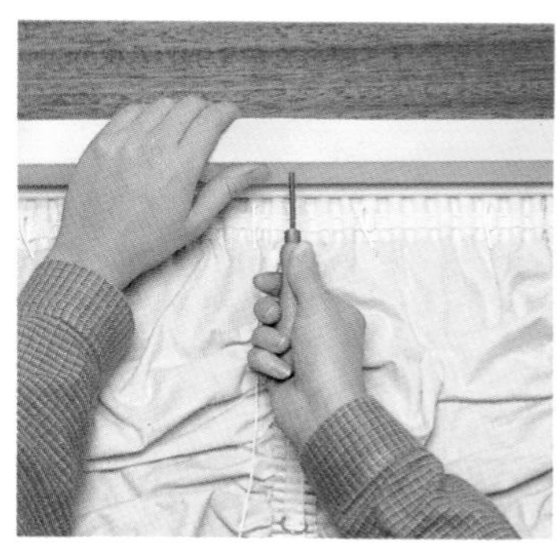

4 Lay the batten, track side down, along the top of the blind with the ends of each aligned. Make pilot holes with a bradawl on the bottom of the batten opposite the centre of each vertical strip of tape.

5 Insert a screw eye in each pilot hole. Several cords will pass through the left-hand eyes and you may need larger eyes there than at the right. Turn each screw eye so that the eye will be at right angles to the window when the batten is in place.

6 Hook the blind on the curtain track gliders.

7 With the blind still spread out flat on the floor with its wrong side up, lead the cords through the screw eyes. Working from the right, thread the first cord from right to left through the screw eye immediately above it on the batten. Continue to thread the cord from right to left along the batten through each screw eye. Repeat with each cord.

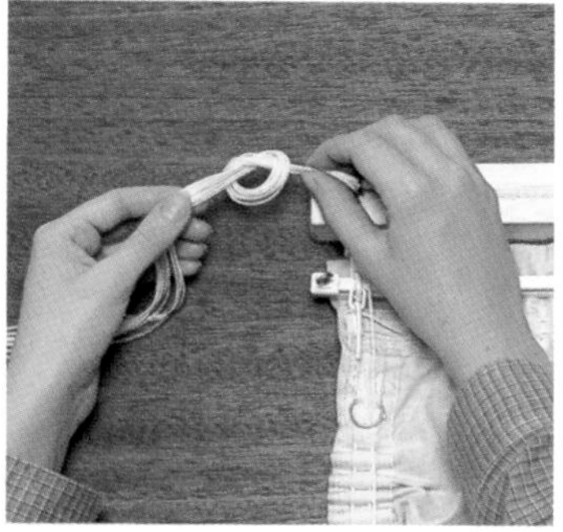

8 Knot all the cords together 1½in (4cm) from the left-hand edge of the wrong side of the blind.

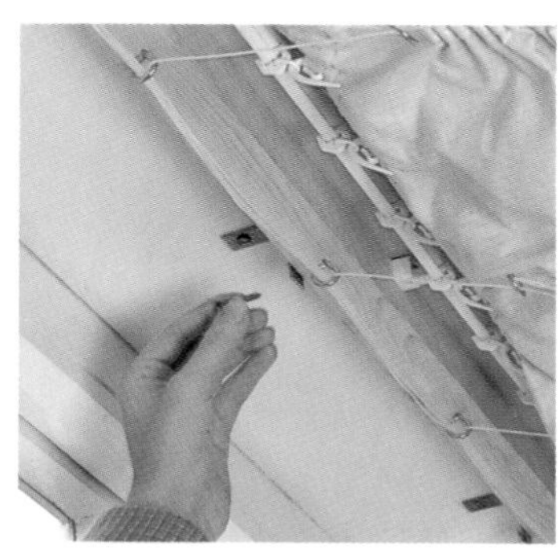

9 Secure the batten to the angle brackets. You will need one or two helpers to hold the batten in place and lift the blind fabric out of the way. Hold the batten, complete with track and blind, against the angle brackets. Drive in 1in (25mm) No. 8 screws through the brackets into the pilot holes in the back of the batten.

10 Plait together the bundle of cords at the side of the blind or knot them together at intervals. Trim the ends to an even length and knot them together.

11 Drill and plug holes for the cleat near the bottom of the window recess at the right-hand side of the window. Screw the cleat in place. To raise the blind, pull steadily on the cord and wind the slack several times round the cleat.

How to make a Roman blind

The construction of a Roman blind is very similar to that of a festoon blind, but instead of forming gathers, the blind draws up in neat, crisp pleats.

You will need almost the same tools and materials. The fabric requirement is much less than for a festoon blind but the blind needs a lining to give it more body. No heading tape or curtain track is needed. Since the vertical tapes are not to be drawn up, you can use plain tape instead of curtain heading tape. If you use plain tape, the curtain rings have to be sewn to the tape by hand because there are no pockets to slot them through. Alternatively, you can use Austrian blind tape, but the choice of positions for the rings is more limited than in curtain tape.

When estimating and cutting the fabric, allow the width required for the finished blind plus 1½in (4cm) for turnings. For the length, allow the length required for the finished blind plus 3in (7.5cm) for the top turning and the same for the bottom hem.

The lining should be the width of the finished blind plus ½in (1.3cm) and the length of the finished blind plus ½in (1.3cm).

If you have to join panels of fabric together to make up the width, use a machine run-and-fell seam (page 411). Arrange the panels so that there is a full width of fabric centred on the window with incomplete widths of fabric at the outer edges.

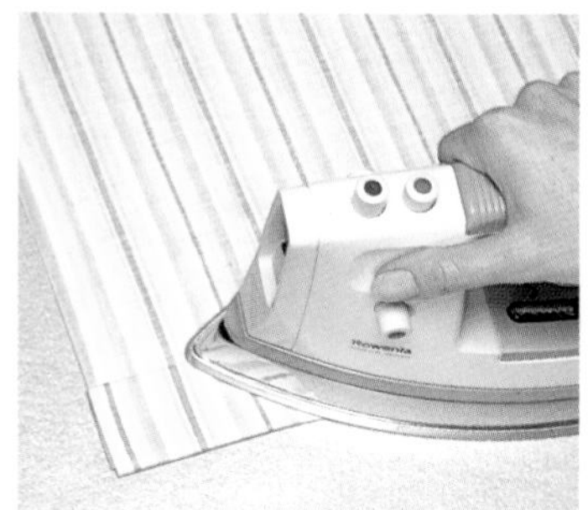

1 Fold in and press a ½in (1.3cm) turning onto the wrong side of the main fabric down each side, and a double 1½in (4cm) turning at top and bottom. Mitres are not needed at the corners because the tape will be at the edge.

2 Fold in and press a ½in (1.3cm) turning onto the wrong side all round the lining.

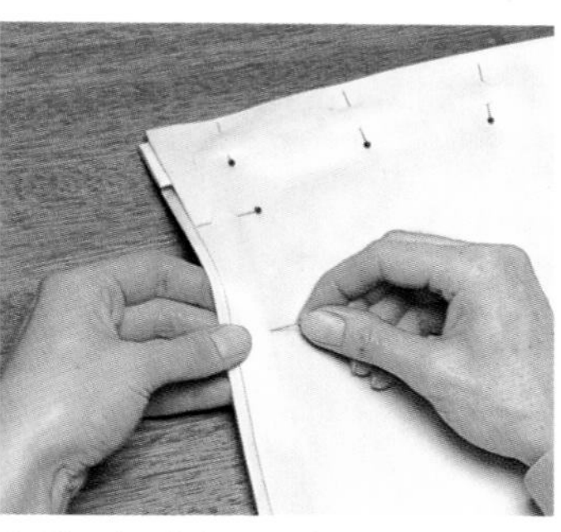

3 Pin the lining to the main fabric, right sides out, with the fabrics aligned at the top and the lining ¼in (6mm) in from the sides of the main fabric.

4 Slipstitch (page 411) the lining to the curtain all round.

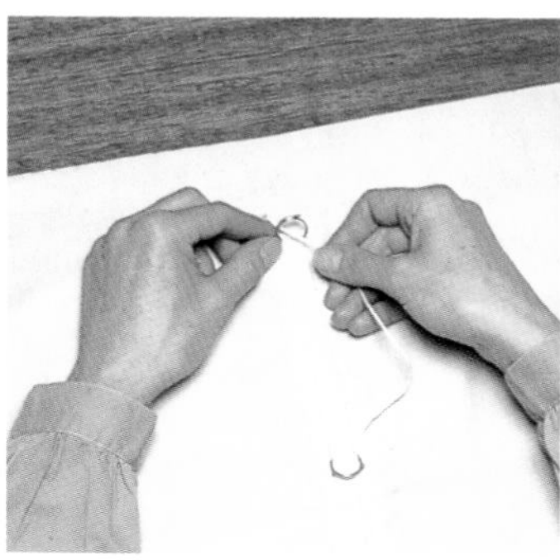

5 Continue as for a festoon blind – apply the vertical tapes; insert the rings, making sure that they are aligned across the rows of tape; and secure and thread the lengths of non-stretch cord.

6 Fit the angle brackets in the window recess; mark the batten and insert screw eyes in it as for a festoon blind.

7 Instead of hooking the blind to a curtain track, fix it direct to the batten with decorative dome-headed upholstery nails driven in at intervals of about 2in (5cm). ALTERNATIVELY, drive in tacks or staples to fix the blind to the batten and conceal them with braid held in place by fabric glue.

8 Finish assembling the blind as for a festoon blind – thread the cords through the screw eyes, working from right to left at the back of the blind. Screw the batten to the angle brackets, with a helper holding it. Plait or knot the cords and wind them round a cleat fitted on the right of the window recess.

How to make simple cushions

A scatter of cushions decorates a sofa or chair, and a large floor cushion or giant bean bag provides extra seating.

Cushions can be made up in a variety of shapes and any size you wish. They may be flat at the edges or welted to give depth at the edges. They can be covered with any type of material; remnants of expensive fabrics can often be bought cheaply and are large enough to cover small cushions. The cushion covers can be plain, piped at the edges, trimmed with braid, or decorated as you wish.

All cushions need the filling, a casing to hold the filling, and an attractive cover. Many department stores and specialist furnishers sell casings ready-made and filled. They are usually square, rectangular or round. You can make your own in these shapes or in hexagons or triangles.

DESIGNING THE CUSHION

Always make a paper pattern for any cushion cover, however small or simple. This allows you to estimate the fabric requirement and to cut out accurately, with any design on the fabric positioned correctly. Make the pattern from brown paper or lining paper for walls. Avoid intricate curves which may be difficult to sew and cause puckering when the cushion is filled.

The opening should be about the length of one side except for an inch at each end. A round cushion needs an opening about a quarter as long as its circumference.

At the opening, fit a zip or strips of touch-and-close tape for the neatest fastening. Hooks and eyes, press-studs or tapes for tying are alternative fastenings, but they do not give such a complete or smooth closure. Some people sew up the opening once the cased filling is inside; but this is much more troublesome to undo and replace when the cover needs washing or dry-cleaning.

MAKING THE PAPER PATTERN

Round cushion

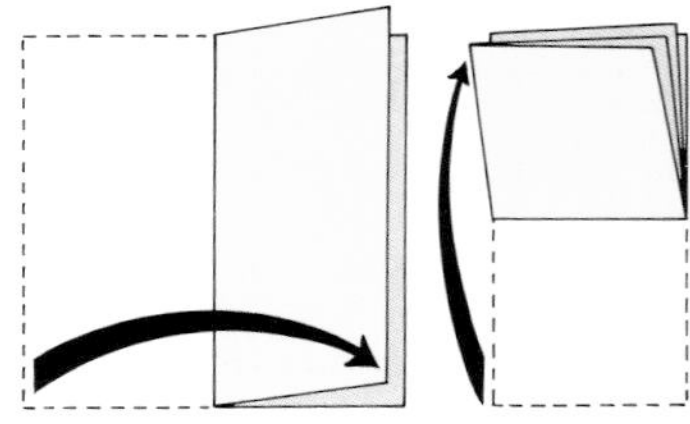

1 Make the pattern from a square sheet of paper that is at least as wide as you want the cushion to be across its diameter. Fold the paper in half then in half again to make a square a quarter the size of the paper.

2 Tie a length of string round a drawing pin at one end and a pencil at the other. The distance between the drawing pin and the pencil should be exactly half the width you want the finished cushion to be.

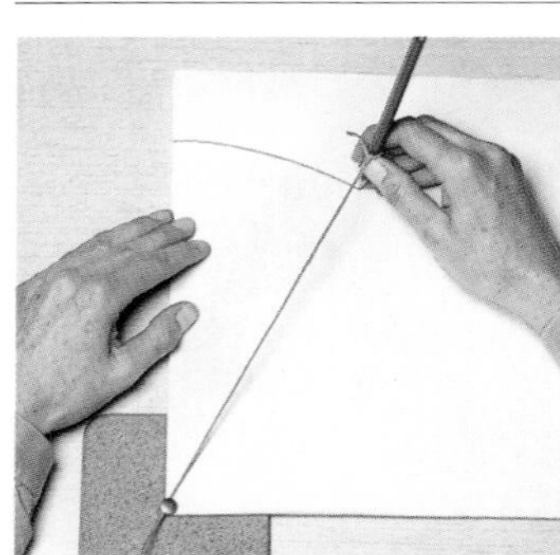

3 Stick the drawing pin into the folded paper at the corner where the folds meet. Put a thick cork mat, cardboard beer mat or piece of hardboard underneath so that the pin does not damage the work surface. With the string held taut and the pencil upright, draw a quarter circle from edge to edge of the paper.

4 Cut along the curved pencil line through all the four thicknesses of paper together so that the four quarters are identical. Open out the paper to give the full circle.

Hexagonal cushion

1 Make a circular paper pattern as described above for a round cushion.

2 With the drawing pin, pencil and string still arranged as for drawing the circle, insert the drawing pin anywhere on the edge of the circle. With the string taut and pencil upright, make a pencil mark on the edge. Put the pin in this mark and make another in the same way farther round the circle. Continue until there are six marks equally spaced round the circle. Remember to protect the work surface before you push in the drawing pin each time.

3 Use a ruler and pencil to join each mark to the one next to it with a straight line.

4 Cut along the six straight lines to give a hexagonal pattern.

Triangular cushion

1 Prepare a circular paper pattern as described above for a round cushion.

2 Make six marks equally spaced round the circle as described above for a hexagonal cushion.

3 Join alternate pencil marks on the circle's edge with straight lines.

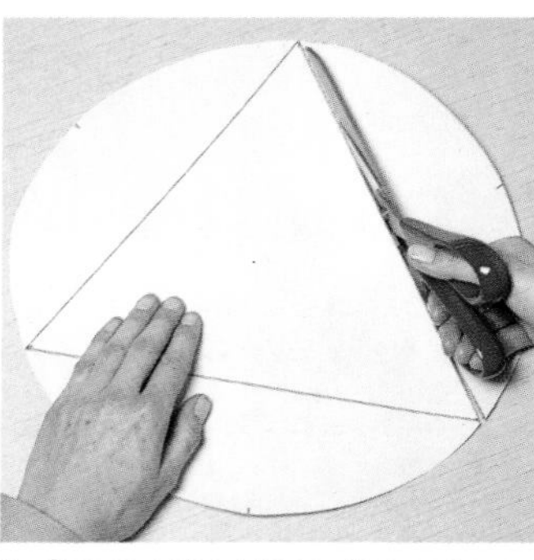

4 Cut out the triangular pattern.

PIPED CUSHIONS

Design the cushion with slightly rounded corners to avoid puckering. Use a saucer or a small round lid as a guide for the corners.

To make your own piping, you need shrink-resistant piping cord and bias binding. If you cannot find shrink-resistant cord, boil ordinary cord in a pan of water for 3 or 4 minutes. Dry it thoroughly.

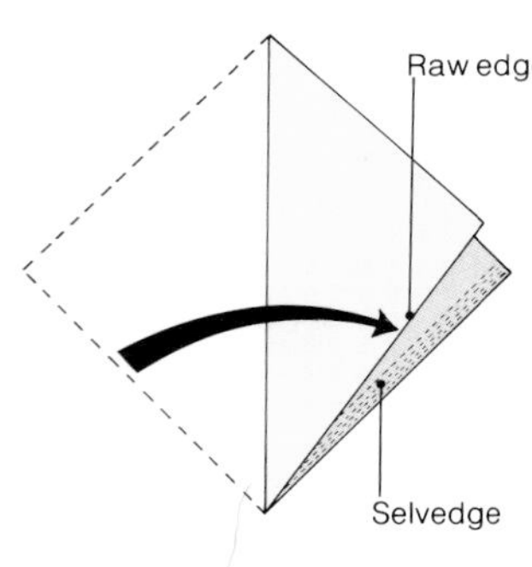

1 To make bias binding, fold the straight raw edge of the fabric back diagonally until it is aligned with the selvedge.

2 Mark the fold with pins.

3 Open out the fabric and cut along the marked diagonal line.

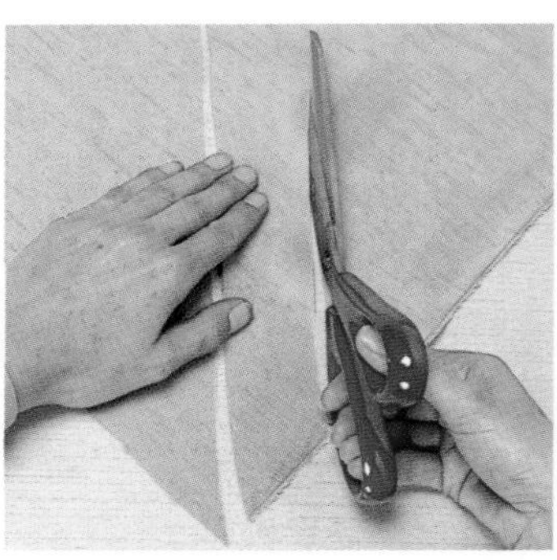

4 Cut strips parallel to the diagonal, making each strip $1\frac{1}{2}$in (4cm) wide.

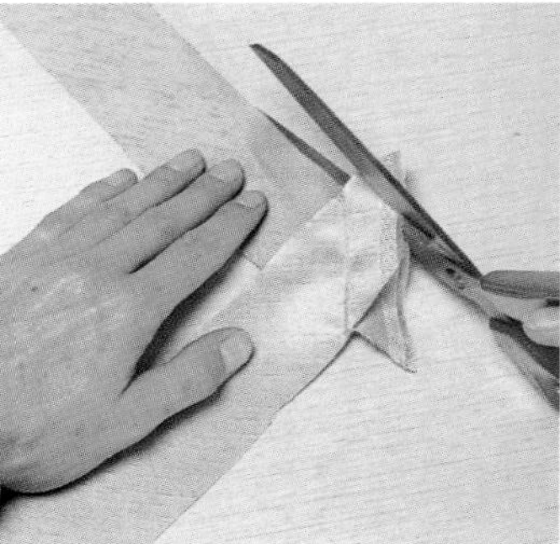

5 To join strips together, place them in a V shape with right sides together. Machine across the bottom of the V and trim off the projecting points.

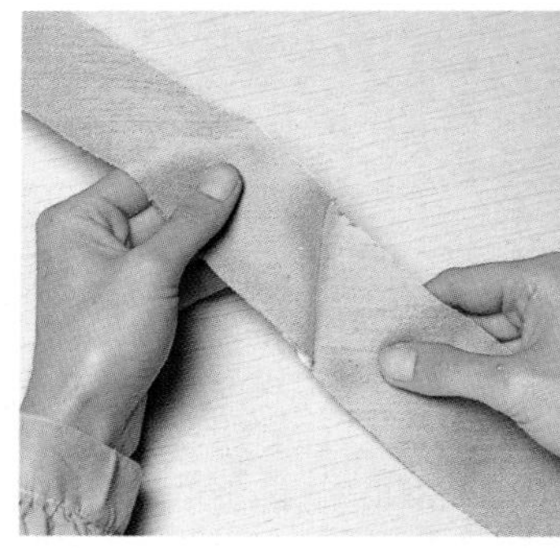

6 Open out the binding and press it flat.

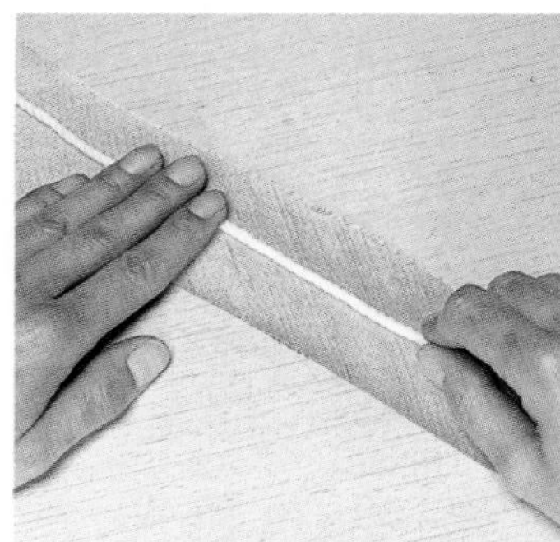

7 Lay out the binding wrong side up and arrange the piping cord along the centre.

HELPFUL TIP
To join cord, overlap the ends, cut through them at an angle, put the angled ends together and bind round them with thread.

8 Draw the edges of the binding together and insert pins close to the cord. Tack the binding in place.

9 Machine with the zipper foot on the machine. Remove the tacking.

MAKING THE CUSHION COVER

A simple square cushion, rounded off at the corners, is given a professional finish with a piped edge.

You will need
Tools Paper pattern; pins; scissors; sewing machine (perhaps with zipper foot); iron.
Materials Fabric; perhaps piping or other trimming; thread; zip fastener or touch-and-close fastener.

1 Pin the pattern on the fabric, making sure that the pattern is centred or accurately aligned on any design on the fabric.

2 Cut out the fabric, making it 1in (2.5cm) larger than the paper pattern all round.

3 Cut another piece of fabric the same size as the first. Again take care about the position of any design on the fabric if you want to be able to use the cushion either side up.

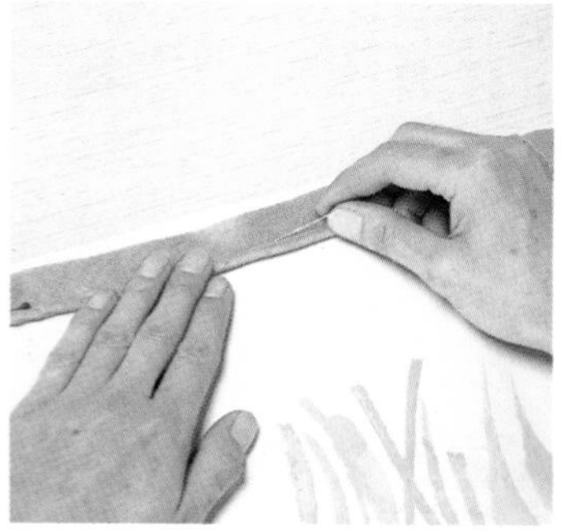

4 If the cushion is to be piped, tack the piping in place on the right side of one of the pieces of fabric 1in (2.5cm) from the edge. At this stage, machine it in place only along the section where the opening is to be; use the zipper foot in the machine and sew close to the piping cord.

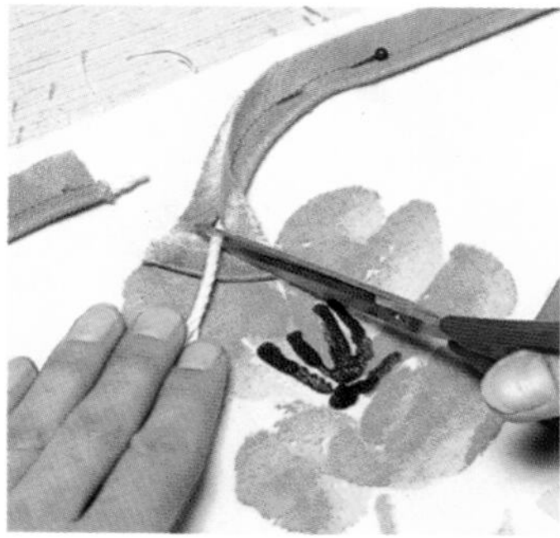

5 Overlap the piping ½in (1.3cm) where it meets; cut off the excess. Undo the stitching at one end for ½in (1.3cm) and cut off that amount of cord. Fold the edge in, lap it onto the other end of the piping and hemstitch (page 411) the join with tiny stitches.

6 Place the two pieces of fabric together with wrong sides out. Mark off the opening with pins.

7 If you are fitting a zip, insert it at this stage (page 431).

8 Pin and tack the edges together round the rest of the cover, 1in (2.5cm) from the edge.

9 Machine the fabric pieces together with a plain seam. If you have fitted piping, use the zipper foot in the machine.

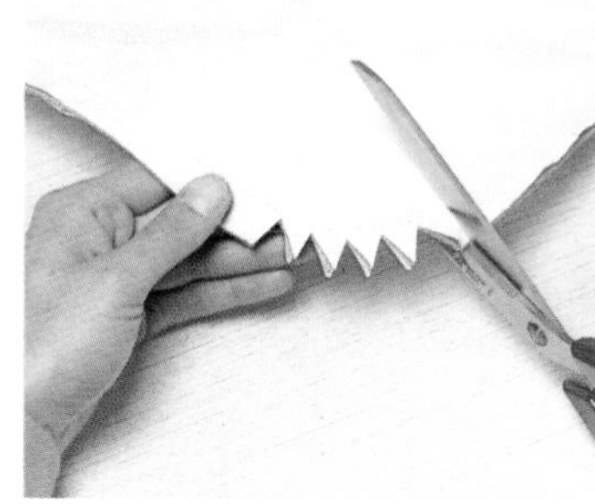

10 If the cover has curved edges, make V-shaped cuts in the seam allowance. At corners, trim off the point diagonally.

11 Oversew (page 411) the raw edges by hand or run a zigzag machine stitch along them. Oversew them separately so that you can press open the seam. After pressing, turn the cover right side out.

12 If you have not fitted a zip in the opening, sew the touch-and-close fastening in place by hand.

13 If the cushion cover is to be trimmed, sew on the trimming by hand using prickstitch (page 411), or fix it in place with iron-on bonding web.

14 Insert the cased filling, pushing it well into the corners of the cover. Close the cover and shake the cushion gently to plump it up.

How to make welted cushions

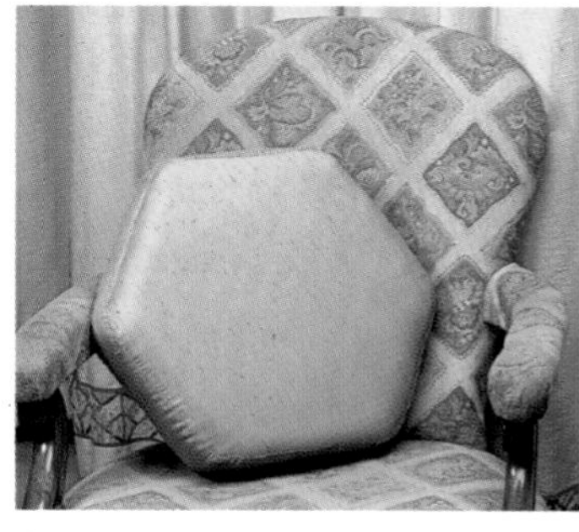

A welt, or strip of fabric running round the sides, gives a cushion depth right to the edge and makes it a more clearly defined shape. The zip is fitted in the welt.

Because of its depth, the cover for a welted cushion takes more fabric, and it requires a longer opening than usual for the bulkier cased filling to be inserted. If you choose to trim the edges, you will need twice as much trimming as for a simple cushion.

Make the pattern for the top and bottom of the cushion exactly as for simple cushions (page 428), choosing from the same variety of shapes.

To make the pattern for the welt, measure with string or ruler round the edge of the pattern for the top; this gives the length. Cut out a paper strip to this length, making the depth what you wish.

Cut off from the paper strip the length required for the opening plus 4in (10cm). On a square, rectangular or triangular cushion, the opening should extend along the whole of one side and 2in (5cm) round the adjoining sides. On a round or hexagonal cushion, the opening should be a third of the circumference. When you have cut off a piece of the right length, cut it in half lengthwise.

You will need
Tools Paper pattern; pins; scissors; sewing machine (perhaps with a zipper foot); iron.
Materials Fabric; perhaps piping or other chosen trimming; thread; zip fastener or touch-and-close fastening tape.

PATTERN PIECES FOR A WELTED HEXAGONAL CUSHION

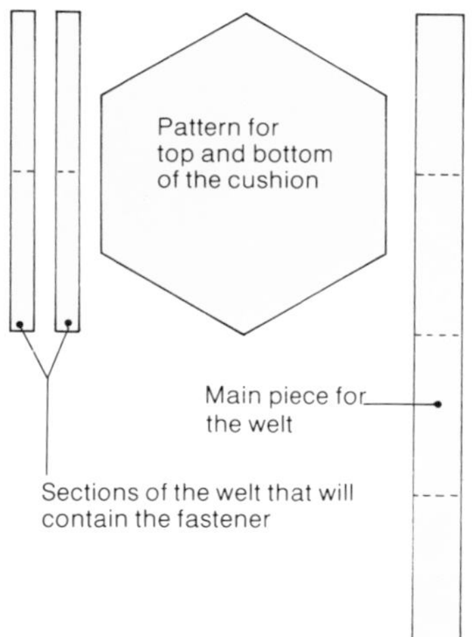

Arrange the pattern pieces on the straight grain of the fabric and leave at least 2in (5cm) between each of the pieces. This gives enough fabric for a seam allowance round each piece.

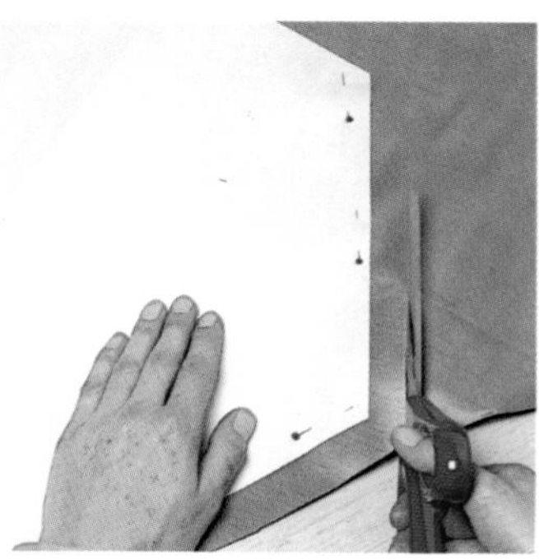

1 Cut out the top and bottom 1in (2.5cm) larger than the pattern all round. Centre or align any design on the fabric accurately. Before you unpin the pattern, put a stitch of bright thread in the fabric at every angle of the pattern. On a round cushion, fold the pattern in four and put a stitch at the four creases at the edge of the pattern.

2 Cut the three pieces for the welt 1in (2.5cm) larger than the pattern all round. You may need to join fabric strips for the main piece.

How to make welted cushions (continued)

3 If you have to join strips of fabric to make up the main piece of the welt, join them with a run-and-fell machine seam (page 411).

4 Sew the zip to the two narrow sections of welt (page 431).

ALTERNATIVELY, sew the touch-and-close fastening in place.

5 Close the zip or touch-and-close fastener and join both ends of the opening section to the main part of the welt with 1in (2.5cm) turning allowances and using run-and-fell machine seams. Put marker stitches at equal intervals 1in (2.5cm) in from each edge of the welt – three markers for a triangular cushion, four for a round or a square one, and six for a hexagonal one.

6 If the cover is to be piped, pin and tack the piping in place round both top and bottom pieces of the cover. Position it so that the line of tacking is 1in (2.5cm) from the edge.

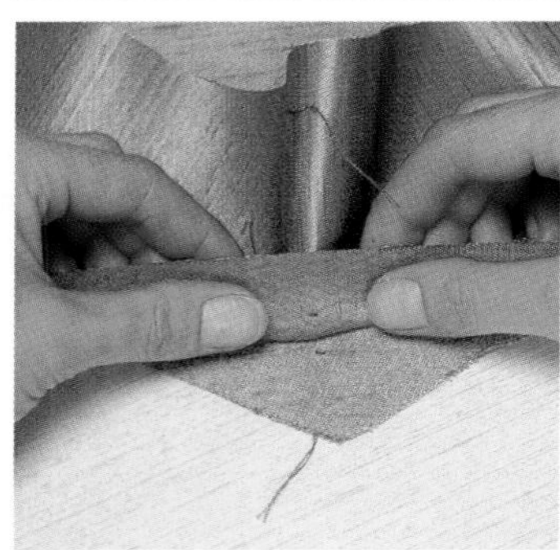

7 With the wrong sides out, pin the welt to the bottom piece of the cover. Match up the marker stitches exactly first of all.

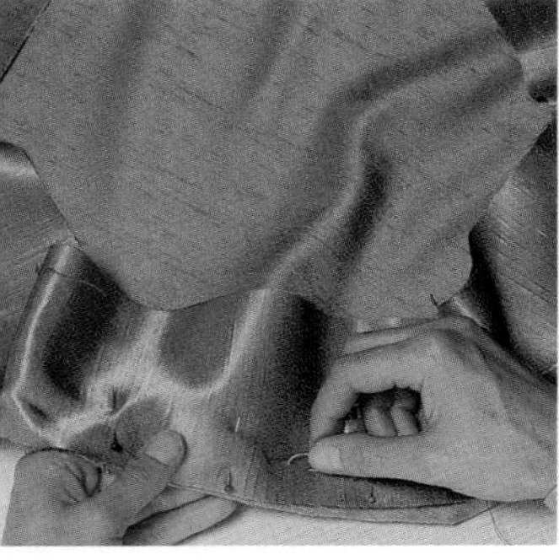

8 Pin together the lengths between the markers 1in (2.5cm) from the edge. Ease or stretch the fabric slightly to make sure there are no puckers. As you work round the cushion, make V-shaped cuts into the seam allowance along any curved edges. This makes it easier to fit the two parts together. The neatness of the finished cushion depends on inserting the welt without puckers.

9 Tack and then machine the welt to the bottom piece of the cover. If you have fitted piping, use the zipper foot. Remove the tacking.

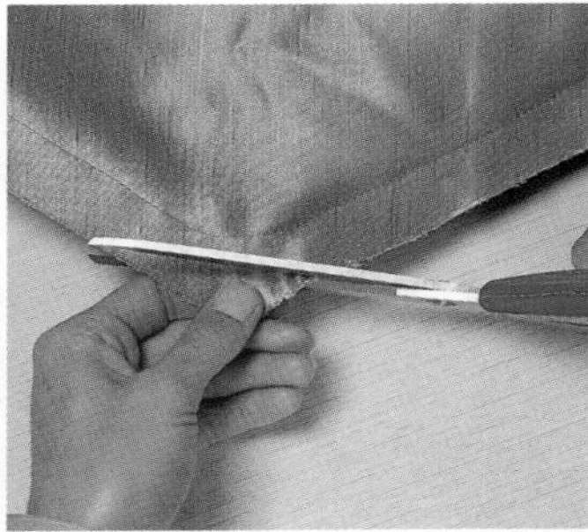

10 Open the fastening. Pin and tack the welt to the top piece of the cover in the same way as you have fitted it to the bottom. Machine it in place. Remove the tacking and snip off the points of any corners.

11 Press all the seam allowances towards the welt so that the top and bottom of the cushion will not show any ridges.

12 Turn the cover right side out and apply any trimming as for a simple cushion.

13 Insert the cased filling and close the fastening.

Making and filling cushion casings

Choose the casing fabric to suit the filling. Use ticking for down or feathers to prevent the quills from working through the fabric. Use foam sheeting for foam chip fillings. For other fillings, use calico, cambric, curtain lining, or casement.

FABRIC CASING

1 Cut out the fabric exactly as for the cushion cover.

2 Pin and tack the pieces together leaving a 6in (15cm) opening in one side. If the casing is for a foam block, leave almost the whole of one end open for a square, rectangular or triangular cushion; leave one-third of the edge open for a round or hexagonal cushion.

3 Use a French seam (page 411) for most casings. For a casing made of ticking, use a plain open seam but stitch round it twice.

4 Turn the casing right side out and insert the filling, pushing it well into any corners.

5 Fold under the edges of the opening. Oversew them firmly together or tack them together and machine along the join.

FOAM CASING

You will need

Tools Small scissors; clothes pegs.
Materials Foam sheeting; foam adhesive.

1 Use the cushion cover pattern to cut out the casing but allow only ¼in (6mm) extra all round.

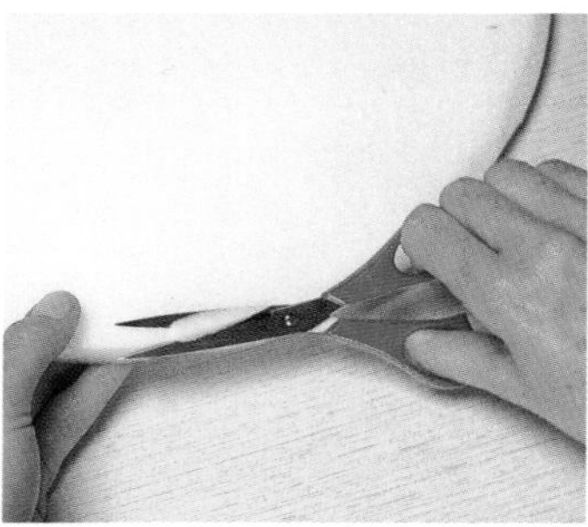

2 Use small, sharp scissors to trim all the edges, giving them an angle of about 45 degrees.

3 Lay out the pieces on a flat surface. Leave 3in (7.5cm) of two adjoining edges bare but apply adhesive to the rest of the edges.

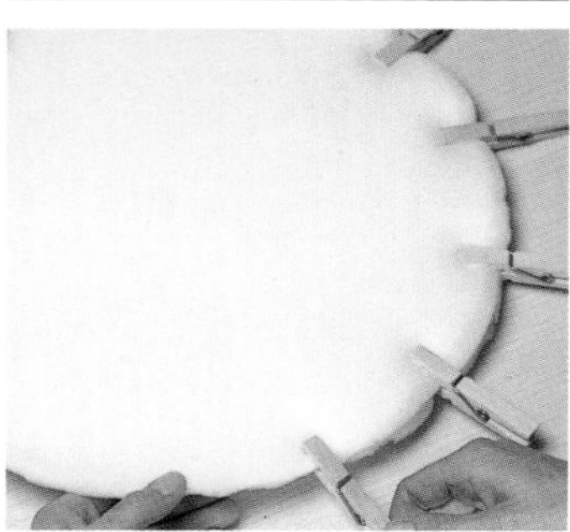

4 Put the edges together and secure them with clothes pegs until completely set.

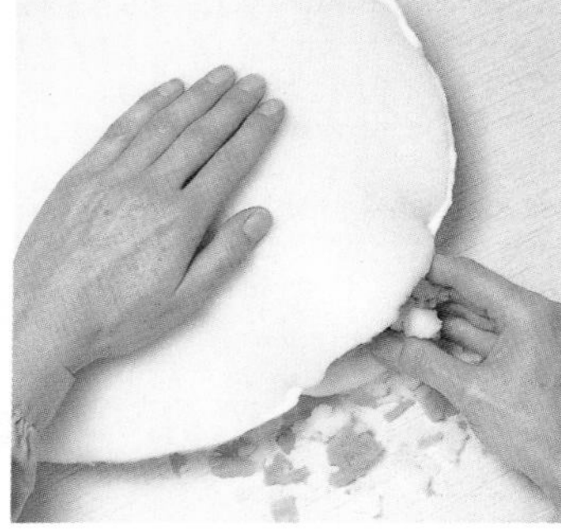

5 Fill the casing with foam chips then apply adhesive to the edges of the opening. Hold them together with clothes pegs until they are securely bonded.

CUSHION FILLINGS

DOWN The softest, most expensive filling is down. It plumps itself up and never loses its springiness. Down can be mixed with feathers to reduce the cost a little.

FEATHERS Although expensive, feathers make a soft filling which keeps its resilience and can be plumped up time and time again. Feathers are readily available in ready-made casings but more difficult to obtain loose. You can re-use feathers from pillows or quilts.

ACRYLIC/POLYESTER WADDING This is relatively cheap and the only washable filling. It must on no account be dry-cleaned because the fibres retain toxic fumes. Pack it firmly into the casing or else it will form lumps. It must meet fire safety regulations and is best used in a fire-retardant interliner.

KAPOK WADDING Kapok is a vegetable fibre filling. It must not be dry-cleaned as it retains toxic fumes. It goes lumpy after a time. It is slightly more expensive than synthetic wadding

FOAM CHIPS The cheapest filling is foam chips. To avoid a lumpy look, pack them firmly in a smooth foam casing. Do not dry-clean them. They are washable but difficult to dry. The foam sheet casing can be sponged gently to clean it. Foam chips must meet fire safety regulations and it is best to use a fire-retardent interliner.

FOAM BLOCKS Use a block to give a sharply defined shape to welted cushions. After several years' wear the blocks begin to crumble. Because of this, it is essential to give the foam block a fabric casing, instead of placing the foam directly inside the main cover. Foam blocks must meet fire safety regulations and should be used with a fire-retardant interliner.

ESTIMATING THE QUANTITY OF FILLING

A simple cushion 18-20in (46-51cm) square would need ¾lb (350g) of down; or 2lb (900g) of feathers; or 1½lb (700g) of synthetic or kapok wadding; or 1¾lb (800g) of foam chips. Double the quantity if you are filling a welted cushion with a 4in (10cm) welt.

How to make a giant bean bag

A large, rounded, squashy floor cushion is easy and inexpensive to make at home. It consists of two bags – an attractive outer cover and an inner lining to contain the polystyrene granules. Use corduroy, canvas or upholstery fabric for the outer cover and sew it with suitably strong thread (page 409). Use a strong fabric for the lining.

You will need
Tools Tape measure; pencil; drawing pin; string; scissors; pins; needles; sewing machine; a cardboard tube, from inside a roll of kitchen foil, for example.
Materials Paper for pattern; adhesive tape; 4⅓yds (4m) of main fabric and lining; thread; a strong zip 15in (38cm) long; ⅔cu yd (0.5cu m) of polystyrene granules.

MAKING THE PATTERN

1 Prepare a pattern for the side sections, which will be petal-shaped. Use pieces of brown paper or wall lining paper taped together to make a sheet 48in (122cm) long and 20in (51cm) wide.

2 Fold the sheet in half lengthwise. Make a pencil mark on the bottom edge 8¼in (21cm) from the fold. On the cut side of the paper make a pencil mark 20in (51cm) from the bottom edge. Make the last pencil mark 12in (30cm) down from the top and 7½in (19cm) from the fold. Draw a curved line up through the marks and sweep it round to finish it at the fold on the top edge.

3 Cut along the line through both layers of paper at once to make the pattern symmetrical. Open out the pattern to give a petal shape

4 For the base, prepare a hexagonal pattern in the same way as for a simple cushion (page 428). Make it with a radius of 16½in (42cm). Cut the hexagon in half from point to point to give two pattern pieces, each with a base 33in (84cm) long and three sides 16½in (42cm) long. On each piece, tape a ¾in (2cm) wide strip of paper on the long side for a turning allowance along the opening.

MAKING THE LINING

1 Pin the pattern to the fabric and cut out the two base sections. Cut the fabric the same size as the pattern; turning allowances are included in the pattern measurements. It is easiest to cut out on a clean floor.

PATTERN PIECES FOR A GIANT BEAN BAG

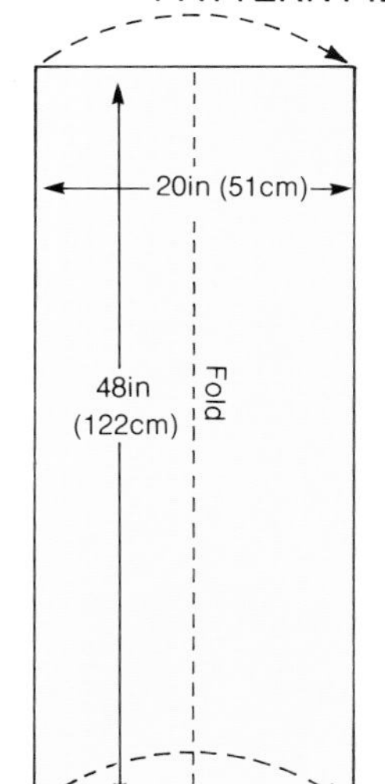

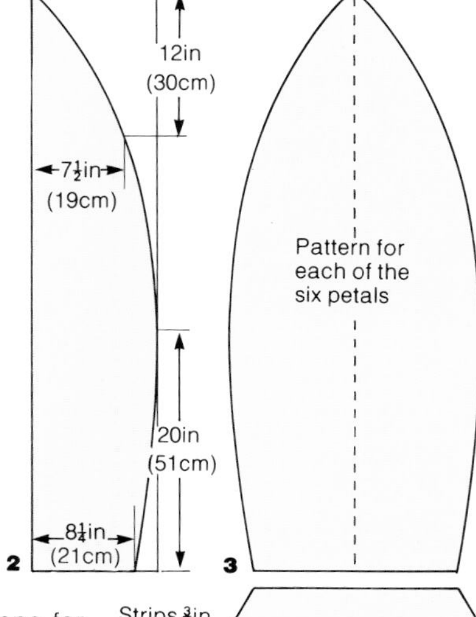

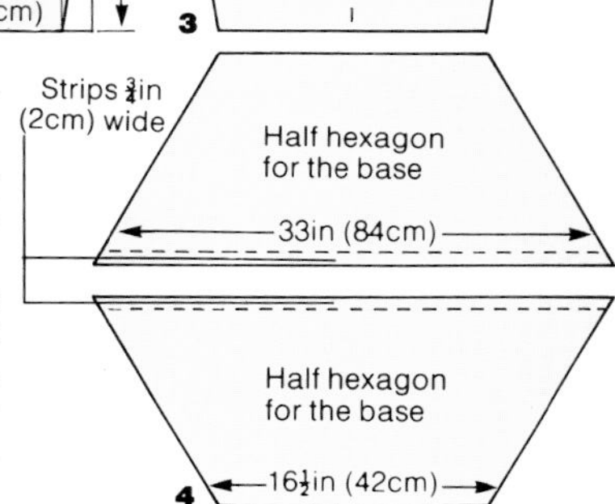

Make up sheets of paper, one for the side and one for the base. Fold the sheet for the side in half lengthwise (1). Measure and draw a pencil curve from the bottom to the top (2). Cut along the curve and open out the petal-shaped pattern (3). Cut out the hexagon for the base, divide it in two and tape on extra strips for the turning allowance at the opening (4).

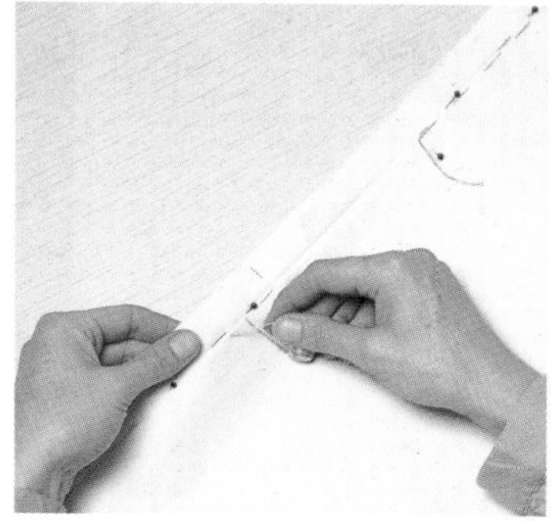

2 Place the two base sections together with wrong sides out. Pin and tack the two long sides together, leaving a ¾in (2cm) seam allowance. Machine the join with a plain open seam leaving a gap of about 3in (7.5cm) at the middle. This is where the filling will be inserted. Remove the tacking.

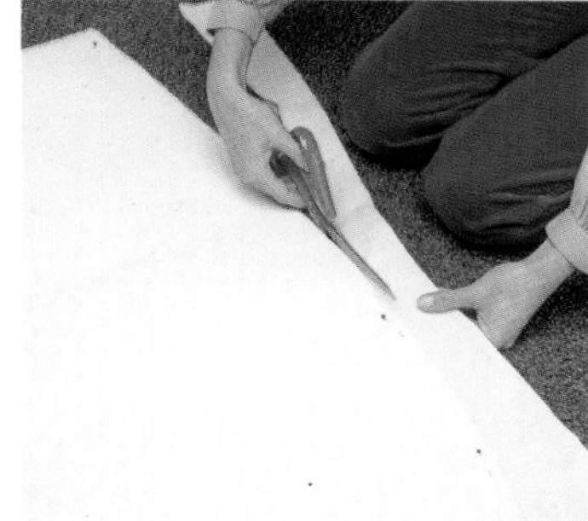

3 Cut out six side sections, each the exact size of the pattern. Pin the long sides of the sections to one another with right sides together. Tack the joins, leaving ⅝in (1.5cm) seam allowances.

4 Snip V-shaped notches in the seam allowances on the curves.

PUTTING IN A ZIP FASTENER

Buy a zip fastener that is suitable for the weight of fabric it will join and for the amount of strain it will take – a tweed-covered giant floor cushion needs a much sturdier zip than a decorative silky cushion on a sofa. Match the colour as closely as possible to that of the fabric you are putting the zip in.

It is much easier to insert a zip while you can spread out flat the sections of fabric it is going to join – before you join the sides to the base of a giant bean bag, for example. You can stitch the zip in place by machine or by hand.

1 Put together the two pieces of fabric that the zip is to join, with wrong sides out and raw edges aligned. Pin, tack and then sew together 2in (5cm) at each end, leaving the recommended seam allowance. Make a plain open machine seam or, if you are sewing by hand, use prickstitch (page 411).

2 Press the seam allowances back along the opening.

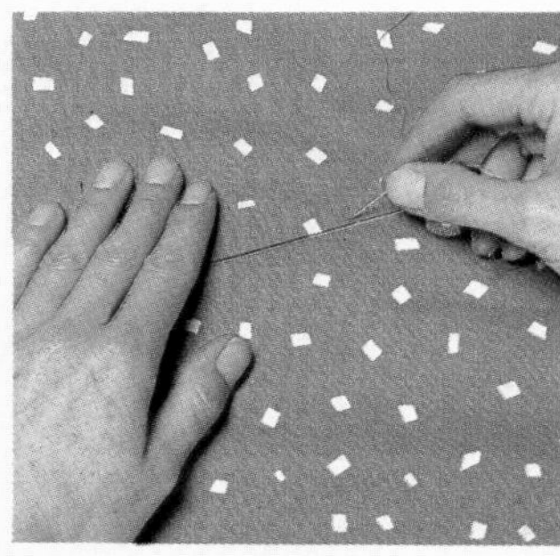

3 On the right side of the fabric, you can slipstitch the opening together while you fit the zip. The stitching is temporary and need not be small or neat.

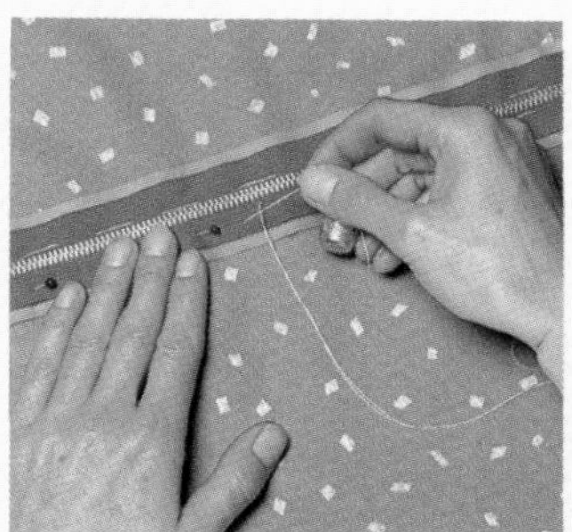

4 On the wrong side of the fabric, position the zip centrally over the opening. Pin and tack it in place, making the stitching ⅛in (3mm) from the teeth of the zip.

5 Turn the material to the right side again. With the zipper foot fitted in the machine, stitch the zip in place down each side as close to the teeth as the zipper foot will allow. Stitch each side in the same direction to avoid puckering. Stitch across the ends of the zip as close to the metal as possible.

ALTERNATIVELY, stitch the zip in place by hand, using prickstitch and following the same order as for machine stitching.

6 Remove the tacking and any slipstitching.

How to make a giant bean bag (continued)

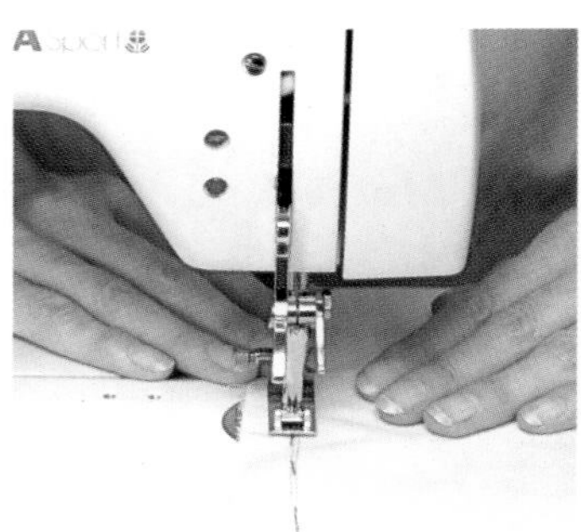

5 Sew the sections together with plain open machine seams. For extra strength, machine two rows of stitching at each seam, making them ⅛in (3mm) apart.

6 Pin and tack the side sections to the base with wrong sides out. Machine two rows of stitching ⅛in (3mm) apart. Remove the tacking.

7 Turn the lining right side out.

MAKING THE OUTER COVER

1 Cut out the fabric as for the lining.

2 Insert the zip (page 431) in the long sides of the base sections making a ¾in (2cm) seam allowance. Finish sewing together the two sides to make a hexagon.

3 Cut out a strip of fabric for the handle. Make it 10in (25cm) long and 7in (18cm) wide. Fold it in half lengthwise and wrong side out.

4 Pin, tack and machine the long sides together ¾in (2cm) from the edge. Remove the tacking.

5 Press the seam allowances back towards the folded edge.

6 Turn the handle right side out. Pin the handle, folded in half, to the right side of one of the side sections, placing it near the pointed top of the section.

7 Pin the sides together, then tack and machine them in the same way as for the lining.

8 Pin, tack and machine the sides to the base in the same way as for the lining. Remember to open the zip before fitting the sides to the base.

ASSEMBLING THE BEAN BAG

1 Place the lining inside the main cover. Make sure both openings coincide at the base.

2 Put the cover on the floor and insert the cardboard tube into the lining opening. Secure the fabric all round the tube with adhesive tape, making sure that there are no gaps.

3 Place the bag of granules on a chair and insert the tube into a small hole in the bag. Again secure the tube with adhesive tape.

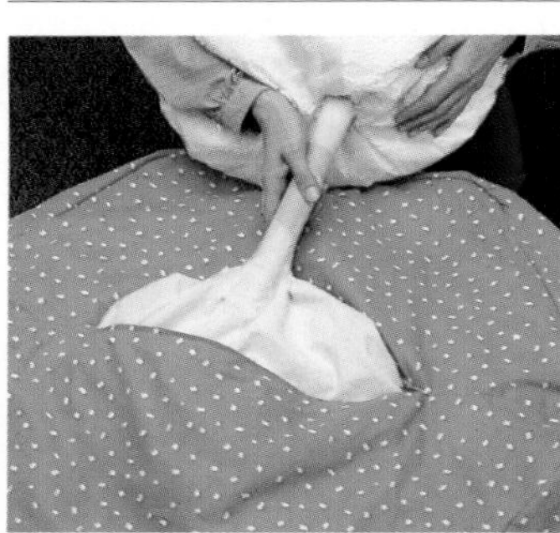

4 Shake the granules through the tube into the inner bag. Make sure that the adhesive tape does not work loose. The cover should be three-quarters full.

5 Sew up the opening in the lining with double thread and small oversewing stitches (page 411). This opening can be undone if necessary for adding more granules as the original ones lose their resilience.

6 Close the zip fastener and shake the bean bag to distribute the granules evenly.

Repairing damaged upholstery

PULLED THREAD

1 Use a thread pulled from the turning under the chair. Undo any hessian to reach it if necessary.

2 Using a semicircular needle, weave in the new thread as near as possible to the pulled one. Do not cut away the old thread yet.

3 Tie the ends of the new thread round one or two cross threads and weave them under the fabric.

4 Snip off the ends of the new thread and cut off the old pulled thread.

TEAR NEAR A SEAM

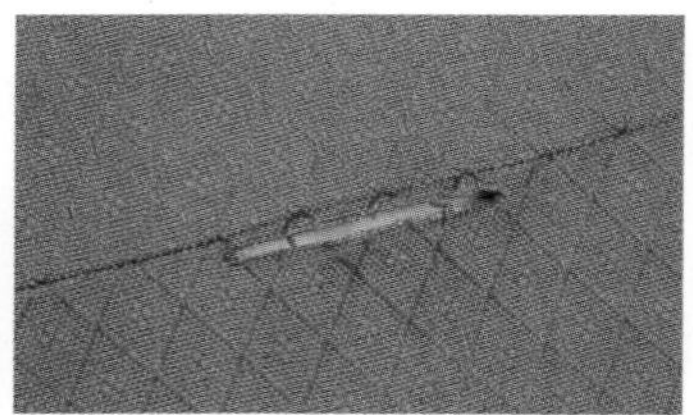

To make the repair, you will have to fold under the torn edge farthest from the seam. Taper off the fold beyond the ends of the tear.

1 Push the fold across to the seam and secure it with large pins.

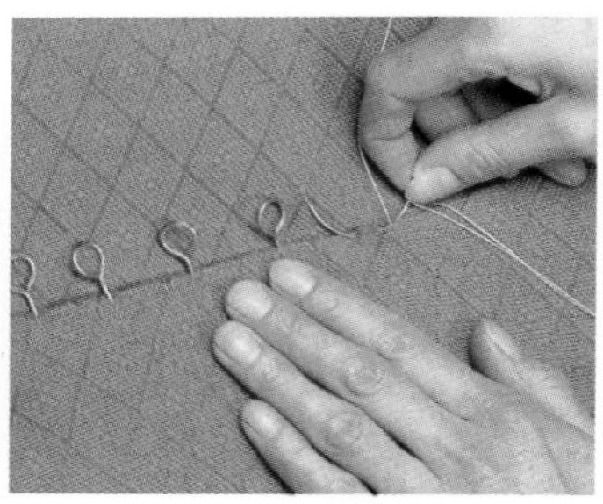

2 With a semicircular needle and strong thread, slipstitch (page 411) the fold to the seam.

TEAR NEAR PIPING

Fold under and pin the tear as for a tear near a seam. Slipstitch the fold to the other side of the seam, taking the needle under the piping with each stitch.

OTHER TEARS

Tears that are not near a seam or piped edge must be patched. Use matching fabric if possible; if not, use fabric of similar weight. The patch must be slightly larger than the tear. You can repair woven fabric or vinyl in this way.

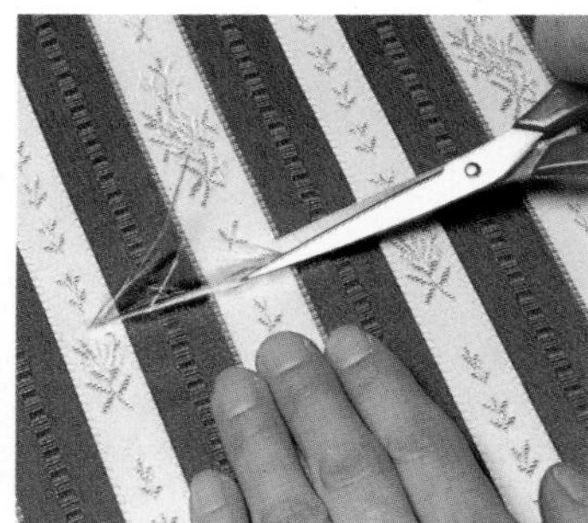

1 Snip away any frayed fibres from the tear.

2 Slip the patch beneath the tear, making sure that it lies flat.

3 Lift the torn edges of fabric – tweezers make this easier – and apply fabric adhesive under them.

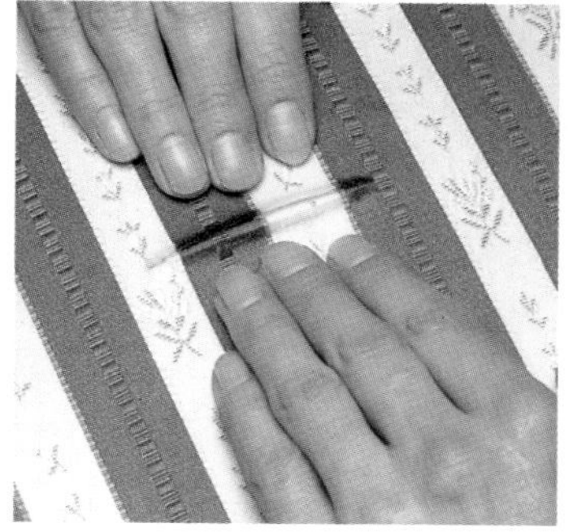

4 Hold the tear against the patch until the adhesive begins to set.

PATCHING A SMALL HOLE

Take the patch from the turning under the seat, undoing any hessian to reach it. For patterned fabric, take the patch from a matching spot. On plain fabrics, trim the hole to a rectangle along the warp and weft and cut a patch running in the same direction as the main fabric.

Fixing with bonding web

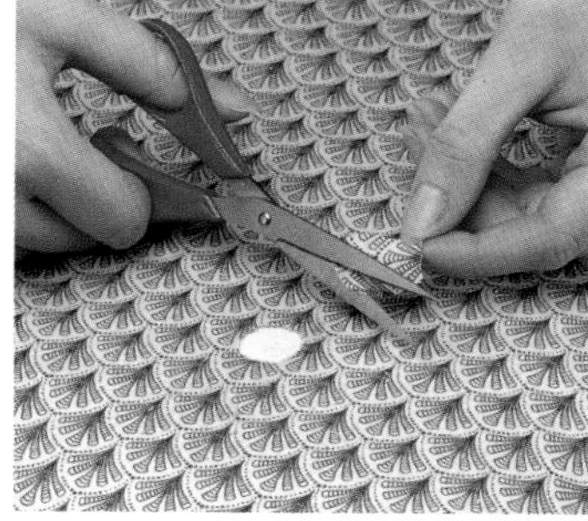

1 Neaten the hole and trim the patch to fit and match it exactly.

2 Use scissor tips to tuck a strip of bonding web under the hole.

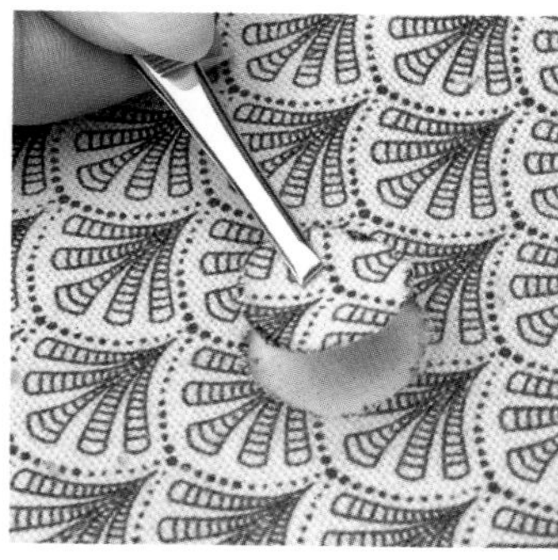

3 Lay the patch in position with the pattern or direction of weave matching the main fabric. Press with a warm iron over a damp cloth until the cloth is dry.

Fixing with adhesive

1 Cut a patch to match the pattern or direction of weave round the hole. Make it ½in (1.3cm) larger than the hole all round to allow for the turning.

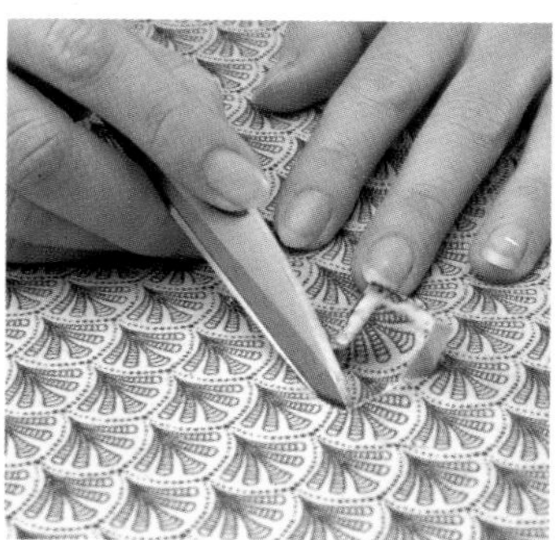

2 Spread fabric adhesive on the margin of the patch and slip it under the hole. Use the tips of scissors to push the edges of the patch flat.

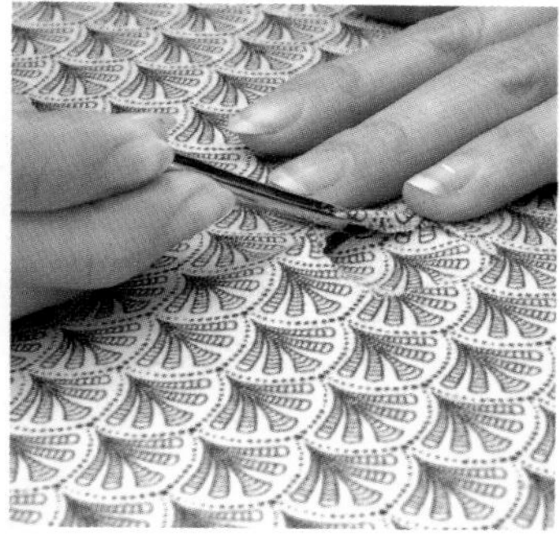

3 Turn under the margin of the hole. Tweezers will help you to do this more easily.

4 Press the folded-under fabric flat. Put a heavy weight over the patched area to press it flat until the adhesive has begun to set.

RE-COVERING A FRONT ARM

1 Carefully snip away any cord or fringing, which is fixed on top of the completed covering. Do not remove piping, which is sewn in as an integral part of the seam.

2 Push any wadding that is sticking out back under the worn fabric.

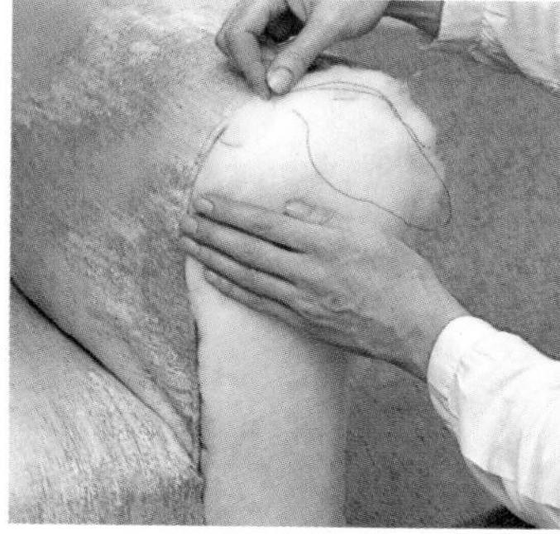

3 Cut to shape a fresh layer of wadding and sew it in place with tacking stitch (page 411).

4 Cut to shape a new front arm section with a ½in (1.3cm) turning allowance all round. If you have no spare fabric, take fabric from under a loose cushion or, if this is not possible, from behind the chair or sofa. Try to match any pattern to that on the other arm.

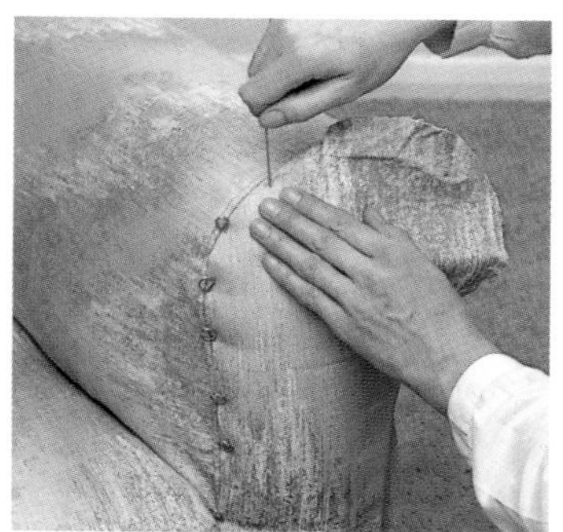

5 Pin the section in place as close as possible to the seam or piping. Fold under the turning allowance as you go.

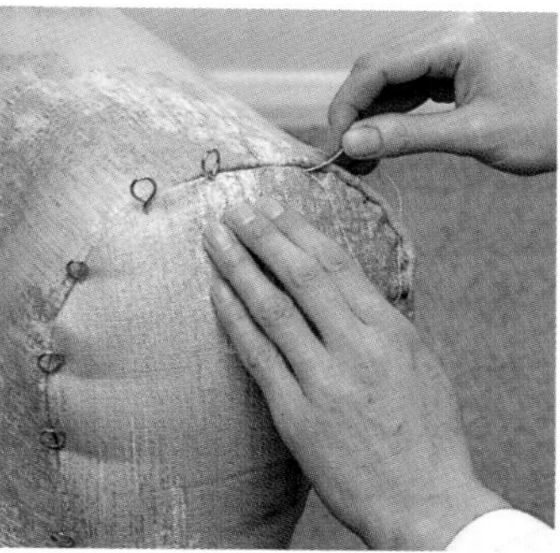

6 Use strong thread and a semicircular needle to slipstitch the section in place, pulling the fabric taut as you work round the section. If there is piping, take the needle under it at each stitch.

7 Sew or glue back any cord or fringing.

RE-COVERING AN INSIDE ARM

1 Leave the old cover in place. Measure the size of fabric needed to reach as far as possible down between the arm and the seat and over the arm to the underside of the curve. Measure the size from front to back, adding on ample turnings. Cut out the fabric.

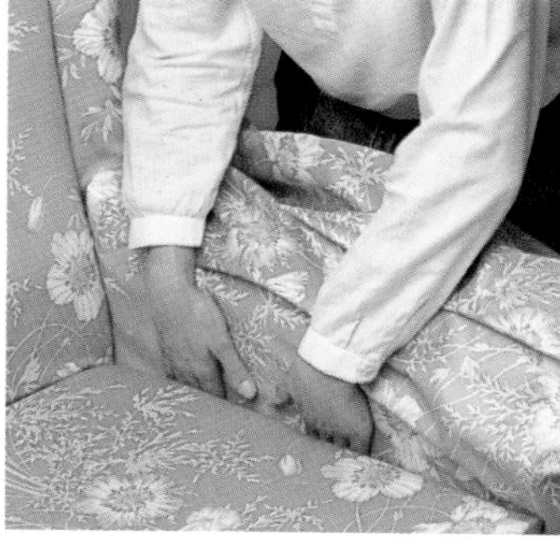

2 Coat the fabric's lower edge with adhesive and push it as far down as you can against the inner arm.

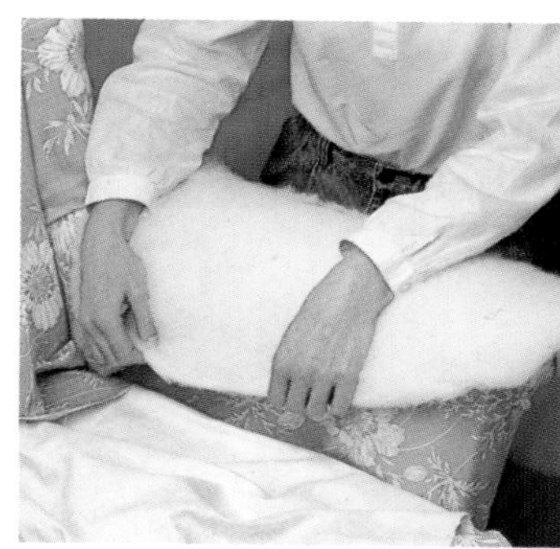

3 When the adhesive is completely set, put a layer of new wadding over the top of the arm.

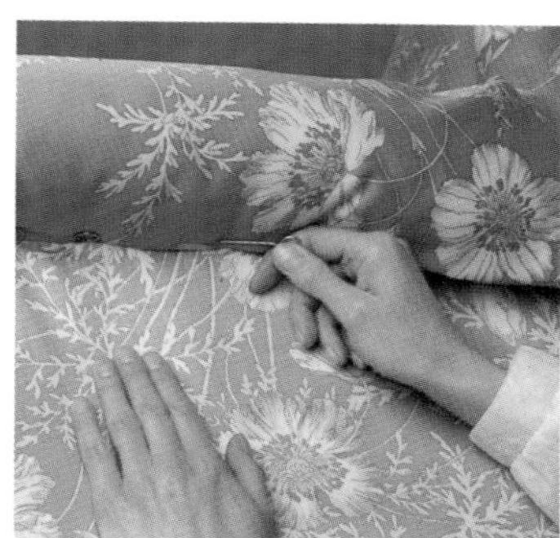

4 Pull the new cover taut up and over the arm and pin it in position with the raw edge turned under.

5 Pin the back and front in place with the edges turned under. If the arm cover is of the type that wraps over the front of the arm, run a gathering thread along the front edge to take in the fullness.

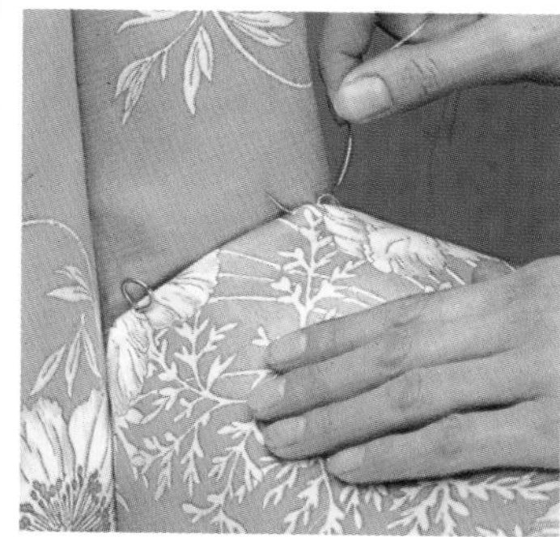

6 Use a semicircular needle and strong thread to slipstitch (page 411) the new cover in place at the back, under the curve of the outside arm, and at the front edge.

Repairing damaged upholstery (continued)

REPLACING A BUTTON

Use a double-pointed upholsterer's needle 6-8in (15-20cm) long, threaded with 12in (30cm) of number 2 twine.

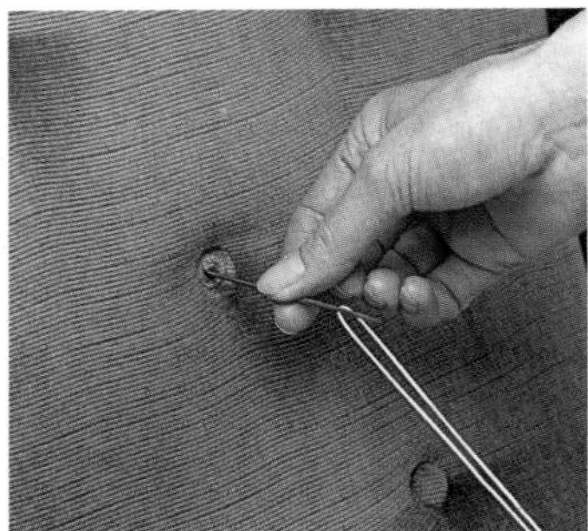

1 Insert the unthreaded end at the button position and push the needle into the padding until the eye disappears and the unthreaded point emerges at the back.

2 Push the needle back to emerge ¼in (6mm) from the entry point.

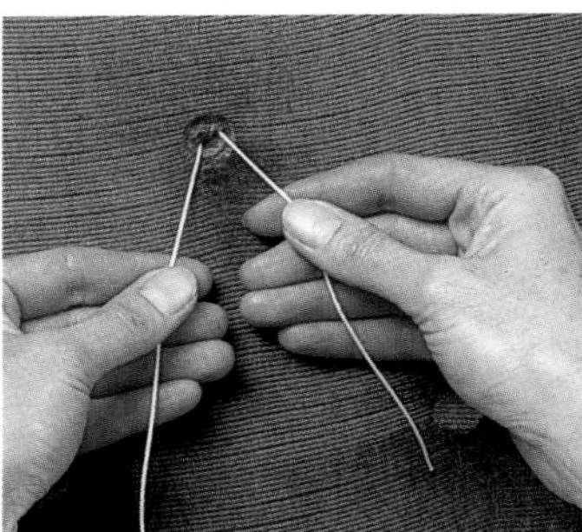

3 Pull out the needle and adjust the twine to make the two lengths equal.

4 Thread one end through the button shank then tie it to the other end in a slip knot (right).

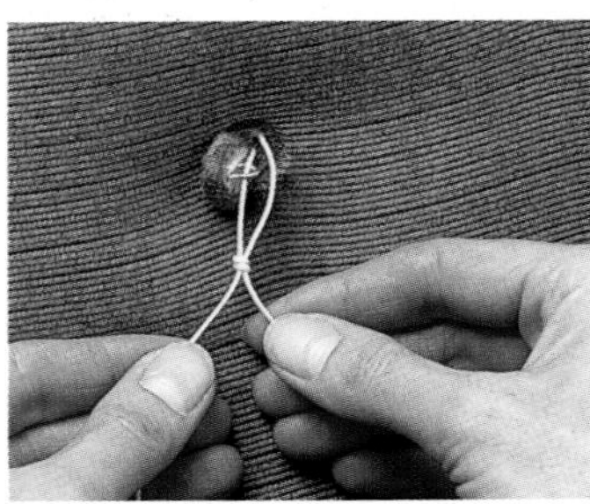

5 Pull the knot tight until the button is in position.

6 Tie the twines together to secure them and cut the ends short enough to be hidden by the button.

7 If the button is lost, buy a button mould and cover it with fabric from the bottom turning; you may have to undo the hessian to reach it.

RENEWING WEBBING

1 Take any hessian off the bottom.

2 If the webbing is attached to the bottom of the seat frame, remove the tacks from worn webbing, snip the twine holding any springs, and remove the webbing. Leave sound webbing in place.

3 Fit the new webbing as for putting new upholstery on a drop-in seat (see facing page), but work with the frame base upwards.

4 If the old webbing was slipped through springs as well as sewn with twine, slip the new webbing through in the same way before tacking the end in place.

5 Sew back any springs (below).

6 Replace any hessian.

7 If the webbing is attached to the upper side of the seat frame, do not remove the entire upholstery. Instead, fit new webbing from below to the inside face of the frame. Interweave it with the original webbing. Put the tacks as close as possible to the top face of the seat frame.

PUTTING SPRINGS IN A CHAIR SEAT

You can give new resilience to a sagging top-padded seat by adding springs to it. Use five springs of 10 gauge wire. About 3-4in (7.5-10cm) is usually high enough; springs too tall will wear the fabric.

1 Invert the chair on a work surface with the back hanging down.

2 With a tack lifter, prise out the tacks holding on the bottom hessian cover and remove it to give access to the webbing. Another layer of hessian may cover the webbing but you can feel where it is.

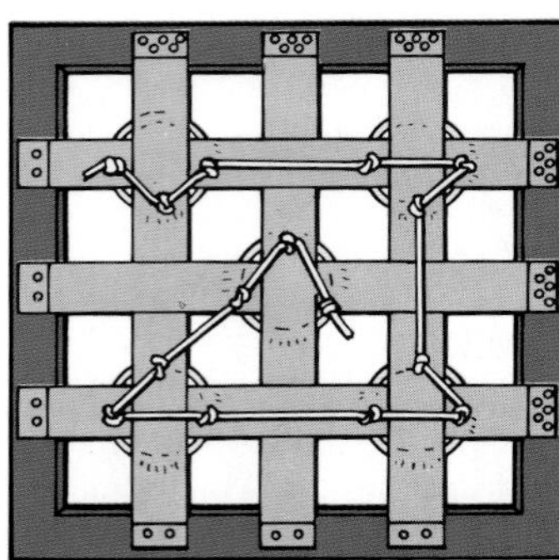

3 Arrange the springs with one dead centre to take the most weight and the others round it in a square. Each spring must be at a point where the webbing strands cross. Use a curved spring needle and one long piece of number 2 twine to sew the springs to the webbing.

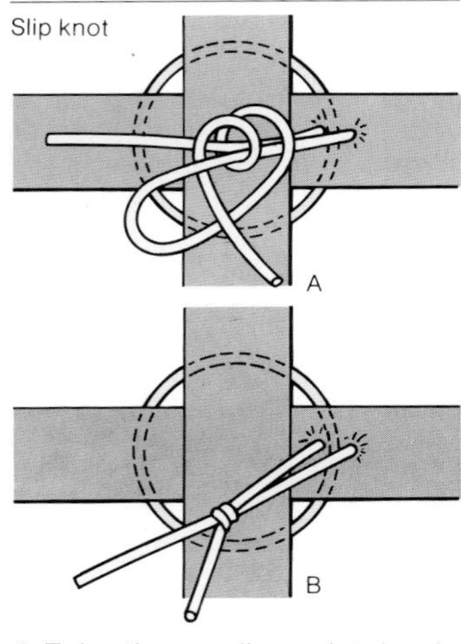

4 Take the needle and twine in and out from left to right under the webbing and central spring, then draw it to the left. Loop it back to pass over and under both strands of twine and then over and under only the lower one (A). Draw the needle tight (B), then slide the knot up close to the spring.

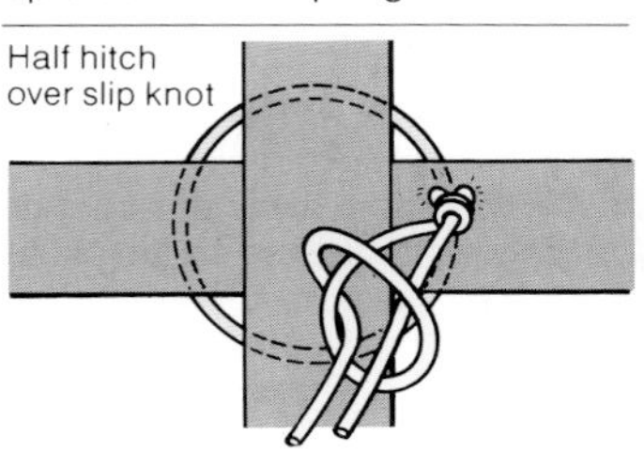

5 Make a half hitch at the same point to secure the slip knot.

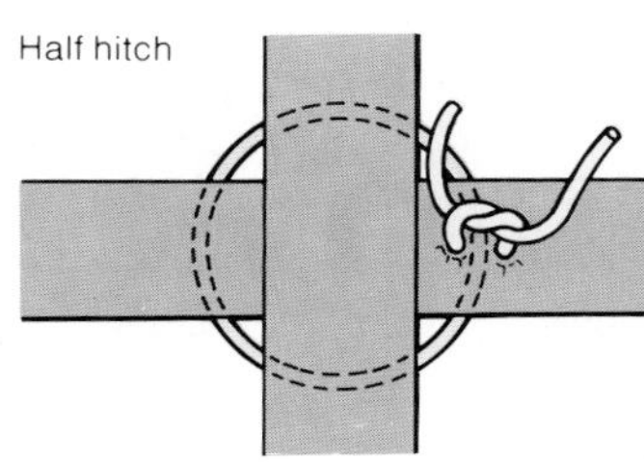

6 Make half hitches at two other points on that spring.

7 Sew a half hitch at three points on each of the other springs.

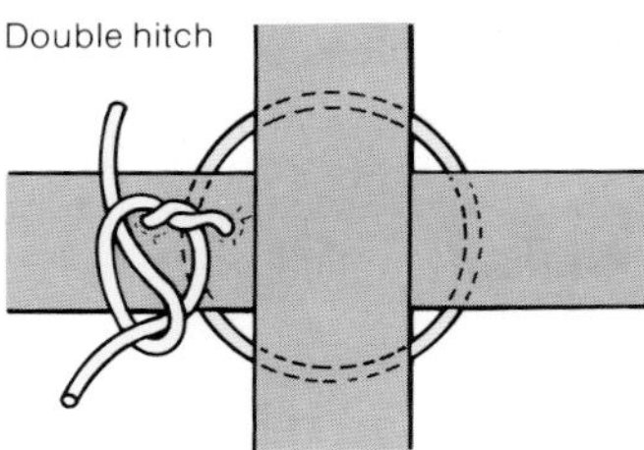

8 Finish off with a double hitch.

9 Tack new webbing to the bottom of the seat frame as for putting new upholstery on a drop-in seat (see facing page).

10 Weave in and fix the cross webbing.

11 Sew the springs in place at the bottom as at the top.

12 Tack the hessian cover back in place on the bottom of the frame.

Putting new upholstery on a drop-in seat

With modern materials you can do many upholstery jobs at home. For repairs to valuable antiques, however, rely on a craftsman who will use traditional methods.

Avoid petrol-based adhesives, which may melt the foam. Use water-based adhesives instead. Copydex and Dunlop L107 are suitable.

You will need

Tools Tack lifter; pincers or pliers; filling knife; plane; abrasive paper; upholsterer's hammer; staple gun; webbing stretcher; measure; scissors; finetoothed hacksaw; firm work surface.

Materials Wood filler; adhesive; strong linen strip to go round the frame; six strips of woven upholstery webbing each the length of the frame plus 8in (20cm); upholstery tacks; hessian the size of the seat plus 1in (2.5cm) all round; sheet of 1in (2.5cm) thick foam the same size as the seat plus $\frac{1}{2}$in (1.3cm) all round; rectangle of $\frac{1}{2}$in (1.3cm) thick hard grade chip foam 2in (5cm) smaller all round than the seat; upholstery wadding the size of the seat; calico and main fabric the size of the seat plus 4in (l0cm) all round.

HELPFUL TIP

If you are reupholstering more than one drop-in seat, number each frame and seat before you lift out the seat. Even in a matching set of chairs the frames differ slightly.

PREPARING THE FRAME

1 Using the tack lifter and pincers or pliers, carefully prise out the tacks from the bottom hessian cover and remove it.

2 Prise out the tacks holding the remaining coverings and discard the coverings.

3 Plane off a shaving of wood for 2in (5cm) at each end of each side of the frame to accommodate the extra thickness of the foam round the corners.

4 Fill old tack holes with wood filler, pressing it in with a filling knife.

5 Sand off any roughness.

6 Glue a strip of strong linen fabric down each side of the frame to provide a smooth surface for the coverings. Leave 2in (5cm) at each end without fabric.

FITTING THE WEBBING SUPPORTS

1 Fold under 1in (2.5cm) at the end of the first webbing strip. Using the staple gun, staple it to the centre back on top of the frame.

2 Thread the webbing through the stretcher with its handle away from you. Lodge the stretcher under the front edge of the frame and press the handle firmly towards you.

3 Secure the webbing with staples and remove the stretcher.

4 Cut the webbing, leaving a 1in (2.5cm) turning allowance. Fold the turning over the staples and staple again to secure it.

5 Fit two more strips of webbing from back to front of the frame, one on each side of the first strip and equally spaced from it.

6 Fit three strips of webbing from side to side of the frame, interweaving them with the strips running from back to front.

7 Lay the hessian over the webbing. Hold it with four temporary tacks, one hammered half in centrally on each side. The hessian should overlap the frame 1in (2.5cm) all round.

8 Fold up the excess hessian along the back of the frame and staple through the fold at the centre back, You will have to remove the temporary tack to do so.

9 Stretch out the fold to each corner and secure it with staples.

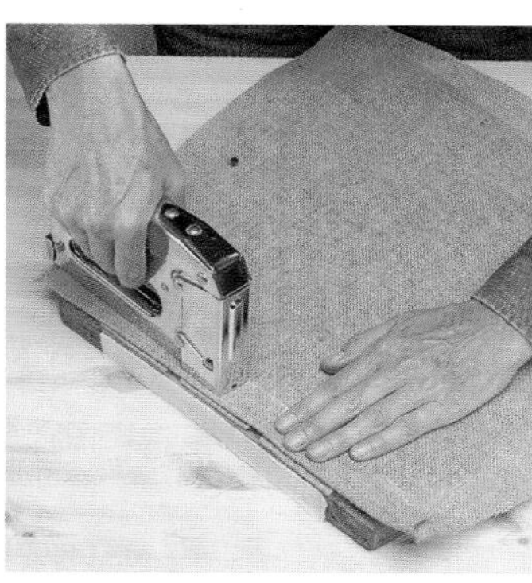

10 Staple at regular intervals along the rest of the fold.

11 Stretch the hessian to the front of the seat frame and fold and staple it in the same way.

12 Fix the other sides of the hessian to the seat frame in the same way.

FITTING THE PADDING

1 Use a hacksaw to trim off the upper edge of the foam sheet at an angle of 45 degrees, but leave a $\frac{1}{4}$in (6mm) lip uncut at the bottom.

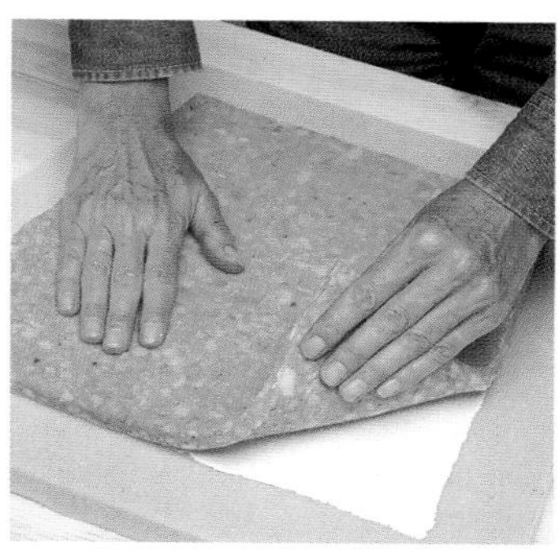

2 Glue the hard foam to the underside of the foam sheet, centring it carefully.

3 Lay the foam sheet on the seat frame and centre it. Tack the $\frac{1}{4}$in (6mm) lip to the top of the outer face of the seat frame, spacing the tacks $\frac{1}{2}$in (1.3cm) apart. On each of the four sides of the seat frame, put the first tack at the centre and work towards the corners, stopping 2in (5cm) from each corner.

4 Cut a $\frac{1}{2}$in (1.3cm) deep V shaped notch out of the foam at each corner. Overlap the sides of the V and secure them to the corner of the frame with one tack; then complete tacking at the sides.

5 Check that all the tacks are hammered in flat with no sharp projections.

FITTING THE COVERING

1 Centre the calico over the foam and hold it in place with four temporary tacks hammered only half in. Position a temporary tack halfway along the outer face of each side of the frame.

2 With the seat base up, staple the calico in place near the outer edge

Putting new upholstery on a drop-in seat (continued)

of the underside of the frame. Turn under the surplus fabric at the raw edges and place the centre staple first as you work on each side.

Work from the centre staple to the corners, drawing the calico taut and making sure the grain of the fabric runs straight. Staple at regular intervals. Work along the four sides of the frame before fixing the corners.

Remove the temporary tacks from the outer frame as you come to them.

3 At each corner smooth the fabric diagonally over the angle of the frame and staple in place. Tuck the excess fabric to each side equally and form pleats to meet at the angle. Overlap the pleats on the base of the frame and secure them with staples.

4 Lay the wadding on the calico.

HELPFUL TIP
To make sure that you fit the main fabric with its grain or pattern square on the seat, cut a notch at the centre of each side of the fabric. Under the seat frame, make a notch at the centre of each side. Match the notches as you fit the cover.

5 Fit the main cover as the calico, but put the staples near the inner edge of the frame's underside. You can trim off some fabric at each pleat fold if the fabric is bulky.

6 Replace the seat in the frame.

Renewing the upholstery on a fixed-seat chair

You can adapt the method for a drop-in seat to renovate a fixed-seat chair. Firm the edge of the upholstery with a pre-formed tack roll, available in different sizes.

1 Strip off the old upholstery as for a drop-in seat. There is no need to plane off any wood or fit linen strips.

2 Use a rasp to chamfer the top outside edge of the frame, making the chamfered surface about ½in (1.3cm) wide.

3 Fill the old tack holes with wood filler and sand the frame smooth.

4 Fit webbing to the upper side of the frame as for a drop-in seat.

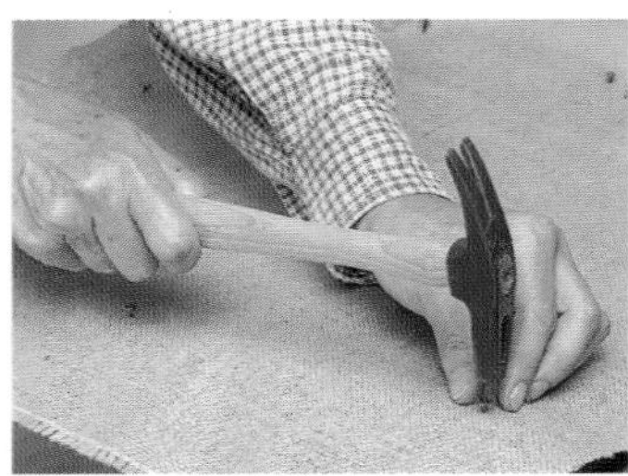

5 Cut a piece of hessian to cover the seat with an overlap of 1in (2.5cm) all round. Centre the hessian on the frame and put a temporary tack centrally in each side of the frame and at each corner. If the back legs are inset in the frame, make a diagonal cut at the back corners of the hessian.

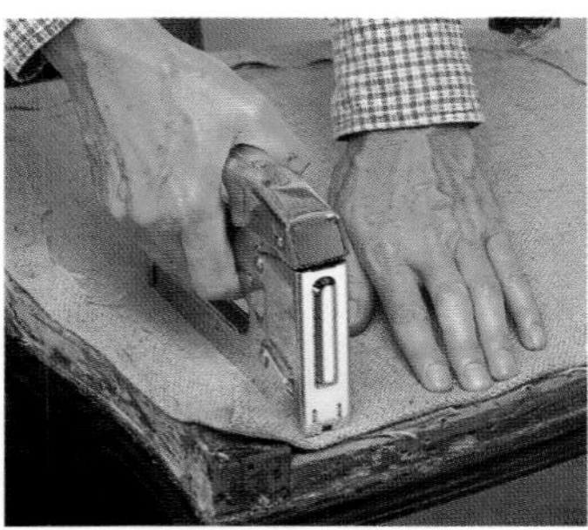

6 Fold under the excess hessian along the back of the frame. Staple through the fold at the centre back, removing the temporary tack to do so. Continue as for a drop-in seat.

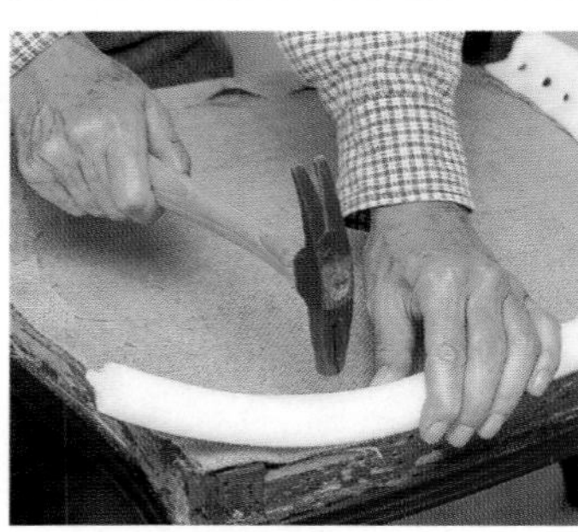

7 Place the lengths of pre-formed tack roll, slightly proud, along the edge of the chair frame and tack it in place at 1in (2.5cm) intervals.

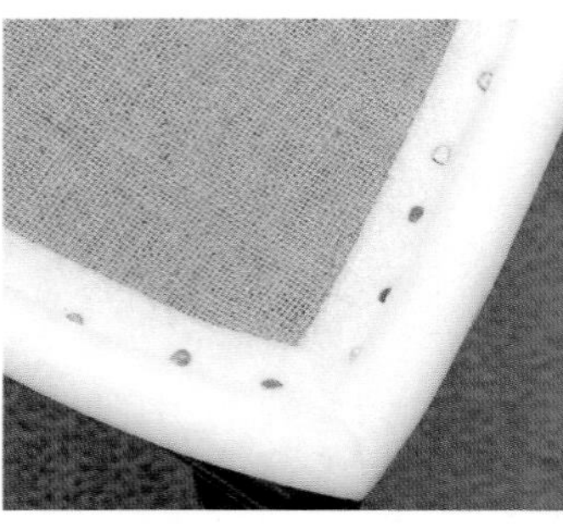

8 Cut the pre-formed tack roll at the corners in order to make it fit smoothly. Cut mitres at the corners if necessary.

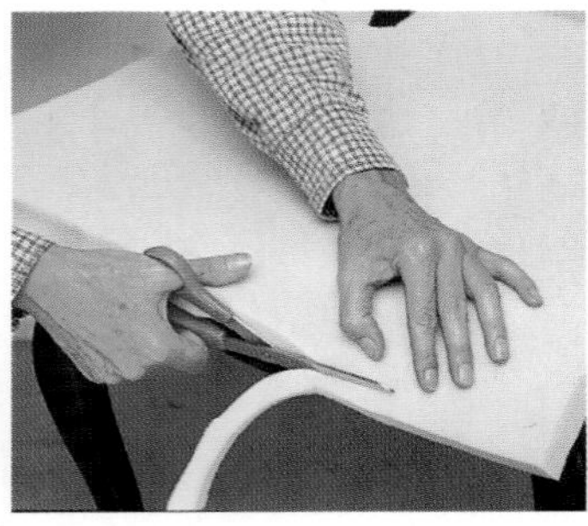

9 Cut the hard foam to fit inside the tack roll and the foam sheeting to go over the tack roll and reach the wood comfortably.

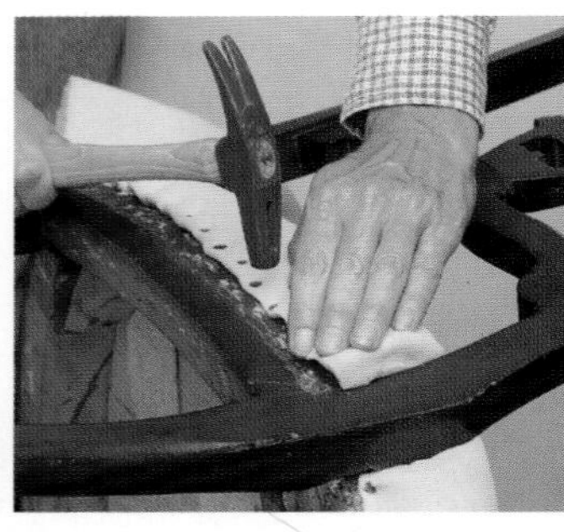

10 Chamfer the edge of the foam sheet, glue on the hard foam, and tack the foam in place as for a drop-in seat. To make the seat more domed, put a layer of stuffing between the hessian and the foam.

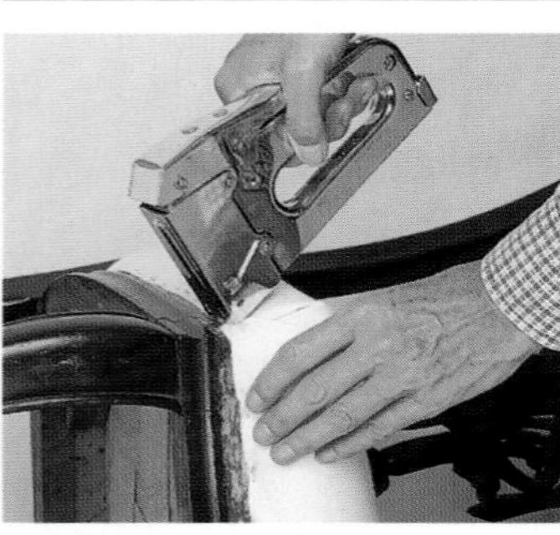

11 Staple the calico in place halfway down the outer face of the seat frame. If the back legs are inset, double under the back corners of the calico and pull it down very tight so that the foam remains hidden when the chair is sat on.

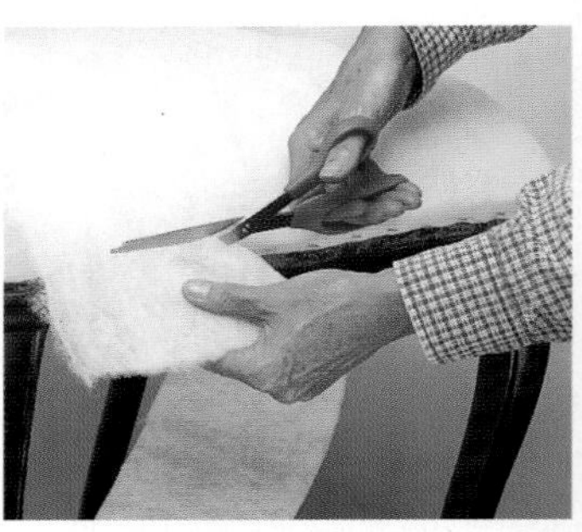

12 Cut the wadding to fit the top of the seat and lay it in place.

13 Fit the main cover in the same way as the calico all round.

14 Use a hot-glue gun to glue on a braid trim to conceal the staples.

14 Roofs, drainage & external walls

Roofs

Drainage

External walls

What can go wrong on the roof

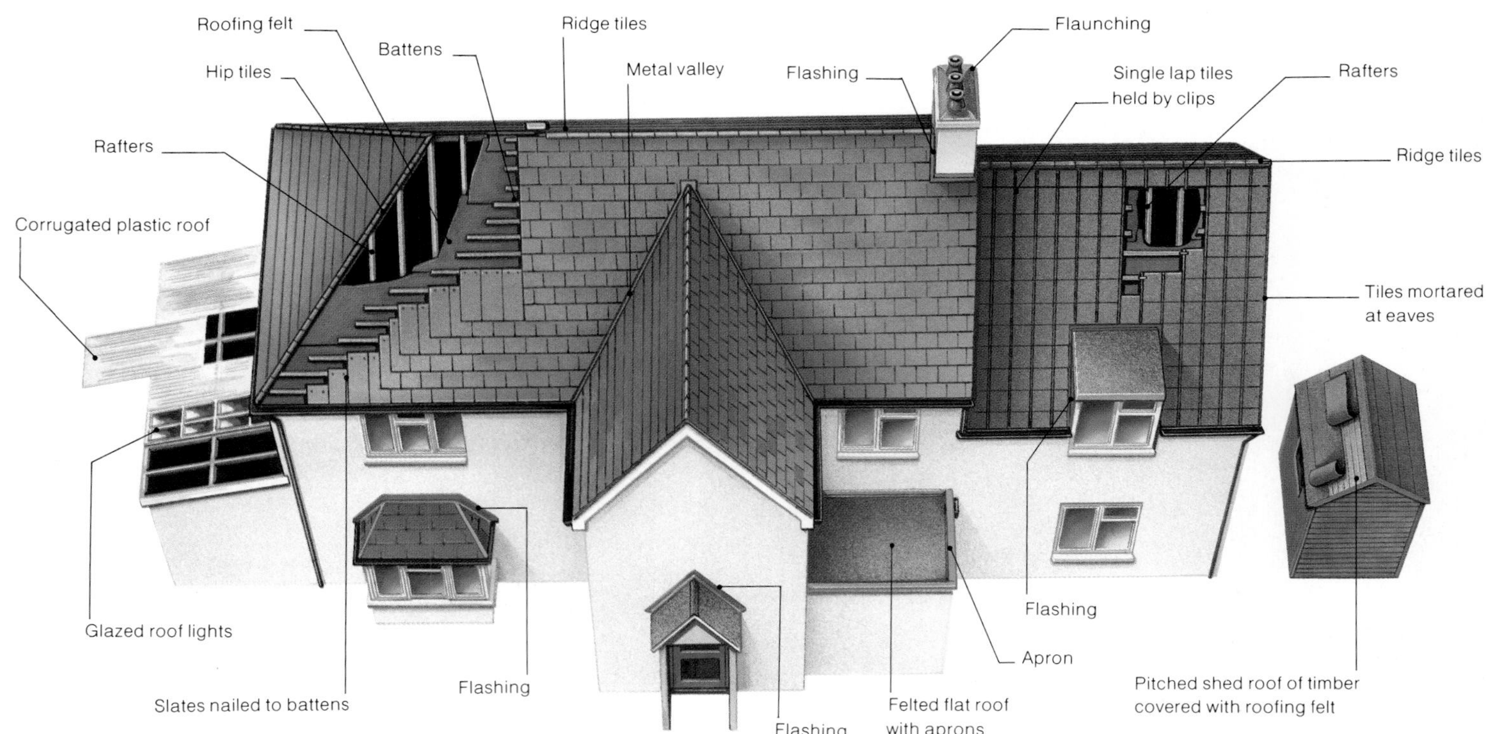

Rain is the main cause of damp in a house. Water will leak through cracks or gaps in a roof and will soak through unprotected wood.

You may discover that the roof needs to be repaired only when stains appear on the ceiling from rain coming into the loft. However, you could discover the need for many repairs earlier by making regular checks in the loft for damp timber and by checking the roof from outside for signs of damage – slipped tiles or slates, or fallen pieces of mortar, for example.

Repair damage as soon as possible after you discover it, so that there is less chance of rain getting into the fabric of the house. Most parts of the house are usually damaged or become faulty for very simple reasons.

To examine the roof thoroughly, set up a ladder which is at least three rungs above the gutter. If you move onto the roof, use a proper roof ladder which hooks over the ridge (see facing page).

Ridge tiles

The mortar which holds these tiles in place may fail with age. It is also likely to fail if it is soaked with rain which freezes – high winds may then dislodge tiles. To replace a ridge tile, see page 443.

Roof tiles

Tiles are usually nailed in place or held by the nibs which project behind each tile and hook over roofing battens. If the nibs are damaged or if the nails rust away, tiles will slide down the roof. Tiles may also be blown off the roof by strong winds or pushed out of place by the weight of a build-up of snow which turns to ice. To replace a roof tile, see page 441.

Slates

There are no nibs on slates, so they need nails to hold them. They may slip out of position if the nails rust. To replace one, see page 442.

Flashings

When roof surfaces meet, the gap between them is sealed with flashing. Lead flashing is more normal in older properties; modern houses tend to have bituminous based strips. Flashings can be displaced when mortar joints fail (the flashing strip is pushed into the joint between bricks or pieces of masonry and sealed with mortar). Cracked flashing is usually caused by slight movement in the building or between neighbouring buildings. This movement is common and depends on the water content in the soil. For how to repair flashings, see page 446. Check all the flashings – around chimney stacks, dormer windows and adjoining flat roofs – when making a repair.

Chimney stacks

Few DIY jobs can be done on a chimney stack – special scaffolding must be erected around the stack and the masonry involved is very heavy. However, you can keep an eye on the condition of the chimney stack and have any repairs carried out quickly to prevent damp.

If a flue is not in use, rain which gets onto the flue lining can cause damp problems. Have the chimney capped with a half-round tile or a cowl to keep rain out. You can only see the edge of the flaunching (the mortar which holds the pots in place) but have it checked if you spot any deterioration. If you notice faults in the brickwork get expert advice.

Flat roofs

Flat roofs are sometimes seen on houses but most are seen on house extensions. They are cheaper than pitched roofs to construct but do not last as long. Even the best felted roof can only be expected to last for about 15 years – but its life can be extended by coating it with a rubber-based compound before it starts to deteriorate.

The main problem with a flat roof is that instead of draining off, water and snow may collect on the surface and will seep through even very small cracks. This can lead to rot in timbers as well as damp patches appearing on the ceilings.

Felt is generally built up in layers on larger roofs, and often the top layer will blister. To repair the damage, see page 448.

Bitumen felt roofs, on small sheds and outhouses, are usually only a single sheet of felt. If this starts to break up, strip off the old covering and replace it (page 452).

Corrugated plastic sheeting may leak at overlaps or where screws or nails pass through the sheets. Seal gaps with silicone rubber sealant. To make a repair with a new piece of sheeting, see page 451.

Glass roofing may leak if the seal fails along glazing bars and rain may be driven up overlaps by strong winds. Use adhesive glazing tape to seal a glazing bar. The type with a foil face looks more in keeping than that with a black face. If a poor overlap cannot be increased, seal the outer gap with silicone rubber sealant.

WHEN SHOULD A WHOLE ROOF BE REPLACED?

It is difficult for an untrained person to judge whether a roof should be completely re-tiled or slated. If a large proportion of the tiles or slates is broken, re-tiling is obviously needed but faults in a roof are usually far less easy to diagnose. Bumps and hollows may be clearly visible and cause anxiety but they may have been caused by movement in the roof timbers years earlier. Movement may long ago have ceased and the roof may be perfectly sound and weatherproof with many more years of life in it. On the other hand movement in the roof timbers may have started recently and be the symptom of faults that need professional work.

If you have doubts about the soundness or safety of your roof, pay an architect or surveyor to give an unbiased report on its condition; a builder's report may not be so unbiased.

Roof repairs: Tools for the job

Roof ladder
Never venture onto a roof without a roof ladder.

A purpose-made roof ladder is fitted at one end with rubber wheels and a large hook. Using the wheels, you can push the ladder up the roof without dislodging slates or tiles. When the top of the ladder reaches the roof ridge, turn it over so that the hook lodges on the ridge securely.

The ladder must reach all the way from the roof ridge to the gutter to allow you to transfer easily from the ordinary ladder on which you have climbed to gutter level. Extension pieces can be added to a roof ladder for a long roof slope.

If you need a roof ladder only rarely, hire rather than buy; or buy the wheels-and-hook section for fitting onto a conventional ladder.

Slate ripper
The steel blade is about 11in-15in (280mm-380mm) long. It is slipped under the tile or slate to be removed until one of the barbs of its arrow-shaped tip can be hooked round a nail that is driven into the roof batten. A sharp tug, or a hammer blow on the curve of the handle, jerks the barb down, and it cuts through the nail. The ripper is then moved to the other edge of the tile or slate to cut the second nail. Slate rippers can be hired.

Slate cutter
When the handles are squeezed together, the steel blades meet and shear off the edge of the slate. Useful for cutting an oversize slate to the right size.

Tinsnips
The scissors action will cut through lead, zinc or other sheet metals used for roof valleys. Snips are made in several sizes – from 8in-14in (200mm-360mm) long.

Soft-faced mallet
A mallet with a head made of rubber, plastic or rawhide is used to tap sheet metal into shape – when renewing a valley, for example.

Plugging chisel
The plugging chisel, also called a seam chisel, is designed to remove mortar from between bricks or pieces of masonry. It can be used when replacing flashing.

The fluted face of the blade allows debris to be cleared quickly.

An alternative tool would be a $\frac{1}{4}$in (6mm) cold chisel, which is really intended for cutting metal.

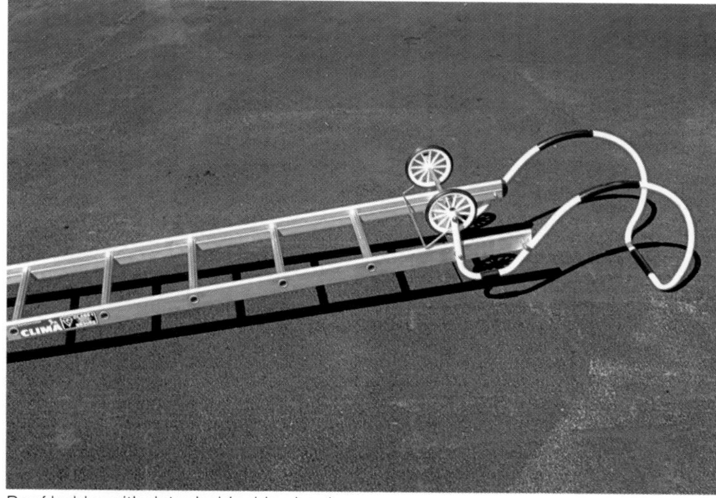

Roof ladder with detachable ridge hook

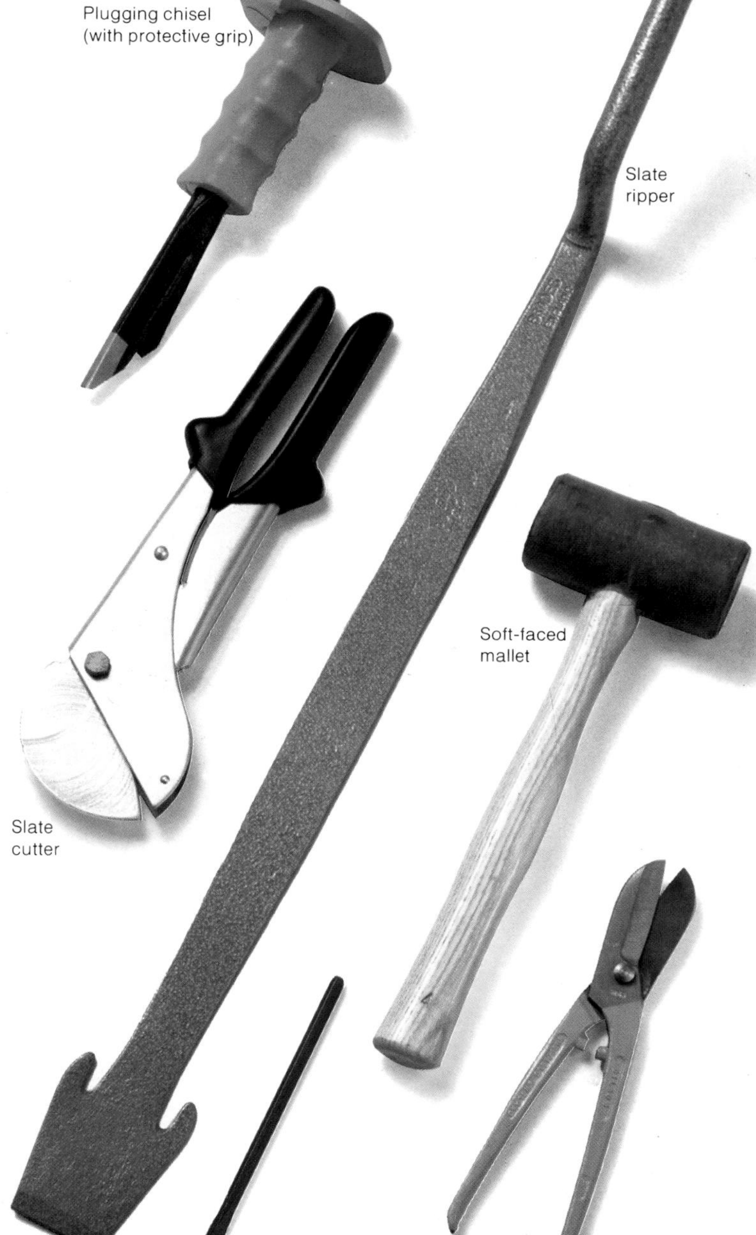

HOW TO WORK SAFELY AT ROOF LEVEL

Ladders
Always make sure that the ladder is set up at the correct angle – 12in (300mm) away from the wall for every 4ft (1.2m) up the wall.

The ladder should be long enough to reach above the working point. When you are going to work on a gutter or the eaves, for example, extend the ladder or scaffold tower enough to reach at least 24in (610mm) above the gutter.

Fit a stand-off bracket to the top of a ladder to make sure it presses against the wall, not against an insecure gutter.

For extra security, you can screw an eye bolt into the fascia board and tie the ladder to it.

Always move the ladder or scaffold tower along the wall to take you within easy reach of the working point. Never lean sideways to reach the work.

Scaffold towers
If you have to work all along the gutter, hire a scaffold tower with locking wheels, guard rail and a firm platform (see page 100).

Safe practices
Always have a helper at least within calling distance when you are working at a height.

Do not attempt to carry heavy items that will unbalance you. You must have a helper to steady the weight.

Have a safe place to put your tools. When working on a ladder you can fix a tray to the ladder to hold the tools; when you are working on the roof hold tools in a bag or pouch slung diagonally across your chest, or in a sturdy apron with a wide pocket, or in a purpose-made belt.

Do not go on the roof without a roof ladder hooked over the ridge and reaching down to the eaves. When you are on the roof, wear a purpose-made safety harness with a tape attached to a firm point – such as a properly secured roof ladder.

Have a stout sack or bucket hooked onto the roof ladder for debris. Lower it on a rope.

Take care not to drop anything; it could cause serious injury to someone below.

CHOOSING TILES FOR ALL PARTS OF THE ROOF

Roof tiles are made in different shapes to cover different parts of the roof. They are made of concrete, or occasionally clay, in a range of red, brown, grey and greenish shades. The finish may be smooth or grainy. Rainwater runs off the smooth finish more easily and because of this smooth tiles need not be sloped as much as grainy tiles.

The slope a tile needs varies with the profile of the tile as well as its finish. Some profiles have more pronounced channels than others to direct rain away from the gaps between tiles. With some tiles, the amount of overlap onto the course of tile below can be increased to compensate for a shallow slope. Manufacturers recommend a minimum angle of slope for each style of tile that they make.

If you have to cut a tile – for a repair at a valley or hip, for example – use an angle grinder (page 484). It gives the neatest cut and greatly reduces the risk of breakage, but take great care – an angle grinder can cause serious injury if not used properly.

PLAIN TILES

The tile surface is slightly convex. There are two nibs behind the top edge to hook over the roofing battens. Nail holes allow every third or fourth course of tiles to be nailed in place for extra stability. Courses of plain tiles are staggered so that each tile overlaps the gap between two tiles in the course below.

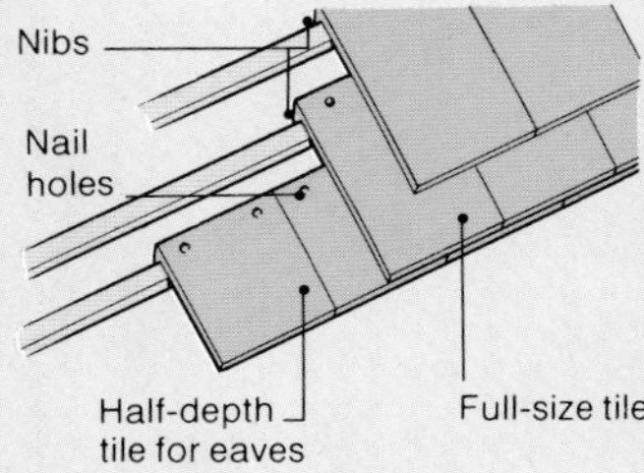

Half-depth tiles are made for the top course and for the underlayer at the eaves. Half-width and one-and-a-half width tiles are made for starting and finishing courses at the gable ends.

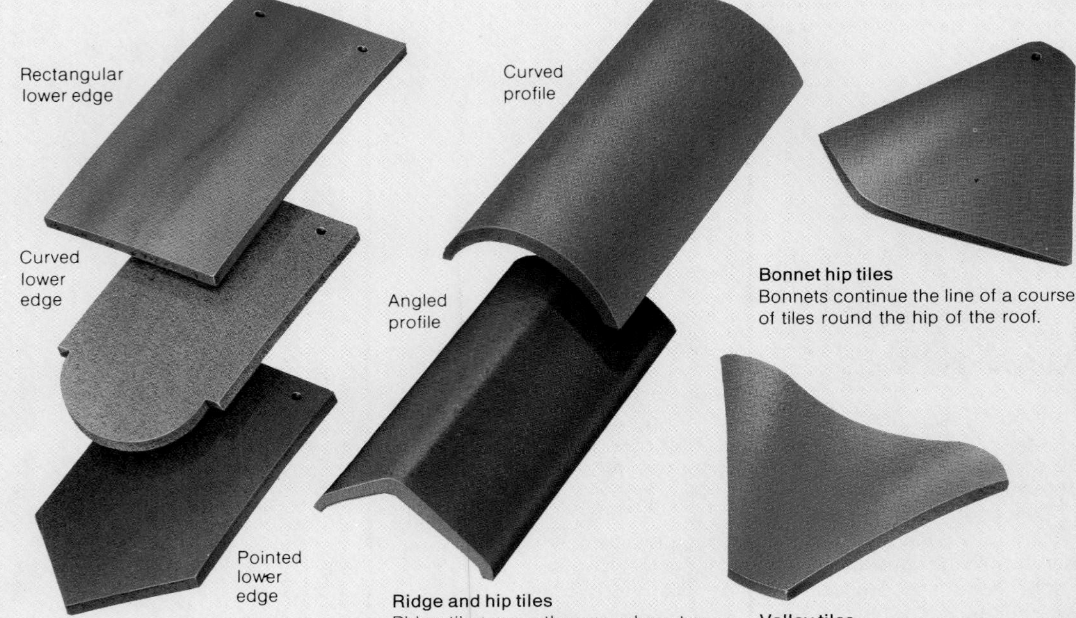

Standard tile
Tiles 10½in (265mm) long and 6½in (165mm) wide cover most of the roof.

Ridge and hip tiles
Ridge tiles cover the gap where two slopes meet at the top. Hip tiles cover the gap where sides of slopes meet. Both types can be curved or angled.

Bonnet hip tiles
Bonnets continue the line of a course of tiles round the hip of the roof.

Valley tiles
Arrow-shaped tiles bridge the gap where two roof slopes meet at the bottom (called the valley).

SINGLE-LAP TILES

Usually the tile surface undulates from side to side so that one or more channels run down the tile. The courses are overlapped, with the tiles in one course aligned exactly with the tiles in the courses above and below so that the channels run all down the roof slope. Each tile in a course interlocks with the tiles on both sides. A few styles have no channels, relying on a firm interlock to make the roof waterproof.

Some styles of single-lap tile hang from the roofing battens on nibs with alternate courses nailed to the battens through holes at the top of the tiles. Others are fixed at the sides with aluminium-alloy tile clips which are nailed to the roofing battens. Ridge and hip tiles are the same types as for plain tiles.

There are no bonnet hip tiles but some firms make trough valley tiles (rectangular valley tiles that are set below the level of the main roof tiles).

Full-size tiles are used for the top course and there is no underlayer at the eaves. Gaps left under the undulating profile at the ridge or hip of the roof are sealed with mortar or by purpose-made profile fillers.

Rounded double-channel profile

Angled double-channel profile

Flat profile

Single lap tile
Tiles 16½in-17in (420mm-430mm) long and 13in (330mm) wide cover most of the roof.

Pantile
15in (380mm) long
9in (230mm) wide
The S-shaped tiles resemble the original clay tiles characteristic of some areas of the country. They are usually made of concrete now.

SIMULATED SLATES

Many houses are roofed with concrete tiles that realistically imitate Cumbrian, Cornish and Welsh slates and Cotswold and Yorkshire stone roofing slabs. They cannot be used to repair real slate or stone roofs. Many are made with nibs and interlock grooves, but some are flat with nail holes for fixing like real slates. There is a wide variety of sizes, some close to other tile sizes, some in the larger sizes of slates.

Lightweight tiles of reconstituted slate are also made.

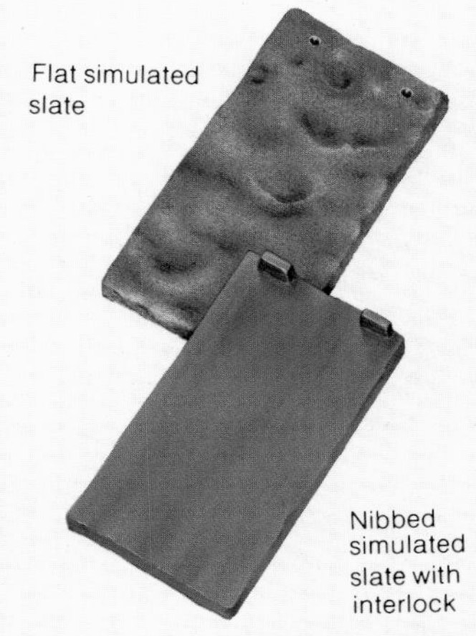

Making a temporary repair to a cracked tile or slate

If rainwater is coming in through a cracked tile or slate and you cannot get a replacement immediately, make a temporary repair to reduce to a minimum the damage done by damp.

You will need
Tools Ladder with stand-off bracket; roof ladder; wooden wedges (panel below); wire brush; paintbrush; sharp knife; old wallpaper seam roller.
Materials Flashing strip primer; self-adhesive flashing strip.

1 Raise the one or two tiles or slates that overlap onto the cracked one to give you better access. Prop them up with wooden wedges.

2 Use the wire brush to clean the surface round the crack.

3 Brush a coat of flashing strip primer into and round the crack, making a strip as wide as the flashing strip. The primer ensures a good bond between tile or slate and flashing strip.

4 Cut a piece of flashing strip from the roll with a sharp knife. Make it long enough to cover all the crack.

5 Press the strip into place and bed it well down. Run a small wallpaper seam roller to and fro over it to firm it down.

REPAIRING A FINE CRACK WITH SEALANT

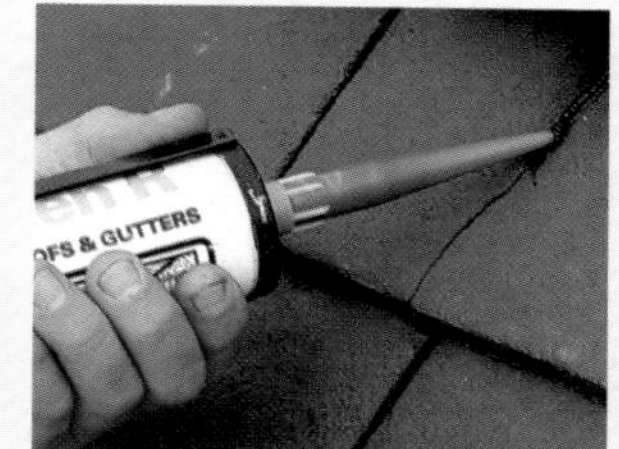

Bituminous sealant in an applicator gun seals a fine crack with very little work.

Prop up the tiles or slates that overlap the cracked one, brush out the crack and then inject sealant.

Replacing one broken plain tile

You will need a tile of the same size and style as the broken one. If you have no spares, a builder's yard may have one or will obtain one for you. Beware of matching the replacement tile to the colour your tiles were when they were new. The tiles may have changed colour considerably and you should try to match the replacement to the colour they are now. If you cannot find a good match, 'steal' a tile from an unobtrusive place on the roof – a side porch, for example. A tile near the end of the bottom course may be the best place. You can put the poor match in its place.

You will need
Tools Ladder with stand-off bracket; roof ladder; wooden wedges; large builder's trowel; perhaps a slate ripper.
Materials Replacement tile.

WEDGES TO PROP TILES UP

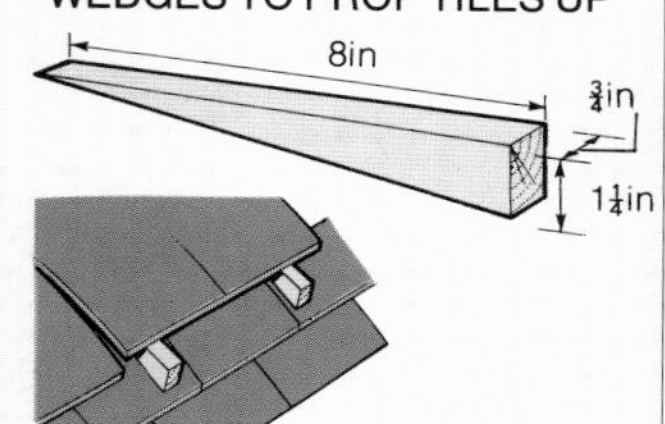

To prop up tiles you will need to prepare two or more wedges from ¾in (19mm) thick wood. Cut them 8in (200mm) long and tapering from 1¼in (32mm) at one end to a point at the other.

1 Lift the two tiles that overlap onto the broken tile from the course above. Tap a wooden wedge under each to hold it up.

2 Slip the large builder's trowel under the broken tile. Lift up the whole tile until its nibs are clear of the batten and you can draw it out towards you.

ALTERNATIVELY, if the broken tile is one that has been nailed to the batten, try to free it by wiggling it from side to side until the nail breaks or comes away.

If this does not free it, you will have to use a slate ripper (page 439) to cut through the nails.

3 Lay the replacement tile on the trowel and slide it up under the two wedged tiles until the nibs hook over the batten. There is no need to nail it, even if the original was nailed. Take out the wedges.

Replacing a group of plain tiles

If you need to replace a group of tiles and have no spares, buy replacements of the same size and style. Buy a colour that matches the tiles now, not the original colour. At some builder's yards you may find weathered tiles or be advised where to find them.

If you cannot match the existing tiles, and the replacement group will be in a noticeable place, take tiles from a part of the roof that is not visible from the street. You can then put the new tiles in this less obtrusive position.

You will need
Tools Ladder with stand-off bracket; roof ladder; wooden wedges (above); large builder's trowel; claw hammer; bucket on a long rope. Perhaps a slate ripper.
Materials Replacement tiles; 1½in (40mm) No. 11 aluminium-alloy nails.

1 Lift the tiles in the course immediately above the highest ones to be replaced. Lift them two at a time and slide the wooden wedges under their outer edges to hold them up. This will allow you to have access to the tile they overlap in the course below.

2 As each tile is exposed, slide the builder's trowel under it and lift it until its nibs clear the batten. Then draw it out towards you. Put it in the bucket and lower it to the ground with the rope.

If a tile is nailed to the batten, see-saw it from side to side to try to dislodge the nails. If you cannot, use a slate ripper (page 439) to cut through the nails.

3 Work along the top course of tiles to be removed and then along the course below that, and so on until all the tiles have been removed.

Once the highest course of tiles has been removed, you can lift the others without using wedges or trowel.

4 To fit the replacement tiles onto the battens, work along the bottom course first.

Hook each tile over the batten by its nibs and make sure that it is centred over the gap between the two tiles below it. Then work along the courses above, fitting all the tiles in place.

5 Nail each tile in every third or fourth course with two nails.

6 To fit the top course, hold up the tiles in the course above in pairs with wedges. Lift each new tile on the trowel and slide it into place. Move one of the wedges to lift the next overlapping tile.

Replacing broken single lap tiles

You will need
Tools Ladder with a stand-off bracket; roof ladder; wooden wedges (page 441). Perhaps a slate ripper, hammer, bucket on a rope.
Materials Replacement tiles. Perhaps tile clips and 1½in (40mm) No. 11 aluminium-alloy nails.

1 Slide up the tiles that overlap onto the broken tile.

ALTERNATIVELY, use wedges to raise the tile to the left of the broken one and that to the right but in the course above.

2 To remove the broken tile, tilt it sideways to separate it from the neighbouring tiles which are interlocked with it. You will be able to free it without disturbing the neighbouring tiles. Lever the tile upwards to release it from any clip that holds it to the batten. If the clip stays in place, the new tile may slip into it. If the clip is dislodged, there is no need to replace it; a few unclipped tiles will not matter. Sometimes alternate courses are nailed in place. If your repair is to a nailed tile, use a slate ripper to cut the nails before you remove the tile.

3 Take the broken tile down to the ground or lower it in a bucket on a rope to a helper.

4 To fit the replacement tile, slide it up into place. You will not be able to nail it or clip it. Pull back into place any tiles that you pushed out of place. Remove any wedges.

REPLACING A GROUP OF TILES

Remove the highest tiles as for a single tile. Lower tiles simply need tilting to free them. Remove the clips wherever you can.

When replacing the tiles, fit the lowest course first and work from right to left. Fit a clip for each tile wherever you are able to nail it to the batten. Lodge the hook of the clip over the ridge at the side of the tile and hammer the nail through the hole in the clip into the top edge of the batten near the bottom edge of the tile you are fitting. You can also nail alternate courses to the battens. The highest course cannot be nailed and the last tile of all cannot be fitted with a clip because the batten will be covered.

Making repairs to slate roofs

Nail-sickness and delamination are the faults most likely to develop in a slate roof – but only after a long life. Slates will last a century or more, but the nails holding them to battens can corrode and break, allowing the slates to slip out of position. The corrosion, or nail-sickness, can affect a large area of a roof within a few years as the nails are the same age and corrode at the same rate. The slates can be re-nailed provided that they are sound.

A more serious problem is delamination, when the surface of the slate becomes flaky or powdery and you can see many cracks and splits. Replacement is the usual solution. Because slates are comparatively expensive, a deteriorating slate roof is often replaced with tiles, which are less expensive. Tiling may spoil the appearance of a house. Simulated slates are made and are much less expensive than real slates. Tiles and many simulated slates are heavier than real slates, so the roof timbers may need strengthening.

If the house is in a terrace, consider how neighbouring roofs are being treated. If they are being renewed with tiles, a new slate roof on your house could look out of place. Another, modern, solution is to weatherproof damaged areas with coats of reinforced bitumen (page 451), but the colour and sheen of the slate are lost.

If you decide on replacing with real slates, you may be able to cut the cost by finding secondhand slates. Many demolition contractors, builders' merchants and roofing companies keep stocks of them. Check that they are the right thickness or they will not bed down properly with re-usable slates from your roof. Check also that their colour matches your slates; slates from different quarries vary in colour. Slates that are smaller than yours are no use to you but larger slates can be cut down to size. The most common sizes are between 9in × 6in (230mm × 150mm) and 24in × 14in (610mm × 355mm). When in place, a slate is more than half covered by the course above.

FIXING SLATES

For fixing a group of replacement slates in several courses you can use 1½in (40mm) No. 11 aluminium alloy or copper nails. If these are hard to find and you only have a small group of slates to nail in place, 1½in (40mm) large-head galvanised clout nails will do.

When you are replacing single slates, you will not be able to nail them because the batten will be covered by the course of slates above. You can secure each slate with a strip of metal cut from lead, zinc, or aluminium that is thin enough to bend. It is fixed from the outside and a small piece shows.

Slates can also be fixed with adhesive expanding foam, which can be applied under a loose slate from outside, or (if the slate is visible) from inside the loft.

HOW TO MAKE HOLES

New slates will not have fixing holes in them; you will have to make the holes. A secondhand slate may have its holes in the wrong place and need drilling. Use the old slate as a pattern to mark drilling spots. The holes are usually about halfway down the sides.

Drill the holes with an electric drill fitted with a No. 6 masonry bit; or make the hole by tapping a nail through the slate with steady, not-too-hard hammer blows. Work from the underside, that is the side without the bevelled edges.

CUTTING A SLATE TO SIZE

Place the slate on a flat board and use a ceramic tile cutter and a metal rule to score a deep cutting line. To complete the cut, use a wide bolster chisel. Tap it along the scored line with gentle hammer blows. Or you can place the slate on a table with the scored line over the table edge and press down to break the slate cleanly.

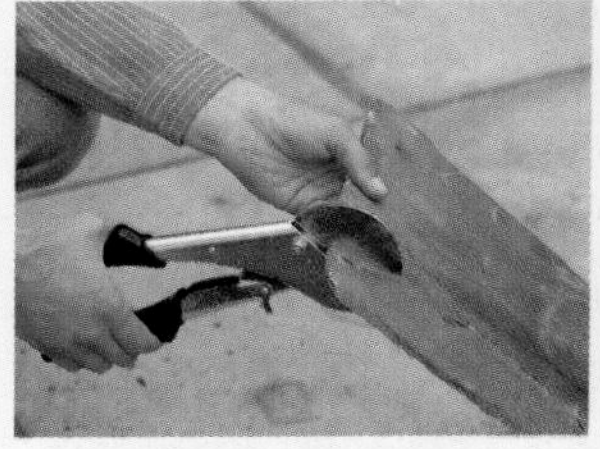

If you have many slates to cut, hire a slate cutter. Cut with the top surface of the slate downwards. On a secondhand slate in particular this ensures that weathering and cutting marks match the other slates. Alternatively, you can hire an electric tile cutter.

Replacing broken slates

If a slate has been cracked – by someone clambering on the roof without using proper access equipment, or by a falling chimney pot for example – you may not be able to obtain a matching replacement slate immediately. Make a temporary repair to prevent water from penetrating. You can make it as for a tile (page 441). Alternatively, you can coat the slate with mastic, cover this with a piece of roofing felt or cooking foil cut to fit, and spread a layer of mastic on top.

Fit the replacement slate when you obtain it.

REPLACING A SINGLE SLATE

You will need
Tools Ladder with a stand-off bracket; roof ladder; slate ripper; a bucket on a long rope; hammer or screwdriver. Perhaps a power drill fitted with No. 6 masonry bit, or nail and hammer.
Materials Replacement slate; strip of lead, zinc, aluminium or copper 1in (25mm) wide, and long enough to reach from the hole in the slate to the bottom plus 4in (100mm); large-head galvanised clout nails 1½in (40mm) long.

1 Cut through the nails that are holding the slate, using the slate ripper.

2 Draw the slate towards you, wiggling it from side to side to ease it from under the slates overlapping it. Take care not to let any broken pieces slide off the roof. They are sharp and can cause damage or injury. Put the pieces in a bucket and take it to the ground or lower it down to a helper.

3 Nail the metal strip to the batten which will just be visible in the gap between the two slates the replacement is going to lap onto. Put the nail in the ready-made hole or about 1in (25mm) down from the top of the strip.

4 Carry the new slate up to the roof in a bucket or put it in a bucket and pull it up with a rope.

5 Slip the new slate, with bevelled edges upwards, under the two slates in the course above. Wiggle it a little to right and left to work it upwards until its lower edge aligns with the slates on each side. Its top edge will fit tightly over the batten to which the course above is nailed.

6 Turn up the end of the metal strip over the lower edge of the slate, then bend it double and press it down flat against the slate. The double thickness prevents snow and ice from forcing the clip open.

REPLACING A GROUP OF SLATES

You will be able to nail the lower courses of slates in place, but the top course and the course below that will have to be fixed with metal strips because the battens to which they should be nailed will be covered by slates (see *Replacing a single slate*, facing page). If necessary, cut the slates to size and drill holes in them.

You will need
Tools Ladder with a stand-off bracket; roof ladder; slate ripper; hammer; a bucket on a long rope and a screwdriver.
Materials Replacement slates; size 6 aluminium alloy or copper nails $1\frac{1}{2}$in (40mm) long; strips of lead, zinc, aluminium or copper 1in (25mm) wide and long enough to reach from the hole in the slate to the bottom plus 4in (100mm).

1 Cut through the nails securing the damaged slates, using a slate ripper. Deal first with the highest course to be removed. Ease each slate out in turn from the overlapping slates and lower it in a bucket to a helper or take it to the ground. Do not let a slate slide from the roof; it is sharp and can cause damage or injury.

Work down course by course, removing the slates. The lower ones will not be overlapped and are easier to remove.

2 Fix the bottom course of replacement slates first. Butt neighbouring slates closely and fit them with the bevelled edges upwards. Nail the slates through the holes to the batten.

3 Work upwards course by course nailing the slates in place. When you can no longer see the battens to nail the slates to, cut metal strips to secure the slates and fit them as described in *Replacing a single slate* (facing page).

Replacing ridge tiles or hip tiles

Both tiled and slate roofs have the gaps at the ridge and hips covered by tiles. The tiles are most often curved, but may be angled. The most common problem at the roof ridge or hip is that the mortar between tiles cracks and crumbles away. Sometimes a tile may then be pushed out of place by a build-up of ice, or occasionally by strong winds. If you spot cracks early while they are narrow, you can fill them with roof-and-gutter sealant. There are coloured sealants which make the repair scarcely noticeable.

If the mortar is crumbling or the tile itself has cracked, you will have to remove the tile and re-fix it or put a new one in its place. If it is the end ridge tile that needs a repair, you must seal up the opening left at the end. Use small pieces of slate or tile bedded in mortar. If the main roof tiles are S-shaped there will be a hollow to seal where the ridge or hip tile meets them.

You will need
Tools Ladder with stand-off bracket; roof ladder; cold chisel; club hammer; brush; paintbrush; small builder's trowel. Perhaps a slate ripper.
Materials Dry mortar mix, or cement and sharp sand; PVA adhesive; bucket of water. Perhaps replacement tiles, narrow pieces of tile or slate, or aluminium-alloy nails.

1 With the chisel and hammer, carefully chip away all cracked or crumbling mortar until the ridge or hip tile is freed and you can lift it off. Make sure that any surrounding mortar you leave in place is sound. Clean the tile.

2 Prepare the mortar (page 481) from a bag of dry mixed material or make your own from one part cement to four parts sharp sand. To improve adhesion, add some PVA adhesive to the water, following the manufacturer's instructions. Do not make the mortar too wet; a firmer mix is easier to work with. Mix enough to half-fill a bucket.

3 Brush all dust away from the area round the repair.

4 Use the paintbrush and water to wet the roof and the existing mortar round the repair. This is especially necessary on a hot day when the mortar would lose its moisture too quickly and crack.

5 Brush PVA adhesive liberally all round the area of the repair to ensure good adhesion between the roof tiles at the ridge or hip and the ridge or hip tile itself.

6 Use the trowel to spread mortar on the roof on both sides of the ridge or hip. Cover the areas where the bottom edges of the tile to be fixed will lie.

Do not use too much mortar; there must be a gap under the ridge or hip tiles so that air can circulate to keep dry the timber below. If you lay too much mortar on the tiles, it could squeeze into the gap and fill it in when you are settling the ridge or hip tile into place.

7 The butt joints where two of the ridge or hip tiles meet can either be pointed with mortar or given a solid bedding of mortar. It is probably best to follow the method already used on the roof. If you make a solid bedding, place a piece of slate or tile across the gap between the two sides of the ridge or hip to prevent mortar falling through.

8 Dip the ridge or hip tile in water, let the water drain off and then set the tile in place. Settle the tile on the mortar carefully so that it makes a smooth line with the neighbouring tiles.

ALTERNATIVELY, if the roof tiles have a curved profile, fill the gap between the down-curve and the ridge or hip tiles with pieces of tile or slate embedded in mortar.

Special 'dentil slips' can be bought for the purpose.

Replacing ridge tiles or hip tiles (continued)

9 Smooth the mortar between tiles and along the bottom edges. There must be no hollows in the mortar between the tiles because they could retain small pockets of rainwater.

10 If the re-fixed tile is at an end of the roof ridge, seal the open end with thin slips of tile or slate bedded in mortar. Smooth the end so that rainwater will flow off readily.

11 If you have been replacing the lowest tile on the hip, make sure the projecting hip iron has not been dislodged; it must be soundly bedded in mortar. Repair the mortar if necessary.

REPLACING A BONNET HIP TILE

Some tiled roofs have bonnet hip tiles to cover the gap at the hip (page 440).

Bonnet hip tiles are nailed to the hip timber as well as being bedded in mortar.

1 Remove a bonnet hip tile by chipping away the mortar above and below it with a cold chisel and club hammer and then sliding a slate ripper under the tile and giving a sharp hammer blow on the handle to cut through the nail. You can then draw out the tile towards you. If you are removing several tiles down the hip, start at the highest one and work down. Clean the tiles of old mortar.

2 Brush away all dust from around the repair, then brush the area with water and with PVA adhesive.

3 If you are replacing a single tile, spread mortar to bed it on. Spread mortar also under the bonnet in the course above. Set the bonnet in place and tap it into alignment with the other tiles in the course before you smooth the mortar and clean away any excess.

4 If you are replacing several bonnets, work from the bottom. Nail each, except the top one, to the timber with an aluminium nail after you have set it on the mortar. Then smooth the mortar and clean away any excess.

Repairs to verges and eaves

A roof with only two main slopes is usually sealed with mortar where it meets the gable ends of the house – the verges. Some styles of tile – curved pantiles, for example – are sealed with mortar and tile slips along the eaves – where the bottom of the roof meets the wall.

You can seal minor cracks in the mortar with roof-and-gutter sealant injected with an applicator gun (page 441). If you choose a sealant to match the mortar, the repair will not be noticeable.

For larger cracks you will have to make the repair with mortar.

You will need
Tools Ladder with stand-off bracket; cold chisel; club hammer; brush; paintbrush; small trowel.
Materials Dry mortar mix, or cement and sharp sand; PVA adhesive; bucket of water. Perhaps narrow slips of tile.

1 With the chisel and hammer, chip away all cracked and crumbling mortar leaving only sound mortar in place.

2 Prepare the mortar (page 481) from a bag of dry mixed material or from one part cement to four parts sharp sand. To improve adhesion, add PVA to the water, following the manufacturer's instructions. Do not make the mortar too wet. Make enough to half-fill a bucket.

3 Brush all dust away, then damp the area with paintbrush and water before brushing on a covering of PVA adhesive.

4 Use the trowel to press mortar well into the areas prepared. Knock it in with the side of the trowel to make sure that there are no air pockets in it.

If the repair is at the eaves under an S-shaped tile, press tile slips into the mortar to make a firmer repair.

5 Smooth the surface of the mortar and clean away any excess. Do not leave any ledges or hollows that could retain rainwater.

Repairs to metal valleys

Where two roof slopes meet at the bottom, the long narrow gap between them is sealed – frequently by a tray of aluminium alloy, lead or zinc. This metal valley is overlapped by the tiles or slates, which drain rainwater into it to be carried down to the gutters at the eaves.

Since valleys are likely to carry a gushing stream of water in heavy rain, they must be kept waterproof and clear of obstructions. If moss, leaves or other debris accumulates, rainwater will build up at the obstruction and spill over the edges of the valley onto the timbers and into the roof space.

If a metal valley has developed a fine crack or is showing the first signs of corrosion, it can be repaired with a liquid bitumen compound. Liquid bitumen can also be used to make a temporary repair if you are waiting for a convenient time to replace the valley.

Holes or splits in a metal valley can be covered with self-adhesive metal-backed flashing strip. If slight corrosion has set in over a large area, flashing strip can be used to cover the entire valley.

MAKING REPAIRS WITH LIQUID BITUMEN

Stir the waterproofer before you apply it. You can use it on a damp, but not a wet, surface. Do not use it, however, if rain or frost is expected within about 24 hours.

You will need
Tools Ladder with a stand-off bracket; roof ladder; wire brush; a spreader for the roof-and-gutter sealant; sharp knife or scissors; soft brush or broom.
Materials Roof-and-gutter sealant; roofing felt or cooking foil; liquid bitumen waterproofing compound; bucket of water.

1 Use the wire brush to clean away dirt and loose metal fragments from the area of the valley that is going to be repaired.

2 Spread roof-and-gutter sealant over the damaged area and at least 2in (50mm) beyond it.

3 Cut out a piece of roofing felt or cooking foil to cover the damage and extend at least 2in (50mm) beyond it. Press the felt or foil down over the sealant.

4 Spread another layer of sealant on top of the felt or foil.

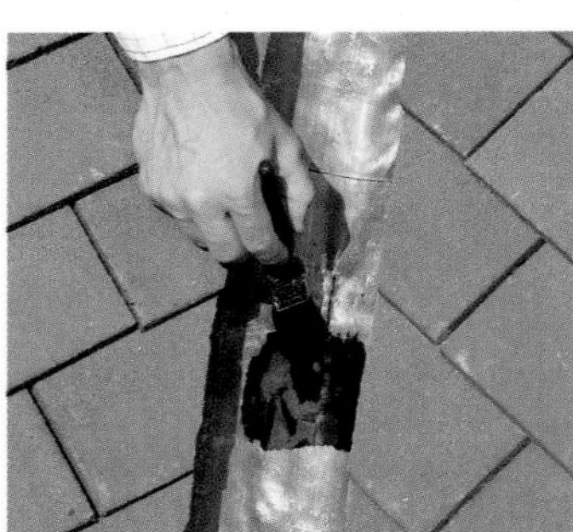

5 Brush the liquid bitumen waterproofing compound over the repair. As a precaution against leaks, you can brush it over the whole valley. Apply it with a soft brush or broom, dipping the brush in water and shaking it dry each time before you load it with the waterproofer. Brush the compound on with even strokes, working in the same direction all the time.

MAKING REPAIRS WITH FLASHING STRIP

You will need
Tools Ladder with stand-off brackets; roof ladder; wire brush; damp cloth; paintbrush; sharp knife or strong scissors; old wallpaper seam roller.
Materials Medium-coarse abrasive paper; flashing-strip primer; self-adhesive metal-backed flashing strip.

1 Use the wire brush to clean away dirt and loose metal fragments from round the crack or hole.

2 Rub over the area with the abrasive paper.

3 Wipe the surface clean with the damp cloth and allow it to dry completely.

4 Use the paintbrush to apply a coat of flashing-strip primer to the area of the repair, extending it at least 2in (50mm) beyond the damage. Leave it to dry for the time recommended by the manufacturer – usually about 30 minutes.

5 Cut out a piece of flashing strip to extend at least 2in (50mm) beyond the crack or hole all round. Cut it with a knife or scissors, then peel off the backing.

6 Press the flashing strip firmly in position, using the wallpaper seam roller to bed it down smoothly.

Laying a new metal roof valley

A valley that is badly holed by corrosion, or wrinkled and pitted too much for flashing strip to bed down smoothly, will have to be replaced.

The metal should be laid over two boards that run down the valley, meeting at the angle. Near the sides, the metal rises over triangular wooden fillets fixed to the boards. The tiles or slates should be sealed to the metal with mortar so that the valley becomes a waterproof channel about 4in (100mm) wide.

When you are fitting the new metal, do not work with strips longer than 5ft (1.5m). A longer piece will expand too much in hot weather.

Nail the strips only at the top. Too many fixing nails will cause the metal to buckle and distort when it expands.

You will need
Tools Ladder with a stand-off bracket; roof ladder; bolster chisel and club hammer; wooden wedges and a large builder's trowel, or a slate ripper, and perhaps all three; chalk; a bucket on a long rope; claw hammer; tinsnips; soft-faced mallet; pointing trowel.
Materials Lead or zinc; No. 11 aluminium alloy nails $1\frac{1}{2}$in (40mm) long; mortar mixed as for replacing ridge or hip tiles (page 443).

1 Use the bolster chisel and club hammer to chip away the mortar sealing the tiles or slates to the metal valley.

2 You will need to remove the cut tiles or slates that edge the valley at each side, and probably also the ones next to these to allow you to fold back the edge of the felt and reach the triangular fillets. You may have to take off pieces of batten to do this.

To remove tiles, push wooden wedges (page 441) under the topmost tile to prop it up. Slide the trowel under the next tile down and lift it until its nibs are clear of the batten. Then draw the tile out towards you.

ALTERNATIVELY, if it is a single-lap interlocked tile, draw it towards you to clear the tile above, then wiggle it slightly from side to side to free it from its neighbour. You will be able to remove the lower tiles without using wedges. Some of the tiles will be nailed to the battens; push the slate ripper under them and strike its handle down with a hammer to cut through the nails.

Take the tiles to the ground a few at a time or lower them in a bucket to a helper.

To remove slates, slide the slate ripper under each one to cut through the nails. As soon as the nails of a slate are cut, lift off the slate and take it to the ground or lower it in a bucket on a rope.

HOW THE VALLEY IS MADE

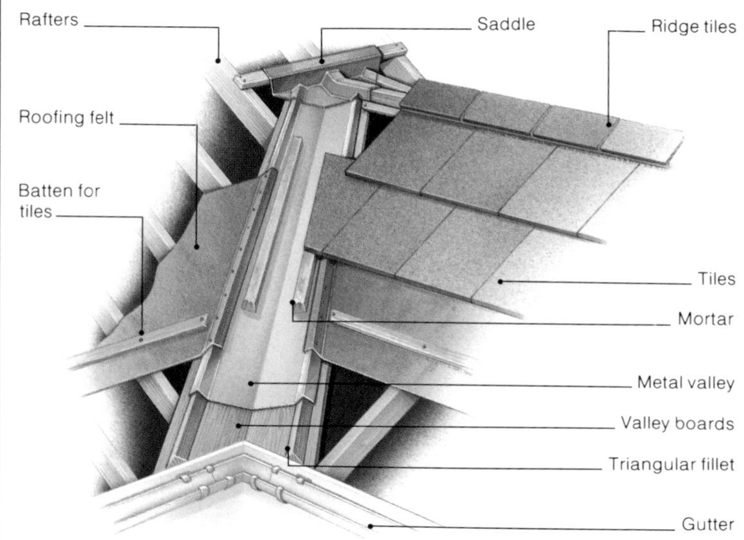

HELPFUL TIP
Number the tiles or slates with chalk as you remove them. Stack them on the ground in the order you take them off the roof. You will then be able to replace them correctly.

3 Use the claw hammer to lever out the nails holding the lead or zinc to the fillets on the valley boards. Again start at the top and remove each piece of metal as you work down.

4 At the very top of the valley the metal is usually fixed under a lead saddle – a piece of lead covering the area where the ridge and the valley meet and shaped to fit snugly over the timbers. Raise the saddle very carefully to free the top of the metal valley.

5 Check the condition of the valley boards and the wooden fillets on them. Treat or repair them as necessary.

6 Use tinsnips to cut new strips of lead or zinc to the same width as the strips used for the old valley and to lengths of not more than 5ft (1.5 metres).

7 Work up from the bottom to fit the new valley. Use the soft-faced mallet to tap the metal gently into the angle of the valley, shaping it to lie closely against the timber. Allow the first piece of metal to overlap into the gutter. At the fillets, tap the metal in place so that it follows the shape of the wood.

8 Nail the metal to the fillets on the slope farthest from the centre of the valley. Use one nail at each side, placing it about $1\frac{1}{2}$in (38mm) from the top of the metal.

9 Continue working up the valley, letting each strip overlap by about 3in (75mm) onto the strip below it.

10 Cut the top strip to length, allowing it to overlap onto the strip below and also to extend under the saddle by at least 2in (50mm).

11 When the top strip is fixed, tap the saddle to fit closely over it.

12 At the bottom of the valley, trim the metal with the tinsnips to cover the bottom edge of the valley boards completely. Tap the metal closely against the boards.

13 Put the felt back in position.

14 Replace the tiles or slates, working from the bottom up and replacing them in the right order. Plain tiles simply have their nibs lodged over the battens. Where a nib has been cut off to make the tile the right shape, nail it securely in place. In any case, nail the tile in every third or fourth course as you work up the valley.

Interlocked tiles must be pressed into the matching grooves firmly. Nail alternate courses to the batten. Slates have to be nailed in every course to the batten.

15 Seal the tiles to the metal with mortar all the way up the sides of the valley. Use mortar also to seal any gaps at the eaves if the tiles you have replaced have curved profiles.

Repairing and replacing valley tiles

Some tiled roofs have tiled valleys, not metal ones. If there is a fine crack in a valley tile, you can follow the method for a temporary repair to a tile (page 441). If one or more tiles are badly damaged, you will have to replace them. Remove tiles from the top down, but replace them from the bottom up.

The tiles may be V-shaped and continue the level and line of the courses on each side. Or they may be rectangular and form a trough. These are called trough valley tiles.

V-SHAPED VALLEY TILES

Follow the method for replacing plain tiles (page 441). Use wedges to raise the surrounding tiles, and lift out the one that needs replacing. Simply place the new tiles in position. They are held in place by those on each side.

TROUGH VALLEY TILES

You will need

Tools Ladder with a stand-off bracket; roof ladder; plugging chisel and club hammer; large builder's trowel; perhaps a slate ripper; pointing trowel.

Materials Trough valley tile to suit the roof pitch; mortar as for replacing a ridge or hip tile (page 443).

1 Chip out the mortar from each side of the damaged tile and from the sides of the tile above it in the valley.

2 Remove the roof tiles (pages 441 and 442) that overlap onto the right-hand side of the valley (as you view it from the eaves).

3 Raise the bottom edge of the damaged valley tile and pull its top edge down to free it from the overlapping valley tile above it. Then slide and tilt the damaged tile to the right to draw it from under the roof tiles overlapping on the left.

4 Reverse the procedure to put the new tile in place, manoeuvring it first under the roof tiles at the left and then sliding it under the tile above it in the valley.

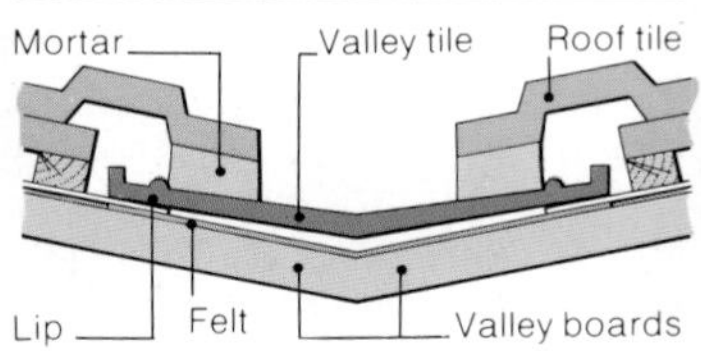

5 Lay new mortar where you removed the old. It must be within the inner lips of the tile.

6 Replace the roof tiles at the right of the valley.

7 Smooth the exposed edge of mortar to leave no water traps.

Repairs to flashings

Where a tile or slate roof meets a wall, there is a flashing to seal the join – for example at the meeting of a roof with a chimney stack and the meeting of a bay window or porch roof with the house wall.

Flashings fitted when the house is built are usually strips of lead which can deteriorate with age.

FINE CRACKS

To repair a fine crack, inject some bituminous sealant or other roof-and-gutter sealant into it with an applicator gun and cartridge. Some sealants are available in different colours so you can choose one that will make the repair less noticeable.

SMALL HOLES OR SLIGHT CORROSION

A patch of self-adhesive flashing strip will make a sound repair over a small hole or where there are first signs of corrosion. Use the method described for a roof valley under *Making repairs with flashing strip*, page 445.

RENEWING FLASHING MORTAR

The top edge of a flashing is sandwiched into the mortar between two courses of bricks. Sometimes it works loose and lets in water.

Repoint the joint (page 460), but first push the edge of the flashing back into the gap between courses of bricks. If the flashing springs out,

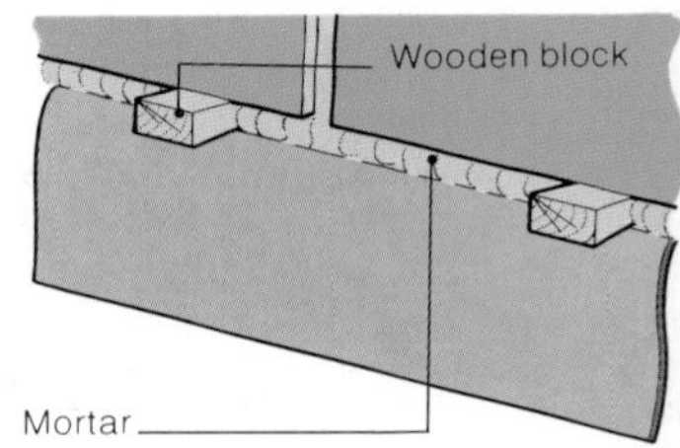

wedge it with blocks of wood until the pointing has hardened. Then withdraw the blocks and fill the holes with mortar.

Replacing a flashing

If a flashing is badly cracked or corroded, replace it with self-adhesive metal-backed flashing strip. Adhesive flashing is not tucked into the mortar joints.

You will need

Tools Ladder with a stand-off bracket; roof ladder; plugging chisel and club hammer; pointing trowel; wire brush; paintbrush; sharp craft knife; old wallpaper seam roller.

Materials Mortar for repointing (page 481); flashing-strip primer; self-adhesive metal-backed flashing strip.

1 Chip out any mortar that is still holding the flashing in the joints between bricks or masonry. Use the plugging chisel and hammer.

2 Strip away the old flashing.

3 Use the wire brush to clean away loose mortar and dirt from the area to be repaired.

4 Repoint the joints between the courses of bricks or masonry (page 460). Let the new pointing dry out overnight.

5 Paint a coat of flashing primer on the wall (or chimney) and roof where the strip is to go. Let it dry for 30 minutes to an hour, according to the manufacturer's instructions.

6 Cut two lengths of flashing strip, each the full length of the area to be sealed.

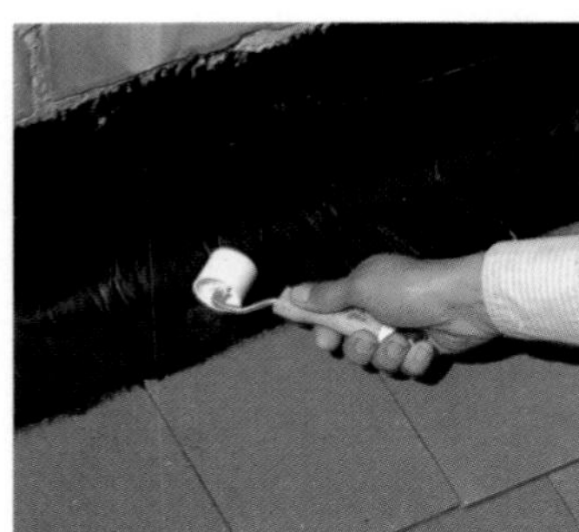

7 Peel off the backing of the first strip and put the strip in position, letting the width lie equally on the roof and the wall (or chimney stack). Roll the strip with the wallpaper seam roller to smooth it out and ensure that it is well stuck.

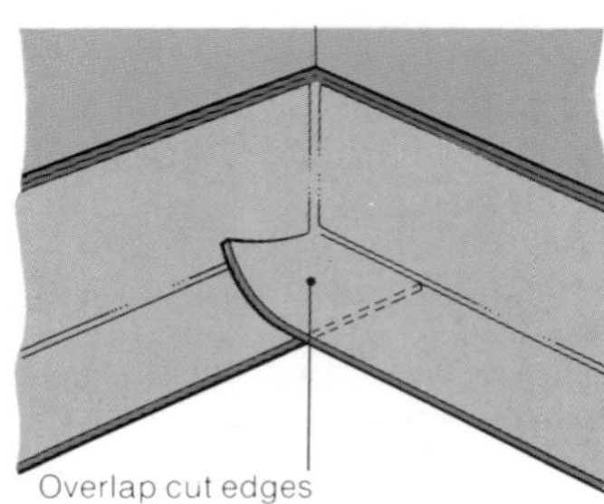

8 At internal corners, make a snip in the lower edge of the strip and overlap the cut edges.

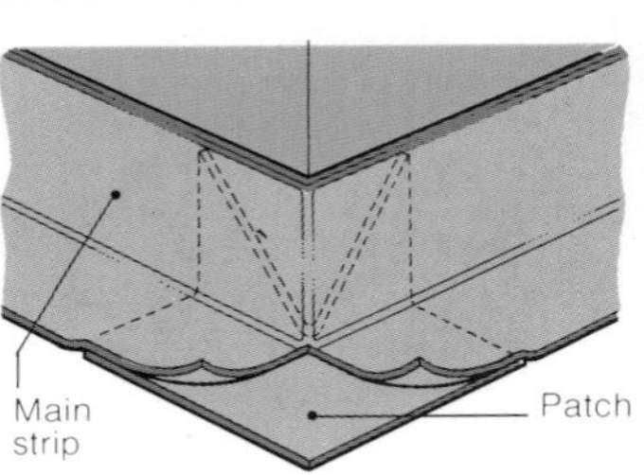

9 At external corners, fit a square patch before the main strip; make a cut from one corner of the patch to the middle. Set the patch with the centre at the point where the wall angle meets the roof and the cut running upwards. Let the cut edges splay out round the angle. In the main strip make a cut in the bottom edge and let the cut edges splay apart over the patch. Trim off any excess at the points.

10 Peel the backing off the second strip and apply it so that its top edge is 2in (50mm) above the top edge of the first layer. Treat any corners as in the first strip. Again smooth the strip out and bed it down well with the wallpaper seam roller.

CHOOSING A TREATMENT FOR A FLAT ROOF OR SHED

Flat roofs are sometimes seen on houses, but most are found on house extensions or garages. They are cheaper than pitched, tiled roofs to construct, but do not last as long. However, DIY repairs are easily carried out with patience and the right choice of material. Several grades of roofing felt are made for different purposes. Roofing felt is sold in rolls about 3ft (1m) wide and 33ft (10m) long. It has some flexibility and is easy to bed down over different shapes. Reinforced bitumen is fairly quick to apply and also makes a sound covering.

MATERIAL	COMBINE WITH	HOW APPLIED	SUGGESTED FOR
Bitumen waterproofing solution	Use with glass-fibre mesh, such as Aquaseal glass-fibre membrane	Brush-on liquid	Parapet flat roof
Asbestos-based roofing felt	Use as two underlayers beneath a top layer of heavy-grade mineral-coated or coarse-grit felt	Nail first layer, stick second layer with roofing-felt adhesive	Flat roof with aprons
Glass-fibre-based felt	Alternative underlayer		
Mineral-coated felt (heavy grade)	Use as top layer over asbestos or glass-fibre-based felt. Also for aprons and flashings	Stick with roofing-felt adhesive	Flat roof with aprons
Coarse-grit felt (heavy grade)	Alternative to mineral-coated felt		
Mineral-coated or coarse-grit felt (medium grade)	Use alone	Roofing nails and roofing-felt adhesive	Roofs of timber garages and garden sheds
Chippings of limestone, granite, gravel or flint	Use over felt	Scatter over brush-on chipping compound	Protection for a felted flat roof in a sunny position.
Liquid rubber	Use alone or with primer, according to manufacturer's instructions	Brush on	Roofs covered with felt, asphalt, asbestos or corrugated iron
Self-adhesive flashing strip	Use over flashing-strip primer	Press on	Repairs to flashing or a hole on a felted or asphalt roof; can also be used to repair a cracked slate
Roof-and-gutter sealant	Use alone	Applicator gun or filling knife	Repairs to cracks in flashing, felt or asphalt
Butyl flat roof covering	Use over felt	Galvanised clout nails through hidden flaps	Flat or pitched roof

Minor repairs to flat roofs

Before carrying out any minor repair, you will have to scrape off any chippings carefully with an old wallpaper scraper.

Small blisters or cracks are the commonest minor defects in felted flat roofs. You can repair them with a roof-and-gutter sealant (see *Repairing a fine crack with sealant*, page 441), with self-adhesive flashing strip (see *Making a temporary repair to a cracked tile or slate*, page 441, or with brush on liquid rubber (right).

Repair damaged flashings as described on the facing page.

A bubble may form in the felt where moisture has seeped under it and swollen in the heat of the sun. Cut a cross in the blister with a sharp knife and fold back the four flaps of felt. Let them dry, then stick them down with a cold felt adhesive before patching the damaged area with a piece of self-adhesive flashing strip or a bitumen mastic repair compound. Replace any chippings when the repairs are complete.

REPAIRING A HOLE OR CRACK WITH LIQUID RUBBER

If cracks develop on a flat roof that is covered with felt or asphalt, treat the whole area with brush-on liquid rubber.

Calculate the area of the roof in square metres and buy the amount of liquid rubber recommended by the manufacturer. It is sold in containers ranging from 1kg to 20kg.

You will need

Tools Ladder; stiff brush and shovel; an old 4in (100mm) paintbrush or a small broom for the liquid rubber. Perhaps a paintbrush for primer.

Materials Liquid rubber. Perhaps primer for liquid rubber.

1 Use the stiff brush and shovel to clear the area of loose chippings and dirt.

2 If the area has previously been treated with a tar-bitumen coating – which gives a black, slightly rough covering – brush on a coat of primer for liquid rubber. Leave it to dry overnight.

3 Brush on a coat of liquid rubber, using all the recommended amount for the area. Leave it to dry thoroughly for 48 hours. After an hour it will be sufficiently dry not to be affected by rain.

4 Brush on a second coat of rubber, using the same amount as before.

REPAIRING A CRACKED FLASHING

Changes in temperature and normal house movement put the flashings under stress and may cause cracks where water can seep in. The resulting wet patch indoors, however, can be several feet away from the crack because the water may run along the roof beams before dripping onto the ceiling. The crack may be difficult to spot. When you have located it, repair it with self-adhesive flashing strip (see *Making repairs with flashing strip*, page 445).

A REPLACEMENT FLASHING

If the flashing has cracked or corroded so much that an adhesive patch may not be able to make firm contact all over the damaged area, strip away the entire flashing and replace it with self-adhesive flashing strip as described in *Replacing a flashing* (facing page).

Seal the joint between roof and parapet (or house wall) with roof-and-gutter sealant before you apply the primer.

If your parapet is the height of only one course of brickwork or masonry, let the second layer of flashing overlap onto the top.

How a flat roof with aprons is made

Timber deck
Flat roofs on house extensions or garages are usually made by nailing planks of tongued-and-grooved softwood or else sheets of exterior grade plywood, chipboard or strawboard to the roof joists and covering them with three layers of roofing felt.

Second flashing
First flashing
Triangular fillet
Raised lip
Capsheet
Second layer
First layer
Apron
Timber deck
Triangular fillet
Fascia
Joist
First flashing
Second flashing
Capsheet
Apron
Second layer
First layer
Gutter
Drip batten
Soffit
Fascia

Flashing
If the roof meets the house walls, there is a flashing at the join.

Chippings
In a sunny place, the felt may be spread with chippings of limestone, granite, gravel or flint over a chipping compound. The chippings are to keep direct sun off the felt, and are not necessary in shade.

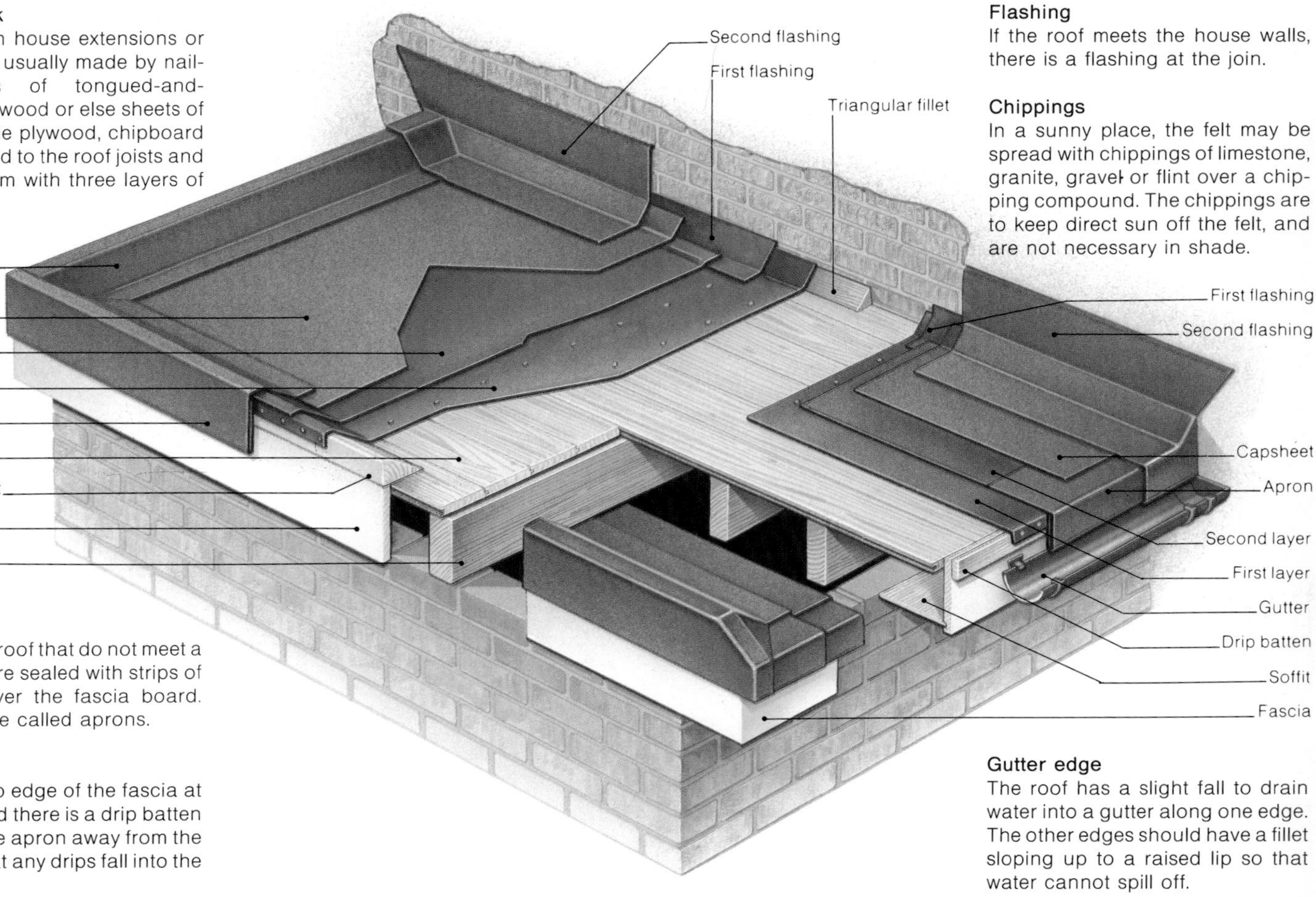

Aprons
Edges of the roof that do not meet a house wall are sealed with strips of felt taken over the fascia board. The strips are called aprons.

Drip batten
Along the top edge of the fascia at the gutter end there is a drip batten that holds the apron away from the board, so that any drips fall into the gutter.

Gutter edge
The roof has a slight fall to drain water into a gutter along one edge. The other edges should have a fillet sloping up to a raised lip so that water cannot spill off.

Renewing the felt on a flat roof with aprons

With age, the felt covering on a roof becomes porous and water will come in at several places. You may be able to extend its life with reinforced bitumen (page 451) but if the felt is badly buckled, has visible cracks, or breaks up when you try to remove any chippings, it will have to be re-covered. Do the work during a dry spell, making a temporary repair in the meantime.

When you have bought suitable felts for the three layers (page 447), do not leave them tightly rolled up. A day or two before laying felt, cut it into strips of the required length, using a sharp knife. Leave the lengths lying flat and weighted down. If space is short, roll the strips loosely in the opposite direction from the original roll.

You will need
Tools Ladder; brush and shovel; sharp knife; claw hammer; batten 1in (25mm) square and about 3ft (1m) long; paintbrush. You may also need an old wallpaper scraper and seam roller; plugging chisel; club hammer; pointing trowel; large cheap paintbrush or soft broom; small shovel; rake.
Materials Suitable types of felt for the underlayers and for the capsheet, aprons and flashings; $\frac{3}{4}$in (20mm) galvanised clout nails; roofing-felt adhesive.

You may also need some of the following: tongued-and-grooved boards or outdoor grade chipboard, plywood, or strawboard with 4in (100mm) wide adhesive sealing tape; 1$\frac{1}{2}$in (40mm) or 2in (50mm) nails for fixing boards or sheets; triangular-section fillet of wood and bituminous sealant; pointing mortar; new chippings and chipping compound.

PREPARATIONS

1 If the roof meets a wall at one edge, remove any existing flashings. Use the plugging chisel and hammer to clean out the first and third joints above the roof to a depth of $\frac{1}{2}$in (13mm).

2 Scrape loose and brush up any chippings and other debris.

3 Tear off all the old felt. If nail heads come off, hammer the shanks right down. If the heads stay on, prise out the nails.

4 Examine the timber deck, fillets and drip battens. Nail down any loose timber. If any is rotten, replace it with new pressure-treated timber. If the deck is strawboard, check the adhesive tape that seals the joints. Replace any that is damaged. Let any damp patches on the existing roof timbers dry out.

FITTING THE FIRST LAYER

1 Position the first length of felt along the gutter end, lapping its long edge over the top of the fascia board and about 1in (25mm) down the drip batten's outside face. Nail the edge of the felt to the drip batten at 2in (50mm) intervals. Start at the middle and work outwards.

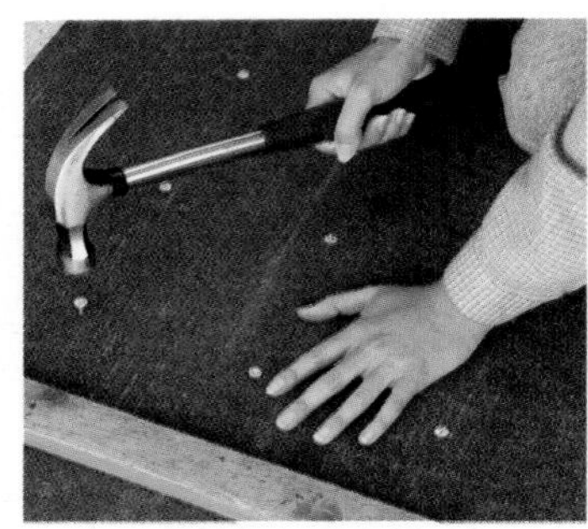

2 On the flat roof surface, run the wooden batten along the felt from the centre to the ends to smooth out wrinkles.

Then drive in clout nails at 6in (150mm) intervals in both directions all over the felt.

As you work along the roof, run the wooden batten along the strip of felt to hold it firm while you hammer in the nails.

3 At the house end of the strip, trim off the felt at the top edge of the triangular fillet.

To fit it neatly, make a small diagonal cut in the felt from the edge upwards to the base of the fillet; let the cut edges splay apart so the felt lies flat on the fillet and the drip batten. Nail the ends of the felt at 2in (50mm) intervals.

4 At the end where the strip meets the raised lip, let the felt lap over the lip and 1in (25mm) down its outer face. Make a diagonal cut up to the base of the fillet and trim off the excess felt at the end of the lip.

5 Overlap the next strip of felt onto the first by 2in (50mm). Nail it at 6in (150mm) intervals over its whole surface, again working out from the middle and using the batten to smooth it out. Nail the overlap at 2in (50mm) intervals.

6 Lap the ends 1in (25mm) onto the outer face of the raised lip. If one end meets the house, run the felt to the top of the fillet. Nail the ends at 1in (25mm) intervals.

7 When the strip is in two parts – because you are starting another roll – make a 4in (100mm) overlap at the join and drive in nails every 2in (50mm) across it.

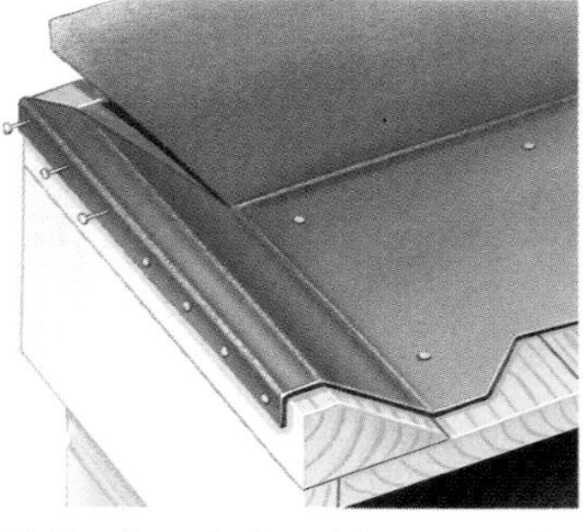

8 Continue laying strips across the roof. On the final strip, at a corner where two raised lips meet, allow for the felt to lap over the lips and 1in (25mm) down their outer faces. Make a diagonal cut from the corner of the felt to where the fillets meet at the base. Trim off the excess to end in the angle where the fillets and then the lips meet. Seal the cut edges down with bituminous sealant.

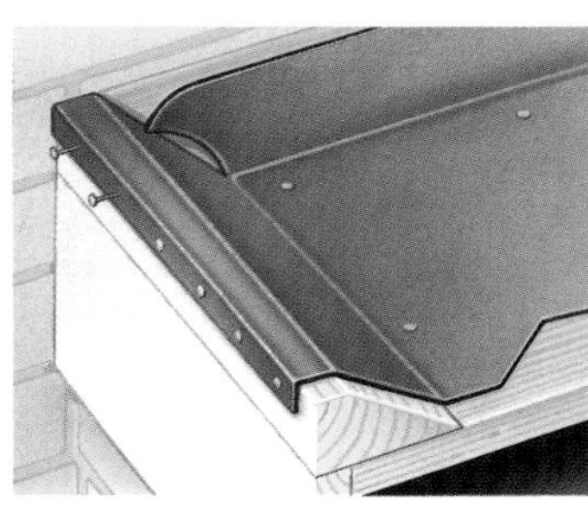

9 Where the roof meets the house wall, trim the end of the felt at the top of the fillet. Let the long edge of the felt lap onto the fascia by 1in (25mm). Make a diagonal cut in the felt where the two fillets meet at the house wall, and trim off the excess felt over the lip to meet the wall neatly.

THE FIRST FLASHING

1 Cut a strip of capsheet felt about 6in (150mm) wide and the full length needed for the flashing. If the roof slopes down the house wall, because the fall runs in that direction, the felt strip will need to widen towards the lower end so that it reaches easily from the first mortar joint to cover a strip of roof 2in (50mm) wide.

2 Lay the flashing in place. Tuck the top edge into the cleaned-out mortar joint and wedge it there with a few small wooden blocks.

3 Nail down the lower edge of the flashing at 6in (150mm) intervals. In the angle between the raised lip and the wall, fold down the excess felt neatly and nail it flat.

4 Where the flashing meets the raised lip, trim it diagonally to lie across the top of the lip and end in the angle where the lip meets the wall, and where the fillets meet.

5 Repoint the mortar joint. If the felt tends to spring out of the joint, leave the wooden blocks in until the pointing is dry, then fill the holes with mortar.

THE GUTTER EDGE APRON

1 To make the apron, cut one continuous strip of capsheet felt the length of the roof edge plus 6in (150mm), and 18in (460mm) wide.

2 Nail the felt, wrong side out, to the outside of the drip batten, so that it hangs down. Let the excess felt project at the lipped end. Nail it at 2in (50mm) intervals.

3 Double the felt back on itself, letting the fold project about 1½in (38mm) below the drip batten. Lap the remaining felt over onto the roof and hold it while you chalk a line against its edge. Release the felt.

4 Brush adhesive along the top of the fascia and onto the roof as far as the chalk line. Leave it for about 30 minutes to become tacky.

5 Fold the felt up again, starting at the centre. Position it on the adhesive and press it down firmly. Make sure no air bubbles are left under it; you can use an old wallpaper seam roller to bed it down. If the apron meets the house wall at one end, make a horizontal cut in it to correspond with the base of the triangular fillet so that the apron will lie smoothly. Press the flaps down smoothly.

ALTERNATIVELY, where the end of the apron is at a raised lip, make vertical cuts in the top edge to correspond to the back and the front edges of the fillet and the outer edge of the lip. Press the flaps down to fit smoothly in place and trim the middle flap at the rim of the fillet.

FITTING THE SECOND LAYER

1 Brush a strip of felt adhesive at least 3in (75mm) wide near the gutter edge of the roof, taking it right to the edge of the apron felt.

2 Brush on adhesive for the other long edge of the felt, measuring the position to make sure the felt's edge will lie on it.

3 At the end that meets the house, paint the adhesive at the edge of the flat surface just before the triangular fillet rises. At the other end, paint the strip along the top of the raised lip.
ALTERNATIVELY, if both ends are at raised lips, paint both strips of adhesive along the tops of the lips.

4 Leave the adhesive for about 30 minutes to become tacky.

5 Lay the length of underfelt in position, press it down and run the batten over it, working from the middle outwards to push out any air bubbles.

6 Brush on adhesive for the next strip of felt, which should overlap 2in (50mm) onto the previous strip. Lay it as the first strip.

7 Continue in the same way across the roof. If a strip has a join, make a 4in (100mm) overlap at the join, apply bitumen adhesive and nail at 2in (50mm) intervals. Joins in layers must not coincide.

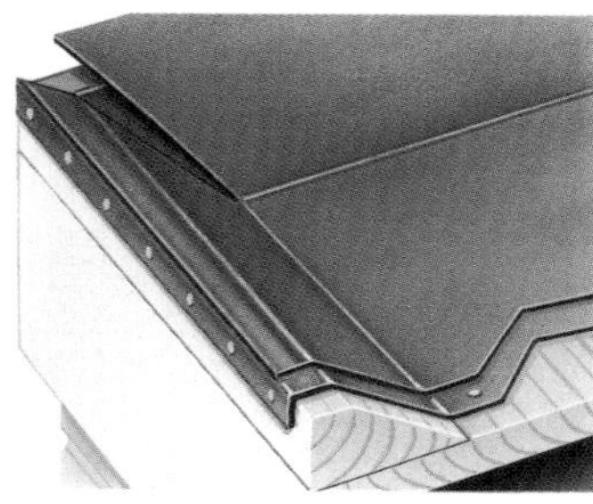

8 Take the last strip to the top outer corner of the raised lip. Make a diagonal cut at the corner if two raised lips meet there, let the cut edges overlap and stick them down well.
ALTERNATIVELY, if the felt's long edge runs parallel to the house wall, trim off and stick the felt where the triangular fillet begins to rise under the first layer of felt.

FIXING THE CAPSHEET

1 Lay the capsheet felt on adhesive in the same way as the second underlayer. At a house end, let the felt lap onto the fillet. At a raised lip, trim each strip at the base of the triangular fillet. Start at the gutter edge, setting the felt 3in (75mm) from the edge.

2 Make sure that any joins where you start another roll of felt do not fall on joins in the layer beneath.

FITTING THE OTHER APRONS

1 For each apron, cut a continuous strip of capsheet felt the length of the roof plus 6in (150mm), and 18in (460mm) wide.

2 Nail the felt, wrong side out, to the outer face of the raised lip. Nail it at 2in (50mm) intervals.

3 Double the felt back on itself about 1½in (38mm) below the bottom of the raised lip. Lap the felt over the raised lip onto the flat surface and draw a chalk line against its edge to show where to put the adhesive. Unfold the felt.

Renewing the felt on a flat roof with aprons (continued)

4 Brush adhesive along the raised lip, the fillet and as far as the chalk line. Leave it to become tacky.

5 Starting at the middle, stick the apron in position, bedding it down with an old wallpaper seam roller.

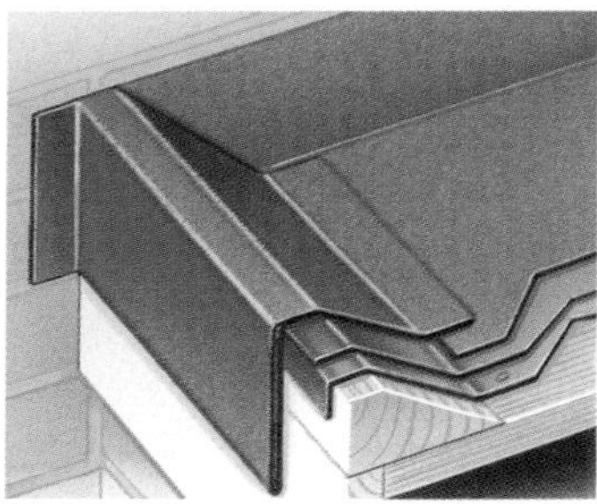

6 At the house wall, let the apron lap 6in (150mm) onto the wall. Cut into it level with the top of the lip. Trim the rest of the end to fit in the angle between lip and wall.

7 At a gutter end make cuts in the end of the strip level with the top outer edge and top inner edge of the lip. Extend them until they meet the lip. Coat under the apron and round the end of the raised lip with adhesive. When the adhesive is tacky, press the flaps down well to drive out any air bubbles.

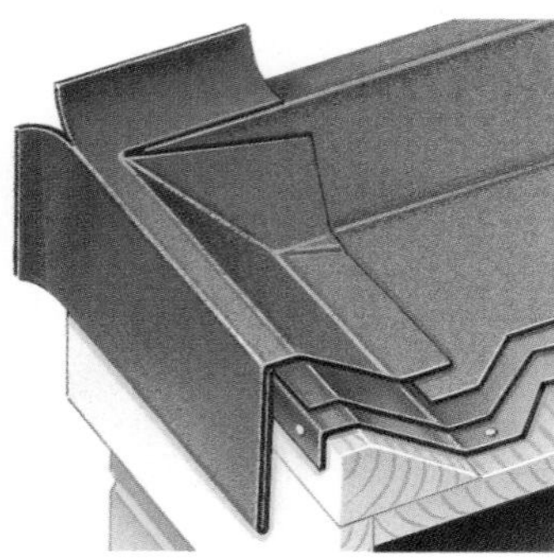

8 At a non-gutter end cut the end of the strip at the level of the outer rim of the raised lip. Cut the top edge along the inner rim of the adjoining lip. Coat under the apron with adhesive and when it is tacky press it down well. Make a small cut in the inner edge to allow a smooth fit where the fillets meet.

THE SECOND FLASHING

1 Cut a continuous strip of cap-sheet felt the length of the roof plus 3in (75mm) at each end and about 15in (380mm) wide; it may have to widen towards one end to allow for any fall.

2 Brush adhesive over the slope where the fillet rises beneath the felt, and 2in (50mm) onto the roof. Leave it to become tacky.

3 Lay the flashing strip in place and press it down, expelling any air bubbles. In the excess felt at the gutter end, make cuts in the end of the strip to meet the top and the bottom of the triangular fillet's slope. In the excess at the non-gutter end, make a cut in the bottom of the flashing to correspond with the top of the raised lip and running to the house wall. Coat under the flaps of felt with adhesive and when they are tacky, seal them down. Let the flashing lap onto the wall and let the cut edges splay apart or overlap to make a snug fit.

Press down the flap from the wall last so that no rim is remaining.

4 Trim the top edge of the flashing to fit neatly into the third mortar joint above the roof. Use the same method to point it in as for the first flashing.

SPREADING ON CHIPPINGS

If the roof is in a sunny position, cover it with chippings. The felt is more likely to blister and deteriorate in sun. If the roof is in a shaded position, there is no need for a covering of chippings.

1 Spread chipping compound over the roof to within 1in (25mm) of the edge. Apply it with a cheap large paintbrush or else use a soft broom.

2 Sprinkle the chippings evenly over the compound from a small shovel. Use the back of a rake to spread them fairly evenly. If the roof is large, treat a section at a time so that you can reach easily to spread the chippings.

How a parapet flat roof is made

Where a flat roof is the main house roof, it is usually of the parapet type. A parapet roof may also be given to a one or two-storey extension or to a detached garage, as an alternative to the more usual flat roof with aprons (page 448).

In a parapet flat roof, the walls continue above the roof level. The parapet may be only one course of brickwork or masonry or it may be several courses. The flat area consists of softwood planks or sheets of outdoor-grade plywood or chipboard nailed to roof beams and covered with asphalt or roofing felt. The roof usually has a slight fall towards an opening in one side with a drainage hopper outside it connected to a downpipe that carries away rainwater.

Where the roof meets the house wall or parapet there is a triangular wooden fillet and a flashing of lead, zinc, aluminium or felt. A cracked or displaced flashing is a frequent source of trouble.

Eventually, cracks may develop in the asphalt or felt covering. You can repair minor damage as described on page 447.

If the roof lets in water in several spots, it is wisest to re-cover the whole area to prevent further damage to the roof timbers or to the rooms below. Layers of rubberised liquid bitumen reinforced with a mesh fabric will make a strong new cover over both the unsound surface and the flashings.

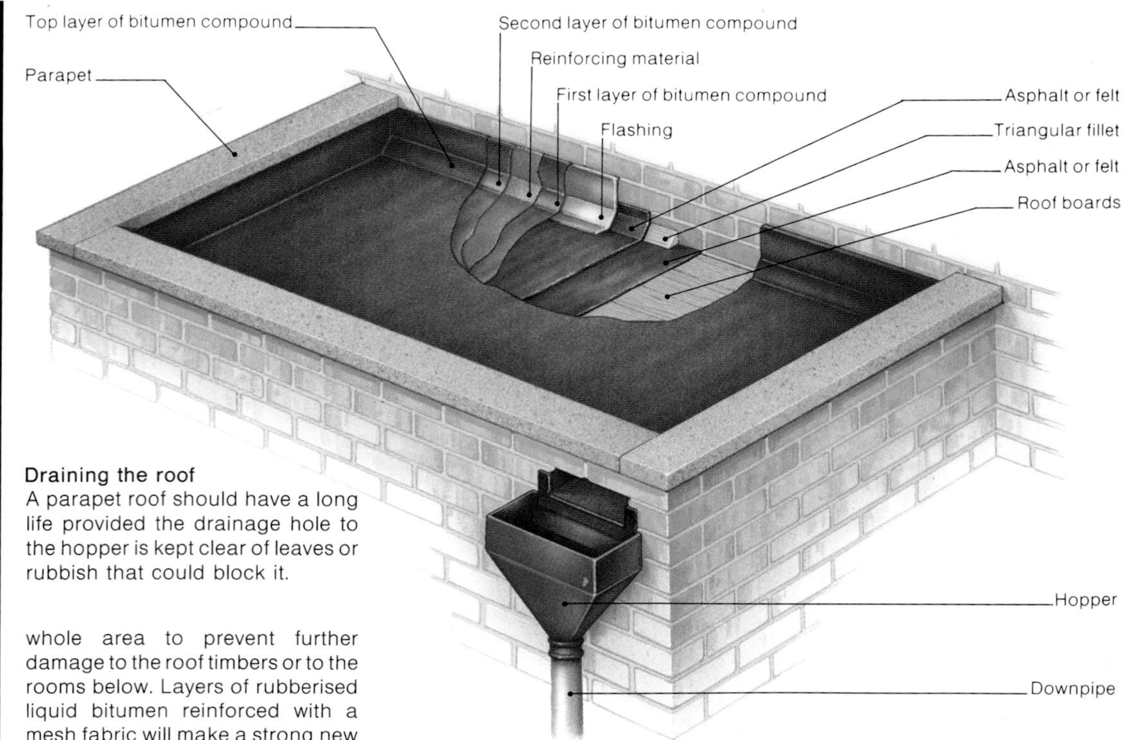

Draining the roof
A parapet roof should have a long life provided the drainage hole to the hopper is kept clear of leaves or rubbish that could block it.

Re-covering a flat roof with reinforced bitumen

The covering consists of a layer of open-meshed reinforcing fabric between layers of a liquid-bitumen waterproofing solution. Both are sold by builders' merchants. The fabric is in rolls; there is no need to overlap the strips.

Wear old shoes which are to be thrown away, or wellington boots which can remain dirty. Change into clean shoes at the parapet before stepping onto the ladder.

You will need

Tools Ladder; stiff brush and shovel; filling knife; paintbrush; sharp knife; wallpaper seam roller; soft broom or large cheap paintbrush for the liquid bitumen.
Materials Roof-and-gutter sealant; flashing-strip primer; self-adhesive flashing strip; bitumen solution; reinforcing fabric, such as Aquaseal glass-fibre membrane.

1 Brush the surface clean of any loose dirt and debris.

2 Press roof-and-gutter sealant into any cracks or holes, using a filling knife to force it well in.

3 Apply a coat of flashing-strip primer to a 6in (150mm) strip at the roof edge and a similar strip of the parapet or house wall adjoining. Let it dry for 30 minutes to an hour.

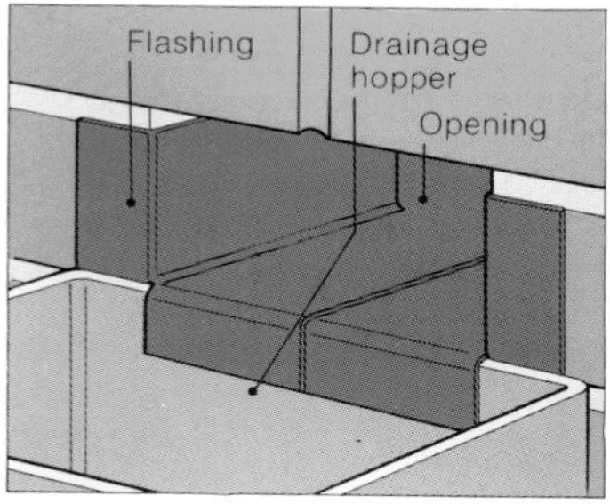

4 Cut and fit lengths of flashing strip as described in *Replacing a flashing* (page 446). Continue the flashing round the sides of the opening for the drainage hopper and let it lap onto the surface of the brick or stonework. Fit a patch under the external angles as shown on page 446.

5 Cut strips of reinforcing fabric to length, allowing for them to extend 6in (150mm) up the wall at each edge. Do not lay them yet.

6 Apply a coat of liquid-bitumen waterproofing solution to the roof with the soft broom or paintbrush. The coat should go about 6in (150mm) up any walls that enclose the roof as well as over the whole flat surface and through the opening to the hopper.

7 After a few minutes, when the surface is tacky, lay the fabric strips side by side over the whole flat area and to the top of the tacky rim round all the walls. At the corners of the parapet fold the excess fabric into a neat pleat and press it flat.

8 Brush a second coat of the liquid-bitumen waterproofing solution over the whole area. Apply it generously, especially at the parapet corners, so that you will dislodge the reinforcing fabric as little as possible. Leave the surface to dry. After about two hours it will be dry enough not to be harmed by rain.

9 Brush a final coat of the liquid-bitumen waterproofing solution all over the flat area and 6in (150mm) up the enclosing walls.

Mending a corrugated plastic roof

Before you buy corrugated plastic to make the repair, measure the profile of the existing plastic on the roof. The sheets may have a round or a box profile and the difference between the lowest and highest points of the profile can vary from $1\frac{1}{2}$in (38mm) to 6in (150mm). If the new plastic does not exactly match the old in profile, it will not make snug overlaps. The length of the screws you use must be the difference between the low and high points of the profile plus at least 1in (25mm) to penetrate the wood.

Overlaps at the sides should finish in a 'valley' of the corrugation, not on a 'peak'. This prevents water from entering at an overlap. If you are renewing a complete panel on the roof, allow the same overlaps as on the rest of the roof.

To reduce the cost of the repair, you can fit a patch. However, the patch will have to be the width of a full sheet and extend over a roof timber at top and bottom to be screwed in place.

Cut sheets to size indoors in cold weather. Plastic becomes brittle in low temperatures and could crack.

Do not walk on the roof. Kneel on scaffold boards secured with sandbags so that they will not slide.

Temporary repairs can be made using clear waterproof tape. Ensure surfaces are clean and dry.

You will need

Tools Sharp knife; tack lifter; screwdriver; fine-toothed saw; hand drill with blunt twist bit, or electric soldering iron with $\frac{3}{16}$in (5mm) bit; steel measuring tape.
Materials Enough corrugated plastic sheeting to make the repair with adequate overlaps; No. 8 galvanised screws of appropriate length; protective screw caps; transparent waterproof glazing tape.

FITTING A WHOLE PANEL

1 Cut away any flashing at the top of the damaged panel.

2 Prise off the screw caps with the tack lifter and take out all the screws securing the panel. Carefully remove the panel.

3 Cut the new panel if necessary to match the length of the old one. Hold the saw at a shallow angle and support the sheet on both sides of the cut. If you have to cut to width, cut along valleys.

4 Place the new panel in position on the roof, overlapping onto the old ones at the sides. If there is another panel above or below it, make sure that the bottom edge of a panel higher up the slope laps onto the panel below.

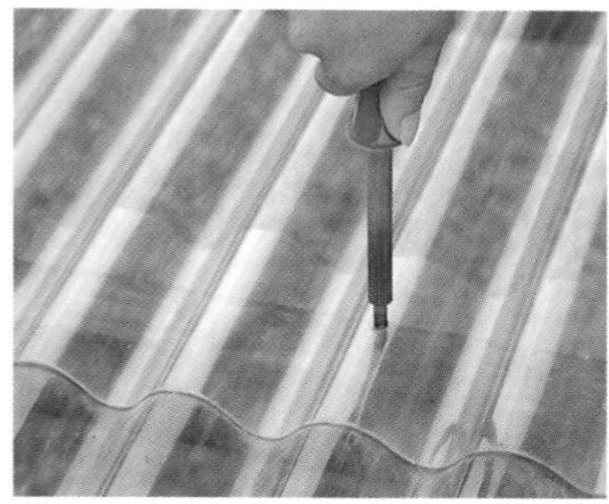

5 Make screw holes through the peaks that are over timbers. Make the holes at intervals of about 18in (460mm) across the panel immediately above the cross timbers. You can either melt the holes with a fine soldering iron, or start them with a bradawl, or use a blunt bit in a drill.

6 Drive in the screws; do not overtighten them or the plastic may split.

7 When the screws are fixed, push on screw caps. They will click into place.

8 Fit new flashing strip (page 446) where the plastic sheet meets the wall. Press it down well into the valleys.

9 Seal the edges where the layers of plastic sheeting overlap at the sides with strips of the glazing tape.

FITTING A PATCH

1 Use a felt pen to mark cutting lines on the damaged panel showing the area for removal. Make the top line just below a timber and the bottom line just above a timber.

2 Remove the whole panel as described on the left.

3 Cut the patch to overlap the guidelines on the old panel by 3in (75mm) at top and bottom. Then cut along the guidelines on the old panel to remove the damaged part. Follow the advice for sawing given in instruction 3 on the left.

4 Lay the plastic for the bottom of the slope in place first. Make screw holes across the bottom if necessary as in instruction 5 on the left. Drive in the screws across the bottom edge. Do not overtighten.

5 Lay the next piece of plastic up the slope; let its bottom edge overlap 3in (75mm) onto the piece below.

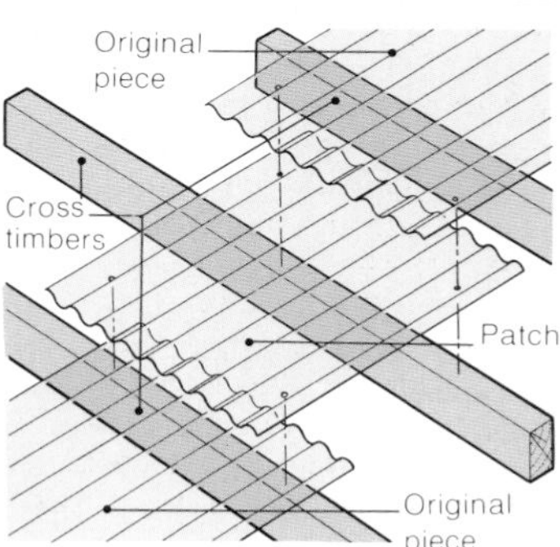

6 Drill screw holes through peaks on the overlap at 18in (460mm) intervals. Drive screws through into the timbers but do not overtighten them.

7 Lay the top piece of plastic sheet in place overlapping the previous piece by 3in (75mm).

8 Drill and screw the bottom edge as for the previous piece.

9 Drill holes if necessary at the top edge and screw it in place.

10 Push caps on all the screws.

11 Fit new flashing and seal the overlaps with glazing tape as for a whole panel.

Re-felting a pitched shed roof

If there is visible damage at several spots on a shed roof, or if water leaks through in places even though you can see no damage, the bituminous felt covering needs replacing. Bituminous felt is sold in green, black and red, and in various grades; the heavier the felt, the longer it usually lasts.

You will usually be able to reach the top of the roof working from a stepladder and moving it along as necessary. If you cannot reach from a stepladder and are not sure that the roof will bear your weight, get someone to help you.

You will need

Tools Stepladder; claw hammer; sharp knife; wooden batten about 3ft (1m) long; old paintbrush. Perhaps also a chisel, saw, plane and screwdriver.

Materials Wood preservative; bituminous roofing felt; ½in (13mm) galvanised clout nails; chalk; cold felt adhesive. Perhaps some new softwood boarding or some outdoor grade plywood or chipboard; fascia boards, ridge board or eaves battens with galvanised nails or screws for fixing.

PREPARATION

1 Tear off all the old felt.

2 Prise out any old nails with the claw hammer. If any heads break off, hammer the shanks down flush so that there are no sharp projections to damage the felt.

3 Check the timber covering of the roof for damage or rot and replace it where necessary. Saturate any replacement wood with preservative and let it dry before use.

If a plywood or chipboard sheet needs replacing, unscrew it and screw a new one in its place with galvanised screws.

If a tongued-and-grooved board needs replacing, cut through the tongue with hammer and chisel so you can ease the board out. You will not be able to fit a tongued-and-grooved replacement unless you remove the tongue. Alternatively, you can plane down a piece of softwood to fit the gap exactly. Nail it in place with galvanised nails.

4 Where a fascia board, a ridge board or an eaves batten is damaged or missing, fit a new one. Treat it first with preservative and fix it with galvanised screws or nails.

5 Treat the remaining roof timber with preservative and let it dry.

6 Cut the felt into strips of the right length with a sharp knife. The strips should run parallel to the ridge and overlap the roof by 1in (25mm) at each end.

FIXING THE FELT

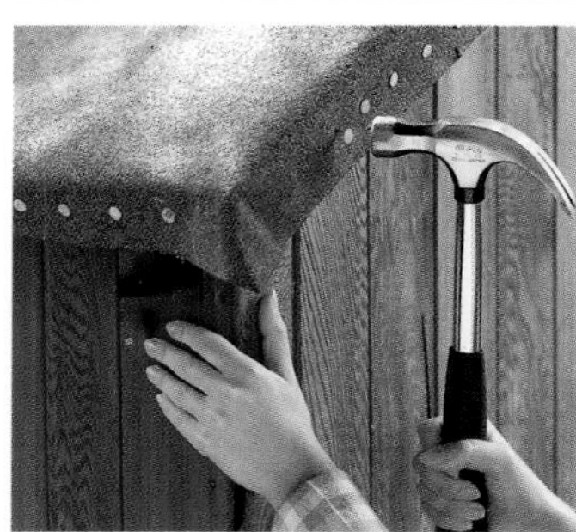

1 Position the first strip with its lower edge overlapping the eaves by 1in (25mm) and its ends overlapping the fascia boards by 1in (25mm) at each end. Run the wooden batten along it – from the centre towards the ends – to smooth out wrinkles. Using the ½in (13mm) galvanised nails, nail the top edge of the felt to the roof timber at 6in (150mm) intervals and the bottom edge to the outside face of the eaves batten at 2in (50mm) intervals. Nail the ends of the felt strip to the outside of the fascia boards at 2in (50mm) intervals.

2 At the corners where the eaves and the fascia boards meet, fold the surplus felt into a neat triangle, bend it flat and drive a nail through.

3 Chalk a line along the length of the felt strip 3in (75mm) below its top edge.

4 Brush a strip of adhesive on the top edge of the felt, taking it down to the chalk line. Take care not to let it spread below the line or a black smear will show on the felt. Leave the adhesive for about 30 minutes to become tacky.

5 Position the next strip of felt carefully over the adhesive. Run the batten over the felt from the middle to the ends to smooth it out. Press down the overlap firmly.

6 Nail the top edge at 6in (150mm) intervals and the ends at 2in (50mm) intervals.

7 If the slope is big enough to need another strip of felt, lay one in the same way. Leave up to 15in (380mm) unfelted at the top.

A TWO-SLOPE SHED ROOF

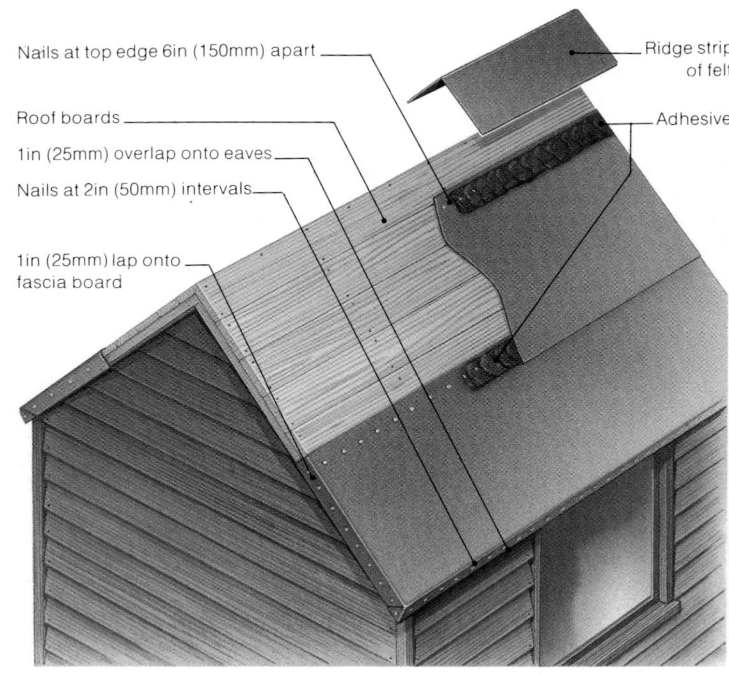

8 Repeat steps 1-7 to felt the other slope of the roof.

9 Measure the gap from the top of the felt on one side over the ridge to the top of the felt on the other side. Measure in several places. Take the highest figure, add on 6in (150mm) and cut a strip of felt this width and the length of the ridge plus 2in (50mm).

10 Lay the felt in place, centred over the ridge, and make a chalk line along each edge to show where to put adhesive. Remove the felt temporarily.

11 Brush strips of adhesive at least 3in (75mm) wide along each slope. Do not let adhesive spread below the chalk lines. Leave the adhesive to become tacky.

12 Lay the felt in place on the adhesive on one slope. Press it down firmly, then smooth it over the ridge and press the other edge in place. Run the batten over the felt on both slopes from the centre outwards to drive out air.

13 Nail the ends to the fascia boards at 2in (50mm) intervals. At the top angle, fold the surplus felt over neatly and drive a nail through the fold.

ONE-SLOPE ROOFS

Pent-style sheds – in which the roof consists of a single slope – can be felted by the same method. At the top of the slope, trim the felt to overlap 1in (25mm) onto the outside face of the batten and nail it there at 2in (50mm) intervals.

PATCHING DAMAGED FELT

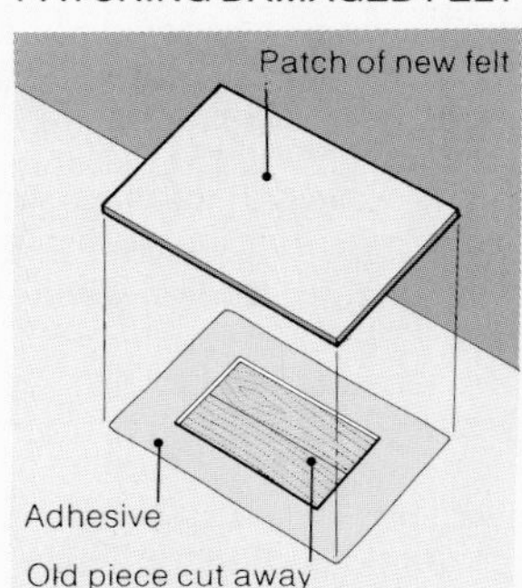

If only a small area of the felt is damaged, you can patch it with bituminous felt and cold felt adhesive.

1 Cut out a rectangle of felt that will cover the damage and extend beyond it by at least 3in (75mm) all round.

2 Position the patch over the damage and run a piece of chalk round it against the edge to mark the area for the adhesive.

3 Brush the adhesive over the marked area with an old paintbrush. Do not let it spread outside the chalked area or smears will show on the roof.

4 Leave the adhesive for 30 minutes to become tacky.

5 Lay the felt patch in position and press it down firmly from the centre to the edges to make sure no air bubbles are trapped under it.

What can go wrong with drainage and walls

GUTTERS

A gutter may leak at the joints between sections; it may become blocked and overflow; or it may sag so that water does not run away properly. In each case, water may soak into the wall and penetrate to the inside, causing damp and damage to the decoration. Even on a cavity wall, water may find a way from the outer to the inner leaf.

Cast-iron gutter sections are usually sealed with putty at joints and then bolted together. The putty may disintegrate in time and in extreme cases the bolts may rust and drop out. A plastic gutter may leak because the clip which seals two sections together has become loose, or because the neoprene gasket has perished, or because the gutter has an incorrect fall, and water spills over.

Sometimes screws holding gutter brackets to the fascia board rust away or the fascia board itself might rot, causing the brackets to move and the gutter sections to sag. For cleaning, aligning and repairing roof gutters, see pages 454–455.

DOWNPIPES

The most common problem with downpipes is that they become blocked – and if they (or the gutters leading to them) overflow or leak, damp may start in the walls.

Most downpipes first get blocked at the top and then are often obstructed farther down as the blockage sinks down the pipe under pressure of rain. For clearing blockages, see page 456.

Cast-iron pipes may crack if damp material stuck inside freezes. When they thaw the pipes will leak and the leaks may cause damage. For repairing cracked downpipes, see page 454.

EXTERNAL WALLS

Rain beating upon an external wall will be partially absorbed. Water from a dripping overflow pipe (page 336) may splash onto a wall.

Faults in a damp-proof course may allow water to rise from the ground and soak the wall. To install a damp-proof course, see page 462. Soil heaped over a damp-proof course can also cause damp.

Defective pointing will allow water to penetrate the outer leaf. For repointing, see page 460.

Excessive damp in an external wall should be dealt with as soon as possible before it can damage the interior. You can usually see the damp patch because the wet brickwork or masonry is a different colour from the dry parts.

BRICK WALLS

Facing brick naturally absorbs a certain amount of rainwater, which penetrates partly into the wall. When the weather dries up, the moisture evaporates and no harm is done. In older houses, some bricks may have become over-porous so that they do not dry completely. This could lead to damp penetrating indoors.

Problems also arise with cavity walls when the wall ties which link the outer and inner leaves are bridged by a build-up of mortar which was dropped during construction of the house. The mortar acts as a wick, carrying moisture across the cavity to form damp patches on the interior wall.

Cavity wall insulation can aggravate the problem because it prevents moisture from evaporating. For this reason, cavity walls should be free of all damp before you have the cavity insulated.

In most cases treating the external face of the wall with a silicone water repellent will cure the damp (page 460).

Mortar between bricks may become highly porous and carry water into the wall. This fault often becomes apparent after a freeze – as the water expands it breaks up the mortar, which will crumble and fall out of joints. for how to repair the damage, see page 460.

RENDERINGS

Cracks and gaps in a rendered surface may allow damp to penetrate and be held in the wall. In extreme cases, this can lead to blisters which must be cut away before the rendering is repaired. For repairing cracks, and patching rendering, see pages 460–461.

CLADDING

Timber cladding, which forms part of an exterior wall, must be protected by preservative or paint if it is not to be affected by damp, otherwise wet rot may set in (page 464). Plastic cladding is not affected by damp but gaps surrounding the cladding must be sealed. Follow the same procedure as for sealing gaps round window frames (page 213).

WINDOW AND DOOR FRAMES

Make sure there are no gaps around window and door frames (page 213). If rain soaks between the masonry and the frame, rot may set into the timber and must be removed (pages 210–211). Maintain the paintwork also (page 123) to prevent rot.

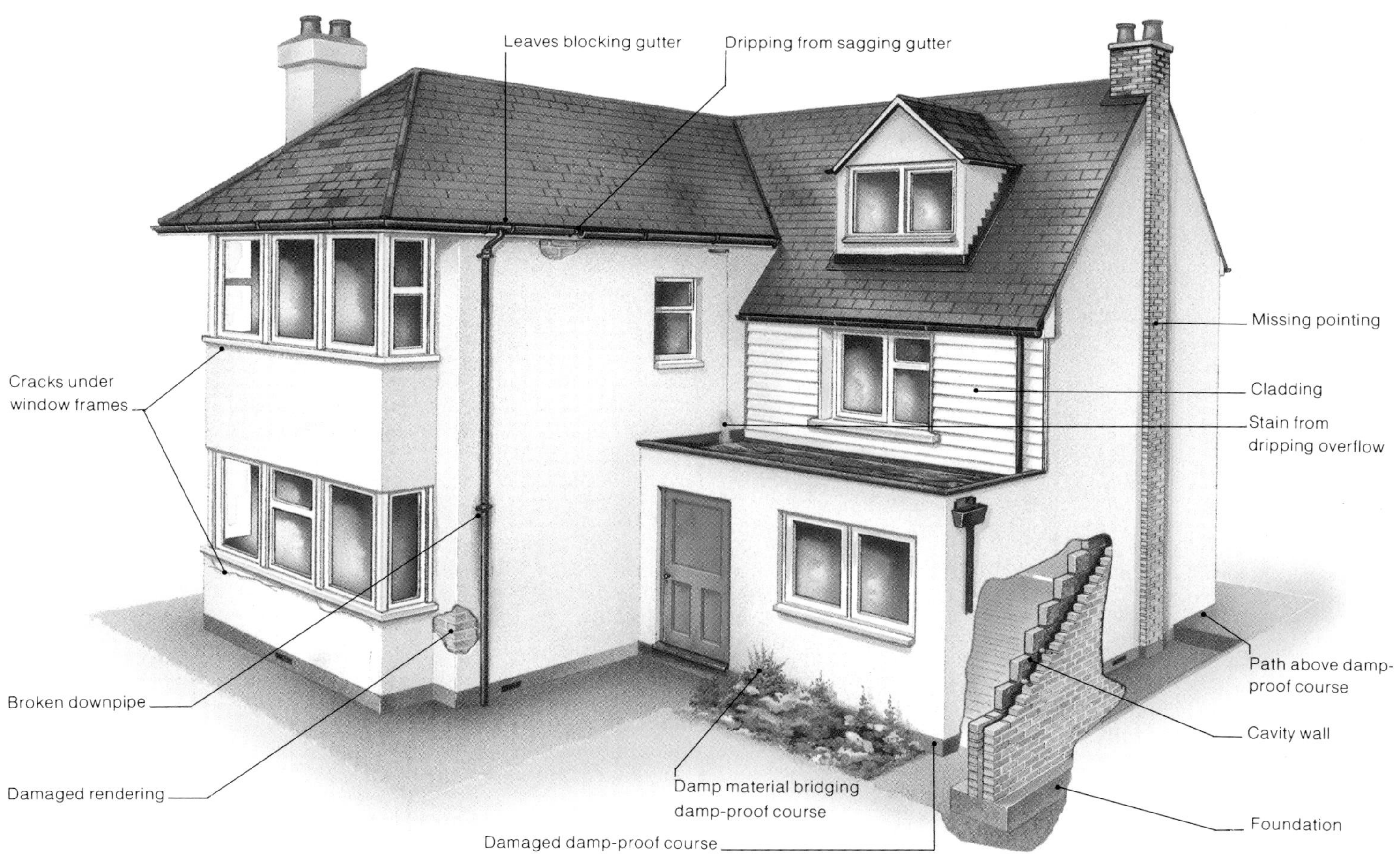

Cleaning an overflowing gutter

Gutters should be cleaned out and checked for damage each year. The job is best done in late autumn after all the leaves have fallen.

Wear sturdy work gloves to avoid scraping your hands on rough or rusty edges or on tiles or slates.

You will need
Tools Ladder with a stand-off bracket; protective gloves; small trowel; bucket; piece of hardboard or a large rag. Possibly a hosepipe.

1 Put the piece of hardboard at the bottom of the downpipe to prevent debris from getting into the gully or the drain, where it could cause a blockage.
ALTERNATIVELY, if the pipe goes direct into the ground, stuff the rag in the top of the downpipe.

2 Scoop out any silt, grit or other debris with the trowel and put it in the bucket. Take care not to let anything drop into the downpipe. Do not let any debris fall down the walls because it may cause stains that are hard to remove.

3 Remove the hardboard or rag and pour three or four buckets of water slowly into the gutter at the end farthest from the downpipe. Alternatively, use a hosepipe to lead water there. The water should flow quickly and smoothly to the downpipe, leaving the gutter empty.

If a pool of water remains, the gutter needs realigning to a correct angle of fall (below).

If the water leaks through cracks or bad joints, repair the gutter (facing page).

If the water starts to overflow at the downpipe, the pipe needs cleaning out (page 456).

4 Inspect metal gutters for signs of rust while you are cleaning them out. If you find any, treat it at once (bottom of this page).

Re-aligning a gutter

If water forms a pool even in a cleaned gutter instead of running away to the downpipe, the fixing screw holding the support bracket or the gutter itself at that point may be loose. Remove the screw, tap a wall plug into the screw hole and re-screw the bracket or gutter with a new zinc-plated screw.

If when you check you find that no screws are loose, or conversely that several are loose, the fall of the gutter needs correcting. You may have to remove a section of gutter to reach the screws.

You will need
Tools Ladder with a stand-off bracket; two or more 6in (150mm) nails; hammer; screwdriver; string and nails; drill with wood bit or high-speed-steel bit, or both.
Materials Wall plugs; zinc-plated No. 8 or 10 screws.

1 Drive a long, strong nail into the fascia board near each end of the loose section of gutter and immediately below it to support it. If the loose section is longer than 7ft (2m) or the gutter is iron, drive in more nails to give it sufficient support.

2 Remove the screws that hold the gutter or its supporting brackets.

3 Fix a string line along the length of the fascia board as described in *Replacing cast-iron guttering with plastic* (page 457), but put it immediately under the guttering. Give it a fall towards the downpipe of $\frac{1}{2}$in-$\frac{3}{4}$in (13mm-19mm) in every 10ft (3m).

4 If the gutter is on brackets, as most gutters are, unscrew those that are letting the gutter sag and move them slightly to new positions so that you can screw into solid wood; make sure the new screw positions align with the string line to give the correct fall.
ALTERNATIVELY, if the gutter is screwed direct to the fascia, raise it to align correctly with the string line and drill new holes through the gutter and into the fascia, about 2in (50mm) to the side of the original holes. Refit the gutter using new zinc-plated screws.
ALTERNATIVELY, if the screws through the gutter have been driven into the ends of the roof rafters, not into a fascia board, fix a string line and adjust the position of the screws to bring the gutter to the correct fall. You may have to remove a tile or slate temporarily so that you can reach the screws (pages 441 and 442).

Treating rusted gutters

Always wear safety spectacles to protect your eyes from flying particles when you are removing rust. Do not rub the metal unnecessarily – just remove the rust; do not try to make the metal shine as new. If the inside of the gutter cannot be seen from any upstairs window, you can use up left-over gloss paint of any colour instead of buying bitumen paint.

You will need
Tools Ladder with a stand-off bracket; safety spectacles; strong work gloves; wire brush or electric drill fitted with wire cup brush or wheel; emery cloth; paintbrush. Perhaps filling knife.
Materials Rust-neutralising primer; black bitumen paint or left-over gloss paint. Perhaps roof-and-gutter sealant or glass-fibre filler.

1 Rub off small rust spots with the emery cloth.

2 Clean away larger patches of rust with the wire brush or brush fitted in the drill.

3 Apply a coat of rust-neutralising primer to the cleaned parts; you can apply it to the rest of the inside of the gutter as well if you wish.

4 Seal any small cracks in the gutter with roof-and-gutter sealant.

5 If there is a larger crack or hole, fill it with a glass-fibre filler of the kind used for car body repairs. Be sure to smooth the filling thoroughly so there is no roughness to hold water or silt.

6 Apply two coats of black bitumen or gloss paint.

REPAIRS WITH EPOXY PASTE

You can make a sound and long-lasting repair to a minor crack in a metal gutter with self-adhesive flashing tape, or with an epoxy-based repair paste. Apply only a little paste to the inside of the gutter and use a filling knife to give it a perfectly smooth finish. If it is not smooth, debris can collect against it and cause the gutter to overflow. Make the repair mainly outside the gutter. You can make it even stronger by applying a patch of glass-fibre reinforcing material to the gutter's underside and fixing it in place with the epoxy paste; work the paste well into the glass-fibre patch and smooth it carefully. You can paint over the repair when it has hardened.

The same method will seal a crack in a metal downpipe. A pipe may be cracked by a heavy accidental blow – or by water freezing and expanding in it after being trapped by a blockage. Apply a thin layer of paste to the pipe, then cut out a strip of glass-fibre reinforcing material, wrap it round the pipe and cover it liberally with epoxy repair paste. Press the paste well into the material and smooth it carefully. Two coats of paint will make the repair almost unnoticeable once the paste has dried.

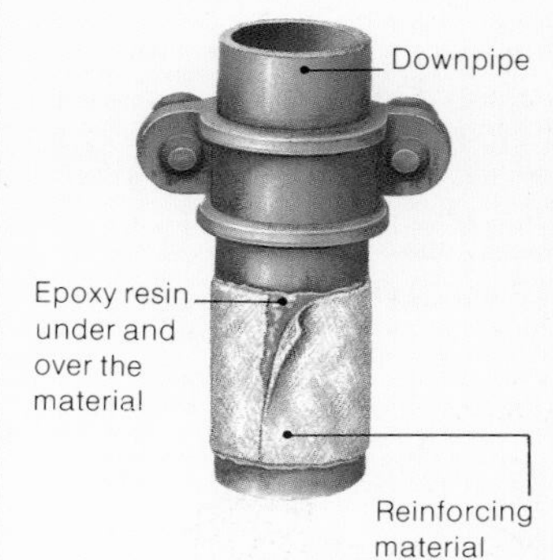

Repairing leaking gutter joints

Rainwater dripping through gutters and splashing the house walls will cause problems outside and in. A water stain will form on the outside wall and after a time moss and algae will grow there, disfiguring the wall. If the leak is not cured, damp will in the end penetrate the walls, causing damage indoors. Damp quickly ruins decorations and would eventually cause rot in timbers.

Sometimes you will spot a dripping gutter from indoors, but occasionally walk round the house during heavy rain to make a check.

LEAKING METAL GUTTERS

A metal gutter is difficult to take apart if the nuts and bolts have corroded, so try first to seal the leak by injecting roof-and-gutter sealant into the joint with an applicator gun. First scrape the joint clean and dry it with a hot-air gun.

If the leak persists, you will have to dismantle and reseal the joint. Wear strong gloves to protect your hands from rough metal.

You will need

Tools Ladder with a stand-off bracket; gloves; safety spectacles; spanner; hammer; wire brush; old chisel; small trowel; paintbrush; narrow-bladed filling knife. Perhaps a junior hacksaw and nail punch.

Materials Metal primer; roof-and-gutter sealant; nut and bolt of correct size.

1 Undo the nut securing the bolt in the joint piece.

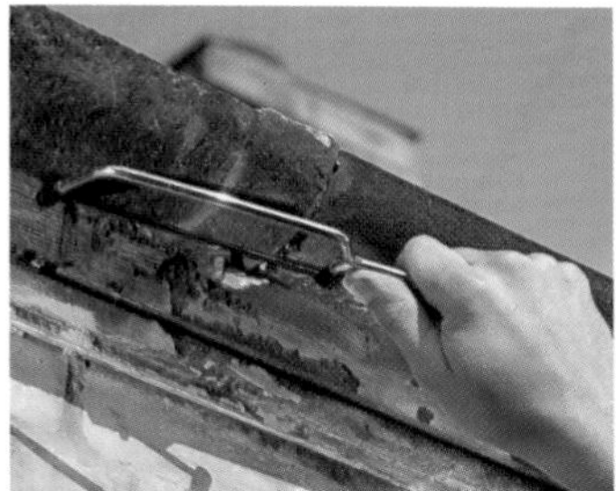

ALTERNATIVELY, if the nut will not move, cut through the bolt with a hacksaw and tap out the shank with the nail punch and hammer.

2 Carefully tap the joint piece with the hammer to separate it from the gutter sections.

3 With the joint dismantled, chisel away the old putty and clean rust from the whole joint area with the wire brush. Scoop away the debris with the trowel.

4 Apply a coat of metal primer to the gutter ends and the joint piece and leave it to dry.

5 Spread roof-and-gutter sealant onto the joint piece and reposition the gutter sections on it.

6 Secure the joint with the new nut and bolt.

LEAKING PLASTIC GUTTERS

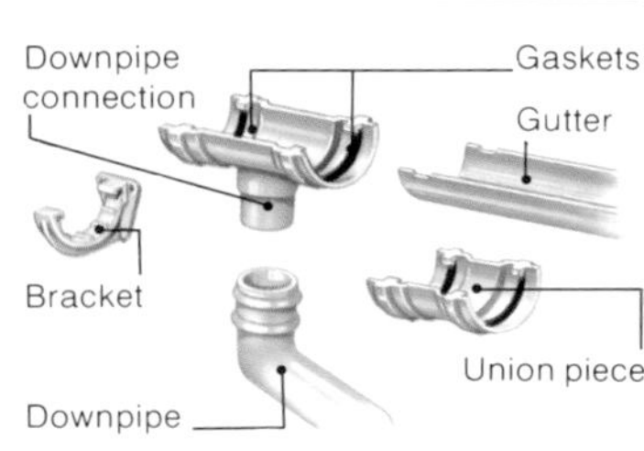

Where pieces of gutter join, or connect with a downpipe, they are clipped to a connector or union piece which has gaskets in it to make the union watertight.

Leakages may be caused by dirt forcing the seal slightly apart; this can be cured by cleaning. Squeeze the sides of the gutter inwards to release it from the union piece. If there is no dirt, the gaskets may need renewing.

You will need

Tools Ladder with a stand-off bracket; filling knife.

Materials New gaskets or roof-and-gutter sealant.

1 Squeeze the sides of the gutter sections to release them from the clips of the union piece.

2 Gently raise the end of each section of gutter in turn until you can see the gasket in the union piece. Peel the gasket away.

3 Fit the new gaskets, pressing them well into place.
ALTERNATIVELY, fill the grooves for the gaskets with sealant.

4 Gently squeeze each gutter section in at the sides to ease it back into the union piece clips.

Securing loose downpipes

A downpipe is held to the wall by retaining clips which are screwed into the mortar joints at intervals of about 3ft (1m). If the pipe is not firmly held, it can vibrate in strong winds, and the vibration can loosen its joints. The sections of downpipe slot loosely one into another; do not seal them together.

CAST-IRON PIPES

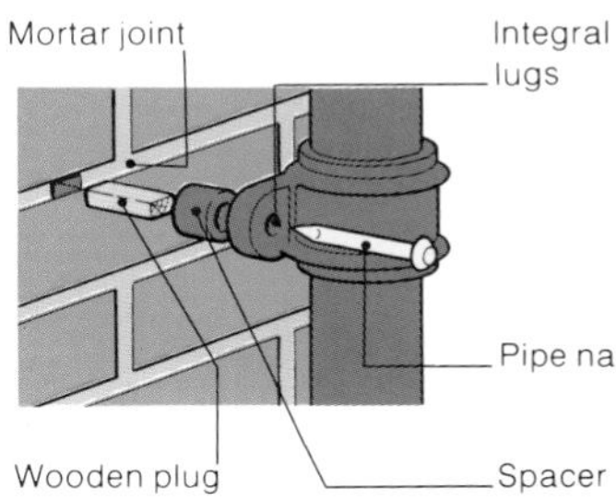

The lugs that hold cast-iron pipes are an integral part of the pipe and are fixed with large nails called pipe nails to wooden plugs inserted in the mortar joints. Either the nails or the plugs can come loose. If only the nails are loose, take them out and fill the hole with wood filler or insert a wall plug into it. Drive the pipe nails back in, or drive in 1½in (38mm) No. 10 galvanised screws instead.

If the wooden plugs in the wall have come loose or rotted; you will have to remove them and fix new ones.

You will need

Tools Ladder with stand-off bracket; pliers; saw; hammer. Perhaps a screwdriver.

Materials Softwood plugs slightly larger than the old ones; wood preservative. Perhaps 1½in (38mm) No. 10 galvanised screws.

1 Pull out the old pipe nails with the pliers. You can use the nails again if they come out undamaged.

2 Remove the spacers that hold the downpipe away from the wall and keep them on one side.

3 Remove one or more sections of pipe to give access to the plugs. Sections are slotted together. Raise one as high as it will go on the section above to free the lower end from the section below.

4 Take out and discard the plugs.

5 Cut new plugs, sawing and planing or chiselling them until they almost fit the holes.

Treat the plugs with wood preservative and tap them into place gently with a hammer.

6 Put back the piece or pieces of downpipe that you have removed.

7 Set the spacers in position behind each pair of lugs and drive the pipe nails through the holes to hold the downpipe securely.
ALTERNATIVELY, set the spacers in position and secure the lugs by driving galvanised screws through the holes.

PLASTIC DOWNPIPES

If a plastic downpipe comes loose from the wall, refix the screws. First

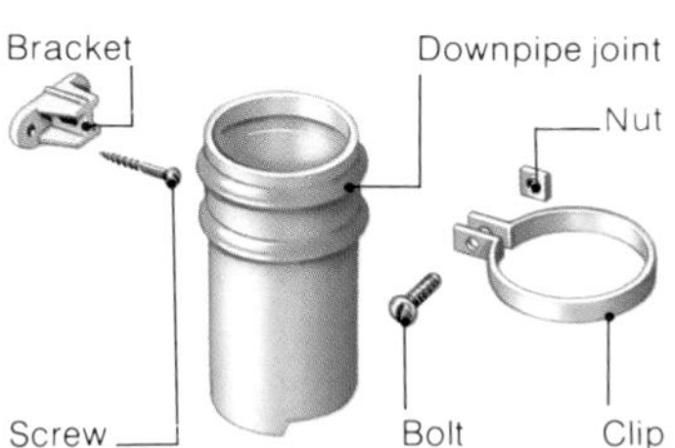

check the plastic or fibre wall plugs to see if they need renewing to give a better fixing. Use 1½in (38mm) No. 10 galvanised screws.

It might be easiest to move the clip up or down a little to a different mortar joint and drill and plug new holes to get a firm fixing. Repair the old holes with mortar or exterior filler. Try to match the colour of the rest of the mortar – using different colour sand or cement – to make the repair inconspicuous.

Do not move a clip fixed at a joint in the downpipe system because it strengthens the joint. You could exchange a one-piece clip for a two-piece clip, or vice-versa, to give different fixing positions for the screws.

Unblocking a downpipe

An overflow from a gutter may sometimes be caused by a blocked downpipe. The blockage could be a ball, a bird's nest or some other object that you can simply lift out. But the most likely obstruction is a collection of wind-blown leaves lodged in the mouth of the downpipe. A pipe with a swan-necked section at the top is more likely to become blocked than a straight downpipe.

Another indication of a blocked downpipe is water seeping out during heavy rain from a joint where sections of downpipe connect. Because the joints are loose, not sealed, you can tell straight away where the blockage is; it is in the section immediately below the leaking joint.

OBSTRUCTIONS NEAR THE TOP

If the downpipe is blocked near the top, you can usually clear it by probing with a length of wire – an opened-out coat hanger, for example. Put a piece of hardboard at the bottom of the pipe first to prevent any debris from falling into the drain. Hook out debris if you can; if you cannot, probe until it becomes looser. Flush away remaining loose debris by pouring buckets of water down the pipe or playing a strong jet of water down it from a hose. If the pipe is straight, not swan-necked, tie rags firmly to the end of a stick (such as a bamboo garden cane) to form a ball and push the obstruction loose with it.

OBSTRUCTIONS OUT OF REACH

Hire a flexible drain rod to clear an obstruction lower down a pipe or in a swan-necked pipe. Or as a last resort, dismantle the lower part of the downpipe.

You will need

Tools Ladder with a stand-off bracket; screwdriver or pliers or box spanner; long stick. Perhaps a cold chisel and claw hammer.

1 On a plastic downpipe, remove the screws that hold the pipe clips to the wall. Work from the bottom and remove the screws and clips up to the point where water seeps from the downpipe. If the pipe is held by two-part brackets, undo the bolts holding the rings to the back plates; leave the back plates in place.

If the pipe is cast-iron, use pliers to pull out the large pipe nails that hold the lugs to the wall. If they are rusted in, use a cold chisel and claw hammer to prise the lugs away from the wall; keep the nails for re-fixing the pipe.

2 As you free the clips or lugs that hold it, raise each section of pipe enough to free it from the section below and lift it away from the wall.

3 Use a long stick to push out any obstructions inside the sections.

4 Replace the pipe section by section, working from the top down, and screw or bolt back in place the clips (or nail the lugs) that hold the section to the wall.

PREVENTING BLOCKAGES

Wire or plastic covers are sold for fitting in the mouths of downpipes. They are made in different sizes, so measure the diameter of the downpipe mouth before buying one.

If there is a hopper at the top of the downpipe, fit fine-mesh wire netting over the top, securing it with fine galvanised wire.

If there are large deciduous trees nearby, it may be worth spending time covering the gutters. You can lay a strip of plastic netting over the gutter to overlap the top by about 2in (50mm) at each side. About every 3ft (1m) along it, thread a length of twine through the overlaps from the underside of the gutter and tie it firmly to hold the mesh taut.

Check the surface of covers or netting regularly during autumn; if wet leaves coat it, rainwater cannot enter the gutter and will spill over it.

Planning a plastic gutter system

Several similar systems of black, white, brown or grey plastic guttering are made; they differ mainly in the way the lengths of gutter are joined. In some systems, lengths of gutter overlap and clip into support brackets; in others, a union piece connects lengths of gutter and may or may not have a bracket.

Gutters are rounded or square in cross-section. Most types are clipped onto brackets which support them from below, but some square styles have brackets fixed above them. Five widths of gutter are made to give different carrying capacities to suit the area of roof draining into it. An undersized gutter will not cope with heavy rain. If you are replacing an old gutter system, use the same size as before, or a size that is slightly larger.

Measure the total length round the fascia to estimate how much guttering to buy. Measure the height from the gutter down to the gully to estimate how much pipe to buy for each downpipe.

You will need a variety of fittings to connect the parts and hold them in place – for example, unions, angled pieces for corners, support brackets, downpipe brackets and downpipe shoes.

Adaptors will link plastic guttering to cast-iron, larger plastic guttering to smaller sizes, and rounded to square section guttering. It is not always possible to link one manufacturer's guttering to another's.

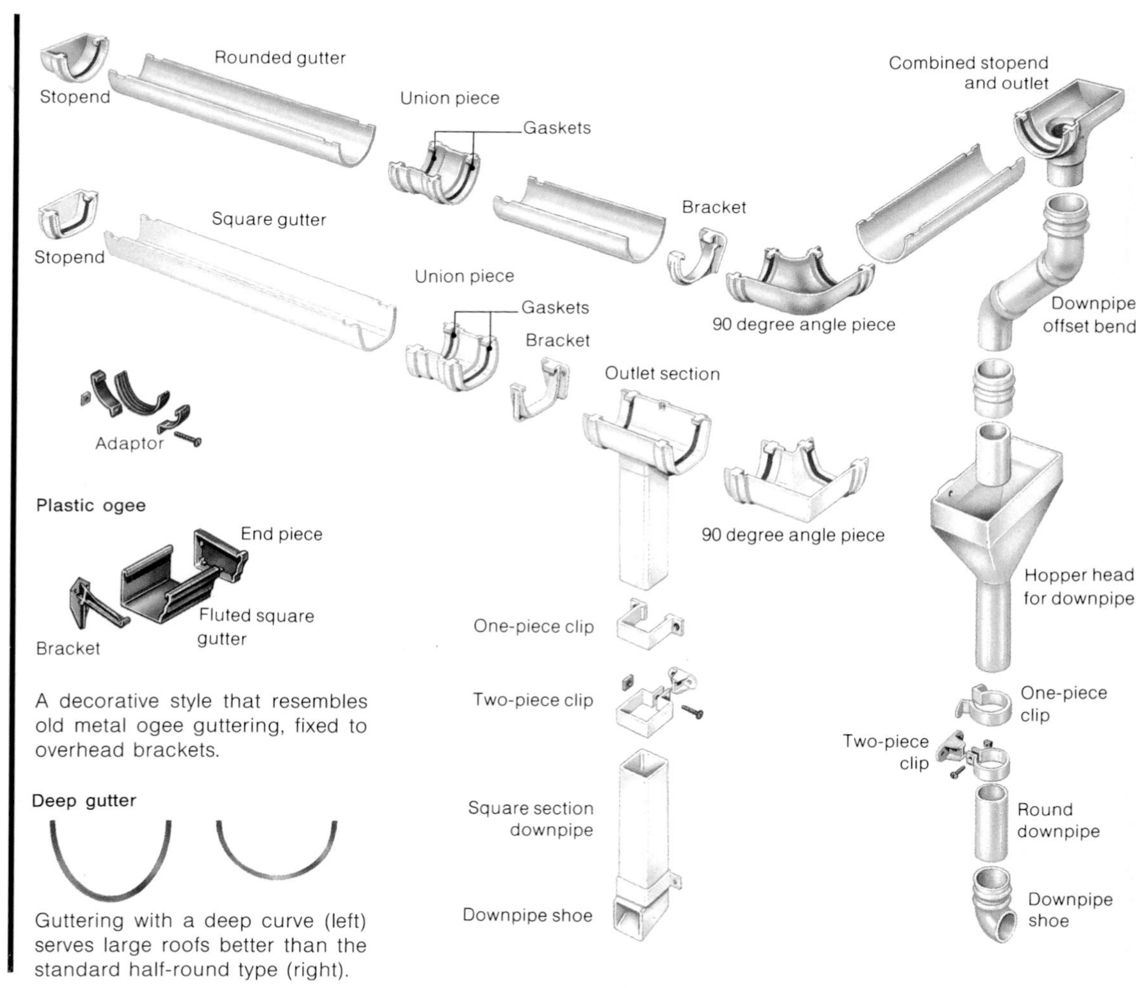

A decorative style that resembles old metal ogee guttering, fixed to overhead brackets.

Guttering with a deep curve (left) serves large roofs better than the standard half-round type (right).

Replacing cast-iron guttering with plastic

When a cast-iron guttering and downpipe system becomes too rusty to repair, you will have to replace it. Plastic guttering is easier and cheaper to fit in its place and needs no painting. Wear strong work gloves to handle the cast-iron; rusty edges can cause nasty cuts.

You will need

Tools Ladder with a stand-off bracket; gloves; spanner; hacksaw; nail punch; claw hammer; rope; large screwdriver; small blowtorch; slim masonry chisel; string line and nails; plumb line; steel measuring tape; file; drill with masonry bit; pointing trowel; filling knife; paintbrush; chalk. Perhaps a gutter notching tool and.a wrecking bar.

Materials Plastic gutter; union pieces; brackets with 1in (25mm) No. 8 galvanised screws; stopends; gutter outlet section; downpipe; offset bends; solvent cement; pipe clips with $1\frac{1}{2}$in (38mm) No. 10 galvanised screws; wall plugs; mortar for pointing; filler and paint for fascia board. Perhaps gutter angle; downpipe shoe.

REMOVING OLD GUTTERS AND PIPES

The cast-iron sections, which may be 7ft-10ft (2m-3m long), are very heavy and difficult to handle when you are standing on a ladder. Take great care and, if possible, have a helper to support each section and help you to lower it to the ground by rope.

1 Try with a spanner to undo the bolts holding the gutter sections together. If you cannot, cut through each bolt with the hacksaw, then tap its shank upwards with a nail punch and hammer to free it.

2 Give sharp hammer taps at the joints where the sections meet. They will be sealed together with old putty or mastic.

3 Tie a rope round the middle of each gutter section as you free it, then lift it off the brackets and lower it to a helper who can steer it clear of windows and walls below.

4 Try with a screwdriver to undo the screws holding the brackets to the fascia board. If they are rusted in, heat the heads with a narrow blowtorch flame to expand the metal and break the grip of the rust. If the screws still will not turn, prise the brackets away from the board and pull the screws out with them. Use a slim masonry chisel and claw hammer to prise them off.

5 Take out the pipe nails holding the downpipe lugs to the wall. Use pliers or, if the nails are rusted in, use a wrecking bar to prise the lugs away from the wall. Work down the wall and as you free each pair of lugs, remove the section of downpipe. It is slotted into the section below and can be lifted out.

6 Use the masonry chisel and hammer to take out the wooden blocks from the wall.

7 If the downpipe goes directly into the ground to connect with a gully, break up the concrete or other surround to free it.

TAKING DOWN OGEE GUTTERING

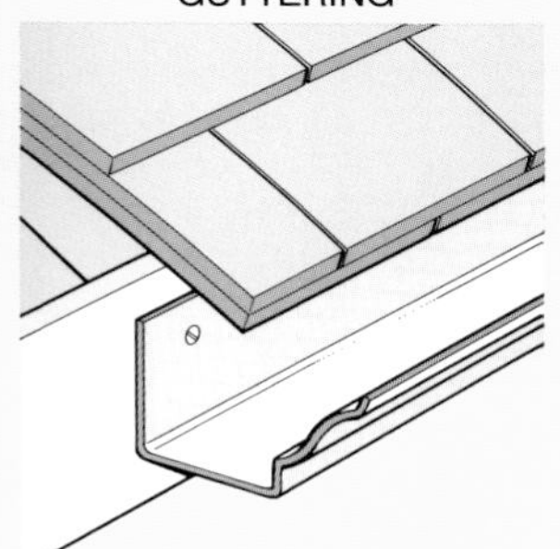

Ogee guttering does not rest on brackets but is screwed direct to the fascia board through its straight back. It is unwise to take it down without a helper. Once you take out the screws from one end, the gutter is unsupported and its weight will unbalance you. Even with a helper to support the gutter section, it is best to work from a scaffold tower, which you can hire. Anchor the tower firmly before tackling each section of gutter. Separate the gutter joints and remove the screws as for other types of cast-iron guttering.

REPAIRS AND PREPARATIONS

1 Repair the fascia board with exterior filler if necessary, before repainting it (page 125).

2 Repair damaged pointing where necessary (see *Repointing a wall*, page 460).

3 Nail a plumb line to drop from the fascia to the gully where the downpipe will discharge. Mark its position with chalk on the fascia and wall, then remove it.

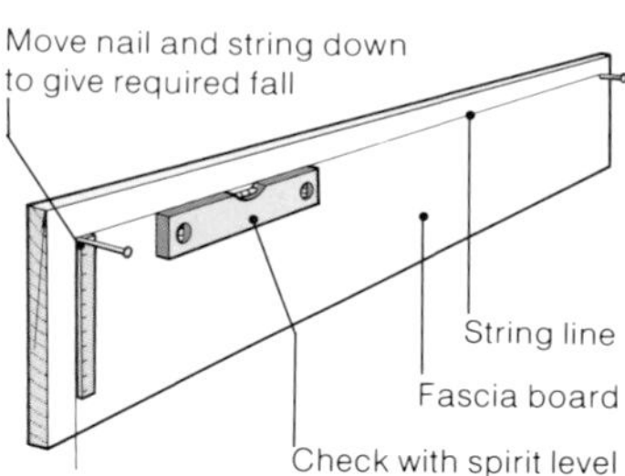

4 Fix a taut string line as a guide for positioning the brackets. Fit it as close up to the tiles or slates as you can. Run it from the downpipe position to the farthest point of the guttering that will drain into it. This may be at the end of the fascia board or at an angle in the guttering. Check with a spirit level that the string is horizontal, and mark its level at the downpipe position with chalk. Then lower the string at the chalk-mark end by the amount needed to give the correct fall and fix it taut with a nail. The fall should be $\frac{1}{2}$in-$\frac{3}{4}$in (13mm-19mm) for every 10ft (3m).

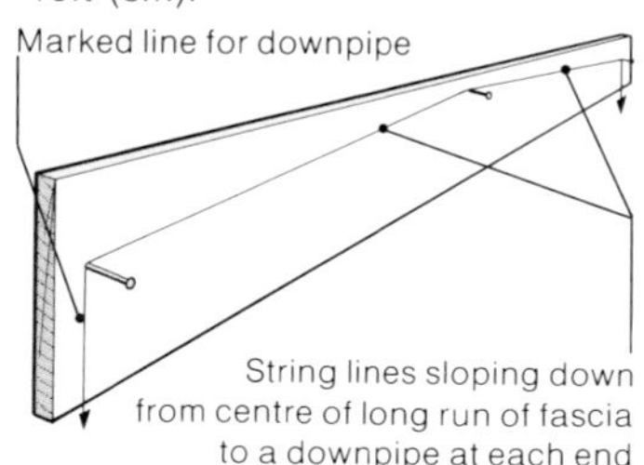

A long stretch of gutter may have a downpipe at each end. Fix the string line with its highest point in the centre and a fall towards each downpipe. If the outlet is in the middle of a run of gutter, fix string lines at both sides of it.

FITTING THE NEW GUTTERING

1 Screw a bracket in place on the fascia 8in (200mm) from the mark at the downpipe position. Align its top with the string line.

2 Screw another bracket in place 6in (150mm) from the other end of the run of guttering, aligning it with the string line at the top.

3 Space out brackets equally between these two at intervals of not more than 24in (610mm).

ALTERNATIVELY, assemble the gutter on the ground and measure exactly the distance from the centre of the downpipe outlet to the centre of the union piece joining the gutter sections – and from this point to the centre of the next union piece. Mark these distances on the fascia and screw brackets there, aligning their tops with the string. Each join will be supported by a bracket and you can then space out the brackets between at intervals of up to 3ft (1m). The measuring has to be very precise and it is often simpler to use more brackets.

4 Clip the gutter, section by section, into the brackets, fitting union pieces where necessary to join the sections. Make sure that the sections are well pressed into place. Lodge the back edge of the gutter under the bracket clip first, then press the front edge down under the other clip.

5 The final section of gutter will have to be cut. Cut it on the ground after measuring off a piece of the right length. If it runs to the end of the fascia, let it extend 2in (50mm) beyond the end of the fascia board. Cut it with a hacksaw and smooth the cut with a file.

Replacing cast-iron guttering with plastic (continued)

6 Use either a gutter notching tool or a file to cut notches in the gutter rims for the stopend clips to engage in. Fit the stopend, and clip the gutter onto its bracket and into the union piece holding it to the adjoining section.

7 If there is guttering at both sides of the outlet, fit the second run in the same way as the first.

FITTING THE DOWNPIPE

1 Measure the length of pipe needed to slope inwards from the gutter outlet to the wall. Cut pipe to this length.

2 Push the offset bends onto the pipe ends and hold this zigzag unit in position at the gutter outlet to test the fit. The lower offset bend should have its outlet the right distance from the wall to accommodate the pipe clip. Saw off more pipe if necessary to achieve the right fit.

3 Clean and wash the pipe ends and the sockets of the bends.

4 With the zigzag section held together again, make a chalk mark along the pipe and onto each offset section to show the correct alignment. Take the unit apart.

5 Apply solvent cement outside the pipe ends and inside the sockets of the bends. Assemble the parts again, lining up the chalk marks.

6 Push the zigzag unit onto the bottom of the gutter outlet.

7 Hold a downpipe section in position over the bottom of the zigzag unit. See whether the top of the downpipe section is in line with a mortar joint. If not, measure how much it needs to be raised. Saw off this amount plus ⅜in (10mm) from the bottom of the zigzag unit. The extra ⅜in (10mm) leaves a gap to allow for expansion of the pipe in hot weather.

8 Mark, drill and plug holes in the mortar joint to screw the pipe clip into. The distance apart of the screw holes depends on the type of clip you are using. Hold the clip against the wall to make marks through the holes as guides for drilling.

9 Measure down the chalk mark on the wall to mark the position for drilling holes for the next pipe clip. You may have to cut the bottom end of the section of downpipe to align the clip with a mortar joint. Remember to cut off the extra ⅜in (10mm) again to create an expansion gap inside the socket.

10 At the bottom, cut the pipe so that the shoe will be about 2in (50mm) clear of the gully. You may need to lift out the drain grid while you fit the shoe. If the pipe goes direct into the ground, allow enough pipe to do this.

11 Drill and plug holes for brackets between the joints of downpipe sections, spacing them equally not more than 3ft (1m) apart and aligning them with mortar joints.

12 When all the holes are drilled and plugged screw the pipe clips in place.

13 If the downpipe goes direct into a gully underground, repair the concrete or other surround.

Cleaning and maintaining a gully

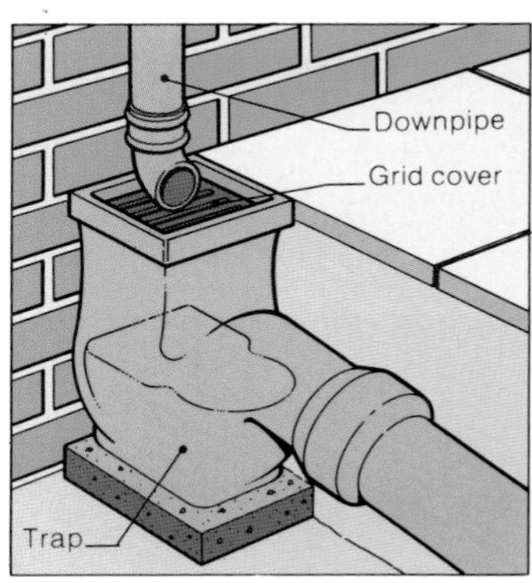

A gully is an underground U-trap – a much larger version of the trap beneath a sink. Anything small enough to pass through the grid cover enters the trap below. A build-up of leaves, silt, grease and other waste can create a blockage and prevent water running away from the gully into the drain.

Sometimes just a choked grid cover is causing the overflow. Try probing with a stick or garden fork to dislodge the blockage. If you cannot move it, wear rubber gloves to lift out the cover, or hook it out with a bent wire. Clean it thoroughly before you replace it.

Prevent future blockages by putting a cover on the gully. Cut it from outdoor-grade plywood ½in-¾in (13mm-19mm) thick. Make a hole for the pipe to pass through. Place the plywood on the brick surround of the gully with a brick or other weight on it to hold it in place. If the pipe stops short of the gully, add a short section to lengthen it enough to pass it through the plywood (see *Fitting the downpipe*, above).

If there is no brick surround to the gully entry, it is worth making one (see *Laying bricks or walling blocks*, page 483). It will serve as a well to retain small amounts of water if there is a minor blockage, and will prevent splashing or flooding of the surrounding area.

If the water does not clear away from an overflowing gully when you remove rubbish from the grid cover, the gully itself may be blocked. Put on a long rubber glove or put your arm in a plastic bag with no holes in it. Take off the grid cover and scoop out the blockage with your protected hand, or use an old soup ladle or an empty food tin as a scoop. If the obstruction is too firm to scoop out, break it down with a bent wire or a small old garden trowel bent to a right angle.

Fitting a cover

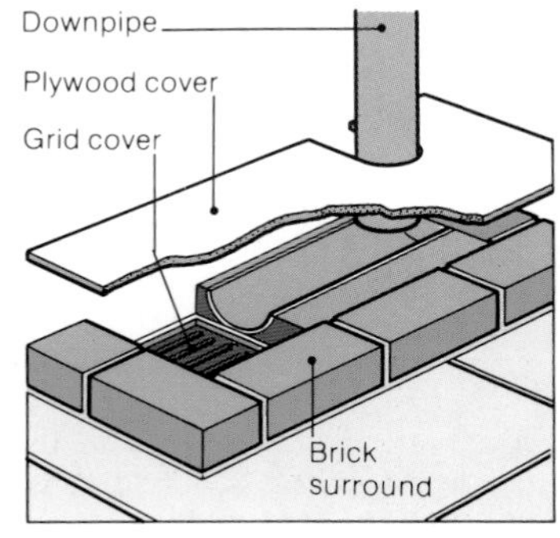

When the gully is cleared, scrub the sides with a disposable nylon pan scrubber and hose them down with a fierce jet of water. Throw away the plastic bag and any tins you have used. Hose down any gloves and the trowel or other tools thoroughly and rub them over with household disinfectant.

If you cannot find an obstruction in the gully, there may be an obstruction farther along the drain; see *Clearing blocked drains*, page 459.

REPAIRING A GULLY CHANNEL

A channel sometimes runs along parallel with the house wall to lead water into a gully entrance or hold water that comes too fast for the gully to take instantly. The channel can crack or become loose. The rendering around it can also crack or develop hollows where water lodges and stagnates.

Repair damaged rendering with a mix of 4 parts sand to 1 part cement, with PVA added for a better bond; or buy a small bag of dry-mix sand-cement mortar to use instead, but add PVA according to the maker's instructions to improve adhesion. Give the repair a smooth finish so water does not collect.

RENEWING A DAMAGED CHANNEL

You will have to chip out the old one and the surrounding brick and rendering. You can cut a glazed earthenware pipe in half for a channel, or you can buy ready-made channelling. Use the same mortar mix as for repairs (left).

You will need

Tools Chalk; cold chisel; club hammer; piece of hardboard; trowel.
Materials Bricks; glazed earthenware pipe or channelling; mortar.

1 To cut the pipe or channelling to length, first measure and mark the length at several points round the pipe and join the marks with a chalk line. Lay the pipe on a heap of sand and use the chisel and hammer to chip round it along the marked line until it breaks off.

2 If you are cutting a pipe in half lengthways, mark two cutting lines along the sides with chalk. Chip along them with the chisel and hammer until the pipe breaks open.

3 Put hardboard over the gully to prevent debris from getting in.

4 Chip out the damaged channel and the mortar and any bricks round it. If the bricks round the gully entrance are damaged, chip these out as well. Brush up the debris.

5 Mix the mortar.

6 Spread a thick layer of mortar where the channel will lie. Bed down the channel on it, setting it so that it slopes slightly towards the gully. Check with a spirit level that it is sloping correctly.

7 Lay a course of bricks (see *Laying bricks or walling blocks*, page 483) on edge to make a little retaining wall round the channel and gully. Set them on a bed of mortar and leave a gap of at least 1in (25mm) between the channel and the bricks alongside it. Nearer the gully the gap may need to be wider.

8 Fill the gap between the channel and the bricks with mortar.

9 Slope the mortar smoothly up to the brick surround and make sure there are no hollows to trap water.

Clearing blocked drains

INSPECTION CHAMBER OVER AN ANGLE IN PIPE

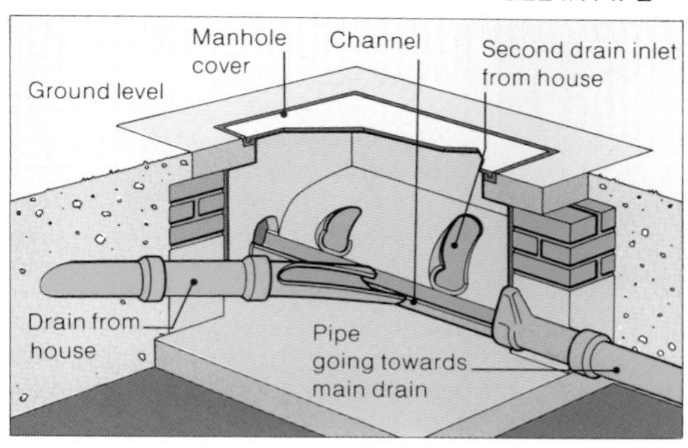

INSPECTION CHAMBER NEAR BOUNDARY

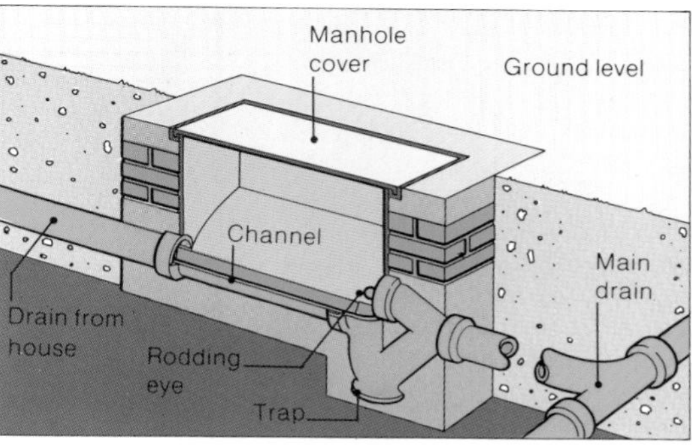

Below ground, pipes carry water and waste from the house to the main drain outside the boundary of the property, or to a cesspool or septic tank. Rainwater may be led separately into the drain or into a soakaway.

The pipes below ground are laid in straight lines for as much of their route as possible. Where a change of direction is needed, the bend should be less than a right angle and there should be an inspection chamber there. There will also be an inspection chamber near your boundary before the house drain joins the main drain. A manhole cover identifies the chambers.

The first sign of a blocked drain may be the failure of lavatories and baths to drain quickly and efficiently, or an overflowing inspection chamber or gully. A gully may be cleared by cleaning (facing page). Otherwise you will have to clear the drain with rods. You can hire rods and various heads. Wear rubber gloves for the work.

You will need
Tools Drain rods fitted with a 4in (100mm) diameter rubber plunger; pair of long rubber gloves; strong garden spade; hose; disinfectant; watering can.

1 Locate the blockage. You will have to lift the manhole covers; a strong garden spade will raise the edge enough for you to grasp the cover. Inspect the chamber that is nearer to the main drain, septic tank or cesspool than the overflowing chamber or gully. If it is empty, the blockage is in the drain between this chamber and the higher one or the gully. If the chamber is full, inspect the chamber next nearest to the main drain or septic tank. If the chamber nearest the main drain is full, the blockage is between it and the main drain. If the drain leads to a septic tank and the last chamber is full, have the tank emptied.

2 To clear the blockage in a main drain system, insert the rod fitted with the plunger into a chamber at one end of the blocked section; it does not matter which of the two. If it is the empty chamber, you can see where the mouth of the pipe is, but if you work from the full chamber, you will have to probe with the plunger until you find the mouth.

3 Add more rods as necessary to work the plunger along the pipe to the blockage. Always turn the rods clockwise as you work; if you turn them anticlockwise, they may unscrew and be left in the drain to cause a greater problem. Keep pushing against the obstruction and then withdrawing the plunger a little way. If this will not shift the blockage, withdraw the rods and exchange the plunger for a corkscrew attachment, which will break up a tightly packed obstruction.

4 Complete the clearance by directing a strong jet of water down the drain from a hosepipe, or by filling the bath and sink and releasing the water in one gush.

5 Hose down the rods and gloves thoroughly and drench them with diluted disinfectant poured from a watering can.

TESTING DRAINS

If the drains are not blocked but a persistent foul smell or unexpectedly wet ground make you suspect that there is a leak somewhere, arrange for the environmental health department to test the drains. You can get in touch with the department at your local authority offices.

CLEARING THROUGH THE RODDING EYE

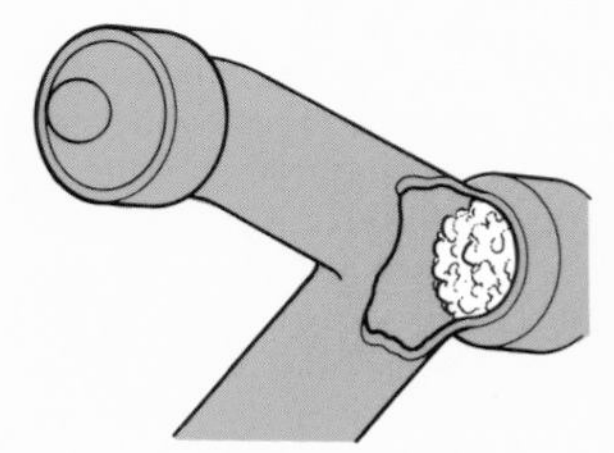

If you have to clear a blockage between the last inspection chamber on your property and the main drain, you will have to insert the rods through the rodding eye. At this chamber, the drain does not simply pass through; it drops through a U-trap similar to the one in a gully. The trap is there to prevent waste from the main drain entering your house drains, but it also prevents you from pushing rods through.

Above the mouth of the trap there is a short projection of pipe with a plug in it. When you locate and pull out the plug, you can insert the drain rods through the hole, which is the rodding eye. The trap, however, may still be blocked and you will have to scoop out the blockage with an empty food can or an old garden trowel bent to a right angle.

When the chamber and trap are clear, hose them down thoroughly to make sure that waste can flow out easily. You can replace the plug but many people prefer not to; if it should fall out accidentally, it could drop into the trap and cause a blockage. Instead, you can mortar a piece of tile over the eye. If you need to open the rodding eye again, the tile will knock off easily with a crowbar and hammer. If the hole has been filled with cement, you can still break through, but it will be difficult.

Minor repairs to walls

REPOINTING A WALL

Where mortar joints in a wall are cracked or crumbling, use a raking-out tool or a club hammer and plugging chisel to take out the old mortar to a depth of about ½in (13mm) ready for repointing.

A problem when you are patching a number of joints is to match the colour of the mortar with that of the surrounding joints. The only way to do this is to experiment with a few different mortar mixes (page 481), using varying amounts of sand and lime. Take a note of each mix and repoint a few joints at a time. Wait a week or two for the mortar to dry thoroughly and show its final colour before you decide on the best mix to complete the job.

Carry out repointing in the same way as pointing (page 484), matching the shape with the surrounding joints. Before you apply new mortar, clean any dust from the joints then brush water into them. If you do not damp them, the joints will soak up moisture from the mortar and cause it to dry out too fast.

DEALING WITH A CRACK

Mortar is intentionally made to be weaker than bricks or masonry so that it offers less resistance if there is any strain on the wall caused by movement beneath the foundations. The mortar will crack before the bricks or masonry.

A single crack confined to a mortar joint, even through several courses, usually indicates a limited amount of soil settlement. A repair can be made by repointing (see left).

A brick or stone may be cracked by a severe blow. You can replace it yourself (see right). If a crack runs through more than the odd brick or stone, there is a more serious strain on the foundations. Get a professional builder to deal with the problem as soon as possible.

RENEWING A BRICK OR STONE

Remove a loose or damaged brick or stone by chipping away the surrounding mortar with a club hammer and cold chisel. It may be difficult to get a matching replacement. You may be able to use the old brick or stone (dressed if necessary) the opposite way round if it is not too badly damaged.

Dampen the cavity by brushing it liberally with water. Spread mortar on the base of the cavity and on the top and sides of the brick or stone.

Tap the brick or stone into the cavity with the trowel handle. When it is properly seated, trim away the excess mortar. Point the joints to match the others on the wall.

DEALING WITH EFFLORESCENCE

The white powdery deposit called efflorescence is caused by dampness, which draws chemical salts from the bricks or mortar to the surface. It is harmless, and will disappear from a newly built wall once it has dried out.

You can discourage efflorescence by coating a wall with a silicone-based water repellent (below). If efflorescence does form, brush it off or treat it with a chemical masonry cleaner available from a builders' merchant. Do not wash off efflorescence; the damp aggravates the problem.

FUNGAL GROWTH

Where a wall has been very damp – perhaps from a neglected leak dripping from a gutter or cracked downpipe – fungal growth may form on the wall. Make sure that the source of the damp has been cured then scrape off the growth with a wire brush. To prevent it from growing again, apply a proprietary fungicide, following the manufacturer's instructions.

Keeping out damp with silicone water repellent

Silicone water repellent will normally cure damp problems on external walls. It prevents rain from getting into the brick and yet it allows the wall to 'breathe' so that moisture already in the material can evaporate.

Efflorescence – salts in the form of white powder which are drawn out of brick and mortar by damp – is also less likely to occur after the wall has been treated.

If damp patches persist after the repellent has been applied, get professional advice. Opening up a wall to clean the wall ties is not a DIY job.

You will need

Tools Bucket of water; wire brush; a clean old paintbrush, 4in-6in (100mm-150mm) wide; paint kettle. Perhaps a ladder.

Materials Silicone water repellent such as Aquaseal 66; white spirit for cleaning brush.

1 Clean the surface with water and the wire brush. Wait until you can see that the surface has dried.

2 Tape paper over the window glass, frame and ledges. You will not be able to remove splashes of silicone from them. Cover any part of a drive or path adjoining the wall you are treating. The silicone could otherwise cause blotches.

3 Pour the repellent into the paint kettle and apply a generous amount of the liquid with an old paintbrush, so that you can see it flowing down the wall.

4 If the surface soaks up all the liquid – because it is very porous – apply a second coat before the first coat dries.

5 Use white spirit to clean the paintbrush and the paint kettle when the job is finished.

Repairing cracks on rendered house walls

Hairline crazing on the surface of rendering does not need filling. Exterior quality wall paint will fill the crazing. Cracks that go deeper than the surface do need filling to keep the wall weatherproof. The repair will show until the wall is repainted; an invisible repair is impossible to achieve.

Fill the cracks with exterior filler or with rendering. Filler is convenient but uneconomical for more than one or two cracks. You can buy dry-mixed rendering in small quantities or you can make your own (page 481), using 6 parts plastering sand to 1 part cement and adding 1 part hydrated lime or PVA (a liquid plasticiser) to keep the mortar pliable.

You will need

Tools Filling knife; brush; wet sponge or cloth; old paintbrush. Perhaps a bolster chisel and club hammer and a ladder.

Materials PVA adhesive; rendering or exterior filler.

1 Draw the edge of a filling knife through the crack to form it into a V with the point of the V at the surface of the rendering and the wider part against the wall.

You can use a bolster chisel and club hammer instead of the filling knife if you find it easier.

The shape will anchor the filler below the surface and the crack is unlikely to open again.

2 Brush out the fragments and dust from the cavity to leave it as clean as possible.

3 Wet the cavity with a sponge or cloth dipped in water.

4 Paint all the inside of the cavity with PVA adhesive to improve adhesion of the filler.

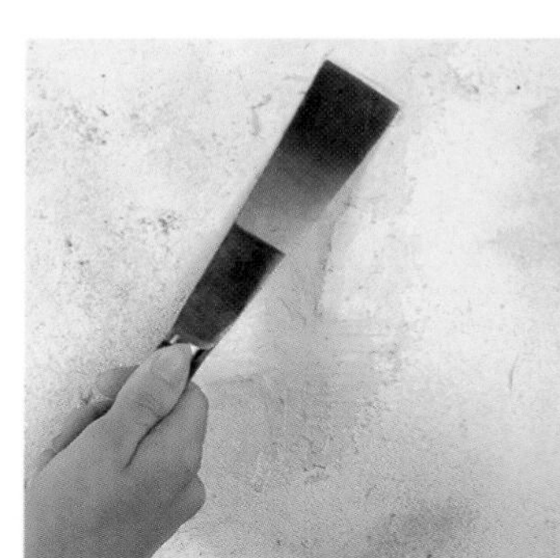

5 Press the filler or rendering into the crack with the filling knife. Prod the knife into the cavity to make sure there are no air pockets in it. Smooth the filling level with the wall surface.

Patching large holes in rendering

When large slabs of rendering fall away from the wall, it is usually because a weak rendering mix has been used and become porous, or because damp has penetrated behind the layer of rendering, perhaps through a crack. Sometimes the rendering may appear intact, when in fact it has separated from the wall behind.

Check the rendering from time to time, tapping it lightly with a hammer; undamaged areas will make a dead sound while defective areas give a hollow sound or fall away.

Carry out rendering work in mild weather. Frost can freeze the water in the rendering, which may cause premature cracking.

PREPARING THE RENDERING

Mix the rendering (page 481) from six parts plastering sand, one part cement and one part hydrated lime. Do not use builders' sand or the rendering will crack when it dries out. Use enough water to make the mixture easy to work with – not too stiff, not too sloppy.

Mix up small batches at a time. The rendering will become too stiff to spread after about 20 minutes. It is applied in two coats – a thick undercoat called the floating coat, and a thinner finishing coat.

You will need

Tools Bolster chisel; club hammer; brush; wet sponge or cloth; steel plastering trowel; old pointed trowel or square of wood with nails driven through to project at about 1½in (38mm) intervals; straight-edged length of wood longer than the width of the patch; damp sponge or clean wooden float. Perhaps a ladder and a plugging chisel.

Materials Rendering.

1 Cut away any loose rendering to leave a sound edge round the patch. Use the bolster chisel and hammer.

2 Clean out any crumbling joints in the brickwork or masonry. Clean them out to a depth of ½in (13mm) with the plugging chisel and club hammer.

3 Brush out all debris and dust.

4 Wet the area to be repaired thoroughly with a sponge or cloth soaked in water. This prevents the rendering from losing moisture into the wall and drying too quickly – which could cause crumbling later.

5 Apply the first coat of rendering. Take some of the mixture on the steel trowel with the handle downwards. Spread it onto the wall, starting from the bottom of the patch and pressing the lower edge of the trowel hard against the wall as you sweep it smoothly upwards. Continue to spread on trowel loads until the rendering is smooth and about ¼in (6mm) below the level of the wall surface. Mix more batches of rendering as necessary.

6 As the rendering begins to stiffen – after about 20 minutes – scratch a criss-cross of lines in it with the old trowel or spiked wood to make a key for the top coat.

7 Leave the first coat to dry for at least 14 hours.

8 Apply the finishing coat. Use the same rendering mixture as for the floating coat. Take some of the rendering on the steel trowel and apply it at the top left of the patch. Sweep the trowel lightly across from left to right to spread the rendering over the area. Leave the rendering standing slightly proud of the surface.

9 Continue applying trowel loads from top to bottom down the patch spreading them from left to right. Mix more small batches of rendering as necessary, but work quickly.

10 Just before the rendering begins to set – about 15 minutes after it has been applied – draw the straight-edged piece of wood upwards over the rendering to level it with the wall. Hold the wood horizontally and make sure that you are pressing its ends firmly against the wall on either side of the patch. If any hollows are showing after levelling off, fill them quickly with more rendering and level them with the straight-edged piece of wood.

11 As the rendering starts to set – 20 minutes after you have applied it – smooth its surface gently with a damp sponge or a damp wooden float. Clean the sponge or float frequently in water.

Repairing pebbledash

It is simple enough to repair damaged pebbledash, but the repair will not be invisible because both the pebbles and the rendering beneath will have changed from their original colour. You can try to recover some of the original pebbles and mix them with the new ones to blend the colours, but painting the whole wall is the only real way of hiding the repair

You will need about 11lb (5kg) of pebbles to cover a square yard.

You will need

Tools Cold chisel; club hammer; brush; wet sponge or cloth; steel trowel; sheet of polythene; small scoop; wooden float. Perhaps a ladder.

Materials Plastering sand; cement; hydrated lime; water; pebbles.

1 Prepare the area for repair as for *Patching large holes in rendering* (above) and mix and lay on a first coat of rendering in the same way, but leave it about ½in (13mm) below the level of the wall surface.

2 Wash the pebbles and drain them. You can use them as soon as they have been drained.

3 Mix the rendering for the top coat, known as the butter coat. Use 5 parts of sand to 1 of cement and 1 of lime. Mix it to a slightly softer consistency than the first coat to make sure that it is still soft when you apply the pebbles. Apply the top coat; if you have a large area to repair, work on a section which you can complete within 20 minutes – before the coat starts to set.

4 Spread a sheet of polythene on the ground below the repair.

5 Throw small scoops of pebbles hard at the rendering until it is evenly covered. Gather up later all the pebbles that fall; wash and drain them to use for a later batch.

6 When you have pebbledashed the area which is spread with top coat, press the wooden float lightly all over it to firm the pebbles into the surface.

7 Continue in the same way until the repair is complete.

Damp-proofing basement and cellar walls

Rooms below ground level are prone to damp – especially in areas where the water table is close to the soil surface. Most damp problems can be solved with DIY methods, but if the walls have been treated and they still weep, seek advice from a surveyor. Water is probably being forced into the room under hydrostatic pressure; this often happens with houses situated in hollows. Land drainage is frequently the only remedy.

TREATING SLIGHT DAMP

If the damp is slight, treat the walls with a bituminous waterproofing compound, such as Aquaseal 77. Prepare the surface so that it is clean and free from old paint or wallpaper, then apply two coats of the treatment.

To provide a tougher barrier against damp, use a moisture-curing polymer, such as Heavy Duty Urethane by Aquaseal. The urethane resin in this liquid sets by the action of moisture upon it and forms a water-resistant film. Again, prepare and clean the surface thoroughly. If you have soaked off old wallpaper, wait for the walls to dry and then apply four coats. Wait about two or three hours between coats – the previous coat should have lost any tacky feel before you brush on the next.

TREATING SEVERE DAMP

If damp is widespread, and if it is not cured by a damp-proofing compound, line the walls with a waterproof lining material, such as Newlath. Remove all the plaster back to the brickwork before you fix the waterproof lining and follow the instructions supplied by the manufacturer. Where a horizontal join has to be made, fix a strip of bituminous felt behind it.

The studded structure of the lining material allows air to circulate over dampness in the wall behind. But to improve the air flow, leave a gap of about $\frac{1}{16}$in (2mm) at the top and about 1in (25mm) at the bottom of the lining.

The surface of the lining material is ideal for plastering; a renovating plaster (page 239) gives the best results. Alternatively, you can fix plasterboard (page 243) to the lining with panel adhesive. Leave a gap at the top and bottom to allow for ventilation. When the new surface is dry, fit skirting and coving to hide (but not seal) the gaps, and then decorate.

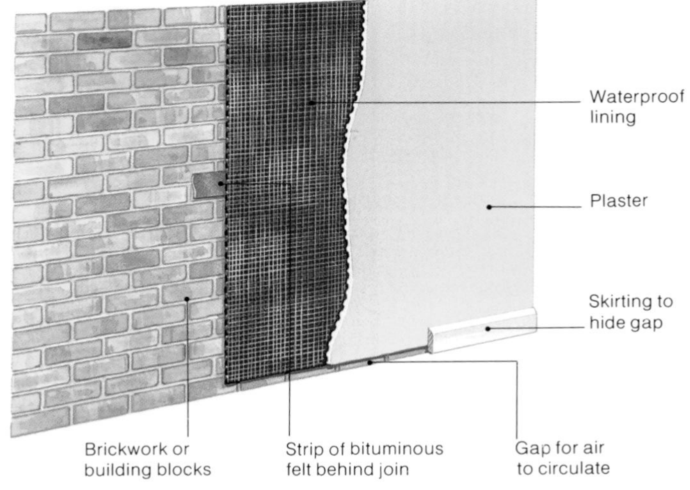
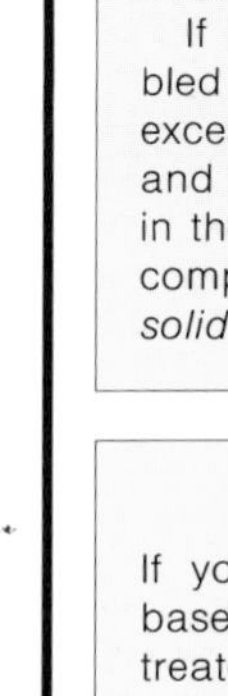

DEALING WITH DAMP IN A CONCRETE FLOOR

Damp rising through a concrete floor indicates that either there is no damp-proof membrane in the concrete or that it has failed at some point – perhaps because the membrane has been punctured during building work.

The easiest way to stop the damp rising is to brush on two coats of a bitumen latex waterproofing emulsion.

For extra protection, lay reflective foil building paper – with the foil side upwards – on the second coat of emulsion while it is still damp.

If the concrete has crumbled because it has become excessively damp, rake it away and brush the floor clean. Fill in the holes with a screeding compound (see *Levelling a solid floor*, page 276).

HELPFUL TIP

If you use any wood in a basement, buy pressure-treated timber which is highly resistant to damp conditions. The extra cost of the wood is money well spent.

Installing a chemical damp-proof course

Damp patches at skirting-board level on an intérior wall, or a tidemark damaging wallpaper, possibly as high as 3ft (1m) from the floor, are two signs of damp rising up from the ground.

DAMP PREVENTION

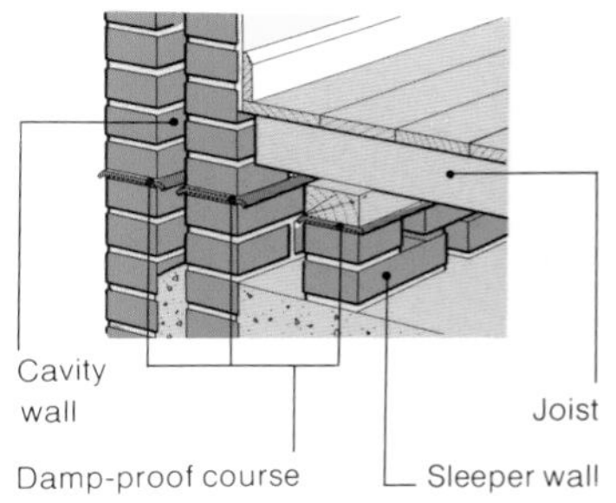

To prevent damp from rising, modern houses are built with a damp-proof course. This can be an impermeable membrane or a chemical solution that acts as a barrier. In most houses, except very old ones, you will see a thicker than usual horizontal line of pointing about 6in (150mm) above the ground right round the external wall. This line indicates a damp-proof membrane.

DEFECTS IN THE DAMP-PROOFING

If the damp-proof course deteriorates or becomes damaged – or if there is no damp-proof course – damp is able to rise through the house walls.

Rising damp will also occur if the damp-proof course is bridged by damp material reaching above it against the outside wall – a rockery, for example, or a flower bed or even a temporary pile of building sand.

Rising damp may occur because a path or drive is too close to, or is higher than, the damp-proof course. Paths and drives must be at least 6in (150mm) below the damp-proof course so that rainwater cannot splash above it. Where necessary, lower the path or drive, either by cutting a deep channel where it meets the outside wall of the house or by re-laying it at a lower level (pages 487–492).

If such alterations are not practicable, you should build a concrete skirting against the foot of the outside wall. Use a waterproofing agent in the concrete to make it impervious to water. Make the skirting reach at least 6in (150mm) higher than the path or drive. Since its top will be above the damp-proof course, make sure that there is no gap between the wall and the skirting, into which water could percolate. Make the top of the skirting slope down from the wall so that water will run off it readily.

A NEW DAMP-PROOF COURSE

Inserting a new membrane between courses of brickwork or masonry is a job for a professional. The best DIY solution is to install a chemical damp-proof course. It consists of a silicone-based water-repellent injected into bricks or stones until they are saturated. Then they become impervious to water and form a damp-proof barrier.

Damp-proof course injection machines can be hired from most tool hire shops (to find your nearest, look in *Yellow Pages* under Hire Services–Tools and Equipment). The shop will supply the injection fluid, power drill and masonry bit of the right size. Ask for an instruction leaflet when you hire the machine and get advice on the amount of fluid. You will need roughly 5 pints for 3ft of wall (3 litres per metre).

HOW TO DIAGNOSE DAMP

Sometimes it is hard to know whether a damp patch is caused by water getting in from outside or by the condensation of moisture-laden air inside. Usually, if the patches appear in mild, wet weather, water is getting in from outside. If the patches appear in cold, dry spells, condensation is the more likely cause.

To get a more accurate diagnosis, make a small raised wall of Plasticine or Blu-tack on the suspect surface to form an enclosed square. Press a piece of glass onto the square so that the glass is within $\frac{1}{4}$in (6mm) of the surface. Alternatively, put a piece of aluminium foil directly on the surface and seal down its edges with sticky tape.

After about 24 hours lift the glass or foil. If moisture has formed on the underside, damp is coming from outside. If the top side is moist, the problem is condensation.

SOLID WALLS

You can inject a solid wall from either side. Less work is involved if you inject from outside. However, if the plaster and skirtings have been badly damaged and need extensive repair, you may choose to work from inside.

If there is no damp-proof course, you will also have to treat internal partition walls.

CAVITY WALLS

Even if only a small area of the damp-proof course is faulty, you will have to tackle the treatment from inside and outside to deal with both leaves of the cavity wall. The upheaval will not be too bad if the area for treatment is small, but if the area is extensive, it is a major undertaking. However, if you do all the preparatory work and drill all the holes in advance, you can inject the average semi-detached house in a weekend.

PREPARING TO INJECT FROM INSIDE

You will have to remove any radiators, electrical appliances, built-in cupboards and pipes that are in the way. Remove the skirting board along the walls to be treated (page 256). Take up floorboards running parallel to the skirting (page 273). If the boards run at right angles to the skirting, take up boards about 20in (510mm) apart.

To give the walls a chance to dry out, remove plaster a few days before you install the damp-proof course. Take the plaster off the walls to expose the bricks or blocks up to about 18in (460mm) above the damp line. Use a hammer and bolster or cold chisel.

Take care not to damage cables, socket connections or pipework. It is safest to switch off the electricity supply to the circuits you are working near. Use an extension lead from another circuit to supply power. Leave the circuits disconnected until the injection is completed and the fluid has dried.

You will need

Tools Percussion drill; masonry bit with depth stop; extension lead and plug-in RCD (page 364); safety goggles; gloves; face mask; damp-proof injection machine.

Materials Injection fluid; paraffin for cleaning machine; mortar (page 481).

1 Drill a horizontal row of holes 3in (75mm) deep into the course of bricks or stones you are going to treat. Use a depth stop or mark the bit with tape to ensure that you do not drill right through a brick or stone. Drill at least 3in (75mm) above any existing damp-proof membrane so that there is no danger of piercing it.

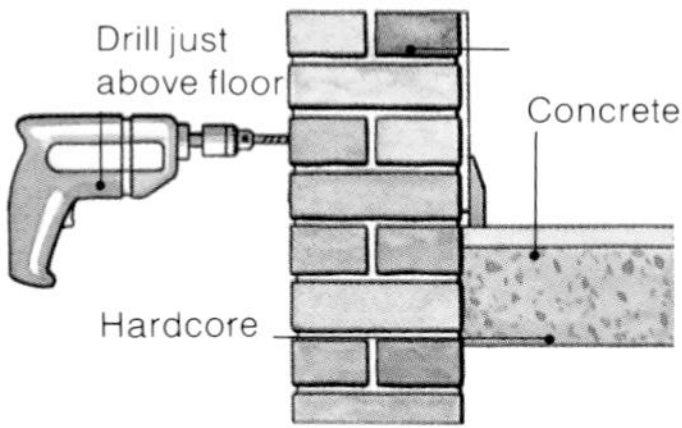

If the floor is made of concrete, drill just above it – probably from the outside if the wall is solid.

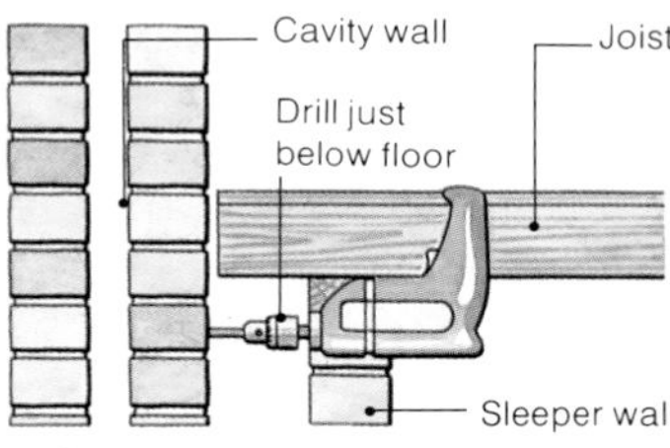

If there is a suspended timber floor, drill just below it – from inside and outside on a cavity wall.

If possible, the new damp-proof course should also be 6in (150mm) above the level of the ground surrounding the house.

For best results, the holes should be about 4½in (115mm) apart. If the bricks are extremely difficult to drill through – or if the walls are made of stone – make the holes in the mortar joints.

2 If necessary, drill the holes in internal partition walls. Walls that are 4½in (115mm) thick require 3in (75mm) holes drilled from one side only. But walls 9in (230mm) thick must be treated twice. After the first injection, either drill through the same holes to a depth of 7½in (190mm), or drill 3in (75mm) holes from the other side of the wall.

Whichever method you choose, take great care not to drill right through the wall; this would weaken it.

3 When all the holes have been drilled, inject the damp-proofing fluid. Follow the instructions supplied with the machine.

Most machines consist of a pump, a suction nozzle and six injecting nozzles. First put the suction nozzle into the container of fluid.

4 Insert all but one of the injection nozzles into prepared holes and tighten the wing nuts to hold them in place.

5 Hold the final nozzle over the container and turn on the pump. When fluid begins to ooze from the nozzle, turn off the pump.

6 Insert the final nozzle in a hole and tighten its wing nut. Turn on the pump. When the bricks or stones joints are saturated, fluid will 'sweat' from the surface. As soon as this happens, turn off the pump and close the nozzles.

7 Undo the wing nuts, move the nozzles to the next set of holes and repeat the procedure. Continue until you have saturated bricks or masonry all round the building. Check regularly to make sure that the container does not empty.

8 Clean the pump with paraffin when you have finished injecting all the holes.

9 Wait for the fluid to dry; it may take two days or more. When the injected course is the same colour as the wall, fill the holes with mortar (page 481).

10 Replace any floorboards.

11 Leave the walls to dry for the period recommended by the fluid manufacturer before plastering.

12 As the walls dry, efflorescence may appear on them (page 460). Brush it off from time to time.

Preventing condensation

Condensation occurs in a room when warm air filled with moisture meets a cold surface, such as an external wall or pane of glass. It has become a more common problem as draughtproofing has improved.

The two main ways to reduce condensation are to reduce the amount of moisture released into the air, or to extract moist air.

In extreme cases a dehumidifier can be used to extract water from the air. Several litres can be collected in a 24 hour period.

REDUCING WATER VAPOUR

Large amounts of water vapour are produced through normal cooking, washing and bathing. Try to reduce the amount of moisture released into the air.

In the kitchen, a hood over the cooker will reduce the problem by removing steam. Cover saucepans with lids when you are cooking and use an automatic kettle, which will switch itself off when the water has boiled. If you have a tumble dryer, make sure that it is vented to the outside unless it is of the condenser type that needs no vent.

Condensation often occurs in bathrooms, especially on cold tiled surfaces. A heated towel rail or electric oil-filled radiator will help to raise the temperature of the room. Less steam will form if you run a little cold water into the bath before turning on the hot water. Keep the bathroom door shut to prevent steam from spreading to other parts of the house.

You can install an extractor fan in the bathroom and the kitchen.

If possible, avoid using a paraffin heater – an amount of water vapour is produced equal to the amount of paraffin you burn.

IMPROVING VENTILATION WITH AN EXTRACTOR FAN

The most effective way of improving ventilation is to install an extractor fan (page 237).

Before buying a fan, find out how much air it can move. Airflow capacity is given in cubic metres per hour, and may range from about 20 to 350 cubic metres.

The numbers of air changes per hour that are recommended for different rooms are: living rooms 4-6, kitchens and toilets 10-15, bathrooms 15-20.

To calculate the required capacity of the fan, multiply the volume of the room (width × length × height) by the recommended number of air changes. For example: Volume of bathroom 2.4m × 2.4m × 2.7m = 15.5cu m. Required fan capacity = 15.5cu m × 15-20 air changes = 233-310cu m per hour.

HELPFUL TIP

Use anti-condensation paint instead of emulsion in very steamy areas. The paint absorbs moisture during periods of high humidity and allows it to evaporate later. It contains a fungicide which reduces the risk of mould.

Raising the temperature of a wall

Condensation will form on a cold wall if warm, moist air hits the surface. You can take the chill off a surface – and reduce the risk of condensation forming – by lining the wall or installing a tubular heater at the base of the wall.

LINING THE WALL

Thermal board (page 243) is the most effective lining for keeping a wall warm. A cheaper alternative is to put up cork wall tiles or expanded polystyrene wall lining.

Expanded polystyrene wall lining is $\frac{1}{16}$in (2mm) thick and available in rolls from most DIY stores. Use an adhesive recommended by the manufacturer and follow the fixing instructions. The lining must be hung and joined like hessian, grasscloth and other special coverings (page 134). You can cover it directly with standard wallpaper, but if you want to fix any other type of wallcovering, such as vinyl or woodchip, first put up ordinary lining paper over the polystyrene to provide a suitable surface.

TUBULAR HEATER

An alternative way to warm a wall is to fit a tubular heater along the skirting board. The heater operates at a low temperature, consuming only 60 watts to 80 watts per foot run. Heaters are available in lengths ranging from 2ft (610mm) to 12ft (3.7m).

You will achieve a similar effect by warming the whole room, but this may prove too expensive if the room is little used.

If spare rooms are unheated, keep doors closed so damp air from other parts of the house cannot get in.

DOUBLE GLAZING

Installing double glazing helps to reduce condensation – the air trapped between the layers of glass acts as an insulator, preventing cold from passing from one layer of glass to the other.

If condensation is forming between the panes in a secondary glazing system, open the secondary glazing (which is usually hinged or slides aside), use a hair dryer to remove the moisture which was trapped, and close the glazing.

Anti-condensation crystals are ineffective. They absorb moisture during cool, cloudy weather, but when the sun heats the crystals the moisture evaporates and condenses on the window panes when it cools again.

How to treat rot, mould and woodworm

If timber becomes damp and does not dry out – perhaps because there is a lack of ventilation – wet rot, dry rot or mould may develop. In sound, seasoned wood, up to 15 per cent of its weight will be moisture. If the moisture content rises by between 6 per cent and 10 per cent, fungi can begin growing rapidly.

To prevent fungi forming, deal with any damp as soon as you find it. It is also essential that the ventilation in the house is adequate.

Check regularly that the airbricks round the outside of the house are clean and free from obstruction. A suspended timber floor needs to be thoroughly ventilated with approximately one airbrick for every 325sq ft (30sq m) of floor. If you discover a damaged airbrick or if you find that an airbrick is missing put one in (page 236). There should also be an airbrick indoors at the base of a chimney breast if the flue has been blocked.

WET ROT

Several different species of fungi attack wood when it becomes very wet (with a 30 per cent moisture content) and cause wet rot. It is most likely to occur outside – at the bottom of a door, window frame or fence, for example – but even inside it is much more common than dry rot, and easier to eradicate since it can spread only over damp timber surfaces. If wood turns dark and shrinks, and sparse dark or white strands become visible on the surface, wet rot may have set in. The wood will crack along the grain. Test the wood by prodding it with a sharp screwdriver, bradawl or knife. If the wood is soft and pulpy, it needs treatment.

Deal with the cause of the damp. When the wood dries out the wet rot will die. Damaged wood should be treated with a wood repair system (page 210) or replaced with some well-seasoned wood.

DRY ROT

Damp, unventilated conditions indoors are perfect for dry rot. It does not occur outside. This is a much more serious condition than wet rot, and the timber need not be as wet before the fungus takes hold.

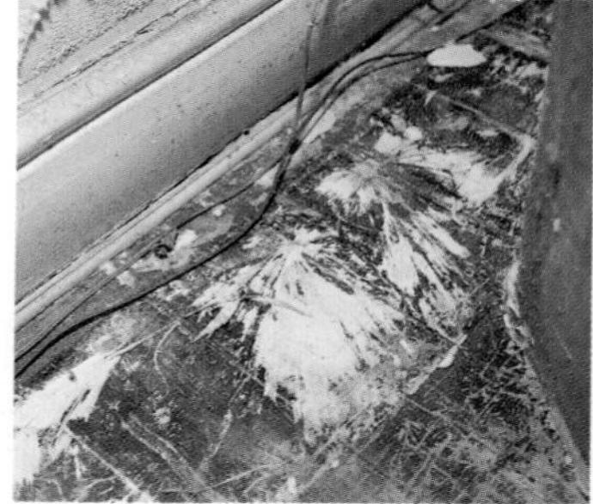

The early growth forms white fluffy strands which later thicken and resemble dirty cotton wool.

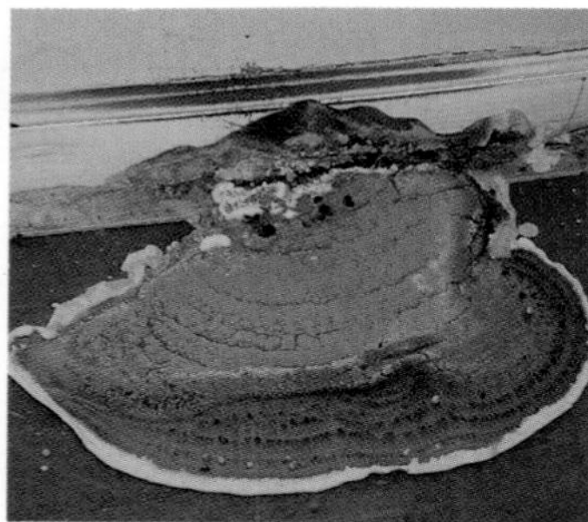

The fruiting body which develops resembles a large, pancake-like lichen, rusty-coloured with a grey-white rim. The fluffy strands will spread across masonry or metalwork seeking out timber. They can extend 40ft (12m) or more. In this way, dry rot can spread rapidly, and it is very difficult to eradicate; every strand must be traced and killed to prevent a new outbreak. If not killed, strands can remain dormant for several years and then start into growth.

Wood which is affected eventually becomes dry, soft and brittle, cracking across the grain. Dry rot smells musty and is often hidden from view – behind skirtings, under floorboards, or behind paint.

Treating dry rot is not a DIY job. It is best to call in a specialist company who will make sure that not the slightest rot is overlooked to spread later to surrounding areas. All affected wood must be burned.

MOULD

Millions of mould spores in the air will establish themselves on a surface in damp, warm conditions. Mould may affect paint and wallpaper and sometimes grout – perhaps if a waterproof grout has not been used to fix tiles in a bathroom or kitchen.

Never use bleach to treat mould. Although this will kill the mould flowers, it will not harm the root and the problem will recur within a few weeks. If mould has ruined a wall covering, strip it off. If paintwork is affected, wash the surface with warm soap or detergent and water. Treat the wall with a proprietary fungicide diluted as instructed by the manufacturer. Wear gloves as protection against the fungicide and brush on two or three coats.

When putting up new wallpaper, use a paste containing fungicide. Most pastes for vinyls are suitable.

WOODWORM

A woodworm attack can be recognised by round holes, $\frac{1}{16}$in (2mm) across, in the surface of wood. Fine wood dust may also be visible. The damage is caused by the larvae of beetles which feed on both softwood and hardwood.

For small attacks, brush all surfaces with two coats of a proprietary woodworm killer. On furniture, also inject the fluid into the holes with a woodworm-fluid applicator.

Extensive outbreaks are best left to a specialist firm; however, it is possible – if unpleasant – to do it yourself. Brush dirt off the timber and spray with woodworm killer, using a garden pressure spray. Wear goggles, face mask and protective cap while spraying. Treat floors by lifting the boards so that the joists can also be sprayed.

HELPFUL TIP

Some specialist companies offer a free survey to check for rot and insect attack. If they find a problem, they will quote for doing the job or they can supply you with the chemicals you need if you want to do the job yourself.

If a building society survey reveals trouble – perhaps dry rot or woodworm – the society will usually insist that the work is carried out by a professional who will give a guarantee. Building societies will not accept DIY work.

15 DIY in the garden

Fences and gates

Garden walls

Drives, paths and steps

Garden ponds

Garage doors

Planning a fence

Whether you want a fence for decoration, to define a boundary, to act as a screen, or for security, consider the nature of the ground on which the fence will be built, not only the use and cost, when choosing the type.

In a very windy spot, for example, an open fence such as post and rails would offer little wind resistance. However, a solid fence would need to be very sturdy. Any solid fence higher than 4ft (1.2m) is at risk of being blown down, no matter how well it is constructed, so it would be best to use open trellis to add any extra height.

If the level of the neighbouring garden is significantly higher than your own and the outside of the fence would be in constant contact with the earth (which would rot timber), you could consider building the fence on a low brick or block retaining wall (page 485), with gaps for concrete spurs to support timber fence posts.

Many types of fencing can be bought in ready-made sections, and matching gates are available for most types.

You must have planning permission to put up a fence more than 3ft 3in (1m) high if it fronts on a public road. Or for any fence more than 6ft 6in (2m) high.

PLASTIC FENCES

Most plastic fencing is sold in kits. The methods of fixing vary with the make, and full instructions are given by the manufacturer.

The commonest type of plastic fence is the post and rail, slotted or screwed into plastic posts with wide or close spaces between rails. The posts are usually concreted into the ground.

Another common type of plastic fence is the post and chain, suitable for a decorative boundary. The chain is generally made of nylon.

Plastic fences are normally white, and need no maintenance apart from occasional washing. They usually last a long time, but they can be expensive.

TYPICAL CONSTRUCTION

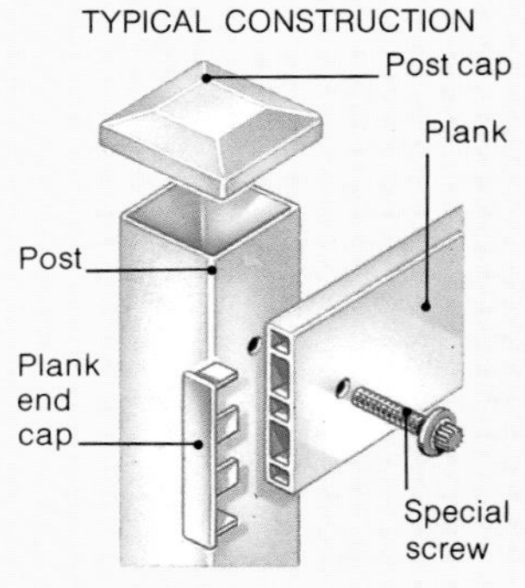

CHOOSING A TIMBER FENCE

TYPE OF FENCE	DESCRIPTION	ADVANTAGES AND DISADVANTAGES
Closeboarded vertical 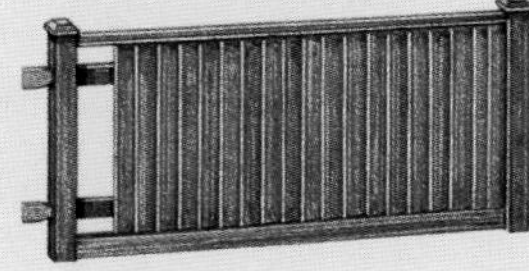	Upright, overlapping feather-edged boards (tapered on one side) nailed to horizontal arris rails secured – often with slot-in joints – between posts. Boards are about 6in (150mm) shorter than the post height above ground, to allow for a horizontal gravel board. Posts are usually 8ft (2.4m) apart.	Excellent for screening or security, but expensive. The timber needs regular preservative treatment (page 473) to prevent shrinking or rotting. Available either in ready-made separate parts, or in panels.
Closeboarded horizontal 	Horizontal boards nailed between posts. The boards are either feather-edged overlapping, or shiplap – with a step-shaped overlap. No arris rails or gravel boards are used. Posts are usually about 4ft (1.2m) apart, with 8ft (2.4m) boards butt-jointed on alternate posts.	As above, but more posts are needed to give the fence strength. It is very solid, but more expensive than vertical closeboard. Shaped, treated, ready-made boards are not generally available except as panels, which are not as strong.
Panel 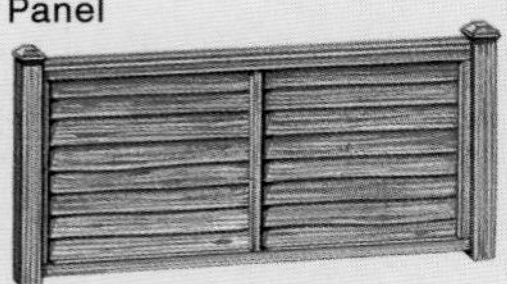	Ready-made panels fixed between posts. Panels may be thin interwoven slats, overlapped horizontal board, or vertical closeboard. Panels are normally 6ft (1.8m) wide; narrower sizes can be made to order. The height range is generally 2ft–6ft (0.6m–1.8m).	Easy to put up. Good for screening or security. The timber needs regular preservative treatment to prevent shrinkage or rotting (page 473). Quality varies widely – cheap, poorly made panels are likely to distort.
Hurdle or wattle 	Thin or half-round interwoven rods formed into 6ft (1.8m) wide panels which can be supported on stakes or between posts. Osier (willow) rods form hurdles, hazel rods form wattle. The height range is about 2ft–7ft (0.6m–2.1m).	Not very long-lasting, but useful as temporary screens for protecting growing plants. Hurdles are more expensive than wattles.
Post and rails (also known as ranch-style or railboard) 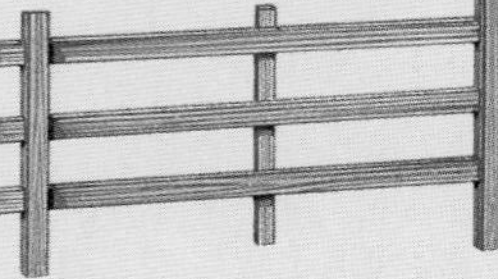	Spaced horizontal rails secured to posts. Rails may be square sawn, half round, or rustic (poles, often with bark attached). Rails can be nailed or slotted into posts. Posts are usually about 6ft (1.8m) apart. Height range about 1ft–6ft (0.3m–1.8m), but normally about 3ft (0.9m) – three rails. See also *Plastic fences* (left).	Suitable for a boundary or for decoration. Not as expensive as closeboard or panel fencing, and not much affected by wind. The timber needs regular painting or preservative treatment (page 473). Children are likely to climb on it.
Square or diamond trellis 	Square trellis is usually made from hardwood battens forming squares of about 6in (150mm), and can be bought in ready-made sections about 6ft 6in (2m) wide with a height range of 1ft–6ft 6in (0.3m–2m), or as panel fencing (see above). Diamond trellis is often expanding, and sold in 6ft (1.8m) lengths with a height range of 1ft–4ft (0.3m–1.2m). Sections can be fixed above each other. Rustic diamond trellis (not expanding) is also available.	Can be nailed to posts or fitted between posts as a screen, or used for decorative fencing. Low trellis can be used to top a wall. High trellis can blow down in a strong wind. The wood needs regular preservative treatment (page 473), or can be painted. Square trellis tends to be the most rigid. Do not thread plants through trellis, they will eventually break it.
Palisade or picket 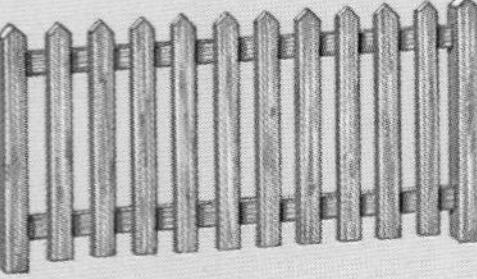	Spaced, upright stakes nailed to horizontal rails slotted into posts. Posts are usually about 8ft (2.4m) apart, and the height range is about 3ft–4ft (0.9m–1.2m). Fencing can be bought in ready-made sections about 6ft (1.8m) long, with brackets supplied for fitting it to posts.	Suitable for a boundary fence. Comparatively cheap. Can be painted or treated with wood preservative (page 473).
Cleft chestnut paling 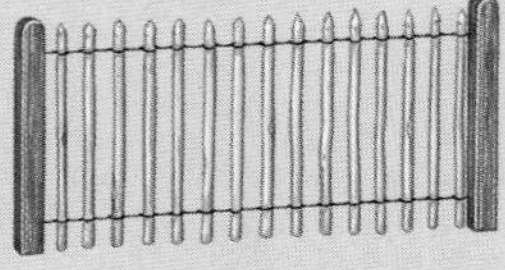	Stakes wired together and stretched between posts. End and corner posts are usually braced with stays. Posts are usually about 9ft (2.7m) apart, and the height range is 2ft 6in–6ft (0.75m–1.8m).	Suitable for a temporary boundary – while a hedge is growing, for example. Easy to put up and take down. Needs no maintenance but wires must be tensioned if the fence is to stay taut.

CHOOSING A WIRE FENCE

TYPE OF FENCE	DESCRIPTION	ADVANTAGES AND DISADVANTAGES
Chain link 	A mesh of thick, interlinked galvanised wire – plain (silver finish) or plastic coated – stretched between concrete or timber end posts by means of metal stretcher bars. The mesh is tied to two or three horizontal wires and also tied or stapled to intermediate posts. Height range from 3ft (0.9m) – the standard height – to 10ft (3m). Mesh normally 2in (50mm) wide. Sold in rolls.	Good for security (especially keeping animals in or out) or boundary fencing. Fairly easy to put up, but will sag unless properly tensioned. Little maintenance is needed, except for painting timber posts, or treating them with wood preservative (page 473).
Wire or plastic netting 	A mesh of galvanised wire or plastic stretched between posts. It is either stapled or wired to posts, or – for greater strength – stretched on horizontal wires. Height range normally 1ft–4ft (0.3m–1.2m). Mesh varies from ½in (13mm) to 3in (75mm) wide.	Suitable for boundary or security fencing. Cheaper than chain link, but not as strong or durable. Plastic is longer lasting.
Post and wire 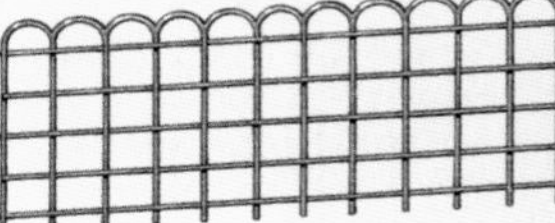	Plain or stranded galvanised wire stretched between posts. Wire is usually sold in coils by weight – from 5kg (11lb) to 25kg (½cwt). Coil length depends on gauge. A 5kg coil of 10g (3.15mm) plain wire is 82m (90yds) long, a 10kg coil twice as long.	Suitable for temporary boundary fencing. Cheap for enclosing a large area.
Decorative wire	Straight or crimped plastic-coated wire welded or interwoven in squares or patterns. The top is usually hooped and the base is usually spiked for sticking into the ground. Taller fencing can be stapled to timber posts. Sold either in rolls or rigid sections, with a height range of about 1ft–3ft (0.3m–0.9m).	Suitable for boundary fencing or decorative edging to flower borders. Easy to put up, cheap, and needs no maintenance. Rolls are cheaper than rigid sections, and can be curved, but rigid sections are stronger.

AN ALTERNATIVE WAY OF DIGGING POST HOLES

If you have a lot of post holes to dig, consider hiring a post-hole borer, which resembles a large corkscrew on a long handle. It saves the hard work of digging, but is less effective where the ground is very stony. To use it, twist it in and out of the ground and continually deposit the soil that gathers on the blades on the ground nearby.

Borers of about 8in (200mm) diameter can be hired from contractors listed in *Yellow Pages* under Hire Services – Tools and Equipment. To hire the borer for the shortest possible period, dig all the holes in one go even though the posts are being put up in pairs.

FENCE POSTS AND ACCESSORIES

Timber post
Usually consists of softwood such as larch or pine. Buy posts ready-treated with preservative, preferably by vacuum/pressure impregnation although this is more expensive.

Posts are available with ready-cut mortises for arris rails. Post sizes are normally 3in (75mm) or 4in (100mm) square; corner posts may be 5in × 4in (125mm × 100mm).

Timber post cap
Flat or bevelled timber cap for shedding rainwater and preventing rot.

Capping strip
Wooden strip nailed across the top of vertical closeboard fencing to keep it in line and prevent rotting or sagging.

Concrete post
Heavier and more expensive than a timber post, but longer lasting and will not rot in the ground. A post 4ft 6in (1.4m) long weighs about 58lb (26kg). Posts are available with ready-made bolt holes, mortises or slots. They are generally 4in (100mm) square, or 4in × 3in (100mm × 75mm).

Concrete spur
Short concrete post with ready-drilled bolt holes – usually ½in (13mm) across – used to support a damaged timber post. Spurs may be 3in (75mm) or 4in (100mm) square. Lengths range from about 3ft 6in (1.1m) to 5ft (1.5m).

Post spike
A spiked steel support driven into the ground as a base for a timber post. The post rests in a square cup above the ground. In some types the post is clamped into the cup. Concreting post spikes have a steel support, for anchoring into concrete. A post spike driven into soil is an unsuitable method of erecting fencing in areas subject to high winds.

Dolly or driving tool
Metal-capped timber block for fitting into a post-spike cup while hammering it in. Side handles allow the cup to be twisted for alignment.

Bolt-down fence base
A square metal cup for supporting a timber post. It has a projecting rim containing holes for bolting the base to a solid surface. Suitable for fixing to concrete or paving slabs fully and firmly bedded in mortar, but not slabs bedded in sand.

Gravel-board clip
Such as Metclip. A clip that can be nailed to a timber post to support a gravel board, particularly where a post is supported by a post spike. It is driven partly into the ground and nailed at the top.

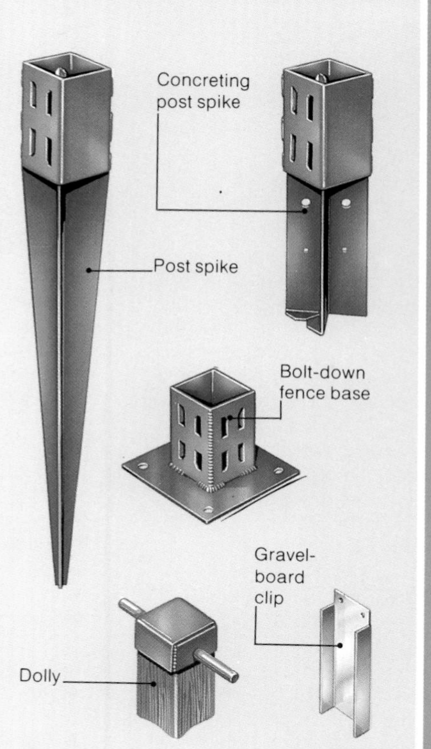

Putting up fence posts

If the distance between fence posts is critical – for example, when fitting ready-made panels – erect posts in pairs and fit the fencing (see below) as you go. If the distance between posts is not critical – such as with a post-and-wire fence – you can put up the posts first.

Posts must be firmly fixed in the ground. The amount of post that should be below ground depends on the fence height. It is advisable to buy new posts pre-treated with preservative.

For fences over 4ft (1.2m) high, sink the bottom of the post at least 24in (610mm) below ground – or 30in (760mm) for tall concrete posts. For lower fences, sink timber posts 18in (460mm), and concrete posts 24in (610mm). Timber posts should have about 6in (150mm) of hardcore below them to provide drainage and lessen the risk of rotting.

Timber posts can either be concreted in or bedded in a mixture of well-compacted hardcore and soil. Concreting ensures a more solid and durable fixing, especially on soft ground, but may slightly increase the risk of rotting. Concrete posts must be concreted in.

Support an end post with one or more stays, unless the post is fixed to a wall. When putting in a solid fence higher than 4ft (1.2m) in a windy spot, strengthen every third post with timber stays. For a lower fence, strengthen every fourth post.

The distance between posts depends on the type of fence (see charts). If the new fence replaces an old one and you want to put the posts in the same positions, you will have to dig out the stumps of the old posts, and possibly the hardcore surrounding them. This is a tough and lengthy job if a lot of posts are involved. Alternatively, you can install a half panel or short section of fencing at each end of the fence so that the new posts fall midway between the old positions.

HANDY HINTS

STOP POSTS ROTTING
Even pre-treated posts will benefit from some extra protection. Soak the part of each fence post that will be buried in the soil, in wood preservative (page 473) for 24 hours.

Lean the posts against a wall in separate containers, or in an improvised trough, such as a shallow pit lined with a thick sheet of polythene. Pour wood preservative into the bottom of each container.

It is not usually practicable to immerse the full 18in or 24in (460mm or 610mm) of post, so brush the preservative up onto the posts from time to time. Allow the posts to dry for 24 hours before using them.

CONCRETE SHORT CUTS
To fix a fence post quickly you can use Supamix Post Fix, which sets in about 10 minutes, instead of rubble and cement. It is sold in 25kg (55lb) bags, each suitable for erecting one fence post.

You will need

Tools Post-hole borer (page 467) or narrow spade – unless using spikes (page 467); string and pegs; spirit level with horizontal and vertical vials; one timber length longer than distance between posts; one timber length as long as distance between posts; timber lengths for temporary post supports; mallet; hammer; timber length or earth rammer (page 490). Possibly also: demolition hammer or pickaxe; sledgehammer; chalk.

Materials Posts of treated timber (see below) or concrete; hardcore (page 487); 2in (50mm) or 3in (75mm) fence nails. Possibly also: fast-set bagged dry mix (page 495) or concrete foundation mix (page 496) – probably 1 bucketful per hole; bolt-down fence base.

1 Mark the inside line of the fence by stretching the pegged string along its length.

2 Use the timber length to measure the distance between each hole, and cut out the area of each hole with a spade. (Or make a chalk mark if the fence crosses a solid surface.)

3 Fix the first post to the wall, if necessary (see facing page).

4 If a hole has to be made in a yard or patio, either take up a slab or bricks, or break a concrete surface with a demolition hammer, and dig below.

Alternatively, for a solid surface use a bolt-down fence base (page 467).

5 Using a post-hole borer or narrow spade, dig each hole to the required depth; remember to include an extra 6in (150mm) for a timber post. Keep the hole as narrow as possible for the size of the post.

6 For a timber post, fill the base of the hole with 6in (150mm) of hardcore, well rammed down.

7 Insert a post so that one side is against the string guideline, and pack some hardcore round the base to keep it upright.

8 Lay a length of timber across the top of each two consecutive posts and use a spirit level to check that the tops are level.

9 Use a spirit level to check that the post is vertical, then pack in more hardcore to support it.

10 To give a stronger temporary support, drive a nail into the post and wedge a length of timber under the nail as a brace.

11 Fill in the hole as soon as possible after erecting the fence. Either fill it with layers of hardcore and a mixture of soil and gravel, ramming the surface well down, or fill the hole with alternate layers of hardcore and concrete rammed well down. Slope the top layer of concrete round a timber post so that the rainwater will run off from round the post.

FIXING A SUPPORT STAY

A post support stay can be fitted against the post either in line with the fence or at right angles to it. Use either a spare fence post or a length of timber 3in x 2in (75mm x 50mm) that has been treated with wood preservative.

The stay should be about three-quarters of the length of the post it supports. Cut it so that it is at an angle of about 35-40 degrees to the

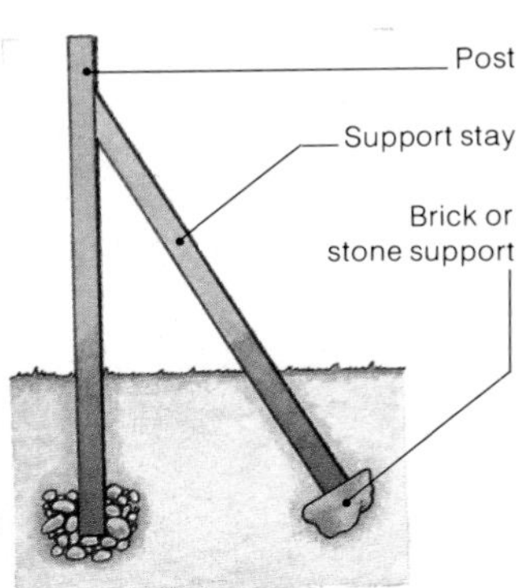

vertical post. Bury the stay to about the same depth as the post, but you will have to dig a wider hole to allow for the angle of the stay. Place a brick or large piece of stone under the angled bottom of the stay to support it. Secure the stay to the post with $2\frac{1}{2}$in or 3in (60mm or 75mm) galvanised nails or floorboard brads (page 161).

USING POSTS SPIKES

Make sure the cup of the spike is the right size for the post. You can trim the bottom of a post to fit into a smaller-sized cup, but this is not advisable as it weakens the post. The post length should be about 2in (50mm) longer than the height of the fence boards or panelling – none of it will be buried below ground.

Fit the driving tool into the cup, press the spike into the earth at the marked spot beside the pegged line, and drive it down using a heavy hammer with slow, firm strokes.

Stop at regular intervals and check with a spirit level that the spike is vertical, otherwise the post will be out of true when fitted. Use the handles of the driving tool to twist or level the spike as necessary to straighten or align it.

The spike will break through small stones, but if you hit a rock, stop and dig it out, or the spike will be pushed out of true. Take care if you are driving a spike where you know there are service pipes. Pipes are normally more than 24in

(610mm) below ground, so should not be in your way.

Continue driving the spike until the bottom of the cup is level with the ground surface. Then fit a post in the cup. Some types have an adjuster nut to level the cup when fitting the post.

FIXING POSTS ON A SLOPE

On a pronounced slope, use fencing such as panels or horizontal rails or boarding, as it can be more easily stepped in sections than upright fencing.

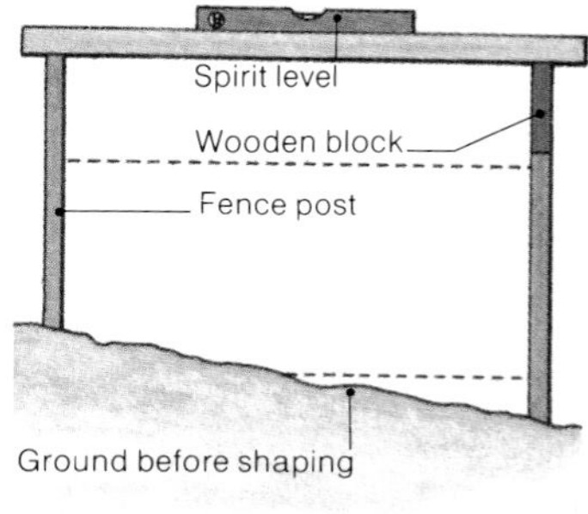

To make even steps, you may have to shape the ground by digging out or building up areas so that there is not too small or too large a gap under each section.

To level each pair of posts, use a wooden block on the lower post to raise the levelling timber to the height of the higher post. How long the block should be depends on the slope – the steeper the slope, the longer it will need to be. By using the same block on each post, you will ensure that the post tops are uniformly stepped.

FIXING A TIMBER POST TO A WALL

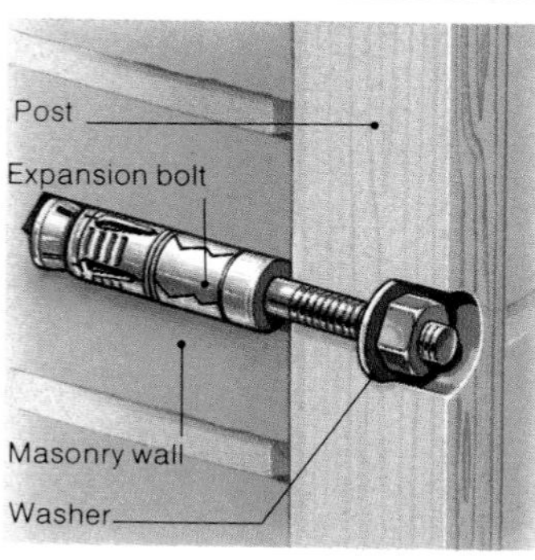

A post fixed against a wall usually rests on the surface of a path or patio, so should be cut shorter than the other fence posts by the amount they are to be buried below ground. Soak the sawn end with wood preservative overnight (facing page).

Secure a post over 4ft (1.2m) high to the wall with three equally spaced expansion or anchor bolts (page 232) at the top, middle and bottom. For shorter posts use only two bolts. Each bolt should be twice as long as the width of the post, as half will be sunk into the brickwork. For panel fencing, the bolt heads must be recessed to lie flush with the edge of the post. On any type of fence, it is neater and safer if they are recessed.

You will need
Tools Steel tape measure; chalk; brace and two auger bits – one of the bolt-hole diameter, one wide enough for the nut recess, allowing for use of a spanner (or use a flat bit for the recess); masonry bit of the recommended diameter for the expansion bolt shield; spirit level with horizontal and vertical vials; 4in (100mm) nail; hammer; box or socket spanner to fit bolt nut.

Materials Sawn post; two or three projecting-type expansion bolts (page 232) – probably for fixing about 2½in (60mm) thickness.

1 Use a steel tape measure and chalk to mark the hole positions on the post.

2 Drill holes of suitable diameter through the post at each marked point, then make a hole for the nut recess about ½in (13mm).

3 Hold the post in position against the wall and use the spirit level to check that it is vertical. Then insert a 4in (100mm) nail through each hole and tap it with a hammer to mark the hole position on the wall.

4 Remove the post and drill holes in the wall of the correct diameter for the bolt shield, and to the depth the bolt will be sunk into the masonry. Remove debris from the hole.

5 Insert the sleeves and bolts (with nuts and washers removed) into the wall holes. Hang the post on the bolts and replace the washers and nuts. Tighten the heads with a box or socket spanner.

Fixing panel fencing to posts

Put up posts in pairs in the manner described on the facing page. You will need a helper to lift and support large panels.

Fix each panel to its first post before positioning the second post. The fixing method depends on whether you are using nails or fence clips on timber posts, or fitting panels into slotted concrete posts. Fit a gravel board in the same way as for a closeboard fence (page 470). If you are not using gravel boards, each panel must be fixed about 3in (75mm) off the ground, or it will quickly rot.

You will need
Tools Power drill; wood bits; hammer. Possibly also: screwdriver; two or three bricks; timber lengths for supporting panels; G-cramp.
Materials Posts (page 467) – one more than the number of panels; panels; either nails – twelve 2in or 3in (50mm or 75mm) galvanised or alloy nails per panel – or fence clips – four per panel, with sufficient screws or nails for each clip. Serrated or barbed nails give the best grip. Possibly also: one 6ft (1.8m) gravel board for each panel; post caps (page 467).

NAILING PANELS DIRECT TO POSTS

1 Drill pilot holes for the nails in each panel, if necessary (some are pre-drilled). Make six holes each end – three on each side through the inner face of the panel frame at the top, middle and bottom. Drill the holes right through.

2 Hold the panel in position against the first post (use a G-cramp if working alone). Allow enough space at the bottom for fitting a 6in (150mm) gravel board, or rest the frame on bricks to leave a gap of about 3in (75mm).

3 Nail the panel to the first post, driving the nails in at a slightly upward or downward angle so that they will not pull straight out if the fence comes under pressure at a later date.

4 Position the second post with the other end of the panel butted to it. Make sure the post tops are level (page 468), then nail the end of the panel in place.

USING FENCE CLIPS

Drill starting holes for nails or screws that are to be driven into the panel frame, otherwise the wood could split.

Some clips are two sided with a post-fixing screw welded to one side. Screw the clips to each post before fitting the panel against it. Place a clip at the top and bottom of each post, facing opposite ways so that each side of the panel is supported. Nail each clip to the panel frame after fitting.

Some clips are three sided, with no built-in screws. Fit them to the post before fitting the panel.

Some clips wrap round one side of the panel frame. Fit them to the top and bottom of the panel on opposite sides of the frame before fitting the panel and nailing the clip to the post.

USING SLOTTED POSTS

Slot the gravel board into the first post, then the panel. Temporarily support the panel with lengths of timber while you position the second post so that it slots onto the other end of the panel.

Fixing closeboard vertical fencing to posts

Posts can be either timber or concrete, and are available with ready-made slots (mortises) for arris rails. Some concrete posts have recesses to which the rails can be bolted. Posts for corners are usually wider than intermediate posts, and are mortised on two adjacent sides.

Put up posts (page 468) in pairs, fitting the arris rails between them. Make sure the posts are the right way round. Some posts are recessed on the bottom front edge to accommodate the gravel board, which fits directly below the overlapping featheredge boards. The back of the fence is the side on which the arris rails are visible. Rails are normally 8ft (2.4m) long, and after they have been slotted into the posts, the length to which boards can be fitted is about 7ft 9in (2.3m).

Use upper and lower arris rails for fencing up to 4ft (1.2m) high, and an extra central rail for a higher fence. Rails may be supplied square sawn and need shaping.

You will need

Tools Spirit level with horizontal and vertical vials; hammer; block of wood about 3½in (90mm) wide as a width gauge for overlapping boards. Possibly also: panel saw; wood plane or shaping tool; power drill with wood bits.

Materials Posts – one for each 8ft (2.4m) section and one extra; two or three arris rails for each section; four 2in (50mm) galvanised or alloy nails for each rail; featheredge boards treated with preservative (probably 27-29 between posts); two 2in (50mm) galvanised or alloy nails per board; one 8ft (2.4m) gravel board for each section. Possibly also: capping strip and nails (page 467); clips or timber battens for fixing gravel boards (page 467).

FITTING ARRIS RAILS

1 With the end post in position (page 468), insert one shaped end of each rail into the post to the full depth of the slot.

2 Hold the second post in position while you fit the other ends of the rails into the post slots to half the depth of the slot (for intermediate posts, there will be a rail fitted in from each side).

HELPFUL TIP

If the featheredge boards need treatment with wood preservative (page 473), treat them before fitting them to the fencing. Do not apply the preservative to the fence after fitting all the boards in position, or the parts that have been overlapped will remain untreated.

SHAPING AN ARRIS RAIL

Use a panel saw to roughly shape the two short sides of the triangular rail so that they slope down to a flat stub of the same width as the fence slot. The third, widest side of the rail – to which the boards are nailed – should remain flat. Plane the surfaces smooth until the stub fits neatly into the slot to the required depth.

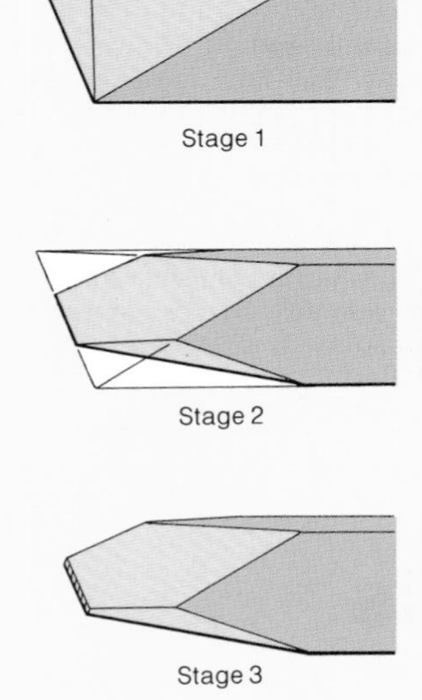

3 Support the post temporarily with timber lengths while you level it with the first post (page 468) and check also that the arris rails are horizontal.

4 Adjust the post as necessary before firming it in (page 468).

5 Nail the arris rails to the posts, driving one nail at an angle through the top of each rail and the other at an angle through the bottom of the rail.

6 Continue fitting posts and rails in the same way until the skeleton of the fence is complete.

FITTING FEATHEREDGE BOARDS

1 Fit the first board with its thicker end butted against the post.

2 Nail it to the centre of the top arris rail, driving the nail at a slight sideways angle.

3 Use a spirit level to check that the board is vertical before driving in the bottom nail – and the central nail, if there is one.

4 Place the width gauge on the first board, aligned with the thick edge, and fit the second board against it. The thick end of the second board should then overlap the thin end of the first board by about ½in (13mm).

5 Nail the second board to the rails, driving each nail through both boards at a slight sideways angle.

6 Continue fixing boards in the same way, checking continually that they are vertical.

7 Before fitting the last three or four boards, measure the gap still remaining to see whether you need to decrease or increase the overlap to fill the rail.

ALTERNATIVELY maintain the ½in (13mm) overlap and fill the last gap with a board fitted backwards – that is, with its thick end butted to the end post.

FITTING A GRAVEL BOARD

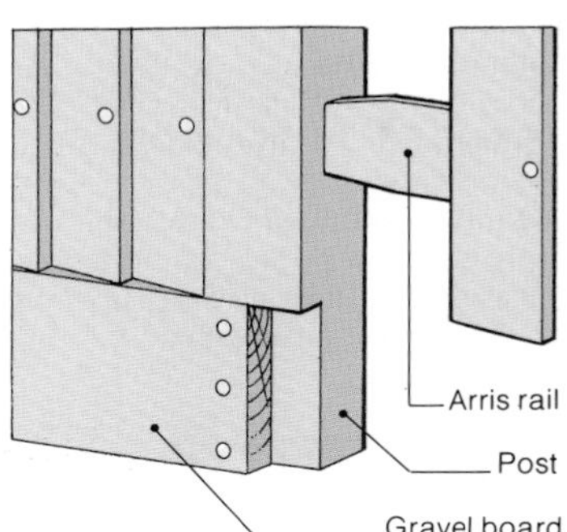

Some timber posts are recessed at the bottom on one side, and the board is nailed into the recess, flush with the front of the post and directly below the overlapping boards. Or the board can be trimmed to fit between the posts and fixed with clips (page 467).

For concrete posts, you may be able to use concrete gravel boards with special fixings. Or wooden gravel boards can be fixed to timber battens set into the ground beside the posts (page 473) while concreting them in.

FITTING A CAPPING STRIP

1 Saw off the fence posts level with the top of the fence boards. If the capping strip is not wide enough to completely cover the post tops, either fit a metal cap to each post (page 467), or slope the uncovered part.

2 Treat the exposed parts with wood preservative (page 473).

3 Place each capping strip to stretch from the centre of one section, across a post to the centre of the next section, with strip ends butted.

4 Nail the strip to the top of a post with 2in (50mm) galvanised or alloy nails.

5 Use 1in (25mm) nails to nail the strip to board tops at each end, and at one or two places in between. Take care not to split the boards. If you find that the nails are tending to split the wood, drill a pilot hole for each nail.

Fixing other types of fencing to posts

TIMBER POSTS AND RAILS

For rails slotted into posts, put up posts in pairs (page 468) and fit the rails between. Nail the rails in the same way as arris rails (facing page), using 2in (50mm) galvanised or alloy nails.

For rails nailed to posts, put up a line of posts before fixing the rails. Allow two posts for each stretch of rails, and one for the end of the run. Butt the rail ends on alternate posts, and stagger the centre rails so they butt on the posts that the other two rails run across. Use 3in (75mm) galvanised or alloy nails.

PALISADE OR PICKET FENCING

Put up posts and arris rails in the same way as for a closeboard fence (facing page). Use 2in (50mm) galvanised or alloy nails to fix the pales – preferably pales with rounded or pointed tops to shed rain – to the rails. With 3in (75mm) spaces between 3in (75mm) pales, you need 15 pales to fill a 7ft 9in (2.3m) run of rail between posts.

CHAIN-LINK FENCING

Concrete straining posts with ready-made holes (usually 15mm diameter) for eyebolts are normally used for chain-link fencing. Narrower intermediate posts have holes of about 9mm for fixing line wires.

Put up straining posts (page 468), at ends and corners, with intermediate posts between them at 10ft (3m) intervals. End posts should each have a support stay (page 468), and corner posts two support stays. Fences up to about 4ft (1.2m) have a line wire at the top and bottom, higher fences an extra wire in the centre.

With timber posts, you can either fit the mesh with stretcher bars as described below, or use eyebolts for line wires only and staple the mesh to the posts. You may have to drill holes for the eyebolts. Corner posts need two sets of bolt holes at right angles to each other, one set slightly higher than the other.

You will need

Tools Spanner; pliers. Possibly also: drill with ½in (13mm) wood bit.
Materials Straining posts and intermediate posts; chain-link mesh together with galvanised line and tie wires; stretcher-bars (one for each end post and two for a corner post), together with eyebolts and angle cleats.

1 With posts in place, thread a stretcher bar through one end of the chain-link roll. Bolt angle cleats to the stretcher bar, and fix each to the first post with an eyebolt (loop end inwards). Leave the roll standing on end.

2 Thread a line wire through each of the eyebolt loops, securing the wire by twisting it with pliers.

3 Run the line wires to the next straining post, and secure them to the post with eyebolts. Do not tauten the wires yet.

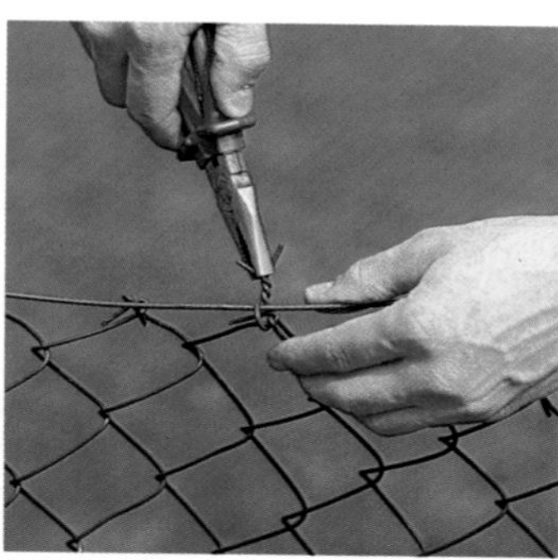

4 Unroll the chain-link mesh along the line wires, keeping it as taut as possible. Secure the mesh to the line wire with tie wires as you go along. Use tie wires at 6in (150mm) intervals on the top wire and at 18in (460mm) intervals on the bottom (and middle) wire.

5 When you reach the straining post, untwist two linked wires at the top and bottom of the mesh and unthread them to separate the secured fencing from the roll.

6 Thread a stretcher bar through the last row of meshes. Undo the eyebolts holding the line wires to the post, fit the bolts through the angle cleats of the stretcher bar, and fasten the bar to the post with the eyebolts.

7 Tauten the line wires by tightening the eyebolt nuts with a spanner as necessary. Do not overtighten, or the line wires may snap and whiplash dangerously.

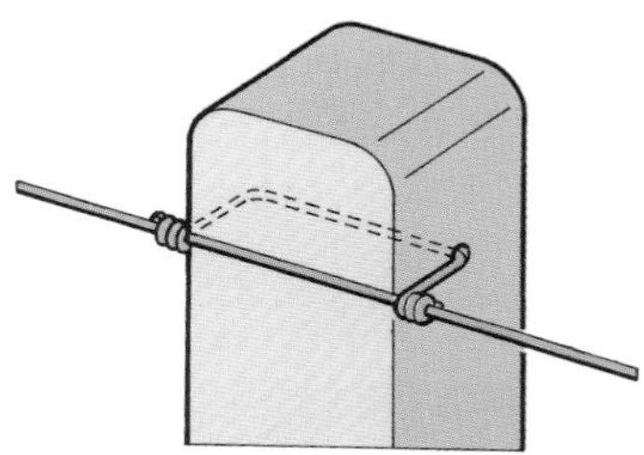

8 Use lengths of wire threaded through the intermediate post holes to secure the line wire stirrup fashion to the post.

WIRE NETTING

Put up posts at about 6ft (1.8m) or 8ft (2.4m) intervals (page 468).

Use eyebolts through the posts to stretch line wires between end and corner posts in the same way as for chain-link fencing (above). The netting can be stapled to timber posts, or tied to concrete posts stirrup fashion. Use tie wires to tie the mesh to the line wires.

To keep out rabbits, bury wire mesh 6-12in (150-300mm) below ground. Mesh of 1½in (38mm) or 1¼in (32mm) is suitable.

POST-AND-WIRE FENCING

Put up straining and intermediate posts (page 468) in the same way as for chain-link fencing (above), and use eyebolts to stretch line wires between the straining posts of the fence.

The line wires can either be threaded through or tied to the bolt holes on intermediate concrete posts, or stapled to intermediate timber posts.

Fence repair and maintenance

All wood is susceptible to rot and attack by wood-boring insects, so treat fences (and other garden woodwork such as sheds and garage doors) with wood preservative regularly to prolong their life.

Timber rots in contact with earth, so whenever possible keep it from direct contact with the ground. Never pile soil against a wooden fence.

Timber fence posts are most likely to rot at the bottom below ground, and will eventually collapse and bring down part of the fence unless reinforced in good time. To prevent a post rotting from the top downwards, slope the top or fit a post cap (page 472).

Featheredged boards often get brittle and start to crack if they are not kept well protected with wood preservative. So do arris rails, which take a lot of strain in supporting featheredged boards or palings, and will quickly get worse unless repaired.

REINFORCING A FENCE POST

If the main part of a rotting post is still sound, it can be supported with a concrete spur (page 467). Alternatively, it can be cut short and refitted with its base in a metal post spike (page 467). If the rot extends higher than the top of the gravel board, you will have to free the fencing from the post on either side before you can cut the rot out. It may be simpler to replace the post.

You will need

Tools Handsaw; old paintbrush; timber lengths for fence supports; timber length for compacting concrete; spade; hammer; brace and ½in (13mm) auger bit; spirit level with horizontal and vertical vials; spanner; hacksaw.
Materials Wood preservative (page 473); concrete spur; two ⅜in diameter coach bolts about 8in (200mm) long; nut and washer for each bolt; concrete foundation mix (page 496).

Fence repair and maintenance (continued)

1 Temporarily support the fence on each side of the post with pieces of timber.

2 Remove the gravel board and cut off the rotting part of the post back to sound wood.

3 Coat the whole post, especially the bottom and end grain, with wood preservative.

4 Dig out a hole alongside the damaged post to a depth of about 18in-24in (460mm-610mm). Make the hole at least 12in (300mm) square.

5 Put the spur in the hole, fitted snugly against the post.

6 Slip the coach bolts through the holes in the spur and strike them firmly with a hammer to mark their positions on the post.

7 Remove the spur and bore holes through the post at the marked spot.

8 Push the bolts through the post and spur so that the tails are on the spur side. Slip on the washers and nuts and tighten the nuts with a spanner.

9 Use a spirit level to check that the post is vertical, pushing it upright as necessary. Then brace it firmly with lengths of timber.

10 Ram hardcore into the bottom of the spur hole, then pour in the mixed concrete, pressing it well down with the end of a piece of timber.

11 Wait 24 hours before moving the timber supports, to give the concrete time to set.

12 Use a hacksaw to cut off the protruding bolt threads slightly proud of the nuts.

REPLACING A TIMBER FENCE POST

You will need

Tools Pincers or claw hammer; narrow spade; spirit level with horizontal and vertical vials; length of timber longer than distance between posts; timber lengths for supporting post; earth rammer (page 490). Possibly also: timber length; nails; strong rope; pile of about five or six bricks.

Materials Treated fence post same size as old one; hardcore (page 487) – probably 3-6 bucketfuls; two or three arris-rail brackets (see below); 2in (50mm) galvanised nails.

1 Support the fence on each side of the post with lengths of timber, wedged under the panel top or upper arris rail.

2 Free the post from the fencing. Undo panels by removing the nails or clips on each side. For vertical closeboard fencing, remove the first board on one side and saw through the arris rails. Remove nails holding the rails to the other side of the post so that they can be pulled out when the post is moved.

> HELPFUL TIP
>
> If the post is difficult to remove, or if it breaks off and leaves a stump, lever it out using a length of timber and a large stone or a pile of bricks about 12in (300mm) high. Lash one end of the timber length to the post or stump, and lay the timber across the stone or brick pile as a balancing point.
>
> 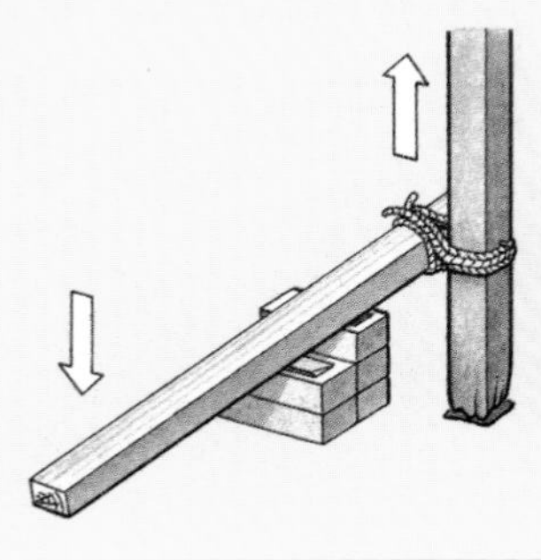

3 Dig down beside the post to free it at the bottom. Then remove the post and clear the hole.

4 Fit the replacement post in the same way as putting up a new post (page 468), but on a closeboard fence, fit the shaped arris rails on one side into the slots as you put the post in. Before you fill in and firm the hole, make sure the fencing will fit flush on both sides.

5 Refit sawn off arris rails to the post using metal arris-rail brackets, but nail shaped arris rails (page 468). Refit panels with nails or clips (page 469).

6 If the post top is square cut, either cut it to a slope or fit a post cap (see below). Treat sawn areas with wood preservative.

REPAIRING A POST TOP

Before repairing the post, probe the top with a sharp knife to find out the extent of the rot. Saw off the rotted area back to sound wood.

Timber or metal post caps are sold ready made. Soak a home-made wooden cap in wood preservative for 24 hours before fitting. The cap should be about ½in (13mm) wider than the post top all round. Nail it to the post with two ring nails driven in on the skew – at an angle from each side. Check wooden caps periodically, and replace any with signs of rot.

A metal post cap can be home-made from a sheet of zinc or aluminium cut about 1in (25mm) wider than the post top and turned down round the edges.

MENDING A CRACKED ARRIS RAIL

Strengthen a rail cracked in the middle with a straight arris rail bracket – a metal bracket about 12in (300mm) long shaped to fit the rail, with ready-made holes for screws or nails. Fasten it with galvanised or alloy 1in (25mm) screws or 2in (50mm) nails.

If the crack is near a post, use a flanged arris-rail bracket. The two flanges – projecting rims at right angles to the bracket – can be fastened to the post. If the post is concrete, use screws and wall plugs (page 232) to fasten the flange to the post.

Tighten a loose arris rail by pinning it with a wooden dowel about 2in (50mm) long. Drill a hole for the dowel through the front of the post about ¾in (19mm) from the edge where the loose rail fits.

Before inserting the dowel, cut a shallow groove along it and coat it all over with waterproof adhesive (page 190). The groove releases excess glue and trapped air.

REPLACING A BROKEN ARRIS RAIL

If the fence posts are concrete, the rails may be bolted to recesses in them, and are easy to replace. Or they may be fitted into mortises in the same way as timber posts, and repaired as described here.

You will need

Tools Panel saw; hammer; plane or shaping tool; pencil.

Materials Arris rail, normally 8ft (2.4m) long, treated with wood preservative; flanged arris-rail bracket (see above); 2in (50mm) galvanised or alloy nails.

1 Hammer the boards or palings away from the damaged rail.

2 Withdraw the nails to pull the damaged rail from the slots at each end. If necessary, saw through the rail flush with the post at one end.

3 Shape one end of the new rail to fit into the post slot (page 470).

4 Fit the new rail into the slot, mark where it will fit flush against the post at the other end, then saw it to length.

5 Refit the rail into the slot, and fix the other end to the post using the flanged bracket.

6 Refit the boards or pales to the rail, making sure they are vertical (page 468).

REPLACING A GRAVEL BOARD

If for any reason a rotting gravel board cannot be replaced without dismantling the fence – if it slots into concrete posts, for example – nail the new board to timber battens fitted beside the posts.

Remove the damaged board by drilling and sawing through flush with the posts at each end. Or, for a closeboard fence, remove a fence board at each end to make room for sawing. Support a panel on bricks.

Treat the new gravel board and the timber battens with wood preservative at least 24 hours before fitting them. For timber posts, use 6in (150mm) battens, which can be nailed to the posts. For concrete posts use battens 24in (610mm) long, driven about 18in (460mm) into the ground beside the posts, as near as any concrete bedding will allow.

Dig a shallow groove under the fence to make way for the new board. Fix the battens so that the board can be fitted flush with the front of a closeboard fence, or centrally under a panel fence. Support the battens from behind while you nail the gravel boards to them. Keep soil away from the board as much as possible.

REPLACING A PANEL

Fence panels are made in standard sizes, so removing a damaged panel and fitting a new one in the same way (page 469) is not usually difficult.

If the new panel is slightly too wide, plane off a small amount of the frame on each side. If, however, it is not wide enough, close the gap

with a narrow fillet of wood inserted between the post and the panel frame. Treat the wood fillet with preservative before fixing it.

REPAIRING FEATHEREDGE BOARDING

Replace damaged or rotten boards with new boards that have been treated with wood preservative (see below).

One nail secures two overlapped boards, so to remove a board you will have to loosen the overlapping board as well and pull out the common nail. Fit the new boards as on page 470.

Undamaged boards sometimes become loose because their nails have rusted. Refit the boards using 2in (50mm) galvanised or alloy nails that will not rust.

If featheredge boards are rotting at the bottom where there is no gravel board, saw them off along the base to leave a gap of at least 3in (75mm).

APPLYING WOOD PRESERVATIVE

Coat existing timber fences with wood preservative regularly, particularly any joints or end grain. The period between treatments depends on the type of wood preservative used and how exposed the fence is. Most modern preservatives will last 2 or 3 years.

Timber for a new fence should be pre-treated with preservative by the manufacturer, preferably by a vacuum/pressure process. Even so, coat it with more preservative before you fix it in place, taking extra care to soak cut edges.

The best time to apply wood preservative is when the wood is thoroughly dry but the sun not too hot – probably in late summer after a dry spell, with no rain expected for a day or two. Damp wood will not absorb the preservative.

Preservative can be applied with an old paintbrush or a garden pressure spray. Or there are kits on the market which pump the liquid from the container to a brush. Always follow any safety precautions given on the container. With some preservatives you should protect your skin and eyes while you are applying them. Coverage is generally around 5-12sq yds (4-10sq m) per litre, but varies according to the type of preservative and the porosity of the wood.

A wide range of wood preservatives is available. One of the best known is creosote, which is made from tar oil. It is cheap but needs yearly application, and its fumes are unpleasant. When wet it is harmful to plants (though it is harmless when dry), and wood treated with it cannot be painted.

Most modern preservatives are either solvent-based or water-based, and contain chemicals or salts that destroy fungi and insects. Solvent-based types give off flammable fumes, and naked flames should be kept away until the preservative is quite dry – until at least 2 days after application. Look for a warning on the container. Water-based types have no smell. Neither type is harmful to plants once dry, but guard against splashing any on plants. Treated wood can be painted, but many brands contain colouring.

Methods of hanging a gate

There are three main ways in which a gate can be hung from timber gateposts. The method depends on the types of fitting used.

Flush between posts
The gate is hung between the posts, with the back of the gate flush with the back of the posts.

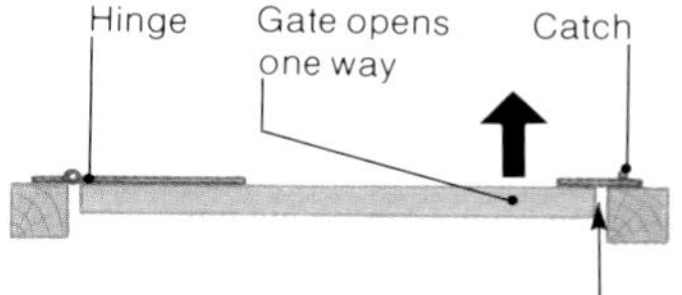

This is the usual method of hanging a timber garden gate with flush-fitting hinges. The gate opens one way only. The clearance for fittings on each side of the gate needs to be about ¼in (6mm).

Centred on posts
The gate is hung between the posts, with the gate width centred

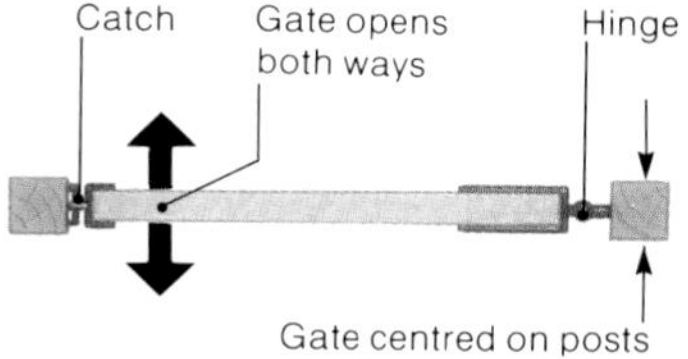

on the gatepost width. This method is common with wrought-iron gates, which usually hook onto a pin, and with double-strap hinges on timber gates. The gate will swing both ways unless there is a stop on the fastener. Depending on the type of catch, the clearance on the hinge side may need to be as much as 4in (100mm), and on the catch side about 2¼in (57mm).

Hung behind posts
The gate is hung on the back of the posts with an overlap of about ½in-1in (13mm-25mm) on each side. This method can be used for a pair of gates, or a wide single gate, hung on double-strap hinges. The

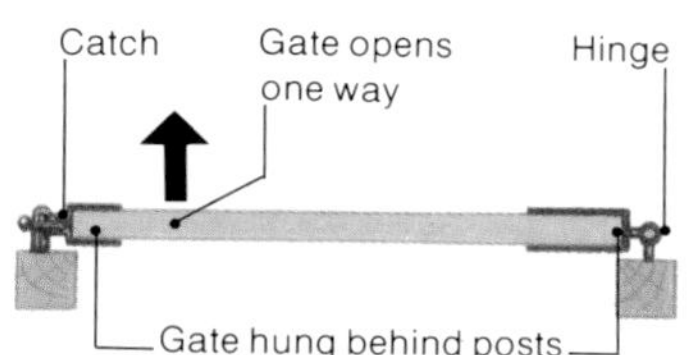

gates can swing inwards only, and slam shut against a post. The types of fastener that can be used are limited (page 476).

CHECKING THE DESIGN

Although some gates look the same both sides, many have supporting framework at the back. They are hung with the back of the gate on the inside.

Gates are often also designed for either right or left hanging. The hanging stile (the upright to which the hinge is fitted) may be wider than the slam or swinging stile (the upright to which the fastener is fitted).

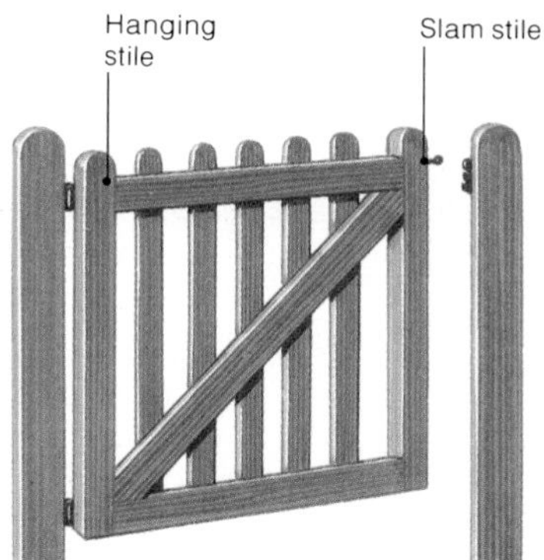

Wooden gates should be braced – with a diagonal strut between the top and bottom rails of the frame – or they will sag. Where there is only one diagonal brace, the gate must be hung with the top of the brace on the swinging side and the bottom of the brace on the hinge side.

Double gates must be a properly matched pair, designed for left and right hanging.

Methods of hanging a gate (continued)

BUYING GATES AND GATEPOSTS

Do not buy a gate until you are sure how wide you want it and how you are going to hang it. The width and fitting method are interdependent. Check also that the gate is designed to hang on whichever side you require – either right or left. If it is to hang across a sloping driveway, it will need to accommodate rising hinges – some types are self-closing. Gates are made in both metric and imperial sizes. Make certain you know the exact width, as conversions are inaccurate. The width range for both systems is generally similar.

Single gates range in width from 3ft (about 900mm) to about 12ft (3.7m), increasing by increments of 1 or 2ft (300 or 600mm). Double gates may range from about 13ft (4m) to 20ft (6m) wide. The height range is typically from 3ft (about 900mm) to 6ft (1.8m), but gates as high as 6ft 6in (2m) and 8ft 6in (2.5m) are available.

If you are buying gateposts as well, make sure timber ones are treated with preservative (page 468). They are generally 6-8ft (1.8-2.4m) long, and range from about 4in (100mm) square to 8in (200mm) square for wide, heavy gates.

Concrete posts may be available with ready-drilled holes for centred gate fittings, or may have top and bottom holes to which a strip of timber can be bolted as a fixing point for fittings. Do not use post spikes for putting up gateposts. They do not give enough support.

There are many different designs of gate available, including matching designs for most types of fencing. Some typical styles are shown below. Most of the types shown are available as double gates.

FITTING A GATE BETWEEN EXISTING SUPPORTS

If the distance between the existing timber posts or brick piers is too wide for the gate and fittings, narrow the gap by fitting timber battens (also called wall plates) on one or both sides. The gate fixings (facing page) can then be fitted to the timber battens. Make sure the battens allow sufficient clearance for the fittings. The gate can then be hung in the way described below. Fixings are also available for fitting gates directly to a brick pier.

If you cannot find a gate narrow enough to fit the gap between existing supports, you may be able to trim a piece off both stiles of a timber gate. Otherwise you will either have to have a gate specially made (more expensive than buying one ready made), or remove the existing gate supports and put up new ones farther apart.

CHOOSING A GATE

Closeboarded (featheredge)
Gates are usually ledged (with cross rails) and braced (with a diagonal bar). The top may be square or rounded.

Panel
In various designs to match panel fencing. Generally 3ft (910mm) wide and 2in (50mm) shorter than the fence height.

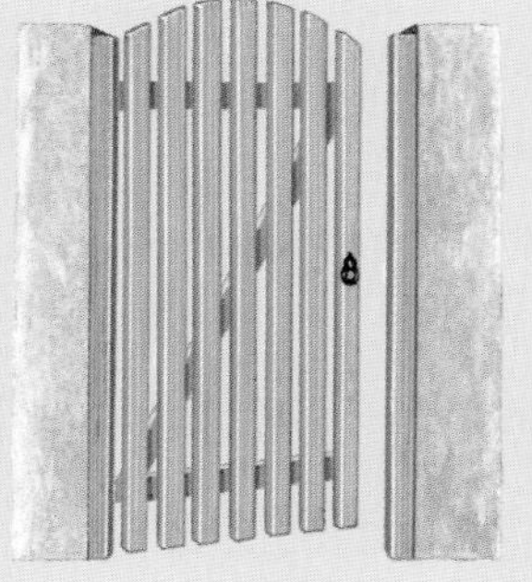

Open-boarded (palisade)
With spaced vertical pales that project above the upper cross rail. Gates are available in tall or short sizes.

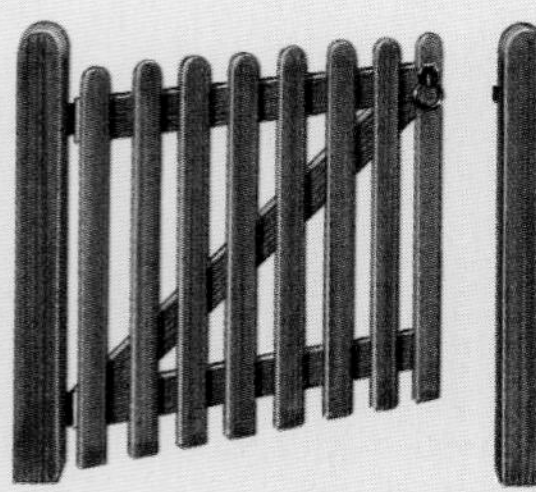

Open-boarded (palisade)
Pale tops may be square, rounded, pointed, or other shapes.

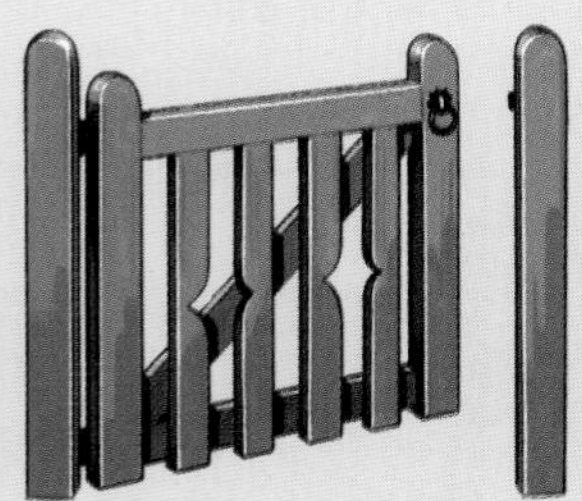

Open-boarded (framed)
With spaced vertical pales that do not protrude above the top bar.

Frame and panel
A timber frame with plywood panels.

Barred (field or country gate)
Usually with five or seven bars and one or more diagonal braces. Available as narrow garden gates or wide single gates suitable for driveways. Some types have a swinging stile with a curved heel at the top. A narrow hunting gate is often partnered with a wide driveway gate.

Wrought iron (single)
Decorative single or double, tall or small gates. Hinge and latch fittings are usually built in, or are on separate metal struts for fitting to gate supports.

Wrought iron (double)
Hinge pins may be downpointing on the gate or upright on the support. To deter thieves, fit a split pin through the hinge pin beyond the eye hook.

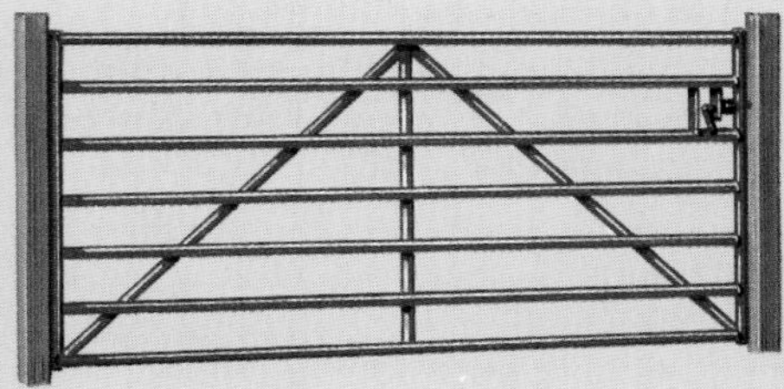

Tubular steel
Usually barred gates, with adjustable built-in forged eye hooks for hinge pins, and a spring-loaded bolt fastening.

CHOOSING GATE HINGES

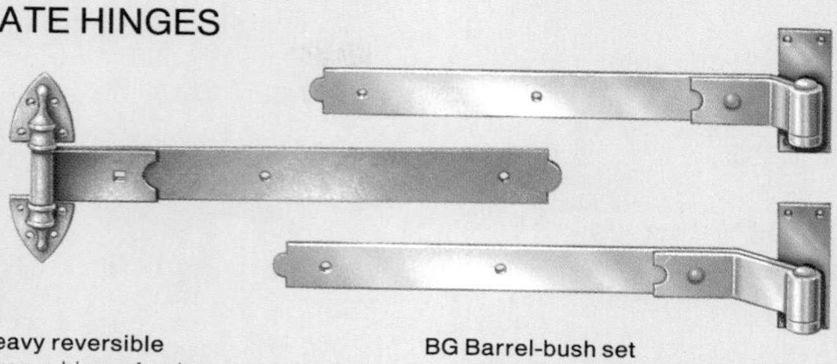

Tee
Commonly used for hanging light or medium-weight gates flush between posts. Heavier types are available.

Strap
For hanging light or medium-weight gates where frame, post and fence rail lie flush. Suitable for left or right hanging.

Heavy reversible
Strong hinge for heavy gates flush between posts. Can be used either way up. Hook held to pin by cups at each end.

BG Barrel-bush set
A cranked strap hinge for smaller gates flush between posts. Bushes between hinge pin and strap give smooth self-closing action.

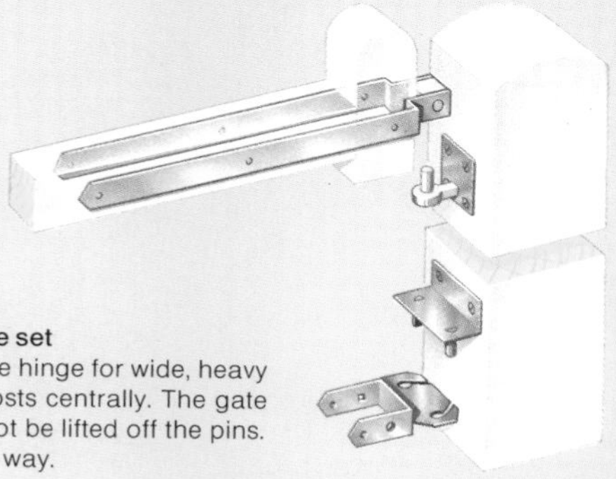

BG Captive rocker hinge set
Double strap or field gate hinge for wide, heavy gates. Hung between posts centrally. The gate is self-closing and cannot be lifted off the pins. It can be opened either way.

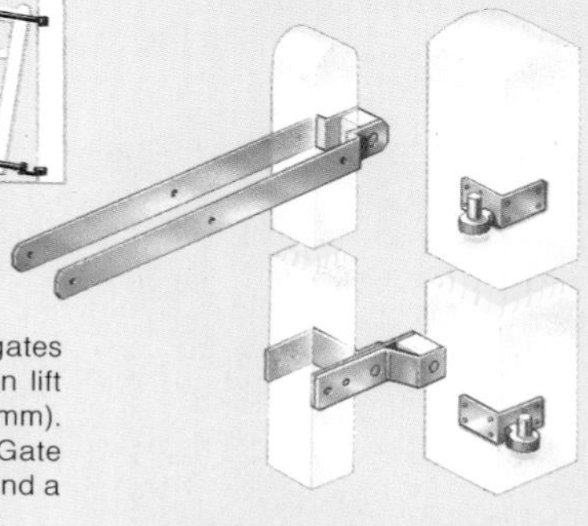

BG Rising hinge set
Double-strap hinges for heavy gates that open against a slope. Can lift gate up to almost 20in (500mm). Lower hinge slightly offset. Gate shuts with self-closing action, and a stop is needed to keep it open.

HINGE PINS FOR HANGING GATES

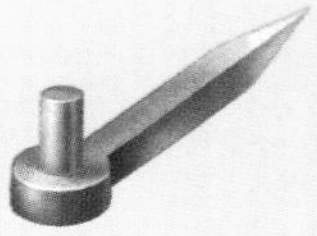

With pointed single prong for fitting into drill hole in post. Usually bottom fitting.

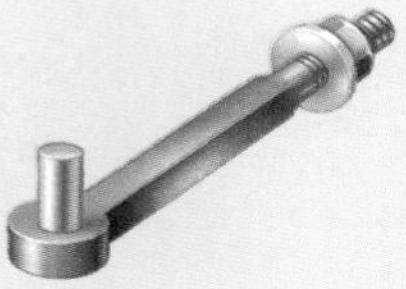

Pin and coach bolt combined for fixing through a post. Usually a top fitting.

Double-pronged fitting for building into the mortar layer of a brick wall or pier.

With broad or narrow fixing plates for screwing onto timber gateposts.

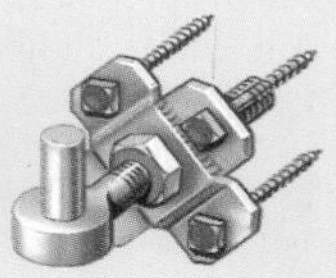

BG Adjustable hook that enables pin to be fitted upright on a leaning post or pier.

Fitting a gate and posts

For a gate to hang snugly between the posts with its base at least 2in (50mm) above the ground, the width between the posts must be accurately measured. Make sure that the bottom of a diagonal brace is on the hinge side.

For small, light gates, gateposts should be about 4in (100mm) square and about 24in (610mm) longer than the gate height. For bigger, heavier gates – over 4ft (1.2m) high or wide – posts should be up to 8in (200mm) square and at least 30in (760mm) longer than the gate height. Post tops should be sloped or fitted with caps to prevent rotting. Buy fittings that are either japanned (black painted) or galvanised to resist rust.

You will need

Tools Length of timber longer than width of gate and posts; pencil; spade or post-hole borer; spirit level with horizontal and vertical vials; builder's square; six timber pieces for temporary post-support stays; pegs to hold stays; timber length for ramming hardcore; two bricks or blocks; about six timber wedges to allow for width of gate fittings; drill and twist bits.

Materials Gate; two gateposts treated with timber preservative; two hinges; gate fastener; galvanised or alloy screws for hinges and fastener; two bricks; rubble or hardcore; concrete – foundation mix or 25kg bag of coarse dry mix (pages 495, 496) to make probably about 1 bucket per hole.

POSITIONING THE POSTS

1 Lay the gateposts parallel on flat ground with the gate face down between them. For flush fitting, raise it as necessary to line up with the back of the posts.

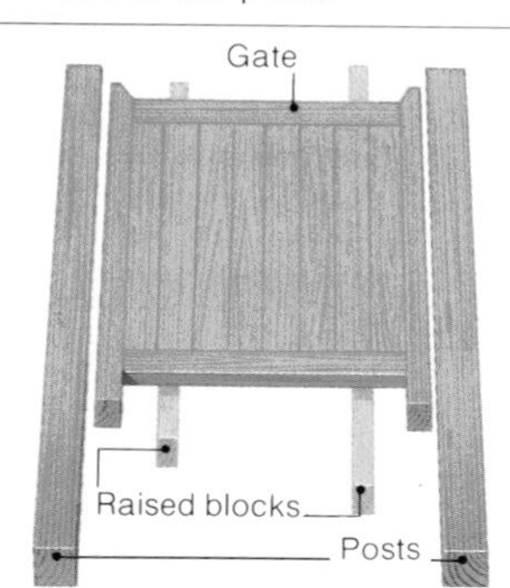

2 Position the gate about 2in (50mm) below the tops of the posts.

3 Use a long piece of timber and a builder's square to make sure the posts are aligned at the top and bottom and are a uniform distance apart.

4 Place the hinges and catches in position. Adjust the posts as necessary to give clearance for the fastenings to operate.

5 Lay a length of timber across the posts about 2-3in (50-75mm) below the bottom of the gate, and use it as a straight-edge to mark a line across each post. This is the depth to which the posts should be sunk.

CHOOSING GATE FASTENERS

FOR GATES HUNG FLUSH BETWEEN POSTS

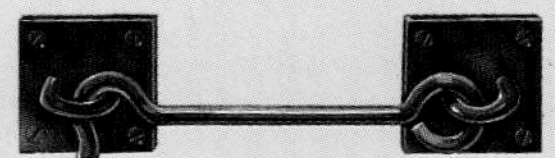

Cabin hook and staple
3in-12in (75mm-305mm) long.

BG Super loop
Loop-over fastener for double gates. Made for 2in (50mm) or 3in (75mm) wide gates.

Locking bar with hasp and staple
For padlock fastening. 4in-12in (100mm-305mm).

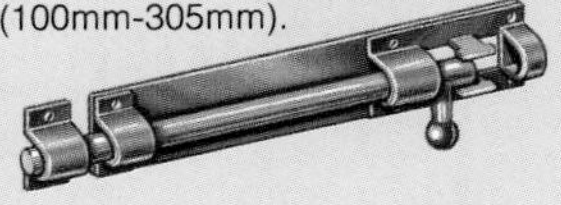

Tower bolt
6in-8in (150mm-200mm) long.

Flat bar and staples
$11\frac{1}{2}$in (292mm) long.

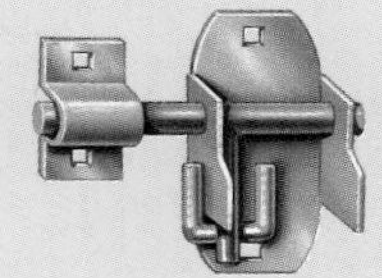

Oval pad bolt
4in (100mm) long bolt plate.

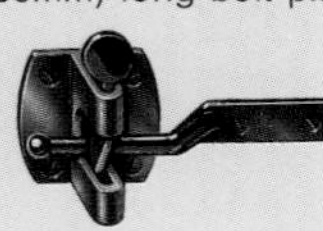

Automatic catch
Fits onto gatepost to receive a cranked bar fitted to the swinging stile of gate.

Suffolk pattern gate latch
Available with knob, ring or lever handles 7in (178mm).

Suffolk latch
Hook and lifting bar that can be raised from both sides; handle and thumb lever on outside. Ornate (Gothic) types and heavy-duty (Barrack) types available. Backplate $7\frac{1}{2}$in-$9\frac{1}{4}$in (191mm-234mm).

FOR GATES CENTRED ON POSTS

Chelsea catch
A bracket-held hook on the swinging stile fits into a catch on the inside of the gatepost.

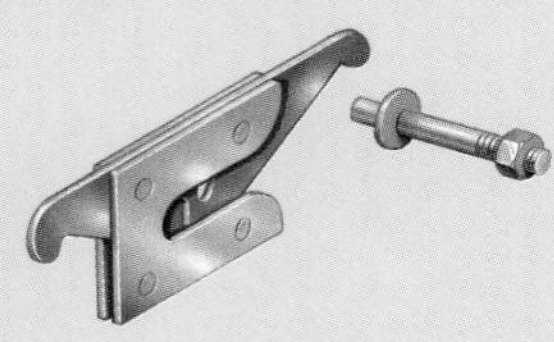

BG slim catch
Fits on the inside of the gatepost to catch a striker bolt on a centred or flush-fitting gate.

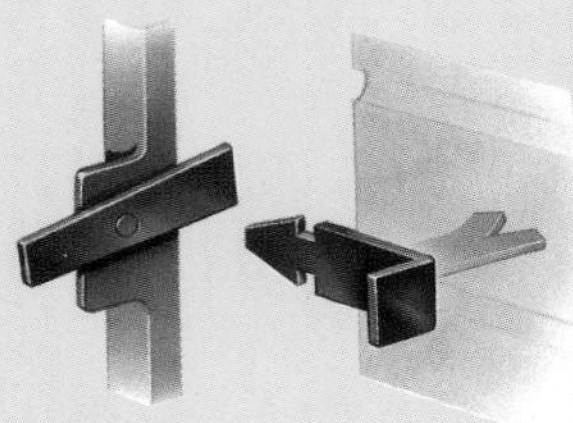

Double-handed catch
With a prong for fixing into the mortar of a brick pier. Suitable for built-in latch on wrought-iron gate. Has a stop to prevent the gate swinging outwards.

FOR GATES HUNG BEHIND POSTS

Automatic catch
Fits onto the back of the gatepost to receive a striker bolt on the swinging stile of the gate.

Spring fastener
A flexible bar on the swinging stile that catches in a hook on the back of the gatepost. The fastener may have a knob handle for pedestrian use (as shown), or a longer, hooked handle for horse riders.

6 Check that the marked lines are at right angles and the same distance from the top of each post.

7 Mark the timber length with the position of each side of each post.

8 Use the timber length as a gauge to mark the post positions on the ground. Dig holes about 12in (300mm) square and 3in (75mm) deeper than the depth marked on the post. Drop removed soil onto a plastic sheet for easy removal.

9 Place a brick flat in the bottom of each hole.

10 Lay the timber gauge across the holes as a guide to positioning the posts. Place each post in the hole on top of the brick and get a helper to hold it upright while you check with a spirit level that it is vertical. Then temporarily support it with timber stays wedged with pegs.

11 Use a flat piece of timber and a spirit level across the top of the gateposts to check they are level.

12 Anchor the post by ramming in rubble or hardcore. Leave the top 4in (100mm) for concrete.

13 Add the concrete, sloping the top to shed rainwater. Leave to set for a week, then remove post supports and hang the gate.

SETTING POSTS IN SOFT GROUND

On soft ground, the gateposts may be pulled inwards by the movement of the gate. To prevent this, dig a trench about 12in (300mm) wide and 8in (200mm) deep between the posts and fill it with concrete.

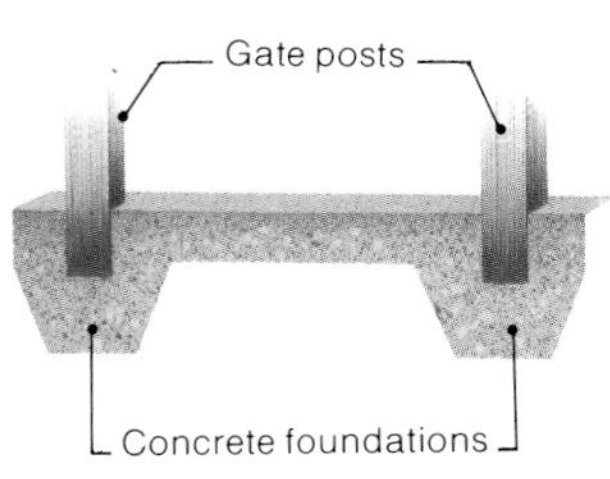

FIXING A GATEPOST TO A WALL

If the gate has to be positioned against a wall, you can buy fixing brackets for securing a post or wall plate to the wall or a brick pier. They comprise right-angled brackets with bolts that are anchored in the wall and plugs that are anchored in the post. A post adequately secured in this way will support the hanging or swinging side of the gate.

HANGING THE GATE

1 Place two blocks or bricks between the gateposts and stand the gate on them. For flush hinges, line the back of the gate with the backs of the posts. For pin fittings, centre the gate on the posts.

2 Use timber wedges to hold the sides of the gate in position with the correct clearance gaps for the fittings. Check with a spirit level that the top rail is horizontal.

3 Hold each hinge in place with the strap along the gate rail while you mark the position of the fixing holes on the post.

4 Drill pilot holes for two screws on each part of each hinge and partially fix each hinge. Then open and close the gate and check that it is level and swinging properly before you finish fitting the hinges.

5 Partially fix the fastener on the gate and post. Then check that it closes properly before you secure the fittings.

6 Fit a post cap to each gatepost unless the post top is sloped or rounded to shed rain. If you cut a square top to a slope, make sure it is protected with wood preservative.

HANGING A PAIR OF GATES

Cramp double gates together and hang them in the same way as a single gate, but with a clearance gap between them.

Use a strip of wood ½in (13mm) wide down the centre, and pack it out at the top to be ¾in (19mm) wide, so that the gap is wider at the top. This allows for initial wear on the hinges, which would otherwise cause the gates to drop at the centre. Use two or three large G-cramps to hold the stiles together, making sure the two gates are level with each other.

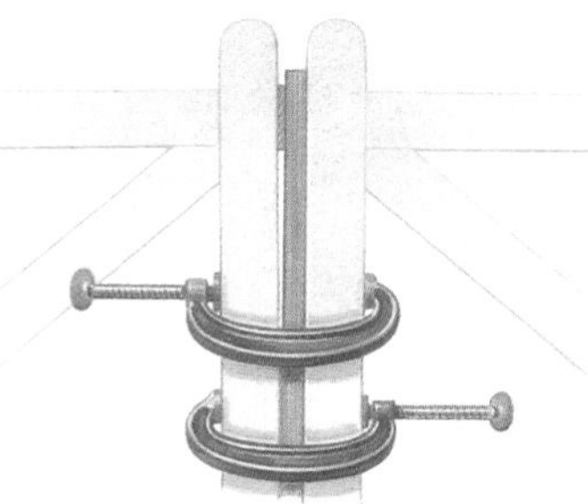

If the gates are cross-braced, make sure that the bottom of each diagonal is on the hinge side, so that the tops of the two diagonals meet in the middle.

CHOOSING GATE ACCESSORIES

Apart from hinges and catches, a gate may need other fittings. Double gates usually need a central ground socket of some sort to fit against, and a hook to hold the gate open is also generally necessary.

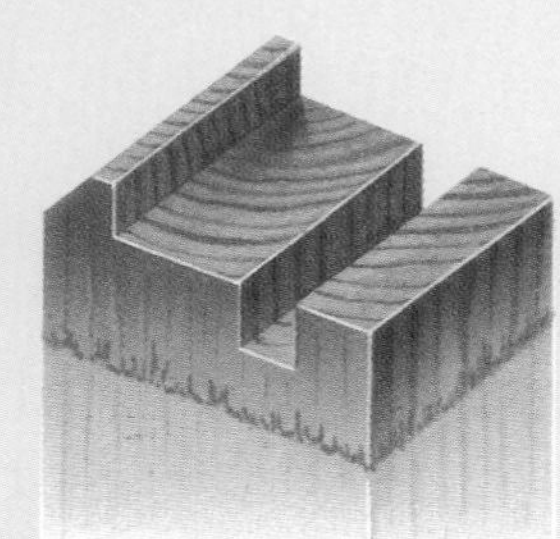

Centre stop block
Sunk into the ground at the meeting point of a pair of gates to stop them from swinging outwards, and to provide a locking point.

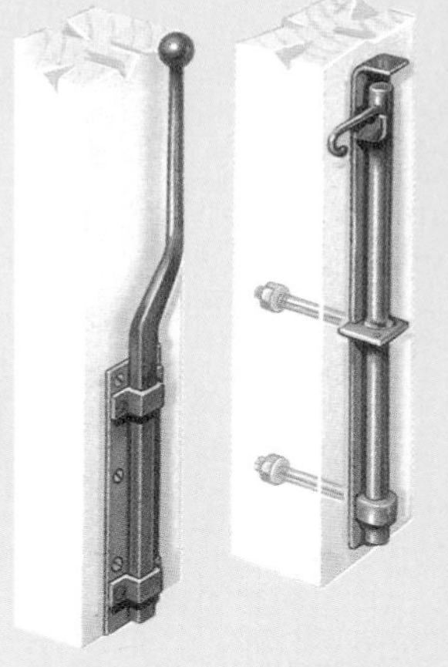

Drop bolts
For use with a centre stop block or a receiver socket or staple. A heavy-duty bolt (right) is best for double gates. A monkey-tail bolt (left) is easy to grasp.

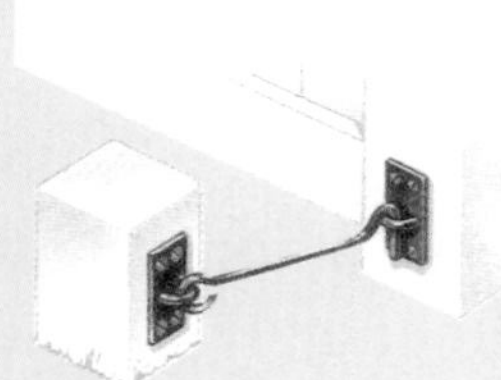

Hook-type hold back
Has to be fastened and unfastened by hand.

Counter-weighted hook
Stops a gate from swinging too far when it is opened, and also holds it open.

Looking after a gate

Keep gates well treated with timber preservative or paint to prevent rotting or rusting. Hinges can be smeared with oil or grease to guard against rust, but for latches, which are constantly handled, paint is preferable, unless they are galvanised or japanned metal.

REPAIRING ROTTEN TIMBER

Cut out small areas of rot on the gate back to sound wood and fill the cavity with a two-part wood-repair filler of the epoxy-resin type (page 106). This sets after about 15 minutes and can be sanded down with medium-grade glasspaper or a power sander to a smooth finish. It will not show after repainting.

Rotting timber parts such as pales or braces can be replaced. Treat new timber with a wood preservative (page 473), using a clear coating if it is to be painted later, or buy pre-treated timber, which will last longer. A rotting or damaged gatepost should be replaced or repaired in the same way as a fence post (page 472); but do not use a post spike. Also repair a rotting post top in the same way as a fence post top (page 472).

DEALING WITH RUST

Keep a look out for rust spots on fittings or metal gates, and remove them with emery cloth. Repaint immediately – rust can recur overnight. Remove severe rusting with a wire brush (wear safety spectacles). Do not use a proprietary remover if you are going to repaint with a rust-inhibiting paint. You can either repaint with a rust-neutralising primer followed by an undercoat and gloss coat, or use a one-coat paint such as Hammerite, which is both a rust-inhibitor and a finishing paint.

REPAIRING A SAGGING GATE

Check whether the hinges are loose. Replace loose hinge screws with longer, galvanised screws if possible. If not, tap wooden dowels (or fibre wall plugs) into the holes and use screws of the same size. Alternatively, if possible refit the hinges slightly higher or lower so that the screws will be biting into firm wood. Replace worn or broken hinges.

If the hinges are all right, the timber joints of the gate may be loose. An isolated loose joint can be repaired with a metal plate – tee, corner or straight – or an angle bracket. Try to force a waterproof adhesive up into the loose joint, then hold it together while you screw the bracket in place.

A very rickety gate should be either replaced or taken apart and remade. Clean away all old adhesive from the joints and reassemble using a waterproof adhesive (page 190). Reinforce mortise-and-tenon joints by drilling into the post and through the tongue of the tenon, then insert a glued dowel. After reassembling the gate, clamp it together while the adhesive dries.

A gate may sag because it has no diagonal brace, or because the brace is not strong enough (or the gate may have been hung on the wrong side). The brace should be firmly fitted between the cross rails on the back of the gate, with the top towards the latch.

Lift and wedge the gate into its proper position and make sure that it is a good fit before fixing the brace with waterproof adhesive and galvanised screws.

Ways of building a wall

A wall is built up of single layers of bricks or blocks, known as courses, cemented together with mortar. The pattern in which the courses are laid is known as a bond. The arrangement of bricks in a bond is designed to give the wall stability and strength by avoiding vertical mortar joints that run through two or more adjoining courses.

Walls built from suitable bricks (page 480) or blocks (page 481) are more expensive than fencing, but last longer, provided that they are built on solid foundations and given adequate frost protection.

Even a low wall can be dangerous if it falls down, and frost damage can cause bricks to disintegrate. Use strong mortar (page 481) and special quality frost-resistant bricks (F grade, page 480), at least for the first two courses.

If you use mainly ordinary bricks that are only moderately frost-resistant (M grade), protect the top course with a damp-proof membrane that has a sanded surface on both sides, sandwiched under coping stones. Use special shaped bricks (page 480) as a capping for frost-resistant bricks only, and fit a damp-proof membrane at least two courses below the wall top, to throw off any water that seeps down through shrunken mortar joints.

Do not use a damp-proof membrane in the lower part of a free-standing wall, as it affects stability.

You need planning permission from the local authority to build a wall higher than 3ft 3in (1m) beside a public highway, or for any free-standing wall over 6ft 6in (2m).

BRICK SIZES AND SHAPES

There is a standard size for bricks, and most are close to it, but sizes do vary slightly. The standard size is 215mm long, 103mm wide and 65mm deep – fractionally smaller than the imperial standard size of 8⅝in × 4⅛in × 2⅝in. The nominal size, which allows for a mortar joint of about ⅜in (10mm) all round, makes it easier to calculate the number of bricks needed. It is 225mm × 113mm × 75mm.

When planning a wall, the design and construction are easier if the dimensions are kept to an exact multiple of the nominal length of the bricks (or blocks) being used.

A brick laid with its long face exposed is called a stretcher. A brick laid with its short face exposed is called a header. Part bricks are cut as required. A brick cut across its width is called a bat, and a brick cut lengthways is called a closer. Many bricks have a V-shaped indentation, known as a frog, on one broad face. This helps to reduce weight. Some bricks are perforated with holes or slits instead.

TYPES OF BOND FOR BRICKS AND BLOCKS

BOND	METHOD OF CONSTRUCTION	QUANTITIES AND FOUNDATIONS NEEDED
Stretcher 	All bricks are laid lengthways, with a half brick at the end of every other course so that each vertical joint (perpend) centres on the bricks above and below. The wall is about 4in (100mm) thick and is known as a half-brick wall. It needs to be stiffened with piers (page 485) at each end and at 6ft (1.8m) intervals. Insert movement joints as for a flemish bond below.	Requires 54 bricks per square yard (0.8sq m), not including piers and capping (top layer). The foundation strip should be about 12in (300mm) wide and 18in (460mm) deep, made up of a 6in (150mm) deep layer of concrete on a 12in (300mm) deep bed of hardcore. Deeper foundations are advisable on a clay soil.
Open (or Honeycomb) 	A decorative stretcher bond with spaces between bricks. The simplest and most solid pattern is with quarter-brick spaces between bricks. Variations are half-brick spaces, or half-brick spaces between header bricks that project about 2¼in (57mm) each side of the wall. The last two spaces at each end or corner of the wall should be narrower to give stability. Piers are needed as for a stretcher bond. Insert movement joints as for a flemish bond below.	Requires 40 bricks per square yard (0.8sq m), for the simplest pattern, not including the piers and capping (see above). Foundations as for a stretcher-bond wall above.
Flemish 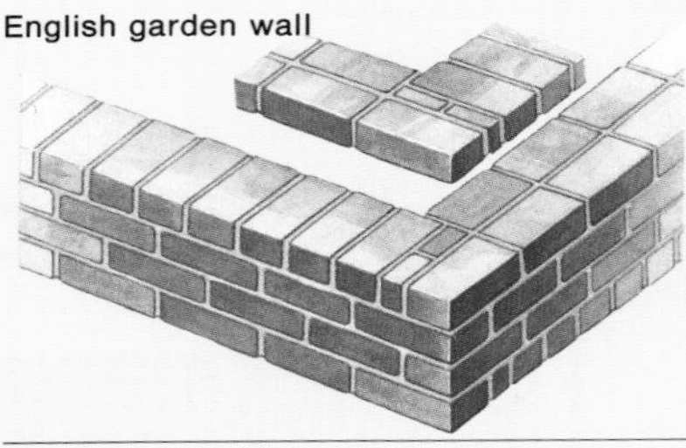	Pairs of parallel stretchers alternated with one header on each course, making a wall 8½in (215mm) thick. Closers are used on alternate courses to stagger the joints. This is known as a one-brick wall. It is more difficult to build than a half-brick wall, but stronger. Insert movement joints (page 485) every 26ft (8m) for clay bricks, or every 13ft (4m) for blocks or calcium-silicate bricks.	Requires 108 bricks per square yard (0.8sq m). Foundations for a wall up to 4ft (1.2m) high should be about 20in (510mm) wide and 20in (510mm) deep, made up of a 9in (230mm) deep layer of concrete on a bed of hardcore about 11in (280mm) deep. For higher walls get professional advice about foundations.
English garden wall 	Three courses of parallel stretchers alternated with one header course. Closers are needed on header courses to stagger the joints. Can be used for a one-brick wall, but is not quite as strong as a flemish bond. Insert movement joints as for flemish bond above.	As above, but cheaper because more of the bricks need be one-faced only (page 480).
Random	With courses made up of blocks of varying heights fitted together. Can be used with walling blocks only. Insert movement joints (page 485) at 13ft (4m) intervals.	Quantity depends on block sizes and patterns (page 481). Foundations as for flemish bond above, but with the strip about three times wider than the wall thickness.
Stack 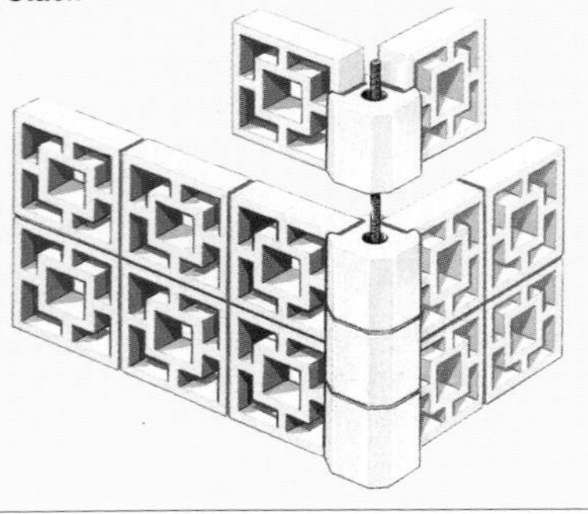	With all joints in line. Used mainly with pierced screen blocks (page 481). Piers (columns) are needed at both ends and at least every 10ft (3m). Insert movement joints (page 485) at 13ft (4m) intervals.	Requires 9 blocks per square yard (0.8sq m). Foundations for a wall up to four blocks high should be about 16in (400mm) wide and as deep as for flemish bond above.

Building tools you will need

Profile board
For marking the edges of strip foundations and walls. Make a uniform pair, or two pairs if the wall turns a corner. For each, use a board about 18–24in (460–610mm) long nailed across two 24in (610mm) battens with pointed ends for driving into the soil.

Notch the top edge of the board at suitable distances to mark each edge of the foundation strip and wall. The notches hold guidelines stretched taut between boards, one at each end of the site. Nails can be used instead of notches.

Spirit level
Used for checking the alignment of walls. It should have both horizontal and vertical vials, and preferably be about 3ft (1m) long.

Plumb line
Useful for checking that the wall is vertical. The line can be tied round and notched into a piece of board placed on the top course, so that it hangs down the wall as a guide while you work.

Builder's square
For checking that square corners are true right angles. A try square is not usually big enough for brick work. Make a square as shown (right). Any three lengths of wood joined in the ratio 3 : 4 : 5 must form a right angle.

Brick (or laying) trowel
A large trowel with a blade 10-13in (250-330mm) long, for spreading mortar when laying bricks.

Pointing trowel
A small trowel with a blade 3-8in (75-200mm) long, used for shaping mortar joints.

Mortar board (hawk)
Useful for holding mortar while working. The wooden, plastic or aluminium surface is about 12in (300mm) square with a central handle underneath. Make one using plywood or oil-tempered hardboard and broom handle. Can also be used when plastering.

Gauge rod
Used to check that each course of bricks is at the correct height. Make one from a length of 3in (75mm) square timber. For brick courses mark the gauge every 3in (75mm). For screen block walling (page 486) mark the gauge every 8in (200mm) for pier pilasters and every 12in (300mm) for blocks. If using other types of walling block (page 481), mark it as for the course heights (including mortar) required.

Line pins and building line
The flat-bladed steel pins are pushed into the mortar joints at the end of each wall once the ends or corners have been built up. The line stretched between them is raised for each course as a levelling guide while laying.

Brick bolster and club hammer
For cutting bricks. The spade-shaped bolster chisel has a 4in (100mm) wide blade, and is used with a $2\frac{1}{2}$lb (1.2kg) hammer.

Pointing tools
For some types of pointing (page 484) you need extra tools for shaping joints. A piece of sacking can be used to smooth flush joints. For concave joints you need either a piece of bent 15mm copper tubing, a piece of $\frac{1}{2}$in hosepipe, or something similar. Alternatively, use a roller pointing and raking tool that has different blades for either shaping various joints or for raking out old mortar.

MAKING A BUILDER'S SQUARE

Use three pieces of wood about 2in (50mm) wide and $\frac{3}{4}$in (19mm) thick, each accurately marked with one of the following lengths: 18in or 450mm (A); 24in or 600mm (B); 30in or 750mm (C).

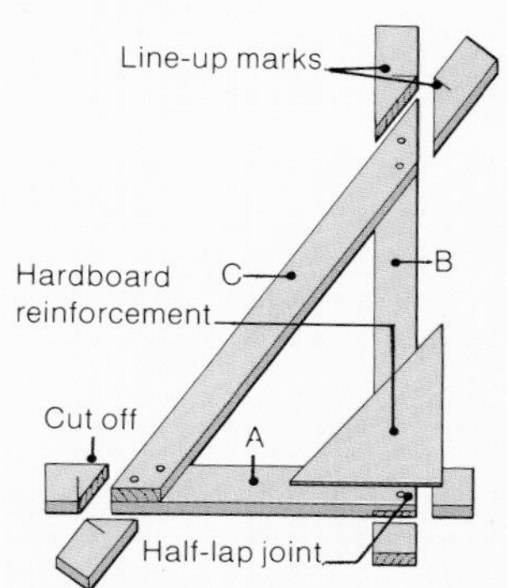

Line up all marks carefully before nailing lengths to each other. Use a half-lap joint for A and B, then overlap C. Check the right angle with a set square, saw off any overlap, then reinforce the corner with a piece of hardboard.

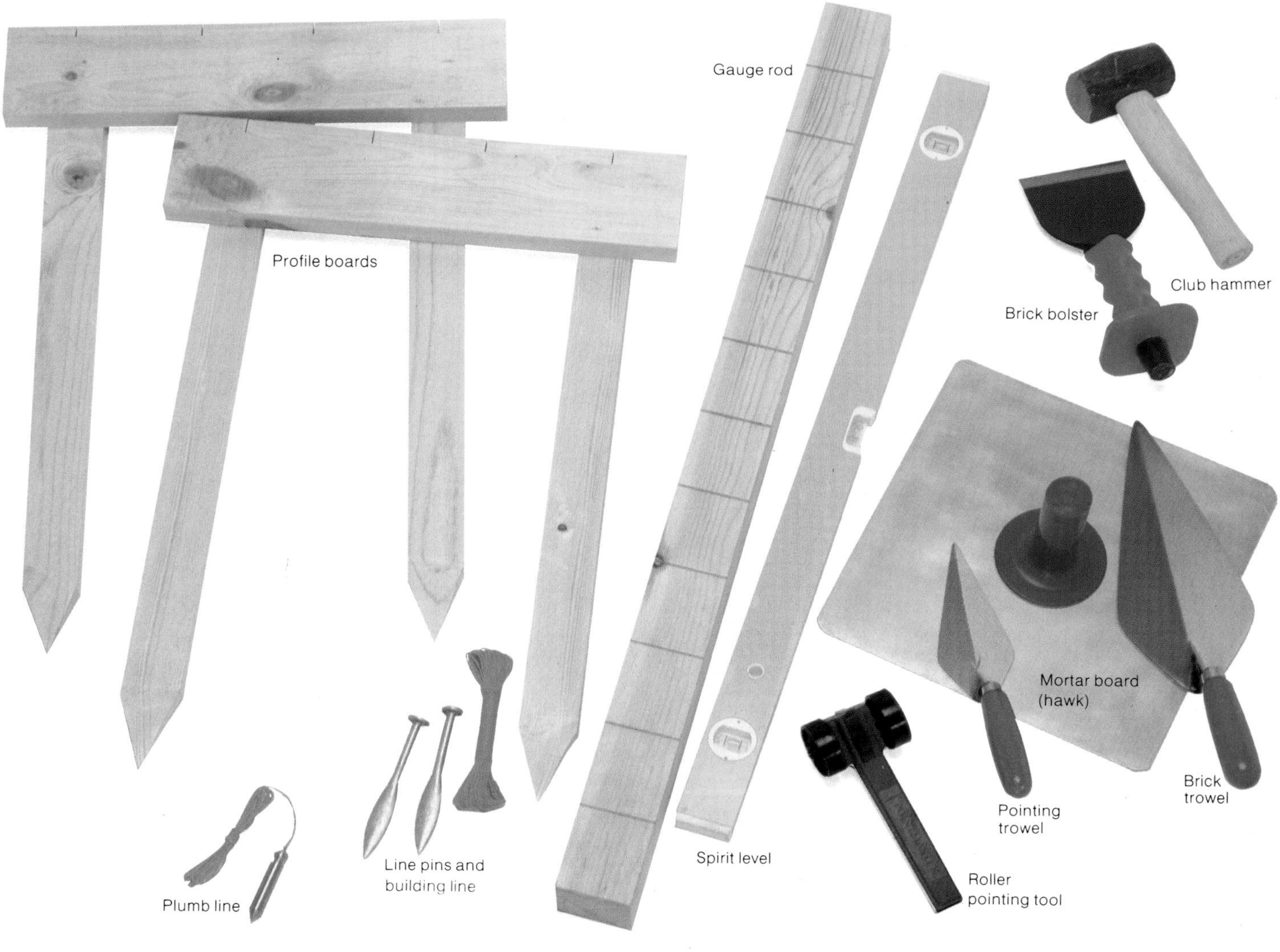

Profile boards
Gauge rod
Club hammer
Brick bolster
Mortar board (hawk)
Brick trowel
Pointing trowel
Spirit level
Roller pointing tool
Line pins and building line
Plumb line

Buying bricks or blocks

Bricks are mostly made from baked clay to a standard size, but some are made from lime mixed with sand or crushed stone or both (these are known as calcium silicate, sand-lime or flintlime bricks). There are also concrete bricks made from cement and aggregates. They resemble clay bricks and are about the same price. Blocks (see facing page) are generally concrete or stone made in various sizes.

Bricks are usually sold by numbers. Small quantities such as 100, 350 or 500 may be available from DIY stores, but builders' merchants normally sell them by the 1000. If transporting bricks, remember that 350 weigh nearly a ton.

GRADES AND TYPES

Bricks are graded according to their quality, which takes into account their frost resistance. The grading system was altered in 1985; new gradings are shown in brackets. F indicates frost-resistant, M moderately frost-resistant. Grades are not marked on bricks, but may be on packs. Check when buying, or with the maker.

INTERNAL QUALITY (now OL, ON) For indoor use only.

ORDINARY QUALITY (now FN, ML, MN) For outdoor use where conditions are not severe.

SPECIAL QUALITY (now FL) With a strong resistance to weather.

Different types are available in each grade, in both standard and special shapes. They include:

COMMONS Bricks for use where their appearance does not matter. They may be any grade, and vary widely in quality.

FACINGS Bricks with an attractive surface finish on one or more sides, and of either ordinary or special grades. They are more expensive than commons, and those faced on more than one side are dearer than one-faced types.

FLETTONS Widely used common or facing bricks made of clay from the Peterborough, Bedfordshire and Buckinghamshire regions.

COLOUR AND TEXTURE

There is a wide range of colours depending on the type of clay used and the manufacturing process; clay varies from area to area – for example, Staffordshire blues, Leicester reds. Multicoloured types are also available. Check the colours stocked by your local brick merchant, and ask to see a catalogue of other colours.

Textures also vary considerably and are either imposed or achieved by the choice of material. They include wirecut bricks, for which the clay has been extruded through a die then cut with wire; sandfaced bricks, which have sand incorporated in the surface during manufacture; and rustic bricks, with a mechanically imposed texture.

HOW TO STORE BRICKS SAFELY

Keep bricks dry. Bricks that are damp right through do not stick well to mortar. Dampness also leads to efflorescence – a white, powdery deposit (page 460).

Stack bricks on planks laid on a hard surface. Cover the planks with plastic sheeting. Build the stack so that the outer walls lean slightly inwards and will not collapse. Cover the stack with more plastic sheeting.

USING SECONDHAND BRICKS

Used bricks with a weathered look can be preferable to new ones for walls or paths in established gardens, or to blend with house walls. Secondhand bricks are generally expensive because of the work involved in handling. Their main drawback is that you do not know their quality – if they are frost-resistant or how strong they are. Bricks are mixed up during demolition, so it is mostly impossible to know their previous use. Do not use secondhand bricks for paving unless you know they are old paving bricks and are therefore likely to be frost-resistant.

Some manufacturers now produce simulated secondhand bricks. These have a weathered appearance and are of known quality, so are safer to use.

Metric-sized bricks are slightly smaller than imperial-sized bricks. Used bricks may be of either type, but not all bricks conform to the standard sizes of either.

The best way to remove the old mortar from uncleaned bricks is with a bolster chisel and club hammer. Wear heavy gloves and safety spectacles. Power tools are difficult to control and scoring or polishing can disfigure a brick.

Proprietary brick cleaners are not suitable for removing mortar, except for stubborn stains from brick faces. Wet the brick before applying the cleaner – this reduces surface absorption and prevents acid penetration.

BRICKS OF SPECIAL SHAPES

Bricks shaped for special use – known as specials – are more expensive than bricks of standard shape, and often more difficult to get. They usually have to be ordered. Many specials are designed for capping or corners.

Special bricks may be designed to lie on edge (65mm wide) or on the flat (103mm wide). Shaped corner bricks are known as internal or external returns.

CAPPING BRICKS

Saddleback coping

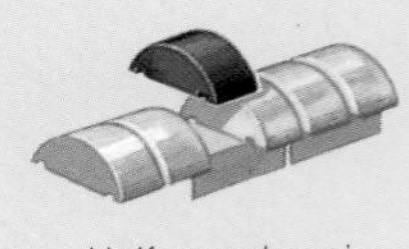

Half-round coping

Bullnose double stretcher

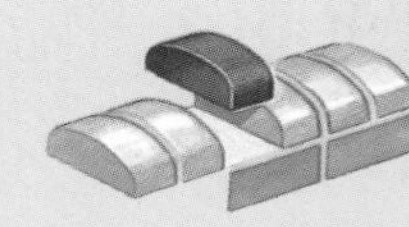

Bullnose double header

Bullnose header

Plinth header

Plinth stretcher

Double cant

CORNER AND END BRICKS

Single bullnose

Bullnose external return

Stop end to double bullnose

Bullnose on end (cownose)

Plinth external return

Plinth internal return (long)

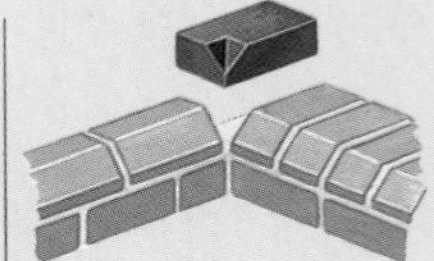

Plinth internal return (short)

Single cant

OTHER TYPES

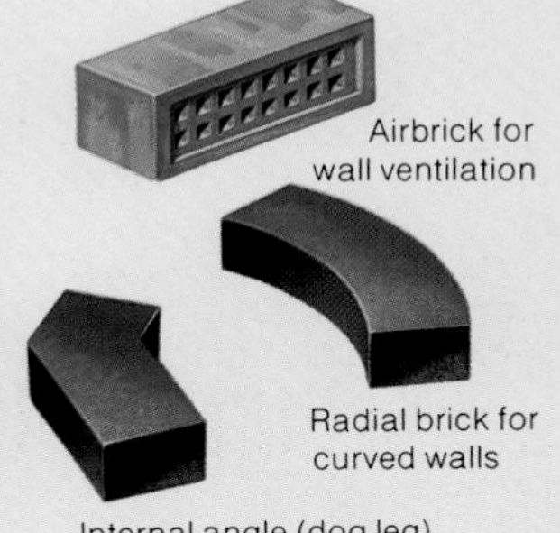

Airbrick for wall ventilation

Radial brick for curved walls

Internal angle (dog leg) for angled bends

CHOOSING DECORATIVE STONE BLOCKS

Natural stone is expensive and not easy to get. Some types of decorative walling block are made from reconstituted stone – that is, concrete made with an aggregate of crushed natural stone. They look very much like stone.

Blocks can generally be laid in the same way as bricks, but follow any special instructions given by the manufacturer. There is no standard block size, it varies according to the manufacturer, but blocks are generally larger than bricks, so wall construction is quicker. Manufacturers usually quote actual rather than nominal sizes, so where necessary allow ⅜in (10mm) for mortar joints when calculating dimensions.

Multistone garden walling
A large block made to look like a number of laid stones, and with textured stone faces resembling dry-stone walling.
Typical size Full block: length 20¾in (527mm), width 4in (100mm), depth 5¾in (147mm); half block: length 10¼in (260mm), widths and depth as for full block.

Single garden walling
Single block that resembles one stone and has one or two textured faces – either on one side and one end, or on both sides. It looks like dry-stone walling.
Typical size Length 12in (300mm), width 6in (150mm), depth 2½in (65mm).

Traditional walling
Blocks simulating various kinds of natural stone, made in a range of sizes for laying random courses (page 478). Jumper blocks (two courses deep) can be used, and L-shaped blocks for corners.
Typical size Nominal course depths: 3in (75mm), 4in (100mm), 5in (125mm) and 6in (150mm). Nominal length range: 8in-13in (200mm-335mm).

Pierced screen block
Square concrete block pierced with an openwork pattern. Used either to build a wall, or incorporated into a brick wall as decoration. Each block may have a complete pattern, or four blocks may be needed for a complete pattern. Special 5½in (140mm) wide, 1in (25mm) thick coping stone (see right) is available for wall tops.
Typical size Nominally 12in (300mm) square and 4in (100mm) thick.

Pilaster block
Grooved hollow block used to build piers (supporting columns) for pierced screen blocks. Grooves may be in one, two or three sides. Piers can be strengthened with iron rods through the centres of pilasters, and sunk into the ground (page 486).
Typical size Nominally 8in (200mm) high and 8in (200mm) square.

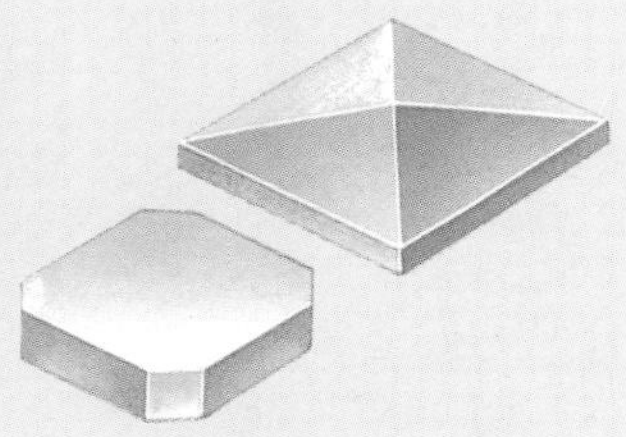

Pier cap
Square or shaped capping stone for brick, stone or pilaster piers (supporting columns). Pier caps usually slope on all four sides. Pilaster caps are generally flat.
Typical sizes Brick or stone piers: 12in (300mm) or 16½in (420mm) square; and 2in (50mm) thick, rising to apex of 3in (75mm). Pilaster caps: 8¾in (222mm) square, 2in (50mm) thick.

Coping stone or course capping
Concrete coping stone for the top of walling to protect it from the weather usually projects 1in (25mm) on each side. It may slope one way or two. Blocks simulating a soldier course (bricks laid upright or as headers on edge), or special-shaped bricks, can also be used.
Typical sizes: Length 18in (460mm), 24in (610mm); width 6in (150mm) or 12in (300mm); thickness 2in (50mm) with 3in (75mm) apex.

How to handle mortar

Cement, sand, and hydrated lime mixed with water make up the mortar used to stick bricks together. The lime acts as a plasticiser, making the mortar smooth and workable and preventing the sand and cement from shrinking and cracking when the mortar dries. Instead of lime, you can use proprietary liquid plasticiser – usually sold in 2½ litre (4½ pint) containers.

You can buy ready-mixed bags of dry bricklaying mortar to which only water has to be added. This is more expensive, but convenient for small jobs. Store ready-mixed bags in the same way as bags of cement (page 498).

Use strong mortar for a garden wall, to withstand strong winds and heavy rain. The standard mix is suitable for more sheltered areas.

PREPARING A MORTAR MIX

Mortar becomes unusable within two hours of mixing (sooner if the weather is hot). It cannot be enlivened by mixing in a little more water, as this would make it too soft to support a brick.

Mix it in small batches to avoid waste. After a time you will be able to gauge how much to make up at a time according to the rate at which you lay bricks.

You will need
Tools Clean mixing surface such as concrete or a mixing board (page 494), two clean shovels, one solely for cement; two heavy-duty polythene measuring buckets of the same size, one solely for

PROPORTIONS FOR MIXING

INGREDIENT	STRONG MIX FOR GARDEN WALL	STANDARD MIX	APPROXIMATE QUANTITIES FOR STRONG MIX
Ordinary Portland cement (usually grey; white or coloured available – page 495)	1 part	1 part	One 50kg bag for every 400–500 bricks
Hydrated lime *Or* mortar plasticiser	¼ part As instructed on container	1 part	Half a 25kg bag for every 400–500 bricks. About 2½fl oz (0.07 litre) for each 50kg bag of cement
Clean building sand (soft sand) (page 495)	3 parts	6 parts bricks 5 parts blocks	0.1cu m (3½cu ft) for every 50kg bag of cement
Bagged bricklaying mortar mix (page 495)	—	—	One 40kg bag for roughly 150 bricks

How to handle mortar (continued)

cement; watering can with fine spray rose.
Materials Ordinary Portland cement; hydrated lime or plasticiser; building sand; water.

1 Measure out the amount of sand you require on the mixing surface. Use a quarter bucketful as a part measure to start with.

2 Use a separate bucket and shovel to measure out the cement and add it to the sand. Do not use the bucket and shovel for other ingredients or mixing, otherwise the cement in the bag could get damp and be spoiled.

3 Mix the sand and cement together thoroughly with the other shovel until they are a consistent greyish colour.

4 Mix in the hydrated lime. Or use a proprietary plasticiser instead, following the instructions on the container for the amount.

5 Make a crater at the top of the pile and pour in a little water from a watering can.

6 Shovel from the outside of the pile into the middle to mix in the water in the crater.

7 Continue adding small amounts of water and turning the pile over with the shovel until the mortar is a stiff mix that falls off the spade cleanly. It is then ready for use.

HELPFUL TIP

One way of speeding up the mixing process is to prepare a batch of sand and lime mix – known as 'coarse stuff' – beforehand and add cement to it as required. Soak the amount of hydrated lime you are likely to need in cold water the night before use. Next morning, pour off the water and mix the lime with the required proportion of sand. Coarse stuff will last a day. It might stiffen up, but can be made workable by adding a little water.

Laying strip foundations

Every wall must be built on a firm, level foundation or it will soon crack and fall down. The usual foundation is a solid layer of concrete on a bed of hardcore; though you need not use hardcore if you are satisfied that the ground beneath is firm. A low wall can be built on a flat, firm surface such as a patio, as long as it has an adequate sub-base and the slabs are set on a full bed of mortar. Set it back from the edge the same distance again as its thickness, but not less than 6in (150mm).

You will need
Tools Spade; profile boards (page 479); string; heavy hammer; earth rammer (page 490) or stout length of timber; pencil or chalk; steel tape measure; spirit level; rake; straight-edged board; mixing platform (page 494); brick trowel.
Materials Hardcore (page 487); marker pegs 18in (460mm) long; concrete (page 495); sharp sand.

1 Mark the edge of each side of the foundation strip using string lines and profile boards (page 479).

2 Remove 2-3in (50-75mm) of topsoil and spread it elsewhere.

3 Measure from the top of each marker peg and mark lines showing the bottom of the concrete layer and the bottom of the hardcore layer (page 487).

4 Drive in marker pegs on each side of the strip at about 3ft 3in (1m) intervals, with their tops at the required height for the surface of the concrete. Generally, the concrete is level with a hard surrounding surface, or 1-2in (25-50mm) below a lawn edge.

5 Level adjacent and opposite pegs using a spirit level, set on a length of board if necessary.

6 Dig a trench as wide as the marked lines and to the required overall depth, using the bottom line on the marker pegs as a guide. If the soil is still soft, dig a little deeper.

7 Fill the bottom of the trench with hardcore to the height of the guideline on the marker peg. Ram the hardcore well down using an earth rammer or a stout length of timber. Cover with a blinding layer of sharp sand (to fill gaps).

8 Mix the concrete (page 496) on a clean surface and shovel it into the trench. Spread it with a rake, making sure it reaches well into the corners and is level with the tops of the marker pegs.

9 Use the edge of a straight-edged board to chop across the concrete to expel air (pages 497–498).

10 Remove the marker pegs and fill the gaps with concrete, smoothing the surface with the board.

11 Leave the profile boards in position and fit string lines to mark wall edges for bricklaying.

12 Mark the positions of the string guidelines for the walls on the concrete strip. Do this either before the concrete sets (a few hours after laying) using a spirit level, straight-edge and brick trowel, or when the concrete is hard, using a chalked string line (page 135).

13 Cover the concrete (page 498) and let it cure and harden for at least three days before building.

Foundation measurements
The width and depth of the foundations depends on the thickness and height of the wall. Guidelines for walls up to about 4ft (1.2m) high are given on page 478. For a higher wall, get professional advice. Foundations need to be a little deeper than recommended where the soil is clay (which shrinks or expands according to the weather) or is soft and loose-knit (such as peaty or sandy soil).

Marker pegs
They indicate the surface level of the concrete while laying, and are removed on completion.

Profile boards
Notches or nails accurately mark the outer edges of the wall and foundation strip.

Taut string line
Used to mark the edges of the strip.

Concrete surface
Provides a firm, level footing for the wall. Set 1–2in (25–50mm) below a lawn surface.

Levelling pegs
Opposite and adjacent marker pegs are levelled to ensure a flat surface.

Corner boards
Profile boards and string lines set at right angles help to ensure accurate corners.

Hardcore layer
Rammed down to form a firm bed for the concrete. The top is also given a blinding layer of sharp sand to fill gaps.

Laying bricks or walling blocks

Before laying any bricks or walling blocks on the strip foundation, work out the bond pattern (page 478) using dry bricks, especially if the wall has any corners or piers (page 485). Take a note of how many part bricks you will need to cut (page 484). Use special-quality frost-resistant bricks either for the whole wall or at least for the first two courses. For an ordinary (M-grade) brick wall, use a damp-proof membrane under coping.

It takes experience to achieve a ⅜in (10mm) thickness of mortar under a brick every time. If you have never done any bricklaying before, practise laying a few bricks with a pseudo mortar of 1 part lime and 3 parts sand. Clean the bricks within two hours so that they can be used in building the wall.

Take particular care in positioning and laying the first course – the most crucial part of the job.

You will need

Tools Brick trowel; spirit level with horizontal and vertical vials; flat, even length of timber; builder's square; gauge rod with 3in (75mm) markings; pointing trowel; line pins and building line; mortar board; jointing tools; straight-edge.

Materials Bricks or walling blocks; coping or capping bricks; strong mortar (page 481); damp-proof membrane about ¾in (19mm) wider than the wall thickness, with sanded surface on both sides.

1 Leave the profile boards and string lines in position as a guide until you have completed the first course.

2 Shape the mortar with the trowel so that it looks like a fat sausage pointed at both ends.

3 Slide the trowel underneath the mortar to lift it off.

4 Tip the mortar onto the building surface between the marked lines (facing page) in position for laying the first brick.

5 Tap the flat of the trowel blade backwards along the mortar to flatten it to a thickness of about ¾in (19mm). The mortar will be pressed down to ⅜in (10mm) thick by the weight of the brick.

6 Lay the first brick in position on the mortar in line with the marked guidelines.

If the brick has a frog (indentation on one side) lay it with the frog facing upwards.

7 Lay another brick in the same way a few feet farther along the line. Do not worry about its position in the bond, it is for levelling only and can be removed later.

8 Place a flat board across the tops of the two bricks and use a spirit level to check that it is horizontal.

Use the trowel handle to tap down the highest brick as necessary until both bricks are level.

BUILDING A FREESTANDING BRICK WALL

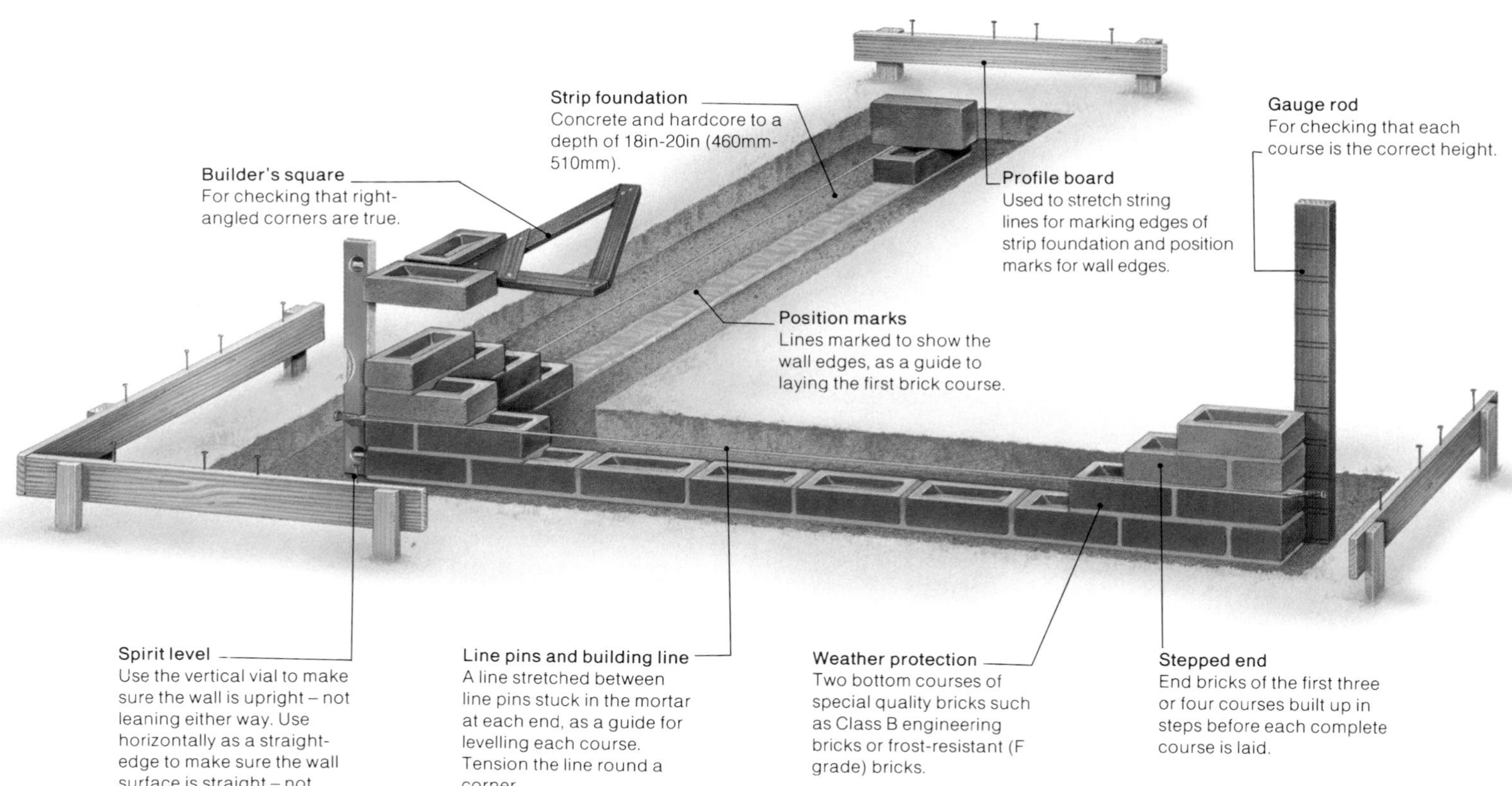

Laying bricks or walling blocks (continued)

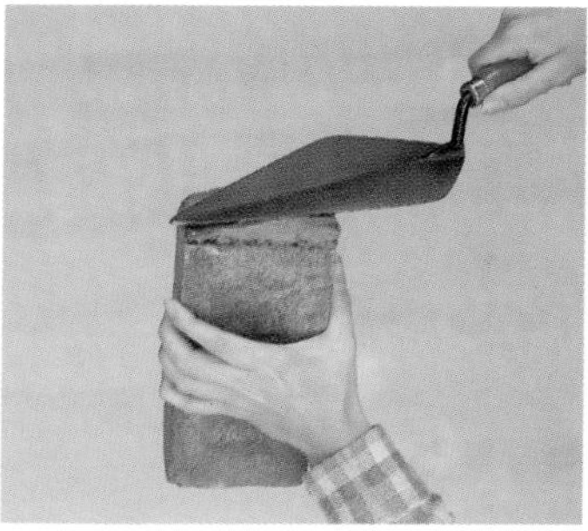

9 Prepare a mortar bed for the second brick of the course. Before laying the brick, hold it upright and spread mortar for the vertical joint on the end to be butted.

10 Squash the mortar down against all four edges, or it will easily fall off.

11 Lay four or five successive bricks of the course in the same way, then place a spirit level along them to check that they are horizontal. Tap bricks down with a trowel handle as necessary. If a brick is too low, remove it and add more mortar.

12 If the course turns a right-angled corner, use a builder's square to make sure it is true.

13 After completing the first course, build up at each end and corner with three or four stepped courses. Use the gauge rod to check that each course is at the correct height.

14 Insert line pins into the mortar at each built-up end. Use the line between them as a guide to levelling the top of the second course. Move it up progressively to check the levels of following courses as you lay the bricks between the stepped ends.

15 Point the bricks after laying three or four courses (see right).

16 From time to time check that the wall is both upright – not leaning – and straight by using a spirit level against it vertically and a straight-edge horizontally.

17 If using a top course of shaped bricks, sandwich the damp-proof membrane into the mortar two courses from the top. If using coping stones, sandwich it into the mortar bed for the coping.

The damp-proof membrane should overhang about ⅜in (10mm) on each side.

HELPFUL TIPS

When levelling bricks, you may have to remove some – either to add more mortar to a low brick, or to scrape some off a high brick that will not tap down to the right level. The replaced brick may not stick well because the mortar has lost some of its adhesion. This does not matter as long as it occurs with only an occasional brick. But if the mortar gives no grip at all, scrape it off and start again.

On a hot day, dip each brick in water to wet the surface before laying it. This makes up for any dryness in the mortar.

CUTTING A BRICK

Cutting bricks in half lengthways (closers) is tricky, as the brick is likely to fracture. It is generally easier to cut two quarter bricks (bats) and lay them end on instead of using a closer. The easiest cutting method is with a brick bolster and club hammer (page 479).

1 Pencil in the cutting line round the brick, then score along it with the bolster, tapping it gently with a club hammer.

2 With the brick laid frog down on sand or grass, rest the bolster in the scored line with its handle tilted slightly towards the waste end of the brick. Then strike it hard with the club hammer. The brick should part neatly in two.

Cutting a block

A walling block can also be cut with a bolster and hammer. Mark the cutting line and continuously score round it, gradually increasing pressure until it breaks cleanly in two. As an alternative, you can use a block splitter (page 493).

Using an angle grinder

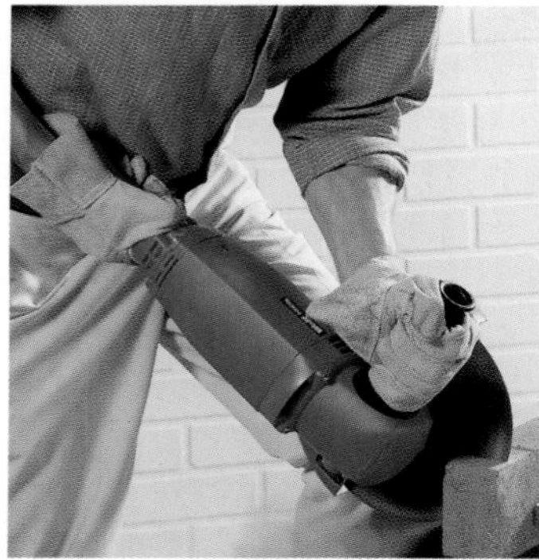

If you have a lot of bricks to cut, hire a power-driven angle grinder masonry cutter, but handle it with care to avoid an accident.

Wear safety spectacles and heavy gloves as a protection from flying fragments.

POINTING THE JOINTS

The mortar joints between bricks are shaped so that they shed rainwater and look neat. The commonest shapes used are flush, concave, and weatherstruck (sloped outwards from a recess at the top of the joint).

The shaping, generally known as pointing, can be done after each course before the mortar dries, or left until later using fresh mortar – of a different colour if desired.

If pointing is to be left until later, when you have laid a few courses, rake out some of the mortar from each joint to leave a ½in (13mm) deep recess.

Flush joint

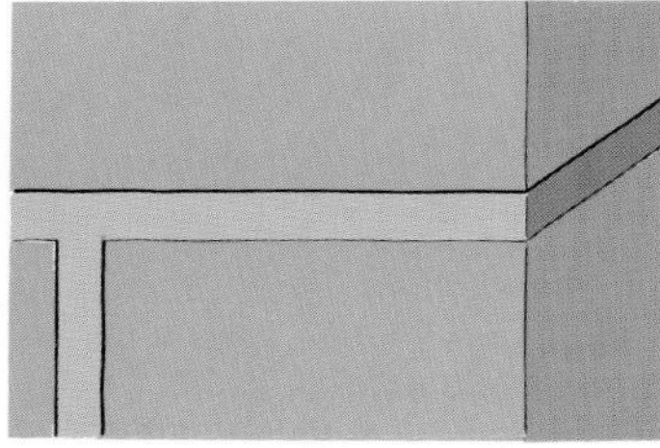

Made by trimming off the excess mortar with a pointing trowel so that it is in line with the adjoining bricks. Rub the joint smooth with a piece of sacking.

Concave joint

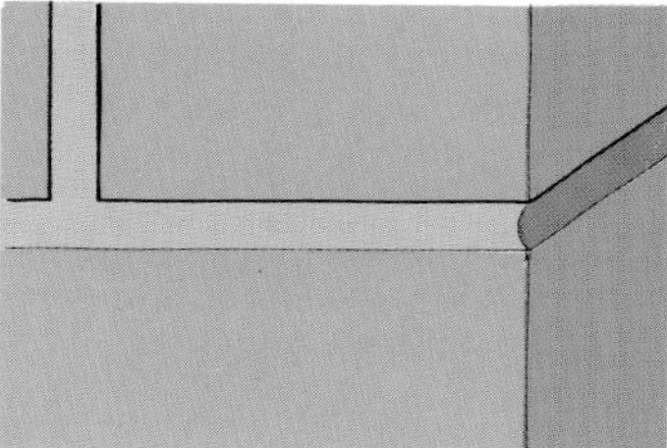

Made by trimming off the excess mortar with a trowel, then drawing a rounded piece of metal along the joint to give it an inward curve. You can use a bent piece of 15mm pipe, or a handle from a bucket may be suitable.

Weatherstruck joint

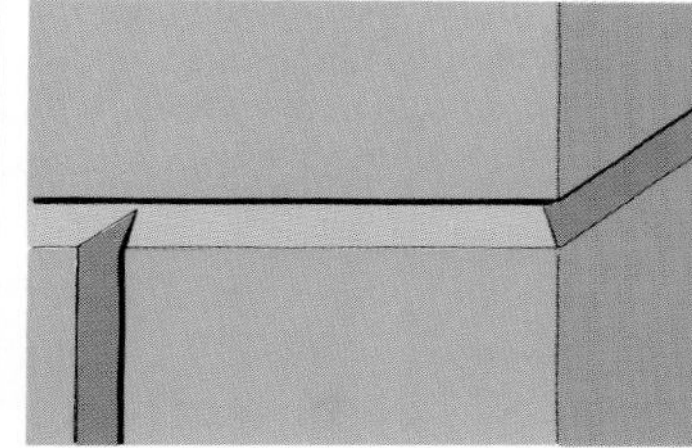

Made by using the pointing trowel to recess the mortar slightly below the upper brick, and then sloping it to project slightly above the lower brick.

Trim off the mortar from the overhang at the base using a straight-edge and the trowel. Shape the vertical joints in the same way, but sloped from side to side, all either to the left or to the right.

Using a roller tool

Pointing can also be done with a roller tool. Different blades can be fitted for shaping different types of joint.

BUILDING A BRICK PIER

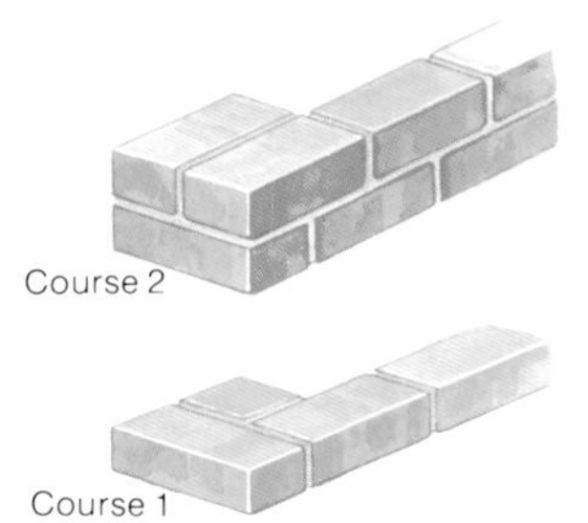

End pier on half-brick wall
A half-brick (stretcher bond) wall is 103mm (about 4in) thick. To make an end pier projecting on one side only, lay a header brick against the end stretcher on the first course, then a half bat butted against the header and parallel to the stretcher.

On the second course of the pier, lay two stretcher bricks, then repeat the pattern for alternate courses.

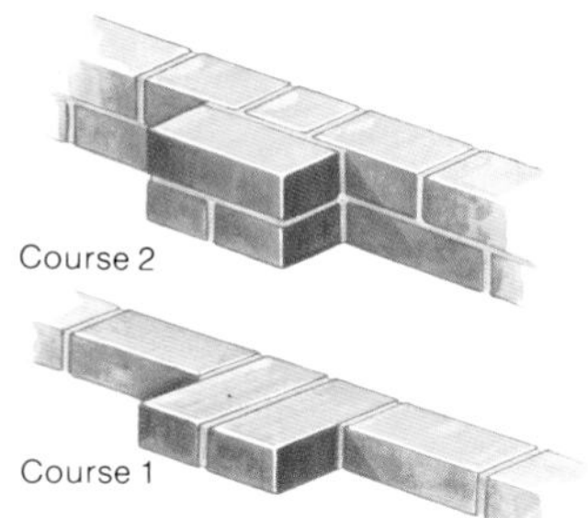

Intermediate pier on half-brick wall
For the first course of an intermediate pier projecting on one side only, lay two header bricks to project from the bond in the place of one of the stretchers at the required positions – at 6ft (1.8m) intervals.

On the second course, the projecting headers are covered with a stretcher, and at the inner end are overlapped by stretchers. To avoid a constant vertical joint on the wall face, use three-quarter bat stretchers with a half bat in between.

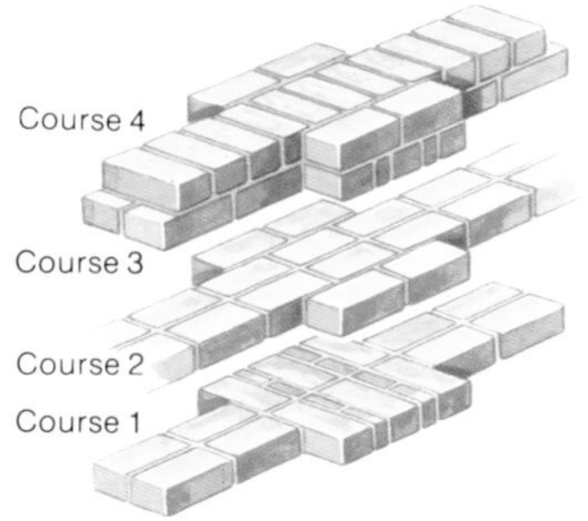

Intermediate double pier on full brick wall
For an intermediate pier projecting both sides from a wall built with an English garden wall bond, interrupt the first stretcher course with three pairs of head-on headers with two pairs of head-on closers (or bats) between them. This will project half a brick on each side of the wall.

For the second course, lay two head-on stretchers on each side on the projecting half bricks. Repeat the pattern for alternate courses. The only variation is that on the fourth (header) course the pier stretchers are alongside headers.

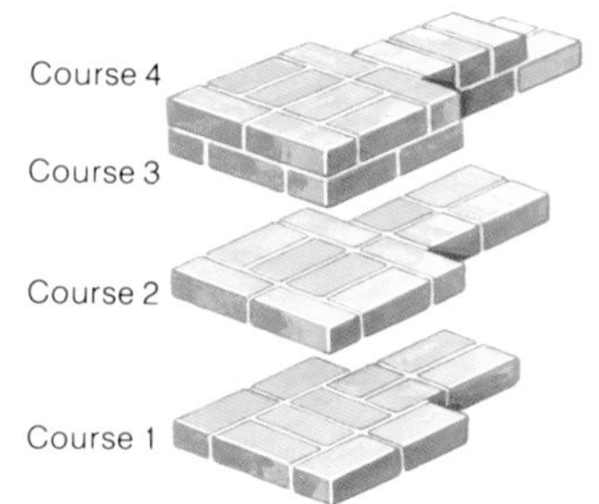

End pier on a full-brick wall
For an end pier on a full-brick wall built with an English garden wall bond, end the course with two three-quarter bat stretchers. Then lay three headers in line with the stretchers. Place two head-on stretchers on each side so that the pier projects half a brick on each side, and runs half a brick beside the three-quarter bats.

End the second course with three-quarter bats, then butt headers across the pier at each end, with four parallel stretchers between. Repeat the pattern for alternate courses. On the fourth (header) course, no three-quarter bats will be needed.

Building a brick retaining wall

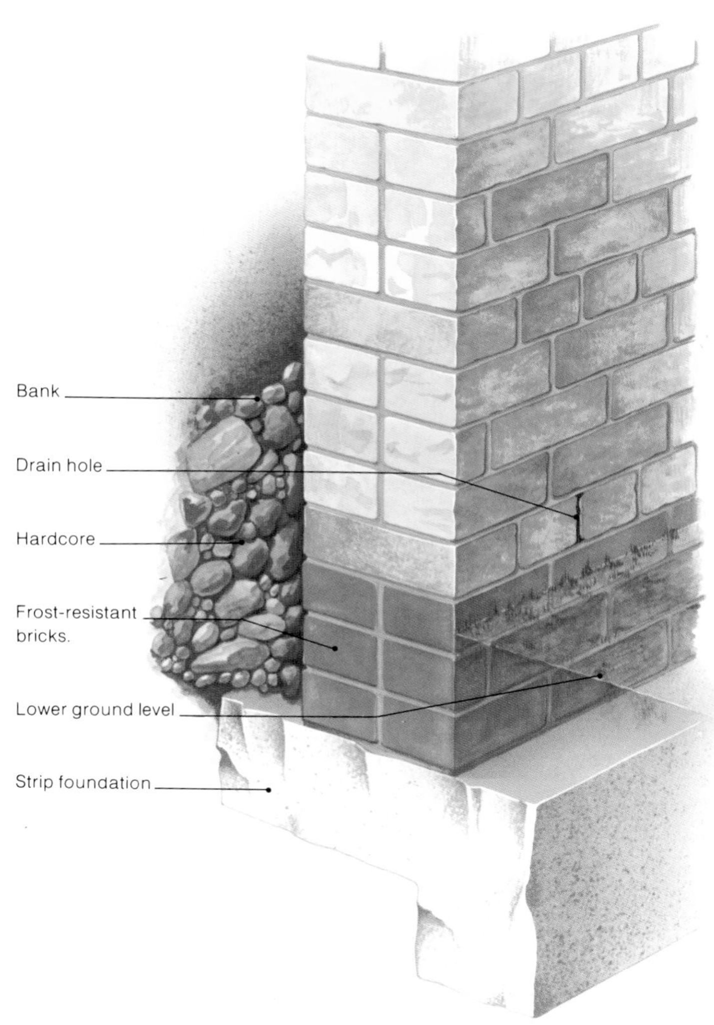

A retaining wall supports a bank of earth on one side, and may be needed in a sloping garden, or as a base for a boundary fence where the neighbouring garden is at a higher level. It can be built of bricks or walling blocks in the usual way, but must be a full-brick wall – about 8½in (215mm) thick – built with a strong bond (page 478) and strong mortar (page 481). If the ground behind the wall either slopes upwards or seems unstable, or if you want to build a wall higher than 3ft 3in (1m), get the advice of a consulting engineer.

The strip foundations (page 482) should be set in a trench with the top of the concrete surface about 9in (230mm) below the level of the lower ground, so that the bottom of the front of the wall is a little below ground level.

To allow for drainage from the banked soil, make drain holes through the wall. One way is to leave out the mortar in every other vertical joint on about the second course above the lower ground level. This is simplest to do between headers. Another way is to angle a plastic or clay pipe through the wall at 3ft 3in (1m) intervals.

MAKING MOVEMENT JOINTS

In a long run of wall, a movement joint is needed to allow for shrinkage or expansion of the materials. The joint is a narrow vertical gap about ⅜in (10mm) wide in the wall and coping, completely separating one length of wall from the next.

Make movement joints at the intervals recommended (page 478). Fill the gap with a strip of plastic foam and seal it on each side with a mastic masonry filler suitable for outside use.

A RAISED PLANT BED

A hollow bed for planting is simply a wall that completely encloses a small area filled with soil. Build a full-brick wall 8½in (215mm) thick (page 478) either on a strip foundation surrounding an area of soil, or on a completely solid surface, such as a patio.

Where there is an earth base to the bed, no drainage is needed in the wall. Where the surface is completely solid, make a series of ⅜in (10mm) drain holes round the base by leaving gaps through the wall on the first course. Choose a bond that includes headers, and leave out alternate mortar joints between them.

A useful height for a raised bed is 24in (610mm). If it is any higher, the pressure of the soil as the weather causes it to expand or shrink could force the walls outwards. Do not make the bed wider than about 3ft (0.9m). Not only will it take a lot of soil to fill it, but it will be difficult to reach plants in the centre.

Building a screen-block wall

Accurate planning of the dimensions of the wall is vital, because part blocks cannot be used to fill spaces. The coping stones, however, can be cut in the same way as bricks, if necessary.

Because of their size and the weakness of the stack bond (page 478), screen blocks are best laid with mortar that is slightly stronger and more pliable than standard brick mortar. It can be made to match the light colour of the blocks by using white Portland cement and light-coloured sand.

It is best to reinforce piers with metal rods, especially for a wall that is high, in an exposed position, or facing a public highway. A wall more than 2ft (610mm) – two blocks – high should have a 4in (100mm) wide strip of steel mesh reinforcement along the top of every other course of blocks, sandwiched in the mortar for the next course.

If you plan to build a screen wall more than 6ft 6in (2m) high, get advice from the screen-block manufacturers.

A screen-block wall built on a slope (in stepped sections if necessary), usually needs to be set on a low base of bricks or solid walling blocks. Screen blocks look rather unsightly if any part of the wall is hidden below ground.

You will need

Tools String lines; spirit level; brick trowel; mortar board; gauge rod with 12in (300mm) and 8in (200mm) markings; length of wood 1in (25mm) thick; steel tape measure; pencil or chalk. Possibly also: 4in (100mm) wide strip of wire mesh; jointing tool; piece of sacking.

Materials Screen blocks; pilasters (page 481); 1 : 1 : 5 mortar, made with plasticiser instead of lime (page 481); sand-cement mortar for filling in piers; pier caps; coping stones. Possibly also: steel rods or lengths of angle iron each about 12in (300mm) longer than the wall height.

1 Prepare a strip foundation about 16in (400mm) wide with scored or chalked guidelines (page 482). If you are going to reinforce the piers, insert rods (see right) while preparing the foundation.

2 Lay the first course using dry blocks and pilasters to ensure that it will fit as planned.

> HELPFUL TIP
> Mortar will stain screen-block surfaces if it accidentally falls on them. Lift it off with the point of the trowel the following day. Then rub the mark very gently with a piece of sacking.

3 Build up piers of pilasters (with reinforcement rods if necessary), using string guidelines to keep the piers in alignment. Bed each pilaster on a layer of 1 : 1 : 5 mortar ½in-¾in (13mm-19mm) thick, in the same way as laying a brick. Make sure that the side grooves of the bottom pilaster are in line with the marked guidelines.

4 Check with a spirit level that piers are level horizontally and vertically. Use the 8in (200mm) marks on the gauge rod to check that the course height is correct.

5 Fill in the central cavity of each pilaster (round any reinforcement rod) with sand-cement mortar.

6 Point the joints (page 484) after completing each pier.

7 Before laying the first screen block, spread a ½in-¾in (13mm-19mm) layer of 1 : 1 : 5 mortar in position on the concrete surface and inside the pilaster grooves to a height of 12in (300mm). The mortar will be compressed by the block to about ⅜in (10mm) thick.

8 Lay the block on the mortar bed in line with the guides, pushing one end to fit snugly into the pilaster grooves.

9 Prepare a mortar bed for the second block. Before laying the block, spread mortar on its vertical butting edge to form the vertical joint.

10 Lay a spirit level across the two blocks to check that they are horizontal.

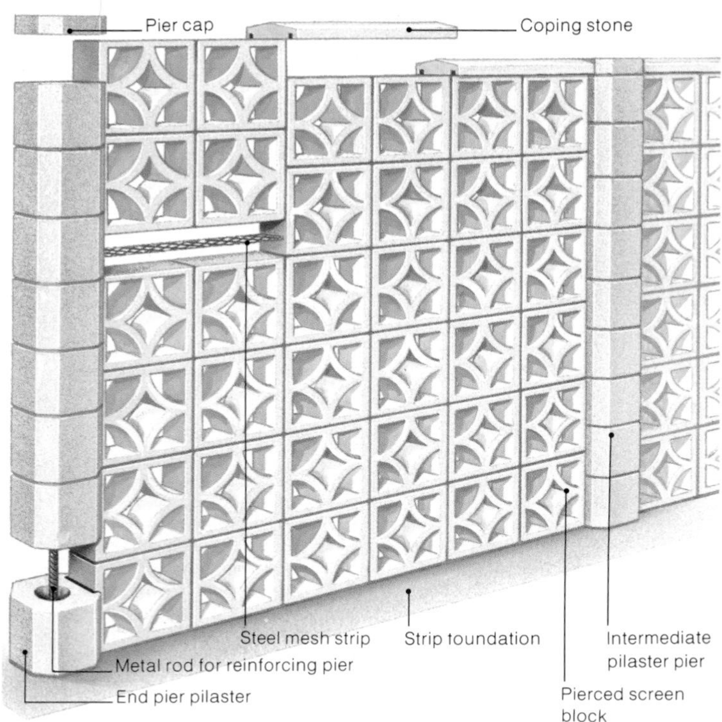

11 If you need to tap a block down with the trowel handle, lay a 1in (25mm) thick piece of wood across the top first. Screen blocks crack easily.

12 Check the height of the course of blocks, using the 12in (300mm) mark on the gauge rod.

13 Point the joints after completing one or two courses. Do not build more than four courses a day. If the wall is higher, allow 24 hours for the mortar to harden before continuing.

14 When the wall is at the required height, fit pier caps and coping stones on a bed of mortar.

REINFORCING A PILASTER PIER

Steel rods or lengths of angle iron for reinforcing piers built from pilasters are inserted in the ground before the strip foundations are filled in. To ensure that the blocks will fit exactly between the piers, the rod positioning must be accurate.

1 Make a scale plan of the first course, marking the centre points of piers, which are sited at each end of the wall and at intervals of about 10ft (3m). Use the nominal screen-block width – which includes ⅜in (10mm) vertical mortar joints – in your calculations, and allow for the depths of the locating grooves in the pilasters.

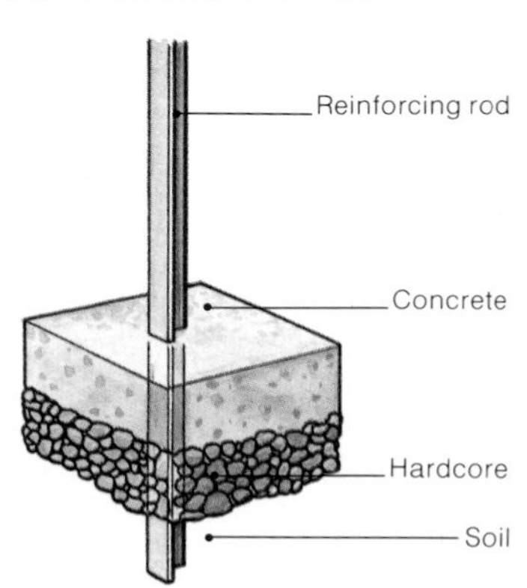

2 When preparing the strip foundation (page 482), set the rods in position, sunk about 3in (75mm) into the ground, before filling in with hardcore and concrete. With a foundation strip 8in (200mm) deep, the rods will need to be 11in-12in (280mm-300mm) longer than the pier height.

3 Before the concrete hardens, use a spirit level to check that each rod is vertical. Check also that the distance between rods is correct, and that the height above the concrete surface is about 2in (50mm) shorter than the finished height of the pier. Adjust if necessary.

Preparing the sub-base for a drive, patio or path

How well a surface will support heavy loads depends to a great extent on the strength of the sub-base. A drive that has to take the weight of one or more cars obviously needs a stronger sub-base than a path.

Some paving materials need a sub-base of hardcore only, others need hardcore topped with a layer of concrete (see chart, page 488). On soft ground or where heavy traffic is likely – where several heavy vehicles will be turning, for example – the sub-base may need to be deeper than recommended on the chart. For soft soil such as peat, you can lay a filter-membrane fabric, such as Terram, as reinforcement under the hardcore.

A drive needs to be at least 10ft (3m) wide for car doors to be opened or for people to walk past a parked car. All drives need to be sloped from side to side (a crossfall) so that rainwater will not lie on the surface. A crossfall of about 1 in 40 is suitable for a drive.

A drive should also slope away from the house, so may need a lengthways slope of 1 in 100 – or steeper if necessary to follow the natural slope of the ground. Consult the local authority if a new driveway needs access onto a main road.

You will need

Tools Pegs and string lines; builder's square; mallet; spade; shovel; steel tape measure; timber pegs about 1in (25mm) square and 18in (460mm) long; chalk or paint for marking; wheelbarrow; spirit level; wooden shims (see below); earth rammer, garden roller or plate vibrator (page 490). Possibly also: sledgehammer; concreting tools (page 494).

Materials Hardcore (see below); ballast (page 495). Possibly also: concrete (page 496).

1 Use taut pegged string lines to mark the edges of the drive area, allowing for permanent edging such as a kerb. Check with a steel tape measure that the width of the site is uniform, and use a builder's square to ensure that right angles are true. For making a curve, see page 490.

2 Decide on the direction of the crossfall. The drive should slope away from the house or garage wall. If the ground slopes naturally towards the house, build up the hardcore base to reverse the slope, if possible. Otherwise build a channel and soakaway (page 491).

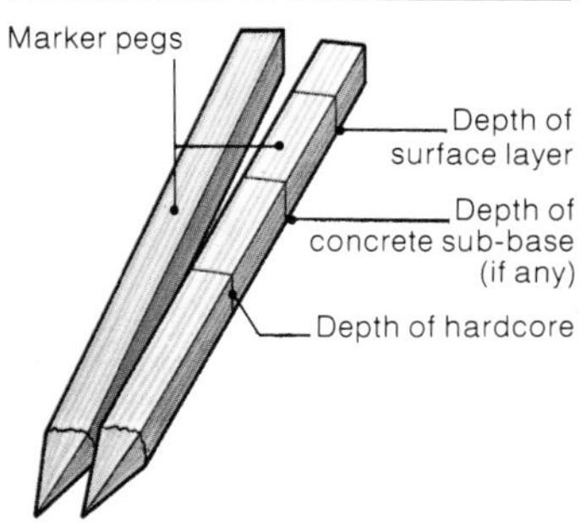

3 Mark the timber pegs from the top to show the depths of the various layers, allowing for any bedding sand or mortar.

4 Drive a marked peg into the ground in the top corner (nearest to the house) of the area to be excavated. Set it with its top at the right level for the drive surface.

5 Drive in a row of pegs at about 5ft (1.5m) intervals across the top of the site, using a spirit level between pairs of pegs to ensure a crossfall of 1 in 40 (see above).

6 Drive in a second row of pegs 5ft (1.5m) farther down the drive. Set the top of each to allow for any lengthways slope necessary from the first rows – for a fall of 1 in 100 use a ⅝in (16mm) shim.

MAKING A SLOPED SURFACE

Place a spirit level – on a length of timber, if necessary – across the pegs marking the surface level. Use a thin piece of wood of the correct thickness (known as a shim) under

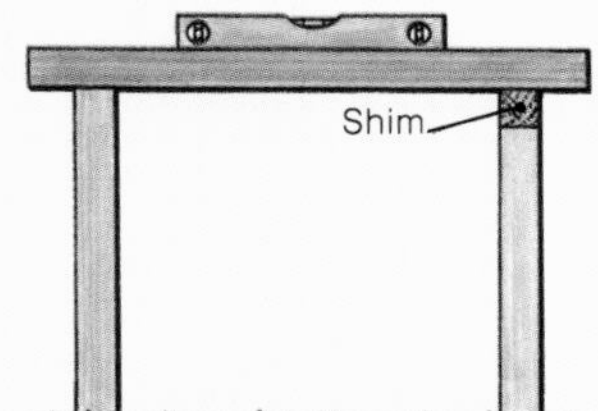

the spirit level or its support on the lower-side pegs. Tap down the lower-side peg until the spirit level is set level with the shim in position.

The thickness of the shim depends on the slope required and the width between pegs. For example, on a path 3ft 3in (1m) wide, you need a ½in (13mm) shim for a crossfall of 1 in 80, ⅝in (16mm) for 1 in 60, or 1in (25mm) for 1 in 40.

For a crossfall of 1 in 40 on a drive with marker pegs spaced at 5ft (1.5m) intervals, you need a 1½in (38mm) shim. The calculation of the shim size need not be precise.

7 Continue with rows of pegs down the drive in this way at similar intervals, adjusting the distances of the last rows as necessary so that the final row is at the bottom edge of the site.

8 Dig out the area within the string lines to the lowest peg mark (the base of the hardcore layer). Spread the top soil on other parts of the garden. Leave the clayey subsoil in a heap for later disposal.

9 Spread hardcore in the excavated area. Ram it well down using an earth rammer (page 490) or, for larger areas, a garden roller or plate vibrator – until it is at the marked level for the hardcore surface. If laying concrete paving blocks (page 493), break up the hardcore as small as possible with a sledgehammer before compacting it with a vibrator.

10 Add a thin layer of ballast to fill in the gaps. Ram it well down.

11 If the base material includes a layer of concrete, spread the concrete (page 496) over the hardcore and blinding layer and tamp it down to the marked level.

Continued on page 490

THE SUB-BASE MATERIAL

Hardcore is made up of broken or crushed bricks, blocks or stone and can be bought from builders' merchants. A ton of hardcore covers roughly 7sq yds (6sq m) if it is laid 4in (100mm) deep.

It must be well broken up, for a drive especially, or it will not bed down properly to form a solid base. Some hardcore may contain demolition rubble, which includes unsuitable material such as wood and plaster. Such hardcore will not bed down well.

Gaps in the hardcore surface are filled with a thin layer of ballast (sand and shingle) – a process known as blinding.

Hoggin is a more expensive form of hardcore, made up of gravel and sandy clay, and will bed down well.

FOUR LAYERS OF A DRIVE

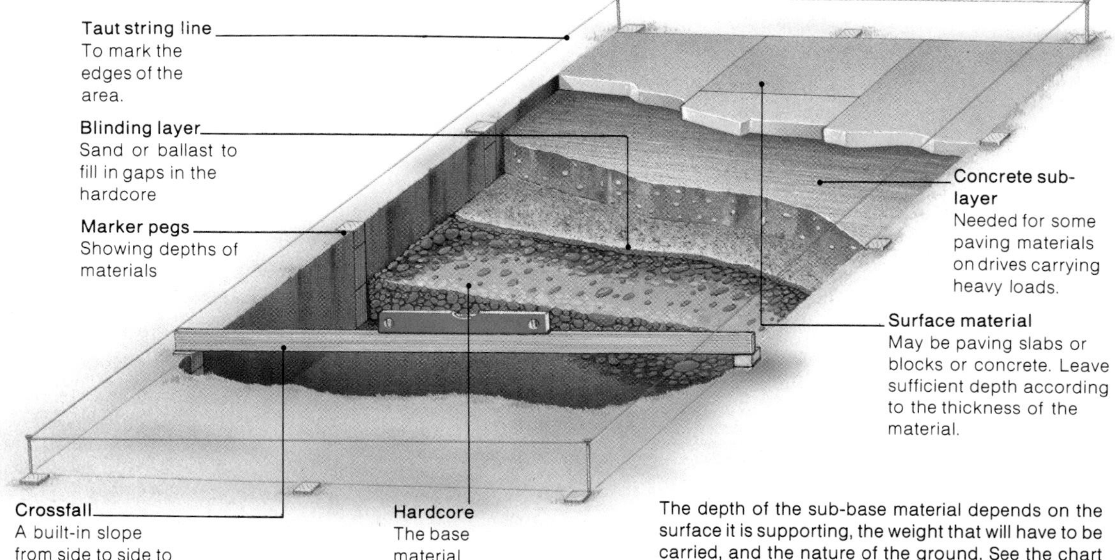

The depth of the sub-base material depends on the surface it is supporting, the weight that will have to be carried, and the nature of the ground. See the chart overleaf. This illustration shows a drive in cross-section.

CHOOSING A PATH OR DRIVE

When choosing material for a path or drive, take into account the amount of wear it is likely to get, as well as the appearance – whether it will blend with the house exterior and garden surroundings. Consider also the amount of work that will be involved in laying the material.

It is worth shopping around. Collect catalogues that illustrate the range of materials and the sizes and cost of those available. The cheapest materials are often those that are quickest and easiest to lay. It may be cost-effective to mix materials, such as paving slabs and bricks or gravel.

In estimating the cost, do not forget to include materials such as mortar, hardcore, or sand as well as the surface material. Also any equipment you may need to hire, such as a plate vibrator.

TYPE OF PATH OR DRIVE	DESCRIPTION	TYPICAL SIZE/COVERING SUB-BASE NEEDED	ADVANTAGES AND DISADVANTAGES
Paving slabs 	Large, flat, pre-cast concrete slabs laid on mortar. Square, rectangular, hexagonal or circular shapes available. Hydraulically pressed types are strongest and should be used for a drive, which has to take the weight of one or more vehicles. Surfaces may be smooth (non-slip), polished, or patterned to appear like cobbles, bricks or tiles in straight or curved designs. Colours include grey, buff and red.	450mm x 450mm x 32mm (about 18in x 18in x $1\frac{1}{4}$in) – 4.9 per sq m; 600mm x 450mm x 32mm (about 24in x 18in x $1\frac{1}{4}$in) – 3.7 per sq m; 600mm x 600mm x 38mm (about 24in x 24in x $1\frac{1}{2}$in) – 2.8 per sq m. Sub-base *Drive:* 4in (100mm) of compacted hardcore topped by 5in (125mm) of concrete. *Path:* 4in (100mm) of hardcore, or firm, well-rolled ground.	Reasonably quick and easy to lay on a straight site, but difficult to form into curves. Careful planning is needed on a slope or an awkwardly shaped site. Can look monotonous in large areas unless colours, shapes or textures are used to enliven the surface.
Crazy paving 	Slabs of irregular shapes fitted together on a bed of mortar. Broken stone or concrete slabs can be bought by the ton, square yard or square metre. Collect your own if you can, so that you can choose your own mixture of colours, shapes and sizes, preferably mostly large and medium pieces because small pieces involve more work.	1 ton covers about 10sq yd (9sq m). Sub-base *Drive:* 4in (100mm) of compacted hardcore topped by 5in (125mm) of concrete. *Path:* 4in (100mm) of hardcore, or firm, well-rolled ground.	Ideal for making a lively looking drive. More difficult to lay than regular slabs because the shapes have to be fitted to a pattern. Also, they are not all the same thickness so need different amounts of mortar to level them. Plenty of time is therefore needed for the job. When filling in the joints, a good way of bringing out the shapes is to draw a well-defined groove in the mortar round each slab using the tip of a brick trowel.
Paving blocks 	Brick-like concrete blocks laid on a bed of thick sand, and held in place between existing walls, edging blocks or kerbing. Commonly rectangular, but interlocking decorative shapes are also available. Internal and external corner blocks allow neat finishing of edges and plant-bed surrounds. Colours include grey, red, charcoal, brown, buff, marigold and red-grey mixtures. Blocks can be laid like brick in various bond patterns (page 478), or patterns such as basket-weave or herringbone. A herringbone pattern is best for drives because it gives blocks the stability to withstand tyre movements when vehicles are manoeuvring.	Rectangular: 200mm x 100mm x 65mm (about 8in x 4in x $2\frac{1}{2}$in) – 50 blocks cover 1 sq m (11 sq ft). Other shapes and sizes are available. Sub-base *Drive:* 4in (100mm) compacted hardcore topped with $2\frac{1}{2}$in (63mm) of sand compacted to 2in (50mm) when the blocks are laid. *Path:* Firm, well-compacted ground and sand bed.	Slower to lay than slabs, but they look well in almost any setting and are easier to fit into awkwardly shaped areas or to form into curves. They can easily be lifted to get at underground pipes. You will need to hire a plate vibrator (page 490) to lay blocks over a large area such as a drive or patio, and a block splitter (page 493) for cutting to size where necessary.
Bricks 	Standard bricks or brick pavers laid on a bed of sand between fixed edging, or on a bed of mortar. Use special-quality F grade bricks (page 480) that withstand hard weather, especially frost. Brick pavers are normally thinner than bricks and are available in square or interlocking shapes. The colour range is very wide in browns, reds, brindles and yellows. Bricks can be laid in walling bond patterns (page 478) or others – typically herringbone and basket weave – and used flat or on edge. Paving is also available resembling old handmade bricks in traditional basket-weave style.	Standard bricks: 215mm x 103mm x 50mm (about $8\frac{5}{8}$in x $4\frac{1}{8}$in x 2in) – laid flat, 40 per sq m, laid on edge, 50 per sq m. Brick-effect paving: 450mm x 450mm x 38mm (about $17\frac{3}{4}$in x $17\frac{3}{4}$in x $1\frac{1}{2}$in) – 4.9 per sq m. Sub-base As for paving blocks, but with the sand layer $2\frac{1}{4}$in (56mm) deep.	A little more difficult to lay than blocks, if bedded on mortar, but similarly flexible and suitable for almost any setting. Bricks bedded in sand have to be tapped down by hand, as they are likely to crack under a plate vibrator.

TYPE OF PATH OR DRIVE	DESCRIPTION	TYPICAL SIZE/COVERING SUB-BASE NEEDED	ADVANTAGES AND DISADVANTAGES
Concrete 	Sand and coarse aggregate (crushed gravel or stone) bound together with cement and water in certain proportions (page 496) and laid while soft between temporary edgings. Hardens to a tough, stone-like surface. Can be mixed as you go along, or delivered in loads for large areas. The surface layer should be 4-6in (100-150mm) thick for a drive or 2-3in (50-75mm) thick for a path. Colouring pigments of yellow, brown or green can be stirred into the mixture – the shade varies with the amount applied, and it is difficult to get a uniform colour.	Available as separate ingredients or in ready-mixed loads. Quantities per cu m are given on page 496. Sub-base *Drive:* 4in (100mm) of well-compacted hardcore and 1-2in (25-50mm) of ballast to fill the gaps. *Path:* Firm well-rolled soil, with hardcore in soft patches or hollows.	Very strong. Cheaper than paving slabs or blocks, and straight-forward to lay. Edging formwork has to be set up in preparation. Mixing to the right consistency is critical, and mixing can be hard work. Hire a small mixer (page 494) if laying about 18cu ft (½cu m) or more. Concrete hardens in about 2 hours – faster in hot weather. The surface can be given various patterned finishes. Large areas can look monotonous.
Edging and kerbing 	For providing fixed edging to an area of paving blocks laid on a sand bed, or to confine loose or soft surfaces such as gravel or asphalt. Paving blocks can be edged with a header course of the same blocks used for the paving (page 493). Path edging is usually available in straight lengths only; standard kerbing, which is thicker and deeper, is also sold in curved lengths. Tops may be flat, chamfered, rounded, bullnosed or scalloped. Kerbing can be laid to finish above the paved surface (to check surface water or stop cars going onto the garden), flush with the paved surface, or just below the paved surface so that it is covered by grass or soil and only the paving shows.	*Edging:* Available in a wide range of sizes and shapes. Size illustrated is 230mm x 210mm x 30mm (about 9in x 8¼in x 1¼in). *Standard kerb:* 24-36in long, 4-6in wide, 10in or 12in deep (610-910mm x 100-150mm x 250mm or 300mm). Sub-base Hardcore from paving base topped by a 3in (75mm) layer of concrete wide enough for the kerb thickness and a generous haunching of bedding mortar or concrete.	Has to be carefully set up in position on its concrete bed to finish at the correct height in relation to the surface, and with the correct crossfall and alignment if laid above or flush with the paving. It must be firmly fixed with a haunching or sand-cement mortar (for edging) or foundation mix concrete (for standard kerbing).
Cold asphalt 	A mixture of bitumen and finely crushed gravel or stone (macadam) spread on top of a thin coat of bitumen emulsion to 'tack' it in place, then compacted between temporary or permanent edging to form a tough, waterproof surface. Normally used to re-surface an existing drive. It is not suitable for making a new drive, but can be used for a new path provided that the hardcore base can be firmly compacted, generally by using a plate vibrator (page 490). Supplied in bags and available in red and black. Decorative stone chippings may be provided with each bag.	One 25kg (½cwt) bag covers about 10sq ft (0.9sq m) laid ¾in (19mm) deep and rolled to ½in (13mm) deep. A 5kg (11lb) can of emulsion covers about 8sq yds (7sq m) on a firm surface. Sub-base *Drive:* An existing surface such as concrete, paving slabs or old asphalt. *Path:* Well-compacted hardcore as for stone chippings below.	Cheaper than paving and simple to lay, but sticky to work with. Wear protective shoes and clothing and protect floor covering if any is likely to be tramped into the house. Useful for covering worn and pitted concrete or paving slabs, or for gravel or ash surfaces. The ground needs to be treated with weedkiller two weeks before the surface is laid. Cold asphalt can be dressed with stone chippings to add interest, but still tends to look monotonous in large areas. The surface can be dented by the weight of a car on a pillar jack.
Stone chippings 	Can be scattered on cold asphalt as a decorative dressing, or used alone as a surface dressing, bound together with a thick coat of bitumen emulsion, to give a firm, waterproof surface. Normally used to re-surface an existing drive, but may be suitable for a new drive provided the hardcore base can be well compacted, generally by using a plate vibrator (page 490). Colours include greyish-white, pink and grey-green.	One 25kg (½cwt) bag covers about 3sq yds (2.5sq m). A 25kg can of bitumen emulsion covers 21sq yds (17.5sq m) on a hard surface, 16sq yds (13.4sq m) on a firm, dense surface or 7½sq yds (6.3sq m) on a loose, open surface. Sub-base *Drive:* Existing surface or 4-6in (100-150mm) of well-compacted hardcore topped with 1-2in (25-50mm) of ballast. *Path:* 3-4in (75-100mm) hardcore topped with ballast.	Cheap and easy to lay. Suitable for light traffic, but loose chippings may be thrown up by tyres. The ground needs to be treated with weedkiller two weeks before the chippings are laid.
Gravel 	A mixture of coarse sand and small stones laid loose on a firm surface, usually between anchored edgings. The stones are normally well-rounded pea gravel of a single size, either 10mm or 20mm. Available in white or various shades of brown.	Half cu yd (0.9 tons) covers about 18sq yds (15sq m) at 1in (25mm) deep. Sub-base *Drive or path:* 4in (100mm) of well-compacted hardcore topped with 1in (25mm) of sand.	Cheap, easy and quick to lay, but can be a difficult surface for walking on or pushing a pram or bicycle across. Stones may be carried into the house on shoes. Needs regular raking or rolling. Not suitable for a drive with a pronounced slope.

Preparing the sub-base for a drive, patio or path (continued)

12 Remove the pegs and fill in the holes with hardcore or hardcore and concrete before laying the paving material.

PREPARING THE SUB-BASE FOR A PATH

A path that will be subject to heavy loads or that is on soft ground will need a well-compacted hardcore sub-base. Prepare it in the same way as for the sub-base for a drive, except that fewer surface marker pegs will be needed.

The path need not slope along its length, but it should have a crossfall of about 1 in 80 away from the wall if it is alongside a house (see *Making a sloped surface*, page 487).

If a hardcore sub-base is necessary, set up string lines and marker pegs and dig out the site only to the depth of the surface material and any bedding needed – a mortar or sand layer (see chart, page 488). Slope the bottom of the excavation to one side and use a spirit level and shim across the bottom to get the required slope.

Fill in any depression in the surface with well-broken hardcore. Use a garden roller to compact the surface until it is firm and even.

MARKING OUT A CURVE

Use a garden hosepipe to mark the outline of the curve on each side by eye. Strips of plastic laminate offcuts are also useful as markers.

It is usually necessary to allow extra width between the curving sides. If they are the same width apart as the straight sides, the path will appear to be narrow at the curve when viewed from a short distance away.

Set up a peg and string line to follow the shape of the marked curve. The pegs will need to be closer together than when using straight string lines.

KEEPING CLEAR OF THE DAMP-PROOF COURSE

If the drive is against a house wall, make sure the base is dug deep enough for the drive surface to be at least 6in (150mm) below the damp-proof course, commonly visible as a thick line of mortar usually two or three brick courses up the wall.

Where it is not possible for the drive surface to be low enough, one alternative is to slope the drive towards the house and build a gully and soakaway. Alternatively, you may be able to build concrete skirting (see *Defects in the damp-proofing*, page 462) between the drive edge and wall.

PLANNING A PATIO

A patio, or paved terrace, is an outside area where a family can eat or relax in good weather. It usually adjoins the house but need not necessarily do so. Locate it in a warm, sunny spot – a site facing south or west is usually best. Make sure there is some shade for at least part of the day, as well as screening from strong winds – or wind tunnels such as a narrow alley between two houses.

Relate the size of the patio to that of the garden. A patio that is too big will tend to dominate the garden, but if it is too small it will look lost. For people to sit on it comfortably, the patio should measure not less than 7ft 6in (2.3m) from front to back. Choose paving materials (page 488) that will blend with the surroundings and not appear monotonous when the terrace is unoccupied.

Draw a scale plan on graph paper before you begin any building work, so that you can work out the positions of any steps or retaining walls that may be needed, or any raised beds you wish to include.

Note whether there are any manhole covers that must be accommodated, and – for a patio adjoining a house – whether there are any airbricks in the wall that might be covered. They are usually above the damp-proof course, but sometimes below it. The patio surface should be at least 6in (150mm) below the damp-proof course in the wall.

Prepare the sub-base in the same way as for a drive, but with hardcore only below the surface material. A slope of 1 in 60 away from the house or towards an existing drain is normally sufficient for drainage, but not severe enough to affect the levels of chairs and tables.

TOOLS FOR A SUB-BASE

Many compacting or demolition tools can be hired. Hire firms are listed in *Yellow Pages* under Hire Services – Tools and Equipment.

Earth rammer
A steel handle with a heavy club end for ramming down hardcore. It can be hired.

Garden roller
A sand or water-filled roller 2cwt (102kg) or heavier can be used instead of an earth rammer for compacting large areas of hardcore (or for rolling cold asphalt surfaces, page 499). A roller can be hired.

Plate vibrator
As an alternative to a roller, you can hire a petrol-driven plate vibrator (also known as a power compactor) for ramming down large areas of hardcore. A light plate vibrator is also used for bedding down concrete paving blocks (page 493).

Demolition or breaker hammer
If you need to break up a concrete surface before laying a new path or drive, the easiest way to tackle a large area is with an electric-powered hammer, which can be hired. It is fitted like a drill with a chisel or point for cutting, and can also be used with a masonry bit for drilling fixing holes into or through concrete.

The tool may be lightweight for concrete up to 4in (100mm) thick, or heavyweight for thicker concrete. Wear safety spectacles and, if possible, steel-tipped boots when using the hammer.

Other useful tools
Two pegs and a string line are needed for marking the outline of an area to be excavated. The stretched string line, taut between the pegs, is also a guide for keeping straight edges.

A garden spade is necessary for digging out soil for the sub-base area. A sledgehammer, may be useful for breaking up hardcore, and a pickaxe for breaking hard ground or small areas of old concrete. Both can be hired.

You will also need concreting tools (page 494) if the sub-base needed includes a layer of concrete above the hardcore.

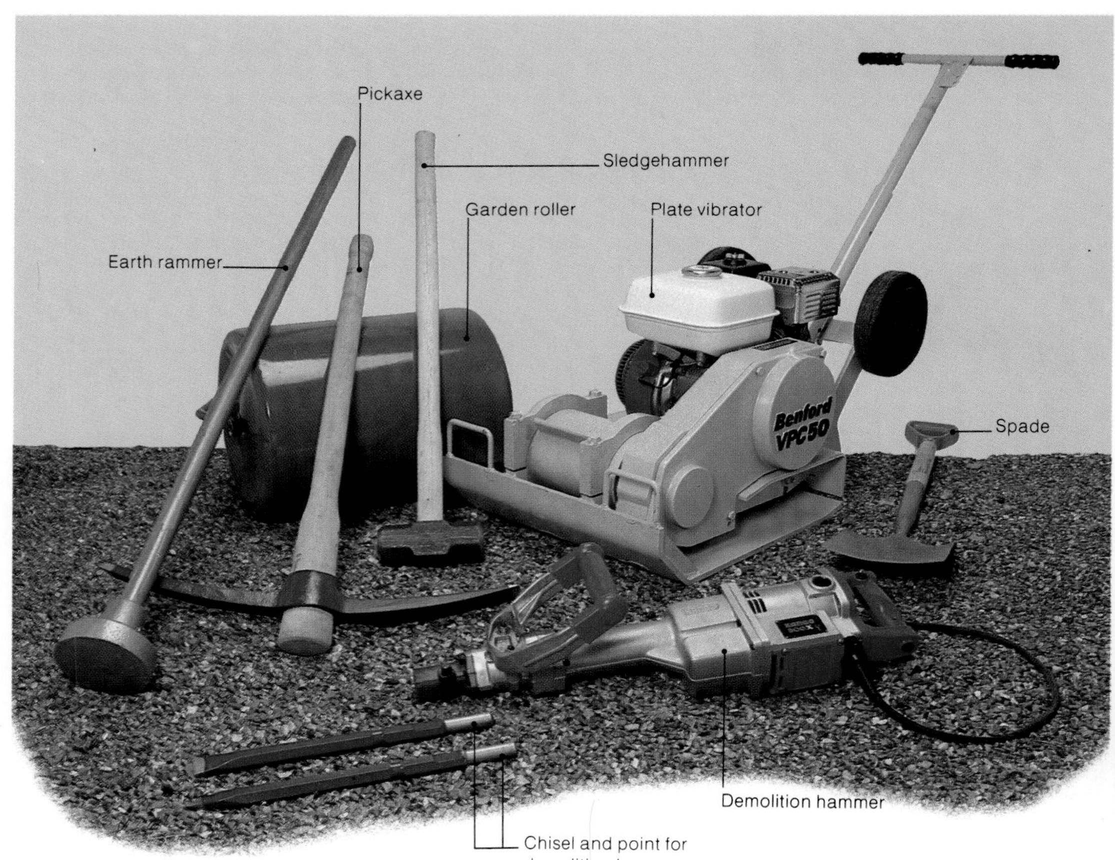

MASKING OR RAISING A MANHOLE COVER

When you build a drive or patio, the ground level is often slightly raised, which means that a manhole cover on an inspection chamber within the paving must be either masked with slabs or raised to fit in at the same level.

The manhole can be masked with a double seal cover, which is available from some builders' merchants. Covers are made of pressed steel and they are commonly 24in × 18in (610mm × 460mm).

There are two types: the skeleton

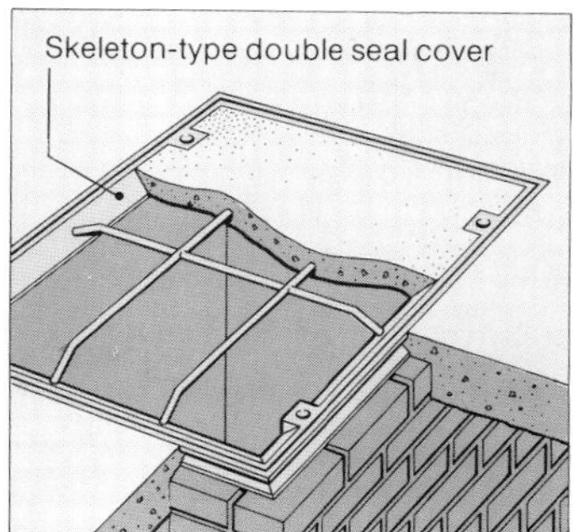

type has a mesh within the edging frame and can be filled in with concrete (apart from the key holes); the recess type has an open tray that can be fitted with loose-laid material. Plan the depth of the terrace so that the masking cover is flush with the surrounding paving.

To raise the height of a manhole cover, remove the lid and put a sheet of polythene over the drains in the chamber to catch the debris.

Then chip away the mortar surrounding the cast-iron frame with a club hammer and cold chisel. Take care not to strike the frame, which shatters easily.

When you have released the frame, clean away the mortar covering the top surface of the brick walls of the chamber.

The material you use to heighten the chamber walls depends on the increase in height required. If the amount is less than the height of a brick – 3in (75mm) including the mortar – use brick slips or strips cut from ½in (13mm) thick concrete roofing tiles, laid in courses in the same way as bricks.

Reset the frame on a bed of sand-cement mortar – 3 parts sand to 1 part cement. Tap it gently into position using a block of wood and a club hammer. Use a spirit level to check that it is level across its width and length.

Slope the mortar round the outside downwards away from the frame to carry away rainwater.

DEALING WITH A LOW AIRBRICK

The drive or patio surface must not cover an airbrick low down in the house wall. If, however, there is no way of arranging the paved surface below the airbrick, one solution is to stop the edge of the paving short to leave a pit at least 12in (300mm) wide in front of it. Keep the pit clear of leaves and debris.

An alternative solution is to run a duct under the surface from the airbrick to an open edge such as a retaining wall.

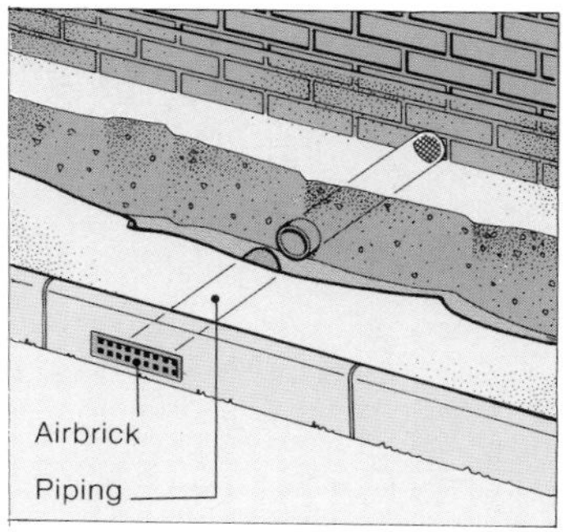

To fit a duct, remove the airbrick (page 460) and cement a length of 4in (100mm) diameter plastic piping for underground drainage into the hole. Use bagged sand-and-cement mortar (page 495) or a 1 : 4 (cement-sand) mix. Run the piping through the hardcore base of the terrace and cement it to a new airbrick at the other end.

Building a drainage channel and soakaway

If you build a drive that follows a natural slope of the ground towards the house, you will have to build a channel at the lowest edge of the drive to carry away rainwater. The channel should run into either an existing drain or a soakaway – a drainage pit sited at least 10ft (3m) from the house.

The channel should be lined with concrete and should have a fall of about 1 in 40 towards the soakaway. Make the channel using a concrete paving mix (page 496) and shape it about 1in (25mm) deep using a length of drainpipe. Make sure there are no ridges.

ALTERNATIVELY, use ready-made concrete channelling, mortared in to the hardcore base. It is available from builders' merchants in about 3ft (910mm) lengths. Enclosed types (as above) are about 10in (250mm) deep and 12in (300mm) wide with a narrow slot or grid in the top. Or you can buy dish channel with a 1in (25mm) deep dish.

MAKING A SOAKAWAY

Any type of soakaway is for dispersing rainwater or surface water only. It must not be used for household drainage water. Get advice from your local authority in case they have specific regulations.

A home-made soakaway

1 To make a soakaway, dig a pit about 4ft (1.2m) across and at least 4ft deep.

If you hit a pan of hard clay that you cannot dig through, make the soakaway longer than 4ft to compensate for the lack of depth.

2 Break up the bottom of the pit with a fork before you fill it to within about 4in (100mm) of the top with rubble, coarser at the bottom. A pit 4ft (1.2m) across and 4ft deep needs about 64cu ft (1.8cu m) of rubble, which is roughly 25-30 wheelbarrow loads.

3 Direct the drainpipe from the channel into the rubble at a gentle slope. Fit a gully trap at the top end.

4 Cover the rubble with a sheet of heavy-gauge polythene, then add a layer of concrete (page 496) 3in (75mm) thick. Finally cover with a thin layer of soil or turf.

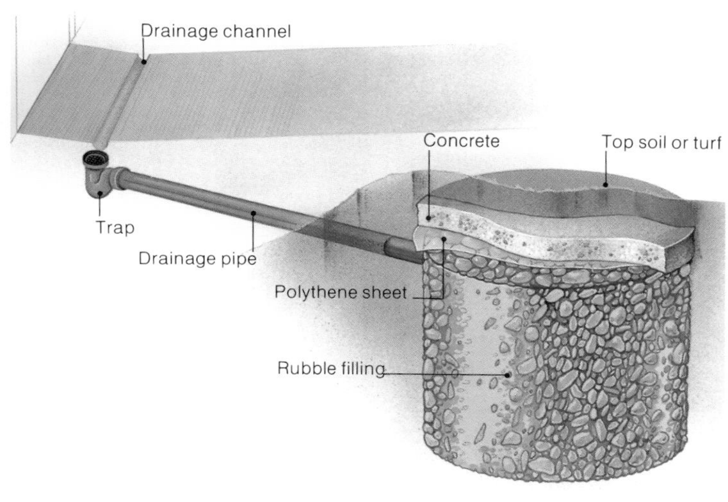

A ready-made soakaway

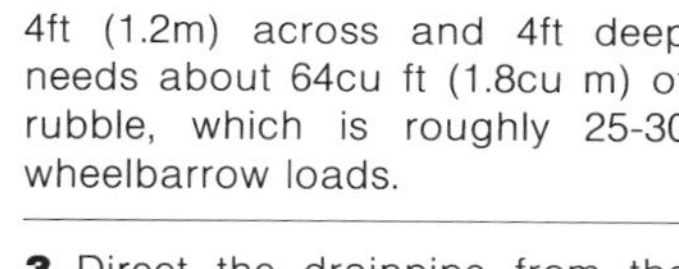

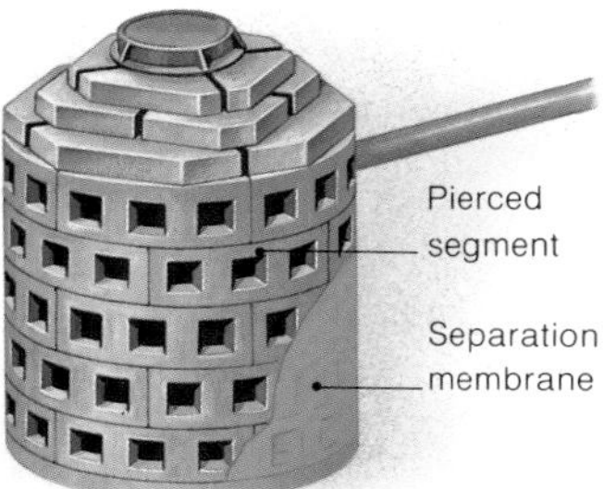

You can buy a ready-made soakaway consisting of pierced concrete segments which build up into rings. They are laid on a strip foundation. Water entering the soakaway seeps out through the rings and through a wrap-round separation membrane into the surrounding soil; there is no rubble filling. Rings are 12in (300mm) or 16½in (420mm) high and 5ft (1.5m) or 7ft (2.1m) across.

Laying slabs for a drive or patio

Plan the area of the site so that it can be divided exactly by the dimensions of the slabs to be used, if possible. It will save you from having to cut too many slabs. Allow for a gap of ⅜in (10mm) between slabs for mortar joints.

Make a scale plan of the site on graph paper, showing the positions and numbers of the slabs – especially if you are mixing different sizes, colours and textures. Where necessary, take up odd dimensions either by using 1in (25mm) wide mortar joints, or fill in with a small-sized unit such as a brick. Use mortar to fill small irregular areas.

Some slab manufacturers supply leaflets showing patterns that can be made using their slabs, and give an estimate of the numbers needed for different patterns.

For a drive, lay slabs on a full bed of mortar. For a path or patio where use is not heavy, lay each slab on five generous dabs of mortar (corners and centre).

You will need

Tools Brick trowel; straight-edge about 6ft (1.8m) long; steel tape measure; marker pegs; builder's square (page 479); spirit level; wooden shim (page 487); club hammer; length of timber 4in × 2in (100mm × 50mm); brick bolster (page 479) or angle grinder/ masonry cutter (page 484); pencil; try square; wooden spacers ⅜in (10mm) thick (probably three or four per slab); piece of wood ⅜in (10mm) thick; two shovels; bucket; fine-rose watering can; mixing platform (page 494); damp sponge.

Materials Paving slabs – use hydraulically pressed 2in (50mm) thick slabs for a drive; bedding mortar mix (page 496) or bagged dry sand-and-cement mortar (page 495) for small areas.

> HELPFUL TIP
> Store paving slabs upright, leaning against a wall. Raise them off the ground on two lengths of wood to keep the bottom edge clean.

1 For a drive, prepare a hardcore and concrete base (page 485), and wait until the concrete is hard (after about three days).

ALTERNATIVELY, for a patio, prepare a hardcore base only, with a blinding layer of sand.

2 Adjust the pegged string lines at the edge of the site as a guide to slab alignment.

Drive in marker pegs as a guide to the height of the slab surface, taking into account the 1in (25mm) depth of bedding mortar, the crossfall, and any lengthways slope. Site the pegs at suitable intervals to be bridged with a spirit level, placed on a straight-edge if necessary.

3 Check the marker peg levels with a spirit level and wooden shims (see *Making a crossfall*, page 487). Check that the corner lines are true with a builder's square.

4 Mix the bedding mortar on a firm surface in the same way as mixing concrete (page 497), but using sharp sand and cement only. Keep one shovel solely for dry cement. Make the mortar to a fairly dry consistency to support the weight of the slab.

5 Use a brick trowel to spread mortar about 1¼in-2in (32mm-50mm) thick for the first slab at one corner of the site. Roughen the mortar surface with the point of the trowel.

6 Lay the slab carefully on the mortar bed so that its outer edges are in line with the string lines.

7 Place a short length of 4in × 2in (100mm × 50mm) thick timber on the slab to cushion it while you tap it down gently with a club hammer until the surface is level with the height pegs. The slab must be bedded down solidly, with no rocking movement. Make sure the compacted mortar bed is about 1in (25mm) thick – adjust the amount if necessary.

8 Use a spirit level and wooden shim to check that the crossfall and lengthways slope of the slab are correct.

9 Lay a row of edge slabs from the corner slab in the same way, in line with the guidelines and pegs. Place wooden spacers at the edge of each slab (unless it has sloped sides) to leave a uniform gap for filling in the joints later.

10 Use a straight-edge to check that the surface of each slab in the row is in line with the one before. If a slab is too high, tap it down if possible, or lift it and re-lay it with less mortar. Or if a slab is too low, lift it, add more mortar, and re-lay it.

11 Lay edge rows out from each corner slab in the same way to form three sides of the area.

12 Fill in between the three edge rows according to your layout pattern. Use a straight-edge to check the surface alignment of each slab with its adjoining slabs.

13 Wait for at least two days before removing wooden spacers and filling in the joints. Mix mortar to a dry, stiff mix, using 1 part cement to 2 parts sharp sand.

14 Force the mortar well into the joints with a piece of wood ⅜in (10mm) thick. For a crisp appearance and to aid drainage, tap the mortar down so that it lies a fraction of an inch (a few millimetres) below the slab surface.

15 Use a damp sponge to clean off excess mortar from the slabs.

CUTTING A SLAB

1 Lay the slab on soft sand and draw a pencil line all round at the cutting point, using a straight-edge and try square.

2 Score the pencil line all round, using either a brick bolster or an angle grinder with a masonry cutting disc – which makes a deep groove.

Using an angle grinder is less strenuous and more accurate, but handle it carefully to avoid accidents. Wear heavy gloves and protect your eyes from flying particles with safety spectacles.

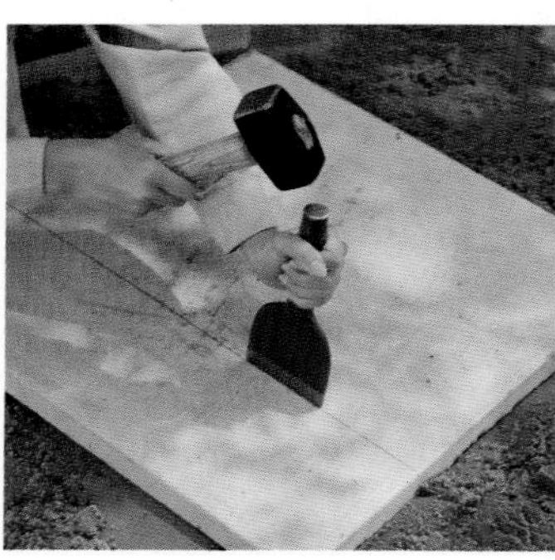

3 To cut the slab, lay it flat (surface upwards). Use the bolster and hammer or the cutting disc to gradually deepen the scored line until the slab breaks cleanly when you tap it.

4 With any cutting method, it is difficult to get a smooth edge. Use cut slabs where the edges will be hidden or not obvious – such as against a lawn edge or mortar joint.

> LAYING CRAZY PAVING
> Because crazy paving comes in many shapes and sizes, it is impossible to make a layout plan before you start. Instead, arrange the slabs in piles of different colours and sizes, and select from the whole range as you go along. Pick out slabs with a straight edge for the borders.
>
> You will need the same tools as for laying standard paving slabs, except for wooden spacers. It is not practicable to maintain uniform joints between slabs, but they should be no wider than 1in (25mm), for mortar economy and good appearance.
>
> The materials needed are also the same, except that the paving material is broken slabs or stones (page 488).
>
> Lay the slabs on a suitable base for a drive or patio and on a full bed of mortar, in the same way as standard slabs.
>
> Not all pieces of crazy paving will be of the same thickness – more mortar will be needed under thinner slabs to maintain a level surface. Check with a straight-edge in all directions to ensure that no pieces are tilted.

Laying paving blocks using a plate vibrator

Block paving needs to be well bedded to give a stable surface for a drive. The best way to do this is with a plate vibrator (page 490), a light compacting machine powered by a petrol-driven motor. This compacts an area of blocks laid on sand to a level, rigid surface, compressing the sand bed from about 2½in (65mm) to 2in (50mm) deep.

You can hire a plate vibrator – be sure to ask for one suitable for compacting paving blocks; some types are too heavy. Pass it over the area as evenly as possible. Do not use it within at least 3ft 3in (1m) of an unsupported edge, where blocks are still being laid.

Paving to be compacted must be laid between firm edges, otherwise the joints will open and the blocks spread. Where there is no adjoining wall or hard edge, lay edging blocks (right) or kerb (page 489).

You will need

Tools Straight-edge; two levelling strips of 2½in (65mm) wide timber as long as the width of the area to be paved; shovel; rake; kneeling board; *either* block splitter (see below) *or* brick bolster (page 479) and club hammer; plate vibrator; soft broom. Possibly also: brick trowel; string line and pegs; builder's square (page 479).

Materials Paving blocks; sharp sand – 1cu m covers about 18sq yds at 2½in deep (about 15sq m at 65mm deep). Possibly also: edging blocks; foundation mix concrete (page 496); water.

1 Prepare a hardcore base for a drive or patio (page 487), wide enough to accommodate a concrete bedding strip for any edging needed (see right). Allow space above the base for the block depth and for a 2in (50mm) layer of sand (the depth after compaction).

2 Lay edging blocks if necessary (see right), allowing for the correct crossfall and any lengthways slope.

Wait three days for the bedding mortar to mature before laying the paving.

3 Place piles of bedding sand, kept as dry as possible, along the site at about 10ft (3m) intervals so that you can spread it in sections without having to walk over it.

4 Lay two 2½in (65mm) deep levelling strips across the site – one where you intend to start laying and one 3ft 3in-6ft 6in (1m-2m) farther down the site. Check their crossfall (page 487) with a spirit level.

5 Spread the sand evenly between the strips, using a shovel and rake. Then lay the straight-edge across the strips and use it to rake off excess sand until the surface is level with the tops of the strips.

6 Prepare two or three sections to give a 10ft-13ft (3m-4m) run for laying. Remove the levelling strips as you go along, carefully filling the depressions with sand.

7 Start laying blocks at one corner of the prepared sand bed, but keep off the bed. As you work forwards, lay a kneeling board across the blocks already laid but not yet compacted.

8 Lay the blocks snugly against each other according to the chosen pattern (page 488), leaving no joint gaps. Lay whole blocks first, and cut and fit half blocks later. Check corners with a builder's square. Blocks laid at the edges should stand about ⅜in (10mm) higher than the edging – they should bed down by this amount when compacted.

9 After laying a run of about 10ft-13ft (3m-4m), use the plate vibrator over the area two or three times, but keep it at least 3ft 3in (1m) back from the last row of newly laid blocks. You can then see how much the blocks are bedding down. The actual amount depends on the moisture content of the sand. If the compacted surface is conspicuously too high or too low, lift the blocks and adjust the level of the sand bed.

10 After laying a satisfactory run of at least 13ft-14ft (4m-4.2m), fill in half blocks and compact the area again with the plate vibrator as before.

11 When all the blocks have been laid and compacted, make sure that the surface is dry then spread a layer of dry, fine sharp sand on it. Use the plate vibrator to work the sand into the crevices between the blocks to lock them in position. Get a helper to brush sand towards the vibrator, as it will be forced away by the vibrations.

LEVELLING THE SAND WITH A NOTCHED BOARD

Where the site has fixed edging on both sides – a footpath, for example – the sand can be levelled with a notched board rested across the edging.

Use a length of 4in × 2in (100mm × 50mm) board with a 6in (150mm) long notch at each end. To allow for the sand compaction, the depth of the board below the notches should be about ¼in (6mm) less than the depth of the paving blocks, unless using a plate vibrator, in which case it should be about ½in (13mm) less.

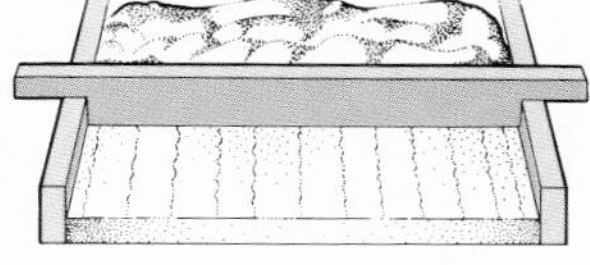

CUTTING PAVING BLOCKS

The easiest and quickest way to cut paving blocks is with a block splitter, a hand-operated hydraulic cutter that can be hired. The alternative is to cut them with a hammer and bolster in the same way as bricks (page 484) – a lengthy job when paving a large area.

LAYING EDGING BLOCKS

A common and reliable edging is a row of flat header paving blocks bedded in stiff sand-and-cement mortar on a layer of concrete (page 496). Use the foundation mix. Allow 8in (200mm) space for each line of edging blocks at the edges of the area to be paved.

Make the concrete layer 3in (75mm) thick and 12in (300mm) wide, to allow 3in (75mm) on the outside and 1in (25mm) on the inside of the line of edging blocks. Make the concrete surface at the correct depth to allow the top of the edging to coincide with the finished level of the compacted paving. Generally the depth is 3¼in (about 82mm) to accommodate the 2½in (65mm) deep block and a ¾in (19mm) layer of bedding mortar.

Wait 24 hours for the concrete to harden before laying the edging on a bed of 3 : 1 sand-cement mortar. Use a taut string line to set the surface level, taking into account the crossfall and any lengthways fall. Slope the bedding mortar a little way up the outside of the edging to make a small haunch. Leave no joints between blocks, unless the edging is curved.

For curved edging use stiff sand-and-cement mortar (2 : 1 mix). Make the joints ⅓in-1in (8mm-25mm) wide and pack them with mortar one day after bedding the blocks. Use a little mortar at a time, packed in with a strip of plywood. Fill to the bottom of the chamfered edge of the block, and sponge off any that smears the surface of the edging.

After completing the edging, wait three days before laying the paving blocks. Check that none of the bedding mortar used for the edging will impede the levelling of the paving blocks. If necessary cut mortar away down to the 1in (25mm) ledge of the concrete bed.

LAYING BRICKS OR BLOCKS WITHOUT A PLATE VIBRATOR

A small area of brick or block paving for a footpath or patio can be laid without using a vibrator, although the surface will not be as stable. Edging can be either paving blocks or timber formwork (page 494) thoroughly coated with wood preservative. The sand layer need be about 2¼in (57mm) deep only, as it will not be compressed as much as with a vibrator.

Before levelling the sand bed, dampen it with a fine-rose watering can until it is moist enough to hold together when you squeeze it.

Concreting: tools and formwork

Mixing platform
Useful if you have no clean, firm surface on which to mix concrete. To make one, use either boards nailed to cross battens, or a sheet of ½in (12mm) thick plywood. A good size is 6ft (1.8m) square, ideally with a 1in (25mm) lip all round to stop concrete spilling off. For small batches, use oil-tempered hardboard or a wheelbarrow. Wash down within two hours of use.

Concrete mixer
You can hire a small concrete mixer. Most types will mix a load of concrete in about three minutes. The capacity of the drum is usually stated for both the volume of dry materials and the approximate volume of mixed concrete. For example: 140/100 litres or 5/3½cu ft. A suitable size for DIY work is 4/3cu ft, which means the mixer takes 4cu ft of sand, cement and coarse aggregate to produce about 3cu ft of concrete.

A mixer may be electric or petrol driven. An electric type is usually more convenient if you have a long enough extension lead. Check the voltage and whether the motor is single phase or three phase. With a single-phase motor, use a transformer to reduce to 110 volts. Check that the leads are in good condition, and avoid damaging them.

A small mixer is likely to be about 30in (760mm) wide. It may be a barrow type (with wheels) or be supplied with a mounting frame so that you can stand a wheelbarrow below it. A barrow type should have a safety bar at the front to stop it going out of control.

Wheelbarrow
A heavy-duty contractor's wheelbarrow – usually 3cu ft (0.08cu m) capacity – can be hired. If it has to be pushed over soft ground or down steps, make a barrow-run – a line of strong planks anchored with pegs or battens. Scaffolding planks 8ft (2.4m) long can be hired.

Shovels, buckets and rake
Use two shovels and two strong, heavy-duty polythene buckets of identical size. Keep one shovel and one bucket for loading and measuring the cement only so that they stay dry and do not get clogged. Use a garden rake to spread the concrete. Wipe the head clean regularly, before the concrete sets.

Tamping beam
A length of straight-edged timber 2in (50mm) thick used on edge to flatten the concrete and expel air before it sets. Use a beam about 12in (300mm) longer than the width of the concrete so that it can rest on the formwork. Tamp a narrow stretch such as a path with a beam about 4in (100mm) deep (use a concave tamping edge if you want a cambered path). For broad sections 6ft-10ft (2m-3m) across, use a 6in (150mm) deep beam with a strong handle at each end. Two people are needed to use a long tamping beam.

Surface-finishing tools
For some types of surface finish you will need either a steel plasterer's finishing trowel or a wood or plastic float – tools that you may be able to hire. You can make a suitable wood float with a piece of flat wood 12in × 5in × ¾in (300mm × 125mm × 19mm). Screw a wooden handle on one side, using two short blocks and one long one with smoothed-off edges.

Arrissing tool
Used to round off the edges of the concrete before it hardens. Hire one, or make your own by bending a piece of sheet metal over a length of round metal rod or dowelling.

TOOLS FOR CONCRETING

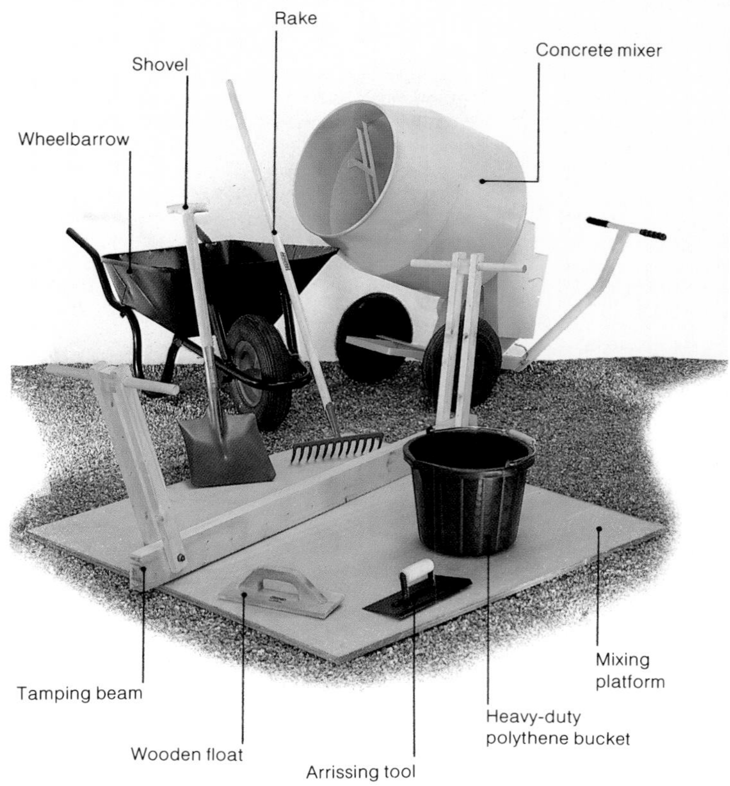

SETTING UP TIMBER EDGING

Timber edging, known as formwork, is needed to contain the soft surface material when making a concrete path or drive. It can be removed once the concrete has hardened. You can use old timber such as fence boards or floorboards.

Timber can also be used as a permanent edging for other types of path such as gravel, asphalt or paving blocks. If timber edging is to be permanent, it should be well soaked with wood preservative – preferably use wood pre-treated with vacuum-pressure impregnation before purchase.

You will need
Tools Spirit level; mallet; hammer; builder's square (page 479); wooden shim (page 487). Possibly also: string and pegs.

Materials Timber lengths as wide as the depth of the surface layer; wooden pegs 1in (25mm) square and about 12in (300mm) long – allow one peg for every 3ft 3in (1m) of edging; 2in (50mm) nails – galvanised for permanent edging.

1 Dig a strip about 6in (150mm) wide along each side of the sub-base surface. The strip should be as deep as the surface layer.

2 Stand a timber length on its side along one side of the sub-base, in line with the string marking line, and drive wooden pegs into the soil to support it from behind. The peg tops should be at the right height above ground for the path or drive surface, and flush with the top of the timber edging.

3 Use a spirit level to check that the edging strip is laid to the correct lengthways fall, if there is one. Then nail it to the pegs.

4 Butt other timber lengths in the same way to form one side of the edging.

5 To allow a slope for drainage, set the timber edging on one side of the path (the side farthest from the house wall, if it is adjoining) slightly lower than the other, according to the crossfall required (see *Making a slope*, page 487).

6 To make a tight corner joint, butt the timbers at right angles, using a builder's square as a check. Nail them together as well as to a peg. There is no need to cut off an overlapping piece of timber on the outside of the corner.

7 On long concrete paths, fit contraction joints across the path at suitable intervals (page 497).

MAKING A CURVE IN FORMWORK

1 Mark out the shape of the curve on the ground and set up pegs and a string line to follow the curve (see *Marking out a curve*, page 490).

2 Use a saw to make cuts in the timber edging for about half its depth on the edge that will form the inside of the curve. Make cuts at about 5in (125mm) intervals, or closer for a sharp curve.

3 Shape the timber by nailing it to the pegs.

4 Check that the timber along each side is at the right height and the correct slope (see *Making a slope*, page 487). Adjust as necessary by tapping it down or levering it up slightly.

CHOOSING MATERIALS FOR MAKING CONCRETE

Concrete is made by mixing sharp sand and small stones (coarse aggregate) with cement and water in certain proportions (page 496). You can make concrete yourself, mixing the ingredients either by hand or with a concrete mixer. Or you can buy it ready-mixed for immediate laying.

Mixing concrete yourself allows you to work at your own pace and lay sections at different times. If you buy ready-mixed concrete, it must be laid quickly all in one go, and you usually need several helpers. But for a large area requiring a full load – likely to be about 70sq yds (60sq m) at 4in (100mm) deep – it can be cheaper than mixing your own.

MATERIAL	DESCRIPTION	HOW SOLD	HOW TO STORE
Cement	Mixed lime and clay processed to a powder that sets hard when mixed with water. Ordinary Portland cement (OPC), which is grey, is used for most concrete. White Portland cement for making decorative white concrete or mortar costs twice as much. Sulphate-resisting cement is for concrete that will be exposed to seawater or soils high in sulphates – most likely on reclaimed land or some types of clay (the local Building Control Officer will advise); it is dearer than OPC and not widely available. Do not use masonry cement, which has additives to increase water-holding and plasticity. Rapid-setting cement is for small repairs underwater or in wet conditions.	Sold mainly in 50kg (1cwt) bags. Smaller bags – down to about 2.5kg (5lb) – are available; they are relatively dearer but are economical for small jobs or repairs. Check the condition of bags when buying – do not buy damp bags or bags in which you can feel lumps, which means that the cement has started to harden. To avoid waste because of hardening during storage, buy at one time only as much as you will use in a week.	Store bags off the ground on a dry, hard surface, stacked flat and close together so that air cannot circulate round them. Moisture in the air can penetrate the paper of the bag and cause the cement to harden (this is known as air-hardening or air-setting). Once cement has hardened, it is useless, even though it can be crumbled in the hand. Store bags under cover if possible. Cover them with plastic sheeting if they are left outside. If you have to store an opened bag for several days, keep it dry and airtight inside a tightly tied plastic bag. Cement can irritate the skin. If any goes in the eye, bathe at once in cold water and get medical advice.
Sand	Sand is classed as fine aggregate – material that will pass through a $\frac{3}{16}$in (5mm) mesh. Use sharp sand for concreting. It is coarser than builder's (or soft) sand, which is used for making mortar (page 481). Silver sand can be used with white Portland cement for making white concrete or mortar. It is finer than sharp sand, so use slightly more cement in the mix to give it sufficient strength.	Large amounts are usually sold loose, either by the ton (about 1000kg) or the cubic metre, (roughly 1500kg or $1\frac{1}{2}$ tons weight) and are available from builders' merchants, sand and gravel suppliers or quarries. Sand is cleaned by washing or dry screening. If you buy it from a quarry, make sure it has been cleaned. Small amounts are sold in 50kg (1cwt) and 25kg ($\frac{1}{2}$cwt) bags at DIY and garden centres and most builders' merchants.	Keep sand as clean as possible, stored on a hard surface or polythene sheeting and covered with waterproof sheeting to keep it as dry as possible. Sand retains moisture, which increases its bulk, and any sand you use is certain to contain some moisture. Quantities for mixing (page 496) are given by volume for dry sand, so if the sand is appreciably damp (but not soaked through) increase the recommended volume by up to 25 per cent. Fully saturated sand has a similar volume to dry sand.
Coarse aggregate	Small stones that are too big to pass through a $\frac{3}{16}$in (5mm) mesh, and which form the bulk of concrete. Well-graded aggregate has a balanced mixture of stone sizes, but is available with different sizes. A $\frac{3}{4}$in (20mm) maximum is used for most DIY concreting. Fine concrete is made with $\frac{3}{8}$in (10mm) maximum stones.	Usually sold either by the ton (about 1000kg) or cubic metre (roughly 1500–1800kg or $1\frac{1}{2}$–2 tons weight), and is available from builders' merchants, sand and gravel suppliers and quarries. Some suppliers sell small amounts such as 50kg (1cwt) in bags; these are easy to keep clean and useful for small jobs, but relatively more expensive than buying in bulk.	Aggregate is unaffected by the weather and can be kept for any length of time, but keep it clean by storing on a hard surface or tarpaulin with a covering sheet. If it contains a lot of dirt or debris, the concrete will be weakened. Protect the material from frost. If you use frozen aggregate ice may form within the concrete.
All-in (combined) aggregate and ballast	A mixture of sizes of aggregate, including sand (fine aggregate). It may either be mixed by the supplier (this is more expensive) or sold as naturally mixed when quarried. Mixed ballast is similar but the term usually refers to gravel types of aggregate. It is often used on top of a layer of hardcore to fill in gaps when making a sub-base (page 487). Avoid unwashed ballast.	Sold in the same way as coarse aggregate (above). Tell the supplier you want it for concrete making, as the quality varies. Poorly graded all-in aggregate is not suitable for making concrete. Well-graded material includes 60 per cent of stones bigger than $\frac{3}{16}$in (5mm). One test of the quality is to squeeze the material in your hand – if it leaves a stain because of the high silt content, avoid it.	Store in the same way as coarse aggregates.
Bagged dry-mixes	Mixtures of cement and aggregates (usually in the proportions 1:2:4) to which only water need be added. The different mixes include: Coarse mix or fast-setting (5 minute) mix – For jobs such as putting up fence posts. Fine mix – For jobs needing smooth surfaces. Sand-and-cement mix (usually 1:3/cement: sharp sand) – For patching or as a bedding mortar for slabs or edging.	Sold in 50kg (1cwt), 40kg ($\frac{3}{4}$cwt), and 25kg ($\frac{1}{2}$cwt) bags by builders' merchants, hardware shops and DIY and garden centres. Convenient for small jobs and repairs, but not for large areas as it can cost ten times as much as mixing the ingredients yourself.	Store in the same way as cement. When using, tip all the material from the bag and mix the dry ingredients together thoroughly. Keep the amount you need for mixing with water to one side and return the remainder to the bag (keep it dry). This ensures that the mix is correctly balanced before you start adding water.
Ready-mixed concrete	The concrete is ready-mixed for laying immediately on delivery, and is supplied from special trucks, often with discharge chutes. The sub-base and formwork must be ready at the time of delivery, and the concrete must be laid within two hours (faster in hot weather). Before delivery, work out the best way to get the concrete from the truck to the laying area. If you need wheelbarrows, specify a retarded load – with chemicals added to slow down setting – to allow for the extra time involved. A retarded load must be laid within four hours of delivery (faster in hot weather).	A full truckload is normally 6cu m (about 8cu yds), but some suppliers do smaller loads for DIY work. Get several quotes before you order. Some firms mix the dry ingredients on site, and you pay only for the amount drawn from the truck. Order at least 24 hours before you intend laying and specify clearly what you want. Find out if there is a time limit by which the load has to be discharged (such as 30 minutes per cu m), if delivery can be postponed in wet weather, if wheelbarrows are supplied (if needed), and what happens if you cancel at short notice because of illness?	

CONCRETE COLOURING AND ADDITIVES

You can colour concrete by adding powdered pigment during mixing, or by staining it after laying. Neither method is very successful – colours can look patchy and fade with weathering.

Additives for waterproofing and frost protection can also be mixed in, but use them with caution following the maker's instructions. Waterproofers make concrete less easy for water to pass through. Frost protectors speed up the reaction between water and cement, and may reduce the risk of frost damage soon after laying, but the concrete should still be protected with sheeting (page 498).

Measuring and mixing concrete

DECIDING THE PROPORTIONS OF INGREDIENTS

The strength of concrete varies with the proportions of the ingredients. Choose the right mix for the job, as shown below. The amount of concrete produced from one bag of cement varies with the type of mix.

With any mix, the quality of the concrete produced goes down if you add more water than the amount essential to compact it fully, using a generous amount of effort.

For laying a large drive, ready-mixed paving concrete is preferable to home-mixed because it can be air entrained – a process that traps microscopic air bubbles which protect concrete from the flaking or cracking caused by frost, especially where de-icing salts are carried in from the road. Home-made paving mix cannot be air entrained, although its high cement content gives some weather protection.

Ready-mixed concrete varies in workability. For most DIY work, medium workability is suitable. But high workability – with a superplasticiser added – can be specified if the concrete will be difficult to lay because the site is awkward to get at – a deep trench, for example. Adding a retarder slows down the tendency of the concrete to lose its workability, whether medium or high.

MIX	USE	INGREDIENTS	PROPORTIONS USING: Separate aggregates	All-in aggregates	APPROXIMATE QUANTITIES TO MAKE: 1cu m	1cu yd	WHAT TO SPECIFY FOR A READY-MIXED LOAD
Foundation mix	An economical mix suitable only for unexposed concrete, such as under a path or drive surface, strip foundations for a wall or for concreting in a fence post.	Cement	1	1	5.6 bags	4.25 bags	Mix C7.5P to BS 5328; medium or high workability; 20mm maximum aggregate. Amount required in cubic metres – including 10 per cent for wastage.
		Sharp sand	2½	—	720kg	10.7cwt	
		Coarse aggregate (20mm)	3½	—	1165kg	17.4cwt	
		All-in aggregates	—	5	1885kg	28cwt	
General-purpose mix	Suitable for most jobs other than foundations – for example, garage or shed bases – but not for surfaces exposed to the weather.	Cement	1	1	6.4 bags	4.9 bags	Mix C20P to BS 5328; medium or high workability; 20mm maximum aggregate. Amount required in cubic metres – including 10 per cent for wastage.
		Sharp sand	2	—	680kg	10cwt	
		Coarse aggregate (20mm)	3	—	1175kg	17.5cwt	
		All-in aggregates	—	4	1855kg	27.6cwt	
Paving mix	A strong mix for surfaces exposed to the weather, such as paths, drives and steps.	Cement	1	1	8 bags	6 bags	Special prescribed mix: minimum cement content 330kg per cu m; 4 per cent air entrained; target slump 75mm (a measurement of workability). Amount required in cubic metres – including 10 per cent for wastage.
		Sharp sand	1½	—	600kg	9cwt	
		Coarse aggregate (20mm)	2½	—	1200kg	17.9cwt	
		All-in aggregates	—	3½	1800kg	26.5cwt	
Bedding mortar mix	For paving slabs. ½cu m gives a full mortar bed for about 135sq ft (13sq m).	Cement	1	—	8 bags	6 bags	—
		Sharp sand	4		1600kg	24cwt	

ESTIMATING HOW MUCH CONCRETE IS NEEDED

To find the cubic measurement of concrete you require, measure the area to be covered and multiply it by the thickness needed.

Measure the thickness exactly by laying the tamper across the formwork and measuring down at different points to allow for unevenness in the sub-base. Then take a mean of the different depths. Add 10 per cent to the measured amount to allow for wastage when mixing and laying. For example:

PATH DIMENSIONS

IMPERIAL:	3ft 3in	33ft	3in
METRIC:	1m	10m	75mm

Calculation

IMPERIAL: 3¼ft × 33ft × ¼ft = 26.8cu ft; 26.8 + 10% (2.68) = 29.48cu ft.
1cu m = 36cu ft, so 29.48 ÷ 36 = 0.8cu m.

METRIC: 1m × 10m × 0.075m = 0.75cu m; 0.75 + 10% (0.075) = 0.8cu m.

Work in either metric or imperial measurements. Do not convert as you go along, it can make an appreciable difference to the total.

If you do not want to do your own sums, tell a builders' merchant the area and depth of finished concrete required. He will usually be able to advise the amounts of materials needed.

To measure an area of irregular shape, make a scale grid of squares of uniform size, then draw an outline of the area, square by square, on the grid. Average out part squares to get a round figure.

GUIDE TO BATCH MIXING

Measure the proportions for the mix by the bucket, and mix them in batches based on one bucket of cement. For a 1 : 2 : 3 general-purpose mix, for example, make a batch of one bucket of cement, two of sharp sand and three of coarse aggregate. Fill whole buckets right to the top.

Keep a separate shovel and bucket for the cement, so that they stay dry and are not clogged with half-set concrete, which could spoil the dry cement in the bag and also the proportions of the mix.

A 3 gallon (14 litre) heavy-duty polythene bucket has a capacity of about 0.5cu ft and will hold about 44lb (20kg) of cement. A mixer drum of 4/3cu ft will therefore take about eight buckets of loose material. A 50kg bag of cement yields about 2½ buckets. Some 44-52 pints of water are needed for each 50kg of cement, so a batch based on one bucket takes 12-18 pints.

The capacity of a wheelbarrow is about 3cu ft (0.08cu m), but a manageable barrowload is generally about half capacity or less. This is 25 or more barrowloads per cubic metre of concrete.

A cubic yard of sand weighs 950-1300kg (19-26 50kg bags). A cubic metre of sand weighs 1250-1750kg (25-30 50kg bags).

MIX	NO. OF BUCKETS OF DRY MATERIAL	CONCRETE YIELD (APPROX.)
Foundation (1 : 2½ : 3½)	7	2.5cu ft
General purpose (1 : 2 : 3)	6	2.1cu ft
Paving (1 : 1½ : 2½)	5	1.7cu ft

GUIDE TO CONCRETE COVERAGE

THICKNESS OF LAYER		APPROXIMATE AREA COVERED BY: 1cu m		1.5cu ft	
mm	in	sq m	sq yds	sq m	sq ft
50	2	18	21	0.28	3.0
75	3	13	15	0.23	2.5
100	4	10	12	0.19	2.1
125	5	8	9.5	0.18	1.9
150	6	6	7	0.16	1.7

MIXING CONCRETE BY HAND

Most people find hand mixing hard work, suitable only for small jobs or for jobs that can be done in easy stages – a long path laid in sections, for example. The alternative is to hire a concrete mixer.

To produce good concrete by hand you need to work carefully and methodically at a steady pace – a rushed job is likely to give poor, disappointing results.

You will need
Tools Mixing platform (page 491); two shovels (one for cement only); two heavy-duty polythene buckets of identical size – normally 3 gallons (14 litres) capacity (keep one for cement only); bucket or watering can.
Materials Sharp sand and coarse aggregates (or all-in aggregate); ordinary Portland cement; water (12-18 pints per 3 gallon bucket of cement) – use mains water, if possible, as water from a butt or pond will contain organic substances that could affect the concrete.

1 Set up a mixing platform as near as possible to the laying area.

2 Measure buckets of sand and coarse aggregates in the required proportions and tip them into a pile on the platform.

3 Use the cement shovel to fill the cement bucket to the top. To make sure the bucket is properly packed, knock it two or three times as you fill it, because the cement fluffs up as it is shovelled.

4 Make a crater in the top of the pile of aggregates and tip the bucket of cement into it.

5 Use the aggregate shovel to mix the pile thoroughly, turning it over until it looks the same colour throughout.

6 Make a crater in the top of the mixed pile and gradually pour in about half the water.

7 Turn the pile again, moving dry material from the edge to the middle, until the water is well mixed in. Aim for an even colour and a dryish, crumbly consistency.

8 Continue adding and mixing in water a little at a time until the pile is a smooth, moist consistency – neither crumbly nor sloppy.

9 Test the consistency by slapping along the top of the pile with the back of the shovel. If water runs out readily it is too wet. Mix it a bit more with the shovel, but if it stays too sloppy you have used too much water. Add a small amount of cement and aggregates (in the correct proportions) and mix again until you get it right.

USING A CONCRETE MIXER

Order the cement and aggregates in time for them to be ready for use when the mixer arrives, to save hiring for longer than necessary.

A machine cuts down the amount of heavy work and speeds up mixing considerably. To avoid long breaks between mixing loads, get some helpers. One person can operate the mixer while others spread and level the mixed concrete. Except for a mixing platform, the tools and materials needed are the same as for hand mixing.

1 Switch on the revolving drum, put in half the sand and coarse aggregate, then add half the water.

2 Allow the drum to spin for half a minute, then put in all the cement and the rest of the sand, coarse aggregate, and water.

3 After two or three minutes more mixing, the concrete is ready for use. Tip it straight onto the site, if possible, or use a wheelbarrow.

4 When you have finished mixing for the day, wash out the drum by mixing coarse gravel and plenty of water. Discharge the washings, then pull out the electric plug and scrub down the outside of the machine, using plenty of water.

Laying an area of concrete

Freshly mixed concrete sets and starts to harden within about two hours – faster in very hot weather – so must be laid, levelled and given a surface finish in sections (or bays) so that it can be completed while the concrete is still workable.

The size of a workable section depends on the rate at which you mix and place it, but is likely to be within the region of 3-4 barrowloads with hand mixing, or 6-8 with machine mixing. (See *Guide to concrete coverage*, facing page.)

With ready-mixed concrete, two people can generally spread and tamp down an area of roughly 10sq yds (8.5sq m) of concrete discharged directly into the laying area before it sets.

Concrete will crack if it is allowed to dry too fast, so has to be 'cured' – that is, kept moist for three days after laying. It takes about a month to set to its full strength, but you can walk or build on it after three days (wait seven days in winter).

> HELPFUL TIP
>
> Delay laying concrete if there is any danger of freezing weather all day. Do not lay concrete on a frozen base or with frozen aggregates.
>
> If, after you have laid fresh concrete, a light frost is likely, cover the curing sheet (see overleaf) with a layer of earth or sand.
>
> Or use a layer of straw with a second polythene sheet over the top to keep it in place.
>
> To prevent fresh-laid concrete from freezing, especially during the first night, cover it with either a 3in (75mm) deep layer of straw, or sheeting kept clear of the surface and closed in on all sides.

DECIDING THE SIZE OF A BAY FOR LAYING CONCRETE

There is a maximum size at which any slab of concrete can be laid in one piece without danger of cracking. A surface larger than this maximum is laid in separate sections (or bays) with joints between to allow for contraction and expansion due to temperature changes.

The maximum intervals between contraction joints varies according to the thickness of the concrete and the site width (see below).

In general joints should be closer as the width gets narrower. So a path, for example, usually needs shorter bays between joints than a drive. Make the bays of equal size and as square as possible. The length can be about one and a half times the width, but no more than twice the width.

Contraction joints can be placed at closer intervals to give smaller bays, if this is convenient for laying workable sections when mixing your own concrete.

CONTRACTION JOINT INTERVALS

Width of site	Depth of concrete: 3in (75mm)	4in (100mm)	6in (150mm)
8–10ft (3m)	10ft (3m)	13ft (4m)	16ft (5m)
3–7ft (1–2m)	8ft (2.4m)	6–10ft (2–3m)	10–13ft (3–4m)
Under 3ft (1m)	6ft (1.8m)	—	—

MAKING A CONTRACTION JOINT

You will need
Tools Mallet or club hammer; piece of softwood 1in (25mm) thick, as deep as the formwork and long enough to fit across the inside of the formwork; wooden pegs; arrissing tool (concrete edging trowel).
Materials Hardboard filler strip as long and as deep as the softwood.

1 Position a hardboard filler strip between the two sides of the formwork and at right angles to them. (If one side of the formwork is curved, bend the filler strip to meet the side at right angles.)

Laying an area of concrete (continued)

2 Support the filler strip on the outside of the first bay to be concreted, using the piece of softwood held in position with pegs.

3 Concrete the bay (see right) right up to the hardboard filler, then concrete about 12in (300mm) into the second bay.

4 Lift out the softwood support and pegs but leave the filler strip in position.

5 Push the concrete against the filler where you have removed the softwood support, then continue laying the second bay.

6 When finishing the concrete surface (see below), use an arrissing tool on each side of the hardboard filler strip.

MAKING A CONCRETE PATH OR DRIVE

Prepare the sub-base and formwork (pages 487, 494), allowing for a suitable drainage slope (page 487). Make the concrete surface layer 3in (75mm) thick for a path, or 4in (100mm) thick for a drive. If the drive is on soft soil such as peat, make the surface layer 6in (150mm) thick; use a filter membrane fabric under the sub-base (page 487).

You will need
Tools Rake; shovel; wheelbarrow; tamping beam; arrissing (concrete-edging) trowel; surface-finishing tools; polythene or hessian sheeting; bricks. Possibly also: watering can; sharp sand.
Materials Freshly made concrete of a suitable mix for the job (pages 495, 496).

1 Pour batches of concrete into the first bay to be laid.

2 Use the back of a rake to draw the concrete together so that it is roughly level and about ½in (13mm) higher than the top of the timber formwork.

3 Press the concrete into all corners and against all edges of the bay with a shovel or your boot. Make sure all cavities are filled, because air pockets will weaken the concrete.

4 Compact the filled bay with a tamping beam laid across the formwork. Use it with a chopping action, moving it along about half its thickness with each chop. This leaves an undulating surface.

5 Go over the high spots again, using the tamper steadily backwards and forwards with a sawing action to remove excess concrete.

6 If any depressions appear in the surface, scoop fresh concrete into them with a shovel.

7 Give a final tamp over the bay – this can be the final finish or you can apply a different finish (see below). To get a near-smooth tamped finish, pass the tamper slowly backwards and forwards with steady strokes.

For a textured finish, use the tamper with a lift and drop action. Depending on the spacing between drops, the appearance can vary from close rippled to wide rippled, like a washboard.

8 Before the concrete hardens, round off the edges by running an arrissing tool along the slight gap between the formwork and the concrete edge.

9 As soon as the concrete is hard enough not to be marked, cover it with polythene or hessian sheeting to stop it drying out too quickly. Weight the edges of the sheeting with bricks to stop it blowing away, and sprinkle some sharp sand over the top, if necessary, to prevent ballooning. If you use hessian or sacking, keep it constantly damp, or use it under polythene sheeting.

10 Remove the covering after not less than three days, and the formwork a day or so later.

FINISHING THE SURFACE

A textured finish helps to give the concrete a non-skid surface. If you leave the surface as tamped (see step 7, left), it will have a rippled appearance. Other ways of finishing the surface are shown below.

For a narrow path, you can apply the finish from the ground alongside. For a wide area such as a drive, work from a bridge across the formwork – lay the tamping beam across on its side, for example.

WAYS OF FINISHING THE CONCRETE SURFACE

Brush finish
For a pronounced brush finish, drag a hard-bristled broom over the surface after tamping near-smooth. Hold the broom at a shallow angle so that the surface is indented but not torn up, and make all strokes in the same direction. Rinse the brush bristles if they get clogged, then shake well.

For a smoother brush finish use a soft broom and apply it with gentle strokes.

Float finish
Use a wood float in overlapping circles to produce a fish-scale finish. For a plain finish, draw the float across the surface as soon as you have tamped it. If you want to coarsen the texture, let some of the concrete build up on the float face.

For a smooth, unmarked finish, skim the surface with a steel plasterer's trowel. For a tight, hard-wearing finish, let the surface stiffen first.

Piped finish/shovel finish
A fairly heavy pipe, such as a scaffolding tube, can be rolled over the surface like a rolling pin to give a somewhat stippled appearance. Or it can be rolled, lifted and dropped to give a ridged finish.

For a shovel finish use the back of a shovel to lightly pat the newly tamped surface using a circular movement. This gives an overlapping, fish-scale finish, as with a wood float.

Exposed stone finish
Scatter a thin layer of single-sized stones after tamping. Tamp again, making sure the stones are well bedded. Let the concrete harden until the stones are well gripped, then spray the surface lightly with a fine-rose can. Use a soft broom to brush away loose material, leaving the stones partly exposed. Next day clean the surface with a stiff broom and water. Cure for about three days.

HELPFUL TIP

When applying a float finish – whether using a wood float or a steel trowel – be careful not to over-use the float on fresh concrete. If you press on the surface too much, the aggregates will sink and the surface will be left weakened, containing too much water. When the concrete hardens, it will have a permanent film of light grey dust as the surface slowly crumbles away.

MAKING A PATH OR DRIVE ALONGSIDE A WALL

Instead of fixing formwork along the wall side of the path, fit a strip of ½in (13mm) thick bitumen-impregnated fibreboard such as Flexcell. This will form a joint between the concrete and the brickwork.

Lay the concrete in alternate bays so that you and your helper can stand on each side of the bay you are concreting and use the tamping beam parallel to the wall.

After three days, when the concrete has hardened enough to stand on, lay concrete in the empty bays. Remove the stop-ends of the formwork from the laid bays and lay the new concrete up to the hardened edge of the set concrete. As it dries out, it will shrink and pull away enough to leave a gap sufficient to serve as a contraction joint.

LAYING A BASE FOR A SHED, GARAGE OR GREENHOUSE

The base for a light building is simply a slab of concrete laid in the same way as a drive. Use the general-purpose mix (page 496).

Prepare the sub-base and formwork in the same way as for a drive. There is no need to make a drainage slope, although for a garage it is a good idea to make a 1 in 80 slope towards the door.

Use a spirit level and builder's square (page 479) to ensure the slab is level and that the corners are right angles.

A small base can be laid in one slab. For a larger base you may need to make bays separated by contraction joints (page 497).

Laying cold asphalt and gravel

Cold asphalt is commonly used to re-surface an existing path or drive, such as old, worn asphalt or paving slabs, or pitted concrete.

Do not use it on cracked concrete without first repairing the crack, or the asphalt may crack at the same spot.

Re-surfacing raises the height by about ½in (13mm). Make sure this does not obstruct the opening of gates or doors, or interfere with a damp-proof course.

Cold asphalt is not suitable for making a new drive, but can be used for a new path on a hardcore sub-base as long as it has been well compacted with a vibrator.

Treat an existing surface with weedkiller about two weeks before you intend laying the asphalt. The best time to lay asphalt is when the weather is dry but not hot. Although rain will not damage the cold asphalt, it will affect the bitumen emulsion used to bind it.

Wear old shoes or wellingtons to protect your feet from splashes of emulsion. Do not tread in the emulsion as it is very sticky. Wash off any from your skin, and if you get some in your eye, bathe it at once in cold water and then get medical advice.

You will need

Tools Spirit level; wooden shim (page 487); garden rake; sharp knife for cutting sacks open; length of straight ¾in (19mm) thick wood about 6ft (1.8m) long as a levelling gauge; garden roller; stiff broom. Possibly also: shovel; old watering can with rose removed; hardboard or plywood sheets for masking; several bricks or large stones; plate vibrator (page 490).

Materials Cold asphalt – about 25kg (½cwt) per 10sq ft (0.9sq m); bitumen emulsion – 5kg (11lb) covers about 75sq ft (7sq m) on a firm, dense surface, but roughly less than half that area on hardcore for a new path. Possibly also: decorative stone chippings.

1 Clear the surface of litter such as dead leaves – sweep concrete with a stiff brush - and fill in potholes (page 500). Mask any drain openings or covers with hardboard or plywood securely weighted down with bricks or stones.

ALTERNATIVELY, for a new path prepare a sub-base (page 487). Use well-compacted hardcore 3-4in (75-100mm) deep topped with 1-2in (25-50mm) layer of ballast to fill gaps.

2 Check the drainage slope of the surface (page 487). If it is less than 1 in 80, build it up while laying the asphalt.

3 Prepare permanent edging such as kerbing or formwork if desired, or temporary edging where the site adjoins a lower surface.

4 Spread the bitumen emulsion from the container, or use an old watering can with the rose removed. Tip over about 30sq ft (2.8sq m) at a time – roughly the area covered by three sacks of asphalt.

5 Spread the emulsion with a stiff broom to an even thickness.

6 Wait about 20 minutes while the emulsion turns from brown to black, then tip the asphalt on it.

7 With the levelling gauge laid across the edge of the laying area as a height guide, rake the asphalt to ¾in (19mm) overall thickness.

8 Dampen a garden roller (to stop the asphalt sticking to it), then roll the asphalt.

9 Add extra asphalt to any depressions formed while rolling, and build up the surface to make a drainage slope, if necessary. Then roll the area again.

10 If you want to decorate the surface with stone chippings, scatter them very thinly over the asphalt with a shovel.

11 Finally, roll the whole area thoroughly in several directions so that the asphalt is compacted to a depth of about ½in (13mm).

LAYING GRAVEL

Prepare a hardcore sub-base 4in (100mm) deep, allowing a depth of about 1in (25mm) for the gravel surface. Make a drainage crossfall (page 487) of about 1 in 80. Top the hardcore with a 1in (25mm) blinding layer of sharp sand – to fill any gaps and make a close, smooth base for the gravel. Use 10mm or 20mm pea gravel.

Unless there are walls or turf edging to contain the gravel, lay permanent edging such as kerbing (page 489) or timber formwork (page 494).

Spread the gravel with a rake over the whole area to a depth of about ½in (13mm), then roll it with a garden roller. Spread a second layer of about ½in (13mm), then roll again.

The surface will need regular raking or rolling as it becomes disturbed, and will probably need to be treated with weedkiller about once a year.

12 Clean the broom and rake with paraffin or white spirit.

13 You can walk on the surface as soon as it is laid, but avoid putting any sharp-edged loads on it, or driving a vehicle over it until it is fully hardened – generally after two days. Remove any temporary edging once the surface is hard.

LAYING STONE CHIPPINGS

Clear the surface in the same way as for asphalt, and prepare permanent edging such as kerbing (page 489) or formwork (page 494). Where wear is hard - on bends or drive entrances – put a layer of cold asphalt (as above) before laying the chippings.

Bitumen emulsion is used to bind the surface and hold the chippings together, so a thicker layer is needed than for asphalt. On a smooth or firm, dense surface, 5kg will cover 30-40sq ft (2.8-3.7sq m), but only about 14sq ft (1.3sq m) on a loose, open surface.

The emulsion takes about 12 hours to set, but may set faster when it is hot, or take longer in cold weather. Rain will affect the emulsion before it sets, so do not spread it if rain is likely. Spreading when the surface or the chippings are damp does not matter.

Spread the emulsion over an area of about 50sq ft (5sq m) at a time – enough for about two bags of chippings. Use a spade to shake the chippings evenly over the sticky area, making sure they do not pile up too thickly.

Roll the chippings after laying two or three sections, then roll the whole area again after completion to make a firm, even surface with a crossfall for drainage of about 1 in 80 (page 487). It can be used to walk or drive over immediately.

After a week or two, when the surface has hardened, gently sweep off loose chippings. Apply more emulsion and chippings to any bare patches. If the original surface was very worn or loose, apply a second coat of emulsion and chippings after two days.

Repairing paths, drives and steps

Small cracks that develop in the surface of a path or drive often result from errors in construction – weaknesses in the sub-base, for example, or faulty concrete mixing or curing. Alternatively, they may be caused by a small amount of movement in the ground below.

It is a waste of time to repair small cracks as soon as they appear. Wait to see if they increase in size and number. If after a year or so there has been little or no increase, it is fair to assume that the ground has settled and repairs can be carried out.

But if the surface develops extensive cracking or sunken areas, take it up and lay it again on a new, firm sub-base. Should the cracking or sinking extend to ground beyond the path or drive surface, get a surveyor to check the cause.

REFITTING A DAMAGED OR LOOSE PAVING SLAB

1 Use a spade to chop through any mortar at edge joints. Push the spade under the slab to lift it and slip a broomstick or pipe under it to roll it out. A sunken or see-sawing slab can be re-laid, but renew a cracked or chipped slab.

2 If the slab was bedded on sand, loosen up the old sand with a trowel, add more sharp sand, and lightly level the surface with a length of wood.

ALTERNATIVELY, if the slab was bedded on mortar, remove the old mortar with a hammer and chisel. Mix new bedding mortar in a dryish mix of 1 part cement to 4 parts sharp sand (or use a bagged sand-cement mix) and spread it over the surface with a brick trowel to a thickness of 1¼in-2in (32mm-50mm). Roughen the surface with the trowel point.

3 Slab edge joints may be flush or with gaps. If there are gaps, place ⅜in (10mm) thick wooden spacers along one long and one short edge before rolling the slab into position on a broomstick or pipe. Then space other side gaps.

4 Lay a 2in (50mm) thick piece of flat wood on the slab as a cushion while you use a club hammer to tap it down flush with the surrounding slabs. Check that it is flush using a length of straight-edged timber.

5 If you cannot tap the slab down flush, lift it again and skim off some of the bedding material. Or, if it sinks down too far, add more of the bedding material.

6 Wait at least two days before filling in the joints in the same way as for laying slabs (page 492).

REPAIRING DAMAGED ASPHALT

Cut round the damaged area with a brick bolster (page 479) and club hammer to make an even hole. If the damage is at the edge of an unedged path, fix a temporary timber edge supported by pegs.

Clear out dust and debris from the hole, then paint the bottom and the sides with bitumen emulsion (page 499).

When the emulsion has turned black, tip in a layer of about ¾in (19mm) of cold asphalt and ram it down. Add more layers of asphalt, ramming each one down firmly, until the hole is filled. A packaged patching material such as Instant Road Repair can be used instead of bitumen and asphalt. Follow the maker's instructions.

DEALING WITH STAINS

Oil, grease and rust stains, or moss, often occur on paths and drives. Most can be removed with one of the wide range of proprietary removers available from DIY, gardening or motoring stores. Cat litter is a good absorbent for spreading on fresh oil spillages.

RENEWING DAMAGED KERBING

1 Use a club hammer to loosen the damaged length of kerbing, then prise it out with a spade.

2 Dig out about 2in (50mm) of the sub-base below the removed stone, then ram the surface well down with a thick piece of timber.

3 Mix bedding mortar using a bagged sand-cement mortar mix to a dryish consistency. Spread it about 3in (75mm) deep in the gap.

4 Damp the new kerbstone and lower it into position. Cushion it with a 2in (50mm) piece of flat timber and tap it down with a club hammer until it is flush with the adjoining kerb.

5 Use a spirit level to check that the sides align with the adjoining kerb, and a straight-edge to check that the surface is also aligned. Support kerbing with 1in (25mm) stakes while the mortar sets.

REPAIRING CRACKS OR HOLES IN CONCRETE

Hairline cracks in concrete can be ignored. They often follow the lines of the contraction joints between sections. A hole can be filled if it is at least ½in (13mm) deep. If the hole is shallower, deepen it first, or the new layer will be too thin to hold firm.

Repair concrete with a filler containing PVA adhesive (see panel) to make a good bond. For potholes, packaged material such as Instant Road Repair can be used instead.

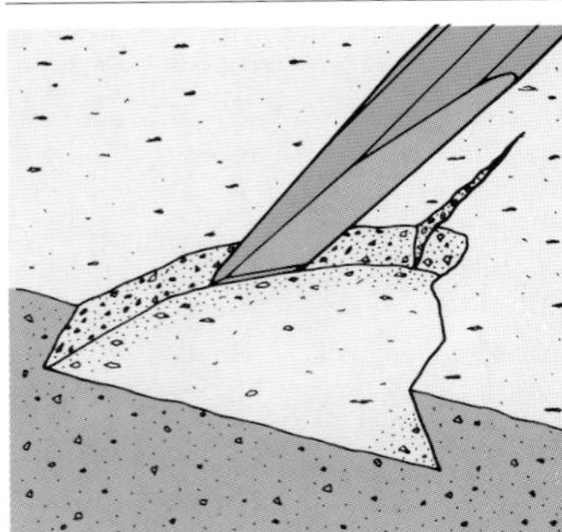

1 Widen the crack or hole below the surface by undercutting the edges with a cold chisel and club hammer. This ensures that the filler will be well anchored.

2 Remove all debris from the hole or crack and brush it with a priming coat of PVA adhesive as instructed on the container – usually 1 part adhesive to 5 parts water.

3 When the priming coat is tacky, fill the crack or hole using concrete filler (see panel). Pack it well down so that there are no air pockets, which will weaken the concrete.

4 Level off the area flush with the surrounding surface using a brick trowel (page 479) or plasterer's steel finishing trowel.

5 Cover the repair with polythene for at least three days.

MAKING CONCRETE FILLER

Prepare a cement and sharp sand mix in the proportions 1:3 by volume, or for small amounts use a bagged sand-cement mix (page 495).

Separately mix equal parts of water and PVA adhesive – a building adhesive such as Evo-Bond or Unibond used to seal or bond various building materials.

Mix the dry material, water and PVA adhesive together in the same way as for making concrete (page 496). Mix until the filler is a smooth, moist consistency – neither crumbly nor too sloppy.

REPAIRING CRUMBLING EDGES ON A CONCRETE PATH

Concrete may crumble at the edges if the edging formwork was removed too soon, or if the wet concrete was not packed well down against the formwork during laying. Air pockets below an apparently solid surface cause the concrete to break up when the edges come under pressure during use.

1 Chip away the damaged concrete back to solid material, using a cold chisel and club hammer.

2 Remove the debris, and if the sub-base is exposed, ram the hardcore well down with a ramming tool or thick length of timber. Add fresh hardcore to any soft spots and ram it well down.

3 Set up timber edging 1in (25mm) thick alongside the damaged area so that the top edge is level with the concrete surface. Support it with pegs driven into the ground.

4 Brush the exposed edge of the concrete with a priming coat of PVA adhesive mixed according to the instructions on the container – usually 1 part adhesive to 5 parts water. Wait for it to dry.

5 Prepare concrete filler (facing page) and use a brick trowel to press it into the exposed area, well down against the edging.

6 Level the surface with the trowel, or use a float (page 494), to give a non-slip finish.

7 Cover the repaired area with polythene to stop it drying too fast. Remove the sheeting after three days. Leave the edging longer if the path is used a lot.

DEALING WITH A DUST FILM ON CONCRETE

Light grey dust that forms continually on concrete and cannot be swept away is caused by the surface crumbling. It is usually the result of over-use of the float when smoothing the surface to a finish.

Seal the surface by brushing on a priming coat of PVA adhesive and water as instructed on the container, usually with 1 part adhesive to 5 parts water.

REPAIRING A CONCRETE STEP

1 Cut back a crumbling edge using a cold chisel and club hammer. If the surface is worn down, score it with a brick bolster (page 479) and hammer to provide a good grip (key) for a new layer of concrete.

2 Fix timber edging round the step using pegs and bricks to keep it firmly in place. If renewing a worn surface, set the edging about ½in (13mm) higher than the surface, with the side pieces allowing a forward slope of about ⅜in (10mm) for water to run off.

3 Brush away dust and debris.

4 Prime the area with a mixture of PVA adhesive and water according to the container instructions – usually 1 part adhesive to 5 parts water. Allow to become tacky.

5 Repair crumbling edges with concrete filler (facing page). Press it well down against the edging.
ALTERNATIVELY, to re-surface the step, use bagged sand-cement mix (page 495) prepared in the normal way, but first coat the surface with a solution of 3 parts PVA adhesive to 1 part water. Before it dries, apply the concrete to lie level with the top of the edging.

6 Level the area. Cover for three days, as for path repairs.

Building garden steps

There are two types of garden step, those built into an existing slope and those that are freestanding – built up from the flat between two different levels.

Whatever the type, for comfort and safety steps should be evenly spaced and not less than 24in (610mm) wide. For two people to walk comfortably abreast, the width must be at least 4ft 6in (1.4m).

Steps are easiest to climb comfortably when long treads (the flat parts) are combined with low risers (the upright parts), or when short treads are used with high risers. The best relationships between the two are shown below.

Choose building materials that blend with their surroundings, and make sure that the treads have a rough, non-slip surface.

TREAD AND RISER COMBINATIONS

Treads should never be less than 12in (300mm) long. Risers should be no lower than 4in (100mm) and no higher than 7in (180mm). Their dimensions are governed to some extent by the gradient of the slope and the building material. Long treads are needed for steps up a gentle slope and short treads for a steep slope.

Brick risers, for example, are limited to multiples of 3in (75mm) – a brick laid flat – or 4½in (113mm) – a brick laid on edge. The height can be adjusted with tiles or brick slips, but this may spoil the look. When using paving slabs as treads, take into account the slab thickness when calculating the riser height.

TREAD	RISER	POSSIBLE RISER MATERIAL
18in (460mm)	4in (100mm)	One course of bricks laid flat, topped with 1in (25mm) thick slab tread.
17in (430mm)	4½in (113mm)	One course of bricks laid on edge. Or one course of bricks laid flat, topped with 1½in (38mm) thick slab tread.
16in (400mm)	5in (125mm)	One course of bricks laid flat, topped with 2in (50mm) thick slab tread.
15in (380mm)	5½in (140mm)	One course of 4in (100mm) walling blocks topped with 1½in (38mm) thick slab tread.
14in (360mm)	6in (150mm)	Two courses of bricks laid flat.
13in (330mm)	6½in (165mm)	One course of bricks laid on edge, topped with 2in (50mm) thick slab tread.
12in (300mm)	7in (180mm)	Two courses of bricks laid flat, topped with 1in (25mm) thick slab tread.

If the steps lead down to a house, make a narrow drainage channel as close as possible to the bottom step (see *Building a drainage channel*, page 491).

WORKING OUT STEP DIMENSIONS

To decide on the number of treads and risers for a flight of steps, measure the following:
a The height difference between the two levels.
b The length of the slope for built-in steps, or the length of ground space available for a freestanding flight to stretch.

For each measurement, calculate the number of steps needed for various combinations of treads and risers until you get more or less the same number for both measurements.

EXAMPLE A: Slope 6ft (1.8m) long with a 24in (610mm) difference in height.
1 Choose a suitable riser height and divide it into the height difference. As the slope is gentle, choose a low riser:
Height difference 24in (610mm) ÷ 4in (100mm) riser = 6 steps.

2 The best tread for a 4in riser is 18in (460mm). Divide this into the slope length:
Slope length 72in (1.8m) ÷ 18in (460mm) tread = 4 steps.

3 To adjust the difference, try again with a higher riser and a shorter tread:
Height 24in ÷ 5in = 4.8.
Length 72in ÷ 16in = 4.5.
So the answer is 5 steps.

EXAMPLE B: Freestanding steps with a height difference of 3ft (0.9m) and ground space of 5ft (1.5m).
1 In a 5ft (1.5m) stretch of ground space, the number of 12in (300mm) treads would be:
Ground space 5ft (1.5m) ÷ 12in (310mm) = 5 steps.
But the final tread could be the top of the higher level, so the actual stretch would be 4ft (1.2m).

2 Treads of 12in (300mm) are best with 7in (180mm) risers:
Height 3ft (0.9m) ÷ 7in (180mm) = 5.1 steps.
The 1in (25mm) height difference can be ignored. Even if the figures divide exactly, minor inaccuracies are bound to occur during the construction.

BUILDING INTO A SLOPE

Roughly shape the slope before you start building the steps. If it is steep, remove some of the soil (it can be spread in other parts of the garden). If you are making steps on an irregular slope, build up where necessary with soil from other parts of the garden.

The layout of the slope may suggest two flights of steps at right angles, with a landing in between. On a long flight, whether or not it turns at an angle, make a landing after about every ten steps to provide a resting place. On flights with high, loose soil at the sides, you will need to build low brick retaining walls (page 485).

The instructions given are for steps built with brick risers and concrete paving slab treads, but the method is similar whatever material you use.

Building garden steps (continued)

You will need

Tools String and pegs; 5m steel tape measure; long length of timber; spirit level; builder's square (page 479); spade; club hammer; brick trowel; mortar mixing board; two heavy-duty polythene buckets and two shovels (for mixing concrete); short tamping beam (page 494); pointing trowel or jointing tool (page 479); earth rammer (page 490); ⅜in (10mm) thick wooden batten. Possibly also: brick bolster.
Materials Hardcore – 1 barrowload fills about 4sq ft (0.4sq m) at 6in (150mm) deep; concrete foundation mix (page 496); bricks; brick mortar (page 481); paving slabs; bedding mortar (page 496); water. Possibly also: sharp sand.

1 Fix two parallel string lines from top to bottom of the slope, as far apart as the required step width.

2 Measure a line to find the length of the slope.

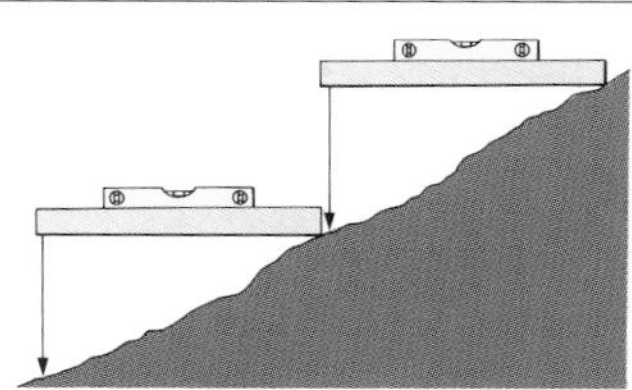

3 To measure the height difference between the levels, rest one end of a length of timber on the top of the slope and place a spirit level on it. Get a helper to hold the timber level while you measure the height of the timber above the lower ground level.

If the timber will not reach the whole way, measure to a point halfway down the slope, then measure from the same point to the lowest level. Add the two heights together for the total fall.

4 Use the height and length measurements to calculate suitable dimensions for treads and risers (page 501).

5 Fix string lines to mark the front edge of each step. Make sure they are evenly spaced, and use a builder's square to check that they are at right angles to the length lines.

6 Use a spade to shape the ground for each step. Begin at the bottom so you always have a flat area to work from.

7 Dig a trench 5in (125mm) deep at the base of the flight to make a footing strip for the first riser – 5in (125mm) wide, for example, for a single line of bricks laid flat.

8 Tip about 1in (25mm) of hardcore into the base of the trench and ram it well down.

9 Fill the trench with concrete, tamp level with the ground and cover (page 498, step 9).

10 Wait three days before building the first riser on the footing strip (see *Laying bricks*, page 483).

11 Wait at least two hours for the mortar to dry before ramming down a layer of hardcore for the first tread behind the riser. Take care not to disturb the bricks and fresh mortar. Slope the hardcore surface to the front for drainage (see right).

12 Lay paving slabs (page 492) for the first tread. Use a full bed of mortar and project the slab about 1in (25mm) in front of the riser.

13 Build the next riser on the back edge of the first tread. Make sure the riser is vertical – use the mortar layer to adjust for the slight drainage slope on the tread.

STEPS BUILT INTO A SLOPE

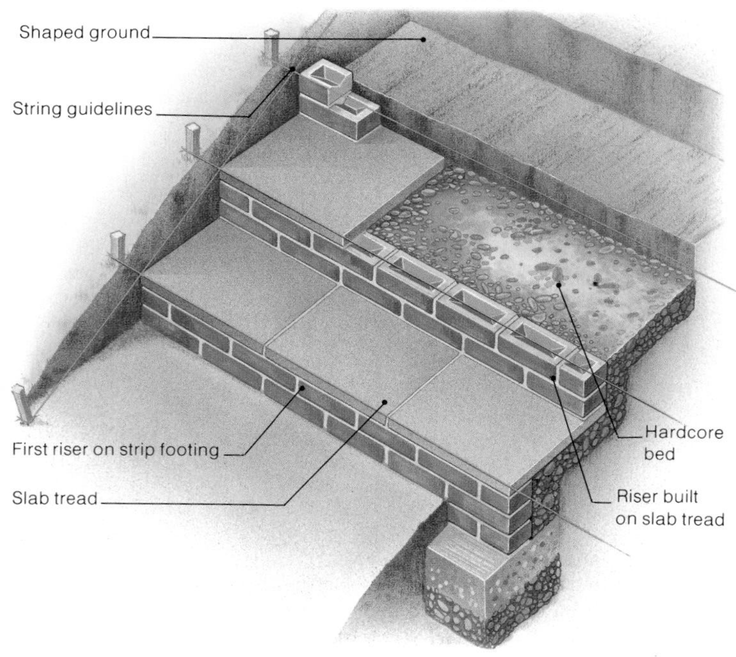

The ground is roughly shaped for the treads and risers. The first riser is built on a footing strip, and each following riser on the back of the previous tread. Treads are bedded on hardcore with a built-in drainage slope.

14 Make sure the top tread is level with the surrounding ground. If necessary, slope the ground towards the tread, or raise the tread slightly – no more than ½in (13mm).

15 Fill in between the tread slabs with mortar (page 492, step 13) or sharp sand. If you use mortar, wait about a week before using the steps, to allow the mortar to set.

SLOPING A TREAD FOR DRAINAGE

1 Build up the hardcore surface a little higher at the back of the step. Slope the surface to level with the top of the riser at the front.

2 To check the slope, lay a spirit level from the back to the front with a ⅜in (10mm) thick wooden batten under the front edge, on the riser. Build up the back of the slope until the spirit level is horizontal with the wooden batten in place.

3 Check that the hardcore area is level from side to side.

> **HELPFUL TIP**
> To save wear on the lawn at the base of a flight of steps, lay a paving slab in front of the bottom step. Cut out an area of turf of a suitable size and depth for bedding the slab on 1in (25mm) deep sharp sand.

BUILDING FREESTANDING STEPS

The treads of freestanding steps are supported on side walls, with the area between filled in with hardcore as a base. For a flight of up to about five steps build the side walls centred on a concrete footing strip. For a higher flight, lay a concrete sub-base for the whole structure.

The risers can be constructed in two ways – either built across the hardcore base or built up from the ground. If they are built across the hardcore base, the hardcore has to be filled in successive layers as a riser and its corresponding side walls are built. This means waiting for the brick mortar to dry out each time. On a high flight it saves considerably on bricks and the waiting may not be inconvenient.

On a low flight, it is generally easier to build up the risers from the ground and fill in all the hardcore at once to save waiting, and few extra bricks are needed. The method given below is for a small flight with risers built up from the ground.

Steps can be built either at right angles to the higher level, or parallel with it. Or the flight can change direction at a landing

STEPS BUILT UP FROM THE GROUND

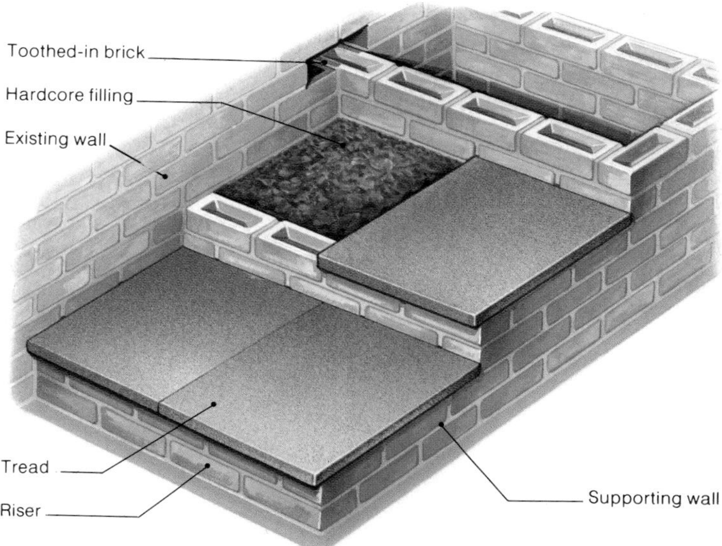

Steps can be built alongside an existing wall, or outwards from it. The supporting walls of the steps and the risers are built up with bricks, like an open box, and the area between them is filled in with hardcore. The treads rest on the walls and the hardcore bed.

about halfway down. A parallel flight often saves space when a lot of steps are needed.

You will need

Tools String and pegs; profile boards (page 479); steel tape measure; spirit level; builder's square (page 479); brick trowel; two heavy-duty polythene buckets and two shovels (for mixing concrete); club hammer; tamping beam (page 494); mortar mixing board; earth rammer (page 490); pointing trowel; gauge rod (page 479); plumb line; line pins and building line (page 479); ⅜in (10mm) thick wooden batten. Possibly also: brick bolster.

Materials Hardcore – 1 barrowload fills about 4sq ft (0.4sq m) at 6in (150mm) deep; concrete foundation mix (page 496); paving slabs; bricks; bedding mortar (page 496); brick mortar (page 481); water. Possibly also: sharp sand.

1 Measure the height difference and the ground space available, then work out the dimensions of treads and risers (page 501).

2 Prepare a concrete sub-base (page 482) either in strips or for the full area. Use a 2in (50mm) layer of hardcore topped with 3in (75mm) of concrete. Strip footing should be twice as wide as the thickness of the supporting wall.

3 Wait for three days for the concrete to harden before building the supporting walls.

4 Build supporting walls course by course (page 483) according to the depths of the risers. The front wall is the riser for the first step. Mark the position of the second and subsequent risers with string and pegs. Anchor courses to an existing terrace as necessary (see below). Check continually that corners are right angles and that walls are vertical, with courses at the right depth (page 483).

5 Wait until the brick mortar has set, then fill the areas between the walls and risers with hardcore well rammed down and with a drainage slope from front to back (see facing page). Take care not to disturb the newly laid bricks and fresh mortar.

6 Lay the paving slabs for each tread (page 492) on a full mortar bed, ensuring they project 1in (25mm) in front of each riser.

7 Fill the gaps between the top of the side wall and the back edge of the sloped slab with mortar.

ANCHORING STEPS TO A WALL

The supporting walls of freestanding steps must be anchored – or toothed in – to the wall they are built against. Half of the last brick in every other course of the step side walls (beginning with the bottom course) is linked into the existing wall. Remove the appropriate bricks (page 460) before you start the steps.

If the flight runs parallel with the existing wall, link in a brick at the end of each riser, and in alternate courses of the back wall.

Building a wooden pergola

A pergola is an open-work roof on columns, designed to support climbing plants. The columns can be brick or metal, but wood is popular. Kits are available with full building instructions.

If you want to design your own pergola, use timber posts at least 3in (75mm) square and about 10ft (3m) long. Sink them 24in (610mm) into the ground, bedded in the same way as fence posts (page 468). On concrete use a bolt-down fence base (page 467).

You can use sawn timber or rustic poles, or rustic poles cut in half lengthways (known as sawn slabs). Whatever timber you use, make sure it is thoroughly treated with wood preservative that is harmless to plants (page 473).

The timbers are commonly joined with halving joints (page 158) or skew nailing (page 165). Or you can use coach bolts (page 163).

A FREESTANDING PERGOLA

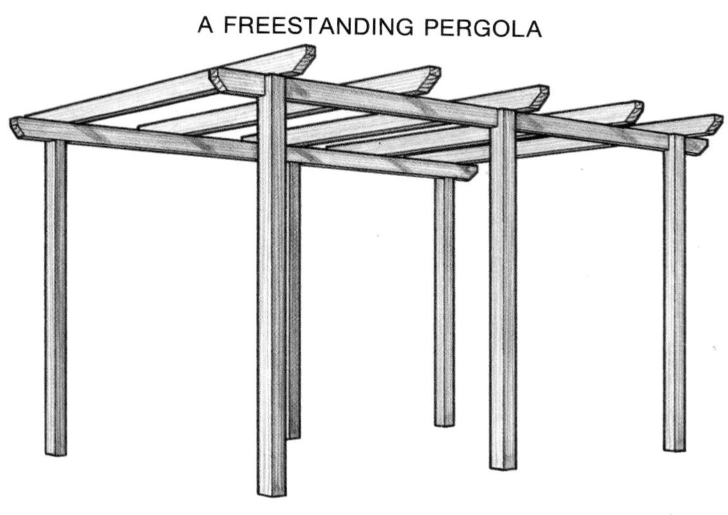

Plants can be trained along the timbers or supported on netting or trellis fixed to the uprights. For a pergola adjoining a house, fit cross rails to the wall with metal joist-hangers fixed into mortar joints.

A READY-MADE BOX JOINT

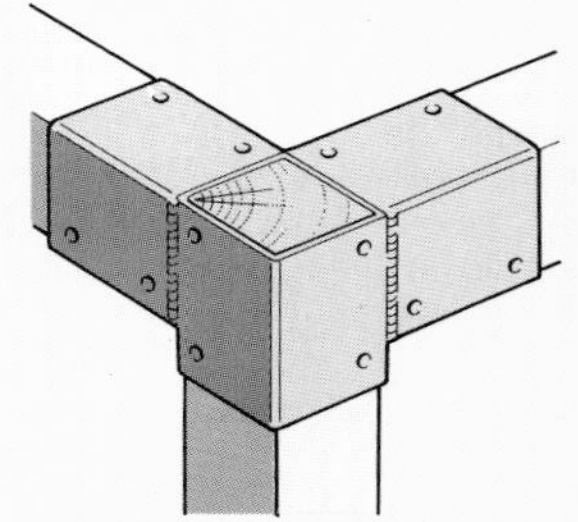

A useful fixing method for garden woodwork – such as a seat or a fruit cage – is a ready-made metal multi-joint such as a Metjoint. It holds three pieces of 2in (50mm) timber together at right angles. The timbers are tapped into each box of the joint with a mallet.

Building a garden pond

Find a patch of level ground, well away from trees. Overhanging trees and bushes not only shade the pond, but tend to fill it with dead leaves which will foul the water when they decay. Ideally, the pond should be in direct sunlight all day, as aquatic plants do not like the shade. If this is impossible, make sure the pond will be in the sun for at least half a day.

If you intend to have a fountain, waterfall or underwater lights, position the pond near the house so that the power supply they need will be easier and more economical to install. Make sure, too, that the pond is within the reach of a garden hose so that it can be filled and also topped up occasionally as the water evaporates.

Wait for about a week after first filling the pond for harmful chemicals to disperse before adding any plants. Do not stock with fish until the pond has been planted for about a month.

If you have small children or they are regular visitors, either fence off the pond securely or cover it with strong protective netting to prevent anyone falling in.

CHOOSING THE TYPE OF POND

A pond can either be shaped with a pre-formed rigid mould or dug out to the shape you want and lined with a flexible liner.

Rigid moulds are easy to install but are more expensive than flexible liners. Fibreglass moulds are the strongest, thickest and most long-lasting. They are self-supporting and can be fitted into a wall surround, as well as sunk into the ground. Plastic moulds are cheaper and may be damaged unless the sides are well-supported and protected from stones.

A flexible liner is a rubber or plastic sheet that is draped into a pond. The most durable types are synthetic butyl rubber, of which laminated types are the thickest and toughest. Cheaper but not as strong are PVC liners, of which the best types are double layered with a reinforcing nylon net between.

Any type of mould or liner should last at least ten years provided that it is properly installed.

DECIDING THE SIZE OF THE POND

A pond that is to be stocked with plants and fish should be at least 40sq ft (3.7sq m) in area to be sure of a balanced relationship and to keep the water clear. The depth required increases in relation to the surface area. If the pond is too shallow, it will get too hot in summer and freeze solid in winter.

Different plants need different depths of water, so ponds normally have a shelf all round the edge.

The smallest pond needs to be at least 16in (400mm) deep at its deepest part. A pond 25-100sq ft (2.3-9.3sq m) in area needs to be about 18in (460mm) deep, a pond 100-200sq ft (9.3-18.6sq m) in area about 24in (610mm) deep, and a pond over 200sq ft in area should be 30in (760mm) deep.

MAKING A POND WITH A FLEXIBLE LINER

Liners are square or rectangular, so avoid making the pond a complicated shape with narrow parts, which wastes material. A broad kidney shape is generally the most economical design.

Whatever the shape, when calculating the size of the liner, add a measurement equal to twice the maximum depth of the pond to both the overall length and overall width measurements. This allows for the overall depth of the pond.

You will need
Tools Garden hose; string and pegs; spade; steel tape measure; a piece of straight-edged timber longer than the pond length; spirit level; trimming knife; bricks for weighting the liner.
Materials Flexible liner; sharp sand.

1 Use a garden hose to outline the shape of the pond on the selected site. View it from all angles and at both sitting and standing heights, and adjust the outline until you are satisfied that the shape fits in with its surroundings.

2 Mark the chosen outline with wooden pegs not more than 3ft (0.9m) apart driven in to lie flush with the ground surface.

3 Use a length of timber and a spirit level to check that the pegs are level with each other all round and across the width and length.

If the pond surround is not level, it will be shown up by the water level, and will mar the appearance of the pond.

4 Dig out the shape of the pond to a depth of about 9in (230mm). Use the excavated soil to build up low areas of the surround to the right level, if necessary.

5 Dig out the centre of the pond, leaving a shelf about 9in (230mm) wide all round at the 9in depth for marginal plants.

6 Slope the sides down from the shelf to the bottom at an angle of about 20 degrees – that is, about 3in (75mm) down for every 9in (230mm) inwards. This is so that if ice forms, its expansion will not create pressure on the sides.

7 When you have dug to the required depth, level the bottom, removing any pointed stones that would damage the liner. Use a spirit level across the width and length to check the level.

8 Compact the soil using the back of a spade, then line the base and sides of the hole with a ¾in (19mm) layer of sharp sand. Damp the sand if necessary to keep it in place, and pat it well down to make a bed for the liner.

9 Drape the liner squarely over the sand-lined hole and weight it round the edges with bricks.

10 Use a garden hose connected to a mains-fed household tap to fill the liner slowly with cold water. The liner will stretch under the pressure of the water to fit snugly into the hole. Move the bricks in as necessary as the pond fills so that the liner can bed down properly.

11 When the pond is full, trim the surplus liner to leave a 6in (150mm) border to fit under the edging slabs. Trim back surrounding turf if necessary, so the slabs lie just below the level of a lawn.

> HELPFUL TIP
>
> As a guide to how much sand you need to line a pond, 1cu ft of sand covers about 15sq ft at ¾in deep (or 0.2cu m covers about 10sq m at 20mm deep). Roughly 3cwt of sand (about three 50kg bags) is equivalent to 4cu ft (0.1cu m).
>
> Consider the surface area of the pond as a rectangle based on the longest and widest parts. To allow for the overall depth, use the formula for estimating the size of a flexible liner – add twice the measurement of the maximum depth to both the length and the width before you multiply them together to find the area.
>
> So for a pond 8ft (2.4m) long, 6ft (1.8m) wide and 16in (406mm) deep, the lining area would be 10ft 8in (3.2m) by 8ft 8in (2.6m) = 92.3sq ft (8.3sq m). At 1cu ft of sand per 15sq ft, you are likely to need roughly 6cu ft (0.17cu m) – about 5cwt (250kg).

INSTALLING A RIGID POND

You will need
Tools Spade; stick; garden hose; spirit level.
Materials Pond mould; sharp sand.

1 Place the mould on the site face up and sprinkle sand or earth round the outline to mark a rough guide for digging. (Do not lay the mould on its face, or the shape will be reversed from left to right.)

2 Dig a hole to take the mould so that its edges are flush with the surrounding ground. Make the hole about 6in (150mm) wider than the mould on all edges, and about 1in (25mm) deeper. From time to time put the mould in the hole to see how much more you need to dig.

3 When the hole is large enough, remove visible large or pointed stones and compact the earth well down using the back of the spade.

4 Line the hole with a ¾in (19mm) deep layer of damp sand to bed the mould on.

5 Put the mould in the hole on the sand bed and use a spirit level (on a length of wood if necessary) to check that the sides are level from end to end and side to side. If the mould slopes, the water will run to one end or one side.

6 Fill the gap round the mould edges with damp sand, pushing it well down with a stick. Or use sifted earth for large gaps. Be careful to fill the area below the underside of the shelf.

7 Check the level of the pond again, in case you have disturbed it while filling round the edges.

8 Fill the pond with cold water using a garden hose connected to a mains-fed household tap.

FINISHING THE SURROUND OF THE POND

Pave the edges of either type of pond with slabs or crazy paving (page 492). Spread bedding mortar

on top of a flexible-lining border. Place the slabs to overhang the pond by at least ½in (13mm) to hide the liner. Do not rest slabs directly on a rigid mould, or it may crack. Some moulded ponds have a preformed edge simulating rocks or crazy paving, which should be left exposed.

Be very careful not to drop any mortar or cement dust into the pond, because it will poison plants or fish. If any does fall in, do not ignore it. Empty the pond (the easiest way is with a small electric pump), clean it out and refill it.

Repairing wooden side-hung garage doors

Doors sag because the hinges are damaged or because the wood in the door or frame is rotten. Unless hinges are regularly oiled and the screws and bolts are painted, they will rust.

Woodwork must also be regularly painted or varnished to protect it. Rain splashing off a drive can cause the wood to rot, particularly at the base of the door and frame. Probe the wood occasionally with a knife to see if it is sound. If the knife blade goes in more than about ⅛in (3mm), treat the wood with a wood preservative.

Replace damaged or rusty hinges and rotten wood as soon as you discover them. The hinges are normally either tee hinges (page 475) or band and hook hinges, and are fitted in the same way as a door hinge (page 196).

REPLACING ROTTEN WOOD

Most side-hung double doors are tongued-and-grooved boarding (matchboarding) on a ledged-and-braced wooden frame, but some have solid panels. Replace rotten wood with pre-treated timber of the same type and thickness as on the existing door.

If the area of rotten wood is too small or difficult to cut out, treat the rot with a wood-repair system (page 210).

You will need

Tools Power jig saw or pad saw; brace and bit; plane; steel tape measure; straight-edge; pencil; hammer; nail punch; paintbrush. Possibly also: tenon saw; hammer and wood chisel.

Materials Pre-treated solid timber or matchboard; galvanised 1½in (38mm) or 2in (50mm) nails; exterior-grade filler; exterior-grade gloss paint. Possibly also: battens or timber piece for back support.

1 Mark on the front of the door the positions of horizontal rails or braces at the back that are near the rotten timber.

2 Outline the area to be removed, making it regular in shape. It should extend at least 3in (75mm) beyond the rotten wood and, if practicable, be backed by part of a support rail.

3 Drill starting holes near the edges of the area marked for removal, avoiding a spot where there is a backing rail.

4 Saw out the rotten wood, working from the starting hole. Use a jig saw or a pad saw. A tenon saw may be best for cutting down between the tongued-and-grooved boards. Where there is a supporting rail, use the tip of a tenon saw to avoid cutting through it, and if necessary finish the cut with a hammer and wood chisel.

5 Measure and cut the new wood to size, using tongued-and-grooved boards fitted together where necessary. Plane it smooth.

6 If there is no supporting rail behind the hole, nail battens across as supports.

7 Nail the new wood in place against its support, then punch the nail heads below the surface.

8 Fill the nail holes and any gaps round the new section with exterior-grade wood filler. Leave it to dry. Rub smooth with abrasive paper.

9 Paint the door with exterior-grade gloss paint to conceal the repair and protect the wood.

REPAIRING A LOOSE DOOR FRAME

To make repairs to the frame, unscrew the hinges and remove the door. If the frame is loose, tighten the screws holding it to the wall, if possible. You may have to scrape paint away to find them. If necessary, use one or two frame fixings (page 232) between the screw positions to secure the frame.

When tightening the screws, use a plumb line or spirit level to ensure that the frame remains vertical. It is easy to force a frame out of true, and if you do the doors will not open and close properly.

If a door frame is out of true, it is usually because the packing (pieces of wood between the frame and the wall) has been dislodged. The only way to find out is to expose the gap between the frame and the wall by chipping away the mortar with a hammer and cold chisel. If necessary, push in new packing pieces of marine-grade plywood to bring the frame vertical before you drive in a frame fixing. Refill the gap between the frame and wall with mastic filler (page 106).

SPLICING A ROTTED DOOR FRAME

Where part of the door frame has rotted, use an angled (scarf) joint when inserting new wood. This gives a wide joining area, which increases the strength of the joint.

Use wood pre-treated with wood preservative and of the same width and thickness as the existing wood. If the frame is rebated (step-shaped), either get a matching piece cut to shape at a woodyard, or glue and screw two pieces of wood together to match the profile of the frame. Remove the door before you start.

1 Mark cutting lines on the frame at each end, at least 3in (75mm) beyond the damaged wood.

2 Saw through the frame at the marked points making a cut at an angle of about 45 degrees.

3 Hold the replacement wood alongside the frame against the gap and carefully mark the angle of the cut at each end.

4 Cut the wood to size and check that it fits.

5 Apply exterior-grade woodworking adhesive to the angle surfaces of the new and old wood and stick it in position. Then screw the two pieces together with the screw driven in at an angle.

6 Use frame fixings (page 232) to secure the new timber to the wall.

CHOOSING AN UP-AND-OVER DOOR

Instead of replacing an old side-hung timber door, consider putting in a more efficient up-and-over door. Manufacturers normally supply good installation instructions.

There are two different lifting systems – tracked and trackless – but both work on counterbalanced weights and springs. With a tracked system, the opened door retracts fully into the garage and is supported on two side tracks either fixed to the walls or hung from the roof.

With a trackless system, the opened door does not retract fully. It is supported on a sub-frame that fits inside the garage opening. The tracked system is the stronger, but the trackless system is cheaper and easier to install.

Doors may be metal (usually galvanised pressed steel or aluminium), wood or plastic. Metal is cheapest. Wood is more expensive and needs more maintenance to protect it from the weather. Plastic tends to be the most expensive, but needs no maintenance apart from washing. A plastic door can be painted if you want to smarten it up or change the colour.

Most doors are made to a standard height – 6ft 6in (1.9m) or 7ft (2.1m). Widths range from about 6ft 6in (1.9m) to 16ft (4.9m).

When measuring your garage opening for a new door, allow space for the sub-frame on a trackless system. If you cannot find a door to fit, it is cheaper to alter the size of the garage opening than to cut a new door to size or have one specially made.

If the opening is too big, fit another frame inside the existing one. If it is too small, remove the existing frame and fit a thinner one to gain a little extra width.

Index

Page numbers in **bold** refer to photographs in chapter one: Ideas for the Home (pages 6-96)

B

C

D

F

IJ

L

M

N

P

U

V

W

Z

Acknowledgments

The publishers gratefully acknowledge the help given by the following organisations in the preparation of the *Reader's Digest Complete D-I-Y Manual.*

3M United Kingdom PLC
Aga-Rayburn
Anodic Castings Ltd
Aquatron Showers Ltd
Arrow Fastener UK Ltd
Ashley Accessories
B & R Electrical Products Ltd
Backer Distribution Ltd
Bahco Record Tools Ltd
Banham's Patent Locks Ltd
Barron Control Gear Ltd
Bartol Ltd
Baxi Heating
Beechwood Brushes Ltd
Benford Ltd
Bennetts British Brushes Ltd
Beta Naco Ltd
BET Plant Services PLC (Clima Holdings)
BICC PLC
Black and Decker
Bogod Machine Co Ltd
Robert Bosch Ltd
Brefco
Brick Development Association
British Gates and Timber Ltd
Briton Chadwick Ltd
Brownhills Sheet Metal and Engineering Co Ltd
Bulldog Tools
Bullfinch (Gas Equipment) Ltd
Burgen & Ball Ltd
Burgess Power Tools Ltd
Can-Corp
Carpet Cleaners' Association
Cement and Concrete Association
Chubb & Sons Lock & Safe Co Ltd
Click Systems Ltd
Conex Sanbra Ltd
Copydex
J B Corrie
Crado International Ltd
Crime Prevention Service, Metropolitan Police
DRG Sellotape Products
Thomas Dudley Ltd
Duet Showers
Dunsley Heating Appliance Co Ltd
Duraflex Products Ltd
Electrak International Ltd
Electrium
Ellistons (Welwyn) Ltd
ERF Plastics
Errut Products Ltd
European Industrial Services Ltd
Every Ready Ltd
Excalibur Hand Tools Ltd
Florin Ltd, Vitrex Tools Div
Fordham Bathrooms and Kitchens Ltd
GEC Vynckier
GKN Crompton Ltd
Glynwed Consumer & Building Products Ltd (Leisure)
Richard Graefe Ltd
Gravity Randall Ltd
Gripperrods International Ltd
Hamilton & Co (London) Ltd
Hansil Ltd
Heuga UK Ltd
Hewetson Floors Ltd
Hiretech
Home Automation
Honeywell Control Systems Ltd
Hoover PLC
Hunter Building Products Ltd
IMI Santon Ltd
IMI Yorkshire Fittings Ltd
C I Jenkinson & Son Ltd
H & R Johnson Tiles Ltd
Douglas Kane Ltd
Kango Wolf Power Tools Ltd
Kay & Co (Engineers) Ltd
Kesteven Copper Cylinders Ltd
Kibblewhite & Blackmur Ltd
Langley London Ltd
J Legge & Co Ltd
Link 51 Ltd
London Fire Brigade
Magnet & Southerns PLC
Mallinson-Denny (Lydney) Ltd
Marley Extrusions Ltd
Marley Floors Ltd
Marshall-Tufflex
Metlex Industries Ltd
Metpost Ltd
Micromark
Millbrook Water Gardens, Crowborough
MK Electric Ltd
Mustang Tools Ltd
Myson Heating Ltd
Neill Tools Ltd
Newman-Tonks Engineering Ltd
W H Newson & Sons Ltd
Oracstar Ltd
Peak Technologies Ltd
Pendock Ltd
Pifco Ltd
Pilkington's Tiles Ltd
Polycell Products Ltd
Preedy Glass Merchants
Randall Electronics Ltd
Respatex
E J Reynolds & Co Ltd
Roberts-Copydex
Rock Electrical Accessories Ltd
Ronson Ltd
Rowenta UK
Sadia Water Heaters Ltd
Sandvik Ltd
George H Scholes PLC
Skarsten Manufacturing Co Ltd
SMC (Sealed Motor Construction Co Ltd)
Smiths Industries Environmental Controls Co Ltd
Spur Systems International Ltd
Stanley Tools
Stelrad Group Ltd
Superswitch Electrical Appliances Ltd
Swedish Finnish Timber Council
Swedal Leisure (U.K.) Ltd
Tebrax Ltd
Tek Cambridge Ltd
The Dripping Tap, Bromley, Kent
Thor Hammer Co Ltd
Thorn EMI Domestic Appliances Ltd
Thunder Screw Anchors Ltd
Timber Research and Development Association
TI Parkray Ltd
Transbyn Ltd (Saniflo)
Trent Valley Plastics Ltd
Trianco Redfyre Ltd
Ernest Turner
Edgar Udny & Co Ltd
Uni-Tubes Ltd
Volex Electrical Products Ltd
Wagner Spraytech (UK) Ltd
Walker Crosweller & Co Ltd (Mira)
The Wednesbury Tube Company
William Whitehouse & Co
Yale Security Products Ltd

Photographic credits

The photographs listed below were provided by the following photographers, agencies and companies. All photographs not listed were specially commissioned by Reader's Digest. Four photographs are from books previously published by The Reader's Digest Association Ltd.

The position of photographs on each page is indicated by the letters after the page number: *T* = top; *B* = bottom; *L* = left; *C* = centre; *R* = right.

8 Elizabeth Whiting & Associates/Spike Powell **9** *T* Camera Press *B* Robert Harding Syndication/Brian Harrison **10** *TL* Camera Press *TR* Camera Press *B* Robert Harding Syndication/Jan Baldwin/Homes & Gardens **11** *T* John Lewis of Hungerford *BL* Robert Harding Syndication/Ideal Home *BR* Robert Harding Syndication/Homes & Ideas **12** *T* Camera Press *B* Elizabeth Whiting & Associates/Tommy Candler **13** *TL* Elizabeth Whiting & Associates/Tom Leighton *TR* Elizabeth Whiting & Associates/Rodney Hyett *B* Robert Harding Syndication/Ideal Home **14** *TL* Jessica Strang *TR* Camera Press *B* Greenwich Wood Works, London SE13 7QS. Tel: 020-8694 8449 **15** *TL* Jessica Strang/Designer, Nic Thomas/Cats painted Mary Komoki *TR* Robert Harding Syndication/Bill Reavell/Homes & Ideas *B* Elizabeth Whiting & Associates/ Rodney Hyett **16** *T* Robert Harding Syndication/Dominic Blackmore/Homes & Ideas *BL* Robert Harding Syndication/Country Homes & Interiors **17** *T* Jessica Strang/Barrie Weaver *BL* Camera Press *BR* Camera Press **18** *T* Elizabeth Whiting & Associates *B* Robert Harding Syndication **19** *TL* Camera Press *TR* Magnet/Shaker Green *B* Magnet/Shaker Blue **20** *TR* Conran Design Group *B* Magnet/Manhattan **21** *TL* Chromagene Ltd *TR* Neff (UK) Limited *CR* Neff (UK) Limited *B* Neff (UK) Limited **22** Robert Harding Syndication/Ideal Home *BL* Camera Press *BR* Robert Harding Syndication/Tim Beddow/Homes & Gardens **23** *T* Elizabeth Whiting & Associates/Jon Bouchier *BL* Robert Harding Syndication/Ideal Home *BR* Camera Press/Bo Appeltofft **24** *T* Robert Harding Syndication/Spike Powell/Ideal Home *B* Elizabeth Whiting & Associates **25** *TL* Jessica Strang/Designer, Nic Thomas *TR* Elizabeth Whiting & Associates/Rodney Hyett *B* Elizabeth Whiting & Associates/Dennis Stone **26** *TL* Camera Press *TR* Elizabeth Whiting & Associates/Neil Lorimer *CL* Elizabeth Whiting & Associates/Brian Harrison *BL* Elizabeth Whiting & Associates *BR* Elizabeth Whiting & Associates/Andreas V. Einsiedel **27** *T* Camera Press *BL* Elizabeth Whiting & Associates *BR* Elizabeth Whiting & Associates **28** *T* Robert Harding Syndication/Bill Reavell/Homes & Ideas *BL* Elizabeth Whiting & Associates *BR* IKEA **29** Zeyko GmbH **30** Elizabeth Whiting & Associates/Spike Powell **31** *T* Robert Harding Syndication/Bill Reavell/Homes & Ideas *B* Robert Harding Syndication/Trevor Richards/Homes & Gardens **32** *T* Robert Harding Syndication/Trevor Richards/Homes & Gardens *BL* Robert Harding Syndication/Peter Woloszynski/Homes & Gardens *BR* Robert Harding Syndication/James Merrell/Country Homes & Interiors **33** *B* Laura Ashley **34** *TR* Elizabeth Whiting & Associates/Spike Powell *BL* Elizabeth Whiting & Associates/Ian Parry *BR* Robert Harding Syndication/Trevor Richards/Homes & Garden **35** *T* Elizabeth Whiting & Associates/Karl-Dietrich Buhler *BL* Stovax Limited *BR* Elizabeth Whiting & Associates/Huntley Hedworth **36** *T* Elizabeth Whiting & Associates/Nick Carter *BL BR* Robert Harding Syndication/ Tom Leighton/Homes & Gardens **37** *TL* Elizabeth Whiting & Associates *TR* Elizabeth Whiting & Associates/Andrew Kolosnikov *BL* Elizabeth Whiting & Associates/Rodney Hyett *BR* Robert Harding Syndication/Trevor Richards/Homes & Gardens **38** *TL* Camera Press *TR* Camera Press *CL* Marks & Spencer *C* Marks & Spencer *B* Robert Harding Syndication/Henry Bourke/Homes & Gardens/IPC Magazines **39** Marks & Spencer **40** Elizabeth Whiting & Associates **41** *T* Camera Press *BL* Robert Harding Syndication/Chris Drake/Country Homes & Interiors Magazines *BR* Elizabeth Whiting & Associates **42** *T* Camera Press *BL* Camera Press *BR* Robert Harding Syndication/Jan Baldwin/Homes & Gardens **43** *T* Elizabeth Whiting & Associates/Dennis Stone *BL* Jessica Strang/Barrie Weaver *BR* Elizabeth Whiting & Associates/June Buck **44** *T* Elizabeth Whiting & Associates/Rodney Hyett *B* Camera Press **45** Camera Press **46** Elizabeth Whiting & Associates/Jon Bouchier **47** *TL* Robert Harding Syndication/Bill Reavell/Homes & Ideas *TR* Elizabeth Whiting & Associates *B* IKEA **48** Camera Press **49** *TL* Elizabeth Whiting & Associates/Rodney Hyett *TR* Robert Harding Syndication/Trevor Richards/Homes & Gardens/ IPC Magazines *B* Elizabeth Whiting & Associates/Dennis Stone **50** *TR* Elizabeth Whiting & Associates/Rodney Hyett *B* Robert Harding Syndication/David Giles/Homes & Ideas **51** *TL* Camera Press *TR* Armitage Shanks Limited *BL* Robert Harding Syndication/Dominic Blackmore/Homes & Ideas **53** *TL* Camera Press *TR* Camera Press **54** Camera Press **55** *TL* Camera Press *TR* Robert Harding Syndication *B* Camera Press **56** *T* Elizabeth Whiting & Associates/Michael Dunne *BL* Robert Harding Syndication/David Montgomery/Homes & Gardens *BR* Robert Harding Syndication **57** *TL* Robert Harding Syndication/James Merrell/Woman's Journal *CL* Elizabeth Whiting & Associates/Tim Beddow *CR* Robert Harding Syndication/Homes & Gardens *BL* Robert Harding Syndication *BR* Elizabeth Whiting & Associates/Mark Nicholson **58** *TL* Robert Harding Syndication/James Merrell/Homes & Gardens *TR* Robert Harding Syndication/Polly Wreford/Country Homes & Interiors *BL* Camera Press *BR* Robert Harding Syndication/Bill Reavell/ Homes and Ideas **59** *T* Robert Harding Syndication/Homes & Gardens *B* Camera Press **60** *T* Robert Harding Syndication/Dominic Blackmore/Homes & Ideas/IPC Magazines *B* Jessica Strang **61** Interior Archive Limited/Fritz von Schulenburg **62** Elizabeth Whiting & Associates/Spike Powell **63** *TL* Camera Press *TR* Robert Harding Syndication/James Merrell/Homes & Gardens *BL* Elizabeth Whiting & Associates/Michael Crockett *BR* Camera Press **64** *T* Camera Press *BL* Robert Harding Syndication/Dominic Blackmore/Homes & Ideas *BR* Elizabeth Whiting & Associates **65** *TL* Camera Press *TR* Elizabeth Whiting & Associates/Nick Carter *BL* Elizabeth Whiting & Associates/Steve Hawkins *BR* Elizabeth Whiting & Associates/Michael Dunne **66** Camera Press **67** *TL* Elizabeth Whiting & Associates/Spike Powell *TR BL* Robert Harding Syndication/James Merrell/Country Homes & Interiors *BR* Robert Harding Syndication/Dominic Blackmore/Ideal Home **68** *TL* Robert Harding Syndication/Homes & Ideas*TR* Laura Ashley *BL* Elizabeth Whiting & Associates/Neil Lorimer *BR* Elizabeth Whiting & Associates/Jerry Tubby **69** Elizabeth Whiting & Associates **70** Camera Press **71** *TL* Camera Press *TR* Jessica Strang *B* Camera Press **72** *TL* Camera Press*TR* Camera Press *B* Camera Press **73** *TL* Camera Press *TR* IKEA *CL* IKEA *BL* Elizabeth Whiting & Associates/Spike Powell *BR* Camera Press **74** *T* Robert Harding Syndication/Tom Leighton/Homes & Gardens *BL* Camera Press *BR* Camera Press **75** *TL* Camera Press *TR* Camera Press *B* Camera Press **76** Elizabeth Whiting & Associates *TL* Elizabeth Whiting & Associates/Huntley Hedworth **77** *TR* Camera Press *B* Elizabeth Whiting & Associates/Steve Hawkins **78** *T* Robert Harding Syndication/Ideal Home *BL* Camera Press *BR* Camera Press **79** *T* Robert Harding Syndication *B* Camera Press **80** Jessica Strang **81** *TL* Elizabeth Whiting & Associates/Michael Nicholson *TR* Jessica Strang *B* Jessica Strang **82** *T* Robert Harding Syndication/Homes & Gardens *B* Robert Harding Syndication **83** *T* Philip Bier/View Pictures *BL* Robert Harding Syndication *BR* Robert Harding Syndication/Hugh Palmer/ Homes & Interiors **84** Eric Crichton **85** *TL* Elizabeth Whiting & Associates/Michael Nicholson *TR* GPL/John Glover *CR* Eric Crichton *B* Eric Crichton **86** *TR* Eric Crichton *TR* GPL/Vaughan Fleming *BL* GPL/Lynne Brotchie *BR* GPL/Lynne Brotchie **87** Eric Crichton **88** *TL* Elizabeth Whiting & Associates/Jerry Harpur *TR* Elizabeth Whiting & Associates/Jerry Harpur *B* GPL/Ron Sutherland **89** *TL* GPL/Steven Wooster *TR* GPL/JS Sira *B* Eric Crichton **90** *TL* Eric Crichton *TR* Eric Crichton *BL* GPL/Steven Wooster *BR* Camera Press **91** *TL* GPL/JS Sira *TR* GPL *B* GPL/Ron Sutherland **92** *T* GPL/Lamontagne *B* Jessica Strang **93** *T* Eric Crichton *CR* GPL/Brigitte Thomas *BL* Eric Crichton *BR* Elizabeth Whiting & Associates/Rodney Hyett **95** Eric Crichton *TL* Elizabeth Whiting & Associates/Jerry Harpur *TR* GPL/JS Sira *CR* GPL/John Baker *BL* GPL/Michael Howes *BC* Eric Crichton *BR* GPL/Ron Sutherland **96** *TL* Eric Crichton *TR* Eric Crichton *CL* Jessica Strang *CR* Eric Crichton *BL* Eric Crichton BR Eric Crichton **488** Elizabeth Whiting & Associates/ Ann Kelley Elizabeth Whiting & Associates/Neil Lorimer John Vigurs Elizabeth Whiting & Associates/Karl-D-Buhler **489** Cement & Concrete Association John Vigurs Elizabeth Whiting & Associates/David Lloyd Elizabeth Whiting & Associates/Jon Bouchier Elizabeth Whiting & Associates/Jerry Tubby

2003 Reprint

i-xii all house facades Edifice **v** *TL* Houses and Interiors/David Copsey, *CL* Houses and Interiors/David Markson, Houses and Interiors/Ed Buziak **ix** *L* Houses and Interiors/David Markson **294** All DIY Photo Library **295** *TL* DIY Photo Library

Reader's Digest Complete DIY Manual was edited and designed by
The Reader's Digest Association Limited, London

First Edition Copyright © 1994
The Reader's Digest Association Limited,
11 Westferry Circus, Canary Wharf,
London E14 4HE
www.readersdigest.co.uk

Typesetting
Vantage Photosetting Co. Ltd, Eastleigh and London
Elite Typesetting, Southampton
Opus Graphics Ltd, London

The typeface used for the main text
of this book is Helvetica light

Separations
Reprocolor Llovet S.A., Barcelona
Grafascan Ltd, Dublin
Litho Origination Ltd, London

Based on Reader's Digest
New D-I-Y Manual, first published in 1987
Revised and updated

This edition, reprinted with amendments 2003

Printing and Binding
Arnoldo Mondadori, Verona

ISBN 0 276 42804 8
BOOK CODE 400-169-01
ORACLE CODE 250007718H.00.24